# Financial and Managerial Accounting
## Information for Decisions

Volume 1 Chapters 1–11
Volume 2 Chapters 12–21

John J. Wild
University of Wisconsin at Madison

Kermit D. Larson
University of Texas at Austin

Barbara Chiappetta
Nassau Community College

McGraw-Hill
Irwin

Boston Burr Ridge, IL Dubuque, IA Madison, WI New York
San Francisco St. Louis Bangkok Bogotá Caracas Kuala Lumpur
Lisbon London Madrid Mexico City Milan Montreal New Delhi
Santiago Seoul Singapore Sydney Taipei Toronto

To my wife **Gail** and children, **Kimberly, Jonathan, Stephanie,** and **Trevor.**
To my wife **Nancy.**
To my husband **Bob,** my sons **Michael** and **David,** and my **mother.**

**McGraw-Hill**
**Irwin**

FINANCIAL AND MANAGERIAL ACCOUNTING: INFORMATION FOR DECISIONS

Published by McGraw-Hill/Irwin, a business unit of The McGraw-Hill Companies, Inc., 1221 Avenue of the Americas, New York, NY, 10020. Copyright © 2005 by The McGraw-Hill Companies, Inc. All rights reserved. No part of this publication may be reproduced or distributed in any form or by any means, or stored in a database or retrieval system, without the prior written consent of The McGraw-Hill Companies, Inc., including, but not limited to, in any network or other electronic storage or transmission, or broadcast for distance learning.

Some ancillaries, including electronic and print components, may not be available to customers outside the United States.

This book is printed on acid-free paper.

1 2 3 4 5 6 7 8 9 0 VNH/VNH 0 9 8 7 6 5 4

ISBN     0-07-304435-0
           0-07-304973-5 (Volume 1)
           0-07-304974-3 (Volume 2)

Vice president and editor-in-chief: *Robin J. Zwettler*
Editorial director: *Brent Gordon*
Publisher: *Stewart Mattson*
Sponsoring editor: *Steve Schuetz*
Developmental editor I: *Kelly Odom*
Marketing manager: *Richard Kolasa*
Senior producer, Media technology: *Ed Przyzycki*
Senior project manager: *Lori Koetters*
Senior production supervisor: *Michael R. McCormick*
Lead designer: *Matthew Baldwin*
Photo research coordinator: *Judy Kausal*
Photo researcher: *Sarah Evertson*
Lead supplement producer: *Becky Szura*
Senior digital content specialist: *Brian Nacik*
Cover designer: *Matthew Baldwin*
Cover image: © *Corbis Images*
Typeface: *10.5/12 Times Roman*
Compositor: *The GTS Companies/York, PA Campus*
Printer: *Von Hoffmann Corporation*

**Library of Congress Control Number: 2004104700**

# CPS
# Classroom Performance System

## What is CPS?

The Classroom Performance System is a revolutionary system that brings ultimate interactivity to the lecture hall or classroom. CPS is a wireless response system that gives you immediate feedback from every student in the class. CPS units include easy-to-use software for creating and delivering questions and assessments to your class. With CPS you can ask subjective and objective questions. Then every student simply responds with their individual, wireless response pad, providing instant results. CPS is the perfect tool for engaging students while gathering important assessment data.

## Features and Benefits:

- Better interactivity- Receive instant feedback on what students have learned
- Increased class discussion – anonymous opinion polls can be used to generate debate
- Improved attendance by "alert" students
- Automatically graded testing
- Simple to install, set up and use
- Low cost
- Reliable technical support available

CPS Receiver Unit

## How do I get CPS?

Please contract you McGraw-Hill textbook representative. The keypads are ordered by your bookstore and the enrollment codes needed to enroll the keypad in your course are packaged with your student's textbook or available online.

# Financial and Managerial Accounting
## Information for Decisions

Over the past several years, the financial and managerial accounting book market has evolved. Departmental decisions between user-oriented books and traditional procedural-oriented books have been greatly debated among faculty. While teaching accounting at their respective colleges, John Wild, Kermit Larson, and Barbara Chiappetta engaged in similar discussions, but found several core aspects of these different perspectives that achieved success for advocates of both.

Everyone agreed, firstly, that students could not relate to the traditional examples and dry companies integrated throughout other accounting books. With our authors' passion for bringing the classroom to life by using examples of exciting, new businesses, it was an obvious choice to use such pedagogy throughout this book.

Second, it was clear that students needed exposure to "real world" accounting data, giving them experience in analyzing and interpreting business performance. The authors therefore integrated real world accounting data throughout the book in a non-intimidating manner. They also formed a relationship with Krispy Kreme and bundled its annual report with every book.

Finally, the ability of students to analyze, interpret, and apply accounting information seemed crucial to both users and preparers of accounting information. As a key model, the authors developed the Decision Center, a pedagogical tool integrated throughout the book allowing students to identify where and how business decisions are made and that draw upon accounting information.

"There is a good balance between accounting from the user perspective and the preparer perspective. [This book] is written by an author who is clearly a classroom teacher."
— **Phillip Stickney, Conchise College**

**John J. Wild** is a professor of accounting and the Robert and Monica Beyer Distinguished Professor at the University of Wisconsin at Madison. He previously held appointments at Michigan State University and the University of Manchester in England. He received his BBA, MS, and PhD from the University of Wisconsin.

Professor Wild teaches accounting courses at both the undergraduate and graduate levels. He has received the Mabel W. Chipman Excellence-in-Teaching Award, the departmental Excellence-in-Teaching Award, and the Teaching Excellence Award from the 2003 graduation class at the University of Wisconsin. He also received the Beta Alpha Psi and Roland F. Salmonson Excellence-in Teaching Award from Michigan State University. Professor Wild is a past KPMG Peat Marwick National Fellow and is a recipient of fellowships from the American Accounting Association and the Ernst and Young Foundation.

Professor Wild is an active member of the American Accounting Association and its sections. He has served on several committees of these organizations, including the Outstanding Accounting Educator Award, Wildman Award, National Program Advisory, Publications, and Research Committees. Professor Wild is author of Fundamental Accounting Principles and Financial Statement Analysis, both published by McGraw-Hill/Irwin. His research appears in The Accounting Review, Journal of Accounting Research, Journal of Accounting and Economics, Contemporary Accounting Research, Journal of Accounting, Auditing and Finance, Journal of Accounting and Public Policy, and other business periodicals. He is past associate editor of Contemporary Accounting Research and has served on several editorial boards including The Accounting Review.

Professor Wild, his wife, and four children enjoy travel, music, sports, and community activities.

**Kermit D. Larson** is the Arthur Andersen & Co. Alumni Professor of Accounting Emeritus at the University of Texas at Austin. He served as chairman of the University of Texas, Department of Accounting and was visiting professor at Tulane University. His scholarly articles have been published in a variety of journals, including The Accounting Review, Journal of Accountancy, and Abacus. He is the author of several books, including Financial Accounting and Fundamental Accounting Principles, both published by McGraw-Hill/Irwin.

Professor Larson is a member of the American Accounting Association, the Texas Society of CPAs, and the American Institute of CPAs. His positions with the AAA have included vice president, southwest regional vice president, and chairperson of several committees, including the Committee of Concepts and Standards. He was a member of the committee that planned the first AAA doctoral consortium and served as its director.

Professor Larson served as president of the Richard D. Irwin Foundation. He also served on the Accounting Accreditation Committee and on the Accounting Standards Committee of the AACSB. He was a member of the Constitutional Drafting Committee of the Federation of Schools of Accountancy and a member of the Commission on Professional Accounting Education. He has been an expert witness on cases involving mergers, antitrust litigation, consolidation criteria, franchise taxes, and expropriation of assets by foreign governments. Professor Larson served on the Board of Directors and Executive Committee of Tekcon, Inc., and on the National Accountants Advisory Board of Safe-Guard Business Systems. In his leisure time, he enjoys skiing and is an avid sailor and golfer.

**Barbara Chiappetta** received her BBA in Accountancy and MS in Education from Hofstra University and is a tenured full professor at Nassau Community College. For the past 17 years, she has been an active executive board member of the Teachers of Accounting at Two-Year Colleges (TACTYC), serving 10 years as vice president and as president from 1993 through 1999. As an active member of the American Accounting Association, she has served on the Northeast Regional Steering Committee, chaired the Curriculum Revision Committee of the Two-Year Section, and participated in numerous national committees.

In 1998, Professor Chiappetta was inducted into the American Accounting Association Hall of Fame for the Northeast Region. She received the Nassau Community College dean of instruction's Faculty Distinguished Achievement Award in 1995. Professor Chiappetta was honored with the State University of New York Chancellor's Award for Teaching Excellence in 1997. As a confirmed believer in the benefits of active learning pedagogy, Professor Chiappetta has authored Student Learning Tools, an active learning workbook for a first-year accounting course, published by McGraw-Hill/Irwin.

In her leisure time, Professor Chiappetta enjoys tennis and participates on a U.S.T.A. team. She also enjoys the challenge of bridge. Her husband, Robert, is an entrepreneur in the leisure sport industry. She has two sons—Michael, a lawyer, specializing in intellectual property law in New York, and David, a composer, pursuing a career in music for film in Los Angeles.

# Financial and Managerial Accounting , Information for Decisions

The financial and managerial accounting courses are crucial for accounting majors and non-majors alike. They are courses that quickly immerse the student in unfamiliar and challenging new concepts and procedures.

Much of your students' future success in both accounting and business is determined by their experiences in the financial and managerial accounting courses. Will your students struggle with this new material? Or will they understand that accounting is a vital discipline relevant to any career, and use that knowledge to achieve new heights of success in business and in their lives?

*Financial and Managerial Accounting: Information for Decisions* presents accounting concepts as key tools that anyone can learn and successfully use. This textbook supplements that focus with additional attention into three areas: **student engagement**, **technology**, and **decision-making**. In sum, *Financial and Managerial Accounting: Information for Decisions* portrays accounting as it truly is — a language of business communication that is crucial to student success.

# New heights in student engagement

Instructors repeatedly raise a common concern: the biggest hurdle they face is getting students interested and motivated in the materials. *Financial and Managerial Accounting* provides solutions. It is more engaging and student-friendly than any competing book, from the book's eye-catching design to its comprehensive and stimulating end-of-chapter material. Each new book includes the actual shareholders' report from Krispy Kreme Doughnuts, which gets real financial data in students' hands. Moreover, engaging chapter-opening vignettes focus on small businesses and entrepreneurs to show how accounting knowledge is a springboard to success.

> "[A feature I like best about this book] is the tie-in to real world situations that are done in every chapter throughout the book."
> — **Jan Mardon, Green River Community College**

# New heights in technology

Compare our technology assets against those of any book, and we're confident you'll agree: *Financial and Managerial Accounting's* technology is, hands-down, the best in the market.

- **Carol Yachts General Ledger and Peachtree Complete Accounting**
- **ALEKS for Financial Accounting and ALEKS for the Accounting Cycle**
- **Mcgraw-Hill's Homework Manager**
- **Topic Tackler**
- **Online Learning Center**
- **Interactive Quizzes**

To learn more about these and other technology enhancements, see page xii.

# New heights in decision-making

*Financial and Managerial Accounting's* Decision Center is a pedagogical tool exclusive to this book. It provides students with a framework enabling them to better understand why and how businesses make strategic decisions with accounting information. Decision icons also make it easy for students to locate relevant material within the chapter, whether a boxed item or end-of-chapter material.

By addressing students in language that speaks to them, by providing your class with market-leading technology support, and by ensuring the textbook package is strong in the areas you rely on most, *Financial and Managerial Accounting: Information for Decisions* helps you *achieve new heights of success* in the classroom—and beyond.

# What are the pedagogical tools for success in learning accounting?

## Decision Center

Whether we prepare, analyze, or apply accounting information, one skill remains essential: decision-making. To help develop good decision-making habits and to illustrate the relevance of accounting, *Financial and Managerial Accounting: Information for Decisions* uses a unique pedagogical framework called the Decision Center. This framework is comprised of a variety of approaches and subject areas, giving students insight into every aspect of business decision-making. Answers to Decision Maker and Decision Ethics boxes are at the end of each chapter.

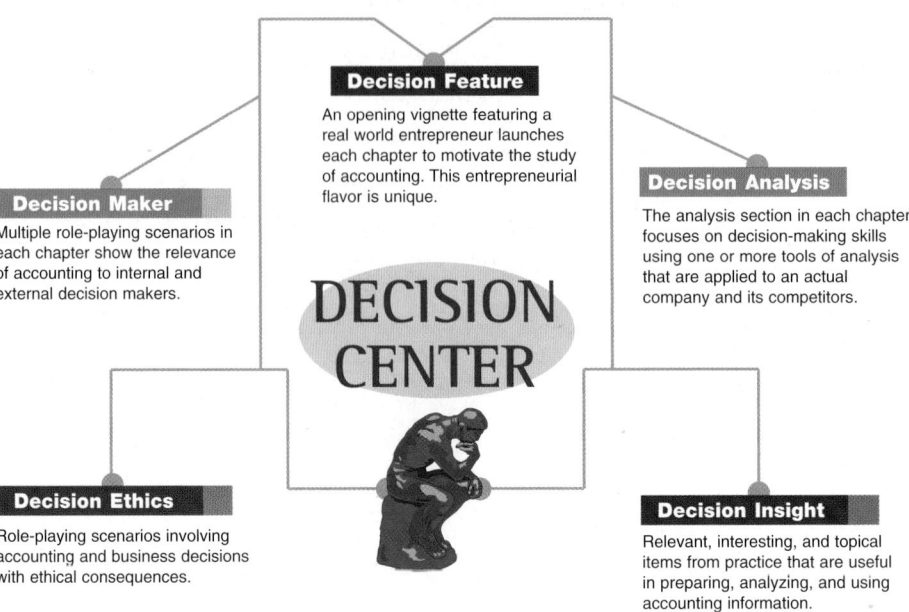

**Decision Feature**

An opening vignette featuring a real world entrepreneur launches each chapter to motivate the study of accounting. This entrepreneurial flavor is unique.

**Decision Maker**

Multiple role-playing scenarios in each chapter show the relevance of accounting to internal and external decision makers.

**Decision Analysis**

The analysis section in each chapter focuses on decision-making skills using one or more tools of analysis that are applied to an actual company and its competitors.

**Decision Ethics**

Role-playing scenarios involving accounting and business decisions with ethical consequences.

**Decision Insight**

Relevant, interesting, and topical items from practice that are useful in preparing, analyzing, and using accounting information.

---

"The Decision sidebars are one of the particular strengths of the text. They help the student stop and think about what he or she has read or can be used by the professor to stimulate discussion when introducing a topic. They are excellent tools!"
— **M. Conway, Kingsborough Community College**

---

## CAP Model

The Conceptual/Analytical/Procedural (CAP) Model allows courses to be specially designed to meet your teaching needs or those of a diverse faculty. This model identifies learning objectives, textual materials, assignments, and test items by C, A, or P. This allows different instructors to teach from the same materials, yet easily customize their courses toward a conceptual, analytical, or procedural approach (or a combination thereof) based on personal preferences.

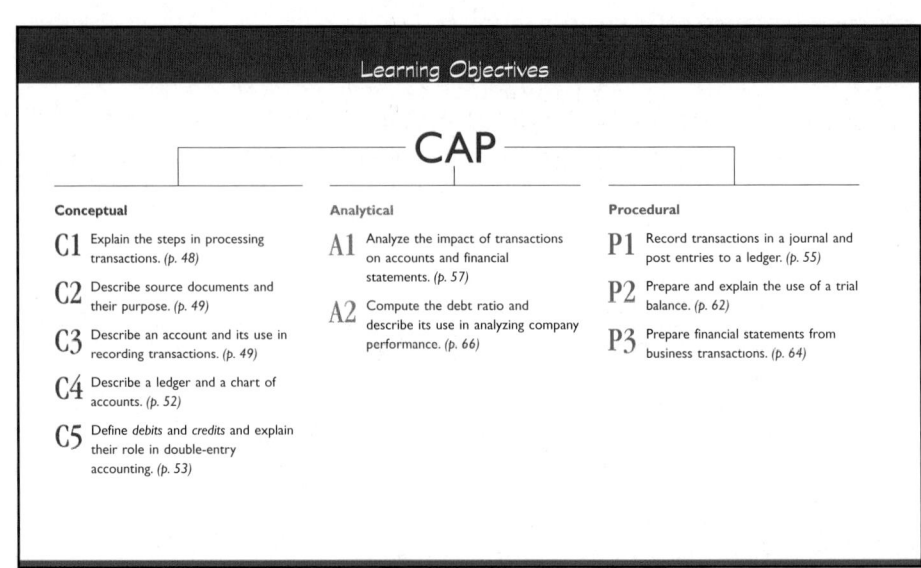

Learning Objectives

### CAP

**Conceptual**

C1 Explain the steps in processing transactions. *(p. 48)*

C2 Describe source documents and their purpose. *(p. 49)*

C3 Describe an account and its use in recording transactions. *(p. 49)*

C4 Describe a ledger and a chart of accounts. *(p. 52)*

C5 Define *debits* and *credits* and explain their role in double-entry accounting. *(p. 53)*

**Analytical**

A1 Analyze the impact of transactions on accounts and financial statements. *(p. 57)*

A2 Compute the debt ratio and describe its use in analyzing company performance. *(p. 66)*

**Procedural**

P1 Record transactions in a journal and post entries to a ledger. *(p. 55)*

P2 Prepare and explain the use of a trial balance. *(p. 62)*

P3 Prepare financial statements from business transactions. *(p. 64)*

# Chapter Preview with Flow Chart

This feature provides a handy textual/visual guide at the start of each chapter. Students can now begin their reading with a clear understanding of what they will learn and when, which allows them to stay more focused and organized along the way.

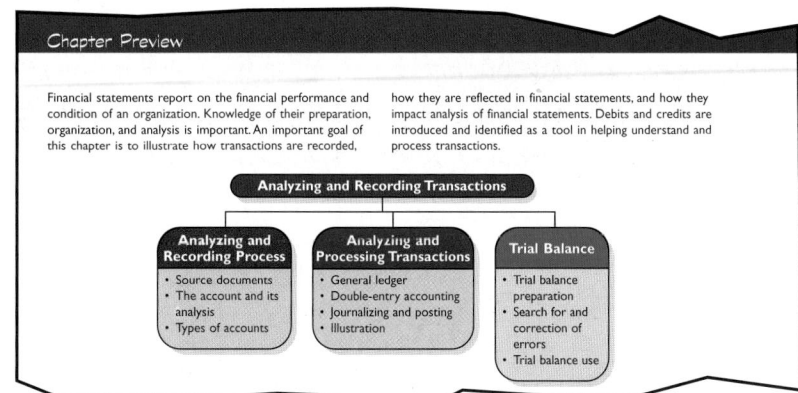

# Quick Check

These short question/answer features reinforce the material immediately preceding them. They allow the reader to pause and reflect on the topics described, then receive immediate feedback before going on to new topics. Answers are provided at the end of each chapter.

### Quick Check

8. What types of transactions increase equity? What types decrease equity?
9. Why are accounting systems called *double entry*?
10. For each transaction, double-entry accounting requires which of the following: (*a*) Debits to asset accounts must create credits to liability or equity accounts, (*b*) a debit to a liability account must create a credit to an asset account, or (*c*) total debits must equal total credits.
11. An owner invests $15,000 cash along with equipment having a market value of $23,000 in a company in exchange for common stock. Prepare the necessary journal entry.
12. Explain what a compound journal entry is.
13. Why are posting reference numbers entered in the journal when entries are posted to ledger accounts?

Answers—p. 72

# FastForward

FastForward is a case that takes students through the Accounting Cycle, chapters 1-3. The FastForward icon is placed in the margin at key points when this case is discussed.

# Marginal Student Annotations

These annotations provide students with additional hints, tips, and examples to help them more fully understand the concepts and retain what they have learned. The annotations also include notes on global implications of accounting and further examples.

cord for each customer, but for now, we and decreases in receivables in a single

itten promise of another entity to pay a the holder of the note. A company hold- s an asset that is recorded in a Note (or

are assets that represent prepayments of expenses are later incurred, the amounts ccounts. Common examples of prepaid

**Point:** A college parking fee is a prepaid account from the student's standpoint. At the beginning of the term, it represents an asset that entitles a student to park on or near campus. The benefits of the parking fee expire as the term progresses. At term-end, prepaid parking (asset) equals zero as it has been entirely recorded as parking expense.

# How are chapter concepts reinforced and mastered?

*Once a student has finished reading the chapter, how well he or she retains the material can depend greatly on the questions, exercises, and problems that reinforce it. This book leads the way in comprehensive, accurate end-of-chapter assignments.*

## Demonstration Problems

present both a problem and a complete solution, allowing students to review the entire problem-solving process and achieve success.

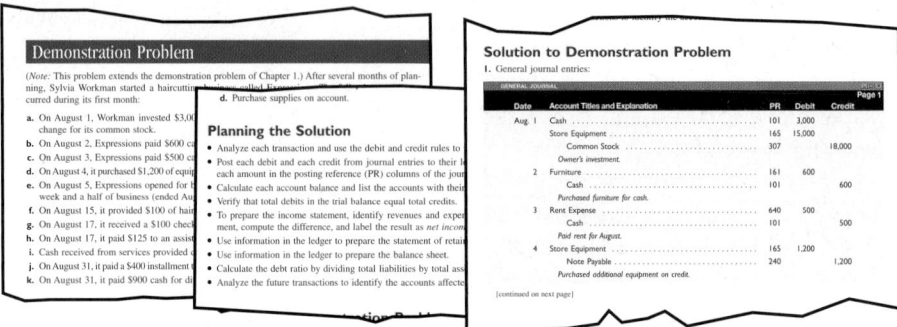

## Chapter Summaries

provide students with a review organized by learning objectives. Chapter Summaries are a component of the CAP model (see page viii), and they recap each conceptual, analytical, and procedural objective.

## Key Terms

are bolded in the text and repeated at the end of the chapter with page numbers indicating their location. The book also includes a complete Glossary of key terms. Key Terms are also available as online flash cards at the book's Website.

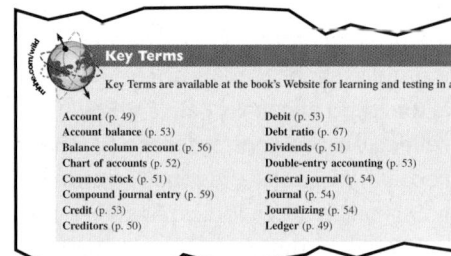

## Quick Study

assignments are short exercises that often focus on one learning objective. All are also included in Homework Manager. There are usually 8-10 Quick Study assignments per chapter.

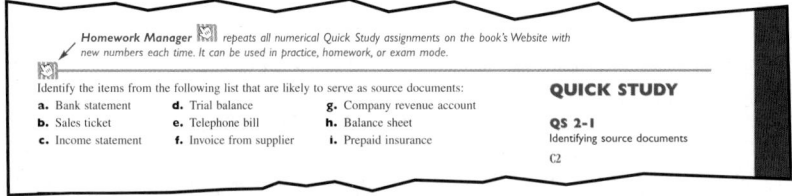

## Exercises

are one of this book's many strengths and a competitive advantage. There are about 10-15 per chapter and all are included in Homework Manager.

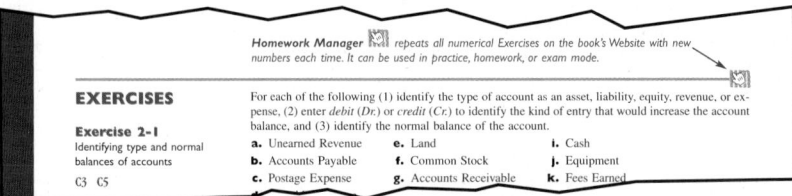

## Problem Sets A, B & C

are proven problems that can be assigned as homework or for in-class projects. Problem Set C is available on the book's Website. All problems are coded according to the CAP model (see page viii), and all are included in Homework Manager.

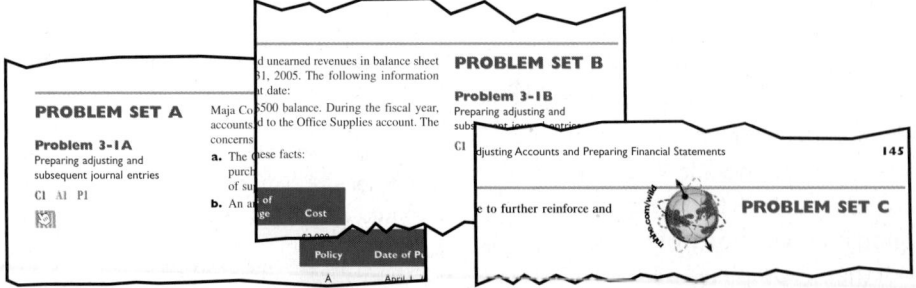

## Beyond the Numbers

**Beyond the Numbers** exercises ask students to use accounting figures and understand their meaning. Students also learn how accounting applies to a variety of business situations. These creative and fun exercises are divided into 10 sections:

- Reporting in Action
- Comparative Analysis
- Ethics Challenge
- Communicating in Practice
- Taking It to The Net

- Teamwork in Action
- Hitting the Road
- Business Week Activity
- Entrepreneurial Decision
- Global Decision

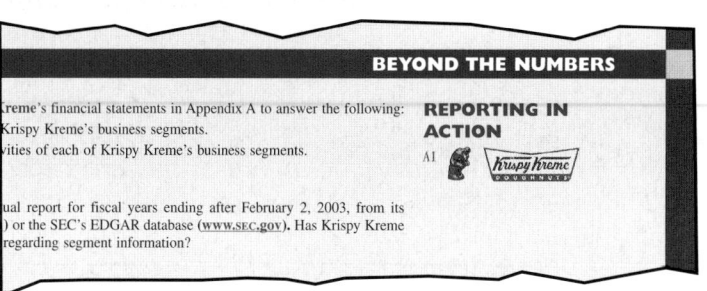

**BEYOND THE NUMBERS**

Kreme's financial statements in Appendix A to answer the following:
Krispy Kreme's business segments.
vities of each of Krispy Kreme's business segments.

**REPORTING IN ACTION**

A1

ual report for fiscal years ending after February 2, 2003, from its ) or the SEC's EDGAR database (www.sec.gov). Has Krispy Kreme regarding segment information?

## Serial Problems

**Serial Problems** use a continuous running case study to illustrate chapter concepts in a familiar context. Serial Problems can be followed continuously from the first chapter or picked up at any later point in the book; enough information is provided to ensure students can get right to work.

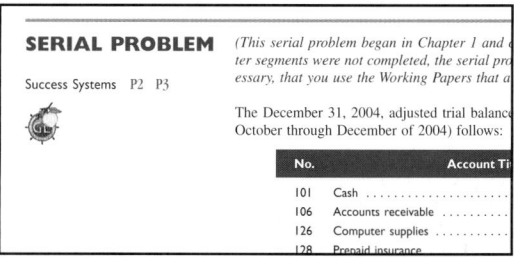

**SERIAL PROBLEM**

Success Systems   P2  P3

*(This serial problem began in Chapter 1 and ter segments were not completed, the serial pr essary, that you use the Working Papers that a*

The December 31, 2004, adjusted trial balance October through December of 2004) follows:

| No. | Account Ti |
| --- | --- |
| 101 | Cash . . . . . . . . . . . . . . . . . . . . |
| 106 | Accounts receivable . . . . . . . . . |
| 126 | Computer supplies . . . . . . . . . . |
| 128 | Prepaid insurance |

> "I like the Beyond the Numbers because it gives an instructor options. For example, in certain chapters you could assign the Ethics Challenge, or Taking It To The Net. This would give students exposure without overwhelming them."
>
> — **Dawn McKinley, William Rainey Harper College**

## The End of the Chapter Is Only the Beginning

Our valuable and proven assignments aren't just confined to the book. From problems that require field visits to materials found exclusively online, this book's end-of-chapter material is fully integrated with its technology package.

- Quick Studies, Exercises, and Problems available on Homework Manager (see page xii) are marked with an icon.

- Problems supported by the all-new General Ledger Application Software or Peachtree are marked with an icon.

- The Online Learning Center (OLC) includes more Taking It To The Net exercises, Personal Interactive Quizzes, more Excel template assignments, and Problem Set C

eXcel

mhhe.com/wild

- Problems supported with Microsoft Excel templates are marked with an icon.

- Material that receives additional coverage (slide shows, videos, audio, etc.) in Topic Tackler is marked with an icon.

### Put Away Your Red Pen

We pride ourselves on the accuracy of this book's assignment materials. Independent research reports that instructors and reviewers point to the accuracy of this book's assignment materials as one of its key competitive advantages.

The authors extend a special thanks to accuracy checkers **Marc Giullian**, Montana State University - Bozeman; **Suzanne King**, University of Charleston; **Barbara Schnathorst**, The Write Solution, Inc.; and **Jo Lynne Koehn**, Central Missouri State University.

# How does technology assist students in assessment and learning?

*In teaching and learning accounting, the book itself is only the beginning. Our comprehensive technology package provides ample opportunity for both assessment and reinforcement, while offering valuable practice in learning and using digital tools in the modern accounting and business workplace.*

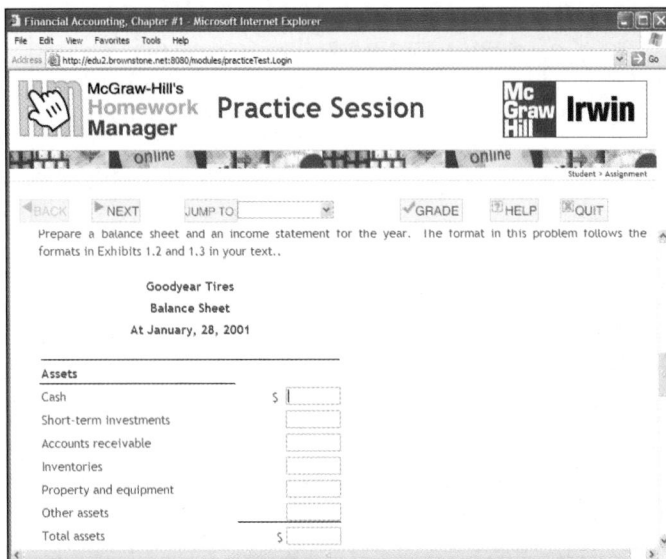

## McGraw-Hill's Homework Manager

This Web-based study and review aid uses a sophisticated algorithm to generate "look-a-like" versions of this book's assignment materials. These exercises and problems contain identical or different values (instructor's choice) to those in the book, allowing students to practice and refine their skills. The algorithm can generate infinite variations of any selected assignments.

Instructors can use Homework Manager to build custom homework assignments, test, or quizzes that can be completed either online or with pencil and paper. Student answers are graded automatically and the results stored in a secure online gradebook. Tests and quizzes prepared from Homework Manager overcome any inconsistencies between the "test bank" and the language and approach in the book — now there is complete consistency!

Homework Manager gives you:

- Textbook quick studies, exercises, and problems in electronic format
- Automatic grading and analysis for instructors (no more collecting homework!)
- Immediate feedback for students <u>and</u> instructors
- Algorithmic-generated quick studies, exercises, and problems
- Instructor course management tools
- 100% consistency in language between test problems and the textbook

 Quick Studies, Exercises, and Problems appearing in the book are reproduced in Homework Manager and often are marked with an icon.

## ALEKS® for the Accounting Cycle and ALEKS® for Financial Accounting

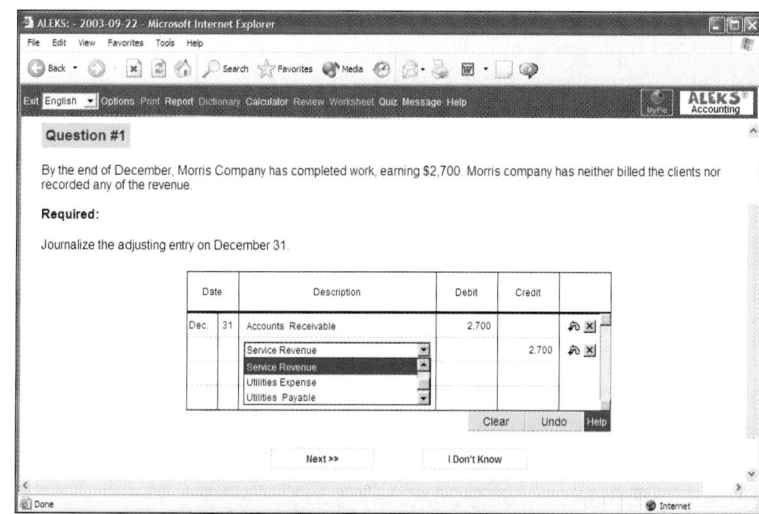

Available from McGraw-Hill over the World Wide Web, ALEKS (Assessment and LEarning in Knowledge Spaces) provides precise assessment and individualized instruction in the fundamental skills your students need to succeed in accounting.

ALEKS motivates your students because ALEKS can tell what a student knows, doesn't know, and is most ready to learn next. ALEKS does this using the ALEKS Assessment and Knowledge Space Theory as an artificial intelligence engine to exactly identify a student's knowledge of accounting. When students focus on precisely what they are ready to learn, they build the confidence and learning momentum that fuel success.

To learn more about adding ALEKS to your accounting course, visit www.business.aleks.com.

## GradeSummit

The online resource GradeSummit tells your students everything they need to know to study effectively. GradeSummit provides a series of practice tests written to coincide with this book's coverage. Once a student has taken a particular test, GradeSummit returns a detailed results page showing exactly where the student did well and where he or she needs to improve. They can compare their results with those of other classmates, or even with those students using the book nationwide.

With that information, students can plan their studying to focus exclusively on their weak areas, without wasting effort on material they've already mastered. And they can come back to take a retest on those subjects later, comparing their new score with their previous efforts.

## Carol Yacht's General Ledger and Peachtree Complete 2004 CD-ROM

Carol Yacht's General Ledger Software is McGraw-Hill/Irwin's custom-built general ledger package for this book. Carol Yacht's General Ledger can help your students master every aspect of the general ledger, from inputting sales and cash receipts to calculating ratios for analysis and computing inventory valuations.

Carol Yacht's General Ledger allows students to review an entire report, and then double-click on any single transaction to review or edit it. All reports immediately reflect the revised figures. When it comes to learning how an individual transaction impacts financial statements no other approach matches that of Carol Yacht's General Ledger.

Also on Carol Yacht's General Ledger CD, students receive the educational version of Peachtree Complete 2004, along with templates containing data for many of this book's exercises and problems. Familiarity with Peachtree Complete is essential for many students entering the job market, and Carol Yacht's Peachtree templates ensure they get plenty of practice.

Students can use Carol Yacht's General Ledger to solve numerous problems from the book; the data for these problems are already included on the General Ledger CD-ROM. You can even populate the General Ledger with your own custom data for your class.

## Online Learning Center (OLC) with PowerWeb
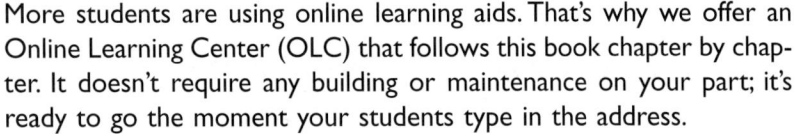
www.mhhe.com/wild

More students are using online learning aids. That's why we offer an Online Learning Center (OLC) that follows this book chapter by chapter. It doesn't require any building or maintenance on your part; it's ready to go the moment your students type in the address.

As your students study and learn from this book, they can visit the OLC Website and work with a multitude of helpful tools that include:

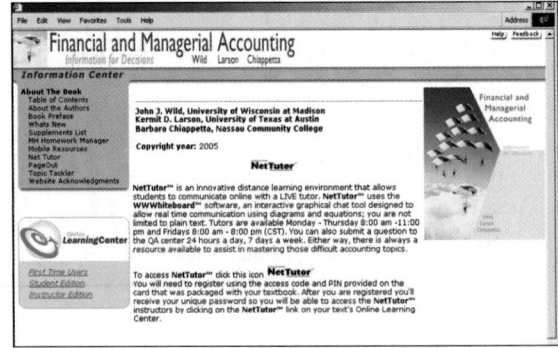

- Tutorial
- Glossary
- NetTutor
- PowerWeb
- Chapter Objectives
- Chapter Overview
- Text Company Links
- Interactive Quizzes A&B
- Key Term Flashcards
- PowerPoint Presentation
- Additional appendices
- Cogg Hill Practice Set
- Updates
- Mobile Resources

- Audio Narrated PowerPoint
- Excel Template Assignments
- More *Taking It To The Net*
- Problem Set C
- *BusinessWeek* Articles

A secured Instructor Resource Center stores your essential course materials to save you prep time before class. Everything you need to run a lively classroom and an efficient course is included:

- Sample Syllabi
- Additional chapter materials
- Transition Notes
- Instructor Manual
- Solutions to Excel Template Assignments
- Cogg Hill Solutions Manual
- Updates

- Solutions Manual
- PowerPoint Presentations
- Textbook Company Links
- More *Taking It To The Net* Solutions
- *BusinessWeek* Articles
- Problem Set C Solutions

## Topic Tackler—<u>FREE</u> with new book

This software is a complete tutorial focusing on those areas in financial and managerial accounting that give students the most trouble. Providing help on at least 2 key topics per chapter, this program delves into the material using the following learning aids:

- Video clips
- PowerPoint slide-shows (many include animations)
- Drag-and-drop, fill-in-the-blank exercises
- Self-test quizzes

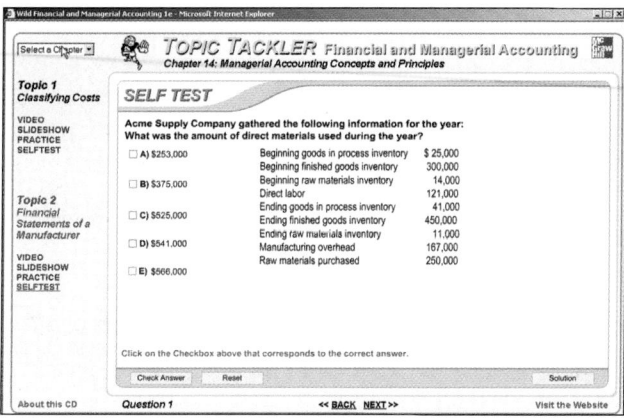

This highly engaging presentation will put your students in control of the most fundamental aspects of financial and managerial accounting.

Concepts appearing in this book that receive additional treatment in Topic Tackler are marked with an icon at the appropriate location in the margin of the page.

## Net Tutor™

### NetTutor

NetTutor allows tutors and students to communicate with each other in a variety of ways:

- The Live Tutor Center via NetTutor's WWWhiteboard enables a tutor to hold an interactive on-line tutorial with several students, whose questions are placed in a queue and answered sequentially.

- The Q&A Center allows students to submit questions at any time and retrieve answers within 24 hours.

- The Archive Center allows students to browse for answers to previously asked questions. They can also search for questions pertinent to a particular topic. If they encounter an answer they do not understand, they can ask a follow-up question.

Students are issued 5 hours of <u>free</u> NetTutor time when they purchase a new copy of this book. Additional time can be purchased in 5-hour increments.

**PowerWeb** provides high quality, peer-reviewed content including up-to-date articles from leading periodicals and journals, current news, weekly updates with assessment, interactive exercises, Web research guide, study tips, and much more. PowerWeb is <u>free</u> with your adoption of this book.

*In today's learning environment, a computer is as indispensible a tool as a blackboard or an overhead projector. McGraw-Hill/Irwin continues to lead in innovative classroom technology, and this book's teaching tools put it far ahead of any book.*

# Course Management

## PageOut
## McGraw-Hill's Course Management System

PageOut is the easiest way to create a Website for your accounting course.

There's no need for HTML coding, graphic design, or a thick how-to book. Just fill in a series of boxes with plain English and click on one of our professional designs. In no time, your course is online with a Website that contains your syllabus!

Should you need assistance in preparing your Website, we can help you. Our team of specialists is ready to take your course materials and build a custom Website to your specifications. Simply call a McGraw-Hill/Irwin PageOut specialist to start the process. (For information on how to do this, see "Superior Service" on page xvii.) Best of all, PageOut is <u>free</u> when you adopt this book! To learn more, please visit www.pageout.net.

## Third-Party Course Management Systems

For the ambitious instructor, we offer this book's content for complete online courses. To make this possible, we have joined forces with the most popular delivery platforms currently available. These platforms are designed for instructors who want complete control over course content and how it is presented to students. You can customize the book's Online Learning Center content and author your own course materials. It's entirely up to you.

Products like WebCT, Blackboard, and eCollege all expand the reach of your course. Online discussion and message boards will now complement your office hours. Thanks to a sophisticated tracking system, you will know which students need more attention – even if they don't ask for help. That's because online testing scores are recorded and automatically placed in your grade book, and if a student is struggling with coursework, a special alert message lets you know.

Remember, this book's content is flexible enough to use with any platform currently available. If your department or school is already using a platform, we can help. For information on McGraw-Hill/Irwin's course management supplements, including Instructor Advantage and Knowledge Gateway, see "Superior Service" on the next page.

**WebCT**

**Bb**
Blackboard
www.blackboard.com

# Superior Service

No matter which online course solution you choose, you can count on the highest level of service. That's what sets McGraw-Hill apart. Once you choose this book, our specialists offer free training and will answer any question you have through the life of your adoption.

## Instructor Advantage and Instructor Advantage Plus

**Instructor Advantage** is a special level of service McGraw-Hill offers in conjunction with WebCT and Blackboard. A team of platform specialists is always available, either by toll-free phone or e-mail, to ensure everything runs smoothly through the life of your adoption. Instructor Advantage is available <u>free</u> to all McGraw-Hill customers.

**Instructor Advantage Plus** is available to qualifying McGraw-Hill adopters (see your representative for details). **IA Plus** guarantees you a full day of on-site training by a Blackboard or WebCT specialist, for yourself and up to nine colleagues. Thereafter, you will enjoy the benefits of unlimited telephone and e-mail support throughout the life of your adoption. **IA Plus** users also have the opportunity to access the **McGraw-Hill Knowledge Gateway**.

## Knowledge Gateway

Developed with the help of our partner Eduprise, the McGraw-Hill Knowledge Gateway is an all-purpose service and resource center for instructors teaching online from this book.

The First Level of **Knowledge Gateway** is available to all professors browsing the McGraw-Hill Higher Education Website, and consists of an introduction to OLC content, access to the first level of the Resource Library, technical support, and information on Instructional Design Services available through Eduprise.

The Second Level is password-protected and provides access to the expanded Resource Library, technical and pedagogical support for WebCT, Blackboard, and TopClass, the online Instructional Design helpdesk and an online discussion forum. The **Knowledge Gateway** provides a considerable advantage for teaching online—and it's only available through McGraw-Hill.

To see how these platforms can assist your online accounting course, visit www.mhhe.com/solutions.

## Instructor's Resource CD-ROM

*ISBN: 0073044458*

This is your all-in-one resource. It allows you to create custom presentations from your own materials or from the following text-specific materials provided in the CD's asset library:

- Instructor's Resource Manual
- Solutions Manual
- Test Bank, Computerized Test Bank
- PowerPoint® Presentations Prepared by Jon A. Booker, Charles W. Caldwell, and Susan C. Galbreath. Presentations allow for revision of lecture slides, and includes a viewer, allowing screens to be shown with or without the software.
- Excel Template Assignments
- Link to PageOut
- Video Clips

## Instructor's Resource Manual

*ISBN: 0073044407*

*Written by Jeannie Folk, College of DuPage, and Barbara Chiappetta, Nassau Community College.*

This manual contains (for each chapter) a Lecture Outline, a chart linking all assignment materials to Learning Objectives, a list of relevant active learning activities, and additional visuals with transparency masters. An electronic version is available on the Website and on the Instructor's Resource CD-ROM.

## Solutions Manual

*ISBN: 0073044415*

*Written by John J. Wild and Jo Lynne Koehn.*

## Test Bank

*ISBN: 0073044423*

*Written by Marilyn Sagrillo and John J. Wild.*

## Brownstone Diploma 6.2 Computerized Test Bank

*Available for Windows only, located on the Instructor's Resource CD-ROM.*

## Financial and Managerial Accounting Video Library

*Financial Videos: 0072376163*

*Managerial Videos: 0072376171*

These short, action-oriented videos, developed by Dallas County Community College for the Accounting in Action distance-learning course, provide an impetus for lively classroom discussion. Tied closely to this book's pedagogical framework, these videos avoid dry talking-head footage in favor of dynamic, documentary-style explorations of how businesses use accounting information.

## Topic Tackler
### (free with new books)

*Prepared by Jeannie Folk, College of DuPage, and Joan Cook and Laura Ruff, Milwaukee Area Technical College.*

See page xv for complete description.

## Carol Yacht's General Ledger & Peachtree Complete 2004 CD-ROM

*ISBN: 007304959X*

*GL Software developed by Jack E. Terry, ComSource Associates, Inc.*

*Peachtree templates prepared by Carol Yacht.*

The CD-ROM includes fully functioning versions of McGraw-Hill's own General Ledger Application software as well as Peachtree Complete 2004. Problem templates are included that allow you to assign text problems for working in either Yacht's General Ledger or Peachtree Complete 2004.

## Study Guide

*ISBN: 007304444X*

*Prepared by Jeannie Folk, College of DuPage, and Barbara Chiappetta, Nassau Community College.*

Covers each chapter and appendix with reviews of the learning objectives, outlines of the chapters, summaries of chapter materials, and additional problems with solutions.

Special thanks to **Joan Cook** and **Laura Ruff**, *Milwaukee Area Technical College,* for their efforts in revising the Topic Tackler CD-ROM, and to **Janice Klimek**, *Central Missouri State University,* for accuracy checking Topic Tackler.

## Working Papers

*ISBN: 0073044431*

*Written by John J. Wild.*

Working Papers are available to help direct students in solving all assignments. Each chapter also contains one set of papers that can be used for either the A or B series of problems.

## Excel Working Papers

*ISBN: 0073044482*

*Written by John J. Wild.*

Working Papers delivered in Excel spreadsheets. Excel Working Papers are available on CD-ROM and can be bundled with or without the printed Working Papers; see your representative for information.

# Acknowledgements

The authors and McGraw-Hill/Irwin would like to recognize the following instructors for their valuable feedback and involvement in the development of *Financial and Managerial Accounting: Information for Decisions*. We are thankful for their suggestions, counsel, and encouragement.

**Survey Participants:**

Christopher Brandon, Indiana University-Purdue University Columbus

Kim Tarantino, California State University–Fullerton

Brandi Roberts, Southeastern Louisiana University

Angelo Luciano, Columbia College–Chicago

Kathy Horton, College of DuPage

Jeff Ritter, St. Norbert College

Lois Mahoney, University of Central Florida

Florence McGovern, Bergen Community College

Sheri Henson, Western Kentucky University

David P. Weiner, University of San Francisco

Catherine Collins, Waubonsee Community College

John Karayan, California State Polytechnic University–Pomona

Leon J. Hanouille, Syracuse University

Pamela Stuerke, Case Western Reserve

Linda Christiansen, Indiana University–Southeast

Carolyn Jean Craig, Ivy Tech State College

Linda Benz, Jefferson Community College

Angela Sandberg, Jacksonville State University

Jeffry Haber, Iona College

John Rossi, Moravian College

Talitha Smith, Auburn University

Ronald Halsac, Community College of Alegheny City

Bruce Oliver, Rochester Institute of Technology

Joseph Morris, Southeastern Louisiana University

Margaret O'Reilly-Allen, Rider University

Lawrence Roman, Cuyahoga Community College

S. Murray Simons, Mount Ida College

Marguerite Savage, Elgin Community College

Kathleen A. Simons, Bryant College

Ernest Marquez, Columbia College–Jacksonville

Kay Carnes, Gonzaga University

Rafik Z. Elias, Cameron University

Dawn Hukai, University of Wisconsin –River Falls

Steven Lafave, Augsburg College

Ed Blocher, University of North Carolina–Chapel Hill

Daniel Gibbons, Columbia College–Crystal Lake

Jan Mardon, Green River Community College

Myra Bruegger, Southeastern Community College

Donald Boone, Lebanon Valley College

Staci Kolb, Samford University

Meg Pollard, American River College–Los Rios

Bill Alexander, Indian Hills Community College

**Focus Group Participants:**

Elaine Eikner, Southwest Texas State University

Paul Jep Robertson, New Mexico State University

Angelo Luciano, Columbia College–Chicago

David Weiner, University of San Francisco

Debra Prendergast, Northwestern Business College

John D. Rossi, Moravian College

**Review Participants:**

Linda Kropp, Modesto Junior College

Philip Stickney, Conchise College

Jan Mardon, Green River Community College

Peter Margaritas, Franklin University

John Roberts, St. John's River Community College

Pat Bouker, North Seattle Community College

Chris Bjornson, Indiana University Southeast

Scott Steinkamp, College of Lake County (IL)

Dawn McKinley, William Rainey Harper College

Laura D. Delaune, Louisiana State University

Janice R. Holmes, Louisiana State University

**Jo Lynne Koehn** received her Ph.D. and Master's of Accountancy from the University of Wisconsin at Madison and is an associate professor at Central Missouri State University. Her scholarly articles have been published in a variety of journals including Issues in Accounting Education, The CPA Journal, The Tax Advisor, and Accounting Enquiries. Professor Koehn is a member of the American Accounting Association and the American Institute of CPAs. She also holds a Certified Financial Planning license and is active in promoting a financial planning curriculum at Central Missouri State University.

**Jeannie M. Folk** teaches financial and managerial accounting at the College of DuPage and mentors accounting students working in cooperative education positions. In addition, she is active in the area of online, distance education. Professor Folk serves on the board of directors and the Scholarship Committee of TACTYC (Teachers of Accounting at Two-Year Colleges) as well as the Illinois CPA Society's Outstanding Educator Award Committee. She is also a member of the American Accounting Association and the American Institute of Certified Public Accountants. She was honored with the Illinois CPA Society's Outstanding Educator Award and was a recipient of the Women in Management, Inc., Charlotte Danstrom Woman of Achievement Award. Before entering academe, Professor Folk was a general practice auditor with Coopers & Lybrand (now PriceWaterhouseCoopers). She received her BBA from Loyola University Chicago and MAS in Accountancy from Northern Illinois University. Professor Folk enjoys travel, camping, hiking, and community activities with her three children.

**Carol Yacht** is a textbook author and educator with a teaching career spanning more than three decades. Carol has taught at Yavapai College; West Los Angeles Community College; California State University, L.A.; and Beverly Hills High School and Adult School. She has worked for IBM Corporation as an educational instruction specialist and currently serves on the Computer Education Task Force for the National Business Education Association. Carol is a frequent speaker at state, regional, and national conventions; teaches school consortium meetings; and is active in Department of Education conferences. Carol earned her AS degree from Temple University, BS degree from the University of New Mexico, and MA degree from California State University, L.A.

---

In addition to the helpful and generous colleagues listed above, we thank the entire McGraw-Hill/Irwin Financial and Managerial Accounting team, including Brent Gordon, Stewart Mattson, Steve Schuetz, Kelly Odom, Lori Koetters, Matthew Baldwin, Michael McCormick, Becky Szura, and Edward Przyzycki. We also thank the great marketing and sales support staff, including Rich Kolasa and Jackie Powers. Many talented educators and professionals worked hard to create the supplements for this book, and for their efforts we're grateful. Finally, many more people we either did not meet or whose efforts we did not personally witness nevertheless helped to make this book everything that it is, and we thank them all.

John J. Wild
Kermit D. Larson
Barbara Chiappetta

# Brief Contents

*Appendixes D & E are available on the book's Website, mhhe.com/wild, and as print copy from a McGraw-Hill representative.

# Contents

**9  Reporting and Analyzing
Current Liabilities 350**

**10  Reporting and
Analyzing
Long-Term
Liabilities 394**

*Appendixes D & E are available on the book's Website, <u>mhhe.com/wild</u>, and as print copy from a McGraw-Hill representative.

# Financial and Managerial Accounting
## Information
## for Decisions

Have You Had Your Chocolate Today?

*"Growing beyond the protected world of a "kid's" business required us to overcome many obstacles"*—Elise and Evan Macmillan

# 1 Introducing Accounting in Business

## A Look at This Chapter

Accounting plays a crucial role in the information age. In this chapter, we discuss the importance of accounting to different types of organizations and describe its many users and uses. We explain that ethics are crucial to accounting. We also describe business transactions and how they are reflected in financial statements.

## A Look Ahead

Chapter 2 further describes and analyzes business transactions. We explain the analysis and recording of transactions, the ledger and trial balance, and the double-entry system. More generally, Chapters 2 and 3 focus on accounting and analysis, and they illustrate (via the accounting cycle) how financial statements reflect business activities.

*Learning Objectives are organized by conceptual, analytical, and procedural.*

# CAP

## Conceptual

**C1** Explain the purpose and importance of accounting in the information age. *(p. 4)*

**C2** Identify users and uses of accounting. *(p. 5)*

**C3** Identify opportunities in accounting and related fields. *(p. 6)*

**C4** Explain why ethics are crucial to accounting. *(p. 8)*

**C5** Explain the meaning of generally accepted accounting principles, and define and apply several key principles of accounting. *(p. 9)*

## Analytical

**A1** Define and interpret the accounting equation and each of its components. *(p. 12)*

**A2** Analyze business transactions using the accounting equation. *(p. 13)*

**A3** Compute and interpret return on assets. *(p. 20)*

## Procedural

**P1** Identify and prepare basic financial statements and explain how they interrelate. *(p. 17)*

---

## Decision Feature

# Sweet Taste of Success

DENVER—Elise and Evan Macmillan—sister and brother entrepreneurs—aim to satisfy. "Our whole business is about customers," says Elise. These young entrepreneurs head **The Chocolate Farm (TheChocolateFarm.com),** which specializes in making chocolates and in helping their customers make them.

"We thought our business was going to be a one-day thing," says Elise, "but it turned into a real business." This meant Elise and Evan had to deal with issues such as organization form, accounting and information systems, transaction analysis, and financial reports. Adds Elise, "I'm kept busy with the company's future plans and new product ideas and everything else that there is to a company."

Special attention is directed at accounting information; because without income, The Chocolate Farm would be knee-deep in cocoa. Elise and Evan were able to set up a transaction-based accounting system to profitably handle customer sales and orders. They also used accounting information to make good business decisions. Relying on sales and expense information, Elise and Evan focused efforts on their best-sellers such as *Brown Cows, Mint Sheep Munch, Pecan Turtles,* and *Pigs in Mud.* Moreover, after an analysis of the accounting information, they decided to expand and now employ more than a dozen people.

Evan admits that even with the best accounting information, one must accept some risk. We "accept the fact that it's a risk," says Evan, but that's the reality of money making. Elise concurs, "I love chocolate, and so I'm having fun making money." The Farm now produces more than $1 million per year in revenues. We could all become chocolate-lovers with results like that!

[Sources: *Ernst & Young Website,* January 2004; *The Chocolate Farm Website,* January 2004; *Entrepreneur,* May 2002; *Denver Business Journal,* January 2002; *MarkED Website,* June 2003; *The Wall Street Journal,* March 2003.]

*A **Decision Feature** launches each chapter showing the relevance of accounting for a real entrepreneur. An **Entrepreneurial Decision** problem at the end of the assignments returns to this feature with a mini-case.*

*A **Preview** opens each chapter with a summary of topics covered.*

Today's world is one of information—its preparation, communication, analysis, and use. Accounting is at the heart of this information age. Knowledge of accounting gives us career opportunities and the insight to take advantage of them. By studying this book, you will learn about concepts, procedures, and analyses that will help you make better decisions throughout your life. In this chapter we describe accounting, the users and uses of accounting information, the forms and activities of organizations, and several accounting principles. We also introduce transaction analysis and financial statements.

**Introducing Accounting in Business**

| **Importance of Accounting** | **Fundamentals of Accounting** | **Transaction Analysis** | **Financial Statements** |
|---|---|---|---|
| • Accounting information users<br>• Opportunities in accounting | • Ethics—key concept<br>• Generally accepted accounting principles | • Accounting equation<br>• Transaction analysis—illustrated | • Income statement<br>• Statement of owner's equity<br>• Balance sheet<br>• Statement of cash flows |

# Importance of Accounting

**C1** Explain the purpose and importance of accounting in the information age.

We live in an information age—a time of communication and immediate access to data, news, facts, and commentary. Information affects how we live, whom we associate with, and the opportunities we have. To fully benefit from the available information, we need knowledge of the information system. An information system involves the collecting, processing, and reporting of information to decision makers.

Providing information about what businesses own, what they owe, and how they perform is an important aim of accounting. **Accounting** is an information and measurement system that identifies, records, and communicates relevant, reliable, and comparable information about an organization's business activities. *Identifying* business activities requires selecting transactions and events relevant to an organization. Examples are the sale of bicycles by **Cannondale** and the receipt of ticket money by **TicketMaster**. *Recording* business activities requires keeping a chronological log of transactions and events measured in dollars and classified and summarized in a useful format. *Communicating* business activities requires preparing accounting reports such as financial statements. It also requires analyzing and interpreting such reports. (The financial statements and notes of **Krispy Kreme** are shown in Appendix A of this book. This appendix also shows the financial statements of **Tastykake** and **Harley-Davidson**.) Exhibit 1.1 summarizes accounting activities.

We must guard against a narrow view of accounting. The most common contact with accounting is through credit approvals, checking accounts, tax forms, and payroll. These

## Exhibit 1.1

Accounting Activities

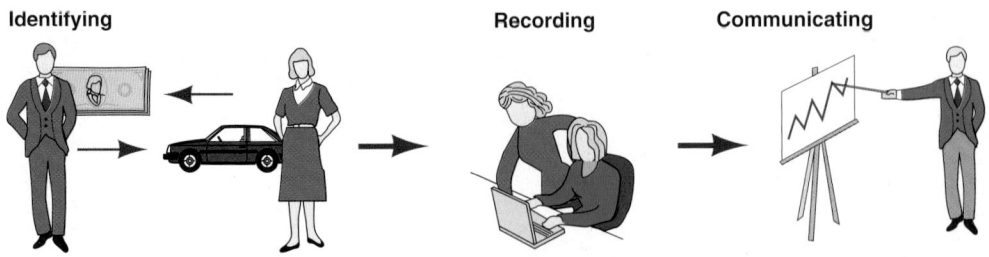

| Identifying | Recording | Communicating |
|---|---|---|
| Select transactions and events | Log, measure and classify | Prepare, analyze and interpret |

experiences are limited and tend to focus on the recordkeeping parts of accounting. **Recordkeeping,** or **bookkeeping,** is the recording of transactions and events, either manually or electronically. This is just one part of accounting. Accounting also identifies and communicates information on transactions and events, and it includes the crucial processes of analysis and interpretation.

*Margin notes further enhance the textual material.*

Technology is a key part of modern business and plays a major role in accounting. Technology reduces the time, effort, and cost of recordkeeping while improving clerical accuracy. Some small organizations continue to perform various accounting tasks manually, but even they are impacted by information technology. As technology has changed the way we store, process, and summarize masses of data, accounting has been freed to expand. Consulting, planning, and other financial services are now closely linked to accounting. These services require sorting through data, interpreting their meaning, identifying key factors, and analyzing their implications.

**Point:** Technology is only as useful as the accounting data available, and users' decisions are only as good as their understanding of accounting. The best software and recordkeeping cannot make up for lack of accounting knowledge.

## Users of Accounting Information

Accounting is often called the *language of business* because all organizations set up an accounting information system to communicate data to help people make better decisions. Exhibit 1.2 shows that the accounting information system serves many kinds of users who can be divided into two groups: external users and internal users.

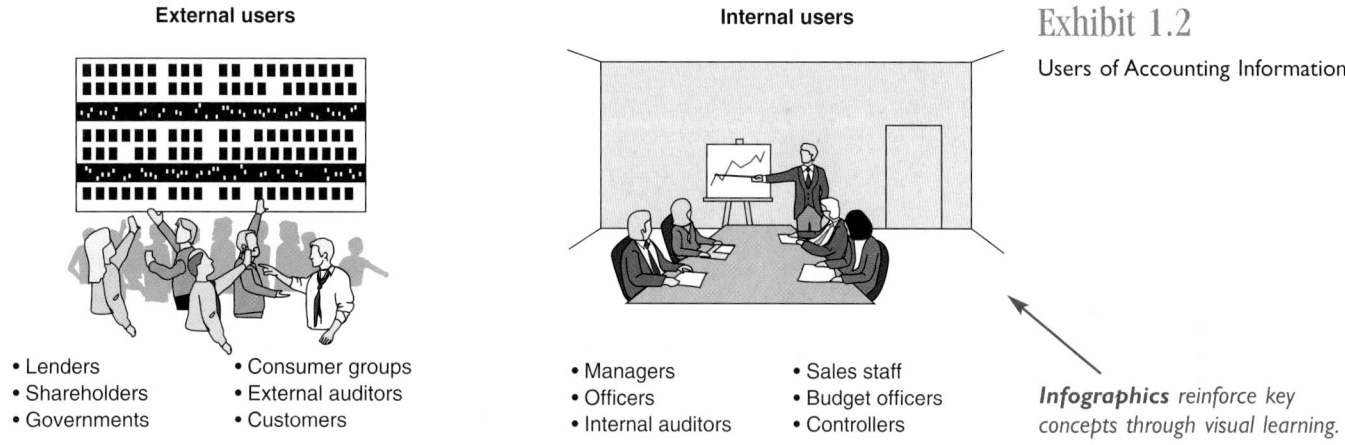

**External users**

- Lenders
- Shareholders
- Governments
- Consumer groups
- External auditors
- Customers

**Internal users**

- Managers
- Officers
- Internal auditors
- Sales staff
- Budget officers
- Controllers

Exhibit 1.2

Users of Accounting Information

*Infographics reinforce key concepts through visual learning.*

**External Information Users**  **External users** of accounting information are *not* directly involved in running the organization. They include shareholders (investors), lenders, directors, customers, suppliers, regulators, lawyers, brokers, and the press. External users have limited access to an organization's information. Yet many of their important decisions depend on information that is reliable, relevant, and comparable.

**C2**  Identify users and uses of accounting.

**Financial accounting** is the area of accounting aimed at serving external users by providing them with financial statements. These statements are known as *general-purpose financial statements.* The term *general-purpose* refers to the broad range of purposes for which external users rely on these statements.

Each external user has special information needs depending on the types of decisions to be made. *Lenders* (creditors) loan money or other resources to an organization. Banks, savings and loans, co-ops, and mortgage and finance companies often are lenders. Lenders look for information to help them assess whether an organization is likely to repay its loans with interest. *Shareholders* (investors) are the owners of a corporation. They use accounting reports in deciding whether to buy, hold, or sell stock. Shareholders typically elect a *board of directors* to oversee their interests in an organization. Since directors are responsible to shareholders, their information needs are similar. *External* (independent) *auditors* examine financial statements to verify that they are prepared according to generally accepted accounting principles. *Employees* and *labor unions* use financial statements to judge the fairness of

**Point:** World Wrestling Entertainment has more than 70 mil. shares of stock outstanding.

wages, assess future job prospects, and bargain for better wages. *Regulators* often have legal authority over certain activities of organizations. For example, the Internal Revenue Service (IRS) and other tax authorities require organizations to file accounting reports in computing taxes. Other regulators include utility boards that use accounting information to set utility rates and securities regulators that require reports for companies that sell their stock to the public.

**Point:** Microsoft's high income levels encouraged antitrust actions against it.

Accounting serves the needs of many other external users. *Voters, legislators,* and *government officials* use accounting information to monitor and evaluate a government's receipts and expenses. *Contributors* to nonprofit organizations use accounting information to evaluate the use and impact of their donations. *Suppliers* use accounting information to judge the soundness of a customer before making sales on credit, and *customers* use financial reports to assess the staying power of potential suppliers.

**Internal Information Users**   **Internal users** of accounting information are those directly involved in managing and operating an organization. They use the information to help improve the efficiency and effectiveness of an organization. **Managerial accounting** is the area of accounting that serves the decision-making needs of internal users. Internal reports are not subject to the same rules as external reports and are designed with the special needs of internal users in mind.

*Decision Insight boxes highlight relevant items from practice.*

There are several types of internal users, and many are managers of key operating activities. *Research and development managers* need information about projected costs and revenues of proposed changes in products and services. *Purchasing managers* need to know what, when, and how much to purchase. *Human resource managers* need information about employees' payroll, benefits, performance, and compensation. *Production managers* depend on information to monitor costs and ensure quality. *Distribution managers* need reports for timely, accurate, and efficient delivery of products and services. *Marketing managers* use reports about sales and costs to target consumers, set prices, and monitor consumer needs, tastes, and price concerns. *Service managers* require information on both the costs and benefits of looking after products and services.

### Decision Insight

**Know-Nothing CEO**   The know-nothing defense of CEOs such as **Global Crossing's** Gary Winnick and **Enron's** Jeffrey Skilling and Kenneth Lay could soon be shattered. Through novel legal moves, prosecutors are achieving convictions provided they prove that the CEO knew the company's internal picture was different than the picture shown to outsiders.

Both internal and external users rely on internal controls to monitor and control company activities. *Internal controls* are procedures set up to protect company property and equipment, ensure reliable accounting reports, promote efficiency, and encourage adherence to company policies. Examples are good records, physical controls (locks, passwords, guards), and independent reviews.

## Opportunities in Accounting

**C3**  Identify opportunities in accounting and related fields.

Accounting information affects many aspects of our lives. When we earn money, pay taxes, invest savings, budget earnings, and plan for the future, we are influenced by accounting. Accounting has four broad areas of opportunities: financial, managerial, taxation, and accounting-related. Exhibit 1.3 lists selected opportunities in each area.

The majority of accounting opportunities are in *private accounting,* as shown in Exhibit 1.4. *Public accounting* offers the next largest number of opportunities. Still other opportunities exist in government (and not-for-profit) agencies, including business regulation and investigation of law violations.

**Point:** The "top 5" greatest investors of the 20th century per a recent survey:
1. Warren Buffett, Berkshire Hathaway
2. Peter Lynch, Fidelity Funds
3. John Templeton, Templeton Group
4. Benjamin Graham & David Dodd, professors
5. George Soros, Soros Fund

Accounting specialists are highly regarded. Their professional standing often is denoted by a certificate. Certified public accountants (CPAs) must meet education and experience requirements, pass an examination, and exhibit ethical character. Many accounting specialists hold certificates in addition to or instead of the CPA. Two of the most common are the

Exhibit 1.3

Accounting Opportunities

certificate in management accounting (CMA) and the certified internal auditor (CIA). Employers also look for specialists with designations such as certified bookkeeper (CB), certified payroll professional (CPP), and personal financial specialist (PFS).

Individuals with accounting knowledge are always in demand as they can help with financial analysis, strategic planning, e-commerce, product feasibility analysis, information technology, and financial management. Benefit packages can include flexible work schedules, telecommuting options, career path alternatives, casual work environments, extended vacation time, and child and elder care.

Demand for accounting specialists is boosting salaries. Exhibit 1.5 reports average annual salaries for several accounting positions. Salary variation depends on location, company size, professional designation, experience, and other factors. For example, salaries for chief financial officers (CFO) range from under $75,000 to more than $1 million per year. Likewise, salaries for bookkeepers range from under $30,000 to more than $80,000.

Exhibit 1.4

Accounting Jobs by Area

Private accounting 60%

Public accounting 25%

Government, not-for-profit and education 15%

**Point:** The firm of Ernst & Young gave its interns a vacation at Disney World.

**Point:** The CFOs of Cisco Systems and Qualcom received an annual salary of more than $20 mil.

| Field | Title (experience) | 2003 Salary | 2008 Estimate* |
|---|---|---|---|
| **Public Accounting:** | Partner | $181,000 | $231,000 |
| | Manager (6–8 years) | 89,500 | 114,000 |
| | Senior (3–5 years) | 68,500 | 87,500 |
| | Junior (0–2 years) | 49,000 | 62,500 |
| **Private Accounting:** | CFO | 221,000 | 282,000 |
| | Controller/Treasurer | 140,000 | 179,000 |
| | Manager (6–8 years) | 83,000 | 106,000 |
| | Senior (3–5 years) | 69,000 | 88,000 |
| | Junior (0–2 years) | 47,000 | 60,000 |
| **Recordkeeping:** | Full-charge bookkeeper | 55,000 | 70,000 |
| | Accounts manager | 48,500 | 62,000 |
| | Payroll manager | 52,000 | 66,000 |
| | Accounting clerk (0–1 years) | 30,500 | 39,000 |

* Estimates assume a 5% compounded annual increase over current levels.

Exhibit 1.5

Accounting Salaries for Selected Fields

**Point:** For updated salary information:
www.AICPA.org
Abbott-Langer.com
Kforce.com

*Quick Check is a chance to stop and reflect on key points.*

Answers—p. 26

## Quick Check

1. What is the purpose of accounting?
2. What is the relation between accounting and recordkeeping?
3. Identify some advantages of technology for accounting.
4. Who are the internal and external users of accounting information?
5. Identify at least five types of managers who are internal users of accounting information.
6. What are internal controls and why are they important?

# Fundamentals of Accounting

Accounting is guided by principles, standards, concepts, and assumptions. This section describes several of these key fundamentals of accounting.

## Ethics—A Key Concept

**C4** Explain why ethics are crucial to accounting.

The goal of accounting is to provide useful information for decisions. For information to be useful, it must be trusted. This demands ethics in accounting. **Ethics** are beliefs that distinguish right from wrong. They are accepted standards of good and bad behavior.

Identifying the ethical path is sometimes difficult. The preferred path is a course of action that avoids casting doubt on one's decisions. For example, accounting users are less likely to trust an auditor's report if the auditor's pay depends on the success of the client. To avoid such concerns, ethics rules are often set. For example, auditors are banned from direct investment in their client and cannot accept pay that depends on figures in the client's reports. Exhibit 1.6 gives guidelines for making ethical decisions.

**Point:** Sarbanes-Oxley Act requires each issuer of securities to disclose whether it has adopted a code of ethics for its senior financial officers and the contents of that code.

## Exhibit 1.6

Guidelines for Ethical Decision Making

| Identify ethical concerns | Analyze options | Make ethical decision |
| --- | --- | --- |
| Use personal ethics to recognize an ethical concern. | Consider all good and bad consequences. | Choose best option after weighing all consequences. |

**Global:** Business ethics differ across countries. This is due to cultural, political, legal, economic, and other important factors.

**Point:** A survey of executives, educators, and legislators showed that 9 of 10 participants believe organizations are troubled by ethical problems.

**Point:** The American Institute of Certified Public Accountants' *Code of Professional Conduct* is available at www.AICPA.org.

Providers of accounting information often face ethical choices as they prepare financial reports. These choices can affect the price a buyer pays and the wages paid to workers. They can even affect the success of products and services. Misleading information can lead to a wrongful closing of a division that harms workers, customers, and suppliers. There is an old saying worth remembering: *Good ethics are good business.*

Some extend ethics to *social responsibility,* which refers to a concern for the impact of actions on society. An organization's social responsibility can include donations to hospitals, colleges, community programs, and law enforcement. It also can include programs to reduce pollution, increase product safety, improve worker conditions, and support continuing education. These programs are not limited to large companies. For example, many independently owned theaters and small businesses offer discounts to students and senior citizens. Still others help sponsor events such as the Special Olympics and summer reading programs.

*Graphical displays are often used to illustrate key points.*

# Generally Accepted Accounting Principles

Financial accounting practice is governed by concepts and rules known as **generally accepted accounting principles (GAAP).** To use and interpret financial statements effectively, we need to understand these principles. A main purpose of GAAP is to make information in financial statements relevant, reliable, and comparable. *Relevant information* affects the decisions of its users. *Reliable information* is trusted by users. *Comparable information* is helpful in contrasting organizations.

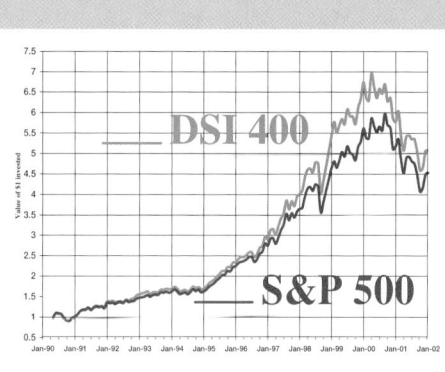

**Decision Insight**

**Virtuous Returns**   Virtue is not always its own reward. Compare the S&P 500 with the Domini Social Index (DSI), which covers 400 companies that have especially good records of social responsibility. Notice that returns for companies with socially responsible behavior are at least as high as those of the S&P 500.

**Setting Accounting Principles**   Two main groups establish generally accepted accounting principles in the United States. The **Financial Accounting Standards Board (FASB)** is the private group that sets both broad and specific principles. The **Securities and Exchange Commission (SEC)** is the government group that establishes reporting requirements for companies that issue stock to the public.

In today's global economy, there is increased demand by external users for comparability in accounting reports. This often arises when companies wish to raise money from lenders and investors in different countries. To that end, the **International Accounting Standards Board (IASB)** issues *International Financial Reporting Standards* (*IFRS*) that identify preferred accounting practices. The IASB hopes to create more harmony among accounting practices of different countries. If standards are harmonized, one company can use a single set of financial statements in all financial markets. Many countries' standard setters support the IASB, and interest in moving U.S. GAAP toward the IASB's practices is growing, yet the IASB does not have the authority to impose its standards on companies.

**Principles of Accounting**   Accounting principles are of two types. *General principles* are the basic assumptions, concepts, and guidelines for preparing financial statements. *Specific principles* are detailed rules used in reporting business transactions and events. General principles stem from long-used accounting practices. Specific principles arise more often from the rulings of authoritative groups.

We need to understand both general and specific principles to effectively use accounting information. Several general principles are described in this section and several others are described in later chapters. General principles are portrayed as building blocks of GAAP in Exhibit 1.7. The specific principles are described as we encounter them.

The **objectivity principle** means that accounting information is supported by independent, unbiased evidence. It demands more than a person's opinion. Information is not reliable if it is based only on what a preparer thinks might be true. A preparer can be too optimistic or pessimistic. The objectivity principle is intended to make financial statements useful by ensuring they report reliable and verifiable information.

The **cost principle** means that accounting information is based on actual cost. Cost is measured on a cash or equal-to-cash basis. This means if cash is given for a service, its cost is measured as the amount of cash paid. If something besides cash is exchanged (such as

**C5**   Explain the meaning of generally accepted accounting principles, and define and apply several key principles of accounting.

**Point:** State ethics codes require CPAs who audit financial statements to disclose areas where those statements fail to comply with GAAP. If CPAs fail to report noncompliance, they can lose their licenses and be subject to criminal action and fines.

**Point:** An audit examines whether financial statements are prepared using GAAP. It does *not* attest to the absolute accuracy of the statements.

**Point:** The largest accounting firms are Deloitte & Touche, Ernst & Young, PricewaterhouseCoopers, and KPMG.

## Exhibit 1.7

Building Blocks for GAAP

**Point:** The cost principle is also called the *historical cost principle.*

**Point:** For currency conversion: **cnnfn.com/markets/currencies**

**Example:** Cadbury Schweppes, a leading beverage and confectionery producer, recently reported sales of £5,500 million. What is the U.S.$ equivalent of these sales if the exchange rate is £1 = $1.50? *Answer:* $8,250 million (£5,500 × $1.50).

**Example:** When a bookstore sells a textbook on credit is its earnings process complete? *Answer:* The bookstore can record sales for these books minus an amount expected for returns.

**Point:** Abuse of the entity principle was a main culprit in the collapse of Enron.

a car traded for a truck), cost is measured as the cash value of what is given up or received. The cost principle emphasizes reliability, and information based on cost is considered objective. To illustrate, suppose a company pays $5,000 for equipment. The cost principle requires that this purchase be recorded at a cost of $5,000. It makes no difference if the owner thinks this equipment is worth $7,000.

The **going-concern principle** means that accounting information reflects an assumption that the business will continue operating instead of being closed or sold. This implies, for example, that property is reported at cost instead of, say, liquidation values that assume closure.

The **monetary unit principle** means that we can express transactions and events in monetary, or money, units. Money is the common denominator in business. Examples of monetary units are the dollar in the United States, Canada, Australia, and Singapore; the pound sterling in the United Kingdom; and the peso in Mexico, the Philippines, and Chile. The monetary unit a company uses in its accounting reports usually depends on the country where it operates, but many companies today are expressing reports in more than one monetary unit.

Revenue (sales) is the amount received from selling products and services. The **revenue recognition principle** provides guidance on when a company must recognize revenue. To *recognize* means to record it. If revenue is recognized too early, a company would look more profitable than it is. If revenue is recognized too late, a company would look less profitable than it is. The following three concepts are important to revenue recognition. (1) *Revenue is recognized when earned.* The earnings process is normally complete when services are rendered or a seller transfers ownership of products to the buyer. (2) *Proceeds from selling products and services need not be in cash.* A common noncash proceed received by a seller is a customer's promise to pay at a future date, called *credit sales.* (3) *Revenue is measured by the cash received plus the cash value of any other items received.*

The **business entity principle** means that a business is accounted for separately from other business entities, including its owner. The reason for this principle is that separate information about each business is necessary for good decisions. A business entity can take one of three legal forms: *sole proprietorship, partnership,* or *corporation.*

1. A **sole proprietorship,** or simply **proprietorship,** is a business owned by one person. No special legal requirements must be met to start a proprietorship. It is a separate entity for accounting purposes, but it is *not* a separate legal entity from its owner. This means, for example, that a court can order an owner to sell personal belongings to pay a proprietorship's debt. This *unlimited liability* of a proprietorship is a disadvantage. However, an advantage is that a proprietorship's income is not subject to a business income tax but is instead reported and taxed on the owner's personal income tax return. Proprietorship characteristics are summarized in Exhibit 1.8.

2. A **partnership** is a business owned by two or more people, called *partners.* Like a proprietorship, no special legal requirements must be met in starting a partnership. The only requirement is an agreement between partners to run a business together. The agreement can be either oral or

| Characteristic | Proprietorship | Partnership | Corporation |
|---|---|---|---|
| Business entity | yes | yes | yes |
| Legal entity | no | no | yes |
| Limited liability | no* | no* | yes |
| Unlimited life | no | no | yes |
| Business taxed | no | no | yes |
| One owner allowed | yes | no | yes |

**Exhibit 1.8**

Characteristics of Businesses

* Proprietorships and partnerships that are set up as LLCs provide limited liability.

written and usually indicates how income and losses are to be shared. A partnership, like a proprietorship, is *not* legally separate from its owners. This means that each partner's share of profits is reported and taxed on that partner's tax return. It also means *unlimited liability* for its partners. However, at least three types of partnerships limit liability. A *limited partnership* (*LP*) includes a general partner(s) with unlimited liability and a limited partner(s) with liability restricted to the amount invested. A *limited liability partnership* (*LLP*) restricts partners' liabilities to their own acts and the acts of individuals under their control. This protects an innocent partner from the negligence of another partner, yet all partners remain responsible for partnership debts. A *limited liability company* (*LLC*), offers the limited liability of a corporation and the tax treatment of a partnership (or proprietorship). Most proprietorships and partnerships are now organized as an LLC.

3. A **corporation** is a business legally separate from its owners, meaning it is responsible for its own acts and its own debts. Separate legal status means that a corporation can conduct business with the rights, duties, and responsibilities of a person. A corporation acts through its managers, who are its legal agents. Separate legal status also means that its owners, who are called **shareholders** (or **stockholders**), are not personally liable for corporate acts and debts. This limited liability is its main advantage. A main disadvantage is what's called *double taxation*—meaning that (1) the corporation income is taxed and (2) any distribution of income to its owners through dividends is taxed as part of the owners' personal income (usually at the 15% rate). An exception to this is an *S corporation*, a corporation with certain characteristics that give it a tax status that removes its corporate income tax. Owners of S corporations report their share of corporate income with their personal income. (*Note:* For lower income taxpayers, the dividend tax is less than 15%, and in some cases zero.) Ownership of corporations is divided into units called **shares** or **stock**. When a corporation issues only one class of stock, we call it **common stock** (or *capital stock*).

**Decision Insight**

**Web Info**   Most organizations maintain Websites that include accounting information—see **Krispy Kreme's** (**KrispyKreme.com**) Website as one example. The SEC keeps an online database called EDGAR (**www.SEC.gov/edgar.shtml**), which has accounting information for thousands of companies that sell their stock to the public.

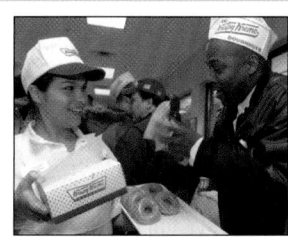

*Lightbulb icon highlights entrepreneurial-related info.*

**Decision Insight**

**New Age**   Entrepreneurship will be the defining trend of business in this century, according to a survey of business leaders. Respondents see the biggest opportunities for entrepreneurship in technology, medicine, food services, hospitality, and information services.

*Decision Ethics boxes are role-playing exercises that stress ethics in accounting and business.*

**Decision Ethics**

**Entrepreneur**   You and a friend develop a new design for in-line skates that improves speed and performance by 25% to 40%. You plan to form a business to manufacture and market these skates. You and your friend want to minimize taxes, but your prime concern is potential lawsuits from individuals who might be injured on these skates. What form of organization do you set up?

Answer—p. 26

## Quick Check

7. What three-step guidelines can help people make ethical decisions?
8. Why are ethics and social responsibility valuable to organizations?
9. Why are ethics crucial in accounting?
10. Who sets U.S. accounting rules?
11. How are U.S. companies affected by international accounting standards?
12. How are the objectivity and cost principles related?
13. Why is the business entity principle important?
14. Why is the revenue recognition principle important?
15. What are the three basic forms of business organization?
16. Identify the owners of corporations and the terminology for ownership units.

Answers—p. 26

# Transaction Analysis and the Accounting Equation

A1  Define and interpret the accounting equation and each of its components.

To understand accounting information, we need to know how an accounting system captures relevant data about transactions, and then classifies, records, and reports data.

## Accounting Equation

The accounting system reflects two basic aspects of a company: what it owns and what it owes. **Assets** are resources with future benefits that are owned or controlled by a company. Examples are cash, supplies, equipment, and land. The claims on a company's assets—what it owes—are separated into owner and nonowner claims. **Liabilities** are what a company owes its nonowners (creditors) in future products or services. **Equity** (also called owners' equity or capital) refers to the claims of its owner(s). Together, liabilities and equity are the source of funds to acquire assets. The relation of assets, liabilities, and equity is reflected in the following **accounting equation:**

$$\text{Assets} = \text{Liabilities} + \text{Equity}$$

Liabilities are usually shown before equity in this equation because creditors' claims must be paid before the claims of owners. (The terms in this equation can be rearranged; for example, Assets − Liabilities = Equity.) The accounting equation applies to all transactions and events, to all companies and forms of organization, and to all points in time. To illustrate, **Krispy Kreme**'s assets equal $410,487, its liabilities equal $137,135, and its equity equals $273,352 ($ in thousands). Let's now look at the accounting equation in more detail.

*Real company names are printed in bold magenta.*

**Point:** The phrase "on credit" implies that the cash payment will occur at a future date.

**Assets**   **Assets** are resources owned or controlled by a company. These resources are expected to yield future benefits. Examples are Web servers for an online services company, musical instruments for a rock band, and land for a vegetable grower. The term *receivable* is used to refer to an asset that promises a future inflow of resources. A company that provides a service or product on credit is said to have an account receivable from that customer.

**Liabilities**   **Liabilities** are creditors' claims on assets. These claims reflect obligations to provide assets, products or services to others. The term *payable* refers to a liability that promises a future outflow of resources. Examples are wages payable to workers, accounts payable to suppliers, notes payable to banks, and taxes payable to the government.

**Equity**   **Equity** is the owner's claim on assets. Equity is equal to assets minus liabilities. This is the reason equity is also called *net assets* or *residual equity* (*interest*).

A corporation's equity—often called stockholders' or shareholders' equity—has two parts: contributed capital and retained earnings. **Contributed capital** refers to the amount that stockholders invest in the company—included under the title **common stock. Retained earnings** refer to income (revenues less expenses) that is not distributed to its stockholders. The distribution of assets to stockholders is called **dividends,** which reduce retained earnings. **Revenues** increase retained earnings and are the assets earned from a company's earnings activities. Examples are consulting services provided, sales of products, facilities rented to others, and commissions from services. **Expenses** decrease retained earnings and are the cost of assets or services used to earn revenues. Examples are costs of employee time, use of supplies, and the advertising, utilities, and insurance services from others. In sum, retained earnings is the accumulated revenues less the accumulated expenses and dividends since the company began. This breakdown of equity yields the following **expanded accounting equation:**

Key **terms** *are printed in bold and defined again in the end-of-book* **glossary.**

**Point:** Revenues and owner investments increase equity. Expenses and owner withdrawals decrease equity.

$$\text{Assets} = \text{Liabilities} + \overbrace{\text{Contributed Capital} + \overbrace{\text{Retained Earnings}}^{\phantom{}}}^{\textbf{Equity}}$$
$$+ \text{Common Stock} - \text{Dividends} + \text{Revenues} - \text{Expenses}$$

**Net income** occurs when revenues exceed expenses. Net income increases equity. A **net loss** occurs when expenses exceed revenues, which decreases equity. The accounting equation can be used to track changes in a company's assets, liabilities, and equity, which is the focus of the next section.

## Transaction Analysis

Business activities can be described in terms of transactions and events. **External transactions** are exchanges of value between two entities, which yield changes in the accounting equation. **Internal transactions** are exchanges within an entity; they can also affect the accounting equation. An example is a company's use of its supplies, which are reported as expenses when used. **Events** refer to those happenings that affect an entity's accounting equation *and* can be reliably measured. They include business events such as changes in the market value of certain assets and liabilities, and natural events such as floods and fires that destroy assets and create losses. They do not include, for example, the signing of service or product contracts, which by themselves do not impact the accounting equation.

A2 Analyze business transactions using the accounting equation.

*Topic Tackler* **icon** *references additional help on the CD.*

Topic Tackler 1-1

This section uses the accounting equation to analyze 11 selected transactions and events of FastForward, a start-up consulting business, in its first month of operations. Remember that each transaction and event leaves the equation in balance and that assets *always* equal the sum of liabilities and equity.

**Transaction 1: Investment by Owner** On December 1, Chuck Taylor forms an athletic shoe consulting business, which he names FastForward. He sets it up as a corporation. Taylor owns and manages the business. The marketing plan for the business is to focus primarily on consulting with sports clubs, amateur athletes, and others who place orders for athletic shoes with manufacturers. Taylor personally invests $30,000 cash in the new company and deposits the cash in a bank account opened under the name of FastForward. After this transaction, the cash (an asset) and the stockholders' equity each equal $30,000. The source of increase in equity is the owner's investment (stock issuance), which is included in the column titled Common Stock. The effect of this transaction on FastForward is reflected in the accounting equation as follows:

**Point:** There are 3 basic types of company operations: (1) **Services**—providing services for profit, (2) **Merchandisers**—buying products and selling them for profit, and (3) **Manufacturers**—creating products and selling them for profit.

| | Assets | = | Liabilities | + | Equity |
|---|---|---|---|---|---|
| | **Cash** | = | | | **Common Stock** |
| **(1)** | **+$30,000** | = | | | **+$30,000** |

**Transaction 2: Purchase Supplies for Cash** FastForward uses $2,500 of its cash to buy supplies of brand name athletic shoes for testing over the next few months. This

transaction is an exchange of cash, an asset, for another kind of asset, supplies. It merely changes the form of assets from cash to supplies. The decrease in cash is exactly equal to the increase in supplies. The supplies of athletic shoes are assets because of the expected future benefits from the test results of their performance. This transaction is reflected in the accounting equation as follows:

| | Assets | | | = | Liabilities | + | Equity |
|---|---|---|---|---|---|---|---|
| | **Cash** | + | **Supplies** | = | | | **Common Stock** |
| Old Bal. | $30,000 | | | = | | | $30,000 |
| (2) | −2,500 | + | $2,500 | | | | |
| New Bal. | $27,500 | + | $ 2,500 | = | | | $30,000 |
| | | | $30,000 | | | $30,000 | |

**Transaction 3: Purchase Equipment for Cash**   FastForward spends $26,000 to acquire equipment for testing athletic shoes. Like transaction 2, transaction 3 is an exchange of one asset, cash, for another asset, equipment. The equipment is an asset because of its expected future benefits from testing athletic shoes. This purchase changes the makeup of assets but does not change the asset total. The accounting equation remains in balance.

| | Assets | | | | | = | Liabilities | + | Equity |
|---|---|---|---|---|---|---|---|---|---|
| | **Cash** | + | **Supplies** | + | **Equipment** | = | | | **Common Stock** |
| Old Bal. | $27,500 | + | $2,500 | | | = | | | $30,000 |
| (3) | −26,000 | | | + | $26,000 | | | | |
| New Bal. | $1,500 | + | $2,500 | + | $ 26,000 | = | | | $30,000 |
| | | | $30,000 | | | | | $30,000 | |

**Example:** If FastForward pays $500 cash in transaction 4, how does this partial payment affect the liability to CalTech? What would be FastForward's cash balance? *Answers:* The liability to CalTech would be reduced to $6,600 and the cash balance would be reduced to $1,000.

**Transaction 4: Purchase Supplies on Credit**   Taylor decides he needs more supplies of athletic shoes. These additional supplies total $7,100, but as we see from the accounting equation in transaction 3, FastForward has only $1,500 in cash. Taylor arranges to purchase them on credit from CalTech Supply Company. Thus, FastForward acquires supplies in exchange for a promise to pay for them later. This purchase increases assets by $7,100 in supplies, and liabilities (called *accounts payable* to CalTech Supply) increase by the same amount. The effects of this purchase on the accounting equation follow:

| | Assets | | | | | = | Liabilities | + | Equity |
|---|---|---|---|---|---|---|---|---|---|
| | **Cash** | + | **Supplies** | + | **Equipment** | = | **Accounts Payable** | + | **Common Stock** |
| Old Bal. | $1,500 | + | $2,500 | + | $26,000 | = | | | $30,000 |
| (4) | | + | 7,100 | | | | +$7,100 | | |
| New Bal. | $1,500 | + | $9,600 | + | $26,000 | = | $ 7,100 | + | $30,000 |
| | | | $37,100 | | | | | $37,100 | |

**Transaction 5: Provide Services for Cash**   FastForward earns revenues by consulting with clients about test results on athletic shoes. It earns net income only if its revenues are greater than its expenses incurred in earning them. In one of its first jobs, FastForward provides consulting services to an athletic club and immediately collects $4,200 cash. The accounting equation reflects this increase in cash of $4,200 and in equity of $4,200. This increase in equity is identified in the far right column under Revenues because the cash is earned by providing consulting services.

| | Assets | | | | | = | Liabilities | + | | | Equity | |
|---|---|---|---|---|---|---|---|---|---|---|---|---|
| | Cash | + | Supplies | + | Equipment | = | Accounts Payable | + | Common Stock | + | Revenues | |
| Old Bal. | $1,500 | + | $9,600 | + | $26,000 | = | $7,100 | + | $30,000 | | | |
| (5) | +4,200 | | | | | | | | | + | $4,200 | |
| New Bal. | $5,700 | + | $9,600 | + | $26,000 | = | $7,100 | + | $30,000 | + | $ 4,200 | |
| | | | $41,300 | | | | | | $41,300 | | | |

**Transactions 6 and 7: Payment of Expenses in Cash**  FastForward pays $1,000 rent to the landlord of the building where its store is located. Paying this amount allows FastForward to occupy the space for the month of December. The rental payment is reflected in the following accounting equation as transaction 6. FastForward also pays the biweekly $700 salary of the company's only employee. This is reflected in the accounting equation as transaction 7. Both transactions 6 and 7 are December expenses for FastForward. The costs of both rent and salary are expenses, as opposed to assets, because their benefits are used in December (they have no future benefits after December). These transactions also use up an asset (cash) in carrying out FastForward's operations. The accounting equation shows that both transactions reduce cash and equity. The far right column identifies these decreases as Expenses.

| | Assets | | | | | = | Liabilities | + | | | Equity | | | |
|---|---|---|---|---|---|---|---|---|---|---|---|---|---|---|
| | Cash | + | Supplies | + | Equipment | = | Accounts Payable | + | Common Stock | + | Revenues | − | Expenses |
| Old Bal. | $5,700 | + | $9,600 | + | $26,000 | = | $7,100 | + | $30,000 | + | $4,200 | | |
| (6) | −1,000 | | | | | | | | | | | − | $1,000 |
| Bal. | 4,700 | + | 9,600 | + | 26,000 | = | 7,100 | + | 30,000 | + | 4,200 | − | 1,000 |
| (7) | − 700 | | | | | | | | | | | − | 700 |
| New Bal. | $4,000 | + | $9,600 | + | $26,000 | = | $7,100 | + | $30,000 | + | $4,200 | − | $ 1,700 |
| | | | $39,600 | | | | | | $39,600 | | | | |

**Transaction 8: Provide Services and Facilities for Credit**  FastForward provides consulting services of $1,600 and rents its test facilities for $300 to an amateur sports club. The rental involves allowing club members to try recommended shoes at FastForward's testing grounds. The sports club is billed for the $1,900 total. This transaction results in a new asset, called *accounts receivable,* from this client. It also yields an increase in equity from the two revenue components reflected in the Revenues column of the accounting equation:

| | Assets | | | | | | | = | Liabilities | + | | | Equity | | | |
|---|---|---|---|---|---|---|---|---|---|---|---|---|---|---|---|---|
| | Cash | + | Accounts Receivable | + | Supplies | + | Equipment | = | Accounts Payable | + | Common Stock | + | Revenues | − | Expenses |
| Old Bal. | $4,000 | + | | | $9,600 | + | $26,000 | = | $7,100 | + | $30,000 | + | $4,200 | − | $1,700 |
| (8) | | + | $1,900 | | | | | | | | | + | 1,600 | | |
| | | | | | | | | | | | | + | 300 | | |
| New Bal. | $4,000 | + | $ 1,900 | + | $9,600 | + | $26,000 | = | $7,100 | + | $30,000 | + | $6,100 | − | $1,700 |
| | | | | | $41,500 | | | | | | | $41,500 | | | |

**Transaction 9: Receipt of Cash from Accounts Receivable**  The client in transaction 8 (the amateur sports club) pays $1,900 to FastForward 10 days after it is billed for consulting services. This transaction 9 does not change the total amount of assets and

**Point:** Receipt of cash is not always a revenue.

does not affect liabilities or equity. It converts the receivable (an asset) to cash (another asset). It does not create new revenue. Revenue was recognized when FastForward rendered the services in transaction 8, not when the cash is now collected. This emphasis on the earnings process instead of cash flows is a goal of the revenue recognition principle and yields useful information to users. The new balances follow:

| | Assets | | | | = | Liabilities | + | | Equity | | |
|---|---|---|---|---|---|---|---|---|---|---|---|
| | Cash | + Accounts Receivable | + Supplies | + Equipment | = | Accounts Payable | + Common Stock | + Revenues | − Expenses |
| Old Bal. | $4,000 | + $1,900 | + $9,600 | + $26,000 | = | $7,100 | + $30,000 | + $6,100 | − $1,700 |
| (9) | +1,900 | − 1,900 | | | | | | | |
| New Bal. | $5,900 | + $ 0 | + $9,600 | + $26,000 | = | $7,100 | + $30,000 | + $6,100 | − $1,700 |
| | | $41,500 | | | | | | $41,500 | |

**Transaction 10: Payment of Accounts Payable**  FastForward pays CalTech Supply $900 cash as partial payment for its earlier $7,100 purchase of supplies (transaction 4), leaving $6,200 unpaid. The accounting equation shows that this transaction decreases FastForward's cash by $900 and decreases its liability to CalTech Supply by $900. Equity does not change. This event does not create an expense even though cash flows out of FastForward (instead the expense is recorded when FastForward derives the benefits from these supplies).

| | Assets | | | | = | Liabilities | + | | Equity | | |
|---|---|---|---|---|---|---|---|---|---|---|---|
| | Cash | + Accounts Receivable | + Supplies | + Equipment | = | Accounts Payable | + Common Stock | + Revenues | − Expenses |
| Old Bal. | $5,900 | + $ 0 | + $9,600 | + $26,000 | = | $7,100 | + $30,000 | + $6,100 | − $1,700 |
| (10) | − 900 | | | | | − 900 | | | |
| New Bal. | $5,000 | + $ 0 | + $9,600 | + $26,000 | = | $6,200 | + $30,000 | + $6,100 | − $1,700 |
| | | $40,600 | | | | | | $40,600 | |

**Transaction 11: Payment of Cash Dividend**  FastForward declares and pays a $600 cash dividend to its owner. Dividends (decreases in equity) are not reported as expenses because they are not part of the company's earnings process. Since dividends are not company expenses, they are not used in computing net income.

| | Assets | | | | = | Liabilities | + | | Equity | | | |
|---|---|---|---|---|---|---|---|---|---|---|---|---|
| | Cash | + Accounts Receivable | + Supplies | + Equipment | = | Accounts Payable | + Common Stock | − Dividends | + Revenues | − Expenses |
| Old Bal. | $5,000 | + $ 0 | + $9,600 | + $26,000 | = | $6,200 | + $30,000 | | + $6,100 | − $1,700 |
| (11) | − 600 | | | | | | | − $600 | | |
| New Bal. | $4,400 | + $ 0 | + $9,600 | + $26,000 | = | $6,200 | + $30,000 | − $600 | + $6,100 | − $1,700 |
| | | $40,000 | | | | | | $40,000 | | |

## Summary of Transactions

**Point:** Knowing how financial statements are prepared improves our analysis of them. We develop the skills for analysis of financial statements throughout the book. Chapter 13 focuses on financial statement analysis.

We summarize in Exhibit 1.9 the effects of these 11 transactions of FastForward using the accounting equation. Two points should be noted. First, the accounting equation remains in balance after each transaction. Second, transactions can be analyzed by their effects on components of the accounting equation. For example, in transactions 2, 3, and 9, one asset increased while another decreased by equal amounts.

## Exhibit 1.9

Summary of Transactions Using the Accounting Equation

| | Cash | + | Accounts Receivable | + | Supplies | + | Equipment | = | Accounts Payable | + | Common Stock | − | Dividends | + | Revenues | − | Expenses |
|---|---|---|---|---|---|---|---|---|---|---|---|---|---|---|---|---|---|
| | **Assets** | | | | | | | = | **Liabilities** | + | | | **Equity** | | | | |
| (1) | $30,000 | | | | | | | = | | | $30,000 | | | | | | |
| (2) | − 2,500 | | | + | $2,500 | | | | | | | | | | | | |
| Bal. | 27,500 | | | + | 2,500 | | | = | | | 30,000 | | | | | | |
| (3) | −26,000 | | | | | + | $26,000 | | | | | | | | | | |
| Bal. | 1,500 | | | + | 2,500 | + | 26,000 | = | | | 30,000 | | | | | | |
| (4) | | | | + | 7,100 | | | | +$7,100 | | | | | | | | |
| Bal. | 1,500 | | | + | 9,600 | + | 26,000 | = | 7,100 | + | 30,000 | | | | | | |
| (5) | + 4,200 | | | | | | | | | | | | | + | $4,200 | | |
| Bal. | 5,700 | | | + | 9,600 | + | 26,000 | = | 7,100 | + | 30,000 | | | + | 4,200 | | |
| (6) | − 1,000 | | | | | | | | | | | | | | | − | $1,000 |
| Bal. | 4,700 | | | + | 9,600 | + | 26,000 | = | 7,100 | + | 30,000 | | | + | 4,200 | − | 1,000 |
| (7) | − 700 | | | | | | | | | | | | | | | − | 700 |
| Bal. | 4,000 | | | + | 9,600 | + | 26,000 | = | 7,100 | + | 30,000 | | | + | 4,200 | − | 1,700 |
| (8) | | + | $1,900 | | | | | | | | | | | + | 1,600 | | |
| | | | | | | | | | | | | | | + | 300 | | |
| Bal. | 4,000 | + | 1,900 | + | 9,600 | + | 26,000 | = | 7,100 | + | 30,000 | | | + | 6,100 | − | 1,700 |
| (9) | + 1,900 | − | 1,900 | | | | | | | | | | | | | | |
| Bal. | 5,900 | + | 0 | + | 9,600 | + | 26,000 | = | 7,100 | + | 30,000 | | | + | 6,100 | − | 1,700 |
| (10) | − 900 | | | | | | | | − 900 | | | | | | | | |
| Bal. | 5,000 | + | 0 | + | 9,600 | + | 26,000 | = | 6,200 | + | 30,000 | | | + | 6,100 | − | 1,700 |
| (11) | − 600 | | | | | | | | | | | − | $600 | | | | |
| Bal. | $ 4,400 | + | $ 0 | + | $ 9,600 | + | $ 26,000 | = | $ 6,200 | + | $ 30,000 | − | $ 600 | + | $6,100 | − | $1,700 |

# Financial Statements

This section shows how financial statements are prepared from the analysis of business transactions. The four financial statements and their purposes are:

**P1** Identify and prepare basic financial statements and explain how they interrelate.

1. *Income statement*—describes a company's revenues and expenses along with the resulting net income or loss over a period of time due to earnings activities.
2. *Statement of retained earnings*—explains changes in retained earnings from net income (or loss) and from any dividends over a period of time.
3. *Balance sheet*—describes a company's financial position (types and amounts of assets, liabilities, and equity) at a point in time.
4. *Statement of cash flows*—identifies cash inflows (receipts) and cash outflows (payments) over a period of time.

We prepare these financial statements using the 11 selected transactions of FastForward. (These statements are technically called *unadjusted*—we explain this in Chapters 2 and 3.)

Topic Tackler 1-2

## Income Statement

**Point:** Net income is sometimes called *earnings* or *profit*.

FastForward's income statement for December is shown at the top of Exhibit 1.10. Information about revenues and expenses is conveniently taken from the Equity columns of Exhibit 1.9. Revenues are reported first on the income statement. They include consulting revenues of $5,800 from transactions 5 and 8 and rental revenue of $300 from transaction 8. Expenses are reported after revenues. (For convenience in this chapter, we list larger amounts first, but we can sort expenses in different ways.) Rent and salary expenses are from transactions 6 and 7. Expenses reflect the costs to generate the revenues reported. Net income (or loss) is reported at the bottom of the statement and is the amount earned in December. Stockholders' investments and dividends are *not* part of income.

**Point:** Decision makers often compare income to the operating section of the statement of cash flows to help assess how much income is in the form of cash.

## Statement of Retained Earnings

**Point:** The statement of retained earnings is also called the *statement of changes in retained earnings*. Note: Beg. Ret. Earnings + Net Income − Dividends = End. Ret. Earnings

The statement of retained earnings reports information about how retained earnings changes over the reporting period. This statement shows beginning retained earnings, events that increase it (net income), and events that decrease it (dividends and net loss). Ending retained earnings is computed in this statement and is carried over and reported on the balance sheet. FastForward's statement of retained earnings is the second report in Exhibit 1.10. The beginning balance is measured as of the start of business on December 1. It is zero because FastForward did not exist before then. An existing business reports the beginning balance as of the end of the prior reporting period (such as from November 30). FastForward's statement shows the $4,400 of net income earned during the period. This links the income statement to the statement of retained earnings (see line ①). The statement also reports the $600 cash dividend and FastForward's end-of-period retained earnings balance.

## Balance Sheet

FastForward's balance sheet is the third report in Exhibit 1.10. This statement refers to FastForward's financial condition at the close of business on December 31. The left side of the balance sheet lists FastForward's assets: cash, supplies, and equipment. The upper right side of the balance sheet shows that FastForward owes $6,200 to creditors. Any other liabilities (such as a bank loan) would be listed here. The equity (capital) balance is $33,800. Note the link between the ending balance of the statement of retained earnings and the retained earnings balance here—see line ②. (This presentation of the balance sheet is called the *account form:* assets on the left and liabilities and equity on the right. Another presentation is the *report form:* assets on top, followed by liabilities and then equity at the bottom. Either presentation is acceptable.)

*Decision Maker boxes are role-playing exercises that stress the relevance of accounting.*

### Decision Maker

**Retailer**   You open a wholesale business selling entertainment equipment to retail outlets. You find that most of your customers demand to buy on credit. How can you use the balance sheets of these customers to help you decide which ones to extend credit to?

Answer—p. 26

## Statement of Cash Flows

**Point:** Statement of cash flows has three main sections: operating, investing, and financing.

**Point:** Payment for supplies is an operating activity because supplies are expected to be used up in short-term operations (typically less than one year).

FastForward's statement of cash flows is the final report in Exhibit 1.10. The first section reports cash flows from *operating activities*. It shows the $6,100 cash received from clients and the cash paid for supplies, rent, and employee salaries. Outflows are in parentheses to denote subtraction. Net cash provided by operating activities for December is $1,000. If cash paid exceeded cash received, we would call it "cash used by operating activities." The second section reports *investing activities*, which involve buying and selling assets such as land and equipment that are held for *long-term use* (typically more than one-year). The only investing activity is the $26,000 purchase of equipment. The third section shows cash flows from *financing activities*, which include the *long-term* borrowing and repaying of cash from lenders and the cash investments from and dividends to stockholders. FastForward reports

Exhibit 1.10

Financial Statements and
Their Links

**FASTFORWARD**
**Income Statement**
**For Month Ended December 31, 2004**

Revenues:

| | | |
|---|---:|---:|
| Consulting revenue ($4,200 + $1,600) . . . . . . . . . . . . . | $ 5,800 | |
| Rental revenue . . . . . . . . . . . . . . . . . . . . . . . . . . . . . . | 300 | |
| Total revenues . . . . . . . . . . . . . . . . . . . . . . . . . . . . | | $ 6,100 |
| Expenses: | | |
| Rent expense . . . . . . . . . . . . . . . . . . . . . . . . . . . . . | 1,000 | |
| Salaries expense . . . . . . . . . . . . . . . . . . . . . . . . . . | 700 | |
| Total expenses . . . . . . . . . . . . . . . . . . . . . . . . . . . . | | 1,700 |
| Net income . . . . . . . . . . . . . . . . . . . . . . . . . . . . . . . . | | $ 4,400 |

**Point:** A statement's heading identifies the company, the statement title, and the date or time period.

**FASTFORWARD**
**Statement of Retained Earnings**
**For Month Ended December 31, 2004**

| | | |
|---|---:|---:|
| Retained earnings, December 1, 2004 . . . . . . . . . . . . . . . . . . . . . . | $ 0 | |
| Plus: Net income . . . . . . . . . . . . . . . . . . . . . . . . . . . . . . . . . | 4,400 | |
| | 4,400 | |
| Less: Dividends . . . . . . . . . . . . . . . . . . . . . . . . . . . . . . . . . . | 600 | |
| Retained earnings, December 31, 2004 . . . . . . . . . . . . . . . . . . . . . | $ 3,800 | |

**Point:** Arrow lines show how the statements are linked. ① Net income is used to compute equity. ② Equity is used to prepare the balance sheet. ③ Cash from the balance sheet is used to reconcile the statement of cash flows.

**FASTFORWARD**
**Balance Sheet**
**December 31, 2004**

| Assets | | Liabilities | |
|---|---:|---|---:|
| Cash . . . . . . . . . | $ 4,400 | Accounts payable . . . . . . . . . . | $ 6,200 |
| Supplies . . . . . . . | 9,600 | Total liabilities . . . . . . . . . . . . | 6,200 |
| Equipment . . . . . . | 26,000 | | |
| | | **Equity** | |
| | | Common stock . . . . . . . . . . . . | 30,000 |
| | | Retained earnings . . . . . . . . . . | 3,800 |
| Total assets . . . . . . | $40,000 | Total liabilities and equity . . . . . | $ 40,000 |

**Point:** The income statement, the statement of retained earnings, and the statement of cash flows are prepared for a *period* of time. The balance sheet is prepared as of a *point* in time.

**FASTFORWARD**
**Statement of Cash Flows**
**For Month Ended December 31, 2004**

| | | |
|---|---:|---:|
| Cash flows from operating activities: | | |
| Cash received from clients ($4,200 + $1,900) . . . . . . . | $ 6,100 | |
| Cash paid for supplies ($2,500 + $900) . . . . . . . . . . . | (3,400) | |
| Cash paid for rent . . . . . . . . . . . . . . . . . . . . . . . . . . | (1,000) | |
| Cash paid to employee . . . . . . . . . . . . . . . . . . . . . . | (700) | |
| Net cash provided by operating activities . . . . . . . . . . | | $ 1,000 |
| Cash flows from investing activities: | | |
| Purchase of equipment . . . . . . . . . . . . . . . . . . . . . . | (26,000) | |
| Net cash used by investing activities . . . . . . . . . . . . . | | (26,000) |
| Cash flows from financing activities: | | |
| Investments by stockholder . . . . . . . . . . . . . . . . . . . | 30,000 | |
| Dividends to stockholder . . . . . . . . . . . . . . . . . . . . . | (600) | |
| Net cash provided by financing activities . . . . . . . . . . | | 29,400 |
| Net increase in cash . . . . . . . . . . . . . . . . . . . . . . . . . | | $ 4,400 |
| Cash balance, December 1, 2004 . . . . . . . . . . . . . . . . . . | | 0 |
| Cash balance, December 31, 2004 . . . . . . . . . . . . . . . . . . | | $ 4,400 |

**Point:** A single ruled line denotes an addition or subtraction. Final totals are double underlined. Negative amounts are often in parentheses.

**Point:** Investing activities refer to long-term asset investments by the company, *not* to owner investments.

$30,000 from the owner's initial investment and the $600 cash dividend. The net cash effect of all transactions is a $29,400 cash inflow. The final part of the statement shows FastForward increased its cash balance by $4,400 in December. Since it started with no cash, the ending balance is also $4,400—see line ③.

---

### Quick Check

**21.** Explain the link between the income statement and the statement of retained earnings.

**22.** Describe the link between the balance sheet and the statement of retained earnings.

**23.** Discuss the three major sections of the statement of cash flows.

Answers—p. 27

---

*Decision Analysis (a section at the end of each chapter) introduces and explains ratios helpful in decision making using real company data. Instructors can skip this section and cover all ratios in Chapter 13.*

## Decision Analysis                                    Return on Assets

A *Decision Analysis* section at the end of each chapter is devoted to financial statement analysis. We organize financial statement analysis into four areas: (1) liquidity and efficiency, (2) solvency, (3) profitability, and (4) market prospects—the back inside cover has a ratio listing with definitions and groupings by area. When analyzing ratios, we need benchmarks to identify good, bad, or average levels. Common benchmarks include the company's prior levels and those of its competitors.

**A3** Compute and interpret return on assets.

This chapter presents a profitability measure, that of return on assets. Return on assets is useful in evaluating management, analyzing and forecasting profits, and planning activities. **Dell Computer** has its marketing department compute return on assets for *every* mailing. *Return on assets (ROA)*, also called *return on investment (ROI)*, is defined in Exhibit 1.11.

**Exhibit 1.11**

Return on Assets

$$\text{Return on assets} = \frac{\text{Net income}}{\text{Average total assets}}$$

Net income is from the annual income statement, and average total assets is computed by adding the beginning and ending amounts for that same period and dividing by 2. To illustrate, **Nike** reports net income of $663.3 million in 2002. At the beginning of fiscal 2002, its total assets are $5,819.6 million and at the end of fiscal 2002, they total $6,443.0 million. Nike's return on assets for 2002 is:

$$\text{Return on assets} = \frac{\$663.3 \text{ mil.}}{(\$5,819.6 \text{ mil.} + \$6,443.0 \text{ mil.})/2} = 10.8\%$$

Is a 10.8% return on assets good or bad for Nike? To help answer this question, we compare (benchmark) Nike's return with its prior performance, the returns of competitors (such as **Reebok, Converse, Skechers,** and **Vans**), and the returns from alternative investments. Nike's return for each of the prior five years is in the second column of Exhibit 1.12, which ranges from 7.4% to 10.8%. These returns show an increase in its productive use of assets in recent years. We also compute Reebok's returns in the third column of Exhibit 1.12. In four of the five years, Nike's return exceeds Reebok's, and its average return is higher for this period. We also compare Nike's return to the normal return for manufacturers of athletic footwear and apparel (fourth column). Industry averages are available from services such as **Dun & Bradstreet**'s *Industry Norms and Key Ratios* and **Robert Morris Associates**' *Annual Statement Studies*. When compared to the industry, Nike performs well.

*Each **Decision Analysis** section ends with a role-playing scenario to show the usefulness of ratios.*

### Decision Maker

**Business Owner**   You own a small winter ski resort that earns a 21% return on its assets. An opportunity to purchase a winter ski equipment manufacturer is offered to you. This manufacturer earns a 19% return on its assets. The industry return for this manufacturer is 14%. Do you purchase this manufacturer?

Answer—p. 26

| Nike Fiscal Year | Return on Assets | | |
|---|---|---|---|
| | Nike | Reebok | Industry |
| 2002 | 10.8% | 6.8% | 3.6% |
| 2001 | 10.1 | 5.3 | 6.4 |
| 2000 | 10.4 | 0.7 | 5.1 |
| 1999 | 8.5 | 1.4 | 6.4 |
| 1998 | 7.4 | 7.7 | 6.1 |

**Exhibit 1.12**

Nike, Reebok, and Industry Returns

*The **Demonstration Problem** is a review of key chapter content. The Planning the Solution offers strategies in solving the problem.*

# Demonstration Problem

After several months of planning, Sylvia Workman started a haircutting business called Expressions. The following events occurred during its first month:

**a.** On August 1, Workman invested $3,000 cash and $15,000 of equipment in Expressions in exchange for its common stock.

**b.** On August 2, Expressions paid $600 cash for furniture for the shop.

**c.** On August 3, Expressions paid $500 cash to rent space in a strip mall for August.

**d.** On August 4, it purchased $1,200 of equipment on credit for the shop (using a long-term note payable).

**e.** On August 5, Expressions opened for business. Cash received from services provided in the first week and a half of business (ended August 15) is $825.

**f.** On August 15, it provided $100 of haircutting services on account.

**g.** On August 17, it received a $100 check for services previously rendered on account.

**h.** On August 17, it paid $125 cash to an assistant for working during the grand opening.

**i.** Cash received from services provided during the second half of August is $930.

**j.** On August 31, it paid a $400 installment toward principal on the note payable entered into on August 4.

**k.** On August 31, it paid $900 cash dividends to Workman.

**Required**

**1.** Arrange the following asset, liability, and equity titles in a table similar to the one in Exhibit 1.9: Cash; Accounts Receivable; Furniture; Store Equipment; Note Payable; Common Stock; Dividends; Revenues; and Expenses. Show the effects of each transaction using the accounting equation.

**2.** Prepare an income statement for August.

**3.** Prepare a statement of retained earnings for August.

**4.** Prepare a balance sheet as of August 31.

**5.** Prepare a statement of cash flows for August.

**6.** Determine the return on assets ratio for August.

## Planning the Solution

- Set up a table like Exhibit 1.9 with the appropriate columns for accounts.
- Analyze each transaction and show its effects as increases or decreases in the appropriate columns. Be sure the accounting equation remains in balance after each transaction.
- Prepare the income statement, and identify revenues and expenses. List those items on the statement, compute the difference, and label the result as *net income* or *net loss*.
- Use information in the Equity columns to prepare the statement of retained earnings.
- Use information in the last row of the transactions table to prepare the balance sheet.
- Prepare the statement of cash flows; include all events listed in the Cash column of the transactions table. Classify each cash flow as operating, investing, or financing.
- Calculate return on assets by dividing net income by average assets.

## Solution to Demonstration Problem

**1.**

| | Cash | + | Accounts Receiv-able | + | Furni-ture | + | Store Equip-ment | = | Note Payable | + | Common Stock | − | Dividends | + | Revenues | − | Expenses |
|---|---|---|---|---|---|---|---|---|---|---|---|---|---|---|---|---|---|
| *a.* | $3,000 | | | | | | $15,000 | | | | $18,000 | | | | | | |
| *b.* | − 600 | | | + | $600 | | | | | | | | | | | | |
| Bal. | 2,400 | + | | + | 600 | + | 15,000 | = | | | 18,000 | | | | | | |
| *c.* | − 500 | | | | | | | | | | | | | | | − | $500 |
| Bal. | 1,900 | + | | + | 600 | + | 15,000 | = | | | 18,000 | | | | | − | 500 |
| *d.* | | | | | | + | 1,200 | | +$1,200 | | | | | | | | |
| Bal. | 1,900 | + | | + | 600 | + | 16,200 | = | 1,200 | + | 18,000 | | | | | − | 500 |
| *e.* | + 825 | | | | | | | | | | | | | + | $ 825 | | |
| Bal. | 2,725 | + | | + | 600 | + | 16,200 | = | 1,200 | + | 18,000 | | | + | 825 | − | 500 |
| *f.* | | + | $100 | | | | | | | | | | | + | 100 | | |
| Bal. | 2,725 | + | 100 | + | 600 | + | 16,200 | = | 1,200 | + | 18,000 | | | + | 925 | − | 500 |
| *g.* | + 100 | − | 100 | | | | | | | | | | | | | | |
| Bal. | 2,825 | + | 0 | + | 600 | + | 16,200 | = | 1,200 | + | 18,000 | | | + | 925 | − | 500 |
| *h.* | − 125 | | | | | | | | | | | | | | | − | 125 |
| Bal. | 2,700 | + | 0 | + | 600 | + | 16,200 | = | 1,200 | + | 18,000 | | | + | 925 | − | 625 |
| *i.* | + 930 | | | | | | | | | | | | | + | 930 | | |
| Bal. | 3,630 | + | 0 | + | 600 | + | 16,200 | = | 1,200 | + | 18,000 | | | + | 1,855 | − | 625 |
| *j.* | − 400 | | | | | | | | − 400 | | | | | | | | |
| Bal. | 3,230 | + | 0 | + | 600 | + | 16,200 | = | 800 | + | 18,000 | | | + | 1,855 | − | 625 |
| *k.* | − 900 | | | | | | | | | | | − | $900 | | | | |
| Bal. | $ 2,330 | + | 0 | + | $600 | + | $ 16,200 | = | $  800 | + | $ 18,000 | − | $900 | + | $1,855 | − | $625 |

**2.**

| EXPRESSIONS |
|---|
| **Income Statement** |
| **For Month Ended August 31** |

| | | |
|---|---|---|
| Revenues: | | |
| Haircutting services revenue . . . . . . . . | | $1,855 |
| Expenses: | | |
| Rent expense . . . . . . . . . . . . . . . . | $500 | |
| Wages expense . . . . . . . . . . . . . . . | 125 | |
| Total expenses . . . . . . . . . . . . . . . | | 625 |
| Net Income . . . . . . . . . . . . . . . . . | | $1,230 |

**3.**

| EXPRESSIONS |
|---|
| **Statement of Retained Earnings** |
| **For Month Ended August 31** |

| | |
|---|---|
| Retained earnings, August 1* . . . . . . . . . . . . . . | $    0 |
| Plus:  Net income . . . . . . . . . . . . . . . . . . . . | 1,230 |
| | 1,230 |
| Less:  Dividend to owner . . . . . . . . . . . . . . . . | 900 |
| Retained earnings, August 31 . . . . . . . . . . . . . . | $  330 |

* If Expressions had been an existing business from a prior period, the beginning retained earnings balance would equal the retained earnings balance from the end of the prior period.

**4.**

| EXPRESSIONS<br>Balance Sheet<br>August 31 | | | |
|---|---|---|---|
| **Assets** | | **Liabilities** | |
| Cash ............... | $ 2,330 | Note payable ............... | $   800 |
| Furniture ............. | 600 | **Equity** | |
| Store equipment ........ | 16,200 | Common stock .............. | 18,000 |
| Total assets .......... | $19,130 | Retained earnings ............ | 330 |
| | | Total liabilities and equity ....... | 19,130 |

**5.**

| EXPRESSIONS<br>Statement of Cash Flows<br>For Month Ended August 31 | | |
|---|---|---|
| Cash flows from operating activities: | | |
| Cash received from customers ................... | $1,855 | |
| Cash paid for rent ......................... | (500) | |
| Cash paid for wages ........................ | (125) | |
| Net cash provided by operating activities ........... | | $1,230 |
| Cash flows from investing activities: | | |
| Cash paid for furniture ..................... | | (600) |
| Cash flows from financing activities: | | |
| Cash from stock issuance ..................... | 3,000 | |
| Cash paid for dividend ....................... | (900) | |
| Partial repayment of (long-term) note payable ........ | (400) | |
| Net cash provided by financing activities ........... | | 1,700 |
| Net increase in cash ....................... | | $2,330 |
| Cash balance, August 1 ........................ | | 0 |
| Cash balance, August 31 ...................... | | $2,330 |

**6.** Return on assets $= \dfrac{\text{Net income}}{\text{Average assets}} = \dfrac{\$1,230}{(\$18,000^* + \$19,130)/2} = \dfrac{\$1,230}{\$18,565} = \underline{\underline{6.63\%}}$

\* Uses the initial $18,000 investment as the begining balance for the startup period only.

# Return and Risk Analysis

This appendix explains return and risk analysis and its role in business and accounting.

Net income is often linked to **return.** Return on assets (ROA) is stated in ratio form as income divided by assets invested. For example, banks report return from a savings account in the form of an interest return such as 4%. If we invest in a savings account or in U.S. Treasury bills, we expect a return of around 2% to 7%. We could also invest in a company's stock, or even start our own business. How do we decide among these investment options? The answer depends on our trade-off between return and risk.

A4    Explain the relation between return and risk.

**Celebrity Investing**   How do fame and fortune translate into return and risk? A poll asked people which celebrity is the best investment. Similar to business investments, many people named performers with years of earning power ahead—see results to the right.

| | |
|---|---|
| Oprah Winfrey | 27% |
| Steven Spielberg | 19 |
| Tiger Woods | 15 |
| Michael Jordan | 14 |
| Tom Cruise | 8 |
| Jerry Seinfeld | 4 |
| Madonna | 2 |

**Risk** is the uncertainty about the return we will earn. All business investments involve risk, but some investments involve more risk than others. The lower the risk of an investment, the lower is our expected return. The reason that savings accounts pay such a low return is the low risk of not being repaid with interest (the government guarantees most savings accounts from default). If we buy a share of Nike or any other company, we might obtain a large return. However, we have no guarantee of any return; there is even the risk of loss.

The bar graph in Exhibit 1A.1 shows recent returns for 30-year bonds with different risks. *Bonds* are written promises by organizations to repay amounts loaned with interest. U.S. Treasury bonds provide a low expected return, but they also offer low risk since they are backed by the U.S. government. High-risk corporate bonds offer a much larger potential return but with much higher risk.

The trade-off between return and risk is a normal part of business. Higher risk implies higher, but riskier, expected returns. To help us make better decisions, we use accounting information to assess both return and risk.

### Exhibit 1A.1

Average Returns for Bonds with Different Risks

### APPENDIX

# 1B   Business Activities and the Accounting Equation

**C6**   Identify and describe the three major activities in organizations.

This appendix explains how the accounting equation is derived from business activities.

There are three major types of business activities: financing, investing, and operating. Each of these requires planning. *Planning* involves defining an organization's ideas, goals, and actions. Most public corporations use the *Management Discussion and Analysis* section in their annual reports to communicate plans. However, planning is not cast in stone. This adds *risk* to both setting plans and analyzing them.

**Point:** Management must understand accounting data to set financial goals, make financing and investing decisions, and evaluate operating performance.

**Point:** Investing (assets) and financing (liabilities plus equity) totals are *always* equal.

**Financing**   *Financing activities* provide the means organizations use to pay for resources such as land, buildings, and equipment to carry out plans. Organizations are careful in acquiring and managing financing activities because they can determine success or failure. The two sources of financing are owner and nonowner. *Owner financing* refers to resources contributed by the owner along with any income the owner leaves in the organization. *Nonowner* (or *creditor*) *financing* refers to resources contributed by creditors (lenders). *Financial management* is the task of planning how to obtain these resources and to set the right mix between owner and creditor financing.

**Investing**   *Investing activities* are the acquiring and disposing of resources (assets) that an organization uses to acquire and sell its products or services. Assets are funded by an organization's financing. Organizations differ on the amount and makeup of assets. Some require land and factories to operate. Others need only an office. Determining the amount and type of assets for operations is called *asset management.*

Invested amounts are referred to as *assets.* Financing is made up of creditor and owner financing, which hold claims on assets. Creditors' claims are called *liabilities,* and the owner's claim is called *equity.* This basic equality is called the *accounting equation* and can be written as: Assets = Liabilities + Equity.

**Operating**  *Operating activities* involve using resources to research, develop, purchase, produce, distribute, and market products and services. Sales and revenues are the inflow of assets from selling products and services. Costs and expenses are the outflow of assets to support operating activities. *Strategic management* is the process of determining the right mix of operating activities for the type of organization, its plans, and its market.

Exhibit 1B.1 summarizes business activities. Planning is part of each activity and gives them meaning and focus. Investing (assets) and financing (liabilities and equity) are set opposite each other to stress their balance. Operating activities are below investing and financing activities to show that operating activities are the result of investing and financing.

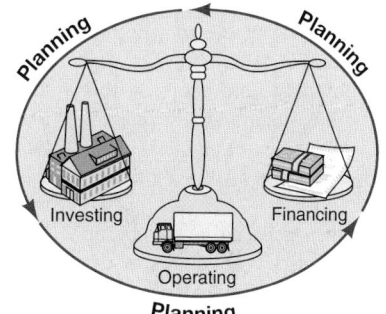

**Exhibit 1B.1**

Activities in Organizations

---

*— A **Summary** organized by learning objectives concludes each chapter.*

## Summary

**C1  Explain the purpose and importance of accounting in the information age.** Accounting is an information and measurement system that aims to identify, record, and communicate relevant, reliable, and comparable information about business activities. It helps assess opportunities, products, investments, and social and community responsibilities.

**C2  Identify users and uses of accounting.** Users of accounting are both internal and external. Some users and uses of accounting include (a) managers in controlling, monitoring, and planning; (b) lenders for measuring the risk and return of loans; (c) shareholders for assessing the return and risk of stock; (d) directors for overseeing management; and (e) employees for judging employment opportunities.

**C3  Identify opportunities in accounting and related fields.** Opportunities in accounting include financial, managerial, and tax accounting. They also include accounting-related fields such as lending, consulting, managing, and planning.

**C4  Explain why ethics are crucial to accounting.** The goal of accounting is to provide useful information for decision making. For information to be useful, it must be trusted. This demands ethical behavior in accounting.

**C5  Explain the meaning of generally accepted accounting principles, and define and apply several key principles of accounting.** Generally accepted accounting principles are a common set of standards applied by accountants. Accounting principles aid in producing relevant, reliable, and comparable information. The business entity principle means that a business is accounted for separately from its owner(s). The objectivity principle means independent, objective evidence supports the information. The cost principle means financial statements are based on actual costs incurred. The monetary unit principle assumes transactions can be reflected in money terms. The going-concern principle means financial statements assume the business will continue. The revenue recognition principle means revenue is recognized when earned.

**C6<sup>B</sup> Identify and describe the three major activities in organizations.** Organizations carry out three major activities: financing, investing, and operating. Financing is the means used to pay for resources such as land, buildings, and machines. Investing refers to the buying and selling of resources used in acquiring and selling products and services. Operating activities are those necessary for carrying out the organization's plans.

**A1  Define and interpret the accounting equation and each of its components.** The accounting equation is: Assets = Liabilities + Equity. Assets are resources owned by a company. Liabilities are creditors' claims on assets. Equity is the owner's claim on assets (*the residual*). The expanded accounting equation is: Assets = Liabilities + [Common Stock − Dividends + Revenues − Expenses].

**A2  Analyze business transactions using the accounting equation.** A *transaction* is an exchange of economic consideration between two parties. Examples include exchanges of products, services, money, and rights to collect money. Transactions always have at least two effects on one or more components of the accounting equation. This equation is always in balance.

**A3  Compute and interpret return on assets.** Return on assets is computed as net income divided by average assets. For example, if we have an average balance of $100 in a savings account and it earns $5 interest for the year, the return on assets is $5/$100, or 5%.

**A4<sup>A</sup> Explain the relation between return and risk.** *Return* refers to income, and *risk* is the uncertainty about the return we hope to make. All investments involve risk. The lower the risk of an investment, the lower is its expected return. Higher risk implies higher, but riskier, expected return.

**P1  Identify and prepare basic financial statements and explain how they interrelate.** Four financial statements report on an organization's activities: balance sheet, income statement, statement of retained earnings, and statement of cash flows.

## Guidance Answers to **Decision Maker** and **Decision Ethics**

**Entrepreneur** (p. 11) You should probably form the business as a corporation if potential lawsuits are of prime concern. The corporate form of organization protects your personal property from lawsuits directed at the business and places only the corporation's resources at risk. A downside of the corporate form is double taxation: The corporation must pay taxes on its income, and you normally must pay taxes on any money distributed to you from the business (even though the corporation already paid taxes on this money). You should also examine the ethical and socially responsible aspects of starting a business in which you anticipate injuries to others. Formation as an LLC or S corp. should also be explored.

**Retailer** (p. 18) You can use the accounting equation (Assets = Liabilities + Equity) to help identify risky customers to whom you would likely not want to extend credit. A balance sheet

provides amounts for each of these key components. The lower a customer's equity is relative to liabilities, the less likely you would extend credit. A low equity means the business has little value that does not already have creditor claims to it.

**Business Owner** (p. 20) The 19% return on assets for the manufacturer exceeds the 14% industry return (and many others). This is a positive factor for a potential purchase. Also, the purchase of this manufacturer is an opportunity to spread your risk over two businesses as opposed to one. Still, you should hesitate to purchase a business whose return of 19% is lower than your current resort's return of 21%. You are probably better off directing efforts to increase investment in your resort, assuming you can continue to earn a 21% return.

## Guidance Answers to **Quick Checks**

1. Accounting is an information and measurement system that identifies, records, and communicates relevant information to help people make better decisions.

2. Recordkeeping, also called *bookkeeping,* is the recording of financial transactions and events, either manually or electronically. Recordkeeping is essential to data reliability; but accounting is this and much more. Accounting includes identifying, measuring, recording, reporting, and analyzing business events and transactions.

3. Technology offers increased accuracy, speed, efficiency, and convenience in accounting.

4. External users of accounting include lenders, shareholders, directors, customers, suppliers, regulators, lawyers, brokers, and the press. Internal users of accounting include managers, officers, and other internal decision makers involved with strategic and operating decisions.

5. Internal users (managers) include those from research and development, purchasing, human resources, production, distribution, marketing, and servicing.

6. Internal controls are procedures set up to protect assets, ensure reliable accounting reports, promote efficiency, and encourage adherence to company policies. Internal controls are crucial for relevant and reliable information.

7. Ethical guidelines are threefold: (1) identify ethical concerns using personal ethics, (2) analyze options considering all good and bad consequences, and (3) make ethical decisions after weighing all consequences.

8. Ethics and social responsibility yield good behavior, and they often result in higher income and a better working environment.

9. For accounting to provide useful information for decisions, it must be trusted. Trust requires ethics in accounting.

10. Two major participants in setting rules include the SEC and the FASB. (*Note:* Accounting rules reflect society's needs, not those of accountants or any other single constituency).

11. Most U.S. companies are not directly affected by international accounting standards. International standards are put forth as preferred accounting practices. However, stock exchanges and

other parties are increasing the pressure to narrow differences in worldwide accounting practices. International accounting standards are playing an important role in that process.

12. The objectivity and cost principles are related in that most users consider information based on cost as objective. Information prepared using both principles is considered highly reliable and often relevant.

13. Users desire information about the performance of a specific entity. If information is mixed between two or more entities, its usefulness decreases.

14. The revenue recognition principle gives preparers guidelines on when to recognize (record) revenue. This is important; for example, if revenue is recognized too early, the statements report revenue sooner than it should and the business looks more profitable than it is. The reverse is also true.

15. The three basic forms of business organization are sole proprietorships, partnerships, and corporations.

16. Owners of corporations are called *shareholders* (or *stockholders*). Corporate ownership is divided into units called *shares* (or *stock*). The most basic of corporate shares is common stock (or capital stock).

17. The accounting equation is: Assets = Liabilities + Equity. This equation is always in balance, both before and after each transaction.

18. A transaction that changes the makeup of assets would not affect liability and equity accounts. FastForward's transactions 2 and 3 are examples. Each exchanges one asset for another.

19. Earning revenue by performing services, as in FastForward's transaction 5, increases equity (and assets). Incurring expenses while servicing clients, such as in transactions 6 and 7, decreases equity (and assets). Other examples include owner investments (stock issuances) that increase equity and dividends that decrease equity.

20. Paying a liability with an asset reduces both asset and liability totals. One example is FastForward's transaction 10 that reduces a payable by paying cash.

**21.** An income statement reports a company's revenues and expenses along with the resulting net income or loss. A statement of retained earnings shows changes in retained earnings, including that from net income or loss. Both statements report transactions occurring over a period of time.

**22.** The balance sheet describes a company's financial position (assets, liabilities, and equity) at a point in time. The retained earnings account in the balance sheet is obtained from the statement of retained earnings.

**23.** Cash flows from operating activities report cash receipts and payments from the primary business the company engages in. Cash flows from investing activities involve cash transactions from buying and selling long-term assets. Cash flows from financing activities include long-term cash borrowings and repayments to lenders and the cash investments from and dividends to the stockholders.

*A list of key terms with page references concludes each chapter (a complete glossary is at the end of the book and also on the book's Website).*

## Key Terms

Key Terms are available at the book's Website for learning and testing in an online Flashcard Format.

| | | |
|---|---|---|
| Accounting (p. 4) | Financial accounting (p. 5) | Partnership (p. 10) |
| Accounting equation (p. 12) | Financial Accounting Standards Board (FASB) (p. 9) | Proprietorship (p. 10) |
| Assets (p. 12) | | Recordkeeping (p. 5) |
| Audit (p. 9) | Generally Accepted Accounting Principles (GAAP) (p. 9) | Retained earnings (p. 13) |
| Balance sheet (p. 17) | | Return (p. 23) |
| Bookkeeping (p. 5) | Going-concern principle (p. 10) | Return on assets (p. 20) |
| Business entity principle (p. 10) | Income (p. 13) | Revenues (p. 13) |
| Common stock (p. 11) | Income statement (p. 17) | Revenue recognition principle (p. 10) |
| Contributed capital (p. 13) | Internal transactions (p. 13) | Risk (p. 24) |
| Corporation (p. 11) | Internal users (p. 6) | Securities and Exchange Commission (SEC) (p. 9) |
| Cost principle (p. 9) | International Accounting Standards Board (IASB) (p. 9) | |
| Dividends (p. 13) | | Shareholders (p. 11) |
| Equity (p. 12) | Liabilities (p. 12) | Shares (p. 11) |
| Ethics (p. 8) | Managerial accounting (p. 6) | Sole proprietorship (p. 10) |
| Events (p. 13) | Monetary unit principle (p. 10) | Statement of cash flows (p. 17) |
| Expanded accounting equation (p. 13) | Net assets (p. 12) | Statement of retained earnings (p. 17) |
| Expenses (p. 13) | Net income (p. 13) | Stock (p. 11) |
| External transactions (p. 13) | Net loss (p. 13) | Stockholders (p. 11) |
| External users (p. 5) | Objectivity principle (p. 9) | |

## Personal Interactive Quiz

Personal Interactive Quizzes A and B are available at the book's Website to reinforce and assess your learning.

*Superscript letter $^A$ ($^B$) denotes assignments based on Appendix 1A (1B).*

## Discussion Questions

**1.** What is the purpose of accounting in society?

**2.** Identify three actual businesses that offer services and three actual businesses that offer products.

**3.** Why do organizations license and monitor accounting and accounting-related professionals?

**4.** Technology is increasingly used to process accounting data. Why then must we study and understand accounting?

**5.** Identify four kinds of external users and describe their uses of accounting information.

**6.** What are at least three questions business owners might be able to answer by looking at accounting information?

**7.** Describe the internal role of accounting for organizations.

**8.** What type of accounting information might be useful to those who carry out the marketing activities of a business?

**9.** Identify three types of services typically offered by accounting professionals.

**10.** Why is accounting described as a service activity?

**11.** Identify at least three tasks you would expect to be performed by government accounting professionals.

**12.** What work do tax accounting professionals perform in addition to preparing tax returns?

**13.** What ethical issues might accounting professionals face in dealing with confidential information?

**14.** Identify the two main categories of accounting principles.

**15.** What does the objectivity principle imply for information reported in financial statements? Why?

**16.** A business reports its own office stationery on the balance sheet at its $430 cost, although it cannot be sold for more than $10 as scrap paper. Which accounting principle(s) justifies this treatment?

**17.** Why is the revenue recognition principle needed? What does it demand?

**18.** Describe the three basic forms of business organization and their key characteristics.

**19.** Identify three types of organizations that can be formed as either profit-oriented entities or government (or non-profit) entities.

**20.** Define (*a*) *assets*, (*b*) *liabilities*, (*c*) *equity*, and (*d*) *net assets*.

**21.** What events or transactions change equity?

**22.** What do accountants mean by the term *revenue?*

**23.** Define *net income* and explain its computation.

**24.** Identify the four basic financial statements of a business.

**25.** What information is reported in an income statement?

**26.** Give two examples of expenses a business might incur.

**27.** What information is reported in a balance sheet?

**28.** The statement of cash flows reports on what major activities?

**29.** Define and explain return on assets.

**30.**ᴬExplain return and risk. Discuss the trade-off between them.

**31.**ᴮDescribe the three major activities in organizations.

**32.**ᴮExplain why investing (assets) and financing (liabilities and equity) totals are always equal.

**33.** Refer to the financial statements of **Krispy Kreme** in Appendix A. To what level of significance are dollar amounts rounded? What time period does its income statement cover?

**34.** Identify the dollar amounts of **Tastykake's** 2002 assets, liabilities, and equity shown in its statements in Appendix A near the end of the book.

**35.** Access the SEC EDGAR database **(www.SEC.gov)** and retrieve **Harley-Davidson's** 2002 10-K (filed 2003-03-28). Identify its auditor. What responsibility does its independent auditor claim regarding its financial statements?    **Harley-Davidson**

### Red numbers denote Discussion Questions that involve decision-making.

*Quick Study exercises give readers a brief test of key elements.*

*Homework Manager* 🖐 *repeats all numerical Quick Study assignments on the book's Website with new numbers each time. It can be used in practice, homework, or exam mode.*

## QUICK STUDY

**QS 1-1**
Identifying accounting users
C2

Identify the following users as either external users (E) or internal users (I).

**a.** Managers     **d.** FBI and CIA     **g.** Consumer group     **j.** Shareholders
**b.** Controllers     **e.** Sales staff     **h.** Customers     **k.** Congress
**c.** Business press     **f.** Brokers     **i.** Lenders     **l.** District attorney

**QS 1-2**
Identifying accounting terms
C1

(*a*) Identify the meaning of these accounting-related acronyms: GAAP, SEC, and FASB, and then briefly explain the importance of each to accounting. (*b*) Identify the international accounting standards setting organization, and then briefly explain its purpose.

**QS 1-3**
Accounting opportunities
C3

Identify at least three main areas of opportunities for accounting professionals. For each area, identify at least three job possibilities linked to accounting.

**QS 1-4**
Identifying ethical concerns
C4

Accounting professionals must sometimes choose between two or more acceptable methods of accounting for business transactions and events. Explain why these situations can involve difficult matters of ethical concern.

*Thinker icon highlights assignments that use decision-making skills.*

Accounting provides information about an organization's business transactions and events that both affect the accounting equation and can be reliably measured. Identify at least two examples of both (*a*) business transactions and (*b*) business events that meet these requirements.

**QS 1-5**
Identifying transactions and events

A2

---

An important responsibility of many accounting professionals is to design and implement internal control procedures for organizations. Explain the purpose of internal control procedures.

**QS 1-6**
Explaining internal control

C1

---

Identify which general accounting principle best describes each of the following practices:

**a.** Marilyn Choi owns both Sailing Passions and Dockside Supplies. In preparing financial statements for Dockside Supplies, Choi makes sure that the expense transactions of Sailing Passions are kept separate from Dockside's statements.

**b.** In December 2004, A-Plus Floors received a customer's order and cash prepayment to install carpet in a new house that would not be ready for installation until March 2005. A-Plus Floors should record the revenue from the customer order in March 2005, not in December 2004.

**c.** If $30,000 cash is paid to buy land, the land is reported on the buyer's balance sheet at $30,000.

**QS 1-7**
Identifying accounting principles

C5

---

**a.** Total assets of HLC Financial Co. equal $40,000 and its equity is $10,000. What is the amount of its liabilities?

**b.** Total assets of Deep Valley Co. equal $55,000 and its liabilities and equity amounts are equal. What is the amount of its liabilities? What is the amount of its equity?

**QS 1-8**
Applying the accounting equation

A1

---

Use the accounting equation to compute the missing financial statement amounts (*a*), (*b*), and (*c*).

| Company | Assets | = | Liabilities | + | Equity |
|---------|--------|---|-------------|---|--------|
| 1 | $30,000 | | $ (a) | | $20,000 |
| 2 | $ (b) | | $50,000 | | $30,000 |
| 3 | $90,000 | | $10,000 | | $ (c) |

**QS 1-9**
Applying the accounting equation

A1

---

Use **Harley-Davidson**'s December 31, 2002, financial statements, in Appendix A near the end of the book, to answer the following:

**a.** Identify the dollar amounts of Harley's 2002 (1) assets, (2) liabilities, and (3) equity.

**b.** Using Harley's amounts from part *a*, verify that Assets = Liabilities + Equity.

**QS 1-10**
Identifying and computing assets, liabilities, and equity

A2  **Harley-**
**Davidson**

---

Indicate in which financial statement each item would most likely appear: income statement (I), balance sheet (B), statement of retained earnings (E), or statement of cash flows (CF).

**a.** Assets      **d.** Equipment      **g.** Total liabilities and equity

**b.** Revenues    **e.** Dividends      **h.** Cash from operating activities

**c.** Liabilities **f.** Expenses       **i.** Net decrease (or increase) in cash

**QS 1-11**
Identifying items by financial statements

P1

---

In a recent year's financial statements, **Boeing Company**, which is the largest aerospace company in the United States, reported the following. Compute and interpret Boeing's return on assets (assume competitors average a 6% return on assets).

**QS 1-12**
Computing and interpreting return on assets

A3

| | |
|---|---|
| Sales . . . . . . . . . . . . . . . . . . | $21,924 million |
| Net income . . . . . . . . . . . . . | 856 million |
| Average total assets . . . . . . . . | 21,463 million |

# EXERCISES

**Exercise 1-1**

Distinguishing business organizations

C5

The following describe several different business organizations. Determine whether the description refers to a sole proprietorship, partnership, or corporation.

**a.** Ownership of Spirit Company is divided into 1,000 shares of stock.

**b.** Delta is owned by Sarah Gomez, who is personally liable for the debts of the business.

**c.** Jo Chen and Al Fitch own Financial Services, a financial services provider. Neither Chen nor Fitch has personal responsibility for the debts of Financial Services.

**d.** Sung Kwon and Frank Heflin own Get-It-There, a courier service. Both are personally liable for the debts of the business.

**e.** XLT Services does not have separate legal existence apart from the one person who owns it.

**f.** BioProducts does not pay income taxes and has one owner.

**g.** Tampa Biz pays its own income taxes and has two owners.

---

**Exercise 1-2**

Identifying accounting principles

C5

Match each of the numbered descriptions with the principle it best reflects. Indicate your answer by writing the letter for the appropriate principle in the blank space next to each description.

**A.** General accounting principle       **E.** Specific accounting principle

**B.** Cost principle                     **F.** Objectivity principle

**C.** Business entity principle          **G.** Going-concern principle

**D.** Revenue recognition principle

_____ **1.** Usually created by a pronouncement from an authoritative body.

_____ **2.** Financial statements reflect the assumption that the business continues operating.

_____ **3.** Derived from long-used and generally accepted accounting practices.

_____ **4.** Financial statement information is supported by evidence other than someone's opinion or belief.

_____ **5.** Every business is accounted for separately from its owner or owners.

_____ **6.** Revenue is recorded only when the earnings process is complete.

_____ **7.** Information is based on actual costs incurred in transactions.

---

**Exercise 1-3**

Describing accounting responsibilities

C2   C3

Many accounting professionals work in one of the following three areas:

**A.** Financial accounting       **B.** Managerial accounting       **C.** Tax accounting

Identify the area of accounting that is most involved in each of the following responsibilities:

_____ **1.** External auditing.          _____ **5.** Planning transactions to minimize taxes.

_____ **2.** Cost accounting.            _____ **6.** Preparing external financial statements.

_____ **3.** Budgeting.                  _____ **7.** Reviewing reports for SEC compliance.

_____ **4.** Internal auditing.          _____ **8.** Investigating violations of tax laws.

---

**Exercise 1-4**

Identifying accounting users and uses

C2

Much of accounting is directed at servicing the information needs of those users that are external to an organization. Identify at least three external users of accounting information and indicate two questions they might seek to answer through their use of accounting information.

---

**Exercise 1-5**

Identifying ethical concerns

C4

Assume the following role and describe a situation in which ethical considerations play an important part in guiding your decisions and actions:

**a.** You are a student in an introductory accounting course.

**b.** You are a manager with responsibility for several employees.

**c.** You are an accounting professional preparing tax returns for clients.

**d.** You are an accounting professional with audit clients that are competitors in business.

Match each of the numbered descriptions with the term or phrase it best reflects. Indicate your answer by writing the letter for the term or phrase in the blank provided.

**A.** Audit     **C.** Ethics     **E.** SEC     **G.** Net income

**B.** GAAP     **D.** Tax accounting     **F.** Public accountants     **H.** IASB

_____ **1.** Amount a business earns after paying all expenses and costs associated with its sales and revenues.

_____ **2.** An examination of an organization's accounting system and records that adds credibility to financial statements.

_____ **3.** Principles that determine whether an action is right or wrong.

_____ **4.** Accounting professionals who provide services to many clients.

_____ **5.** An accounting area that includes planning future transactions to minimize taxes paid.

**Exercise 1-6**

Learning the language of business

C1–C4

---

Answer the following questions. (*Hint:* Use the accounting equation.)

**a.** Fong's Medical Supplies has assets equal to $123,000 and liabilities equal to $53,000 at year-end. What is the total equity for Fong's business at year-end?

**b.** At the beginning of the year, Beyonce Company's assets are $200,000 and its equity is $150,000. During the year, assets increase $70,000 and liabilities increase $30,000. What is the equity at the end of the year?

**c.** At the beginning of the year, New Wave Company's liabilities equal $60,000. During the year, assets increase by $80,000, and at year-end assets equal $180,000. Liabilities decrease $10,000 during the year. What are the beginning and ending amounts of equity?

**Exercise 1-7**

Using the accounting equation

A1  A2

**Check** (c) Beg. equity, $40,000

---

Determine the missing amount from each of the separate situations a, b, and c below.

| | Assets | = | Liabilities | + | Equity |
|---|---|---|---|---|---|
| a. | ? | = | $30,000 | + | $65,000 |
| b. | $ 89,000 | = | $22,000 | + | ? |
| c. | $132,000 | = | ? | + | $20,000 |

**Exercise 1-8**

Using the accounting equation

A1

---

Provide an example of a transaction that creates the described effects for the separate cases *a* through *g*.

**a.** Decreases an asset and decreases equity.

**b.** Increases an asset and increases a liability.

**c.** Decreases a liability and increases a liability.

**d.** Decreases an asset and decreases a liability.

**e.** Increases an asset and decreases an asset.

**f.** Increases a liability and decreases equity.

**g.** Increases an asset and increases equity.

**Exercise 1-9**

Identifying effects of transactions on the accounting equation

A1  A2

---

Mulan began a new consulting firm on January 5. The accounting equation showed the following balances after each of the company's first five transactions. Analyze the accounting equation for each transaction and describe each of the five transactions with their amounts.

**Exercise 1-10**

Analysis using the accounting equation

A1  A2

| | | | Assets | | | | | | = | Liabilities | + | | Equity | |
|---|---|---|---|---|---|---|---|---|---|---|---|---|---|---|
| Trans-action | Cash | + | Accounts Receiv-able | + | Office Sup-plies | + | Office Furni-ture | = | Accounts Payable | + | Common Stock | + | Revenues |
| a. | $20,000 | + | $ 0 | + | $ 0 | + | $ 0 | = | $ 0 | + | $20,000 | + | $ 0 |
| b. | 19,000 | + | 0 | + | 1,500 | + | 0 | = | 500 | + | 20,000 | + | 0 |
| c. | 11,000 | + | 0 | + | 1,500 | + | 8,000 | = | 500 | + | 20,000 | + | 0 |
| d. | 11,000 | + | 3,000 | + | 1,500 | + | 8,000 | = | 500 | + | 20,000 | + | 3,000 |
| e. | 11,500 | + | 3,000 | + | 1,500 | + | 8,000 | = | 500 | + | 20,000 | + | 3,500 |

## Exercise 1-11

Identifying effects of
transactions on accounting
equation

A1   A2

The following table shows the effects of five transactions (*a* through *e*) on the assets, liabilities, and
equity of Bonita Boutique. Write short descriptions of the probable nature of each transaction.

|   | Assets | | | | = Liabilities + | | Equity | |
|---|---|---|---|---|---|---|---|---|
|   | Cash | + Accounts Receivable | + Office Supplies | + Land | = Accounts Payable | + Common Stock | + Revenues | |
|   | $ 10,500 | + $ 0 | + $1,500 | + $ 9,500 | = $ 0 | + $21,500 | + $ 0 | |
| a. | − 2,000 | | | + 2,000 | | | | |
| b. | | | + 500 | | +500 | | | |
| c. | | + 950 | | | | | + 950 | |
| d. | − 500 | | | | −500 | | | |
| e. | + 950 | − 950 | | | | | | |
|   | $ 8,950 | + $ 0 | + $2,000 | + $ 11,500 | = $ 0 | + $21,500 | + $950 | |

## Exercise 1-12

Identifying effects of
transactions on the
accounting equation and
computing return on assets

A1   A2

Pamela Maben began a professional practice on June 1 and plans to prepare financial statements at
the end of each month. During June, Maben (the owner) completed these transactions:

**a.** Owner invested $50,000 cash along with equipment that had a $10,000 market value in exchange
for common stock.

**b.** Paid $1,600 cash for rent of office space for the month.

**c.** Purchased $12,000 of additional equipment on credit (due within 30 days).

**d.** Completed work for a client and immediately collected the $2,000 cash earned.

**e.** Completed work for a client and sent a bill for $7,000 to be paid within 30 days.

**f.** Purchased additional equipment for $8,000 cash.

**g.** Paid an assistant $2,400 cash as wages for the month.

**h.** Collected $5,000 cash on the amount owed by the client described in transaction *e*.

**i.** Paid $12,000 cash to settle the liability created in transaction *c*.

**j.** Paid $500 cash dividends to the owner.

**Required**

**Check**   Net income, $5,000

Create a table like the one in Exhibit 1.9, using the following headings for columns: Cash; Accounts
Receivable; Equipment; Accounts Payable; Common Stock; Dividends; Revenues; and Expenses. Then
use additions and subtractions to show the effects of the transactions on individual items of the accounting equation. Show new balances after each transaction.

## Exercise 1-13

Preparing an income
statement

P1

On October 1, Sasha Shandi organized Best Answers a new consulting firm. On October 31, the company's records show the following items and amounts. Use this information to prepare an October income statement for the business.

| | | | |
|---|---|---|---|
| Cash .................. | $ 2,000 | Cash dividends ............. | $ 3,360 |
| Accounts receivable ....... | 13,000 | Consulting fees earned ........ | 15,000 |
| Office supplies ........... | 4,250 | Rent expense ............... | 2,550 |
| Land ................... | 36,000 | Salaries expense ............. | 6,000 |
| Office equipment ......... | 28,000 | Telephone expense ........... | 660 |
| Accounts payable ........ | 7,500 | Miscellaneous expenses ....... | 680 |
| Common stock ........... | 74,000 | | |

**Check**   Net income, $5,110

## Exercise 1-14

Preparing a statement of
retained earnings   P1

Use the information in Exercise 1-13 to prepare an October statement of retained earnings for Best
Answers.

Use the information in Exercise 1-13 (if completed, you can also use your solution to Exercise 1-14) to prepare an October 31 balance sheet for Best Answers.

**Exercise 1-15**
Preparing a balance sheet   P1

Use the information in Exercise 1-13 to prepare an October 31 statement of cash flows for Best Answers. Also assume the following:

**a.** The owner's initial investment consists of $38,000 cash and $36,000 in land in exchange for common stock.

**b.** The $28,000 equipment purchase is paid in cash.

**c.** The accounts payable balance of $7,500 consists of the $4,250 office supplies purchase and $3,250 in employee salaries yet to be paid.

**d.** The rent, telephone, and miscellaneous expenses are paid in cash.

**e.** Only $2,000 cash has been collected for the $15,000 consulting services provided.

**Exercise 1-16**
Preparing a statement of cash flows

P1

**Check**   Net increase in cash, $2,000

Indicate the section where each of the following would appear on the statement of cash flows.
**A.** Cash flows from operating activity
**B.** Cash flows from investing activity
**C.** Cash flows from financing activity

**Exercise 1-17**
Identifying sections of the statement of cash flows

P1

_____ **1.** Cash paid for wages
_____ **2.** Cash paid for dividends
_____ **3.** Cash purchase of equipment
_____ **4.** Cash paid for advertising

_____ **5.** Cash paid on an account payable
_____ **6.** Cash received from stock issued
_____ **7.** Cash received from clients
_____ **8.** Cash paid for rent

Geneva Group reports net income of $20,000 for 2005. At the beginning of 2005, Geneva Group had $100,000 in assets. By the end of 2005, assets had grown to $150,000. What is Geneva Group's 2005 return on assets? How would you assess its performance if competitors average a 10% return on assets?

**Exercise 1-18**
Analysis of return on assets

A3

Match each transaction or event to one of the following activities of an organization: financing activities (F), investing activities (I), or operating activities (O).

**a.** _____ An owner contributes resources to the business in exchange for stock.
**b.** _____ An organization purchases equipment.
**c.** _____ An organization advertises a new product.
**d.** _____ The organization borrows money from a bank.
**e.** _____ An organization sells some of its land.

**Exercise 1-19ᴮ**
Identifying business activities

C6

> *Problem Set B* located at the end of *Problem Set A* is provided for <u>each</u> problem to reinforce the learning process. *Problem Set C* (with solutions for instructors) is provided on this book's Website.

The following financial statement information is from five separate companies:

**PROBLEM SET A**

**Problem 1-1A**
Computing missing information using accounting knowledge

A1   A2

| | Company A | Company B | Company C | Company D | Company E |
|---|---|---|---|---|---|
| **December 31, 2004:** | | | | | |
| Assets . . . . . . . . . . . . . . . | $45,000 | $35,000 | $29,000 | $80,000 | $123,000 |
| Liabilities . . . . . . . . . . . . . | 23,500 | 22,500 | 14,000 | 38,000 | ? |
| **December 31, 2005:** | | | | | |
| Assets . . . . . . . . . . . . . . . | 48,000 | 41,000 | ? | 125,000 | 112,500 |
| Liabilities . . . . . . . . . . . . . | ? | 27,500 | 19,000 | 64,000 | 75,000 |
| **During year 2005:** | | | | | |
| Stock issuances . . . . . . . . . | 5,000 | 1,500 | 7,750 | ? | 4,500 |
| Net income . . . . . . . . . . . . | 7,500 | ? | 9,000 | 12,000 | 18,000 |
| Cash dividends . . . . . . . . . . | 2,500 | 3,000 | 3,875 | 0 | 9,000 |

**Required**

**1.** Answer the following questions about Company A:

   **a.** What is the equity amount on December 31, 2004?

   **b.** What is the equity amount on December 31, 2005?

   **c.** What is the amount of liabilities on December 31, 2005?

**2.** Answer the following questions about Company B:

   **a.** What is the equity amount on December 31, 2004?

   **b.** What is the equity amount on December 31, 2005?

   **c.** What is net income for year 2005?

**3.** Calculate the amount of assets for Company C on December 31, 2005.

**4.** Calculate the amount of stock issuances for Company D during year 2005.

**5.** Calculate the amount of liabilities for Company E on December 31, 2004.

---

**Problem 1-2A**

Identifying effects of transactions on financial statements

A1   A2

Identify how each of the following separate transactions affects financial statements. For the balance sheet, identify how each transaction affects total assets, total liabilities, and total equity. For the income statement, identify how each transaction affects net income. For the statement of cash flows, identify how each transaction affects cash flows from operating activities, cash flows from financing activities, and cash flows from investing activities. For increases, place a "+" in the column or columns. For decreases, place a "−" in the column or columns. If both an increase and a decrease occur, place a "+/−" in the column or columns. The first transaction is completed as an example.

| | | **Balance Sheet** | | | **Income Statement** | **Statement of Cash Flows** | | |
| | **Transaction** | **Total Assets** | **Total Liab.** | **Total Equity** | **Net Income** | **Operating Activities** | **Financing Activities** | **Investing Activities** |
|---|---|---|---|---|---|---|---|---|
| 1 | Owner invests cash for stock | + | | + | | | + | |
| 2 | Receives cash for services provided | | | | | | | |
| 3 | Pays cash for employee wages | | | | | | | |
| 4 | Incurs legal costs on credit | | | | | | | |
| 5 | Borrows cash by signing long-term note payable | | | | | | | |
| 6 | Pays cash dividend | | | | | | | |
| 7 | Buys land by signing note payable | | | | | | | |
| 8 | Provides services on credit | | | | | | | |
| 9 | Buys office equipment for cash | | | | | | | |
| 10 | Collects cash on receivable from (8) | | | | | | | |

---

**Problem 1-3A**

Preparing an income statement

P1

The following is selected financial information for Valdez Energy Company for the year ended December 31, 2005: revenues, $65,000; expenses, $50,000; net income, $15,000.

**Required**

Prepare the 2005 calendar-year income statement for Valdez Energy Company.

---

**Problem 1-4A**

Preparing a balance sheet

P1

The following is selected financial information for Amico as of December 31, 2005: liabilities, $34,000; equity, $56,000; assets, $90,000.

**Required**

Prepare the balance sheet for Amico as of December 31, 2005.

The following is selected financial information of Trimark for the year ended December 31, 2005:

**Problem 1-5A**
Preparing a statement of cash flows

P1

| | |
|---|---|
| Cash used by investing activities . . . . . . . . | $(3,000) |
| Net increase in cash . . . . . . . . . . . . . . . | 200 |
| Cash used by financing activities . . . . . . . . | (3,800) |
| Cash from operating activities . . . . . . . . . | 7,000 |
| Cash, December 31, 2004 . . . . . . . . . . . . | 3,300 |

**Required**

Prepare the 2005 calendar-year statement of cash flows for Trimark.

---

The following is selected financial information for Boardwalk for the year ended December 31, 2005:

**Problem 1-6A**
Preparing a statement of retained earnings

P1

| | | | |
|---|---|---|---|
| Retained earnings, Dec. 31, 2005 . . . . . . | $15,000 | Cash dividends . . . . . . . . . . . . . . . . . | $2,000 |
| Net income . . . . . . . . . . . . . . . . . . . . | 9,000 | Retained earnings, Dec. 31, 2004 . . . . . . | 8,000 |

**Required**

Prepare the 2005 calendar-year statement of retained earnings for Boardwalk.

---

J. D. Simpson started The Simpson Co., a new business that began operations on May 1. Simpson Co. completed the following transactions during that first month:

**Problem 1-7A**
Analyzing transactions and preparing financial statements

C5 A2 P1

mhhe.com/wild3e

| May | 1 | J. D. Simpson invested $60,000 cash in the business in exchange for common stock. |
|---|---|---|
| | 1 | Rented a furnished office and paid $3,200 cash for May's rent. |
| | 3 | Purchased $1,680 of office equipment on credit. |
| | 5 | Paid $800 cash for this month's cleaning services. |
| | 8 | Provided consulting services for a client and immediately collected $4,600 cash. |
| | 12 | Provided $3,000 of consulting services for a client on credit. |
| | 15 | Paid $850 cash for an assistant's salary for the first half of this month. |
| | 20 | Received $3,000 cash payment for the services provided on May 12. |
| | 22 | Provided $2,800 of consulting services on credit. |
| | 25 | Received $2,800 cash payment for the services provided on May 22. |
| | 26 | Paid $1,680 cash for the office equipment purchased on May 3. |
| | 27 | Purchased $60 of advertising in this month's (May) local paper on credit; cash payment is due June 1. |
| | 28 | Paid $850 cash for an assistant's salary for the second half of this month. |
| | 30 | Paid $200 cash for this month's telephone bill. |
| | 30 | Paid $480 cash for this month's utilities. |
| | 31 | Paid $1,200 cash for dividends. |

**Required**

1. Arrange the following asset, liability, and equity titles in a table like Exhibit 1.9: Cash; Accounts Receivable; Office Equipment; Accounts Payable; Common Stock; Dividends; Revenues; and Expenses.

2. Show effects of the transactions on the accounts of the accounting equation by recording increases and decreases in the appropriate columns. Do not determine new account balances after each transaction. Determine the final total for each account and verify that the equation is in balance.

3. Prepare an income statement for May, a statement of retained earnings for May, a May 31 balance sheet, and a statement of cash flows for May.

**Check** (2) Ending balances: Cash, $61,140; Expenses, $6,440

(3) Net income, $3,960; Total assets, $62,820

## Problem 1-8A

Analyzing transactions and
preparing financial statements

C5   A2   P1

mhhe.com/wild3e

Curtis Hamilton started a new business and completed these transactions during December:

Dec. 1   Curtis Hamilton transferred $56,000 cash from a personal savings account to a checking
account in the name of Hamilton Electric in exchange for common stock.
2   Rented office space and paid $800 cash for the December rent.
3   Purchased $14,000 of electrical equipment by paying $3,200 cash and agreeing to pay the
$10,800 balance in 30 days.
5   Purchased office supplies by paying $900 cash.
6   Completed electrical work and immediately collected $1,000 cash for the work.
8   Purchased $3,800 of office equipment on credit.
15   Completed electrical work on credit in the amount of $4,000.
18   Purchased $500 of office supplies on credit.
20   Paid $3,800 cash for the office equipment purchased on December 8.
24   Billed a client $600 for electrical work completed; the balance is due in 30 days.
28   Received $4,000 cash for the work completed on December 15.
29   Paid the assistant's salary of $1,200 cash for this month.
30   Paid $440 cash for this month's utility bill.
31   Paid $700 cash for dividends.

### Required

1. Arrange the following asset, liability, and equity titles in a table like Exhibit 1.9: Cash; Accounts
Receivable; Office Supplies; Office Equipment; Electrical Equipment; Accounts Payable; Common
Stock; Dividends; Revenues; and Expenses.

**Check**   (2) Ending balances: Cash,
$49,960, Accounts Payable, $11,300

(3) Net income, $3,160;
Total assets, $69,760

2. Use additions and subtractions to show the effects of each transaction on the accounts in the accounting equation. Show new balances after each transaction.

3. Use the increases and decreases in the columns of the table from part 2 to prepare an income
statement, a statement of retained earnings, and a statement of cash flows for the month. Also prepare a balance sheet as of the end of the month.

### Analysis Component

4. Assume that the owner investment transaction on December 1 was $40,000 cash instead of $56,000
and that Hamilton Electric obtained the $16,000 difference by borrowing it from a bank. Explain
the effect of this change on total assets, total liabilities, and total equity.

## Problem 1-9A

Analyzing effects of transactions

C5   P1   A1   A2

Miranda Right started Right Consulting, a new business, and completed the following transactions
during its first year of operations:

**a.** M. Right invests $60,000 cash and office equipment valued at $30,000 in exchange for common
stock.

**b.** Purchased a $300,000 building to use as an office. Right paid $50,000 in cash and signed a note
payable promising to pay the $250,000 balance over the next ten years.

**c.** Purchased office equipment for $6,000 cash.

**d.** Purchased $4,000 of office supplies and $1,000 of office equipment on credit.

**e.** Paid a local newspaper $1,000 cash for printing an announcement of the office's opening.

**f.** Completed a financial plan for a client and billed that client $4,000 for the service.

**g.** Designed a financial plan for another client and immediately collected an $8,000 cash fee.

**h.** Paid $1,800 cash for dividends.

**i.** Received a $3,000 partial cash payment from the client described in transaction *f*.

**j.** Made a $500 cash payment on the equipment purchased in transaction *d*.

**k.** Paid $2,500 cash for the office secretary's wages.

### Required

1. Create a table like the one in Exhibit 1.9, using the following headings for the columns: Cash;
Accounts Receivable; Office Supplies; Office Equipment; Building; Accounts Payable; Notes
Payable; Common Stock; Dividends; Revenues; and Expenses.

**Check**   (2) Ending balances:
Cash, $9,200; Expenses, $3,500

(3) Net income, $8,500

2. Use additions and subtractions to show the effects of these transactions on individual items of the
accounting equation. Show new balances after each transaction.

3. Once you have completed the table, determine the company's net income.

Coca-Cola and PepsiCo both produce and market beverages that are direct competitors. Key financial figures (in $ millions) for these businesses over the past year follow:

| Key Figures | Coca-Cola | PepsiCo |
|---|---|---|
| Sales ...................... | 400 | $250.0 |
| Net income ................ | 50 | 37.5 |
| Average invested (assets) ....... | 625 | 312.5 |

**Problem 1-10A**
Computing and interpreting return on assets

A3

**Required**

**1.** Compute return on assets for (*a*) Coca-Cola and (*b*) PepsiCo.

**2.** Which company is more successful in its total amount of sales to consumers?

**3.** Which company is more successful in returning net income from its amount invested?

*Analysis Component*

**4.** Write a one-paragraph memorandum explaining which company you would invest your money in and why. (Limit your explanation to the information provided.)

**Check**   (1*a*) 8%; (1*b*) 12%

---

Zia manufactures, markets, and sells cellular telephones. The average total assets for Zia is $250,000. In its most recent year, Zia reported net income of $55,000 on revenues of $455,000.

**Required**

**1.** What is Zia's return on assets?

**2.** Does return on assets seem satisfactory for Zia given that its competitors average a 12% return on assets?

**3.** What are total expenses for Zia in its most recent year?

**4.** What is the average total amount of liabilities plus equity for Zia?

**Problem 1-11A**
Determining expenses, liabilities, equity and return on assets

A1   A3

**Check**   (3) $400,000
          (4) $250,000

---

All business decisions involve aspects of risk and return.

**Required**

Identify both the risk and the return in each of the following activities:

**1.** Investing $1,000 in a 4% savings account.

**2.** Placing a $1,000 bet on your favorite sports team.

**3.** Investing $10,000 in Yahoo! stock.

**4.** Taking out a $10,000 college loan to earn an accounting degree.

**Problem 1-12A**<sup>A</sup>
Identifying risk and return

A4

---

A startup company often engages in the following transactions in its first year of operations. Classify these transactions in one of the three major categories of an organization's business activities.

**A.** Financing     **B.** Investing     **C.** Operating

_____ **1.** Owner investing land in business.     _____ **5.** Purchasing equipment.
_____ **2.** Purchasing a building.     _____ **6.** Selling and distributing products.
_____ **3.** Purchasing land.     _____ **7.** Paying for advertising.
_____ **4.** Borrowing cash from a bank.     _____ **8.** Paying employee wages.

**Problem 1-13A**<sup>B</sup>
Describing organizational activities

C6

---

An organization undertakes various activities in pursuit of business success. Identify an organization's three major business activities, and describe each activity.

**Problem 1-14A**<sup>B</sup>
Describing organizational activities   C6

## PROBLEM SET B

### Problem 1-1B

Computing missing information using accounting knowledge

A1  A2

The following financial statement information is from five separate companies:

|  | Company V | Company W | Company X | Company Y | Company Z |
|---|---|---|---|---|---|
| **December 31, 2004:** | | | | | |
| Assets . . . . . . . . . . . . . . . | $45,000 | $70,000 | $121,500 | $82,500 | $124,000 |
| Liabilities . . . . . . . . . . . . . | 30,000 | 50,000 | 58,500 | 61,500 | ? |
| **December 31, 2005:** | | | | | |
| Assets . . . . . . . . . . . . . . . | 49,000 | 90,000 | 136,500 | ? | 160,000 |
| Liabilities . . . . . . . . . . . . . | 26,000 | ? | 55,500 | 72,000 | 52,000 |
| **During year 2005:** | | | | | |
| Stock issuances . . . . . . . . . | 6,000 | 10,000 | ? | 38,100 | 40,000 |
| Net income . . . . . . . . . . . . | ? | 30,000 | 16,500 | 24,000 | 32,000 |
| Cash dividends . . . . . . . . . | 4,500 | 2,000 | 0 | 18,000 | 6,000 |

### Required

**1.** Answer the following questions about Company V:

**a.** What is the amount of equity on December 31, 2004?

**Check** (1*b*) $23,000

**b.** What is the amount of equity on December 31, 2005?

**c.** What is net income for year 2005?

**2.** Answer the following questions about Company W:

**a.** What is the amount of equity on December 31, 2004?

**b.** What is the amount of equity on December 31, 2005?

(2*c*) $32,000

**c.** What is the amount of liabilities on December 31, 2005?

**3.** Calculate the amount of stock issuances for Company X during 2005.

(4) $137,100

**4.** Calculate the amount of assets for Company Y on December 31, 2005.

**5.** Calculate the amount of liabilities for Company Z on December 31, 2004.

### Problem 1-2B

Identifying effects of transactions on financial statements

A1  A2

Identify how each of the following separate transactions affects financial statements. For the balance sheet, identify how each transaction affects total assets, total liabilities, and total equity. For the income statement, identify how each transaction affects net income. For the statement of cash flows, identify how each transaction affects cash flows from operating activities, cash flows from financing activities, and cash flows from investing activities. For increases, place a "+" in the column or columns. For decreases, place a "−" in the column or columns. If both an increase and a decrease occur, place "+/−" in the column or columns. The first transaction is completed as an example.

| | | **Balance Sheet** | | | **Income Statement** | **Statement of Cash Flows** | | |
|---|---|---|---|---|---|---|---|---|
| | Transaction | Total Assets | Total Liab. | Total Equity | Net Income | Operating Activities | Financing Activities | Investing Activities |
| 1 | Owner invests cash for stock | + | | + | | | + | |
| 2 | Buys building by signing note payable | | | | | | | |
| 3 | Pays cash for salaries incurred | | | | | | | |
| 4 | Provides services for cash | | | | | | | |
| 5 | Pays cash for rent incurred | | | | | | | |
| 6 | Incurs utilities costs on credit | | | | | | | |
| 7 | Buys store equipment for cash | | | | | | | |
| 8 | Pays cash dividend | | | | | | | |
| 9 | Provides services on credit | | | | | | | |
| 10 | Collects cash on receivable from (9) | | | | | | | |

Selected financial information for Online Co. for the year ended December 31, 2005, follows:

| | | | | | |
|---|---|---|---|---|---|
| Revenues . . . . . . . | $58,000 | Expenses . . . . . . . | $30,000 | Net income . . . . . . . | $28,000 |

**Problem 1-3B**
Preparing an income statement

P1

**Required**

Use the information provided to prepare the 2005 calendar-year income statement for Online Co.

---

The following is selected financial information for RWB Company as of December 31, 2005:

| | | | | | |
|---|---|---|---|---|---|
| Liabilities . . . . . . . | $74,000 | Equity . . . . . . . | $40,000 | Assets . . . . . . . | $114,000 |

**Problem 1-4B**
Preparing a balance sheet

P1

**Required**

Use the information provided to prepare the balance sheet for RWB as of December 31, 2005.

---

Selected financial information of BuyRight Co. for the year ended December 31, 2005, follows:

| | |
|---|---|
| Cash from investing activities . . . . . . . . | $2,600 |
| Net increase in cash . . . . . . . . . . . . . | 1,400 |
| Cash from financing activities . . . . . . . . | 2,800 |
| Cash used by operating activities . . . . . | (4,000) |
| Cash, December 31, 2004 . . . . . . . . . . | 1,300 |

**Problem 1-5B**
Preparing a statement of cash flows

P1

**Required**

Use this information to prepare the 2005 calendar-year statement of cash flows for BuyRight.

---

The following is selected financial information of ComEx for the year ended December 31, 2005:

| | | | |
|---|---|---|---|
| Retained earnings, Dec. 31, 2005 . . . . . | $47,000 | Cash dividends . . . . . . . . . . . . . . . . | $ 8,000 |
| Net income . . . . . . . . . . . . . . . . . . . | 6,000 | Retained earnings, Dec. 31, 2004 . . . . . | 49,000 |

**Problem 1-6B**
Preparing a statement of retained earnings

P1

**Required**

Prepare the 2005 calendar-year statement of retained earnings for ComEx.

---

Ken Stone launched a new business, Ken's Maintenance Co., that began operations on June 1. The following transactions were completed by the company during that first month:

June  1  K. Stone invested $120,000 cash in the business in exchange for common stock.
     2  Rented a furnished office and paid $4,500 cash for June's rent.
     4  Purchased $2,400 of equipment on credit.
     6  Paid $1,125 cash for the next week's advertising of the opening of the business.
     8  Completed maintenance services for a customer and immediately collected $750 cash.
    14  Completed $6,300 of maintenance services for First Union Center on credit.
    16  Paid $900 cash for an assistant's salary for the first half of the month.
    20  Received $6,300 cash payment for services completed for First Union Center on June 14.
    21  Completed $3,500 of maintenance services for Skyway Co. on credit.
    24  Completed $825 of maintenance services for Comfort Motel on credit.
    25  Received $3,500 cash payment from Skyway Co. for the work completed on June 21.
    26  Made payment of $2,400 cash for the equipment purchased on June 4.
    28  Paid $900 cash for an assistant's salary for the second half of this month.
    29  Paid $2,000 cash for dividends.
    30  Paid $120 cash for this month's telephone bill.
    30  Paid $525 cash for this month's utilities.

**Problem 1-7B**
Analyzing transactions and preparing financial statements

C5  A2  P1

**Required**

1. Arrange the following asset, liability, and equity titles in a table like Exhibit 1.9: Cash; Accounts Receivable; Equipment; Accounts Payable; Common Stock; Dividends; Revenues; and Expenses.

**2.** Show the effects of the transactions on the accounts of the accounting equation by recording increases and decreases in the appropriate columns. Do not determine new account balances after each transaction. Determine the final total for each account and verify that the equation is in balance.

**3.** Prepare a June income statement, a June statement of retained earnings, a June 30 balance sheet, and a June statement of cash flows.

---

**Problem 1-8B**

Analyzing transactions and preparing financial statements

C5  A2  P1

Swender Excavating Co., owned by Patrick Swender, began operations in July and completed these transactions during that first month:

July  1   P. Swender invested $60,000 cash in the business in exchange for common stock.
      2   Rented office space and paid $500 cash for the July rent.
      3   Purchased excavating equipment for $4,000 by paying $800 cash and agreeing to pay the $3,200 balance in 30 days.
      6   Purchased office supplies for $500 cash.
      8   Completed work for a customer and immediately collected $2,200 cash for the work.
     10   Purchased $3,800 of office equipment on credit.
     15   Completed work for a customer on credit in the amount of $2,400.
     17   Purchased $1,920 of office supplies on credit.
     23   Paid $3,800 cash for the office equipment purchased on July 10.
     25   Billed a customer $5,000 for work completed; the balance is due in 30 days.
     28   Received $2,400 cash for the work completed on July 15.
     30   Paid an assistant's salary of $1,260 cash for this month.
     31   Paid $260 cash for this month's utility bill.
     31   Paid $1,200 cash for dividends.

**Required**

**1.** Arrange the following asset, liability, and equity titles in a table like Exhibit 1.9: Cash; Accounts Receivable; Office Supplies; Office Equipment; Excavating Equipment; Accounts Payable; Common Stock; Dividends; Revenues; and Expenses.

**2.** Use additions and subtractions to show the effects of each transaction on the accounts in the accounting equation. Show new balances after each transaction.

**3.** Use the increases and decreases in the columns of the table from part 2 to prepare an income statement, a statement of retained earnings, and a statement of cash flows for the month. Also prepare a balance sheet as of the end of the month.

*Analysis Component*

**4.** Assume that the $4,000 purchase of excavating equipment on July 3 was financed from an owner investment of another $4,000 cash in the business in exchange for more common stock (instead of the purchase conditions described in the transaction). Explain the effect of this change on total assets, total liabilities, and total equity.

---

**Problem 1-9B**

Analyzing effects of transactions

C5  P1  A1  A2

Tiana Moore started a new business, Tiana's Solutions, that completed the following transactions during its first year of operations:

**a.** T. Moore invests $95,000 cash and office equipment valued at $20,000 in exchange for common stock.

**b.** Purchased a $120,000 building to use as an office. Moore paid $20,000 in cash and signed a note payable promising to pay the $100,000 balance over the next ten years.

**c.** Purchased office equipment for $20,000 cash.

**d.** Purchased $1,400 of office supplies and $3,000 of office equipment on credit.

**e.** Paid a local newspaper $400 cash for printing an announcement of the office's opening.

**f.** Completed a financial plan for a client and billed that client $1,800 for the service.

**g.** Designed a financial plan for another client and immediately collected a $2,000 cash fee.

**h.** Paid $5,000 cash for dividends.

**i.** Received $1,800 cash from the client described in transaction *f*.

**j.** Made a $2,000 cash payment on the equipment purchased in transaction *d*.

**k.** Paid $2,000 cash for the office secretary's wages.

**Required**

**1.** Create a table like the one in Exhibit 1.9, using the following headings for the columns: Cash; Accounts Receivable; Office Supplies; Office Equipment; Building; Accounts Payable; Notes Payable; Common Stock; Dividends; Revenues; and Expenses.

**2.** Use additions and subtractions to show the effects of these transactions on individual items of the accounting equation. Show new balances after each transaction.

**3.** Once you have completed the table, determine the company's net income.

**Check**  (2) Ending balances: Cash, $49,400; Expenses, $2,400

(3) Net income, $1,400

---

AT&T and GTE produce and market telecommunications products and are competitors. Key financial figures (in $ millions) for these businesses over the past year follow:

**Problem 1-10B**
Computing and interpreting return on assets

A3

| Key Figures | AT&T | GTE |
|---|---|---|
| Sales . . . . . . . . . . . . . . . . | $79,609 | $19,957 |
| Net income  . . . . . . . . . . . | 139 | 2,538 |
| Average invested (assets) . . . | 87,261 | 37,019 |

**Required**

**1.** Compute return on assets for (*a*) AT&T and (*b*) GTE.

**2.** Which company is more successful in the total amount of sales to consumers?

**3.** Which company is more successful in returning net income from its amount invested?

**Check**  (1a) 0.16%; (1b) 6.9%

*Analysis Component*

**4.** Write a one-paragraph memorandum explaining which company you would invest your money in and why. (Limit your explanation to the information provided.)

---

Aspen Company manufactures, markets, and sells snowmobile equipment. The average total assets for Aspen Company is $2,000,000. In its most recent year, Aspen reported net income of $100,000 on revenues of $1,200,000.

**Problem 1-11B**
Determining expenses, liabilities, equity, and return on assets

A1  A3

**Required**

**1.** What is Aspen Company's return on assets?

**2.** Does return on assets seem satisfactory for Aspen given that its competitors average a 9.5% return on assets?

**3.** What are the total expenses for Aspen Company in its most recent year?

**4.** What is the average total amount of liabilities plus equity for Aspen Company?

**Check**  (3) $1,100,000

(4) $2,000,000

---

All business decisions involve aspects of risk and return.

**Problem 1-12B^A**
Identifying risk and return

A4

**Required**

Identify both the risk and the return in each of the following activities:

**1.** Stashing $1,000 under your mattress.

**2.** Placing a $500 bet on a horse running in the Kentucky Derby.

**3.** Investing $10,000 in Nike stock.

**4.** Investing $10,000 in U.S. Savings Bonds.

---

A startup company often engages in the following activities during its first year of operations. Classify each of the following activities into one of the three major activities of an organization:

**A.** Financing     **B.** Investing     **C.** Operating

**Problem 1-13B^B**
Describing organizational activities

C6

_____ **1.** Providing client services.

_____ **2.** Obtaining a bank loan.

_____ **3.** Purchasing machinery.

_____ **4.** Researching products.

_____ **5.** Supervising workers.

_____ **6.** Owner investing money in business.

_____ **7.** Renting office space.

_____ **8.** Paying utilities expenses.

---

**Problem 1-14B<sup>B</sup>**
Describing organizational
activities   C6

Identify in outline format the three major business activities of an organization. For each of these activities, identify at least two specific transactions or events normally undertaken by the business's owners or managers.

---

**PROBLEM SET C**

Problem Set C is available at the book's Website to further reinforce and assess your learning.

---

*This serial problem starts in this chapter and continues throughout most chapters of the book. It is most readily solved if you use the Working Papers that accompany this book.*

---

**SERIAL PROBLEM**

Success Systems

On October 1, 2004, Kay Breeze launched a computer services company, **Success Systems,** that is organized as a corporation and provides consulting services, computer system installations, and custom program development. Breeze adopts the calendar year for reporting purposes and expects to prepare the company's first set of financial statements on December 31, 2004.

**Required**

Create a table like the one in Exhibit 1.9 using the following headings for columns: Cash; Accounts Receivable; Computer Supplies; Office Equipment; Accounts Payable; Common Stock; Dividends; Revenues; and Expenses. Then use additions and subtractions to show the effects of the October transactions for Success Systems on the individual items of the accounting equation. Show new balances after each transaction.

Oct.  1   Kay Breeze invested $55,000 cash, a $20,000 computer system, and $8,000 of office equipment in the business in exchange for common stock.
      3   Purchased $1,420 of computer supplies on credit from Cain Office Products.
      6   Billed Easy Leasing $4,800 for services performed in installing a new Web server.
      8   Paid $1,420 cash for the computer supplies purchased from Cain Office Products on October 3.
      10  Hired Sherry Adams as a part-time assistant for $125 per day, as needed.
      12  Billed Easy Leasing another $1,400 for services performed.
      15  Received $4,800 cash from Easy Leasing on its account.
      17  Paid $805 cash to repair computer equipment damaged when moving it.
      20  Paid $1,940 cash for an advertisement in the local newspaper.
      22  Received $1,400 cash from Easy Leasing on its account.
      28  Billed Clark Company $5,208 for services performed.
      31  Paid $875 cash for Sherry Adam's wages for seven days of work.
      31  Paid $3,600 cash for dividends.

**Check**  Ending balances: Cash, $52,560; Revenues, $11,408; Expenses, $3,620

---

*Beyond the Numbers (BTN) is a special problem section aimed to refine communication, conceptual, analysis, and research skills. It includes many activities helpful in developing an active learning environment.*

## BEYOND THE NUMBERS

**REPORTING IN ACTION**

A1  A3  A4

**BTN 1-1**   Key financial figures for **Krispy Kreme's** fiscal year ended February 2, 2003, follow:

| Key Figure | In Thousands |
|---|---|
| Liabilities + Equity | $410,487 |
| Net income | 33,478 |
| Revenues | 491,549 |

**Required**

1. What is the total amount of assets invested in Krispy Kreme?
2. What is Krispy Kreme's return on assets? Its assets at February 3, 2002, equal $255,376 (in thousands).
3. How much are total expenses for Krispy Kreme?
4. Does Krispy Kreme's return on assets seem satisfactory if competitors average a 3% return?

**Check**   (2) 10.1%

*Roll On*

5. Access Krispy Kreme's financial statements (Form 10-K) for fiscal years ending after February 2, 2003, from its Website (**KrispyKreme.com**) or from the SEC Website (**www.sec.gov**) and compute its return on assets for those fiscal years. Compare the February 2, 2003, fiscal year-end return on assets to any subsequent years' returns you are able to compute, and interpret the results.

---

**BTN 1-2**   Key comparative figures ($ thousands) for both **Krispy Kreme** and **Tastykake** follow:

| Key Figure | Krispy Kreme | Tastykake |
|---|---|---|
| Liabilities + Equity | $410,487 | $116,560 |
| Net income | 33,478 | 2,000* |
| Revenues (sales) | 491,549 | 162,263 |

* Restructuring charges are removed.

**COMPARATIVE ANALYSIS**

A1  A3  A4

**Required**

1. What is the total amount of assets invested in (*a*) Krispy Kreme and (*b*) Tastykake?
2. What is the return on assets for (*a*) Krispy Kreme and (*b*) Tastykake? Krispy Kreme's beginning-year assets equal $255,376 (in thousands) and Tastykake's beginning-year assets equal $116,137 (in thousands).
3. How much are expenses for (*a*) Krispy Kreme and (*b*) Tastykake?
4. Is return on assets satisfactory for (*a*) Krispy Kreme and (*b*) Tastykake? (Assume competitors average a 3% return.)
5. What can you conclude about Krispy Kreme and Tastykake from these computations?

**Check**   (2b) 1.7%

---

**BTN 1-3**   Juanita Cruz works in a public accounting firm and hopes to eventually be a partner. The management of Allnet Company invites Cruz to prepare a bid to audit Allnet's financial statements. In discussing the audit fee, Allnet's management suggests a fee range in which the amount depends on the reported profit of Allnet. The higher its profit, the higher will be the audit fee paid to Cruz's firm.

**ETHICS CHALLENGE**

C4  C5

**Required**

1. Identify the parties potentially affected by this audit and the fee plan proposed.
2. What are the ethical factors in this situation? Explain.
3. Would you recommend that Cruz accept this audit fee arrangement? Why or why not?
4. Describe some ethical considerations guiding your recommendation.

---

**BTN 1-4**   Refer to this chapter's opening feature about **The Chocolate Farm**. Assume that the Macmillans wish to expand The Chocolate Farm to include a store devoted to selling food decorations related to the main business. They meet with a loan officer of a Denver bank to discuss a loan.

**COMMUNICATING IN PRACTICE**

A1  C2

**Required**

1. Prepare a half-page report outlining the information you would request from the Macmillans if you were the loan officer.
2. Indicate whether the information you request and your loan decision are affected by the form of business organization for the proposed Chocolate Farm store.

## TAKING IT TO THE NET

A3

mhhe.com/wild3e

**BTN 1-5**    Visit the EDGAR database at (www.sec.gov). Access the Form 10-K report of World Wrestling Entertainment (ticker WWE) filed on July 26, 2002.

**Required**

**1.** On page 16 of the 10-K report you will find comparative income statements of WWE for the years 1998–2002. How would you describe the revenue trend for WWE over this five-year period?

**2.** Has the WWE been profitable (see net income) over this five-year period?

## TEAMWORK IN ACTION

C1

**BTN 1-6**    Teamwork is important in today's business world. Successful teams schedule convenient meetings, maintain regular communications, and cooperate with and support their members. This assignment aims to establish support/learning teams, initiate discussions, and set meeting times.

**Required**

**1.** Form teams and open a team discussion to determine a regular time and place for your team to meet between each scheduled class meeting. Notify your instructor via a memorandum or e-mail message as to when and where your team will hold regularly scheduled meetings.

**2.** Develop a list of telephone numbers and/or e-mail addresses of your teammates.

Book's Website provides free and easy access to all articles for every Business Week Activity.

## BUSINESS WEEK ACTIVITY    C1

mhhe.com/wild3e

**BTN 1-7**    *Business Week* publishes a ranking of the top 1,000 companies based on several performance measures. This issue is called the *Business Week Global 1000*. Obtain the July 14, 2003, publication of this issue—this book's Website maintains free access to this article.

**Required**

**1.** What are the top 10 companies on the basis of market value?

**2.** Are any of the top 10 companies in the same industry?

**3.** How many of the top 10 based on market capitalization are not U.S. companies?

## ENTREPRENEURIAL DECISION

A1    A2

**Check** (2) 25%

**BTN 1-8**    Refer to this chapter's opening feature about **The Chocolate Farm**. Assume the Macmillans decide to open a small retail store to supplement their chocolate operations.

**Required**

**1.** The Macmillans obtain a $50,000 bank loan and contribute $30,000 of their own assets in exchange for common stock to support the opening of the new store.

  **a.** What is the new store's total amount of liabilities plus equity?

  **b.** What is the new store's total amount of assets?

**2.** If the Macmillans earn $20,000 of income in the first year the retail store operates, compute the store's return on assets (assume average assets equal $80,000). Assess its performance if competitors average a 10% return.

## HITTING THE ROAD

C2

**BTN 1-9**    You are to interview a local business owner. (This can be a friend or relative.) Opening lines of communication with members of the business community can provide personal benefits of business networking. If you do not know the owner, you should call ahead to introduce yourself and explain your position as a student and your assignment requirements. You should request a thirty minute appointment for a face-to-face or phone interview to discuss the form of organization and operations of the business. Be prepared to make a good impression.

**Required**

**1.** Identify and describe the main operating activities and the form of organization for this business.

**2.** Determine and explain why the owner(s) chose this particular form of organization.

**3.** Identify any special advantages and/or disadvantages the owner(s) experiences in operating with this form of business organization.

**BTN 1-10** Grupo Bimbo (<u>GrupoBimbo.com</u>) is a leader in the baking industry and also competes with both **Krispy Kreme** and **Tastykake**. Key financial figures for Grupo Bimbo follow:

**GLOBAL DECISION**

A1 A3 A4

| Key Figure* | Pesos in Millions |
|---|---|
| Average assets ......... | 27,750 |
| Net income .......... | 1,003 |
| Revenues ............ | 41,373 |
| Return on assets ........ | 3.6% |

\* Figures prepared in accordance with Generally Accepted Accounting Principles in Mexico.

**Required**

1. Identify any concerns you have in comparing Grupo Bimbo's income, revenue, liabilities, and equity figures to those of Krispy Kreme and Tastykake (in BTN 1-2) for purposes of making business decisions.

2. Identify any concerns you have in comparing Grupo Bimbo's return on assets ratio to those of Krispy Kreme and Tastykake (in BTN 1-2) for purposes of making business decisions.

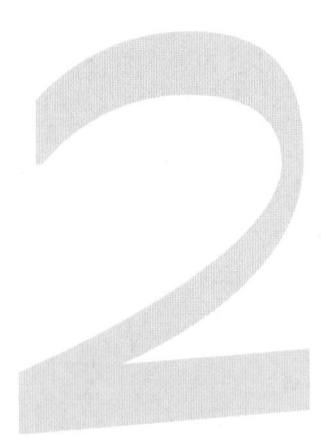

*"I want everything done . . . like, yesterday"*—Tanya York

# 2

# Analyzing and Recording Business Transactions

### A Look Back

Chapter 1 considered the role of accounting in the information age and introduced financial statements. We described different forms of organizations and identified users and uses of accounting. We explained the accounting equation and applied it to transaction analysis.

### A Look at This Chapter

This chapter focuses on the accounting process. We describe transactions and source documents as inputs for analysis. We explain the analysis and recording of transactions. The accounting equation, T-account, general ledger, trial balance, and debits and credits are shown as useful tools in the accounting process.

### A Look Ahead

Chapter 3 extends our focus on processing information. We explain the importance of adjusting accounts and the procedures in preparing financial statements.

# CAP

## Conceptual

**C1** Explain the steps in processing transactions. *(p. 48)*

**C2** Describe source documents and their purpose. *(p. 49)*

**C3** Describe an account and its use in recording transactions. *(p. 49)*

**C4** Describe a ledger and a chart of accounts. *(p. 52)*

**C5** Define *debits* and *credits* and explain their role in double-entry accounting. *(p. 53)*

## Analytical

**A1** Analyze the impact of transactions on accounts and financial statements. *(p. 56)*

**A2** Compute the debt ratio and describe its use in analyzing company performance. *(p. 67)*

## Procedural

**P1** Record transactions in a journal and post entries to a ledger. *(p. 54)*

**P2** Prepare and explain the use of a trial balance. *(p. 63)*

**P3** Prepare financial statements from business transactions. *(p. 64)*

## Decision Feature

# Against Long Odds

LOS ANGELES—Tanya York produced her first film at 19. Since then she has produced hundreds of films with her company **York Entertainment (YorkEntertainment.com).** York's company has become an urban powerhouse and distributes its titles under the York Urban, York Latino, and York En Espanol labels. Says York, "I'm Jamaican myself, so I can kind of relate to being a minority in a world where so much is aimed at the majority, so, in that way I'm happy to be able to offer films with an urban appeal."

York insists that the business and accounting side of production is as important as the artistic side. "With producing you're involved in all aspects of the entertainment industry," she says, "the creative side as well as the business side." York knows that attention to financial statements and know-how of the accounting system of debits and credits is crucial to success. An understanding of the accounting details enabled York to assess and enhance her company's profitability and financial position.

York relies on the financial numbers in devising strategies to enhance income. At the same time, she does not lose sight of giving the public what they want. Adds York, "I don't see my job as changing the public [demands]." Instead she fulfills them. This includes filling her movies with stars like Ice T, Kurupt, Destiny's Child, Kool Mo Dee, and Mac 10.

York continues to grow her company. With revenues near $20 million, she shows a keen understanding of accounting information in making good business decisions. Still, she insists anyone can use such information in a business to achieve similar success. "I came to America and through hard work built a company."

Without a doubt, Tanya York has not only tasted success but is living it. Adds York, "I like to always have new challenges in front of me."

[Sources: *York Entertainment Website,* January 2004; *Cinescape,* 2002; *Rolling Out Urban Style,* January 2002; *Entrepreneur,* November 2002; *Los Angeles Daily News,* February 2003.]

Financial statements report on the financial performance and condition of an organization. Knowledge of their preparation, organization, and analysis is important. A main goal of this chapter is to illustrate how transactions are recorded, how they are reflected in financial statements, and how they impact analysis of financial statements. Debits and credits are introduced and identified as a tool in helping understand and process transactions.

## Analyzing and Recording Business Transactions

### Analyzing and Recording Process
- Source documents
- The account and its analysis
- Types of accounts

### Analyzing and Processing Transactions
- General ledger
- Double-entry accounting
- Journalizing and posting
- An Illustration

### Trial Balance
- Trial balance preparation
- Search for and correction of errors
- Trial balance use

# Analyzing and Recording Process

The accounting process identifies business transactions and events, analyzes and records their effects, and summarizes and presents information in reports and financial statements. These reports and statements are used for making investing, lending, and other business decisions. The steps in the accounting process that focus on *analyzing and recording* transactions and events are shown in Exhibit 2.1.

**Exhibit 2.1**

The Analyzing and Recording Process

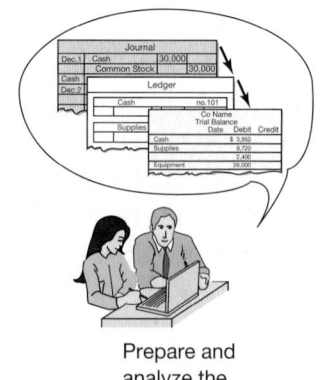

Analyze each transaction and event from source documents

Record relevant transactions and events in a journal

Post journal information to ledger accounts

Prepare and analyze the trial balance

**C1** Explain the steps in processing transactions.

Business transactions and events are the starting points. Relying on source documents, transactions and events are analyzed using the accounting equation to understand how they affect company performance and financial position. These effects are recorded in accounting records, informally referred to as the *accounting books,* or simply the *books.* Additional steps such as posting and then preparing a trial balance help summarize and classify the effects of transactions and events. Ultimately, the accounting process provides information in useful reports or financial statements to decision makers.

## Source Documents

**Source documents** identify and describe transactions and events entering the accounting process. They are the sources of accounting information and can be in either hard copy or electronic form. Examples are sales tickets, checks, purchase orders, bills from suppliers, employee earnings records, and bank statements. To illustrate, when an item is purchased on credit, the seller usually prepares at least two copies of a sales invoice. One copy is given to the buyer. Another copy, often sent electronically, results in an entry in the seller's information system to record the sale. Sellers use invoices for recording sales and for control; buyers use them for recording purchases and for monitoring purchasing activity. Note that many cash registers record information for each sale on a tape or electronic file locked inside the register. This record can be used as a source document for recording sales in the accounting records. Source documents, especially if obtained from outside the organization, provide objective and reliable evidence about transactions and events and their amounts.

**C2**  Describe source documents and their purpose.

**Point:** To ensure that all sales are rung up on the register, most sellers require customers to have their receipts to exchange or return purchased items.

### Decision Ethics

**Cashier**  Your manager requires that you, as cashier, immediately enter each sale. Recently, lunch hour traffic has increased and the assistant manager asks you to avoid delays by taking customers' cash and making change without entering sales. The assistant manager says she will add up cash and enter sales after lunch. She says that, in this way, the register will always match the cash amount when the manager arrives at three o'clock. What do you do?

Answer—p. 71

## The Account and Its Analysis

An **account** is a record of increases and decreases in a specific asset, liability, equity, revenue, or expense item. Information from an account is analyzed, summarized, and presented in reports and financial statements. The **general ledger,** or simply **ledger,** is a record containing all accounts used by a company. The ledger is often in electronic form. While most companies' ledgers contain similar accounts, a company may use one or more unique accounts because of its type of operations. Accounts are arranged into three general categories (based on the accounting equation), as shown in Exhibit 2.2.

**C3**  Describe an account and its use in recording transactions.

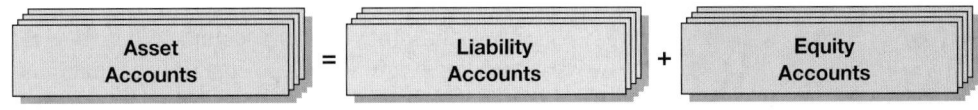

**Exhibit 2.2**

Accounts Organized by the Accounting Equation

**Asset Accounts**  Assets are resources owned or controlled by a company and that have expected future benefits. Most accounting systems include (at a minimum) separate accounts for the assets described here.

A *Cash* account reflects a company's cash balance. All increases and decreases in cash are recorded in the Cash account. It includes money and any medium of exchange that a bank accepts for deposit (coins, checks, money orders, and checking account balances).

*Accounts receivable* are held by a seller and refer to promises of payment from customers to sellers. These transactions are often called *credit sales* or *sales on account* (or *on credit*). Accounts receivable are increased by credit sales and are decreased by customer payments. A company needs a separate record for each customer, but for now, we use the simpler practice of recording all increases and decreases in receivables in a single account called Accounts Receivable.

A *note receivable,* or promissory note, is a written promise of another entity to pay a definite sum of money on a specified future date to the holder of the note. A company holding a promissory note signed by another entity has an asset that is recorded in a Note (or Notes) Receivable account.

*Prepaid accounts* (also called *prepaid expenses*) are assets that represent prepayments of future expenses (*not* current expenses). When the expenses are later incurred, the amounts in prepaid accounts are transferred to expense accounts. Common examples of prepaid

**Point:** Customers and others who owe a company are called its **debtors.**

**Point:** A college parking fee is a prepaid account from the student's standpoint. At the beginning of the term, it represents an asset that entitles a student to park on or near campus. The benefits of the parking fee expire as the term progresses. At term-end, prepaid parking (asset) equals zero as it has been entirely recorded as parking expense.

**Point:** Prepaid accounts that apply to current *and* future periods are assets. These assets are adjusted at the end of each period to reflect only those amounts that have not yet expired and to record as expenses those amounts that have expired.

accounts include prepaid insurance, prepaid rent, and prepaid services (such as club memberships). Prepaid accounts expire with the passage of time (such as with rent) or through use (such as with prepaid meal tickets). When financial statements are prepared, prepaid accounts are adjusted so that (1) all expired and used prepaid accounts are recorded as regular expenses and (2) all unexpired and unused prepaid accounts are recorded as assets (reflecting future use in future periods). To illustrate, when an insurance fee, called a *premium,* is paid in advance, the cost is typically recorded in the asset account Prepaid Insurance. Over time, the expiring portion of the insurance cost is removed from this asset account and reported in expenses on the income statement. Any unexpired portion remains in Prepaid Insurance and is reported on the balance sheet as an asset. (An exception exists for prepaid accounts that will expire or be used before the end of the current accounting period when financial statements are prepared. In this case, the prepayments *can* be recorded immediately as expenses.)

*Supplies* are assets until they are used. When they are used up, their costs are reported as expenses. The costs of unused supplies are recorded in a Supplies asset account. Supplies are often grouped by purpose—for example office supplies and store supplies. *Office supplies* include stationery, paper, toner, and pens. *Store supplies* include packaging materials, plastic and paper bags, gift boxes and cartons, and cleaning materials. The costs of these unused supplies can be recorded in an Office Supplies or a Store Supplies asset account. When supplies are used, their costs are transferred from the asset accounts to expense accounts.

**Point:** Some assets are described as *intangible* because they do not have physical existence or their benefits are highly uncertain. A recent balance sheet for Coca-Cola Company shows nearly $3.5 billion in intangible assets.

*Equipment* is an asset. When equipment is used and gets worn down its cost is gradually reported as an expense (called depreciation). Equipment is often grouped by its purpose—for example, office equipment and store equipment. *Office equipment* includes computers, printers, desks, chairs, shelves, and other office equipment. Costs incurred for these items are recorded in an Office Equipment asset account. The Store Equipment account includes the costs of assets used in a store such as counters, showcases, ladders, hoists, and cash registers.

*Buildings* such as stores, offices, warehouses, and factories are assets because they provide expected future benefits to those who control or own them. Their costs are recorded in a Buildings asset account. When several buildings are owned, separate accounts are sometimes kept for each of them.

The cost of *land* owned by a business is recorded in a Land account. The cost of buildings located on the land is separately recorded in one or more building accounts.

### Decision Insight

**Boss-Aid**  Entrepreneurs were asked whom they would want—if they could have anyone—to help run their businesses for a week. Bill Gates led, with 24%, followed by Donald Trump and Warren Buffet—see selected survey results.

| | |
|---|---|
| Bill Gates | 24% |
| Donald Trump | 6.8 |
| Warren Buffet | 5.8 |
| Lee Iacocca | 5.2 |
| Ross Perot | 3.1 |
| Hillary Clinton | 1.4 |

**Liability Accounts**  Liabilities are claims (by creditors) against assets, which means they are obligations to transfer assets or provide products or services to other entities. **Creditors** are individuals and organizations that own the right to receive payments from a company. If a company fails to pay its obligations, the law gives creditors a right to force the sale of that company's assets to obtain the money to meet creditors' claims. When assets are sold under these conditions, creditors are paid first, but only up to the amount of their claims. Any remaining money, the residual, goes to the owners of the company. Creditors often use a balance sheet to help decide whether to loan money to a company. A loan is less risky if the borrower's liabilities are small in comparison to assets because there are more resources than claims on resources. The more common liability accounts are described here.

**Point:** Accounts Payable are also called *Trade Payables.*

*Accounts payable* refer to oral or implied promises to pay later, which commonly arise from purchases of merchandise. Payables can also arise from purchases of supplies, equipment, and services. Accounting systems keep separate records about each creditor. We describe these individual records in Chapter 4.

A *note payable* refers to a formal promise, usually denoted by the signing of a promissory note, to pay a future amount. It is recorded in either a Short-Term Note Payable account or a Long-Term Note Payable account, depending on when it must be repaid. We explain details of short- and long-term classification in Chapter 3.

**Unearned Revenue** refers to a liability that is settled in the future when a company delivers its products or services. When customers pay in advance for products or services (before revenue is earned), the revenue recognition principle requires that the seller consider this payment as unearned revenue. Examples of unearned revenue include magazine subscriptions collected in advance by a publisher, sales of gift certificates by stores, and season ticket sales by sports teams. The seller would record these in liability accounts such as Unearned Subscriptions, Unearned Store Sales, and Unearned Ticket Revenue. When products and services are later delivered, the earned portion of the unearned revenue is transferred to revenue accounts such as Subscription Fees, Store Sales, and Ticket Sales.[1]

> **Decision Insight**
>
> **Cash Spread**  The **Green Bay Packers** have *Unearned Revenues* of nearly $40 million in advance ticket sales. When the team plays its regular season home games, it settles this liability to its ticket holders and transfers the amount earned to *Ticket Revenues*.

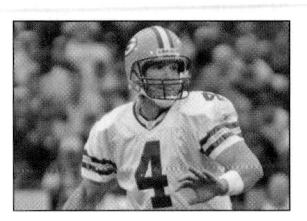

**Point:** If a subscription is cancelled the publisher should refund the unused portion to the subscriber.

*Accrued liabilities* are amounts owed that are not yet paid. Examples are wages payable, taxes payable, and interest payable. These are often recorded in separate liability accounts by the same title. If they are not large in amount, one or more ledger accounts can be added and reported as a single amount on the balance sheet. (Financial statements often have amounts reported that are a summation of several ledger accounts.)

**Equity Accounts**    The owner's claim on a corporation's assets is called *equity, stockholders' equity,* or *shareholders' equity.* Equity is the owners' *residual interest* in the assets of a business after deducting liabilities. There are four subcategories of equity: common stock, dividends, revenues, and expenses. We show this visually in Exhibit 2.3 by expanding the accounting equation.

**Point:** Equity is also called *net assets.*

## Exhibit 2.3

**Expanded Accounting Equation**

| Asset Accounts | = | Liability Accounts | + | Equity Accounts |
|---|---|---|---|---|

+ Common Stock  −  Dividends  +  Revenues  −  Expenses

When an owner invests in a company in exchange for common stock, the invested amount is recorded in an account titled **Common Stock.** Any further owner investments are recorded in this account. When the company pays any cash dividends it decreases both the company's assets and its total equity. Dividends are not expenses of the business. They are simply the opposite of owner investments. A **Dividends** account is used in recording asset distributions to stockholders (owners).

Revenues and expenses are the final two categories of equity. Examples of revenue accounts are Sales, Commissions Earned, Professional Fees Earned, Rent Earned, and Interest Revenue. *Revenues increase equity* and result from products or services provided to customers. Examples of expense accounts are Advertising Expense, Store Supplies Expense, Office Salaries Expense, Office Supplies Expense, Rent Expense, Utilities Expense, and Insurance Expense. *Expenses decrease equity* and result from assets or services used in a

**Point:** The Dividends account is sometimes referred to as a *contra equity* account because it reduces the normal balance of equity.

**Point:** The withdrawal of assets by the owners of a corporation is called a *dividend.*

---

[1] In practice, account titles vary. As one example, Subscription Fees is sometimes called Subscription Fees Revenue, Subscription Fees Earned, or Earned Subscription Fees. As another example, Rent Earned is sometimes called Rent Revenue, Rental Revenue, or Earned Rent Revenue. We must use good judgment when reading financial statements because titles can differ even within the same industry. For example, product sales are called *revenues* at **Krispy Kreme,** but *net sales* at **Tastykake.** Generally, the term *revenues* or *fees* is more commonly used with service businesses, and *net sales* or *sales* with product businesses.

company's operations. The variety of revenues
and expenses can be seen by looking at the *chart
of accounts* that follows the index at the back
of this book. (Different companies sometimes
use different account titles than those in this
book's chart of accounts. For example, some
might use Interest Revenue instead of Interest
Earned, or Rental Expense instead of Rent
Expense. It is important only that an account
title describe the item it represents.)

# Analyzing and Processing Transactions

This section explains several crucial tools and processes that comprise an accounting system. These include a ledger, T-accounts, debits and credits, double-entry accounting, journalizing, and posting.

## Ledger and Chart of Accounts

**C4**   Describe a ledger and a
chart of accounts.

The collection of all accounts for an information system is called a *ledger* (or *general ledger*).
If accounts are in files on a hard drive, the sum of those files is the ledger. If the accounts
are pages in a file, that file is the ledger. A company's size and diversity of operations affect the number of accounts needed. A small
company can get by with as few as 20 or 30
accounts; a large company can require several
thousand. The **chart of accounts** is a list of all
accounts a company uses and includes an identification number assigned to each account. A
small business might use the following numbering system for its accounts:

| | |
|---|---|
| 101–199 | Asset accounts |
| 201–299 | Liability accounts |
| 301–399 | Equity accounts |
| 401–499 | Revenue accounts |
| 501–699 | Expense accounts |

These numbers provide a three-digit code that is useful in recordkeeping. In this case, the
first digit assigned to asset accounts is a 1, the first digit assigned to liability accounts is a
2, and so on. The second and third digits relate to the accounts' subcategories. Exhibit 2.4
shows a partial chart of accounts for FastForward.

**Exhibit 2.4**

Partial Chart of Accounts
for FastForward

| Account Number | Account Name | Account Number | Account Name |
|---|---|---|---|
| 101 | Cash | 307 | Common stock |
| 106 | Accounts receivable | 319 | Dividends |
| 126 | Supplies | 403 | Consulting revenue |
| 128 | Prepaid insurance | 406 | Rental revenue |
| 167 | Equipment | 622 | Salaries expense |
| 201 | Accounts payable | 637 | Insurance expense |
| 236 | Unearned consulting revenue | 640 | Rent expense |
| | | 652 | Supplies expense |
| | | 690 | Utilities expense |

## Debits and Credits

A **T-account** represents a ledger account and is a tool used to understand the effects of one or more transactions. Its name comes from its shape like the letter *T*. The layout of a T-account (shown in Exhibit 2.5) is (1) the account title on top, (2) a left, or debit side, and (3) a right, or credit, side.

The left side of an account is called the **debit** side, often abbreviated *Dr*. The right side is called the **credit** side, abbreviated *Cr*.[2] To enter amounts on the left side of an account is to *debit* the account. To enter

| Account Title | |
|---|---|
| (Left side) | (Right side) |
| *Debit* | *Credit* |

amounts on the right side is to *credit* the account. Do not make the error of thinking that the terms *debit* and *credit* mean increase or decrease. Whether a debit or a credit is an increase or decrease depends on the account. In an account where a debit is an increase, the credit is a decrease; in an account where a debit is a decrease, the credit is an increase. The difference between total debits and total credits for an account, including any beginning balance, is the **account balance.** When the sum of debits exceeds the sum of credits, the account has a *debit balance*. It has a *credit balance* when the sum of credits exceeds the sum of debits. When the sum of debits equals the sum of credits, the account has a *zero balance*.

## Double-Entry Accounting

**Double-entry accounting** requires that each transaction affect, and be recorded in, at least two accounts. It also means the *total amount debited must equal the total amount credited* for each transaction. Thus, the sum of the debits for all entries must equal the sum of the credits for all entries, and the sum of debit account balances in the ledger must equal the sum of credit account balances.

The system for recording debits and credits follows from the usual accounting equation—see Exhibit 2.6. Two points are important here. First, like any simple mathematical relation, net increases or decreases on one side have equal net effects on the other side. For example, a net increase in assets must be accompanied by an identical net increase on the liabilities and

| Assets | | = | Liabilities | | + | Equity | |
|---|---|---|---|---|---|---|---|
| Debit for increases | Credit for decreases | | Debit for decreases | Credit for increases | | Debit for decreases | Credit for increases |
| + | − | | − | + | | − | + |

equity side. Recall that some transactions affect only one side of the equation, meaning that two or more accounts on one side are affected, but their net effect on this one side is zero. Second, the left side is the *normal balance* side for assets, and the right side is the *normal balance* side for liabilities and equity. This matches their layout in the accounting equation where assets are on the left side of this equation, and liabilities and equity are on the right.

Equity increases from revenues and stock issuances and it decreases from expenses and dividends. These important equity relations are conveyed by expanding the accounting equation to include debits and credits in double-entry form as shown in Exhibit 2.7.

Increases (credits) to common stock and revenues *increase* equity; increases (debits) to dividends and expenses *decrease* equity. The normal balance of each account (asset, liability, common stock, dividends, revenue, or expense) refers to the left or right (debit or credit) side where *increases* are recorded. Understanding these diagrams and rules is required to prepare, analyze, and interpret financial statements.

---

[2] These abbreviations are remnants of 18th-century English recordkeeping practices where the terms *debitor* and *creditor* were used instead of *debit* and *credit*. The abbreviations use the first and last letters of these terms, just as we still do for Saint (St.) and Doctor (Dr.).

C5 Define *debits* and *credits* and explain their role in double-entry accounting.

**Exhibit 2.5**

The T-Account

**Point:** Think of *debit* and *credit* as accounting directions for left and right.

"Total debits equal total credits for each entry."

**Exhibit 2.6**

Debits and Credits in the Accounting Equation

**Point:** Debits and credits do not mean favorable or unfavorable. A debit to an asset increases it, as does a debit to an expense. A credit to a liability increases it, as does a credit to a revenue.

## Exhibit 2.7

Debit and Credit Effects for Component Accounts

The T-account for FastForward's Cash account, reflecting its first 11 transactions (from Exhibit 1.9), is shown in Exhibit 2.8. The total increases in its Cash account are $36,100, the total decreases are $31,700, and the account's debit balance is $4,400.

## Exhibit 2.8

Computing the Balance for a T-Account

| Cash | | | |
|---|---|---|---|
| Investment by owner for stock | 30,000 | Purchase of supplies | 2,500 |
| Consulting services revenue earned | 4,200 | Purchase of equipment | 26,000 |
| Collection of account receivable | 1,900 | Payment of rent | 1,000 |
| | | Payment of salary | 700 |
| | | Payment of account payable | 900 |
| | | Payment of cash dividend | 600 |
| Balance | 4,400 | | |

**Point:** The ending balance is on the side with the largest dollar amount.

## Quick Check

1. Identify examples of accounting source documents.

2. Explain the importance of source documents.

3. Identify each of the following as either an asset, a liability, or equity: (*a*) Prepaid Rent, (*b*) Unearned Fees, (*c*) Building, (*d*) Wages Payable, and (*e*) Office Supplies.

4. What is an account? What is a ledger?

5. What determines the number and types of accounts a company uses?

6. Does *debit* always mean increase and *credit* always mean decrease?

7. Describe a chart of accounts.

Answers—p. 72

## Journalizing and Posting Transactions

**P1** Record transactions in a journal and post entries to a ledger.

Processing transactions is a crucial part of accounting. The four usual steps of this process are depicted in Exhibit 2.9. Steps 1 and 2—involving transaction analysis and double-entry accounting—were introduced in prior sections. This section extends that discussion and focuses on steps 3 and 4 of the accounting process. Step 3 is to record each transaction in a journal. A **journal** gives a complete record of each transaction in one place. It also shows debits and credits for each transaction. The process of recording transactions in a journal is called **journalizing.** Step 4 is to transfer (or *post*) entries from the journal to the ledger. The process of transferring journal entry information to the ledger is called **posting.**

**Journalizing Transactions**    The process of journalizing transactions requires an understanding of a journal. While companies can use various journals, every company uses a **general journal.** It can be used to record any transaction and includes the following information about each transaction: (1) date of transaction, (2) titles of affected accounts,

**Step 1**: Analyze transactions and
      source documents.

| Services Contract | | |
|---|---|---|
| Client Billing | | |
| Note Payable | | |
| Purchase Ticket | | |
| Bank Statement | | |
| 1 | Deposit | 30,000 |
| | | |
| | | |
| | TOTAL | |

**Step 2**: Apply double-entry accounting.

Cash

Assets = Liability + Equity

**Step 3**: Record journal entry.

| General Journal | | |
|---|---|---|
| Dec. 1 | Cash | 30,000 | |
| | Taylor, Capital | | 30,000 |
| | | | |
| Dec. 2 | Supplies | 2,500 | |
| | Cash | | 2,500 |

**Step 4**: Post entry to ledger.

General Journal

Ledger

Exhibit 2.9

Steps in Processing Transactions

(3) dollar amount of each debit and credit, and (4) explanation of the transaction. Exhibit 2.10 shows how the first two transactions of FastForward are recorded in a general journal. This process is similar for manual and computerized systems. Computerized journals are often designed to look like a manual journal page, and also include error-checking routines that ensure debits equal credits for each entry. Shortcuts allow recordkeepers to select account names and numbers from pull-down menus.

**GENERAL JOURNAL**                                                                                        Page 1

| Date | Account Titles and Explanation | PR | Debit | Credit |
|---|---|---|---|---|
| 2004 Dec. 1 | Cash | | 30,000 | |
| | C. Taylor, Capital | | | 30,000 |
| | *Investment by owner.* | | | |
| | | | | |
| Dec. 2 | Supplies | | 2,500 | |
| | Cash | | | 2,500 |
| | *Purchased supplies for cash.* | | | |

Exhibit 2.10

Partial General Journal for
FastForward

To record entries in a general journal, apply these steps; refer to the entries in Exhibit 2.10 when reviewing these steps. ① Date the transaction: Enter the year at the top of the first column and the month and day on the first line of each journal entry. ② Enter titles of accounts debited and then enter amounts in the Debit column on the same line. Account titles are taken from the chart of accounts and are aligned with the left margin of the Account Titles and Explanation column. ③ Enter titles of accounts credited and then enter amounts in the Credit column on the same line. Account titles are from the chart of accounts and are indented from the left margin of the Account Titles and Explanation column to distinguish them from debited accounts. ④ Enter a brief explanation of the transaction on the line below the entry (it often references a source document). This explanation is indented about half as far as the credited account titles to avoid confusing it with accounts, and it is italicized.

A blank line is left between each journal entry for clarity. When a transaction is first recorded, the **posting reference (PR) column** blank is left blank (in a manual system). Later, when posting entries to the ledger, the identification numbers of the individual ledger accounts are entered in the PR column.

**Balance Column Account**   T-accounts are simple and direct means to show how the accounting process works. However, actual accounting systems need more structure and therefore use **balance column accounts,** as in Exhibit 2.11.

**Exhibit 2.11**

Cash Account in Balance Column Format

| Cash | | | | | Account No. 101 |
|---|---|---|---|---|---|
| Date | Explanation | PR | Debit | Credit | Balance |
| 2004 | | | | | |
| Dec.  1 | | G1 | 30,000 | | 30,000 |
| Dec.  2 | | G1 | | 2,500 | 27,500 |
| Dec.  3 | | G1 | | 26,000 | 1,500 |
| Dec. 10 | | G1 | 4,200 | | 5,700 |

The balance column account format is similar to a T-account in having columns for debits and credits. It is different in including transaction date and explanation columns. It also has a column with the balance of the account after each entry is recorded. To illustrate, FastForward's Cash account in Exhibit 2.11 is debited on December 1 for the $30,000 owner investment, yielding a $30,000 debit balance. The account is credited on December 2 for $2,500, yielding a $27,500 debit balance. On December 3, it is credited again, this time for $26,000, and its debit balance is reduced to $1,500. The Cash account is debited for $4,200 on December 10, and its debit balance increases to $5,700; and so on.

The heading of the Balance column does not show whether it is a debit or credit balance. Instead, an account is assumed to have a *normal balance.* Unusual events can sometimes temporarily give an account an abnormal balance. An *abnormal balance* refers to a balance on the side where decreases are recorded. For example, a customer might mistakenly overpay a bill. This gives that customer's account receivable an abnormal (credit) balance. An abnormal balance is often identified by circling it or by entering it in red or some other unusual

**Exhibit 2.12**

Posting an Entry to the Ledger

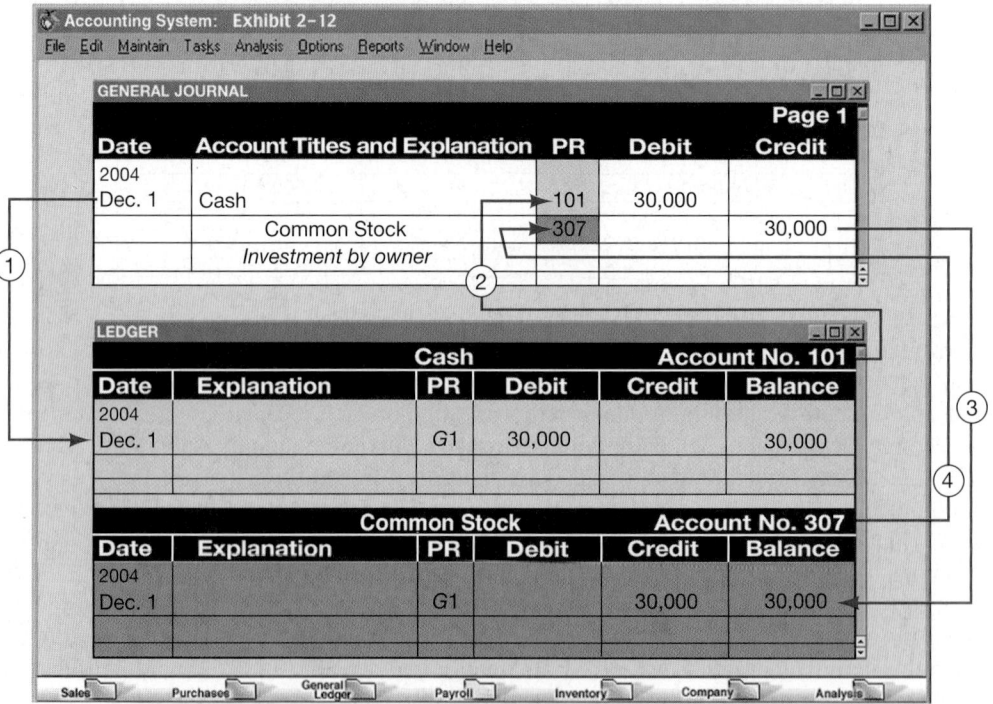

Key:   ① Identify debit account in Ledger: enter date, journal page, amount, and balance.
        ② Enter the debit account number from the Ledger in the PR column of the journal.
        ③ Identify credit account in Ledger: enter date, journal page, amount, and balance.
        ④ Enter the credit account number from the Ledger in the PR column of the journal.

color. A zero balance for an account is usually shown by writing zeros or a dash in the Balance column to avoid confusion between a zero balance and one omitted in error.

**Posting Journal Entries**   Step 4 of processing transactions is to post journal entries to ledger accounts (see Exhibit 2.9). To ensure that the ledger is up-to-date, entries are posted as soon as possible. This might be daily, weekly, or when time permits. All entries must be posted to the ledger before financial statements are prepared to ensure that account balances are up-to-date. When entries are posted to the ledger, the debits in journal entries are transferred into ledger accounts as debits, and credits are transferred into ledger accounts as credits. Exhibit 2.12 shows the four steps to post a journal entry. First, identify the ledger account that is debited in the entry; then, in the ledger, enter the entry date, the journal and page in its PR column, the debit amount, and the new balance of the ledger account. (The letter *G* shows it came from the General Journal.) Second, enter the ledger account number in the PR column of the journal. Steps three and four repeat the first two steps for credit entries and amounts. The posting process creates a link between the ledger and the journal entry. This link is a useful cross-reference for tracing an amount from one record to another.

**Point:** Computerized systems often provide a code beside a balance such as *dr.* or *cr.* to identify its balance.

**Point:** A journal is often referred to as the *book of original entry*. The ledger is referred to as the *book of final entry* because financial statements are prepared from it.

**Point:** Posting is automatic and immediate with accounting software.

**Point:** Explanations are typically included in ledger accounts only for unusual transactions or events.

## Analyzing Transactions—An Illustration

We return to the activities of FastForward to show how double-entry accounting is useful in analyzing and processing transactions. Analysis of each transaction follows the four steps of Exhibit 2.9. First, we review the transaction and any source documents. Second, we analyze the transaction using the accounting equation. Third, we use double-entry accounting to record the transaction in journal entry form. Fourth, the entry is posted (for simplicity, we use T-accounts to represent ledger accounts). We also identify the financial statements affected by each transaction. Study each transaction thoroughly before proceeding to the next. The first 11 transactions are from Chapter 1, and we analyze five additional December transactions of FastForward (numbered 12 through 16) that were omitted earlier.

A1   Analyze the impact of transactions on accounts and financial statements.

Topic Tackler 2-1

### 1. Investment by Owner

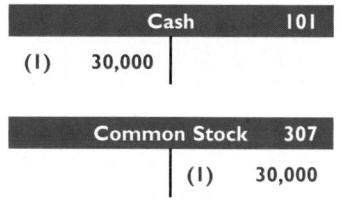

*Transaction:*  Chuck Taylor invests $30,000 cash in FastForward in exchange for common stock.

*Analysis:*

| Assets | = | Liabilities | + | Equity |
|---|---|---|---|---|
| **Cash** | | | | **Common Stock** |
| +30,000 | = | 0 | + | 30,000 |

*Double entry:*

| (1) | Cash | 101 | 30,000 | |
|---|---|---|---|---|
| | Common Stock | 307 | | 30,000 |

*Statements affected:*[3]  BLS and SCF

### 2. Purchase Supplies for Cash

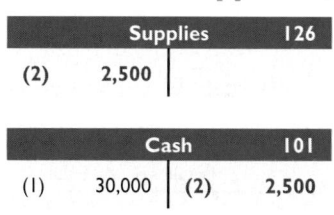

*Transaction:*  FastForward pays $2,500 cash for supplies.

*Analysis:*

| Assets | | = | Liabilities | + | Equity |
|---|---|---|---|---|---|
| **Cash** | **Supplies** | | | | |
| −2,500 | +2,500 | = | 0 | + | 0 |

Changes the composition of assets but not the total.

*Double entry:*

| (2) | Supplies | 126 | 2,500 | |
|---|---|---|---|---|
| | Cash | 101 | | 2,500 |

*Statements affected:*  BLS and SCF

---

[3] We use abbreviations for the statements: income statement (IS), balance sheet (BLS), statement of cash flows (SCF), and statement of retained earnings (SRE).

### 3. Purchase Equipment for Cash

| Equipment | 167 |
|---|---|
| (3) 26,000 | |

| Cash | 101 |
|---|---|
| (1) 30,000 | (2) 2,500 |
| | (3) 26,000 |

*Transaction:* FastForward pays $26,000 cash for equipment.

*Analysis:*

| Assets | | = | Liabilities | + | Equity |
|---|---|---|---|---|---|
| **Cash** | **Equipment** | | | | |
| −26,000 | +26,000 | = | 0 | + | 0 |

Changes the composition of assets but not the total.

*Double entry:*

| (3) | Equipment | 167 | 26,000 | |
|---|---|---|---|---|
| | Cash | 101 | | 26,000 |

*Statements affected:* BLS and SCF

### 4. Purchase Supplies on Credit

| Supplies | 126 |
|---|---|
| (2) 2,500 | |
| (4) 7,100 | |

| Accounts Payable | 201 |
|---|---|
| | (4) 7,100 |

*Transaction:* FastForward purchases $7,100 of supplies on credit from a supplier.

*Analysis:*

| Assets | = | Liabilities | + | Equity |
|---|---|---|---|---|
| **Supplies** | | **Accounts Payable** | | |
| +7,100 | = | +7,100 | + | 0 |

*Double entry:*

| (4) | Supplies | 126 | 7,100 | |
|---|---|---|---|---|
| | Accounts Payable | 201 | | 7,100 |

*Statements affected:* BLS

### 5. Provide Services for Cash

| Cash | 101 |
|---|---|
| (1) 30,000 | (2) 2,500 |
| (5) 4,200 | (3) 26,000 |

| Consulting Revenue | 403 |
|---|---|
| | (5) 4,200 |

*Transaction:* FastForward provides consulting services and immediately collects $4,200 cash.

*Analysis:*

| Assets | = | Liabilities | + | Equity |
|---|---|---|---|---|
| **Cash** | | | | **Consulting Revenue** |
| +4,200 | = | 0 | | +4,200 |

*Double entry:*

| (5) | Cash | 101 | 4,200 | |
|---|---|---|---|---|
| | Consulting Revenue | 403 | | 4,200 |

*Statements affected:* BLS, IS, SCF, and SRE

### 6. Payment of Expense in Cash

| Rent Expense | 640 |
|---|---|
| (6) 1,000 | |

| Cash | 101 |
|---|---|
| (1) 30,000 | (2) 2,500 |
| (5) 4,200 | (3) 26,000 |
| | (6) 1,000 |

*Transaction:* FastForward pays $1,000 cash for December rent.

*Analysis:*

| Assets | = | Liabilities | + | Equity |
|---|---|---|---|---|
| **Cash** | | | | **Rent Expense** |
| −1,000 | = | 0 | | −1,000 |

*Double entry:*

| (6) | Rent Expense | 640 | 1,000 | |
|---|---|---|---|---|
| | Cash | 101 | | 1,000 |

*Statements affected:* BLS, IS, SCF, and SRE

### 7. Payment of Expense in Cash

| Salaries Expense | 622 |
|---|---|
| (7) 700 | |

| Cash | 101 |
|---|---|
| (1) 30,000 | (2) 2,500 |
| (5) 4,200 | (3) 26,000 |
| | (6) 1,000 |
| | (7) 700 |

*Transaction:* FastForward pays $700 cash for employee salary.

*Analysis:*

| Assets | = | Liabilities | + | Equity |
|---|---|---|---|---|
| **Cash** | | | | **Salaries Expense** |
| −700 | = | 0 | | −700 |

*Double entry:*

| (7) | Salaries Expense | 622 | 700 | |
|---|---|---|---|---|
| | Cash | 101 | | 700 |

*Statements affected:* BLS, IS, SCF, and SRE

## 8. Provide Consulting and Rental Services on Credit

| Accounts Receivable 106 | |
|---|---|
| (8)    1,900 | |

| Consulting Revenue 403 | |
|---|---|
| | (5)    4,200 |
| | (8)    1,600 |

| Rental Revenue 406 | |
|---|---|
| | (8)    300 |

*Transaction:* FastForward provides consulting services of $1,600 and rents its test facilities for $300. The customer is billed $1,900 for these services.

*Analysis:*

| Assets | = | Liabilities | + | | Equity | |
|---|---|---|---|---|---|---|
| **Accounts Receivable** | | | | **Consulting Revenue** | **Rental Revenue** | |
| +1,900 | = | 0 | | +1,600 | +300 | |

*Double entry:*

| (8) | Accounts Receivable | 106 | 1,900 | |
|---|---|---|---|---|
| | Consulting Revenue | 403 | | 1,600 |
| | Rental Revenue | 406 | | 300 |

*Statements affected:* BLS, IS, and SRE

**Point:** Transaction 8 is a **compound journal entry,** which affects three or more accounts.

## 9. Receipt of Cash on Account

| Cash | | 101 | |
|---|---|---|---|
| (1)    30,000 | (2) | 2,500 | |
| (5)    4,200 | (3) | 26,000 | |
| (9)    1,900 | (6) | 1,000 | |
| | (7) | 700 | |

| Accounts Receivable 106 | |
|---|---|
| (8)    1,900 | (9)    1,900 |

*Transaction:* FastForward receives $1,900 cash from the client billed in transaction 8.

*Analysis:*

| Assets | | = | Liabilities | + | Equity |
|---|---|---|---|---|---|
| | **Accounts** | | | | |
| **Cash** | **Receivable** | | | | |
| +1,900 | −1,900 | = | 0 | + | 0 |

*Double entry:*

| (9) | Cash | 101 | 1,900 | |
|---|---|---|---|---|
| | Accounts Receivable | 106 | | 1,900 |

*Statements affected:* BLS and SCF

**Point:** The *revenue recognition principle* requires revenue to be recognized when earned, which is when the company provides products or services to a customer. This is not necessarily the same time that the customer pays. A customer can pay before or after products or services are provided.

## 10. Partial Payment of Accounts Payable

| Accounts Payable    201 | |
|---|---|
| (10)    900 | (4)    7,100 |

| Cash | | 101 | |
|---|---|---|---|
| (1)    30,000 | (2) | 2,500 | |
| (5)    4,200 | (3) | 26,000 | |
| (9)    1,900 | (6) | 1,000 | |
| | (7) | 700 | |
| | (10) | 900 | |

*Transaction:* FastForward pays CalTech Supply $900 cash toward the payable of transaction 4.

*Analysis:*

| Assets | = | Liabilities | + | Equity |
|---|---|---|---|---|
| **Cash** | | **Accounts Payable** | | |
| −900 | = | −900 | + | 0 |

*Double entry:*

| (10) | Accounts Payable | 201 | 900 | |
|---|---|---|---|---|
| | Cash | 101 | | 900 |

*Statements affected:* BLS and SCF

## 11. Payment of Cash Dividend

| Dividends    319 | |
|---|---|
| (11)    600 | |

| Cash | | 101 | |
|---|---|---|---|
| (1)    30,000 | (2) | 2,500 | |
| (5)    4,200 | (3) | 26,000 | |
| (9)    1,900 | (6) | 1,000 | |
| | (7) | 700 | |
| | (10) | 900 | |
| | (11) | 600 | |

*Transaction:* FastForward pays $600 cash for dividends.

*Analysis:*

| Assets | = | Liabilities | + | Equity |
|---|---|---|---|---|
| **Cash** | | | | **Dividends** |
| −600 | = | 0 | | −600 |

*Double entry:*

| (11) | Dividends | 319 | 600 | |
|---|---|---|---|---|
| | Cash | 101 | | 600 |

*Statements affected:* BLS, SCF, and SRE

## 12. Receipt of Cash for Future Services

| Cash | | | 101 |
|---|---|---|---|
| (1) | 30,000 | (2) | 2,500 |
| (5) | 4,200 | (3) | 26,000 |
| (9) | 1,900 | (6) | 1,000 |
| (12) | 3,000 | (7) | 700 |
| | | (10) | 900 |
| | | (11) | 600 |

| Unearned Consulting Revenue | | 236 |
|---|---|---|
| | (12) | 3,000 |

*Transaction:* FastForward receives $3,000 cash in advance of providing consulting services to a customer.

*Analysis:*

| Assets | = | Liabilities | + | Equity |
|---|---|---|---|---|
| | | **Unearned** | | |
| **Cash** | | **Consulting Revenue** | | |
| +3,000 | = | +3,000 | + | 0 |

Accepting $3,000 cash obligates FastForward to perform future services and is a liability. No revenue is earned until services are provided.

*Double entry:*

| (12) | Cash | 101 | 3,000 | |
|---|---|---|---|---|
| | Unearned Consulting Revenue | 236 | | 3,000 |

*Statements affected:* BLS and SCF

---

## 13. Pay Cash for Future Insurance Coverage

| Prepaid Insurance | | 128 |
|---|---|---|
| (13) | 2,400 | |

| Cash | | | 101 |
|---|---|---|---|
| (1) | 30,000 | (2) | 2,500 |
| (5) | 4,200 | (3) | 26,000 |
| (9) | 1,900 | (6) | 1,000 |
| (12) | 3,000 | (7) | 700 |
| | | (10) | 900 |
| | | (11) | 600 |
| | | (13) | 2,400 |

*Transaction:* FastForward pays $2,400 cash (insurance premium) for a 24-month insurance policy. Coverage begins on December 1.

*Analysis:*

| Assets | | = | Liabilities | + | Equity |
|---|---|---|---|---|---|
| | **Prepaid** | | | | |
| **Cash** | **Insurance** | | | | |
| −2,400 | +2,400 | = | 0 | + | 0 |

Changes the composition of assets from cash to prepaid insurance. Expense is incurred as insurance coverage expires.

*Double entry:*

| (13) | Prepaid Insurance | 128 | 2,400 | |
|---|---|---|---|---|
| | Cash | 101 | | 2,400 |

*Statements affected:* BLS and SCF

---

## 14. Purchase Supplies for Cash

| Supplies | | 126 |
|---|---|---|
| (2) | 2,500 | |
| (4) | 7,100 | |
| (14) | 120 | |

| Cash | | | 101 |
|---|---|---|---|
| (1) | 30,000 | (2) | 2,500 |
| (5) | 4,200 | (3) | 26,000 |
| (9) | 1,900 | (6) | 1,000 |
| (12) | 3,000 | (7) | 700 |
| | | (10) | 900 |
| | | (11) | 600 |
| | | (13) | 2,400 |
| | | (14) | 120 |

*Transaction:* FastForward pays $120 cash for supplies.

*Analysis:*

| Assets | | = | Liabilities | + | Equity |
|---|---|---|---|---|---|
| **Cash** | **Supplies** | | | | |
| −120 | +120 | = | 0 | + | 0 |

*Double entry:*

| (14) | Supplies | 126 | 120 | |
|---|---|---|---|---|
| | Cash | 101 | | 120 |

*Statements affected:* BLS and SCF

## 15. Payment of Expense in Cash

| Utilities Expense | | 690 |
|---|---|---|
| (15) | 230 | |

| Cash | | | 101 |
|---|---|---|---|
| (1) | 30,000 | (2) | 2,500 |
| (5) | 4,200 | (3) | 26,000 |
| (9) | 1,900 | (6) | 1,000 |
| (12) | 3,000 | (7) | 700 |
| | | (10) | 900 |
| | | (11) | 600 |
| | | (13) | 2,400 |
| | | (14) | 120 |
| | | (15) | 230 |

*Transaction:* FastForward pays $230 cash for December utilities expense.

*Analysis:*

| Assets | = | Liabilities | + | Equity |
|---|---|---|---|---|
| **Cash** | | | | **Utilities Expense** |
| −230 | = | 0 | | −230 |

*Double entry:*

| (15) | Utilities Expense | 690 | 230 | |
|---|---|---|---|---|
| | Cash | 101 | | 230 |

*Statements affected:* BLS, IS, SCF, and SRE

## 16. Payment of Expense in Cash

| Salaries Expense | | 622 |
|---|---|---|
| (7) | 700 | |
| (16) | 700 | |

| Cash | | | 101 |
|---|---|---|---|
| (1) | 30,000 | (2) | 2,500 |
| (5) | 4,200 | (3) | 26,000 |
| (9) | 1,900 | (6) | 1,000 |
| (12) | 3,000 | (7) | 700 |
| | | (10) | 900 |
| | | (11) | 600 |
| | | (13) | 2,400 |
| | | (14) | 120 |
| | | (15) | 230 |
| | | (16) | 700 |

*Transaction:* FastForward pays $700 cash in employee salary for work performed in the latter part of December.

*Analysis:*

| Assets | = | Liabilities | + | Equity |
|---|---|---|---|---|
| **Cash** | | | | **Salaries Expense** |
| −700 | = | 0 | | −700 |

*Double entry:*

| (16) | Salaries Expense | 622 | 700 | |
|---|---|---|---|---|
| | Cash | 101 | | 700 |

*Statements affected:* BLS, IS, SCF, and SRE

**Point:** We could merge transactions 15 and 16 into one *compound entry.*

# Accounting Equation Analysis

Exhibit 2.13 shows the accounts (in T-account form) of FastForward after all 16 transactions are recorded, posted and the balances computed. The accounts are grouped into three major columns corresponding to the accounting equation: assets, liabilities, and equity. Note several important points. First, as with each transaction, the totals for the three columns must obey the accounting equation. Specifically, assets equal $42,070 ($3,950 + $0 + $9,720 + $2,400 + $26,000); liabilities equal $9,200 ($6,200 + $3,000); and equity equals $32,870 ($30,000 − $600 + $5,800 + $300 − $1,400 − $1,000 − $230). These numbers prove the accounting equation: Assets of $42,070 = Liabilities of $9,200 + Equity of $32,870. Second, the common stock, dividends, revenue, and expense accounts reflect the transactions that change equity. The latter three accounts underlie the statement of retained earnings. Third, the revenue and expense account balances will be summarized and reported in the income statement. Fourth, increases and decreases in the cash account make up the elements reported in the statement of cash flows.

**Summary of debit and credit rules:**

| Accounts | Increase (normal bal.) | Decrease |
|---|---|---|
| Asset | Debit | Credit |
| Liability | Credit | Debit |
| Common stock | Credit | Debit |
| Dividends | Debit | Credit |
| Revenue | Credit | Debit |
| Expense | Debit | Credit |

**Point:** Technology does not provide the judgment required to analyze most business transactions. Analysis requires the expertise of skilled and ethical professionals.

Exhibit 2.13

Ledger for FastForward (in T-Account Form)

| Assets | | | | = | Liabilities | | | + | Equity | | |
|---|---|---|---|---|---|---|---|---|---|---|---|

**Cash          101**

| (1) | 30,000 | (2) | 2,500 |
|---|---|---|---|
| (5) | 4,200 | (3) | 26,000 |
| (9) | 1,900 | (6) | 1,000 |
| (12) | 3,000 | (7) | 700 |
| | | (10) | 900 |
| | | (11) | 600 |
| | | (13) | 2,400 |
| | | (14) | 120 |
| | | (15) | 230 |
| | | (16) | 700 |
| Balance | **3,950** | | |

**Accounts Receivable          106**

| (8) | 1,900 | (9) | 1,900 |
|---|---|---|---|
| Balance | **0** | | |

**Supplies          126**

| (2) | 2,500 | | |
|---|---|---|---|
| (4) | 7,100 | | |
| (14) | 120 | | |
| Balance | **9,720** | | |

**Prepaid Insurance          128**

| (13) | **2,400** | | |
|---|---|---|---|

**Equipment          167**

| (3) | **26,000** | | |
|---|---|---|---|

**Accounts Payable          201**

| (10) | 900 | (4) | 7,100 |
|---|---|---|---|
| | | Balance | **6,200** |

**Unearned Consulting Revenue   236**

| | | (12) | **3,000** |
|---|---|---|---|

**Common Stock          307**

| | | (1) | **30,000** |
|---|---|---|---|

**Dividends          319**

| (11) | **600** | | |
|---|---|---|---|

**Consulting Revenue          403**

| | | (5) | 4,200 |
|---|---|---|---|
| | | (8) | 1,600 |
| | | Balance | **5,800** |

**Rental Revenue          406**

| | | (8) | **300** |
|---|---|---|---|

**Salaries Expense          622**

| (7) | 700 | | |
|---|---|---|---|
| (16) | 700 | | |
| Balance | **1,400** | | |

**Rent Expense          640**

| (6) | **1,000** | | |
|---|---|---|---|

**Utilities Expense          690**

| (15) | **230** | | |
|---|---|---|---|

Accounts in this white area reflect those reported on the income statement.

| **$42,070** | = | **$9,200** | + | **$32,870** |
|---|---|---|---|---|

## Quick Check

**8.** What types of transactions increase equity? What types decrease equity?

**9.** Why are accounting systems called *double entry*?

**10.** For each transaction, double-entry accounting requires which of the following: (*a*) Debits to asset accounts must create credits to liability or equity accounts, (*b*) a debit to a liability account must create a credit to an asset account, or (*c*) total debits must equal total credits.

**11.** An owner invests $15,000 cash along with equipment having a market value of $23,000 in a company in exchange for common stock. Prepare the necessary journal entry.

**12.** Explain what a compound journal entry is.

**13.** Why are posting reference numbers entered in the journal when entries are posted to ledger accounts?

Answers—p. 72

# Trial Balance

Double-entry accounting requires the sum of debit account balances to equal the sum of credit account balances. A trial balance is used to verify this. A **trial balance** is a list of accounts and their balances at a point in time. Account balances are reported in the appropriate debit or credit column of a trial balance. Exhibit 2.14 shows the trial balance for FastForward after its 16 entries have been posted to the ledger. (This is an *unadjusted* trial balance—Chapter 3 will explain the necessary adjustments.)

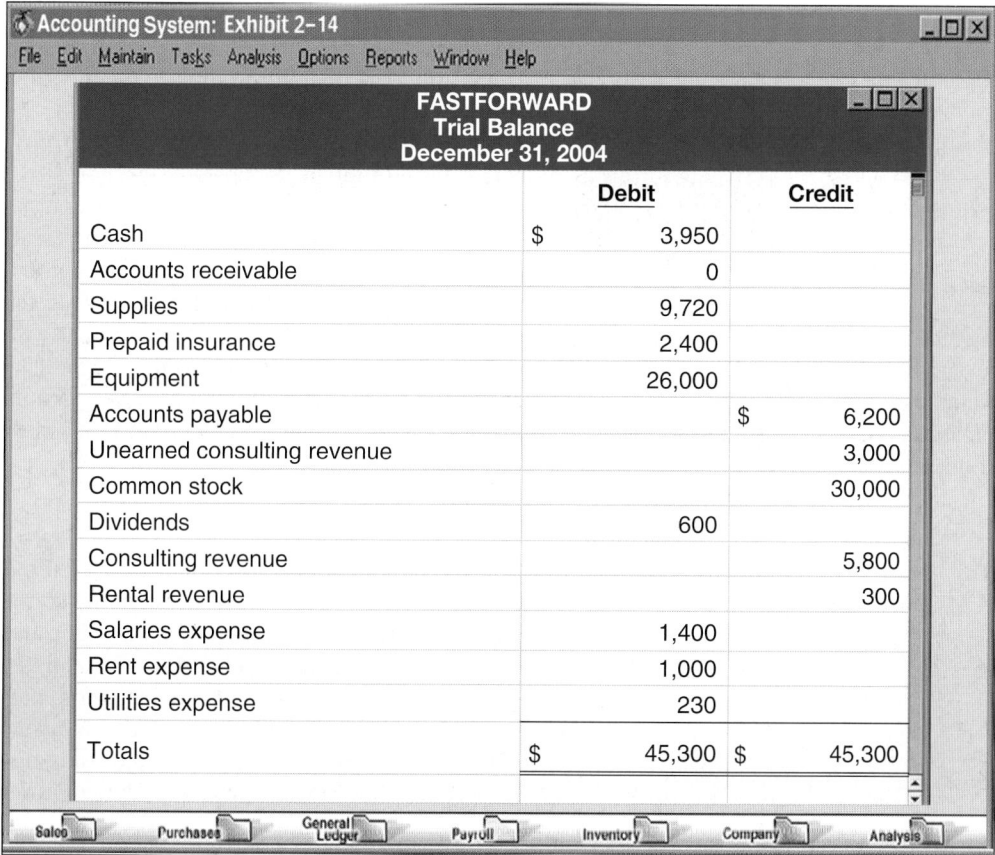

**Exhibit 2.14**

Trial Balance (unadjusted)

| FASTFORWARD Trial Balance December 31, 2004 | Debit | Credit |
|---|---|---|
| Cash | $ 3,950 | |
| Accounts receivable | 0 | |
| Supplies | 9,720 | |
| Prepaid insurance | 2,400 | |
| Equipment | 26,000 | |
| Accounts payable | | $ 6,200 |
| Unearned consulting revenue | | 3,000 |
| Common stock | | 30,000 |
| Dividends | 600 | |
| Consulting revenue | | 5,800 |
| Rental revenue | | 300 |
| Salaries expense | 1,400 | |
| Rent expense | 1,000 | |
| Utilities expense | 230 | |
| Totals | $ 45,300 | $ 45,300 |

## Preparing a Trial Balance

Preparing a trial balance involves three steps:

1. List each account title and its amount (from ledger) in the trial balance. If an account has a zero balance, list it with a zero in its normal balance column (or omit it entirely).
2. Compute the total of debit balances and the total of credit balances.
3. Verify (*prove*) total debit balances equal total credit balances.

**P2** Prepare and explain the use of a trial balance.

**Point:** The ordering of accounts in a trial balance typically follows their identification number from the chart of accounts.

The total of debit balances equals the total of credit balances for the trial balance in Exhibit 2.14. Note that equality of these two totals does not guarantee that no errors were made. For example, the column totals still will be equal when a debit or credit of a correct amount is made to a wrong account. Another error that does not cause unequal column totals is when equal debits and credits of an incorrect amount are entered.

**Searching for and Correcting Errors**  If the trial balance does not balance (when its columns are not equal), the error (or errors) must be found and corrected. An efficient way to search for an error is to check the journalizing, posting, and trial balance preparation in *reverse order*. Step 1 is to verify that the trial balance columns are correctly added. If

**Point:** A trial balance is *not* a financial statement but a mechanism for checking equality of debits and credits in the ledger. Financial statements do not have debit and credit columns.

**Example:** If a credit to Unearned Revenue were incorrectly posted from the journal as a credit to the Revenue ledger account, would the ledger still balance? Would the financial statements be correct? *Answers:* The ledger would balance, but liabilities would be understated, equity would be overstated, and income would be overstated (all because of overstated revenues).

step 1 fails to find the error, step 2 is to verify that account balances are accurately entered from the ledger. Step 3 is to see whether a debit (or credit) balance is mistakenly listed in the trial balance as a credit (or debit). A clue to this error is when the difference between total debits and total credits equals twice the amount of the incorrect account balance. If the error is still undiscovered, Step 4 is to recompute each account balance in the ledger. Step 5 is to verify that each journal entry is properly posted. Step 6 is to verify that the original journal entry has equal debits and credits. At this point, the errors should be uncovered.[4]

If an error in a journal entry is discovered before the error is posted, it can be corrected in a manual system by drawing a line through the incorrect information. The correct information is written above it to create a record of change for the auditor. Many computerized systems allow the operator to replace the incorrect information directly.

### Decision Insight

**Gorge'em** *Disgorgement* is one of the government's strongest weapons for going after shady executives. When the SEC wins a court order or settles a case against executives, it can require them to give back their salaries, including stock gains.

If an error in a journal entry is not discovered until after it is posted, do not strike through both erroneous entries in the journal and ledger. Instead, correct this error by creating a *correcting entry* that removes the amount from the wrong account and records it to the correct account. As an example, suppose a $100 purchase of supplies is journalized with an incorrect debit to Equipment, and then this incorrect entry is posted to the ledger. The Supplies ledger account balance is understated by $100, and the Equipment ledger account balance is overstated by $100. The correcting entry is: debit Supplies and credit Equipment (both for $100).

**Point:** The IRS requires companies to keep records that can be audited.

## Using a Trial Balance to Prepare Financial Statements

**P3**   Prepare financial statements from business transactions.

This section shows how to prepare *financial statements* from the trial balance in Exhibit 2.14 and information on the December transactions of FastForward. The statements differ from those in Chapter 1 because of several additional transactions. These statements are also more precisely called *unadjusted statements* because we need to make some further accounting adjustments (described in Chapter 3).

### Exhibit 2.15

Links between Financial Statements Across Time

How financial statements are linked in time is illustrated in Exhibit 2.15. A balance sheet reports on an organization's financial position at a *point in time*. The income statement, statement of retained earnings, and statement of cash flows report on financial performance over a *period of time*. The

Topic Tackler 2-2

---

[4] *Transposition* occurs when two digits are switched, or transposed, within a number. If transposition is the only error, it yields a difference between the two trial balance totals that is evenly divisible by 9. For example, assume that a $691 debit in an entry is incorrectly posted to the ledger as $619. Total credits in the trial balance are then larger than total debits by $72 ($691 − $619). The $72 error is *evenly* divisible by 9 (72/9 = 8). The first digit of the quotient (in our example it is 8) equals the difference between the digits of the two transposed numbers (the 9 and the 1). The number of digits in the quotient also tells the location of the transposition, starting from the right. The quotient in our example had only one digit (8), so it tells us the transposition is in the first digit. Consider another example where a transposition error involves posting $961 instead of the correct $691. The difference in these numbers is $270, and its quotient is 30 (270/9). The quotient has two digits, so it tells us to check the second digit from the right for a transposition of two numbers that have a difference of 3.

three statements in the middle column of Exhibit 2.15 link balance sheets from the beginning to the end of a reporting period. They explain how financial position changes from one point to another.

Preparers and users (including regulatory agencies) determine the length of the reporting period. A one-year, or annual, reporting period is common, as are semiannual, quarterly, and monthly periods. The one-year reporting period is known as the *accounting,* or *fiscal, year.* Businesses whose accounting year begins on January 1 and ends on December 31 are known as *calendar-year* companies. Many companies choose a fiscal year ending on a date other than December 31. **Krispy Kreme** is a *noncalendar-year* company as reflected in the headings of its February 2 year-end financial statements in Appendix A near the end of the book.

**Point:** A statement's heading lists the 3 W's: **W**ho—name of organization, **W**hat—name of statement, **W**hen— statement's point in time or period of time.

**Income Statement**    An income statement reports the revenues earned less the expenses incurred by a business over a period of time. FastForward's income statement for December is shown at the top of Exhibit 2.16. Information about revenues and expenses is conveniently taken from the trial balance in Exhibit 2.14. Net income of $3,470 is reported at the bottom of the statement. Owner investments and dividends are *not* part of income.

**Statement of Retained Earnings**    The statement of retained earnings reports information about how retained earnings changes over the reporting period. FastForward's statement of retained earnings is the second report in Exhibit 2.16. It shows the $3,470 of net income, the $600 dividend, and the $2,870 end-of-period balance. (The beginning balance in the statement of retained earnings is rarely zero. An exception is for the first period of operations. The beginning retained earnings balance in January 2005 is $2,870, which is December's ending balance.)

HARVARD BUSINESS REVIEW, JUNE 2002

"I'LL TELL YOU, HARRIS, THEY DON'T MAKE ACCOUNTANTS LIKE THEY USED TO. THOSE I HAD IN THE '90's, NEVER BROUGHT ME FIGURES LIKE THESE."

**Balance Sheet**    The balance sheet reports the financial position of a company at a point in time, usually at the end of a month, quarter, or year. FastForward's balance sheet is the third report in Exhibit 2.16. This statement refers to financial condition at the close of business on December 31. The left side of the balance sheet lists its assets: cash, supplies, prepaid insurance, and equipment. The upper right side of the balance sheet shows that it owes $6,200 to creditors and $3,000 in services to customers who paid in advance. The equity section shows an ending balance of $32,870. Note the link between the ending balance of the statement of retained earnings and the retained earnings balance here. (Recall that this presentation of the balance sheet is called the *account form:* assets on the left and liabilities and equity on the right. Another presentation is the *report form:* assets on top, followed by liabilities and then equity. Either presentation is acceptable.)

**Point:** Knowing how financial statements are prepared improves our analysis of them.

**Point:** An income statement is also called an *earnings statement, a statement of operations,* or a *P&L (profit and loss) statement.* A balance sheet is also called a *statement of financial position.*

**Decision Maker**

**Entrepreneur**    You open a wholesale business selling entertainment equipment to retail outlets. You find that most of your customers demand to buy on credit. How can you use the balance sheets of these customers to decide which ones to extend credit to?

Answer—p. 71

**Presentation Issues**    Dollar signs are not used in journals and ledgers. They do appear in financial statements and other reports such as trial balances. The usual practice is to put dollar signs beside only the first and last numbers in a column. **Krispy Kreme**'s financial statements in Appendix A show this. When amounts are entered in a journal, ledger, or trial balance, commas are optional to indicate thousands, millions, and so forth. However, commas are always used in financial statements. Companies also commonly round amounts in reports to the nearest dollar, or even to a higher level. Krispy Kreme is typical of many companies in that it rounds its financial statement amounts to the nearest thousand. This decision is based on the perceived impact of rounding for users' business decisions.

**Point:** While revenues increase equity and expenses decrease equity, the amounts are not reported in detail in the statement of retained earnings. Instead, their effects are reflected through net income.

## Exhibit 2.16

Financial Statements and
Their Links

**FASTFORWARD**
**Income Statement**
**For Month Ended December 31, 2004**

| | | |
|---|---:|---:|
| Revenues | | |
| Consulting revenue ($4,200 + $1,600) . . . . . . . | $ 5,800 | |
| Rental revenue . . . . . . . . . . . . . . . . . . . . . . . | 300 | |
| Total revenues . . . . . . . . . . . . . . . . . . . . . . . | | $ 6,100 |
| Expenses | | |
| Rent expense . . . . . . . . . . . . . . . . . . . . . . . . | 1,000 | |
| Salaries expense . . . . . . . . . . . . . . . . . . . . . | 1,400 | |
| Utilities expense . . . . . . . . . . . . . . . . . . . . | 230 | |
| Total expenses . . . . . . . . . . . . . . . . . . . . . . . | | 2,630 |
| Net income . . . . . . . . . . . . . . . . . . . . . . . . . | | **$ 3,470** ◄ |

**Point:** Arrow lines show how the statements are linked.

**FASTFORWARD**
**Statement of Retained Earnings**
**For Month Ended December 31, 2004**

| | | |
|---|---:|---:|
| Retained earnings, December 1, 2004 . . . . . . . . . . | $ 0 | |
| Plus: Net income . . . . . . . . . . . . . . . . . . . . . . | **3,470** ◄ |
| | 3,470 | |
| Less: Cash dividends . . . . . . . . . . . . . . . . . . . | 600 | |
| Retained earnings, December 31, 2004 . . . . . . . . | **$ 2,870** ◄ |

**FASTFORWARD**
**Balance Sheet**
**December 31, 2004**

| **Assets** | | **Liabilities** | |
|---|---:|---|---:|
| Cash . . . . . . . . . . . | $ 3,950 | Accounts payable . . . . . . . | $ 6,200 |
| Supplies . . . . . . . . . | 9,720 | Unearned revenue . . . . . . | 3,000 |
| Prepaid insurance . . | 2,400 | Total liabilities . . . . . . . . . | 9,200 |
| Equipment . . . . . . . | 26,000 | **Equity** | |
| | | Common stock . . . . . . . . | 30,000 |
| | | Retained earnings . . . . . . . | **2,870** ◄ |
| Total assets . . . . . . | $42,070 | Total liabilities and equity . | $42,070 |

**Point:** To *foot* a column of numbers is to add them.

**Example:** How would the balance sheet in Exhibit 2.16 change if FastForward pays $2,000 of its payable on December 31 using its Cash account? What would be the new amount of total assets? Would the balance sheet still balance? *Answers:* Cash would be $1,950, accounts payable would be $4,200, total assets (and liabilities plus equity) would be $40,070, and the balance sheet would still balance.

## Quick Check

**14.** Where are dollar signs typically entered in financial statements?

**15.** If a $4,000 debit to Equipment in a journal entry is incorrectly posted to the ledger as a $4,000 credit, and the ledger account has a resulting debit balance of $20,000, what is the effect of this error on the Trial Balance column totals?

**16.** Describe the link between the income statement and the statement of retained earnings.

**17.** Explain the link between the balance sheet and the statement of retained earnings.

**18.** Define and describe revenues and expenses.

**19.** Define and describe assets, liabilities, and equity.

Answers—p. 72

## Debt Ratio

An important business objective is gathering information to help assess a company's risk of failing to pay its debts. Companies finance their assets with either liabilities or equity. A company that finances a relatively large portion of its assets with liabilities is said to have a high degree of *financial leverage*. Higher financial leverage involves greater risk because liabilities must be repaid and often require regular interest payments (equity financing does not). The risk that a company might not be able to meet such required payments is higher if it has more liabilities (is more highly leveraged). One way to assess the risk associated with a company's use of liabilities is to compute the **debt ratio** as in Exhibit 2.17.

**A2** Compute the debt ratio and describe its use in analyzing company performance.

$$\text{Debt ratio} = \frac{\text{Total liabilities}}{\text{Total assets}}$$

To see how to apply the debt ratio, let's look at **Stride Rite**'s liabilities and assets. Stride Rite makes Keds, Pro-Keds, and other footwear. Exhibit 2.18 computes and reports its debt ratio at the end of each year from 1998 to 2002.

## Exhibit 2.17

Debt Ratio

**Point:** Compare the equity amount to the liability amount to assess the extent of owner versus nonowner financing.

## Exhibit 2.18

Computation and Analysis of Debt Ratio

| | 2002 | 2001 | 2000 | 1999 | 1998 |
|---|---|---|---|---|---|
| Total liabilities (in mil.) ....... | $ 82 | $100 | $110 | $101 | $102 |
| Total assets (in mil.) ......... | $335 | $362 | $359 | $351 | $347 |
| **Debt ratio** .............. | **0.24** | **0.28** | **0.31** | **0.29** | **0.29** |
| Industry debt ratio ......... | 0.45 | 0.49 | 0.48 | 0.46 | 0.52 |

Stride Rite's debt ratio ranges from a low of 0.24 to a high of 0.31. Its ratio is low compared with the industry ratio. Stride Rite reports that it carries no long-term debt, which is unusual. This analysis implies a low risk from its financial leverage. Is this good or bad? To answer that question we need to compare the company's return on the borrowed money to the rate it is paying creditors. If the company's return is higher, it is successfully borrowing money to make more money. Be aware that a company's success with making money from borrowed money can quickly turn unprofitable if its own return drops below the rate it is paying creditors.

### Decision Maker

**Investor** You consider buying stock in **Converse**. As part of your analysis, you compute its debt ratio for 2001, 2002, and 2003 as: 0.35, 0.74, and 0.94, respectively. Based on the debt ratio, is Converse a low-risk investment? Has the risk of buying Converse stock changed over this period? (*Note:* The industry ratio averages 0.40.)

Answer—p. 71

## Demonstration Problem

(*Note:* This problem extends the demonstration problem of Chapter 1.) After several months of planning, Sylvia Workman started a haircutting business called Expressions. The following events occurred during its first month:

**a.** On August 1, Workman invested $3,000 cash and $15,000 of equipment in Expressions in exchange for its common stock.

**b.** On August 2, Expressions paid $600 cash for furniture for the shop.

**c.** On August 3, Expressions paid $500 cash to rent space in a strip mall for August.

**d.** On August 4, it purchased $1,200 of equipment on credit for the shop (using a long-term note payable).

**e.** On August 5, Expressions opened for business. Cash received from services provided in the first week and a half of business (ended August 15) is $825.

**f.** On August 15, it provided $100 of haircutting services on account.

**g.** On August 17, it received a $100 check for services previously rendered on account.

**h.** On August 17, it paid $125 to an assistant for working during the grand opening.

**i.** Cash received from services provided during the second half of August is $930.

**j.** On August 31, it paid a $400 installment toward principal on the note payable entered into on August 4.

**k.** On August 31, it paid $900 cash for dividends.

**Required**

1. Open the following ledger accounts in balance column format (account numbers are in parentheses): Cash (101); Accounts Receivable (102); Furniture (161); Store Equipment (165); Note Payable (240); Common Stock (307); Dividends (319); Haircutting Services Revenue (403); Wages Expense (623); and Rent Expense (640). Prepare general journal entries for the transactions.

2. Post the journal entries from (1) to the ledger accounts.

3. Prepare a trial balance as of August 31.

4. Prepare an income statement for August.

5. Prepare a statement of retained earnings for August.

6. Prepare a balance sheet as of August 31.

7. Determine the debt ratio as of August 31.

**Extended Analysis**

8. In the coming months, Expressions will experience a greater variety of business transactions. Identify which accounts are debited and which are credited for the following transactions. (*Hint:* You need to use some accounts not opened in part 1.)

    a. Purchase supplies with cash.

    b. Pay cash for future insurance coverage.

    c. Receive cash for services to be provided in the future.

    d. Purchase supplies on account.

# Planning the Solution

- Analyze each transaction and use the debit and credit rules to prepare a journal entry for each.
- Post each debit and each credit from journal entries to their ledger accounts and cross-reference each amount in the posting reference (PR) columns of the journal and ledger.
- Calculate each account balance and list the accounts with their balances on a trial balance.
- Verify that total debits in the trial balance equal total credits.
- To prepare the income statement, identify revenues and expenses. List those items on the statement, compute the difference, and label the result as *net income* or *net loss*.
- Use information in the ledger to prepare the statement of retained earnings.
- Use information in the ledger to prepare the balance sheet.
- Calculate the debt ratio by dividing total liabilities by total assets.
- Analyze the future transactions to identify the accounts affected and apply debit and credit rules.

# Solution to Demonstration Problem

1. General journal entries:

**GENERAL JOURNAL**

Page 1

| Date | Account Titles and Explanation | PR | Debit | Credit |
|------|-------------------------------|-----|-------|--------|
| Aug. 1 | Cash | 101 | 3,000 | |
| | Store Equipment | 165 | 15,000 | |
| |     Common Stock | 307 | | 18,000 |
| | *Owner's investment.* | | | |
| 2 | Furniture | 161 | 600 | |
| |     Cash | 101 | | 600 |
| | *Purchased furniture for cash.* | | | |
| 3 | Rent Expense | 640 | 500 | |
| |     Cash | 101 | | 500 |
| | *Paid rent for August.* | | | |
| 4 | Store Equipment | 165 | 1,200 | |
| |     Note Payable | 240 | | 1,200 |
| | *Purchased additional equipment on credit.* | | | |

[continued on next page]

[continued from previous page]

| | | | | | |
|---|---|---|---|---|---|
| 15 | Cash ........................................ | 101 | 825 | |
| | Haircutting Services Revenue .................. | 403 | | 825 |
| | *Cash receipts from 10 days of operations.* | | | |
| 15 | Accounts Receivable ........................... | 102 | 100 | |
| | Haircutting Services Revenue .................. | 403 | | 100 |
| | *To record revenue for services provided on account.* | | | |
| 17 | Cash ........................................ | 101 | 100 | |
| | Accounts Receivable ...................... | 102 | | 100 |
| | *To record cash received as payment on account.* | | | |
| 17 | Wages Expense ............................. | 623 | 125 | |
| | Cash .................................. | 101 | | 125 |
| | *Paid wages to assistant.* | | | |
| 31 | Cash ........................................ | 101 | 930 | |
| | Haircutting Services Revenue .................. | 403 | | 930 |
| | *Cash receipts from second half of August.* | | | |
| 31 | Note Payable ................................ | 240 | 400 | |
| | Cash .................................. | 101 | | 400 |
| | *Paid an installment on the note payable.* | | | |
| 31 | Dividends .................................... | 319 | 900 | |
| | Cash .................................. | 101 | | 900 |
| | *Paid cash dividend.* | | | |

**2.** Post journal entries from (part 1) to the ledger accounts:

## General Ledger

**Cash**                Account No. 101

| Date | PR | Debit | Credit | Balance |
|---|---|---|---|---|
| Aug. 1 | G1 | 3,000 | | 3,000 |
| 2 | G1 | | 600 | 2,400 |
| 3 | G1 | | 500 | 1,900 |
| 15 | G1 | 825 | | 2,725 |
| 17 | G1 | 100 | | 2,825 |
| 17 | G1 | | 125 | 2,700 |
| 31 | G1 | 930 | | 3,630 |
| 31 | G1 | | 400 | 3,230 |
| 31 | G1 | | 900 | 2,330 |

**Accounts Receivable**        Account No. 102

| Date | PR | Debit | Credit | Balance |
|---|---|---|---|---|
| Aug. 15 | G1 | 100 | | 100 |
| 17 | G1 | | 100 | 0 |

**Furniture**                Account No. 161

| Date | PR | Debit | Credit | Balance |
|---|---|---|---|---|
| Aug. 2 | G1 | 600 | | 600 |

**Store Equipment**            Account No. 165

| Date | PR | Debit | Credit | Balance |
|---|---|---|---|---|
| Aug. 1 | G1 | 15,000 | | 15,000 |
| 4 | G1 | 1,200 | | 16,200 |

**Note Payable**                Account No. 240

| Date | PR | Debit | Credit | Balance |
|---|---|---|---|---|
| Aug. 4 | G1 | | 1,200 | 1,200 |
| 31 | G1 | 400 | | 800 |

**Common Stock**                Account No. 307

| Date | PR | Debit | Credit | Balance |
|---|---|---|---|---|
| Aug. 1 | G1 | | 18,000 | 18,000 |

**Dividends**                Account No. 319

| Date | PR | Debit | Credit | Balance |
|---|---|---|---|---|
| Aug. 31 | G1 | 900 | | 900 |

**Haircutting Services Revenue** Account No. 403

| Date | PR | Debit | Credit | Balance |
|---|---|---|---|---|
| Aug. 15 | G1 | | 825 | 825 |
| 15 | G1 | | 100 | 925 |
| 31 | G1 | | 930 | 1,855 |

**Wages Expense**                Account No. 623

| Date | PR | Debit | Credit | Balance |
|---|---|---|---|---|
| Aug. 17 | G1 | 125 | | 125 |

**Rent Expense**                Account No. 640

| Date | PR | Debit | Credit | Balance |
|---|---|---|---|---|
| Aug. 3 | G1 | 500 | | 500 |

**3.** Prepare a trial balance from the ledger:

| EXPRESSIONS Trial Balance August 31 | Debit | Credit |
|---|---|---|
| Cash . . . . . . . . . . . . . . . . . . . . . . | $ 2,330 | |
| Accounts receivable . . . . . . . . . . . . . | 0 | |
| Furniture . . . . . . . . . . . . . . . . . . . | 600 | |
| Store equipment . . . . . . . . . . . . . . | 16,200 | |
| Note payable . . . . . . . . . . . . . . . . . | | $   800 |
| Common stock . . . . . . . . . . . . . . . . | | 18,000 |
| Dividends . . . . . . . . . . . . . . . . . . . | 900 | |
| Haircutting services revenue . . . . . . . | | 1,855 |
| Wages expense . . . . . . . . . . . . . . . | 125 | |
| Rent expense . . . . . . . . . . . . . . . . | 500 | |
| Totals . . . . . . . . . . . . . . . . . . . . . | $20,655 | $20,655 |

**4.**

| EXPRESSIONS Income Statement For Month Ended August 31 | | |
|---|---|---|
| Revenues | | |
| Haircutting services revenue . . . . . . . | | $1,855 |
| Operating expenses | | |
| Rent expense . . . . . . . . . . . . . . . . . | $500 | |
| Wages expense . . . . . . . . . . . . . . . | 125 | |
| Total operating expenses . . . . . . . . . | | 625 |
| Net Income . . . . . . . . . . . . . . . . . . . | | $1,230 |

**5.**

| EXPRESSIONS Statement of Retained Earnings For Month Ended August 31 | |
|---|---|
| Retained earnings, August 1 . . . . . . . . | $   0 |
| Plus:  Net income . . . . . . . . . . . . . | 1,230 |
| | 1,230 |
| Less:  Cash dividends . . . . . . . . . . . | 900 |
| Retained earnings, August 31 . . . . . . . | $ 330 |

**6.**

| EXPRESSIONS Balance Sheet August 31 | | | |
|---|---|---|---|
| **Assets** | | **Liabilities** | |
| Cash . . . . . . . . . . . . . . . | $ 2,330 | Note payable . . . . . . . . . . . . . . | $   800 |
| Furniture . . . . . . . . . . . . | 600 | **Equity** | |
| Store equipment . . . . . . . | 16,200 | Common stock . . . . . . . . . . . . . | 18,000 |
| Total assets . . . . . . . . . . | $19,130 | Retained earnings . . . . . . . . . . . . | 330 |
| | | Total liabilities and equity . . . . . . . | $19,130 |

**7.** Debt ratio $= \dfrac{\text{Total liabilities}}{\text{Total assets}} = \dfrac{\$800}{\$19,130} = \underline{\underline{\textbf{4.18}\%}}$

**8a.** Supplies *debited*
      Cash *credited*

**8b.** Prepaid Insurance *debited*
      Cash *credited*

**8c.** Cash *debited*
      Unearned Services Revenue *credited*

**8d.** Supplies *debited*
      Accounts Payable *credited*

## Summary

**C1  Explain the steps in processing transactions.** The accounting process identifies business transactions and events, analyzes and records their effects, and summarizes and prepares information useful in making decisions. Transactions and events are the starting points in the accounting process. Source documents help in their analysis. The effects of transactions and events are recorded in journals. Posting along with a trial balance helps summarize and classify these effects.

**C2  Describe source documents and their purpose.** Source documents identify and describe transactions and events. Examples are sales tickets, checks, purchase orders, bills, and bank statements. Source documents provide objective and reliable evidence, making information more useful.

**C3  Describe an account and its use in recording transactions.** An account is a detailed record of increases and decreases in a specific asset, liability, equity, revenue, or expense. Information from accounts is analyzed, summarized, and presented in reports and financial statements for decision makers.

**C4  Describe a ledger and a chart of accounts.** The ledger (or general ledger) is a record containing all accounts used by a company and their balances. It is referred to as the *books*. The chart of accounts is a list of all accounts and usually includes an identification number assigned to each account.

**C5  Define *debits* and *credits* and explain their role in double-entry accounting.** *Debit* refers to left, and *credit* refers to right. Debits increase assets, expenses, and dividends while credits decrease them. Credits increase liabilities, common stock, and revenues; debits decrease them. Double-entry accounting means each transaction affects at least two accounts and has at least one debit and one credit. The system for recording debits and credits follows from the accounting equation. The left side of an account is the normal balance for assets, dividends, and expenses, and the right side is the normal balance for liabilities, common stock, and revenues.

**A1  Analyze the impact of transactions on accounts and financial statements.** We analyze transactions using concepts of double-entry accounting. This analysis is performed by determining a transaction's effects on accounts. These effects are recorded in journals and posted to ledgers.

**A2  Compute the debt ratio and describe its use in analyzing company performance.** A company's debt ratio is computed as total liabilities divided by total assets. It reveals how much of the assets are financed by creditor (nonowner) financing. The higher this ratio, the more risk a company faces because liabilities must be repaid at specific dates.

**P1  Record transactions in a journal and post entries to a ledger.** Transactions are recorded in a journal. Each entry in a journal is posted to the accounts in the ledger. This provides information that is used to produce financial statements. Balance column accounts are widely used and include columns for debits, credits, and the account balance.

**P2  Prepare and explain the use of a trial balance.** A trial balance is a list of accounts from the ledger showing their debit or credit balances in separate columns. The trial balance is a summary of the ledger's contents and is useful in preparing financial statements and in revealing recordkeeping errors.

**P3  Prepare financial statements from business transactions.** The balance sheet, the statement of retained earnings, the income statement, and the statement of cash flows use data from the trial balance (and other financial statements) for their preparation.

## Guidance Answers to **Decision Maker** and **Decision Ethics**

**Cashier**  The advantages to the process proposed by the assistant manager include improved customer service, fewer delays, and less work for you. However, you should have serious concerns about internal control and the potential for fraud. In particular, the assistant manager could steal cash and simply enter fewer sales to match the remaining cash. You should reject her suggestion without the manager's approval. Moreover, you should have an ethical concern about the assistant manager's suggestion to ignore store policy.

**Entrepreneur**  We can use the accounting equation (Assets = Liabilities + Equity) to help us identify risky customers to whom we would likely not want to extend credit. A balance sheet provides amounts for each of these key components. The lower a customer's equity is relative to liabilities, the less likely you would extend credit. A low equity means the business has little value that does not already have creditor claims to it.

**Investor**  The debt ratio suggests the stock of Converse is of higher risk than normal and that this risk is rising. The average industry ratio of 0.40 further supports this conclusion. The 2003 debt ratio for Converse is twice the industry norm. Also, a debt ratio approaching 1.0 indicates little to no equity.

## Guidance Answers to **Quick Checks**

**1.** Examples of source documents are sales tickets, checks, purchase orders, charges to customers, bills from suppliers, employee earnings records, and bank statements.

**2.** Source documents serve many purposes, including record-keeping and internal control. Source documents, especially if obtained from outside the organization, provide objective and reliable evidence about transactions and their amounts.

**3.**

| Assets | Liabilities | Equity |
|--------|-------------|--------|
| a,c,e | b,d | — |

**4.** An account is a record in an accounting system that records and stores the increases and decreases in a specific asset, liability, equity, revenue, or expense. The ledger is a collection of all the accounts of a company.

**5.** A company's size and diversity affect the number of accounts in its accounting system. The types of accounts depend on information the company needs to both effectively operate and report its activities in financial statements.

**6.** No. Debit and credit both can mean increase or decrease. The particular meaning in a circumstance depends on the *type of account*. For example, a debit increases the balance of asset, dividends, and expense accounts, but it decreases the balance of liability, common stock, and revenue accounts.

**7.** A chart of accounts is a list of all of a company's accounts and their identification numbers.

**8.** Equity is increased by revenues and by owner investments. Equity is decreased by expenses and dividends.

**9.** The name *double entry* is used because all transactions affect at least two accounts. There must be at least one debit in one account and at least one credit in another account.

**10.** Answer is (*c*).

**11.**

| | | |
|---|---|---|
| Cash . . . . . . . . . . . . . . . . . . . . . . . . . . . . | 15,000 | |
| Equipment . . . . . . . . . . . . . . . . . . . . . . . | 23,000 | |
|     Common Stock . . . . . . . . . . . . . . . . | | 38,000 |
| *Investment by owner of cash and equipment.* | | |

**12.** A compound journal entry affects three or more accounts.

**13.** Posting reference numbers are entered in the journal when posting to the ledger as a cross-reference that allows the record-keeper or auditor to trace debits and credits from one record to another.

**14.** At a minimum, dollar signs are placed beside the first and last numbers in a column. It is also common to place dollar signs beside any amount that appears after a ruled line to indicate that an addition or subtraction has occurred.

**15.** The Equipment account balance is incorrectly reported at $20,000—it should be $28,000. The effect of this error understates the trial balance's Debit column total by $8,000. This results in an $8,000 difference between the column totals.

**16.** An income statement reports a company's revenues and expenses along with the resulting net income or loss. A statement of retained earnings reports changes in retained earnings, including that from net income or loss. Both statements report transactions occurring over a period of time.

**17.** The balance sheet describes a company's financial position (assets, liabilities, and equity) at a point in time. The retained earnings amount in the balance sheet is obtained from the statement of retained earnings.

**18.** Revenues are inflows of assets in exchange for products or services provided to customers as part of the main operations of a business. Expenses are outflows or the using up of assets that result from providing products or services to customers.

**19.** Assets are the resources a business owns or controls that carry expected future benefits. Liabilities are the obligations of a business, representing the claims of others against the assets of a business. Equity reflects the owner's claims on the assets of the business after deducting liabilities.

## Key Terms

Key Terms are available at the book's Website for learning and testing in an online Flashcard Format.

| | | |
|---|---|---|
| **Account** (p. 49) | **Debit** (p. 53) | **Posting** (p. 54) |
| **Account balance** (p. 53) | **Debt ratio** (p. 67) | **Posting reference (PR) column** (p. 55) |
| **Balance column account** (p. 56) | **Dividends** (p. 51) | **Source documents** (p. 49) |
| **Chart of accounts** (p. 52) | **Double-entry accounting** (p. 53) | **T-account** (p. 53) |
| **Common stock** (p. 51) | **General journal** (p. 54) | **Trial balance** (p. 63) |
| **Compound journal entry** (p. 59) | **Journal** (p. 54) | **Unearned revenue** (p. 51) |
| **Credit** (p. 53) | **Journalizing** (p. 54) | |
| **Creditors** (p. 50) | **Ledger** (p. 49) | |

## Personal Interactive Quiz

Personal Interactive Quizzes A and B are available at the book's Website to reinforce and assess your learning.

## Discussion Questions

**1.** Provide the names of two (*a*) asset accounts, (*b*) liability accounts, and (*c*) equity accounts.

**2.** What is the difference between a note payable and an account payable?

**3.** Discuss the steps in processing business transactions.

**4.** What kinds of transactions can be recorded in a general journal?

**5.** Are debits or credits typically listed first in general journal entries? Are the debits or the credits indented?

**6.** If assets are valuable resources and asset accounts have debit balances, why do expense accounts have debit balances?

**7.** Should a transaction be recorded first in a journal or the ledger? Why?

**8.** Why does the recordkeeper prepare a trial balance?

**9.** If a wrong amount is journalized and posted to the accounts, how should the error be corrected?

**10.** Identify the four financial statements of a business.

**11.** What information is reported in an income statement?

**12.** Why does the user of an income statement need to know the time period that it covers?

**13.** What information is reported in a balance sheet?

**14.** Define (*a*) *assets,* (*b*) *liabilities,* (*c*) *equity,* and (*d*) *net assets.*

**15.** Which financial statement is sometimes called the *statement of financial position?*

**16.** Review the **Krispy Kreme** balance sheet in Appendix A. Identify three accounts on its balance sheet that carry debit balances and three accounts on its balance sheet that carry credit balances.

**17.** Review the **Tastykake** balance sheet in Appendix A. Identify two different liability accounts that include the word *payable* in the account title.

**18.** Locate **Harley-Davidson**'s income statement in Appendix A. What is the title of its revenue account?   **Harley-Davidson**

*Red numbers denote Discussion Questions that involve decision-making.*

*Homework Manager* 👆 *repeats all numerical Quick Study assignments on the book's Website with new numbers each time. It can be used in practice, homework, or exam mode.*

---

Identify the items from the following list that are likely to serve as source documents:

**a.** Bank statement
**b.** Sales ticket
**c.** Income statement

**d.** Trial balance
**e.** Telephone bill
**f.** Invoice from supplier

**g.** Company revenue account
**h.** Balance sheet
**i.** Prepaid insurance

**QUICK STUDY**

**QS 2-1**
Identifying source documents

C2

---

Identify the financial statement(s) where each of the following items appears. Use I for income statement, E for statement of retained earnings, and B for balance sheet:

**a.** Service fees earned
**b.** Cash dividends
**c.** Office equipment

**d.** Accounts payable
**e.** Cash
**f.** Utilities expenses

**g.** Office supplies
**h.** Prepaid rent
**i.** Unearned fees

**QS 2-2**
Identifying financial statement items

C3   P3

---

Indicate whether a debit or credit *decreases* the normal balance of each of the following accounts:

**a.** Office Supplies
**b.** Repair Services Revenue
**c.** Interest Payable
**d.** Accounts Receivable

**e.** Salaries Expense
**f.** Common Stock
**g.** Prepaid Insurance
**h.** Buildings

**i.** Interest Revenue
**j.** Dividends
**k.** Unearned Revenue
**l.** Accounts Payable

**QS 2-3**
Linking debit or credit with normal balance

C5

**QS 2-4**

Analyzing debit or credit by account

C5 A1

Identify whether a debit or credit yields the indicated change for each of the following accounts:

**a.** To increase Store Equipment
**b.** To increase Dividends
**c.** To decrease Cash
**d.** To increase Utilities Expense
**e.** To increase Fees Earned
**f.** To decrease Unearned Revenue
**g.** To decrease Prepaid Insurance
**h.** To increase Notes Payable
**i.** To decrease Accounts Receivable
**j.** To increase Common Stock

**QS 2-5**

Identifying normal balance

C5

Identify whether the normal balances (in parentheses) assigned to the following accounts are correct or incorrect.

**a.** Office supplies (Debit)
**b.** Dividends (Credit)
**c.** Fees Earned (Debit)
**d.** Wages Expense (Credit)
**e.** Cash (Debit)
**f.** Prepaid Insurance (Credit)
**g.** Wages Payable (Credit)
**h.** Building (Debit)

**QS 2-6**

Preparing journal entries

P1

Prepare journal entries for each of the following selected transactions:

**a.** On January 13, Chico Chavez opens a landscaping business called Showcase Yards by investing $70,000 cash along with equipment having a $30,000 value in exchange for common stock.
**b.** On January 21, Showcase Yards purchases office supplies on credit for $280.
**c.** On January 29, Showcase Yards receives $7,800 cash for performing landscaping services.
**d.** On January 30, Showcase Yards receives $1,000 cash in advance of providing landscaping services to a customer.

**QS 2-7**

Identifying a posting error

P2

A trial balance has total debits of $20,000 and total credits of $24,500. Which one of the following errors would create this imbalance? Explain.

**a.** A $2,250 debit to Rent Expense in a journal entry is incorrectly posted to the ledger as a $2,250 credit, leaving the Rent Expense account with a $3,000 debit balance.
**b.** A $4,500 debit to Salaries Expense in a journal entry is incorrectly posted to the ledger as a $4,500 credit, leaving the Salaries Expense account with a $750 debit balance.
**c.** A $2,250 credit to Consulting Fees Earned in a journal entry is incorrectly posted to the ledger as a $2,250 debit, leaving the Consulting Fees Earned account with a $6,300 credit balance.

**QS 2-8**

Classifying accounts in financial statements

P3

Indicate the financial statement on which each of the following items appears. Use I for income statement, E for statement of retained earnings, and B for balance sheet:

**a.** Office Supplies
**b.** Services Revenue
**c.** Interest Payable
**d.** Accounts Receivable
**e.** Salaries Expense
**f.** Equipment
**g.** Prepaid Insurance
**h.** Buildings
**i.** Interest Revenue
**j.** Dividends

*Homework Manager*  *repeats all numerical Exercises on the book's Website with new numbers each time. It can be used in practice, homework, or exam mode.*

# EXERCISES

**Exercise 2-1**

Identifying type and normal balances of accounts

C3   C5

For each of the following (1) identify the type of account as an asset, liability, equity, revenue, or expense, (2) enter *debit* (*Dr.*) or *credit* (*Cr.*) to identify the kind of entry that would increase the account balance, and (3) identify the normal balance of the account.

**a.** Unearned Revenue
**b.** Accounts Payable
**c.** Postage Expense
**d.** Prepaid Insurance
**e.** Land
**f.** Common Stock
**g.** Accounts Receivable
**h.** Dividends
**i.** Cash
**j.** Equipment
**k.** Fees Earned
**l.** Wages Expense

Tavon Co. recently notified a client that it must pay a $48,000 fee for services provided. Tavon agreed to accept the following three items in full payment: (1) $7,500 cash, (2) computer equipment worth $75,000, and (3) assume responsibility for a $34,500 note payable related to the computer equipment. The entry Tavon makes to record this transaction includes which one or more of the following?

**a.** $34,500 increase in a liability account

**d.** $48,000 increase in an asset account

**b.** $7,500 increase in the Cash account

**e.** $48,000 increase in a revenue account

**c.** $7,500 increase in a revenue account

**Exercise 2-2**
Analyzing effects of transactions on accounts

A1

---

Use the information in each of the following separate cases to calculate the unknown amount:

**a.** During October, Shandra Company had $97,500 of cash receipts and $101,250 of cash disbursements. The October 31 Cash balance was $16,800. Determine how much cash the company had at the close of business on September 30.

**b.** On September 30, Li Ming Co. had a $97,500 balance in Accounts Receivable. During October, the company collected $88,950 from its credit customers. The October 31 balance in Accounts Receivable was $100,500. Determine the amount of sales on account that occurred in October.

**c.** Nasser Co. had $147,000 of accounts payable on September 30 and $136,500 on October 31. Total purchases on account during October were $270,000. Determine how much cash was paid on accounts payable during October.

**Exercise 2-3**
Analyzing account entries and balances

A1

---

Prepare general journal entries for the following transactions of a new business called Pose-for-Pics.

Aug.  1    Hashim Paris, the owner, invested $7,500 cash and $32,500 of photography equipment in the business in exchange for its common stock.
  1    Paid $3,000 cash for an insurance policy covering the next 24 months.
  5    Purchased office supplies for $1,400 cash.
  20    Received $2,650 cash in photography fees earned.
  31    Paid $875 cash for August utilities.

**Exercise 2-4**
Preparing general journal entries

A1  P1

---

Use the information in Exercise 2-4 to prepare an August 31 trial balance for Pose-for-Pics. Open these T-accounts: Cash; Office Supplies; Prepaid Insurance; Photography Equipment; Common Stock; Photography Fees Earned; and Utilities Expense. Post the general journal entries to these T-accounts (which will serve as the ledger), and prepare a trial balance.

**Exercise 2-5**
Preparing T-accounts and a trial balance

C3  P2

---

Record the transactions below for Dejonge Company by recording the debit and credit entries directly in the following T-accounts: Cash; Accounts Receivable; Office Supplies; Office Equipment; Accounts Payable; Common Stock; Dividends; Fees Earned; and Rent Expense. Use the letters beside each transaction to identify entries. Determine the ending balance of each T-account.

**a.** Robert Dejonge invested $12,750 cash in the business in exchange for its common stock.

**b.** Purchased office supplies for $375 cash.

**c.** Purchased $7,050 of office equipment on credit.

**d.** Received $1,500 cash as fees for services provided to a customer.

**e.** Paid $7,050 cash to settle the payable for the office equipment purchased in transaction *c*.

**f.** Billed a customer $2,700 as fees for services provided.

**g.** Paid the monthly rent with $525 cash.

**h.** Collected $1,125 cash toward the account receivable created in transaction *f*.

**i.** Paid $1,000 cash for dividends.

**Exercise 2-6**
Recording effects of transactions in T-accounts

C5  A1

**Check**   Cash ending balance, $6,425

---

After recording the transactions of Exercise 2-6 in T-accounts and calculating the balance of each account, prepare a trial balance. Use May 31, 2005, as its report date.

**Exercise 2-7**
Preparing a trial balance   P2

**Exercise 2-8**
Analyzing and journalizing
revenue transactions

A1  P1

Examine the following transactions and identify those that create revenues for Jade Services, a company owned by Mia Jade. Prepare general journal entries to record those transactions and explain why the other transactions did not create revenues.

**a.** Mia Jade invests $38,250 cash in the business in exchange for its common stock.

**b.** Provided $1,350 of services on credit.

**c.** Provided services to a client and received $1,575 cash.

**d.** Received $9,150 cash from a client in payment for services to be provided next year.

**e.** Received $4,500 cash from a client in partial payment of an account receivable.

**f.** Borrowed $150,000 cash from the bank by signing a promissory note.

**Exercise 2-9**
Analyzing and journalizing
expense transactions

A1  P1

Examine the following transactions and identify those that create expenses for Jade Services. Prepare general journal entries to record those transactions and explain why the other transactions did not create expenses.

**a.** Paid $14,100 cash for office supplies that were purchased more than 1 year ago.

**b.** Paid $1,125 cash for the two-week salary of the receptionist.

**c.** Paid $45,000 cash for equipment.

**d.** Paid $930 cash for monthly utilities.

**e.** Paid $5,000 cash for dividends.

**Exercise 2-10**
Preparing an income
statement

C4  P3

On October 1, Ming Lue organized a new consulting firm called Tech Today. On October 31, the company's records show the following items and amounts. Use this information to prepare an October income statement for the business.

| | | | | |
|---|---|---|---|---|
| Cash | $ 8,360 | | Dividends | $ 3,000 |
| Accounts receivable | 17,000 | | Consulting fees earned | 17,000 |
| Office supplies | 3,250 | | Rent expense | 4,550 |
| Patents | 46,000 | | Salaries expense | 8,000 |
| Office equipment | 18,000 | | Telephone expense | 560 |
| Accounts payable | 8,000 | | Miscellaneous expenses | 280 |
| Common stock | 84,000 | | | |

**Check**   Net income, $3,610

**Exercise 2-11**
Preparing a statement
of retained earnings   P3

Use the information in Exercise 2-10 to prepare an October statement of retained earnings for Tech Today.

**Exercise 2-12**
Preparing a balance sheet   P3

Use the information in Exercise 2-10 (if completed, you can also use your solution to Exercise 2-11) to prepare an October 31 balance sheet for Tech Today.

**Exercise 2-13**
Computing net income

A1  P3

A corporation had the following assets and liabilities at the beginning and end of a recent year:

| | Assets | Liabilities |
|---|---|---|
| Beginning of the year | $ 70,000 | $30,000 |
| End of the year | 115,000 | 46,000 |

Determine the net income earned or net loss incurred by the business during the year for each of the following *separate* cases:

**a.** Owner made no investments in the business and no dividends were paid during the year.

**b.** Owner made no investments in the business but dividends were $1,250 cash per month.

**c.** No dividends were paid during the year but the owner invested an additional $45,000 cash in exchange for common stock.

**d.** Dividends were $1,250 cash per month and the owner invested an additional $25,000 cash in exchange for common stock.

---

Compute the missing amount in each of the following separate companies *a* through *d*:

**Exercise 2-14**
Analyzing changes in a company's equity

C5  P3

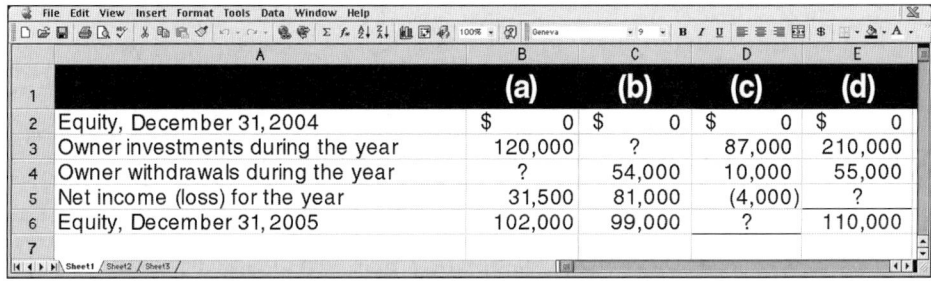

| | (a) | (b) | (c) | (d) |
|---|---|---|---|---|
| Equity, December 31, 2004 | $ 0 | $ 0 | $ 0 | $ 0 |
| Owner investments during the year | 120,000 | ? | 87,000 | 210,000 |
| Owner withdrawals during the year | ? | 54,000 | 10,000 | 55,000 |
| Net income (loss) for the year | 31,500 | 81,000 | (4,000) | ? |
| Equity, December 31, 2005 | 102,000 | 99,000 | ? | 110,000 |

---

Assume the following T-accounts reflect Joy Co.'s general ledger and that seven transactions *a* through *g* are posted to them. Provide a short description of each transaction. Include the amounts in your descriptions.

**Exercise 2-15**
Interpreting and describing transactions from T-accounts

C1  A1

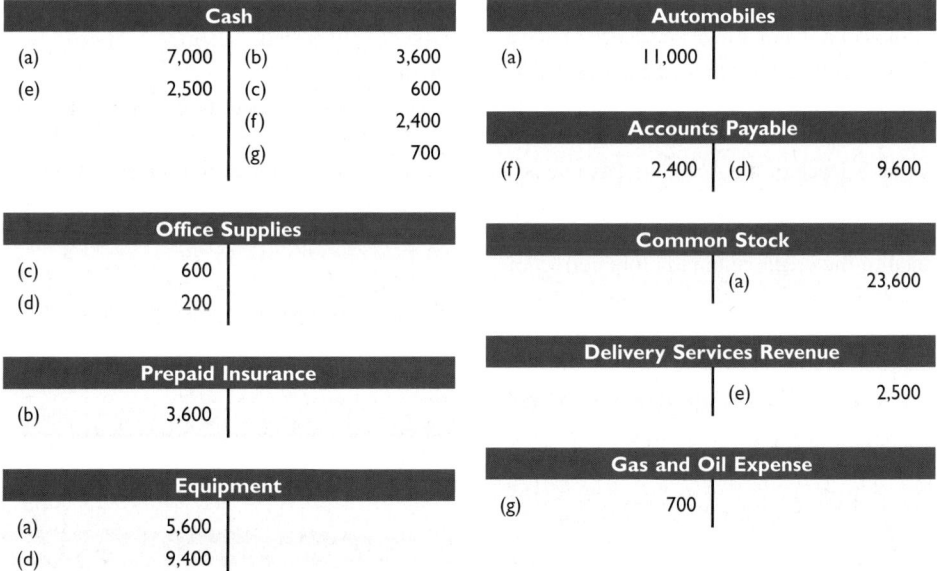

---

Use information from the T-accounts in Exercise 2-15 to prepare general journal entries for each of the seven transaction *a* through *g*.

**Exercise 2-16**
Preparing general journal entries  A1  P1

---

Posting errors are identified in the following table. In column (1), enter the amount of the difference between the two (debit and credit) trial balance columns due to the error. In column (2), identify the trial balance column (debit or credit) with the larger amount if they are not equal. In column (3), identify the account(s) affected by the error. In column (4), indicate the amount by which the account(s) in column (3) is (are) under- or overstated. Answers for the first error are given.

**Exercise 2-17**
Identifying effects of posting errors on the trial balance  A1  P2

| | Description of Posting Error | (1)<br>Difference between<br>Debit and Credit<br>Columns | (2)<br>Column with<br>the Larger<br>Total | (3)<br>Identify<br>Account(s)<br>Incorrectly<br>Stated | (4)<br>Amount that<br>Account(s) is<br>Over- or<br>Understated |
|---|---|---|---|---|---|
| a. | $2,400 debit to Rent Expense is posted as a $1,590 debit. | $810 | Credit | Rent Expense | Rent Expense understated $810 |
| b. | $4,050 credit to Cash is posted twice as two credits to Cash. | | | | |
| c. | $9,900 debit to the Dividends account is debited to Common Stock. | | | | |
| d. | $2,250 debit to Prepaid Insurance is posted as a debit to Insurance Expense. | | | | |
| e. | $42,000 debit to Machinery is posted as a debit to Accounts Payable. | | | | |
| f. | $4,950 credit to Services Revenue is posted as a $495 credit. | | | | |
| g. | $1,440 debit to Store Supplies is not posted. | | | | |

### Exercise 2-18
Analyzing a trial
balance error

A1  P2

You are told the column totals in a trial balance are not equal. After careful analysis, you discover only one error. Specifically, a correctly journalized credit purchase of a computer for $16,950 is posted from the journal to the ledger with a $16,950 debit to Office Equipment and another $16,950 debit to Accounts Payable. The balance of the Office Equipment account has a debit balance of $40,100 on the trial balance. Answer each of the following questions and compute the dollar amount of any misstatement:

**a.** Is the debit column total of the trial balance overstated, understated, or correctly stated?

**b.** Is the credit column total of the trial balance overstated, understated, or correctly stated?

**c.** Is the balance of the Office Equipment account overstated, understated, or correctly stated in the trial balance?

**d.** Is the balance of the Accounts Payable account overstated, understated, or correctly stated in the trial balance?

**e.** If the debit column total of the trial balance is $360,000 before correcting the error, what is the total of the credit column before correction?

### Exercise 2-19
Interpreting the debt ratio
and return on assets

A2

**a.** Calculate the debt ratio and the return on assets using the year-end information for each of the following six separate companies ($ in thousands):

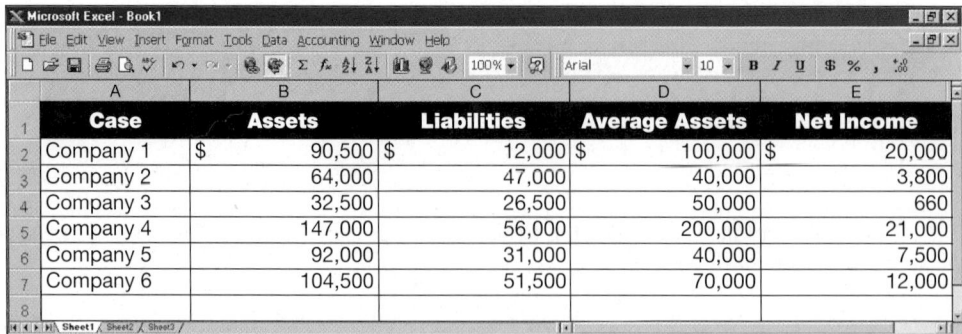

| Case | Assets | Liabilities | Average Assets | Net Income |
|---|---|---|---|---|
| Company 1 | $ 90,500 | $ 12,000 | $ 100,000 | $ 20,000 |
| Company 2 | 64,000 | 47,000 | 40,000 | 3,800 |
| Company 3 | 32,500 | 26,500 | 50,000 | 660 |
| Company 4 | 147,000 | 56,000 | 200,000 | 21,000 |
| Company 5 | 92,000 | 31,000 | 40,000 | 7,500 |
| Company 6 | 104,500 | 51,500 | 70,000 | 12,000 |

**b.** Of the six companies, which business relies most heavily on creditor financing?

**c.** Of the six companies, which business relies most heavily on equity financing?

**d.** Which two companies indicate the greatest risk?

**e.** Which two companies earn the highest return on assets?

**f.** Which one company would investors likely prefer based on the risk–return relation?

Roberto Ricci opens a computer consulting business called Viva Consultants and completes the following transactions in its first month of operations:

April 1   Ricci invests $100,000 cash along with office equipment valued at $24,000 in the business in exchange for its common stock.

2   Prepaid $7,200 cash for twelve months' rent for office space. (*Hint:* Debit Prepaid Rent for $7,200.)

3   Made credit purchases for $12,000 in office equipment and $2,400 in office supplies. Payment is due within 10 days.

6   Completed services for a client and immediately received $2,000 cash.

9   Completed an $8,000 project for a client, who must pay within 30 days.

13   Paid $14,400 cash to settle the account payable created on April 3.

19   Paid $6,000 cash for the premium on a 12-month insurance policy. (*Hint:* Debit Prepaid Insurance for $6,000.)

22   Received $6,400 cash as partial payment for the work completed on April 9.

25   Completed work for another client for $2,640 on credit.

28   Paid $6,200 cash for dividends.

29   Purchased $800 of additional office supplies on credit.

30   Paid $700 cash for this month's utility bill.

### Required

**1.** Prepare general journal entries to record these transactions (use account titles listed in part 2).

**2.** Open the following ledger accounts—their account numbers are in parentheses (use the balance column format): Cash (101); Accounts Receivable (106); Office Supplies (124); Prepaid Insurance (128); Prepaid Rent (131); Office Equipment (163); Accounts Payable (201); Common Stock (307); Dividends (319); Services Revenue (403); and Utilities Expense (690). Post journal entries from part 1 to the ledger accounts and enter the balance after each posting.

**3.** Prepare a trial balance as of the end of this month's operations.

## PROBLEM SET A

### Problem 2-1A
Preparing and posting general journal entries; preparing a trial balance

C4  C5  A1  P1  P2

**Check**   (2) Ending balances: Cash, $73,900; Accounts Receivable, $4,240; Accounts Payable, $800

(3) Total debits, $137,440

---

Shelton Engineering completed the following transactions in the month of June.

**a.** Shania Shelton, the owner, invested $105,000 cash, office equipment with a value of $6,000, and $45,000 of drafting equipment to launch the business in exchange for its common stock.

**b.** Purchased land worth $54,000 for an office by paying $5,400 cash and signing a long-term note payable for $48,600.

**c.** Purchased a portable building with $75,000 cash and moved it onto the land acquired in *b*.

**d.** Paid $6,000 cash for the premium on an 18-month insurance policy.

**e.** Completed and delivered a set of plans for a client and collected $5,700 cash.

**f.** Purchased $22,500 of additional drafting equipment by paying $10,500 cash and signing a long-term note payable for $12,000.

**g.** Completed $12,000 of engineering services for a client. This amount is to be received in 30 days.

**h.** Purchased $2,250 of additional office equipment on credit.

**i.** Completed engineering services for $18,000 on credit.

**j.** Received a bill for rent of equipment that was used on a recently completed job. The $1,200 rent must be paid within 30 days.

**k.** Collected $7,200 cash in partial payment from the client described in transaction *g*.

**l.** Paid $1,500 cash for wages to a drafting assistant.

**m.** Paid $2,250 cash to settle the account payable created in transaction *h*.

**n.** Paid $675 cash for minor repairs to the drafting equipment.

**o.** Paid $9,360 cash for dividends.

**p.** Paid $1,500 cash for wages to a drafting assistant.

**q.** Paid $3,000 cash for advertisements in the local newspaper during June.

### Problem 2-2A
Preparing and posting journal entries; preparing a trial balance

C4  C5  A1  P1  P2

**Required**

**1.** Prepare general journal entries to record these transactions (use the account titles listed in part 2).

**2.** Open the following accounts—their account numbers are in parentheses (use the balance column format): Cash (101); Accounts Receivable (106); Prepaid Insurance (108); Office Equipment (163); Drafting Equipment (164); Building (170); Land (172); Accounts Payable (201); Notes Payable (250); Common Stock (307); Dividends (319); Engineering Fees Earned (402); Wages Expense (601); Equipment Rental Expense (602); Advertising Expense (603); and Repairs Expense (604). Post the journal entries from part 1 to the accounts and enter the balance after each posting.

**3.** Prepare a trial balance as of the end of this month's operations.

---

## Problem 2-3A

Preparing and posting general journal entries; preparing a trial balance

C4  C5  A1  P1  P2

mhhe.com/wild3e

Santo Birch opens a Web consulting business called Show-Me-the-Money Consultants and completes the following transactions in March:

March  1  Birch invested $150,000 cash along with $22,000 of office equipment in the business in exchange for its common stock.
      2  Prepaid $6,000 cash for six months' rent for an office. (*Hint:* Debit Prepaid Rent for $6,000.)
      3  Made credit purchases of office equipment for $3,000 and office supplies for $1,200. Payment is due within 10 days.
      6  Completed services for a client and immediately received $4,000 cash.
      9  Completed a $7,500 project for a client, who must pay within 30 days.
     10  Paid $4,200 cash to settle the account payable created on March 3.
     19  Paid $5,000 cash for the premium on a 12-month insurance policy.
     22  Received $3,500 cash as partial payment for the work completed on March 9.
     25  Completed work for another client for $3,820 on credit.
     29  Paid $5,100 cash for dividends.
     30  Purchased $600 of additional office supplies on credit.
     31  Paid $200 cash for this month's utility bill.

**Required**

**1.** Prepare general journal entries to record these transactions (use the account titles listed in part 2).

**2.** Open the following accounts—their account numbers are in parentheses (use the balance column format): Cash (101); Accounts Receivable (106); Office Supplies (124); Prepaid Insurance (128); Prepaid Rent (131); Office Equipment (163); Accounts Payable (201); Common Stock (307); Dividends (319); Services Revenue (403); and Utilities Expense (690). Post the journal entries from part 1 to the accounts and enter the balance after each posting.

**3.** Prepare a trial balance as of the end of this month's operations.

---

## Problem 2-4A

Computing net income from equity analysis, preparing a balance sheet, and calculating the debt ratio

C3  A1  A2  P3

mhhe.com/wild3e

The accounting records of Crist Crate Services show the following assets and liabilities as of December 31, 2004, and 2005:

|  | December 31 | |
| --- | --- | --- |
|  | **2004** | **2005** |
| Cash ................. | $ 52,500 | $ 18,750 |
| Accounts receivable ....... | 28,500 | 22,350 |
| Office supplies .......... | 4,500 | 3,300 |
| Office equipment ........ | 138,000 | 147,000 |
| Trucks ................ | 54,000 | 54,000 |
| Building .............. | 0 | 180,000 |
| Land ................. | 0 | 45,000 |
| Accounts payable ........ | 7,500 | 37,500 |
| Note payable ........... | 0 | 105,000 |

Late in December 2005, the business purchased a small office building and land for $225,000. It paid $120,000 cash toward the purchase and a $105,000 note payable was signed for the balance. Crist had to invest $35,000 cash in the business (in exchange for stock) to enable it to pay the $120,000 cash. The business pays $3,000 cash per month for dividends.

**Required**

**1.** Prepare balance sheets for the business as of December 31, 2004, and 2005. (*Hint:* You need only report total equity on the balance sheet, and remember that total equity equals the difference between assets and liabilities.)

**2.** By comparing equity amounts from the balance sheets and using the additional information presented in this problem, prepare a calculation to show how much net income was earned by the business during 2005.

**Check**  (2) Net income, $58,900

**3.** Compute the 2005 year-end debt ratio for the business.

(3) Debt ratio, 30.29%

---

Carlos Beltran started an engineering firm called Beltran Engineering. He began operations and completed seven transactions in May, which included his initial investment of $17,000 cash. After these transactions, the ledger included the following accounts with normal balances:

**Problem 2-5A**
Analyzing account balances and reconstructing transactions

C1  C4  A1  P2

| | |
|---|---:|
| Cash ................... | $26,660 |
| Office supplies ............. | 660 |
| Prepaid insurance ........... | 3,200 |
| Office equipment ........... | 16,500 |
| Accounts payable ........... | 16,500 |
| Common stock ............ | 17,000 |
| Dividends ................ | 3,740 |
| Engineering fees earned ....... | 24,000 |
| Rent expense ............. | 6,740 |

**Required**

**1.** Prepare a trial balance for this business at the end of May.

**Check**  (1) Trial balance totals, $57,500

*Analysis Components*

**2.** Analyze the accounts and their balances and prepare a list that describes each of the seven most likely transactions and their amounts.

**3.** Prepare a report of cash received and cash paid showing how the seven transactions in part 2 yield the $26,660 ending Cash balance.

(3) Cash paid, $14,340

---

Business transactions completed by Eric Piburn during the month of September are as follows:

**Problem 2-6A**
Recording transactions; posting to ledger; preparing a trial balance

C4  A1  P1  P2

**a.** Piburn invested $23,000 cash along with office equipment valued at $12,000 in exchange for common stock of a new business named EP Consulting.

**b.** Purchased land valued at $8,000 and a building valued at $33,000. The purchase is paid with $15,000 cash and a long-term note payable for $26,000.

**c.** Purchased $600 of office supplies on credit.

**d.** Piburn invested his personal automobile in the business in exchange for more common stock. The automobile has a value of $7,000 and is to be used exclusively in the business.

**e.** Purchased $1,100 of additional office equipment on credit.

**f.** Paid $800 cash salary to an assistant.

**g.** Provided services to a client and collected $2,700 cash.

**h.** Paid $430 cash for this month's utilities.

**i.** Paid $600 cash to settle the account payable created in transaction *c*.

**j.** Purchased $4,000 of new office equipment by paying $2,400 cash and trading in old equipment with a recorded net cost and value of $1,600. (*Hint:* Credit Office Equipment (old) for $1,600.)

**k.** Completed $2,400 of services for a client, who must pay within 30 days.

**l.** Paid $800 cash salary to an assistant.

**m.** Received $1,000 cash on the receivable created in transaction *k*.

**n.** Paid $1,050 cash for dividends.

**Required**

**1.** Prepare general journal entries to record these transactions (use the account titles listed in part 2).

**Check**　(2) Ending balances: Cash, $5,620; Office Equipment, $15,500

**2.** Open the following accounts—their account numbers are in parentheses (use the balance column format): Cash (101); Accounts Receivable (106); Office Supplies (108); Office Equipment (163); Automobiles (164); Building (170); Land (172); Accounts Payable (201); Notes Payable (250); Common Stock (307); Dividends (319); Fees Earned (402); Salaries Expense (601); and Utilities Expense (602). Post the journal entries from part 1 to the accounts and enter the balance after each posting.

(3) Trial balance totals, $74,200

**3.** Prepare a trial balance as of the end of this month's operations.

---

# PROBLEM SET B

## Problem 2-1B

Preparing and posting general journal entries; preparing a trial balance

C4　C5　A1　P1　P2

Lummus Management Services opens for business and completes these transactions in September:

Sept.　1　Rhonda Lummus, the owner, invests $28,000 cash along with office equipment valued at $25,000 in the business in exchange for its common stock.

　　　　2　Prepaid $10,500 cash for twelve months' rent for office space. (*Hint:* Debit Prepaid Rent for $10,500.)

　　　　4　Made credit purchases for $9,000 in office equipment and $1,200 in office supplies. Payment is due within 10 days.

　　　　8　Completed work for a client and immediately received $2,600 cash.

　　　　12　Completed a $13,400 project for a client, who must pay within 20 days.

　　　　13　Paid $10,200 cash to settle the account payable created on September 4.

　　　　19　Paid $5,200 cash for the premium on an 18-month insurance policy. (*Hint:* Debit Prepaid Insurance for $5,200.)

　　　　22　Received $7,800 cash as partial payment for the work completed on September 12.

　　　　24　Completed work for another client for $1,900 on credit.

　　　　28　Paid $5,300 cash for dividends.

　　　　29　Purchased $1,700 of additional office supplies on credit.

　　　　30　Paid $460 cash for this month's utility bill.

**Required**

**1.** Prepare general journal entries to record these transactions (use account titles listed in part 2).

**Check**　(2) Ending balances: Cash, $6,740; Accounts Receivable, $7,500; Accounts Payable, $1,700

**2.** Open the following ledger accounts—their account numbers are in parentheses (use the balance column format): Cash (101); Accounts Receivable (106); Office Supplies (124); Prepaid Insurance (128); Prepaid Rent (131); Office Equipment (163); Accounts Payable (201); Common Stock (307); Dividends (319); Service Fees Earned (401); and Utilities Expense (690). Post journal entries from part 1 to the ledger accounts and enter the balance after each posting.

(3) Total debits, $72,600

**3.** Prepare a trial balance as of the end of this month's operations.

---

## Problem 2-2B

Preparing and posting journal entries; preparing a trial balance

C4　C5　A1　P1　P2　

At the beginning of April, Brooke Grechus launched a custom computer programming company called Softways. The company had the following transactions during April:

**a.** Brooke Grechus invested $45,000 cash, office equipment with a value of $4,500, and $28,000 of computer equipment in the company in exchange for its common stock.

**b.** Purchased land worth $24,000 for an office by paying $4,800 cash and signing a long-term note payable for $19,200.

**c.** Purchased a portable building with $21,000 cash and moved it onto the land acquired in *b*.

**d.** Paid $6,600 cash for the premium on a two-year insurance policy.

**e.** Provided services to a client and collected $3,200 cash.

**f.** Purchased $3,500 of additional computer equipment by paying $700 cash and signing a long-term note payable for $2,800.

**g.** Completed $3,750 of services for a client. This amount is to be received within 30 days.

**h.** Purchased $750 of additional office equipment on credit.

**i.** Completed client services for $9,200 on credit.

**j.** Received a bill for rent of a computer testing device that was used on a recently completed job. The $320 rent must be paid within 30 days.

**k.** Collected $4,600 cash from the client described in transaction *i.*

**l.** Paid $1,600 cash for wages to an assistant.

**m.** Paid $750 cash to settle the account payable created in transaction *h.*

**n.** Paid $425 cash for minor repairs to the computer equipment.

**o.** Paid $3,875 cash for dividends.

**p.** Paid $1,600 cash for wages to an assistant.

**q.** Paid $800 cash for advertisements in the local newspaper during April.

**Required**

**1.** Prepare general journal entries to record these transactions (use the account titles listed in part 2).

**2.** Open the following accounts—their account numbers are in parentheses (use the balance column format): Cash (101); Accounts Receivable (106); Prepaid Insurance (108); Office Equipment (163); Computer Equipment (164); Building (170); Land (172); Accounts Payable (201); Notes Payable (250); Common Stock (307); Dividends (319); Fees Earned (402); Wages Expense (601); Computer Rental Expense (602); Advertising Expense (603); and Repairs Expense (604). Post the journal entries from part 1 to the accounts and enter the balance after each posting.

**3.** Prepare a trial balance as of the end of this month's operations.

**Check**   (2) Ending balances: Cash, $10,650; Accounts Receivable, $8,350; Accounts Payable, $320

(3) Trial balance totals, $115,970

---

Shaw Management Services opens for business and completes these transactions in November:

**Problem 2-3B**
Preparing and posting general journal entries; preparing a trial balance

C4   C5   A1   P1   P2

Nov.  1   Kita Shaw, the owner, invested $30,000 cash along with $15,000 of office equipment in the business in exchange for its common stock.

2   Prepaid $4,500 cash for six months' rent for an office. (*Hint:* Debit Prepaid Rent for $4,500.)

4   Made credit purchases of office equipment for $2,500 and of office supplies for $600. Payment is due within 10 days.

8   Completed work for a client and immediately received $3,400 cash.

12   Completed a $10,200 project for a client, who must pay within 30 days.

13   Paid $3,100 cash to settle the account payable created on November 4.

19   Paid $1,800 cash for the premium on a 24-month insurance policy.

22   Received $5,200 cash as partial payment for the work completed on November 12.

24   Completed work for another client for $1,750 on credit.

28   Paid $5,300 cash for dividends.

29   Purchased $249 of additional office supplies on credit.

30   Paid $531 cash for this month's utility bill.

**Required**

**1.** Prepare general journal entries to record these transactions (use account titles listed in part 2).

**2.** Open the following accounts—their account numbers are in parentheses (use the balance column format): Cash (101); Accounts Receivable (106); Office Supplies (124); Prepaid Insurance (128); Prepaid Rent (131); Office Equipment (163); Accounts Payable (201); Common Stock (307); Dividends (319); Services Revenue (403); and Utilities Expense (690). Post the journal entries from part 1 to the accounts and enter the balance after each posting.

**3.** Prepare a trial balance as of the end of this month's operations.

**Check**   (2) Ending balances: Cash, $23,369; Accounts Receivable, $6,750; Accounts Payable, $249

(3) Total debits, $60,599

## Problem 2-4B

Computing net income from equity analysis, preparing a balance sheet, and computing the debt ratio

C3   A1   A2   P3

The accounting records of Schmit Co. show the following assets and liabilities as of December 31, 2004, and 2005:

|  | December 31 | |
| --- | --- | --- |
|  | **2004** | **2005** |
| Cash . . . . . . . . . . . . . . . . . | $14,000 | $ 10,000 |
| Accounts receivable . . . . . . . | 25,000 | 30,000 |
| Office supplies . . . . . . . . . . | 10,000 | 12,500 |
| Office equipment . . . . . . . . . | 60,000 | 60,000 |
| Machinery . . . . . . . . . . . . . . | 30,500 | 30,500 |
| Building . . . . . . . . . . . . . . | 0 | 260,000 |
| Land . . . . . . . . . . . . . . . . . | 0 | 65,000 |
| Accounts payable . . . . . . . . . | 5,000 | 15,000 |
| Note payable . . . . . . . . . . . | 0 | 260,000 |

Late in December 2005, the business purchased a small office building and land for $325,000. It paid $65,000 cash toward the purchase and a $260,000 note payable was signed for the balance. Schmit had to invest an additional $25,000 cash (in exchange for stock) to enable it to pay the $65,000 cash. The business pays $1,000 cash per month in dividends.

### Required

**1.** Prepare balance sheets for the business as of December 31, 2004, and 2005. (*Hint:* You need only report total equity on the balance sheet, and remember that total equity equals the difference between assets and liabilities.)

**Check**   (2) Net income, $45,500

**2.** By comparing equity amounts from the balance sheets and using the additional information presented in the problem, prepare a calculation to show how much net income was earned by the business during 2005.

(3) Debt ratio, 58.76%

**3.** Calculate the December 31, 2005, debt ratio for the business.

## Problem 2-5B

Analyzing account balances and reconstructing transactions

C1   C4   A1   P2

Miguel Gould started a Web consulting firm called Gould Solutions. He began operations and completed seven transactions in April that resulted in the following accounts, which all have normal balances:

| | |
| --- | --- |
| Cash . . . . . . . . . . . . . . . . . . . . . | $12,485 |
| Office supplies . . . . . . . . . . . . . . | 560 |
| Prepaid rent . . . . . . . . . . . . . . . | 1,500 |
| Office equipment . . . . . . . . . . . . | 11,450 |
| Accounts payable . . . . . . . . . . . . | 11,450 |
| Common Stock . . . . . . . . . . . . . | 10,000 |
| Dividends . . . . . . . . . . . . . . . . . | 6,200 |
| Consulting fees earned . . . . . . . . | 16,400 |
| Operating expenses . . . . . . . . . . | 5,655 |

### Required

**Check**   (1) Trial balance total, $37,850

**1.** Prepare a trial balance for this business at the end of April.

*Analysis Component*

**2.** Analyze the accounts and their balances and prepare a list that describes each of the seven most likely transactions and their amounts.

(3) Cash paid, $13,915

**3.** Present a report that shows how the seven transactions in part 2 yield the $12,485 Cash balance.

## Problem 2-6B

Recording transactions; posting to ledger; preparing a trial balance

C4   A1   P1   P2

Czekai Consulting completed the following transactions during June:

**a.** Chris Czekai, the owner, invested $80,000 cash along with office equipment valued at $30,000 in the new business in exchange for common stock.

**b.** Purchased land valued at $30,000 and a building valued at $170,000. The purchase is paid with $40,000 cash and a long-term note payable for $160,000.

**c.** Purchased $2,400 of office supplies on credit.

**d.** Czekai invested her personal automobile in the business in exchange for more common stock. The automobile has a value of $18,000 and is to be used exclusively in the business.

**e.** Purchased $6,000 of additional office equipment on credit.

**f.** Paid $1,500 cash salary to an assistant.

**g.** Provided services to a client and collected $6,000 cash.

**h.** Paid $800 cash for this month's utilities.

**i.** Paid $2,400 cash to settle the account payable created in transaction *c*.

**j.** Purchased $20,000 of new office equipment by paying $18,600 cash and trading in old equipment with a recorded net cost and value of $1,400. (*Hint:* Credit Office Equipment (old) for $1,400.)

**k.** Completed $5,200 of services for a client, who must pay within 30 days.

**l.** Paid $1,500 cash salary to an assistant.

**m.** Received $3,800 cash on the receivable created in transaction *k*.

**n.** Paid $6,400 cash for dividends.

### Required

**1.** Prepare general journal entries to record these transactions (use the account titles listed in part 2).

**2.** Open the following accounts—their account numbers are in parentheses (use the balance column format): Cash (101); Accounts Receivable (106); Office Supplies (108); Office Equipment (163); Automobiles (164); Building (170); Land (172); Accounts Payable (201); Notes Payable (250); Common Stock (307); Dividends (319); Fees Earned (402); Salaries Expense (601); and Utilities Expense (602). Post the journal entries from part 1 to the accounts and enter the balance after each posting.

**3.** Prepare a trial balance as of the end of this month's operations.

**Check**  (2) Ending balances: Cash, $18,600; Office Equipment, $54,600

(3) Trial balance totals, $305,200

---

Problem Set C is available at the book's Website to further reinforce and assess your learning.

## PROBLEM SET C

---

*(This serial problem started in Chapter 1 and continues through most of the chapters. If the Chapter 1 segment was not completed, the problem can begin at this point. It is helpful, but not necessary, to use the Working Papers that accompany this book.)*

## SERIAL PROBLEM

Success Systems

On October 1, 2004, Kay Breeze launched a computer services company called Success Systems, which provides consulting services, computer system installations, and custom program development. Breeze adopts the calendar year for reporting purposes and expects to prepare the company's first set of financial statements on December 31, 2004. The company's initial chart of accounts follows:

| Account | No. | Account | No. |
|---|---|---|---|
| Cash | 101 | Common Stock | 307 |
| Accounts Receivable | 106 | Dividends | 319 |
| Computer Supplies | 126 | Computer Services Revenue | 403 |
| Prepaid Insurance | 128 | Wages Expense | 623 |
| Prepaid Rent | 131 | Advertising Expense | 655 |
| Office Equipment | 163 | Mileage Expense | 676 |
| Computer Equipment | 167 | Miscellaneous Expenses | 677 |
| Accounts Payable | 201 | Repairs Expense—Computer | 684 |

**Required**

**1.** Prepare journal entries to record each of the following transactions for Success Systems.

Oct.  1   Breeze invested $55,000 cash, a $20,000 computer system, and $8,000 of office equipment in the business in exchange for its common stock.
      2   Paid $3,300 cash for four months' rent. (*Hint:* Debit Prepaid Rent for $3,300.)
      3   Purchased $1,420 of computer supplies on credit from Cain Office Products.
      5   Paid $2,220 cash for one year's premium on a property and liability insurance policy. (*Hint:* Debit Prepaid Insurance for $2,220.)
      6   Billed Easy Leasing $4,800 for services performed in installing a new Web server.
      8   Paid $1,420 cash for the computer supplies purchased from Cain Office Products on October 3.
     10   Hired Sherry Adams as a part-time assistant for $125 per day, as needed.
     12   Billed Easy Leasing another $1,400 for services performed.
     15   Received $4,800 cash from Easy Leasing on its account.
     17   Paid $805 cash to repair computer equipment damaged when moving it.
     20   Paid $1,940 cash for an advertisement in the local newspaper.
     22   Received $1,400 cash from Easy Leasing on its account.
     28   Billed Clark Company $5,208 for services performed.
     31   Paid $875 cash for Sherry Adams' wages for seven days' work.
     31   Paid $3,600 cash for dividends.
Nov.  1   Reimbursed Breeze in cash for business automobile mileage allowance (Breeze logged 1,000 miles at $0.32 per mile).
      2   Received $4,633 cash from Chang Corporation for computer services performed.
      5   Purchased computer supplies for $1,125 cash from Cain Office Products.
      8   Billed Gomez Co. $5,668 for services performed.
     13   Received notification from Alex's Engineering Co. that Success Systems' bid of $3,950 for an upcoming project is accepted.
     18   Received $2,208 cash from Clark Company as partial payment of the October 28 bill.
     22   Donated $250 cash to the United Way in the company's name.
     24   Completed work for Alex's Engineering Co. and sent it a bill for $3,950.
     25   Sent another bill to Clark Company for the past-due amount of $3,000.
     28   Reimbursed Breeze in cash for business automobile mileage (1,200 miles at $0.32 per mile).
     30   Paid $1,750 cash for Sherry Adams' wages for 14 days' work.
     30   Paid $2,000 cash for dividends.

**2.** Open ledger accounts (in balance column format) and post the journal entries from part 1 to them.

**3.** Prepare a trial balance as of the end of November.

# BEYOND THE NUMBERS

## REPORTING IN ACTION

A1  A2

**BTN 2-1**   Refer to **Krispy Kreme**'s financial statements in Appendix A for the following questions.

**Required**

**1.** What amount of total liabilities does it report for each of the fiscal years ended 2002 and 2003?

**2.** What amount of total assets does it report for each of the fiscal years ended 2002 and 2003?

**3.** Calculate its debt ratio for each of the fiscal years ended 2002 and 2003.

**4.** In which fiscal year did it employ more financial leverage (2002 or 2003)? Explain.

*Roll On*

**5.** Access its financial statements (10-K report) for a fiscal year ending after February 2, 2003, from its Website (**KrispyKreme.com**) or the SEC's EDGAR database (**www.sec.gov**). Recompute its debt ratio for any subsequent year's data and compare it with the February 2, 2003, debt ratio.

**BTN 2-2**   Key comparative figures ($ thousands) for both **Krispy Kreme** and **Tastykake** follow:

| Key Figures | Krispy Kreme | | Tastykake | |
| --- | --- | --- | --- | --- |
| | Current Year | Prior Year | Current Year | Prior Year |
| Total liabilities ....... | $131,942 | $ 65,218 | $ 69,035 | $ 61,072 |
| Total assets ......... | 410,487 | 255,376 | 116,560 | 116,137 |

**1.** What is the debt ratio for Krispy Kreme in the current year and the prior year?

**2.** What is the debt ratio for Tastykake in the current year and the prior year?

**3.** Which of the two companies has a higher degree of financial leverage? What does this imply?

**BTN 2-3**   Review the *Decision Ethics* case from the first part of this chapter involving the cashier. The guidance answer suggests that you should not comply with the assistant manager's request.

**Required**

Propose and evaluate two other courses of action you might consider, and explain why.

**BTN 2-4**   Amy Renkmeyer is an aspiring entrepreneur and your friend. She is having difficulty understanding the purposes of financial statements and how they fit together across time.

**Required**

Write a one-page memorandum to Renkmeyer explaining the purposes of the four financial statements and how they are linked across time.

**BTN 2-5**   Access EDGAR online (www.sec.gov) and locate the 10-K report of **Amazon.com** (ticker AMZN) filed on January 24, 2002. Review its financial statements reported for fiscal years ended 1999, 2000, and 2001 to answer the following questions:

**Required**

**1.** What are the amounts of its net losses reported for each of these three years?

**2.** Does Amazon's operations provide cash or use cash for each of these three years?

**3.** If Amazon has a 2000 net loss and a net use of cash in operations in 2000, how is it possible that its cash balance at December 31, 2000, shows an increase relative to its balance at January 1, 2000?

**BTN 2-6**   The expanded accounting equation consists of assets, liabilities, common stock, dividends, revenues, and expenses. It can be used to reveal insights into changes in a company's financial position.

**Required**

**1.** Form *learning teams* of six (or more) members. Each team member must select one of the six components and each team must have at least one expert on each component: (*a*) assets, (*b*) liabilities, (*c*) common stock, (*d*) dividends, (*e*) revenues, and (*f*) expenses.

**2.** Form *expert teams* of individuals who selected the same component in part 1. Expert teams are to draft a report that each expert will present to his or her learning team addressing the following:

   **a.** Identify for its component the (i) increase and decrease side of the account and (ii) normal balance side of the account.

   **b.** Describe a transaction, with amounts, that increases its component.

    **c.** Using the transaction and amounts in (*b*), verify the equality of the accounting equation and then explain any effects on the income statement and statement of cash flows.

    **d.** Describe a transaction, with amounts, that decreases its component.

    **e.** Using the transaction and amounts in (*d*), verify the equality of the accounting equation and then explain any effects on the income statement and statement of cash flows.

**3.** Each expert should return to his/her learning team. In rotation, each member presents his/her expert team's report to the learning team. Team discussion is encouraged.

---

## BUSINESS WEEK ACTIVITY

A2

mhhe.com/wild3e

**BTN 2-7**    Read the article "Leveraged for Success" in the April 18, 2002, issue of *Business Week*.

**Required**

**1.** Explain why debt financing can be a less expensive alternative than equity financing.

**2.** What can happen if a company takes on too much debt?

**3.** Name five companies cited by the article that are using a high degree of leverage but still maintaining top credit ratings.

---

## ENTREPRENEURIAL DECISION

A1  A2  P3

**BTN 2-8**    Liang Lu is a young entrepreneur who operates Lu Music Services, offering singing lessons and instruction on musical instruments. Lu wishes to expand but needs a loan. The bank requests Lu to prepare a balance sheet and key financial ratios. Lu has not kept formal records but is able to provide the following accounts and their amounts as of December 31, 2005:

| | | | | | |
|---|---|---|---|---|---|
| Cash . . . . . . . . . . . . . | $ 1,800 | Accounts Receivable . . . . . | $4,800 | Prepaid Insurance . . | $ 750 |
| Prepaid Rent . . . . . . . | 4,700 | Store Supplies . . . . . . . . . . | 3,300 | Equipment . . . . . . . . | 25,000 |
| Accounts Payable . . . | 1,100 | Unearned Lesson Fees . . . . | 7,800 | Total Equity* . . . . . . | 31,450 |
| Annual net income . . | 20,000 | | | | |

*The total equity amount reflects all owner investments, dividends, revenues, and expenses as of December 31, 2005.

**Required**

**1.** Prepare a balance sheet as of December 31, 2005, for Lu Music Services. (You need only report the total equity amount on the balance sheet.)

**2.** Compute Lu's debt ratio and its return on assets (from Chapter 1). Assume average assets equal its ending balance.

**3.** Do you think the prospects of a $15,000 bank loan are good? Why or why not?

A1  A2  P3

**BTN 2-9**    Assume that Tanya York of **York Entertainment** wants to grow company revenues by 10% each year for the next five years. York has determined that achieving that revenue growth will require additional financing. Accordingly, the company has sought and been offered a $5 million dollar line of credit by a Los Angeles bank to help fund current operations and new movie projects. York is not required to use the line of credit, but it does have preapproval to use the line of credit as needed. If the line of credit is used, an annual interest rate of 8% will be charged on the money borrowed.

**Required**

**1.** What will York's annual revenues be in five years if the revenue growth target rate is achieved?

**2.** If York decides to borrow against the line of credit, what must it do to successfully employ financial leverage?

---

## HITTING THE ROAD

C1

**BTN 2-10**    Obtain a recent copy of the most prominent newspaper distributed in your area. Research the classified section and prepare a report answering the following questions (attach relevant classified clippings to your report). Alternatively, you may want to search the Web for the required information. One suitable Website is **America's Job Bank (www.AJB.org).** For documentation, you should print copies of Websites accessed.

**1.** Identify the number of listings for accounting positions and the various accounting job titles.

**2.** Identify the number of listings for other job titles, with examples, that require or prefer accounting knowledge/experience but are not specifically accounting positions.

**3.** Specify the salary range for the accounting and accounting-related positions if provided.

**4.** Indicate the job that appeals to you, the reason for its appeal, and its requirements.

---

**BTN 2-11** Grupo Bimbo (GrupoBimbo.com) competes with several companies, including Krispy Kreme and Tastykake. Key financial ratios for the current fiscal year follow:

**GLOBAL DECISION**

A2

| Key Figure | Grupo Bimbo | Krispy Kreme | Tastykake |
|---|---|---|---|
| Return on assets . . . . . . . . | 3.6% | 10.1% | 1.7% |
| Debt ratio . . . . . . . . . . . | 56.0% | 32.1% | 59.2% |

**Required**

**1.** Which company is most profitable according to return on assets?

**2.** Which company is most risky according to the debt ratio?

**3.** Which company deserves increased investment based on a joint analysis of return on assets and the debt ratio?

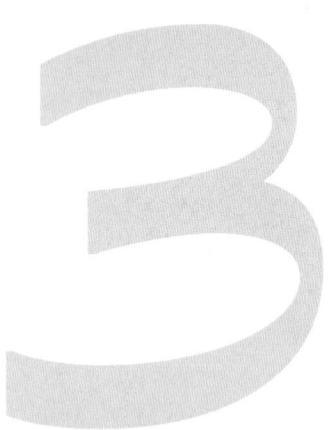

*"Snowskates let you live out your skateboarding fantasies on the snow"*—Andy Wolf

# 3 Adjusting Accounts and Preparing Financial Statements

## A Look Back

Chapter 2 explained the analysis and recording of transactions. We showed how to apply and interpret company accounts, T-accounts, double-entry accounting, ledgers, postings, and trial balances.

## A Look at This Chapter

This chapter explains the timing of reports and the need to adjust accounts. Adjusting accounts is important for recognizing revenues and expenses in the proper period. We describe how to prepare financial statements from an adjusted trial balance, and how the closing process works. A classified balance sheet is also introduced and applied.

## A Look Ahead

Chapter 4 looks at accounting for merchandising activities. We describe the sale and purchase of merchandise and the implications of merchandising activities for preparing and analyzing financial statements.

# CAP

## Conceptual

**C1** Explain the importance of periodic reporting and the time period principle. *(p. 92)*

**C2** Explain accrual accounting and how it makes financial statements more useful. *(p. 93)*

**C3** Identify the types of adjustments and their purpose. *(p. 95)*

**C4** Explain why temporary accounts are closed each period. *(p. 138)*

**C5** Identify steps in the accounting cycle. *(p. 143)*

**C6** Explain and prepare a classified balance sheet. *(p. 144)*

## Analytical

**A1** Explain how accounting adjustments link to financial statements. *(p. 102)*

**A2** Compute profit margin and describe its use in analyzing company performance. *(p. 106)*

**A3** Compute the current ratio and describe what it reveals about a company's financial condition. *(p. 146)*

## Procedural

**P1** Prepare and explain adjusting entries. *(p. 95)*

**P2** Explain and prepare an adjusted trial balance. *(p. 103)*

**P3** Prepare financial statements from an adjusted trial balance. *(p. 104)*

**P4** Describe and prepare closing entries. *(p. 139)*

**P5** Explain and prepare a post-closing trial balance. *(p. 141)*

---

## Decision Feature

# Snowskate on Upstart

PORTLAND—Andy Wolf was a frustrated skateboarder when he moved to Portland a few years ago because of its snow-covered surroundings for much of the year. Wolf toyed with the idea of making a skateboard for snow. His answer was the "snowskate"—similar in size and shape to a skateboard but ridden without bindings to allow *shove-its* and *flip tricks* that aren't possible with snowboards. He now heads the upstart **Premier Snowskate (PremierSnowsk8.com),** the maker of snowskates.

Wolf says his early business experiences were tough as people reacted to him as if "all he knows how to do is ride a snowboard and play Nintendo." People were wrong. One of Wolf's first goals was to control costs. "I wanted to keep the price under $100 retail," says Wolf; "that's how I sourced my materials." He also monitored revenues and kept track of financial performance. Closing procedures were important in helping identify the proper costs and revenues for specific periods. He also relied on classified balance sheets so that he would know what was due and when.

Still, it was tough. "It was still a job," says Wolf. "I had to handle my business, do my own deals, set up my traveling, and work with reps." Accounting work sheets helped Wolf identify temporary and permanent accounts, make crucial adjustments, and prepare and analyze financial reports. Yet the final business decisions were his to make.

Today, his decisions look good as forward-thinking resorts are building snowskate parks. "We're finding that resorts are totally into it," says Wolf. "Either embrace it or have it run them over."

Now for Wolf: How is he dealing with success? "I kind of hate to admit it," says Wolf, "but snowskates are going mainstream." From skateboarder to entrepreneur who uses accounting data—that must hurt. However, with annual sales projected to top $3 million this year, the hurt is tolerable. Admits Wolf, "I'm pretty damn lucky."

[Sources: *Premier Snowskates Website,* January 2004; *Entrepreneur Magazine,* May 2002; *Snowskates Underground,* May 2001; *USA Today,* January 2003; *Sports Guide,* December 2002; *Transworld Snowboarding,* February 2003.]

Financial statements reflect revenues when earned and expenses when incurred. Many of the important steps leading to financial statements were explained in Chapters 1 and 2. We described how transactions and events are analyzed, journalized, and posted. This chapter describes important adjustments that are often necessary to properly reflect revenues when earned and expenses when incurred. This chapter also describes financial statement preparation. It explains the closing process that readies revenue, expense, and dividends accounts for the next reporting period and updates retained earnings. It also explains how accounts are classified on a balance sheet to increase their usefulness to decision makers.

**Adjusting Accounts and Preparing Financial Statements**

| Timing and Reporting | Adjusting Accounts | Preparing Financial Statements | Closing Process | Classified Balance Sheet |
|---|---|---|---|---|
| • Accounting period<br>• Accrual versus cash<br>• Recognition of revenues and expenses | • Prepaid expenses<br>• Unearned revenues<br>• Accrued expenses<br>• Accrued revenues<br>• Adjusted trial balance | • Income statement<br>• Statement of retained earnings<br>• Balance sheet | • Temporary and permanent accounts<br>• Closing entries<br>• Post-closing trial balance<br>• Accounting cycle summary | • Classification structure<br>• Classification categories |

# Timing and Reporting

This section describes the impact on the accounting process of the point in time or the period of time that a report refers to.

## The Accounting Period

**C1** Explain the importance of periodic reporting and the time period principle.

"Krispy Kreme announces earnings per share of . . ."

The value of information is often linked to its timeliness. Useful information must reach decision makers frequently and promptly. To provide timely information, accounting systems prepare reports at regular intervals. This results in an accounting process impacted by the time period (or periodicity) principle. The **time period principle** assumes that an organization's activities can be divided into specific time periods such as a month, a three-month quarter, a six-month interval, or a year. Exhibit 3.1 shows various **accounting,** or *reporting,*

**Exhibit 3.1**

Accounting Periods

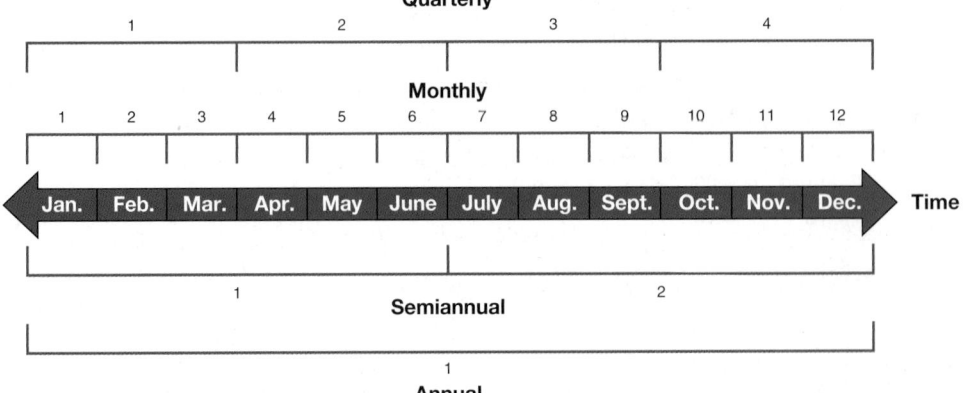

**periods.** Most organizations use a year as their primary accounting period. Reports covering a one-year period are known as **annual financial statements.** Many organizations also prepare **interim financial statements** covering one, three, or six months of activity.

The annual reporting period is not always a calendar year ending on December 31. An organization can adopt a **fiscal year** consisting of any 12 consecutive months. It is also acceptable to adopt an annual reporting period of 52 weeks. For example, **Gap**'s fiscal year consistently ends the final week of January or the first week of February each year.

Companies with little seasonal variation in sales often choose the calendar year as their fiscal year. For example, the financial statements of **Marvel Enterprises** reflect a fiscal year that ends on December 31. Companies experiencing seasonal variations in sales often choose a **natural business year** end, which is when sales activities are at their lowest level for the year. The natural business year for retailers such as **Wal-Mart**, **Dell**, and **FUBU** usually ends around January 31, after the holiday season.

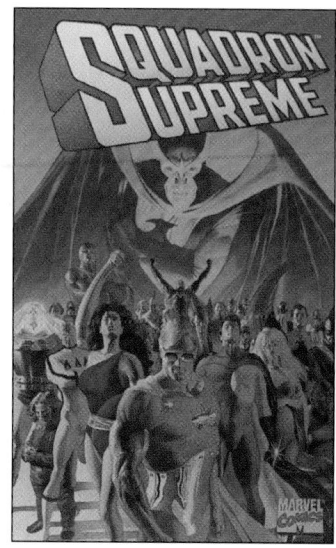

## Accrual Basis versus Cash Basis

After external transactions and events are recorded, several accounts still need adjustments before their balances appear in financial statements. This need arises because internal transactions and events remain unrecorded. **Accrual basis accounting** uses the adjusting process to recognize revenues when earned and to match expenses with revenues.

**Cash basis accounting** recognizes revenues when cash is received and records expenses when cash is paid. This means that cash basis net income for a period is the difference between cash receipts and cash payments. Cash basis accounting is not consistent with generally accepted accounting principles.

It is commonly held that accrual accounting better reflects business performance than information about cash receipts and payments. Accrual accounting also increases the *comparability* of financial statements from one period to another. Yet cash basis accounting is useful for several business decisions—which is the reason companies must report a statement of cash flows.

To see the difference between these two accounting systems, let's consider FastForward's Prepaid Insurance account. FastForward paid $2,400 for 24 months of insurance coverage beginning on December 1, 2004. Accrual accounting requires that $100 of insurance expense be reported on December's income statement. Another $1,200 of expense is reported in year 2005, and the remaining $1,100 is reported as expense in the first 11 months of 2006. Exhibit 3.2 illustrates this allocation of insurance cost across these three years. The accrual basis balance sheet reports any unexpired premium as a Prepaid Insurance asset.

**C2** Explain accrual accounting and how it makes financial statements more useful.

**Point:** IBM's revenues from services to customers are recorded when services are performed. Its revenues from product sales are recorded when products are shipped.

## Exhibit 3.2

Accrual Basis Accounting for Allocating Prepaid Insurance to Expense

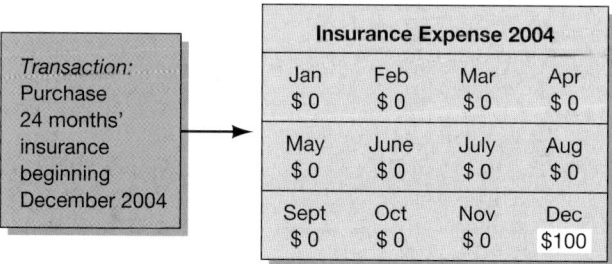

| Transaction: Purchase 24 months' insurance beginning December 2004 | | Insurance Expense 2004 | | | | Insurance Expense 2005 | | | | Insurance Expense 2006 | | | |
|---|---|---|---|---|---|---|---|---|---|---|---|---|---|
| | | Jan $0 | Feb $0 | Mar $0 | Apr $0 | Jan $100 | Feb $100 | Mar $100 | Apr $100 | Jan $100 | Feb $100 | Mar $100 | Apr $100 |
| | | May $0 | June $0 | July $0 | Aug $0 | May $100 | June $100 | July $100 | Aug $100 | May $100 | June $100 | July $100 | Aug $100 |
| | | Sept $0 | Oct $0 | Nov $0 | Dec $100 | Sept $100 | Oct $100 | Nov $100 | Dec $100 | Sept $100 | Oct $100 | Nov $100 | Dec $0 |

A cash basis income statement for December 2004 reports insurance expense of $2,400, as shown in Exhibit 3.3. The cash basis income statements for years 2005 and 2006 report no insurance expense. The cash basis balance sheet never reports an insurance asset because it is immediately expensed. Note that reported income for 2004–2006 fails to match the cost of insurance with the insurance benefits received for those years and months.

**Point:** Recording revenue early overstates current-period revenue and income; recording it late understates current-period revenue and income.

**Point:** Recording expense early overstates current-period expense and understates current-period income; recording it late understates current-period expense and overstates current-period income.

## Recognizing Revenues and Expenses

We use the time period principle to divide a company's activities into specific time periods, but not all activities are complete when financial statements are prepared. Thus, adjustments often are required to get correct account balances.

## Exhibit 3.3

Cash Basis Accounting for Allocating Prepaid Insurance to Expense

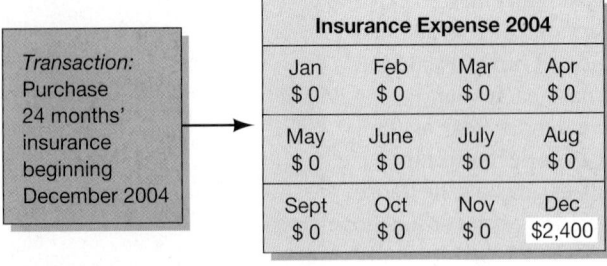

*Transaction:*
Purchase
24 months'
insurance
beginning
December 2004

| Insurance Expense 2004 | | | |
|---|---|---|---|
| Jan $0 | Feb $0 | Mar $0 | Apr $0 |
| May $0 | June $0 | July $0 | Aug $0 |
| Sept $0 | Oct $0 | Nov $0 | Dec $2,400 |

| Insurance Expense 2005 | | | |
|---|---|---|---|
| Jan $0 | Feb $0 | Mar $0 | Apr $0 |
| May $0 | June $0 | July $0 | Aug $0 |
| Sept $0 | Oct $0 | Nov $0 | Dec $0 |

| Insurance Expense 2006 | | | |
|---|---|---|---|
| Jan $0 | Feb $0 | Mar $0 | Apr $0 |
| May $0 | June $0 | July $0 | Aug $0 |
| Sept $0 | Oct $0 | Nov $0 | Dec $0 |

### Decision Insight

**Numbers Game** **Ascential Software**, a software provider, recorded revenue when products were passed to distributors. It admits now that there were "errors in the way revenues had been recorded," and its CEO is in jail. **Centennial Technologies**, a computer manufacturer, recognized revenue when it shipped products. What is not common is that Centennial's CEO shipped products to the warehouses of friends and reported it as revenue. Risky or improper revenue recognition practices are often revealed by a large increase in the *Accounts Receivable to Sales* ratio.

We rely on two principles in the adjusting process: revenue recognition and matching. Chapter 1 explained that the *revenue recognition principle* requires that revenue be recorded when earned, not before and not after. Most companies earn revenue when they provide services and products to customers. A major goal of the adjusting process is to have revenue recognized (reported) in the time period when it is earned.

The **matching principle** aims to record expenses in the same accounting period as the revenues that are earned as a result of these expenses. This matching of expenses with the revenue benefits is a major part of the adjusting process.

Matching expenses with revenues often requires us to predict certain events. When we use financial statements, we must understand that they require estimates and therefore include measures that are not precise. **Walt Disney**'s annual report explains that its production costs from movies are matched to revenues based on a ratio of current revenues from the movie divided by its predicted total revenues.

### Quick Check

1. Describe a company's annual reporting period.
2. Why do companies prepare interim financial statements?
3. What two accounting principles most directly drive the adjusting process?
4. Is cash basis accounting consistent with the matching principle? Why or why not?
5. If your company pays a $4,800 premium on April 1, 2004, for two years' insurance coverage, how much insurance expense is reported in 2005 using cash basis accounting?

Answers—p. 125

## Adjusting Accounts

**C3** Identify the types of adjustments and their purpose.

Topic Tackler 3-1

The process of adjusting accounts involves analyzing each account balance and the transactions and events that affect it to determine any needed adjustments. An **adjusting entry** is recorded to bring an asset or liability account balance to its proper amount. This entry also updates a related expense or revenue account.

### Framework for Adjustments

Adjustments are necessary for transactions and events that extend over more than one period. It is helpful to group adjustments by the timing of cash receipt or cash payment in relation to the recognition of the related revenues or expenses. Exhibit 3.4 identifies four types of adjustments.

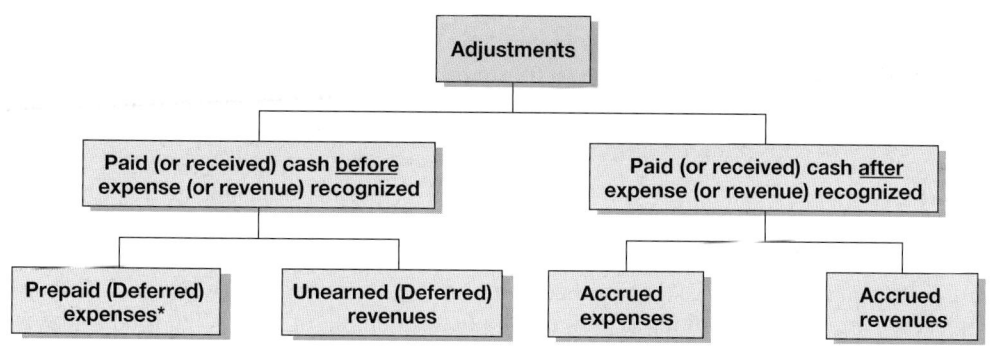

Exhibit 3.4

Types of Adjustments

The left side of this exhibit shows prepaid expenses (including depreciation) and unearned revenues, which reflect transactions when cash is paid or received *before* a related expense or revenue is recognized. They are also called *deferrals* because the recognition of an expense (or revenue) is *deferred* until after the related cash is paid (or received). The right side of this exhibit shows accrued expenses and accrued revenues, which reflect transactions when cash is paid or received *after* a related expense or revenue is recognized. Adjusting entries are necessary for each of these so that revenues, expenses, assets, and liabilities are correctly reported. It is helpful to remember that each adjusting entry affects one or more income statement accounts *and* one or more balance sheet accounts (but not the Cash account).

**Point:** Adjusting is a 3-step process: (1) Compute current account balance, (2) Compute what current account balance should be, and (3) Record entry to get from step 1 to step 2.

## Prepaid (Deferred) Expenses

**Prepaid expenses** refer to items *paid for* in advance of receiving their benefits. Prepaid expenses are assets. When these assets are used, their costs become expenses. Adjusting entries for prepaids increase expenses and decrease assets as shown in the T-accounts of Exhibit 3.5. Such adjustments reflect transactions and events that use up prepaid expenses (including passage of time). To illustrate the accounting for prepaid expenses, this section focuses on prepaid insurance, supplies, and depreciation.

**P1** Prepare and explain adjusting entries.

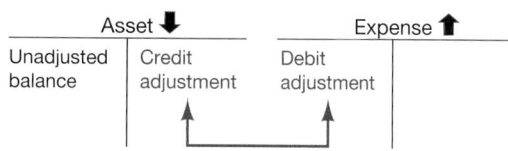

Exhibit 3.5

Adjusting for Prepaid Expenses

**Prepaid Insurance**   We illustrate prepaid insurance using FastForward's payment of $2,400 for 24 months of insurance benefits beginning on December 1, 2004. With the passage of time, the benefits of the insurance gradually expire and a portion of the Prepaid Insurance asset becomes expense. For instance, one month's insurance coverage expires by December 31, 2004. This expense is $100, or 1/24 of $2,400. The adjusting entry to record this expense and reduce the asset, along with T-account postings, follows:

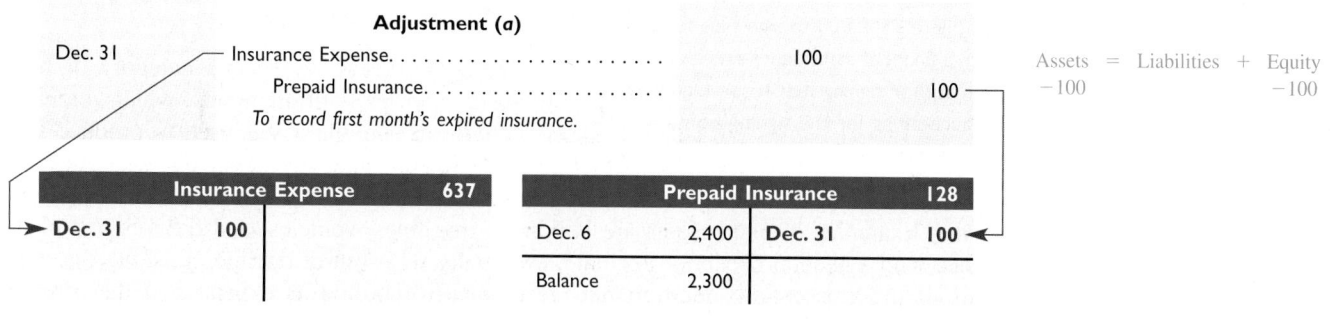

After adjusting and posting, the $100 balance in Insurance Expense and the $2,300 balance in Prepaid Insurance are ready for reporting in financial statements. *Not* making the adjustment on or before December 31 would (1) understate expenses by $100 and overstate net income by $100 for the December income statement and (2) overstate both prepaid insurance (assets) and equity (because of net income) by $100 in the December 31 balance sheet. It is also evident from Exhibit 3.2 that 2005's adjustments must transfer a total of $1,200 from Prepaid Insurance to Insurance Expense, and 2006's adjustments must transfer the remaining $1,100 to Insurance Expense.

**Supplies**   Supplies are a prepaid expense often requiring adjustment. To illustrate, FastForward purchased $9,720 of supplies in December and used some of them. When financial statements are prepared at December 31, the cost of supplies used during December must be recognized. When FastForward computes (takes inventory of) its remaining unused supplies at December 31, it finds $8,670 of supplies remaining of the $9,720 total supplies. The $1,050 difference between these two amounts is December's supplies expense. The adjusting entry to record this expense and reduce the Supplies asset account, along with T-account postings, follows:

Assets = Liabilities + Equity
−1,050              −1,050

The balance of the Supplies account is $8,670 after posting—equaling the cost of the remaining supplies. *Not* making the adjustment on or before December 31 would (1) understate expenses by $1,050 and overstate net income by $1,050 for the December income statement and (2) overstate both supplies and equity (because of net income) by $1,050 in the December 31 balance sheet.

**Other Prepaid Expenses**   Other prepaid expenses, such as Prepaid Rent, are accounted for exactly as Insurance and Supplies are. We should also note that some prepaid expenses are both paid for and fully used up within a single accounting period. One example is when a company pays monthly rent on the first day of each month. This payment creates a prepaid expense on the first day of each month that fully expires by the end of the month. In these special cases, we can record the cash paid with a debit to an expense account instead of an asset account. This practice is described more completely later in the chapter.

**Depreciation**   A special category of prepaid expenses is **plant assets,** which refers to long-term tangible assets used to produce and sell products and services. Plant assets are expected to provide benefits for more than one period. Examples of plant assets are buildings, machines, vehicles, and fixtures. All plant assets, with a general exception for land, eventually wear out or decline in usefulness. The costs of these assets are deferred but are gradually reported as expenses in the income

---

## Decision Maker

**Investor**   A small publishing company signs a well-known athlete to write a book. The company pays the athlete $500,000 to sign plus future book royalties. A note to the company's financial statements says that "prepaid expenses include $500,000 in author signing fees to be matched against future expected sales." Is this accounting for the signing bonus acceptable? How does it affect your analysis?

Answer—p. 125

statement over the assets' useful lives (benefit periods). **Depreciation** is the process of allocating the costs of these assets over their expected useful lives. Depreciation expense is recorded with an adjusting entry similar to that for other prepaid expenses.

**Point:** Depreciation does not necessarily measure the decline in market value.

To illustrate, recall that FastForward purchased equipment for $26,000 in early December to use in earning revenue. This equipment's cost must be depreciated. The equipment is expected to have a useful life (benefit period) of four years and to be worth about $8,000 at the end of four years. This means the *net* cost of this equipment over its useful life is $18,000 ($26,000 − $8,000). We can use any of several methods to allocate this $18,000 net cost to expense. FastForward uses a method called **straight-line depreciation,** which allocates equal amounts of an asset's net cost to depreciation during its useful life. Dividing the $18,000 net cost by the 48 months in the asset's useful life gives a monthly cost of $375 ($18,000/48). The adjusting entry to record monthly depreciation expense, along with T-account postings, follows:

**Point:** An asset's expected value at the end of its useful life is called *salvage value.*

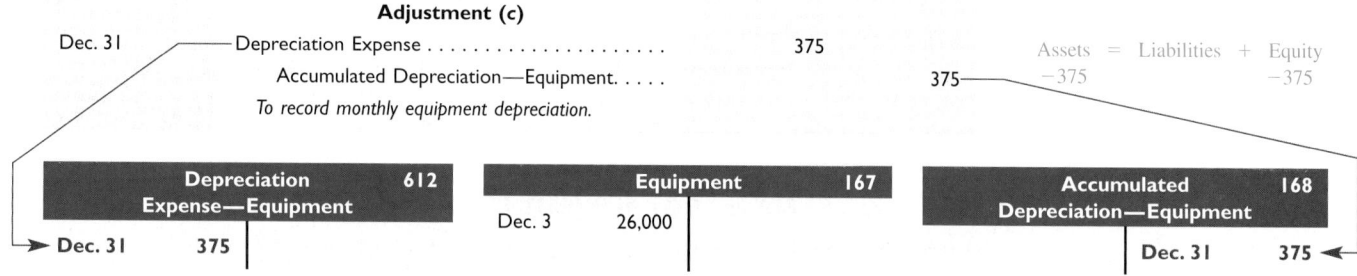

After posting the adjustment, the Equipment account ($26,000) less its Accumulated Depreciation ($375) account equals the $25,625 net cost of the 47 remaining months in the benefit period. The $375 balance in the Depreciation Expense account is reported in the December income statement. *Not* making the adjustment at December 31 would (1) understate expenses by $375 and overstate net income by $375 for the December income statement and (2) overstate both assets and equity (because of income) by $375 in the December 31 balance sheet.

Notice the accumulated depreciation is kept in a separate contra account. A **contra account** is an account linked with another account, it has an opposite normal balance, and it is reported as a subtraction from that other account's balance. For instance, FastForward's contra account of Accumulated Depreciation—Equipment is subtracted from the Equipment account in the balance sheet (see Exhibit 3.7).

**Point:** The cost principle requires an asset to be initially recorded at acquisition cost. Depreciation causes the asset's book value (cost less accumulated depreciation) to decline over time.

A contra account allows balance sheet readers to know both the full costs of assets and the total amount of depreciation. By knowing both these amounts, decision makers can better assess a company's capacity and its need to replace assets. For example, FastForward's balance sheet shows both the $26,000 original cost of equipment and the $375 balance in the accumulated depreciation contra account. This in-

> **Decision Maker**
>
> **Entrepreneur**   You are preparing an offer to purchase a family-run restaurant. The depreciation schedule for the restaurant's building and equipment shows costs of $175,000 and accumulated depreciation of $155,000. This leaves a net for building and equipment of $20,000. Is this information useful in helping you decide on a purchase offer?
>
> Answer—p. 125

formation reveals that the equipment is close to new. If FastForward reports equipment only at its net amount of $25,625, users cannot assess the equipment's age or its need for replacement. The title of the contra account, *Accumulated Depreciation,* indicates that this account includes total depreciation expense for all prior periods for which the asset was used. To illustrate, the Equipment and the Accumulated Depreciation accounts appear as in Exhibit 3.6 on February 28, 2005, after three months of adjusting entries.

The $1,125 balance in the accumulated depreciation account can be subtracted from its related $26,000 asset cost. The difference ($24,875) between these two balances is the cost of the asset that has not yet been depreciated. This difference is called the **book value,** or

**Point:** The net cost of equipment is also called the *depreciable basis.*

## Exhibit 3.6

Accounts after Three Months of Depreciation Adjustments

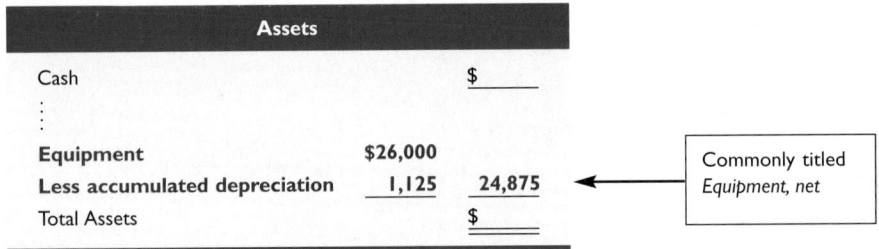

*net amount,* which equals the asset's costs less its accumulated depreciation. These account balances are reported in the assets section of the February 28 balance sheet in Exhibit 3.7.

## Exhibit 3.7

Equipment and Accumulated Depreciation on February 28 Balance Sheet

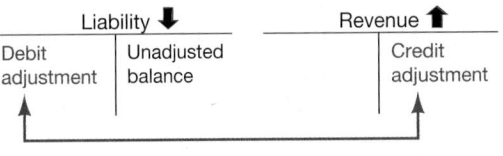

| Assets | | |
|---|---|---|
| Cash | | $ |
| ⋮ | | |
| Equipment | $26,000 | |
| Less accumulated depreciation | 1,125 | 24,875 ← Commonly titled *Equipment, net* |
| Total Assets | | $ |

## Unearned (Deferred) Revenues

The term **unearned revenues** refers to cash received in advance of providing products and services. Unearned revenues, also called *deferred revenues,* are liabilities. When cash is accepted, an obligation to provide products or services is accepted. As products or services are provided, the unearned revenues become *earned* revenues. Adjusting entries for unearned revenues involve increasing revenues and decreasing unearned revenues, as shown in Exhibit 3.8.

## Exhibit 3.8

Adjusting for Unearned Revenues

**Point:** To *defer* is to postpone. We postpone reporting amounts received as revenues until they are earned.

An example of unearned revenues is from **The New York Times Company**, which reports unexpired (unearned) subscriptions of more than $60 million: "Proceeds from . . . subscriptions are deferred at the time of sale and are recognized in earnings on a pro rata basis over the terms of the subscriptions." Unearned revenues are more than 10% of the current liabilities for the Times. Another example comes from the **Boston Celtics**. When the Celtics receive cash from advance ticket sales and broadcast fees, they record it in an unearned revenue account called *Deferred Game Revenues.* The Celtics recognize this unearned revenue with adjusting entries on a game-by-game basis. Since the NBA regular season begins in October and ends in April, revenue recognition is mainly limited to this period. For a recent season, the Celtics' quarterly revenues were $0 million for July–September; $34 million for October–December; $48 million for January–March; and $17 million for April–June.

FastForward has unearned revenues. It agreed on December 26 to provide consulting services to a client for a fixed fee of $3,000 for 60 days. On that same day, this client paid the 60-day fee in advance, covering the period December 27 to February 24. The entry to record the cash received in advance is

Assets = Liabilities + Equity
+3,000     +3,000

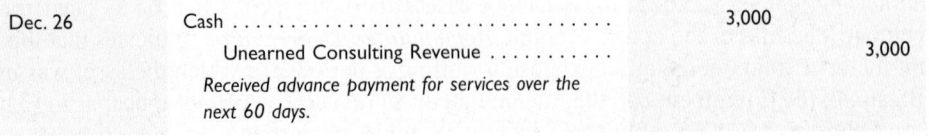

| Dec. 26 | Cash . . . . . . . . . . . . . . . . . . . . . . . . . . . . . . . . | 3,000 | |
|---|---|---|---|
| | Unearned Consulting Revenue . . . . . . . . . . | | 3,000 |
| | *Received advance payment for services over the next 60 days.* | | |

This advance payment increases cash and creates an obligation to do consulting work over the next 60 days. As time passes, FastForward will earn this payment through consulting.

By December 31, it has provided five days' service and earned 5/60 of the $3,000 unearned revenue. This amounts to $250 ($3,000 × 5/60). The *revenue recognition principle* implies that $250 of unearned revenue must be reported as revenue on the December income statement. The adjusting entry to reduce the liability account and recognize earned revenue, along with T-account postings, follows:

The adjusting entry transfers $250 from unearned revenue (a liability account) to a revenue account. *Not* making the adjustment (1) understates revenue and net income by $250 in the December income statement and (2) overstates unearned revenue and understates equity by $250 on the December 31 balance sheet.

## Accrued Expenses

**Accrued expenses** refer to costs that are incurred in a period but are both unpaid and unrecorded. Accrued expenses must be reported on the income statement of the period when incurred. Adjusting entries for recording accrued expenses involves increasing expenses and increasing liabilities as shown in Exhibit 3.9. This adjustment recognizes expenses incurred in a period but not yet paid. Common examples of accrued expenses are salaries, interest, rent, and taxes. We use salaries and interest to show how to adjust accounts for accrued expenses.

**Exhibit 3.9**

Adjusting for Accrued Expenses

**Point:** Accrued expenses are also called *accrued liabilities*.

**Accrued Salaries Expense**   FastForward's employee earns $70 per day, or $350 for a five-day workweek beginning on Monday and ending on Friday. This employee is paid every two weeks on Friday. On December 12 and 26, the wages are paid, recorded in the journal, and posted to the ledger. The calendar in Exhibit 3.10 shows three working days

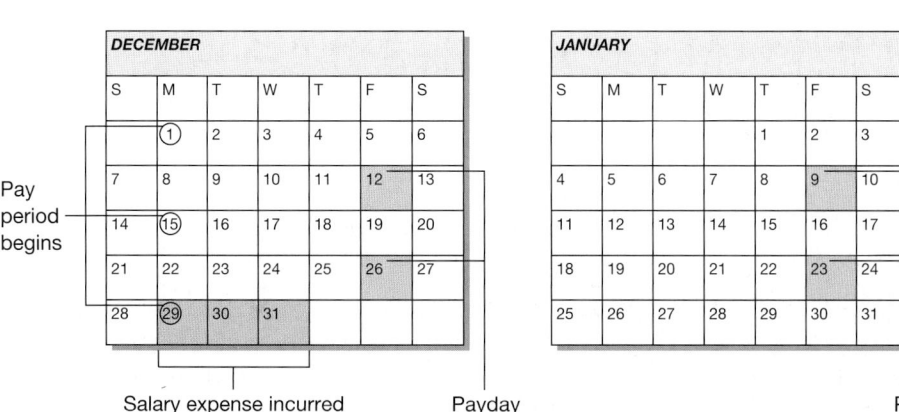

**Exhibit 3.10**

Salary Accrual and Paydays

**Point:** Assume: (1) the last payday for the year is December 19, (2) the next payday is January 2, and (3) December 25 is a paid holiday. Record the December 31 adjusting entry. *Answer:* We must accrue pay for eight working days (8 × $70):
Salaries Expense . . . 560
  Salaries Payable . . . . 560

Assets = Liabilities + Equity
         +210        −210

after the December 26 payday (29, 30, and 31). This means the employee has earned three days' salary by the close of business on Wednesday, December 31, yet this salary cost is not paid or recorded.

The financial statements would be incomplete if FastForward fails to report the added expense and liability to the employee for unpaid salary from December 29–31. The adjusting entry to account for accrued salaries, along with T-account postings, follows:

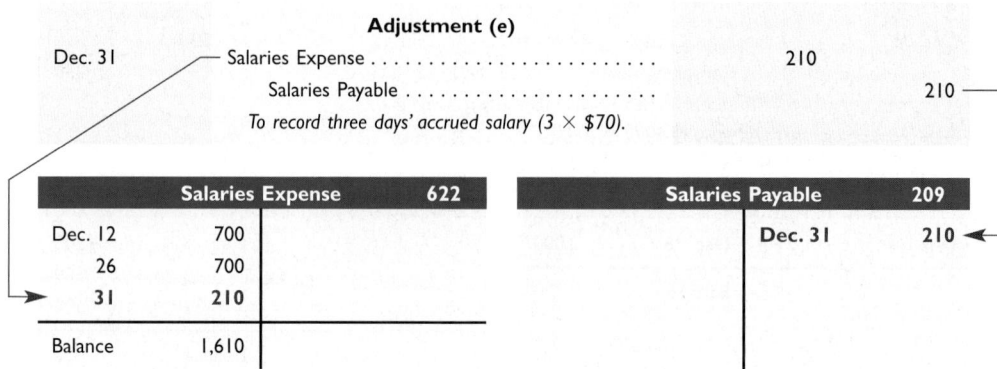

**Point:** An employer records salaries expense and a vacation pay liability when employees earn vacation pay.

Salaries expense of $1,610 is reported on the December income statement and $210 of salaries payable (liability) is reported in the balance sheet. *Not* making the adjustment (1) understates salaries expense and overstates net income by $210 in the December income statement and (2) understates salaries payable (liabilities) and overstates equity by $210 on the December 31 balance sheet.

**Accrued Interest Expense**   Companies commonly have accrued interest expense on notes payable and other long-term liabilities at the end of a period. Interest expense is incurred with the passage of time. Unless interest is paid on the last day of an accounting period, we need to adjust for interest expense incurred but not yet paid. This means we must accrue interest cost from the most recent payment date up to the end of the period. The formula for computing accrued interest is:

**Principal amount owed × Annual interest rate × Fraction of year since last payment date.**

**Point:** Interest computations assume a 360-day year.

To illustrate, if a company has a $6,000 loan from a bank at 6% annual interest, then 30 days' accrued interest expense is $30—computed as $6,000 × 0.06 × 30/360. The adjusting entry would be to debit Interest Expense for $30 and credit Interest Payable for $30.

**Future Payment of Accrued Expenses**   Adjusting entries for accrued expenses foretell cash transactions in future periods. Specifically, accrued expenses at the end of one accounting period result in *cash payments* in a *future* period(s). To illustrate, recall that FastForward recorded accrued salaries of $210. On January 9, the first payday of the next period, the following entry settles the accrued liability (salaries payable) and records salaries expense for seven days of work in January:

Assets = Liabilities + Equity
−700      −210        −490

| Jan. 9 | Salaries Payable (3 days at $70 per day) . . . . . . . . | 210 | |
| | Salaries Expense (7 days at $70 per day) . . . . . . . | 490 | |
| |    Cash. . . . . . . . . . . . . . . . . . . . . . . . . . . . | | 700 |
| | *Paid two weeks' salary including three days accrued in December.* | | |

The $210 debit reflects the payment of the liability for the three days' salary accrued on December 31. The $490 debit records the salary for January's first seven working days (including the New Year's Day holiday) as an expense of the new accounting period. The $700 credit records the total amount of cash paid to the employee.

# Accrued Revenues

The term **accrued revenues** refers to revenues earned in a period that are both unrecorded and not yet received in cash (or other assets). An example is a technician who bills customers only when the job is done. If one-third of a job is complete by the end of a period, then the technician must record one-third of the expected billing as revenue in that period—even though there is no billing or collection. The adjusting entries for accrued revenues increase assets and increase revenues as shown in Exhibit 3.11.

**Point:** Accrued revenues are also called *accrued assets*.

Accrued revenues commonly arise from services, products, interest, and rent. We use service fees and interest to show how to adjust for accrued revenues.

## Exhibit 3.11

Adjusting for Accrued Revenues

**Accrued Services Revenue**   Accrued revenues are not recorded until adjusting entries are made at the end of the accounting period. These accrued revenues are earned but unrecorded because either the buyer has not yet paid for them or the seller has not yet billed the buyer. FastForward provides an example. In the second week of December, it agreed to provide 30 days of consulting services to a local sports club for a fixed fee of $2,700. The terms of the initial agreement call for FastForward to provide services from December 12, 2004, through January 10, 2005, or 30 days of service. The club agrees to pay FastForward $2,700 on January 10, 2005, when the service period is complete. At December 31, 2004, 20 days of services have already been provided. Since the contracted services are not yet entirely provided, FastForward has neither billed the club nor recorded the services already provided. Still, FastForward has earned two-thirds of the 30-day fee, or $1,800 ($2,700 × 20/30). The *revenue recognition principle* implies that it must report the $1,800 on the December income statement. The balance sheet also must report that the club owes FastForward $1,800. The year-end adjusting entry to account for accrued services revenue is

**Adjustment (f)**

| | | |
|---|---|---|
| Dec. 31 | Accounts Receivable . . . . . . . . . . . . . . . . . . . . . . | 1,800 |
| | Consulting Revenue . . . . . . . . . . . . . . . . . . . | 1,800 |
| | *To record 20 days' accrued revenue.* | |

Assets  =  Liabilities  +  Equity
+1,800                         +1,800

| **Accounts Receivable** | | | 106 |
|---|---|---|---|
| Dec. 12 | 1,900 | Dec. 22 | 1,900 |
| 31 | 1,800 | | |
| Balance | 1,800 | | |

| **Consulting Revenue** | | 403 |
|---|---|---|
| | Dec.  5 | 4,200 |
| | 12 | 1,600 |
| | 31 | 250 |
| | 31 | 1,800 |
| | Balance | 7,850 |

Accounts receivable are reported on the balance sheet at $1,800, and the $7,850 of consulting revenue is reported on the income statement. *Not* making the adjustment would understate (1) both consulting revenue and net income by $1,800 in the December income statement and (2) both accounts receivable (assets) and equity by $1,800 on the December 31 balance sheet.

**Example:** What is the adjusting entry if the 30-day consulting period began on December 22? *Answer:* One-third of the fee is earned:
Accounts Receivable. . . 900
    Consulting Revenue . . . 900

**Accrued Interest Revenue**   In addition to the accrued interest expense we described earlier, interest can yield an accrued revenue when a debtor owes money (or other assets) to a company. If a company is holding notes or accounts receivable that produce interest revenue, we must adjust the accounts to record any earned and yet uncollected interest revenue. The adjusting entry is similar to the one for accruing services revenue. Specifically, we debit Interest Receivable (asset) and credit Interest Revenue.

**Decision Maker**

**Loan Officer**   The owner of an electronics store applies for a business loan. The store's financial statements reveal large increases in current-year revenues and income. Analysis shows that these increases are due to a promotion that let consumers buy now and pay nothing until January 1 of next year. The store recorded these sales as accrued revenue. Does your analysis raise any concerns?

Answer—p. 125

**Future Receipt of Accrued Revenues** Accrued revenues at the end of one accounting period result in *cash receipts* in a *future* period(s). To illustrate, recall that FastForward made an adjusting entry for $1,800 to record 20 days' accrued revenue earned from its consulting contract. When FastForward receives $2,700 cash on January 10 for the entire contract amount, it makes the following entry to remove the accrued asset (accounts receivable) and recognize the revenue earned in January. The $2,700 debit reflects the cash received. The $1,800 credit reflects the removal of the receivable, and the $900 credit records the revenue earned in January.

| Assets = Liabilities + Equity |
| :--- |
| +2,700           +900 |
| −1,800 |

| Jan. 10 | Cash .................................. | 2,700 | |
| | Accounts Receivable (20 days at $90 per day) | | 1,800 |
| | Consulting Revenue (10 days at $90 per day) | | 900 |
| | *Received cash for the accrued asset and recorded earned consulting revenue.* | | |

## Links to Financial Statements

**A1** Explain how accounting adjustments link to financial statements.

The process of adjusting accounts is intended to bring an asset or liability account balance to its correct amount. It also updates a related expense or revenue account. These adjustments are necessary for transactions and events that extend over more than one period. (Adjusting entries are posted like any other entry.)

Exhibit 3.12 summarizes the four types of transactions requiring adjustment. Understanding this exhibit is important to understanding the adjusting process and its importance to financial statements. Remember that each adjusting entry affects one or more income statement accounts *and* one or more balance sheet accounts (but not cash).

**Exhibit 3.12**

Summary of Adjustments and Financial Statement Links

| | Before Adjusting | | |
| :--- | :--- | :--- | :--- |
| **Category** | **Balance Sheet** | **Income Statement** | **Adjusting Entry** |
| **Prepaid expenses**[†] | Asset overstated | Expense understated | Dr. Expense |
| | Equity overstated | | Cr. Asset* |
| **Unearned revenues**[†] | Liability overstated | Revenue understated | Dr. Liability |
| | Equity understated | | Cr. Revenue |
| **Accrued expenses** | Liability understated | Expense understated | Dr. Expense |
| | Equity overstated | | Cr. Liability |
| **Accrued revenues** | Asset understated | Revenue understated | Dr. Asset |
| | Equity understated | | Cr. Revenue |

*For depreciation, the credit is to Accumulated Depreciation (contra asset).

[†]Exhibit assumes that prepaid expenses are initially recorded as assets and that unearned revenues are initially recorded as liabilities.

Information about some adjustments is not always available until several days or even weeks after the period-end. This means that some adjusting and closing entries are recorded later than, but dated as of, the last day of the period. One example is a company that receives a utility bill on January 10 for costs incurred for the month of December. When it receives the bill, the company records the expense and the payable as of December 31. Other examples include long-distance phone usage and costs of many Web billings. The December income statement reflects these additional expenses incurred, and the December 31 balance sheet includes these payables, although the amounts were not actually known on December 31.

Answers—p. 125

> ## Quick Check
>
> **6.** If an adjusting entry for accrued revenues of $200 at year-end is omitted, what is this error's effect on the year-end income statement and balance sheet?
>
> **7.** What is a contra account? Explain its purpose.
>
> **8.** What is an accrued expense? Give an example.
>
> **9.** Describe how an unearned revenue arises. Give an example.

## Adjusted Trial Balance

An **unadjusted trial balance** is a list of accounts and balances prepared *before* adjustments are recorded. An **adjusted trial balance** is a list of accounts and balances prepared *after* adjusting entries have been recorded and posted to the ledger.

**P2**  Explain and prepare an adjusted trial balance.

Exhibit 3.13 shows both the unadjusted and the adjusted trial balances for FastForward at December 31, 2004. The order of accounts in the trial balance is usually set up to match the order in the chart of accounts. Notice that several new accounts arise from the adjusting entries.

Each adjustment is identified by a letter in parentheses that links it to an adjusting entry explained earlier. Each amount in the Adjusted Trial Balance columns is computed by taking that account's amount from the Unadjusted Trial Balance columns and adding or subtracting any adjustment(s). To illustrate, Supplies has a $9,720 Dr. balance in the unadjusted columns. Subtracting the $1,050 Cr. amount shown in the adjustments columns yields an

## Exhibit 3.13

Unadjusted and Adjusted Trial Balances

**FASTFORWARD**
**Trial Balances**
**December 31, 2004**

| Acct. No. | Account Title | Unadjusted Trial Balance Dr. | Unadjusted Trial Balance Cr. | Adjustments Dr. | Adjustments Cr. | Adjusted Trial Balance Dr. | Adjusted Trial Balance Cr. |
|---|---|---|---|---|---|---|---|
| 101 | Cash | $ 3,950 | | | | $ 3,950 | |
| 106 | Accounts receivable | 0 | | (f) $1,800 | | 1,800 | |
| 126 | Supplies | 9,720 | | | (b) $1,050 | 8,670 | |
| 128 | Prepaid insurance | 2,400 | | | (a)    100 | 2,300 | |
| 167 | Equipment | 26,000 | | | | 26,000 | |
| 168 | Accumulated depreciation—Equip. | | $    0 | | (c)    375 | | $    375 |
| 201 | Accounts payable | | 6,200 | | | | 6,200 |
| 209 | Salaries payable | | 0 | | (e)    210 | | 210 |
| 236 | Unearned consulting revenue | | 3,000 | (d)    250 | | | 2,750 |
| 307 | Common stock | | 30,000 | | | | 30,000 |
| 318 | Retained earnings | | 0 | | | | 0 |
| 319 | Dividends | 600 | | | | 600 | |
| 403 | Consulting revenue | | 5,800 | | (d)    250 | | 7,850 |
|     |                   |   |       |   | (f)  1,800 |   |       |
| 406 | Rental revenue | | 300 | | | | 300 |
| 612 | Depreciation expense—Equip. | 0 | | (c)    375 | | 375 | |
| 622 | Salaries expense | 1,400 | | (e)    210 | | 1,610 | |
| 637 | Insurance expense | 0 | | (a)    100 | | 100 | |
| 640 | Rent expense | 1,000 | | | | 1,000 | |
| 652 | Supplies expense | 0 | | (b)  1,050 | | 1,050 | |
| 690 | Utilities expense | 230 | | | | 230 | |
|     | Totals | $45,300 | $45,300 | $3,785 | $3,785 | $47,685 | $47,685 |

adjusted $8,670 Dr. balance for Supplies. An account can have more than one adjustment, such as for Consulting Revenue. Also, some accounts might not require adjustment for this period, such as Accounts Payable.

# Preparing Financial Statements

**P3**   Prepare financial statements from an adjusted trial balance.

We can prepare financial statements directly from information in the *adjusted* trial balance. An adjusted trial balance (see the right-most two columns in Exhibit 3.13) includes all accounts and balances appearing in financial statements, and is easier to work from than the entire ledger when preparing financial statements.

Exhibit 3.14 shows how revenue and expense balances are transferred from the adjusted trial balance to the income statement (red lines). The net income, retained earnings, and dividends are then used to prepare the statement of retained earnings (black lines). Asset, liability, and common stock balances on the adjusted trial balance are then transferred to the balance sheet (blue lines). The ending retained earnings is determined on the statement of retained earnings and transferred to the balance sheet (green line).

**Point: Sarbanes-Oxley Act** requires that financial statements filed with the SEC be certified by the CEO and CFO, including a declaration that the statements fairly present the issuer's operations and financial condition. Violators can receive a $5,000,000 fine and/or 20 years imprisonment.

We usually prepare financial statements in the following order: income statement, statement of retained earnings, and balance sheet. This order makes sense since the balance sheet uses information from the statement of retained earnings, which in turn uses information from the income statement. The statement of cash flows is usually the final statement prepared.

## Quick Check

10. Music-Mart records $1,000 of accrued salaries on December 31. Five days later, on January 5 (the next payday), salaries of $7,000 are paid. What is the January 5 entry?

11. Jordan Air has the following information in its unadjusted and adjusted trial balances:

|  | Unadjusted | | Adjusted | |
|---|---|---|---|---|
|  | Debit | Credit | Debit | Credit |
| Prepaid insurance ........ | $6,200 |  | $5,900 |  |
| Salaries payable .......... |  | $   0 |  | $1,400 |

What are the adjusting entries that Jordan Air likely recorded?

12. What accounts are taken from the adjusted trial balance to prepare an income statement?

13. In preparing financial statements from an adjusted trial balance, what statement is usually prepared second?

Answers—p. 125

# Closing Process

**C4**   Explain why temporary accounts are closed each period.

The **closing process** is an important step at the end of an accounting period *after* financial statements have been completed. It prepares accounts for recording the transactions and the events of the *next* period. In the closing process we must (1) identify accounts for closing, (2) record and post the closing entries, and (3) prepare a post-closing trial balance. The purpose of the closing process is twofold. First, it resets revenue, expense, and dividends account balances to zero at the end of each period. This is done so that these accounts can properly measure income and dividends for the next period. Second, it helps in summarizing a period's revenues and expenses. This section explains the closing process.

## Temporary and Permanent Accounts

**Temporary** (or *nominal*) **accounts** accumulate data related to one accounting period. They include all income statement accounts, the dividends account, and the Income Summary

# Exhibit 3.14

Preparing the Financial Statements (Adjusted Trial Balance from Exhibit 3.13)

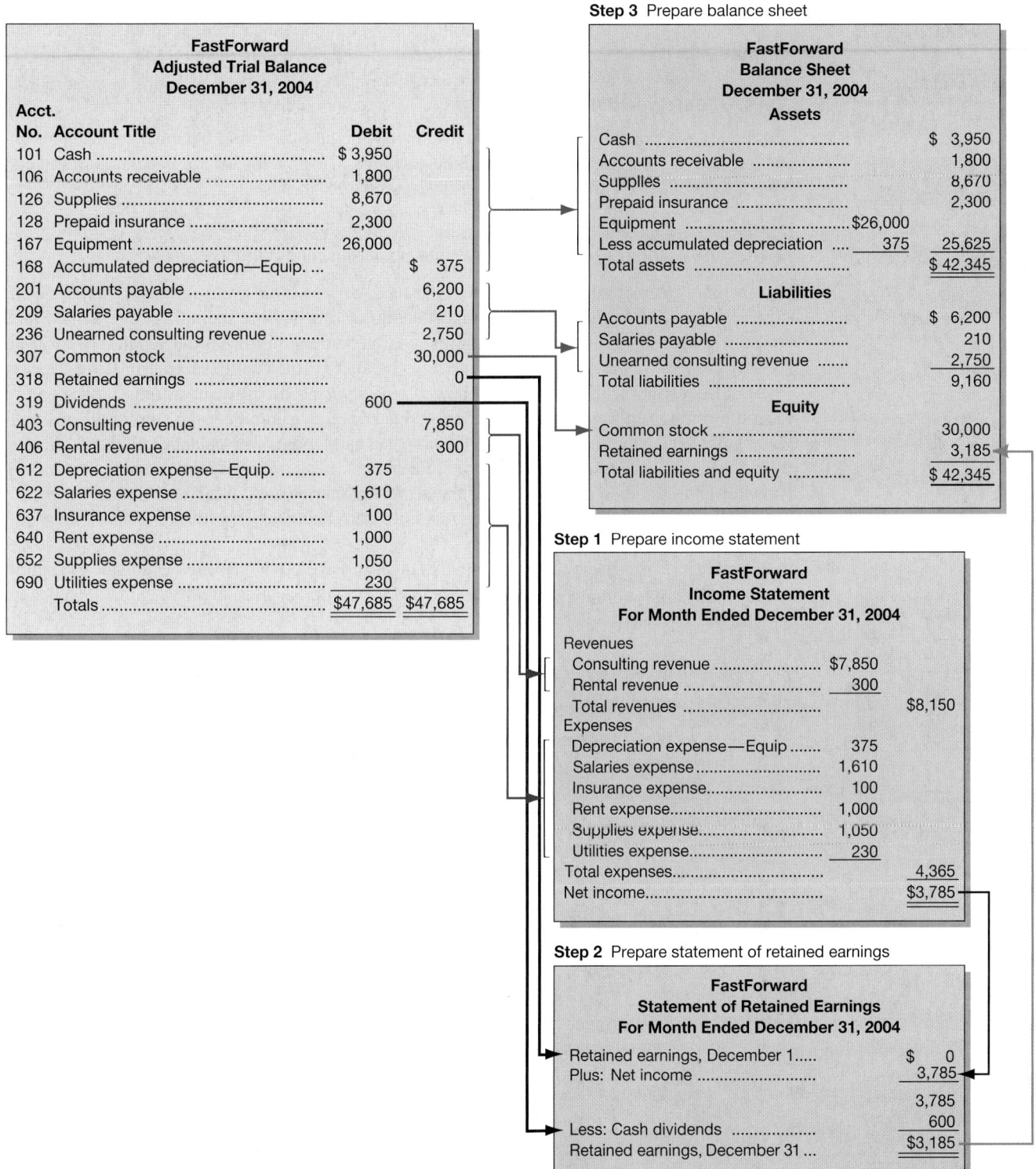

**Temporary Accounts**

| |
|---|
| Revenues |
| Expenses |
| Dividends |
| Income Summary |

**Permanent Accounts**

| |
|---|
| Assets |
| Liabilities |
| Common Stock |
| Retained Earnings |

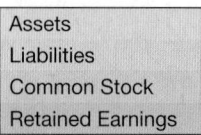

Topic Tackler 3-2

**Point:** To understand the closing process, focus on its *outcomes—updating* the retained earnings account balance to its proper ending balance, and getting *temporary accounts* to show *zero balances* for purposes of accumulating data for the next period.

account. They are temporary because the accounts are opened at the beginning of a period, used to record transactions and events for that period, and then closed at the end of the period. *The closing process applies only to temporary accounts.* **Permanent** (or *real*) **accounts** report on activities related to one or more future accounting periods. They carry their ending balances into the next period and generally consist of all balance sheet accounts. These asset, liability, and equity accounts are not closed.

## Recording Closing Entries

To record and post **closing entries** is to transfer the end-of-period balances in revenue, expense, and dividends accounts to retained earnings. Closing entries are necessary at the end of each period after financial statements are prepared because

■ Revenue, expense, and dividends accounts must begin each period with zero balances.

■ Retained earnings must reflect revenues, expenses, and dividends.

An income statement aims to report revenues and expenses for a *specific accounting period.* The statement of retained earnings reports similar information, including dividends. Since revenue, expense, and dividends accounts must accumulate information separately for each period, they must start each period with zero balances. To close these accounts, we transfer their balances first to an account called *Income Summary.* **Income Summary** is a temporary account (only used for the closing process) that contains a credit for the sum of all revenues (and gains) and a debit for the sum of all expenses (and losses). Its balance equals net income or net loss and it is transferred to retained earnings. Next, the dividends account balance is transferred to retained earnings. After these closing entries are posted, the revenue, expense, dividends, and Income Summary accounts have zero balances. These accounts are then said to be *closed* or *cleared.*

Exhibit 3.15 uses the adjusted account balances of FastForward (from the left side of Exhibit 3.14) to show the four steps necessary to close its temporary accounts. We explain each step.

## Exhibit 3.15

Four-Step Closing Process

**Step 1: Close Credit Balances in Revenue Accounts to Income Summary**
The first closing entry transfers credit balances in revenue (and gain) accounts to the Income Summary account. We bring accounts with credit balances to zero by debiting them. For

FastForward, this journal entry is step 1 in Exhibit 3.16. This entry closes revenue accounts and leaves them with zero balances. The accounts are now ready to record revenues when they occur in the next period. The $8,150 credit entry to Income Summary equals total revenues for the period.

Exhibit 3.16

Preparing Closing Entries

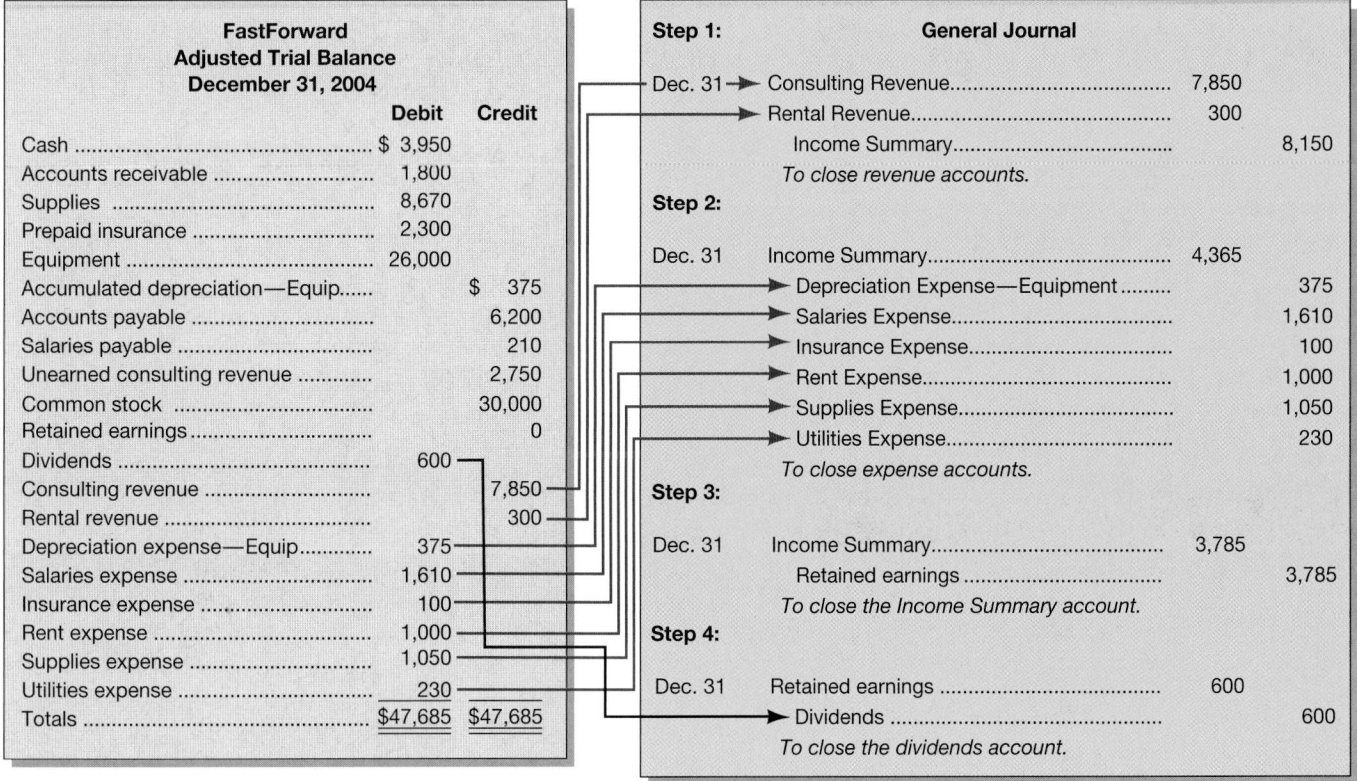

**Step 2: Close Debit Balances in Expense Accounts to Income Summary**
The second closing entry transfers debit balances in expense (and loss) accounts to the Income Summary account. We bring expense accounts' debit balances to zero by crediting them. With a balance of zero, these accounts are ready to accumulate a record of expenses for the next period. This second closing entry for FastForward is step 2 in Exhibit 3.16. Exhibit 3.15 shows that posting this entry gives each expense account a zero balance.

**Point:** It is possible to close revenue and expense accounts directly to retained earnings. Computerized accounting systems do this.

**Step 3: Close Income Summary to Retained Earnings** After steps 1 and 2, the balance of Income Summary is equal to December's net income of $3,785. The third closing entry transfers the balance of the Income Summary account to retained earnings. This entry closes the Income Summary account and is step 3 in Exhibit 3.16. The Income Summary account has a zero balance after posting this entry. It continues to have a zero balance until the closing process again occurs at the end of the next period. (If a net loss occurred because expenses exceeded revenues, the third entry is reversed: debit Retained Earnings and credit Income Summary.)

**Point:** The Income Summary is used only for closing entries.

**Step 4: Close Dividends Account to Retained Earnings** The fourth closing entry transfers any debit balance in the dividends account to retained earnings—see step 4 in Exhibit 3.16. This entry gives the dividends account a zero balance, and the account is now ready to accumulate next period's dividends. This entry also reduces the retained earnings balance to the $3,185 amount reported on the balance sheet.

**Decision Insight**

**Instant Numbers** Quantum leaps in technology are increasing the importance of accounting analysis and interpretation. We are moving toward what some call the "virtual financial statement"—up-to-date financials with the click of a mouse. This reality increases the value of those individuals with the skills to use accounting data.

# Exhibit 3.17

General Ledger after the Closing Process for FastForward

## Asset Accounts

**Cash**    Acct. No. 101

| Date | Explan. | PR | Debit | Credit | Balance |
|---|---|---|---|---|---|
| 2004 | | | | | |
| Dec. 1 | | G1 | 30,000 | | 30,000 |
| 2 | | G1 | | 2,500 | 27,500 |
| 3 | | G1 | | 26,000 | 1,500 |
| 5 | | G1 | 4,200 | | 5,700 |
| 6 | | G1 | | 2,400 | 3,300 |
| 12 | | G1 | | 1,000 | 2,300 |
| 12 | | G1 | | 700 | 1,600 |
| 22 | | G1 | 1,900 | | 3,500 |
| 24 | | G1 | | 900 | 2,600 |
| 24 | | G1 | | 600 | 2,000 |
| 26 | | G1 | 3,000 | | 5,000 |
| 26 | | G1 | | 120 | 4,880 |
| 26 | | G1 | | 230 | 4,650 |
| 26 | | G1 | | 700 | **3,950** |

**Accounts Receivable**    Acct. No. 106

| Date | Explan. | PR | Debit | Credit | Balance |
|---|---|---|---|---|---|
| 2004 | | | | | |
| Dec. 12 | | G1 | 1,900 | | 1,900 |
| 22 | | G1 | | 1,900 | 0 |
| 31 | Adj. | G1 | 1,800 | | **1,800** |

**Supplies**    Acct. No. 126

| Date | Explan. | PR | Debit | Credit | Balance |
|---|---|---|---|---|---|
| 2004 | | | | | |
| Dec. 2 | | G1 | 2,500 | | 2,500 |
| 6 | | G1 | 7,100 | | 9,600 |
| 26 | | G1 | 120 | | 9,720 |
| 31 | Adj. | G1 | | 1,050 | **8,670** |

**Prepaid Insurance**    Acct. No. 128

| Date | Explan. | PR | Debit | Credit | Balance |
|---|---|---|---|---|---|
| 2004 | | | | | |
| Dec. 6 | | G1 | 2,400 | | 2,400 |
| 31 | Adj. | G1 | | 100 | **2,300** |

**Equipment**    Acct. No. 167

| Date | Explan. | PR | Debit | Credit | Balance |
|---|---|---|---|---|---|
| 2004 | | | | | |
| Dec. 3 | | G1 | 26,000 | | **26,000** |

**Accumulated Depreciation— Equipment**    Acct. No. 168

| Date | Explan. | PR | Debit | Credit | Balance |
|---|---|---|---|---|---|
| 2004 | | | | | |
| Dec. 31 | Adj. | G1 | | 375 | **375** |

## Liability and Equity Accounts

**Accounts Payable**    Acct. No. 201

| Date | Explan. | PR | Debit | Credit | Balance |
|---|---|---|---|---|---|
| 2004 | | | | | |
| Dec. 6 | | G1 | | 7,100 | 7,100 |
| 24 | | G1 | 900 | | **6,200** |

**Salaries Payable**    Acct. No. 209

| Date | Explan. | PR | Debit | Credit | Balance |
|---|---|---|---|---|---|
| 2004 | | | | | |
| Dec. 31 | Adj | G1 | | 210 | **210** |

**Unearned Consulting Revenue**    Acct. No. 236

| Date | Explan. | PR | Debit | Credit | Balance |
|---|---|---|---|---|---|
| 2004 | | | | | |
| Dec. 26 | | G1 | | 3,000 | 3,000 |
| 31 | Adj. | G1 | 250 | | **2,750** |

**Common Stock**    Acct. No. 307

| Date | Explan. | PR | Debit | Credit | Balance |
|---|---|---|---|---|---|
| 2004 | | | | | |
| Dec. 1 | | G1 | | 30,000 | **30,000** |

**Retained Earnings**    Acct. No. 318

| Date | Explan. | PR | Debit | Credit | Balance |
|---|---|---|---|---|---|
| 2004 | | | | | |
| Dec. 31 | Closing | G1 | | 3,785 | 3,785 |
| 31 | Closing | G1 | 600 | | 3,185 |

**Dividends**    Acct. No. 319

| Date | Explan. | PR | Debit | Credit | Balance |
|---|---|---|---|---|---|
| 2004 | | | | | |
| Dec. 24 | | G1 | 600 | | 600 |
| 31 | Closing | G1 | | 600 | 0 |

## Revenue and Expense Accounts (including Income Summary)

**Consulting Revenue**    Acct. No. 403

| Date | Explan. | PR | Debit | Credit | Balance |
|---|---|---|---|---|---|
| 2004 | | | | | |
| Dec. 5 | | G1 | | 4,200 | 4,200 |
| 12 | | G1 | | 1,600 | 5,800 |
| 31 | Adj. | G1 | | 250 | 6,050 |
| 31 | Adj. | G1 | | 1,800 | 7,850 |
| 31 | Closing | G1 | 7,850 | | 0 |

**Rental Revenue**    Acct. No. 406

| Date | Explan. | PR | Debit | Credit | Balance |
|---|---|---|---|---|---|
| 2004 | | | | | |
| Dec. 12 | | G1 | | 300 | 300 |
| 31 | Closing | G1 | 300 | | 0 |

**Depreciation Expense— Equipment**    Acct. No. 612

| Date | Explan. | PR | Debit | Credit | Balance |
|---|---|---|---|---|---|
| 2004 | | | | | |
| Dec. 31 | Adj. | G1 | 375 | | 375 |
| 31 | Closing | G1 | | 375 | 0 |

**Salaries Expense**    Acct. No. 622

| Date | Explan. | PR | Debit | Credit | Balance |
|---|---|---|---|---|---|
| 2004 | | | | | |
| Dec. 12 | | G1 | 700 | | 700 |
| 26 | | G1 | 700 | | 1,400 |
| 31 | Adj. | G1 | 210 | | 1,610 |
| 31 | Closing | G1 | | 1,610 | 0 |

**Insurance Expense**    Acct. No. 637

| Date | Explan. | PR | Debit | Credit | Balance |
|---|---|---|---|---|---|
| 2004 | | | | | |
| Dec. 31 | Adj. | G1 | 100 | | 100 |
| 31 | Closing | G1 | | 100 | 0 |

**Rent Expense**    Acct. No. 640

| Date | Explan. | PR | Debit | Credit | Balance |
|---|---|---|---|---|---|
| 2004 | | | | | |
| Dec. 12 | | G1 | 1,000 | | 1,000 |
| 31 | Closing | G1 | | 1,000 | 0 |

**Supplies Expense**    Acct. No. 652

| Date | Explan. | PR | Debit | Credit | Balance |
|---|---|---|---|---|---|
| 2004 | | | | | |
| Dec. 31 | Adj. | G1 | 1,050 | | 1,050 |
| 31 | Closing | G1 | | 1,050 | 0 |

**Utilities Expense**    Acct. No. 690

| Date | Explan. | PR | Debit | Credit | Balance |
|---|---|---|---|---|---|
| 2004 | | | | | |
| Dec. 26 | | G1 | 230 | | 230 |
| 31 | Closing | G1 | | 230 | 0 |

**Income Summary**    Acct. No. 901

| Date | Explan. | PR | Debit | Credit | Balance |
|---|---|---|---|---|---|
| 2004 | | | | | |
| Dec. 31 | Closing | G1 | | 8,150 | 8,150 |
| 31 | Closing | G1 | 4,365 | | 3,785 |
| 31 | Closing | G1 | 3,785 | | 0 |

Notice that we can select the accounts and amounts needing to be closed by identifying individual revenue, expense, and dividends accounts in the ledger. This is illustrated in Exhibit 3.16. (Information for closing entries is also in the financial statement columns of the work sheet—see Appendix 3B.)

## Post-Closing Trial Balance

Exhibit 3.17 shows the entire ledger of FastForward as of December 31 after adjusting and closing entries are posted. Note that the temporary accounts (revenues, expenses, and dividends) have balances equal to zero.

**P5**  Explain and prepare a post-closing trial balance.

A **post-closing trial balance** is a list of permanent accounts and their balances from the ledger after all closing entries have been journalized and posted. It lists the balances for all accounts not closed. These accounts comprise a company's assets, liabilities, and equity, which are identical to those in the balance sheet. The aim of a post-closing trial balance is to verify that (1) total debits equal total credits for permanent accounts and (2) all temporary accounts have zero balances. FastForward's post-closing trial balance is shown in Exhibit 3.18. The post-closing trial balance usually is the last step in the accounting process.

| FASTFORWARD<br>Post-Closing Trial Balance<br>December 31, 2004 | Debit | Credit |
|---|---|---|
| Cash | $ 3,950 | |
| Accounts receivable | 1,800 | |
| Supplies | 8,670 | |
| Prepaid insurance | 2,300 | |
| Equipment | 26,000 | |
| Accumulated depreciation—Equipment | | $   375 |
| Accounts payable | | 6,200 |
| Salaries payable | | 210 |
| Unearned consulting revenue | | 2,750 |
| Common stock | | 30,000 |
| Retained earnings | | 3,185 |
| Totals | $42,720 | $42,720 |

**Exhibit 3.18**

Post-Closing Trial Balance

Answers—p. 125

### Quick Check

**14.** What are the major steps in preparing closing entries?

**15.** Why are revenue and expense accounts called *temporary?* Can you identify and list any other temporary accounts?

**16.** What accounts are listed on the post-closing trial balance?

## Accounting Cycle Summary

The term **accounting cycle** refers to the steps in preparing financial statements. It is called a *cycle* because the steps are repeated each reporting period. Exhibit 3.19 shows the 10 steps in the cycle, beginning with analyzing transactions and ending with a post-closing trial balance or reversing entries. Steps 1 through 3 usually occur regularly as a company enters into transactions. Steps 4 through 9 are done at the end of a period. Reversing entries in step 10 are optional and are explained in Appendix 3C.

**C5**  Identify steps in the accounting cycle.

### Decision Insight

**Data Dash**   A few years ago **Sun Microsystems** took a month to prepare statements after its year-end. Today, it takes less than 24 hours to deliver preliminary figures to key decision makers. What is Sun's secret? Transactions are entered into a network of computerized systems.

## Exhibit 3.19

Steps in the Accounting Cycle*

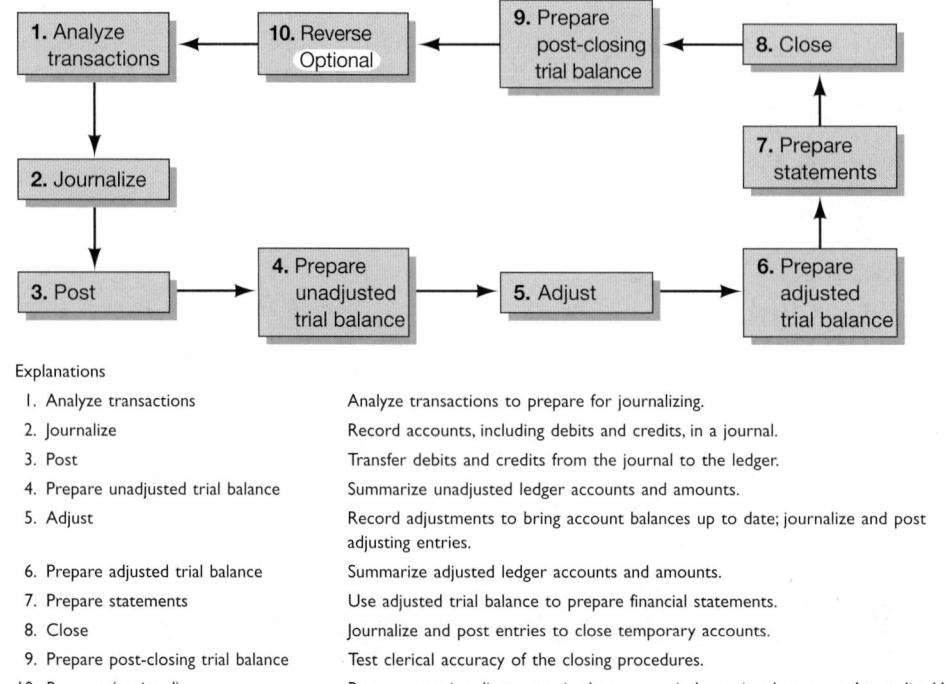

Explanations

| 1. | Analyze transactions | Analyze transactions to prepare for journalizing. |
|---|---|---|
| 2. | Journalize | Record accounts, including debits and credits, in a journal. |
| 3. | Post | Transfer debits and credits from the journal to the ledger. |
| 4. | Prepare unadjusted trial balance | Summarize unadjusted ledger accounts and amounts. |
| 5. | Adjust | Record adjustments to bring account balances up to date; journalize and post adjusting entries. |
| 6. | Prepare adjusted trial balance | Summarize adjusted ledger accounts and amounts. |
| 7. | Prepare statements | Use adjusted trial balance to prepare financial statements. |
| 8. | Close | Journalize and post entries to close temporary accounts. |
| 9. | Prepare post-closing trial balance | Test clerical accuracy of the closing procedures. |
| 10. | Reverse (optional) | Reverse certain adjustments in the next period—optional step; see Appendix 4A. |

*Steps 4, 6, and 9 can be done on a work sheet. A work sheet is useful in planning adjustments, but adjustments (step 5) must always be journalized and posted. Steps 3, 4, 6, and 9 are automatic with a computerized system.

# Classified Balance Sheet

**C6**  Explain and prepare a classified balance sheet.

Our discussion to this point has been limited to unclassified financial statements. This section describes a classified balance sheet. Chapter 4 describes a classified income statement. An **unclassified balance sheet** is one whose items are broadly grouped into assets, liabilities, and equity. One example is FastForward's balance sheet in Exhibit 3.14. A **classified balance sheet** organizes assets and liabilities into important subgroups that provide more information to decision makers.

## Classification Structure

A classified balance sheet has no required layout, but it usually contains the categories in Exhibit 3.20. One of the more important classifications is the separation between current and noncurrent items for both assets and liabilities. Current items are those expected to come due (either collected or owed) within one year or the company's operating cycle, whichever is longer. The **operating cycle** is the time span from when *cash is used* to acquire goods and services until *cash is received* from the sale of those goods and services. "Operating" refers to company operations and "cycle" refers to the circular flow of cash used for company inputs and then cash received from its outputs. The length of a company's operating cycle depends on its activities. For a service company, the operating cycle is the time span between (1) paying employees who perform the services and (2) receiving cash from customers. For a merchandiser selling products, the operating cycle is the time span between (1) paying suppliers for merchandise and (2) receiving cash from customers.

Most operating cycles are less than one year. This means most companies use a one-year period in deciding which assets and liabilities are current. A few companies have an operating

## Exhibit 3.20

Typical Categories in a Classified Balance Sheet

| Assets | Liabilities and Equity |
|---|---|
| Current assets | Current liabilities |
| Noncurrent assets | Noncurrent liabilities |
|    Long-term investments | Equity |
|    Plant assets | |
|    Intangible assets | |

**Point:** Current is also called *short term*, and noncurrent is also called *long term*.

cycle longer than one year. For instance, producers of certain beverages (wine) and products (ginseng) that require aging for several years have operating cycles longer than one year. A balance sheet lists current assets before noncurrent assets and current liabilities before noncurrent liabilities. This consistency in presentation allows users to quickly identify current assets that are most easily converted to cash and current liabilities that are shortly coming due. Items in current assets and current liabilities are listed in the order of how quickly they will be converted to, or paid in, cash.

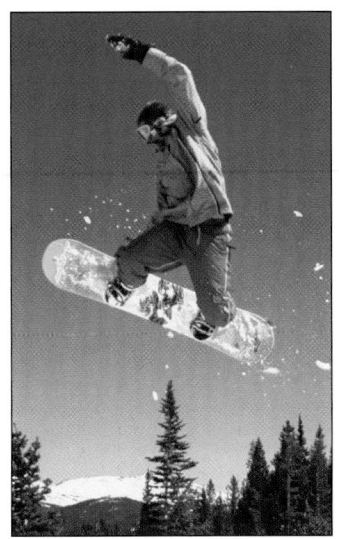

## Classification Categories

This section describes the most common categories in a classified balance sheet. The balance sheet for Snowboarding Components in Exhibit 3.21 shows these typical categories. Its assets are classified as either current or noncurrent. Its noncurrent assets include three main categories: long-term investments, plant assets, and intangible assets. Its liabilities are classified as either current or long term. Not all companies use the same categories of assets

| SNOWBOARDING COMPONENTS Balance Sheet January 31, 2005 | | |
|---|---:|---:|
| **Assets** | | |
| **Current assets** | | |
| Cash | $ 6,500 | |
| Short-term investments | 2,100 | |
| Accounts receivable | 4,400 | |
| Merchandise inventory | 27,500 | |
| Prepaid expenses | 2,400 | |
| Total current assets | | $ 42,900 |
| **Long-term investments** | | |
| Notes receivable | 1,500 | |
| Investments in stocks and bonds | 18,000 | |
| Land held for future expansion | 48,000 | |
| Total long-term investments | | 67,500 |
| **Plant assets** | | |
| Store equipment | $ 33,200 | |
| Less accumulated depreciation | 8,000 | 25,200 |
| Buildings | 170,000 | |
| Less accumulated depreciation | 45,000 | 125,000 |
| Land | | 73,200 |
| Total plant assets | | 223,400 |
| **Intangible assets** | | 10,000 |
| Total assets | | $343,800 |
| **Liabilities** | | |
| **Current liabilities** | | |
| Accounts payable | $15,300 | |
| Wages payable | 3,200 | |
| Notes payable | 3,000 | |
| Current portion of long-term liabilities | 7,500 | |
| Total current liabilities | | $ 29,000 |
| **Long-term liabilities** (net of current portion) | | 150,000 |
| Total liabilities | | 179,000 |
| **Equity** | | |
| Common stock | | 50,000 |
| Retained earnings | | 114,800 |
| Total liabilities and equity | | $343,800 |

**Exhibit 3.21**

Example of a Classified Balance Sheet

and liabilities for their balance sheets. **K2**'s balance sheet lists only three asset classes: current assets; property, plant and equipment; and other assets.

**Current Assets**    **Current assets** are cash and other resources that are expected to be sold, collected, or used within one year or the company's operating cycle, whichever is longer. Examples are cash, short-term investments, accounts receivable, short-term notes receivable, goods for sale (called *merchandise* or *inventory*), and prepaid expenses. The individual prepaid expenses of a company are usually small in amount compared to many other assets and are often combined and shown as a single item. The prepaid expenses in Exhibit 3.21 likely include items such as prepaid insurance, prepaid rent, office supplies, and store supplies. Prepaid expenses are usually listed last because they will not be converted to cash (instead, they are used).

**Point:** Short-term investments maturing within three months are combined with cash on both the balance sheet and cash flow statement. This combination is called *cash and cash equivalents*.

**Long-Term Investments**    A second major balance sheet classification is **long-term** (or *noncurrent*) **investments.** Notes receivable and investments in stocks and bonds are long-term assets when they are expected to be held for more than the longer of one year or the operating cycle. Land held for future expansion is a long-term investment because it is *not* used in operations.

**Global:** In the U.K. and many countries influenced by U.K. reporting, noncurrent assets are listed first and current assets are listed second.

**Plant Assets**    Plant assets are tangible assets that are both *long lived* and *used to produce* or *sell products and services*. Examples are equipment, machinery, buildings, and land that are used to produce or sell products and services. The order listing for plant assets is usually from most liquid to least liquid such as equipment and machinery to buildings and land.

**Point:** Plant assets are also called **fixed assets; property, plant and equipment;** or **long-lived assets.**

**Intangible Assets**    **Intangible assets** are long-term resources that benefit business operations. They usually lack physical form and have uncertain benefits. Examples are patents, trademarks, copyrights, franchises, and goodwill. Their value comes from the privileges or rights granted to or held by the owner. **Huffy Corporation** reports intangible assets of $48.1 million, which is more than 15 percent of its total assets. Its intangibles include trademarks, patents, and licensing agreements.

**Current Liabilities**    **Current liabilities** are obligations due to be paid or settled within one year or the operating cycle, whichever is longer. They are usually settled by paying out current assets such as cash. Current liabilities often include accounts payable, notes payable, wages payable, taxes payable, interest payable, and unearned revenues. Also, any portion of a long-term liability due to be paid within one year or the operating cycle, whichever is longer, is a current liability. Unearned revenues are current liabilities when they will be settled by delivering products or services within one year or the operating cycle, whichever is longer. Current liabilities are reported in the order of those to be settled first.

**Point:** Many financial ratios are distorted if accounts are not classified correctly. We must be especially careful when analyzing accounts whose balances are separated into short and long term.

**Long-Term Liabilities**    **Long-term liabilities** are obligations *not* due within one year or the operating cycle, whichever is longer. Notes payable, mortgages payable, bonds payable, and lease obligations are common long-term liabilities. If a company has both short- and long-term items in each of these categories, they are commonly separated into two accounts in the ledger.

**Point:** Many companies report two or more subgroups for long-term liabilities. See the balance sheets in Appendix A for examples.

**Equity**    Equity is the owner's claim on assets. The equity section for a corporation is divided into two main subsections, common stock (or contributed capital) and retained earnings.

---

### Quick Check

**17.** Identify which of the following assets are classified as (1) current assets or (2) plant assets: (*a*) land used in operations, (*b*) office supplies, (*c*) receivables from customers due in 10 months, (*d*) insurance protection for the next nine months, (*e*) trucks used to provide services to customers, (*f*) trademarks.

**18.** Cite two examples of assets classified as investments on the balance sheet.

**19.** Explain the operating cycle for a service company.

**Profit Margin and Current Ratio**

## Profit Margin

A useful measure of a company's operating results is the ratio of its net income to net sales. This ratio is called **profit margin,** or *return on sales,* and is computed as in Exhibit 3.22.

$$\text{Profit margin} = \frac{\text{Net income}}{\text{Net sales}}$$

A2 Compute profit margin and describe its use in analyzing company performance.

Exhibit 3.22

Profit Margin

This ratio is interpreted as reflecting the percent of profit in each dollar of sales. To illustrate how we compute and use profit margin, let's look at the results of **Limited Brands, Inc.,** in Exhibit 3.23 for the period 2000–2003.

|  | 2003 | 2002 | 2001 | 2000 |
|---|---|---|---|---|
| Net income (in mil.) . . . . . . . . . . . | $ 502 | $ 519 | $ 428 | $ 461 |
| Net sales (in mil.) . . . . . . . . . . . . | $8,445 | $8,423 | $9,080 | $8,765 |
| **Profit margin** . . . . . . . . . . . . . . | 5.9% | 6.2% | 4.7% | 5.3% |
| **Industry profit margin** . . . . . . . | 1.8% | 1.5% | 2.5% | 2.9% |

Exhibit 3.23

Limited Brands's Profit Margin

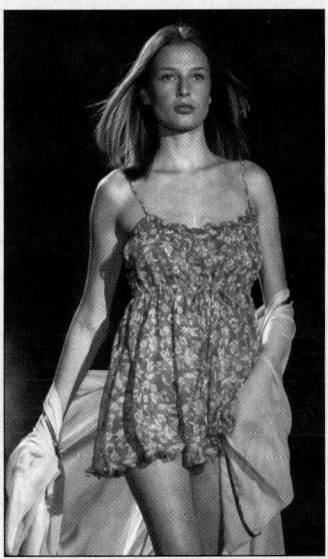

The Limited's average profit margin is 5.5% during this period. This favorably compares to the average industry profit margin of 2.2%. Moreover, Limited's most recent two years' profit margins are markedly better than earlier years. Thus, while 2001 was a difficult year for Limited in generating profits on its sales, its performance has slightly improved in 2002–2003. Future success depends on Limited maintaining and preferably increasing its profit margin.

## Current Ratio

An important use of financial statements is to help assess a company's ability to pay its debts in the near future. Such analysis affects decisions by suppliers when allowing a company to buy on credit. It also affects decisions by creditors when lending money to a company, including loan terms such as interest rate, due date, and collateral requirements. It can also affect a manager's decisions about using cash to pay existing debts when they come due. The **current ratio** is an important measure of a company's ability to pay its short-term obligations. It is defined in Exhibit 3.24 as current assets divided by current liabilities:

A3 Compute the current ratio and describe what it reveals about a company's financial condition.

$$\text{Current ratio} = \frac{\text{Current assets}}{\text{Current liabilities}}$$

Exhibit 3.24

Current Ratio

Using financial information from Limited Brands, Inc., we compute its current ratio for the recent four-year period. The results are in Exhibit 3.25.

| Fiscal Year ($ Millions) | 2003 | 2002 | 2001 | 2000 |
|---|---|---|---|---|
| Current assets . . . . . . . . . . . . . | $3,606 | $2,784 | $2,068 | $2,285 |
| Current liabilities . . . . . . . . . . . | $1,259 | $1,454 | $1,000 | $1,236 |
| **Current ratio** . . . . . . . . . . . . | 2.9 | 1.9 | 2.1 | 1.8 |
| Industry current ratio . . . . . . . . | 2.8 | 2.9 | 3.3 | 3.4 |

Exhibit 3.25

Limited Brands's Current Ratio

**Decision Maker**

**Analyst**   You are analyzing the financial condition of a fitness club to assess its ability to meet upcoming loan payments. You compute its current ratio as 1.2. You also find that a major portion of accounts receivable is due from one client who has not made any payments in the past 12 months. Removing this receivable from current assets drops the current ratio to 0.7. What do you conclude?

Answer—p. 125

Limited Brands's current ratio rose to 2.9 in 2003 compared to lower ratios for prior years. Still, the current ratio for each of these years suggests that the company's short-term obligations can be covered with its short-term assets. However, if its ratio would approach 1.0, Limited would expect to face challenges in covering liabilities. If the ratio were *less* than 1.0, current liabilities would exceed current assets, and the company's ability to pay short-term obligations would be in doubt.

# Demonstration Problem 1

The following information relates to Fanning's Electronics on December 31, 2005. The company, which uses the calendar year as its annual reporting period, initially records prepaid and unearned items in balance sheet accounts (assets and liabilities, respectively).

a. The company's weekly payroll is $8,750, paid each Friday for a five-day workweek. December 31, 2005, falls on a Monday, but the employees will not be paid their wages until Friday, January 4, 2006.

b. Eighteen months earlier, on July 1, 2004, the company purchased equipment that cost $20,000. Its useful life is predicted to be five years, at which time the equipment is expected to be worthless (zero salvage value).

c. On October 1, 2005, the company agreed to work on a new housing development. The company is paid $120,000 on October 1 in advance of future installation of similar alarm systems in 24 new homes. That amount was credited to the Unearned Services Revenue account. Between October 1 and December 31, work on 20 homes was completed.

d. On September 1, 2005, the company purchased a 12-month insurance policy for $1,800. The transaction was recorded with an $1,800 debit to Prepaid Insurance.

e. On December 29, 2005, the company performed a $7,000 service that has not been billed and not recorded as of December 31, 2005.

### Required

1. Prepare any necessary adjusting entries on December 31, 2005, in relation to transactions and events *a* through *e*.

2. Prepare T-accounts for the accounts affected by adjusting entries, and post the adjusting entries. Determine the adjusted balances for the Unearned Revenue and the Prepaid Insurance accounts.

3. Complete the following table and determine the amounts and effects of your adjusting entries on the year 2005 income statement and the December 31, 2005, balance sheet. Use up (down) arrows to indicate an increase (decrease) in the Effect columns.

| Entry | Amount in the Entry | Effect on Net Income | Effect on Total Assets | Effect on Total Liabilities | Effect on Total Equity |
|---|---|---|---|---|---|
| | | | | | |

## Planning the Solution

- Analyze each situation to determine which accounts need to be updated with an adjustment.
- Calculate the amount of each adjustment and prepare the necessary journal entries.
- Show the amount of each adjustment in the designated accounts, determine the adjusted balance, and identify the balance sheet classification of the account.
- Determine each entry's effect on net income for the year and on total assets, total liabilities, and total equity at the end of the year.

# Solution to Demonstration Problem 1

**1.** Adjusting journal entries.

| | | | | |
|---|---|---|---|---|
| (a) Dec. 31 | Wages Expense. . . . . . . . . . . . . . . . . . . . . . . . | | 1,750 | |
| | Wages Payable. . . . . . . . . . . . . . . . . . . . . | | | 1,750 |
| | *To accrue wages for the last day of the year* | | | |
| | *($8,750 × 1/5).* | | | |
| (b) Dec. 31 | Depreciation Expense—Equipment . . . . . . . . . . . | | 4,000 | |
| | Accumulated Depreciation—Equipment. . . . . | | | 4,000 |
| | *To record depreciation expense for the year* | | | |
| | *($20,000/5 years = $4,000 per year).* | | | |
| (c) Dec. 31 | Unearned Services Revenue. . . . . . . . . . . . . . . . | | 100,000 | |
| | Services Revenue. . . . . . . . . . . . . . . . . . . . | | | 100,000 |
| | *To recognize services revenue earned* | | | |
| | *($120,000 × 20/24).* | | | |
| (d) Dec. 31 | Insurance Expense. . . . . . . . . . . . . . . . . . . . . . | | 600 | |
| | Prepaid Insurance. . . . . . . . . . . . . . . . . . . | | | 600 |
| | *To adjust for expired portion of insurance* | | | |
| | *($1,800 × 4/12).* | | | |
| (e) Dec. 31 | Accounts Receivable. . . . . . . . . . . . . . . . . . . . . | | 7,000 | |
| | Services Revenue. . . . . . . . . . . . . . . . . . . . | | | 7,000 |
| | *To record services revenue earned.* | | | |

**2.** T-accounts for adjusting journal entries *a* through *e*.

| Wages Expense | | | | Wages Payable | | |
|---|---|---|---|---|---|---|
| (a) | 1,750 | | | | (a) | 1,750 |

| Depreciation Expense—Equipment | | | | Accumulated Depreciation—Equipment | | |
|---|---|---|---|---|---|---|
| (b) | 4,000 | | | | (b) | 4,000 |

| Unearned Revenue | | | | Services Revenue | | |
|---|---|---|---|---|---|---|
| | | Unadj. Bal. | 120,000 | | (c) | 100,000 |
| (c) | 100,000 | | | | (e) | 7,000 |
| | | Adj. Bal. | 20,000 | | Adj. Bal. | 107,000 |

| Insurance Expense | | | | Prepaid Insurance | | |
|---|---|---|---|---|---|---|
| (d) | 600 | | | Unadj. Bal. | 1,800 | |
| | | | | | (d) | 600 |

| Accounts Receivable | | | | | |
|---|---|---|---|---|---|
| (e) | 7,000 | | Adj. Bal. | 1,200 | |

**3.** Financial statement effects of adjusting journal entries.

| Entry | Amount in the Entry | Effect on Net Income | Effect on Total Assets | Effect on Total Liabilities | Effect on Total Equity |
|---|---|---|---|---|---|
| a | $ 1,750 | $ 1,750 ↓ | No effect | $ 1,750 ↑ | $ 1,750 ↓ |
| b | 4,000 | 4,000 ↓ | $4,000 ↓ | No effect | 4,000 ↓ |
| c | 100,000 | 100,000 ↑ | No effect | $100,000 ↓ | 100,000 ↑ |
| d | 600 | 600 ↓ | $ 600 ↓ | No effect | 600 ↓ |
| e | 7,000 | 7,000 ↑ | $7,000 ↑ | No effect | 7,000 ↑ |

# Demonstration Problem 2

Use the following adjusted trial balance to answer questions 1–4.

| CHOI COMPANY<br>Adjusted Trial Balance<br>December 31 | Debit | Credit |
|---|---|---|
| Cash | $ 3,050 | |
| Accounts receivable | 400 | |
| Prepaid insurance | 830 | |
| Supplies | 80 | |
| Equipment | 217,200 | |
| Accumulated depreciation—Equipment | | $ 29,100 |
| Wages payable | | 880 |
| Interest payable | | 3,600 |
| Unearned rent | | 460 |
| Long-term notes payable | | 150,000 |
| Common stock | | 10,000 |
| Retained earnings | | 30,340 |
| Dividends | 21,000 | |
| Rent earned | | 57,500 |
| Wages expense | 25,000 | |
| Utilities expense | 1,900 | |
| Insurance expense | 3,200 | |
| Supplies expense | 250 | |
| Depreciation expense—Equipment | 5,970 | |
| Interest expense | 3,000 | |
| Totals | $281,880 | $281,880 |

**1.** Prepare the annual income statement from the adjusted trial balance of Choi Company.

*Answer:*

| CHOI COMPANY<br>Income Statement<br>For Year Ended December 31 | | |
|---|---|---|
| Revenues | | |
| Rent earned | | $57,500 |
| Expenses | | |
| Wages expense | $25,000 | |
| Utilities expense | 1,900 | |
| Insurance expense | 3,200 | |
| Supplies expense | 250 | |
| Depreciation expense—Equipment | 5,970 | |
| Interest expense | 3,000 | |
| Total expenses | | 39,320 |
| Net income | | $18,180 |

**2.** Prepare a statement of retained earnings from the adjusted trial balance of Choi Company.

*Answer:*

| CHOI COMPANY<br>Statement of Retained Earnings<br>For Year Ended December 31 | |
|---|---|
| Retained earnings, December 31 (prior year) | $30,340 |
| Plus:  Net income | 18,180 |
| | 48,520 |
| Less:  Cash dividends | 21,000 |
| Retained earnings, December 31 (current year) | $27,520 |

**3.** Prepare a classified balance sheet from the adjusted trial balance of Choi Company.

*Answer:*

<table>
<tr><td colspan="3" style="text-align:center">CHOI COMPANY<br>Balance Sheet<br>December 31</td></tr>
<tr><td colspan="3" style="text-align:center">Assets</td></tr>
<tr><td>Current assets</td><td></td><td></td></tr>
<tr><td>Cash .........................</td><td></td><td>$  3,050</td></tr>
<tr><td>Accounts receivable ..............</td><td></td><td>400</td></tr>
<tr><td>Prepaid insurance ................</td><td></td><td>830</td></tr>
<tr><td>Supplies ......................</td><td></td><td>80</td></tr>
<tr><td>Total current assets ..............</td><td></td><td>4,360</td></tr>
<tr><td>Plant assets</td><td></td><td></td></tr>
<tr><td>Equipment .....................</td><td>$217,200</td><td></td></tr>
<tr><td>Less accumulated depreciation .......</td><td>29,100</td><td></td></tr>
<tr><td>Total plant assets ...............</td><td></td><td>188,100</td></tr>
<tr><td>Total assets ....................</td><td></td><td>$192,460</td></tr>
<tr><td colspan="3" style="text-align:center">Liabilities</td></tr>
<tr><td>Current liabilities</td><td></td><td></td></tr>
<tr><td>Wages payable ..................</td><td></td><td>$     880</td></tr>
<tr><td>Interest payable ................</td><td></td><td>3,600</td></tr>
<tr><td>Unearned rent ..................</td><td></td><td>460</td></tr>
<tr><td>Total current liabilities ...........</td><td></td><td>4,940</td></tr>
<tr><td>Long-term liabilities</td><td></td><td></td></tr>
<tr><td>Long-term note payable ............</td><td></td><td>150,000</td></tr>
<tr><td>Total liabilities ...................</td><td></td><td>154,940</td></tr>
<tr><td colspan="3" style="text-align:center">Equity</td></tr>
<tr><td>Common stock ...................</td><td></td><td>10,000</td></tr>
<tr><td>Retained earnings .................</td><td></td><td>27,520</td></tr>
<tr><td>Total liabilities and equity ............</td><td></td><td>$192,460</td></tr>
</table>

**4.** Prepare the closing entries for Choi Company.

| | | | |
|---|---|---|---|
| Dec. 31 | Rent Earned............................ | 57,500 | |
| | Income Summary..................... | | 57,500 |
| | *To close revenue accounts.* | | |
| Dec. 31 | Income Summary ....................... | 39,320 | |
| | Wages Expense ..................... | | 25,000 |
| | Utilities Expense .................... | | 1,900 |
| | Insurance Expense................... | | 3,200 |
| | Supplies Expense .................... | | 250 |
| | Depreciation Expense—Equip. ........... | | 5,970 |
| | Interest Expense .................... | | 3,000 |
| | *To close expense accounts.* | | |
| Dec. 31 | Income Summary ...................... | 18,180 | |
| | Retained Earnings.................... | | 18,180 |
| | *To close Income Summary account.* | | |
| Dec. 31 | Retained Earnings ....................... | 21,000 | |
| | Dividends ......................... | | 21,000 |
| | *To close the Dividends account.* | | |

# 3A Alternative Accounting for Prepayments

This appendix explains an alternative in accounting for prepaid expenses and unearned revenues.

## Recording the Prepayment of Expenses in Expense Accounts

**P6** Identify and explain alternatives in accounting for prepaids.

An alternative method is to record *all* prepaid expenses with debits to expense accounts. If any prepaids remain unused or unexpired at the end of an accounting period, then adjusting entries must transfer the cost of the unused portions from expense accounts to prepaid expense (asset) accounts. This alternative method is acceptable. The financial statements are identical under either method, but the adjusting entries are different. To illustrate the differences between these two methods, let's look at FastForward's cash payment of December 6 for 24 months of insurance coverage beginning on December 1. FastForward recorded that payment with a debit to an asset account, but it could have recorded a debit to an expense account. These alternatives are shown in Exhibit 3A.1.

**Exhibit 3A.1**

Alternative Initial Entries for Prepaid Expenses

| | | Payment Recorded as Asset | Payment Recorded as Expense |
|---|---|---|---|
| Dec. 6 | Prepaid Insurance . . . . . . . . . . . | 2,400 | |
| | Cash . . . . . . . . . . . . . . . . | 2,400 | |
| Dec. 6 | Insurance Expense . . . . . . . . . . | | 2,400 |
| | Cash . . . . . . . . . . . . . . . . | | 2,400 |

At the end of its accounting period on December 31, insurance protection for one month has expired. This means $100 ($2,400/24) of insurance coverage expired and is an expense for December. The adjusting entry depends on how the original payment was recorded. This is shown in Exhibit 3A.2.

**Exhibit 3A.2**

Adjusting Entry for Prepaid Expenses for the Two Alternatives

| | | Payment Recorded as Asset | Payment Recorded as Expense |
|---|---|---|---|
| Dec. 31 | Insurance Expense . . . . . . . . . . | 100 | |
| | Prepaid Insurance . . . . . . . . | 100 | |
| Dec. 31 | Prepaid Insurance . . . . . . . . . . . | | 2,300 |
| | Insurance Expense . . . . . . . | | 2,300 |

When these entries are posted to the accounts in the ledger, we can see that these two methods give identical results. The December 31 adjusted account balances in Exhibit 3A.3 show Prepaid Insurance of $2,300 and Insurance Expense of $100 for both methods.

**Exhibit 3A.3**

Account Balances under Two Alternatives for Recording Prepaid Expenses

| Payment Recorded as Asset | | | | Payment Recorded as Expense | | | |
|---|---|---|---|---|---|---|---|
| **Prepaid Insurance** | | | 128 | **Prepaid Insurance** | | | 128 |
| Dec. 6 | 2,400 | Dec. 31 | 100 | Dec. 31 | 2,300 | | |
| Balance | 2,300 | | | | | | |

| Payment Recorded as Asset | | | | Payment Recorded as Expense | | | |
|---|---|---|---|---|---|---|---|
| **Insurance Expense** | | | 637 | **Insurance Expense** | | | 637 |
| Dec. 31 | 100 | | | Dec. 6 | 2,400 | Dec. 31 | 2,300 |
| | | | | Balance | 100 | | |

## Recording the Prepayment of Revenues in Revenue Accounts

As with prepaid expenses, an alternative method is to record *all* unearned revenues with credits to revenue accounts. If any revenues are unearned at the end of an accounting period, then adjusting entries must transfer the unearned portions from revenue accounts to unearned revenue (liability) accounts. This alternative method is acceptable. The adjusting entries are different for these two alternatives, but the financial statements are identical. To illustrate the accounting differences between these two methods, let's look at FastForward's December 26 receipt of $3,000 for consulting services covering the period December 27 to February 24. FastForward recorded this transaction with a credit to a liability account. The alternative is to record it with a credit to a revenue account, as shown in Exhibit 3A.4.

| | | | Receipt Recorded as Liability | Receipt Recorded as Revenue |
|---|---|---|---|---|
| Dec. 26 | Cash . . . . . . . . . . . . . . . . . . . . . . . . . . . . | | 3,000 | |
| | Unearned Consulting Revenue . . . . . . . . | | 3,000 | |
| Dec. 26 | Cash . . . . . . . . . . . . . . . . . . . . . . . . . . . . | | | 3,000 |
| | Consulting Revenue . . . . . . . . . . . . . . | | | 3,000 |

**Exhibit 3A.4**

Alternative Initial Entries for Unearned Revenues

By the end of its accounting period on December 31, FastForward has earned $250 of this revenue. This means $250 of the liability has been satisfied. Depending on how the initial receipt is recorded, the adjusting entry is as shown in Exhibit 3A.5.

| | | | Receipt Recorded as Liability | Receipt Recorded as Revenue |
|---|---|---|---|---|
| Dec. 31 | Unearned Consulting Revenue . . . . . . . . . . . | | 250 | |
| | Consulting Revenue . . . . . . . . . . . . . . . | | 250 | |
| Dec. 31 | Consulting Revenue . . . . . . . . . . . . . . . . . . . | | | 2,750 |
| | Unearned Consulting Revenue . . . . . . . . | | | 2,750 |

**Exhibit 3A.5**

Adjusting Entry for Unearned Revenues for the Two Alternatives

After adjusting entries are posted, the two alternatives give identical results. The December 31 adjusted account balances in Exhibit 3A.6 show unearned consulting revenue of $2,750 and consulting revenue of $250 for both methods.

| Receipt Recorded as Liability | | | | Receipt Recorded as Revenue | | | |
|---|---|---|---|---|---|---|---|
| **Unearned Consulting Revenue** | | **236** | | **Unearned Consulting Revenue** | | **236** | |
| Dec. 31 | 250 | Dec. 26 | 3,000 | | | Dec. 31 | 2,750 |
| | | Balance | 2,750 | | | | |
| **Consulting Revenue** | | **403** | | **Consulting Revenue** | | **403** | |
| | | Dec. 31 | 250 | Dec. 31 | 2,750 | Dec. 26 | 3,000 |
| | | | | | | Balance | 250 |

**Exhibit 3A.6**

Account Balances under Two Alternatives for Recording Unearned Revenues

---

**APPENDIX**

# Work Sheet as a Tool

# 3B

Information preparers use various analyses and internal documents when organizing information for internal and external decision makers. Internal documents are often called **working papers.** One widely used working paper is the **work sheet,** which is a useful tool for preparers in working with accounting information. It is usually not available to external decision makers.

P7 Prepare a work sheet and explain its usefulness.

## Benefits of a Work Sheet

A work sheet is *not* a required report, yet using a manual or electronic work sheet has several potential benefits. Specifically, a work sheet:

- Aids the preparation of financial statements.
- Reduces the possibility of errors when working with many accounts and adjustments.
- Links accounts and adjustments to their impacts in financial statements.
- Assists in planning and organizing an audit of financial statements—as it can be used to reflect any adjustments necessary.
- Helps in preparing interim (monthly and quarterly) financial statements when the journalizing and posting of adjusting entries are postponed until the year-end.
- Shows the effects of proposed or "what if" transactions.

## Use of a Work Sheet

**Point:** Since a work sheet is *not* a required report or an accounting record, its format is flexible and can be modified by its user to fit his/her preferences.

When a work sheet is used to prepare financial statements, it is constructed at the end of a period before the adjusting process. The complete work sheet includes a list of the accounts, their balances and adjustments, and their sorting into financial statement columns. It provides two columns each for the unadjusted trial balance, the adjustments, the adjusted trial balance, the income statement, and the balance sheet (including the statement of owner's equity). To describe and interpret the work sheet, we use the information from FastForward. Preparing the work sheet has five important steps. Each step, 1 through 5, is color-coded and explained with reference to Exhibit 3B.1.

### ① Step 1. Enter Unadjusted Trial Balance

The first step in preparing a work sheet is to list the title of every account and its account number that is expected to appear on its financial statements. This includes all accounts in the ledger plus any new ones from adjusting entries. Most adjusting entries—including expenses from salaries, supplies, depreciation, and insurance—are predictable and recurring. The unadjusted balance for each account is then entered in the appropriate Debit or Credit column of the unadjusted trial balance columns. The totals of these two columns must be equal. Exhibit 3B.1 shows FastForward's work sheet after completing this first step. Sometimes blank lines are left on the work sheet based on past experience to indicate where lines will be needed for adjustments to certain accounts. Exhibit 3B.1 shows Consulting Revenue as one example. An alternative is to squeeze adjustments on one line or to combine the effects of two or more adjustments in one amount. In the unusual case when an account is not predicted, we can add a new line for such an account following the *Totals* line.

### ② Step 2. Enter Adjustments

**Point:** A recordkeeper often can complete the procedural task of journalizing and posting adjusting entries by using a work sheet and the guidance that *keying* provides.

The second step in preparing a work sheet is to enter adjustments in the Adjustments columns. The adjustments shown are the same ones shown in Exhibit 3.13. An identifying letter links the debit and credit of each adjusting entry. This is called *keying* the adjustments. After preparing a work sheet, adjusting entries must still be entered in the journal and posted to the ledger. The Adjustments columns provide the information for those entries.

### ③ Step 3. Prepare Adjusted Trial Balance

**Point:** To avoid omitting the transfer of an account balance, start with the first line (cash) and continue in account order.

The adjusted trial balance is prepared by combining the adjustments with the unadjusted balances for each account. As an example, the Prepaid Insurance account has a $2,400 debit balance in the Unadjusted Trial Balance columns. This $2,400 debit is combined with the $100 credit in the Adjustments columns to give Prepaid Insurance a $2,300 debit in the Adjusted Trial Balance columns. The totals of the Adjusted Trial Balance columns confirm the equality of debits and credits.

### ④ Step 4. Sort Adjusted Trial Balance Amounts to Financial Statements

This step involves sorting account balances from the adjusted trial balance to their proper financial statement columns. Expenses go to the Income Statement Debit column and revenues to the Income Statement Credit column. Assets and Dividends go to the Balance Sheet Debit column. Liabilities, Retained Earnings, and Common Stock go to the Balance Sheet Credit column.

### ⑤ Step 5. Total Statement Columns, Compute Income or Loss, and Balance Columns

Each financial statement column (from Step 4) is totaled. The difference between the totals of the Income Statement columns is net income or net loss. This occurs because revenues are entered in the

# Exhibit 3B.1

Work Sheet

File Edit View Insert Format Tools Data Window Help

**FastForward**
**Work Sheet**
**For Month Ended December 31, 2004**

| No. | Account | Unadjusted Trial Balance Dr. | Cr. | Adjustments Dr. | Cr. | Adjusted Trial Balance Dr. | Cr. | Income Statement Dr. | Cr. | Balance Sheet Dr. | Cr. |
|---|---|---|---|---|---|---|---|---|---|---|---|
| 101 | Cash | 3,950 | | | | 3,950 | | | | 3,950 | |
| 106 | Accounts receivable | 0 | | (f)1,800 | | 1,800 | | | | 1,800 | |
| 126 | Supplies | 9,720 | | | (b)1,050 | 8,670 | | | | 8,670 | |
| 128 | Prepaid insurance | 2,400 | | | (a) 100 | 2,300 | | | | 2,300 | |
| 167 | Equipment | 26,000 | | | | 26,000 | | | | 26,000 | |
| 168 | Accumulated depreciation—Equip. | | 0 | | (c) 375 | | 375 | | | | 375 |
| 201 | Accounts payable | | 6,200 | | | | 6,200 | | | | 6,200 |
| 209 | Salaries payable | | 0 | | (e) 210 | | 210 | | | | 210 |
| 236 | Unearned consulting revenue | | 3,000 | (d) 250 | | | 2,750 | | | | 2,750 |
| 307 | Common stock | | 30,000 | | | | 30,000 | | | | 30,000 |
| 318 | Retained earnings | | 0 | | | | 0 | | | | 0 |
| 319 | Dividends | 600 | | | | 600 | | | | 600 | |
| 403 | Consulting revenue | | 5,800 | | (d) 250 | | 7,850 | | 7,850 | | |
| | | | | | (f)1,800 | | | | | | |
| 406 | Rental revenue | | 300 | | | | 300 | | 300 | | |
| 612 | Depreciation expense—Equip. | 0 | | (c) 375 | | 375 | | 375 | | | |
| 622 | Salaries expense | 1,400 | | (e) 210 | | 1,610 | | 1,610 | | | |
| 637 | Insurance expense | 0 | | (a) 100 | | 100 | | 100 | | | |
| 640 | Rent expense | 1,000 | | | | 1,000 | | 1,000 | | | |
| 652 | Supplies expense | 0 | | (b)1,050 | | 1,050 | | 1,050 | | | |
| 690 | Utilities expense | 230 | | | | 230 | | 230 | | | |
| | Totals | 45,300 | 45,300 | 3,785 | 3,785 | 47,685 | 47,685 | 4,365 | 8,150 | 43,320 | 39,535 |
| | Net income | | | | | | | 3,785 | | | 3,785 |
| | Totals | | | | | | | 8,150 | 8,150 | 43,320 | 43,320 |

Sheet1 / Sheet2 / Sheet3 /

List all accounts from the ledger and those expected to arise from adjusting entries.

Enter all amounts available from ledger accounts. Column totals must be equal.

A work sheet collects and summarizes information used to prepare adjusting entries, financial statements, and closing entries.

Credit column and expenses in the Debit column. If the Credit total exceeds the Debit total, there is net income. If the Debit total exceeds the Credit total, there is a net loss. For FastForward, the Credit total exceeds the Debit total, giving a $3,785 net income.

The net income from the Income Statement columns is then entered in the Balance Sheet Credit column. Adding net income to the last Credit column implies that it is to be added to retained earnings. If a loss occurs, it is added to the Debit column. This implies that it is to be subtracted from retained earnings. The ending balance of retained earnings does not appear in the last two columns as a single amount, but it is computed in the statement of retained earnings using these account balances. When net income or net loss is added to the proper Balance Sheet column, the totals of the last two columns must balance. If they do not, one or more errors have been made. The error can either be mathematical or involve sorting one or more amounts to incorrect columns.

## Work Sheet Applications and Analysis

A work sheet does not substitute for financial statements. It is a tool we can use at the end of an accounting period to help organize data and prepare financial statements. FastForward's financial statements are shown in Exhibit 3.14. Its income statement amounts are taken from the Income Statement columns of the work sheet. Similarly, amounts for its balance sheet and its statement of retained earnings are taken from the Balance Sheet columns of the work sheet.

Work sheets are also useful in analyzing the effects of proposed, or what-if, transactions. This is done by entering financial statement amounts in the Unadjusted (what-if) columns. Proposed transactions are then entered in the Adjustments columns. We then compute "adjusted" amounts from these proposed transactions. The extended amounts in the financial statement columns show the effects of these proposed transactions. These financial statement columns yield **pro forma financial statements** because they show the statements *as if* the proposed transactions occurred.

---

## APPENDIX

# 3C Reversing Entries

**Reversing entries** are optional. They are recorded in response to accrued assets and accrued liabilities that were created by adjusting entries at the end of a reporting period. The purpose of reversing entries is to simplify a company's recordkeeping. Exhibit 3C.1 shows an example of FastForward's reversing entries. The top of the exhibit shows the adjusting entry FastForward recorded on December 31 for its employee's earned but unpaid salary. The entry recorded three days' salary of $210, which increased December's total salary expense to $1,610. The entry also recognized a liability of $210. The expense is reported on December's income statement. The expense account is then closed. The ledger on January 1, 2005, shows a $210 liability and a zero balance in the Salaries Expense account. At this point, the choice is made between using or not using reversing entries.

**Point:** As a general rule, adjusting entries that create new asset or liability accounts are likely candidates for reversing.

## Accounting *without* Reversing Entries

The path down the left side of Exhibit 3C.1 is described in the chapter. To summarize here, when the next payday occurs on January 9, we record payment with a compound entry that debits both the expense and liability accounts and credits Cash. Posting that entry creates a $490 balance in the expense account and reduces the liability account balance to zero because the debt has been settled. The disadvantage of this approach is the slightly more complex entry required on January 9. Paying the accrued liability means that this entry differs from the routine entries made on all other paydays. To construct the proper entry on January 9, we must recall the effect of the December 31 adjusting entry. Reversing entries overcome this disadvantage.

## Accounting *with* Reversing Entries

**P8** Prepare reversing entries and explain their purpose.

The right side of Exhibit 3C.1 shows how a reversing entry on January 1 overcomes the disadvantage of the January 9 entry when not using reversing entries. A reversing entry is the exact opposite of an adjusting entry. For FastForward, the Salaries Payable liability account is debited for $210, meaning that

*Accrue salaries expense on December 31, 2004*

**Exhibit 3C.1**

Reversing Entries for an Accrued Expense

Salaries Expense .............. 210
        Salaries Payable .............. 210

**Salaries Expense**

| Date | Expl. | Debit | Credit | Balance |
|---|---|---|---|---|
| 2004 | | | | |
| Dec. 12 | (7) | 700 | | 700 |
| 26 | (16) | 700 | | 1,400 |
| 31 | (e) | 210 | | 1,610 |

**Salaries Payable**

| Date | Expl. | Debit | Credit | Balance |
|---|---|---|---|---|
| 2004 | | | | |
| Dec. 31 | (e) | | 210 | 210 |

— OR —

*No reversing entry recorded on January 1, 2005*

NO ENTRY

**Salaries Expense**

| Date | Expl. | Debit | Credit | Balance |
|---|---|---|---|---|
| 2005 | | | | |

**Salaries Payable**

| Date | Expl. | Debit | Credit | Balance |
|---|---|---|---|---|
| 2004 | | | | |
| Dec. 31 | (e) | | 210 | 210 |
| 2005 | | | | |

*Reversing entry recorded on January 1, 2005*

Salaries Payable .............. 210
        Salaries Expense .............. 210

**Salaries Expense***

| Date | Expl. | Debit | Credit | Balance |
|---|---|---|---|---|
| 2005 | | | | |
| Jan. 1 | | | 210 | (210) |

**Salaries Payable**

| Date | Expl. | Debit | Credit | Balance |
|---|---|---|---|---|
| 2004 | | | | |
| Dec. 31 | (e) | | 210 | 210 |
| 2004 | | | | |
| Jan. 1 | | 210 | | 0 |

*Pay the accrued and current salaries on January 9, the first payday in 2005*

Salaries Expense .............. 490
Salaries Payable .............. 210
        Cash .............. 700

**Salaries Expense**

| Date | Expl. | Debit | Credit | Balance |
|---|---|---|---|---|
| 2005 | | | | |
| Jan. 9 | | 490 | | 490 |

**Salaries Payable**

| Date | Expl. | Debit | Credit | Balance |
|---|---|---|---|---|
| 2004 | | | | |
| Dec. 31 | (e) | | 210 | 210 |
| 2005 | | | | |
| Jan. 9 | | 210 | | 0 |

Salaries Expense .............. 700
        Cash .............. 700

**Salaries Expense***

| Date | Expl. | Debit | Credit | Balance |
|---|---|---|---|---|
| 2005 | | | | |
| Jan. 1 | | | 210 | (210) |
| Jan. 9 | | 700 | | 490 |

**Salaries Payable**

| Date | Expl. | Debit | Credit | Balance |
|---|---|---|---|---|
| 2004 | | | | |
| Dec. 31 | (e) | | 210 | 210 |
| 2005 | | | | |
| Jan. 1 | | 210 | | 0 |

Under both approaches, the expense and liability accounts have identical balances after the cash payment on January 9.

| Salaries Expense .............. | $490 |
|---|---|
| Salaries Payable .............. | $ 0 |

*Circled numbers in the *Balance* column indicate abnormal balances.

this account now has a zero balance after the entry is posted. The Salaries Payable account temporarily understates the liability, but this is not a problem since financial statements are not prepared before the liability is settled on January 9. The credit to the Salaries Expense account is unusual because it gives the account an *abnormal credit balance*. We highlight an abnormal balance by circling it. Because of the reversing entry, the January 9 entry to record payment is straightforward. This entry debits the Salaries Expense account and credits Cash for the full $700 paid. It is the same as all other entries made to record 10 days' salary for the employee. Notice that after the payment entry is posted, the Salaries Expense account has a $490 balance that reflects seven days' salary of $70 per day (see the lower right side of Exhibit 3C.1). The zero balance in the Salaries Payable account is now correct. The lower section of Exhibit 3C.1 shows that the expense and liability accounts have exactly the same balances whether reversing entries are used or not. This means that both approaches yield identical results.

## Summary

**C1** **Explain the importance of periodic reporting and the time period principle.** The value of information is often linked to its timeliness. To provide timely information, accounting systems prepare periodic reports at regular intervals. The time period principle assumes that an organization's activities can be divided into specific time periods for periodic reporting.

**C2** **Explain accrual accounting and how it makes financial statements more useful.** Accrual accounting recognizes revenue when earned and expenses when incurred—not necessarily when cash inflows and outflows occur. This information is valuable in assessing a company's financial position and performance.

**C3** **Identify the types of adjustments and their purpose.** Adjustments can be grouped according to the timing of cash receipts and cash payments relative to when they are recognized as revenues or expenses as follows: prepaid expenses, unearned revenues, accrued expenses, and accrued revenues. Adjusting entries are necessary so that revenues, expenses, assets, and liabilities are correctly reported.

**C4** **Explain why temporary accounts are closed each period.** Temporary accounts are closed at the end of each accounting period for two main reasons. First, the closing process updates the retained earnings account to include the effects of all transactions and events recorded for the period. Second, it prepares revenue, expense, and dividends accounts for the next reporting period by giving them zero balances.

**C5** **Identify steps in the accounting cycle.** The accounting cycle consists of 10 steps: (1) analyze transactions, (2) journalize, (3) post, (4) prepare an unadjusted trial balance, (5) adjust accounts, (6) prepare an adjusted trial balance, (7) prepare statements, (8) close, (9) prepare a post-closing trial balance, and (10) prepare (optional) reversing entries.

**C6** **Explain and prepare a classified balance sheet.** Classified balance sheets report assets and liabilities in two categories: current and noncurrent. Noncurrent assets often include long-term investments, plant assets, and intangible assets. A corporation separates equity into common stock and retained earnings.

**A1** **Explain how accounting adjustments link to financial statements.** Accounting adjustments bring an asset or liability account balance to its correct amount. They also update related expense or revenue accounts. Every adjusting entry affects one or more income statement accounts *and* one or more balance sheet accounts. An adjusting entry never affects cash.

**A2** **Compute profit margin and describe its use in analyzing company performance.** *Profit margin* is defined as the reporting period's net income divided by its net sales. Profit margin reflects on a company's earnings activities by showing how much income is in each dollar of sales.

**A3** **Compute the current ratio and describe what it reveals about a company's financial condition.** A company's current ratio is defined as current assets divided by current liabilities. We use it to evaluate a company's ability to pay its current liabilities out of current assets.

**P1** **Prepare and explain adjusting entries.** *Prepaid expenses* refer to items paid for in advance of receiving their benefits. Prepaid expenses are assets. Adjusting entries for prepaids involve increasing (debiting) expenses and decreasing (crediting) assets. *Unearned* (or *prepaid*) *revenues* refer to cash received in advance of providing products and services. Unearned revenues are liabilities. Adjusting entries for unearned revenues involves increasing (crediting) revenues and decreasing (debiting) unearned revenues. *Accrued expenses* refer to costs incurred in a period that are both unpaid and unrecorded. Adjusting entries for recording accrued expenses involve increasing (debiting) expenses and increasing (crediting) liabilities. *Accrued revenues* refer to revenues earned in a period that are both unrecorded and not yet received in cash. Adjusting entries for recording accrued revenues involve increasing (debiting) assets and increasing (crediting) revenues.

**P2** **Explain and prepare an adjusted trial balance.** An adjusted trial balance is a list of accounts and balances prepared after recording and posting adjusting entries. Financial statements are often prepared from the adjusted trial balance.

**P3** **Prepare financial statements from an adjusted trial balance.** Revenue and expense balances are reported on the income statement. Asset, liability, and equity balances are reported on the balance sheet. We usually prepare statements in the following order: income statement, statement of retained earnings, balance sheet, and statement of cash flows.

**P4** **Describe and prepare closing entries.** Closing entries involve four steps: (1) close credit balances in revenue (and gain) accounts to Income Summary, (2) close debit balances in expense (and loss) accounts to Income Summary, (3) close Income Summary to Retained Earnings, and (4) close Dividends account to Retained Earnings.

**P5** **Explain and prepare a post-closing trial balance.** A post-closing trial balance is a list of permanent accounts and their balances after all closing entries have been journalized and posted. Its purpose is to verify that (1) total debits equal total credits for permanent accounts and (2) all temporary accounts have zero balances.

**P6**[A] **Identify and explain alternatives in accounting for prepaids.** Charging all prepaid expenses to expense accounts when they are purchased is acceptable. When this is done, adjusting entries must transfer any unexpired amounts from expense accounts to asset accounts. Crediting all unearned revenues to revenue accounts when cash is received is also acceptable. In this case, the adjusting entries must transfer any unearned amounts from revenue accounts to unearned revenue accounts.

**P7**[B] **Prepare a work sheet and explain its usefulness.** A work sheet can be a useful tool in preparing and analyzing financial statements. It is helpful at the end of a period in preparing adjusting entries, an adjusted trial balance, and financial statements. A work sheet usually contains five pairs of columns: Unadjusted Trial Balance, Adjustments, Adjusted Trial Balance, Income Statement, and Balance Sheet.

**P8**[C] **Prepare reversing entries and explain their purpose.** Reversing entries are an optional step. They are applied to accrued expenses and revenues. The purpose of reversing entries is to simplify subsequent journal entries. Financial statements are unaffected by the choice to use or not use reversing entries.

## Guidance Answers to **Decision Maker** and **Decision Ethics**

**Investor**   Prepaid expenses are items paid for in advance of receiving their benefits. They are assets and are expensed as they are used up. The publishing company's treatment of the signing bonus is acceptable provided future book sales can at least match the $500,000 expense. As an investor, you are concerned about the risk of future book sales. The riskier the likelihood of future book sales is, the more likely your analysis is to treat the $500,000, or a portion of it, as an expense, not a prepaid expense (asset).

**Entrepreneur**   Depreciation is a process of cost allocation, not asset valuation. Knowing the depreciation schedule is not especially useful in your estimation of what the building and equipment are currently worth. Your own assessment of the age, quality, and usefulness of the building and equipment is more important.

**Loan Officer**   Your concern in lending to this store arises from analysis of current-year sales. While increased revenues and income are fine, your concern is with collectibility of these promotional sales. If the owner sold products to customers with poor records of

paying bills, then collectibility of these sales is low. Your analysis must assess this possibility and recognize any expected losses.

**Financial Officer**   Omitting accrued expenses and recognizing revenue early can mislead financial statement users. One action is to request a second meeting with the president so you can explain that accruing expenses when incurred and recognizing revenue when earned are required practices. If the president persists, you might discuss the situation with legal counsel and any auditors involved. Your ethical action might cost you this job, but the potential pitfalls for falsification of statements, reputation loss, personal integrity, and other costs are too great.

**Analyst**   A current ratio of 1.2 suggests that current assets are sufficient to cover current liabilities, but it implies a minimal buffer in case of errors in measuring current assets or current liabilities. Removing tardy receivables reduces the current ratio to 0.7. Your assessment is that the club will have some difficulty meeting its loan payments.

## Guidance Answers to **Quick Checks**

**1.** An annual reporting (or accounting) period covers one year and refers to the preparation of annual financial statements. The annual reporting period is not always a calendar year that ends on December 31. An organization can adopt a fiscal year consisting of any consecutive 12 months or 52 weeks.

**2.** Interim financial statements (covering less than one year) are prepared to provide timely information to decision makers.

**3.** The revenue recognition principle and the matching principle lead most directly to the adjusting process.

**4.** No. Cash basis accounting is not consistent with the matching principle because it reports expenses when paid, not in the period when revenue is earned as a result of those expenses.

**5.** No expense is reported in 2005. Under cash basis accounting, the entire $4,800 is reported as an expense in April 2004 when the premium is paid.

**6.** If the accrued revenues adjustment of $200 is not made, then both revenues and net income are understated by $200 on the current year's income statement, and both assets and equity are understated by $200 on the balance sheet.

**7.** A contra account is an account that is subtracted from the balance of a related account. Use of a contra account provides more information than simply reporting a net amount.

**8.** An accrued expense is a cost incurred in a period that is both unpaid and unrecorded prior to adjusting entries. One example is salaries earned but not yet paid at period-end.

**9.** An unearned revenue arises when a firm receives cash (or other assets) from a customer before providing the services or products to the customer. A magazine subscription paid in advance is one example; season ticket sales is another.

**10.** Salaries Payable . . . . . . . . . . . . . . . . . .   1,000
   Salaries Expense . . . . . . . . . . . . . . . .   6,000
      Cash . . . . . . . . . . . . . . . . . . . . . .          7,000
   *Paid salary including accrual from December.*

**11.** The probable adjusting entries of Jordan Air are:
   Insurance Expense . . . . . . . . . . . . . . . .   300
      Prepaid Insurance . . . . . . . . . . . . .          300
   *To record insurance expired.*
   Salaries Expense . . . . . . . . . . . . . . . . .   1,400
      Salaries Payable . . . . . . . . . . . . . .          1,400
   *To record accrued salaries.*

**12.** Revenue accounts and expense accounts.

**13.** Statement of retained earnings.

**14.** The major steps in preparing closing entries are to close (1) credit balances in revenue accounts to Income Summary, (2) debit balances in expense accounts to Income Summary, (3) Income Summary to Retained Earnings, and (4) any Dividends account to Retained Earnings.

**15.** Revenue (and gain) and expense (and loss) accounts are called *temporary* because they are opened and closed each period. The Income Summary and Dividends accounts are also temporary.

**16.** Permanent accounts make up the post-closing trial balance. These accounts are asset, liability, and equity accounts.

**17.** Current assets: (*b*), (*c*), (*d*). Plant assets: (*a*), (*e*). Item (*f*) is an intangible asset.

**18.** Investment in common stock, investment in bonds, and land held for future expansion.

**19.** For a service company, the operating cycle is the usual time between (1) paying employees who do the services and (2) receiving cash from customers for services provided.

## Key Terms

Key Terms are available at the book's Website for learning and testing in an online Flashcard Format.

| | | |
|---|---|---|
| **Accounting cycle** (p. 109) | **Current assets** (p. 112) | **Plant assets** (p. 97) |
| **Accounting period** (p. 92) | **Current liabilities** (p. 112) | **Post-closing trial balance** (p. 109) |
| **Accrual basis accounting** (p. 93) | **Current ratio** (p. 113) | **Prepaid expenses** (p. 95) |
| **Accrued expenses** (p. 99) | **Depreciation** (p. 97) | **Profit margin** (p. 106) |
| **Accrued revenues** (p. 101) | **Fiscal year** (p. 93) | **Pro forma financial statements** (p. 122) |
| **Adjusted trial balance** (p. 103) | **Income Summary** (p. 106) | **Reversing entries** (p. 122) |
| **Adjusting entry** (p. 95) | **Intangible assets** (p. 112) | **Straight-line depreciation method** (p. 97) |
| **Annual financial statements** (p. 93) | **Interim financial statements** (p. 93) | **Temporary accounts** (p. 104) |
| **Book value** (p. 98) | **Long-term investments** (p. 112) | **Time period principle** (p. 92) |
| **Cash basis accounting** (p. 93) | **Long-term liabilities** (p. 112) | **Unadjusted trial balance** (p. 103) |
| **Classified balance sheet** (p. 110) | **Matching principle** (p. 94) | **Unclassified balance sheet** (p. 110) |
| **Closing entries** (p. 106) | **Natural business year** (p. 93) | **Unearned revenues** (p. 98) |
| **Closing process** (p. 104) | **Operating cycle** (p. 110) | **Working papers** (p. 119) |
| **Contra account** (p. 97) | **Permanent accounts** (p. 106) | **Work sheet** (p. 119) |

## Personal Interactive Quiz

Personal Interactive Quizzes A and B are available at the book's Website to reinforce and assess your learning.

*Superscript letter $^A$ ($^B$ and $^C$) denotes assignments based on Appendix 3A (3B and 3C).*

## Discussion Questions

1. What is the difference between the cash basis and the accrual basis of accounting?

2. Why is the accrual basis of accounting generally preferred over the cash basis?

3. What type of business is most likely to select a fiscal year that corresponds to its natural business year instead of the calendar year?

4. Where is a prepaid expense reported in the financial statements?

5. What type of asset(s) requires adjusting entries to record depreciation?

6. What contra account is used when recording and reporting the effects of depreciation? Why is it used?

7. Where is unearned revenue reported in financial statements?

8. What is an accrued revenue? Give an example.

9.$^A$If a company initially records prepaid expenses with debits to expense accounts, what type of account is debited in the adjusting entries for those prepaid expenses?

10. Review the balance sheet of **Krispy Kreme** in Appendix A. Identify two asset accounts that require adjustment before annual financial statements can be prepared. What would be the effect on the income statement if these two asset accounts were not adjusted?

11. Review the balance sheet of **Tastykake** in Appendix A. In addition to Prepayments, identify two accounts (either assets or liabilities) requiring adjusting entries.

12. Refer to **Harley-Davidson**'s balance sheet in Appendix A. If it made an adjustment for unpaid wages at year-end, where would the Accrued Wages Expense be reported on its balance sheet?

13. What accounts are affected by closing entries? What accounts are not affected?

14. What two purposes are accomplished by recording closing entries?

15. What are the steps in recording closing entries?

16. What is the purpose of the Income Summary account?

17. Explain whether an error has occurred if a post-closing trial balance includes a Depreciation Expense account.

18.$^B$What tasks are aided by a work sheet?

19.$^B$Why are the debit and credit entries in the Adjustments columns of the work sheet identified with letters?

**20.** What is a company's operating cycle?

**21.** What classes of assets and liabilities are shown on a typical classified balance sheet?

**22.** How is unearned revenue classified on the balance sheet?

**23.** What are the characteristics of plant assets?

**24.**<sup>c</sup> How do reversing entries simplify recordkeeping?

**25.**<sup>c</sup> If a company recorded accrued salaries expense of $500 at the end of its fiscal year, what reversing entry could be made? When would it be made?

**26.** Refer to the balance sheet for **Krispy Kreme** in Appendix A. What five noncurrent asset categories are used on its classified balance sheet?

**27.** Refer to **Tastykake**'s balance sheet in Appendix A. Identify the accounts listed as current liabilities.

**28.** Refer to **Harley-Davidson**'s financial statements in Appendix A. What journal entry was likely recorded as of December 31, 2002, to close its Income Summary account.  **Harley-Davidson**

 **Red numbers denote Discussion Questions that involve decision-making.**

*Homework Manager* 🖱 *repeats all numerical Quick Study assignments on the book's Website with new numbers.*

Classify the following adjusting entries as involving prepaid expenses (PE), unearned revenues (UR), accrued expenses (AE), or accrued revenues (AR).

**a.** _____ To record revenue earned that was previously received as cash in advance.

**b.** _____ To record annual depreciation expense.

**c.** _____ To record wages expense incurred but not yet paid (nor recorded).

**d.** _____ To record revenue earned but not yet billed (nor recorded).

**e.** _____ To record expiration of prepaid insurance.

**QUICK STUDY**

**QS 3-1**
Identifying accounting adjustments

C3

---

**a.** On July 1, 2005, Beyonce Company paid $1,800 for six months of insurance coverage. No adjustments have been made to the Prepaid Insurance account, and it is now December 31, 2005. Prepare the journal entry to reflect expiration of the insurance as of December 31, 2005.

**b.** Tyrell Company has a Supplies account balance of $1,000 on January 1, 2005. During 2005, it purchased $3,000 of supplies. As of December 31, 2005, a supplies inventory shows $1,300 of supplies available. Prepare the adjusting journal entry to correctly report the balance of the Supplies account and the Supplies Expense account as of December 31, 2005.

**QS 3-2**
Adjusting prepaid expenses

P1

---

**a.** Carlos Company purchases $30,000 of equipment on January 1, 2005. The equipment is expected to last five years and be worth $5,000 at the end of that time. Prepare the entry to record one year's depreciation expense for the equipment as of December 31, 2005.

**b.** Chavez Company purchases $40,000 of land on January 1, 2005. The land is expected to last indefinitely. What depreciation adjustment, if any, should be made with respect to the Land account as of December 31, 2005?

**QS 3-3**
Adjusting for depreciation

P1

---

**a.** Eager receives $20,000 cash in advance for 4 months of legal services on October 1, 2005, and records it by debiting Cash and crediting Unearned Revenue both for $20,000. It is now December 31, 2005, and Eager has provided legal services as planned. What adjusting entry should Eager make to account for the work performed from October 1 through December 31, 2005?

**b.** S. Morford started a new publication called *Contest News*. Her subscribers pay $48 to receive 12 issues. With every new subscriber, Morford debits Cash and credits Unearned Subscription Revenue for the amounts received. Morford has 100 new subscribers as of July 1, 2005. She sends *Contest News* to each of these subscribers every month from July through December. Assuming no changes in subscribers, prepare the journal entry that Morford must make as of December 31, 2005, to adjust the Subscription Revenue account and the Unearned Subscription Revenue account.

**QS 3-4**
Adjusting for unearned revenues

A1  P1

---

Matia Mouder employs one college student every summer in her coffee shop. The student works the five weekdays and is paid on the following Monday. (For example, a student who works Monday through Friday, June 1 through June 5, is paid for that work on Monday, June 8.) Mouder adjusts her books monthly, if needed, to show salaries earned but unpaid at month-end. The student works the last week of July—Friday is August 1. If the student earns $100 per day, what adjusting entry must Mouder make on July 31 to correctly record accrued salaries expense for July?

**QS 3-5**
Accruing salaries

A1  P1

**QS 3-6**

Recording and analyzing
adjusting entries

A1

Adjusting entries affect at least one balance sheet account and at least one income statement account. For the following entries, identify the account to be debited and the account to be credited. Indicate which of the accounts is the income statement account and which is the balance sheet account.

**a.** Entry to record revenue earned that was previously received as cash in advance.

**b.** Entry to record annual depreciation expense.

**c.** Entry to record wage expenses incurred but not yet paid (nor recorded).

**d.** Entry to record revenue earned but not yet billed (nor recorded).

**e.** Entry to record expiration of prepaid insurance.

---

**QS 3-7**

Preparing adjusting entries

C3  P1

During the year, Lola Co. recorded prepayments of expenses in asset accounts, and cash receipts of unearned revenues in liability accounts. At the end of its annual accounting period, the company must make three adjusting entries: (1) accrue salaries expense, (2) adjust the Unearned Services Revenue account to recognize earned revenue, and (3) record services revenue earned for which cash will be received the following period. For each of these adjusting entries (1), (2), and (3), indicate the account from a through g to be debited and the account to be credited.

**a.** Accounts Receivable      **e.** Unearned Services Revenue

**b.** Prepaid Salaries        **f.** Salaries Expense

**c.** Cash                  **g.** Services Revenue

**d.** Salaries Payable

---

**QS 3-8**

Interpreting adjusting entries

C2  P2

The following information is taken from Cruz Company's unadjusted and adjusted trial balances:

|  | Unadjusted | | Adjusted | |
|---|---|---|---|---|
|  | **Debit** | **Credit** | **Debit** | **Credit** |
| Prepaid insurance ....... | $4,100 |  | $3,700 |  |
| Interest payable ......... |  | $ 0 |  | $800 |

Given this information, which of the following is likely included among its adjusting entries?

**a.** A $400 credit to Prepaid Insurance and an $800 debit to Interest Payable.

**b.** A $400 debit to Insurance Expense and an $800 debit to Interest Payable.

**c.** A $400 debit to Insurance Expense and an $800 debit to Interest Expense.

---

**QS 3-9**

Computing accrual and cash
income

C1  C2

In its first year of operations, Harden Co. earned $39,000 in revenues and received $33,000 cash from these customers. The company incurred expenses of $22,500 but had not paid $2,250 of them at year-end. Harden also prepaid $3,750 cash for expenses that would be incurred the next year. Calculate the first year's net income under both the cash basis and the accrual basis of accounting.

---

**QS 3-10**

Determining effects of
adjusting entries

C3  A1

In making adjusting entries at the end of its accounting period, Gomez Consulting failed to record $1,600 of insurance coverage that had expired. This $1,600 cost had been initially debited to the Prepaid Insurance account. The company also failed to record accrued salaries expense of $1,000. As a result of these two oversights, the financial statements for the reporting period will [choose one] (1) understate assets by $1,600; (2) understate expenses by $2,600; (3) understate net income by $1,000; or (4) overstate liabilities by $1,000.

---

**QS 3-11**

Determining effects of
closing entries

C4  P4

Argosy Company began the current period with a $14,000 credit balance in the Retained Earnings account. At the end of the period, the company's adjusted account balances include the following temporary accounts with normal balances:

| | | | |
|---|---|---|---|
| Service fees earned ......... | $35,000 | Interest revenue ........ | $3,500 |
| Salaries expense ........... | 19,000 | Dividends ............ | 6,000 |
| Depreciation expense ....... | 4,000 | Utilities expense ....... | 2,300 |

After closing the revenue and expense accounts, what will be the balance of the Income Summary account? After all closing entries are journalized and posted, what will be the balance of the Retained Earnings account?

List the following steps of the accounting cycle in their proper order:

**a.** Preparing the post-closing trial balance.

**b.** Posting the journal entries.

**c.** Journalizing and posting adjusting entries.

**d.** Preparing the adjusted trial balance.

**e.** Journalizing and posting closing entries.

**f.** Analyzing transactions and events.

**g.** Preparing the financial statements.

**h.** Preparing the unadjusted trial balance.

**i.** Journalizing transactions and events.

**QS 3-12**
Identifying the accounting cycle
C5

---

The following are common categories on a classified balance sheet:

**A.** Current assets

**B.** Long-term investments

**C.** Plant assets

**D.** Intangible assets

**E.** Current liabilities

**F.** Long-term liabilities

For each of the following items, select the letter that identifies the balance sheet category where the item typically would appear.

_____ **1.** Trademarks

_____ **2.** Accounts receivable

_____ **3.** Land not currently used in operations

_____ **4.** Notes payable (due in three years)

_____ **5.** Cash

_____ **6.** Wages payable

_____ **7.** Store equipment

_____ **8.** Accounts payable

**QS 3-13**
Classifying balance sheet items
C6

---

The ledger of Avril Company includes the following accounts with normal balances: Retained Earnings $6,000; Dividends $400; Services Revenue $10,000; Wages Expense $5,200; and Rent Expense $800. Prepare the necessary closing entries at December 31.

**QS 3-14**
Prepare closing entries from the ledger   P4

---

Identify the accounts listed in QS 3-14 that would be included in a post-closing trial balance.

**QS 3-15**
Identify post-closing accounts   P5

---

Yang Company reported net income of $37,925 and net sales of $390,000 for the current year. Calculate Yang's profit margin and interpret the result. Assume that Yang's competitors' average profit margin is 15%.

**QS 3-16**
Analyzing profit margin

A2

---

Compute Jamar Company's current ratio using the following information:

| | | | |
|---|---|---|---|
| Accounts receivable | $15,000 | Long-term notes payable | $20,000 |
| Accounts payable | 10,000 | Office supplies | 1,800 |
| Buildings | 42,000 | Prepaid insurance | 2,500 |
| Cash | 6,000 | Unearned services revenue | 4,000 |

**QS 3-17**
Identifying current accounts and computing the current ratio
C6   A3

---

Diego Consulting initially records prepaid and unearned items in income statement accounts. Given Diego Consulting's accounting practices, which of the following applies to the preparation of adjusting entries at the end of its first accounting period?

**a.** Earned but unbilled (and unrecorded) consulting fees are recorded with a debit to Unearned Consulting Fees and a credit to Consulting Fees Earned.

**b.** Unpaid salaries are recorded with a debit to Prepaid Salaries and a credit to Salaries Expense.

**c.** The cost of unused office supplies is recorded with a debit to Supplies Expense and a credit to Office Supplies.

**d.** Unearned fees (on which cash was received in advance earlier in the period) are recorded with a debit to Consulting Fees Earned and a credit to Unearned Consulting Fees.

**QS 3-18ᴬ**
Preparing adjusting entries
C3   P6

---

In preparing a work sheet, indicate the financial statement Debit column to which a normal balance in the following accounts should be extended. Use IS for the Income Statement Debit column and BS for the Balance Sheet Debit column.

_____ **a.** Insurance expense

_____ **b.** Equipment

_____ **c.** Dividends

_____ **d.** Depreciation expense—Equipment

_____ **e.** Prepaid rent

_____ **f.** Accounts receivable

**QS 3-19ᴮ**
Applying a work sheet
P7

**QS 3-20<sup>B</sup>**

Preparing a partial work sheet

P7

The ledger of Terrel Company includes the following unadjusted normal balances: Prepaid Rent $800, Services Revenue $11,600, and Wages Expense $5,000. Adjusting entries are required for (a) accrued rent expense $240; (b) accrued services revenue $180; and (c) accrued wages expense $160. Enter these unadjusted balances and the necessary adjustments on a work sheet and complete the work sheet for these accounts. *Note:* You must include the following accounts: Accounts Receivable, Wages Payable, and Rent Expense.

**QS 3-21<sup>C</sup>**

Reversing entries

P8

On December 31, 2004, Yates Co. prepared an adjusting entry for $6,700 of earned but unrecorded management fees. On January 16, 2005, Yates received $15,500 cash in management fees, which included the accrued fees earned in 2004. Assuming the company uses reversing entries, prepare the January 1, 2005, reversing entry and the January 16, 2005, cash receipt entry.

*Homework Manager*  *repeats all numerical Exercises on the book's Website with new numbers.*

# EXERCISES

**Exercise 3-1**

Preparing adjusting entries

P1

For each of the following separate cases, prepare adjusting entries required for financial statements for the year ended (or date of) December 31, 2005. (Assume that prepaid expenses are initially recorded in asset accounts and that fees collected in advance of work are initially recorded as liabilities.)

**a.** One-third of the work related to $30,000 cash received in advance is performed this period.

**b.** Wages of $9,000 are earned by workers but not paid as of December 31, 2005.

**c.** Depreciation on the company's equipment for 2005 is $19,127.

**d.** The Office Supplies account had a $480 debit balance on December 31, 2004. During 2005, $5,349 of office supplies is purchased. A physical count of supplies at December 31, 2005, shows $587 of supplies available.

**Check** (e) Dr. Insurance Expense, $2,800; (f) Cr. Interest Revenue, $750

**e.** The Prepaid Insurance account had a $5,000 balance on December 31, 2004. An analysis of insurance policies shows that $2,200 of unexpired insurance benefits remain at December 31, 2005.

**f.** The company has earned (but not recorded) $750 of interest from investments in CDs for the year ended December 31, 2005. The interest revenue will be received on January 10, 2006.

**g.** The company has a bank loan and has incurred (but not recorded) interest expenses of $3,500 for the year ended December 31, 2005. The company must pay the interest on January 2, 2006.

**Exercise 3-2**

Preparing adjusting entries

P1

Prepare adjusting journal entries for the year ended (or date of) December 31, 2005, for each of these separate situations. Assume that prepaid expenses are initially recorded in asset accounts. Also assume that fees collected in advance of work are initially recorded as liabilities.

**a.** Depreciation on the company's equipment for 2005 is computed to be $16,000.

**b.** The Prepaid Insurance account had a $7,000 debit balance at December 31, 2005, before adjusting for the costs of any expired coverage. An analysis of the company's insurance policies showed that $1,040 of unexpired insurance coverage remains.

**Check** (c) Dr. Office Supplies Expense, $2,626; (e) Dr. Insurance Expense, $4,600

**c.** The Office Supplies account had a $300 debit balance on December 31, 2004; and $2,680 of office supplies was purchased during the year. The December 31, 2005, physical count showed $354 of supplies available.

**d.** One-half of the work related to $10,000 cash received in advance was performed this period.

**e.** The Prepaid Insurance account had a $5,600 debit balance at December 31, 2005, before adjusting for the costs of any expired coverage. An analysis of insurance policies showed that $4,600 of coverage had expired.

**f.** Wage expenses of $4,000 have been incurred but are not paid as of December 31, 2005.

**Exercise 3-3**

Adjusting and paying accrued wages

C1   P1

Pablo Management has five part-time employees, each of whom earns $100 per day. They are normally paid on Fridays for work completed Monday through Friday of the same week. They were paid in full on Friday, December 28, 2005. The next week, the five employees worked only four days because New Year's Day was an unpaid holiday. Show (*a*) the adjusting entry that would be recorded on Monday, December 31, 2005, and (*b*) the journal entry that would be made to record payment of the employees' wages on Friday, January 4, 2006.

The following three separate situations require adjusting journal entries to prepare financial statements as of April 30. For each situation, present both the April 30 adjusting entry and the subsequent entry during May to record the payment of the accrued expenses.

**a.** On April 1, the company retained an attorney at a flat monthly fee of $2,500. This amount is payable on the 12th of the following month.

**b.** A $780,000 note payable requires 9.6% annual interest, or $6,240 to be paid at the end of each 30 days. The interest was last paid on April 20 and the next payment is due on May 20. As of April 30, $2,080 of interest has accrued.

**c.** Total weekly salaries expense for all employees is $9,000. This amount is paid at the end of the day on Friday of each five-day workweek. April 30 falls on Tuesday of this year, which means that the employees had worked two days since the last payday. The next payday is May 3.

**Exercise 3-4**
Adjusting and paying accrued expenses

A1  P1

**Check**   (b) May 20 Dr. Interest Expense, $4,160

On March 1, 2003, a company paid a $16,200 premium on a 36-month insurance policy for coverage beginning on that date. Refer to that policy and fill in the blanks in the following table:

**Exercise 3-5**
Determining assets and expenses for accrual and cash accounting

C2

| Balance Sheet Insurance Asset Using | | Insurance Expense Using | | |
|---|---|---|---|---|
| | Accrual Basis | Cash Basis | | Accrual Basis | Cash Basis |
| Dec. 31, 2003  $____ | $____ | 2003  $____ | $____ |
| Dec. 31, 2004  ____ | ____ | 2004  ____ | ____ |
| Dec. 31, 2005  ____ | ____ | 2005  ____ | ____ |
| Dec. 31, 2006  ____ | ____ | 2006  ____ | |
| | | Total  $____ | $____ |

**Check**   2005 insurance expense: Accrual, $5,400; Cash, $0. Dec. 31, 2005, asset: Accrual, $900; Cash, $0.

The following adjusted trial balance contains the accounts and balances of Showers Company as of December 31, 2005, the end of its fiscal year. (1) Prepare the December 31, 2005, closing entries for Showers Company. (2) Prepare the December 31, 2005, post-closing trial balance for Showers Company.

**Exercise 3-6**
Preparing closing entries and a post-closing trial balance

C4  P4  P5

| No. | Account Title | Debit | Credit |
|---|---|---|---|
| 101 | Cash | $18,000 | |
| 126 | Supplies | 12,000 | |
| 128 | Prepaid insurance | 2,000 | |
| 167 | Equipment | 23,000 | |
| 168 | Accumulated depreciation—Equipment | | $ 6,500 |
| 307 | Common stock | | 10,000 |
| 318 | Retained earnings | | 36,600 |
| 319 | Dividends | 6,000 | |
| 404 | Services revenue | | 36,000 |
| 612 | Depreciation expense—Equipment | 2,000 | |
| 622 | Salaries expense | 21,000 | |
| 637 | Insurance expense | 1,500 | |
| 640 | Rent expense | 2,400 | |
| 652 | Supplies expense | 1,200 | |
| | Totals | $89,100 | $89,100 |

**Check**   (2) Retained Earnings (ending), $38,500; Total debits, $55,000

Use the following adjusted trial balance of Webb Trucking Company to prepare a classified balance sheet as of December 31, 2005.

**Exercise 3-7**
Preparing a classified balance sheet

C6

| Account Title | Debit | Credit |
|---|---|---|
| Cash | $ 7,000 | |
| Accounts receivable | 16,500 | |
| Office supplies | 2,000 | |
| Trucks | 170,000 | |
| Accumulated depreciation—Trucks | | $ 35,000 |
| Land | 75,000 | |
| Accounts payable | | 11,000 |
| Interest payable | | 3,000 |

[continued on next page]

[continued from previous page]

| | | |
|---|---:|---:|
| Long-term notes payable ............... | | 52,000 |
| Common stock ...................... | | 60,000 |
| Retained earnings .................... | | 101,000 |
| Dividends ......................... | 19,000 | |
| Trucking fees earned .................. | | 128,000 |
| Depreciation expense—Trucks ........... | 22,500 | |
| Salaries expense .................... | 60,000 | |
| Office supplies expense ............... | 7,000 | |
| Repairs expense—Trucks .............. | 11,000 | |
| Totals ............................ | $390,000 | $390,000 |

**Check**  Total assets, $235,500;
Retained Earnings (ending), $109,500

---

### Exercise 3-8
Preparing the financial statements

C5

Use the information in the adjusted trial balance reported in Exercise 3-7 to prepare Webb Trucking Company's (1) income statement, and (2) statement of retained earnings.

---

### Exercise 3-9
Computing and interpreting profit margin

A2

Use the following information to compute profit margin for each separate company *a* through *e:*

| | Net Income | Net Sales | | Net Income | Net Sales |
|---|---|---|---|---|---|
| **a.** | $ 5,390 | $ 44,830 | **d.** | $55,234 | $1,458,999 |
| **b.** | 87,644 | 398,954 | **e.** | 70,158 | 435,925 |
| **c.** | 93,385 | 257,082 | | | |

Which of the five companies is the most profitable according to the profit margin ratio? Interpret that company's profit margin ratio.

---

### Exercise 3-10
Computing the current ratio

A3

Use the information in the adjusted trial balance reported in Exercise 3-7 to compute the current ratio as of the balance sheet date. Interpret the current ratio for this company. (Assume that the industry norm for the current ratio is 1.5.)

---

### Exercise 3-11
Computing and analyzing the current ratio

A3

Calculate the current ratio in each of the following separate cases. Identify the company case with the strongest liquidity position. (These cases represent competing companies in the same industry.)

| | Current Assets | Current Liabilities |
|---|---:|---:|
| Case 1 ........ | $ 78,000 | $31,000 |
| Case 2 ........ | 104,000 | 75,000 |
| Case 3 ........ | 44,000 | 48,000 |
| Case 4 ........ | 84,500 | 80,600 |
| Case 5 ........ | 60,000 | 99,000 |

---

### Exercise 3-12^A
Adjusting for prepaids recorded as expenses and unearned revenues recorded as revenues

P6

**Check**  (*f*) Cr. Insurance Expense,
$1,200; (*g*) Dr. Remodeling Fees Earned,
$9,300

On-The-Mark Construction began operations on December 1. In setting up its accounting procedures, the company decided to debit expense accounts when it prepays its expenses and to credit revenue accounts when customers pay for services in advance. Prepare journal entries for items *a* through *d* and the adjusting entries as of its December 31 period-end for items *e* through *g.*

**a.** Supplies are purchased on December 1 for $3,000 cash.

**b.** The company prepaid its insurance premiums for $1,440 cash on December 2.

**c.** On December 15, the company receives an advance payment of $12,000 cash from a customer for remodeling work.

**d.** On December 28, the company receives $3,600 cash from another customer for remodeling work to be performed in January.

**e.** A physical count on December 31 indicates that On-The-Mark has $1,920 of supplies available.

**f.** An analysis of the insurance policies in effect on December 31 shows that $240 of insurance coverage had expired.

**g.** As of December 31, only one remodeling project has been worked on and completed. The $6,300 fee for this project had been received in advance.

Cosmo Company experienced the following events and transactions during July:

July   1   Received $2,000 cash in advance of performing work for Jill Dwyer.
       6   Received $8,400 cash in advance of performing work for Lisa Poe.
      12   Completed the job for Dwyer.
      18   Received $7,500 cash in advance of performing work for Vern Hillsman.
      27   Completed the job for Poe.
      31   None of the work for Hillsman has been performed.

**a.** Prepare journal entries (including any adjusting entries as of the end of the month) to record these events using the procedure of initially crediting the Unearned Fees account when payment is received from a customer in advance of performing services.

**b.** Prepare journal entries (including any adjusting entries as of the end of the month) to record these events using the procedure of initially crediting the Fees Earned account when payment is received from a customer in advance of performing services.

**c.** Under each method, determine the amount of earned fees reported on the income statement for July and the amount of unearned fees reported on the balance sheet as of July 31.

**Exercise 3-13**[A]
Recording and reporting revenues received in advance

P6

**Check**   (c) Fees Earned, $10,400

---

The following unadjusted trial balance contains the accounts and balances of Dalton Delivery Company as of December 31, 2005, its first year of operations. (1) Use the following information about the company's adjustments to complete a 10-column work sheet for Dalton.

**a.** Unrecorded depreciation on the trucks at the end of the year is $35,000.

**b.** The total amount of accrued interest expense at year-end is $8,000.

**c.** The cost of unused office supplies still available the year-end is $1,000.

(2) Prepare the year-end closing entries for Dalton, and determine the retained earnings to be reported on the year-end balance sheet.

**Exercise 3-14**[B]
Preparing a work sheet and recording closing entries

P4   P7

File Edit View Insert Format Tools Data Accounting Window Help

| Account Title | Debit | Credit |
|---|---|---|
| Cash | $ 14,000 | |
| Accounts receivable | 33,000 | |
| Office supplies | 4,000 | |
| Trucks | 340,000 | |
| Accumulated depreciation—Trucks | | $ 70,000 |
| Land | 150,000 | |
| Accounts payable | | 22,000 |
| Interest payable | | 6,000 |
| Long-term notes payable | | 104,000 |
| Common stock | | 100,000 |
| Retained earnings | | 222,000 |
| Dividends | 38,000 | |
| Delivery fees earned | | 256,000 |
| Depreciation expense—Truck | 45,000 | |
| Salaries expense | 120,000 | |
| Office supplies expense | 14,000 | |
| Interest expense | 6,000 | |
| Repairs expense—trucks | 16,000 | |
| Totals | $780,000 | $780,000 |

Sheet1 / Sheet2 / Sheet3 /

**Check**   Adj. trial balance totals, $817,000; Net income, $15,000

---

The following two events occurred for Totten Co. on October 31, 2005, the end of its fiscal year:

**a.** Totten rents a building from its owner for $3,200 per month. By a prearrangement, the company delayed paying October's rent until November 5. On this date, the company paid the rent for both October and November.

**b.** Totten rents space in a building it owns to a tenant for $750 per month. By prearrangement, the tenant delayed paying the October rent until November 8. On this date, the tenant paid the rent for both October and November.

**Exercise 3-15**[C]
Preparing reversing entries

P8

**Required**

1. Prepare adjusting entries that Totten must record for these events as of October 31.

2. Assuming Totten does *not* use reversing entries, prepare journal entries to record Totten's payment of rent on November 5 and the collection of rent on November 8 from Totten's tenant.

3. Assuming that Totten uses reversing entries, prepare reversing entries on November 1 and the journal entries to record Totten's payment of rent on November 5 and the collection of rent on November 8 from Totten's tenant.

---

**Exercise 3-16<sup>c</sup>**

Preparing reversing entries

P8

Hinson Company records prepaid assets and unearned revenues in balance sheet accounts. The following information was used to prepare adjusting entries for Hinson Company as of August 31, the end of the company's fiscal year:

**a.** The company has earned $5,000 in unrecorded service fees.

**b.** The expired portion of prepaid insurance is $2,700.

**c.** The company has earned $1,900 of its Unearned Service Fees account balance.

**d.** Depreciation expense for office equipment is $2,300.

**e.** Employees have earned but have not been paid salaries of $2,400.

Prepare any necessary reversing entries for the accounting adjustments *a* through *e* assuming that Hinson uses reversing entries in its accounting system.

---

# PROBLEM SET A

**Problem 3-1A**

Preparing adjusting and subsequent journal entries

C1  A1  P1

Maja Co. follows the practice of recording prepaid expenses and unearned revenues in balance sheet accounts. Maja's annual accounting period ends on December 31, 2005. The following information concerns the adjusting entries to be recorded as of that date:

**a.** The Office Supplies account started the year with a $3,000 balance. During 2005, the company purchased supplies for $12,400, which was added to the Office Supplies account. The inventory of supplies available at December 31, 2005, totaled $2,640.

**b.** An analysis of the company's insurance policies provided these facts:

| Policy | Date of Purchase | Months of Coverage | Cost |
|--------|------------------|--------------------|------|
| A | April 1, 2004 | 24 | $15,840 |
| B | April 1, 2005 | 36 | 13,068 |
| C | August 1, 2005 | 12 | 2,700 |

The total premium for each policy was paid in full (for all months) at the purchase date, and the Prepaid Insurance account was debited for the full cost. (Note that year-end adjusting entries for Prepaid Insurance were properly recorded in all prior years.)

**c.** The company has 15 employees, who earn a total of $2,100 in salaries each working day. They are paid each Monday for their work in the five-day workweek ending on the previous Friday. Assume that December 31, 2005, is a Tuesday, and all 15 employees worked the first two days of that week. Because New Year's Day is a paid holiday, they will be paid salaries for five full days on Monday, January 6, 2006.

**d.** The company purchased a building on January 1, 2005. It cost $855,000 and is expected to have a $45,000 salvage value at the end of its predicted 30-year life.

**e.** Since the company is not large enough to occupy the entire building it owns, it rented space to a tenant at $2,400 per month, starting on November 1, 2005. The rent was paid on time on November 1, and the amount received was credited to the Rent Earned account. However, the tenant has not paid the December rent. The company has worked out an agreement with the tenant, who has promised to pay both December and January rent in full on January 15. The tenant has agreed not to fall behind again.

**f.** On November 1, the company rented space to another tenant for $2,175 per month. The tenant paid five months' rent in advance on that date. The payment was recorded with a credit to the Unearned Rent account.

**Required**

**1.** Use the information to prepare adjusting entries as of December 31, 2005.

**2.** Prepare journal entries to record the first subsequent cash transaction in 2006 for parts *c* and *e*.

**Check**   (1*b*) Dr. Insurance Expense, $12,312 (1*d*) Dr. Depreciation Expense, $27,000

Watson Technical Institute (WTI), a school owned by Tom Watson, provides training to individuals who pay tuition directly to the school. WTI also offers training to groups in off-site locations. Its unadjusted trial balance as of December 31, 2005, follows. WTI initially records prepaid expenses and unearned revenues in balance sheet accounts. Descriptions of items *a* through *h* that require adjusting entries on December 31, 2005, follow.

**Problem 3-2A**

Preparing adjusting entries, adjusted trial balance, and financial statements

A1  P1  P2  P3

mhhe.com/wild3e

**Additional Information Items**

**a.** An analysis of the school's insurance policies shows that $3,000 of coverage has expired.

**b.** An inventory count shows that teaching supplies costing $2,600 are available at year-end 2005.

**c.** Annual depreciation on the equipment is $12,000.

**d.** Annual depreciation on the professional library is $6,000.

**e.** On November 1, the school agreed to do a special six-month course (starting immediately) for a client. The contract calls for a monthly fee of $2,200, and the client paid the first five months' fees in advance. When the cash was received, the Unearned Training Fees account was credited. The fee for the sixth month will be recorded when it is collected in 2006.

**f.** On October 15, the school agreed to teach a four-month class (beginning immediately) for an individual for $3,000 tuition per month payable at the end of the class. The services are being provided as agreed, and no payment has yet been received.

**g.** The school's two employees are paid weekly. As of the end of the year, two days' wages have accrued at the rate of $100 per day for each employee.

**h.** The balance in the Prepaid Rent account represents rent for December.

| WATSON TECHNICAL INSTITUTE Unadjusted Trial Balance December 31, 2005 | | |
|---|---|---|
| | **Debit** | **Credit** |
| Cash | $ 26,000 | |
| Accounts receivable | 0 | |
| Teaching supplies | 10,000 | |
| Prepaid insurance | 15,000 | |
| Prepaid rent | 2,000 | |
| Professional library | 30,000 | |
| Accumulated depreciation—Professional library | | $  9,000 |
| Equipment | 70,000 | |
| Accumulated depreciation—Equipment | | 16,000 |
| Accounts payable | | 36,000 |
| Salaries payable | | 0 |
| Unearned training fees | | 11,000 |
| Common stock | | 10,000 |
| Retained earnings | | 53,600 |
| Dividends | 40,000 | |
| Tuition fees earned | | 102,000 |
| Training fees earned | | 38,000 |
| Depreciation expense—Professional library | 0 | |
| Depreciation expense—Equipment | 0 | |
| Salaries expense | 48,000 | |
| Insurance expense | 0 | |
| Rent expense | 22,000 | |
| Teaching supplies expense | 0 | |
| Advertising expense | 7,000 | |
| Utilities expense | 5,600 | |
| Totals | $275,600 | $275,600 |

**Required**

**1.** Prepare T-accounts (representing the ledger) with balances from the unadjusted trial balance.

**2.** Prepare the necessary adjusting journal entries for items *a* through *h* and post them to the T-accounts. Assume that adjusting entries are made only at year-end.

**3.** Update balances in the T-accounts for the adjusting entries and prepare an adjusted trial balance.

**4.** Prepare Watson Technical Institute's income statement and statement of retained earnings for the year 2005 and prepare its balance sheet as of December 31, 2005.

## Problem 3-3A

Preparing trial balances, closing entries, and financial statements

C6 P4 P5

The adjusted trial balance of Lakia Repairs on December 31, 2005, follows:

| No. | Account Title | Debit | Credit |
|---|---|---|---|
| | **LAKIA REPAIRS** | | |
| | **Adjusted Trial Balance** | | |
| | **December 31, 2005** | | |
| 101 | Cash | $ 13,000 | |
| 124 | Office supplies | 1,200 | |
| 128 | Prepaid insurance | 1,950 | |
| 167 | Equipment | 48,000 | |
| 168 | Accumulated depreciation—Equipment | | $ 4,000 |
| 201 | Accounts payable | | 12,000 |
| 210 | Wages payable | | 500 |
| 307 | Common stock | | 10,000 |
| 318 | Retained earnings | | 30,000 |
| 319 | Dividends | 15,000 | |
| 401 | Repair fees earned | | 77,750 |
| 612 | Depreciation expense—Equipment | 4,000 | |
| 623 | Wages expense | 36,500 | |
| 637 | Insurance expense | 700 | |
| 640 | Rent expense | 9,600 | |
| 650 | Office supplies expense | 2,600 | |
| 690 | Utilities expense | 1,700 | |
| | Totals | $134,250 | $134,250 |

**Required**

**1.** Prepare an income statement and a statement of retained earnings for the year 2005, and a classified balance sheet at December 31, 2005.

**2.** Enter the adjusted trial balance in the first two columns of a six-column table. Use columns three and four for closing entry information and the last two columns for a post-closing trial balance. Insert an Income Summary account as the last item in the trial balance.

**3.** Enter closing entry information in the six-column table and prepare journal entries for them.

*Analysis Component*

**4.** Assume for this part only that:

**a.** None of the $700 insurance expense had expired during the year. Instead, assume it is a prepayment of the next period's insurance protection.

**b.** There are no earned and unpaid wages at the end of the year. (*Hint:* Reverse the $500 wages payable accrual.)

Describe the financial statement changes that would result from these two assumptions.

## Problem 3-4A

Applying the accounting cycle

C4 C5 P4 P5

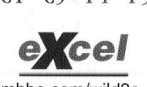

mhhe.com/wild3e

On April 1, 2005, Jennifer Stafford created a new travel agency, See-It-Now Travel. The following transactions occurred during the company's first month:

April 1 Stafford invested $20,000 cash and computer equipment worth $40,000 in the business in exchange for its common stock.

2 Rented furnished office space by paying $1,700 cash for the first month's (April) rent.

3 Purchased $1,100 of office supplies for cash.

10 Paid $3,600 cash for the premium on a 12-month insurance policy. Coverage begins on April 11.

14 Paid $1,800 cash for two weeks' salaries earned by employees.

24 Collected $7,900 cash on commissions from airlines on tickets obtained for customers.

28 Paid another $1,800 cash for two weeks' salaries earned by employees.

29 Paid $250 cash for minor repairs to the company's computer.

30 Paid $650 cash for this month's telephone bill.

30 Paid $1,500 cash for dividends.

The company's chart of accounts follows:

| | | | |
|---|---|---|---|
| 101 | Cash | 405 | Commissions Earned |
| 106 | Accounts Receivable | 612 | Depreciation Expense—Computer Equip. |
| 124 | Office Supplies | 622 | Salaries Expense |
| 128 | Prepaid Insurance | 637 | Insurance Expense |
| 167 | Computer Equipment | 640 | Rent Expense |
| 168 | Accumulated Depreciation—Computer Equip. | 650 | Office Supplies Expense |
| 209 | Salaries Payable | 684 | Repairs Expense |
| 307 | Common Stock | 688 | Telephone Expense |
| 318 | Retained Earnings | 901 | Income Summary |
| 319 | Dividends | | |

**Required**

**1.** Use the balance column format to set up each ledger account listed in its chart of accounts.

**2.** Prepare journal entries to record the transactions for April and post them to the ledger accounts. The company records prepaid and unearned items in balance sheet accounts.

**3.** Prepare an unadjusted trial balance as of April 30.

**4.** Use the following information to journalize and post adjusting entries for the month:

  **a.** Two-thirds of one month's insurance coverage has expired.

  **b.** At the end of the month, $700 of office supplies are still available.

  **c.** This month's depreciation on the computer equipment is $600.

  **d.** Employees earned $320 of unpaid and unrecorded salaries as of month-end.

  **e.** The company earned $1,650 of commissions that are not yet billed at month-end.

**5.** Prepare the income statement and the statement of retained earnings for the month of April and the balance sheet at April 30, 2005.

**6.** Prepare journal entries to close the temporary accounts and post these entries to the ledger.

**7.** Prepare a post-closing trial balance.

**Check** (3) Unadj. trial balance totals, $67,900

(4a) Dr. Insurance Expense, $200

(5) Net income, $1,830; Retained Earnings (ending), $330; Total assets, $60,650

(7) P-C trial balance totals, $61,250

---

In the blank space beside each numbered balance sheet item, enter the letter of its balance sheet classification. If the item should not appear on the balance sheet, enter a Z in the blank.

**Problem 3-5A**
Determining balance sheet classifications

C6

**A.** Current assets    **D.** Intangible assets    **F.** Long-term liabilities

**B.** Long-term investments    **E.** Current liabilities    **G.** Equity

**C.** Plant assets

_____ **1.** Accumulated depreciation—Trucks

_____ **2.** Cash

_____ **3.** Buildings

_____ **4.** Store supplies

_____ **5.** Office equipment

_____ **6.** Land (used in operations)

_____ **7.** Repairs expense

_____ **8.** Office supplies

_____ **9.** Current portion of long-term note payable

_____ **10.** Long-term investment in stock

_____ **11.** Depreciation expense—Building

_____ **12.** Prepaid rent

_____ **13.** Interest receivable

_____ **14.** Taxes payable

_____ **15.** Automobiles

_____ **16.** Notes payable (due in 3 years)

_____ **17.** Accounts payable

_____ **18.** Prepaid insurance

_____ **19.** Common stock

_____ **20.** Unearned services revenue

## Problem 3-6A[A]

Recording prepaid expenses and unearned revenues

P1   P6

Quisp Co. had the following transactions in the last two months of its year ended December 31:

Nov.   1   Paid $1,500 cash for future newspaper advertising.
       1   Paid $2,160 cash for 12 months of insurance through October 31 of the next year.
      30   Received $3,300 cash for future services to be provided to a customer.
Dec.   1   Paid $2,700 cash for a consultant's services to be received over the next three months.
      15   Received $7,650 cash for future services to be provided to a customer.
      31   Of the advertising paid for on November 1, $900 worth is not yet used.
      31   A portion of the insurance paid for on November 1 has expired. No adjustment was made in November to Prepaid Insurance.
      31   Services worth $1,200 are not yet provided to the customer who paid on November 30.
      31   One-third of the consulting services paid for on December 1 have been received.
      31   The company has performed $3,000 of services that the customer paid for on December 15.

### Required

**1.** Prepare entries for these transactions under the method that records prepaid expenses as assets and records unearned revenues as liabilities. Also prepare adjusting entries at the end of the year.

**2.** Prepare entries for these transactions under the method that records prepaid expenses as expenses and records unearned revenues as revenues. Also prepare adjusting entries at the end of the year.

### Analysis Component

**3.** Explain why the alternative sets of entries in requirements 1 and 2 do not result in different financial statement amounts.

## Problem 3-7A[B]

Preparing a work sheet, adjusting and closing entries, and financial statements

C6   P4   P7

The following unadjusted trial balance is for Adams Construction Co. as of the end of its 2005 fiscal year. The owner invested $25,000 cash in the company in exchange for stock during the 2005 fiscal year.

| File   Edit   View   Insert   Format   Tools   Data   Window   Help | | |
|---|---|---|
| **ADAMS CONSTRUCTION CO.** | | |
| **Unadjusted Trial Balance** | | |
| **June 30, 2005** | | |
| **No.     Account Title** | **Debit** | **Credit** |
| 101   Cash | $ 17,500 | |
| 126   Supplies | 8,900 | |
| 128   Prepaid insurance | 6,200 | |
| 167   Equipment | 131,000 | |
| 168   Accumulated depreciation—Equipment | | $ 25,250 |
| 201   Accounts payable | | 5,800 |
| 203   Interest payable | | 0 |
| 208   Rent payable | | 0 |
| 210   Wages payable | | 0 |
| 213   Property taxes payable | | 0 |
| 251   Long-term notes payable | | 24,000 |
| 307   Common stock | | 40,000 |
| 318   Retained earnings | | 37,660 |
| 319   Dividends | 30,000 | |
| 401   Construction fees earned | | 134,000 |
| 612   Depreciation expense—Equipment | 0 | |
| 623   Wages expense | 45,860 | |
| 633   Interest expense | 2,640 | |
| 637   Insurance expense | 0 | |
| 640   Rent expense | 13,200 | |
| 652   Supplies expense | 0 | |
| 683   Property taxes expense | 4,600 | |
| 684   Repairs expense | 2,810 | |
| 690   Utilities expense | 4,000 | |
| Totals | $266,710 | $266,710 |

**Required**

**1.** Prepare a 10-column work sheet for fiscal year 2005, starting with the unadjusted trial balance and including adjustments based on these additional facts:

    **a.** The supplies available at the end of fiscal year 2005 had a cost of $3,200.

    **b.** The cost of expired insurance for the fiscal year is $3,900.

    **c.** Annual depreciation on equipment is $8,500.

    **d.** The June utilities expense of $550 is not included in the unadjusted trial balance because the bill arrived after the trial balance was prepared. The $550 amount owed needs to be recorded.

    **e.** The company's employees have earned $1,600 of accrued wages at fiscal year-end.

    **f.** The rent expense incurred and not yet paid or recorded at fiscal year-end is $200.

    **g.** Additional property taxes of $900 have been assessed for this fiscal year but have not been paid or recorded in the accounts.

    **h.** The long-term note payable bears interest at 12% per year. The unadjusted Interest Expense account equals the amount paid for the first 11 months of the 2005 fiscal year. The $240 accrued interest for June has not yet been paid or recorded. (Note that the company is required to make a $5,000 payment toward the note payable during the 2006 fiscal year.)

**2.** Use the work sheet to enter the adjusting and closing entries; then journalize them.

**3.** Prepare the income statement and the statement of retained earnings for the year ended June 30 and the classified balance sheet at June 30, 2005.

**Check**   (3) Total assets, $120,250; current liabilities, $14,290; Net income, $39,300

*Analysis Component*

**4.** Analyze the following separate errors and describe how each would affect the 10-column work sheet. Explain whether the error is likely to be discovered in completing the work sheet and, if not, the effect of the error on the financial statements.

    **a.** Assume that the adjustment for supplies used consisted of a credit to Supplies for $3,200 and a debit for $3,200 to Supplies Expense.

    **b.** When the adjusted trial balance in the work sheet is completed, the $17,500 Cash balance is incorrectly entered in the Credit column.

---

Nomo Co. follows the practice of recording prepaid expenses and unearned revenues in balance sheet accounts. Nomo's annual accounting period ends on October 31, 2005. The following information concerns the adjusting entries that need to be recorded as of that date:

**a.** The Office Supplies account started the fiscal year with a $500 balance. During the fiscal year, the company purchased supplies for $3,650, which was added to the Office Supplies account. The supplies available at October 31, 2005, totaled $700.

**b.** An analysis of the company's insurance policies provided these facts:

**PROBLEM SET B**

**Problem 3-1B**
Preparing adjusting and subsequent journal entries

C1  A1  P1

| Policy | Date of Purchase | Months of Coverage | Cost |
|--------|------------------|--------------------|------|
| A | April 1, 2004 | 24 | $3,000 |
| B | April 1, 2005 | 36 | 3,600 |
| C | August 1, 2005 | 12 | 660 |

The total premium for each policy was paid in full (for all months) at the purchase date, and the Prepaid Insurance account was debited for the full cost. (Note that year-end adjusting entries for Prepaid Insurance were properly recorded in all prior fiscal years.)

**c.** The company has four employees, who earn a total of $800 for each workday. They are paid each Monday for their work in the five-day workweek ending on the previous Friday. Assume that October 31, 2005, is a Monday, and all five employees worked the first day of that week. They will be paid salaries for five full days on Monday, November 7, 2005.

**d.** The company purchased a building on November 1, 2004, that cost $155,000 and is expected to have a $20,000 salvage value at the end of its predicted 25-year life.

**e.** Since the company does not occupy the entire building it owns, it rented space to a tenant at $600 per month, starting on September 1, 2005. The rent was paid on time on September 1, and the amount received was credited to the Rent Earned account. However, the October rent has not been paid. The company has worked out an agreement with the tenant, who has promised to pay both October and November rent in full on November 15. The tenant has agreed not to fall behind again.

**f.** On September 1, the company rented space to another tenant for $525 per month. The tenant paid five months' rent in advance on that date. The payment was recorded with a credit to the Unearned Rent account.

### Required

**1.** Use the information to prepare adjusting entries as of October 31, 2005.

**2.** Prepare journal entries to record the first subsequent cash transaction in 2006 for parts *c* and *e*.

---

**Problem 3-2B**

Preparing adjusting entries, adjusted trial balance, and financial statements

A1  P1  P2  P3

Following is the unadjusted trial balance for Alcorn Institute as of December 31, 2005, which initially records prepaid expenses and unearned revenues in balance sheet accounts. The Institute provides one-on-one training to individuals who pay tuition directly to the business and offers extension training to groups in off-site locations. Shown after the trial balance are items *a* through *h* that require adjusting entries as of December 31, 2005.

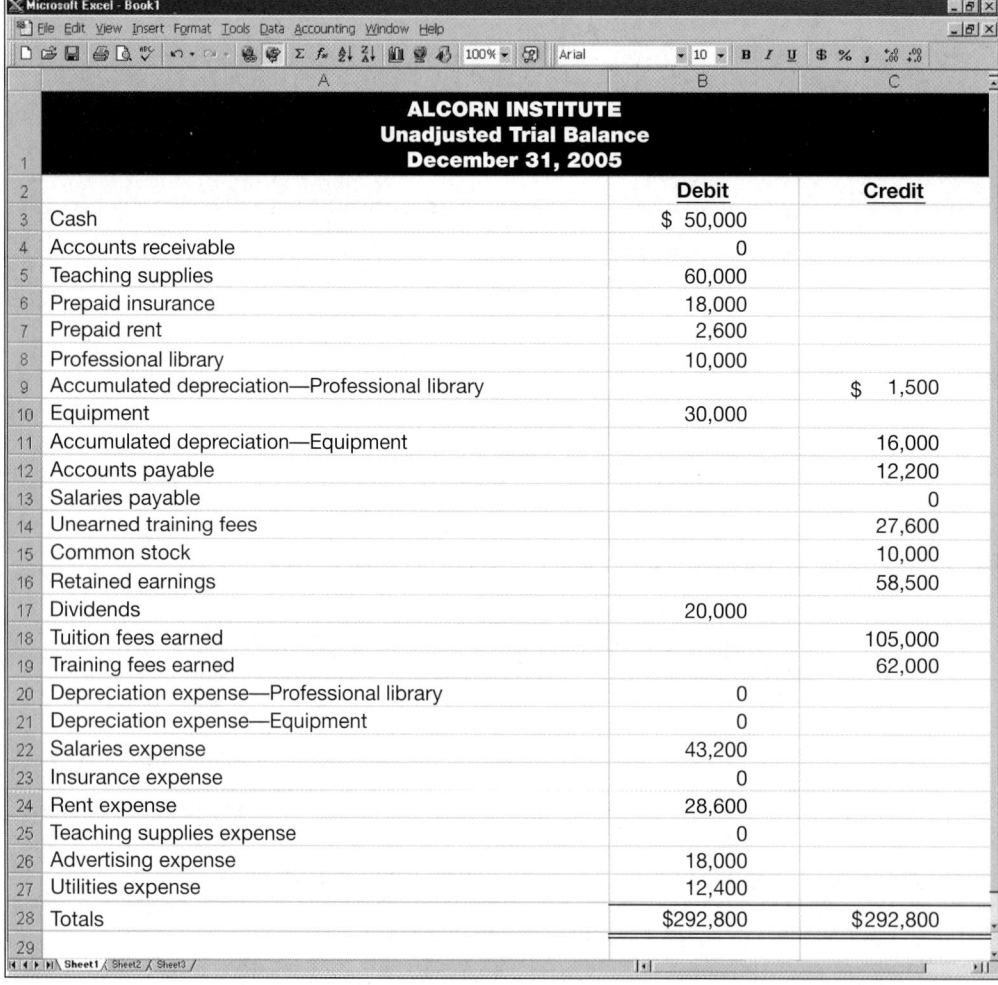

| ALCORN INSTITUTE Unadjusted Trial Balance December 31, 2005 | Debit | Credit |
|---|---|---|
| Cash | $ 50,000 | |
| Accounts receivable | 0 | |
| Teaching supplies | 60,000 | |
| Prepaid insurance | 18,000 | |
| Prepaid rent | 2,600 | |
| Professional library | 10,000 | |
| Accumulated depreciation—Professional library | | $ 1,500 |
| Equipment | 30,000 | |
| Accumulated depreciation—Equipment | | 16,000 |
| Accounts payable | | 12,200 |
| Salaries payable | | 0 |
| Unearned training fees | | 27,600 |
| Common stock | | 10,000 |
| Retained earnings | | 58,500 |
| Dividends | 20,000 | |
| Tuition fees earned | | 105,000 |
| Training fees earned | | 62,000 |
| Depreciation expense—Professional library | 0 | |
| Depreciation expense—Equipment | 0 | |
| Salaries expense | 43,200 | |
| Insurance expense | 0 | |
| Rent expense | 28,600 | |
| Teaching supplies expense | 0 | |
| Advertising expense | 18,000 | |
| Utilities expense | 12,400 | |
| Totals | $292,800 | $292,800 |

### Additional Information Items

**a.** An analysis of the Institute's insurance policies shows that $6,400 of coverage has expired.

**b.** An inventory count shows that teaching supplies costing $2,500 are available at year-end 2005.

**c.** Annual depreciation on the equipment is $4,000.

**d.** Annual depreciation on the professional library is $2,000.

**e.** On November 1, the Institute agreed to do a special four-month course (starting immediately) for a client. The contract calls for a $4,600 monthly fee, and the client paid the first two months' fees in advance. When the cash was received, the Unearned Training Fees account was credited. The last two months' fees will be recorded when collected in 2006.

**f.** On October 15, the Institute agreed to teach a four-month class (beginning immediately) to an individual for $2,200 tuition per month payable at the end of the class. The class started on October 15, but no payment has yet been received.

**g.** The Institute's only employee is paid weekly. As of the end of the year, three days' wages have accrued at the rate of $180 per day.

**h.** The balance in the Prepaid Rent account represents rent for December.

**Required**

**1.** Prepare T-accounts (representing the ledger) with balances from the unadjusted trial balance.

**2.** Prepare the necessary adjusting journal entries for items *a* through *h*, and post them to the T-accounts. Assume that adjusting entries are made only at year-end.

**3.** Update balances in the T-accounts for the adjusting entries and prepare an adjusted trial balance.

**4.** Prepare Alcorn Institute's income statement and statement of retained earnings for the year 2005, and prepare its balance sheet as of December 31, 2005.

**Check** (2e) Cr. Training Fees Earned, $9,200; (2f) Cr. Tuition Fees Earned, $5,500; (3) Adj. trial balance totals, $304,840; (4) Net income, $6,460; Ending Retained Earnings, $44,960

---

Heel-To-Toe-Shoes' adjusted trial balance on December 31, 2005, follows:

**Problem 3-3B**

Preparing trial balances, closing entries, and financial statements

C6  P4  P5

| | HEEL-TO-TOE SHOES<br>Adjusted Trial Balance<br>December 31, 2005 | | |
|---|---|---|---|
| **No.** | **Account Title** | **Debit** | **Credit** |
| 101 | Cash ................................ | $ 13,450 | |
| 125 | Store supplies ......................... | 4,140 | |
| 128 | Prepaid insurance ..................... | 2,200 | |
| 167 | Equipment .......................... | 33,000 | |
| 168 | Accumulated depreciation—Equipment ....... | | $ 9,000 |
| 201 | Accounts payable ...................... | | 1,000 |
| 210 | Wages payable ........................ | | 3,200 |
| 307 | Common stock ......................... | | 10,000 |
| 318 | Retained earnings ...................... | | 21,650 |
| 319 | Dividends ............................ | 16,000 | |
| 401 | Repair fees earned ..................... | | 62,000 |
| 612 | Depreciation expense—Equipment ......... | 3,000 | |
| 623 | Wages expense ........................ | 28,400 | |
| 637 | Insurance expense ...................... | 1,100 | |
| 640 | Rent expense ......................... | 2,400 | |
| 651 | Store supplies expense .................. | 1,300 | |
| 690 | Utilities expense ....................... | 1,860 | |
| | Totals ............................... | $106,850 | $106,850 |

**Required**

**1.** Prepare an income statement and a statement of retained earnings for the year 2005, and a classified balance sheet at December 31, 2005.

**2.** Enter the adjusted trial balance in the first two columns of a six-column table. Use the middle two columns for closing entry information and the last two columns for a post-closing trial balance. Insert an Income Summary account as the last item in the trial balance.

**3.** Enter closing entry information in the six-column table and prepare journal entries for them.

**Check** (1) Ending Retained Earnings, $29,590

(2) P-C trial balance totals, $52,790

*Analysis Component*

**4.** Assume for this part only that:

    **a.** None of the $1,100 insurance expense had expired during the year. Instead, assume it is a prepayment of the next period's insurance protection.

    **b.** There are no earned and unpaid wages at the end of the year. (*Hint:* Reverse the $3,200 wages payable accrual.)

    Describe the financial statement changes that would result from these two assumptions.

---

**Problem 3-4B**

Applying the accounting cycle

C4  C5  P4  P5

On July 1, 2005, Lucinda Fogle created a new self-storage business, KeepSafe Co. The following transactions occurred during the company's first month:

July  1  Fogle invested $20,000 cash and buildings worth $120,000 in the business in exchange for its common stock.

     2  Rented equipment by paying $1,800 cash for the first month's (July) rent.

     5  Purchased $2,300 of office supplies for cash.

   10  Paid $5,400 cash for the premium on a 12-month insurance policy. Coverage begins on July 11.

   14  Paid an employee $900 cash for two weeks' salary earned.

   24  Collected $8,800 cash for storage fees from customers.

   28  Paid another $900 cash for two weeks' salary earned by an employee.

   29  Paid $850 cash for minor repairs to a leaking roof.

   30  Paid $300 cash for this month's telephone bill.

   31  Paid $1,600 cash for dividends.

The company's chart of accounts follows:

| | | | | |
|---|---|---|---|---|
| 101 | Cash | | 401 | Storage Fees Earned |
| 106 | Accounts Receivable | | 606 | Depreciation Expense—Buildings |
| 124 | Office Supplies | | 622 | Salaries Expense |
| 128 | Prepaid Insurance | | 637 | Insurance Expense |
| 173 | Buildings | | 640 | Rent Expense |
| 174 | Accumulated Depreciation—Buildings | | 650 | Office Supplies Expense |
| 209 | Salaries Payable | | 684 | Repairs Expense |
| 307 | Common Stock | | 688 | Telephone Expense |
| 318 | Retained Earnings | | 901 | Income Summary |
| 319 | Dividends | | | |

**Required**

**1.** Use the balance column format to set up each ledger account listed in its chart of accounts.

**2.** Prepare journal entries to record the transactions for July and post them to the ledger accounts. Record prepaid and unearned items in balance sheet accounts.

**Check** (3) Unadj. trial balance totals, $148,800

**3.** Prepare an unadjusted trial balance as of July 31.

**4.** Use the following information to journalize and post adjusting entries for the month:

    **a.** Two-thirds of one month's insurance coverage has expired.

(4a) Dr. Insurance Expense, $300

    **b.** At the end of the month, $1,550 of office supplies are still available.

    **c.** This month's depreciation on the buildings is $1,200.

    **d.** An employee earned $180 of unpaid and unrecorded salary as of month-end.

    **e.** The company earned $950 of storage fees that are not yet billed at month-end.

(5) Net income, $2,570; Retained Earnings (ending), $970; Total assets, $141,150

**5.** Prepare the income statement and the statement of retained earnings for the month of July and the balance sheet at July 31, 2005.

**6.** Prepare journal entries to close the temporary accounts and post these entries to the ledger.

(7) P-C trial balance totals, $142,350

**7.** Prepare a post-closing trial balance.

In the blank space beside each numbered balance sheet item, enter the letter of its balance sheet classification. If the item should not appear on the balance sheet, enter a Z in the blank.

**Problem 3-5B**
Determining balance sheet classifications

C6

**A.** Current assets
**B.** Long-term investments
**C.** Plant assets
**D.** Intangible assets

**E.** Current liabilities
**F.** Long-term liabilities
**G.** Equity

_____  **1.** Machinery
_____  **2.** Prepaid insurance
_____  **3.** Current portion of long term note payable
_____  **4.** Interest receivable
_____  **5.** Rent receivable
_____  **6.** Land (used in operations)
_____  **7.** Copyrights
_____  **8.** Rent revenue
_____  **9.** Depreciation expense—Trucks
_____  **10.** Long-term investment in stock
_____  **11.** Office supplies

_____  **12.** Interest payable
_____  **13.** Retained Earnings
_____  **14.** Notes receivable (due in 120 days)
_____  **15.** Accumulated depreciation— Trucks
_____  **16.** Salaries payable
_____  **17.** Commissions earned
_____  **18.** Interest payable
_____  **19.** Office equipment
_____  **20.** Notes payable (due in 5 years)

---

Quake Co. had the following transactions in the last two months of its fiscal year ended May 31:

**Problem 3-6B**<sup>A</sup>
Recording prepaid expenses and unearned revenues

P6  P1

Apr.  1   Paid $3,450 cash for future consulting services.
      1   Paid $2,700 cash for 12 months of insurance through March 31 of the next year.
      30  Received $7,500 cash for future services to be provided to a customer.
May   1   Paid $3,450 cash for future newspaper advertising.
      23  Received $9,450 cash for future services to be provided to a customer.
      31  Of the consulting services paid for on April 1, $1,500 worth has been received.
      31  A portion of the insurance paid for on April 1 has expired. No adjustment was made in April to Prepaid Insurance.
      31  Services worth $3,600 are not yet provided to the customer who paid on April 30.
      31  Of the advertising paid for on May 1, $1,050 worth is not yet used.
      31  The company has performed $4,500 of services that the customer paid for on May 23.

**Required**

**1.** Prepare entries for these transactions under the method that records prepaid expenses and unearned revenues in balance sheet accounts. Also prepare adjusting entries at the end of the year.

**2.** Prepare entries for these transactions under the method that records prepaid expenses and unearned revenues in income statement accounts. Also prepare adjusting entries at the end of the year.

*Analysis Component*

**3.** Explain why the alternative sets of entries in parts 1 and 2 do not result in different financial statement amounts.

---

The following unadjusted trial balance is for Crush Demolition Company as of the end of its April 30, 2005, fiscal year. The owner invested $30,000 cash in the company in exchange for stock during the 2005 fiscal year.

**Problem 3-7B**
Preparing a work sheet, adjusting and closing entries, and financial statements

C6  P4  P7

The following additional facts are collected for use in making adjusting entries prior to preparing financial statements for the company's first three months:

**a.** The December 31 inventory count of computer supplies shows $580 still available.

**b.** Three months have expired since the 12-month insurance premium was paid in advance.

**c.** As of December 31, Sherry Adams has not been paid for four days of work at $125 per day.

**d.** The company's computer is expected to have a four-year life with no salvage value.

**e.** The office equipment is expected to have a five-year life with no salvage value.

**f.** Prepaid rent for three of the four months has expired.

### Required

**1.** Prepare journal entries to record each of the December transactions and events for Success Systems. Post these entries to the accounts in the ledger.

**2.** Prepare adjusting entries to reflect *a* through *f.* Post these entries to the accounts in the ledger.

**Check** (3) Adjusted trial balance totals, $119,034

**3.** Prepare an adjusted trial balance as of December 31, 2004.

(4) Total assets, $93,248

**4.** Prepare an income statement and a statement of retained earnings for the three months ended December 31, 2004. Prepare a balance sheet as of December 31, 2004.

(6) Post-closing trial balance totals, $94,898

**5.** Record and post the necessary closing entries for Success Systems.

**6.** Prepare a post-closing trial balance as of December 31, 2004.

# BEYOND THE NUMBERS

## REPORTING IN ACTION

C1 C2 C4 A1 A2 P4

**BTN 3-1**   Refer to **Krispy Kreme**'s financial statements in Appendix A to answer the following:

**1.** Identify and write down the revenue recognition principle as explained in the chapter.

**2.** Research Krispy Kreme's footnotes to discover how it applies the revenue recognition principle. Report what you discover.

**3.** What is Krispy Kreme's profit margin for 2003 and for 2002?

**4.** For the fiscal year ended February 2, 2003, what amount will be credited to Income Summary to summarize its revenues earned?

**5.** For the fiscal year ended February 2, 2003, what amount will be debited to Income Summary to summarize its expenses incurred?

**6.** For the fiscal year ended February 2, 2003, what will be the balance of its Income Summary account before it is closed?

### Roll On

**7.** Access Krispy Kreme's annual report (10-K) for fiscal years ending after February 2, 2003, at its Website (**KrispyKreme.com**) or the SEC's EDGAR database (**www.sec.gov**). Compare the February 2, 2003, fiscal year profit margin to any subsequent year's profit margin that you are able to calculate.

## COMPARATIVE ANALYSIS

A2 A3

**BTN 3-2**   Key figures for the recent two years of both **Krispy Kreme** and **Tastykake** follow:

| Key Figures | Krispy Kreme | | Tastykake | |
|---|---|---|---|---|
| ($ thousands) | Current Year | Prior Year | Current Year | Prior Year |
| Net income ........... | $ 33,478 | $ 26,378 | $ 2,000* | $ 8,048 |
| Net sales ............. | 491,549 | 394,354 | 162,263 | 166,245 |
| Current assets ........ | 141,128 | 101,769 | 36,095 | 35,169 |
| Current liabilities ....... | 59,687 | 52,533 | 19,307 | 16,885 |

\* Net income without restructuring charges.

**Required**

1. Compute profit margins for (*a*) Krispy Kreme and (*b*) Tastykake for the two years of data shown.
2. Which company is more successful on the basis of profit margin? Explain.
3. Compute the current ratio for both years and both companies.
4. Which has the better ability to pay short-term obligations according to the current ratio?
5. Analyze and comment on each company's current ratios for the past two years.
6. How do Krispy Kreme's and Tastykake's current ratios compare to their industry average ratio of about 1.0 to 1.2?

---

**BTN 3-3**   On January 20, 2005, Jennifer Nelson, the accountant for Travon Enterprises, is feeling pressure to complete the annual financial statements. The company president has said he needs up-to-date financial statements to share with the bank on January 21 at a dinner meeting that has been called to discuss Travon's obtaining loan financing for a special building project. Jennifer knows that she will not be able to gather all the needed information in the next 24 hours to prepare the entire set of adjusting entries that must be posted before the financial statements accurately portray the company's performance and financial position for the fiscal period ended December 31, 2004. Jennifer ultimately decides to estimate several expense accruals at the last minute. When deciding on estimates for the expenses, she uses low estimates because she does not want to make the financial statements look worse than they are. Jennifer finishes the financial statements before the deadline and gives them to the president without mentioning that several accounts use estimated balances.

**ETHICS CHALLENGE**

C5

**Required**

1. Identify several courses of action that Jennifer could have taken instead of the one she took.
2. If you were in Jennifer's situation, what would you have done? Briefly justify your response.

---

**BTN 3-4**   Assume that one of your classmates states that a company's books should be ongoing and therefore not closed until that business is terminated: Write a one-half page memo to this classmate explaining the concept of the closing process by drawing analogies between (1) a scoreboard for an athletic event and the revenue and expense accounts of a business or (2) a sports team's record book and the capital account. (*Hint:* Think about what would happen if the scoreboard is not cleared before the start of a new game.)

**COMMUNICATING IN PRACTICE**

C4   P4

---

**BTN 3-5**   Access the **Cannondale** promotional Website (**Cannondale.com**).

1. What is the primary product that Cannondale sells?
2. Review its form 10-K. You can access this from the EDGAR system (**www.sec.gov**). You must scroll down the form to find the financial statements.
3. What is Cannondale's fiscal year-end?
4. What are Cannondale's net sales for the annual period ended June 29, 2002?
5. What is Cannondale's net income for the annual period ended June 29, 2002?
6. Compute Cannondale's profit margin ratio for the annual period ended June 29, 2002.
7. Do you think its decision to use a year-end of late June or early July relates to its natural business year?

**TAKING IT TO THE NET**

C1   A2

mhhe.com/wild3e

**BTN 3-6**   Access **Motley Fool**'s discussion of the current ratio at Fool.com/School/Valuation/CurrentAndQuickRatio.htm. (Note that if the page changed, search the site for the *current ratio*.)

A3

**Required**

1. What level for the current ratio is generally regarded as sufficient to meet near-term operating needs?
2. Once you have calculated the current ratio for a company, what should you compare it against?
3. What are the implications for a company that has a current ratio that is too high?

## TEAMWORK IN ACTION

C3   A1   P1

**BTN 3-7**   Four types of adjustments are described in the chapter: (1) prepaid expenses, (2) unearned revenues, (3) accrued expenses, and (4) accrued revenues.

**Required**

1. Form *learning teams* of four (or more) members. Each team member must select one of the four adjustments as an area of expertise (each team must have at least one expert in each area).

2. Form *expert teams* from the individuals who have selected the same area of expertise. Expert teams are to discuss and write a report that each expert will present to his or her learning team addressing the following:

   a. Description of the adjustment and why it's necessary.

   b. Example of a transaction or event, with dates and amounts, that requires adjustment.

   c. Adjusting entry(ies) for the example in requirement *b*.

   d. Status of the affected account(s) before and after the adjustment in requirement *c*.

   e. Effects on financial statements of not making the adjustment.

3. Each expert should return to his or her learning team. In rotation, each member should present his or her expert team's report to the learning team. Team discussion is encouraged.

## BUSINESS WEEK ACTIVITY

C2

**BTN 3-8**   Read the article "It's Like When Someone Robs a Bank," in the August 19, 2002, issue of *Business Week*. (Access the book's Website for a free link.)

**Required**

1. Describe the type of overall accounting reform that FASB Chairman Herz favors.

2. What does Herz assert as being at the core of most recent scandals in corporate America?

3. What is meant by "principles-based accounting"?

4. Why is "principles-based accounting" controversial?

C6   A3

**BTN 3-9**   Read the article "Weighing the Balance Sheet" in the April 1, 2002, issue of *Business Week*.

**Required**

1. This article explains how to evaluate whether a company has a financially strong balance sheet. What does the author of this article look for when evaluating the debt level carried by companies?

2. The article reports a table showing 12 companies that passed the test for strong balance sheets. Identify the range of the current ratio for these 12 companies and name the company with the highest and the company with the lowest current ratios.

3. What is the range of the return on assets ratio for the 12 companies with attractive numbers according to the article? Identify the company with highest and the company with the lowest return on assets.

4. Some investors will not buy tobacco or asbestos-related companies even if they have a very strong balance sheet. What risk factor are these investors concerned with so that it is more important for these companies than the level of debt on their balance sheets?

mhhe.com/wild3e

## HITTING THE ROAD

C5

**BTN 3-10**   Select a company that you can visit in person or interview on the telephone. Call ahead to the company to arrange a time when you can interview an employee (preferably an accountant) who helps prepare the annual financial statements. Inquire about the following aspects of its *accounting cycle:*

1. Does it prepare interim financial statements? What time period(s) is used for interim statements?

2. Does the company use the cash or accrual basis of accounting?

3. Does the company use a work sheet in preparing financial statements? Why or why not?

4. Does the company use a spreadsheet program? If so, which software program is used?

5. How long does it take after the end of its reporting period to complete annual statements?

**BTN 3-11**   Review this chapter's opening feature involving Andy Wolf and his startup company, Premier Snowskates.

**ENTREPRENEURIAL DECISION**

A3   C6   P4

**Required**

1. What is a conservative estimate for the units of snowskates that will be sold if annual sales are $3 million and Andy Wolf meets his targeted retail price?
2. What ratios studied in Chapters 1 through 3 do you recommend that Andy use to monitor the financial performance of his company?
3. What portions of the classified balance sheet do you believe are most relevant in assisting Andy in discovering what obligations are due and when?
4. What objectives are met when Andy applies closing procedures each fiscal year?

**BTN 3-12**   Grupo Bimbo is a major producer and distributor of bakery products. Access its 2002 annual financial report at the company's Website (**GrupoBimbo.com**) to answer the following questions.

**GLOBAL DECISION**

A2   C1   C2

**Required**

1. Identify and report the revenue recognition policy applied by Grupo Bimbo?
2. What are the five types of assets depreciated by Grupo Bimbo? Which two assets classified as property, plant, and equipment are not depreciated?
3. What is Grupo Bimbo's profit margin for both fiscal years ended 2002 and 2001?
4. Compute the current ratio for Grupo Bimbo for both the current and prior years.
5. Comment on the level and the change in the current ratios computed in part 1.

*"I felt we should go into something that we had some connection to"*—Dwayne Lewis (standing; Michael Cherry sitting)

# 4 Reporting and Analyzing Merchandising Operations

## A Look Back

Chapter 3 focused on the final steps of the accounting process. We explained the importance of proper revenue and expense recognition and described the adjusting and closing processes. We also showed how to prepare and interpret financial statements.

## A Look at This Chapter

This chapter emphasizes merchandising activities. We explain how reporting merchandising activities differs from reporting service activities. We also analyze and record merchandise purchases and sales transactions and explain the adjustments and closing process for merchandisers.

## A Look Ahead

Chapter 5 extends our analysis of merchandising activities and focuses on the valuation of inventory. Topics include the items in inventory, costs assigned, costing methods used, and inventory estimation techniques.

# CAP

## Conceptual

**C1** Describe merchandising activities and identify income components for a merchandising company. *(p. 152)*

**C2** Identify and explain the inventory asset of a merchandising company. *(p. 153)*

**C3** Describe both perpetual and periodic inventory systems. *(p. 153)*

**C4** Analyze and interpret cost flows and operating activities of a merchandising company. *(p. 161)*

## Analytical

**A1** Compute the acid-test ratio and explain its use to assess liquidity. *(p. 167)*

**A2** Compute the gross margin ratio and explain its use to assess profitability. *(p. 167)*

## Procedural

**P1** Analyze and record transactions for merchandise purchases using a perpetual system. *(p. 154)*

**P2** Analyze and record transactions for merchandise sales using a perpetual system. *(p. 159)*

**P3** Prepare adjustments and close accounts for a merchandising company. *(p. 162)*

**P4** Define and prepare multiple-step and single-step income statements. *(p. 164)*

## Decision Feature

# Dada, Dada, Dada . . .

EL SEGUNDO, CA—Dwayne Lewis and Michael Cherry had a dream—a dream to own and run a company. With one lone product (a five-panel polo hat) and $1,000 in pooled paychecks, they launched **Damani Dada (DamaniDada.com).** The two dreamed that Damani Dada would bring an ultra-hip style to the urban fashion scene. A mere seven years after its launch, Dada projects annual sales of more than $50 million.

The early days, however, were far from easy as Lewis and Cherry struggled alone against long odds. "It was very tricky to try and learn the business without a mentor," recalls Lewis. "We always struggled with the task of maintaining a strong financial backing, and we had to learn a lot by making mistakes." Among those struggles was implementing and learning a merchandising system—one that could capture and communicate the costs and sales information so desperately needed by the young entrepreneurs.

A crucial part of their success was tracking merchandising activities. This was necessary for setting prices and making policies for everything from discounts and allowances to returns on both sales and purchases. Also, use of a perpetual inventory system enabled them to stock the right type and amount of merchandise and to avoid the costs of out-of-stock and excess inventory. This chapter describes how the accounting system captures merchandising information for these and other business decisions. It also introduces analysis tools for assessing the financial condition and performance of merchandisers.

Damani Dada successfully weathered the storm and now offers a full line of both men's and women's apparel and footwear. NBA star Chris Webber's chrome Dada shoes were the talk of the 2003 All-Star Game. But it's still a battle. "Business is war," says Lewis. "You have to be mentally strong, willing to sacrifice, and willing to accept delayed gratification."

[Sources: *Damani Dada Website,* January 2004; *Entrepreneur,* November 2000; *ESPN Sports Business,* February 2003.]

Merchandising activities are a major part of modern business. Consumers expect a wealth of products, discount prices, inventory on demand, and high quality. This chapter introduces the business and accounting practices used by companies engaged in merchandising activities. We show how financial statements reflect these merchandising activities and explain the new financial statement items created by merchandising activities. We also analyze and record merchandise purchases and sales, and explain the adjustments and the closing process for merchandising companies.

## Merchandising Activities

**C1**  Describe merchandising activities and identify income components for a merchandising company.

**Point:** Fleming, SuperValu, and SYSCO are wholesalers. Gap, Oakley, and Wal-Mart are retailers.

Previous chapters emphasized the accounting and reporting activities of service companies. A merchandising company's activities differ from those of a service company. **Merchandise** consists of products, also called *goods,* that a company acquires to resell to customers. A **merchandiser** earns net income by buying and selling merchandise. Merchandisers are often identified as either wholesalers or retailers. A **wholesaler** is an *intermediary* that buys products from manufacturers or other wholesalers and sells them to retailers or other wholesalers. A **retailer** is an intermediary that buys products from manufacturers or wholesalers and sells them to consumers. Many retailers sell both products and services.

### Reporting Income for a Merchandiser

Net income to a merchandiser equals revenues from selling merchandise minus both the cost of merchandise sold to customers and the cost of other expenses for the period (see Exhibit 4.1). The usual accounting term for revenues from selling merchandise is *sales,* and

Exhibit 4.1

Computing Income for a Merchandising Company versus a Service Company

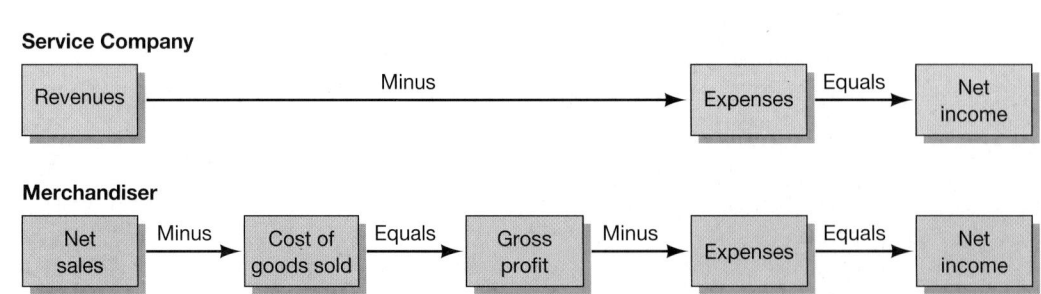

the term used for the expense of buying and preparing the merchandise is **cost of goods sold.** (Note that many service companies use the term *sales* instead of revenues, and cost of goods sold is also called *cost of sales*.)

| **Z-MART**<br>**Income Statement**<br>**For Year Ended December 31, 2005** | |
| --- | ---: |
| Net sales . . . . . . . . . . . . . . | $314,700 |
| Cost of goods sold . . . . . . . . | 230,400 |
| Gross profit . . . . . . . . . . . . | 84,300 |
| Expenses . . . . . . . . . . . . . . | 71,400 |
| Net income . . . . . . . . . . . . . | $ 12,900 |

Exhibit 4.2

Merchandiser's Income Statement

The income statement for Z-Mart in Exhibit 4.2 illustrates these key components of a merchandiser's net income. The first two lines show that products are acquired at a cost of $230,400 and sold for $314,700. The third line shows an $84,300 **gross profit,** also called **gross margin,** which equals net sales less cost of goods sold. Finally, $71,400 of other expenses are reported, which leaves $12,900 in net income.

**Point:** Analysis of gross profit is important to effective business decisions, and is described later in the chapter.

## Reporting Inventory for a Merchandiser

A merchandiser's balance sheet includes a current asset called *merchandise inventory,* an item not on a service company's balance sheet. **Merchandise inventory,** or simply *inventory,* refers to products that a company owns and intends to sell. The cost of this asset includes the cost incurred to buy the goods, ship them to the store, and make them ready for sale.

**C2**   Identify and explain the inventory asset of a merchandising company.

## Operating Cycle for a Merchandiser

A merchandising company's operating cycle begins by purchasing merchandise and ends by collecting cash from selling the merchandise. The length of an operating cycle differs across the types of businesses. Department stores often have operating cycles of two to five months. Operating cycles for grocery merchants usually range from two to eight weeks.

Exhibit 4.3

Merchandiser's Operating Cycle

Exhibit 4.3 illustrates an operating cycle for a merchandiser with credit sales. The cycle moves from (*a*) cash purchases of merchandise to (*b*) inventory for sale to (*c*) credit sales to (*d*) accounts receivable to (*e*) cash. Companies try to keep their operating cycles short because assets tied up in inventory and receivables are not productive.

**Point:** Cash sales shorten operating cycles. Credit purchases lengthen operating cycles.

## Inventory Systems

**Cost of goods sold** is the cost of merchandise sold to customers during a period. It is often the largest single expense on a merchandiser's income statement. **Inventory** refers to products a company owns and expects to sell in its normal operations. Exhibit 4.4 shows that a company's merchandise available for sale consists of what it begins with (beginning inventory) and what it purchases (net cost of purchases). The merchandise available is either sold (cost of goods sold) or kept for future sales (ending inventory).

Exhibit 4.4

Merchandiser's Cost Flow for a Single Time Period

Two alternative inventory accounting systems can be used to collect information about cost of goods sold and cost of inventory: *perpetual system* or *periodic system.* The **perpetual**

**C3**   Describe both perpetual and periodic inventory systems.

**inventory system** continually updates accounting records for merchandising transactions—specifically, for those records of inventory available for sale and inventory sold. The **periodic inventory system** updates the accounting records for merchandise transactions only at the *end of a period*. Technological advances and competitive pressures have dramatically increased the use of the perpetual system.

**Quick Check**

1. Describe a merchandiser's cost of goods sold.
2. What is gross profit for a merchandising company?
3. Explain why use of the perpetual inventory system has dramatically increased.

Answers—p. 178

---

*The following sections on purchasing, selling, and adjusting merchandise use the perpetual system. Appendix 4A uses the periodic system (with the perpetual results on the side). An instructor can choose to cover either one or both inventory systems.*

---

# Accounting for Merchandise Purchases

The cost of merchandise purchased for resale is recorded in the Merchandise Inventory asset account. To illustrate, Z-Mart records a $1,200 cash purchase of merchandise on November 2 as follows:

Assets = Liabilities + Equity
+1,200
−1,200

| Nov. 2 | Merchandise Inventory . . . . . . . . . . . . . . . . . . . . | 1,200 | |
| | Cash . . . . . . . . . . . . . . . . . . . . . . . . . . . | | 1,200 |
| | *Purchased merchandise for cash.* | | |

**P1** Analyze and record transactions for merchandise purchases using a perpetual system.

The invoice for this merchandise is shown in Exhibit 4.5. The buyer usually receives the original invoice, and the seller keeps a copy. This *source document* serves as the purchase invoice of Z-Mart (buyer) and the sales invoice for Trex (seller). The amount recorded for merchandise inventory includes its purchase cost, shipping fees, taxes, and any other costs necessary to make it ready for sale. This section explains how we compute the recorded cost of merchandise purchases.

Topic Tackler 4-1

## Trade Discounts

When a manufacturer or wholesaler prepares a catalog of items it has for sale, it usually gives each item a **list price,** also called a *catalog price.* However, an item's intended *selling price* equals list price minus a given percent called a **trade discount.** The amount of trade discount usually depends on whether a buyer is a wholesaler, retailer, or final consumer. A wholesaler buying in large quantities is often granted a larger discount than a retailer buying in smaller quantities. Note that a buyer records the net amount of list price minus trade discount. For example, in the November 2 purchase of merchandise by Z-Mart, the merchandise was listed in the seller's catalog at $2,000 and Z-Mart received a 40% trade discount. This meant that Z-Mart's purchase price was $1,200, computed as $2,000 − (40% × $2,000).

**Point:** The Merchandise Inventory account reflects the cost of goods available for resale.

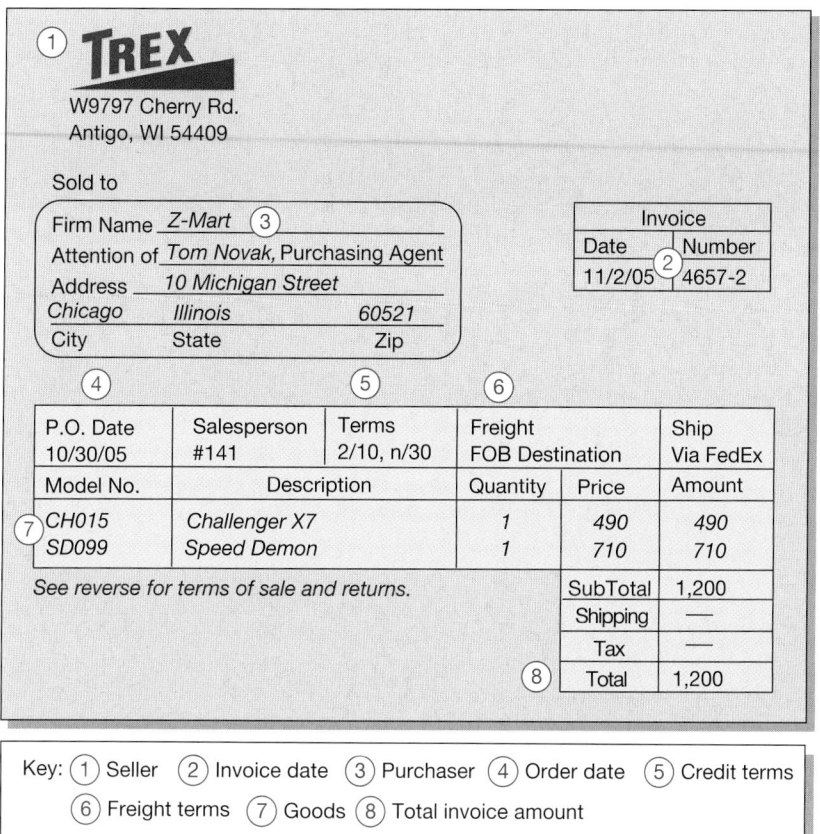

Exhibit 4.5

Invoice

## Purchase Discounts

The purchase of goods on credit requires a clear statement of expected future payments and dates to avoid misunderstandings. **Credit terms** for a purchase include the amounts and timing of payments from a buyer to a seller. Credit terms usually reflect an industry's practices. To illustrate, when sellers require payment within 10 days after the end of the month of the invoice date, the invoice will show credit terms as "n/10 EOM," which stands for net 10 days after end of month (**EOM**). When sellers require payment within 30 days after the invoice date, the invoice shows credit terms of "n/30," which stands for *net 30 days*.

Exhibit 4.6 portrays credit terms. The amount of time allowed before full payment is due is called the **credit period.** Sellers can grant a **cash discount** to encourage buyers to pay earlier. A buyer views a cash discount as a **purchase discount.** A seller views a cash discount as a **sales discount.** Any cash discounts are described in the credit terms on the invoice. For example, credit terms of "2/10, n/60" mean that full payment is due within a 60-day credit period, but the buyer can deduct 2% of the invoice amount if payment is made within 10 days of the invoice date. This reduced payment applies only for the **discount period.**

**Point:** Since both the buyer and seller know the invoice date, this date is used in determining the discount and credit periods.

Exhibit 4.6

Credit Terms

*Discount refers to a purchase discount for a buyer and a sales discount for a seller.

**Point:** Appendix 4A repeats journal entries *a* through *f* using a periodic inventory system.

Assets = Liabilities + Equity
+1,200      +1,200

To illustrate how a buyer accounts for a purchase discount, assume that Z-Mart's $1,200 purchase of merchandise is on credit with terms of 2/10, n/30. Its entry is

| | | | |
|---|---|---|---|
| **(a)** Nov. 2 | Merchandise Inventory . . . . . . . . . . . . . . . . . . . . | 1,200 | |
| | Accounts Payable . . . . . . . . . . . . . . . . . . . . | | 1,200 |
| | *Purchased merchandise on credit, invoice dated Nov. 2, terms 2/10, n/30.* | | |

If Z-Mart pays the amount due on (or before) November 12, the entry is

Assets = Liabilities + Equity
−24         −1,200
−1,176

| | | | |
|---|---|---|---|
| **(b)** Nov. 12 | Accounts Payable . . . . . . . . . . . . . . . . . . . . . . . | 1,200 | |
| | Merchandise Inventory . . . . . . . . . . . . . . . . | | 24 |
| | Cash . . . . . . . . . . . . . . . . . . . . . . . . . . . . . | | 1,176 |
| | *Paid for the $1,200 purchase of Nov. 2 less the discount of $24 (2% × $1,200).* | | |

**Point:** These entries illustrate what is called the *gross method* of accounting for purchases with discount terms.

The Merchandise Inventory account after these entries reflects the net cost of merchandise purchased, and the Accounts Payable account shows a zero balance. Both ledger accounts, in T-account form, follow:

| Merchandise Inventory | | | | | Accounts Payable | | | |
|---|---|---|---|---|---|---|---|---|
| Nov. 2 | 1,200 | Nov. 12 | 24 | | Nov. 12 | 1,200 | Nov. 2 | 1,200 |
| Balance | 1,176 | | | | | | Balance | 0 |

**Decision Maker**

**Entrepreneur**  You purchase a batch of products on terms of 3/10, n/90, but your company has limited cash and you must borrow funds at an 11% annual rate if you are to pay within the discount period. Do you take advantage of the purchase discount?

Answer—p. 177

A buyer's failure to pay within a discount period can be expensive. To illustrate, if Z-Mart does not pay within the 10-day 2% discount period, it can delay payment by 20 more days. This delay costs Z-Mart $24, computed as 2% × $1,200. Most buyers take advantage of a purchase discount because of the usually high interest rate implied from not taking it.[1] Also, good cash management means that no invoice is paid until the last day of the discount or credit period.

## Purchase Returns and Allowances

*Purchase returns* refer to merchandise a buyer acquires but then returns to the seller. A *purchase allowance* is a reduction in the cost of defective or unacceptable merchandise that a buyer acquires. Buyers often keep defective but still marketable merchandise if the seller grants an acceptable allowance.

**Point:** The sender (maker) of a *debit memorandum* will debit the account of the memo's receiver. The memo's receiver will credit the account of the sender.

When a buyer returns or takes an allowance on merchandise, the buyer issues a **debit memorandum** to inform the seller of a debit made to the seller's account in the buyer's records. To illustrate, on November 15 Z-Mart (buyer) issues a $300 debit memorandum for

---

[1] The *implied annual interest rate* formula is:

$$(365 \text{ days} \div [\text{Credit period} - \text{Discount period}]) \times \text{Cash discount rate.}$$

For terms of 2/10, n/30, missing the 2% discount for an additional 20 days is equal to an annual interest rate of 36.5%, computed as (365 days/[30 days − 10 days]) × 2% discount rate. *Favorable purchase discounts* are those with implied annual interest rates that exceed the purchaser's annual rate for borrowing money.

an allowance from Trex for defective merchandise. Z-Mart's November 15 entry to update its Merchandise Inventory account to reflect the purchase allowance is

| (c) Nov. 15 | Accounts Payable . . . . . . . . . . . . . . . . . . . . . . . | 300 | | Assets = Liabilities + Equity |
|---|---|---|---|---|
| | Merchandise Inventory . . . . . . . . . . . . . . . . . | | 300 | −300       −300 |
| | *Allowance for defective merchandise.* | | | |

If this had been a return, then the total *recorded cost* (all costs less any discounts) of the defective merchandise would be entered. The buyer's cost of returned and defective merchandise is usually offset against the buyer's current account payable balance to the seller. When cash is refunded, the Cash account is debited instead of Accounts Payable.

When goods are returned, a buyer can take a purchase discount on only the remaining balance of the invoice. For example, suppose Z-Mart purchases $1,000 of merchandise offered with a 2% cash discount. Two days later, Z-Mart returns $100 of goods before paying the invoice. When Z-Mart later pays within the discount period, it takes the 2% discount only on the $900 remaining balance. The discount is $18 (2% × $900) and the cash payment is $882 ($900 − $18).

**Example:** Z-Mart pays $980 cash for $1,000 of merchandise purchased within its 2% discount period. Later, Z-Mart returns $100 of the original $1,000 merchandise. The return entry is

Cash . . . . . . . . . . . . . . . . . . 98
    Merchandise Inventory . . . 98

## Transportation Costs and Ownership Transfer

The buyer and seller must agree on who is responsible for paying any freight costs and who bears the risk of loss during transit for merchandising transactions. This is essentially the same as asking at what point ownership transfers from the seller to the buyer. The point of transfer is called the **FOB** (*free on board*) point, which determines who pays transportation costs (and often other incidental costs of transit such as insurance).

Exhibit 4.7 identifies two alternative points of transfer. (1) *FOB shipping point,* also called *FOB factory,* means the buyer accepts ownership when the goods depart the seller's place of business. The buyer is then responsible for paying shipping costs and bearing the risk of damage or loss when goods are in transit. The goods are part of the buyer's inventory when they are in transit since ownership has transferred to the buyer. **Cannondale**, a major bike manufacturer, uses FOB shipping point. (2) *FOB destination* means ownership of goods transfers to the buyer when the goods arrive at the buyer's place of business. The seller is responsible for paying shipping charges and bears the risk of damage or loss in transit. The

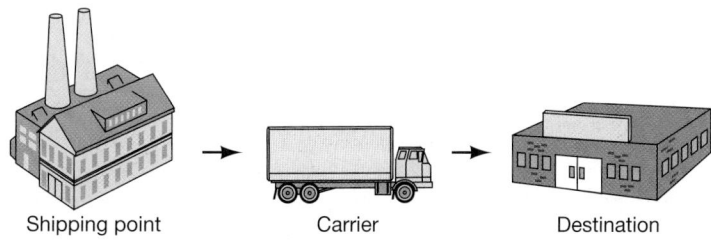

| | Ownership Transfers when Goods Passed to | Transportation Costs Paid by |
|---|---|---|
| FOB shipping point | Carrier | Buyer |
| FOB destination | Buyer | Seller |

## Exhibit 4.7

Ownership Transfer and Transportation Costs

**Point: Compaq Computer** at one time shipped its products FOB shipping point, but it found delivery companies unreliable. Compaq then changed its agreements to FOB destination, took control of shipping, and eliminated its problems.

**Point:** The party not responsible for shipping costs sometimes pays the carrier. In these cases, the party paying these costs either bills the party responsible or, more commonly, adjusts its account payable or account receivable with the other party. For example, a buyer paying a carrier when terms are FOB destination can decrease its account payable to the seller by the amount of shipping cost.

seller does not record revenue from this sale until the goods arrive at the destination because this transaction is not complete before that point.

Z-Mart's $1,200 purchase on November 2 is on terms of FOB destination. This means Z-Mart is not responsible for paying transportation costs. When a buyer is responsible for paying transportation costs, the payment is made to a carrier or directly to the seller depending on the agreement. The cost principle requires that any necessary transportation costs of a buyer (often called *transportation-in* or *freight-in*) be included as part of the cost of purchased merchandise. To illustrate, Z-Mart's entry to record a $75 freight charge from an independent carrier for merchandise purchased FOB shipping point is

Assets = Liabilities + Equity
+75
−75

| (d) Nov. 24 | Merchandise Inventory . . . . . . . . . . . . . . . . . . . . | 75 | |
|---|---|---|---|
| | Cash . . . . . . . . . . . . . . . . . . . . . . . . . . . | | 75 |
| | *Paid freight costs on purchased merchandise.* | | |

A seller records the costs of shipping goods to customers in a Delivery Expense account when the seller is responsible for these costs. Delivery Expense, also called *transportation-out* or *freight-out,* is reported as a selling expense in the seller's income statement.

In summary, purchases are recorded as debits to Merchandise Inventory. Any later purchase discounts, returns, and allowances are credited (decreases) to Merchandise Inventory. Transportation-in is debited (added) to Merchandise Inventory. Z-Mart's itemized costs of merchandise purchases for year 2005 are in Exhibit 4.8.

## Exhibit 4.8

Itemized Costs of
Merchandise Purchases

| Z-MART<br>Itemized Costs of Merchandise Purchases<br>For Year Ended December 31, 2005 | |
|---|---|
| Invoice cost of merchandise purchases . . . . . . . . . . | $ 235,800 |
| Less: Purchase discounts received . . . . . . . . . . . . . | (4,200) |
| Purchase returns and allowances . . . . . . . . . . | (1,500) |
| Add: Costs of transportation-in . . . . . . . . . . . . . . | 2,300 |
| **Total cost of merchandise purchases** . . . . . . . | **$232,400** |

**Point:** Some companies have separate accounts for purchase discounts, returns and allowances, and transportation-in. These accounts are then transferred to Merchandise Inventory at period-end. This is a *hybrid system* of perpetual and periodic. That is, Merchandise Inventory is updated on a perpetual basis but only for purchases and cost of goods sold.

The accounting system described here does not provide separate records (accounts) for total purchases, total purchase discounts, total purchase returns and allowances, and total transportation-in. Yet nearly all companies collect this information in supplementary records because managers need this information to evaluate and control each of these cost elements. **Supplementary records,** also called *supplemental records,* refer to information outside the usual general ledger accounts.

### Quick Check

4. How long are the credit and discount periods when credit terms are 2/10, n/60?

5. Identify which items are subtracted from the *list* amount and not recorded when computing purchase price: (*a*) freight-in; (*b*) trade discount; (*c*) purchase discount; (*d*) purchase return.

6. What does *FOB* mean? What does *FOB destination* mean?

Answers—p. 178

# Accounting for Merchandise Sales

Merchandising companies also must account for sales, sales discounts, sales returns and allowances, and cost of goods sold. A merchandising company such as Z-Mart reflects these items in its gross profit computation, as shown in Exhibit 4.9. This section explains how this information is derived from transactions.

Exhibit 4.9

Gross Profit Computation

| Z-MART Computation of Gross Profit For Year Ended December 31, 2005 | | |
|---|---|---|
| Sales ............................... | | $321,000 |
| Less: Sales discounts ................. | $4,300 | |
| Sales returns and allowances ....... | 2,000 | 6,300 |
| Net sales ......................... | | 314,700 |
| Cost of goods sold ................. | | 230,400 |
| **Gross profit** ...................... | | **$ 84,300** |

## Sales of Merchandise

Each sales transaction for a seller of merchandise involves two parts. One part is the revenue received in the form of an asset from a customer. The second part is the recognition of the cost of merchandise sold to a customer. Accounting for a sales transaction under the perpetual system requires recording information about both parts. This means that each sales transaction for merchandisers, whether for cash or on credit, requires two entries: one for revenue and one for cost. To illustrate, Z-Mart sold $2,400 of merchandise on credit on November 3. The revenue part of this transaction is recorded as

**P2** Analyze and record transactions for merchandise sales using a perpetual system.

**Point:** Growth of superstores such as **Price Club** and **Costco** is fed by the efficient use of perpetual inventory.

| **(e)** Nov. 3 | Accounts Receivable..................... | 2,400 | |
| | Sales............................... | | 2,400 |
| | *Sold merchandise on credit.* | | |

Assets = Liabilities + Equity
+2,400                        +2,400

This entry reflects an increase in Z-Mart's assets in the form of an accounts receivable. It also shows the increase in revenue (Sales). If the sale is for cash, the debit is to Cash instead of Accounts Receivable.

The cost part of each sales transaction ensures that the Merchandise Inventory account under a perpetual inventory system reflects the updated cost of the merchandise available for sale. For example, the cost of the merchandise Z-Mart sold on November 3 is $1,600, and the entry to record the cost part of this sales transaction is

Topic Tackler 4-2

| **(e)** Nov. 3 | Cost of Goods Sold ..................... | 1,600 | |
| | Merchandise Inventory................ | | 1,600 |
| | *To record the cost of Nov. 3 sale.* | | |

Assets = Liabilities + Equity
−1,600                        −1,600

**Point:** The Cost of Goods Sold account is only used in a perpetual system.

## Sales Discounts

*Sales discounts* on credit sales can benefit a seller by decreasing the delay in receiving cash and reducing future collection efforts.

At the time of a credit sale, a seller does not know whether a customer will pay within the discount period and take advantage of a purchases discount. This means the seller usually

### Decision Insight

**Suppliers and Demands** Merchandising companies often bombard suppliers with demands. These include special discounts for new stores, payment of fines for shipping errors, and free samples. Merchandisers' goals are to reduce inventories, shorten lead times, and eliminate errors.

does not record a sales discount until a customer actually pays within the discount period. To illustrate, Z-Mart completes a credit sale for $1,000 on November 12 with terms of 2/10, n/60. The entry to record the revenue part of this sale is

| Nov. 12 | Accounts Receivable..................... | 1,000 | |
| | Sales............................... | | 1,000 |
| | *Sold merchandise under terms of 2/10, n/60.* | | |

Assets = Liabilities + Equity
+1,000                        +1,000

This entry records the receivable and the revenue as if the customer will pay the full amount. The customer has two options, however. One option is to wait 60 days until January 11 and pay the full $1,000. In this case, Z-Mart records that payment as

Assets = Liabilities + Equity
+1,000
−1,000

| Jan. 11 | Cash ................................... | 1,000 | |
| | Accounts Receivable .................. | | 1,000 |
| | *Received payment for Nov. 12 sale.* | | |

The customer's second option is to pay $980 within a 10-day period ending November 22. If the customer pays on (or before) November 22, Z-Mart records the payment as

**Point:** Sales discounts is seldom reported on income statements distributed to external users.

Assets = Liabilities + Equity
+980              −20
−1,000

| Nov. 22 | Cash ................................... | 980 | |
| | Sales Discounts ......................... | 20 | |
| | Accounts Receivable .................. | | 1,000 |
| | *Received payment for Nov. 12 sale less discount.* | | |

Sales Discounts is a contra revenue account, meaning the Sales Discounts account is deducted from the Sales account when computing a company's net sales (see Exhibit 4.9). Management monitors Sales Discounts to assess the effectiveness and cost of its discount policy.

## Sales Returns and Allowances

*Sales returns* refer to merchandise that customers return to the seller after a sale. Many companies allow customers to return merchandise for a full refund. *Sales allowances* refer to reductions in the selling price of merchandise sold to customers. This can occur with damaged or defective merchandise that a customer is willing to purchase with a decrease in selling price. Sales returns and allowances usually involve dissatisfied customers and the possibility of lost future sales, and managers need information about returns and allowances to monitor these problems.

**Point:** Published income statements rarely disclose Sales Returns and Allowances.

To illustrate, recall Z-Mart's sale of merchandise on November 3 for $2,400 that had cost $1,600. Assume that the customer returns part of the merchandise on November 6, and the returned items sell for $800 and cost $600. The revenue part of this transaction must reflect the decrease in sales from the customer's return of merchandise as follows:

Assets = Liabilities + Equity
−800              −800

| **(f)** Nov. 6 | Sales Returns and Allowances .............. | 800 | |
| | Accounts Receivable .................. | | 800 |
| | *Customer returns merchandise of Nov. 3 sale.* | | |

If the merchandise returned to Z-Mart is not defective and can be resold to another customer, Z-Mart returns these goods to its inventory. The entry to restore the cost of such goods to the Merchandise Inventory account is

Assets = Liabilities + Equity
+600              +600

| Nov. 6 | Merchandise Inventory ................... | 600 | |
| | Cost of Goods Sold................... | | 600 |
| | *Returned goods added to inventory.[2]* | | |

---

[2] This entry changes if the goods returned are defective—that is, the returned inventory is recorded at its estimated value, not its cost. To illustrate, if the goods (costing $600) returned to Z-Mart are defective and estimated to be worth $150, the following entry is made: Dr. Merchandise Inventory for $150, Dr. Loss from Defective Merchandise for $450, and Cr. Cost of Goods Sold for $600.

To illustrate sales allowances, assume that $800 of the merchandise Z-Mart sold on November 3 is defective but the buyer decides to keep it because Z-Mart offers a $100 price reduction. Z-Mart records the allowance and decreases expected assets as follows:

| | | |
|---|---|---|
| Nov. 6 | Sales Returns and Allowances . . . . . . . . . . . . . . . | 100 |
| | Accounts Receivable . . . . . . . . . . . . . . . . . | | 100 |
| | *To record sales allowance on Nov. 3 sale.* | |

Assets = Liabilities + Equity
−100                        −100

The seller usually prepares a credit memorandum to confirm a buyer's return or allowance. A seller's **credit memorandum** informs a buyer of the seller's credit to the buyer's Account Receivable (on the seller's books).

**Point:** The sender (maker) of a credit memorandum will *credit* the account of the receiver. The receiver of a credit memorandum will *debit* the account of the sender.

## Quick Check

**7.** Why are sales discounts and sales returns and allowances recorded in contra revenue accounts instead of directly in the Sales account?

**8.** Under what conditions are two entries necessary to record a sales return?

**9.** When merchandise is sold on credit and the seller notifies the buyer of a price allowance, does the seller create and send a credit memorandum or a debit memorandum?

Answers—p. 178

# Completing the Accounting Cycle

Exhibit 4.10 shows the flow of merchandising costs during a period and where these costs are reported at period-end. This chapter already discussed how a merchandiser's purchases and sales transactions during a period are analyzed, recorded, and reported. Specifically, beginning inventory plus the net cost of purchases is the merchandise available for sale. As inventory is sold, its cost is recorded in cost of goods sold on the income statement; what remains is ending inventory on the balance sheet. Note that a period's ending inventory is the next period's beginning inventory.

Each of the steps in the accounting cycle described in Chapter 3 for a service company applies to a merchandiser. This section extends that discussion to three remaining steps of the accounting cycle for a merchandiser—adjustments, statement preparation, and closing.

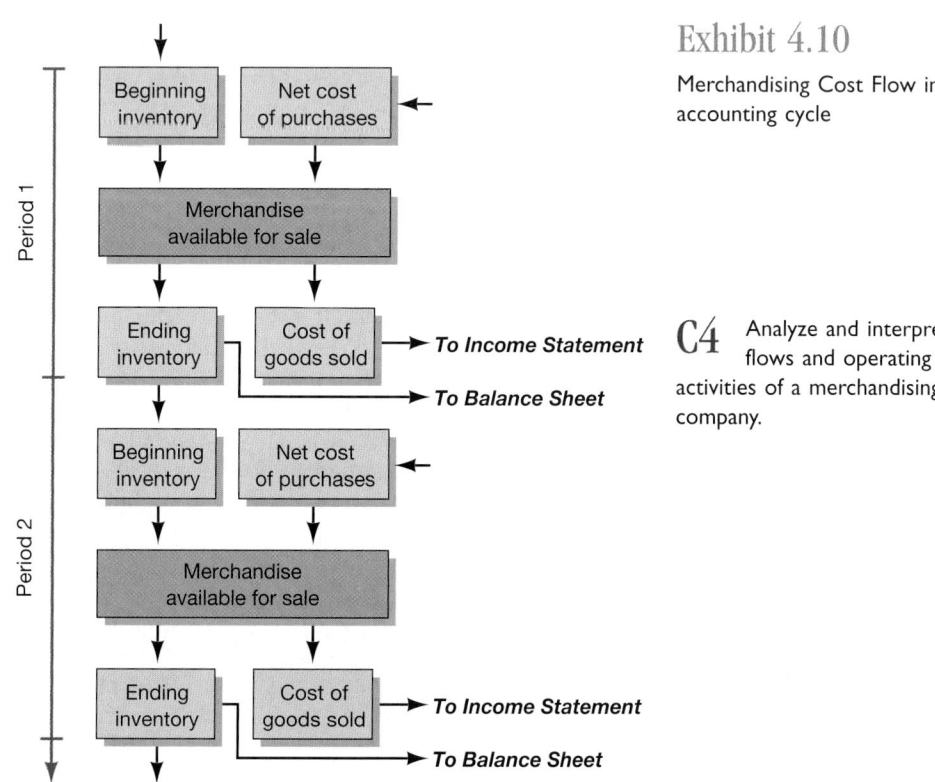

**Exhibit 4.10**

Merchandising Cost Flow in the accounting cycle

C4   Analyze and interpret cost flows and operating activities of a merchandising company.

## Adjusting Entries for Merchandisers

**P3**  Prepare adjustments and close accounts for a merchandising company.

Adjusting entries are generally the same for merchandising companies and service companies, including those for prepaid expenses (including depreciation), accrued expenses, unearned revenues, and accrued revenues. However, a merchandiser using a perpetual inventory system is usually required to make another adjustment to update the Merchandise Inventory account to reflect any loss of merchandise, including theft and deterioration. **Shrinkage** is the term used to refer to the loss of inventory and it is computed by comparing a physical count of inventory with recorded amounts. A physical count is usually performed at least once annually.

**Point:** About two-thirds of shoplifting losses are thefts by employees.

To illustrate, Z-Mart's Merchandise Inventory account at the end of year 2005 has a balance of $21,250, but a physical count reveals that only $21,000 of inventory exists. The adjusting entry to record this $250 shrinkage is

Assets = Liabilities + Equity
−250                      −250

| Dec. 31 | Cost of Goods Sold . . . . . . . . . . . . . . . . . . . . . . | 250 | |
| | Merchandise Inventory . . . . . . . . . . . . . . . . | | 250 |
| | *To adjust for $250 shrinkage revealed by a physical count of inventory.* | | |

## Preparing Financial Statements

The financial statements of a merchandiser, and their preparation, are similar to those for a service company described in Chapters 2 and 3. The income statement mainly differs by the inclusion of *cost of goods sold* and *gross profit*. Also, net sales is affected by discounts, returns, and allowances, and some additional expenses are possible such as delivery expense and loss from defective merchandise. The balance sheet mainly differs by the inclusion of *merchandise inventory* as part of current assets. The statement of retained earnings is unchanged. A work sheet can be used to help prepare these statements, and one is illustrated in Appendix 4B for Z-Mart.

**Point: CompUSA's** costs of shipping merchandise to its stores is included in the costs of its inventories as required by the cost principle.

## Closing Entries for Merchandisers

**Point:** The Inventory account is not affected by the closing process under a perpetual system.

Closing entries are similar for service companies and merchandising companies using a perpetual system. The difference is that we must close some new temporary accounts that arise from merchandising activities. Z-Mart has several temporary accounts unique to merchandisers: Sales (of goods), Sales Discounts, Sales Returns and Allowances, and Cost of Goods Sold. Their existence in the ledger means that the first two closing entries for a merchandiser are slightly different from the ones described in Chapter 3 for a service company. These differences are set in boldface in the closing entries of Exhibit 4.11.

## Summary of Merchandising Entries

Exhibit 4.12 summarizes the key adjusting and closing entries of a merchandiser (using a perpetual inventory system) that are different from those of a service company described in prior chapters (the Demonstration Problem 2 illustrates these merchandising entries).

Exhibit 4.11

Closing Entries for a
Merchandiser

## Step 1: Close Credit Balances in Temporary Accounts to Income Summary.

Z-Mart has one temporary account with a credit balance; it is closed with this entry:

| Dec. 31 | Sales ............................... | 321,000 | |
| |     Income Summary ................... | | 321,000 |
| |     *To close credit balances in temporary accounts.* | | |

## Step 2: Close Debit Balances in Temporary Accounts to Income Summary.

The second entry closes temporary accounts having debit balances such as Cost of Goods Sold, Sales Discounts, and Sales Returns and Allowances and is shown here:

| Dec. 31 | Income Summary ...................... | 308,100 | |
| |     **Sales Discounts** ................... | | **4,300** |
| |     **Sales Returns and Allowances** ........ | | **2,000** |
| |     **Cost of Goods Sold** ............... | | **230,400** |
| |     Depreciation Expense—Store Equipment ... | | 3,000 |
| |     Depreciation Expense—Office Equipment ... | | 700 |
| |     Office Salaries Expense ............... | | 25,300 |
| |     Sales Salaries Expense ................ | | 18,500 |
| |     Insurance Expense.................... | | 600 |
| |     Rent Expense—Office Space ............ | | 900 |
| |     Rent Expense—Selling Space ............ | | 8,100 |
| |     Office Supplies Expense ............... | | 1,800 |
| |     Store Supplies Expense ................ | | 1,200 |
| |     Advertising Expense .................. | | 11,300 |
| |     *To close debit balances in temporary accounts.* | | |

## Step 3: Close Income Summary to Retained Earnings.

The third closing entry is exactly the same for a merchandising company and a service company. It updates the Retained Earnings account for the net income or loss and is shown here:

| Dec. 31 | Income Summary ...................... | 12,900 | |
| |     Retained Earnings.................... | | 12,900 |
| |     *To close the Income Summary account.* | | |

The $12,900 amount in the entry is net income reported on the income statement in Exhibit 4.2.

## Step 4: Close Dividends Account to Retained Earnings.

The fourth closing entry is exactly the same for a merchandising company and a service company. It closes the Dividends account and adjusts the Retained Earnings account balance to the amount shown on the balance sheet. This entry for Z-Mart is

| Dec. 31 | Retained Earnings ..................... | 4,000 | |
| |     Dividends ......................... | | 4,000 |
| |     *To close the dividends account.* | | |

When these entries are posted, all temporary accounts are set to zero and are ready to record events for the next period. The Retained Earnings account is now updated to reflect all current and prior period transactions.

## Single-Step Income Statement

A **single-step income statement** is another widely used format, and is shown in Exhibit 4.14 for Z-Mart. It lists cost of goods sold as another expense and shows only one subtotal for total expenses. Expenses are grouped into very few, if any, categories. Many companies use formats that combine features of both the single- and multiple-step statements. Provided that income statement items are shown sensibly, management can choose the format. (In later chapters, we describe some items, such as extraordinary gains and losses, that must be reported in certain locations on the income statement.) Similar presentation options are available for the statement of retained earnings and statement of cash flows.

**Point:** Many companies report interest expense and interest income in separate categories after income from operations and before subtracting income taxes expense. As one example, see Krispy Kreme's income statement in Appendix A.

### Exhibit 4.14

Single-Step Income Statement

| Z-MART<br>Income Statement<br>For Year Ended December 31, 2005 | | |
|---|---:|---:|
| **Revenues** | | |
| Net sales .......................... | | $314,700 |
| Interest revenue ...................... | | 1,000 |
| Gain on sale of building ................ | | 2,500 |
| Total revenues ....................... | | 318,200 |
| **Expenses** | | |
| Cost of goods sold ................... | $230,400 | |
| Selling expenses ..................... | 42,100 | |
| General and administrative expenses ....... | 29,300 | |
| Interest expense ..................... | 1,500 | |
| Total expenses ...................... | | 303,300 |
| **Net income** .......................... | | $ 14,900 |

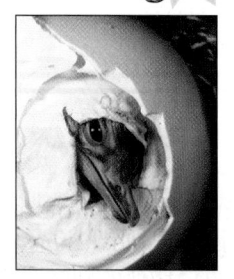

## Classified Balance Sheet

The merchandiser's classified balance sheet reports merchandise inventory as a current asset, usually after accounts receivable according to an asset's nearness to liquidity. Inventory is usually less liquid than accounts receivable because receivables must first be sold before cash is received, but more liquid than supplies and prepaid expenses. Exhibit 4.15 shows the current asset section of Z-Mart's classified balance sheet (other sections are as shown in Chapter 3).

### Exhibit 4.15

Classified Balance Sheet (partial) of a Merchandiser

| Z-MART<br>Balance Sheet (partial)<br>December 31, 2005 | |
|---|---:|
| **Assets** | |
| Current assets | |
| Cash ........................ | $ 8,200 |
| Accounts receivable ............. | 11,200 |
| **Merchandise inventory** ....... | **21,000** |
| Office supplies ................ | 550 |
| Store supplies ................ | 250 |
| Prepaid insurance ............. | 300 |
| Total current assets ........... | $ 41,500 |

| **Acid-Test and Gross Margin Ratios** | **Decision Analysis** |

## Acid-Test Ratio

For many merchandisers, inventory makes up a large portion of current assets. Inventory must be sold and any resulting accounts receivable must be collected before cash is available. Chapter 3 explained that the current ratio, defined as current assets divided by current liabilities, is useful in assessing a company's ability to pay current liabilities. Since it is sometimes unreasonable to assume that inventories are a source of payment for current liabilities, we look to other measures.

One measure of a merchandiser's ability to pay its current liabilities (its *liquidity*) is the acid-test ratio. It differs from the current ratio by excluding less liquid current assets such as inventory and prepaid expenses that take longer to be converted to cash. The **acid-test ratio,** also called *quick ratio,* is defined as *quick assets* (cash, short-term investments, and current receivables) divided by current liabilities—see Exhibit 4.16.

**A1**  Compute the acid-test ratio and explain its use to assess liquidity.

$$\text{Acid-test ratio} = \frac{\text{Cash and equivalents} + \text{Short-term investments} + \text{Current receivables}}{\text{Current liabilities}}$$

**Exhibit 4.16**

Acid-Test (Quick) Ratio

Exhibit 4.17 shows both the acid-test and current ratios of retailer **JCPenney** for fiscal years 1999 through 2003. JCPenney's acid-test ratio reveals a decline in 2000–2001 that exceeds the decline in the retailing industry. Still, JCPenney's current ratio (never less than 1.7) suggests that its short-term obligations can be covered with short-term assets.

**Exhibit 4.17**

JCPenney's Acid-Test and Current Ratios

| ($ in millions) | 2003 | 2002 | 2001 | 2000 | 1999 |
|---|---|---|---|---|---|
| Total quick assets . . . . . . . . . . . | $3,179 | $3,538 | $1,837 | $2,076 | $ 4,779 |
| Total current assets . . . . . . . . . . | $8,353 | $8,677 | $7,257 | $8,174 | $11,007 |
| Total current liabilities . . . . . . . . | $4,159 | $4,499 | $4,235 | $4,272 | $ 5,912 |
| **Acid-test ratio** . . . . . . . . . . . . | **0.76** | **0.79** | **0.43** | **0.49** | **0.81** |
| **Current ratio** . . . . . . . . . . . . . | **2.01** | **1.93** | **1.71** | **1.91** | **1.86** |
| Industry acid-test ratio . . . . . . . . | 0.5 | 0.5 | 0.8 | 0.8 | 0.9 |
| Industry current ratio . . . . . . . . | 2.5 | 2.6 | 3.0 | 2.8 | 3.1 |

An acid-test ratio less than 1.0 means that current liabilities exceed quick assets. A rule of thumb is that the acid-test ratio should have a value of, or higher than, 1.0 to conclude that a company is unlikely to face near-term liquidity problems. A value less than 1.0 raises liquidity concerns unless a company can generate enough cash from inventory sales or if much of its liabilities are not due until late in the next period. Similarly, a value greater than 1.0 can hide a liquidity problem if payables are due shortly and receivables are not collected until late in the next period. Analysis of JCPenney reveals a slight concern with its liquidity in 2000–2001, especially when benchmarked against the industry ratio. However, in 2002–2003 JCPenney raised its acid-test ratio to a reasonable level (and its inventory is fairly liquid).

**Point:** Successful use of a just-in-time inventory system can narrow the gap between the acid-test ratio and the current ratio.

**Decision Maker**

**Supplier**  A retailer requests to purchase supplies on credit from your company. You have no prior experience with this retailer. The retailer's current ratio is 2.1, its acid-test ratio is 0.5, and inventory makes up most of its current assets. Do you extend credit?

Answer—p. 177

## Gross Margin Ratio

The cost of goods sold makes up much of expenses for merchandisers. Without sufficient gross profit, a merchandiser will likely fail. Users often compute the gross margin ratio to help understand this relation. It differs from the profit margin ratio in that it excludes all costs except cost of goods sold. The **gross margin ratio** is defined as *gross margin* (net sales minus cost of goods sold) divided by net sales—see Exhibit 4.18.

**A2**  Compute the gross margin ratio and explain its use to assess profitability.

$$\text{Gross margin ratio} = \frac{\text{Net sales} - \text{Cost of goods sold}}{\text{Net sales}}$$

**Exhibit 4.18**

Gross Margin Ratio

### Decision Maker

**Financial Officer**   Your company has a 36% gross margin ratio and a 17% net profit margin ratio. Industry averages are 44% for gross margin and 16% for net profit margin. Do these comparative results concern you?

Answer—p. 177

**Point:** The power of a ratio is often its ability to identify areas for more detailed analysis.

Exhibit 4.19 shows the gross margin ratio of **JCPenney** for fiscal years 1999–2003. For JCPenney, each $1 of sales in 2003 yielded about 30¢ in gross margin to cover all other expenses and still produce a profit. This 30¢ margin is up from 29¢ in 2002 and from 28¢ in 2001. This rebound is an important (and positive) development. Success for merchandisers such as JCPenney depends on adequate gross margin. Overall, both the acid-test ratio and the gross margin ratio suggest that the financial condition and performance of JCPenney has markedly improved over the past two years.

## Exhibit 4.19

JCPenney's Gross Margin Ratio

| ($ in millions) | 2003 | 2002 | 2001 | 2000 | 1999 |
|---|---|---|---|---|---|
| Gross margin .............. | $ 9,774 | $ 9,215 | $ 8,815 | $ 9,457 | $ 9,140 |
| Net sales ................. | $32,347 | $32,004 | $31,846 | $31,743 | $29,761 |
| **Gross margin ratio** ........ | 30.2% | 28.8% | 27.7% | 29.8% | 30.7% |

# Demonstration Problem 1

Use the following adjusted trial balance and additional information to complete the requirements:

**KC ANTIQUES**
**Adjusted Trial Balance**
**December 31, 2005**

| | Debit | Credit |
|---|---|---|
| Cash ................................. | $ 20,000 | |
| Merchandise inventory ...................... | 60,000 | |
| Store supplies ........................... | 1,500 | |
| Equipment ............................. | 45,600 | |
| Accumulated depreciation—Equipment .......... | | $ 16,600 |
| Accounts payable ........................ | | 9,000 |
| Salaries payable .......................... | | 2,000 |
| Common stock .......................... | | 20,000 |
| Retained earnings ....................... | | 59,000 |
| Dividends .............................. | 10,000 | |
| Sales .................................. | | 343,250 |
| Sales discounts ......................... | 5,000 | |
| Sales returns and allowances ................ | 6,000 | |
| Cost of goods sold ....................... | 159,900 | |
| Depreciation expense—Store equipment ........ | 4,100 | |
| Depreciation expense—Office equipment ........ | 1,600 | |
| Sales salaries expense ..................... | 30,000 | |
| Office salaries expense .................... | 34,000 | |
| Insurance expense ........................ | 11,000 | |
| Rent expense (70% is store, 30% is office) ....... | 24,000 | |
| Store supplies expense .................... | 5,750 | |
| Advertising expense ...................... | 31,400 | |
| Totals ................................. | $449,850 | $449,850 |

KC Antiques' *supplementary records* for 2005 reveal the following itemized costs for merchandising activities:

| | |
|---|---|
| Invoice cost of merchandise purchases ....... | $150,000 |
| Purchase discounts received .............. | 2,500 |
| Purchase returns and allowances ........... | 2,700 |
| Cost of transportation-in ................ | 5,000 |

**Required**

1. Use the supplementary records to compute the total cost of merchandise purchases for 2005.
2. Prepare a 2005 multiple-step income statement. (Inventory at December 31, 2004, is $70,100.)
3. Prepare a single-step income statement for 2005.
4. Prepare closing entries for KC Antiques at December 31, 2005.
5. Compute the acid-test ratio and the gross margin ratio. Explain the meaning of each ratio and interpret them for KC Antiques.

## Planning the Solution

- Compute the total cost of merchandise purchases for 2005.
- To prepare the multiple-step statement, first compute net sales. Then, to compute cost of goods sold, add the net cost of merchandise purchases for the year to beginning inventory and subtract the cost of ending inventory. Subtract cost of goods sold from net sales to get gross profit. Then classify expenses as selling expenses or general and administrative expenses.
- To prepare the single-step income statement, begin with net sales. Then list and subtract the expenses.
- The first closing entry debits all temporary accounts with credit balances and opens the Income Summary account. The second closing entry credits all temporary accounts with debit balances. The third entry closes the Income Summary account to the retained earnings account, and the fourth entry closes the dividends account to the retained earnings account.
- Identify the quick assets on the adjusted trial balance. Compute the acid-test ratio by dividing quick assets by current liabilities. Compute the gross margin ratio by dividing gross profit by net sales.

## Solution to Demonstration Problem 1

**1.**

| | |
|---|---:|
| Invoice cost of merchandise purchases . . . . . . . | $150,000 |
| Less: Purchases discounts received . . . . . . . . . . | 2,500 |
| Purchase returns and allowances . . . . . . . . | 2,700 |
| Add: Cost of transportation-in . . . . . . . . . . . . . | 5,000 |
| Total cost of merchandise purchases . . . . . . . . . | $149,800 |

**2.** Multiple-step income statement

| KC ANTIQUES<br>Income Statement<br>For Year Ended December 31, 2005 | | |
|---|---:|---:|
| Sales . . . . . . . . . . . . . . . . . . . . . . . . . . . . . . . . . . | | $343,250 |
| Less: Sales discounts . . . . . . . . . . . . . . . . . . . . . . . . | $ 5,000 | |
| Sales returns and allowances . . . . . . . . . . . . . . . | 6,000 | 11,000 |
| Net sales . . . . . . . . . . . . . . . . . . . . . . . . . . . . . . | | 332,250 |
| Cost of goods sold* . . . . . . . . . . . . . . . . . . . . . . . . | | 159,900 |
| Gross profit . . . . . . . . . . . . . . . . . . . . . . . . . . . . | | 172,350 |
| Expenses | | |
| Selling expenses | | |
| Depreciation expense—Store equipment . . . . . . . . | 4,100 | |
| Sales salaries expense . . . . . . . . . . . . . . . . . . . . | 30,000 | |
| Rent expense—Selling space . . . . . . . . . . . . . . . | 16,800 | |
| Store supplies expense . . . . . . . . . . . . . . . . . . . | 5,750 | |
| Advertising expense . . . . . . . . . . . . . . . . . . . . . | 31,400 | |
| Total selling expenses . . . . . . . . . . . . . . . . . . . . | 88,050 | |

[continued on next page]

[continued from previous page]

General and administrative expenses

| | | |
|---|---:|---:|
| Depreciation expense—Office equipment ....... | 1,600 | |
| Office salaries expense .................... | 34,000 | |
| Insurance expense ...................... | 11,000 | |
| Rent expense—Office space ............... | 7,200 | |
| Total general and administrative expenses ........ | 53,800 | |
| Total operating expenses ..................... | | 141,850 |
| Net income .................................. | | $ 30,500 |

\* Cost of goods sold can also be directly computed (applying concepts from Exhibit 4.4):

| | |
|---|---:|
| Merchandise inventory, December 31, 2004 ............. | $ 70,100 |
| Total cost of merchandise purchases (from part 1) ......... | 149,800 |
| Goods available for sale .......................... | 219,900 |
| Merchandise inventory, December 31, 2005 ............. | 60,000 |
| Cost of goods sold ............................. | $159,900 |

## 3. Single-step income statement

**KC ANTIQUES**
**Income Statement**
**For Year Ended December 31, 2005**

| | | |
|---|---:|---:|
| Net sales ............................. | | $332,250 |
| Expenses | | |
| Cost of goods sold .................... | $159,900 | |
| Selling expenses ..................... | 88,050 | |
| General and administrative expenses ....... | 53,800 | |
| Total expenses ..................... | | 301,750 |
| Net income .......................... | | $ 30,500 |

## 4.

| | | | |
|---|---|---:|---:|
| Dec. 31 | Sales ................................... | 343,250 | |
| | Income Summary.................... | | 343,250 |
| | *To close credit balances in temporary accounts.* | | |
| Dec. 31 | Income Summary ......................... | 312,750 | |
| | Sales Discounts ...................... | | 5,000 |
| | Sales Returns and Allowances............ | | 6,000 |
| | Cost of Goods Sold .................. | | 159,900 |
| | Depreciation Expense—Store Equipment ... | | 4,100 |
| | Depreciation Expense—Office Equipment ... | | 1,600 |
| | Sales Salaries Expense ................ | | 30,000 |
| | Office Salaries Expense ............... | | 34,000 |
| | Insurance Expense.................... | | 11,000 |
| | Rent Expense ....................... | | 24,000 |
| | Store Supplies Expense ............... | | 5,750 |
| | Advertising Expense .................. | | 31,400 |
| | *To close debit balances in temporary accounts.* | | |
| Dec. 31 | Income Summary ....................... | 30,500 | |
| | Retained Earnings ................... | | 30,500 |
| | *To close the Income Summary account.* | | |
| Dec. 31 | Retained Earnings ...................... | 10,000 | |
| | Dividends .......................... | | 10,000 |
| | *To close the dividends account.* | | |

**5.** Acid-test ratio = (Cash and equivalents + Short-term investments + Current receivables)/
        Current liabilities

    = Cash/(Accounts payable + Salaries payable)

    = \$20,000/(\$9,000 + \$2,000) = \$20,000/\$11,000 = $\underline{1.82}$

Gross margin ratio = Gross profit/Net sales = \$172,350/\$332,250 = $\underline{0.52}$ (or 52%)

KC Antiques has a healthy acid-test ratio of 1.82. This means it has more than $1.80 in liquid assets to satisfy each $1.00 in current liabilities. The gross margin of 0.52 shows that KC Antiques spends 48¢ ($1.00 − $0.52) of every dollar of net sales on the costs of acquiring the merchandise it sells. This leaves 52¢ of every dollar of net sales to cover other expenses incurred in the business and to provide a profit.

# Demonstration Problem 2

Prepare journal entries to record the following merchandising transactions for both the seller (BMX) and buyer (Sanuk).

May 4 BMX sold $1,500 of merchandise on account to Sanuk, terms FOB shipping point, n/45, invoice dated May 4. The cost of the merchandise was $900.

May 6 Sanuk paid transportation charges of $30 on the May 4 purchase from BMX.

May 8 BMX sold $1,000 of merchandise on account to Sanuk, terms FOB destination, n/30, invoice dated May 8. The cost of the merchandise was $700.

May 10 BMX paid transportation costs of $50 for delivery of merchandise sold to Sanuk on May 8.

May 16 BMX issued Sanuk a $200 credit memorandum for merchandise returned. The merchandise was purchased by Sanuk on account on May 8. The cost of the merchandise returned was $140.

May 18 BMX received payment from Sanuk for purchase of May 8.

May 21 BMX sold $2,400 of merchandise on account to Sanuk, terms FOB shipping point, 2/10, n/EOM. BMX prepaid transportation costs of $100, which were added to the invoice. The cost of the merchandise was $1,440.

May 31 BMX received payment from Sanuk for purchase of May 21, less discount (2% × $2,400).

## Solution to Demonstration Problem 2

| | BMX (Seller) | | | Sanuk (Buyer) | | |
|---|---|---|---|---|---|---|
| May 4 | Accounts Receivable—Sanuk .... | 1,500 | | Merchandise Inventory ........ | 1,500 | |
| | Sales ................. | | 1,500 | Accounts Payable—BMX ... | | 1,500 |
| | Cost of Goods Sold .......... | 900 | | | | |
| | Merchandise Inventory ..... | | 900 | | | |
| 6 | No entry. | | | Merchandise Inventory ........ | 30 | |
| | | | | Cash ................. | | 30 |
| 8 | Accounts Receivable—Sanuk .... | 1,000 | | Merchandise Inventory ........ | 1,000 | |
| | Sales ................. | | 1,000 | Accounts Payable—BMX .... | | 1,000 |
| | Cost of Goods Sold .......... | 700 | | | | |
| | Merchandise Inventory ..... | | 700 | | | |
| 10 | Delivery Expense ............ | 50 | | No entry. | | |
| | Cash ................. | | 50 | | | |
| 16 | Sales Returns & Allowances ..... | 200 | | Accounts Payable—BMX ...... | 200 | |
| | Accounts Receivable—Sanuk . | | 200 | Merchandise Inventory ...... | | 200 |
| | Merchandise Inventory ........ | 140 | | | | |
| | Cost of Goods Sold ....... | | 140 | | | |
| 18 | Cash ..................... | 800 | | Accounts Payable—BMX ...... | 800 | |
| | Accounts Receivable—Sanuk . | | 800 | Cash ................. | | 800 |
| 21 | Accounts Receivable—Sanuk .... | 2,400 | | Merchandise Inventory ........ | 2,500 | |
| | Sales ................. | | 2,400 | Accounts Payable—BMX ... | | 2,500 |
| | Accounts Receivable—Sanuk .... | 100 | | | | |
| | Cash ................. | | 100 | | | |
| | Cost of Goods Sold .......... | 1,440 | | | | |
| | Merchandise Inventory ..... | | 1,440 | | | |
| 31 | Cash ..................... | 2,452 | | Accounts Payable—BMX ...... | 2,500 | |
| | Sales Discounts .............. | 48 | | Merchandise Inventory ..... | | 48 |
| | Accounts Receivable—Sanuk . | | 2,500 | Cash ................. | | 2,452 |

## APPENDIX

# 4A

# Periodic (and Perpetual) Inventory System

A **periodic inventory system** requires updating the inventory account only at the *end of a period* to reflect the quantity and cost of both the goods available and the goods sold. Thus, during the period, the Merchandise Inventory balance remains unchanged. It reflects the beginning inventory balance until it is updated at the end of the period. During the period the cost of merchandise is recorded in a temporary *Purchases* account. When a company sells merchandise, it records revenue but not the cost of the goods sold. At the end of the period when a company prepares financial statements, it takes a *physical count of inventory* by counting the quantities and costs of merchandise available. The cost of goods sold is then computed by subtracting the ending inventory amount from the cost of merchandise available for sale.

## Recording Merchandise Transactions

**P5** Record and compare merchandising transactions using both periodic and perpetual inventory systems.

Under a periodic system, each purchase, purchase return and allowance, purchase discount, and transportation-in transaction is recorded in a separate temporary account. At period-end, each of these temporary accounts is closed and the Merchandise Inventory account is updated. To illustrate, journal entries under the periodic inventory system are shown for the most common transactions (codes *a* through *f* link these transactions to those in the chapter, and we drop explanations for simplicity). For comparison, perpetual system journal entries are shown to the right of each periodic entry.

**Purchases**   The periodic system uses a temporary *Purchases* account that accumulates the cost of all purchase transactions during each period. Z-Mart's November 2 entry to record the purchase of merchandise for $1,200 on credit with terms of 2/10, n/30 is

| (a) | *Periodic* | | | *Perpetual* | | |
|---|---|---|---|---|---|---|
| Purchases . . . . . . . . . . . . . | 1,200 | | Merchandise Inventory . . . . . . | 1,200 | |
| Accounts Payable . . . . | | 1,200 | Accounts Payable . . . . . . . | | 1,200 |

**Purchase Discounts**   The periodic system uses a temporary *Purchase Discounts* account that accumulates discounts taken on purchase transactions during the period. If payment in (*a*) is delayed until after the discount period expires, the entry is to debit Accounts Payable and credit Cash for $1,200 each. However, if Z-Mart pays the supplier for the previous purchase in (*a*) within the discount period, the required payment is $1,176 ($1,200 × 98%) and is recorded as

| (b) | *Periodic* | | | *Perpetual* | | |
|---|---|---|---|---|---|---|
| Accounts Payable . . . . . . . | 1,200 | | Accounts Payable . . . . . . . . . . | 1,200 | |
| Purchase Discounts . . . | | 24 | Merchandise Inventory . . . | | 24 |
| Cash . . . . . . . . . . . . . | | 1,176 | Cash . . . . . . . . . . . . . . . | | 1,176 |

**Purchase Returns and Allowances**   Z-Mart returned merchandise purchased on November 2 because of defects. In the periodic system, the temporary *Purchase Returns and Allowances* account accumulates the cost of all returns and allowances during a period. The recorded cost (including discounts) of the defective merchandise is $300, and Z-Mart records the November 15 return with this entry:

| (c) | *Periodic* | | | *Perpetual* | | |
|---|---|---|---|---|---|---|
| Accounts Payable . . . . . . . | 300 | | Accounts Payable . . . . . . . . . . | 300 | |
| Purchase Returns and Allowances . . . . . | | 300 | Merchandise Inventory . . . | | 300 |

**Transportation-In**  Z-Mart paid a $75 freight charge to transport merchandise to its store. In the periodic system, this cost is charged to a temporary *Transportation-In* account.

(d)

| Periodic | | | Perpetual | | |
|---|---|---|---|---|---|
| Transportation-In ....... | 75 | | Merchandise Inventory ....... | 75 | |
| Cash ............. | | 75 | Cash ................ | | 75 |

**Sales**  Under the periodic system, the cost of goods sold is *not* recorded at the time of each sale. (We later show how to compute total cost of goods sold at the end of a period.) Z-Mart's November 3 entry to record sales of $2,400 in merchandise on credit (when its cost is $1,600) is:

(e)

| Periodic | | | Perpetual | | |
|---|---|---|---|---|---|
| Accounts Receivable ..... | 2,400 | | Accounts Receivable ........ | 2,400 | |
| Sales ............. | | 2,400 | Sales ................ | | 2,400 |
| | | | Cost of Goods Sold ........ | 1,600 | |
| | | | Merchandise Inventory ... | | 1,600 |

**Sales Returns**  A customer returned part of the merchandise from the transaction in (e), where the returned items sell for $800 and cost $600. (*Recall:* The periodic system records only the revenue effect, not the cost effect, for sales transactions.) Z-Mart restores the merchandise to inventory and records the November 6 return as

(f)

| Periodic | | | Perpetual | | |
|---|---|---|---|---|---|
| Sales Returns and | | | Sales Returns and | | |
| Allowances ............ | 800 | | Allowances .............. | 800 | |
| Accounts Receivable . | | 800 | Accounts Receivable ..... | | 800 |
| | | | Merchandise Inventory ....... | 600 | |
| | | | Cost of Goods Sold ..... | | 600 |

## Adjusting and Closing Entries

The periodic and perpetual inventory systems have slight differences in adjusting and closing entries. The period-end Merchandise Inventory balance (unadjusted) is $19,000 under the periodic system and $21,250 under the perpetual system. Since the periodic system does not update the Merchandise Inventory balance during the period, the $19,000 amount is the beginning inventory. However, the $21,250 balance under the perpetual system is the recorded ending inventory before adjusting for any inventory shrinkage.

A physical count of inventory taken at the end of the period reveals $21,000 of merchandise available. The adjusting and closing entries for the two systems are shown in Exhibit 4A.1. The periodic

**Exhibit 4A.1**

Comparison of Adjusting and Closing Entries—Periodic and Perpetual

| Periodic | | | Perpetual | | |
|---|---|---|---|---|---|
| **Adjusting Entry—Shrinkage** | | | **Adjusting Entry—Shrinkage** | | |
| None | | | Cost of Goods Sold ................. | 250 | |
| | | | Merchandise Inventory ........... | | 250 |
| **Closing Entries** | | | **Closing Entries** | | |
| (1) Sales ......................... | 321,000 | | (1) Sales ............................ | 321,000 | |
| Merchandise Inventory ............. | 21,000 | | Income Summary ............... | | 321,000 |
| Purchase Discounts ............... | 4,200 | | | | |
| Purchase Returns and Allowances .... | 1,500 | | | | |
| Income Summary ............... | | 347,700 | | | |

[continued on next page]

[continued from previous page]

| (2) Income Summary | 334,800 | | | (2) Income Summary . . . . . . . . . . . . . . . . . . . | 308,100 | |
|---|---|---|---|---|---|---|
| Sales Discounts . . . . . . . . . . . . . . . . . | | 4,300 | | Sales Discounts . . . . . . . . . . . . . . . . . | | 4,300 |
| Sales Returns and Allowances . . . . . . . | | 2,000 | | Sales Returns and Allowances . . . . . . . | | 2,000 |
| **Merchandise Inventory** . . . . . . . . . | | **19,000** | | | | |
| **Purchases** . . . . . . . . . . . . . . . . . . . . | | **235,800** | | **Cost of Goods Sold** . . . . . . . . . . . . | | **230,400** |
| **Transportation-In** . . . . . . . . . . . . . . | | **2,300** | | | | |
| Depreciation Expense—Store eq. . . . . | | 3,000 | | Depreciation Expense—Store eq. . . . . | | 3,000 |
| Depreciation Expense—Office eq. . . . | | 700 | | Depreciation Expense—Office eq. . . . | | 700 |
| Office Salaries Expense . . . . . . . . . . . . | | 25,300 | | Office Salaries Expense . . . . . . . . . . . . | | 25,300 |
| Sales Salaries Expense . . . . . . . . . . . . | | 18,500 | | Sales Salaries Expense . . . . . . . . . . . . . | | 18,500 |
| Insurance Expense . . . . . . . . . . . . . . . | | 600 | | Insurance Expense . . . . . . . . . . . . . . . | | 600 |
| Rent Expense—Office space . . . . . . . | | 900 | | Rent Expense—Office space . . . . . . . | | 900 |
| Rent Expense—Selling space . . . . . . . | | 8,100 | | Rent Expense—Selling space . . . . . . . | | 8,100 |
| Office Supplies Expense . . . . . . . . . . . | | 1,800 | | Office Supplies Expense . . . . . . . . . . . | | 1,800 |
| Store Supplies Expense . . . . . . . . . . . | | 1,200 | | Store Supplies Expense . . . . . . . . . . . | | 1,200 |
| Advertising Expense . . . . . . . . . . . . . | | 11,300 | | Advertising Expense . . . . . . . . . . . . . | | 11,300 |
| (3) Income Summary . . . . . . . . . . . . . . . . . . | 12,900 | | | (3) Income Summary . . . . . . . . . . . . . . . . . . | 12,900 | |
| Retained Earnings . . . . . . . . . . . . . . | | 12,900 | | Retained Earnings . . . . . . . . . . . . . . | | 12,900 |
| (4) Retained Earnings . . . . . . . . . . . . . . . . . | 4,000 | | | (4) Retained Earnings . . . . . . . . . . . . . . . . . | 4,000 | |
| Dividends . . . . . . . . . . . . . . . . . . . . | | 4,000 | | Dividends . . . . . . . . . . . . . . . . . . . . | | 4,000 |

system records the ending inventory of $21,000 in the Merchandise Inventory account (which includes shrinkage) in the first closing entry and removes the $19,000 beginning inventory balance from the account in the second closing entry.*

By updating Merchandise Inventory and closing Purchases, Purchase Discounts, Purchase Returns and Allowances, and Transportation-In, the periodic system transfers the cost of goods sold amount to Income Summary. Review the periodic side of Exhibit 4A.1 and notice that the boldface items affect Income Summary as follows:

| | |
|---|---|
| Credit to Income Summary in the first closing entry includes amounts from: | |
| Merchandise inventory (ending) . . . . . . . . . . . . . . . . . . . . . . . . . . . . . . . . . . . . . | $ 21,000 |
| Purchase discounts . . . . . . . . . . . . . . . . . . . . . . . . . . . . . . . . . . . . . . . . . . . . . . | 4,200 |
| Purchase returns and allowances . . . . . . . . . . . . . . . . . . . . . . . . . . . . . . . . . . . | 1,500 |
| Debit to Income Summary in the second closing entry includes amounts from: | |
| Merchandise inventory (beginning) . . . . . . . . . . . . . . . . . . . . . . . . . . . . . . . . . . | (19,000) |
| Purchases . . . . . . . . . . . . . . . . . . . . . . . . . . . . . . . . . . . . . . . . . . . . . . . . . . . . | (235,800) |
| Transportation-in . . . . . . . . . . . . . . . . . . . . . . . . . . . . . . . . . . . . . . . . . . . . . . | (2,300) |
| **Net effect on Income Summary** . . . . . . . . . . . . . . . . . . . . . . . . . . . . . . . . . . . | **$(230,400)** |

This $230,400 effect on Income Summary is the cost of goods sold amount. The periodic system transfers cost of goods sold to the Income Summary account but without using a Cost of Goods Sold account. Also, the periodic system does not separately measure shrinkage. Instead, it computes cost of goods available for sale, subtracts the cost of ending inventory, and defines the difference as cost of goods sold, which includes shrinkage.

---

* (This approach is called the *closing entry method*. An alternative approach, referred to as the *adjusting entry method,* would not make any entries to Merchandise Inventory in the closing entries of Exhibit 4A.1, but instead would make two adjusting entries. Using Z-Mart data, the two adjusting entries would be: (1) Dr. Income Summary and Cr. Merchandise Inventory for $19,000 each, and (2) Dr. Merchandise Inventory and Cr. Income Summary for $21,000 each. The first entry removes the beginning balance of Merchandise Inventory, and the second entry records the actual ending balance.)

# Preparing Financial Statements

The financial statements of a merchandiser using the periodic system are similar to those for a service company described in prior chapters. The income statement mainly differs by the inclusion of *cost of goods sold* and *gross profit*—of course, net sales is affected by discounts, returns, and allowances. The cost of goods sold section under the periodic system follows

| Calculation of Cost of Goods Sold<br>For Year Ended December 31, 2005 | |
|---|---|
| Beginning inventory . . . . . . . . . . . . . . . . | $ 19,000 |
| Cost of goods purchased . . . . . . . . . . . . | 232,400 |
| Cost of goods available for sale . . . . . . . | 251,400 |
| Less ending inventory . . . . . . . . . . . . . . | 21,000 |
| Cost of goods sold . . . . . . . . . . . . . . . | $230,400 |

The balance sheet mainly differs by the inclusion of *merchandise inventory* in current assets—see Exhibit 4.15. The statement of retained earnings is unchanged. Finally, a work sheet can be used to help prepare these statements. The only differences under the periodic system from the worksheet illustrated in Appendix 4B using the perpetual system follow:

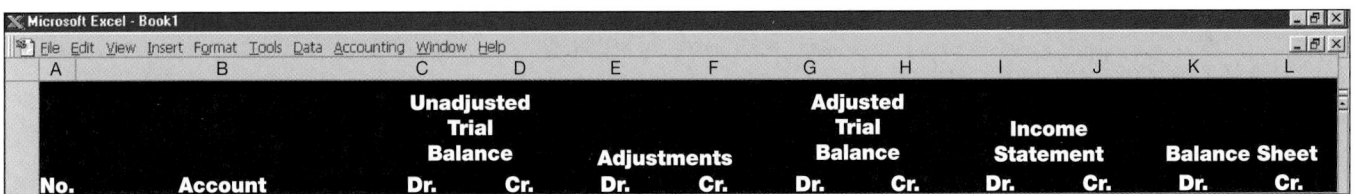

| No. | Account | Unadjusted Trial Balance Dr. | Cr. | Adjustments Dr. | Cr. | Adjusted Trial Balance Dr. | Cr. | Income Statement Dr. | Cr. | Balance Sheet Dr. | Cr. |
|---|---|---|---|---|---|---|---|---|---|---|---|

(1) Delete the following row for Merchandise Inventory

| 5 | 119 | Merchandise Inventory | 21,250 | | | (g) 250 | 21,000 | | | | 21,000 | |

and substitute the following row:

| 5 | 119 | Merchandise Inventory | 19,000 | | | | 19,000 | | 19,000 | 21,000 | 21,000 | |

(2) Delete the following cost of goods sold row

| 20 | 502 | Cost of goods sold | 230,150 | | (g) 250 | | 230,400 | | 230,400 | | | |

and substitute the following 4 rows:

| 20a | 505 | Purchases | 235,800 | | | | 235,800 | | 235,800 | | | |
| 20b | 506 | Purchases returns & allow. | | 1,500 | | | | 1,500 | | 1,500 | | |
| 20c | 507 | Purchases discounts | | 4,200 | | | | 4,200 | | 4,200 | | |
| 20d | 508 | Transportation-In | 2,300 | | | | 2,300 | | 2,300 | | | |

Of course, the worksheet column totals will slightly differ, but not the net income amount.

## Quick Check

**13.** What account is used in a perpetual inventory system but not in a periodic system?

**14.** Which of the following accounts are temporary accounts under a periodic system?
(*a*) Merchandise Inventory; (*b*) Purchases; (*c*) Transportation-In.

**15.** How is cost of goods sold computed under a periodic inventory system?

**16.** Do reported amounts of ending inventory and net income differ if the adjusting entry method of recording the change in inventory is used instead of the closing entry method?

Answer—p. 178

**APPENDIX**

# 4B    Work Sheet—Perpetual System

Exhibit 4B.1 shows the work sheet for preparing financial statements of a merchandiser. It differs slightly from the work sheet layout in Chapter 3—the differences are in bold. Also, the adjustments in the work sheet reflect the following: (*a*) Expiration of $600 of prepaid insurance. (*b*) Use of $1,200 of store supplies. (*c*) Use of $1,800 of office supplies. (*d*) Depreciation of $3,000 for store equipment. (*e*) Depreciation of $700 for office equipment. (*f*) Accrual of $300 of unpaid office salaries and $500 of unpaid store salaries. (*g*) Inventory shrinkage of $250. Once the adjusted amounts are extended into the financial statement columns, the information is used to develop financial statements.

## Exhibit 4B.1

Work Sheet for Merchandiser (using a perpetual system)

| No. | Account | Unadjusted Trial Balance Dr. | Cr. | Adjustments Dr. | Cr. | Adjusted Trial Balance Dr. | Cr. | Income Statement Dr. | Cr. | Balance Sheet Dr. | Cr. |
|---|---|---|---|---|---|---|---|---|---|---|---|
| 101 | Cash | 8,200 | | | | 8,200 | | | | 8,200 | |
| 106 | Accounts receivable | 11,200 | | | | 11,200 | | | | 11,200 | |
| 119 | **Merchandise Inventory** | 21,250 | | | (g) 250 | 21,000 | | | | 21,000 | |
| 124 | Office supplies | 2,350 | | | (c) 1,800 | 550 | | | | 550 | |
| 125 | Store supplies | 1,450 | | | (b) 1,200 | 250 | | | | 250 | |
| 128 | Prepaid insurance | 900 | | | (a) 600 | 300 | | | | 300 | |
| 163 | Office equipment | 4,200 | | | | 4,200 | | | | 4,200 | |
| 164 | Accum. depr.—Office equip. | | 700 | | (e) 700 | | 1,400 | | | | 1,400 |
| 165 | Store equipment | 30,000 | | | | 30,000 | | | | 30,000 | |
| 166 | Accum. depr.—Store equip. | | 3,000 | | (d) 3,000 | | 6,000 | | | | 6,000 |
| 201 | Accounts payable | | 16,000 | | | | 16,000 | | | | 16,000 |
| 209 | Salaries payable | | | | (f) 800 | | 800 | | | | 800 |
| 307 | Common stock | | 10,000 | | | | 10,000 | | | | 10,000 |
| 318 | Retained earnings | | 32,600 | | | | 32,600 | | | | 32,600 |
| 319 | Dividends | 4,000 | | | | 4,000 | | | | 4,000 | |
| 413 | **Sales** | | 321,000 | | | | 321,000 | | 321,000 | | |
| 414 | **Sales returns and allowances** | 2,000 | | | | 2,000 | | 2,000 | | | |
| 415 | **Sales discounts** | 4,300 | | | | 4,300 | | 4,300 | | | |
| 502 | **Cost of goods sold** | 230,150 | | (g) 250 | | 230,400 | | 230,400 | | | |
| 612 | Depr. expense—Store equip. | | | (d) 3,000 | | 3,000 | | 3,000 | | | |
| 613 | Depr. expense—Office equip. | | | (e) 700 | | 700 | | 700 | | | |
| 620 | Office salaries expense | 25,000 | | (f) 300 | | 25,300 | | 25,300 | | | |
| 621 | Sales salaries expense | 18,000 | | (f) 500 | | 18,500 | | 18,500 | | | |
| 637 | Insurance expense | | | (a) 600 | | 600 | | 600 | | | |
| 641 | Rent expense—Office space | 900 | | | | 900 | | 900 | | | |
| 642 | Rent expense—Selling space | 8,100 | | | | 8,100 | | 8,100 | | | |
| 650 | Office supplies expense | | | (c) 1,800 | | 1,800 | | 1,800 | | | |
| 651 | Store supplies expense | | | (b) 1,200 | | 1,200 | | 1,200 | | | |
| 655 | Advertising expense | 11,300 | | | | 11,300 | | 11,300 | | | |
| | Totals | 383,300 | 383,300 | 8,350 | 8,350 | 387,800 | 387,800 | 308,100 | 321,000 | 79,700 | 66,800 |
| | Net income | | | | | | | 12,900 | | | 12,900 |
| | Totals | | | | | | | 321,000 | 321,000 | 79,700 | 79,700 |

## Summary

**C1  Describe merchandising activities and identify income components for a merchandising company.** Merchandisers buy products and resell them. Examples of merchandisers include Wal-Mart, Home Depot, The Limited, and Barnes & Noble. A merchandiser's costs on the income statement include an amount for cost of goods sold. Gross profit, or gross margin, equals sales minus cost of goods sold.

**C2  Identify and explain the inventory asset of a merchandising company.** The current asset section of a merchandising company's balance sheet includes *merchandise inventory,* which refers to the products a merchandiser sells and are available for sale at the balance sheet date.

**C3  Describe both perpetual and periodic inventory systems.** A perpetual inventory system continuously tracks the cost of goods available for sale and the cost of goods sold. A periodic system accumulates the cost of goods purchased during the period and does not compute the amount of inventory or the cost of goods sold until the end of a period.

**C4  Analyze and interpret cost flows and operating activities of a merchandising company.** Cost of merchandise purchases flows into Merchandise Inventory and from there to Cost of Goods Sold on the income statement. Any remaining inventory is reported as a current asset on the balance sheet.

**A1  Compute the acid-test ratio and explain its use to assess liquidity.** The acid-test ratio is computed as quick assets (cash, short-term investments, and current receivables) divided by current liabilities. It indicates a company's ability to pay its current liabilities with its existing quick assets. An acid-test ratio equal to or greater than 1.0 is often adequate.

**A2  Compute the gross margin ratio and explain its use to assess profitability.** The gross margin ratio is computed as gross margin (net sales minus cost of goods sold) divided by net sales. It indicates a company's profitability before considering other expenses.

**P1  Analyze and record transactions for merchandise purchases using a perpetual system.** For a perpetual inventory system, purchases of inventory (net of trade discounts) are added to the Merchandise Inventory account. Purchase discounts and purchase returns and allowances are subtracted from Merchandise Inventory, and transportation-in costs are added to Merchandise Inventory.

**P2  Analyze and record transactions for merchandise sales using a perpetual system.** A merchandiser records sales at list price less any trade discounts. The cost of items sold is transferred from Merchandise Inventory to Cost of Goods Sold. Refunds or credits given to customers for unsatisfactory merchandise are recorded in Sales Returns and Allowances, a contra account to Sales. If merchandise is returned and restored to inventory, the cost of this merchandise is removed from Cost of Goods Sold and transferred back to Merchandise Inventory. When cash discounts from the sales price are offered and customers pay within the discount period, the seller records Sales Discounts, a contra account to Sales.

**P3  Prepare adjustments and close accounts for a merchandising company.** With a perpetual system, it is often necessary to make an adjustment for inventory shrinkage. This is computed by comparing a physical count of inventory with the Merchandise Inventory balance. Shrinkage is normally charged to Cost of Goods Sold. Temporary accounts closed to Income Summary for a merchandiser include Sales, Sales Discounts, Sales Returns and Allowances, and Cost of Goods Sold.

**P4  Define and prepare multiple-step and single-step income statements.** Multiple-step income statements include greater detail for sales and expenses than do single-step income statements. They also show details of net sales and report expenses in categories reflecting different activities.

**P5^A  Record and compare merchandising transactions using both periodic and perpetual inventory systems.** Transactions involving the sale and purchase of merchandise are recorded and analyzed under both the periodic and perpetual inventory systems. Adjusting and closing entries for both inventory systems are illustrated and explained.

## Guidance Answers to **Decision Maker** and **Decision Ethics**

**Entrepreneur**  For terms of 3/10, n/90, missing the 3% discount for an additional 80 days equals an implied annual interest rate of 13.69% computed as (365 days ÷ 80 days) × 3%. Since you can borrow funds at 11% (assuming no other processing costs), it is better to borrow and pay within the discount period. You save 2.69% (13.69% − 11%) in interest costs by paying early.

**Credit Manager**  Your decision is whether to comply with prior policy or to create a new policy and not abuse discounts offered by suppliers. Your first step should be to meet with your superior to find out if the late payment policy is the actual policy and, if so, its rationale. If it is the policy to pay late, you must apply your own sense of ethics. One point of view is that the late payment policy is unethical. A deliberate plan to make late payments means the company lies when it pretends to make payment within the discount period. Another view is that the late payment policy is acceptable. In some markets, attempts to take discounts through late payments are accepted as a continued phase of "price negotiation." Also, your company's suppliers can respond by billing your company for the discounts not accepted because of late payments. However, this is a dubious viewpoint, especially since the prior manager proposes that you explain late payments as computer or mail problems and since some suppliers have complained.

**Supplier**  A current ratio of 2.1 suggests sufficient current assets to cover current liabilities. An acid-test ratio of 0.5 suggests, however, that quick assets can cover only about one-half of current liabilities. This implies that the retailer depends on money from sales of inventory to pay current liabilities. If sales of inventory decline or profit margins decrease, the likelihood that this retailer will default on its payments increases. Your decision is probably not to extend credit. If you do extend credit, you are likely to closely monitor the retailer's financial condition. (It is better to hold unsold inventory than uncollectible receivables.)

**Financial Officer**   Your company's net profit margin is about equal to the industry average and suggests typical industry performance. However, gross margin reveals that your company is paying far more in cost of goods sold or receiving far less in sales price than competitors. Your attention must be directed to finding the problem with cost of goods sold, sales, or both. One positive note is that your company's expenses make up 19% of sales (36% − 17%). This favorably compares with competitors' expenses that make up 28% of sales (44% − 16%).

## Guidance Answers to **Quick Checks**

1. Cost of goods sold is the cost of merchandise purchased from a supplier that is sold to customers during a specific period.

2. Gross profit (or gross margin) is the difference between net sales and cost of goods sold.

3. Widespread use of computing and related technology has dramatically increased the use of the perpetual inventory system.

4. Under credit terms of 2/10, n/60, the credit period is 60 days and the discount period is 10 days.

5. (*b*) trade discount.

6. *FOB* means "free on board." It is used in identifying the point when ownership transfers from seller to buyer. *FOB destination* means that the seller transfers ownership of goods to the buyer when they arrive at the buyer's place of business. It also means that the seller is responsible for paying shipping charges and bears the risk of damage or loss during shipment.

7. Recording sales discounts and sales returns and allowances separately from sales gives useful information to managers for internal monitoring and decision making.

8. When a customer returns merchandise *and* the seller restores the merchandise to inventory, two entries are necessary. One entry records the decrease in revenue and credits the customer's account. The second entry debits inventory and reduces cost of goods sold.

9. Credit memorandum—seller credits accounts receivable from buyer.

10. Merchandise Inventory may need adjusting to reflect shrinkage.

11. Sales (of goods), Sales Discounts, Sales Returns and Allowances, and Cost of Goods Sold (and maybe Delivery Expense).

12. Four closing entries: (1) close credit balances in temporary accounts to Income Summary, (2) close debit balances in temporary accounts to Income Summary, (3) close Income Summary to Retained Earnings, and (4) close Dividends account to Retained Earnings.

13. Cost of Goods Sold.

14. (*b*) Purchases and (*c*) Transportation-In.

15. Under a periodic inventory system, the cost of goods sold is determined at the end of an accounting period by adding the net cost of goods purchased to the beginning inventory and subtracting the ending inventory.

16. Both methods report the same ending inventory and income.

## Key Terms

Key Terms are available at the book's Website for learning and testing in an online Flashcard Format.

| | | |
|---|---|---|
| **Acid-test ratio** (p. 167) | **Gross margin** (p. 153) | **Purchase discount** (p. 155) |
| **Cash discount** (p. 155) | **Gross margin ratio** (p. 167) | **Retailer** (p. 152) |
| **Cost of goods sold** (p. 153) | **Gross profit** (p. 153) | **Sales discount** (p. 155) |
| **Credit memorandum** (p. 161) | **Inventory** (p. 153) | **Selling expenses** (p. 165) |
| **Credit period** (p. 155) | **List price** (p. 154) | **Shrinkage** (p. 162) |
| **Credit terms** (p. 155) | **Merchandise** (p. 152) | **Single-step income statement** (p. 166) |
| **Debit memorandum** (p. 156) | **Merchandise inventory** (p. 153) | **Supplementary records** (p. 158) |
| **Discount period** (p. 155) | **Merchandiser** (p. 152) | **Trade discount** (p. 154) |
| **EOM** (p. 155) | **Multiple-step income statement** (p. 164) | **Wholesaler** (p. 152) |
| **FOB** (p. 157) | **Periodic inventory system** (p. 154) | |
| **General and administrative expenses** (p. 165) | **Perpetual inventory system** (p. 153) | |

## Personal Interactive Quiz

Personal Interactive Quizzes A and B are available at the book's Website to reinforce and assess your learning.

*Superscript letter* ^A (^B) *denotes assignments based on Appendix 4A (4B).*

## Discussion Questions

**1.** In comparing the accounts of a merchandising company with those of a service company, what additional accounts would the merchandising company likely use, assuming it employs a perpetual inventory system?

**2.** What items appear in financial statements of merchandising companies but not in the statements of service companies?

**3.** Explain how a business can earn a positive gross profit on its sales and still have a net loss.

**4.** Why do companies offer a cash discount?

**5.** How does a company that uses a perpetual inventory system determine the amount of inventory shrinkage?

**6.** Distinguish between cash discounts and trade discounts. Is the amount of a trade discount on purchased merchandise recorded in the accounts?

**7.** What is the difference between a sales discount and a purchase discount?

**8.** Why would a company's manager be concerned about the quantity of its purchase returns if its suppliers allow unlimited returns?

**9.** Does the sender (maker) of a debit memorandum record a debit or a credit in the recipient's account? What entry (debit or credit) does the recipient record?

**10.** What is the difference between the single-step and multiple-step income statement formats?

**11.** Refer to the income statement for **Krispy Kreme** in Appendix A. What term is used instead of cost of goods sold? Does the company present a detailed calculation of its cost of goods sold?

**12.** Refer to the balance sheet for **Tastykake** in Appendix A. What does Tastykake call its inventory account? What alternate name could it use?

**13.** Refer to the income statement of **Harley-Davidson** in Appendix A. Does its income statement report a gross profit figure? If yes, what is the amount?

**14.** Buyers negotiate purchase contracts with suppliers. What type of shipping terms should a buyer attempt to negotiate to minimize freight-in costs?

### Red numbers denote Discussion Questions that involve decision-making.

*Homework Manager repeats all numerical Quick Study assignments on the book's Website with new numbers.*

Prepare journal entries to record each of the following purchases transactions of a merchandising company. Show supporting calculations and assume a perpetual inventory system.

Mar.  5   Purchased 500 units of product with a list price of $5 per unit. The purchaser is granted a trade discount of 20%; terms of the sale are 2/10, n/60; invoice is dated March 5.

Mar.  7   Returned 50 defective units from the March 5 purchase and received full credit.

Mar. 15   Paid the amount due from the March 5 purchase, less the return on March 7.

**QUICK STUDY**

**QS 4-1**
Recording purchases—perpetual system

P1

Prepare journal entries to record each of the following sales transactions of a merchandising company. Show supporting calculations and assume a perpetual inventory system.

Apr.  1   Sold merchandise for $2,000, granting the customer terms of 2/10, EOM; invoice dated April 1. The cost of the merchandise is $1,400.

Apr.  4   The customer in the April 1 sale returned merchandise and received credit for $500. The merchandise, which had cost $350, is returned to inventory.

Apr. 11   Received payment for the amount due from the April 1 sale less the return on April 4.

**QS 4-2**
Recording sales—perpetual system

P2

**QS 4-3**

Computing and analyzing
gross margin

C1   A2

Compute net sales, gross profit, and the gross margin ratio for each separate case *a* through *d*. Interpret the gross margin ratio for case *a*.

|  | a | b | c | d |
|---|---|---|---|---|
| Sales ......................... | $130,000 | $512,000 | $35,700 | $245,700 |
| Sales discounts ................. | 4,200 | 16,500 | 400 | 3,500 |
| Sales returns and allowances ....... | 17,000 | 5,000 | 5,000 | 700 |
| Cost of goods sold .............. | 76,600 | 326,700 | 21,300 | 125,900 |

**QS 4-4**

Accounting for shrinkage—
perpetual system

P3

Nix'It Company's ledger on July 31, its fiscal year-end, includes the following selected accounts that have normal balances (Nix'It uses the perpetual inventory system):

| | | | |
|---|---|---|---|
| Merchandise inventory ....... | $ 34,800 | Sales returns and allowances ........ | $ 3,500 |
| Common stock ............ | 20,000 | Cost of goods sold .............. | 102,000 |
| Retained earnings ........... | 95,300 | Depreciation expense ............ | 7,300 |
| Dividends ................ | 7,000 | Salaries expense ................ | 29,500 |
| Sales .................... | 157,200 | Miscellaneous expenses ........... | 2,000 |
| Sales discounts ............ | 1,700 | | |

A physical count of its July 31 year-end inventory discloses that the cost of the merchandise inventory still available is $32,900. Prepare the entry to record any inventory shrinkage.

**QS 4-5**

Closing entries   P3

Refer to QS 4-4 and prepare journal entries to close the balances in temporary revenue and expense accounts. Remember to consider the entry for shrinkage that is made to solve QS 4-4.

**QS 4-6**

Computing and interpreting
acid-test ratio

A1

Use the following information on current assets and current liabilities to compute and interpret the acid-test ratio. Explain what the acid-test ratio of a company measures.

| | | | |
|---|---|---|---|
| Cash ................. | $1,200 | Prepaid expenses ............ | $ 600 |
| Accounts receivable ....... | 2,700 | Accounts payable ............ | 4,750 |
| Inventory ............... | 5,000 | Other current liabilities ....... | 950 |

**QS 4-7**

Contrasting liquidity ratios   A1

Identify similarities and differences between the acid-test ratio and the current ratio. Compare and describe how the two ratios reflect a company's ability to meet its current obligations.

**QS 4-8ᴬ**

Contrasting periodic and
perpetual systems

C3

Identify whether each description best applies to a periodic or a perpetual inventory system.
**a.** Provides more timely information to managers.
**b.** Requires an adjusting entry to record inventory shrinkage.
**c.** Markedly increased in frequency and popularity in business within the past decade.
**d.** Records cost of goods sold each time a sales transaction occurs.

**QS 4-9ᴬ**

Recording purchases—
periodic system   P5

Refer to QS 4-1 and prepare journal entries to record each of the merchandising transactions assuming that the periodic inventory system is used.

**QS 4-10ᴬ**

Recording purchases—
periodic system   P5

Refer to QS 4-2 and prepare journal entries to record each of the merchandising transactions assuming that the periodic inventory system is used.

_Homework Manager repeats all numerical Exercises on the book's Website with new numbers._

Prepare journal entries to record the following transactions for a retail store. Assume a perpetual inventory system.

Apr.  2   Purchased merchandise from Blue Company under the following terms: $3,600 price, invoice dated April 2, credit terms of 2/15, n/60, and FOB shipping point.
       3   Paid $200 for shipping charges on the April 2 purchase.
       4   Returned to Blue Company unacceptable merchandise that had an invoice price of $600.
      17   Sent a check to Blue Company for the April 2 purchase, net of the discount and the returned merchandise.
      18   Purchased merchandise from Fox Corp. under the following terms: $7,500 price, invoice dated April 18, credit terms of 2/10, n/30, and FOB destination.
      21   After negotiations, received from Fox a $2,100 allowance on the April 18 purchase.
      28   Sent a check to Fox paying for the April 18 purchase, net of the discount and allowance.

**EXERCISES**

**Exercise 4-1**
Recording entries for merchandise purchases

P1

**Check**  April 28, Cr. Cash $5,292

---

Taos Company purchased merchandise for resale from Tucson Company with an invoice price of $22,000 and credit terms of 3/10, n/60. The merchandise had cost Tucson $15,000. Taos paid within the discount period. Assume that both buyer and seller use a perpetual inventory system.

**1.** Prepare entries that the buyer should record for the purchase and the cash payment.
**2.** Prepare entries that the seller should record for the sale and the cash collection.
**3.** Assume that the buyer borrowed enough cash to pay the balance on the last day of the discount period at an annual interest rate of 8% and paid it back on the last day of the credit period. Compute how much the buyer saved by following this strategy. (Assume a 365-day year and round dollar amounts to the nearest cent.)

**Exercise 4-2**
Analyzing and recording merchandise transactions—both buyer and seller

P1  P2

**Check**  (3) $426 savings

---

Insert the letter for each term in the blank space beside the definition that it most closely matches:

**A.** Cash discount        **E.** FOB shipping point      **H.** Purchase discount
**B.** Credit period        **F.** Gross profit            **I.** Sales discount
**C.** Discount period      **G.** Merchandise inventory    **J.** Trade discount
**D.** FOB destination

_____  **1.** Ownership of goods is transferred when delivered to the buyer's place of business.
_____  **2.** Time period in which a cash discount is available.
_____  **3.** Difference between net sales and the cost of goods sold.
_____  **4.** Reduction in a receivable or payable if it is paid within the discount period.
_____  **5.** Purchaser's description of a cash discount received from a supplier of goods.
_____  **6.** Ownership of goods is transferred when the seller delivers goods to the carrier.
_____  **7.** Reduction below list or catalog price that is negotiated in setting the price of goods.
_____  **8.** Seller's description of a cash discount granted to buyers in return for early payment.
_____  **9.** Time period that can pass before a customer's payment is due.
_____  **10.** Goods a company owns and expects to sell to its customers.

**Exercise 4-3**
Applying merchandising terms

C1

---

Spare Parts was organized on May 1, 2005, and made its first purchase of merchandise on May 3. The purchase was for 1,000 units at a price of $10 per unit. On May 5, Spare Parts sold 600 of the units for $14 per unit to DeSoto Co. Terms of the sale were 2/10, n/60. Prepare entries for Spare Parts to record the May 5 sale and each of the following separate transactions _a_ through _c_ using a perpetual inventory system.

**a.** On May 7, DeSoto returns 200 units because they did not fit the customer's needs. Spare Parts restores the units to its inventory.

**b.** On May 8, DeSoto discovers that 50 units are damaged but of some use and, therefore, keeps the units. Spare Parts sends DeSoto a credit memorandum for $300 to compensate for the damage.

**c.** On May 15, DeSoto returns 100 defective units and Spare Parts concludes that these units cannot be resold. As a result, Spare Parts discards them—it removes these units' cost from cost of good sold and records a loss from defective merchandise.

**Exercise 4-4**
Recording sales returns and allowances

P2

**Check**  (c) Cr. Cost of Good Sold $1,000

**Exercise 4-5**

Recording purchase returns and allowances   P1

Refer to Exercise 4-4 and prepare the appropriate journal entries for DeSoto Co. to record the May 5 purchase and each of the three separate transactions *a* through *c*. DeSoto is a retailer that uses a perpetual inventory system and purchases these units for resale.

**Exercise 4-6**

Analyzing and recording merchandise transactions—both buyer and seller

P1   P2

**Check**   (1) May 20, Cr. Cash $27,936

On May 11, Smythe Co. accepts delivery of $30,000 of merchandise it purchases for resale from Hope Corporation. With the merchandise is an invoice dated May 11, with terms of 3/10, n/90, FOB shipping point. The cost of the goods for Hope is $20,000. When the goods are delivered, Smythe pays $335 to Express Shipping for delivery charges on the merchandise. On May 12, Smythe returns $1,200 of goods to Hope, who receives them one day later and restores them to inventory. The returned goods had cost Hope $800. On May 20, Smythe mails a check to Hope Corporation for the amount owed. Hope receives it the following day. (Both Smythe and Hope use a perpetual inventory system)

**1.** Prepare journal entries that Smythe Co. records for these transactions.

**2.** Prepare journal entries that Hope Corporation records for these transactions.

**Exercise 4-7**

Sales returns and allowances

C1   P2

Explain why a company's manager wants the accounting system to record customers' returns of unsatisfactory goods in the Sales Returns and Allowances account instead of the Sales account. In addition, explain whether this information would be useful for external decision makers.

**Exercise 4-8**

Recording effects of merchandising activities

C4

**Check**   Merchandise Inventory
(12/31/2005), $29,200

The following supplementary records summarize Titus Company's merchandising activities for year 2005. Set up T-accounts for Merchandise Inventory and Cost of Goods Sold. Then record the summarized activities in those T-accounts and compute account balances.

| | |
|---|---:|
| Cost of merchandise sold to customers in sales transactions . . . . . . . . . . . . . . | $186,000 |
| Merchandise inventory, December 31, 2004 . . . . . . . . . . . . . . . . . . . . . . . . . . | 27,000 |
| Invoice cost of merchandise purchases  . . . . . . . . . . . . . . . . . . . . . . . . . . . . . | 190,500 |
| Shrinkage determined on December 31, 2005 . . . . . . . . . . . . . . . . . . . . . . . . . | 700 |
| Cost of transportation-in . . . . . . . . . . . . . . . . . . . . . . . . . . . . . . . . . . . . . . . | 1,900 |
| Cost of merchandise returned by customers and restored to inventory  . . . . . . . | 2,200 |
| Purchase discounts received . . . . . . . . . . . . . . . . . . . . . . . . . . . . . . . . . . . . . | 1,600 |
| Purchase returns and allowances . . . . . . . . . . . . . . . . . . . . . . . . . . . . . . . . . . | 4,100 |

**Exercise 4-9**

Calculating revenues, expenses, and income

C1   C4

Fill in the blanks in the following separate income statements *a* through *e*. Identify any negative amount by putting it in parentheses.

| | a | b | c | d | e |
|---|---:|---:|---:|---:|---:|
| Sales . . . . . . . . . . . . . . . . . . . . . . . . . . . . . | $60,000 | $42,500 | $36,000 | $ ? | $23,600 |
| Cost of goods sold | | | | | |
| Merchandise inventory (beginning) . . . . . . . . . . | 6,000 | 17,050 | 7,500 | 7,000 | 2,560 |
| Total cost of merchandise purchases  . . . . . . . | 36,000 | ? | ? | 32,000 | 5,600 |
| Merchandise inventory (ending) . . . . . . . . . . . | ? | (2,700) | (9,000) | (6,600) | ? |
| Cost of goods sold . . . . . . . . . . . . . . . . . . . . | 34,050 | 15,900 | ? | ? | 5,600 |
| Gross profit  . . . . . . . . . . . . . . . . . . . . . . . . | ? | ? | 3,750 | 45,600 | ? |
| Expenses . . . . . . . . . . . . . . . . . . . . . . . . . . . | 9,000 | 10,650 | 12,150 | 2,600 | 6,000 |
| Net income (loss) . . . . . . . . . . . . . . . . . . . . | $ ? | $15,950 | $ (8,400) | $43,000 | $ ? |

**Exercise 4-10**

Preparing adjusting and closing entries for a merchandiser   P3

The following list includes some permanent accounts and all of the temporary accounts from the December 31, 2005, unadjusted trial balance of Deacon Co., a business owned by Julie Deacon. Use these account balances along with the additional information to journalize (*a*) adjusting entries and (*b*) closing entries. Deacon Co. uses a perpetual inventory system.

|  | Debit | Credit |
|---|---|---|
| Merchandise inventory . . . . . . . . . . . . | $ 28,000 | |
| Prepaid selling expenses . . . . . . . . . . . | 5,000 | |
| Dividends . . . . . . . . . . . . . . . . . . . | 2,200 | |
| Sales . . . . . . . . . . . . . . . . . . . . . . . | | $429,000 |
| Sales returns and allowances . . . . . . . | 16,500 | |
| Sales discounts . . . . . . . . . . . . . . . . | 4,000 | |
| Cost of goods sold . . . . . . . . . . . . . . | 211,000 | |
| Sales salaries expense . . . . . . . . . . . . | 47,000 | |
| Utilities expense . . . . . . . . . . . . . . . | 14,000 | |
| Selling expenses . . . . . . . . . . . . . . . . | 35,000 | |
| Administrative expenses . . . . . . . . . . . | 95,000 | |

**Additional Information**

Accrued sales salaries amount to $1,600. Prepaid selling expenses of $2,000 have expired. A physical count of year-end merchandise inventory shows $27,450 of goods still available.

**Check** Entry to close Income Summary: Cr. Retained Earnings $2,350

---

A retail company recently completed a physical count of ending merchandise inventory to use in preparing adjusting entries. In determining the cost of the counted inventory, company employees failed to consider that $2,000 of incoming goods had been shipped by a supplier on December 31 under an FOB shipping point agreement. These goods had been recorded in Merchandise Inventory as a purchase, but they were not included in the physical count because they were in transit. Explain how this overlooked fact affects the company's financial statements and the following ratios: return on assets, debt ratio, current ratio, profit margin ratio, and acid-test ratio.

**Exercise 4-11**

Interpreting a physical count error as inventory shrinkage

A1  A2  P3

---

Compute the current ratio and acid-test ratio for each of the following separate cases. Which company case is in the best position to meet short-term obligations? Explain.

**Exercise 4-12**

Computing and analyzing acid-test and current ratios

A1

|  | Case X | Case Y | Case Z |
|---|---|---|---|
| Cash . . . . . . . . . . . . . . . . . . | $ 800 | $ 910 | $1,100 |
| Short-term investments . . . . . . . | 0 | 0 | 500 |
| Current receivables . . . . . . . . . | 0 | 990 | 800 |
| Inventory . . . . . . . . . . . . . . . . | 2,000 | 1,000 | 4,000 |
| Prepaid expenses . . . . . . . . . . . | 1,200 | 600 | 900 |
| Total current assets . . . . . . . . . | $4,000 | $3,500 | $7,300 |
| Current liabilities . . . . . . . . . . . | $2,200 | $1,100 | $3,650 |

---

Journalize the following merchandising transactions for CSI Systems assuming it uses (a) a periodic inventory system and (b) a perpetual inventory system.

1. On November 1, CSI Systems purchases merchandise for $1,400 on credit with terms of 2/5, n/30, FOB shipping point; invoice dated November 1.
2. On November 5, CSI Systems pays cash for the November 1 purchase.
3. On November 7, CSI Systems discovers and returns $100 of defective merchandise purchased on November 1 for a cash refund.
4. On November 10, CSI Systems pays $80 cash for transportation costs with the November 1 purchase.
5. On November 13, CSI Systems sells merchandise for $1,500 on credit. The cost of the merchandise is $750.
6. On November 16, the customer returns merchandise from the November 13 transaction. The returned items sell for $200 and cost $100.

**Exercise 4-13[A]**

Preparing journal entries for both the periodic and perpetual systems

P1  P2  P5

---

### Exercise 4-14[A]
Recording purchases—
periodic system   P5

Refer to Exercise 4-1 and prepare journal entries to record each of the merchandising transactions assuming that the periodic inventory system is used.

---

### Exercise 4-15[A]
Recording purchases and
sales—periodic system   P5

Refer to Exercise 4-2 and prepare journal entries to record each of the merchandising transactions assuming that the periodic inventory system is used by both the buyer and the seller. (Skip the part 3 requirement.)

---

### Exercise 4-16[A]
Buyer and seller transactions—
periodic system   P5

Refer to Exercise 4-6 and prepare journal entries to record each of the merchandising transactions assuming that the periodic inventory system is used by both the buyer and the seller.

---

## PROBLEM SET A

### Problem 4-1A
Preparing journal entries for
merchandising activities—
perpetual system

P1   P2

**Check** Aug. 9, Dr. Delivery
Expense, $120

Aug. 18, Cr. Cash $4,695

Aug. 29, Dr. Cash $2,970

Prepare journal entries to record the following merchandising transactions of Stone Company, which applies the perpetual inventory system. (*Hint:* It will help to identify each receivable and payable; for example, record the purchase on August 1 in Accounts Payable—Abilene.)

Aug.  1   Purchased merchandise from Abilene Company for $6,000 under credit terms of 1/10, n/30, FOB destination, invoice dated August 1.
      4   At Abilene's request, Stone paid $100 cash for freight charges on the August 1 purchase, reducing the amount owed to Abilene.
      5   Sold merchandise to Lux Corp. for $4,200 under credit terms of 2/10, n/60, FOB destination, invoice dated August 5. The merchandise had cost $3,000.
      8   Purchased merchandise from Welch Corporation for $5,300 under credit terms of 1/10, n/45, FOB shipping point, invoice dated August 8. The invoice showed that at Stone's request, Welch paid the $240 shipping charges and added that amount to the bill.
      9   Paid $120 cash for shipping charges related to the August 5 sale to Lux Corp.
     10   Lux returned merchandise from the August 5 sale that had cost Stone $500 and been sold for $700. The merchandise was restored to inventory.
     12   After negotiations with Welch Corporation concerning problems with the merchandise purchased on August 8, Stone received a credit memorandum from Welch granting a price reduction of $800.
     15   Received balance due from Lux Corp. for the August 5 sale less the return on August 10.
     18   Paid the amount due Welch Corporation for the August 8 purchase less the price reduction granted.
     19   Sold merchandise to Trax for $3,600 under credit terms of 1/10, n/30, FOB shipping point, invoice dated August 19. The merchandise had cost $2,500.
     22   Trax requested a price reduction on the August 19 sale because the merchandise did not meet specifications. Stone sent Trax a $600 credit memorandum to resolve the issue.
     29   Received Trax's cash payment for the amount due from the August 19 purchase.
     30   Paid Abilene Company the amount due from the August 1 purchase.

---

### Problem 4-2A
Preparing journal entries for
merchandising activities—
perpetual system

P1   P2

Prepare journal entries to record the following merchandising transactions of Bask Company, which applies the perpetual inventory system. (*Hint:* It will help to identify each receivable and payable; for example, record the purchase on July 1 in Accounts Payable—Black.)

July  1   Purchased merchandise from Black Company for $6,000 under credit terms of 1/15, n/30, FOB shipping point, invoice dated July 1.
      2   Sold merchandise to Coke Co. for $800 under credit terms of 2/10, n/60, FOB shipping point, invoice dated July 2. The merchandise had cost $500.
      3   Paid $100 cash for freight charges on the purchase of July 1.
      8   Sold merchandise that had cost $1,200 for $1,600 cash.
      9   Purchased merchandise from Lane Co. for $2,300 under credit terms of 2/15, n/60, FOB destination, invoice dated July 9.
     11   Received a $200 credit memorandum from Lane Co. for the return of part of the merchandise purchased on July 9.

12    Received the balance due from Coke Co. for the invoice dated July 2, net of the discount.

16    Paid the balance due to Black Company within the discount period.

19    Sold merchandise that cost $900 to AKP Co. for $1,250 under credit terms of 2/15, n/60, FOB shipping point, invoice dated July 19.

21    Issued a $150 credit memorandum to AKP Co. for an allowance on goods sold on July 19.

24    Paid Lane Co. the balance due after deducting the discount.

30    Received the balance due from AKP Co. for the invoice dated July 19, net of discount.

31    Sold merchandise that cost $3,200 to Coke Co. for $5,000 under credit terms of 2/10, n/60, FOB shipping point, invoice dated July 31.

**Check**   July 12, Dr. Cash $784
July 16, Cr. Cash $5,940

July 24, Cr. Cash $2,058
July 30, Dr. Cash $1,078

---

The following unadjusted trial balance is prepared at fiscal year-end for Rex Company:

**Problem 4-3A**

Preparing adjusting entries and income statements; and computing gross margin, acid-test, and current ratios

A1   A2   P3   P4

mhhe.com/wild3e

| File Edit View Insert Format Tools Data Accounting Window Help | | |
| --- | --- | --- |
| **REX COMPANY** Unadjusted Trial Balance January 31, 2005 | | |
| 1 | Debit | Credit |
| 2   Cash | $   2,200 | |
| 3   Merchandise inventory | 11,500 | |
| 4   Store supplies | 4,800 | |
| 5   Prepaid insurance | 2,300 | |
| 6   Store equipment | 41,900 | |
| 7   Accumulated depreciation—Store equipment | | $  15,000 |
| 8   Accounts payable | | 9,000 |
| 9   Common stock | | 5,000 |
| 10  Retained earnings | | 27,000 |
| 11  Dividends | 2,000 | |
| 12  Sales | | 104,000 |
| 13  Sales discounts | 1,000 | |
| 14  Sales returns and allowances | 2,000 | |
| 15  Cost of good sold | 37,400 | |
| 16  Depreciation expense—Store equipment | 0 | |
| 17  Salaries expense | 31,000 | |
| 18  Insurance expense | 0 | |
| 19  Rent expense | 14,000 | |
| 20  Store supplies expense | 0 | |
| 21  Advertising expense | 9,900 | |
| 22  Totals | $160,000 | $160,000 |
| 23 | | |

Rent expense and salaries expense are equally divided between selling activities and the general and administrative activities. Rex Company uses a perpetual inventory system.

**Required**

**1.** Prepare adjusting journal entries to reflect each of the following:

   **a.** Store supplies still available at fiscal year-end amount to $1,650.

   **b.** Expired insurance, an administrative expense, for the fiscal year is $1,500.

   **c.** Depreciation expense on store equipment, a selling expense, is $1,400 for the fiscal year.

   **d.** To estimate shrinkage, a physical count of ending merchandise inventory is taken. It shows $11,100 of inventory is still available at fiscal year-end.

**2.** Prepare a multiple-step income statement for fiscal year 2005.

**3.** Prepare a single-step income statement for fiscal year 2005.

**4.** Compute the current ratio, acid-test ratio, and gross margin ratio as of January 31, 2005.

**Check**   (2) Gross profit, $63,200;
(3) Total expenses, $98,750; Net income, $2,250

## Problem 4-4A

Computing merchandising amounts and formatting income statements

C4  P4

BizKid Company's adjusted trial balance on August 31, 2005, its fiscal year-end, follows:

|  | Debit | Credit |
|---|---|---|
| Merchandise inventory . . . . . . . . . . . | $ 31,000 | |
| Other (noninventory) assets . . . . . . . | 120,400 | |
| Total liabilities . . . . . . . . . . . . . . . . . | | $ 35,000 |
| Common stock . . . . . . . . . . . . . . . . | | 20,000 |
| Retained earnings . . . . . . . . . . . . . . | | 81,650 |
| Dividends . . . . . . . . . . . . . . . . . . . . | 8,000 | |
| Sales . . . . . . . . . . . . . . . . . . . . . . . | | 212,000 |
| Sales discounts . . . . . . . . . . . . . . . . | 3,250 | |
| Sales returns and allowances . . . . . . . | 14,000 | |
| Cost of goods sold . . . . . . . . . . . . . | 82,600 | |
| Sales salaries expense . . . . . . . . . . . | 29,000 | |
| Rent expense—Selling space . . . . . . . | 10,000 | |
| Store supplies expense . . . . . . . . . . . | 2,500 | |
| Advertising expense . . . . . . . . . . . . . | 18,000 | |
| Office salaries expense . . . . . . . . . . . | 26,500 | |
| Rent expense—Office space . . . . . . . | 2,600 | |
| Office supplies expense . . . . . . . . . . | 800 | |
| Totals . . . . . . . . . . . . . . . . . . . . . . | $348,650 | $348,650 |

On August 31, 2004, merchandise inventory was $25,000. Supplementary records of merchandising activities for the year ended August 31, 2005, reveal the following itemized costs:

| | |
|---|---|
| Invoice cost of merchandise purchases . . . . . . . | $91,000 |
| Purchase discounts received . . . . . . . . . . . . . . | 1,900 |
| Purchase returns and allowances . . . . . . . . . . . | 4,400 |
| Costs of transportation-in . . . . . . . . . . . . . . . | 3,900 |

### Required

**Check**  (2) $88,600;

(3) Gross profit, $112,150;
Net income, $22,750;

(4) Total expenses, $172,000

**1.** Compute the company's net sales for the year.

**2.** Compute the company's total cost of merchandise purchased for the year.

**3.** Prepare a multiple-step income statement that includes separate categories for selling expenses and for general and administrative expenses.

**4.** Prepare a single-step income statement that includes these expense categories: cost of goods sold, selling expenses, and general and administrative expenses.

## Problem 4-5A

Preparing closing entries and interpreting information about discounts and returns

C4  P3

**Check**  (1) $22,750 Dr. to close
Income Summary

(3) Current-year rate, 6.6%

Use the data for BizKid Company in Problem 4-4A to complete the following requirements:

### Required

**1.** Prepare closing entries as of August 31, 2005 (the perpetual inventory system is used).

### Analysis Component

**2.** The company makes all purchases on credit, and its suppliers uniformly offer a 3% sales discount. Does it appear that the company's cash management system is accomplishing the goal of taking all available discounts? Explain.

**3.** In prior years, the company experienced a 5% returns and allowance rate on its sales, which means approximately 5% of its gross sales were eventually returned outright or caused the company to grant allowances to customers. How do this year's results compare to prior years' results?

Refer to the data and information in Problem 4-3A.

**Required**

Prepare and complete the entire 10-column work sheet for Rex Company. Follow the structure of Exhibit 4B.1 in Appendix 4B.

**Problem 4-6A**[B]
Preparing a work sheet for a merchandiser

---

Prepare journal entries to record the following merchandising transactions of Wave Company, which applies the perpetual inventory system. (*Hint:* It will help to identify each receivable and payable; for example, record the purchase on July 3 in Accounts Payable—CAP.)

July  3   Purchased merchandise from CAP Corp. for $15,000 under credit terms of 1/10, n/30, FOB destination, invoice dated July 3.

     4   At CAP's request, Wave paid $250 cash for freight charges on the July 3 purchase, reducing the amount owed to CAP.

     7   Sold merchandise to Morris Co. for $10,500 under credit terms of 2/10, n/60, FOB destination, invoice dated July 7. The merchandise had cost $7,500.

    10   Purchased merchandise from Murdock Corporation for $14,200 under credit terms of 1/10, n/45, FOB shipping point, invoice dated July 10. The invoice showed that at Wave's request, Murdock paid the $600 shipping charges and added that amount to the bill.

    11   Paid $300 cash for shipping charges related to the July 7 sale to Morris Co.

    12   Morris returned merchandise from the July 7 sale that had cost Wave $1,250 and been sold for $1,750. The merchandise was restored to inventory.

    14   After negotiations with Murdock Corporation concerning problems with the merchandise purchased on July 10, Wave received a credit memorandum from Murdock granting a price reduction of $2,000.

    17   Received balance due from Morris Co. for the July 7 sale less the return on July 12.

    20   Paid the amount due Murdock Corporation for the July 10 purchase less the price reduction granted.

    21   Sold merchandise to Ulsh for $9,000 under credit terms of 1/10, n/30, FOB shipping point, invoice dated July 21. The merchandise had cost $6,250.

    24   Ulsh requested a price reduction on the July 21 sale because the merchandise did not meet specifications. Wave sent Ulsh a credit memorandum for $1,500 to resolve the issue.

    30   Received Ulsh's cash payment for the amount due from the July 21 purchase.

    31   Paid CAP Corp. the amount due from the July 3 purchase.

**PROBLEM SET B**

**Problem 4-1B**
Preparing journal entries for merchandising activities—perpetual system

P1  P2

**Check**  July 17, Dr. Cash $8,575
July 20, Cr. Cash $12,678

July 30, Dr. Cash $7,425

---

Prepare journal entries to record the following merchandising transactions of Yang Company, which applies the perpetual inventory system. (*Hint:* It will help to identify each receivable and payable; for example, record the purchase on May 2 in Accounts Payable—Bots.)

May  2   Purchased merchandise from Bots Co. for $9,000 under credit terms of 1/15, n/30, FOB shipping point, invoice dated May 2.

     4   Sold merchandise to Chase Co. for $1,200 under credit terms of 2/10, n/60, FOB shipping point, invoice dated May 4. The merchandise had cost $750.

     5   Paid $150 cash for freight charges on the purchase of May 2.

     9   Sold merchandise that had cost $1,800 for $2,400 cash.

    10   Purchased merchandise from Snyder Co. for $3,450 under credit terms of 2/15, n/60, FOB destination, invoice dated May 10.

    12   Received a $300 credit memorandum from Snyder Co. for the return of part of the merchandise purchased on May 10.

    14   Received the balance due from Chase Co. for the invoice dated May 4, net of the discount.

    17   Paid the balance due to Bots Co. within the discount period.

    20   Sold merchandise that cost $1,450 to Tex Co. for $2,800 under credit terms of 2/15, n/60, FOB shipping point, invoice dated May 20.

    22   Issued a $400 credit memorandum to Tex Co. for an allowance on goods sold from May 20.

    25   Paid Snyder Co. the balance due after deducting the discount.

    30   Received the balance due from Tex Co. for the invoice dated May 20, net of discount and allowance.

    31   Sold merchandise that cost $4,800 to Chase Co. for $7,500 under credit terms of 2/10, n/60, FOB shipping point, invoice dated May 31.

**Problem 4-2B**
Preparing journal entries for merchandising activities—perpetual system

P1  P2

**Check**  May 14, Dr. Cash $1,176
May 17, Cr. Cash $8,910

May 30, Dr. Cash $2,352

**Problem 4-3B**

Preparing adjusting entries and income statements; and computing gross margin, acid-test, and current ratios

A1   A2   P3   P4

The following unadjusted trial balance is prepared at fiscal year-end for FAB Products Company:

| FAB PRODUCTS COMPANY Unadjusted Trial Balance October 31, 2005 | | |
|---|---|---|
| | Debit | Credit |
| Cash | $ 4,400 | |
| Merchandise inventory | 23,000 | |
| Store supplies | 9,600 | |
| Prepaid insurance | 4,600 | |
| Store equipment | 83,800 | |
| Accumulated depreciation—Store equipment | | $ 30,000 |
| Accounts payable | | 16,000 |
| Common stock | | 10,000 |
| Retained earnings | | 54,000 |
| Dividends | 2,000 | |
| Sales | | 208,000 |
| Sales discounts | 2,000 | |
| Sales returns and allowances | 4,000 | |
| Cost of good sold | 74,800 | |
| Depreciation expense—Store equipment | 0 | |
| Salaries expense | 62,000 | |
| Insurance expense | 0 | |
| Rent expense | 28,000 | |
| Store supplies expense | 0 | |
| Advertising expense | 19,800 | |
| Totals | $318,000 | $318,000 |

Rent expense and salaries expense are equally divided between selling activities and the general and administrative activities. FAB Products Company uses a perpetual inventory system.

**Required**

1. Prepare adjusting journal entries to reflect each of the following:
   a. Store supplies still available at fiscal year-end amount to $3,300.
   b. Expired insurance, an administrative expense, for the fiscal year is $3,000.
   c. Depreciation expense on store equipment, a selling expense, is $2,800 for the fiscal year.
   d. To estimate shrinkage, a physical count of ending merchandise inventory is taken. It shows $22,200 of inventory is still available at fiscal year-end.

**Check**   (2) Gross profit, $126,400; (3) Total expenses, $197,500; Net income, $4,500

2. Prepare a multiple-step income statement for fiscal year 2005.
3. Prepare a single-step income statement for fiscal year 2005.
4. Compute the current ratio, acid-test ratio, and gross margin ratio as of October 31, 2005.

**Problem 4-4B**

Computing merchandising amounts and formatting income statements

C1   C4   P4

Albin Company's adjusted trial balance on March 31, 2005, its fiscal year-end, follows:

| | Debit | Credit |
|---|---|---|
| Merchandise inventory | $ 46,500 | |
| Other (noninventory) assets | 190,600 | |
| Total liabilities | | $ 52,500 |
| Common stock | | 20,000 |
| Retained earnings | | 132,475 |
| Dividends | 2,000 | |
| Sales | | 318,000 |
| Sales discounts | 4,875 | |
| Sales returns and allowances | 21,000 | |
| Cost of goods sold | 123,900 | |
| Sales salaries expense | 43,500 | |

[continued on next page]

[continued from previous page]

| | |
|---|---|
| Rent expense—Selling space . . . . . . . | 15,000 |
| Store supplies expense . . . . . . . . . . . | 3,750 |
| Advertising expense . . . . . . . . . . . . . | 27,000 |
| Office salaries expense . . . . . . . . . . . | 39,750 |
| Rent expense—Office space . . . . . . . | 3,900 |
| Office supplies expense . . . . . . . . . . | 1,200 |
| Totals . . . . . . . . . . . . . . . . . . . . . . | $522,975   $522,975 |

On March 31, 2004, merchandise inventory was $37,500. Supplementary records of merchandising activities for the year ended March 31, 2005, reveal the following itemized costs:

| | |
|---|---|
| Invoice cost of merchandise purchases . . . . . . . | $136,500 |
| Purchase discounts received . . . . . . . . . . . . . . | 2,850 |
| Purchase returns and allowances . . . . . . . . . . . | 6,600 |
| Costs of transportation-in . . . . . . . . . . . . . . | 5,850 |

**Required**

1. Calculate the company's net sales for the year.

2. Calculate the company's total cost of merchandise purchased for the year.

3. Prepare a multiple-step income statement that includes separate categories for selling expenses and for general and administrative expenses.

4. Prepare a single-step income statement that includes these expense categories: cost of goods sold, selling expenses, and general and administrative expenses.

**Check** (2) $132,900;

(3) Gross profit, $168,225;
Net income, $34,125;

(4) Total expenses, $258,000

---

Use the data for Albin Company in Problem 4-4B to complete the following requirements:

**Required**

1. Prepare closing entries as of March 31, 2005 (the perpetual inventory system is used).

*Analysis Component*

2. The company makes all purchases on credit, and its suppliers uniformly offer a 3% sales discount. Does it appear that the company's cash management system is accomplishing the goal of taking all available discounts? Explain.

3. In prior years, the company experienced a 5% returns and allowance rate on its sales, which means approximately 5% of its gross sales were eventually returned outright or caused the company to grant allowances to customers. How do this year's results compare to prior years' results?

**Problem 4-5B**
Preparing closing entries and interpreting information about discounts and returns

C4 P3

**Check** (1) $34,125 Dr. to close Income Summary

(3) Current-year rate, 6.6%

---

Refer to the data and information in Problem 4-3B.

**Required**

Prepare and complete the entire 10-column work sheet for FAB Products Company. Follow the structure of Exhibit 4B.1 in Appendix 4B.

**Problem 4-6B**[B]
Preparing a work sheet for a merchandiser

---

Problem Set C is available at the book's Website to further reinforce and assess your learning.

**PROBLEM SET C**

---

*(This serial problem began in Chapter 1 and continues through most of the book. If previous chapter segments were not completed, the serial problem can begin at this point. It is helpful, but not necessary, that you use the Working Papers that accompany the book.)*

Kay Breeze created Success Systems on October 1, 2004. The company has been successful, and its list of customers has grown. To accommodate the growth, the accounting system is modified to set up separate accounts for each customer. The following chart of accounts includes the account number used for each account and any balance as of December 31, 2004. Breeze decided to add a fourth digit with a decimal point to the 106 account number that had been used for the single Accounts Receivable account. This modification allows the company to continue using the existing chart of accounts.

**SERIAL PROBLEM**

Success Systems

| No. | Account Title | Dr. | Cr. |
|-----|--------------|-----|-----|
| 101 | Cash | 58,160 | |
| 106.1 | Alex's Engineering Co. | 0 | |
| 106.2 | Wildcat Services | 0 | |
| 106.3 | Easy Leasing | 0 | |
| 106.4 | Clark Co. | 3,000 | |
| 106.5 | Chang Corp. | 0 | |
| 106.6 | Gomez Co. | 2,668 | |
| 106.7 | Delta Co. | 0 | |
| 106.8 | KC, Inc. | 0 | |
| 106.9 | Dream, Inc. | 0 | |
| 119 | Merchandise inventory | 0 | |
| 126 | Computer supplies | 580 | |
| 128 | Prepaid insurance | 1,665 | |
| 131 | Prepaid rent | 825 | |
| 163 | Office equipment | 8,000 | |
| 164 | Accumulated depreciation—Office equipment | | 400 |
| 167 | Computer equipment | 20,000 | |
| 168 | Accumulated depreciation—Computer equipment | | 1,250 |
| 201 | Accounts payable | | 1,100 |

| No. | Account Title | Dr. | Cr. |
|-----|--------------|-----|-----|
| 210 | Wages payable | | 500 |
| 236 | Unearned computer services revenue | | 1,500 |
| 307 | Common stock | | 83,000 |
| 318 | Retained earnings | | 7,148 |
| 319 | Dividends | 0 | |
| 403 | Computer services revenue | | 0 |
| 413 | Sales | | 0 |
| 414 | Sales returns and allowances | 0 | |
| 415 | Sales discounts | 0 | |
| 502 | Cost of goods sold | 0 | |
| 612 | Depreciation expense—Office equipment | 0 | |
| 613 | Depreciation expense—Computer equipment | 0 | |
| 623 | Wages expense | 0 | |
| 637 | Insurance expense | 0 | |
| 640 | Rent expense | 0 | |
| 652 | Computer supplies expense | 0 | |
| 655 | Advertising expense | 0 | |
| 676 | Mileage expense | 0 | |
| 677 | Miscellaneous expenses | 0 | |
| 684 | Repairs expense—Computer | 0 | |

In response to requests from customers, Breeze will begin selling computer software. The company will extend credit terms of 1/10, n/30, FOB shipping point, to all customers who purchase this merchandise. However, no cash discount is available on consulting fees. Note that additional accounts (Nos. 119, 413, 414, 415, and 502) are added to its general ledger to accommodate the company's new merchandising activities. Also, Success Systems does not use reversing entries and, therefore, all revenue and expense accounts have zero balances as of January 1, 2005. Its transactions for January through March follow:

Jan. 4   Paid cash to Sherry Adams for five days' work at the rate of $125 per day. Four of the five days relate to wages payable that were accrued in the prior year.

5   Kay Breeze invested an additional $25,000 cash in the business in exchange for more common stock.

7   Purchased $5,800 of merchandise from Kansas Corp. with terms of 1/10, n/30, FOB shipping point, invoice dated January 7.

9   Received $2,668 cash from Gomez Co. as full payment on its account.

**Check** Jan. 11, Dr. Unearned Computer Services Revenue $1,500

11   Completed a five-day project for Alex's Engineering Co. and billed it $5,500, which is the total price of $7,000 less the advance payment of $1,500.

13   Sold merchandise with a retail value of $5,200 and a cost of $3,560 to Chang Corp., invoice dated January 13.

15   Paid $600 cash for freight charges on the merchandise purchased on January 7.

16   Received $4,000 cash from Delta Co. for computer services provided.

17   Paid Kansas Corp. for the invoice dated January 7, net of the discount.

**Check** Jan. 20, No entry to Cost of Goods Sold

20   Chang Corp. returned $500 of defective merchandise from its invoice dated January 13. The returned merchandise, which had a $320 cost, is discarded. (The policy of Success Systems is to leave the cost of defective products in cost of goods sold.)

22   Received the balance due from Chang Corp., net of both the discount and the credit for the returned merchandise.

24   Returned defective merchandise to Kansas Corp. and accepted a credit against future purchases. The defective merchandise invoice cost, net of the discount, was $496.

26   Purchased $9,000 of merchandise from Kansas Corp. with terms of 1/10, n/30, FOB destination, invoice dated January 26.

26   Sold merchandise with a $4,640 cost for $5,800 on credit to KC, Inc., invoice dated January 26.

29   Received a $496 credit memorandum from Kansas Corp. concerning the merchandise returned on January 24.

31   Paid cash to Sherry Adams for 10 days' work at $125 per day.

Feb. 1   Paid $2,475 cash to Summit Mall for another three months' rent in advance.

3   Paid Kansas Corp. for the balance due, net of the cash discount, less the $496 amount in the credit memorandum.

5   Paid $600 cash to the local newspaper for an advertising insert in today's paper.

11   Received the balance due from Alex's Engineering Co. for fees billed on January 11.

15  Paid $4,800 cash for dividends.

23  Sold merchandise with a $2,660 cost for $3,220 on credit to Delta Co., invoice dated February 23.

26  Paid cash to Sherry Adams for eight days' work at $125 per day.

27  Reimbursed Kay Breeze for business automobile mileage (600 miles at $0.32 per mile).

Mar.  8  Purchased $2,730 of computer supplies from Cain Office Products on credit, invoice dated March 8.

9  Received the balance due from Delta Co. for merchandise sold on February 23.

11  Paid $960 cash for minor repairs to the company's computer.

16  Received $5,260 cash from Dream, Inc., for computing services provided.

19  Paid the full amount due to Cain Office Products, including amounts created on December 15 and March 8.

24  Billed Easy Leasing for $8,900 of computing services provided.

25  Sold merchandise with a $2,002 cost for $2,800 on credit to Wildcat Services, invoice dated March 25.

30  Sold merchandise with a $1,100 cost for $2,220 on credit to Clark Company, invoice dated March 30.

31  Reimbursed Kay Breeze for business automobile mileage (400 miles at $0.32 per mile).

The following additional facts are available for preparing adjustments on March 31 prior to financial statement preparation:

**a.** The March 31 amount of computer supplies still available totals $2,005.

**b.** Three more months have expired since the company purchased its annual insurance policy at a $2,220 cost for 12 months of coverage.

**c.** Sherry Adams has not been paid for seven days of work at the rate of $125 per day.

**d.** Three months have passed since any prepaid rent has been transferred to expense. The monthly rent expense is $825.

**e.** Depreciation on the computer equipment for January 1 through March 31 is $1,250.

**f.** Depreciation on the office equipment for January 1 through March 31 is $400.

**g.** The March 31 amount of merchandise inventory still available totals $704.

### Required

**1.** Prepare journal entries to record each of the January through March transactions.

**2.** Post the journal entries in part 1 to the accounts in the company's general ledger. (*Note:* Begin with the ledger's post-closing adjusted balances as of December 31, 2004.)

**3.** Prepare a partial work sheet consisting of the first six columns (similar to the one shown in Exhibit 4B.1) that includes the unadjusted trial balance, the March 31 adjustments (*a*) through (*g*), and the adjusted trial balance. Do not prepare closing entries and do not journalize the adjustments or post them to the ledger.

**4.** Prepare an income statement (from the adjusted trial balance in part 3) for the three months ended March 31, 2005. Use a single-step format. List all expenses without differentiating between selling expenses and general and administrative expenses.

**5.** Prepare a statement of retained earnings (from the adjusted trial balance in part 3) for the three months ended March 31, 2005.

**6.** Prepare a classified balance sheet (from the adjusted trial balance) as of March 31, 2005.

**Check**  (2) Ending balances: Cash, $77,845; Sales, $19,240;

(3) Unadj. totals, $161,198; Adj. totals, $163,723;

(4) Net income, $18,686;

(5) Retained Earnings (3/31/05), $21,034;

(6) Total assets, $129,909

## BEYOND THE NUMBERS

**BTN 4-1**  Refer to **Krispy Kreme**'s financial statements in Appendix A to answer the following.

### Required

**1.** Assume that the amounts reported for inventories and cost of sales reflect items purchased in a form ready for resale. Compute the net cost of goods purchased for the fiscal year ended February 2, 2003.

**2.** Compute the current ratio and acid-test ratio as of February 2, 2003, and February 3, 2002. Interpret and comment on the ratio results.

*Roll On*

**3.** Access Krispy Kreme's financial statements (form 10-K) for fiscal years ending after February 2, 2003, from its Website (**KrispyKreme.com**) or the SEC's EDGAR database (**www.sec.gov**). Recompute and interpret the current ratio and acid-test ratio for these current fiscal years.

**REPORTING IN ACTION**

C4  A1

## COMPARATIVE ANALYSIS

A2

**BTN 4-2**   Key comparative figures ($ thousands) for both **Krispy Kreme** and **Tastykake** follow:

| Key Figures | Krispy Kreme | | Tastykake | |
| --- | --- | --- | --- | --- |
| | Current Year | Prior Year | Current Year | Prior Year |
| Revenues (net sales) ....... | $491,549 | $394,354 | $162,263 | $166,245 |
| Cost of sales ............. | 381,489 | 316,946 | 111,187 | 103,297 |

### Required

1. Compute the dollar amount of gross margin and the gross margin ratio for the two years shown for both companies.
2. Which company earns more in gross margin for each dollar of net sales?
3. Did the gross margin ratio improve or decline for these companies?

## ETHICS CHALLENGE

C1  P2

**BTN 4-3**   Amy Martinez is a student who plans to attend approximately four professional events a year at her college. Each event necessitates a financial outlay of $100–$200 for a new suit and accessories. After incurring a major hit to her savings for the first event, Amy developed a different approach. She buys the suit on credit the week before the event, wears it to the event, and returns it the next week to the store for a full refund on her charge card.

### Required

1. Comment on the ethics exhibited by Amy and possible consequences of her actions.
2. How does the merchandising company account for the suits that Amy returns?

## COMMUNICATING IN PRACTICE

C3  C4  P3

**BTN 4-4**   You are the financial officer for Music Plus, a retailer that sells goods for home entertainment needs. The business owner, Vic Velakturi, recently reviewed the annual financial statements you prepared and sent you an e-mail stating that he thinks you overstated net income. He explains that although he has invested a great deal in security, he is sure shoplifting and other forms of inventory shrinkage have occurred, but he does not see any deduction for shrinkage on the income statement. The store uses a perpetual inventory system.

### Required

Prepare a brief memorandum that responds to the owner's concerns.

## TAKING IT TO THE NET

A2  C1

mhhe.com/wild3e

**BTN 4-5**   Access the SEC's EDGAR database (www.sec.gov) and obtain the April 22, 2003, filing of its fiscal 2003 10-K report (for the year ended February 1, 2003) for **J. Crew Group, Inc**.

### Required

Prepare a table that reports the gross margin ratios for J. Crew using the revenues and cost of goods sold data from J. Crew's income statement for each of its most recent four years. Analyze and comment on the trend in its gross margin ratio.

## TEAMWORK IN ACTION

C1  C4

**BTN 4-6**   Best Brands' general ledger and supplementary records at the end of its current period reveal the following:

| | | | | |
| --- | --- | --- | --- | --- |
| Sales ................. | $430,000 | Merchandise inventory (beginning of period) .... | $ 49,000 |
| Sales returns ........... | 18,000 | Invoice cost of merchandise purchases ........ | 180,000 |
| Sales discounts .......... | 6,600 | Purchase discounts received ................ | 4,500 |
| Cost of transportation-in .... | 11,000 | Purchase returns and allowances ............ | 5,500 |
| Operating expenses ....... | 20,000 | Merchandise inventory (end of period) ........ | 42,000 |

### Required

1. *Each* member of the team is to assume responsibility for computing *one* of the following items. You are not to duplicate your teammates' work. Get any necessary amounts to compute your item from the appropriate teammate. Each member is to explain his or her computation to the team in preparation for reporting to the class.

**Point:** In teams of four, assign the same student *a* and *e*. Rotate teams for reporting on a different computation and the analysis in step 3.

   a. Net sales
   b. Total cost of merchandise purchases
   c. Cost of goods sold

   d. Gross profit
   e. Net income

**2.** Check your net income with the instructor. If correct, proceed to step 3.

**3.** Assume that a physical inventory count finds that actual ending inventory is $38,000. Discuss how this affects previously computed amounts in step 1.

---

**BTN 4-7**   Read the article, "The End of Fuzzy Math?" in the December 11, 2000, issue of *Business Week*. The book's Website provides free access to the article.

**BUSINESS WEEK ACTIVITY**

C1  C4

mhhe.com/wild3e

**Required**

**1.** How does the article define *fulfillment costs?*

**2.** Where does **Amazon.com** account for fulfillment costs on its income statement?

**3.** Where do similar companies, such as catalog companies and direct marketers, account for fulfillment costs on their income statements?

**4.** Does the FASB specify how to account for fulfillment costs? Explain.

**5.** Why is the issue of accounting for fulfillment costs important to investors?

---

**BTN 4-8**   Dwayne Lewis and Michael Cherry have earned well beyond the $1,000 they used to launch **Damani Dada** (see chapter's opening feature). Good entrepreneurs continually rethink and refine business strategies. Assume that Damani Dada's most recent income statement follows:

**ENTREPRENEURIAL DECISION**

C1  C4  P4

| DAMANI DADA | |
|---|---|
| **Income Statement ($ thousands)** | |
| **For Year Ended April 30, 2005** | |
| Net sales | $50,000 |
| Cost of sales | 35,000 |
| Expenses | 4,000 |
| Net income | $11,000 |

To increase income, Lewis and Cherry are proposing to offer sales discounts of 3/10, n/30, and to ship merchandise FOB shipping point. Assume that Damani Dada presently offers no discounts and ships merchandise FOB destination. The sales discounts are predicted to increase net sales by 14%, and the ratio of cost of sales divided by net sales is expected to remain unchanged. Since delivery expenses are zero under this proposal, the expenses are predicted to increase by only 10%.

**Required**

**1.** Prepare a forecasted income statement for the year ended April 30, 2006, based on this proposal.

**2.** Do you recommend that it implement the proposal given your analysis in part 1? Explain.

**3.** Identify any concerns you might express to Lewis and Cherry regarding their proposal.

---

**BTN 4-9**   Arrange an interview (in person or by phone) with the manager of a retail shop in a mall or in the downtown area of your community. Explain to the manager that you are a student studying merchandising activities and the accounting for sales returns and sales allowances. Ask the manager what the store policy is regarding returns. Also find out if the sales allowances are ever negotiated with customers. Inquire whether management perceives that customers are abusing return policies and what actions management takes to counter potential abuses. Be prepared to discuss your findings in class.

**HITTING THE ROAD**

C1

**Point:** This activity complements the Ethics Challenge assignment.

---

**BTN 4-10**   **Grupo Bimbo (GrupoBimbo.com)**, **Krispy Kreme**, and **Tastykake** are all competitors in the global marketplace. Key comparative figures for each company follow:

**GLOBAL DECISION**

A2  P4

| | Net Sales | Cost of Sales |
|---|---|---|
| Grupo Bimbo* | 41,373,269 | 19,155,865 |
| Krispy Kreme** | $ 491,549 | $ 381,489 |
| Tastykake** | $ 162,263 | $ 111,187 |

\* Thousands of pesos (Grupo Bimbo).
\*\* Thousands of dollars (Krispy Kreme and Tastykake).

**Required**

**1.** Rank the three companies (highest to lowest) based on the gross margin ratio.

**2.** Which of the companies uses a multiple-step income statement format? (Access their annual reports.)

**3.** Which company's income statement would likely be most easily interpreted by potential investors? Provide a brief justification for your choice.

"I am the COF—Chairman of Fun!"—Mike Becker

# 5 Reporting and Analyzing Inventories

## A Look Back

Chapter 4 focused on merchandising activities and how they are reported and analyzed. We also analyzed and recorded merchandise purchases and sales and explained accounting adjustments and the closing process for merchandising companies.

## A Look at This Chapter

This chapter emphasizes accounting for inventory. We describe the methods available for assigning costs to inventory and explain the items and costs making up merchandise inventory. We also analyze the effects of inventory on both financial and tax reporting, and we discuss other methods of estimating and measuring inventory.

## A Look Ahead

Chapter 6 focuses on internal controls and accounting for cash and cash equivalents. We explain good internal control procedures and their importance for accounting and analysis.

# CAP

| Conceptual | Analytical | Procedural |
|---|---|---|

**Conceptual**

**C1** Identify the items making up merchandise inventory. *(p. 196)*

**C2** Identify the costs of merchandise inventory. *(p. 197)*

**Analytical**

**A1** Analyze the effects of inventory methods for both financial and tax reporting. *(p. 203)*

**A2** Analyze the effects of inventory errors on current and future financial statements. *(p. 206)*

**A3** Assess inventory management using both inventory turnover and days' sales in inventory. *(p. 207)*

**Procedural**

**P1** Compute inventory in a perpetual system using the methods of specific identification, FIFO, LIFO, and weighted average. *(p. 198)*

**P2** Compute the lower of cost or market amount of inventory. *(p. 205)*

---

**Decision Feature**

# Wacky Inventor of Wobblers

SNOHOMISH, WA—Mike Becker long collected nostalgia-based toys from his childhood. Becker imagined that "there's got to be people like me out there [who love such toys], where I could have a cool little business based on that love."

Drawing on his life savings of $35,000, Becker started **FunKo (Funko.com)** making Wacky Wobblers (bobbleheads) out of his garage. His Wobblers are based on characters and personalities from his youth. "It's about invoking a feeling," says Becker. "We want people to say, 'Oh, I remember that!'" Becker has now sold more than 600,000 of 50 different Wobblers (selling for about $15 each) in the past 5 years. He projects sales this year of more than $2 million.

Still, the road to the top was shaky. Becker struggled with purchases and sales and had to confront discounts, returns, and allowances. One of his biggest obstacles, and continuing challenges, is maintaining the right inventories and controlling costs of sales. "It was kind of by trial and error," says Becker. "I didn't understand what the heck I was doing. I didn't have any distribution networks, sales reps, employees, or even a place of business." Success is more than good products, says Becker; it depends on assigning and monitoring costs of inventory and applying sound inventory management procedures.

With business booming, he continues to keep watch over inventory turnover and days' sales in inventory. This chapter focuses on these issues, including measuring, monitoring and managing such inventories. Yet Becker keeps all in perspective. "I guess we totally underestimated the possibility that there were so many other weirdos like us out there."

[Sources: *FunKo Website,* January 2004; *Entrepreneur,* November 2002; *Puget Sound Business Journal,* June 8, 2001; *Tri-City Herald,* January 2002; *Seattle Times,* April 13, 2002.]

Merchandisers' activities include the purchasing and reselling of merchandise. We explained accounting for merchandisers in Chapter 4, including that for purchases and sales. In this chapter, we extend the study and analysis of inventory by explaining the methods used to assign costs to merchandise inventory *and* to cost of goods sold. Retailers, wholesalers, and other merchandising companies that purchase products for resale use the principles and methods described. Understanding inventory accounting helps in the analysis and interpretation of financial statements, and in helping people run their own businesses.

**Reporting and Analyzing Inventories**

**Inventory Basics**

- Determining inventory items
- Determining inventory costs
- Internal control of inventory and taking a physical count

**Inventory Costing Under a Perpetual System**

- Inventory cost flow assumptions
- Specific identification
- First-in, first-out
- Last-in, first-out
- Weighted average
- Financial statement effects
- Consistent use of methods

**Inventory Valuation and Errors**

- Inventory valuation at lower of cost or market
- Financial statement effects of inventory errors

# Inventory Basics

This section identifies the items and costs making up merchandise inventory. It also describes the importance of internal controls in taking a physical count of inventory.

## Determining Inventory Items

**C1** Identify the items making up merchandise inventory.

Merchandise inventory includes all goods that a company owns and holds for sale. This rule holds regardless of where the goods are located when inventory is counted. Certain inventory items require special attention, including goods in transit, goods on consignment, and goods that are damaged or obsolete.

**Goods in Transit** Does a purchaser's inventory include goods in transit from a supplier? The answer is that if ownership has passed to the purchaser, the goods are included in the purchaser's inventory. We determine this by reviewing the shipping terms: *FOB destination* or *FOB shipping point*. If the purchaser is responsible for paying freight, ownership passes when goods are loaded on the transport vehicle. If the seller is responsible for paying freight, ownership passes when goods arrive at their destination.

**Goods on Consignment** Goods on consignment are goods shipped by the owner, called the **consignor,** to another party, the **consignee.** A consignee sells goods for the owner. The consignor continues to own the consigned goods and reports them in its inventory. **Upper Deck**, for instance, pays sports celebrities such as Tiger Woods to sign memorabilia, which are offered to shopping networks on consignment. Upper Deck, the consignor, must report these items in its inventory until sold.

**Goods Damaged or Obsolete** Damaged and obsolete (and deteriorated) goods are not counted in inventory if they cannot be sold. If these goods can be sold at a reduced price, they are included in inventory at a conservative estimate of their **net realizable value.** Net realizable value is sales price minus the cost of making the sale. The period when damage or obsolescence (or deterioration) occurs is the period when the loss in value is reported.

## Determining Inventory Costs

Merchandise inventory includes costs of expenditures necessary, directly or indirectly, to bring an item to a salable condition and location. This means that the cost of an inventory item includes its invoice cost minus any discount, and plus any added or incidental costs necessary to put it in a place and condition for sale. Added or incidental costs can include import duties, freight, storage, insurance, and costs incurred in an aging process (for example, aging wine or cheese).

Accounting principles prescribe that incidental costs be assigned to inventory. Also, the *matching principle* states that inventory costs should be recorded against revenue in the period when inventory is sold. However, some companies use the *materiality principle* (*cost-to-benefit constraint*) to avoid assigning incidental costs of acquiring merchandise to inventory. These companies argue either that incidental costs are immaterial or that the effort in assigning these costs to inventory outweighs the benefit.

**C2**   Identify the costs of merchandise inventory.

> ### Decision Insight
>
> A wireless portable computer with a two-way radio allows clerks to quickly record inventory by scanning bar codes and to instantly send and receive data. It gives managers access to up-to-date information on inventory and its location.
>
>

> ### Decision Insight
>
> Some retailers are adding bar code readers on shopping carts for customers to swipe products over the reader, charging it to a credit card. There is no need to stand in a checkout line. Customers simply pass through a gate to verify that everything in the cart is scanned.

## Internal Controls and Taking a Physical Count

The Inventory account under a perpetual system is updated for each purchase and sale, but events can cause the account balance to be different from the actual inventory available. Such events include theft, loss, damage, and errors. Thus, nearly all companies take a *physical count of inventory* at least once each year—informally called *taking an inventory*. This often occurs at the end of a fiscal year or when inventory amounts are low. This physical count is used to adjust the Inventory account balance to the actual inventory available.

A business must apply internal controls when taking a physical count of inventory that would usually include the following:

■ *Prenumbered inventory tickets* are prepared and distributed to *counters*—each ticket must be accounted for.

■ Counters of inventory are assigned that do not include those responsible for the inventory.

■ Counters confirm the validity of inventory, including its existence, amounts, quality, and so forth.

■ A second count should occur by a different counter.

■ A manager confirms that all inventories are ticketed once, and only once.

**Point:** The Inventory account is a controlling account for the inventory subsidiary ledger. This *subsidiary ledger* contains a separate record (units and costs) for each separate product, and it can be in electronic or paper form. Subsidiary records assist managers in planning and monitoring inventory.

> ### Quick Check
>
> 1. What accounting principle most guides the allocation of cost of goods available for sale between ending inventory and cost of goods sold?
>
> 2. If **Skechers** sells goods to **Target** with terms FOB shipping point, which company reports these goods in its inventory while they are in transit?
>
> 3. An art gallery purchases a painting for $11,400 on terms FOB shipping point. Additional costs in obtaining and offering the artwork for sale include $130 for transportation-in, $150 for import duties, $100 for insurance during shipment, $180 for advertising, $400 for framing, and $800 for office salaries. For computing inventory, what cost is assigned to the painting?

Answers—p. 219

# Inventory Costing Under a Perpetual System

Accounting for inventory affects both the balance sheet and the income statement. A major goal in accounting for inventory is to properly match costs with sales. We use the *matching principle* to decide how much of the cost of the goods available for sale is deducted from sales and how much is carried forward as inventory and matched against future sales.

Management decisions in accounting for inventory involve the following

- Costing method (specific identification, FIFO, LIFO, or weighted average).
- Inventory system (perpetual or periodic).
- Items included in inventory and their costs.
- Use of market values or other estimates.

Decisions on these points affect the reported amounts for inventory, cost of goods sold, gross profit, income, current assets, and other accounts.

One of the most important issues in accounting for inventory is determining the per unit costs assigned to inventory items. When all units are purchased at the same unit cost, this process is simple. When identical items are purchased at different costs, however, a question arises as to which amounts to record in cost of goods sold and which amounts remain in inventory.

Four methods are commonly used to assign costs to inventory and to cost of goods sold: (1) specific identification; (2) first-in, first-out; (3) last-in, first-out; and (4) weighted average. Exhibit 5.1 shows the frequency in the use of these methods.

**Exhibit 5.1**

Frequency in Use of
Inventory Methods

LIFO 32%     FIFO 44%

Weighted Average 20%     Other* 4%

*Includes specific identification.

Each method assumes a particular pattern for how costs flow through inventory. Each of these four methods is acceptable whether or not the actual physical flow of goods follows the cost flow assumption. Physical flow of goods depends on the type of product and the way it is stored. (Perishable goods such as fresh fruit demand that a business attempt to sell them in a first-in, first-out physical flow. Other products such as crude oil and minerals such as coal, gold, decorative stone can be sold in a last-in, first-out physical flow.) **Physical flow and cost flow need not be the same.**

## Inventory Cost Flow Assumptions

**P1**  Compute inventory in a perpetual system using the methods of specific identification, FIFO, LIFO, and weighted average.

This section introduces inventory cost flow assumptions. Assume that three identical units are purchased at the following three dates and costs: May 1 at $45, May 3 at $65, and May 6 at $70. One unit is then sold on May 7 for $100. Exhibit 5.2 gives a visual layout of the flow of costs to either the gross profit section of the income statement or the inventory reported on the balance sheet for FIFO, LIFO, and weighted average.

(1) *FIFO assumes costs flow in the order incurred.* The unit purchased on May 1 for $45 is the earliest cost incurred—it is sent to cost of goods sold on the income statement. The remaining two units ($65 and $70) are reported in inventory on the balance sheet.

(2) *LIFO assumes costs flow in the reverse order incurred.* The unit purchased on May 6 for $70 is the most recent cost incurred—it is sent to cost of goods sold on the income statement. The remaining two units ($45 and $65) are reported in inventory on the balance sheet.

(3) *Weighted average assumes costs flow at an average of the costs available.* The units available at the May 7 sale average $60 in cost, computed as ($45 + $65 + $70)/3. One unit's $60 average cost is sent to cost of goods sold on the income statement. The remaining two units' average costs are reported in inventory at $120 on the balance sheet.

Cost flow assumptions can markedly impact gross profit and inventory. Exhibit 5.2 shows that gross profit as a percent of net sales ranges from 30% to 55% due to nothing else but the cost flow assumption.

**Exhibit 5.2**

Cost Flow Assumptions

The following sections on inventory costing methods use the perpetual system. Appendix 5A uses the periodic system. An instructor can choose to cover either one or both inventory systems.

## Inventory Costing Illustration

This section provides a comprehensive illustration of inventory costing methods. We use information from Trekking, a sporting goods store. Among its many products, Trekking carries one type of mountain bike whose sales are directed at resorts that provide inexpensive mountain bikes for complimentary guest use. Its customers usually purchase in amounts of 10 or more bikes. We use Trekking's data from August 2005. Its mountain bike (unit) inventory at the beginning of August and its purchases and sales during August are shown in Exhibit 5.3. It ends August with 12 bikes remaining in inventory.

**Point:** Inventories are a large portion of current assets for most wholesalers, retailers, and manufacturers. Accounting for inventories is key to determining cost of goods sold and gross profit.

| Date | Activity | Units Acquired at Cost | | Units Sold at Retail | Unit Inventory |
|------|----------|------------------------|---|----------------------|----------------|
| Aug. 1 | Beginning inventory . | 10 units @ $ 91 = $ 910 | | | 10 units |
| Aug. 3 | Purchases . . . . . . . . | 15 units @ $106 = $1,590 | | | 25 units |
| Aug. 14 | Sales . . . . . . . . . . . | | | 20 units @ $130 | 5 units |
| Aug. 17 | Purchases . . . . . . . . | 20 units @ $115 = $2,300 | | | 25 units |
| Aug. 28 | Purchases . . . . . . . . | 10 units @ $119 = $1,190 | | | 35 units |
| Aug. 31 | Sales . . . . . . . . . . . | | | 23 units @ $150 | **12 units** |
| | Totals . . . . . . . . . . | **55 units** | **$5,990** | **43 units** | |

**Exhibit 5.3**

Purchases and Sales of Goods

Trekking uses the perpetual inventory system, which means that its merchandise inventory account is continually updated to reflect purchases and sales. **(Appendix 5A describes the assignment of costs to inventory using a periodic system.)** Regardless of what inventory method or system is used, cost of goods available for sale must be allocated between cost of goods sold and ending inventory.

**Point:** The perpetual inventory system is now the most dominant system across U.S. businesses.

**Point:** Cost of goods sold plus ending inventory equals cost of goods available for sale.

## Specific Identification

When each item in inventory can be identified with a specific purchase and invoice, we can use **specific identification** (also called *specific invoice inventory pricing*) to assign costs.

**Point:** Three key variables determine the dollar value of ending inventory: (1) inventory quantity, (2) costs of inventory, and (3) cost flow assumption.

We also need sales records that identify exactly which items were sold and when. Trekking's internal documents reveal that 7 of the 12 unsold units in ending inventory were from the August 28 purchase and 5 were from the August 17 purchase. We use this information and the specific identification method to assign costs to the 12 units in ending inventory and to the 43 units sold as shown in Exhibit 5.4. Carefully study this exhibit to see the flow of costs both in and out of inventory. Notice that each unit, whether sold or remaining in inventory, has its own specific cost attached to it.

## Exhibit 5.4

### Specific Identification Computations

For the 20 units sold on Aug. 14, the company specifically identified that 8 of those had cost $91 and 12 had cost $106.

For the 23 units sold on Aug. 31, the company specifically identified each bike sold and its acquisition cost from prior purchases.

\* Identification of items sold (and their costs) is obtained from internal documents that track each unit from its purchase to its sale.

**Point:** Specific identification is usually only practical for companies with expensive, custom-made inventory.

When using specific identification, Trekking's cost of goods sold reported on the income statement totals **$4,582**, the sum of $2,000 and $2,582 from the third column of Exhibit 5.4. Trekking's ending inventory reported on the balance sheet is **$1,408**, which is the final inventory balance from the fourth column of Exhibit 5.4.

The purchases and sales entries for Exhibit 5.4 follow (the boldface numbers are those determined by the cost flow assumption):

| | **Purchases** | | | | **Sales** | | |
|---|---|---|---|---|---|---|---|
| Aug. 3 | Merchandise Inventory | 1,590 | | Aug. 14 | Accounts Receivable | 2,600 | |
| | Accounts Payable | | 1,590 | | Sales | | 2,600 |
| 17 | Merchandise Inventory | 2,300 | | 14 | Cost of Goods Sold | **2,000** | |
| | Accounts Payable | | 2,300 | | Merchandise Inventory | | **2,000** |
| 28 | Merchandise Inventory | 1,190 | | 31 | Accounts Receivable | 3,450 | |
| | Accounts Payable | | 1,190 | | Sales | | 3,450 |
| | | | | 31 | Cost of Goods Sold | **2,582** | |
| | | | | | Merchandise Inventory | | **2,582** |

## First-In, First-Out

The **first-in, first-out (FIFO)** method of assigning costs to both inventory and cost of goods sold assumes that inventory items are sold in the order acquired. When sales occur, the costs of the earliest units acquired are charged to cost of goods sold. This leaves the costs from the most recent purchases in ending inventory. Use of FIFO for computing the cost of inventory and cost of goods sold is shown in Exhibit 5.5.

**Point:** The "Goods Purchased" column is identical for all methods. Data are taken from Exhibit 5.3.

| Date | Goods Purchased | Cost of Goods Sold | Inventory Balance |
|------|-----------------|--------------------|-------------------|
| Aug. 1 | Beginning balance | | 10 @ $ 91    = $ 910 |
| Aug. 3 | 15 @ $106 = $1,590 | | 10 @ $ 91 ⎫<br>15 @ $106 ⎬ = $2,500 |
| Aug. 14 | | 10 @ $ 91 = $ 910 ⎫<br>10 @ $106 = $1,060 ⎬ = $1,970 | 5 @ $106    = $ 530 |
| Aug. 17 | 20 @ $115 = $2,300 | | 5 @ $106 ⎫<br>20 @ $115 ⎬ = $2,830 |
| Aug. 28 | 10 @ $119 = $1,190 | | 5 @ $106 ⎫<br>20 @ $115 ⎬ = $4,020<br>10 @ $119 ⎭ |
| Aug. 31 | | 5 @ $106 = $ 530 ⎫<br>18 @ $115 = $2,070 ⎬ = $2,600<br>$4,570 | 2 @ $115 ⎫<br>10 @ $119 ⎬ = $1,420 |

**Exhibit 5.5**

FIFO Computations— Perpetual System

> For the 20 units sold on Aug. 14, the first 10 sold are assigned the earliest cost of $91 (from beg. bal.). The next 10 sold are assigned the next earliest cost of $106.

> For the 23 units sold on Aug. 31, the first 5 sold are assigned the earliest available cost of $106 (from Aug. 3 purchase). The next 18 sold are assigned the next earliest cost of $115 (from Aug. 17 purchase).

Trekking's FIFO cost of goods sold reported on its income statement (reflecting the 43 units sold) is **$4,570** ($1,970 + $2,600), and its ending inventory reported on the balance sheet (reflecting the 12 units unsold) is **$1,420**.

The purchases and sales entries for Exhibit 5.5 follow (the boldface numbers are those affected by the cost flow assumption):

**Point:** Under FIFO, a unit sold is assigned the earliest (oldest) cost from inventory. This leaves the most recent costs in ending inventory.

| Purchases | | | | Sales | | | |
|-----------|--|--|--|-------|--|--|--|
| Aug. 3 | Merchandise Inventory | 1,590 | | Aug. 14 | Accounts Receivable | 2,600 | |
| | Accounts Payable | | 1,590 | | Sales | | 2,600 |
| 17 | Merchandise Inventory | 2,300 | | 14 | Cost of Goods Sold | **1,970** | |
| | Accounts Payable | | 2,300 | | Merchandise Inventory | | **1,970** |
| 28 | Merchandise Inventory | 1,190 | | 31 | Accounts Receivable | 3,450 | |
| | Accounts Payable | | 1,190 | | Sales | | 3,450 |
| | | | | 31 | Cost of Goods Sold | **2,600** | |
| | | | | | Merchandise Inventory | | **2,600** |

## Last-In, First-Out

The **last-in, first-out (LIFO)** method of assigning costs assumes that the most recent purchases are sold first. These more recent costs are charged to the goods sold, and the costs of the earliest purchases are assigned to inventory. As with other methods, LIFO is acceptable even when the physical flow of goods does not follow a last-in, first-out pattern. One appeal of LIFO is that by assigning costs from the most recent purchases to cost of goods sold, LIFO comes closest to matching current costs of goods sold with revenues (compared to FIFO or weighted average). Exhibit 5.6 shows how LIFO assigns the costs of mountain bikes to the 12 units in ending inventory and to the 43 units sold.

Topic Tackler 5-1

**Point:** Under LIFO, a unit sold is assigned the most recent (latest) cost from inventory. This leaves the oldest costs in inventory.

## Exhibit 5.6

LIFO Computations—
Perpetual System

For the 20 units sold on Aug. 14, the first 15 sold are assigned the most recent cost of $106. The next 5 sold are assigned the next most recent cost of $91.

For the 23 units sold on Aug. 31, the first 10 sold are assigned the most recent cost of $119. The next 13 sold are assigned the next most recent cost of $115.

| Date | Goods Purchased | Cost of Goods Sold | Inventory Balance |
|---|---|---|---|
| Aug. 1 | Beginning balance | | 10 @ $ 91 = $ 910 |
| Aug. 3 | 15 @ $106 = $1,590 | | 10 @ $ 91 }<br>15 @ $106 } = $ 2,500 |
| Aug. 14 | | 15 @ $106 = $1,590 }<br>5 @ $ 91 = $ 455 } = $2,045 | 5 @ $ 91 = $ 455 |
| Aug. 17 | 20 @ $115 = $2,300 | | 5 @ $ 91 }<br>20 @ $115 } = $ 2,755 |
| Aug. 28 | 10 @ $119 = $1,190 | | 5 @ $ 91 }<br>20 @ $115 } = $ 3,945<br>10 @ $119 } |
| Aug. 31 | | 10 @ $119 = $1,190 }<br>13 @ $115 = $1,495 } = $2,685<br>$4,730 | 5 @ $ 91 }<br>7 @ $115 } = $1,260 |

Trekking's LIFO cost of goods sold reported on the income statement is **$4,730** ($2,045 + $2,685), and its ending inventory reported on the balance sheet is **$1,260**.

The purchases and sales entries for Exhibit 5.6 follow (the boldface numbers are those affected by the cost flow assumption):

| Purchases | | | | Sales | | | |
|---|---|---|---|---|---|---|---|
| Aug. 3 | Merchandise Inventory....... | 1,590 | | Aug. 14 | Accounts Receivable ....... | 2,600 | |
| | Accounts Payable....... | | 1,590 | | Sales ............... | | 2,600 |
| 17 | Merchandise Inventory....... | 2,300 | | 14 | Cost of Goods Sold ....... | **2,045** | |
| | Accounts Payable....... | | 2,300 | | Merchandise Inventory .. | | **2,045** |
| 28 | Merchandise Inventory....... | 1,190 | | 31 | Accounts Receivable ....... | 3,450 | |
| | Accounts Payable....... | | 1,190 | | Sales ............... | | 3,450 |
| | | | | 31 | Cost of Goods Sold ....... | **2,685** | |
| | | | | | Merchandise Inventory .. | | **2,685** |

## Weighted Average

The **weighted average** (also called **average cost**) method of assigning cost requires that we compute the weighted average cost per unit of inventory at the time of each sale. Weighted average cost per unit at the time of each sale equals the cost of goods available for sale divided by the units available. The results using weighted average for Trekking are shown in Exhibit 5.7.

**Point:** Under weighted average, a unit sold is assigned the average cost of all items currently available for sale at the date of each sale.

Trekking's cost of goods sold reported on the income statement (reflecting the 43 units sold) is **$4,622** ($2,000 + $2,622), and its ending inventory reported on the balance sheet (reflecting the 12 units unsold) is **$1,368**.

The purchases and sales entries for Exhibit 5.7 follow (the boldface numbers are those affected by the cost flow assumption):

| Purchases | | | | Sales | | | |
|---|---|---|---|---|---|---|---|
| Aug. 3 | Merchandise Inventory....... | 1,590 | | Aug. 14 | Accounts Receivable ....... | 2,600 | |
| | Accounts Payable ....... | | 1,590 | | Sales ............... | | 2,600 |
| 17 | Merchandise Inventory....... | 2,300 | | 14 | Cost of Goods Sold........ | **2,000** | |
| | Accounts Payable ....... | | 2,300 | | Merchandise Inventory... | | **2,000** |
| 28 | Merchandise Inventory....... | 1,190 | | 31 | Accounts Receivable ....... | 3,450 | |
| | Accounts Payable ....... | | 1,190 | | Sales ............... | | 3,450 |
| | | | | 31 | Cost of Goods Sold........ | **2,622** | |
| | | | | | Merchandise Inventory... | | **2,622** |

| Date | Goods Purchased | Cost of Goods Sold | Inventory Balance | |
|---|---|---|---|---|
| Aug. 1 | Beginning balance | | 10 @ $ 91 = $ 910 | |
| Aug. 3 | 15 @ $106 = $1,590 | | 10 @ $ 91 ⎫ = $2,500 (or $100 per unit)ᵃ <br> 15 @ $106 ⎭ | |
| Aug. 14 | | 20 @ $100 = $2,000 | 5 @ $100 = $ 500 (or $100 per unit)ᵇ | For the 20 units sold on Aug. 14, the cost assigned is the $100 *average cost* per unit from the inventory balance column at the time of sale. |
| Aug. 17 | 20 @ $115 = $2,300 | | 5 @ $100 ⎫ = $2,800 (or $112 per unit)ᶜ <br> 20 @ $115 ⎭ | |
| Aug. 28 | 10 @ $119 = $1,190 | | 5 @ $100 ⎫ <br> 20 @ $115 ⎬ = $3,990 (or $114 per unit)ᵈ <br> 10 @ $119 ⎭ | For the 23 units sold on Aug. 31, the cost assigned is the $114 *average cost* per unit from the inventory balance column at the time of sale. |
| Aug. 31 | | 23 @ $114 = $2,622 | 12 @ $114 = $1,368 (or $114 per unit)ᵉ | |
| | | $4,622 | | |

Exhibit 5.7

Weighted Average
Computations—Perpetual System

ᵃ $100 per unit = ($2,500 inventory balance ÷ 25 units in inventory).

ᵇ $100 per unit = ($500 inventory balance ÷ 5 units in inventory).

ᶜ $112 per unit = ($2,800 inventory balance ÷ 25 units in inventory).

ᵈ $114 per unit = ($3,990 inventory balance ÷ 35 units in inventory).

ᵉ $114 per unit = ($1,368 inventory balance ÷ 12 units in inventory).

Advances in technology have greatly reduced the cost of a perpetual inventory system. Many companies are now asking whether they can afford *not* to have a perpetual inventory system because timely access to inventory information is a competitive advantage and it can help reduce the level of inventory, which reduces costs.

**Decision Insight**

**Inventory War**  The Pentagon applies accounting tools to shrink inventories and speed deliveries. Use of bar codes, laser cards, radio tags, and perpetual accounting systems speeds delivery from factory to foxhole.

## Financial Statement Effects of Costing Methods

When purchase prices do not change, each inventory costing method assigns the same cost amounts to inventory and to cost of goods sold. When purchase prices are different, however, the methods nearly always assign different cost amounts. We show these differences in Exhibit 5.8 using Trekking's data.

A1  Analyze the effects of inventory methods for both financial and tax reporting.

| | Specific Identification | FIFO | LIFO | Weighted Average |
|---|---|---|---|---|
| **TREKKING COMPANY** <br> **For Month Ended August 31** | | | | |
| **Income Statement** | | | | |
| Sales ..................... | $6,050 | $6,050 | $6,050 | $6,050 |
| Cost of goods sold ........... | 4,582 | 4,570 | 4,730 | 4,622 |
| Gross profit ............... | 1,468 | 1,480 | 1,320 | 1,428 |
| Expenses .................... | 450 | 450 | 450 | 450 |
| Income before taxes ........... | 1,018 | 1,030 | 870 | 978 |
| Income tax expense (30%) ....... | 305 | 309 | 261 | 293 |
| **Net income** ................. | $ 713 | $ 721 | $ 609 | $ 685 |
| **Balance Sheet** | | | | |
| **Inventory** .................. | $1,408 | $1,420 | $1,260 | $1,368 |

Exhibit 5.8

Financial Statement Effects of
Inventory Costing Methods

When purchase costs *regularly rise,* as in Trekking's case, note the following:

**Point:** FIFO is preferred when costs are rising and managers have incentives to report higher income for reasons such as bonus plans, job security, and reputation.

■ FIFO assigns the lowest amount to cost of goods sold—yielding the highest gross profit and net income.

■ LIFO assigns the highest amount to cost of goods sold—yielding the lowest gross profit and net income, which also yields a temporary tax advantage by postponing payment of some income tax.

■ Weighted average yields results between FIFO and LIFO.

■ Specific identification always yields results that depend on which units are sold.

**Point:** LIFO inventory is often less than the inventory's replacement cost because LIFO inventory is valued using the oldest inventory purchase costs.

When costs *regularly decline,* the reverse occurs for FIFO and LIFO.

All four inventory costing methods are acceptable. However, a company must disclose the inventory method it uses in its financial statements or notes. Each method offers certain advantages as follows:

■ FIFO assigns an amount to inventory on the balance sheet that approximates its current cost; it also mimics the actual flow of goods for most businesses.

■ LIFO assigns an amount to cost of goods sold on the income statement that approximates its current cost; it also better matches current costs with revenues in computing gross profit.

■ Weighted average tends to smooth out erratic changes in costs.

■ Specific identification exactly matches the costs of items with the revenues they generate.

### Decision Maker

**Financial Planner**   One of your clients asks if the inventory account of a company using FIFO needs any "adjustments" for analysis purposes in light of recent inflation. What is your advice? Does your advice depend on changes in the costs of these inventories?

Answer—p. 219

### Decision Insight

**Giving for Growth**   A recent survey found 76% of consumers saying they'd switch from their current product to one with a "good cause" if price and quality are equal. Many entrepreneurs combine their business ventures with their social passions for a win-win situation.

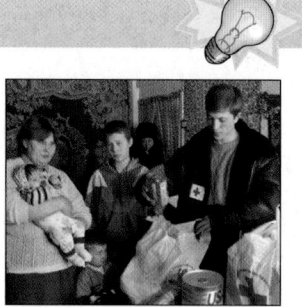

**Tax Effects of Costing Methods**
Trekking's segment income statement in Exhibit 5.8 includes income tax expense (at a rate of 30%) because it was formed as a corporation. Since inventory costs affect net income, they have potential tax effects. Trekking gains a temporary tax advantage by using LIFO. Many companies use LIFO for this reason.

Companies can and often do use different costing methods for financial reporting and tax reporting. *The only exception is when LIFO is used for tax reporting; in this case, the IRS requires that it also be used in financial statements.*

## Consistency in Using Costing Methods

**Global:** LIFO is acceptable under international accounting standards.

The **consistency principle** prescribes that a company use the same accounting methods period after period so that financial statements are comparable across periods—the only exception is when a change from one method to another will improve its financial reporting. The *full-disclosure principle* prescribes that the notes to the statements report this type of change, its justification, and its effect on net income.

The consistency principle does *not* require a company to use one method exclusively. For example, it can use different methods to value different categories of inventory.

### Decision Ethics

**Inventory Manager**   Your compensation as inventory manager includes a bonus plan based on gross profit. Your superior asks your opinion on changing the inventory costing method from FIFO to LIFO. Since costs are expected to continue to rise, your superior predicts that LIFO would match higher current costs against sales, thereby lowering taxable income (and gross profit). What do you recommend?

Answer—p. 219

## Quick Check

4. Describe one advantage for each of the inventory costing methods: specific identification, FIFO, LIFO, and weighted average.

5. When costs are rising, which method reports higher net income—LIFO or FIFO?

6. When costs are rising, what effect does LIFO have on a balance sheet compared to FIFO?

7. A company takes a physical count of inventory at the end of 2005 and finds that ending inventory is understated by $10,000. Would this error cause cost of goods sold to be overstated or understated in 2005? In year 2006? If so, by how much?

Answers—pp. 219–220

# Valuing Inventory at LCM and the Effects of Inventory Errors

This section examines the role of market costs in determining inventory on the balance sheet and also the financial statement effects of inventory errors.

## Lower of Cost or Market

We explained how to assign costs to ending inventory and cost of goods sold using one of four costing methods (FIFO, LIFO, weighted average, or specific identification). However, *accounting principles require that inventory be reported at the market value (cost) of replacing inventory when market value is lower than cost.* Merchandise inventory is then said to be reported on the balance sheet at the **lower of cost or market (LCM).**

**P2** Compute the lower of cost or market amount of inventory.

**Computing the Lower of Cost or Market**   *Market* in the term *LCM* is defined as the current replacement cost of purchasing the same inventory items in the usual manner. A decline in replacement cost reflects a loss of value in inventory. When the recorded cost of inventory is higher than the replacement cost, a loss is recognized. When the recorded cost is lower, no adjustment is made.

LCM is applied in one of three ways: (1) to each individual item separately, (2) to major categories of items, or (3) to the entire inventory. The less similar the items that make up inventory, the more likely companies are to apply LCM to individual items. To illustrate, we apply LCM to the ending inventory of a motorsports retailer in Exhibit 5.9.

**Point:** Advances in technology encourage the individual-item approach for LCM.

| Inventory Items | Units | Per Unit Cost | Per Unit Market | Total Cost | Total Market | LCM Applied to Items | LCM Applied to Categories | LCM Applied to Whole |
|---|---|---|---|---|---|---|---|---|
| **Cycles** | | | | | | | | |
| Roadster ..... | 20 | $8,000 | $7,000 | $160,000 | $140,000 | $ 140,000 | | |
| Sprint ....... | 10 | 5,000 | 6,000 | 50,000 | 60,000 | 50,000 | | |
| Category subtotal | | | | 210,000 | 200,000 | | $ 200,000 | |
| **Off-Road** | | | | | | | | |
| Trax-4 ....... | 8 | 5,000 | 6,500 | 40,000 | 52,000 | 40,000 | | |
| Blazer ....... | 5 | 9,000 | 7,000 | 45,000 | 35,000 | 35,000 | | |
| Category subtotal | | | | 85,000 | 87,000 | | 85,000 | |
| Totals | | | | $295,000 | $287,000 | $265,000 | $285,000 | $287,000 |

**Exhibit 5.9**

Lower of Cost or Market Computations

When LCM is applied to the *entire* inventory, the market amount is $287,000. Since this market amount is $8,000 lower than the $295,000 recorded cost, the $287,000 amount is reported for inventory on the balance sheet. When LCM is applied to the major *categories* of inventory, the market is $285,000. When LCM is applied to individual *items* of inventory, the market is $265,000. Since market amounts for these cases is less than the $295,000 recorded cost, the market amount is reported for inventory. Any one of these three applications of LCM is acceptable. The retailer **Best Buy** applies LCM and reports that its "merchandise inventories are recorded at the lower of average cost or market."

**Global:** In Canada, the Netherlands, and the United Kingdom, the *market* in LCM is defined as "net realizable value" (selling price less costs to complete and sell).

**Recording the Lower of Cost or Market**   Inventory must be adjusted downward when market is less than cost. To illustrate, if LCM is applied to the individual items of inventory in Exhibit 5.9, the Merchandise Inventory account must be adjusted from the $295,000 recorded cost down to the $265,000 market amount as follows

| | | |
|---|---|---|
| Cost of Goods Sold . . . . . . . . . . . . . . . . . . . . . | 30,000 | |
| Merchandise Inventory . . . . . . . . . . . . . . . . | | 30,000 |
| *To adjust inventory cost to market.* | | |

Accounting rules require that inventory be adjusted to market when market is less than cost, but inventory usually cannot be written up to market when market exceeds cost. If recording inventory down to market is acceptable, why are companies not allowed to record inventory up to market? One view is that a gain from a market increase should not be realized until a sales transaction verifies the gain. However, this problem also applies when market is less than cost. A second and primary reason is the **conservatism principle,** which prescribes the use of the less optimistic amount when more than one estimate of the amount to be received or paid exists and these estimates are about equally likely.

## Financial Statement Effects of Inventory Errors

A2   Analyze the effects of inventory errors on current and future financial statements.

Topic Tackler 5-2

Companies must take care in both taking a physical count of inventory and in assigning a cost to it. An inventory error causes misstatements in cost of goods sold, gross profit, net income, current assets, and equity. It also causes misstatements in the next period's statements because ending inventory of one period is the beginning inventory of the next.

**Income Statement Effects**   Exhibit 5.10 shows the effects of inventory errors on key amounts in the current period's income statement. Notice that inventory errors yield opposite effects in cost of goods sold and net income. Inventory errors also carry over to the next period, yielding reverse effects.

**Exhibit 5.10**

Effects of Inventory Errors on the Current Period's Income Statement

| Inventory Error | Cost of Goods Sold | Net Income |
|---|---|---|
| Understate ending inventory | Overstated | Understated |
| Understate beginning inventory | Understated | Overstated |
| Overstate ending inventory* | Understated | Overstated |
| Overstate beginning inventory* | Overstated | Understated |

\* These errors are less likely under a perpetual system because they imply more inventory than is recorded (or less shrinkage than expected). Thus, management will normally follow up and discover and correct these errors before they impact any accounts.

To illustrate, consider an inventory error for a company with $100,000 in sales for each of the years 2004, 2005, and 2006. If this company maintains a steady $20,000 inventory level during this period and makes $60,000 in purchases in each of these years, its cost of goods sold is $60,000 and its gross profit is $40,000 each year. What if this company errs in computing its 2004 ending inventory and reports $16,000 instead of the correct amount of $20,000? The effects of this error are shown in Exhibit 5.11. The $4,000 understatement of the year 2004 ending inventory causes a $4,000 overstatement in year 2004 cost of goods sold and a $4,000 understatement in both gross profit and net income for year 2004. Since year 2004 ending inventory becomes year 2005 beginning inventory, this error causes an understatement in 2005 cost of goods sold and a $4,000 overstatement in both gross profit and net income for year 2005. Notice that an inventory error in period 1 (2004) does not affect the period 3, year 2006. An inventory error is said to be *self-correcting* because it always yields an offsetting error in the next period. This, however, does not make inventory errors less serious. Managers, lenders, owners, and other users make important decisions from analysis of changes in net income and cost of goods sold.

**Point:** A former internal auditor at Coca-Cola alleges that just before midnight at the 2002 period-end, fully loaded Coke trucks were ordered to drive about 2 feet away from the loading dock so that Coke could record millions of dollars in extra sales.

Exhibit 5.11

Effects of Inventory Errors on Three Periods' Income Statements

| Income Statements | | | | | |
|---|---|---|---|---|---|
| | 2004 | | 2005 | | 2006 |
| Sales .................... | | $100,000 | | $100,000 | $100,000 |
| Cost of goods sold | | | | | |
| Beginning inventory ........ | $20,000 | | →$16,000* | | →$20,000 |
| Cost of goods purchased ..... | 60,000 | | 60,000 | | 60,000 |
| Goods available for sale ..... | 80,000 | | 76,000 | | 80,000 |
| Ending inventory .......... | 16,000* | | 20,000 | | 20,000 |
| Cost of goods sold ........ | | 64,000† | | 56,000† | 60,000 |
| Gross profit .............. | | 36,000 | | 44,000 | 40,000 |
| Expenses ................ | | 10,000 | | 10,000 | 10,000 |
| Net income .............. | | $ 26,000 | | $ 34,000 | $ 30,000 |

\* Correct amount is $20,000.      † Correct amount is $60,000.

**Balance Sheet Effects**   Balance sheet effects of an inventory error can be seen by considering the components of the accounting equation: Assets = Liabilities + Equity. For example, understating ending inventory understates both current and total assets. An understatement in ending inventory also yields an understatement in equity because of the understatement in net income. Exhibit 5.12 shows the effects of inventory errors on the current period's balance sheet amounts. Errors in *beginning* inventory do not yield misstatements in the end-of-period balance sheet, but they do affect that current period's income statement.

**Example:** If year 2004 ending inventory in Exhibit 5.11 is overstated by $3,000, what is the effect on cost of goods sold, gross profit, assets, and equity? *Answer:* Cost of goods sold is understated by $3,000 in 2004 and overstated by $3,000 in 2005. Gross profit and net income are overstated in 2004 and understated in 2005. Assets and equity are overstated in 2004.

Exhibit 5.12

Effects of Inventory Errors on Current Period's Balance Sheet

| Inventory Error | Assets | Equity |
|---|---|---|
| Understate ending inventory | Understated | Understated |
| Overstate ending inventory | Overstated | Overstated |

## Quick Check

**8.** Use LCM applied separately to individual items to compute ending inventory if the data are as follows:

| Product | Units | Unit Recorded Cost | Unit Market Cost |
|---|---|---|---|
| A .......... | 20 | $ 6 | $ 5 |
| B .......... | 40 | 9 | 8 |
| C .......... | 10 | 12 | 15 |

Answer—p. 220

## Inventory Turnover and Days' Sales in Inventory                    Decision Analysis

### Inventory Turnover

Earlier chapters described two important ratios useful in evaluating a company's short-term liquidity: current ratio and acid-test ratio. A merchandiser's ability to pay its short-term obligations also depends on how quickly it sells its merchandise inventory. **Inventory turnover,** also called *merchandise inventory turnover,* is one ratio used to assess this and is defined in Exhibit 5.13.

**A3** Assess inventory management using both inventory turnover and days' sales in inventory.

Exhibit 5.13

Inventory Turnover

$$\text{Inventory turnover} = \frac{\text{Cost of goods sold}}{\text{Average inventory}}$$

**Point:** We must take care when comparing turnover ratios across companies that use different costing methods (such as FIFO and LIFO).

This ratio reveals how many *times* a company turns over (sells) its inventory during a period. If a company's inventory greatly varies within a year, average inventory amounts can be computed from interim periods such as quarters or months.

Users apply inventory turnover to help analyze short-term liquidity and to assess whether management is doing a good job controlling the amount of inventory available. A low ratio compared to that of competitors suggests inefficient use of assets. The company may be holding more inventory than it needs to support its sales volume. Similarly, a very high ratio compared to that of competitors suggests inventory might be too low. This can cause lost sales if customers must back order merchandise. Inventory turnover has no simple rule except to say *a high ratio is preferable provided inventory is adequate to meet demand.*

### Decision Insight

**Dell-ocity**   From its roots in a college dorm room, **Dell** now sells 50 million dollars' worth of computers each day from its Website. The speed of Web technology has allowed Dell to slash inventories. Dell's operating cycle is less than 15 hours and its days' sales in inventory is 3 days. Michael Dell asserts, "Speed is everything in this business."

## Days' Sales in Inventory

**Point:** Inventory turnover is higher and days' sales in inventory is lower for industries such as foods and other perishable products. The reverse holds for nonperishable product industries.

To better interpret inventory turnover, many users measure the adequacy of inventory to meet sales demand. **Days' sales in inventory,** also called *days' stock on hand,* is a ratio that reveals how much inventory is available in terms of the number of days' sales. It can be interpreted as the number of days one can sell from inventory if no new items are purchased. This ratio is often viewed as a measure of the buffer against out-of-stock inventory and is useful in evaluating liquidity of inventory. It is defined in Exhibit 5.14.

**Exhibit 5.14**

Days' Sales in Inventory

$$\text{Days' sales in inventory} = \frac{\text{Ending inventory}}{\text{Cost of goods sold}} \times 365$$

Days' sales in inventory focuses on ending inventory and it estimates how many days it will take to convert inventory at the end of a period into accounts receivable or cash. Notice that days' sales in inventory focuses on *ending* inventory whereas inventory turnover focuses on *average* inventory.

## Analysis of Inventory Management

Inventory management is a major emphasis for merchandisers. They must both plan and control inventory purchases and sales. **Toys "R" Us** is one of those merchandisers. Its inventory in fiscal year 2003 was $2,190 million. This inventory constituted 62% of its current assets and 23% of its total assets. We apply the analysis tools in this section to Toys "R" Us, as shown in Exhibit 5.15.

**Exhibit 5.15**

Inventory Turnover and Days' Sales in Inventory for Toys "R" Us

| ($ in millions) | 2003 | 2002 | 2001 |
|---|---|---|---|
| Cost of goods sold . . . . . . . . . . . . . . . . | $7,799 | $7,604 | $7,815 |
| Ending inventory . . . . . . . . . . . . . . . . . . | $2,190 | $2,041 | $2,307 |
| **Inventory turnover** . . . . . . . . . . . . . . | 3.7 times | 3.5 times | 3.6 times |
| *Industry* inventory turnover . . . . . . . . . . | 2.6 times | 2.5 times | 2.8 times |
| **Days' sales in inventory** . . . . . . . . . . . | 102 days | 98 days | 108 days |
| *Industry* days' sales in inventory . . . . . . . | 139 days | 146 days | 130 days |

### Decision Maker

**Entrepreneur**   Analysis of your retail store yields an inventory turnover of 5.0 and a days' sales in inventory of 73 days. The industry norm for inventory turnover is 4.4 and for days' sales in inventory is 74 days. What is your assessment of inventory management?

Answer—p. 219

Its 2003 inventory turnover of 3.7 times means that Toys "R" Us turns over its inventory 3.7 times per year, or once every 99 days (365 days ÷ 3.7). We prefer inventory turnover to be high provided inventory is not out of stock and the company is not losing customers. The 2003 days' sales in inventory of 102 days reveals that it is carrying 102 days of sales in inventory. This inventory buffer seems more than adequate. Toys "R" Us would benefit from further management efforts to increase inventory turnover and reduce inventory levels.

# Demonstration Problem

Craig Company uses a perpetual inventory system for its one product. Its beginning inventory, purchases, and sales during year 2005 follow:

| Date | | Activity | Units Acquired at Cost | Units Sold at Retail | Unit Inventory |
|---|---|---|---|---|---|
| Jan. | 1 | Beg. Inventory .. | 400 units @ $14 = $5,600 | | 400 units |
| Jan. | 15 | Sale ......... | | 200 units @ $30 | 200 units |
| March | 10 | Purchase ...... | 200 units @ $15 = $3,000 | | 400 units |
| April | 1 | Sale ......... | | 200 units @ $30 | 200 units |
| May | 9 | Purchase ...... | 300 units @ $16 = $4,800 | | 500 units |
| Sept. | 22 | Purchase ...... | 250 units @ $20 = $5,000 | | 750 units |
| Nov. | 1 | Sale ......... | | 300 units @ $35 | 450 units |
| Nov. | 28 | Purchase ...... | 100 units @ $21 = $2,100 | | 550 units |
| | | Totals ........ | 1,250 units    $20,500 | 700 units | |

*Additional tracking data for applying specific identification:* (1) January 15 sale—200 units @ $14, (2) April 1 sale—200 units @ $15, and (3) November 1 sale—200 units @ $14 and 100 units @ $20.

**Required**

1. Calculate the cost of goods available for sale.
2. Apply the four different methods of inventory costing (FIFO, LIFO, weighted average, and specific identification) to calculate ending inventory and cost of goods sold under each method.
3. In preparing financial statements for year 2005, the financial officer was instructed to use FIFO but failed to do so and instead computed cost of goods sold according to LIFO. Determine the impact on year 2005's income from the error. Also determine the effect of this error on year 2006's income. Assume no income taxes.
4. Management wants a report that shows how changing from FIFO to another method would change net income. Prepare a table showing (1) the cost of goods sold amount under each of the four methods, (2) the amount by which each cost of goods sold total is different from the FIFO cost of goods sold, and (3) the effect on net income if another method is used instead of FIFO.

## Planning the Solution

- Compute cost of goods available for sale by multiplying the units of beginning inventory and each purchase by their unit costs to determine the total cost of goods available for sale.
- Prepare a perpetual FIFO table starting with beginning inventory and showing how inventory changes after each purchase and after each sale (see Exhibit 5.5).
- Prepare a perpetual LIFO table starting with beginning inventory and showing how inventory changes after each purchase and after each sale (see Exhibit 5.6).
- Make a table of purchases and sales recalculating the average cost of inventory prior to each sale to arrive at the weighted average cost of ending inventory. Total the average costs associated with each sale to determine cost of goods sold (see Exhibit 5.7).
- Prepare a table showing the computation of cost of goods sold and ending inventory using the specific identification method (see Exhibit 5.4).
- Compare the year-end 2005 inventory amounts under FIFO and LIFO to determine the misstatement of year 2005 income that results from using LIFO. The errors for year 2005 and 2006 are equal in amount but opposite in effect.
- Create a table showing cost of goods sold under each method and how net income would differ from FIFO net income if an alternate method is adopted.

## Solution to Demonstration Problem

1. Cost of goods available for sale (this amount is the same for all methods):

| Date | | Units | Unit Cost | Total Cost |
|---|---|---|---|---|
| Jan. 1 | Beg. Inventory . . . . . . . . | 400 | $14 | $ 5,600 |
| March 10 | Purchase . . . . . . . . . . . | 200 | 15 | 3,000 |
| May 9 | Purchase . . . . . . . . . . . | 300 | 16 | 4,800 |
| Sept. 22 | Purchase . . . . . . . . . . . | 250 | 20 | 5,000 |
| Nov. 28 | Purchase . . . . . . . . . . . | 100 | 21 | 2,100 |
| Total cost of goods available for sale . . . . . . . . . . . . . . . . . . . | | | | $20,500 |

**2a.** FIFO perpetual method:

| Date | Goods Purchased | Cost of Goods Sold | Inventory Balance |
|---|---|---|---|
| Jan. 1 | Beginning balance | | 400 @ $14    = $ 5,600 |
| Jan. 15 | | 200 @ $14 = $2,800 | 200 @ $14    = $ 2,800 |
| Mar. 10 | 200 @ $15 = $3,000 | | 200 @ $14 <br> 200 @ $15 } = $ 5,800 |
| April 1 | | 200 @ $14 = $2,800 | 200 @ $15    = $ 3,000 |
| May 9 | 300 @ $16 = $4,800 | | 200 @ $15 <br> 300 @ $16 } = $ 7,800 |
| Sept. 22 | 250 @ $20 = $5,000 | | 200 @ $15 <br> 300 @ $16 <br> 250 @ $20 } = $12,800 |
| Nov. 1 | | 200 @ $15 = $3,000 <br> 100 @ $16 = $1,600 | 200 @ $16 <br> 250 @ $20 } = $ 8,200 |
| Nov. 28 | 100 @ $21 = $2,100 | | 200 @ $16 <br> 250 @ $20 <br> 100 @ $21 } = $10,300 |
| Total cost of goods sold | | $10,200 | |

*Note to students:* **In a classroom situation,** once we compute cost of goods available for sale, we can compute the amount for either cost of goods sold or ending inventory—it is a matter of preference. **In practice,** the costs of items sold are identified as sales are made and immediately transferred from the inventory account to the cost of goods sold account. The previous solution showing the line-by-line approach illustrates actual application in practice. The following alternate solutions illustrate that, once the concepts are understood, other solution approaches are available—although this is only shown for FIFO, it could be shown for all methods.

**Alternate Methods to Compute FIFO Perpetual Numbers**

[FIFO Alternate No. 1: Computing cost of goods sold first]

| | | | |
|---|---|---|---|
| Cost of goods available for sale (from part 1) . . . . . . . . . | | | $ 20,500 |
| **Cost of goods sold** | | | |
| Jan. 15 | Sold (200 @ $14) . . . . . . . . . . . . . . . . . . . | $2,800 | |
| April 1 | Sold (200 @ $14) . . . . . . . . . . . . . . . . . . . | 2,800 | |
| Nov. 1 | Sold (200 @ $15 and 100 @ $16) . . . . . . . | 4,600 | 10,200 |
| **Ending inventory** . . . . . . . . . . . . . . . . . . . . . . . . . . . . . | | | $10,300 |

[FIFO Alternate No. 2: Computing ending inventory first]

| | | |
|---|---|---|
| Cost of goods available for sale (from part 1) ....... | | $ 20,500 |
| Ending inventory* | | |
| Nov. 28   Purchase (100 @ $21) ............. | $2,100 | |
| Sept. 22   Purchase (250 @ $20) ............. | 5,000 | |
| May   9   Purchase (200 @ $16) ............. | 3,200 | |
| Ending inventory ......................... | | 10,300 |
| Cost of goods sold ...................... | | $10,200 |

\* Since FIFO assumes that the earlier costs are the first to flow out, we determine ending inventory by assigning the most recent costs to the remaining items.

**2b.** LIFO perpetual method:

| Date | Goods Purchased | Cost of Goods Sold | Inventory Balance | |
|---|---|---|---|---|
| Jan.   1 | Beginning balance | | 400 @ $14 | = $ 5,600 |
| Jan.   15 | | 200 @ $14 = $2,800 | 200 @ $14 | = $ 2,800 |
| Mar.   10 | 200 @ $15 = $3,000 | | 200 @ $14<br>200 @ $15 | = $ 5,800 |
| April   1 | | 200 @ $15 = $3,000 | 200 @ $14 | = $ 2,800 |
| May   9 | 300 @ $16 = $4,800 | | 200 @ $14<br>300 @ $16 | = $ 7,600 |
| Sept. 22 | 250 @ $20 = $5,000 | | 200 @ $14<br>300 @ $16<br>250 @ $20 | = $12,600 |
| Nov.   1 | | 250 @ $20 = $5,000<br>50 @ $16 = $  800 | 200 @ $14<br>250 @ $16 | = $ 6,800 |
| Nov. 28 | 100 @ $21 = $2,100 | | 200 @ $14<br>250 @ $16<br>100 @ $21 | = $ 8,900 |
| | **Total cost of goods sold** | **$11,600** | | |

**2c.** Weighted average perpetual method:

| Date | Goods Purchased | Cost of Goods Sold | Inventory Balance | |
|---|---|---|---|---|
| Jan.   1 | Beginning balance | | 400 @ $14 | = $  5,600 |
| Jan.   15 | | 200 @ $14   = $2,800 | 200 @ $14 | = $  2,800 |
| Mar.   10 | 200 @ $15 = $3,000 | | 200 @ $14<br>200 @ $15<br>(avg. cost is $14.5) | = $  5,800 |
| April   1 | | 200 @ $14.5   = $2,900 | 200 @ $14.5 | = $  2,900 |
| May   9 | 300 @ $16 = $4,800 | | 200 @ $14.5<br>300 @ $16<br>(avg. cost is $15.4) | = $  7,700 |

[continued on next page]

[continued from previous page]

| | | | |
|---|---|---|---|
| Sept. 22 | 250 @ $20 = $5,000 | | 200 @ $14.5 <br> 300 @ $16 <br> 250 @ $20 $\Big\}$ = $ 12,700 <br> (avg. cost is $16.93) |
| Nov.  1 | | 300 @ $16.93 = $5,079 | 450 @ $16.93   = $ 7,618.5 |
| Nov. 28 | 100 @ $21 = $2,100 | | 450 @ $16.93 <br> 100 @ $21 $\Big\}$ = **$9,718.5** |
| **Total cost of goods sold*** | | **$10,779** | |

\* The cost of goods sold ($10,779) plus ending inventory ($9,718.5) is $2.5 less than the cost of goods available for sale ($20,500) due to rounding.

**2d.** Specific identification method:

| Date | Goods Purchased | Cost of Goods Sold | Inventory Balance |
|---|---|---|---|
| Jan.  1 | Beginning balance | | 400 @ $14   = $ 5,600 |
| Jan.  15 | | 200 @ $14 = $2,800 | 200 @ $14   = $ 2,800 |
| Mar. 10 | 200 @ $15 = $3,000 | | 200 @ $14 <br> 200 @ $15 $\Big\}$ = $ 5,800 |
| April  1 | | 200 @ $15 = $3,000 | 200 @ $14   = $ 2,800 |
| May  9 | 300 @ $16 = $4,800 | | 200 @ $14 <br> 300 @ $16 $\Big\}$ = $ 7,600 |
| Sept. 22 | 250 @ $20 = $5,000 | | 200 @ $14 <br> 300 @ $16 <br> 250 @ $20 $\Big\}$ = $12,600 |
| Nov.  1 | | 200 @ $14 = $2,800 <br> 100 @ $20 = $2,000 | 300 @ $16 <br> 150 @ $20 $\Big\}$ = $ 7,800 |
| Nov. 28 | 100 @ $21 = $2,100 | | 300 @ $16 <br> 150 @ $20 <br> 100 @ $21 $\Big\}$ = **$ 9,900** |
| **Total cost of goods sold** | | **$10,600** | |

**3.** Mistakenly using LIFO when FIFO should have been used overstates cost of goods sold in year 2005 by $1,400, which is the difference between the FIFO and LIFO amounts of ending inventory. It understates income in 2005 by $1,400. In year 2006, income is overstated by $1,400 because of the understatement in beginning inventory.

**4.** Analysis of the effects of alternative inventory methods:

| | Cost of Goods Sold | Difference from FIFO Cost of Goods Sold | Effect on Net Income if Adopted Instead of FIFO |
|---|---|---|---|
| FIFO .................. | $10,200 | — | — |
| LIFO .................. | 11,600 | +$1,400 | $1,400 lower |
| Weighted average ......... | 10,779 | +   579 | 579 lower |
| Specific identification ........ | 10,600 | +   400 | 400 lower |

# Inventory Costing Under a Periodic System

# 5A

The basic aim of the periodic system and the perpetual system is the same: to assign costs to inventory and cost of goods sold. The same four methods are used to assign costs under both systems: specific identification; first-in, first-out; last-in, first-out; and weighted average. We use information from Trekking to show how to assign costs using these four methods with a periodic system. Data for sales and purchases are reported in the chapter (see Exhibit 5.3). Recall that we explained the accounting under a periodic system in Appendix 4A.

**P3** Compute inventory in a periodic system using the methods of specific identification, FIFO, LIFO, and weighted average.

## Specific Identification

We use the information in Exhibit 5.3 and the specific identification method to assign costs to the 12 units in ending inventory and to the 43 units sold as shown in Exhibit 5A.1. Carefully study Exhibit 5A.1 to see the flow of costs both in and out of inventory. Notice that each unit, whether sold or remaining in inventory, has its own specific cost attached to it.

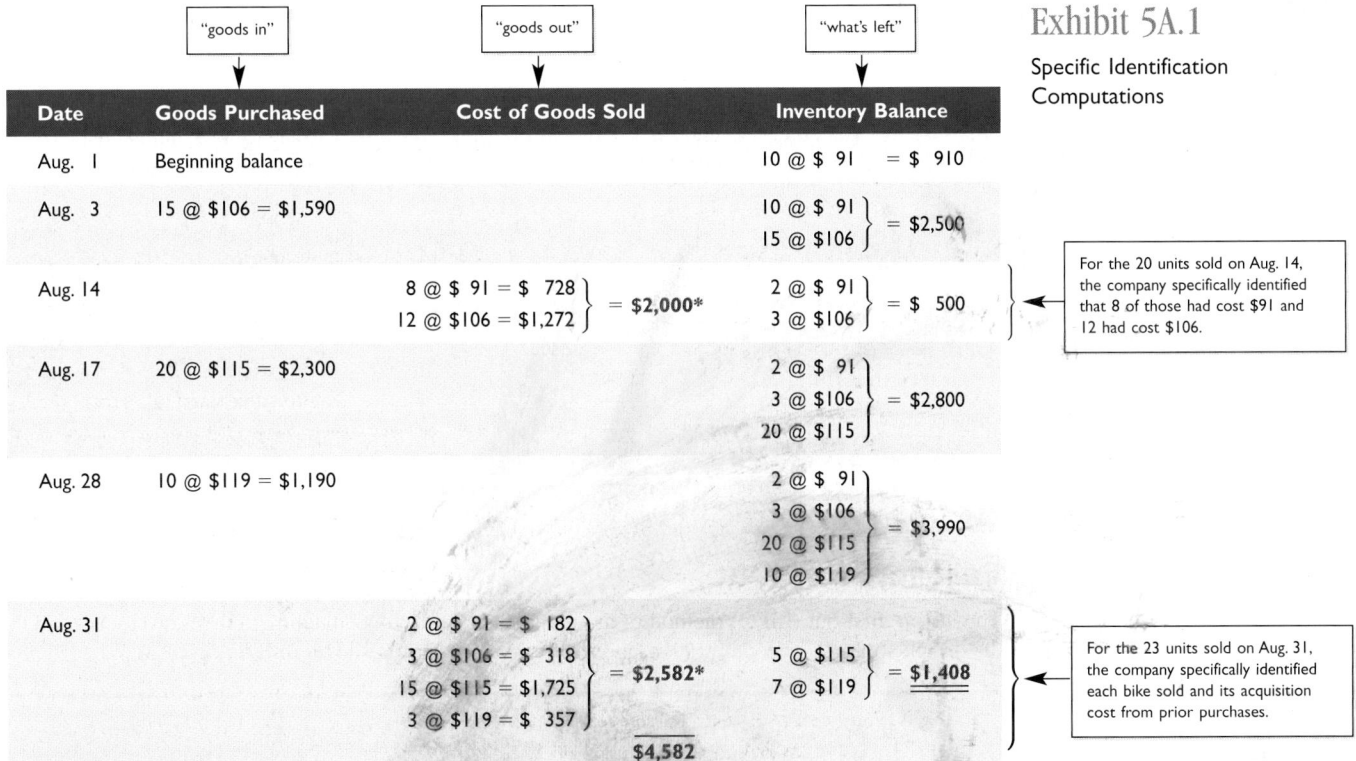

**Exhibit 5A.1**

Specific Identification Computations

* Identification of items sold (and their costs) is obtained from internal documents that track each unit from its purchase to its sale.

When using specific identification, Trekking's cost of goods sold reported on the income statement totals $4,582, the sum of $2,000 and $2,582 from the third column of Exhibit 5A.1. Trekking's ending inventory reported on the balance sheet is **$1,408**, which is the final inventory balance from the fourth column of Exhibit 5A.1. The purchases and sales entries for Exhibit 5A.1 follow (the

**Point:** The assignment of costs to the goods sold and to inventory using specific identification is the same for both the perpetual and periodic systems.

boldface numbers are those affected by the cost flow assumption):

| Purchases | | | | Sales | | |
|---|---|---|---|---|---|---|
| Aug. 3 | Purchases . . . . . . . . . . . . . . | 1,590 | | Aug. 14 | Accounts Receivable . . . . . . . . | 2,600 | |
| | Accounts Payable . . . . . . | | 1,590 | | Sales. . . . . . . . . . . . . . . | | 2,600 |
| 17 | Purchases . . . . . . . . . . . . . . | 2,300 | | 31 | Accounts Receivable . . . . . . . . | 3,450 | |
| | Accounts Payable . . . . . . | | 2,300 | | Sales. . . . . . . . . . . . . . . | | 3,450 |
| 28 | Purchases . . . . . . . . . . . . . . | 1,190 | | | **Adjusting Entry** | | |
| | Accounts Payable . . . . . . | | 1,190 | 31 | Merchandise Inventory . . . . . . . | **1,408** | |
| | | | | | Income Summary . . . . . . | | 498 |
| | | | | | Merchandise Inventory. . . | | 910 |

## First-In, First-Out

The first-in, first-out (FIFO) method of assigning cost to both inventory and cost of goods sold using the periodic system is shown in Exhibit 5A.2.

**Exhibit 5A.2**

FIFO Computations—
Periodic System

Exhibit 5.3 shows that the 12 units in ending inventory consist of 10 units from the latest purchase on Aug. 28 and 2 units from the next latest purchase on Aug. 17.

**Point:** The assignment of costs to the goods sold and to inventory using FIFO is the same for both the perpetual and periodic systems.

| | | |
|---|---|---|
| Total cost of 55 units available for sale (from Exhibit 5.3) . . . . . . . | | $5,990 |
| Less ending inventory priced using FIFO | | |
| 10 units from August 28 purchase at $119 each . . . . . . . . . . . . | $1,190 | |
| 2 units from August 17 purchase at $115 each . . . . . . . . . . . . | 230 | |
| **Ending inventory** . . . . . . . . . . . . . . . . . . . . . . . . . . . . . . . . | | **1,420** |
| **Cost of goods sold** . . . . . . . . . . . . . . . . . . . . . . . . . . . . . . | | **$4,570** |

Trekking's ending inventory reported on the balance sheet is **$1,420**, and its cost of goods sold reported on the income statement is **$4,570**. These amounts are the same as those computed using the perpetual system. This always occurs because the most recent purchases are in ending inventory under both systems. The purchases and sales entries for Exhibit 5A.2 follow (the boldface numbers are those affected by the cost flow assumption):

| Purchases | | | | Sales | | |
|---|---|---|---|---|---|---|
| Aug. 3 | Purchases . . . . . . . . . . . . . . | 1,590 | | Aug. 14 | Accounts Receivable . . . . . . . . | 2,600 | |
| | Accounts Payable . . . . . . . | | 1,590 | | Sales . . . . . . . . . . . . . . . | | 2,600 |
| 17 | Purchases . . . . . . . . . . . . . . | 2,300 | | 31 | Accounts Receivable . . . . . . . . | 3,450 | |
| | Accounts Payable . . . . . . . | | 2,300 | | Sales . . . . . . . . . . . . . . . | | 3,450 |
| 28 | Purchases . . . . . . . . . . . . . . | 1,190 | | | **Adjusting Entry** | | |
| | Accounts Payable . . . . . . . | | 1,190 | 31 | Merchandise Inventory . . . . . . | **1,420** | |
| | | | | | Income Summary . . . . . | | 510 |
| | | | | | Merchandise Inventory . . | | 910 |

## Last-In, First-Out

The last-in, first-out (LIFO) method of assigning costs to the 12 remaining units in inventory (and to the 43 units in cost of goods sold) using the periodic system is shown in Exhibit 5A.3.

**Exhibit 5A.3**

LIFO Computations—
Periodic System

Exhibit 5.3 shows that the 12 units in ending inventory consist of 10 units from the earliest purchase (beg. inv.) and 2 units from the next earliest purchase on Aug. 3.

| | | |
|---|---|---|
| Total cost of 55 units available for sale (from Exhibit 5.3) . . . . . . . . | | $5,990 |
| Less ending inventory priced using LIFO | | |
| 10 units in beginning inventory at $91 each . . . . . . . . . . . . . . . . | $910 | |
| 2 units from August 3 purchase at $106 each . . . . . . . . . . . . . | 212 | |
| **Ending inventory** . . . . . . . . . . . . . . . . . . . . . . . . . . . . . . . . | | **1,122** |
| **Cost of goods sold** . . . . . . . . . . . . . . . . . . . . . . . . . . . . . . | | **$4,868** |

Trekking's ending inventory reported on the balance sheet is **$1,122**, and its cost of goods sold reported on the income statement is **$4,868**. When LIFO is used with the periodic system, cost of goods sold is assigned costs from the most recent purchases for the period. With a perpetual system, cost of goods sold is assigned costs from the most recent purchases at the point of *each sale*. The purchases and sales entries for Exhibit 5A.3 follow (the boldface numbers are those affected by the cost flow assumption):

| Purchases | | | Sales | | |
|---|---|---|---|---|---|
| Aug. 3 Purchases ............... | 1,590 | | Aug. 14 Accounts Receivable ........ | 2,600 | |
| Accounts Payable ...... | | 1,590 | Sales ................ | | 2,600 |
| 17 Purchases ............... | 2,300 | | 31 Accounts Receivable ........ | 3,450 | |
| Accounts Payable ...... | | 2,300 | Sales ............... | | 3,450 |
| 28 Purchases ............... | 1,190 | | **Adjusting Entry** | | |
| Accounts Payable ....... | | 1,190 | 31 Merchandise Inventory ....... | **1,122** | |
| | | | Income Summary ....... | | 212 |
| | | | Merchandise Inventory.... | | 910 |

# Weighted Average

The weighted average method of assigning cost involves three important steps. The first two steps are shown in Exhibit 5A.4. First, multiply the per unit cost for beginning inventory and each particular purchase by the corresponding number of units (from Exhibit 5.3). Second, add these amounts and divide by the total number of units available for sale to find the weighted average cost per unit.

Exhibit 5A.4

**Weighted Average Cost per Unit**

| Step 1: | 10 units @ $ 91 = $ 910 |
|---|---|
| | 15 units @ $106 = 1,590 |
| | 20 units @ $115 = 2,300 |
| | 10 units @ $119 = 1,190 |
| | 55          $5,990 |
| Step 2: | $5,990/55 units = **$108.91** weighted average cost per unit |

**Example:** In Exhibit 5A.4, if 5 more units had been purchased at $120 each, what would be the weighted average cost per unit?
*Answer:* $109.83 ($6,590/60)

The third step is to use the weighted average cost per unit to assign costs to inventory and to the units sold as shown in Exhibit 5A.5.

Exhibit 5A.5

**Weighted Average Computations—Periodic**

| Step 3: | Total cost of 55 units available for sale (from Exhibit 5.3) ........ | $ 5,990 |
|---|---|---|
| | Less **ending inventory** priced on a weighted average cost basis: 12 units at $108.91 each (from Exhibit 5A.4) ......... | 1,307 |
| | **Cost of goods sold** ................................. | $4,683 |

Trekking's ending inventory reported on the balance sheet is **$1,307**, and its cost of goods sold reported on the income statement is **$4,683** when using the weighted average (periodic) method. The purchases and sales entries for Exhibit 5A.5 follow (the boldface numbers are those affected by the cost flow assumption):

**Point:** Weighted average usually yields different results for the perpetual and the periodic systems because under a perpetual system it recomputes the per unit cost prior to each sale, whereas under a periodic system, the per unit cost is computed only at the end of a period.

| Purchases | | | Sales | | |
|---|---|---|---|---|---|
| Aug. 3 Purchases ............... | 1,590 | | Aug. 14 Accounts Receivable ........ | 2,600 | |
| Accounts Payable ....... | | 1,590 | Sales ............... | | 2,600 |
| 17 Purchases ............... | 2,300 | | 31 Accounts Receivable ........ | 3,450 | |
| Accounts Payable ....... | | 2,300 | Sales ............... | | 3,450 |
| 28 Purchases ............... | 1,190 | | **Adjusting Entry** | | |
| Accounts Payable ....... | | 1,190 | 31 Merchandise Inventory ...... | **1,307** | |
| | | | Income Summary ....... | | 397 |
| | | | Merchandise Inventory... | | 910 |

# Financial Statement Effects

When purchase prices do not change, each inventory costing method assigns the same cost amounts to inventory and to cost of goods sold. When purchase prices are different, however, the methods nearly always assign different cost amounts. We show these differences in Exhibit 5A.6 using Trekking's data. When purchase costs *regularly rise,* as in Trekking's case, note the following:

**Point:** LIFO inventory is often less than the inventory's replacement cost because LIFO inventory is valued using the oldest inventory purchase costs.

## Exhibit 5A.6

Financial Statement Effects of
Inventory Costing Methods

| | TREKKING COMPANY For Month Ended August 31 | | | |
|---|---|---|---|---|
| | Specific Identification | FIFO | LIFO | Weighted Average |
| **Income Statement** | | | | |
| Sales | $ 6,050 | $ 6,050 | $ 6,050 | $ 6,050 |
| **Cost of goods sold** | 4,582 | 4,570 | 4,868 | 4,683 |
| Gross profit | 1,468 | 1,480 | 1,182 | 1,367 |
| Expenses | 450 | 450 | 450 | 450 |
| Income before taxes | 1,018 | 1,030 | 732 | 917 |
| Income tax expense (30%) | 305 | 309 | 220 | 275 |
| Net income | $ 713 | $ 721 | $ 512 | $ 642 |
| **Balance Sheet** | | | | |
| Inventory | $1,408 | $1,420 | $1,122 | $1,307 |

■ FIFO assigns the lowest amount to cost of goods sold—yielding the highest gross profit and net income.

■ LIFO assigns the highest amount to cost of goods sold—yielding the lowest gross profit and net income, which also yields a temporary tax advantage by postponing payment of some income tax.

■ Weighted average yields results between FIFO and LIFO.

■ Specific identification always yields results that depend on which units are sold.

When costs *regularly decline,* the reverse occurs for FIFO and LIFO.

All four inventory costing methods are acceptable in practice. A company must disclose the inventory method it uses. Each method offers certain advantages as follows:

■ FIFO assigns an amount to inventory on the balance sheet that approximates its current cost; it also mimics the actual flow of goods for most businesses.

■ LIFO assigns an amount to cost of goods sold on the income statement that approximates its current cost; it also better matches current costs with revenues in computing gross profit.

■ Weighted average tends to smooth out erratic changes in costs.

■ Specific identification exactly matches the costs of items with the revenues they generate.

While Dilbert's suggestion may be easier said than done, it does reinforce the importance of inventory management. This includes attention to inventory turnover, days' sales in inventory, and other measures.

DILBERT reprinted by permission of United Feature Syndicate, Inc.

### Quick Check

**9.** A company reports the following beginning inventory and purchases, and it ends the period with 30 units in inventory.

| | |
|---|---|
| Beginning Inventory | 100 units at $10 cost per unit |
| Purchase 1 | 40 units at $12 cost per unit |
| Purchase 2 | 20 units at $14 cost per unit |

**a.** Compute ending inventory using the FIFO periodic system.

**b.** Compute cost of goods sold using the LIFO periodic system.

# Inventory Estimation Methods

# 5B

Inventory sometimes requires estimation for two reasons. First, companies may require **interim statements** (financial statements prepared for periods of less than one year), but they only annually take a physical count of inventory. Second, companies may require an inventory estimate if some casualty such as fire or flood makes taking a physical count impossible. Note that estimates are usually only required for companies that use the periodic system. Companies using a perpetual system would presumably have updated inventory data.

This appendix describes two methods to estimate inventory.

**P4** Apply both the retail inventory and gross profit methods to estimate inventory.

## Retail Inventory Method

To avoid the time-consuming and expensive process of taking a physical inventory each month or quarter, some companies use the **retail inventory method** to estimate cost of goods sold and ending inventory. Some companies even use the retail inventory method to prepare the annual statements. **Home Depot**, for instance, says in its recent annual report: "Inventories are stated at the lower of cost (first-in, first-out) or market, as determined by the retail inventory method." A company may also estimate inventory for audit purposes or when inventory is damaged or destroyed.

The retail inventory method uses a three-step process to estimate ending inventory. We need to know the amount of inventory a company had at the beginning of the period in both *cost* and *retail* amounts. We already explained how to compute the cost of inventory. The *retail amount of inventory* refers to its dollar amount measured using selling prices of inventory items. We also need to know the net amount of goods purchased (minus returns, allowances, and discounts) in the period, both at cost and at retail. The amount of net sales at retail is also needed. The process is shown in Exhibit 5B.1.

The reasoning behind the retail inventory method is that if we can get a good estimate of the cost-to-retail ratio, we can multiply ending inventory at retail by this ratio to estimate ending inventory at cost. We show in Exhibit 5B.2 how these steps are applied to estimate ending inventory for

**Point:** When a retailer takes a physical inventory, it can restate the retail value of inventory to a cost basis by applying the cost-to-retail ratio. It can also estimate the amount of shrinkage by comparing the inventory computed with the amount from a physical inventory.

Exhibit 5B.1

Retail Inventory Method of Inventory Estimation

| | At Cost | At Retail |
|---|---|---|
| Goods available for sale | | |
| Beginning inventory | $ 20,500 | $ 34,500 |
| Cost of goods purchased | 39,500 | 65,500 |
| **Step 1:** Goods available for sale | 60,000 | 100,000 |
| Deduct net sales at retail | | 70,000 |
| Ending inventory at retail | | $ 30,000 |
| **Step 2:** Cost-to-retail ratio: ($60,000 ÷ $100,000) = 60% | | |
| **Step 3:** Estimated ending inventory at cost ($30,000 × 60%) | $18,000 | |

Exhibit 5B.2

Estimated Inventory Using the Retail Inventory Method

**Example:** What is the cost of ending inventory in Exhibit 5B.2 if the cost of beginning inventory is $22,500 and its retail value is $34,500? *Answer:* $30,000 × 62% = $18,600

a typical company. First, we find that $100,000 of goods (at retail selling prices) was available for sale. We see that $70,000 of these goods were sold, leaving $30,000 (retail value) of merchandise in ending inventory. Second, the cost of these goods is 60% of the $100,000 retail value. Third, since cost for these goods is 60% of retail, the estimated cost of ending inventory is $18,000.

## Gross Profit Method

The **gross profit method** estimates the cost of ending inventory by applying the gross profit ratio to net sales (at retail). This type of estimate often is needed when inventory is destroyed, lost, or stolen. These cases require an inventory estimate so that a company can file a claim with its insurer. Users also apply this method to see whether inventory amounts from a physical count are reason-

### Exhibit 5B.3

Gross Profit Method of Inventory Estimation

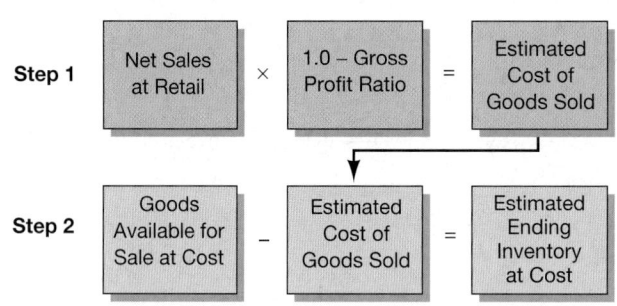

able. This method uses the historical relation between cost of goods sold and net sales to estimate the proportion of cost of goods sold making up current sales. This cost of goods sold estimate is then subtracted from cost of goods available for sale to estimate the ending inventory at cost. These two steps are shown in Exhibit 5B.3.

To illustrate, assume that a company's inventory is destroyed by fire in March 2005. When the fire occurs, the company's accounts show the following balances for January through March: sales, $31,500; sales returns, $1,500; inventory (January 1, 2005), $12,000; and cost of goods purchased, $20,500. If this company's gross profit ratio is 30%, then 30% of each net sales dollar is gross profit and 70% is cost of goods sold. We show in Exhibit 5B.4 how this 70% is used to estimate lost inventory of $11,500. To understand this exhibit, think of subtracting cost of goods sold from the goods available for sale to get ending inventory.

**Point:** A fire or other catastrophe can result in an insurance claim for lost inventory or income. Backup and off-site storage of data help ensure coverage for such losses.

**Point:** Reliability of the gross profit method depends on a good estimate of the gross profit ratio.

### Exhibit 5B.4

Estimated Inventory Using the Gross Profit Method

| | | |
|---|---|---|
| Goods available for sale | | |
| Inventory, January 1, 2005 . . . . . . . . . . . . . . . . . . . . . . . . . | $12,000 | |
| Cost of goods purchased . . . . . . . . . . . . . . . . . . . . . | 20,500 | |
| Goods available for sale (at cost) . . . . . . . . . . . . . . . . . . | 32,500 | |
| Net sales at retail ($31,500 − $1,500) . . . . . . . . . . . . . . . . . | | $30,000 ⌐ |
| **Step 1:** **Estimated cost of goods sold ($30,000 × 70%)** . . . . . . . | **(21,000)** ← ⌐× 0.70⌐ |
| **Step 2:** **Estimated March inventory at cost** . . . . . . . . . . . . . . . | **$11,500** | |

## Quick Check

**10.** Using the retail method and the following data, estimate the cost of ending inventory.

| | Cost | Retail |
|---|---|---|
| Beginning inventory . . . . . . . . . . . . | $324,000 | $530,000 |
| Cost of goods purchased . . . . . . . . | 195,000 | 335,000 |
| Net sales . . . . . . . . . . . . . . . . . . . . | | 320,000 |

Answers—p. 220

## Summary

**C1**  **Identify the items making up merchandise inventory.**
Merchandise inventory refers to goods owned by a company and held for resale. Three special cases merit our attention. Goods in transit are reported in inventory of the company that holds ownership rights. Goods on consignment are reported in the consignor's inventory. Goods damaged or obsolete are reported in inventory at their net realizable value.

**C2**  **Identify the costs of merchandise inventory.** Costs of merchandise inventory include expenditures necessary to bring an item to a salable condition and location. This includes its invoice cost minus any discount plus any added or incidental costs necessary to put it in a place and condition for sale.

**A1**  **Analyze the effects of inventory methods for both financial and tax reporting.** When purchase costs are rising or falling, the inventory costing methods are likely to assign different costs to inventory. Specific identification exactly matches costs and revenues. Weighted average smooths out cost changes. FIFO assigns an amount to inventory closely approximating current replacement cost. LIFO assigns the most recent costs incurred to cost of goods sold and likely better matches current costs with revenues.

A2  **Analyze the effects of inventory errors on current and future financial statements.** An error in the amount of ending inventory affects assets (inventory), net income (cost of goods sold), and equity for that period. Since ending inventory is next period's beginning inventory, an error in ending inventory affects next period's cost of goods sold and net income. Inventory errors in one period are offset in the next period.

A3  **Assess inventory management using both inventory turnover and days' sales in inventory.** We prefer a high inventory turnover, provided that goods are not out of stock and customers are not turned away. We use days' sales in inventory to assess the likelihood of goods being out of stock. We prefer a small number of days' sales in inventory if we can serve customer needs and provide a buffer for uncertainties.

P1  **Compute inventory in a perpetual system using the methods of specific identification, FIFO, LIFO, and weighted average.** Costs are assigned to the cost of goods sold account *each time* a sale occurs in a perpetual system. Specific identification assigns a cost to each item sold by referring to its actual cost (for example, its net invoice cost). Weighted average assigns a cost to items sold by dividing the current balance in the inventory account by the total items available for sale to determine cost per unit. We then multiply the number of units sold by this cost per unit to get the cost of each sale. FIFO assigns cost to items sold assuming that the earliest units purchased are the

first units sold. LIFO assigns cost to items sold assuming that the most recent units purchased are the first units sold.

P2  **Compute the lower of cost or market amount of inventory.** Inventory is reported at market cost when market is *lower* than recorded cost, called the *lower of cost or market (LCM) inventory*. Market is typically measured as replacement cost. Lower of cost or market can be applied separately to each item, to major categories of items, or to the entire inventory.

P3[A]  **Compute inventory in a periodic system using the methods of specific identification, FIFO, LIFO, and weighted average.** Periodic inventory systems allocate the cost of goods available for sale between cost of goods sold and ending inventory *at the end of a period*. Specific identification and FIFO give identical results whether the periodic or perpetual system is used. LIFO assigns costs to cost of goods sold assuming the last units purchased for the period are the first units sold. The weighted average cost per unit is computed by dividing the total cost of beginning inventory and net purchases for the period by the total number of units available. Then, it multiplies cost per unit by the number of units sold to give cost of goods sold.

P4[B]  **Apply both the retail inventory and gross profit methods to estimate inventory.** The retail inventory method involves three steps: (1) goods available at retail minus net sales at retail equals ending inventory at retail, (2) goods available at cost divided by goods available at retail equals the cost-to-retail ratio, and (3) ending inventory at retail multiplied by the cost-to-retail ratio equals estimated ending inventory at cost. The gross profit method involves two steps: (1) net sales at retail multiplied by 1 minus the gross profit ratio equals estimated cost of goods sold, and (2) goods available at cost minus estimated cost of goods sold equals estimated ending inventory at cost.

## Guidance Answers to **Decision Maker** and **Decision Ethics**

**Financial Planner**   The FIFO method implies that the oldest costs are the first ones assigned to cost of goods sold. This leaves the most recent costs in ending inventory. You report this to your client and note that in most cases, the ending inventory of a company using FIFO is reported at or near its replacement cost. This means that your client need not in most cases adjust the reported value of inventory. Your answer changes only if there are major increases in replacement cost compared to the cost of recent purchases reported in inventory. When major increases in costs occur, your client might wish to adjust inventory (for internal reports) for the difference between the reported cost of inventory and its replacement cost. (*Note:* Decreases in costs of purchases are recognized under the lower of cost or market adjustment.)

**Inventory Manager**   It seems your company can save (or at least postpone) taxes by switching to LIFO, but the switch is likely to reduce bonus money that you think you have earned and deserve.

Since the U.S. tax code requires companies that use LIFO for tax reporting also to use it for financial reporting, your options are further constrained. Your best decision is to tell your superior about the tax savings with LIFO. You also should discuss your bonus plan and how this is likely to hurt you unfairly. You might propose to compute inventory under the LIFO method for reporting purposes but use the FIFO method for your bonus calculations. Another solution is to revise the bonus plan to reflect the company's use of the LIFO method.

**Entrepreneur**   Your inventory turnover is markedly higher than the norm, whereas days' sales in inventory approximates the norm. Since your turnover is already 14% better than average, you are probably best served by directing attention to days' sales in inventory. You should see whether you can reduce the level of inventory while maintaining service to customers. Given your higher turnover, you should be able to hold less inventory.

## Guidance Answers to **Quick Checks**

**1.** The matching principle.
**2.** **Target** reports these goods in its inventory.
**3.** Total cost assigned to the painting is $12,180, computed as $11,400 + $130 + $150 + $100 + $400.

**4.** Specific identification exactly matches costs and revenues. Weighted average tends to smooth out cost changes. FIFO assigns an amount to inventory that closely approximates current replacement cost. LIFO assigns the most recent costs incurred to cost of goods sold and likely better matches current costs with revenues.

**5.** FIFO—it gives a lower cost of goods sold, a higher gross profit, and a higher net income when costs are rising.

**6.** When costs are rising, LIFO gives a lower inventory figure on the balance sheet as compared to FIFO. FIFO's inventory amount approximates current replacement costs.

**7.** Cost of goods sold would be overstated by $10,000 in 2005 and understated by $10,000 in year 2006.

**8.** The reported LCM inventory amount (using items) is $540, computed as $[(20 \times \$5) + (40 \times \$8) + (10 \times \$12)]$.

**9.$^{A}$a.** FIFO periodic inventory $= (20 \times \$14) + (10 \times \$12)$
$$= \$400$$

**b.** LIFO periodic cost of goods sold
$$= (20 \times \$14) + (40 \times \$12) + (70 \times \$10)$$
$$= \$1,460$$

**10.$^{B}$**Estimated ending inventory (at cost) is $327,000. It is computed as follows:

Step 1: $(\$530,000 + \$335,000) - \$320,000 = \$545,000$

Step 2: $\dfrac{\$324,000 + \$195,000}{\$530,000 + \$335,000} = 60\%$

Step 3: $\$545,000 \times 60\% = \underline{\$327,000}$

## Key Terms

Key Terms are available at the book's Website for learning and testing in an online Flashcard Format.

**Average cost** (p. 202)
**Conservatism principle** (p. 206)
**Consignee** (p. 196)
**Consignor** (p. 196)
**Consistency principle** (p. 204)
**Days' sales in inventory** (p. 208)

**First-in, first-out (FIFO)** (p. 201)
**Gross profit method** (p. 218)
**Interim statements** (p. 217)
**Inventory turnover** (p. 207)
**Last-in, first-out (LIFO)** (p. 201)
**Lower of cost or market (LCM)** (p. 205)

**Net realizable value** (p. 196)
**Retail inventory method** (p. 217)
**Specific identification** (p. 199)
**Weighted average** (p. 202)

## Personal Interactive Quiz

Personal Interactive Quizzes A and B are available at the book's Website to reinforce and assess your learning.

*Superscript letter $^{A}$ ($^{B}$) denotes assignments based on Appendix 5A (5B).*

## Discussion Questions

**1.** Describe the flow of costs from inventory to cost of goods sold for the following methods: (*a*) FIFO and (*b*) LIFO.

**2.** Where is the amount of merchandise inventory disclosed in the financial statements?

**3.** Why are incidental costs sometimes ignored in inventory costing? Under what principle is this permitted?

**4.** If costs are declining, will the LIFO or FIFO method of inventory valuation result in the lower cost of goods sold?

**5.** What does the full-disclosure principle prescribe if a company changes from one acceptable accounting method to another?

**6.** Can a company change its inventory method each accounting period? Explain.

**7.** Does the accounting principle of consistency preclude any changes from one accounting method to another?

**8.** If inventory errors are said to correct themselves, why are accounting users concerned when such errors are made?

**9.** Explain the following statement: "Inventory errors correct themselves."

**10.** What is the meaning of *market* as it is used in determining the lower of cost or market for inventory?

**11.** What guidance does the principle of conservatism offer?

**12.** What factors contribute to (or cause) inventory shrinkage?

**13.$^{A}$**What accounts are used in a periodic inventory system but not in a perpetual inventory system?

**14.$^{B}$**When preparing interim financial statements, what two methods can companies utilize to estimate cost of goods sold and ending inventory?

**15.** Refer to **Krispy Kreme**'s financial statements in Appendix A. On February 2, 2003, what percent of current assets are represented by inventory?

**16.** Refer to **Tastykake**'s financial statements in Appendix A. Compute its cost of goods available for sale for the year ended December 28, 2002.

**17.** What percent of **Harley-Davidson**'s current assets are inventory as of December 31, 2002, and as of December 31, 2001? **Harley-Davidson**

*Red numbers denote Discussion Questions that involve decision-making.*

*Homework Manager repeats all numerical Quick Study assignments on the book's Website with new numbers.*

Tevin Trader starts a merchandising business on December 1 and enters into three inventory purchases:

**QUICK STUDY**

**QS 5-1**
Assigning costs to inventory—
perpetual systems

P1

| December 7 | 10 units @ $ 6 cost |
| December 14 | 20 units @ $12 cost |
| December 21 | 15 units @ $14 cost |

Trader sells 15 units for $25 each on December 15. Eight of the sold units are from the December 7 purchase and seven are from the December 14 purchase. Trader uses a perpetual inventory system. Determine the costs assigned to the December 31 ending inventory when costs are assigned based on (a) FIFO, (b) LIFO, (c) weighted average, and (d) specific identification.

**Check**  (c) $360

---

Senona Company reports beginning inventory of 10 units at $50 each. Every week for four weeks it purchases an additional 10 units at respective costs of $51, $52, $55, and $60 per unit for weeks 1 through 4. Calculate the cost of goods available for sale and the units available for sale for this four-week period.

**QS 5-2**
Computing goods available for sale

P1

---

A company reports the following beginning inventory and purchases for January. On January 26, 345 units were sold. What is the cost of the 140 units that remain in ending inventory, assuming costs are assigned based on (a) FIFO, (b) LIFO, and (c) weighted average? (Round unit costs to the nearest cent.)

**QS 5-3**
Inventory costing methods

P1

| | Units | Unit Cost |
| --- | --- | --- |
| Beginning inventory on January 1 ....... | 310 | $3.00 |
| Purchase on January 9 ............... | 75 | 3.20 |
| Purchase on January 25 ............. | 100 | 3.35 |

---

Identify the inventory costing method best described by each of the following separate statements. Assume a period of increasing costs.

**1.** The preferred method when each unit of product has unique features that markedly affect cost.

**2.** Matches recent costs against net sales.

**3.** Provides a tax advantage (deferral) to a corporation.

**4.** Yields a balance sheet inventory amount often markedly less than its replacement cost.

**5.** Results in a balance sheet inventory amount approximating replacement cost.

**QS 5-4**
Contrasting inventory costing methods

A1

---

**1.** At year-end, Jolie Co. had shipped $850 of merchandise FOB destination to China Co. Which company should include the $850 of merchandise in transit as part of its year-end inventory?

**2.** Jolie Company has shipped $500 of goods to China Co., and China Co. has arranged to sell the goods for Jolie. Identify the consignor and the consignee. Which company should include any unsold goods as part of its inventory?

**QS 5-5**
Inventory ownership

C1

---

Crafts Galore, a distributor of handmade gifts, operates out of owner Jenny Finn's house. At the end of the current period, Jenny reports she has 1,500 units (products) in her basement, 30 of which were damaged by water and cannot be sold. She also has another 250 units in her van, ready to deliver per a customer order, terms FOB destination, and another 70 units out on consignment to a friend who owns a retail store. How many units should Jenny include in her company's period-end inventory?

**QS 5-6**
Inventory ownership

C1

---

A car dealer acquires a used car for $3,000, terms FOB shipping point. Additional costs in obtaining and offering the car for sale include $150 for transportation-in, $200 for import duties, $50 for insurance during shipment, $25 for advertising, and $250 for sales staff salaries. For computing inventory, what cost is assigned to the used car?

**QS 5-7**
Inventory costs

C2

**QS 5-8**
Inventory costs
C2

Duke & Son, antique dealers, purchased the contents of an estate for $37,500. Terms of the purchase were FOB shipping point, and the cost of transporting the goods to Duke & Son's warehouse was $1,200. Duke & Son insured the shipment at a cost of $150. Prior to putting the goods up for sale, they cleaned and refurbished them at a cost of $490. Determine the cost of the inventory acquired from the estate.

**QS 5-9**
Applying LCM to inventories
P2

Talisman Trading Co. has the following products in its ending inventory. Compute lower of cost or market for inventory (*a*) as a whole and (*b*) applied separately to each product.

| Product | Quantity | Cost per Unit | Market per Unit |
|---|---|---|---|
| Mountain bikes ........ | 9 | $360 | $330 |
| Skateboards .......... | 12 | 210 | 270 |
| Gliders ............. | 25 | 480 | 420 |

**QS 5-10**
Inventory errors
A2

In taking a physical inventory at the end of year 2005, Nadir Company erroneously forgot to count certain units. Explain how this error affects the following: (*a*) 2005 cost of goods sold, (*b*) 2005 gross profit, (*c*) 2005 net income, (*d*) 2006 net income, (*e*) the combined two-year income, and (*f*) income for years after 2006.

**QS 5-11**
Analyzing inventory  A3

Market Company begins the year with $200,000 of goods in inventory. At year-end, the amount in inventory has increased to $230,000. Cost of goods sold for the year is $1,600,000. Compute Market's inventory turnover and days' sales in inventory. Assume that there are 365 days in the year.

**QS 5-12**[A]
Costing methods—
periodic system  P3

Refer to QS 5-1 and assume the periodic inventory system is used. Determine the costs assigned to the December 31 ending inventory when costs are assigned based on (*a*) FIFO, (*b*) LIFO, (*c*) weighted average, and (*d*) specific identification.

**QS 5-13**[A]
Costing methods—
periodic system  P3

Refer to QS 5-3 and assume the periodic inventory system is used. Determine the costs assigned to the ending inventory when costs are assigned based on (*a*) FIFO, (*b*) LIFO, and (*c*) weighted average. (Round unit costs to the nearest cent.)

**QS 5-14**[B]
Estimating inventories—gross
profit method
P4

Dooling Store's inventory is destroyed by a fire on September 5, 2005. The following data for year 2005 are available from the accounting records. Estimate the cost of the inventory destroyed.

| | |
|---|---|
| Jan. 1 inventory ...................... | $180,000 |
| Jan. 1 through Sept. 5 purchases (net) ........ | $342,000 |
| Jan. 1 through Sept. 5 sales (net) ........... | $675,000 |
| Year 2005 estimated gross profit rate ....... | 42% |

*Homework Manager repeats all numerical Exercises on the book's Website with new numbers.*

# EXERCISES

Lakia Corporation reported the following current-year purchases and sales data for its only product:

**Exercise 5-1**
Inventory costing
methods—perpetual
P1

| Date | Activities | Units Acquired at Cost | Units Sold at Retail |
|---|---|---|---|
| Jan. 1 | Beginning inventory ....... | 120 units @ $6.00 = $ 720 | |
| Jan. 10 | Sales ................ | | 70 units @ $15 |
| Mar. 7 | Purchase ............. | 200 units @ $5.50 = 1,100 | |
| Mar. 15 | Sales ................ | | 125 units @ $15 |
| July 28 | Purchase ............. | 500 units @ $5.00 = 2,500 | |
| Oct. 3 | Purchase ............. | 375 units @ $4.40 = 1,650 | |
| Oct. 5 | Sales ................ | | 600 units @ $15 |
| Dec. 19 | Purchase ............. | 100 units @ $4.10 = 410 | |
| | Totals ................ | 1,295 units    $6,380 | 795 units |

Lakia uses a perpetual inventory system. Ending inventory consists of 500 units, 400 from the July 28 purchase and 100 from the December 19 purchase. Determine the cost assigned to ending inventory and to cost of goods sold using (a) specific identification, (b) weighted average, (c) FIFO, and (d) LIFO.

**Check**  Ending inventory: LIFO, $2,498; WA, $2,350

Use the data in Exercise 5-1 to prepare comparative income statements for Lakia Corporation (calendar year-end 2005) similar to those shown in Exhibit 5.8 for the four inventory methods. Assume expenses are $1,250. The applicable income tax rate is 30%.

**1.** Which method yields the highest net income?

**2.** Does net income using weighted average fall between that using FIFO and LIFO?

**3.** If costs are rising instead of declining, which method would yield the highest net income?

**Exercise 5-2**
Income effects of inventory methods

A1

Henin Co. reported the following current-year purchases and sales data for its only product:

**Exercise 5-3**
Inventory costing methods (perpetual)—FIFO and LIFO

P1

| Date | Activities | Units Acquired at Cost | Units Sold at Retail |
|---|---|---|---|
| Jan. 1 | Beginning inventory ....... | 100 units @ $10 = $ 1,000 | |
| Jan. 10 | Sales ................. | | 90 units @ $40 |
| Mar. 14 | Purchase .............. | 250 units @ $15 = 3,750 | |
| Mar. 15 | Sales ................. | | 140 units @ $40 |
| July 30 | Purchase .............. | 400 units @ $20 = 8,000 | |
| Oct. 5 | Sales ................. | | 300 units @ $40 |
| Oct. 26 | Purchase .............. | 600 units @ $25 = 15,000 | |
| | Totals ............... | 1,350 units     $27,750 | 530 units |

Henin uses a perpetual inventory system. Determine the costs assigned to ending inventory and to cost of goods sold using (a) FIFO and (b) LIFO. Compute the gross margin for each method.

**Check**  Ending inventory: LIFO, $18,750

Refer to the data in Exercise 5-3. Assume that ending inventory is made up of 200 units from the March 14 purchase, 20 units from the July 30 purchase, and all the units of the October 26 purchase. Using the specific identification method, calculate (a) the cost of goods sold and (b) the gross margin.

**Exercise 5-4**
Specific Identification   P1

Tanzy Company's ending inventory includes the following items. Compute the lower of cost or market for ending inventory (a) as a whole and (b) applied separately to each product.

**Exercise 5-5**
Lower of cost or market

P2

| | | Per Unit | |
|---|---|---|---|
| **Product** | **Units** | **Cost** | **Market** |
| Helmets ........ | 22 | $50 | $54 |
| Bats ........... | 15 | 78 | 72 |
| Shoes ......... | 36 | 95 | 91 |
| Uniforms ....... | 40 | 36 | 36 |

**Check**  (b) $6,896

Ringo Company had $900,000 of sales in each of three consecutive years 2004–2006, and it purchased merchandise costing $500,000 in each of those years. It also maintained a $200,000 inventory from the beginning to the end of the three-year period. In accounting for inventory, it made an error at the end of year 2004 that caused its year-end 2004 inventory to appear on its statements as $180,000 rather than the correct $200,000.

**1.** Determine the correct amount of the company's gross profit in each of the years 2004–2006.

**2.** Prepare comparative income statements as in Exhibit 5.11 to show the effect of this error on the company's cost of goods sold and gross profit for each of the years 2004–2006.

**Exercise 5-6**
Analysis of inventory errors

A2

**Check**  2004 gross profit, $380,000

## Problem 5-2A
Analysis of inventory errors

A2

mhhe.com/wild3e

Stover Company's financial statements report the following. Stover recently discovered that in making physical counts of inventory, it had made the following errors: Inventory on December 31, 2004, is understated by $66,000, and inventory on December 31, 2005, is overstated by $30,000.

| | | For Year Ended December 31 | | |
|---|---|---|---|---|
| **Key Figures** | | **2004** | **2005** | **2006** |
| (a) | Cost of goods sold ........ | $ 715,000 | $ 847,000 | $ 770,000 |
| (b) | Net income ............. | 220,000 | 275,000 | 231,000 |
| (c) | Total current assets ........ | 1,155,000 | 1,265,000 | 1,100,000 |
| (d) | Total equity ............. | 1,287,000 | 1,430,000 | 1,232,000 |

### Required

**1.** For each key financial statement figure—(a), (b), (c), and (d) above—prepare a table similar to the following to show the adjustments necessary to correct the reported amounts.

| Figure: _____ | **2004** | **2005** | **2006** |
|---|---|---|---|
| Reported amount ................... | _____ | _____ | _____ |
| Adjustments for: 12/31/2004 error ........ | _____ | _____ | _____ |
| 12/31/2005 error ....... | _____ | _____ | _____ |
| Corrected amount ................... | _____ | _____ | _____ |

**Check** (1) Corrected net income:
2004, $286,000; 2005, $179,000;
2006, $261,000

### Analysis Component

**2.** What is the error in total net income for the combined three-year period resulting from the inventory errors? Explain.

**3.** Explain why the understatement of inventory by $66,000 at the end of 2004 results in an understatement of equity by the same amount in that year.

## Problem 5-3A
Lower of cost or market

P2

A physical inventory of Ireland Unlimited taken at December 31 reveals the following:

| | | Per Unit | |
|---|---|---|---|
| **Item** | **Units** | **Cost** | **Market** |
| Audio equipment | | | |
| Receivers | 335 | $ 90 | $ 98 |
| CD players | 250 | 111 | 100 |
| DVD players | 316 | 86 | 95 |
| Speakers | 194 | 52 | 41 |
| Video equipment | | | |
| Televisions | 470 | 150 | 125 |
| VCRs | 281 | 93 | 84 |
| Video cameras | 202 | 310 | 322 |
| Car audio equipment | | | |
| DVD radios | 175 | 70 | 84 |
| CD radios | 160 | 97 | 105 |

### Required

**Check** (b) $270,332; (c) $263,024

Calculate the lower of cost or market for the inventory (a) as a whole, (b) by major category, and (c) applied separately to each item.

Viper Company began year 2005 with 20,000 units of product in its January 1 inventory costing $15 each. It made successive purchases of its product in year 2005 as follows:

| Mar. 7 | 28,000 units @ $18 each |
|---|---|
| May 25 | 30,000 units @ $22 each |
| Aug. 1 | 20,000 units @ $24 each |
| Nov. 10 | 33,000 units @ $27 each |

**Problem 5-4A**[A]

Alternative cost flows—periodic

P3

The company uses a periodic inventory system. On December 31, 2005, a physical count reveals that 35,000 units of its product remain in inventory.

### Required

**1.** Compute the number and total cost of the units available for sale in year 2005.

**2.** Compute the amounts assigned to the 2005 ending inventory and the cost of goods sold using (*a*) FIFO, (*b*) LIFO, and (*c*) weighted average.

**Check**   (2) Cost of goods sold: FIFO, $1,896,000; LIFO, $2,265,000; WA, $2,077,557

---

True Blue Corp. sold 5,500 units of its product at $45 per unit in year 2005 and incurred operating expenses of $6 per unit in selling the units. It began the year with 600 units in inventory and made successive purchases of its product as follows:

| Jan. 1 | Beginning inventory | 600 units @ $18 per unit |
|---|---|---|
| Feb. 20 | Purchase | 1,500 units @ $19 per unit |
| May 16 | Purchase | 700 units @ $20 per unit |
| Oct. 3 | Purchase | 400 units @ $21 per unit |
| Dec. 11 | Purchase | 3,300 units @ $22 per unit |
| | Total | 6,500 units |

**Problem 5-5A**[A]

Income comparisons and cost flows—periodic

A1   P3

### Required

**1.** Prepare comparative income statements similar to Exhibit 5.8 for the three inventory costing methods of FIFO, LIFO, and weighted average. Include a detailed cost of goods sold section as part of each statement. The company uses a periodic inventory system, and its income tax rate is 30%.

**2.** How would the financial results from using the three alternative inventory costing methods change if True Blue had been experiencing declining costs in its purchases of inventory?

**3.** What advantages and disadvantages are offered by using (*a*) LIFO and (*b*) FIFO? Assume the continuing trend of increasing costs.

**Check**   (1) Net income: LIFO, $69,020; FIFO, $71,540; WA, $70,603

---

The records of Nilson Company provide the following information for the year ended December 31:

|  | At Cost | At Retail |
|---|---|---|
| January 1 beginning inventory | $ 471,350 | $ 927,150 |
| Cost of goods purchased | 3,276,030 | 6,279,350 |
| Sales | | 5,495,700 |
| Sales returns | | 44,600 |

**Problem 5-6A**[B]

Retail inventory method

P4

mhhe.com/wild3e

### Required

**1.** Use the retail inventory method to estimate the company's year-end inventory.

**2.** A year-end physical inventory at retail prices yields a total inventory of $1,675,800. Prepare a calculation showing the company's loss from shrinkage at cost and at retail.

**Check**   (1) Inventory, $912,808 cost;
        (2) Inventory shortage at
cost, $41,392

## Problem 5-7A[B]
Gross profit method

P4

Wayman Company wants to prepare interim financial statements for the first quarter. The company wishes to avoid making a physical count of inventory. Wayman's gross profit rate averages 35%. The following information for the first quarter is available from its records:

| | |
|---|---|
| January 1 beginning inventory . . . . . . . | $ 300,260 |
| Cost of goods purchased . . . . . . . . . . . | 939,050 |
| Sales . . . . . . . . . . . . . . . . . . . . . . . | 1,191,150 |
| Sales returns . . . . . . . . . . . . . . . . . . | 9,450 |

**Check**  Estimated ending inventory,
$471,205

### Required

Use the gross profit method to estimate the company's first-quarter ending inventory.

# PROBLEM SET B

## Problem 5-1B
Alternative cost flows—perpetual

P1

Venus Company uses a perpetual inventory system. It entered into the following calendar-year 2005 purchases and sales transactions:

| Date | Activities | Units Acquired at Cost | Units Sold at Retail |
|---|---|---|---|
| Jan.  1 | Beginning inventory . . . . . . . | 600 units @ $55/unit | |
| Jan. 10 | Purchase . . . . . . . . . . . . . . | 450 units @ $56/unit | |
| Feb. 13 | Purchase . . . . . . . . . . . . . . | 200 units @ $57/unit | |
| Feb. 15 | Sales . . . . . . . . . . . . . . . . . | | 430 units @ $90/unit |
| July 21 | Purchase . . . . . . . . . . . . . . | 230 units @ $58/unit | |
| Aug.  5 | Purchase . . . . . . . . . . . . . . | 345 units @ $59/unit | |
| Aug. 10 | Sales . . . . . . . . . . . . . . . . . | | 335 units @ $90/unit |
| | Total . . . . . . . . . . . . . . . . . | 1,825 units | 765 units |

### Required

**1.** Compute cost of goods available for sale and the number of units available for sale.

**2.** Compute the number of units in ending inventory.

**Check**  (3) Ending inventory: FIFO,
$61,055; LIFO, $59,250; WA, $60,293;

**3.** Compute the cost assigned to ending inventory using (a) FIFO, (b) LIFO, (c) specific identification (*Note:* The units sold consist of 600 units from beginning inventory and 165 units from the February 13 purchase), and (d) weighted average.

(4) LIFO gross profit, $24,805

**4.** Compute gross profit earned by the company for each of the four costing methods in part 3.

*Analysis Component*

**5.** If the company's manager earns a bonus based on a percent of gross profit, which method of inventory costing will the manager likely prefer?

## Problem 5-2B
Analysis of inventory errors

A2

Hector Company's financial statements report the following. Hector recently discovered that in making physical counts of inventory, it had made the following errors: Inventory on December 31, 2004, is overstated by $17,000, and inventory on December 31, 2005, is understated by $25,000.

| | | For Year Ended December 31 | | |
|---|---|---|---|---|
| **Key Figures** | | **2004** | **2005** | **2006** |
| (a) | Cost of goods sold . . . . . . . | $205,200 | $212,800 | $196,030 |
| (b) | Net income . . . . . . . . . . . . . | 174,800 | 211,270 | 183,910 |
| (c) | Total current assets . . . . . . . | 266,000 | 276,500 | 262,950 |
| (d) | Total equity . . . . . . . . . . . . . | 304,000 | 316,000 | 336,000 |

### Required

**1.** For each key financial statement figure—(a), (b), (c), and (d) above—prepare a table similar to the following to show the adjustments necessary to correct the reported amounts.

| Figure: _____ | 2004 | 2005 | 2006 |
|---|---|---|---|
| Reported amount . . . . . . . . . . . . . . . . . . | _____ | _____ | _____ |
| Adjustments for: 12/31/2004 error . . . . . . . . | _____ | _____ | _____ |
| 12/31/2005 error . . . . . . . | _____ | _____ | _____ |
| Corrected amount . . . . . . . . . . . . . . . . . . | _____ | _____ | _____ |

**Check**  (1) Corrected net income:
2004, $157,800; 2005, $253,270;
2006, $158,910

*Analysis Component*

**2.** What is the error in total net income for the combined three-year period resulting from the inventory errors? Explain.

**3.** Explain why the overstatement of inventory by $17,000 at the end of 2004 results in an overstatement of equity by the same amount in that year.

---

A physical inventory of Office Deals taken at December 31 reveals the following:

**Problem 5-3B**
Lower of cost or market
P2

| | | Per Unit | |
|---|---|---|---|
| **Item** | **Units** | **Cost** | **Market** |
| Office furniture | | | |
|   Desks | 436 | $261 | $305 |
|   Credenzas | 295 | 227 | 256 |
|   Chairs | 587 | 49 | 43 |
|   Bookshelves | 321 | 93 | 82 |
| Filing cabinets | | | |
|   Two-drawer | 214 | 81 | 70 |
|   Four-drawer | 398 | 135 | 122 |
|   Lateral | 175 | 104 | 118 |
| Office equipment | | | |
|   Fax machines | 430 | 168 | 200 |
|   Copiers | 545 | 317 | 288 |
|   Telephones | 352 | 125 | 117 |

**Required**

Calculate the lower of cost or market for the inventory (*a*) as a whole, (*b*) by major category, and (*c*) applied separately to each item.

**Check** (*b*) $607,707; (*c*) $584,444

---

Elfrink Co. began year 2005 with 6,300 units of product in its January 1 inventory costing $35 each. It made successive purchases of its product in year 2005 as follows:

**Problem 5-4B**[A]
Alternative cost flows—periodic
P3

| | | |
|---|---|---|
| Jan. 4 | ....... | 10,500 units @ $33 each |
| May 18 | ....... | 13,000 units @ $32 each |
| July 9 | ....... | 12,000 units @ $29 each |
| Nov. 21 | ....... | 15,500 units @ $26 each |

The company uses a periodic inventory system. On December 31, 2005, a physical count reveals that 16,500 units of its product remain in inventory.

**Required**

**1.** Compute the number and total cost of the units available for sale in year 2005.

**2.** Compute the amounts assigned to the 2005 ending inventory and the cost of goods sold using (*a*) FIFO, (*b*) LIFO, and (*c*) weighted average.

**Check** (2) Cost of goods sold: FIFO, $1,302,000; LIFO, $1,176,900; WA, $1,234,681

---

Rikkers Corp. sold 2,500 units of its product at $98 per unit in year 2005 and incurred operating expenses of $14 per unit in selling the units. It began the year with 740 units in inventory and made successive purchases of its product as follows:

**Problem 5-5B**[A]
Income comparisons and cost flows—periodic
A1 P3

| | | | |
|---|---|---|---|
| Jan. 1 | Beginning inventory | ....... | 740 units @ $58 per unit |
| April 2 | Purchase | ............. | 700 units @ $59 per unit |
| June 14 | Purchase | ............. | 600 units @ $61 per unit |
| Aug. 29 | Purchase | ............. | 500 units @ $64 per unit |
| Nov. 18 | Purchase | ............. | 800 units @ $65 per unit |
| | Total | ................. | 3,340 units |

**Required**

**1.** Prepare comparative income statements similar to Exhibit 5.8 for the three inventory costing methods of FIFO, LIFO, and weighted average. Include a detailed cost of goods sold section as part of each statement. The company uses a periodic inventory system, and its income tax rate is 25%.

**2.** How would the financial results from using the three alternative inventory costing methods change if Rikkers had been experiencing decreasing prices in its purchases of inventory?

**3.** What advantages and disadvantages are offered by using (*a*) LIFO and (*b*) FIFO? Assume the continuing trend of increasing costs.

## Problem 5-6B$^B$
Retail inventory method

P4

The records of Alaina Co. provide the following information for the year ended December 31:

|  | At Cost | At Retail |
| --- | --- | --- |
| January 1 beginning inventory ....... | $ 81,670 | $114,610 |
| Cost of goods purchased ........... | 492,250 | 751,730 |
| Sales ....................... |  | 786,120 |
| Sales returns ................... |  | 4,480 |

**Required**

**1.** Use the retail inventory method to estimate the company's year-end inventory.

**2.** A year-end physical inventory at retail prices yields a total inventory of $78,550. Prepare a calculation showing the company's loss from shrinkage at cost and at retail.

## Problem 5-7B$^B$
Gross profit method

P4

Ernst Equipment Co. wants to prepare interim financial statements for the first quarter. The company wishes to avoid making a physical count of inventory. Ernst's gross profit rate averages 30%. The following information for the first quarter is available from its records:

| | |
| --- | --- |
| January 1 beginning inventory ....... | $  752,880 |
| Cost of goods purchased ........... | 2,159,630 |
| Sales ....................... | 3,710,250 |
| Sales returns ................... | 74,200 |

**Required**

Use the gross profit method to estimate the company's first quarter ending inventory.

# PROBLEM SET C

Problem Set C is available at the book's Website to further reinforce and assess your learning.

# SERIAL PROBLEM

Success Systems

*(This serial problem began in Chapter 1 and continues through most of the book. If previous chapter segments were not completed, the serial problem can begin at this point.)*

Selected accounts and balances for the three months ended March 31, 2005, for Success Systems follows:

| | |
| --- | --- |
| January 1 beginning inventory ....... | $    0 |
| Cost of goods sold .............. | 14,052 |
| March 31 ending inventory ......... | 704 |

**Required**

**1.** Compute inventory turnover and days' sales in inventory for the three months ended March 31, 2005.

**2.** Assess its performance if competitors average 10 times for inventory turnover and 29 days for days' sales in inventory.

## BEYOND THE NUMBERS

**BTN 5-1** Refer to **Krispy Kreme**'s financial statements in Appendix A to answer the following:

**Required**

1. What amount of inventories did Krispy Kreme hold as a current asset on February 2, 2003? On February 3, 2002?
2. Inventories represent what percent of total assets on February 2, 2003? On February 3, 2002?
3. Comment on the relative size of Krispy Kreme's inventories compared to its other types of assets.
4. What accounting method did Krispy Kreme use to compute inventory amounts on its balance sheet?
5. Compute inventory turnover for fiscal year ended February 2, 2003, and days' sales in inventory as of February 2, 2003. (*Note:* Cost of goods sold is titled operating expenses for Krispy Kreme.)

*Roll On*

6. Access Krispy Kreme's financial statements for fiscal years ended after February 2, 2003, from its Website (**KrispyKreme.com**) or the SEC's EDGAR database (**www.sec.gov**). Answer questions 1 through 5 using the current Krispy Kreme information and compare results to those prior years.

**REPORTING IN ACTION**

C2 A3

**BTN 5-2** Key comparative figures ($ thousands) for both **Krispy Kreme** and **Tastykake** follow:

| Key Figures | Krispy Kreme | | | Tastykake | | |
| --- | --- | --- | --- | --- | --- | --- |
| | Current Year | One Year Prior | Two Years Prior | Current Year | One Year Prior | Two Years Prior |
| Inventory .......... | $ 24,365 | $ 16,159 | $ 12,031 | $ 6,777 | $ 8,412 | $ 5,930 |
| Cost of sales ........ | 381,489 | 316,946 | 250,690 | 111,187 | 103,297 | 105,036 |

**Required**

1. Calculate inventory turnover for both companies for the most recent two years shown.
2. Calculate days' sales in inventory for both companies for the three years shown.
3. Comment on and interpret your findings from parts 1 and 2.

**COMPARATIVE ANALYSIS**

A3

**BTN 5-3** Golf Away Corp. is a retail sports store carrying golf apparel and equipment. The store is at the end of its second year of operation and is struggling. A major problem is that its cost of inventory has continually increased in the past two years. In the first year of operations, the store assigned inventory costs using LIFO. A loan agreement the store has with its bank, its prime source of financing, requires the store to maintain a certain profit margin and current ratio. The store's owner is currently looking over Golf Away's preliminary financial statements for its second year. The numbers are not favorable. The only way the store can meet the required financial ratios agreed on with the bank is to change from LIFO to FIFO. The store originally decided on LIFO because of its tax advantages. The owner recalculates ending inventory using FIFO and submits those numbers and statements to the loan officer at the bank for the required bank review. The owner thankfully reflects on the available latitude in choosing the inventory costing method.

**Required**

1. How does Golf Away's use of FIFO improve its net profit margin and current ratio?
2. Is the action by Golf Away's owner ethical? Explain.

**ETHICS CHALLENGE**

A1

**BTN 5-4** You are a financial adviser with a client in the wholesale produce business that just completed its first year of operations. Due to weather conditions, the cost of acquiring produce to resell has escalated during the later part of this period. Your client, Jariah Gish, mentions that because the business sells perishable goods, she has striven to maintain a FIFO flow of goods. Although sales are good, the increasing cost of inventory has put the business in a tight cash position. Gish has expressed concern regarding the ability of the business to meet income tax obligations.

**Required**

Prepare a memorandum that identifies, explains, and justifies the inventory method you recommend your client, Ms. Gish, adopt.

**COMMUNICATING IN PRACTICE**

A1

## TAKING IT TO THE NET

A3

mhhe.com/wild3e

**BTN 5-5**    Access the 2002 annual 10-K report for **Oakley, Inc.** (Ticker OO), filed on March 31, 2003, from the EDGAR filings at www.sec.gov.

**Required**

1. What product does Oakley sell that is especially popular with college students?
2. What inventory method does Oakley use? (*Hint:* See the notes to its financial statements.)
3. Compute Oakley's gross margin and gross margin ratio for the current year.
4. Compute Oakley's inventory turnover and days' sales in inventory for the current year.

## TEAMWORK IN ACTION

A1  P1

**Point:** Step 1 allows four choices or areas for expertise. Larger teams will have some duplication of choice, but the specific identification method should not be duplicated.

**BTN 5-6**    Each team member has the responsibility to become an expert on an inventory method. This expertise will be used to facilitate teammates' understanding of the concepts relevant to that method.

1. Each learning team member should select an area for expertise by choosing one of the following inventory methods: specific identification, LIFO, FIFO, or weighted average.
2. Form expert teams made up of students who have selected the same area of expertise. The instructor will identify where each expert team will meet.
3. Using the following data, each expert team must collaborate to develop a presentation that illustrates the relevant concepts and procedures for its inventory method. Each team member must write the presentation in a format that can be shown to the learning team.

**Data**

Wiseman Corp. uses a perpetual inventory system. It had the following beginning inventory and current year purchases of its product:

| | | | |
|---|---|---|---|
| Jan.  1 | Beginning inventory ....... | 50 units @ $10 = | $  500 |
| Jan. 14 | Purchase ............... | 150 units @ $12 = | 1,800 |
| Apr. 30 | Purchase ............... | 200 units @ $15 = | 3,000 |
| Sept. 26 | Purchase ............... | 300 units @ $20 = | 6,000 |

Wiseman Corp. transacted sales on the following dates at a $35 per unit sales price:

| | | |
|---|---|---|
| Jan. 10 | 30 units | (specific cost: 30 @ $10) |
| Feb. 15 | 100 units | (specific cost: 100 @ $12) |
| Oct. 5 | 350 units | (specific cost: 100 @ $15 and 250 @ $20) |

**Concepts and Procedures to Illustrate in Expert Presentation**

a. Identify and compute the costs to assign to the units sold.
b. Identify and compute the costs to assign to the units in ending inventory.
c. How likely is it that this inventory costing method will reflect the actual physical flow of goods? How relevant is that factor in determining whether this is an acceptable method to use?
d. What is the impact of this method versus others in determining net income and income taxes?
e. How closely does the ending inventory amount reflect replacement cost?

4. Re-form learning teams. In rotation, each expert is to present to the team the presentation developed in part 3. Experts are to encourage and respond to questions.

## BUSINESS WEEK ACTIVITY

A3

mhhe.com/wild3e

**BTN 5-7**    Read the article "iPod: A Seed for Growth?" from the August 27, 2002, issue of *Business Week*. (The book's Website provides a free link.)

**Required**

1. What percent of the U.S. market for digital music players does **Apple** have?
2. What firms are emerging with products to compete with the Apple iPod?
3. Why might the **Toshiba** product hold an inventory cost edge over the Apple iPod?
4. How does Apple expect its unit sales of the iPod to grow from 2002 to 2006?

**BTN 5-8** Review the chapter's opening feature highlighting Mike Becker and his company, **FunKo**. Assume that FunKo consistently maintains an inventory level of $500,000, meaning that its average and ending inventory levels are the same. Also assume its annual cost of sales is $1,050,000. To cut costs, Becker proposes to slash inventory to a constant level of $125,000 with no impact on cost of sales.

**ENTREPRENEURIAL DECISION**

A3

**Required**

1. Compute the company's inventory turnover and its days' sales in inventory under (*a*) current conditions and (*b*) proposed conditions.

2. Evaluate and comment on the merits of Becker's proposal given your analysis in part 1. Identify any concerns you would express about the proposal.

**BTN 5-9** Visit four retail stores with another classmate. In each store, identify whether the store uses a bar-coding system to help manage its inventory. Try to find at least one store that does not use bar-coding. If a store does not use bar-coding, ask the store's manager or clerk whether he or she knows which type of inventory method the store employs. Create a table that shows columns for the name of store visited, type of merchandise sold, use or nonuse of bar-coding, and the inventory method used if bar-coding is not employed. You might also inquire as to what the store's inventory turnover is and how often physical inventory is taken.

**HITTING THE ROAD**

C1  C2

**BTN 5-10** Key figures (pesos millions) for **Grupo Bimbo** (GrupoBimbo.com) follow:

| Key Figures | Current Year | One Year Prior | Two Years Prior |
|---|---|---|---|
| Inventory . . . . . . . . . . | 905 | 767 | 725 |
| Cost of sales . . . . . . . . | 19,156 | 15,708 | 13,939 |

**GLOBAL DECISION**

A3

**Required**

1. Use these data and those from BTN 5-2 to compute (*a*) inventory turnover and (*b*) days' sales in inventory for the most recent two years shown for **Grupo Bimbo**, **Krispy Kreme**, and **Tastykake**.

2. Comment on and interpret your findings from part 1.

"They [customers] love that it's very childhood, nostalgic"—Dylan Lauren (on right, Jeff Rubin on left)

# 6

# Reporting and Analyzing Cash and Internal Controls

## A Look Back

Chapters 4 and 5 focused on merchandising activities and accounting for inventory. We explained both the perpetual and periodic inventory systems, accounting for inventory transactions, and methods for assigning costs to inventory.

## A Look at This Chapter

This chapter extends our study of accounting to the area of internal control and the analysis of cash. We describe procedures that are good for internal control. We also explain the control of and the accounting for cash, including control features of banking activities.

## A Look Ahead

Chapter 7 focuses on receivables, which are some of the most liquid assets other than cash. We explain how to account and report on receivables and their related accounts. This includes estimating uncollectible receivables and computing interest earned.

# CAP

| Conceptual | Analytical | Procedural |
|---|---|---|

**Conceptual**

**C1** Define internal control and identify its purpose and principles. *(p. 236)*

**C2** Define cash and cash equivalents and explain how to report them. *(p. 240)*

**C3** Identify control features of banking activities. *(p. 247)*

**Analytical**

**A1** Compute the days' sales uncollected ratio and use it to assess liquidity. *(p. 253)*

**Procedural**

**P1** Apply internal control to cash receipts and disbursements. *(p. 241)*

**P2** Explain and record petty cash fund transactions. *(p. 244)*

**P3** Prepare a bank reconciliation. *(p. 250)*

---

**Decision Feature**

# Sweet Success

NEW YORK—A 10-foot chocolate bunny named Jeffrey greets you as you enter the store—that should be warning enough! This elite designer candy store, christened **Dylan's Candy Bar (DylansCandyBar.com),** is the brainchild of co-founders Dylan Lauren and Jeff Rubin (the bunny is named for him). This sweet-lovers heaven offers more than 5,000 different choices of sweets from all over the world. In just under two years of operation, it has become a hip hangout for locals and tourists—and it has made candy cool. Says Lauren, "Park Avenue women come in, and the first thing they ask for is Gummi bears. They love that it's very childhood, nostalgic."

The New York store projects more than $5 million in sales this year. While marketing is an important part of its success, Lauren and Rubin's management of internal controls and cash is equally impressive. Several control procedures monitor its business activities and safeguard its assets. An example is the biometric time and attendance control system using fingerprint characteristics. Says Rubin,

"There's no fooling the system! It is going to help us remotely manage our employees while eliminating human error and dishonesty. [It] is a cost effective and important business management tool." Similar controls are applied throughout the store. Rubin notes that such controls raise productivity and cut expenses.

The store's cash management practices are equally impressive, including controls over cash receipts, disbursements, and petty cash. The use of bank reconciliations further helps with the store's control and management of cash.

Internal controls are crucial when on a busy day its store brings in more than 8,000 customers, and their cash. Moreover, expansion is already underway in Orlando, Houston, Chicago, Toronto, and Las Vegas. Through it all, Lauren says it is "totally fun." And how is it that Lauren maintains her slim figure. "I work out a lot!" she exclaims.

[Sources: *Dylan's Candy Bar Website,* January 2004; *Entrepreneur,* December 2002; *USA Today,* October 26, 2001; *PR Newswire,* November 2001; ECommerce-Guide.com, June 2003.]

We all are aware of reports and experiences involving theft and fraud. These occurrences affect us in several ways: We lock doors, chain bikes, review sales receipts, and acquire alarm systems. A company also takes actions to safeguard, control, and manage what it owns. Experience tells us that small companies are most vulnerable, usually due to weak internal controls. It is management's responsibility to set up policies and procedures to safeguard a company's assets,

especially cash. To do so, management *and* employees must understand and apply principles of internal control. This chapter describes these principles and how to apply them. It focuses special attention on cash because it is easily transferable and often at high risk of loss. An understanding of these controls and procedures makes us more secure in carrying out business activities and in assessing the activities of other companies.

### Reporting and Analyzing Cash and Internal Controls

**Internal Control**
- Purpose of controls
- Principles of controls
- Technology and controls
- Limitations of controls

**Control of Cash**
- Cash, cash equivalents, and liquidity
- Control of receipts
- Control of disbursements

**Banking Activities as Controls**
- Basic bank services
- Bank statement
- Bank reconciliation

# Internal Control

This section describes internal control and its fundamental principles. We also discuss the impact of technology on internal control and the limitations of control procedures.

## Purpose of Internal Control

**C1** Define internal control and identify its purpose and principles.

Managers (or owners) of small businesses often control the entire operation. These managers usually purchase all assets, hire and manage employees, negotiate all contracts, and sign all checks. They know from personal contact and observation whether the business is actually receiving the assets and services paid for. Most companies, however, cannot maintain this close personal supervision. They must delegate responsibilities and rely on formal procedures rather than personal contact in controlling business activities.

Managers use an internal control system to monitor and control business activities. An **internal control system** consists of the policies and procedures managers use to

**Point:** With company growth comes increased reporting and controls to safeguard assets and manage operations.

- Protect assets.
- Ensure reliable accounting.
- Promote efficient operations.
- Urge adherence to company policies.

### Decision Insight

**What's the Password?** Good internal control prevents unauthorized access to assets and accounting records by requiring passwords. It takes a password, for instance, to boot up most office PCs, log onto a network, and access voice mail, e-mail, and online services—not to mention personal ID numbers on credit and cash cards.

A properly designed internal control system is a key part of systems design, analysis, and performance. Managers place a high priority on internal control systems because they can prevent avoidable losses, help managers plan operations, and monitor company and employee performance. Internal controls do not provide guarantees, but they lower the company's risk of loss.

# Principles of Internal Control

Internal control policies and procedures vary from company to company according to such factors as the nature of the business and its size. Certain fundamental internal control principles apply to all companies. The **principles of internal control** are to

Topic Tackler 6-1

1. Establish responsibilities.
2. Maintain adequate records.
3. Insure assets and bond key employees.
4. Separate recordkeeping from custody of assets.
5. Divide responsibility for related transactions.
6. Apply technological controls.
7. Perform regular and independent reviews.

This section explains these seven principles and describes how internal control procedures minimize the risk of fraud and theft. These procedures also increase the reliability and accuracy of accounting records.

**Point: Sarbanes-Oxley Act** requires that each annual report contain an *internal control report*, which must: (1) state managers' responsibility for establishing and maintaing adequate internal controls for financial reporting; and (2) assess the effectiveness of those controls.

**Establish Responsibilities**    Proper internal control means that responsibility for a task is clearly established and assigned to one person. When a problem occurs in a company where responsibility is not identified, determining who is at fault is difficult. For instance, if two salesclerks share the same cash register and there is a cash shortage, neither clerk can be held accountable. To prevent this problem, one clerk might be given responsibility for handling all cash sales. Alternately, a company can use a register with separate cash drawers for each clerk. Most of us have waited at a retail counter during a shift change while employees swap cash drawers.

**Point:** Many companies have a mandatory vacation policy for employees who handle cash. When another employee must cover for the one on vacation, it is more difficult to hide cash frauds.

**Maintain Adequate Records**    Good recordkeeping is part of an internal control system. It helps protect assets and ensures that employees use prescribed procedures. Reliable records are also a source of information that managers use to monitor company activities. When detailed records of equipment are kept, for instance, items are unlikely to be lost or stolen without detection. Similarly, transactions are less likely to be entered in wrong accounts if a chart of accounts is set up and carefully used. Many preprinted forms and internal documents are also designed for use in a good internal control system. When sales slips are properly designed, for instance, sales personnel can record needed information efficiently with less chance of errors or delays to customers. When sales slips are prenumbered and controlled, each one issued is the responsibility of one salesperson, preventing the salesperson from pocketing cash by making a sale and destroying the sales slip. Computerized point-of-sale systems achieve the same control results.

**Point:** The Association of Certified Fraud Examiners (cfenet.com) estimates that employee fraud costs small companies an average of about $130,000 per incident.

**Insure Assets and Bond Key Employees**    Good internal control means that assets are adequately insured against casualty and that employees handling large amounts of cash and easily transferable assets are bonded. An employee is *bonded* when a company purchases an insurance policy, or a bond, against losses from theft by that employee. Bonding reduces the risk of loss. It also discourages theft because bonded employees know an independent bonding company will be involved when theft is uncovered and is unlikely to be sympathetic with an employee involved in theft.

**Decision Insight**

**Check It Out**    What lurks behind that spiffy résumé you just reviewed? The Association of Certified Fraud Examiners (**cfenet.com**) provides links to search engines to verify Social Security numbers, addresses, and phone numbers. Also, **KnowX.com** lets you check lawsuits and bankruptcies, and **EmployeeScreen.com** offers background searches, including employment verification.

**Separate Recordkeeping from Custody of Assets**    A person who controls or has access to an asset must not keep that asset's accounting records. This principle reduces the risk of theft or waste of an asset because the person with control over it knows that another person keeps its records. Also, a recordkeeper who does not have access to the asset

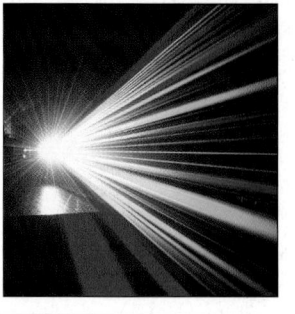

has no reason to falsify records. This means that to steal an asset and hide the theft from the records, two or more people must *collude*—or agree in secret to commit the fraud.

**Divide Responsibility for Related Transactions**   Good internal control divides responsibility for a transaction or a series of related transactions between two or more individuals or departments. This is to ensure that the work of one individual acts as a check on the other. This principle, often called *separation of duties*, is not a call for duplication of work. Each employee or department should perform unduplicated effort. Examples of transactions with divided responsibility are placing purchase orders, receiving merchandise, and paying vendors. These tasks should not be given to one individual or department. Assigning responsibility for two or more of these tasks to one party increases mistakes and perhaps fraud. Having an independent person, for example, check incoming goods for quality and quantity encourages more care and attention to detail than having the person who placed the order do the checking. Added protection can result from identifying a third person to approve payment of the invoice. A company can even designate a fourth person with authority to write checks as another protective measure.

**Point:** Evidence of any internal control failure for a company reduces user reliance on its financial statements.

**Apply Technological Controls**   Cash registers, check protectors, time clocks, and personal identification scanners are examples of devices that can improve internal control. Technology often improves the effectiveness of controls. A cash register with a locked-in tape or electronic file makes a record of each cash sale. A check protector perforates the amount of a check into its face and makes it difficult to alter the amount. A time clock registers the exact time an employee both arrives at and departs from the job. Mechanical change and currency counters quickly and accurately count amounts, and personal scanners limit access to only authorized individuals. Each of these and other technological controls are an effective part of many internal control systems.

**Perform Regular and Independent Reviews**   Changes in personnel, stress of time pressures, and technological advances present opportunities for shortcuts and lapses. To counter these factors, regular reviews of internal control systems are needed to ensure that procedures are followed. These reviews are preferably done by internal auditors not directly involved in the activities. Their impartial perspective encourages an evaluation of the efficiency as well as the effectiveness of the internal control system. Many companies also pay for audits by independent, external auditors. These external auditors test the company's financial records to give an opinion as to whether its financial statements are presented fairly. Before external auditors decide on how much testing is needed, they evaluate the effectiveness of the internal control system. This evaluation is often helpful to a client.

**Point:** Information on Internet fraud can be found at these Websites: ftc.gov/ftc/consumer.htm sec.gov/investor/pubs/cyberfraud.htm www.fraud.org

## Technology and Internal Control

The fundamental principles of internal control are relevant no matter what the technological state of the accounting system, from purely manual to fully automated systems. Technology impacts an internal control system in several important ways. Perhaps the most obvious is that technology allows us quicker access to databases and information. Used effectively, technology greatly improves managers' abilities to monitor and control business activities. This section describes some technological impacts we must be alert to.

**Reduced Processing Errors** Technologically advanced systems reduce the number of errors in processing information. Provided the software and data entry are correct, the risk of mechanical and mathematical errors is nearly eliminated. However, we must remember that erroneous software or data entry does exist. Also, less human involvement in data processing can cause data entry errors to go undiscovered. Moreover, errors in software can produce consistent but erroneous processing of transactions. Continually checking and monitoring all types of systems are important.

**More Extensive Testing of Records** A company's review and audit of electronic records can include more extensive testing when information is easily and rapidly accessed. When accounting records are kept manually, auditors and others likely select only small samples of data to test. When data are accessible with computer technology, however, auditors can quickly analyze large samples or even the entire database.

**Limited Evidence of Processing** Many data processing steps are increasingly done by computer. Accordingly, fewer hard-copy items of documentary evidence are available for review. Yet technologically advanced systems can provide new evidence. They can, for instance, record who made the entries, the date and time, the source of the entry, and so on. Technology can also be designed to require the use of passwords or other identification before access to the system is granted. This means that internal control depends more on the design and operation of the information system and less on the analysis of its resulting documents.

**Crucial Separation of Duties** Technological advances in accounting information systems often yield some job eliminations or consolidations. While those who remain have the special skills necessary to operate advanced programs and equipment, a company with a reduced workforce risks losing its crucial separation of duties. The company must establish ways to control and monitor employees to minimize risk of error and fraud. For instance, the person who designs and programs the information system must not be the one who operates it. The company must also separate control over programs and files from the activities related to cash receipts and disbursements. For instance, a computer operator should not control check-writing activities. Achieving acceptable separation of duties can be especially difficult and costly in small companies with few employees.

**Point:** There's a new security device—a person's ECG (electrocardiogram) reading, which is as unique as a fingerprint and a lot harder to lose or steal than a PIN. An ECG also shows that a living person is actually there, whereas fingerprint and facial recognition software can be fooled. ECGs can be read through fingertip touches.

**Point:** External decision makers look to several sources when assessing a company's internal controls. Sources include the auditor's report, management report on controls (if available), management discussion and analysis, and financial press.

### Decision Insight

**Hot Prospects** A recent survey cites the shortage of accounting techies as one barrier to company growth. The most prized recruits are those adept at enterprise software, the Web, intranets, and accounting.

## Limitations of Internal Control

All internal control policies and procedures have limitations which usually arise from either (1) the human element, or (2) the cost-benefit principle.

Internal control policies and procedures are applied by people. This human element creates several potential limitations that we can categorize as either (1) human error or (2) human fraud. *Human error* can occur from negligence, fatigue, misjudgment, or confusion. *Human fraud* involves intent by people to defeat internal controls, such as *management override,* for personal gain. Fraud also includes collusion to thwart the separation of duties. The human element highlights the importance of establishing an *internal control environment* to convey management's commitment to internal control policies and procedures.

**Point:** When the electronic manufacturer Casio (**Casio.com**) started an e-commerce site, it found 13% of its first-year customer purchases were fraudulent.

**Point:** <u>Cybercrime.gov</u> pursues computer and intellectual property crimes, including that of e-commerce.

The second major limitation on internal control is the *cost-benefit principle,* which dictates that the costs of internal controls must not exceed their benefits. Analysis of costs and benefits must consider all factors, including the impact on morale. Most companies, for instance, have a legal right to read employees' e-mails, yet companies seldom exercise that right unless they are confronted with evidence of potential harm to the company. The same holds for drug testing, phone tapping, and hidden cameras. The bottom line is that managers must establish internal control policies and procedures with a net benefit to the company.

## Quick Check

**I.** Principles of internal control suggest that (choose one): (*a*) Responsibility for a series of related transactions (such as placing orders, receiving and paying for merchandise) should be assigned to one employee; (*b*) Responsibility for individual tasks should be shared by more than one employee so that one serves as a check on the other; or (*c*) Employees who handle considerable cash and easily transferable assets should be bonded.

**2.** What are some impacts of computing technology on internal control?

Answers—p. 261

# Control of Cash

*Cash* is a necessary asset of every company. Most companies also own *cash equivalents* (defined below), which are assets similar to cash. Cash and cash equivalents are the most liquid of all assets and are easily hidden and moved. An effective system of internal controls protects these assets and it should meet three basic guidelines:

1. Handling cash is separate from recordkeeping of cash.
2. Cash receipts are promptly deposited in a bank.
3. Cash disbursements are made by check.

The first guideline applies separation of duties to minimize errors and fraud. When duties are separated, two or more people must collude to steal cash and conceal this action in the accounting records. The second guideline uses immediate (say, daily) deposits of all cash receipts to produce a timely independent record of the cash received. It also reduces the likelihood of cash theft (or loss) and the risk that an employee could personally use the money before depositing it. The third guideline uses payments by check to develop an independent bank record of cash disbursements. This guideline also reduces the risk of cash theft (or loss).

This section begins with definitions of cash and cash equivalents. Discussion then focuses on controls and accounting for both cash receipts and disbursements. The exact procedures used to achieve control over cash vary across companies. They depend on factors such as company size, number of employees, volume of cash transactions, and sources of cash.

## Cash, Cash Equivalents, and Liquidity

C2   Define cash and cash equivalents and explain how to report them.

Good accounting systems help in managing the amount of cash and controlling who has access to it. Cash is the usual means of payment when paying for assets, services, or liabilities. **Liquidity** refers to a company's ability to pay for its near-term obligations. Cash and similar assets are called **liquid assets** because they can be readily used to settle such obligations. A company needs liquid assets to effectively operate.

**Cash** includes currency and coins along with the amounts on deposit in bank accounts, checking accounts (called *demand deposits*), and many savings accounts (called *time deposits*). Cash also includes items that are acceptable for deposit in these accounts such as customer checks, cashier checks, certified checks, and money orders. **Cash equivalents** are short-term, highly liquid investment assets meeting two criteria: (1) readily convertible to a known cash

**Point:** The most liquid assets are usually reported first on a balance sheet; the least liquid assets are reported last.

amount and (2) sufficiently close to their due date so that their market value is not sensitive to interest rate changes. Only investments purchased within three months of their due date usually satisfy these criteria. Examples of cash equivalents are short-term investments in assets such as U.S. Treasury bills and money market funds. To increase their return, many companies invest idle cash in cash equivalents. Most companies combine cash equivalents with cash as a single item on the balance sheet.

**Point:** The e-commerce company i2 Technologies reports cash and cash equivalents of $538 million in its recent balance sheet. This amount makes up nearly one-third of its total assets.

## Control of Cash Receipts

Internal control of cash receipts ensures that cash received is properly recorded and deposited. Cash receipts can arise from transactions such as cash sales, collections of customer accounts, receipts of interest earned, bank loans, sales of assets, and owner investments. This section explains internal control over two important types of cash receipts: over-the-counter and by mail.

**P1**   Apply internal control to cash receipts and disbursements.

**Over-the-Counter Cash Receipts**   For purposes of internal control, over-the-counter cash receipts from sales should be recorded on a cash register at the time of each sale. To help ensure that correct amounts are entered, each register should be located so customers can read the amounts entered. Clerks also should be required to enter each sale before wrapping merchandise and to give the customer a receipt for each sale. The design of each cash register should provide a permanent, locked-in record of each transaction. In many systems, the register is directly linked with computing and accounting services. Less advanced registers simply print a record of each transaction on a paper tape or electronic file locked inside the register.

Proper internal control prescribes that custody over cash should be separate from its recordkeeping. For over-the-counter cash receipts, this separation begins with the cash sale. The clerk who has access to cash in the register should not have access to its locked-in record. At the end of the clerk's work period, the clerk should count the cash in the register, record the amount, and turn over the cash and a record of its amount to the company cashier. The cashier, like the clerk, has access to the cash but should not have access to accounting records (or the register tape or file). A third employee compares the record of total register transactions (or the register tape or file) with the cash receipts reported by the cashier. This record is the basis for a journal entry recording over-the-counter cash receipts. The third employee has access to the records for cash but not to the actual cash. The clerk and the cashier have access to cash but not to the accounting records. None of them can make a mistake or divert cash without the difference being revealed.

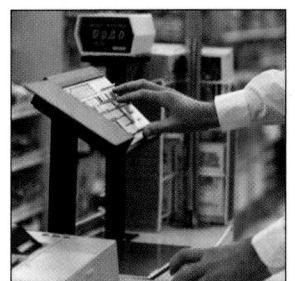

***Cash over and short.***   Sometimes errors in making change are discovered from differences between the cash in a cash register and the record of the amount of cash receipts. Although a clerk is careful, one or more customers can be given too much or too little change. This means that at the end of a work period, the cash in a cash register might not equal the record of cash receipts. This difference is reported in the **Cash Over and Short**

**Point:** Retailers often require cashiers to restrictively endorse checks immediately on receipt by stamping them "For deposit only."

account, also called *Cash Short and Over*, which is an income statement account recording the income effects of cash overages and cash shortages. To illustrate, if a cash register's record shows $550 but the count of cash in the register is $555, the entry to record cash sales and its overage is

| Cash . . . . . . . . . . . . . . . . . . . . . . . . . . . . . . . . . | 555 | |
| **Cash Over and Short** . . . . . . . . . . . . . . | | 5 |
| Sales . . . . . . . . . . . . . . . . . . . . . . . . . . . . | | 550 |

*To record cash sales and a cash overage.*

On the other hand, if a cash register's record shows $625 but the count of cash in the register is $621, the entry to record cash sales and its shortage is:

| Cash . . . . . . . . . . . . . . . . . . . . . . . . . . . . . . . . . | 621 | |
| **Cash Over and Short** . . . . . . . . . . . . . . . . . . | 4 | |
| Sales . . . . . . . . . . . . . . . . . . . . . . . . . . . . | | 625 |

*To record cash sales and a cash shortage.*

Since customers are more likely to dispute being shortchanged than being given too much change, the Cash Over and Short account usually has a debit balance at the end of an accounting period. A debit balance reflects an expense. It can be shown on the income statement as part of general and administrative expenses. (Note that since the amount is usually small, it is often combined with other small expenses and reported as part of *miscellaneous expenses;* or as part of *miscellaneous revenues* if it has a credit balance.)

**Cash Receipts by Mail**    Control of cash receipts that arrive through the mail starts with the person who opens the mail. Preferably, two people are assigned the task of, and are present for, opening the mail. In this case, theft of cash receipts by mail requires collusion between these two employees. Specifically, the person(s) opening the mail enters a list (in triplicate) of money received. This list should contain a record of each sender's name, the amount, and an explanation of why the money is sent. The first copy is sent with the money to the cashier. A second copy is sent to the recordkeeper in the accounting area. A third copy is kept by the clerks who opened the mail. The cashier deposits the money in a bank, and the recordkeeper records the amounts received in the accounting records.

This process reflects good internal control. That is, when the bank balance is reconciled by another person (explained later in the chapter), errors or acts of fraud by the mail clerks, the cashier, or the recordkeeper are revealed. They are revealed because the bank's record of cash deposited must agree with the records from each of the three. Moreover, if the mail clerks do not report all receipts correctly, customers will question their account balances. If the cashier does not deposit all receipts, the bank balance does not agree with the recordkeeper's cash balance. The recordkeeper and the person who reconciles the bank balance do not have access to cash and therefore have no opportunity to divert cash to themselves. This system makes errors and fraud highly unlikely. The exception is employee collusion.

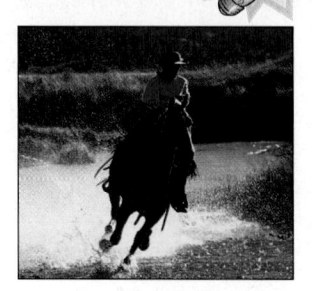

**Decision Insight**

**Look West**    In the annual Small Business Survival Index (**SBSC.org**), the first 4 of the top 5 states ranked as most entrepreneur friendly are west of the Mississippi: (1) South Dakota, (2) Nevada, (3) Wyoming, (4) Texas, and (5) Florida. Factors considered included taxes, regulations, costs, and crime.

## Control of Cash Disbursements

Control of cash disbursements is especially important as most large thefts occur from payment of fictitious invoices. One key to controlling cash disbursements is to require all expenditures to be made by check. The only exception is small payments made from petty cash.

Another key is to deny access to the accounting records to anyone other than the owner who has the authority to sign checks. A small business owner often signs checks and knows from personal contact that the items being paid for are actually received. This arrangement is impossible in large businesses. Instead, internal control procedures must be substituted for personal contact. Such procedures are designed to assure the check signer that the obligations recorded are properly incurred and should be paid. This section describes these and other internal control procedures, including the voucher system and petty cash system. The management of cash disbursements for purchases is described in Appendix 6B.

### Decision Insight

**Hidden Risks** The basic purposes of paper and electronic documents are similar. However, the internal control system must change to reflect different risks, including confidential and competitive-sensitive information that is at greater risk in electronic systems.

**Voucher System of Control** A **voucher system** is a set of procedures and approvals designed to control cash disbursements and the acceptance of obligations. The voucher system of control establishes procedures for

- Verifying, approving, and recording obligations for eventual cash disbursement.
- Issuing checks for payment of verified, approved, and recorded obligations.

A reliable voucher system follows standard procedures for every transaction. This applies even when multiple purchases are made from the same supplier.

A voucher system's control over cash disbursements begins when a company incurs an obligation that will result in payment of cash. A key factor in this system is that only approved departments and individuals are authorized to incur such obligations. The system often limits the type of obligations that a department or individual can incur. In a large retail store, for instance, only a purchasing department should

### Decision Insight

**Cyber Setup** The FTC is on the cutting edge of cybersleuthing. Opportunists in search of easy money are lured to **WeMarket4U.net/netops**. Take the bait and you get warned—and possibly targeted. (The top 4 fraud complaints as compiled by the Internet Fraud Complaint Center are shown to the right.)

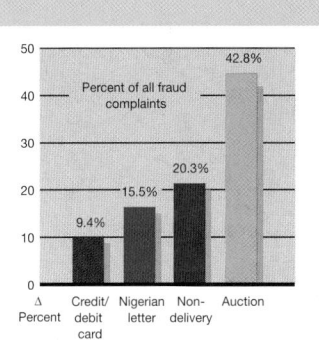

be authorized to incur obligations for merchandise inventory. Another key factor is that procedures for purchasing, receiving, and paying for merchandise are divided among several departments (or individuals). These departments include the one requesting the purchase, the purchasing department, the receiving department, and the accounting department. To coordinate and control responsibilities of these departments, a company uses several different business documents. Exhibit 6.1 shows how documents are accumulated in a **voucher,** which is an internal document (or file) used to accumulate information to control cash

## Exhibit 6.1

Document Flow in a Voucher System

**Point:** MCI, formerly WorldCom, paid a whopping $500 million in SEC fines for accounting fraud. Among the charges were that it inflated earnings by as much as $10 billion.

disbursements and to ensure that a transaction is properly recorded. This specific example begins with a *purchase requisition* and concludes with a *check* drawn against cash. Appendix 8A describes each document entering and leaving a voucher system. It also describes the internal control objective served by each document.

A voucher system should be applied not only to purchases of inventory but to all expenditures. To illustrate, when a company receives a monthly telephone bill, it should review and verify the charges, prepare a voucher (file), and insert the bill. This transaction is then recorded with a journal entry. If the amount is currently due, a check is issued. If not, the voucher is filed for payment on its due date. If no voucher is prepared, verifying the invoice and its amount after several days or weeks can be difficult. Also, without records, a dishonest employee could collude with a dishonest supplier to get more than one payment for an obligation, payment for excessive amounts, or payment for goods and services not received. An effective voucher system helps prevent such frauds.

### Decision Insight

**Hoodwinked**   Fictitious sales receipts and altered inventory tags deceived auditors, investors, and creditors of **Centennial Technologies**. Its CEO was eventually indicted on five counts of fraud. Many of these shenanigans could have been avoided with internal controls.

**Point:** A *voucher* is an internal document (or file).

### Quick Check

3. Why must a company hold liquid assets?

4. Why does a company hold cash equivalent assets in addition to cash?

5. Identify at least two assets that are classified as cash equivalents.

6. Good internal control procedures for cash include which of the following? (*a*) All cash disbursements, other than those for very small amounts, are made by check; (*b*) One employee should count cash received from sales and promptly deposit cash receipts; or (*c*) Cash receipts by mail should be opened by one employee who is then responsible for recording and depositing receipts.

7. Should all companies require a voucher system? At what point in a company's growth would you recommend a voucher system?

Answers—p. 261

**P2**   Explain and record petty cash fund transactions.

**Petty Cash System of Control**   A basic principle for controlling cash disbursements is that all payments must be made by check. An exception to this rule is made for *petty cash disbursements,* which are the small payments required for items such as postage, courier fees, minor repairs, and low-cost supplies. To avoid the time and cost of writing checks for small amounts, a company sets up a petty cash fund to make small payments. (**Petty cash** activities are part of an *imprest system,* which designates advance money to establish the fund, to withdraw from the fund, and to reimburse the fund.)

*Operating a petty cash fund.*   Establishing a petty cash fund requires estimating the total amount of small payments likely to be made during a short period such as a week or month. A check is then drawn by the company cashier for an amount slightly in excess of this estimate. This check is recorded with a debit to the Petty Cash account (an asset) and a credit to Cash. The check is cashed, and the currency is given to an employee designated as the *petty cashier* or *petty cash custodian.* The petty cashier is responsible for keeping this cash safe, making payments from the fund, and keeping records of it in a secure place referred to as the *petty cashbox.*

For example, when each cash disbursement is made, the person receiving payment should sign a prenumbered *petty cash receipt,* also called *petty cash ticket*—see Exhibit 6.2. The petty cash receipt is then placed in the petty cashbox with the remaining money. Under this system, the sum of all receipts plus the remaining cash equals the total fund amount. A $100 petty cash fund, for instance, contains any combination of cash and petty cash receipts that totals

**Point:** A petty cash fund is used only for business expenses.

**Petty Cash Receipt** No. 9
**Z-Mart**

For _____ Freight charges _____     Date _____ 11/5/05 _____

Charge to _____ Merchandise Inventory _____     Amount _____ $6.75 _____

Approved by _____ Jim Gilla _____     Received by _____ Dick Pitch _____

**Exhibit 6.2**

Petty Cash Receipt

$100 (examples are $80 cash plus $20 in receipts, or $10 cash plus $90 in receipts). Each disbursement reduces cash and increases the amount of receipts in the petty cashbox.

The petty cash fund should be reimbursed when it is nearing zero and at the end of an accounting period when financial statements are prepared. For this purpose, the petty cashier sorts the paid receipts by the type of expense or account and then totals the receipts. The petty cashier presents all paid receipts to the company cashier, who stamps all receipts *paid* so they cannot be reused, files them for recordkeeping, and gives the petty cashier a check for their sum. When this check is cashed and the money placed in the cashbox, the total money in the cashbox is restored to its original amount. The fund is now ready for a new cycle of petty cash payments.

**Point:** Petty cash receipts with either no signature or a forged signature usually indicate misuse of petty cash. Companies respond with surprise petty cash counts for verification.

***Illustrating a petty cash fund.*** To illustrate, assume Z-Mart establishes a petty cash fund on November 1 and designates one of its office employees as the petty cashier. A $75 check is drawn, cashed, and the proceeds given to the petty cashier. The entry to record the setup of this petty cash fund is

| Nov. I | Petty Cash . . . . . . . . . . . . . . . . . . . . . . . . . . . . . . . . | 75 | |
| | Cash . . . . . . . . . . . . . . . . . . . . . . . . . . . . . . . . | | 75 |
| | *To establish a petty cash fund.* | | |

Assets = Liabilities + Equity
+75
−75

After the petty cash fund is established, the *Petty Cash account is not debited or credited again unless the amount of the fund is changed.* (A fund probably should be increased if it requires reimbursement too frequently. On the other hand, if the fund is too large, some of its money should be redeposited in the Cash account.)

Next, assume that Z-Mart's petty cashier makes several November payments from petty cash. Each person who received payment is required to sign a receipt. On November 27, after making a $26.50 cash payment for tile cleaning, only $3.70 cash remains in the fund. The petty cashier then summarizes and totals the petty cash receipts as shown in Exhibit 6.3.

**Point:** Reducing or eliminating a petty cash fund would require a credit to Petty Cash.

**Point:** Although *individual* petty cash disbursements are not evidenced by a check, the initial petty cash fund is evidenced by a check, and later petty cash expenditures are evidenced by a check to replenish them *in total.*

| **Z-MART** | | |
|---|---|---|
| **Petty Cash Payments Report** | | |
| **Miscellaneous Expenses** | | |
| Nov. 2 Washing windows . . . . . . . . . . . . . . . . . . . . . . . . . . | $20.00 | |
| Nov. 27 Tile cleaning . . . . . . . . . . . . . . . . . . . . . . . . . . . | 26.50 | $ 46.50 |
| **Merchandise Inventory (transportation-in)** | | |
| Nov. 5 Transport of merchandise purchased . . . . . . . . . . . . . | 6.75 | |
| Nov. 20 Transport of merchandise purchased . . . . . . . . . . . . . | 8.30 | 15.05 |
| **Delivery Expense** | | |
| Nov. 18 Customer's package delivered . . . . . . . . . . . . . . . . . | | 5.00 |
| **Office Supplies Expense** | | |
| Nov. 15 Purchase of office supplies immediately used . . . . . . . | | 4.75 |
| **Total** . . . . . . . . . . . . . . . . . . . . . . . . . . . . . . . . . . . . . | | **$71.30** |

**Exhibit 6.3**

Petty Cash Payments Report

**Point:** This report can also include receipt number and names of those who approved and received cash payment (see Demo Problem 2).

The petty cash payments report and all receipts are given to the company cashier in exchange for a $71.30 check to reimburse the fund. The petty cashier cashes the check and puts the $71.30 cash in the petty cashbox. The company records this reimbursement as follows:

Assets = Liabilities + Equity
−71.30          −46.50
                −15.05
                − 5.00
                − 4.75

| Nov. 27 | Miscellaneous Expenses...................... | 46.50 | |
| | Merchandise Inventory ..................... | 15.05 | |
| | Delivery Expense ........................ | 5.00 | |
| | Office Supplies Expense.................... | 4.75 | |
| | Cash............................ | | 71.30 |
| | *To reimburse petty cash.* | | |

**Point:** To avoid errors in recording petty cash reimbursement, follow these steps: (1) prepare payments report, (2) compute cash needed by subtracting cash remaining from total fund amount, (3) record entry, and (4) check "Dr. = Cr." in entry—any difference is Cash Over and Short.

A petty cash fund is usually reimbursed at the end of an accounting period so that expenses are recorded in the proper period, even if the fund is not low on money. If the fund is not reimbursed at the end of a period, the financial statements would show both an overstated cash asset and understated expenses (or assets) that were paid out of petty cash. Some companies do not reimburse the petty cash fund at the end of each period under the principle that this amount is immaterial to users of financial statements.

***Increasing or decreasing a petty cash fund.*** A decision to increase or decrease a petty cash fund is often made when reimbursing it. To illustrate, assume Z-Mart decides to *increase* its petty cash fund from $75 to $100 on November 27 when it reimburses the fund. The entries required are to (1) reimburse the fund as usual (see the preceding November 27 entry, and (2) increase the fund amount as follows:

| Nov. 27 | Petty Cash ............................ | 25 | |
| | Cash............................ | | 25 |
| | *To increase the petty cash fund amount.* | | |

**Internal Auditor** You make a surprise count of a $300 petty cash fund. You arrive at the petty cashier when she is on the telephone. She politely asks that you return after lunch so that she can finish her business on the telephone. You agree and return after lunch. In the petty cashbox, you find 14 new $20 bills with consecutive serial numbers plus receipts totaling $20. What is your evaluation?

Answer—p. 261

| Event | Petty Cash | Cash | Expenses |
| --- | --- | --- | --- |
| Set up fund | Dr. | Cr. | — |
| Reimburse fund | — | Cr. | Dr. |
| Increase fund | Dr. | Cr. | — |
| Decrease fund | Cr. | Dr. | — |

Alternatively, if Z-Mart *decreases* the petty cash fund from $75 to $55 on November 27, the entry is to (1) credit Petty Cash for $20 (decreasing the fund from $75 to $55) and (2) debit Cash for $20 (reflecting the $20 transfer from Petty Cash to Cash).

***Cash over and short.*** Sometimes a petty cashier fails to get a receipt for payment or overpays for the amount due. When this occurs and the fund is later reimbursed, the petty cash payments report plus the cash remaining will not total to the fund balance. This mistake causes the fund to be *short*. This shortage is recorded as an expense in the reimbursing entry with a debit to the Cash Over and Short account. (An overage in the petty cash fund is recorded with a credit to Cash Over and Short in the reimbursing entry.) To illustrate, prepare the entry to reimburse a $200 petty cash fund when its payments report shows $178 in miscellaneous expenses and $15 cash remains.

| Miscellaneous Expenses..................................... | 178 | |
| Cash Over and Short ...................................... | 7 | |
| Cash.......................................... | | 185 |
| *To reimburse petty cash.* | | |

### Quick Check

**8.** Why are some cash payments made from a petty cash fund, and not by check?

**9.** Why should a petty cash fund be reimbursed at the end of an accounting period?

**10.** Identify at least two results of reimbursing a petty cash fund.

Answers—p. 261

# Banking Activities as Controls

Banks (and other financial institutions) provide many services, including helping companies control cash. Banks safeguard cash, provide detailed and independent records of cash transactions, and are a source of cash financing. This section describes these services and the documents provided by banking activities that increase managers' control over cash.

## Basic Bank Services

This section explains basic bank services—such as the bank account, the bank deposit, and checking—that contribute to the control of cash.

**C3** Identify control features of banking activities.

**Bank Account, Deposit, and Check**   A *bank account* is a record set up by a bank for a customer. It permits a customer to deposit money for safekeeping and helps control withdrawals. To limit access to a bank account, all persons authorized to write checks on the account must sign a **signature card,** which bank employees use to verify signatures on checks. Many companies have more than one bank account to serve different needs and to handle special transactions such as payroll.

Each bank deposit is supported by a **deposit ticket,** which lists items such as currency, coins, and checks deposited along with their corresponding dollar amounts. The bank gives the customer a copy of the deposit ticket or a deposit receipt as proof of the deposit. Exhibit 6.4 shows one type of deposit ticket.

**Exhibit 6.4**

Deposit Ticket

To withdraw money from an account, the depositor can use a **check,** which is a document signed by the depositor instructing the bank to pay a specified amount of money to a designated recipient. A check involves three parties: a *maker* who signs the check, a *payee* who is the recipient, and a *bank* (or *payer*) on which the check is drawn. The bank provides a depositor the checks

**Decision Insight**

**Web-bank**   Many companies balance checkbooks and pay bills via the Web. Customers value the convenience and low cost of banking services anytime, anywhere. Services include the ability to stop payment on a check, move money between accounts, get up-to-date balances, and identify cleared checks and deposits.

that are serially numbered and imprinted with the name and address of both the depositor and bank. Both checks and deposit tickets are imprinted with identification codes in magnetic ink for computer processing. Exhibit 6.5 shows one type of check. It is accompanied with an optional *remittance advice* explaining the payment. When a remittance advice is unavailable, the *memo* line is often used for a brief explanation.

## Exhibit 6.5

Check with Remittance Advice

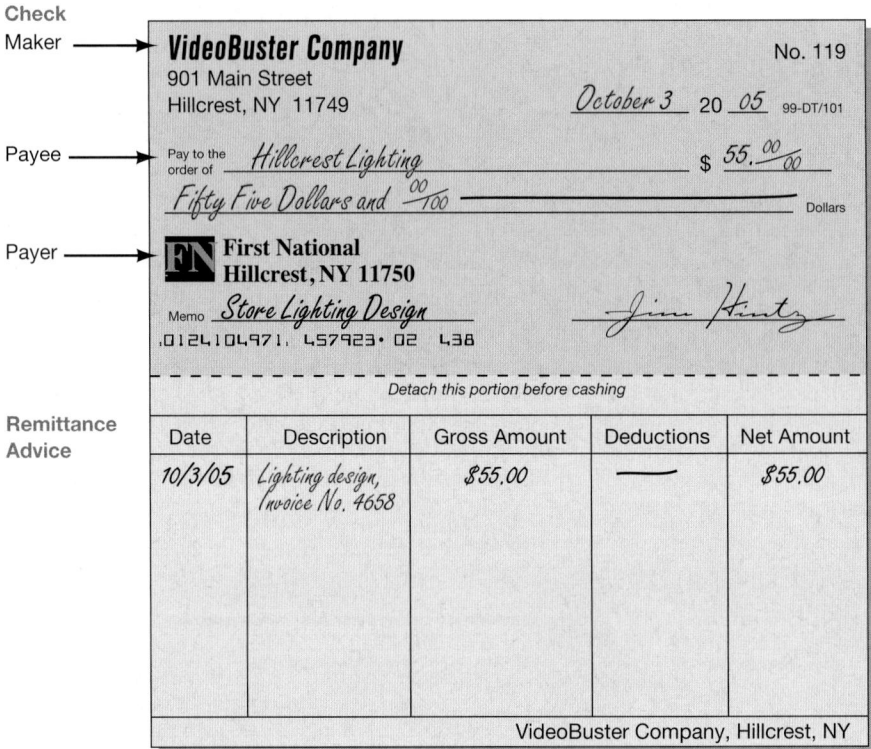

**Electronic Funds Transfer**    **Electronic funds transfer (EFT)** is the electronic communication transfer of cash from one party to another. No paper documents are necessary. Banks simply transfer cash from one account to another with a journal entry. Companies are increasingly using EFT because of its convenience and low cost. For instance, it can cost up to 50 cents to process a check through the banking system, whereas EFT cost is near zero. We now commonly see items such as payroll, rent, utilities, insurance, and interest payments being handled by EFT. The bank statement lists cash withdrawals by EFT with the checks and other deductions. Cash receipts by EFT are listed with deposits and other additions. A bank statement is sometimes a depositor's only notice of an EFT.

## Bank Statement

**Point:** Good internal control is to deposit all cash receipts daily and make all payments for goods and services by check. This controls access to cash and creates an independent record of all cash activities.

Usually once a month, the bank sends each depositor a **bank statement** showing the activity in the account. Different banks use different formats for their bank statements, but all of them include the following items of information:

1.  Beginning-of-period balance of the depositor's account.
2.  Checks and other debits decreasing the account during the period.
3.  Deposits and other credits increasing the account during the period.
4.  End-of-period balance of the depositor's account.

This information reflects the bank's records. Exhibit 6.6 shows one type of bank statement. Identify each of these four items in that statement. Part Ⓐ of Exhibit 6.6 summarizes changes

Exhibit 6.6

Bank Statement

| Member FDIC | | **FN First National** Hillcrest, NY 11750 | | Bank Statement | |
|---|---|---|---|---|---|

VideoBuster Company
901 Main Street
Hillcrest, NY 11749

October 31, 2005
Statement Date

494 504 2
Account Number

Ⓐ

| Previous Balance | Total Checks and Debits | Total Deposits and Credits | Current Balance |
|---|---|---|---|
| 1,609.58 | 723.00 | 1,163.42 | 2,050.00 |

Ⓑ Ⓒ Ⓓ

| Checks and Debits | | | Deposits and Credits | | Daily Balance | |
|---|---|---|---|---|---|---|
| Date | No. | Amount | Date | Amount | Date | Amount |
| 10/03 | 119 | 55.00 | 10/02 | 240.00 | 10/01 | 1,609.58 |
| 10/09 | 120 | 200.00 | 10/09 | 180.00 | 10/02 | 1,849.58 |
| 10/10 | 121 | 120.00 | 10/15 | 100.00 | 10/03 | 1,794.58 |
| 10/12 | | 23.00 DM | 10/16 | 150.00 | 10/09 | 1,774.58 |
| 10/14 | 122 | 70.00 | 10/23 | 485.00 CM | 10/10 | 1,654.58 |
| 10/16 | 123 | 25.00 | 10/31 | 8.42 IN | 10/12 | 1,631.58 |
| 10/23 | 125 | 15.00 | | | 10/14 | 1,561.58 |
| 10/25 | | 20.00 NSF | | | 10/15 | 1,661.58 |
| | | 10.00 DM | | | 10/16 | 1,786.58 |
| 10/26 | 127 | 50.00 | | | 10/23 | 2,256.58 |
| 10/29 | 128 | 135.00 | | | 10/25 | 2,226.58 |
| | | | | | 10/26 | 2,176.58 |
| | | | | | 10/29 | 2,041.58 |
| | | | | | 10/31 | 2,050.00 |

| Symbols: | **CM**–Credit Memo | **EC**–Error Correction | **NSF**–Non-Sufficient Funds | **SC**–Service Charge |
|---|---|---|---|---|
| | **DM**–Debit Memo | **IN**–Interest Earned | **OD**–Overdraft | |

< Reconcile the account immediately. >

in the account. Part Ⓑ lists paid checks along with other debits. Part Ⓒ lists deposits and credits to the account, and part Ⓓ shows the daily account balances.

In reading a bank statement note that a depositor's account is a liability on the bank's records. This is so because the money belongs to the depositor, not the bank. When a depositor increases the account balance, the bank records it with a *credit* to that liability account. This means that debit memos from the bank produce *credits* on the depositor's books, and credit memos from the bank produce *debits* on the depositor's books.

Enclosed with a bank statement is a list of the depositor's canceled checks (or the actual canceled checks) along with any debit or credit memoranda affecting the account. **Canceled checks** are checks the bank has paid and deducted from the customer's account during the period. Other deductions that can appear on a bank statement include (1) service charges and fees assessed by the bank, (2) checks deposited that are uncollectible, (3) corrections of previous errors, (4) withdrawals through automated teller machines (ATMs), and (5) periodic payments arranged in advance by a depositor. (Most company checking accounts do not allow ATM withdrawals because of the company's desire to make all disbursements by check.) Except for service charges, the bank notifies the depositor of each deduction with a debit memorandum when the bank reduces the balance. A copy of each debit memorandum is usually sent with the statement.

Transactions that increase the depositor's account include amounts the bank collects on behalf of the depositor and the corrections of previous errors. Credit memoranda notify the depositor of all increases when they are recorded. A copy of each credit memorandum is often sent with the bank statement. Banks that pay interest on checking accounts often compute the amount of interest earned on the average cash balance and would credit it to the depositor's account each period. In Exhibit 6.6, the bank credits $8.42 of interest to the account.

**Global:** If cash is in more than one currency, a company usually translates these amounts into U.S. dollars using the exchange rate as of the balance sheet date.

**Global:** A company must disclose any restrictions on cash accounts located outside the United States.

# Bank Reconciliation

P3   Prepare a bank
reconciliation.

When a company deposits all cash receipts and makes all cash payments (except petty cash) by check, it can use the bank statement for proving the accuracy of its cash records. This is done using a **bank reconciliation,** which is a report explaining any differences between the checking account balance according to the depositor's records and the balance reported on the bank statement.

Topic Tackler 6-2

**Purpose of Bank Reconciliation**   The balance of a checking account reported on the bank statement rarely equals the balance in the depositor's accounting records. This is usually due to information that one party has that the other does not. We must therefore prove the accuracy of both the depositor's records and those of the bank. This means we must *reconcile* the two balances and explain or account for any differences in them. Among the factors causing the bank statement balance to differ from the depositor's book balance are these:

■ **Outstanding checks. Outstanding checks** are checks written (or drawn) by the depositor, deducted on the depositor's records, and sent to the payees but not yet received by the bank for payment at the bank statement date.

■ **Deposits in transit** (also called **outstanding deposits**). **Deposits in transit** are deposits made and recorded by the depositor but not yet recorded on the bank statement. For example, companies can make deposits (in the night depository) at the end of a business day after the bank is closed. If such a deposit occurred on a bank statement date, it would not appear on this period's statement. The bank would record such a deposit on the next business day, and it would appear on the next period's bank statement. Deposits mailed to the bank near the end of a period also can be in transit and unrecorded when the statement is prepared.

■ **Deductions for uncollectible items and for services.** A company sometimes deposits another party's check that is uncollectible (usually meaning the balance in such an account is not large enough to cover the check). This check is called a *non-sufficient funds (NSF)* check. The bank would have initially credited the depositor's account for the amount of the check. When the bank learns the check is uncollectible, it debits (reduces) the depositor's account for the amount of that check. The bank may also charge the depositor a fee for processing an uncollectible check and notify the depositor of the deduction by sending a debit memorandum. The depositor should record each deduction when a debit memorandum is received, but an entry is sometimes not made until the bank reconciliation is prepared. Other possible bank charges to a depositor's account that are first reported on a bank statement include printing new checks and service fees.

■ **Additions for collections and for interest.** Banks sometimes act as collection agents for their depositors by collecting notes and other items. Banks can also receive electronic funds transfers to the depositor's account. When a bank collects an item, it is added to the depositor's account, less any service fee. The bank also sends a credit memorandum to notify the depositor of the transaction. When the memorandum is received, the depositor should record it; yet it sometimes remains unrecorded until the bank reconciliation is prepared. The bank statement also includes a credit for any interest earned.

■ **Errors.** Both banks and depositors can make errors. Bank errors might not be discovered until the depositor prepares the bank reconciliation. Also, depositor errors are sometimes discovered when the bank balance is reconciled. Error testing includes: (a) comparing deposits on the bank statement with deposits in the accounting records and (b) comparing canceled checks on the bank statement with checks recorded in the accounting records.

**Point:** Small businesses with few employees often allow recordkeepers to both write checks and keep the general ledger. If this is done, it is essential that the owner do the bank reconciliation.

**Point:** The person preparing the bank reconciliation should not be responsible for processing cash receipts, managing checks, or maintaining cash records.

**Illustration of a Bank Reconciliation**   We follow nine steps in preparing the bank reconciliation. It is helpful to refer to the bank reconciliation in Exhibit 6.7 when studying steps ❶ through ❾.

① Identify the bank statement balance of the cash account (*balance per bank*). VideoBuster's bank balance is $2,050.

② Identify and list any unrecorded deposits and any bank errors understating the bank balance. Add them to the bank balance. VideoBuster's $145 deposit placed in the bank's night depository on October 31 is not recorded on its bank statement.

③ Identify and list any outstanding checks and any bank errors overstating the bank balance. Deduct them from the bank balance. VideoBuster's comparison of canceled checks with its books shows two checks outstanding: No. 124 for $150 and No. 126 for $200.

④ Compute the *adjusted bank balance,* also called the *corrected* or *reconciled balance.*

⑤ Identify the company's book balance of the cash account (*balance per book*). VideoBuster's book balance is $1,404.58.

⑥ Identify and list any unrecorded credit memoranda from the bank, any interest earned, and errors understating the book balance. Add them to the book balance. Enclosed with VideoBuster's bank statement is a credit memorandum showing the bank collected a note receivable for the company on October 23. The note's proceeds of $500 (minus a $15 collection fee) are credited to the company's account. VideoBuster's bank statement also shows a credit of $8.42 for interest earned on the average cash balance. There was no prior notification of this item, and it is not yet recorded.

⑦ Identify and list any unrecorded debit memoranda from the bank, any service charges, and errors overstating the book balance. Deduct them from the book balance. Debits on VideoBuster's bank statement that are not yet recorded include (a) a $23 charge for check printing and (b) an NSF check for $20 plus a related $10 processing fee. (The NSF check is dated October 16 and was included in the book balance.)

⑧ Compute the *adjusted book balance,* also called *corrected* or *reconciled balance.*

⑨ Verify that the two adjusted balances from steps 4 and 8 are equal. If so, they are reconciled. If not, check for accuracy and missing data to achieve reconciliation.

**Point:** Outstanding checks are identified by comparing canceled checks on the bank statement with checks recorded. This includes identifying any outstanding checks listed on the *previous* period's bank reconciliation that are not included in the canceled checks on this period's bank statement.

**Adjusting Entries from a Bank Reconciliation** A bank reconciliation often identifies unrecorded items that need recording by the company. In VideoBuster's reconciliation, the adjusted balance of $1,845 is the correct balance as of October 31. But the company's accounting records show a $1,404.58 balance. We must prepare journal entries to adjust the book balance to the correct balance. *It is important to remember that only the items reconciling the book balance require adjustment.* A review of Exhibit 6.7 indicates that four entries are required for VideoBuster.

**Point:** The adjusting entries could be combined into one compound entry.

## Exhibit 6.7

Bank Reconciliation

| | **VIDEOBUSTER** Bank Reconciliation October 31, 2005 | | | | | | |
|---|---|---|---|---|---|---|---|
| ① | Bank statement balance . . . . . . . . . . | | $ 2,050.00 | ⑤ | Book balance . . . . . . . . . . . . . . . . | | $ 1,404.58 |
| ② | Add | | | ⑥ | Add | | |
| | Deposit of Oct. 31 in transit . . . . . | | 145.00 | | Collect $500 note less $15 fee . . . . | $485.00 | |
| | | | 2,195.00 | | Interest earned . . . . . . . . . . . . . . | 8.42 | 493.42 |
| ③ | Deduct | | | | | | 1,898.00 |
| | Outstanding checks | | | ⑦ | Deduct | | |
| | No. 124 . . . . . . . . . . . . . . . . . | $150.00 | | | Check printing charge . . . . . . . . . | 23.00 | |
| | No. 126 . . . . . . . . . . . . . . . . . | 200.00 | 350.00 | | NSF check plus service fee . . . . . . . | 30.00 | 53.00 |
| ④ | **Adjusted bank balance** | | **$1,845.00** | ⑧ | **Adjusted book balance** . . . . . . . . | | **$1,845.00** |

⑨ Balances are equal (reconciled)

***Collection of note.***   The first entry is to record the proceeds of its note receivable collected by the bank less the expense of having the bank perform that service.

Assets = Liabilities + Equity
+485                      −15
−500

| Oct. 31 | Cash . . . . . . . . . . . . . . . . . . . . . . . . . . . . . . . . . . . | 485 | |
| | Collection Expense . . . . . . . . . . . . . . . . . . . . . . . | 15 | |
| | Notes Receivable. . . . . . . . . . . . . . . . . . . . | | 500 |
| | *To record the collection fee and proceeds for a note collected by the bank.* | | |

***Interest earned.***   The second entry records interest credited to its account by the bank.

Assets = Liabilities + Equity
+8.42                    +8.42

| Oct. 31 | Cash . . . . . . . . . . . . . . . . . . . . . . . . . . . . . . . . | 8.42 | |
| | Interest Revenue . . . . . . . . . . . . . . . . . . . . . | | 8.42 |
| | *To record interest earned on the cash balance in the checking account.* | | |

***Check printing.***   The third entry records expenses for the check printing charge.

Assets = Liabilities + Equity
−23                      −23

| Oct. 31 | Miscellaneous Expenses. . . . . . . . . . . . . . . . . . . | 23 | |
| | Cash. . . . . . . . . . . . . . . . . . . . . . . . . . . . . . . . | | 23 |
| | *Check printing charge.* | | |

***NSF check.***   The fourth entry records the NSF check that is returned as uncollectible. The $20 check was originally received from F. Heflin in payment of his account and then deposited. The bank charged $10 for handling the NSF check and deducted $30 total from VideoBuster's account. This means the entry must reverse the effects of the original entry made when the check was received and must record (add) the $10 bank fee.

**Point:** The company will try to collect the entire NSF amount of $30.

Assets = Liabilities + Equity
+30
−30

| Oct. 31 | Accounts Receivable—F. Heflin . . . . . . . . . . . . . | 30 | |
| | Cash. . . . . . . . . . . . . . . . . . . . . . . . . . . . . . . . | | 30 |
| | *To charge Heflin's account for $20 NSF check and $10 bank fee.* | | |

**Point:** The Demo Problem I shows an adjusting entry for an error correction.

After these four entries are recorded, the book balance of cash is adjusted to the correct amount of $1,845 (computed as $1,404.58 + $485 + $8.42 − $23 − $30).

## Quick Check

11. What is a bank statement?
12. What is the meaning of the phrase *to reconcile a bank balance?*
13. Why do we reconcile the bank statement balance of cash and the depositor's book balance of cash?
14. List at least two items affecting the bank balance side of a bank reconciliation and indicate whether the items are added or subtracted.
15. List at least three items affecting the book balance side of a bank reconciliation and indicate whether the items are added or subtracted.

Answers—pp. 261–262

## Days' Sales Uncollected

Many companies attract customers by selling to them on credit. This means that cash receipts from customers are delayed until accounts receivable are collected. Users of accounting information often want to know how quickly a company can convert its accounts receivable into cash. This is important for evaluating a company's liquidity. One measure of the receivables' nearness to cash is the **days' sales uncollected,** also called *days' sales in receivables*. This measure is computed by dividing the current balance of receivables by net credit sales over the year just completed and then multiplying by 365 (number of days in a year). Since net credit sales usually are not reported to external users, the net sales (or revenues) figure is commonly used in the computation as in Exhibit 6.8.

A1 Compute the days' sales uncollected ratio and use it to assess liquidity.

$$\text{Days' sales uncollected} = \frac{\text{Accounts receivable}}{\text{Net sales}} \times 365$$

**Exhibit 6.8**

Days' Sales Uncollected

We use days' sales uncollected to estimate how much time is likely to pass before the current amount of accounts receivable is received in cash. For evaluation purposes, we need to compare this estimate to that for other companies in the same industry. We also make comparisons between current and prior periods.

To illustrate, we select data from the annual reports of two toy manufacturers, **Hasbro** and **Mattel**. Their days' sales uncollected figures are shown in Exhibit 6.9.

**Exhibit 6.9**

Analysis using Days' Sales Uncollected

| Company | Figure ($ millions) | 2002 | 2001 | 2000 |
|---------|--------------------|------|------|------|
| **Hasbro** | Accounts receivable | $555 | $572 | $686 |
| | Net sales | $2,816 | $2,856 | $3,787 |
| | **Days' sales uncollected** | **72 days** | **73 days** | **66 days** |
| **Mattel** | Accounts receivable | $491 | $666 | $840 |
| | Net sales | $4,885 | $4,688 | $4,565 |
| | **Days' sales uncollected** | **37 days** | **52 days** | **67 days** |

Days' sales uncollected for Hasbro in 2002 is computed as ($555/$2,816) × 365 days = 72 days. This means that it will take about 72 days to collect cash from ending accounts receivable. This number reflects one or more of the following factors: a company's ability to collect receivables, customer financial health, customer payment strategies, and discount terms. To further assess days' sales uncollected for Hasbro, we compare it to two prior years and to those of Mattel. We see that Hasbro's days' sales uncollected has slightly increased from 66 days in 2000 to 72 days in 2002, which is not good for its liquidity. In comparison, Mattel has improved on this factor. Specifically, Mattel's days' sales uncollected has declined from 67 days in 2000 to 37 days in 2002. The less time that money is tied up in receivables often translates into increased profitability.

### Decision Maker

**Sales Representative**  The sales staff is told to take action to help reduce days' sales uncollected. What can you, a salesperson, do to reduce days' sales uncollected?

Answer—p. 261

# Demonstration Problem 1

Prepare a bank reconciliation for Jamboree Enterprises for the month ended November 30, 2005. The following information is available to reconcile Jamboree Enterprises' book balance of cash with its bank statement balance as of November 30, 2005:

**a.** After all posting is complete on November 30, the company's book balance of Cash has a $16,380 debit balance, but its bank statement shows a $38,520 balance.

**b.** Checks No. 2024 for $4,810 and No. 2036 for $5,000 are outstanding.

**c.** In comparing the canceled checks on the bank statement with the entries in the accounting records, it is found that Check No. 2025 in payment of rent is correctly drawn for $1,000 but is erroneously entered in the accounting records as $880.

**d.** The November 30 deposit of $17,150 was placed in the night depository after banking hours on that date, and this amount does not appear on the bank statement.

**e.** In reviewing the bank statement, a check written by Jumbo Enterprises in the amount of $160 was erroneously drawn against Jamboree's account.

**f.** A credit memorandum enclosed with the bank statement indicates that the bank collected a $30,000 note and $900 of related interest on Jamboree's behalf. This transaction was not recorded by Jamboree prior to receiving the statement.

**g.** A debit memorandum for $1,100 lists a $1,100 NSF check received from a customer, Marilyn Welch. Jamboree had not recorded the return of this check before receiving the statement.

**h.** Bank service charges for November total $40. These charges were not recorded by Jamboree before receiving the statement.

## Planning the Solution

- Set up a bank reconciliation with a bank side and a book side (as in Exhibit 6.7). Leave room to both add and deduct items. Each column will result in a reconciled, equal balance.
- Examine each item *a* through *h* to determine whether it affects the book or the bank balance and whether it should be added or deducted from the bank or book balance.
- After all items are analyzed, complete the reconciliation and arrive at a reconciled balance between the bank side and the book side.
- For each reconciling item on the book side, prepare an adjusting entry. Additions to the book side require an adjusting entry that debits Cash. Deductions on the book side require an adjusting entry that credits Cash.

## Solution to Demonstration Problem I

**JAMBOREE ENTERPRISES**
**Bank Reconciliation**
**November 30, 2005**

| | | | | | | |
|---|---|---|---|---|---|---|
| Bank statement balance . . . . . . . . . . . . | | $ 38,520 | Book balance . . . . . . . . . . . . . . . . | | | $ 16,380 |
| Add | | | Add | | | |
| Deposit of Nov. 30 . . . . . | $17,150 | | Collection of note . . . | $30,000 | | |
| Bank error . . . . . . . . . . | 160 | 17,310 | Interest earned . . . . . . | 900 | 30,900 | |
| | | 55,830 | | | | 47,280 |
| Deduct | | | Deduct | | | |
| Outstanding checks . . . . . . . . . . . . | | 9,810 | NSF check . . . . . . . . . | 1,100 | | |
| | | | Recording error . . . . . | 120 | | |
| | | | Service charge . . . . . . | 40 | 1,260 | |
| **Adjusted bank balance** | | **$46,020** | **Adjusted book balance** | | | **$46,020** |

**Required Adjusting Entries for Jamboree**

| | | | |
|---|---|---|---|
| Nov. 30 | Cash . . . . . . . . . . . . . . . . . . . . . . . . . . . . . . . . | | 30,900 | |
| |     Notes Receivable . . . . . . . . . . . . . . . . . . . | | 30,000 |
| |     Interest Earned . . . . . . . . . . . . . . . . . . . . | | 900 |
| |   *To record collection of note with interest.* | | |
| Nov. 30 | Accounts Receivable—M. Welch . . . . . . . . . . . . | 1,100 | |
| |     Cash. . . . . . . . . . . . . . . . . . . . . . . . . . . . | | 1,100 |
| |   *To reinstate account due from an NSF check.* | | |

[continued on next page]

[continued from previous page]

| | | | |
|---|---|---|---|
| Nov. 30 | Rent Expense .......................... | 120 | |
| | Cash .............................. | | 120 |
| | *To correct recording error on check no. 2025.* | | |
| Nov. 30 | Bank Service Charges ..................... | 40 | |
| | Cash............................... | | 40 |
| | *To record bank service charges.* | | |

## Demonstration Problem 2

Bacardi Company established a $150 petty cash fund with Dean Martin as the petty cashier. When the fund balance reached $19 cash, Martin prepared a petty cash payment report, which follows:

| Petty Cash Payments Report | | | | |
|---|---|---|---|---|
| **Receipt No.** | **Account Charged** | | **Approved by** | **Received by** |
| 12 | Delivery Expense ........... | $ 29 | Martin | A. Smirnoff |
| 13 | Merchandise Inventory ........ | 18 | Martin | J. Daniels |
| 15 | (Omitted) ............... | 32 | Martin | C. Carlsberg |
| 16 | Miscellaneous Expense ........ | 41 | (Omitted) | J. Walker |
| | Total .................. | $120 | | |

### Required

1. Identify four internal control weaknesses from the payment report.
2. Prepare general journal entries to record:
   a. Establishment of the petty cash fund.
   b. Reimbursement of the fund. (Assume for this part only that petty cash receipt no. 15 was issued for  miscellaneous expenses.)
3. What is the Petty Cash account balance immediately before reimbursement? Immediately after reimbursement?

## Solution to Demonstration Problem 2

1. Four internal control weaknesses are
   a. Petty cash ticket no. 14 is missing. Its omission raises questions about the petty cashier's management of the fund.
   b. The $19 cash balance means that $131 has been withdrawn ($150 − $19 = $131). However, the total amount of the petty cash receipts is only $120 ($29 + $18 + $32 + $41). The fund is $11 short of cash ($131 − $120 = $11). Was petty cash receipt no. 14 issued for $11? Management should investigate.
   c. The petty cashier (Martin) did not sign petty cash receipt no. 16. This omission could have been an oversight on his part or he might not have authorized the payment. Management should investigate.
   d. Petty cash receipt no. 15 does not indicate which account to charge. This omission could have been an oversight on the petty cashier's part. Management could check with C. Carlsberg and the petty cashier (Martin) about the transaction. Without further information, debit Miscellaneous Expense.
2. Petty cash general journal entries:
   a. Entry to establish the petty cash fund:

| | | |
|---|---|---|
| Petty Cash ................. | 150 | |
| Cash ................ | | 150 |

   b. Entry to reimburse the fund:

| | | |
|---|---|---|
| Delivery Expense ................ | 29 | |
| Merchandise Inventory ............ | 18 | |
| Miscellaneous Expense ($41 + $32) ... | 73 | |
| Cash Over and Short ............. | 11 | |
| Cash ..................... | | 131 |

3. The Petty Cash account balance *always* equals its fund balance, in this case $150. This account balance does not change unless the fund is increased or decreased.

# Documents in a Voucher System

P4   Describe the voucher system to control cash disbursements.

This appendix describes the important business documents of a voucher system of control.

**Purchase Requisition**   Department managers are usually not allowed to place orders directly with suppliers for control purposes. Instead, a department manager must inform the purchasing department of its needs by preparing and signing a **purchase requisition,** which lists the merchandise needed and requests that it be purchased—see Exhibit 6A.1. Two copies of the purchase requisition are sent to the purchasing department, which then sends one copy to the accounting department. When the accounting department receives a purchase requisition, it creates and maintains a voucher for this transaction. The requesting department keeps the third copy.

## Exhibit 6A.1

Purchase Requisition

| Purchase Requisition | | No. 917 |
| --- | --- | --- |
| **Z-Mart** | | |

**From** ___ Sporting Goods Department ___         **Date** ___ October 28, 2005 ___
**To** ___ Purchasing Department ___         **Preferred Vendor** ___ Trex ___

Request purchase of the following item(s):

| Model No. | Description | Quantity |
| --- | --- | --- |
| CH 015 | Challenger X7 | 1 |
| SD 099 | SpeedDemon | 1 |

**Reason for Request** ___ Replenish inventory ___
**Approval for Request** ___ *J.Z.* ___

For Purchasing Department use only: Order Date _10/30/05_   P.O. No. ___ P98 ___

**Point:** It is important to note that a voucher system is designed to uniquely meet the needs of a specific business. Thus, you should read this appendix as one example of a common voucher system design, but *not* the only design.

**Purchase Order**   A **purchase order** is a document the purchasing department uses to place an order with a **vendor** (seller or supplier). A purchase order authorizes a vendor to ship ordered merchandise at the stated price and terms—see Exhibit 6A.2. When the purchasing department receives a purchase requisition, it prepares at least five copies of a purchase order. The copies are distributed as follows: *copy 1* to the vendor as a purchase request and as authority to ship merchandise; *copy 2*, along with a copy of the purchase requisition, to the accounting department, where it is entered in the voucher and used in approving payment of the invoice; *copy 3* to the requesting department to inform its manager that action is being taken; *copy 4* to the receiving department without order quantity so it can compare with goods received and provide independent count of goods received; and *copy 5* retained on file by the purchasing department.

**Invoice**   An **invoice** is an itemized statement of goods prepared by the vendor listing the customer's name, items sold, sales prices, and terms of sale. An invoice is also a bill sent to the buyer from the supplier. From the vendor's point of view, it is a *sales invoice.* The buyer, or **vendee,** treats it as a *purchase invoice.* When receiving a purchase order, the vendor ships the ordered merchandise to the buyer and includes or mails a copy of the invoice covering the shipment to the buyer. The invoice is sent to the buyer's accounting department where it is placed in the voucher. (Refer back to Exhibit 4.5, which shows Z-Mart's purchase invoice.)

| Purchase Order | | | No. P98 |
|---|---|---|---|
| **Z-Mart** | | | |
| **10 Michigan Street** | | | |
| **Chicago, Illinois 60521** | | | |

**To:** Trex
W9797 Cherry Road
Antigo, Wisconsin 54409

**Date** _____ 10/30/05 _____
**FOB** _____ Destination _____
**Ship by** __ As soon as possible __
**Terms** _____ 2/15, n/30 _____

Request shipment of the following item(s):

| Model No. | Description | Quantity | Price | Amount |
|---|---|---|---|---|
| CH 015 | Challenger X7 | 1 | 490 | 490 |
| SD 099 | SpeedDemon | 1 | 710 | 710 |

All shipments and invoices must include purchase order number

Ordered by
*J.W.*

**Exhibit 6A.2**

Purchase Order

**Receiving Report**   Many companies maintain a separate department to receive all merchandise and purchased assets. When each shipment arrives, this receiving department counts the goods and checks them for damage and agreement with the purchase order. It then prepares four or more copies of a **receiving report,** which is used within the company to notify the appropriate persons that ordered goods have been received and to describe the quantities and condition of the goods. One copy is sent to accounting and placed in the voucher. Copies are also sent to the requesting department and the purchasing department to notify them that the goods have arrived. The receiving department retains a copy in its files.

**Invoice Approval**   When a receiving report arrives, the accounting department should have copies of the following documents in the voucher: purchase requisition, purchase order, and invoice. With the information in these documents, the accounting department can record the purchase and approve its payment. In approving an invoice for payment, it checks and compares information across all documents. To facilitate this checking and to ensure that no step is omitted, it often uses an **invoice approval,** also called *check authorization*—see Exhibit 6A.3. An invoice approval is a checklist of steps necessary for approving an invoice for recording and payment. It is a separate document either filed in the voucher or preprinted (or stamped) on the voucher.

| Invoice Approval | | By | Date |
|---|---|---|---|
| Document | | | |
| Purchase requisition | 917 | 72 | 10/28/05 |
| Purchase order | P98 | 9W | 10/30/05 |
| Receiving report | R85 | SK | 11/3/05 |
| Invoice: | 4657 | | 11/12/05 |
| Price | | 9L | 11/12/05 |
| Calculations | | 9L | 11/12/05 |
| Terms | | 9L | 11/12/05 |
| Approved for payment | | BC | |

**Exhibit 6A.3**

Invoice Approval

As each step in the checklist is approved, the person initials the invoice approval and records the current date. Final approval implies the following steps have occurred:

1. **Requisition check:** Items on invoice are requested per purchase requisition.
2. **Purchase order check:** Items on invoice are ordered per purchase order.
3. **Receiving report check:** Items on invoice are received, per receiving report.
4. **Invoice check: Price:** Invoice prices are as agreed with the vendor.
    **Calculations:** Invoice has no mathematical errors.
    **Terms:** Terms are as agreed with the vendor.

**Point:** Recording a purchase is initiated by an invoice approval, not an invoice. An invoice approval verifies that the amount is consistent with that requested, ordered, and received. This controls and verifies purchases and related liabilities.

**Voucher**   Once an invoice has been checked and approved, the voucher is complete. A complete voucher is a record summarizing a transaction. Once the voucher certifies a transaction, it authorizes recording an obligation. A voucher also contains approval for paying the obligation on an appropriate date. The physical form of a voucher varies across companies. Many are designed so that the invoice and other related source documents are placed inside the voucher, which can be a folder.

Completion of a voucher usually requires a person to enter certain information on both the inside and outside of the voucher. Typical information required on the inside of a voucher is shown in Exhibit 6A.4, and that for the outside is shown in Exhibit 6A.5. This information is taken from the invoice and the supporting documents filed in the voucher. A complete voucher is sent to an authorized individual (often called an *auditor*). This person performs a final review, approves the accounts and amounts for debiting (called the *accounting distribution*), and authorizes recording of the voucher.

**Exhibit 6A.4**

Inside of a Voucher

After a voucher is approved and recorded (in a journal called a **voucher register**), it is filed by its due date. A check is then sent on the payment date from the cashier, the voucher is marked "paid", and the voucher is sent to the accounting department and recorded (in a journal called the **check register**). The person issuing checks relies on the approved voucher and its signed supporting documents as proof that an obligation has been incurred and must be paid. The purchase requisition and purchase order confirm the purchase was authorized. The receiving report shows that items have been received, and the invoice approval form verifies that the invoice has been checked for errors. There is little chance for error and even less chance for fraud without collusion unless all the documents and signatures are forged.

**Exhibit 6A.5**

Outside of a Voucher

**APPENDIX**

# Control of Purchase Discounts

# 6B

This appendix explains how a company can better control its cash *disbursements* to take advantage of favorable purchases discounts. Chapter 4 described the entries to record the receipt and payment of an invoice for a merchandise purchase with and without discount terms. Those entries were prepared under what is called the **gross method** of recording purchases, which initially records the invoice at its *gross* amount ignoring any cash discount.

The **net method** is another means of recording purchases, which initially records the invoice at its *net* amount of any cash discount. The net method gives management an advantage in controlling and monitoring cash payments involving purchase discounts.

**P5**  Apply the net method to control purchase discounts.

To explain, when invoices are recorded at *gross* amounts, the amount of any discounts taken is deducted from the balance of the Merchandise Inventory account when cash payment is made. This means that the amount of any discounts lost is not reported in any account or on the income statement. Lost discounts recorded in this way are unlikely to come to the attention of management. When purchases are recorded at *net* amounts, a **Discounts Lost** expense account is recorded and brought to management's attention. Management can then seek to identify the reason for discounts lost such as oversight, carelessness, or unfavorable terms. (Chapter 4 explains how managers assess whether a discount is favorable or not.)

**Perpetual Inventory System**   To illustrate, assume that a company purchases merchandise on November 2 at a $1,200 invoice price with terms of 2/10, n/30. Its November 2 entries under the gross and net methods are

| Gross Method | | | Net Method | | |
|---|---|---|---|---|---|
| Merchandise Inventory | 1,200 | | Merchandise Inventory | 1,176 | |
| Accounts Payable | | 1,200 | Accounts Payable | | 1,176 |

If the invoice is paid on November 12 within the discount period, it records the following

| Gross Method | | | Net Method | | |
|---|---|---|---|---|---|
| Accounts Payable | 1,200 | | Accounts Payable | 1,176 | |
| Merchandise Inventory | | 24 | Cash | | 1,176 |
| Cash | | 1,176 | | | |

If the invoice is *not* paid within the discount period, it records the following November 12 entry (which is the date corresponding to the end of the discount period)

| Gross Method | | | Net Method | | |
|---|---|---|---|---|---|
| No entry | | | Discounts Lost | 24 | |
| | | | Accounts Payable | | 24 |

Then, when the invoice is later paid on December 2, outside the discount period, it records the following

| Gross Method | | | Net Method | | |
|---|---|---|---|---|---|
| Accounts Payable | 1,200 | | Accounts Payable | 1,200 | |
| Cash | | 1,200 | Cash | | 1,200 |

(Note that the discount lost can be recorded when the cash payment is made with a single entry. However, in this case, when financial statements are prepared after a discount is lost and before the cash payment is made, an adjusting entry is required to recognize any unrecorded discount lost in the period when incurred.)

**Periodic Inventory System**   The preceding entries assume a perpetual inventory system. If a company is using a *periodic system*, its November 2 entries under the gross and net methods are

| Gross Method—Periodic | | | Net Method—Periodic | | |
|---|---|---|---|---|---|
| Purchases . . . . . . . . . . . . . . . . . . | 1,200 | | Purchases . . . . . . . . . . . . . . . . . . | 1,176 | |
|     Accounts Payable . . . . . . . . . | | 1,200 |     Accounts Payable . . . . . . . . . | | 1,176 |

If the invoice is paid on November 12 within the discount period, it records the following

| Gross Method—Periodic | | | Net Method—Periodic | | |
|---|---|---|---|---|---|
| Accounts Payable . . . . . . . . . . . . . | 1,200 | | Accounts Payable . . . . . . . . . . . . . | 1,176 | |
|     Purchases Discounts . . . . . . . | | 24 |     Cash . . . . . . . . . . . . . . . . . . | | 1,176 |
|     Cash . . . . . . . . . . . . . . . . . . | | 1,176 | | | |

If the invoice is *not* paid within the discount period, it records the following November 12 entry

| Gross Method—Periodic | | | Net Method—Periodic | | |
|---|---|---|---|---|---|
| No entry | | | Discounts Lost . . . . . . . . . . . . . . | 24 | |
| | | |     Accounts Payable . . . . . . . . . | | 24 |

Then, when the invoice is later paid on December 2, outside the discount period, it records the following

| Gross Method—Periodic | | | Net Method—Periodic | | |
|---|---|---|---|---|---|
| Accounts Payable . . . . . . . . . . . . . | 1,200 | | Accounts Payable . . . . . . . . . . . . . | 1,200 | |
|     Cash . . . . . . . . . . . . . . . . . . | | 1,200 |     Cash . . . . . . . . . . . . . . . . . . | | 1,200 |

## Summary

**C1**   **Define internal control and identify its purpose and principles.** An internal control system consists of the policies and procedures managers use to protect assets, ensure reliable accounting, promote efficient operations, and urge adherence to company policies. It can prevent avoidable losses and help managers both plan operations and monitor company and human performance. Principles of good internal control include establishing responsibilities, maintaining adequate records, insuring assets and bonding employees, separating recordkeeping from custody of assets, dividing responsibilities for related transactions, applying technological controls, and performing regular independent reviews.

**C2**   **Define cash and cash equivalents and explain how to report them.** Cash includes currency, coins, and amounts on (or acceptable for) deposit in checking and savings accounts. Cash equivalents are short-term, highly liquid investment assets readily convertible to a known cash amount and sufficiently close to their maturity date so that market value is not sensitive to interest rate changes. Cash and cash equivalents are liquid assets because they are readily converted into other assets or can be used to pay for goods, services, or liabilities.

**C3**   **Identify control features of banking activities.** Banks offer several services that promote the control and safeguarding of cash. A bank account is a record set up by a bank permitting a customer to deposit money for safekeeping and to draw checks on it. A bank deposit is money contributed to the account with a deposit ticket as proof. A check is a document signed by the depositor instructing the bank to pay a specified amount of money to a designated recipient.

**A1**   **Compute the days' sales uncollected ratio and use it to assess liquidity.** Many companies attract customers by selling to them on credit. This means that cash receipts from customers are delayed until accounts receivable are collected. Users want to know how quickly a company can convert its accounts receivable into cash. The days' sales uncollected ratio, one measure reflecting company liquidity, is computed by dividing the ending balance of receivables by annual net sales, and then multiplying by 365.

**P1**   **Apply internal control to cash receipts and disbursements.** Internal control of cash receipts ensures that all cash received is properly recorded and deposited. Attention focuses on two important types of cash receipts: over-the-counter and by mail. Good internal control for over-the-counter cash receipts includes use of a cash register, customer review, use of receipts, a permanent transaction record, and separation of the custody of cash from its recordkeeping. Good internal control for cash receipts by mail includes at least two people assigned to open mail and a listing of each sender's name, amount, and explanation.

**P2**  **Explain and record petty cash fund transactions.** Petty cash disbursements are payments of small amounts for items such as postage, courier fees, minor repairs, and supplies. A company usually sets up one or more petty cash funds. A petty fund cashier is responsible for safekeeping the cash, making payments from this fund, and keeping receipts and records. A Petty Cash account is debited only when the fund is established or increased in amount. When the fund is replenished, petty cash disbursements are recorded with debits to expense (or asset) accounts and a credit to cash.

**P3**  **Prepare a bank reconciliation.** A bank reconciliation proves the accuracy of the depositor's and the bank's records. The bank statement balance is adjusted for items such as outstanding checks and unrecorded deposits made on or before the bank statement date but not reflected on the statement. The book balance is adjusted for items such as service charges, bank collections for the depositor, and interest earned on the account.

**P4ᴬ**  **Describe the voucher system to control cash disbursements.** A voucher system is a set of procedures and approvals designed to control cash disbursements and acceptance of obligations. The voucher system of control relies on several important documents, including the voucher and its supporting files. A key factor in this system is that only approved departments and individuals are authorized to incur certain obligations.

**P5ᴮ**  **Apply the net method to control purchase discounts.** The net method aids management in monitoring and controlling purchase discounts. When invoices are recorded at gross amounts, the amount of discounts taken is deducted from the balance of the Inventory account. This means that the amount of any discounts lost is not reported in any account and is unlikely to come to the attention of management. When purchases are recorded at net amounts, a Discounts Lost account is brought to management's attention as an operating expense. Management can then seek to identify the reason for discounts lost, such as oversight, carelessness, or unfavorable terms.

---

## Guidance Answers to **Decision Maker** and **Decision Ethics**

**Entrepreneur**  A forced vacation policy is part of a good system of internal controls. When employees are forced to take vacations, their ability to hide any fraudulent behavior decreases because others must perform the vacationers' duties. A replacement employee potentially can uncover fraudulent behavior or falsified records. A forced vacation policy is especially important for employees in sensitive positions of handling money or in control of easily transferable assets.

**Internal Auditor**  Since you were asked to postpone your count, along with the fact the fund consists of 14 new $20 bills, you have legitimate concerns about whether money is being used for personal use. It is possible the most recent reimbursement of the fund was for $280 (14 × $20) or more. In that case, this reimbursement can leave the fund with sequentially numbered $20 bills. But if the most recent reimbursement was for less than $280, the presence of 14 sequentially numbered $20 bills suggests that the new bills were obtained from a bank as replacement for bills that had been removed. Neither situation shows that the cashier is stealing money, but the second case indicates that the cashier "borrowed" the cash and later replaced it after the auditor showed up. In writing your report, you must not conclude that the cashier is unethical unless other evidence supports it. You should consider additional surprise counts of this petty cashier over the next few weeks.

**Sales Representative**  A salesperson can take several steps to reduce days' sales uncollected. These include (1) decreasing the ratio of sales on account to total sales by encouraging more cash sales, (2) identifying customers most delayed in their payments and encouraging earlier payments or cash sales, and (3) applying stricter credit policies to eliminate credit sales to customers that never pay.

---

## Guidance Answers to **Quick Checks**

**1.** (*c*)

**2.** Technology reduces processing errors. It also allows more extensive testing of records, limits the amount of hard evidence, and highlights the importance of separation of duties.

**3.** A company holds liquid assets so that it can purchase other assets, buy services, and pay obligations.

**4.** It owns cash equivalents because they yield a return greater than what cash earns (and are readily exchanged for cash).

**5.** Examples of cash equivalents are 90-day U.S. Treasury bills, money market funds, and commercial paper (notes).

**6.** (*a*)

**7.** A voucher system is used when an owner/manager can no longer control purchasing procedures through personal supervision and direct participation.

**8.** If all cash payments are made by check, numerous checks for small amounts must be written. Since this practice is expensive and time-consuming, a petty cash fund is often established for making small (immaterial) cash payments.

**9.** If the petty cash fund is not reimbursed at the end of an accounting period, the transactions involving petty cash are not yet recorded and the petty cash asset is overstated.

**10.** First, petty cash transactions are recorded when the petty cash fund is reimbursed. Second, reimbursement provides cash to allow the fund to continue being used. Third, reimbursement identifies any cash shortage or overage in the fund.

**11.** A bank statement is a report prepared by the bank describing the activities in a depositor's account.

**12.** To reconcile a bank balance means to explain the difference between the cash balance in the depositor's accounting records and the cash balance on the bank statement.

**13.** The purpose of the bank reconciliation is to determine whether the bank or the depositor has made any errors and whether the bank has entered any transactions affecting the account that the depositor has not recorded.

**14.** Outstanding checks—subtracted
Unrecorded deposits—added

**15.** Debit memos—subtracted          Interest earned—added
NSF checks—subtracted          Credit memos—added
Bank service charges—subtracted

## Key Terms

Key Terms are available at the book's Website for learning and testing in an online Flashcard Format.

Bank reconciliation (p. 250)
Bank statement (p. 248)
Canceled checks (p. 249)
Cash (p. 240)
Cash equivalents (p. 240)
Cash Over and Short (p. 241)
Check (p. 247)
Check register (p. 258)
Days' sales uncollected (p. 253)
Deposits in transit (p. 250)
Deposit ticket (p. 247)

Discounts Lost (p. 259)
Electronic funds transfer (EFT) (p. 248)
Gross method (p. 259)
Internal control system (p. 236)
Invoice (p. 256)
Invoice approval (p. 257)
Liquid assets (p. 240)
Liquidity (p. 240)
Net method (p. 259)
Outstanding checks (p. 250)
Petty cash (p. 244)

Principles of internal control (p. 237)
Purchase order (p. 256)
Purchase requisition (p. 256)
Receiving report (p. 257)
Signature card (p. 247)
Vendee (p. 256)
Vendor (p. 256)
Voucher (p. 243)
Voucher register (p. 258)
Voucher system (p. 243)

## Personal Interactive Quiz

Personal Interactive Quizzes A and B are available at the book's Website to reinforce and assess your learning.

*Superscript letter $^A$ ($^B$) denotes assignments based on Appendix 6A (6B).*

## Discussion Questions

**1.** List the seven broad principles of internal control.

**2.** Why should responsibility for related transactions be divided among different departments or individuals?

**3.** Internal control procedures are important in every business, but at what stage in the development of a business do they become especially critical?

**4.** Which of the following assets is most liquid? Which is least liquid? Inventory, building, accounts receivable, or cash.

**5.** Why should the person who keeps the records of an asset not be the person responsible for its custody?

**6.** When a store purchases merchandise, why are individual departments not allowed to directly deal with suppliers?

**7.** What is a petty cash receipt? Who should sign it?

**8.** Why should cash receipts be deposited on the day of receipt?

**9.** **Krispy Kreme**'s statement of cash flows in Appendix A describes changes in cash and cash equivalents for the year ended February 2, 2003. What amount is provided (used) by investing activities? What amount is provided (used) by financing activities?

**10.** Refer to **Tastykake**'s balance sheet in Appendix A. Compare and discuss the amount of its cash with its other current assets (both in amount and percent) as of December 28, 2002. Compare and assess the cash amount at December 28, 2002, with its amount at December 29, 2001.

**11.** **Harley-Davidson**'s balance sheet in Appendix A reports that cash and equivalents decreased during the fiscal year ended December 31, 2002. Identify at least three major causes of this change in cash and equivalents.

### *Red numbers denote Discussion Questions that involve decision-making.*

*Homework Manager repeats all numerical Quick Studies on the book's Website with new numbers.*

## QUICK STUDY

An internal control system consists of all policies and procedures used to protect assets, ensure reliable accounting, promote efficient operations, and urge adherence to company policies.

**1.** What is the main objective of internal control procedures, and how is it achieved?

**2.** Why should recordkeeping for assets be separated from custody over the assets?

**3.** Why should the responsibility for a transaction be divided between two or more individuals or departments?

**QS 6-1**
Internal control objectives

C1

---

A good system of internal control for cash provides adequate procedures for protecting both cash receipts and cash disbursements.

**1.** What are three basic guidelines that help achieve this protection?

**2.** Identify two control systems or procedures for cash disbursements.

**QS 6-2**
Internal control for cash

P1

---

Good accounting systems help with the management and control of cash and cash equivalents.

**1.** Define and contrast the terms *liquid asset* and *cash equivalent*.

**2.** Why would companies invest their idle cash in cash equivalents?

**QS 6-3**
Cash, liquidity, and return

C1   C2

---

Good accounting systems help in managing cash and controlling who has access to it.

**1.** What items are included in the category of cash?

**2.** What items are included in the category of cash equivalents?

**3.** What does the term *liquidity* refer to?

**QS 6-4**
Cash and equivalents

C2

---

**1.** The petty cash fund of the Rio Agency is established at $75. At the end of the current period, the fund contained $14 and had the following receipts: film rentals, $19, and refreshments for meetings, $23 (both expenditures to be classified as Entertainment Expense); postage, $6; and printing, $13. Prepare journal entries to record (*a*) establishment of the fund and (*b*) reimbursement of the fund at the end of the current period.

**2.** Identify the two events that cause a Petty Cash account to be credited in a journal entry.

**QS 6-5**
Petty cash accounting

P2

---

**1.** For each of the following items, indicate whether its amount (i) affects the bank or book side of a bank reconciliation and (ii) represents an addition or a subtraction in a bank reconciliation:

    **a.** Outstanding checks     **d.** Unrecorded deposits     **g.** Bank service charges

    **b.** Debit memos     **e.** Interest on cash balance

    **c.** NSF checks     **f.** Credit memos

**2.** Which of the items in part 1 require an adjusting journal entry?

**QS 6-6**
Bank reconciliation

P3

---

The following annual account balances are taken from Next Level Sports at December 31:

| | 2005 | 2004 |
|---|---|---|
| Accounts receivable ....... | $ 75,692 | $ 70,484 |
| Net sales .............. | 2,591,933 | 2,296,673 |

What is the change in the number of days' sales uncollected between years 2005 and 2004? According to this analysis, is the company's collection of receivables improving? Explain your answer.

**QS 6-7**
Days' sales uncollected

A1

---

An important part of cash management is knowing when, and if, to take purchase discounts. (*a*) Which accounting method uses a Discounts Lost account? (*b*) What is the advantage of this method for management?

**QS 6-8**B
Purchase discounts

P5

*Homework Manager* repeats all numerical Exercises on the book's Website with new numbers.

# EXERCISES

### Exercise 6-1
Internal control recommendations

C1

What internal control procedures would you recommend in each of the following situations?

**1.** A concession company has one employee who sells T-shirts and sunglasses at the beach. Each day, the employee is given enough shirts and sunglasses to last through the day and enough cash to make change. The money is kept in a box at the stand.

**2.** An antique store has one employee who is given cash and sent to garage sales each weekend. The employee pays cash for this merchandise that the antique store resells.

### Exercise 6-2
Control of cash receipts by mail

P1

Some of Castel Co.'s cash receipts from customers are sent to the company with the regular mail. Castel's recordkeeper opens these letters and deposits the cash received each day. (*a*) Identify any internal control problem(s) in this arrangement. (*b*) What changes do you recommend?

### Exercise 6-3
Analyzing internal control

C1

Bemis Company is a rapidly growing start-up business. Its recordkeeper, who was hired one year ago, left town after the company's manager discovered that a large sum of money had disappeared over the past six months. An audit disclosed that the recordkeeper had written and signed several checks made payable to her fiancé and then recorded the checks as salaries expense. The fiancé, who cashed the checks but never worked for the company, left town with the recordkeeper. As a result, the company incurred an uninsured loss of $84,000. Evaluate Bemis's internal control system and indicate which principles of internal control appear to have been ignored.

### Exercise 6-4
Petty cash fund with a shortage

P2

**Check**   (2) Cr. Cash $234 and Dr. Cash $100

Gannon Company establishes a $400 petty cash fund on September 9. On September 30, the fund shows $166 in cash along with receipts for the following expenditures: transportation-in, $32; postage expenses, $113; and miscellaneous expenses, $87. The petty cashier could not account for a $2 shortage in the fund. Gannon uses the perpetual system in accounting for merchandise inventory. Prepare (1) the September 9 entry to establish the fund and (2) the September 30 entry to both reimburse the fund and reduce it to $300.

### Exercise 6-5
Petty cash fund accounting

P2

**Check**   (3) Cr. Cash $472 (total)

Dane Co. establishes a $200 petty cash fund on January 1. One week later, the fund shows $28 in cash along with receipts for the following expenditures: postage, $64; transportation-in, $19; delivery expenses, $36; and miscellaneous expenses, $53. Dane uses the perpetual system in accounting for merchandise inventory. Prepare journal entries to (1) establish the fund on January 1, (2) reimburse it on January 8, and (3) both reimburse the fund and increase it to $500 on January 8, assuming no entry in part 2.

### Exercise 6-6
Bank reconciliation and adjusting entries

P3

Prepare a table with the following headings for a monthly bank reconciliation dated September 30:

| Bank Balance | | Book Balance | | | Not Shown on the Reconciliation |
|---|---|---|---|---|---|
| Add | Deduct | Add | Deduct | Adjust | |

For each item 1 through 12, place an *x* in the appropriate column to indicate whether the item should be added to or deducted from the book or bank balance, or whether it should not appear on the reconciliation. If the book balance is to be adjusted, place a *Dr.* or *Cr.* in the Adjust column to indicate whether the Cash balance should be debited or credited. At the left side of your table, number the items to correspond to the following list.

**1.** Bank service charge.

**2.** Checks written and mailed to payees on October 2.

**3.** Checks written by another depositor but charged against this company's account.

**4.** Principal and interest on a note collected by the bank but not yet recorded by the company.

**5.** Special bank charge for collection of note in part 4 on this company's behalf.

**6.** Check written against the company's account and cleared by the bank; erroneously not recorded by the company's recordkeeper.

**7.** Interest earned on the cash balance in the bank.

**8.** Night deposit made on September 30 after the bank closed.

**9.** Checks outstanding on August 31 that cleared the bank in September.

**10.** NSF check from customer returned on September 25 but not yet recorded by this company.

**11.** Checks written by the company and mailed to payees on September 30.

**12.** Deposit made on September 5 and processed by the bank on September 6.

---

The voucher system of control is designed to control cash disbursements and the acceptance of obligations.

**1.** The voucher system of control establishes procedures for what two processes?

**2.** What types of expenditures should be overseen by a voucher system of control?

**3.** When is the voucher initially prepared? Explain.

**Exercise 6-7**
Voucher system

P1

---

Cruz Clinic deposits all cash receipts on the day when they are received and makes all cash payments by check. At the close of business on June 30, 2004, its Cash account shows an $11,352 debit balance. Cruz Clinic's June 30 bank statement shows $10,332 on deposit in the bank on that day. Prepare a bank reconciliation for Cruz Clinic using the following information:

**a.** Outstanding checks as of June 30 total $1,713.

**b.** The June 30 bank statement included an $18 debit memorandum for bank services.

**c.** Check No. 919, listed with the canceled checks, was correctly drawn for $489 in payment of a utility bill on June 15. Cruz Clinic mistakenly recorded it with a debit to Utilities Expense and a credit to Cash in the amount of $498.

**d.** The June 30 cash receipts of $2,724 were placed in the bank's night depository after banking hours and were not recorded on the June 30 bank statement.

**Exercise 6-8**
Bank reconciliation

P3

**Check**   Reconciled bal., $11,343

---

Prepare the adjusting journal entries that Cruz Clinic must record as a result of preparing the bank reconciliation in Exercise 6-8.

**Exercise 6-9**
Adjusting entries from
bank reconciliation   P3

---

Deacon Co. reported annual net sales for 2004 and 2005 of $565,000 and $647,000, respectively. Its year-end balances of accounts receivable follow: December 31, 2004, $51,000; and December 31, 2005, $83,000. (*a*) Calculate its days' sales uncollected at the end of each year. (*b*) Evaluate and comment on any changes in the amount of liquid assets tied up in receivables.

**Exercise 6-10**
Liquid assets and
accounts receivable

A1

---

Management uses a voucher system to help control and monitor cash disbursements. Identify at least four key documents that are part of a voucher system of control. Explain each document's purpose, where it originates, and how it flows through the voucher system (including its copies).

**Exercise 6-11**[A]
Documents in a voucher system

P4

---

Trade Imports uses the perpetual system in accounting for merchandise inventory and had the following transactions during the month of October. Prepare entries to record these transactions assuming that Trade Imports records invoices (*a*) at gross amounts and (*b*) at net amounts.

**Exercise 6-12**[B]
Record invoices at
gross or net amounts   P5

Oct.  2  Purchased merchandise at a $4,000 price, invoice dated October 2, terms 2/10, n/30.
   10  Received a $400 credit memorandum (at full invoice price) for the return of merchandise that it purchased on October 2.
   17  Purchased merchandise at a $4,400 price, invoice dated October 16, terms 2/10, n/30.
   26  Paid for the merchandise purchased on October 17, less the discount.
   31  Paid for the merchandise purchased on October 2. Payment was delayed because the invoice was mistakenly filed for payment today. This error caused the discount to be lost.

## PROBLEM SET A

### Problem 6-1A
Analyzing internal control

C1

For each of these five separate cases, identify the principle of internal control that is violated. Recommend what the business should do to ensure adherence to principles of internal control.

**1.** Heather Flatt records all incoming customer cash receipts for her employer and posts the customer payments to their respective accounts.

**2.** At Netco Company, Jeff and Jose alternate lunch hours. Jeff is the petty cash custodian, but if someone needs petty cash when he is at lunch, Jose fills in as custodian.

**3.** Nadine Cox posts all patient charges and payments at the P-Town Medical Clinic. Each night Nadine backs up the computerized accounting system to a tape and stores the tape in a locked file at her desk.

**4.** Barto Sayles prides himself on hiring quality workers who require little supervision. As office manager, Barto gives his employees full discretion over their tasks and for years has seen no reason to perform independent reviews of their work.

**5.** Desi West's manager has told her to reduce costs. Desi decides to raise the deductible on the plant's property insurance from $5,000 to $10,000. This cuts the property insurance premium in half. In a related move, she decides that bonding the plant's employees is a waste of money since the company has not experienced any losses due to employee theft. Desi saves the entire amount of the bonding insurance premium by dropping the bonding insurance.

### Problem 6-2A
Establish, reimburse, and adjust petty cash

P2

Shawnce Co. set up a petty cash fund for payments of small amounts. The following transactions involving the petty cash fund occurred in May (the last month of the company's fiscal year):

May  1  Prepared a company check for $250 to establish the petty cash fund.
   15  Prepared a company check both to replenish the fund for the following expenditures made since May 1 and to increase the fund to $450.
      *a.*  Paid $78 for janitorial services.
      *b.*  Paid $63.68 for miscellaneous expenses.
      *c.*  Paid postage expenses of $43.50.
      *d.*  Paid $57.15 to *The County Gazette* (the local newspaper) for an advertisement.
      *e.*  Counted $11.15 remaining in the petty cash box.
   31  The petty cashier reports that $293.39 cash remains in the fund and decides that the May 15 increase in the fund was too large. A company check is drawn both to replenish the fund for the following expenditures made since May 15 and to reduce the fund to $400.
      *f.*  Paid postage expenses of $48.36.
      *g.*  Reimbursed the office manager for business mileage, $38.50.
      *h.*  Paid $39.75 to deliver merchandise to a customer, terms FOB destination.

**Required**

**Check**  (1) Total Cr. to Cash: May 15, $438.85; May 31, $106.61

**1.** Prepare journal entries to establish the fund on May 1, to replenish it on May 15 and on May 31, and to reflect any increase or decrease in the fund balance on those dates.

*Analysis Component*

**2.** Explain how the company's financial statements are affected if the petty cash fund is not replenished and no entry is made on May 31.

Inoke Gallery had the following petty cash transactions in February of the current year:

Feb.  2  Wrote a $300 check, cashed it, and gave the proceeds and the petty cashbox to Bo Brown, the petty cashier.

5  Purchased bond paper for the copier for $10.13 that is immediately used.

9  Paid $22.50 COD shipping charges on merchandise purchased for resale, terms FOB shipping point. Metro uses the perpetual system to account for merchandise inventory.

12  Paid $9.95 postage to express mail a contract to a client.

14  Reimbursed Alli Buck, the manager, $58 for business mileage on her car.

20  Purchased stationery for $77.76 that is immediately used.

23  Paid a courier $18 to deliver merchandise sold to a customer, terms FOB destination.

25  Paid $15.10 COD shipping charges on merchandise purchased for resale, terms FOB shipping point.

27  Paid $64 for postage expenses.

28  The fund had $21.23 remaining in the petty cash box. Sorted the petty cash receipts by accounts affected and exchanged them for a check to reimburse the fund for expenditures. The fund amount is also increased to $400.

### Required

**1.** Prepare the journal entry to establish the petty cash fund.

**2.** Prepare a petty cash payments report for February with these categories: delivery expense, mileage expense, postage expense, merchandise inventory (for transportation-in), and office supplies expense. Sort the payments into the appropriate categories and total the expenditures in each category.

**3.** Prepare the journal entries for part 2 to both (*a*) reimburse and (*b*) increase the fund amount.

The following information is available to reconcile Clark Company's book balance of cash with its bank statement cash balance as of July 31, 2005:

**a.** After all posting is complete on July 31, the company's Cash account has a $26,193 debit balance, but its July bank statement shows a $28,020 cash balance.

**b.** Check No. 3031 for $1,380 and Check No. 3040 for $552 were outstanding on the June 30 bank reconciliation. Check No. 3040 is listed with the July canceled checks, but Check No. 3031 is not. Also, Check No. 3065 for $336 and Check No. 3069 for $2,148, both written in July, are not among the canceled checks on the July 31 statement.

**c.** In comparing the canceled checks on the bank statement with the entries in the accounting records, it is found that Check No. 3056 for July rent was correctly written and drawn for $1,250 but was erroneously entered in the accounting records as $1,230.

**d.** A credit memorandum enclosed with the July bank statement indicates the bank collected $9,000 cash on a noninterest-bearing note for Clark, deducted a $45 collection fee, and credited the remainder to its account. Clark had not recorded this event before receiving the statement.

**e.** A debit memorandum for $805 lists a $795 NSF check plus a $10 NSF charge. The check had been received from a customer, Jim Shaw. Clark has not yet recorded this check as NSF.

**f.** Enclosed with the July statement is a $15 debit memorandum for bank services. It has not yet been recorded because no previous notification had been received.

**g.** Clark's July 31 daily cash receipts of $10,152 were placed in the bank's night depository on that date, but do not appear on the July 31 bank statement.

### Required

**1.** Prepare the bank reconciliation for this company as of July 31, 2005.

**2.** Prepare the journal entries necessary to bring the company's book balance of cash into conformity with the reconciled cash balance as of July 31, 2005.

### Analysis Component

**3.** Assume that the July 31, 2005, bank reconciliation for this company is prepared and some items are treated incorrectly. For each of the following errors, explain the effect of the error on (i) the adjusted bank statement cash balance and (ii) the adjusted cash account book balance.

**a.** The company's unadjusted cash account balance of $26,193 is listed on the reconciliation as $26,139.

**b.** The bank's collection of the $9,000 note less the $45 collection fee is added to the bank statement cash balance on the reconciliation.

**Problem 6-3A**
Establish, reimburse, and increase petty cash
P2

**Check**  (3a & 3b) Cr. Cash $378.77

**Problem 6-4A**
Prepare a bank reconciliation and record adjustments
P3

mhhe.com/wild3e

**Check**  (1) Reconciled balance, $34,308; (2) Cr. Note Receivable $9,000

## Problem 6-5A
Prepare a bank reconciliation and record adjustments

P3

mhhe.com/wild3e

Els Company most recently reconciled its bank statement and book balances of cash on August 31 and it reported two checks outstanding, No. 5888 for $1,038.05 and No. 5893 for $484.25. The following information is available for its September 30, 2005, reconciliation:

### From the September 30 Bank Statement

| Previous Balance | Total Checks and Debits | Total Deposits and Credits | Current Balance |
|---|---|---|---|
| 16,800.45 | 9,620.05 | 11,182.85 | 18,363.25 |

| Checks and Debits | | | Deposits and Credits | | Daily Balance | |
|---|---|---|---|---|---|---|
| Date | No. | Amount | Date | Amount | Date | Amount |
| 09/03 | 5888 | 1,038.05 | 09/05 | 1,103.75 | 08/31 | 16,800.45 |
| 09/04 | 5902 | 731.90 | 09/12 | 2,226.90 | 09/03 | 15,762.40 |
| 09/07 | 5901 | 1,824.25 | 09/21 | 4,093.00 | 09/04 | 15,030.50 |
| 09/17 | | 588.25 NSF | 09/25 | 2,351.70 | 09/05 | 16,134.25 |
| 09/20 | 5905 | 937.00 | 09/30 | 22.50 IN | 09/07 | 14,310.00 |
| 09/22 | 5903 | 399.10 | 09/30 | 1,385.00 CM | 09/12 | 16,536.90 |
| 09/22 | 5904 | 2,080.00 | | | 09/17 | 15,948.65 |
| 09/28 | 5907 | 213.85 | | | 09/20 | 15,011.65 |
| 09/29 | 5909 | 1,807.65 | | | 09/21 | 19,104.65 |
| | | | | | 09/22 | 16,625.55 |
| | | | | | 09/25 | 18,977.25 |
| | | | | | 09/28 | 18,763.40 |
| | | | | | 09/29 | 16,955.75 |
| | | | | | 09/30 | 18,363.25 |

### From Els Company's Accounting Records

| Cash Receipts Deposited | | | | Cash Disbursements | | |
|---|---|---|---|---|---|---|
| Date | | Cash Debit | | Check No. | | Cash Credit |
| Sept. | 5 | 1,103.75 | | 5901 | | 1,824.25 |
| | 12 | 2,226.90 | | 5902 | | 731.90 |
| | 21 | 4,093.00 | | 5903 | | 399.10 |
| | 25 | 2,351.70 | | 5904 | | 2,050.00 |
| | 30 | 1,582.75 | | 5905 | | 937.00 |
| | | 11,358.10 | | 5906 | | 859.30 |
| | | | | 5907 | | 213.85 |
| | | | | 5908 | | 276.00 |
| | | | | 5909 | | 1,807.65 |
| | | | | | | 9,099.05 |

| Cash | | | | | | Acct. No. 101 |
|---|---|---|---|---|---|---|
| Date | | Explanation | PR | Debit | Credit | Balance |
| Aug. | 31 | Balance | | | | 15,278.15 |
| Sept. | 30 | Total receipts | R12 | 11,358.10 | | 26,636.25 |
| | 30 | Total disbursements | D23 | | 9,099.05 | 17,537.20 |

## Additional Information

Check No. 5904 is correctly drawn for $2,080 to pay for computer equipment; however, the record-keeper misread the amount and entered it in the accounting records with a debit to Computer Equipment and a credit to Cash of $2,050. The NSF check shown in the statement was originally received from a customer, S. Nilson, in payment of her account. Its return has not yet been recorded by the company. The credit memorandum is from the collection of a $1,400 note for Els Company by the bank. The bank deducted a $15 collection fee. The collection and fee are not yet recorded.

## Required

**1.** Prepare the September 30, 2005, bank reconciliation for this company.

**2.** Prepare the journal entries to adjust the book balance of cash to the reconciled balance.

**Check** (1) Reconciled balance, $18,326.45 (2) Cr. Note Receivable $1,400

*Analysis Component*

**3.** The bank statement reveals that some of the prenumbered checks in the sequence are missing. Describe three situations that could explain this.

---

For each of these five separate cases, identify the principle of internal control that is violated. Recommend what the business should do to ensure adherence to principles of internal control.

**1.** Latoya Tally is the company's computer specialist and oversees its computerized payroll system. Her boss recently asked her to put password protection on all office computers. Latoya has put a password in place that allows only the boss access to the file where pay rates are changed and personnel are added or deleted from the payroll.

**2.** Lake Theater has a computerized order-taking system for its tickets. The system is active all week and backed up every Friday night.

**3.** X2U Company has two employees handling acquisitions of inventory. One employee places purchase orders and pays vendors. The second employee receives the merchandise.

**4.** The owner of Super-Aid uses a check protector to perforate checks, making it difficult for anyone to alter the amount of the check. The check protector sits on the owner's desk in an office that contains company checks and is often unlocked.

**5.** LeAnn Company is a small business that has separated the duties of cash receipts and cash disbursements. The employee responsible for cash disbursements reconciles the bank account monthly.

## PROBLEM SET B

**Problem 6-1B**
Analyzing internal control

C1

---

Pepco Co. establishes a petty cash fund for payments of small amounts. The following transactions involving the petty cash fund occurred in January (the last month of the company's fiscal year).

Jan. 3  A company check for $150 is written and made payable to the petty cashier to establish the petty cash fund.

14  A company check is written both to replenish the fund for the following expenditures made since January 3 and to increase the fund to $175.
   *a.* Purchased office supplies for $16.29 that are immediately used up.
   *b.* Paid $17.60 COD shipping charges on merchandise purchased for resale, terms FOB shipping point. Pepco uses the perpetual system to account for inventory.
   *c.* Paid $36.57 to All-Tech for minor repairs to a computer.
   *d.* Paid $14.82 for items classified as miscellaneous expenses.
   *e.* Counted $62.28 remaining in the petty cash box.

31  The petty cashier reports that $17.35 remains in the fund and decides that the February 14 increase in the fund was not large enough. A company check is written both to replenish the fund for the following expenditures made since January 14 and to increase it to $250.
   *f.* Paid $40 to *The Smart Shopper* for an advertisement in January's newsletter.
   *g.* Paid $38.19 for postage expenses.
   *h.* Paid $58 to Take-You-There for delivery of merchandise, terms FOB destination.

**Problem 6-2B**
Establishing, reimbursing, and adjusting petty cash

P2

**Required**

1. Prepare journal entries to establish the fund on January 3, to replenish it on January 14 and January 31, and to reflect along with any increase or decrease in the fund balance on those dates.

*Analysis Component*

2. Explain how the company's financial statements are affected if the petty cash fund is not replenished and no entry is made on January 31.

---

**Problem 6-3B**

Establish, reimburse, and increase petty cash

P2

RPM Music Center had the following petty cash transactions in March of the current year:

March  5  Wrote a $200 check, cashed it, and gave the proceeds and the petty cashbox to Liz Buck, the petty cashier.

　　　 6  Paid $14.50 COD shipping charges on merchandise purchased for resale, terms FOB shipping point. RPM uses the perpetual system to account for merchandise inventory.

　　　11  Paid $8.75 delivery charges on merchandise sold to a customer, terms FOB destination.

　　　12  Purchased file folders for $12.13 that are immediately used.

　　　14  Reimbursed Will Nelson, the manager, $9.65 for office supplies purchased and used.

　　　18  Purchased printer paper for $22.54 that is immediately used.

　　　27  Paid $47.10 COD shipping charges on merchandise purchased for resale, terms FOB shipping point.

　　　28  Paid postage expenses of $16.

　　　30  Reimbursed Nelson $58.80 for business car mileage.

　　　31  Cash of $11.53 remained in the fund. Sorted the petty cash receipts by accounts affected and exchanged them for a check to reimburse the fund for expenditures. The fund amount is also increased to $250.

**Required**

1. Prepare the journal entry to establish the petty cash fund.

2. Prepare a petty cash payments report for March with these categories: delivery expense, mileage expense, postage expense, merchandise inventory (for transportation-in), and office supplies expense. Sort the payments into the appropriate categories and total the expenses in each category.

3. Prepare the journal entries for part 2 to both (*a*) reimburse and (*b*) increase the fund amount.

---

**Problem 6-4B**

Prepare a bank reconciliation and record adjustments

P3

The following information is available to reconcile Style Co.'s book balance of cash with its bank statement cash balance as of December 31, 2005:

a. After posting is complete, the December 31 cash balance according to the accounting records is $31,743.70, and the bank statement cash balance for that date is $45,091.80.

b. Check No. 1273 for $1,084.20 and Check No. 1282 for $390.00, both written and entered in the accounting records in December, are not among the canceled checks. Two checks, No. 1231 for $2,289.00 and No. 1242 for $370.50, were outstanding on the most recent November 30 reconciliation. Check No. 1231 is listed with the December canceled checks, but Check No. 1242 is not.

c. When the December checks are compared with entries in the accounting records, it is found that Check No. 1267 had been correctly drawn for $2,435 to pay for office supplies but was erroneously entered in the accounting records as $2,453.

d. Two debit memoranda are enclosed with the statement and are unrecorded at the time of the reconciliation. One debit memorandum is for $749.50 and dealt with an NSF check for $732 received from a customer, Titus Industries, in payment of its account. The bank assessed a $17.50 fee for processing it. The second debit memorandum is a $79.00 charge for check printing. Style did not record these transactions before receiving the statement.

e. A credit memorandum indicates that the bank collected $20,000 cash on a note receivable for the company, deducted a $20 collection fee, and credited the balance to the company's Cash account. Style did not record this transaction before receiving the statement.

f. Style's December 31 daily cash receipts of $7,666.10 were placed in the bank's night depository on that date, but do not appear on the December 31 bank statement.

**Required**

**1.** Prepare the bank reconciliation for this company as of December 31, 2005.

**2.** Prepare the journal entries necessary to bring the company's book balance of cash into conformity with the reconciled cash balance as of December 31, 2005.

*Analysis Component*

**3.** Explain the nature of the communications conveyed by a bank when the bank sends the depositor (*a*) a debit memorandum and (*b*) a credit memorandum.

**Check** (1) Reconciled balance, $50,913.20; (2) Cr. Note Receivable $20,000

---

Safe Systems Co. most recently reconciled its bank balance on April 30 and reported two checks outstanding at that time, No. 1771 for $781.00 and No. 1780 for $1,325.90. The following information is available for its May 31, 2005, reconciliation:

**Problem 6-5B**

Prepare a bank reconciliation and record adjustments

P3

### From the May 31 Bank Statement

| Previous Balance | Total Checks and Debits | Total Deposits and Credits | Current Balance |
|---|---|---|---|
| 18,290.70 | 12,898.90 | 16,416.80 | 21,808.60 |

| Checks and Debits | | | Deposits and Credits | | Daily Balance | |
|---|---|---|---|---|---|---|
| Date | No. | Amount | Date | Amount | Date | Amount |
| 05/01 | 1771 | 781.00 | 05/04 | 2,438.00 | 04/30 | 18,290.70 |
| 05/02 | 1783 | 195.30 | 05/14 | 2,898.00 | 05/01 | 17,509.70 |
| 05/04 | 1782 | 1,285.50 | 05/22 | 1,801.80 | 05/02 | 17,314.40 |
| 05/11 | 1784 | 1,449.60 | 05/25 | 7,200.00 CM | 05/04 | 18,466.90 |
| 05/18 | | 431.80 NSF | 05/26 | 2,079.00 | 05/11 | 17,017.30 |
| 05/25 | 1787 | 8,032.50 | | | 05/14 | 19,915.30 |
| 05/26 | 1785 | 157.20 | | | 05/18 | 19,483.50 |
| 05/29 | 1788 | 554.00 | | | 05/22 | 21,285.30 |
| 05/31 | | 12.00 SC | | | 05/25 | 20,452.80 |
| | | | | | 05/26 | 22,374.60 |
| | | | | | 05/29 | 21,820.60 |
| | | | | | 05/31 | 21,808.60 |

### From Safe Systems' Accounting Records

| Cash Receipts Deposited | | | | Cash Disbursements | | |
|---|---|---|---|---|---|---|
| Date | | Cash Debit | | Check No. | | Cash Credit |
| May | 4 | 2,438.00 | | 1782 | | 1,285.50 |
| | 14 | 2,898.00 | | 1783 | | 195.30 |
| | 22 | 1,801.80 | | 1784 | | 1,449.60 |
| | 26 | 2,079.00 | | 1785 | | 157.20 |
| | 31 | 2,526.30 | | 1786 | | 353.10 |
| | | 11,743.10 | | 1787 | | 8,032.50 |
| | | | | 1788 | | 544.00 |
| | | | | 1789 | | 639.50 |
| | | | | | | 12,656.70 |

| Cash | | | | | | Acct. No. 101 |
|---|---|---|---|---|---|---|
| Date | | Explanation | PR | Debit | Credit | Balance |
| Apr. | 30 | Balance | | | | 16,183.80 |
| May | 31 | Total receipts | R7 | 11,743.10 | | 27,926.90 |
| | 31 | Total disbursements | D8 | | 12,656.70 | 15,270.20 |

## Additional Information

Check No. 1788 is correctly drawn for $554 to pay for May utilities; however, the recordkeeper mis-read the amount and entered it in the accounting records with a debit to Utilities Expense and a credit to Cash for $544. The bank paid and deducted the correct amount. The NSF check shown in the statement was originally received from a customer, S. Bax, in payment of her account. The company has not yet recorded its return. The credit memorandum is from a $7,300 note that the bank collected for the company. The bank deducted a $100 collection fee and deposited the remainder in the company's account. The collection and fee have not yet been recorded.

## Required

**Check**  (1) Reconciled balance, $22,016.40; (2) Cr. Note Receivable $7,300

**1.** Prepare the May 31, 2005, bank reconciliation for Safe Systems.

**2.** Prepare the journal entries to adjust the book balance of cash to the reconciled balance.

*Analysis Component*

**3.** The bank statement reveals that some of the prenumbered checks in the sequence are missing. Describe three possible situations to explain this.

---

# PROBLEM SET C

Problem Set C is available at the book's Website to further reinforce and assess your learning.

---

# SERIAL PROBLEM

Success Systems

P3

*(This serial problem began in Chapter 1 and continues through most of the book. If previous chapter segments were not completed, the serial problem can begin at this point. It is helpful, but not necessary, that you use the Working Papers that accompany the book.)*

Kay Breeze receives the March bank statement for Success Systems on April 11, 2005. The March 31 bank statement shows an ending cash balance of $77,354. A comparison of the bank statement with the general ledger Cash account, No. 101, reveals the following:

**a.** Breeze notices that the bank erroneously cleared a $500 check against her account that she did not issue. The check documentation included with the bank statement shows that this check was actually issued by a company named Sierra Systems.

**b.** On March 25, the bank issues a $50 debit memorandum for the safety deposit box that Success Systems agreed to rent from the bank beginning March 25.

**c.** On March 26, the bank issues a $102 debit memorandum for printed checks that Success Systems ordered from the bank.

**d.** On March 31, the bank issues a credit memorandum for $33 interest earned on Success Systems's checking account for the month of March.

**e.** Breeze notices that the check she issued for $128 on March 31, 2005, has not yet cleared the bank.

**f.** Breeze verifies that all deposits made in March do appear on the March bank statement.

**g.** The general ledger Cash account, No. 101, shows an ending cash balance per books as $77,845 (prior to any reconciliation).

## Required

**1.** Prepare a bank reconciliation in good form (refer to Exhibit 6.7) for Success Systems for the month ended March 31, 2005.

**2.** Prepare any necessary adjusting entries. Use Miscellaneous Expenses, No. 677, for any bank charges. Use Interest Revenue, No. 404, for any interest earned on the checking account for the month of March.

**BTN 6-1** Refer to **Krispy Kreme**'s financial statements in Appendix A to answer the following:

**REPORTING IN ACTION**

C2 A1

1. For both fiscal year-end 2003 and 2002, identify the total amount of cash and cash equivalents. Determine the percent this amount represents of total current assets, total current liabilities, total shareholders' equity, and total assets for both years. Comment on any trends.

2. For both fiscal 2003 and 2002, use the information in the statement of cash flows to determine the percent change between the beginning and ending year amounts of cash and cash equivalents.

3. Compute the days' sales uncollected as of February 2, 2003, and February 3, 2002. Has the collection of receivables improved?

**Roll On**

4. Access Krispy Kreme's financial statements for fiscal years ending after February 2, 2003, from its Website (**KrispyKreme.com**) or the SEC's EDGAR database (**www.sec.gov**). Recompute its days' sales uncollected for fiscal years ending after February 2, 2003. Compare this to the days' sales uncollected for 2003 and 2002.

---

**BTN 6-2** Key comparative figures ($ thousands) for both **Krispy Kreme** and **Tastykake** follow:

**COMPARATIVE ANALYSIS**

A1

| Key Figures | Krispy Kreme | | Tastykake | |
|---|---|---|---|---|
| | Current Year | Prior Year | Current Year | Prior Year |
| Accounts receivable ....... | $ 34,373 | $ 26,894 | $ 20,882 | $ 22,233 |
| Net sales ............... | 491,549 | 394,354 | 162,263 | 166,244 |

**Required**

Compute days' sales uncollected for both companies for each of the two years shown. Comment on any trends for both companies. Which company has the larger percent change in days' sales uncollected?

---

**BTN 6-3** Carol Benton, Sue Knox, and Marcia Diamond work for a family physician, Dr. Gwen Conrad, who is in private practice. Dr. Conrad is knowledgeable about office management practices and has segregated the cash receipt duties as follows. Benton opens the mail and prepares a triplicate list of money received. She sends one copy of the list to Knox, the cashier, who deposits the receipts daily in the bank. Diamond, the recordkeeper, receives a copy of the list and posts payments to patients' accounts. About once a month the office clerks have an expensive lunch they pay for as follows. First, Knox endorses a patient's check in Dr. Conrad's name and cashes it at the bank. Benton then destroys the remittance advice accompanying the check. Finally, Diamond posts payment to the customer's account as a miscellaneous credit. The three justify their actions by their relatively low pay and knowledge that Dr. Conrad will likely never miss the money.

**ETHICS CHALLENGE**

C1

**Required**

1. Who is the best person in Dr. Conrad's office to reconcile the bank statement?

2. Would a bank reconciliation uncover this office fraud?

3. What are some ways to detect this type of fraud?

4. Suggest additional internal controls that Dr. Conrad could implement.

---

**BTN 6-4**[B] Assume you are a business consultant. The owner of a company sends you an e-mail expressing concern that the company is not taking advantage of its discounts offered by vendors. The company currently uses the gross method of recording purchases. The owner is considering a review of all invoices and payments from the previous period. Due to the volume of purchases, however, the owner recognizes this is time-consuming and costly. The owner seeks your advice about monitoring purchase discounts in the future. Provide a response in memorandum form.

**COMMUNICATING IN PRACTICE**

P5

**BTN 6-5**   Visit the Association of Certified Fraud Examiners Website at **cfenet.com**. Research the fraud facts (see media center—fraud statistics) presented at this site and fill in the blanks in the following statements.

1.   It is estimated that ____% of revenues will be lost in 2002 as a result of occupational fraud and abuse. Applied to the U.S. gross domestic product, this translates to losses of approximately $____ billion, or about $____ per employee.

2.   Organizations with fraud hotlines cut their fraud losses by approximately ____% per scheme. Internal audits, external audits, and background checks also significantly reduce fraud losses.

3.   Small businesses are the most vulnerable to occupational fraud and abuse. The average scheme in a small business causes $____ in losses. The average scheme in the largest companies costs $____.

4.   The most common method for detecting occupational fraud is through tips from ____, customers, vendors, and anonymous sources. The second most common method of discovery is ____.

5.   The typical occupational fraud perpetrator is a first-time offender. Only ____% of occupational fraudsters in this study were known to have prior convictions for fraud-related offenses.

6.   All occupational frauds fall into one of three categories: ____, corruption, or ____statements.

7.   Over ____% of occupational frauds involve asset misappropriations. Cash is the targeted asset ____% of the time.

8.   Corruption schemes account for ____% of all occupational frauds, and they cause over $____ in losses, on average.

9.   Fraudulent statements are the most costly form of occupational fraud with median losses of $____ million per scheme.

10.   Frauds committed by employees cause median losses of $____, while frauds committed by managers and executives cause median losses of $____. When managers and employees conspire in a fraud scheme, the median loss rises to $____.

11.   Losses caused by perpetrators older than 60 are ____times higher than losses caused by employees 25 and younger.

12.   The average fraud scheme lasted ____ months before it was detected.

**BTN 6-6**   Organize the class into teams. Each team must prepare a list of 10 internal controls a consumer could observe in a typical retail department store. When called upon, the team's spokesperson must be prepared to share controls identified by the team that have not been shared by another team's spokesperson.

**BTN 6-7**   Read the article "To Cure Fraud, Start at the Top" in the October 18, 2002, issue of *Business Week*. (The book's Website provides a free link.)

**Required:**

1.   Which fraud case does Pergola (the interviewee) state was the most significant?

2.   What are the character traits of individuals who might be more likely to commit fraud?

3.   Which corporate structures make it easier for fraud to thrive?

4.   How do corporate recruiters keep potential fraudsters from joining the company?

5.   What role can co-workers play in stopping fraud?

**BTN 6-8**   Refer to the chapter's opening feature, "Sweet Success," describing the entrepreneurial efforts of Dylan Lauren and Jeff Rubin with **Dylan's Candy Bar**.

**Required**

List the seven principles of internal control. For each principle, identify how Lauren and Rubin could implement it in their candy store.

**BTN 6-9**    Visit a part of your college that serves the student community with either products or services. Some examples are food services, libraries, and book stores. Identify and describe between four and eight internal controls being implemented.

**HITTING THE ROAD**

C1

**BTN 6-10**    Review the consolidated statement of changes in financial position for **Grupo Bimbo** for the year ended December 31, 2002, at <u>GrupoBimbo.com</u>.

**GLOBAL DECISION**

C2

### Required

1. What item caused the largest change (excluding net income) in the Operations section of the statement?
2. What item caused the largest change in the Financing section of the statement?
3. What item caused the largest change in the Investing section of the statement?
4. Did the cash and marketable securities as of December 31, 2002, increase or decrease relative to December 31, 2001?
5. Calculate the percentage change in both the cash and the marketable securities balances between December 31, 2001 and December 31, 2002.
6. At December 31, 2002, what percentage of current assets is comprised of cash and marketable securities?

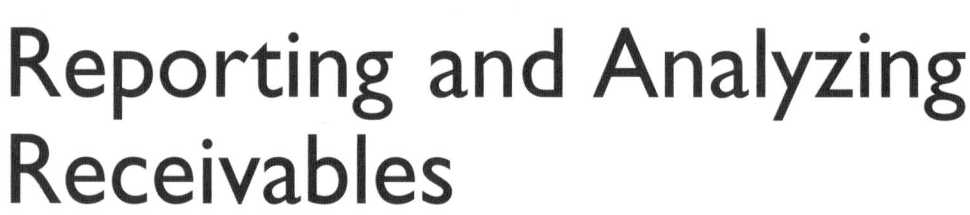

"My goal is to become the Oprah of raw materials"—Barbara Manzi

# 7 Reporting and Analyzing Receivables

## A Look Back

Chapter 6 focused on internal control and reporting for cash. We described procedures that are good for internal control, and we explained the accounting for and management of cash.

## A Look at This Chapter

This chapter emphasizes receivables. We explain that they are liquid assets and describe how companies account for and report them. We also discuss the importance of estimating uncollectibles.

## A Look Ahead

Chapter 8 focuses on plant assets, natural resources, and intangible assets. We explain how to account for, report, and analyze these long-term assets.

# CAP

## Conceptual

**C1** Describe accounts receivable and how they occur and are recorded. *(p. 278)*

**C2** Describe a note receivable and the computation of its maturity date and interest. *(p. 287)*

**C3** Explain how receivables can be converted to cash before maturity. *(p. 291)*

## Analytical

**A1** Compute accounts receivable turnover and use it to help assess financial condition. *(p. 292)*

## Procedural

**P1** Apply the direct write-off and allowance methods to account for accounts receivable. *(p. 282)*

**P2** Estimate uncollectibles using methods based on sales and accounts receivable. *(p. 284)*

**P3** Record the receipt of a note receivable. *(p. 289)*

**P4** Record the honoring and dishonoring of a note and adjustments for interest. *(p. 289)*

## Decision Feature

# Heavy into Metals

BROOKSVILLE, FL—"When you're an African-American entrepreneur, and a woman in a male-dominated industry, you learn some lessons very quickly, " says Barbara Manzi. Manzi launched **Manzi Metals** (**ManziMetals.com**) from her home eight years ago. Her lessons learned have translated into an annual $3 million in revenues as a distributor of aluminum, steel, titanium, brass, and other alloys.

Manzi, who runs Manzi Metals along with her son Louis, had to overcome long odds in achieving success. "There were 12 children in our family," she says. "But if I had listened to [those]... who told me I'd never do anything except get married, I would have gone astray." Instead, Manzi pursued her dreams.

Today, Manzi Metals is a major distributor of all types of metals in any shapes or sizes. Manzi strives for the highest quality service but maintains competitive prices. This includes special attention to customers and keeping control over receivables. Decisions such as selling on credit or not, and setting policies and criteria for extending credit, can make or break a startup.

Manzi, who has "a passion for people," never loses sight of the personal touch when making these business decisions. Recognizing economic downturns and adjusting past due accounts when appropriate are as much people decisions as accounting applications. Still, keeping an eye on accounts receivable turnover and uncollectible accounts is part of good business operations. This chapter focuses on these and related issues. Such factors, says Manzi, must be studied and carefully interpreted. "You have to get it right the first time," she says. "There's no room for mistakes!"

[Sources: *Manzi Metals Website,* January 2004; *Business Week,* January 2003; *Entre World,* February 2003.]

## Exhibit 7.4

General Ledger and
the Accounts Receivable Ledger
(after July 1 transactions)

**General Ledger**

Accounts Receivable

| Date | PR | Debit | Credit | Balance |
|------|----|-------|--------|---------|
| June 30 | | 3,000 | | 3,000 |
| July 1 | | 950 | | 3,950 |
| July 1 | | | 720 | 3,230 |

**Accounts Receivable Ledger**

RDA Electronics

| Date | PR | Debit | Credit | Balance |
|------|----|-------|--------|---------|
| June 30 | | 1,000 | | 1,000 |
| July 1 | | | 720 | 280 |

CompStore

| Date | PR | Debit | Credit | Balance |
|------|----|-------|--------|---------|
| June 30 | | 2,000 | | 2,000 |
| July 1 | | 950 | | 2,950 |

**Schedule of
Accounts Receivable**

| | |
|---|---|
| RDA Electronics .... | $  280 |
| CompStore ........... | 2,950 |
| Total..................... | $3,230 |

except for the possibility of added interest revenue. If a customer owes interest on a bill, we debit Interest Receivable and credit Interest Revenue for that amount.

**Credit Card Sales**   Many companies allow their customers to pay for products and services using third-party credit cards such as **Visa**, **MasterCard**, or **American Express**, and debit cards (also called bankcards). This practice gives customers the ability to make purchases without cash or checks. Once credit is established with a credit card company or bank, the customer does not have to open an account with each store. Customers using these cards can make single monthly payments instead of several payments to different creditors and can defer their payments.

Sellers allow customers to use third-party credit cards and debit cards instead of granting credit directly for several reasons. First, the seller does not have to evaluate each customer's credit standing or make decisions about who gets credit and how much. Second, the seller avoids the risk of extending credit to customers who cannot or do not pay. This risk is transferred to the card company. Third, the seller typically receives cash from the card company sooner than had it granted credit directly to customers. Fourth, a variety of credit options for customers offers a potential increase in sales volume. **Sears** historically offered credit only to customers using a Sears card but later changed its policy to permit customers to charge purchases to third-party credit card companies in a desire to increase sales. It reported: "SearsCharge increased its share of Sears retail sales even as the company expanded the payment options available to its customers with the acceptance . . . of [Visa,] MasterCard, and American Express in addition to the Discover Card."

There are guidelines in how companies account for credit card and debit card sales. Some credit cards, but mostly debit cards, credit a seller's Cash account immediately upon deposit. In this case the seller deposits a copy of each card sales receipt in its bank account just as it deposits a customer's check. Some other cards require the seller to remit a copy (often electronically) of each receipt to the card company. Until payment is received, the seller has an account receivable from the card company. In both cases, the seller pays a fee for services provided by the card company, often ranging

**Point:** Visa USA transacted more than $1 trillion in 2003 from its credit, debit, and prepaid cards.

### Decision Maker

**Entrepreneur**   As a small retailer, you are considering allowing customers to purchase merchandise using credit cards. Until now, your store accepted only cash and checks. What form of analysis do you use to make this decision?

Answer—p. 295

from 1% to 5% of card sales. This charge is deducted from the credit to the seller's account or the cash payment to the seller.

The procedures used in accounting for credit card sales depend on whether cash is received immediately on deposit or cash receipt is delayed until the credit card company makes the payment. To illustrate, if TechCom has $100 of credit card sales with a 4% fee, and its $96 cash is received immediately on deposit, the entry is

| July 15 | Cash | 96 | |
| | Credit Card Expense | 4 | |
| | Sales | | 100 |
| | *To record credit card sales less a 4% credit card expense.** | | |

Assets = Liabilities + Equity
+96                          +100
                             −4

\* We omit the entry to Dr. Cost of Sales and Cr. Merchandise Inventory to focus on credit card expense.

However, if instead TechCom must remit the credit card sales receipts to the credit card company and wait for the $96 cash payment, the entry on the date of sale is

| July 15 | **Accounts Receivable—Credit Card Co.** | 96 | |
| | Credit Card Expense | 4 | |
| | Sales | | 100 |
| | *To record credit card sales less 4% credit card expense.** | | |

Assets = Liabilities + Equity
+96                          +100
                             −4

\* We omit the entry to Dr. Cost of Sales and Cr. Merchandise Inventory to focus on credit card expense.

When cash is later received from the credit card company, the entry is

| July 25 | Cash | 96 | |
| | Accounts Receivable—Credit Card Co. | | 96 |
| | *To record cash receipt.* | | |

Assets = Liabilities + Equity
+96
−96

Some firms report credit card expense in the income statement as a type of discount deducted from sales to get net sales. Other companies classify it as a selling expense or even as an administrative expense. Arguments can be made for each alternative.

**Installment Sales and Receivables**  Many companies allow their credit customers to make periodic payments over several months. For example, **Harley-Davidson** holds more than $400 million in installment receivables. The seller refers to such assets as *installment accounts receivable,* which are amounts owed by customers from credit sales for which payment is required in periodic amounts over an extended time period. Source documents for installment accounts receivable include sales slips or invoices describing the sales transactions. The customer is usually charged interest. Although installment accounts receivable may have credit periods of more than one year, they are classified as current assets if the seller regularly offers customers such terms.

**Point:** Web merchants pay twice as much in credit card association fees as other retailers because they suffer 10 times as much fraud.

**Point:** Third-party credit card costs can be large. JCPenney recently reported sales exceeding $30,000 million along with third-party credit card costs of nearly $100 million.

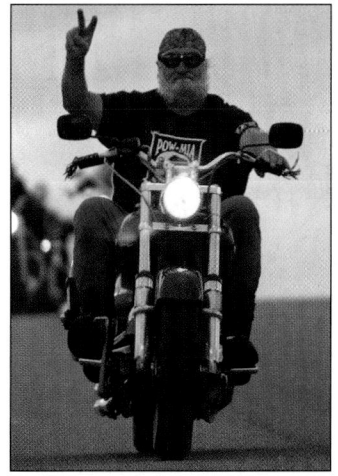

### Quick Check

1. In recording credit card sales, when do you debit Accounts Receivable and when do you debit Cash?

2. A company accumulates sales receipts and remits them to the credit card company for payment. When are the credit card expenses recorded? When are these expenses incurred?

Answers—p. 296

## Valuing Accounts Receivable

When a company directly grants credit to its customers, it expects that some customers will not pay what they promised. The accounts of these customers are *uncollectible accounts,* commonly called **bad debts.** The total amount of uncollectible accounts is an expense of selling on credit. Why do companies sell on credit if they expect some accounts

**Bad Debts** Costs are rising for credit card issuers owing to default rates. Much of this is the fault of issuers who offer credit cards with low "teaser" rates. In response, credit card users have increased their debts, and many are unable to pay them.

| Credit Card Default Rates | |
| --- | --- |
| Banc One . . . . . . . . . | 6.8% |
| First Chicago . . . . . . | 6.7 |
| Discover . . . . . . . . . | 6.1 |
| Citicorp . . . . . . . . . | 5.5 |
| Chase . . . . . . . . . . . | 5.1 |
| Capital One . . . . . . | 5.1 |
| Advanta . . . . . . . . . | 5.1 |

to be uncollectible? The answer is that companies believe that granting credit will increase total sales and net income enough to offset bad debts. Companies use two methods to account for uncollectible accounts: (1) direct write-off method and (2) allowance method. We describe both.

**Direct Write-Off Method** The **direct write-off method** of accounting for bad debts records the loss from an uncollectible account receivable when it is determined to be uncollectible. No attempt is made to predict bad debts expense. To illustrate, if TechCom determines on January 23 that it cannot collect $520 owed to it by its customer J. Kent, it recognizes the loss using the direct write-off method as follows:

**P1** Apply the direct write-off and allowance methods to account for accounts receivable.

Assets = Liabilities + Equity
−520              −520

| Jan. 23 | Bad Debts Expense. . . . . . . . . . . . . . . . . . . . . . | 520 | |
| |      Accounts Receivable—J. Kent. . . . . . . . . . . | | 520 |
| | *To write off an uncollectible account.* | | |

The debit in this entry charges the uncollectible amount directly to the current period's Bad Debts Expense account. The credit removes its balance from the Accounts Receivable account in the general ledger (and its subsidiary ledger).

Sometimes an account written off is later collected. This can be due to factors such as continual collection efforts or a customer's good fortune. If the account of J. Kent that was written off directly to Bad Debts Expense is later collected in full, the following two entries record this recovery:

**Point:** Managers realize that some portion of credit sales will be uncollectible, but which credit sales are uncollectible is unknown.

Assets = Liabilities + Equity
+520              +520

Assets = Liabilities + Equity
+520              +520
−520

| Mar. 11 | Accounts Receivable—J. Kent . . . . . . . . . . . . . . | 520 | |
| |      Bad Debts Expense . . . . . . . . . . . . . . . . . . | | 520 |
| | *To reinstate account previously written off.* | | |
| Mar. 11 | Cash . . . . . . . . . . . . . . . . . . . . . . . . . . . . . . . . | 520 | |
| |      Accounts Receivable—J. Kent . . . . . . . . . . . | | 520 |
| | *To record full payment of account.* | | |

**Point:** If a customer fails to pay within the credit period, most companies send out repeated billings and make other efforts to collect.

Companies must weigh at least two accounting principles when considering the use of the direct write-off method: the (1) matching principle and (2) materiality principle.

***Matching principle applied to bad debts.*** The **matching principle** requires expenses to be reported in the same accounting period as the sales they helped produce. This means that if extending credit to customers helped produce sales, the bad debts expense linked to those sales is matched and reported in the same period. The direct write-off method usually does not best match sales and expenses because bad debts expense is not recorded until an account becomes uncollectible, which often occurs in a period after that of the credit sale. To match bad debts expense with the sales it produces therefore requires a company to estimate future uncollectibles.

**Point:** Pier 1 Imports reports $7 million of bad debts expense matched against $413 million of credit sales in a recent fiscal year.

***Materiality principle applied to bad debts.*** The **materiality principle** states that an amount can be ignored if its effect on the financial statements is unimportant to users' business decisions. The materiality principle permits the use of the direct write-off method when bad debts expenses are very small in relation to a company's other financial statement items such as sales and net income.

**Point:** Under the direct write-off method, expense is recorded each time an account is written off. Under the allowance method, expense is recorded with an adjusting entry equal to the total estimated uncollectibles for that period's sales.

**Allowance Method** The **allowance method** of accounting for bad debts matches the *estimated* loss from uncollectible accounts receivable against the sales they helped produce. We must use estimated losses because when sales occur, management does not know which customers will not pay their bills. This means that at the end of each period, the allowance method requires an estimate of the total bad debts expected to result from that period's sales. This method has two advantages over the direct write-off method: (1) it records estimated bad debts expense in the period when the related sales are recorded and (2) it reports accounts receivable on the balance sheet at the estimated amount of cash to be collected.

Topic Tackler 7-1

**Recording bad debts expense.**   The allowance method estimates bad debts expense at the end of each accounting period and records it with an adjusting entry. TechCom, for instance, had credit sales of $300,000 during its first year of operations. At the end of the first year, $20,000 of credit sales remained uncollected. Based on the experience of similar businesses, TechCom estimated that $1,500 of its accounts receivable would be uncollectible. This estimated expense is recorded with the following adjusting entry:

**Point:** The Office of the Comptroller of the Currency reported that losses from bad debts are a major factor when banks fail.

| Dec. 31 | Bad Debts Expense . . . . . . . . . . . . . . . . . . . . . | 1,500 | |
|---------|---------------------------------------------------------|-------|-------|
|         | Allowance for Doubtful Accounts . . . . . . . . |       | 1,500 |
|         | *To record estimated bad debts.*                        |       |       |

Assets = Liabilities + Equity
−1,500                  −1,500

The estimated Bad Debts Expense of $1,500 is reported on the income statement (as either a selling expense or an administrative expense) and offsets the $300,000 credit sales it helped produce. The **Allowance for Doubtful Accounts** is a contra asset account. A contra account is used instead of reducing accounts receivable directly because at the time of the adjusting entry, the company does not know which customers will not pay. After the bad debts adjusting entry is posted, TechCom's account balances for Accounts Receivable and its Allowance for Doubtful Accounts are as shown in Exhibit 7.5.

**Point:** Credit approval is usually not assigned to the selling department because its main goal is to increase sales, and it may approve customers at the expense of increased bad debts. Instead, approval is assigned to a separate credit-granting or administrative department.

| Accounts Receivable | | | Allowance for Doubtful Accounts | | |
|---------|--------|--|---------|--------|--|
| Dec. 31 | 20,000 | | | Dec. 31 | 1,500 |

**Exhibit 7.5**

General Ledger Balances after Bad Debts Adjusting Entry

The Allowance for Doubtful Accounts credit balance of $1,500 has the effect of reducing accounts receivable to its estimated realizable value. **Realizable value** refers to the expected proceeds from converting an asset into cash. Although credit customers owe $20,000 to TechCom, only $18,500 is expected to be realized in cash collections from these customers. In the balance sheet, the Allowance for Doubtful Accounts is subtracted from Accounts Receivable and is often reported as shown in Exhibit 7.6.

**Point:** Bad Debts Expense is also called *Uncollectible Accounts Expense.* The Allowance for Doubtful Accounts is also called *Allowance for Uncollectible Accounts.*

| Current assets | | |
|----------------|--------|---------|
| Accounts receivable  . . . . . . . . . . . . . . . . . . . . . . . . . | $20,000 | |
| Less allowance for doubtful accounts  . . . . . . . . . . . . | 1,500 | $18,500 |

**Exhibit 7.6**

Balance Sheet Presentation of the Allowance for Doubtful Accounts

Sometimes the Allowance for Doubtful Accounts is not reported separately. This alternative presentation is shown in Exhibit 7.7 (also see Appendix A).

| Current assets | |
|----------------|---------|
| Accounts receivable (net of $1,500 doubtful accounts)  . . . . . . . | $18,500 |

**Exhibit 7.7**

Alternative Presentation of the Allowance for Doubtful Accounts

**Writing off a bad debt.**   When specific accounts are identified as uncollectible, they are written off against the Allowance for Doubtful Accounts. To illustrate, TechCom decides that J. Kent's $520 account is uncollectible and makes the following entry to write it off:

| Jan. 23 | Allowance for Doubtful Accounts . . . . . . . . . . . . | 520 | |
|---------|---------------------------------------------------------|-----|-----|
|         | Accounts Receivable—J. Kent . . . . . . . . . . . |     | 520 |
|         | *To write off an uncollectible account.*                |     |     |

Assets = Liabilities + Equity
+520
−520

**Point:** The Bad Debts Expense account is not debited in the write-off entry because it was recorded in the period when sales occurred.

## Exhibit 7.8

General Ledger Balances after Write-Off

**Point:** In posting a write-off, the ledger's Explanation column indicates the reason for this credit so it is not misinterpreted as payment in full.

## Exhibit 7.9

Realizable Value before and after Write-Off of a Bad Debt

Posting this write-off entry to the Accounts Receivable account removes the amount of the bad debt from the general ledger (it is also posted to the accounts receivable subsidiary ledger). The general ledger accounts now appear as in Exhibit 7.8 (assuming no other transactions affecting these accounts).

| Accounts Receivable | | | | Allowance for Doubtful Accounts | | | |
|---|---|---|---|---|---|---|---|
| Dec. 31 | 20,000 | | | | | Dec. 31 | 1,500 |
| | | Jan. 23 | **520** | Jan. 23 | **520** | | |

The write-off does not affect the realizable value of accounts receivable as shown in Exhibit 7.9. Neither total assets nor net income is affected by the write-off of a specific account. Instead, both assets and net income are affected in the period when bad debts expense is predicted and then recorded with an adjusting entry.

| | Before Write-Off | After Write-Off |
|---|---|---|
| Accounts receivable . . . . . . . . . . . . . . . . . . . . . . . . . . . | $ 20,000 | $ 19,480 |
| Less allowance for doubtful accounts . . . . . . . . . . . . . . | 1,500 | 980 |
| **Estimated realizable accounts receivable**  . . . . . . . | **$18,500** | **$18,500** |

***Recovering a bad debt.***   When a customer fails to pay and the account is written off as uncollectible, his or her credit standing is jeopardized. To help restore credit standing, a customer sometimes volunteers to pay all or part of the amount owed. A company makes two entries when collecting an account previously written off by the allowance method. The first is to reverse the write-off and reinstate the customer's account. The second entry records the collection of the reinstated account. To illustrate, if on March 11 Kent pays in full his account previously written off, the entries are

Assets = Liabilities + Equity
+520
−520

Assets = Liabilities + Equity
+520
−520

| | | | |
|---|---|---|---|
| Mar. 11 | Accounts Receivable—J. Kent . . . . . . . . . . . . . . . | 520 | |
| | Allowance for Doubtful Accounts . . . . . . . . . | | 520 |
| | *To reinstate account previously written off.* | | |
| Mar. 11 | Cash . . . . . . . . . . . . . . . . . . . . . . . . . . . . . . . . . | 520 | |
| | Accounts Receivable—J. Kent . . . . . . . . . . . | | 520 |
| | *To record full payment of account.* | | |

**Example:** If TechCom used a collection agency and paid a 35% commission on $520 collected from Kent, how is this recorded? *Answer:*
Cash . . . . . . . . . . . . . . . . 338
Collection Expense . . . . . . 182
  Accts. Recble.—J. Kent . . . . . . . 520

In this illustration, Kent paid the entire amount previously written off, but sometimes a customer pays only a portion of the amount owed. A question then arises as to whether the entire balance of the account or just the amount paid is returned to accounts receivable. This is a matter of judgment. If we believe this customer will later pay in full, we return the entire amount owed to accounts receivable, but if we expect no further collection, we return only the amount paid.

## Estimating Bad Debts Expense

**P2**   Estimate uncollectibles using methods based on sales and accounts receivable.

Companies with direct credit sales must attempt to estimate bad debts expense to both manage their receivables and set credit policies. The allowance method also requires an estimate of bad debts expense to prepare an adjusting entry at the end of each accounting period. There are two common methods. One is based on the income statement relation between bad debts expense and sales. The second is based on the balance sheet relation between accounts receivable and the allowance for doubtful accounts.

**Point:** The focus is on *credit* sales because cash sales do not produce bad debts. If cash sales are a small or stable percent of credit sales, total sales can be used.

**Percent of Sales Method**   The *percent of sales method* uses income statement relations to estimate bad debts. It is based on the idea that a given percent of a company's credit sales for the period are uncollectible. To illustrate, assume that Musicland has credit sales of $400,000 in year 2005. Based on past experience, Musicland estimates 0.6% of credit sales to be uncollectible. This implies that Musicland expects $2,400 of bad debts expense from its sales (computed as $400,000 \times 0.006 = 2,400$). The adjusting entry to record this estimated expense is

| Dec. 31 | Bad Debts Expense ..................... | 2,400 | |
| | Allowance for Doubtful Accounts ......... | | 2,400 |
| | *To record estimated bad debts.* | | |

Assets = Liabilities + Equity
−2,400                 −2,400

The allowance account ending balance on the balance sheet for this method would rarely equal the bad debts expense on the income statement. This is so because unless a company is in its first period of operations, its allowance account has a zero balance only if the prior amounts written off as uncollectible *exactly* equal the prior estimated bad debts expenses. (When computing bad debts expense as a percent of sales, managers monitor and adjust the percent so it is not too high or too low.)

**Point:** When using the *percent of sales method* for estimating uncollectibles, the estimate of bad debts is the number used in the adjusting entry.

**Accounts Receivable Methods**   The *accounts receivable methods* use balance sheet relations to estimate bad debts—mainly the relation between accounts receivable and the allowance amount. The goal of the bad debts adjusting entry for these methods is to make the Allowance for Doubtful Accounts balance equal to the portion of accounts receivable that is estimated to be uncollectible. The estimated balance for the allowance account is obtained in one of two ways: (1) computing the percent uncollectible from the total accounts receivable or (2) aging accounts receivable.

**Point:** When using an accounts receivable method for estimating uncollectibles, the allowance account balance is adjusted to equal the estimate of uncollectibles.

***Percent of accounts receivable method.***   The *percent of accounts receivable method* assumes that a given percent of a company's receivables is uncollectible. This percent is based on past experience and is impacted by current conditions such as economic trends and customer difficulties. The total dollar amount of all receivables is multiplied by this percent to get the estimated dollar amount of uncollectible accounts—reported in the balance sheet as the Allowance for Doubtful Accounts.

To illustrate, assume that Musicland has $50,000 of accounts receivable on December 31, 2005. Experience suggests 5% of its receivables are uncollectible. This means that after the adjusting entry is posted, we want the Allowance for Doubtful Accounts to show a $2,500 credit balance (5% of $50,000). (*Note:* Its beginning balance is $2,200, which is 5% of the $44,000 accounts receivable on December 31, 2004—see Exhibit 7.10.) Also during 2005, accounts of customers are written off on February 6, July 10, and November 20. Thus, the account has a $200 credit balance prior to the December 31, 2005, adjustment. The adjusting entry to give the allowance account the estimated $2,500 balance is

**Global:** In China, government regulation constrains the *percents* used to estimate bad debts.

| Dec. 31 | Bad Debts Expense ..................... | 2,300 | |
| | Allowance for Doubtful Accounts ......... | | 2,300 |
| | *To record estimated bad debts.* | | |

Assets = Liabilities + Equity
−2,300                 −2,300

Exhibit 7.10 shows the effects of these transactions and adjustments on the allowance amount.

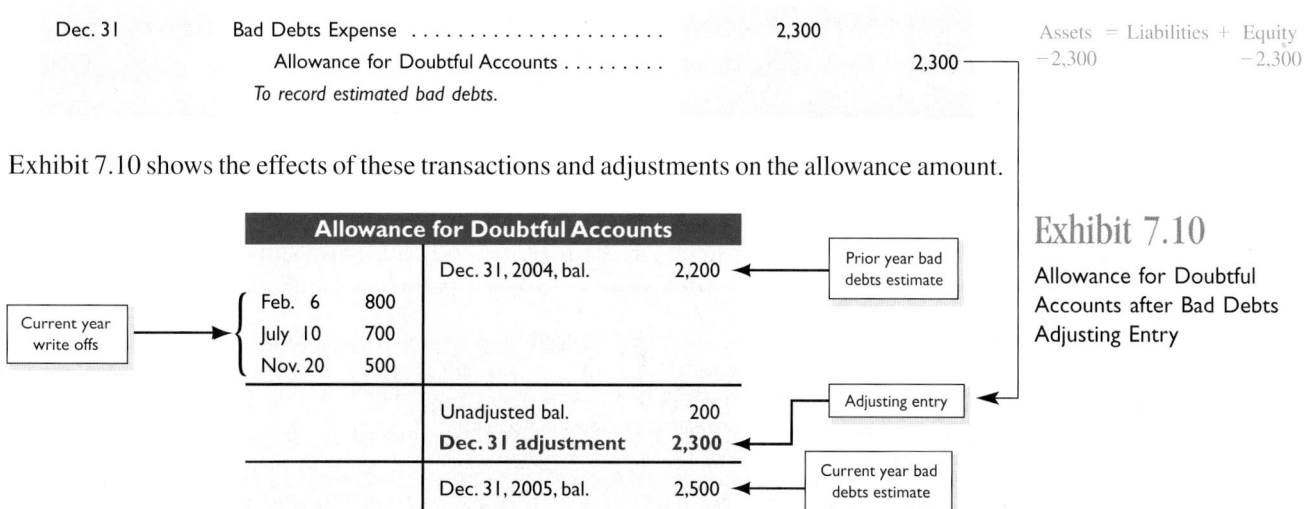

**Exhibit 7.10**

Allowance for Doubtful Accounts after Bad Debts Adjusting Entry

***Aging of accounts receivable method.*** The **aging of accounts receivable** method uses both past and current receivables information to estimate the allowance amount. Specifically, each receivable is classified by how long it is past its due date. Then estimates of uncollectible amounts are made assuming that the longer an amount is past due, the more likely it is to be uncollectible. Classifications are often based on 30-day periods. After the amounts are classified (or aged), experience is used to estimate the percent of each uncollectible class. These percents are applied to the amounts in each class and then totaled to get the estimated balance of the Allowance for Doubtful Accounts. This computation is performed by setting up a schedule such as Exhibit 7.11.

**Decision Insight**

When you buy online with a credit card, you put your account number at risk. If, however, you slide a smart card into a reader on your PC and enter your password, the merchant never gets your account number but only a code authorizing the sale.

## Exhibit 7.11

Aging of Accounts Receivable

Each receivable is grouped by how long it is past its due date

Each age group is multiplied by its estimated bad debts percent

Estimated bad debts for each group are totaled

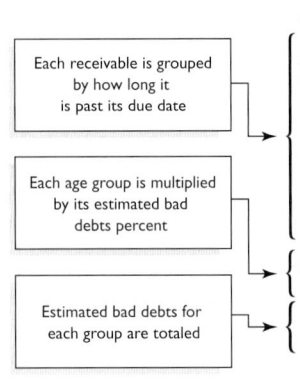

**MUSICLAND**
**Schedule of Accounts Receivable by Age**

| Customer | Totals | Not Yet Due | 1 to 30 Days Past Due | 31 to 60 Days Past Due | 61 to 90 Days Past Due | Over 90 Days Past Due |
|---|---|---|---|---|---|---|
| Carlos Abbot | $ 450 | $ 450 | | | | |
| Jaime Allen | 710 | | | $ 710 | | |
| Chavez Andres | 500 | 300 | $ 200 | | | |
| Belicia Co. | 740 | | | | $ 100 | $ 640 |
| Zamora Services | 1,000 | 810 | 190 | | | |
| Totals | $ 49,900 | $ 37,000 | $ 6,500 | $ 3,500 | $ 1,900 | $ 1,000 |
| Percent uncollectible | | x 2% | x 5% | x 10% | x 25% | x 40% |
| Estimated uncollectible | $ 2,290 | $ 740 | $ 325 | $ 350 | $ 475 | $ 400 |

**Point:** Experience shows the longer a receivable is past due, the lower is the likelihood of collection. An aging schedule exploits this relation.

**Point:** Spreadsheet software is especially useful for estimating bad debts. Using both current and past data, estimates of bad debts are obtained under different assumptions.

Exhibit 7.11 lists each customer's individual balances assigned to one of five classes based on its days past due. The amounts in each class are totaled and multiplied by the estimated percent of uncollectible accounts for each class. The percents used are regularly reviewed to reflect changes in the company and economy.

To explain, notice that Musicland has $3,500 in accounts receivable that are 31 to 60 days past due. Its management estimates 10% of the amounts in this age class are uncollectible, or a total of $350 (computed as $3,500 × 10%). Similar analysis is done for each of the other four classes. The final total of $2,290($740 + $325 + $350 + $475 + $400) shown in the first column is the estimated balance for the Allowance for Doubtful Accounts. Exhibit 7.12 shows that since the allowance account has an unadjusted credit balance of $200, the required adjustment to the Allowance for Doubtful Accounts is $2,090. This yields the following end-of-period adjusting entry:

## Exhibit 7.12

Computation of the Required Adjustment for an Accounts Receivable Method

| | |
|---|---|
| Unadjusted balance . . . . . . . . . . | $ 200 credit |
| Estimated balance . . . . . . . . . . . | 2,290 credit |
| **Required adjustment** . . . . . . . . | **$2,090 credit** |

Assets = Liabilities + Equity
−2,090              −2,090

| Dec. 31 | Bad Debts Expense. . . . . . . . . . . . . . . . . . . . . . | 2,090 | |
| | Allowance for Doubtful Accounts . . . . . . . . | | 2,090 |
| | *To record estimated bad debts.* | | |

Alternatively, if the allowance account had an unadjusted *debit* balance of $500 (instead of the $200 credit balance), its required adjustment would be computed as follows:

| | | |
|---|---|---|
| Unadjusted balance . . . . . . . | $    500 | debit |
| Estimated balance . . . . . . . | 2,290 | credit ← Current year bad debts estimate |
| Adjusting entry → **Required adjustment . . . .** | **$ 2,790** | **credit** |

The entry to record the end-of-period adjustment for this alternative case is

| Dec. 31 | Bad Debts Expense. . . . . . . . . . . . . . . . . . . . . . | 2,790 | | Assets = Liabilities + Equity |
|---|---|---|---|---|
| | Allowance for Doubtful Accounts . . . . . . . . . | | 2,790 | −2,790            −2,790 |
| | *To record estimated bad debts.* | | | |

The aging of accounts receivable method is a more detailed examination of specific accounts and is usually the most reliable of the estimation methods.

Exhibit 7.13 summarizes the principles guiding all three estimation methods and their focus of analysis.

**Decision Maker**

**Labor Union Chief**   One week prior to labor contract negotiations, financial statements are released showing no income growth. A 10% growth was predicted. Your analysis finds that the company increased its allowance for uncollectibles from 1.5% to 4.5% of receivables. Without this change, income would show a 9% growth. Does this analysis impact negotiations?

Answer—p. 296

**Exhibit 7.13**

Methods to Estimate Bad Debts

| Income Statement Focus |
|---|
| Percent of Sales |
| Emphasis on Matching  Sales ←→ Bad Debts Expense |

| Balance Sheet Focus |
|---|
| Percent of Receivables |
| Emphasis on Realizable Value  Accounts ←→ Allowance  Receivable      for Doubtful  (total)          Accounts |

| Balance Sheet Focus |
|---|
| Aging of Receivables |
| Emphasis on Realizable Value  Accounts ←→ Allowance  Receivable      for Doubtful  (individual)      Accounts |

**Quick Check**

3. Why must bad debts expense be estimated if such an estimate is possible?

4. What term describes the balance sheet valuation of Accounts Receivable less the Allowance for Doubtful Accounts?

5. Why is estimated bad debts expense credited to a contra account (Allowance for Doubtful Accounts) rather than to the Accounts Receivable account?

6. SnoBoard Company's year-end balance in its Allowance for Doubtful Accounts is a credit of $440. By aging accounts receivable, it estimates that $6,142 is uncollectible. Prepare SnoBoard's year-end adjusting entry for bad debts.

7. Record entries for these transactions assuming the allowance method is used:

   Jan.   10   The $300 account of customer Cool Jam is determined uncollectible.

   April 12   Cool Jam unexpectedly pays in full the account that was deemed uncollectible on January 10.

Answers—p. 296

# Notes Receivable

A **promissory note** is a written promise to pay a specified amount of money, usually with interest, either on demand or at a definite future date. Promissory notes are used in many transactions, including paying for products and services, and lending and borrowing money. Sellers sometimes ask for a note to replace an account receivable when a customer requests

**C2**   Describe a note receivable and the computation of its maturity date and interest.

additional time to pay a past-due account. For legal reasons, sellers generally prefer to receive notes when the credit period is long and when the receivable is for a large amount. If a lawsuit is needed to collect from a customer, a note is the buyer's written acknowledgment of the debt, its amount, and its terms.

Exhibit 7.14 shows a simple promissory note dated July 10, 2005. For this note, Julia Browne promises to pay TechCom or to its order (according to TechCom's instructions) a specified amount of money ($1,000), called the **principal of a note,** at a definite future date (October 8, 2005). As the one who signed the note and promised to pay it at maturity, Browne is the **maker of the note.** As the person to whom the note is payable, TechCom is the **payee of the note.** To Browne, the note is a liability called a *note payable.* To TechCom, the same note is an asset called a *note receivable.* This note bears interest at 12%, as written on the note. **Interest** is the charge for using (not paying) the money until a later date. To a borrower, interest is an expense. To a lender, it is revenue.

Topic Tackler 7-2

**Exhibit 7.14**

Promissory Note

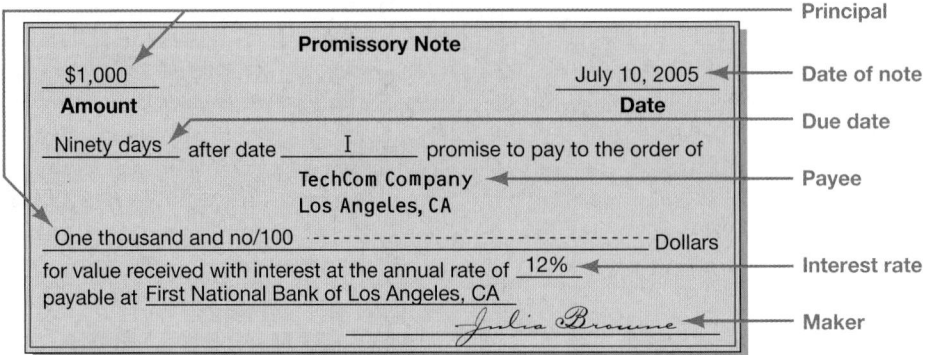

## Computing Maturity and Interest

This section describes key computations for notes including the determination of maturity date, period covered, and interest computation.

**Maturity Date and Period**   The **maturity date of a note** is the day the note (principal and interest) must be repaid. The *period* of a note is the time from the note's (contract) date to its maturity date. Many notes mature in less than a full year, and the period they cover is often expressed in days. When the time of a note is expressed in days, its maturity date is the specified number of days after the note's date. As an example, a five-day note dated June 15 matures and is due on June 20. A 90-day note dated July 10 matures on October 8. This October 8 due date is computed as shown in Exhibit 7.15. The period of a note is sometimes expressed in months or years. When months are used, the note matures and is payable in the month of its maturity on the *same day of the month* as its original date. A nine-month note dated July 10, for instance, is payable on April 10. The same analysis applies when years are used.

**Exhibit 7.15**

Maturity Date Computation

| | |
|---|---|
| Days in July ........................................ | 31 |
| Minus the date of the note ........................ | 10 |
| Days remaining in July ............................. | 21 |
| Add days in August ................................ | 31 |
| Add days in September ............................. | 30 |
| Days to equal 90 days, or **maturity date of October 8** ....... | 8 |
| Period of the note in days .......................... | 90 |

**Interest Computation**   *Interest* is the cost of borrowing money for the borrower or, alternatively, the profit from lending money for the lender. Unless otherwise stated, the rate of interest on a note is the rate charged for the use of the principal for one year. The formula for computing interest on a note is shown in Exhibit 7.16.

$$\text{Principal of the note} \times \text{Annual interest rate} \times \text{Time expressed in years} = \text{Interest}$$

**Exhibit 7.16**

Computation of Interest Formula

To simplify interest computations, a year is commonly treated as having 360 days (called the *banker's rule*). **We treat a year as having 360 days for interest computations in the examples and assignments.** Using the promissory note in Exhibit 7.14 where we have a 90-day, 12%, $1,000 note, the total interest is computed as follows:

$$\$1,000 \times 12\% \times \frac{90}{360} = \$1,000 \times 0.12 \times 0.25 = \$30$$

## Recognizing Notes Receivable

Notes receivable are usually recorded in a single Notes Receivable account to simplify record-keeping. The original notes are kept on file, including information on the maker, rate of interest, and due date. (When a company holds a large number of notes, it sometimes sets up a controlling account and a subsidiary ledger for notes. This is similar to the handling of accounts receivable.) To illustrate the recording for the receipt of a note, we use the $1,000, 90-day, 12% promissory note in Exhibit 7.14. TechCom received this note at the time of a product sale to Julia Browne. This transaction is recorded as follows:

**P3** Record the receipt of a note receivable.

| July 10* | Notes Receivable . . . . . . . . . . . . . . . . . . . . . . . | 1,000 | |
| | Sales . . . . . . . . . . . . . . . . . . . . . . . . . . . . . . | | 1,000 |
| | *Sold goods in exchange for a 90-day, 12% note.* | | |

Assets = Liabilities + Equity
+1,000                    +1,000

\* We omit the entry to Dr. Cost of Sales and Cr. Merchandise Inventory to focus on sales and receivables.

When a seller accepts a note from an overdue customer as a way to grant a time extension on a past-due account receivable, it will often collect part of the past-due balance in cash. This partial payment forces a concession from the customer, reduces the customer's debt (and the seller's risk), and produces a note for a smaller amount. To illustrate, assume that TechCom agreed to accept $232 in cash along with a $600, 60-day, 15% note from Jo Cook to settle her $832 past-due account. TechCom made the following entry to record receipt of this cash and note:

**Point:** Notes receivable often are a major part of a company's assets. Likewise, notes payable often are a large part of a company's liabilities.

| Oct. 5 | Cash . . . . . . . . . . . . . . . . . . . . . . . . . . . . . . . | 232 | |
| | Notes Receivable . . . . . . . . . . . . . . . . . . . . . . . | 600 | |
| | Accounts Receivable—J. Cook . . . . . . . . . . . | | 832 |
| | *Received cash and note to settle account.* | | |

Assets = Liabilities + Equity
+232
+600
−832

## Valuing and Settling Notes

**Recording an Honored Note**  The principal and interest of a note are due on its maturity date. The maker of the note usually *honors* the note and pays it in full. To illustrate, when J. Cook pays the note above on its due date, TechCom records it as follows:

**P4** Record the honoring and dishonoring of a note and adjustments for interest.

| Dec. 4 | Cash . . . . . . . . . . . . . . . . . . . . . . . . . . . . . . . | 615 | |
| | Notes Receivable . . . . . . . . . . . . . . . . . . . | | 600 |
| | Interest Revenue . . . . . . . . . . . . . . . . . . . . | | 15 |
| | *Collect note with interest of $600 × 15% × 60/360.* | | |

Assets = Liabilities + Equity
+615                         +15
−600

Interest Revenue, also called *Interest Earned,* is reported on the income statement.

**Recording a Dishonored Note**     When a note's maker is unable or refuses to pay at maturity, the note is *dishonored*. The act of dishonoring a note does not relieve the maker of the obligation to pay. The payee should use every legitimate means to collect. How do companies report this event? The balance of the Notes Receivable account should include only those notes that have not matured. Thus, when a note is dishonored, we remove the amount of this note from the Notes Receivable account and charge it back to an account receivable from its maker. To illustrate, TechCom holds an $800, 12%, 60-day note of Greg Hart. At maturity, Hart dishonors the note. TechCom records this dishonoring of the note as follows:

**Point:** When posting a dishonored note to a customer's account, an explanation is included so as not to misinterpret the debit as a sale on account.

Assets = Liabilities + Equity
+816                  +16
−800

| Oct. 14 | Accounts Receivable—G. Hart . . . . . . . . . . . . . | 816 | |
| | Interest Revenue . . . . . . . . . . . . . . . . . . . . | | 16 |
| | Notes Receivable . . . . . . . . . . . . . . . . . . . | | 800 |
| | *To charge account of G. Hart for a dishonored note and interest of $800 × 12% × 60/360.* | | |

Charging a dishonored note back to the account of its maker serves two purposes. First, it removes the amount of the note from the Notes Receivable account and records the dishonored note in the maker's account. Second, and more important, if the maker of the dishonored note applies for credit in the future, his or her account will reveal all past dealings, including the dishonored note. Restoring the account also reminds the company to continue collection efforts from Hart for both principal and interest. The entry records the full amount, including interest, to ensure that it is included in collection efforts.

**Point:** Reporting the details of notes is consistent with the **full disclosure principle,** which requires financial statements (including footnotes) to report all relevant information.

**Recording End-of-Period Interest Adjustment**     When notes receivable are outstanding at the end of a period, any accrued interest earned is computed and recorded. To illustrate, on December 16, TechCom accepts a $3,000, 60-day, 12% note from a customer in granting an extension on a past-due account. When TechCom's accounting period ends on December 31, $15 of interest has accrued on this note ($3,000 × 12% × 15/360). The following adjusting entry records this revenue:

Assets = Liabilities + Equity
+15                    +15

| Dec. 31 | Interest Receivable . . . . . . . . . . . . . . . . . . . . . | 15 | |
| | Interest Revenue . . . . . . . . . . . . . . . . . . . . | | 15 |
| | *To record accrued interest earned.* | | |

Interest Revenue appears on the income statement, and Interest Receivable appears on the balance sheet as a current asset. When the December 16 note is collected on February 14, TechCom's entry to record the cash receipt is

Assets = Liabilities + Equity
+3,060                 +45
−15
−3,000

| Feb. 14 | Cash . . . . . . . . . . . . . . . . . . . . . . . . . . . . . . | 3,060 | |
| | Interest Revenue . . . . . . . . . . . . . . . . . . . . | | 45 |
| | Interest Receivable . . . . . . . . . . . . . . . . . | | 15 |
| | Notes Receivable . . . . . . . . . . . . . . . . . . . | | 3,000 |
| | *Received payment of note and its interest.* | | |

Total interest earned on the 60-day note is $60. The $15 credit to Interest Receivable on February 14 reflects the collection of the interest accrued from the December 31 adjusting entry. The $45 interest earned reflects TechCom's revenue from holding the note from January 1 to February 14 of the current period.

## Quick Check

8. Irwin purchases $7,000 of merchandise from Stamford on December 16, 2005. Stamford accepts Irwin's $7,000, 90-day, 12% note as payment. Stamford's accounting period ends on December 31, and it does not make reversing entries. Prepare entries for Stamford on December 16, 2005, and December 31, 2005.

9. Using the information in Quick Check 8, prepare Stamford's March 16, 2006, entry if Irwin dishonors the note.

Answers—p. 296

# Disposing of Receivables

Companies can convert receivables to cash before they are due. Reasons for this include the need for cash or the desire not to be involved in collection activities. Converting receivables is usually done either by (1) selling them or (2) using them as security for a loan. A recent survey shows that about 20% of companies obtain cash from either selling receivables or pledging them as security. In some industries such as textiles, apparel and furniture, this is common practice.

## Selling Receivables

A company can sell all or a portion of its receivables to a finance company or bank. The buyer, called a *factor,* charges the seller a *factoring fee* and then the buyer takes ownership of the receivables and receives cash when they come due. By incurring a factoring fee, the seller receives cash earlier and can pass the risk of bad debts to the factor. The seller can also choose to avoid costs of billing and accounting for the receivables. To illustrate, if TechCom sells $20,000 of its accounts receivable and is charged a 4% factoring fee, it records this sale as follows:

**C3** Explain how receivables can be converted to cash before maturity.

**Global:** Firms in export sales increasingly sell their receivables to factors.

| | | | |
|---|---|---:|---:|
| Aug. 15 | Cash ................................. | 19,200 | |
| | Factoring Fee Expense ................... | 800 | |
| | Accounts Receivable .................. | | 20,000 |
| | *Sold accounts receivable for cash, less 4% fee.* | | |

| Assets | = Liabilities + Equity |
|---|---|
| +19,200 | −800 |
| −20,000 | |

The accounting for sales of notes receivable is similar to that for accounts receivable. The detailed entries are covered in advanced courses.

## Pledging Receivables

A company can raise cash by borrowing money and *pledging* its receivables as security for the loan. Pledging receivables does not transfer the risk of bad debts to the lender because the borrower retains ownership of the receivables. If the borrower defaults on the loan, the lender has a right to be paid from the cash receipts of the receivable when collected. To illustrate, when TechCom borrows $35,000 and pledges its receivables as security, it records this transaction as follows:

**Point:** When accounts receivable are sold, each subsidiary ledger account is credited along with the controlling account for the total.

**Point: Chock Full O'Nuts** reports, "Outstanding borrowings . . . are collateralized by, among other things, the trade accounts receivable."

| | | | |
|---|---|---:|---:|
| Aug. 20 | Cash ................................. | 35,000 | |
| | Notes Payable ..................... | | 35,000 |
| | *Borrowed money with a note secured by pledging receivables.* | | |

| Assets | = Liabilities + Equity |
|---|---|
| +35,000 | +35,000 |

Since pledged receivables are committed as security for a specific loan, the borrower's financial statements disclose the pledging of them. TechCom, for instance, includes the following note with its statements: *Accounts receivable of $40,000 are pledged as security for a $35,000 note payable.*

## Decision Analysis                                    Accounts Receivable Turnover

**A1**  Compute accounts receivable turnover and use it to help assess financial condition.

For a company selling on credit, we want to assess both the quality and liquidity of its accounts receivable. *Quality* of receivables refers to the likelihood of collection without loss. Experience shows that the longer receivables are outstanding beyond their due date, the lower the likelihood of collection. *Liquidity* of receivables refers to the speed of collection. **Accounts receivable turnover** is a measure of both the quality and liquidity of accounts receivable. It indicates how often, on average, receivables are received and collected during the period. The formula for this ratio is shown in Exhibit 7.17.

### Exhibit 7.17

Accounts Receivable Turnover

$$\text{Accounts receivable turnover} = \frac{\text{Net sales}}{\text{Average accounts receivable}}$$

We prefer to use net *credit* sales in the numerator because cash sales do not create receivables. However, since financial statements rarely report net credit sales, our analysis uses net sales. The denominator is the *average* accounts receivable balance, computed as (Beginning balance + Ending balance) ÷ 2. TechCom has an accounts receivable turnover of 5.1. This indicates its average accounts receivable balance is converted into cash 5.1 times during the period. Exhibit 7.18 shows graphically this turnover activity for TechCom.

### Exhibit 7.18

Rate of Accounts Receivable Turnover for TechCom

5.1 times per year

Jan.   Feb.   March   Apr.   May   June   July   Aug.   Sept.   Oct.   Nov.   Dec.

Accounts receivable turnover also reflects how well management is doing in granting credit to customers in a desire to increase sales. A high turnover in comparison with competitors suggests that management should consider using more liberal credit terms to increase sales. A low turnover suggests management should consider stricter credit terms and more aggressive collection efforts to avoid having its resources tied up in accounts receivable.

**Point:** Credit risk ratio is computed by dividing the Allowance for Doubtful Accounts by Accounts Receivable. The higher this ratio, the higher is credit risk.

To illustrate, we take data from two competitors: **Dell Computer** and **Apple Computer**. Exhibit 7.19 shows accounts receivable turnover for both companies.

### Exhibit 7.19

Analysis Using Accounts Receivable Turnover

| Company | Figure ($ millions) | 2002 | 2001 | 2000 |
|---------|---------------------|------|------|------|
| **Dell** | Net sales ......................... | $35,404 | $31,168 | $31,888 |
| | Average accounts receivable ............ | $ 2,428 | $ 2,347 | $ 2,752 |
| | **Accounts receivable turnover** ........ | 14.6 | 13.3 | 11.6 |
| **Apple** | Net sales ......................... | $ 5,742 | $ 5,363 | $ 7,983 |
| | Average accounts receivable ............ | $  516 | $  710 | $  817 |
| | **Accounts receivable turnover** ........ | 11.1 | 7.6 | 9.8 |

Dell's 2002 turnover is computed ($ millions) as $35,404/$2,428 = 14.6. This means that Dell's average accounts receivable balance was converted into cash 14.6 times in 2002. Also, its turnover improved in 2002 (versus its prior two years), and it is superior to that of Apple. Is Dell's turnover too high? Since sales are markedly growing over this time period, Dell's turnover does not appear to be too high. Instead, it seems to be doing well in managing receivables. Similarly, Apple has improved its management of receivables during this period. Turnover for competitors is generally in the range of 7 to 11 for this same period.[1]

### Decision Maker

**Family Physician** Your practice is less profitable, so you hire a health care analyst. The analyst highlights several points including the following: *"Accounts receivable turnover is too low. Tighter credit policies are recommended along with discontinuing service to those most delayed in payments."* How do you interpret these recommendations? What actions do you take?

Answer—p. 296

# Demonstration Problem

Clayco Company completes the following selected transactions during year 2005:

July 14 Writes off a $750 account receivable arising from a sale to Briggs Company that dates to 10 months ago. (Clayco Company uses the allowance method.)

30 Clayco Company receives a $1,000, 90-day, 10% note in exchange for merchandise sold to Sumrell Company (the merchandise cost $600).

Aug. 15 Receives $2,000 cash plus a $10,000 note from JT Co. in exchange for merchandise that sells for $12,000 (its cost is $8,000). The note is dated August 15, bears 12% interest, and matures in 120 days.

Nov. 1 Completed a $200 credit card sale with a 4% fee (the cost of sales is $150). The cash is received immediately from the credit card company.

3 Sumrell Company refuses to pay the note that was due to Clayco Company on October 28. Prepare the journal entry to charge the dishonored note plus accrued interest to Sumrell Company's accounts receivable.

5 Completed a $500 credit card sale with a 5% fee (the cost of sales is $300). The payment from the credit card company is received on Nov. 9.

15 Received the full amount of $750 from Briggs Company that was previously written off on July 14. Record the bad debts recovery.

Dec. 13 Received payment of principal plus interest from JT for the August 15 note.

### Required

**1.** Prepare journal entries to record these transactions on Clayco Company's books.

**2.** Prepare an adjusting journal entry as of December 31, 2005, assuming the following:

**a.** Bad debts expense is estimated to be $20,400 by aging accounts receivable. The unadjusted balance of the Allowance for Doubtful Accounts is $1,000 debit.

**b.** Alternatively, assume that bad debts expense is estimated using the percent of sales method. The Allowance for Doubtful Accounts had a $1,000 debit balance before adjustment, and the company estimates bad debts to be 1% of its credit sales of $2,000,000.

## Planning the Solution

- Examine each transaction to determine the accounts affected, and then record the entries.
- For the year-end adjustment, record the bad debts expense for the two approaches.

---

[1] As an estimate of *average days' sales uncollected,* we compute how many days (*on average*) it takes to collect receivables as follows: 365 days ÷ accounts receivable turnover. An increase in this *average collection period* can signal a decline in its customers' financial condition.

## Solution to Demonstration Problem

1.

| | | | | |
|---|---|---|---:|---:|
| July 14 | Allowance for Doubtful Accounts . . . . . . . . . . . . . | | 750 | |
| |     Accounts Receivable—Briggs Co. . . . . . . . . . | | | 750 |
| | *Wrote off an uncollectible account.* | | | |
| July 30 | Notes Receivable—Sumrell Co. . . . . . . . . . . . . | | 1,000 | |
| |     Sales . . . . . . . . . . . . . . . . . . . . . . . . . . | | | 1,000 |
| | *Sold merchandise for a 90-day, 10% note.* | | | |
| July 30 | Cost of Goods Sold . . . . . . . . . . . . . . . . . . . . . | | 600 | |
| |     Merchandise Inventory . . . . . . . . . . . . . . . . | | | 600 |
| | *To record the cost of July 30 sale.* | | | |
| Aug. 15 | Cash . . . . . . . . . . . . . . . . . . . . . . . . . . . . . . | | 2,000 | |
| | Notes Receivable—JT Co. . . . . . . . . . . . . . . . | | 10,000 | |
| |     Sales . . . . . . . . . . . . . . . . . . . . . . . . . . | | | 12,000 |
| | *Sold merchandise to customer for $2,000* | | | |
| | *cash and $10,000 note.* | | | |
| Aug. 15 | Cost of Goods Sold . . . . . . . . . . . . . . . . . . . . . | | 8,000 | |
| |     Merchandise Inventory . . . . . . . . . . . . . . . . | | | 8,000 |
| | *To record the cost of Aug. 15 sale.* | | | |
| Nov. 1 | Cash . . . . . . . . . . . . . . . . . . . . . . . . . . . . . . | | 192 | |
| | Credit Card Expense . . . . . . . . . . . . . . . . . . . . | | 8 | |
| |     Sales . . . . . . . . . . . . . . . . . . . . . . . . . . | | | 200 |
| | *To record credit card sale less a 4% credit* | | | |
| | *card expense.* | | | |
| Nov. 1 | Cost of Goods Sold . . . . . . . . . . . . . . . . . . . . . | | 150 | |
| |     Merchandise Inventory . . . . . . . . . . . . . . . . | | | 150 |
| | *To record the cost of Nov. 1 sale.* | | | |
| Nov. 3 | Accounts Receivable—Sumrell Co. . . . . . . . . . . | | 1,025 | |
| |     Interest Revenue . . . . . . . . . . . . . . . . . . . . | | | 25 |
| |     Notes Receivable—Sumrell Co. . . . . . . . . . | | | 1,000 |
| | *To charge account of Sumrell Company for* | | | |
| | *a $1,000 dishonored note and interest of* | | | |
| | *$1,000 × 10% × 90/360.* | | | |
| Nov. 5 | Accounts Receivable—Credit Card Co. . . . . . . . . | | 475 | |
| | Credit Card Expense. . . . . . . . . . . . . . . . . . . . | | 25 | |
| |     Sales . . . . . . . . . . . . . . . . . . . . . . . . . . | | | 500 |
| | *To record credit card sale less a 5% credit* | | | |
| | *card expense.* | | | |
| Nov. 5 | Cost of Goods Sold . . . . . . . . . . . . . . . . . . . . . | | 300 | |
| |     Merchandise Inventory . . . . . . . . . . . . . . . . | | | 300 |
| | *To record the cost of Nov. 5 sale.* | | | |
| Nov. 9 | Cash . . . . . . . . . . . . . . . . . . . . . . . . . . . . . . | | 475 | |
| |     Accounts Receivable—Credit Card Co. . . . . | | | 475 |
| | *To record cash receipt from Nov. 5 sale.* | | | |
| Nov. 15 | Accounts Receivable—Briggs Co. . . . . . . . . . . . | | 750 | |
| |     Allowance for Doubtful Accounts . . . . . . . . | | | 750 |
| | *To reinstate the account of Briggs Company* | | | |
| | *previously written off.* | | | |
| Nov. 15 | Cash . . . . . . . . . . . . . . . . . . . . . . . . . . . . . . | | 750 | |
| |     Accounts Receivable—Briggs Co. . . . . . . . . | | | 750 |
| | *Cash received in full payment of account.* | | | |
| Dec. 13 | Cash . . . . . . . . . . . . . . . . . . . . . . . . . . . . . . | | 10,400 | |
| |     Interest Revenue . . . . . . . . . . . . . . . . . . . . | | | 400 |
| |     Note Receivable—JT Co. . . . . . . . . . . . . . | | | 10,000 |
| | *Collect note with interest of* | | | |
| | *$10,000 × 12% × 120/360.* | | | |

**2a.** Aging of accounts receivable method:

| Dec. 31 | Bad Debts Expense...................... | 21,400 | |
|---|---|---|---|
| | Allowance for Doubtful Accounts ......... | | 21,400 |
| | *To adjust allowance account from a $1,000 debit balance to a $20,400 credit balance.* | | |

**2b.** Percent of sales method:*

| Dec. 31 | Bad Debts Expense...................... | 20,000 | |
|---|---|---|---|
| | Allowance for Doubtful Accounts ......... | | 20,000 |
| | *To provide for bad debts as 1% × $2,000,000 in credit sales.* | | |

---

\* For the income statement approach, which requires estimating bad debts as a percent of sales or credit sales, the Allowance account balance is *not* considered when making the adjusting entry.

## Summary

**C1  Describe accounts receivable and how they occur and are recorded.** Accounts receivable are amounts due from customers for credit sales. A subsidiary ledger lists amounts owed by each customer. Credit sales arise from at least two sources: (1) sales on credit and (2) credit card sales. *Sales on credit* refers to a company's granting credit directly to customers. Credit card sales involve customers' use of third-party credit cards.

**C2  Describe a note receivable and the computation of its maturity date and interest.** A note receivable is a written promise to pay a specified amount of money at a definite future date. The maturity date is the day the note (principal and interest) must be repaid. Interest rates are normally stated in annual terms. The amount of interest on the note is computed by expressing time as a fraction of one year and multiplying the note's principal by this fraction and the annual interest rate.

**C3  Explain how receivables can be converted to cash before maturity.** Receivables can be converted to cash before maturity in three ways. First, a company can sell accounts receivable to a factor, who charges a factoring fee. Second, a company can borrow money by signing a note payable that is secured by pledging the accounts receivable. Third, notes receivable can be discounted at (sold to) a financial institution.

**A1  Compute accounts receivable turnover and use it to help assess financial condition.** Accounts receivable turnover is a measure of both the quality and liquidity of accounts receivable. The accounts receivable turnover measure indicates how often, on average, receivables are received and collected during the period. Accounts receivable turnover is computed as net sales divided by average accounts receivable.

**P1  Apply the direct write-off and allowance methods to account for accounts receivable.** The direct write-off method charges Bad Debts Expense when accounts are written off as uncollectible. This method is acceptable only when the amount of bad debts expense is immaterial. Under the allowance method, bad debts expense is recorded with an adjustment at the end of each accounting period that debits the Bad Debts Expense account and credits the Allowance for Doubtful Accounts. The uncollectible accounts are later written off with a debit to the Allowance for Doubtful Accounts.

**P2  Estimate uncollectibles using methods based on sales and accounts receivable.** Uncollectibles are estimated by focusing on either (1) the income statement relation between bad debts expense and credit sales or (2) the balance sheet relation between accounts receivable and the allowance for doubtful accounts. The first approach emphasizes the matching principle using the income statement. The second approach emphasizes realizable value of accounts receivable using the balance sheet.

**P3  Record the receipt of a note receivable.** A note received is recorded at its principal amount by debiting the Notes Receivable account. The credit amount is to the asset, product, or service provided in return for the note.

**P4  Record the honoring and dishonoring of a note and adjustments for interest.** When a note is honored, the payee debits the money received and credits both Notes Receivable and Interest Revenue. Dishonored notes are credited to Notes Receivable and debited to Accounts Receivable (to the account of the maker in an attempt to collect), and Interest Revenue is recorded for interest earned for the time the note is held.

## Guidance Answers to **Decision Maker** and **Decision Ethics**

**Entrepreneur**  Analysis of credit card sales should weigh the benefits against the costs. The primary benefit is the potential to increase sales by attracting customers who prefer the convenience of credit cards. The primary cost is the fee charged by the credit card company for providing this service. Analysis should therefore estimate the expected increase in dollar sales from allowing credit card sales and then subtract (1) the normal costs and expenses and (2) the credit card fees associated with this expected increase in dollar sales. If your analysis shows an increase in profit from allowing credit card sales, your store should probably accept them.

**Labor Union Chief**   Yes, this information is likely to impact your negotiations. The obvious question is why the company markedly increased this allowance. The large increase in this allowance means a substantial increase in bad debts expense *and* a decrease in earnings. This change (coming immediately prior to labor contract discussions) also raises concerns since it reduces the union's bargaining power for increased compensation. You want to ask management for supporting documentation justifying this increase. You also want data for two or three prior years and

similar data from competitors. These data should give you some sense of whether the change in the allowance for uncollectibles is justified.

**Family Physician**   The recommendations are twofold. First, the analyst suggests more stringent screening of patients' credit standing. Second, the analyst suggests dropping patients who are most overdue in payments. You are likely bothered by both suggestions. They are probably financially wise recommendations, but you are troubled by eliminating services to those less able to pay. One alternative is to follow the recommendations while implementing a care program directed at patients less able to pay for services. This allows you to continue services to patients less able to pay and lets you discontinue services to patients able but unwilling to pay.

## Guidance Answers to **Quick Checks**

**1.** If cash is immediately received when credit card sales receipts are deposited, the company debits Cash at the time of sale. If the company does not receive payment until after it submits receipts to the credit card company, it debits Accounts Receivable at the time of sale. (Cash is later debited when payment is received from the credit card company.)

**2.** Credit card expenses are usually *recorded* and *incurred* at the time of their related sales, not when cash is received from the credit card company.

**3.** If possible, bad debts expense must be matched with the sales that gave rise to the accounts receivable. This requires that companies estimate future bad debts at the end of each period before they learn which accounts are uncollectible.

**4.** Realizable value (also called *net realizable value*).

**5.** The estimated amount of bad debts expense cannot be credited to the Accounts Receivable account because the specific customer accounts that will prove uncollectible cannot yet be identified and removed from the accounts receivable subsidiary ledger. Moreover, if only the Accounts Receivable account is credited, its balance would not equal the sum of its subsidiary account balances.

**6.**

| | | | | |
|---|---|---|---|---|
| Dec. 31 | Bad Debts Expense. . . . . . . . . . . . . . . . | 5,702 | |
| | Allowance for Doubtful Accounts. . . . | | 5,702 |

**7.**

| | | | | |
|---|---|---|---|---|
| Jan. 10 | Allowance for Doubtful Accounts . . . . . . . | 300 | |
| | Accounts Receivable—Cool Jam . . . . | | 300 |
| Apr. 12 | Accounts Receivable—Cool Jam . . . . . . . . | 300 | |
| | Allowance for Doubtful Accounts. . . . | | 300 |
| Apr. 12 | Cash . . . . . . . . . . . . . . . . . . . . . . . . . | 300 | |
| | Accounts Receivable—Cool Jam . . . . | | 300 |

**8.**

| | | | | |
|---|---|---|---|---|
| Dec. 16 | Note Receivable—Irwin . . . . . . . . . . . . . . | 7,000 | |
| | Sales. . . . . . . . . . . . . . . . . . . . . . . | | 7,000 |
| Dec. 31 | Interest Receivable . . . . . . . . . . . . . . . . . | 35 | |
| | Interest Revenue . . . . . . . . . . . . . . . | | 35 |
| | ($7,000 × 12% × 15/360) | | |

**9.**

| | | | | |
|---|---|---|---|---|
| Mar. 16 | Accounts Receivable—Irwin . . . . . . . . . . | 7,210 | |
| | Interest Revenue . . . . . . . . . . . . . . . | | 175 |
| | Interest Receivable . . . . . . . . . . . . . | | 35 |
| | Notes Receivable—Irwin . . . . . . . . . | | 7,000 |

## Key Terms

Key Terms are available at the book's Website for learning and testing in an online Flashcard Format.

**Accounts receivable** (p. 278)

**Accounts receivable turnover** (p. 292)

**Aging of accounts receivable** (p. 286)

**Allowance for Doubtful Accounts** (p. 283)

**Allowance method** (p. 282)

**Bad debts** (p. 281)

**Direct write-off method** (p. 282)

**Interest** (p. 288)

**Maker of the note** (p. 288)

**Matching principle** (p. 282)

**Materiality principle** (p. 282)

**Maturity date of a note** (p. 288)

**Payee of the note** (p. 288)

**Principal of a note** (p. 288)

**Promissory note** (or **note**) (p. 287)

**Realizable value** (p. 283)

## Personal Interactive Quiz

Personal Interactive Quizzes A and B are available at the book's Website to reinforce and assess your learning.

## Discussion Questions

1. How do sellers benefit from allowing their customers to use credit cards?

2. Why does the direct write-off method of accounting for bad debts usually fail to match revenues and expenses?

3. Explain the accounting principle of materiality.

4. Explain why writing off a bad debt against the Allowance for Doubtful Accounts does not reduce the estimated realizable value of a company's accounts receivable.

5. Why does the Bad Debts Expense account usually not have the same adjusted balance as the Allowance for Doubtful Accounts?

6. Why might a business prefer a note receivable to an account receivable?

7. Refer to **Krispy Kreme**'s balance sheet in Appendix A. What percent of accounts receivable at February 2, 2003, has been set aside as an allowance for doubtful accounts? How does this percent compare to the prior year?

8. Refer to the balance sheet of **Tastykake** in Appendix A. Does it use the direct write-off method or allowance method to account for doubtful accounts? What is the realizable value of its accounts receivable as of December 28, 2002? What is another name for the Allowance for Doubtful Accounts?

9. Refer to the balance sheet of **Harley-Davidson** in Appendix A. What two types of receivables does Harley show in its current asset section of the balance sheet?

**Harley-Davidson**

*Red numbers denote Discussion Questions that involve decision-making.*

 — *Homework Manager repeats all numerical Quick Studies on the book's Website with new numbers.*

Prepare journal entries for the following credit card sales transactions (the company uses the perpetual inventory system):

1. Sold $10,000 of merchandise, that cost $7,500, on MasterCard credit cards. The net cash receipts from sales are immediately deposited in the seller's bank account. MasterCard charges a 5% fee.

2. Sold $3,000 of merchandise, that cost $1,500, on an assortment of credit cards. Net cash receipts are received 7 days later, and a 4% fee is charged.

## QUICK STUDY

**QS 7-1**
Credit card sales

C1

---

Milner Corp. uses the allowance method to account for uncollectibles. On October 31, it wrote off a $1,000 account of a customer, C. Schaub. On December 9, it receives a $200 payment from Schaub.

1. Prepare the journal entry or entries for October 31.

2. Prepare the journal entry or entries for December 9; assume no additional money is expected from Schaub.

**QS 7-2**
Allowance method for bad debts

P1

---

Wecker Company's year-end unadjusted trial balance shows accounts receivable of $89,000, allowance for doubtful accounts of $500 (credit), and sales of $270,000. Uncollectibles are estimated to be 1.5% of accounts receivable.

1. Prepare the December 31 year-end adjusting entry for uncollectibles.

2. What amount would have been used in the year-end adjusting entry if the allowance account had a year-end unadjusted debit balance of $200?

3. Assume the same facts as in part 1, except that Wecker estimates uncollectibles as 1.0% of sales. Prepare the December 31 year-end adjusting entry for uncollectibles.

**QS 7-3**
Percent of accounts receivable and percent of sales methods

P1  P2

---

On August 2, 2005, JLK Co. receives a $5,500, 90-day, 12% note from customer Tom Menke as payment on his $5,500 account. Prepare JLK's journal entries for August 2 and for the note's maturity date assuming the note is honored by Menke.

**QS 7-4**
Note receivable

P3  P4

---

Dekon Company's December 31 year-end unadjusted trial balance shows an $8,000 balance in Notes Receivable. This balance is from one 6% note dated December 1, with a period of 45 days. Prepare journal entries for December 31 and for the note's maturity date assuming it is honored.

**QS 7-5**
Note receivable

C2  P4

## QS 7-6
Accounts receivable turnover

A1

The following data are taken from the comparative balance sheets of Fulton Company. Compute and interpret its accounts receivable turnover for year 2005 (competitors average a turnover of 7.5).

|  | 2005 | 2004 |
|---|---|---|
| Accounts receivable ....... | $152,900 | $133,700 |
| Net sales .............. | 754,200 | 810,600 |

*Homework Manager repeats all numerical Exercises on the book's Website with new numbers.* →

# EXERCISES

## Exercise 7-1
Accounting for credit card sales

C1

Petri Company allows customers to use two credit cards in charging purchases. With the Omni Card, Petri receives an immediate credit to its account when it deposits sales receipts. Omni Card assesses a 4% service charge for credit card sales. The second credit card that Petri accepts is the Continental Bank Card. Petri sends its accumulated receipts to Continental Bank on a weekly basis and is paid by Continental about a week later. Continental Bank assesses a 2.5% charge on sales for using its card. Prepare journal entries to record the following selected credit card transactions of Petri Company:

Apr.  8  Sold merchandise for $9,200 (that had cost $6,800) and accepted the customer's Omni Card. The Omni receipts are immediately deposited in Petri's bank account.
12  Sold merchandise for $5,400 (that had cost $3,500) and accepted the customer's Continental Bank Card. Transferred $5,400 of credit card receipts to Continental Bank, requesting payment.
20  Received Continental Bank's check for the April 12 billing, less the service charge.

## Exercise 7-2
Accounts receivable subsidiary ledger; schedule of accounts receivable

C1

Sami Company recorded the following selected transactions during November 2005:

| Nov. 5 | Accounts Receivable—Surf Shop . . . . . . . . . . . . . | 4,417 | |
|---|---|---|---|
| | Sales . . . . . . . . . . . . . . . . . . . . . . . . . . . . . | | 4,417 |
| 10 | Accounts Receivable—Yum Enterprises . . . . . . . . | 1,250 | |
| | Sales . . . . . . . . . . . . . . . . . . . . . . . . . . . . . | | 1,250 |
| 13 | Accounts Receivable—Matt Albin. . . . . . . . . . . . | 733 | |
| | Sales . . . . . . . . . . . . . . . . . . . . . . . . . . . . . | | 733 |
| 21 | Sales Returns and Allowances . . . . . . . . . . . . . . | 189 | |
| | Accounts Receivable—Matt Albin . . . . . . . . . | | 189 |
| 30 | Accounts Receivable—Surf Shop . . . . . . . . . . . . | 2,606 | |
| | Sales . . . . . . . . . . . . . . . . . . . . . . . . . . . . . | | 2,606 |

**1.** Open a general ledger having T-accounts for Accounts Receivable, Sales, and Sales Returns and Allowances. Also open an accounts receivable subsidiary ledger having a T-account for each customer. Post these entries to both the general ledger and the accounts receivable ledger.

**Check**   Accounts Receivable ending balance, $8,817

**2.** Prepare a schedule of accounts receivable (see Exhibit 7.4) and compare its total with the balance of the Accounts Receivable controlling account as of November 30.

## Exercise 7-3
Percent of sales method; write-off

P1  P2

At year-end (December 31), Alvare Company estimates its bad debts as 0.5% of its annual credit sales of $875,000. Alvare records its Bad Debts Expense for that estimate. On the following February 1, Alvare decides that the $420 account of P. Coble is uncollectible and writes it off as a bad debt. On June 5, Coble unexpectedly pays the amount previously written off. Prepare the journal entries of Alvare to record these transactions and events of December 31, February 1, and June 5.

## Exercise 7-4
Percent of accounts receivable method

P1  P2

At each calendar year-end, Cabool Supply Co. uses the percent of accounts receivable method to estimate bad debts. On December 31, 2005, it has outstanding accounts receivable of $53,000, and it estimates that 4% will be uncollectible. Prepare the adjusting entry to record bad debts expense for year 2005 under the assumption that the Allowance for Doubtful Accounts has (*a*) a $915 credit balance before the adjustment and (*b*) a $1,332 debit balance before the adjustment.

On June 30, Peña Co. has $125,900 of accounts receivable. Prepare journal entries to record the following selected July transactions. Also prepare any footnotes to the July 31 financial statements that result from these transactions. (The company uses the perpetual inventory system.)

July  4   Sold $6,295 of merchandise (that had cost $4,000) to customers on credit.
       9   Sold $18,000 of accounts receivable to Center Bank. Center charges a 4% factoring fee.
      17   Received $3,436 cash from customers in payment on their accounts.
      27   Borrowed $10,000 cash from Center Bank, pledging $13,000 of accounts receivable as security for the loan.

**Exercise 7-5**
Selling and pledging accounts receivable

C3

---

Prepare journal entries to record these selected transactions for Eduardo Company:

Nov.  1   Accepted a $5,000, 180-day, 6% note dated November 1 from Melosa Allen in granting a time extension on her past-due account receivable.
Dec. 31   Adjusted the year-end accounts for the accrued interest earned on the Allen note.
Apr. 30   Allen honors her note when presented for payment.

**Exercise 7-6**
Honoring a note

P4

---

Prepare journal entries to record the following selected transactions of Paloma Company:

Mar. 21   Accepted a $3,100, 180-day, 10% note dated March 21 from Salma Hernandez in granting a time extension on her past-due account receivable.
Sept. 17  Hernandez dishonors her note when it is presented for payment.
Dec. 31   After exhausting all legal means of collection, Paloma Company writes off Hernandez account against the Allowance for Doubtful Accounts.

**Exercise 7-7**
Dishonoring a note

P4

---

Prepare journal entries for the following selected transactions of Deshawn Company:

**2004**

Dec. 13   Accepted a $10,000, 60-day, 8% note dated December 13 in granting Latisha Clark a time extension on her past-due account receivable.
      31   Prepared an adjusting entry to record the accrued interest on the Clark note.

**2005**

Feb. 11   Received Clark's payment for principal and interest on the note dated December 13.
Mar.  3   Accepted a $4,000, 10%, 90-day note dated March 3 in granting a time extension on the past-due account receivable of Shandi Company.
      17   Accepted a $2,000, 30-day, 9% note dated March 17 in granting Juan Torres a time extension on his past-due account receivable.
Apr. 16   Torres dishonors his note when presented for payment.
May   1   Wrote off the Torres account against the Allowance for Doubtful Accounts.
June  1   Received the Shandi payment for principal and interest on the note dated March 3.

**Exercise 7-8**
Notes receivable transactions and entries

C2  P3  P4

**Check**  Dec. 31, Cr. Interest Revenue $40

**Check**  Feb. 11, Dr. Cash $10,133

**Check**  June 1, Dr. Cash $4,100

---

The following information is from the annual financial statements of Waseem Company. Compute its accounts receivable turnover for 2004 and 2005. Compare the two years results and give a possible explanation for any change (competitors average a turnover of 11).

|  | 2005 | 2004 | 2003 |
| --- | --- | --- | --- |
| Net sales . . . . . . . . . . . . . . . . . . . . . . . . | $305,000 | $236,000 | $288,000 |
| Accounts receivable (December 31) . . . . . . . | 22,900 | 20,700 | 17,400 |

**Exercise 7-9**
Accounts receivable turnover

A1

---

Atlas Co. allows select customers to make purchases on credit. Its other customers can use either of two credit cards: Zisa or Access. Zisa deducts a 3% service charge for sales on its credit card and credits the bank account of Atlas immediately when credit card receipts are deposited. Atlas deposits the Zisa credit card receipts each business day. When customers use Access credit cards, Atlas accumulates the receipts for several days before submitting them to Access for payment. Access deducts a 2% service charge and usually pays within one week of being billed. Atlas completes the

**PROBLEM SET A**

**Problem 7-1A**
Sales on account and credit card sales

C1

following transactions in June. (The terms of all credit sales are 2/15, n/30, and all sales are recorded at the gross price.)

June  4  Sold $750 of merchandise (that had cost $500) on credit to Anne Cianci.
        5  Sold merchandise for $5,900 (that had cost $3,200) to customers who used their Zisa credit cards.
        6  Sold merchandise for $4,800 (that had cost $2,800) to customers who used their Access credit cards.
        8  Sold merchandise for $3,200 (that had cost $1,900) to customers who used their Access credit cards.
        10  Submitted Access card receipts accumulated since June 6 to the credit card company for payment.
        13  Wrote off the account of Nakia Wells against the Allowance for Doubtful Accounts. The $329 balance in Wells' account stemmed from a credit sale in October of last year.

**Check**  June 17, Dr. Cash $7,840
        17  Received the amount due from Access.
        18  Received Cianci's check paying for the purchase of June 4.

**Required**

Prepare journal entries to record the preceding transactions and events. (The company uses the perpetual inventory system.)

---

**Problem 7-2A**

Accounts receivable transactions and bad debts adjustments

C1  P1  P2

Lopez Company began operations on January 1, 2004. During its first two years, the company completed a number of transactions involving sales on credit, accounts receivable collections, and bad debts. These transactions are summarized as follows:

*2004*

a. Sold $1,803,750 of merchandise (that had cost $1,475,000) on credit, terms n/30.

b. Wrote off $20,300 of uncollectible accounts receivable.

c. Received $789,200 cash in payment of accounts receivable.

**Check**  (d) Dr. Bad Debts Expense $35,214

d. In adjusting the accounts on December 31, the company estimated that 1.5% of accounts receivable will be uncollectible.

*2005*

e. Sold $1,825,700 of merchandise (that had cost $1,450,000) on credit, terms n/30.

f. Wrote off $28,800 of uncollectible accounts receivable.

g. Received $1,304,800 cash in payment of accounts receivable.

**Check**  (h) Dr. Bad Debts Expense $36,181

h. In adjusting the accounts on December 31, the company estimated that 1.5% of accounts receivable will be uncollectible.

**Required**

Prepare journal entries to record Lopez's 2004 and 2005 summarized transactions and its year-end adjustments to record bad debts expense. (The company uses the perpetual inventory system.)

---

**Problem 7-3A**

Estimating and reporting bad debts

P1  P2

On December 31, 2005, Ethan Co. records show the following results for the calendar-year:

| | |
|---|---|
| Cash sales . . . . . . . . . | $1,803,750 |
| Credit sales . . . . . . . . | 3,534,000 |

In addition, its unadjusted trial balance includes the following items:

| | |
|---|---|
| Accounts receivable . . . . . . . . . . . . . . . . . | $1,070,100 debit |
| Allowance for doubtful accounts . . . . . . . . | 15,750 debit |

**Required**

1. Prepare the adjusting entry for Ethan Co. to recognize bad debts under each of the following independent assumptions:

    a. Bad debts are estimated to be 2% of credit sales.

    b. Bad debts are estimated to be 1% of total sales.

**Check**  Bad Debts Expense:
(1a) $70,680, (1c) $69,255

    c. An aging analysis estimates that 5% of year-end accounts receivable are uncollectible.

**2.** Show how Accounts Receivable and the Allowance for Doubtful Accounts appear on the December 31, 2005, balance sheet given the facts in part 1*a*.

**3.** Show how Accounts Receivable and the Allowance for Doubtful Accounts appear on the December 31, 2005, balance sheet given the facts in part 1*c*.

---

Carmack Company has credit sales of $2.6 million for year 2005. On December 31, 2005, the company's Allowance for Doubtful Accounts has an unadjusted credit balance of $13,400. Carmack prepares a schedule of its December 31, 2005, accounts receivable by age. On the basis of past experience, it estimates the percent of receivables in each age category that will become uncollectible. This information is summarized here:

**Problem 7-4A**
Aging accounts receivable and accounting for bad debts

P1   P2

| December 31, 2005 Accounts Receivable | Age of Accounts Receivable | Expected Percent Uncollectible |
|---|---|---|
| $730,000 | Not yet due | 1.25% |
| 354,000 | 1 to 30 days past due | 2.00 |
| 76,000 | 31 to 60 days past due | 6.50 |
| 48,000 | 61 to 90 days past due | 32.75 |
| 12,000 | Over 90 days past due | 68.00 |

**Required**

**1.** Estimate the required balance of the Allowance for Doubtful Accounts at December 31, 2005, using the aging of accounts receivable method.

**2.** Prepare the adjusting entry to record bad debts expense at December 31, 2005.

**Check**  (2) Dr. Bad Debts Expense $31,625

*Analysis Component*

**3.** On June 30, 2006, Carmack Company concludes that a customer's $3,750 receivable (created in 2005) is uncollectible and that the account should be written off. What effect will this action have on Carmack's 2006 net income? Explain.

---

The following selected transactions are from Ohlde Company:

**2004**

Dec. 16   Accepted a $9,600, 60-day, 9% note dated this day in granting Todd Duke a time extension on his past-due account receivable.

31   Made an adjusting entry to record the accrued interest on the Duke note.

**2005**

Feb. 14   Received Duke's payment of principal and interest on the note dated December 16.

Mar.  2   Accepted a $4,120, 8%, 90-day note dated this day in granting a time extension on the past-due account receivable from Mare Co.

17   Accepted a $2,400, 30-day, 7% note dated this day in granting Jolene Halaam a time extension on her past-due account receivable.

Apr. 16   Halaam dishonored her note when presented for payment.

June  2   Mare Co. refuses to pay the note that was due to Ohlde Co. on May 31. Prepare the journal entry to charge the dishonored note plus accrued interest to Mare Co.'s accounts receivable.

July 17   Received payment from Mare Co. for the maturity value of its dishonored note plus interest for 46 days beyond maturity at 8%.

Aug.  7   Accepted a $5,440, 90-day, 10% note dated this day in granting a time extension on the past-due account receivable of Birch and Byer Co.

**Problem 7-5A**
Analyzing and journalizing notes receivable transactions

C2   C3   P3   P4

**Check**  Feb. 14, Cr. Interest Revenue $108

**Check**  June 2, Cr. Interest Revenue $82

Sept.   3   Accepted a $2,080, 60-day, 10% note dated this day in granting Kevin York a time exten-
            sion on his past-due account receivable.

Nov.    2   Received payment of principal plus interest from York for the September 3 note.

Nov.    5   Received payment of principal plus interest from Birch and Byer for the August 7 note.

Dec.    1   Wrote off the Jolene Halaam account against Allowance for Doubtful Accounts.

**Required**

**1.** Prepare journal entries to record these transactions and events.

*Analysis Component*

**2.** What reporting is necessary when a business pledges receivables as security for a loan and the
    loan is still outstanding at the end of the period? Explain the reason for this requirement and the
    accounting principle being satisfied.

# PROBLEM SET B

## Problem 7-1B

Sales on account and credit
card sales

C1

Able Co. allows select customers to make purchases on credit. Its other customers can use either of
two credit cards: Commerce Bank or Aztec. Commerce Bank deducts a 3% service charge for sales
on its credit card and immediately credits the bank account of Able when credit card receipts are deposited. Able deposits the Commerce Bank credit card receipts each business day. When customers
use the Aztec card, Able accumulates the receipts for several days and then submits them to Aztec
for payment. Aztec deducts a 2% service charge and usually pays within one week of being billed.
Able completed the following transactions in August (terms of all credit sales are 2/10, n/30; and all
sales are recorded at the gross price).

Aug.    4   Sold $2,780 of merchandise (that had cost $1,750) on credit to Stacy Dalton.
       10   Sold merchandise for $3,248 (that had cost $2,456) to customers who used their Commerce
            Bank credit cards.
       11   Sold merchandise for $1,575 (that had cost $1,150) to customers who used their Aztec cards.
       14   Received Dalton's check paying for the purchase of August 4.
       15   Sold merchandise for $2,960 (that had cost $1,758) to customers who used their Aztec cards.
       18   Submitted Aztec card receipts accumulated since August 11 to the credit card company for
            payment.
       22   Wrote off the account of Ness City against the Allowance for Doubtful Accounts. The $398
            balance in Ness City's account stemmed from a credit sale in November of last year.

       25   Received the amount due from Aztec.

**Required**

Prepare journal entries to record the preceding transactions and events. (The company uses the perpetual inventory system.)

## Problem 7-2B

Accounts receivable transactions
and bad debts adjustments

C1  P1  P2

Crist Co. began operations on January 1, 2004, and completed several transactions during 2004 and
2005 that involved sales on credit, accounts receivable collections, and bad debts. These transactions
are summarized as follows:

*2004*

**a.** Sold $673,490 of merchandise (that had cost $500,000) on credit, terms n/30.

**b.** Received $437,250 cash in payment of accounts receivable.

**c.** Wrote off $8,330 of uncollectible accounts receivable.

**d.** In adjusting the accounts on December 31, the company estimated that 1% of accounts receivable
    will be uncollectible.

*2005*

**e.** Sold $930,100 of merchandise (that had cost $650,000) on credit, terms n/30.

**f.** Received $890,220 cash in payment of accounts receivable.

**g.** Wrote off $10,090 of uncollectible accounts receivable.

**h.** In adjusting the accounts on December 31, the company estimated that 1% of accounts receivable
    will be uncollectible.

**Required**

Prepare journal entries to record Crist's 2004 and 2005 summarized transactions and its year-end adjusting entry to record bad debts expense. (The company uses the perpetual inventory system.)

On December 31, 2005, Klimek Co.'s records show the following results for the year:

**Problem 7-3B**
Estimating and reporting
bad debts

P1   P2

| | |
|---|---|
| Cash sales . . . . . . . . . | $1,015,000 |
| Credit sales . . . . . . . | 1,241,000 |

In addition, its unadjusted trial balance includes the following items:

| | |
|---|---|
| Accounts receivable . . . . . . . . . . . . . . . . | $475,000 debit |
| Allowance for doubtful accounts . . . . . . . | 5,200 credit |

**Required**

**1.** Prepare the adjusting entry for Klimek Co. to recognize bad debts under each of the following independent assumptions:

   **a.** Bad debts are estimated to be 2.5% of credit sales.

   **b.** Bad debts are estimated to be 1.5% of total sales.

   **c.** An aging analysis estimates that 6% of year-end accounts receivable are uncollectible.

**Check**  Bad debts expense:
(1*b*) $33,840, (1*c*) $23,300

**2.** Show how Accounts Receivable and the Allowance for Doubtful Accounts appear on the December
31, 2005, balance sheet given the facts in part 1*a*.

**3.** Show how Accounts Receivable and the Allowance for Doubtful Accounts appear on the December
31, 2005, balance sheet given the facts in part 1*c*.

---

Quisp Company has credit sales of $3.5 million for year 2005. On December 31, 2005, the company's
Allowance for Doubtful Accounts has an unadjusted debit balance of $4,100. Quisp prepares a schedule
of its December 31, 2005, accounts receivable by age. On the basis of past experience, it estimates
the percent of receivables in each age category that will become uncollectible. This information is
summarized here:

**Problem 7-4B**
Aging accounts receivable and
accounting for bad debts

P1   P2

| File Edit View Insert Format Tools Data Accounting Window Help | | |
|---|---|---|
| | | |
| **A** | **B** | **C** |
| **December 31, 2005 Accounts Receivable** | **Age of Accounts Receivable** | **Expected Percent Uncollectible** |
| $296,400 | Not yet due | 2.0% |
| 177,800 | 1 to 30 days past due | 4.0 |
| 58,000 | 31 to 60 days past due | 8.5 |
| 7,600 | 61 to 90 days past due | 39.0 |
| 3,700 | Over 90 days past due | 82.0 |

**Required**

**1.** Compute the required balance of the Allowance for Doubtful Accounts at December 31, 2005, using the aging of accounts receivable method.

**2.** Prepare the adjusting entry to record bad debts expense at December 31, 2005.

**Check**  (2) Dr. Bad Debts Expense
$28,068

*Analysis Component*

**3.** On July 31, 2006, Quisp concludes that a customer's $2,345 receivable (created in 2005) is un-
collectible and that the account should be written off. What effect will this action have on Quisp's
2006 net income? Explain.

## Problem 7-5B
Analyzing and journalizing notes
receivable transactions

C2   C3   P3   P4

The following selected transactions are from Seeker Company:

**2004**

Nov.  1   Accepted a $4,800, 90-day, 8% note dated this day in granting Julie Stephens a time extension on her past-due account receivable.

Dec.  31   Made an adjusting entry to record the accrued interest on the Stephens note.

**2005**

**Check**   Jan. 30, Cr. Interest
Revenue $32

Jan.  30   Received Stephens's payment for principal and interest on the note dated November 1.

Feb.  28   Accepted a $12,600, 6%, 30-day note dated this day in granting a time extension on the past-due account receivable from Kramer Co.

Mar.  1   Accepted a $6,200, 60-day, 8% note dated this day in granting Shelly Myers a time extension on her past-due account receivable.

      30   The Kramer Co. dishonored its note when presented for payment.

**Check**   April 30, Cr. Interest
Revenue $83

April 30   Received payment of principal plus interest from Myers for the March 1 note.

June  15   Accepted a $2,000, 60-day, 10% note dated this day in granting a time extension on the past-due account receivable of Rhonda Rye.

      21   Accepted a $9,500, 90-day, 12% note dated this day in granting Jack Striker a time extension on his past-due account receivable.

Aug.  14   Received payment of principal plus interest from R. Rye for the note of June 15.

**Check**   Sep. 19, Cr. Interest
Revenue $285

Sep.  19   Received payment of principal plus interest from J. Striker for the June 21 note.

Nov.  30   Wrote off Kramer Co.'s account against Allowance for Doubtful Accounts.

### Required

**1.** Prepare journal entries to record these transactions and events.

### Analysis Component

**2.** What reporting is necessary when a business pledges receivables as security for a loan and the loan is still outstanding at the end of the period? Explain the reason for this requirement and the accounting principle being satisfied.

# PROBLEM SET C

Problem Set C is available at the book's Website to further reinforce and assess your learning.

# SERIAL PROBLEM

Success Systems

*(This serial problem began in Chapter 1 and continues through most of the book. If previous chapter segments were not completed, the serial problem can begin at this point. It is helpful, but not necessary, that you use the Working Papers that accompany the book.)*

Kay Breeze, owner of Success Systems, realizes that she needs to begin accounting for bad debts expense. Assume that Success Systems has total revenues of $43,853 during the first three months of 2005. The Accounts Receivable balance on March 31, 2005, is $22,720.

### Required

**1.** Prepare the adjusting entry needed for Success Systems to recognize bad debts expense on March 31, 2005, under each of the following independent assumptions (assume a zero balance in the Allowance for Doubtful Accounts at March 31).

   **a.** Bad debts are estimated to be 1% of total revenues.

   **b.** Bad debts are estimated to be 2% of accounts receivable.

**2.** Assume that Success Systems's Accounts Receivable balance at June 30, 2005, is $20,250 and that one account of $100 has been written off against the Allowance for Doubtful Accounts since March 31, 2005. If Breeze uses the method prescribed in Part 1*b*, what adjusting journal entry must be made to recognize bad debts expense on June 30, 2005?

**3.** Should Breeze consider adopting the direct write-off method of accounting for bad debts expense rather than one of the allowance methods considered in part 1?

## BEYOND THE NUMBERS

**BTN 7-1**   Refer to **Krispy Kreme**'s financial statements in Appendix A to answer the following:

**1.** What is the amount of its accounts receivable (net) on February 2, 2003?

**2.** Krispy Kreme's most liquid assets include (a) Cash and Cash Equivalents, (b) Short-Term Investments, (c) Accounts Receivable, (d) Accounts Receivable, Affiliates, and (e) Other Receivables. Compute the percent that liquid assets are of current liabilities as of February 2, 2003. Do the same for February 3, 2002. Comment on the company's ability to satisfy current liabilities at the end of the fiscal year 2003 as compared to the end of fiscal year 2002.

**3.** What criteria did Krispy Kreme's use to classify items as cash equivalents?

**4.** Compute Krispy Kreme's accounts receivable turnover as of February 2, 2003.

*Roll On*

**5.** Access Krispy Kreme's financial statements for fiscal years ending after February 2, 2003, at its Website (**KrispyKreme.com**) or the SEC's EDGAR database (**www.sec.gov**). Recompute parts 2 and 4 and comment on any changes since February 2, 2003.

**REPORTING IN ACTION**

A1

---

**BTN 7-2**   Key comparative figures ($ thousands) for both **Krispy Kreme** and **Tastykake** follow:

| Key Figures | Krispy Kreme | | | Tastykake | | |
| --- | --- | --- | --- | --- | --- | --- |
| | Current Year | One-Year Prior | Two-Years Prior | Current Year | One-Year Prior | Two-Years Prior |
| Allowance for doubtful accounts . . . . . . . . . . . | $ 1,453 | $ 1,182 | $ 1,302 | $ 3,606 | $ 3,752 | $ 3,329 |
| Accounts receivable, net .. | 34,373 | 26,894 | 19,855 | 20,882 | 22,233 | 20,772 |
| Net sales . . . . . . . . . . . . | 491,549 | 394,354 | 300,715 | 162,263 | 166,245 | 162,877 |

**COMPARATIVE ANALYSIS**

A1  P2

**Required**

**1.** Compute the accounts receivable turnover for both Krispy Kreme and Tastykake for each of the two most recent years using the data shown.

**2.** Using results from part 1, compute how many days it takes each company, *on average,* to collect receivables.

**3.** Which company is more efficient in collecting its accounts receivable?

**4.** Which company estimates a higher percent of uncollectible accounts receivable?

**Hint:** Average collection period equals 365 divided by the accounts receivable turnover.

---

**BTN 7-3**   Kelly Steinman is the manager of a medium-size company. A few years ago, Steinman persuaded the owner to base a part of her compensation on the net income the company earns each year. Each December she estimates year-end financial figures in anticipation of the bonus she will receive. If the bonus is not as high as she would like, she offers several recommendations to the accountant for year-end adjustments. One of her favorite recommendations is for the controller to reduce the estimate of doubtful accounts.

**ETHICS CHALLENGE**

P1  P2

**Required**

**1.** What effect does lowering the estimate for doubtful accounts have on the income statement and balance sheet?

**2.** Do you think Steinman's recommendation to adjust the allowance for doubtful accounts is within her right as manager, or do you think this action is an ethics violation? Justify your response.

**3.** What type of internal control(s) might be useful for this company in overseeing the manager's recommendations for accounting changes?

## COMMUNICATING IN PRACTICE

P1    P2

**BTN 7-4**    As the accountant for Pure-Air Distributing, you attend a sales managers' meeting devoted to a discussion of credit policies. At the meeting, you report that bad debts expense is estimated to be $59,000 and accounts receivable at year-end amount to $1,750,000 less a $43,000 allowance for doubtful accounts. Sid Omar, a sales manager, expresses confusion over why bad debts expense and the allowance for doubtful accounts are different amounts. Write a one-page memorandum to him explaining why a difference in bad debts expense and the allowance for doubtful accounts is not unusual. The company estimates bad debts expense as 2% of sales.

## TAKING IT TO THE NET

C1

mhhe.com/wild3e

**BTN 7-5**    Access **Surg II, Inc.**'s, February 7, 2003, filing of its 10-KSB (small business 10-K) for the fiscal year-end of December 31, 2002 at **www.sec.gov**.

### Required

**1.** How does its accounts receivable balance for the fiscal year-end 2002 compare with its fiscal year-end 2001 balance?

**2.** What event accounts for its 2002 accounts receivable balance being zero?

## TEAMWORK IN ACTION

P2

**BTN 7-6**    Each member of a team is to participate in estimating uncollectibles using the aging schedule and percents shown in Problem 7-4A. The division of labor is up to the team. Your goal is to accurately complete this task as soon as possible. After estimating uncollectibles, check your estimate with the instructor. If the estimate is correct, the team then should prepare the adjusting entry and the presentation of accounts receivable (net) for the December 31, 2005, balance sheet.

## BUSINESS WEEK ACTIVITY

C1    P1

mhhe.com/wild3e

**BTN 7-7**    Read the article "How Plastic Put **Sears** in a Pickle" in the October 30, 2002, issue of *Business Week*. (The book's Website provides a free link.)

### Required

**1.** What two types of credit cards does Sears issue to its customers?

**2.** What is Sears' overall bad-debt charge-off rate as a percent of its receivables?

**3.** How many years does it usually take before a retailer's charge-off rates on new charge card programs peak?

**4.** What are the average balances carried by customers on the Sears MasterCard and on the Sears card? How do these balances compare to balances carried by consumers on general-purchase cards?

## ENTREPRENEURIAL DECISION

C1

**BTN 7-8**    The chapter's opening feature introduces Barbara Manzi and her business, **Manzi Metals**, a distributor of aluminum, steel, titanium, brass, and other alloys. Manzi Metals generates $3 million in annual sales. Assume that all sales are cash sales and that Manzi's net profit margin is 30%. Manzi's buyers would like to either use credit cards with their purchases or buy on credit. Therefore, Manzi has decided to pursue one of two plans (neither plan will impact cash sales nor alter current costs as a percent of sales):

**Plan A.** *Manzi accepts credit cards.* This plan is expected to yield new credit sales equal to 20% of current cash sales. Cost estimates of this plan as a percent of net credit sales are: credit card fee, 4.8%; recordkeeping, 1.2%.

**Plan B.** *Manzi grants credit directly to qualified buyers.* This plan is expected to yield new credit sales equal to 24% of current cash sales. Cost estimates of this plan as a percent of net credit sales are: uncollectibles, 6.7%; collection expenses, 1.3%; recordkeeping, 2.0%.

**Check**    (1b) Net income, $12,000

### Required

**1.** Compute the *added* monthly net income (loss) expected under (*a*) Plan A and (*b*) Plan B.

**2.** Should Manzi pursue either plan? Discuss the financial and nonfinancial factors relevant to this decision.

**BTN 7-9**  Many commercials include comments similar to the following: "Bring your **VISA**" or "We do not accept **American Express**." Conduct your own research by contacting at least five companies via interviews, phone calls, or the Internet to determine the reason(s) companies discriminate in their use of credit cards. (The instructor may assign this as a team activity.)

**HITTING THE ROAD**

C1

**BTN 7-10**  **Grupo Bimbo**, **Krispy Kreme**, and **Tastykake**, are all competitors in the global marketplace. Review the Consolidated Balance Sheet for Grupo Bimbo for the year ended December 31, 2002, at **GrupoBimbo.com**.

**GLOBAL DECISION**

C1  P1

### Required

1. Contrast the presentation of the accounts receivable balance on the Grupo Bimbo balance sheet with that of both Krispy Kreme and Tastykake on their balance sheets in Appendix A.

2. As a potential investor in these companies, which presentation do you prefer: Grupo Bimbo's or that of Krispy Kreme and Tastykake? Explain.

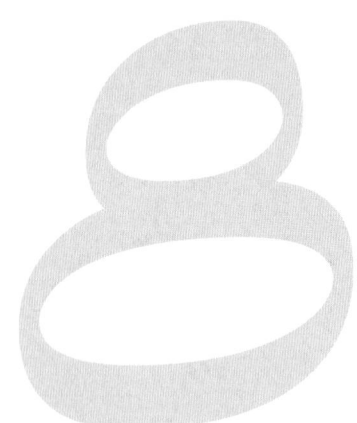

*"There are well over 2 million Hispanic owned businesses in the U.S. today"*—Tina Cordova

# 8 Reporting and Analyzing Long-Term Assets

## A Look Back

Chapters 6 and 7 focused on short-term assets: cash, cash equivalents, and receivables. We explained why they are known as liquid assets and described how companies account and report for them.

## A Look at This Chapter

This chapter introduces us to long-term assets, including plant assets, natural resource assets, and intangible assets. We explain how to account for a long-term asset's cost, the allocation of an asset's cost to periods benefiting from it, the recording of additional costs after an asset is purchased, and the disposal of an asset.

## A Look Ahead

Chapter 9 focuses on current liabilities. We explain how they are computed, recorded, and reported in financial statements. We also explain the accounting for company payroll and contingencies.

# CAP

**Conceptual**

**C1** Describe plant assets and issues in accounting for them. *(p. 310)*

**C2** Explain depreciation and the factors affecting its computation. *(p. 313)*

**C3** Explain depreciation for partial years and changes in estimates. *(p. 318)*

**Analytical**

**A1** Compare and analyze alternative depreciation methods. *(p. 317)*

**A2** Compute total asset turnover and apply it to analyze a company's use of assets. *(p. 329)*

**Procedural**

**P1** Apply the cost principle to compute the cost of plant assets. *(p. 311)*

**P2** Compute and record depreciation using the straight-line, units-of-production, and declining-balance methods. *(p. 314)*

**P3** Distinguish between revenue and capital expenditures, and account for them. *(p. 320)*

**P4** Account for asset disposal through discarding, selling, and exchanging an asset. *(p. 322)*

**P5** Account for natural resource assets and their depletion. *(p. 325)*

**P6** Account for intangible assets. *(p. 326)*

---

**Decision Feature**

# Climbing the Ladder

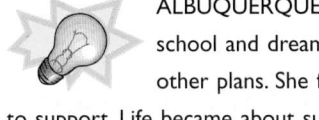

ALBUQUERQUE—Tina Cordova attended medical school and dreamed of being a doctor, but life had other plans. She found herself divorced with a child to support. Life became about survival. Cordova waited tables but something inside told her life had more to offer.

With her life savings of $5,000, she launched **Queston Construction**, a company devoted to roofing and commercial construction. When Cordova sat for the contractor's license exam, she was the only woman among more than 100 men. "Not one of them was particularly glad to see me," she laughs. Cordova soon found herself working with a crew of two men while removing old roofing, laying new roofing, and driving the dump truck. "I figured that the worst thing that could happen was that I'd have to go back to working for someone else," says Cordova. Her first-year sales of $50,000 was meager but enough to continue.

Today, Cordova oversees a crew of 28—swelling to 40 during high season—and reports annual sales of more than $3 million.

One of her greatest challenges is maintaining the right kind, size, and amount of plant assets necessary to maintain her business. Cordova says that maintaining a strong sales to assets ratio is crucial. This includes monitoring and controlling asset costs ranging from expensive construction equipment and trucks to building and land costs. To be successful, Cordova's sales must cover these plant asset costs as well as yield a return adequate to pay other expenses and meet income goals. This chapter focuses on these and other crucial issues related to long-term assets. Cordova says that effective acquisition, use, and disposal of long-term assets are keys to business success.

Cordova doesn't look back at her dreams and what might have been. "Never in a million years," insists Cordova. "I have found my place." That place is at the top of the ladder.

[Sources: *Hispanic Magazine*, April 2003; *Small Business Association Website*, October 2002; *House of Representatives Committee on Small Business*, August 2001.]

This chapter focuses on long-term assets used to operate a company. These assets can be grouped into plant assets, natural resource assets, and intangible assets. Plant assets are a major investment for most companies. They make up a large part of assets on most balance sheets, and they yield depreciation, often one of the largest expenses on income statements. The acquisition or building of a plant asset is often referred to as a *capital expenditure*. Capital expenditures

are important events because they impact both the short- and long-term success of a company. Natural resource assets and intangible assets have similar impacts. This chapter describes the purchase and use of these assets. We also explain what distinguishes these assets from other types of assets, how to determine their cost, how to allocate their costs to periods benefiting from their use, and how to dispose of them.

## Section 1—Plant Assets

**Plant assets** are tangible assets used in a company's operations that have a useful life of more than one accounting period. Plant assets are also called *plant and equipment; property, plant, and equipment;* or *fixed assets.* For many companies, plant assets make up the single largest class of assets they own. Exhibit 8.1 shows plant assets as a percent of total assets for several companies. Not only do they make up a large percent of these companies' assets but also their dollar values are large. **McDonald's** plant assets, for instance, are reported at more than $18 billion, and **Wal-Mart** reports plant assets of more than $48 billion.

**Exhibit 8.1**

Plant Assets of Selected Companies

As a percent of total assets

**C1** Describe plant assets and issues in accounting for them.

Plant assets are set apart from other assets by two important features. First, *plant assets are used in operations.* This makes them different from, for instance, inventory that is held for sale and not used in operations. The distinctive feature here is use, not type of asset. A company that purchases a computer to resell it, reports it on the balance sheet as inventory. If the same company purchases this computer to use in operations, however, it is a plant asset. Another example is land held for future expansion, which is reported as a long-term investment. However, if this land holds a factory used in operations, the land is part of plant assets. Another example is equipment held for use in the event of a breakdown or for peak periods of production, which is reported in plant assets. If this same equipment is removed from use and held for sale, however, it is not reported in plant assets.

The second important feature is that *plant assets have useful lives extending over more than one accounting period.* This makes plant assets different from current assets such as supplies that are normally consumed in a short time period after they are placed in use.

**Point:** Amazon.com's plant assets of $239 million make up 12% of its total assets.

The accounting for plant assets reflects these two features. Since plant assets are used in operations, we try to match their costs against the revenues they generate. Also, since their useful lives extend over more than one period, our matching of costs and revenues must extend over several periods. Specifically, we value plant assets (balance sheet effect) and then allocate their costs to periods benefiting from their use (income statement effect).

Exhibit 8.2 shows four main issues in accounting for plant assets: (1) computing the costs of plant assets, (2) allocating the costs of plant assets (less any salvage amounts) against revenues for the periods they benefit, (3) accounting for expenditures such as repairs and improvements to plant assets, and (4) recording the disposal of plant assets. The following sections discuss these issues.

**Point:** It can help to view plant assets as prepaid expenses that benefit several future accounting periods.

Topic Tackler 8-1

## Exhibit 8.2

Issues in Accounting for Plant Assets

Decline in asset value over its useful life

**Acquisition**
1. Compute cost

**Use**
2. Allocate cost to periods benefited
3. Account for subsequent expenditures

**Disposal**
4. Record disposal

## Cost Determination

Plant assets are recorded at cost when acquired. This is consistent with the *cost principle.* **Cost** includes all normal and reasonable expenditures necessary to get the asset in place and ready for its intended use. The cost of a factory machine, for instance, includes its invoice cost less any cash discount for early payment, plus any necessary freight, unpacking, assembling, installing, and testing costs. Examples are the costs of building a base or foundation for a machine, providing electrical hook-ups, and testing the asset before using it in operations.

To be recorded as part of the cost of a plant asset, an expenditure must be normal, reasonable, and necessary in preparing it for its intended use. If an asset is damaged during unpacking, the repairs are not added to its cost. Instead, they are charged to an expense account. Nor is a paid traffic fine for moving heavy machinery on city streets without a proper permit part of the machinery's cost; but payment for a proper permit is included in the cost of machinery. Charges are sometimes incurred to modify or customize a new plant asset. These charges are added to the asset's cost. We explain in this section how to determine the cost of plant assets for each of its four major classes.

**Global:** International accounting standards encourage use of the cost principle for plant assets. Plant asset revaluation is permitted if it is consistently applied across periods.

### Land

When land is purchased for a building site, its cost includes the total amount paid for the land, including any real estate commissions, title insurance fees, legal fees, and any accrued property taxes paid by the purchaser. Payments for surveying, clearing, grading, and draining also are included in the cost of land. Other costs include government assessments, whether incurred at the time of purchase or later, for items such as public roadways, sewers, and sidewalks. These assessments are included because they permanently add to the land's value. Land purchased as a building site sometimes includes structures that must be removed. In such cases, the total purchase price is charged to the Land account as is the cost of removing the structures, less any amounts recovered through sale of salvaged materials. To illustrate, assume the **Hockey Co.** paid $167,000 cash to acquire land for a retail

**P1** Apply the cost principle to compute the cost of plant assets.

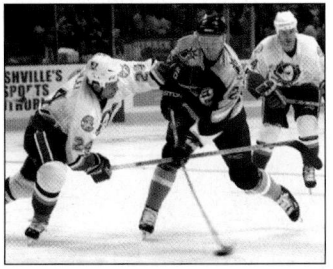

**Exhibit 8.3**

Computing Cost of Land

| | |
|---|---|
| Cash price of land . . . . . . . . . . . . . | $ 167,000 |
| Net cost of garage removal . . . . . . . | 13,000 |
| Closing costs . . . . . . . . . . . . . . . . | 10,000 |
| **Cost of land** . . . . . . . . . . . . . . . . | **$190,000** |

store. This land had an old service garage that was removed at a net cost of $13,000 ($15,000 in costs less $2,000 proceeds from salvaged materials). Additional closing costs total $10,000, consisting of brokerage fees ($8,000), legal fees ($1,500), and title costs ($500). The cost of this land to Hockey Co. is $190,000 and is computed as shown in Exhibit 8.3.

## Land Improvements

Land has an unlimited life and is not usually used up over time. **Land improvements** such as parking lot surfaces, driveways, fences, shrubs, and lighting systems, however, have limited useful lives and are used up. While the costs of these improvements increase the usefulness of the land, they are charged to a separate Land Improvement account so that their costs can be allocated to the periods they benefit.

## Buildings

A Building account is charged for the costs of purchasing or constructing a building that is used in operations. When purchased, a building's costs usually include its purchase price, brokerage fees, taxes, title fees, and attorney fees. Its costs also include all expenditures to ready it for its intended use, including any necessary repairs or renovations such as wiring, lighting, flooring, and wall coverings. When a company constructs a building or any plant asset for its own use, its costs include materials and labor plus a reasonable amount of indirect overhead cost. Overhead includes the costs of items such as heat, lighting, power, and depreciation on machinery used to construct the asset. Costs of construction also include design fees, building permits, and insurance during construction. However, costs such as insurance to cover the asset *after* it is placed in use are operating expenses.

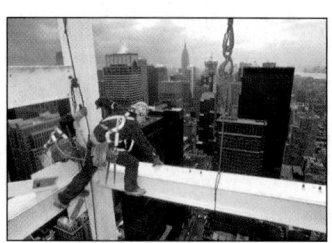

## Machinery and Equipment

The costs of machinery and equipment consist of all costs normal and necessary to purchase them and prepare them for their intended use. These include the purchase price, taxes, transportation charges, insurance while in transit, and the installing, assembling, and testing of the machinery and equipment.

## Lump-Sum Purchase

**Example:** If appraised values in Exhibit 8.4 are land, $24,000; land improvements, $12,000; and building, $84,000, what cost is assigned to the building? *Answer:*
(1) $24,000 + $12,000 + $84,000 = $120,000 (total appraisal)
(2) $84,000/$120,000 = 70% (building's percent of total)
(3) 70% × $90,000 = $63,000 (building's apportioned cost)

Plant assets sometimes are purchased as a group in a single transaction for a lump-sum price. This transaction is called a *lump-sum purchase,* or *group, bulk,* or *basket purchase.* When this occurs, we allocate the cost of the purchase among the different types of assets acquired based on their *relative market values,* which can be estimated by appraisal or by using the tax-assessed valuations of the assets. To illustrate, Oakley paid $90,000 cash to acquire a group of items consisting of land appraised at $30,000, land improvements appraised at $10,000, and a building appraised at $60,000. The $90,000 cost is allocated on the basis of these appraised values as shown in Exhibit 8.4.

**Exhibit 8.4**

Computing Costs in a Lump-Sum Purchase

| | Appraised Value | Percent of Total | Apportioned Cost |
|---|---|---|---|
| Land . . . . . . . . . . . . . . . | $ 30,000 | 30% ($30,000/$100,000) | **$27,000** ($90,000 × 30%) |
| Land improvements . . . . . . | 10,000 | 10   ($10,000/$100,000) | **9,000** ($90,000 × 10%) |
| Building . . . . . . . . . . . . . | 60,000 | 60   ($60,000/$100,000) | **54,000** ($90,000 × 60%) |
| Totals . . . . . . . . . . . . . . | $100,000 | 100% | $ 90,000 |

## Quick Check

1. Identify the asset class for each of the following: (*a*) supplies, (*b*) office equipment, (*c*) inventory, (*d*) land for future expansion, and (*e*) trucks used in operations.

2. Identify the account charged for each of the following: (*a*) purchase price of a vacant lot to be used in operations and (*b*) cost of paving that same vacant lot.

3. Calculate the amount recorded as the cost of a new machine given the following payments related to its purchase: gross purchase price, $700,000; sales tax, $49,000; purchase discount taken, $21,000; freight cost—terms FOB shipping point, $3,500; normal assembly costs, $3,000; cost of necessary foundation for machine, $2,500; cost of parts used in maintaining the machine, $4,200.

Answers—p. 334

# Depreciation

**Depreciation** is the process of allocating the cost of a plant asset to expense in the accounting periods benefiting from its use. Depreciation does not measure the decline in the asset's market value each period, nor does it measure the asset's physical deterioration. Since depreciation reflects the cost of using a plant asset, depreciation charges are only recorded when the asset is actually in service. This section describes the factors we must consider in computing depreciation, the depreciation methods used, revisions in depreciation, and depreciation for partial periods.

Topic Tackler 8-2

## Factors in Computing Depreciation

Factors that determine depreciation are (1) cost, (2) salvage value, and (3) useful life.

**C2** Explain depreciation and the factors affecting its computation.

**Cost**   The **cost** of a plant asset consists of all necessary and reasonable expenditures to acquire it and to prepare it for its intended use.

**Salvage Value**   The total amount of depreciation to be charged off over an asset's benefit period equals the asset's cost minus its salvage value. **Salvage value,** also called *residual value* or *scrap value,* is an estimate of the asset's value at the end of its benefit period. This is the amount the owner expects to receive from disposing the asset at the end of its benefit period. If the asset is expected to be traded in on a new asset, its salvage value is the expected trade-in value.

**Point:** If we expect additional costs in preparing a plant asset for disposal, the salvage value equals the expected amount from disposal less any disposal costs.

**Useful Life**   The **useful life** of a plant asset is the length of time it is productively used in a company's operations. Useful life, also called *service life,* might not be as long as the asset's total productive life. For example, the productive life of a computer can be eight years or more. Some companies, however, trade in old computers for new ones every two years. In this case, these computers have a two-year useful life, meaning the cost of these computers (less their expected trade-in values) is charged to depreciation expense over a two-year period.

**Point:** Useful life and salvage value are estimates. Estimates require judgment based on consideration of all available information.

Several variables often make the useful life of a plant asset difficult to predict. A major variable is the wear and tear from use in operations. Two other variables, inadequacy and obsolescence, also demand consideration. **Inadequacy** refers to the insufficient capacity of a company's plant assets to meet its growing productive demands. **Obsolescence** refers to a plant asset that is no longer useful in producing goods or services with a competitive advantage because of new inventions and improvements. Both inadequacy and obsolescence

### Decision Insight

**Life Line**   Life expectancy of plant assets is often in the eye of the beholder. For instance, **Converse** and **Stride Rite** are competitors, yet their buildings' life expectancies are quite different. Converse depreciates buildings over 5 to 10 years, but Stride Rite depreciates them over 10 to 40 years. Such differences markedly impact financial statements.

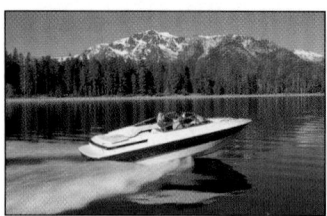

are difficult to predict because of demand changes, new inventions, and improvements. A company usually disposes of an inadequate or obsolete asset before it wears out.

A company is often able to better predict a new asset's useful life when it has past experience with a similar asset. When it has no such experience, a company relies on the experience of others or on engineering studies and judgment. In note 1 of its annual report, **Brunswick**, a manufacturer of boats and motors, reports the following useful lives:

Estimated useful lives of buildings and equipment;
Buildings . . . . . . . . .   5–40 years
Equipment . . . . . . . .   2–20 years

## Depreciation Methods

*Depreciation methods* are used to allocate a plant asset's cost over the accounting periods in its useful life. The most frequently used method of depreciation is the straight-line method. Another common depreciation method is the units-of-production method. We explain both of these methods in this section. This section also describes accelerated depreciation methods, with a focus on the declining-balance method.

The computations in this section use information about a machine that inspects athletic shoes before packaging. Manufacturers such as **Converse, Reebok, Adidas**, and **Fila** use this machine. Data for this machine are in Exhibit 8.5.

**Exhibit 8.5**

Data for Athletic Shoe-Inspecting Machine

| | |
|---|---|
| Cost . . . . . . . . . . . . . . . . . . . | $10,000 |
| Salvage value . . . . . . . . . . . . . | 1,000 |
| Depreciable cost . . . . . . . . . . | $ 9,000 |
| Useful life | |
|    Accounting periods . . . . . . . | 5 years |
|    Units inspected . . . . . . . . . | 36,000 shoes |

**P2**  Compute and record depreciation using the straight-line, units-of-production, and declining-balance methods.

**Straight-Line Method**   **Straight-line depreciation** charges the same amount of expense to each period of the asset's useful life. A two-step process is used. We first compute the *depreciable cost* of the asset; this amount is also called the *cost to be depreciated*. It is computed by subtracting the asset's salvage value from its total cost. Second, depreciable cost is divided by the number of accounting periods in the asset's useful life. The formula for straight-line depreciation, along with its computation for the inspection machine described above, is shown in Exhibit 8.6.

**Exhibit 8.6**

Straight-Line Depreciation Formula and Example

$$\frac{\textbf{Cost} - \textbf{Salvage value}}{\textbf{Useful life in periods}} = \frac{\$10,000 - \$1,000}{5 \text{ years}} = \$1,800 \text{ per year}$$

If this machine is purchased on December 31, 2003, and used throughout its predicted useful life of five years, the straight-line method allocates an equal amount of depreciation to each of the years 2004 through 2008. We make the following adjusting entry at the end of each of the five years to record straight-line depreciation of this machine:

Assets  = Liabilities + Equity
−1,800                    −1,800

| Dec. 31 | Depreciation Expense . . . . . . . . . . . . . . . . . . . . . | 1,800 | |
| |    Accumulated Depreciation—Machinery . . . . . | | 1,800 |
| | *To record annual depreciation.* | | |

The $1,800 Depreciation Expense is reported on the income statement among operating expenses. The $1,800 Accumulated Depreciation is a contra asset account to the Machinery account in the balance sheet. The graph on the left in Exhibit 8.7 shows the $1,800 per year expenses reported in each of the five years. The graph on the right shows the amounts reported on each of the six December 31 balance sheets while the company owns the asset.

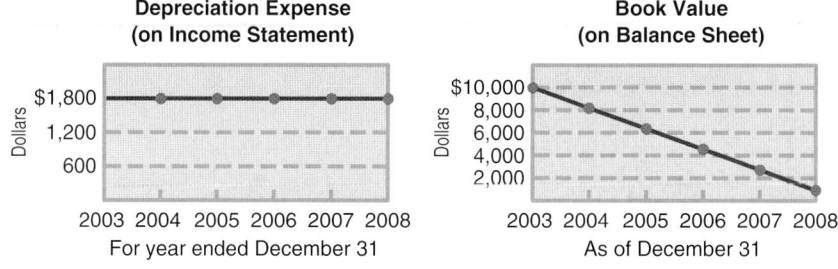

**Exhibit 8.7**

Financial Statement Effects of Straight-Line Depreciation

The net balance sheet amount is the asset's **book value** and is computed as the asset's total cost less its accumulated depreciation. For example, at the end of year 2 (December 31, 2005), its book value is $6,400 and is reported in the balance sheet as follows:

| | | |
|---|---|---|
| Machinery . . . . . . . . . . . . . . . . . . . . . . | $10,000 | |
| Less accumulated depreciation . . . . . . . | 3,600 | $6,400 |

The book value of this machine declines by $1,800 each year due to depreciation. From the graphs in Exhibit 8.7 we can see why this method is called straight line.

We also can compute the *straight-line depreciation rate,* defined as 100% divided by the number of periods in the asset's useful life. For the inspection machine, this rate is 20% (100% ÷ 5 years). We use this rate, along with other information, to compute the machine's *straight-line depreciation schedule* shown in Exhibit 8.8. Note three points in Exhibit 8.8. First, depreciation expense is the same each period. Second, accumulated depreciation is the sum of current and prior periods' depreciation expense. Third, book value declines each period until it equals salvage value at the end of the machine's useful life.

**Point:** Depreciation requires estimates for salvage value and useful life. Decision ethics are relevant when managers might be tempted to choose estimates to achieve desired results on financial statements.

| Annual Period | Depreciation for the Period | | | End of Period | |
|---|---|---|---|---|---|
| | Depreciable Cost* | Depreciation Rate | Depreciation Expense | Accumulated Depreciation | Book Value† |
| 2003 | — | — | — | — | $10,000 |
| 2004 | $9,000 | 20% | **$1,800** | $1,800 | 8,200 |
| 2005 | 9,000 | 20 | **1,800** | 3,600 | 6,400 |
| 2006 | 9,000 | 20 | **1,800** | 5,400 | 4,600 |
| 2007 | 9,000 | 20 | **1,800** | 7,200 | 2,800 |
| 2008 | 9,000 | 20 | **1,800** | 9,000 | **1,000** |

**Exhibit 8.8**

Straight-Line Depreciation Schedule

\* $10,000 − $1,000.      † Book value is total cost minus accumulated depreciation.

**Units-of-Production Method**   The straight-line method charges an equal share of an asset's cost to each period. If plant assets are used up in about equal amounts each accounting period, this method produces a reasonable matching of expenses with revenues. However, the use of some plant assets varies greatly from one period to the next. A builder, for instance, might use a piece of construction equipment for a month and then not use it again for several months. When equipment use varies from period to period, the units-of-production depreciation method can better match expenses with revenues. **Units-of-production depreciation** charges a varying amount to expense for each period of an asset's useful life depending on its usage.

A two-step process is used to compute units-of-production depreciation. We first compute *depreciation per unit* by subtracting the asset's salvage value from its total cost and then dividing by the total number of units expected to be produced during its useful life. Units of production can be expressed in product or other units such as hours used or miles driven. The second step is to compute depreciation expense for the period by multiplying the units produced in the period by the depreciation per unit. The formula for units-of-production depreciation, along with its computation for the machine described in Exhibit 8.5, is shown in Exhibit 8.9. (*Note:* 7,000 shoes are inspected and sold in its first year.)

## Exhibit 8.9

Units-of-Production Depreciation Formula and Example

**Step 1**

$$\text{Depreciation per unit} = \frac{\text{Cost} - \text{Salvage value}}{\text{Total units of production}} = \frac{\$10,000 - \$1,000}{36,000 \text{ shoes}} = \$0.25 \text{ per shoe}$$

**Step 2**

$$\text{Depreciation expense} = \text{Depreciation per unit} \times \text{Units produced in period}$$
$$\$0.25 \text{ per shoe} \times 7,000 \text{ shoes} = \$1,750$$

Using data on the number of shoes inspected by the machine, we can compute the *units-of-production depreciation schedule* shown in Exhibit 8.10. For example, depreciation for the first year is $1,750 (7,000 shoes at $0.25 per shoe). Depreciation for the second year is $2,000 (8,000 shoes at $0.25 per shoe). Other years are similarly computed. Notice in Exhibit 8.10 that (1) depreciation expense depends on unit output, (2) accumulated depreciation is the sum of current and prior periods' depreciation expense, and (3) book value declines each period until it equals salvage value at the end of the asset's useful life. **Boise Cascade** is one of many companies using the units-of-production depreciation method. It reports that most of its "paper and wood products manufacturing facilities determine depreciation by a units-of-production method."

**Example:** Refer to Exhibit 8.10. If the number of shoes inspected in 2008 is 5,500, what is depreciation expense for that year?
*Answer:* $1,250 (never depreciate below salvage value)

## Exhibit 8.10

Units-of-Production Depreciation Schedule

| Annual Period | Depreciation for the Period | | | End of Period | |
| --- | --- | --- | --- | --- | --- |
| | Number of Units | Depreciation per Unit | Depreciation Expense | Accumulated Depreciation | Book Value |
| 2003 | — | — | — | — | $10,000 |
| 2004 | 7,000 | $0.25 | **$1,750** | $1,750 | 8,250 |
| 2005 | 8,000 | 0.25 | **2,000** | 3,750 | 6,250 |
| 2006 | 9,000 | 0.25 | **2,250** | 6,000 | 4,000 |
| 2007 | 7,000 | 0.25 | **1,750** | 7,750 | 2,250 |
| 2008 | 5,000 | 0.25 | **1,250** | 9,000 | **1,000** |

**Declining-Balance Method**   An **accelerated depreciation method** yields larger depreciation expenses in the early years of an asset's life and less depreciation in later years. Of several accelerated methods, the most common is the **declining-balance method** of depreciation, which uses a depreciation rate that is a multiple of the straight-line rate and applies it to the asset's beginning-of-period book value. The amount of depreciation declines each period because book value declines each period.

A common depreciation rate for the declining-balance method is double the straight-line rate. This is called the *double-declining-balance (DDB)* method. This method is applied in three steps: (1) compute the asset's straight-line depreciation rate, (2) double the straight-line rate, and (3) compute depreciation expense by multiplying this rate by the asset's beginning-of-period book value. To illustrate, let's return to the machine in Exhibit 8.5 and

**Global:** German firms commonly apply accelerated depreciation of up to three times the straight-line rate.

**Point:** In the DDB method, *double* refers to the rate and *declining balance* refers to book value. The rate is applied to beginning book value each period.

apply the double-declining-balance method to compute depreciation expense. Exhibit 8.11 shows the first-year depreciation computation for the machine. The three-step process is to (1) divide 100% by five years to determine the straight-line rate of 20% per year, (2) double this 20% rate to get the declining-balance rate of 40% per year, and (3) compute depreciation expense as 40% multiplied by the beginning-of-period book value.

**Exhibit 8.11**

Double-Declining-Balance Depreciation Formula

**Step 1**

**Straight-line rate = 100% ÷ Useful life** = 100% ÷ 5 years = 20%

**Step 2**

**Double-declining-balance rate = 2 × Straight-line rate** = 2 × 20% = 40%

**Step 3**

**Depreciation expense = Double-declining-balance rate × Beginning-period book value**

40% × $10,000 = $4,000 (for 2004)

The *double-declining-balance depreciation schedule* is shown in Exhibit 8.12. The schedule follows the formula except for year 2008, when depreciation expense is $296. This $296 is not equal to 40% × $1,296, or $518.40. If we had used the $518.40 for depreciation expense in 2008, ending book value would equal $777.60, which is less than the $1,000 salvage value. Instead, the $296 is computed by subtracting the $1,000 salvage value from the $1,296 book value at the beginning of the fifth year (the year when DDB depreciation cuts into salvage value).

**Example:** What is DDB depreciation expense in year 2007 if the salvage value is $2,000? *Answer:* $2,160 − $2,000 = $160

**Exhibit 8.12**

Double-Declining-Balance Depreciation Schedule

| Annual Period | Depreciation for the Period | | | End of Period | |
|---|---|---|---|---|---|
| | Beginning of Period Book Value | Depreciation Rate | Depreciation Expense | Accumulated Depreciation | Book Value |
| 2003 | — | — | — | — | $10,000 |
| 2004 | $10,000 | 40% | **$4,000** | $4,000 | 6,000 |
| 2005 | 6,000 | 40 | **2,400** | 6,400 | 3,600 |
| 2006 | 3,600 | 40 | **1,440** | 7,840 | 2,160 |
| 2007 | 2,160 | 40 | **864** | 8,704 | 1,296 |
| 2008 | 1,296 | 40 | **296\*** | 9,000 | **1,000** |

\* Year 2008 depreciation is $1,296 − $1,000 = $296 (never depreciate book value below salvage value).

**Comparing Depreciation Methods** Exhibit 8.13 shows depreciation expense for each year of the machine's useful life under each of the three depreciation methods.

**A1** Compare and analyze alternative depreciation methods.

**Exhibit 8.13**

Depreciation Expense for the Different Methods

| Period | Straight-Line | Units-of-Production | Double-Declining-Balance |
|---|---|---|---|
| 2004 | $1,800 | $1,750 | $4,000 |
| 2005 | 1,800 | 2,000 | 2,400 |
| 2006 | 1,800 | 2,250 | 1,440 |
| 2007 | 1,800 | 1,750 | 864 |
| 2008 | 1,800 | 1,250 | 296 |
| Totals | $9,000 | $9,000 | $9,000 |

While the amount of depreciation expense per period differs for different methods, total depreciation expense is the same over the machine's useful life. Each method starts with a total cost of $10,000 and ends with a salvage value of $1,000. The difference is the pattern

**Global:** Some Canadian companies use an "increasing charge" depreciation (the opposite of accelerated).

**Vogue** About 83% of companies use straight-line depreciation for plant assets, 5% use units-of-production, and 4% use declining-balance. Another 8% use an unspecified accelerated method—most likely declining-balance.

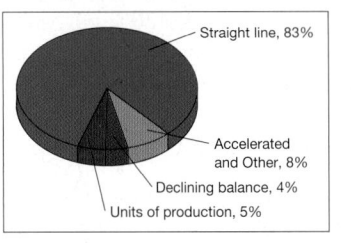

Straight line, 83%

Accelerated and Other, 8%

Declining balance, 4%

Units of production, 5%

in depreciation expense over the useful life. The book value of the asset when using straight-line is always greater than the book value from using double-declining-balance, except at the beginning and end of the asset's useful life, when it is the same. Also, the straight-line method yields a steady pattern of depreciation expense while the units-of-production depreciation depends on the number of units produced. Each of these methods is acceptable because it allocates cost in a systematic and rational manner.

**Depreciation for Tax Reporting** The records a company keeps for financial accounting purposes are usually separate from the records it keeps for tax accounting purposes. This is so because financial accounting aims to report useful information on financial performance and position, whereas tax accounting reflects government objectives in raising revenues. Differences between these two accounting systems are normal and expected. Depreciation is a common example of how the records differ. For example, many companies use accelerated depreciation in computing taxable income. Reporting higher depreciation expense in the early years of an asset's life reduces the company's taxable income in those years and increases it in later years, when the depreciation expense is lower. The company's goal here is to *postpone* its tax payments. This means the company can use these resources now to earn additional income before payment is due.

**Point:** Understanding depreciation for financial accounting will help in learning MACRS for tax accounting. Rules for MACRS are available from www.IRS.com.

**Global:** A few countries require the depreciation method chosen for financial reporting to match the method chosen for tax reporting.

The U.S. federal income tax law has rules for depreciating assets. These rules include the **Modified Accelerated Cost Recovery System (MACRS),** which allows straight-line depreciation for some assets, but it requires accelerated depreciation for most kinds of assets. MACRS separates depreciable assets into different classes and defines the depreciable life and rate for each class. MACRS is not acceptable for financial reporting because it often allocates costs over an arbitrary period that is less than the asset's useful life. Details of MACRS are covered in tax accounting courses.

**Instant Numbers** Computer technology greatly simplifies depreciation computations and revisions. Many inexpensive, off-the-shelf software packages and business calculators allow a user to choose from a variety of depreciation methods and quickly produce depreciation schedules.

## Partial-Year Depreciation

**C3** Explain depreciation for partial years and changes in estimates.

Plant assets are purchased and disposed of at various times. When an asset is purchased (or disposed of) at a time other than the beginning or end of an accounting period, depreciation is recorded for part of a year. This is done so that the year of purchase or the year of disposal is charged with its share of the asset's depreciation.

To illustrate, assume that the machine in Exhibit 8.5 is purchased and placed in service on October 8, 2003, and the annual accounting period ends on December 31. Since this machine is purchased and used for nearly three months in 2003, the calendar-year income statement should report depreciation expense on the machine for that part of the year. Normally, depreciation assumes that the asset is purchased on the first day of the month nearest the actual date of purchase. In this case, since the purchase occurred on October 8, we assume an October 1 purchase date. This means that three months' depreciation is recorded in 2003. Using straight-line depreciation, we compute three months' depreciation of $450 as follows:

$$\frac{\$10,000 - \$1,000}{5 \text{ years}} \times \frac{3}{12} = \$450$$

**Example:** If the machine's salvage value is zero and purchase occurs on Oct. 8, 2003, how much depreciation is recorded at Dec. 31, 2003? *Answer:* $10,000/5 × 3/12 = $500

A similar computation is necessary when an asset disposal occurs during a period. To illustrate, assume that the machine is sold on June 24, 2008. Depreciation is recorded for the period January 1 through June 24 when it is disposed of. This partial year's depreciation,

computed to the nearest whole month, is

$$\frac{\$10,000 - \$1,000}{5 \text{ years}} \times \frac{6}{12} = \$900$$

## Change in Estimates for Depreciation

Depreciation is based on estimates of salvage value and useful life. During the useful life of an asset, new information may indicate that these estimates are inaccurate. If our estimate of an asset's useful life and/or salvage value changes, what should we do? The answer is to use the new estimate to compute depreciation for current and future periods. This means that we revise the depreciation expense computation by spreading the cost yet to be depreciated over the remaining useful life. This approach is used for all depreciation methods.

Let's return to the machine described in Exhibit 8.8 using straight-line depreciation. At the beginning of this asset's third year, its book value is $6,400, computed as $10,000 minus $3,600. Assume that at the beginning of its third year, the estimated number of years remaining in its useful life changes from three to four years *and* its estimate of salvage value changes from $1,000 to $400. Straight-line depreciation for each of the four remaining years is computed as shown in Exhibit 8.14.

**Point:** Remaining depreciable cost equals book value less revised salvage value at the point of revision.

**Point:** Income is overstated (and depreciation understated) when useful life is too high; a useful life that is too low yields opposite results.

$$\frac{\textbf{Book value} - \textbf{Revised salvage value}}{\textbf{Revised remaining useful life}} = \frac{\$6,400 - \$400}{4 \text{ years}} = \$1,500 \text{ per year}$$

**Exhibit 8.14**

Computing Revised Straight-Line Depreciation

Thus, $1,500 of depreciation expense is recorded for the machine at the end of the third through sixth years—each year of its remaining useful life. Since this asset was depreciated at $1,800 per year for the first two years, it is tempting to conclude that depreciation expense was overstated in the first two years. However, these expenses reflected the best information available at that time. We do not go back and restate prior years' financial statements for this type of new information. Instead, we adjust the current and future periods' statements to reflect this new information. Revising an estimate of the useful life or salvage value of a plant asset is referred to as a **change in an accounting estimate** and is reflected in current and future financial statements, not in prior statements.

**Example:** If at the beginning of its second year the machine's remaining useful life changes from four to three years and salvage value from $1,000 to $400, how much straight-line depreciation is recorded in remaining years? *Answer:* Revised depreciation = ($8,200 − $400)/3 = $2,600.

## Reporting Depreciation

Both the cost and accumulated depreciation of plant assets are reported on the balance sheet or in its notes. **Titan Motorcycle**, for instance, reports the following:

| Property and equipment: | |
|---|---|
| Land, building, and vehicles . . . . . . . . . . . . . . . | $ 689,748 |
| Machinery and equipment . . . . . . . . . . . . . . . . | 1,116,318 |
| Displays and leasehold improvements . . . . . . . | 837,414 |
| Gross property and equipment . . . . . . . . . | 2,643,480 |
| Less accumulated depreciation . . . . . . . . . . . | 629,575 |
| Net property and equipment . . . . . . . . . . . | $2,013,905 |

Many companies also show plant assets on one line with the net amount of cost less accumulated depreciation. When this is done, the amount of accumulated depreciation is disclosed in a note. **Krispy Kreme** reports only the net amount of its property and equipment in its balance sheet in Appendix A. To satisfy the full-disclosure principle, Krispy Kreme describes its depreciation methods in its Note 2 and the amounts comprising plant assets in its Note 5.

Reporting both the cost and accumulated depreciation of plant assets helps users compare the assets of different companies. For example, a company holding assets costing $50,000 and accumulated depreciation of $40,000 is likely in a situation different from a company

**Point:** A company usually keeps records for each asset showing its cost and depreciation to date. The combined records for individual assets are a type of *plant asset subsidiary ledger.*

## Decision Ethics

**Controller**   You are the controller for a struggling company. Its operations require regular investments in equipment, and depreciation is its largest expense. Its competitors frequently replace equipment—often depreciated over three years. The company president instructs you to revise useful lives of equipment from three to six years and to use a six-year life on all new equipment. What actions do you take?

Answer—p. 334

**Point:** Depreciation is higher and income lower in the short run when using accelerated versus straight-line methods.

with new assets costing $10,000. While the net undepreciated cost of $10,000 is the same in both cases, the first company may have more productive capacity available but likely is facing the need to replace older assets. These insights are not provided if the two balance sheets report only the $10,000 book values.

Users must remember that plant assets are reported on a balance sheet at their undepreciated costs (book value), not at market values. This emphasis on costs rather than market values is based on the *going-concern principle* described in Chapter 1. This principle states that, unless there is evidence to the contrary, we assume that a company continues in business. This implies that plant assets are held and used long enough to recover their cost through the sale of products and services. Since plant assets are not for sale, their market values are not reported.

Accumulated Depreciation is a contra asset account with a normal credit balance. It does *not* reflect funds accumulated to buy new assets when the assets currently owned are replaced. If a company has funds available to buy assets, the funds are shown on the balance sheet among liquid assets such as Cash or Investments.

## Quick Check

4. On January 1, 2005, a company pays $77,000 to purchase office furniture with a zero salvage value. The furniture's useful life is somewhere between 7 and 10 years. What is the year 2005 straight-line depreciation on the furniture using (*a*) a 7-year useful life and (*b*) a 10-year useful life?

5. What does the term *depreciation* mean in accounting?

6. A company purchases a machine for $96,000 on January 1, 2005. Its useful life is five years or 100,000 units of product, and its salvage value is $8,000. During 2005, 10,000 units of product are produced. Compute the book value of this machine on December 31, 2005, assuming (*a*) straight-line depreciation and (*b*) units-of-production depreciation.

7. In early January 2005, a company acquires equipment for $3,800. The company estimates this equipment to have a useful life of three years and a salvage value of $200. Early in 2007, the company changes its estimates to a total four-year useful life and zero salvage value. Using the straight-line method, what is depreciation for the year ended 2007?

Answers—p. 334

# Additional Expenditures

**P3**   Distinguish between revenue and capital expenditures, and account for them.

**Point:** When an amount is said to be *capitalized* to an account, the amount is added to the account's normal balance.

| Financial Statement Effect | | | |
|---|---|---|---|
| Cost Category | Accounting | Expense Timing | Current Income |
| Revenue expenditure | Income stmt. account debited | Expensed currently | Lower |
| Capital expenditure | Balance sheet account debited | Expensed in future | Higher |

After a company acquires a plant asset and puts it into service, it often makes additional expenditures for that asset's operation, maintenance, repair, and improvement. In recording these expenditures, it must decide whether to capitalize or expense them (to capitalize an expenditure is to debit the asset account). The issue is whether more useful information is provided by reporting these expenditures as current period expenses or by adding them to the plant asset's cost and depreciating them over its remaining useful life.

**Revenue expenditures,** also called *income statement expenditures,* are additional costs of plant assets that do not materially increase the asset's life or productive capabilities. They are recorded as expenses and deducted from revenues in the current period's income statement. Examples of revenue expenditures are cleaning, repainting, adjustments, and lubricants. **Capital expenditures,** also called *balance sheet expenditures,* are additional costs of plant assets that provide benefits extending beyond the current period. They are debited to asset accounts and reported on the balance sheet. Capital expenditures increase or improve the type or amount of service an asset provides. Examples are roofing replacement, plant expansion, and major overhauls of machinery and equipment.

Financial statements are affected for several years by the accounting choice of recording costs as either revenue expenditures or capital expenditures. Managers must be careful in classifying them. This classification decision is based on whether these expenditures are identified as either ordinary repairs or as betterments and extraordinary repairs.

## Ordinary Repairs

**Ordinary repairs** are expenditures to keep an asset in normal, good operating condition. They are necessary if an asset is to perform to expectations over its useful life. Ordinary repairs do not extend an asset's useful life beyond its original estimate or increase its productivity beyond original expectations. Examples are normal costs of cleaning, lubricating, adjusting, and replacing small parts of a machine. Ordinary repairs are treated as *revenue expenditures*. This means their costs are reported as expenses on the current period income statement. Following this rule, **Brunswick** reports that "maintenance and repair costs are expensed as incurred."

**Point:** Many companies apply the *materiality principle* to treat *low-cost plant assets* (say, less than $500) as revenue expenditures.

## Betterments and Extraordinary Repairs

Accounting for betterments and extraordinary repairs is similar. **Betterments,** also called *improvements,* are expenditures that make a plant asset more efficient or productive. A betterment often involves adding a component to an asset or replacing one of its old components with a better one, and does not always increase an asset's useful life. An example is replacing manual controls on a machine with automatic controls. One special type of betterment is an *addition,* such as adding a new wing or dock to a warehouse. Since a betterment benefits future periods, it is debited to the asset account as a capital expenditure. The new book value (less salvage value) is then depreciated over the asset's remaining useful life. To illustrate, suppose a company pays $8,000 for a machine with an eight-year useful life and no salvage value. After three years and $3,000 of depreciation, it adds an automated control system to the machine at a cost of $1,800. This results in reduced labor costs in future periods. The cost of the betterment is added to the Machinery account with this entry:

**Example:** Assume a company owns a Web server. Identify each item as a revenue or capital expenditure: (1) purchase price, (2) necessary wiring, (3) platform for operation, (4) circuits to increase capacity, (5) cleaning after each three months of use, (6) repair of a faulty connection, and (7) replaced a worn cooling fan. *Answer:* Capital expenditures: 1, 2, 3, 4; Revenue expenditures: 5, 6, 7.

| | | | |
|---|---|---|---|
| Jan. 2 | Machinery ............................. | 1,800 | |
| | Cash ............................. | | 1,800 |
| | *To record installation of automated system.* | | |

Assets = Liabilities + Equity
+1,800
−1,800

After the betterment, the remaining cost to be depreciated is $6,800, computed as $8,000 − $3,000 + $1,800. Depreciation expense for the remaining five years is $1,360 per year, computed as $6,800/5 years.

**Point:** Both extraordinary repairs and betterments demand revised depreciation schedules.

**Extraordinary repairs** are expenditures extending the asset's useful life beyond its original estimate. Extraordinary repairs are *capital expenditures* because they benefit future periods. Their costs are debited to the asset account. For example, **America West Airlines** reports: "the cost of major scheduled airframe, engine and certain component overhauls are capitalized (and expensed) . . . over the periods benefited."

### Decision Maker

**Entrepreneur** Your start-up Internet services company needs cash, and you are preparing financial statements to apply for a short-term loan. A friend suggests that you treat as many expenses as possible as capital expenditures. What are the impacts on financial statements of this suggestion? What do you think is the aim of this suggestion?

Answer—p. 334

## Disposals of Plant Assets

Plant assets are disposed of for several reasons. Some are discarded because they wear out or become obsolete. Others are sold because of changing business plans. Regardless of the reason, disposals of plant assets occur in one of three basic ways: discarding, sale, or exchange. The general steps in accounting for a disposal of plant assets is described in Exhibit 8.15.

## Exhibit 8.15

Accounting for Disposals of Plant Assets

1. Record depreciation up to the date of disposal—this also updates Accumulated Depreciation.
2. Record the removal of the disposed asset's account balances—including its Accumulated Depreciation.
3. Record any cash (and/or other assets) received or paid in the disposal.
4. Record any gain or loss—computed by comparing the disposed asset's book value with the market value of any assets received.*

\* One exception to step 4 is the case of a gain on a similar asset exchange—it is described later in this section.

## Discarding Plant Assets

**P4**  Account for asset disposal through discarding, selling, and exchanging an asset.

A plant asset is *discarded* when it is no longer useful to the company and it has no market value. To illustrate, assume that a machine costing $9,000 with accumulated depreciation of $9,000 is discarded. When accumulated depreciation equals the asset's cost, it is said to be *fully depreciated* (zero book value). The entry to record the discarding of this asset is

Assets = Liabilities + Equity
+9,000
−9,000

| June 5 | Accumulated Depreciation—Machinery . . . . . . . . | 9,000 | |
| | Machinery . . . . . . . . . . . . . . . . . . . . . . . . . | | 9,000 |
| | *To discard fully depreciated machinery.* | | |

This entry reflects all four steps of Exhibit 8.15. Step 1 is unnecessary since the machine is fully depreciated. Step 2 is reflected in the debit to Accumulated Depreciation and credit to Machinery. Since no other asset is involved, step 3 is irrelevant. Finally, since book value is zero and no other asset is involved, no gain or loss is recorded in step 4.

How do we account for discarding an asset that is not fully depreciated or one whose depreciation is not up-to-date? To answer this, consider equipment costing $8,000 with accumulated depreciation of $6,000 on December 31 of the prior fiscal year-end. This equipment is being depreciated using the straight-line method over eight years with zero salvage. On July 1 of the current year it is discarded. Step 1 is to bring depreciation up-to-date:

**Point:** Recording depreciation expense up-to-date gives an up-to-date book value for determining gain or loss.

Assets = Liabilities + Equity
−500           −500

| July 1 | Depreciation Expense . . . . . . . . . . . . . . . . . . . | 500 | |
| | Accumulated Depreciation—Equipment . . . . | | 500 |
| | *To record 6 months' depreciation ($1,000 × 6/12).* | | |

Steps 2 through 4 of Exhibit 8.15 are reflected in the second (and final) entry:

Assets = Liabilities + Equity
+6,500        −1,500
−8,000

| July 1 | Accumulated Depreciation—Equipment . . . . . . . . | 6,500 | |
| | Loss on Disposal of Equipment . . . . . . . . . . . . . | 1,500 | |
| | Equipment . . . . . . . . . . . . . . . . . . . . . . . . . | | 8,000 |
| | *To discard equipment with a $1,500 book value.* | | |

**Point:** Gain or loss is determined by comparing "value given" (book value) to "value received."

The loss is computed by comparing the equipment's $1,500 book value ($8,000 − $6,000 − $500) with the zero net cash proceeds. This loss is reported in the Other Expenses and Losses section of the income statement. Discarding an asset can sometimes require a cash payment that would increase the loss. The income statement reports any loss from discarding an asset, and the balance sheet reflects the changes in the asset and accumulated depreciation accounts.

## Selling Plant Assets

Companies often sell plant assets when they restructure or downsize operations. To illustrate the accounting for selling plant assets, we consider BTO's March 31 sale of equipment that cost $16,000 and has accumulated depreciation of $12,000 at December 31 of the prior calendar year-end. Annual depreciation on this equipment is $4,000 computed using straight-line depreciation. Step 1 of this sale is to record depreciation expense and update accumulated depreciation to March 31 of the current year:

| March 31 | Depreciation Expense . . . . . . . . . . . . . . . . . . . . . | 1,000 | |
|---|---|---|---|
| | Accumulated Depreciation—Equipment. . . . . | | 1,000 |
| | *To record 3 months' depreciation ($4,000 × 3/12).* | | |

Assets = Liabilities + Equity
−1,000                         −1,000

Steps 2 through 4 of Exhibit 8.15 can be reflected in one final entry that depends on the amount received from the asset's sale. We consider three different possibilities.

**Sale at Book Value**  If BTO receives $3,000, an amount equal to the equipment's book value as of March 31, no gain or loss occurs on disposal. The entry is

| March 31 | Cash . . . . . . . . . . . . . . . . . . . . . . . . . . . . . . | 3,000 | |
|---|---|---|---|
| | Accumulated Depreciation—Equipment . . . . . . . . | 13,000 | |
| | Equipment . . . . . . . . . . . . . . . . . . . . . . . | | 16,000 |
| | *To record sale of equipment for no gain or loss.* | | |

Assets = Liabilities + Equity
+3,000
+13,000
−16,000

**Sale above Book Value**  If BTO receives $7,000, an amount that is $4,000 above the equipment's book value as of March 31, a gain on disposal occurs. The entry is

| March 31 | Cash . . . . . . . . . . . . . . . . . . . . . . . . . . . . . . | 7,000 | |
|---|---|---|---|
| | Accumulated Depreciation—Equipment . . . . . . . . | 13,000 | |
| | Gain on Disposal of Equipment. . . . . . . . . . . | | 4,000 |
| | Equipment . . . . . . . . . . . . . . . . . . . . . . . | | 16,000 |
| | *To record sale of equipment for a $4,000 gain.* | | |

Assets = Liabilities + Equity
+7,000                         +4,000
+13,000
−16,000

**Sale below Book Value**  If BTO receives $2,500, an amount that is $500 below the equipment's book value as of March 31, a loss on disposal occurs. The entry is

| March 31 | Cash . . . . . . . . . . . . . . . . . . . . . . . . . . . . . . | 2,500 | |
|---|---|---|---|
| | Loss on Disposal of Equipment . . . . . . . . . . . . . | 500 | |
| | Accumulated Depreciation—Equipment . . . . . . . . | 13,000 | |
| | Equipment. . . . . . . . . . . . . . . . . . . . . . . . | | 16,000 |
| | *To record sale of equipment for a $500 loss.* | | |

Assets = Liabilities + Equity
+2,500                         −500
+13,000
−16,000

# Exchanging Plant Assets

Many plant assets such as machinery, automobiles, and office equipment are disposed of by exchanging them for newer assets. In a typical exchange of plant assets, a *trade-in allowance* is received on the old asset and the balance is paid in cash. Accounting for the exchange of assets depends on whether the old and the new assets are similar or dissimilar in the functions they perform. Trading an old truck for a new truck is an exchange of similar assets, whereas trading a truck for a machine is an exchange of dissimilar assets. This section describes the accounting for the exchange of similar assets. Similar asset exchanges are common, whereas dissimilar asset exchanges are not (the latter are discussed in advanced courses).

Accounting for exchanges of similar assets depends on whether the book value of the asset given up is less or more than the market value of the asset received. When the market value of the asset received is less than the book value of the asset given up, the difference is recognized as a loss. However, when the value of the asset received is more than the asset's book value given up, the gain is *not* recognized.

**Receiving Less in Exchange: A Loss**  Let's assume that a company exchanges both old equipment and $33,000 in cash for new equipment. The old equipment originally cost

**Point:** Trade-in allowance minus book value equals the gain (or loss if negative) on exchange.

$36,000 and has accumulated depreciation of $20,000 at the time of exchange. The new equipment has a market value of $42,000. These details are reflected in the middle (Loss) columns of Exhibit 8.16.

**Exhibit 8.16**

Computing Gain or Loss on *Similar* Asset Exchange

| Similar Plant Asset Exchange | | Loss | | Gain | |
|---|---|---|---|---|---|
| Market value of assets received . . . . . . . . . . | | | $ 42,000 | | $ 52,000 |
| Book value of assets given up: | | | | | |
| Equipment ($36,000 − $20,000) . . . . . . . | $16,000 | | | $16,000 | |
| Cash . . . . . . . . . . . . . . . . . . . . . . . . . | 33,000 | 49,000 | | 33,000 | 49,000 |
| **Gain (loss) on exchange** . . . . . . . . . . . . . | | | $(7,000) | | $ 3,000 |

The entry to record this similar asset exchange is

Assets  = Liabilities +  Equity
+42,000                   −7,000
+20,000
−36,000
−33,000

| | Jan. 3 | Equipment (**new**) . . . . . . . . . . . . . . . . . . . . . . . | 42,000 | |
|---|---|---|---|---|
| | | Loss on Exchange of Assets . . . . . . . . . . . . . . . . | 7,000 | |
| | | Accumulated Depreciation—Equipment (**old**) . . . . | 20,000 | |
| | | Equipment (**old**) . . . . . . . . . . . . . . . . . . . . | | 36,000 |
| | | Cash . . . . . . . . . . . . . . . . . . . . . . . . . . . | | 33,000 |
| | | *To record exchange of old equipment and cash for new equipment.* | | |

**Point:** Parenthetical journal entry notes to "new" and "old" equipment are for illustration only. Both the debit and credit are to the same Equipment account in the general ledger.

The book value of the assets given up consists of the $33,000 cash and the $16,000 ($36,000 − $20,000) book value of the old equipment. The total $49,000 book value of assets given up is compared to the $42,000 market value of the new equipment received. This yields a loss of $7,000 ($42,000 − $49,000).

**Receiving More in Exchange: A Gain**   Let's assume the same facts as in the preceding similar asset exchange *except* that the new equipment received has a market value of $52,000 instead of $42,000. The entry to record this similar asset exchange is

Assets  = Liabilities +  Equity
+49,000
+20,000
−36,000
−33,000

| | Jan. 3 | Equipment (**new**) . . . . . . . . . . . . . . . . . . . . . . . | 49,000 | |
|---|---|---|---|---|
| | | Accumulated Depreciation—Equipment (**old**) . . . . | 20,000 | |
| | | Equipment (**old**) . . . . . . . . . . . . . . . . . . . . | | 36,000 |
| | | Cash . . . . . . . . . . . . . . . . . . . . . . . . . . . | | 33,000 |
| | | *To record exchange of old equipment and cash for new equipment.* | | |

**Point:** No gain is recognized for similar asset exchanges.

Exhibit 8.16 shows that there is a "gain" from this exchange in the far right (Gain) columns. This gain is *not* recognized in the entry because of a rule prohibiting recognizing a gain on similar asset exchanges.[1] The $49,000 recorded for the new equipment equals its cash price ($52,000) less the unrecognized gain ($3,000) on the exchange. The $49,000 cost recorded is called the *cost basis* of the new machine. This cost basis is the amount we use to compute depreciation and its book value. The cost basis of the new asset also can be computed by summing the book values of the assets given up as shown in Exhibit 8.17.

**Exhibit 8.17**

Cost Basis of New Asset when Gain Not Recognized

| | |
|---|---|
| Cost of old equipment . . . . . . . . . . . | $ 36,000 |
| Less accumulated depreciation . . . . . . | 20,000 |
| Book value of old equipment . . . . . . . | 16,000 |
| Cash paid in the exchange  . . . . . . . . | 33,000 |
| **Cost recorded for new equipment** . . . . . . . . . . . . . . . . | **$49,000** |

---

[1] The reason a gain from a similar asset exchange is not recognized is that the earnings process is not considered complete for the exchanged asset. The decision to recognize a loss from a similar asset exchange is an application of *accounting conservatism* in measuring and recording asset values.

Answers—pp. 334–335

## Quick Check

**8.** Early in the fifth year of a machine's six-year useful life, it is overhauled, and its useful life is extended to nine years. This machine originally cost $108,000 and the overhaul cost is $12,000. Prepare the entry to record the overhaul cost.

**9.** Explain the difference between revenue expenditures and capital expenditures and how both are recorded.

**10.** What is a betterment? How is a betterment recorded?

**11.** A company acquires equipment on January 10, 2005, at a cost of $42,000. Straight-line depreciation is used with a five-year life and $7,000 salvage value. On June 27, 2006, the company sells this equipment for $32,000. Prepare the entry(ies) for June 27, 2006.

**12.** A company trades an old Web server for a new one. The cost of the old server is $30,000, and its accumulated depreciation at the time of the trade is $23,400. The new server has a cash price of $45,000. Prepare entries to record the trade under two different assumptions where the company receives a trade-in allowance of (*a*) $3,000 and (*b*) $7,000.

**Example:** Assume the old equipment in Exh. 8.17 is sold for $19,000 and, in a *separate* transaction, new equipment is bought for $52,000. Record both transactions. *Answer:*

| | | |
|---|---|---|
| Cash . . . . . . . . . . . . . | 19,000 | |
| Accum. Depr — Eq. . . . | 20,000 | |
| Equipment (old) . . . . . . . . . . | | 36,000 |
| Gain on Sale of Eq. . . . . . . . | | 3,000 |
| Equipment (new) . . . . . | 52,000 | |
| Cash . . . . . . . . . . . . . . . . | | 52,000 |

# Section 2—Natural Resources

**Natural resources** are assets that are physically consumed when used. Examples are standing timber, mineral deposits, and oil and gas fields. Since they are consumed when used, they are often called *wasting assets*. These assets represent soon-to-be inventories of raw materials that will be converted into one or more products by cutting, mining, or pumping. Until that conversion takes place, they are noncurrent assets and are shown in a balance sheet using titles such as timberlands, mineral deposits, or oil reserves. Natural resources are reported under either plant assets or its own separate category. **Alcoa**, for instance, reports its natural resources under the balance sheet title *Properties, plants and equipment*. In a note to its financial statements, Alcoa reports a separate amount for *Land and land rights, including mines*. **Weyerhaeuser**, on the other hand, reports its timber holdings in a separate balance sheet category titled *Timber and timberlands*.

## Cost Determination and Depletion

Natural resources are recorded at cost, which includes all expenditures necessary to acquire the resource and prepare it for its intended use. **Depletion** is the process of allocating the cost of a natural resource to the period when it is consumed. Natural resources are reported on the balance sheet at cost less *accumulated depletion*. The depletion expense per period is usually based on units extracted from cutting, mining, or pumping. This is similar to units-of-production depreciation. **Exxon Mobil** uses this approach to amortize the costs of discovering and operating its oil wells.

**P5** Account for natural resource assets and their depletion.

To illustrate depletion of natural resources, let's consider a mineral deposit with an estimated 250,000 tons of available ore. It is purchased for $500,000, and we expect zero salvage value. The depletion charge per ton of ore mined is $2, computed as $500,000 ÷ 250,000 tons. If 85,000 tons are mined and sold in the first year, the depletion charge for that year is $170,000. These computations are detailed in Exhibit 8.18. Depletion expense for the first year is recorded as follows:

| Dec. 31 | Depletion Expense—Mineral Deposit. . . . . . . . . | 170,000 | |
|---|---|---|---|
| | Accumulated Depletion—Mineral Deposit. . . | | 170,000 |
| | *To record depletion of the mineral deposit.* | | |

| Assets | = Liabilities + | Equity |
|---|---|---|
| −170,000 | | −170,000 |

**Exhibit 8.18**

Depletion Formula and
Example

**Step 1**

$$\text{Depletion per unit} = \frac{\text{Cost} - \text{Salvage value}}{\text{Total units of capacity}} = \frac{\$500,000 - \$0}{250,000 \text{ tons}} = \$2 \text{ per ton}$$

**Step 2**

$$\text{Depletion expense} = \text{Depletion per unit} \times \text{Units extracted and sold in period}$$
$$= \$2 \times 85,000 = \$170,000$$

The period-end balance sheet reports the mineral deposit as shown in Exhibit 8.19.

**Exhibit 8.19**

Balance Sheet Presentation of
Natural Resources

| | | |
|---|---|---|
| Mineral deposit . . . . . . . . . . . . . . . . . . | $500,000 | |
| **Less accumulated depletion** . . . . . . . | **170,000** | $330,000 |

Since all 85,000 tons of the mined ore are sold during the year, the entire $170,000 of depletion is reported on the income statement. If some of the ore remains unsold at year-end, however, the depletion related to the unsold ore is carried forward on the balance sheet and reported as Ore Inventory, a current asset.

## Plant Assets Used in Extracting Resources

The conversion of natural resources by mining, cutting, or pumping usually requires machinery, equipment, and buildings. When the usefulness of these plant assets is directly related to the depletion of a natural resource, their costs are depreciated using the units-of-production method in proportion to the depletion of the natural resource. For example, if a machine is permanently installed in a mine and 10% of the ore is mined and sold in the period, then 10% of the machine's cost (less any salvage value) is allocated to depreciation expense. The same procedure is used when a machine is abandoned once resources have been extracted. If, however, a machine will be moved to and used at another site when extraction is complete, the machine is depreciated over its own useful life.

# Section 3—Intangible Assets

**P6**  Account for intangible
assets.

**Intangible assets** are nonphysical assets (used in operations) that confer on their owners long-term rights, privileges, or competitive advantages. Examples are patents, copyrights, licenses, leaseholds, franchises, goodwill, and trademarks. Lack of physical substance does not necessarily make an asset intangible. Notes and accounts receivable, for instance, lack physical substance, but they are not intangibles. This section identifies the more common types of intangible assets and explains the accounting for them.

## Cost Determination and Amortization

An intangible asset is recorded at cost when purchased. Its cost is systematically allocated to expense over its estimated useful life through the process of **amortization.** If an intangible asset has an **indefinite useful life**—meaning that no legal, regulatory, contractual, competitive, economic, or other factors limit its useful life—it should not be amortized. (If an intangible with an indefinite useful life is later judged to have a limited useful life, it is amortized over that limited useful life.) Amortization of intangible assets is similar to depreciation of plant assets and the depletion of natural resources in that it is a process of cost allocation. However, only the straight-line method is used for amortizing intangibles *unless* the company can show that another method is preferred. The effects of amortization are recorded in a contra account (Accumulated Amortization). The gross acquisition cost of intangible assets is disclosed in the balance sheet along with their accumulated amortization (these

**Point:** Goodwill is not amortized; instead, it is annually tested for impairment.

**Point:** The cost to acquire a Website address is an intangible asset.

disclosures are new per *SFAS 142*). The eventual disposal of an intangible asset involves removing its book value, recording any other asset(s) received or given up, and recognizing any gain or loss for the difference.

Many intangibles have limited useful lives due to laws, contracts, or other asset characteristics. Examples are patents, copyrights, and leaseholds. Other intangibles such as goodwill, trademarks, and trade names have useful lives that cannot be easily determined. The cost of intangible assets is amortized over the periods expected to benefit by their use, but in no case can this period be longer than the asset's legal existence. The values of some intangible assets such as goodwill continue indefinitely into the future and are not amortized. (An intangible asset that is not amortized is tested annually for **impairment**—if necessary, an impairment loss is recorded. Details for this test are in advanced courses.)

Intangible assets are often shown in a separate section of the balance sheet immediately after plant assets. **Callaway Golf**, for instance, follows this approach in reporting more than $100 million of intangible assets in its recent balance sheet. Companies usually disclose their amortization periods for intangibles. The remainder of our discussion focuses on accounting for specific types of intangible assets.

## Types of Intangibles

**Patents**   The federal government grants patents to encourage the invention of new technology, mechanical devices, and production processes. A **patent** is an exclusive right granted to its owner to manufacture and sell a patented item or to use a process for 20 years. When patent rights are purchased, the cost to acquire the rights is debited to an account called Patents. If the owner engages in lawsuits to successfully defend a patent, the cost of lawsuits is debited to the Patents account. However, the costs of research and development leading to a new patent are expensed when incurred.

A patent's cost is amortized over its estimated useful life (not to exceed 20 years). If we purchase a patent costing $25,000 with a useful life of 10 years, we make the following adjusting entry at the end of each of the 10 years to amortize one-tenth of its cost:

### Decision Insight

Mention "drug war" and most people think of fighting cocaine or heroin use. But another drug war is under way: Brand-name drugmakers are fighting to stop generic copies of their products from hitting the market once their patents expire. Successfully delaying a generic rival can mean hundreds of millions of dollars in extra sales.

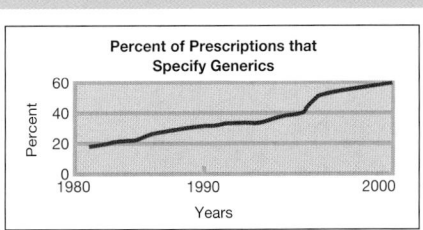

| | | |
|---|---|---|
| Dec. 31 | Amortization Expense—Patents . . . . . . . . . . . . . | 2,500 | |
| | Accumulated Amortization—Patents . . . . . . | | 2,500 |
| | *To amortize patent costs over its useful life.* | | |

Assets = Liabilities + Equity
−2,500                  −2,500

The $2,500 debit to Amortization Expense appears on the income statement as a cost of the product or service provided under protection of the patent. The Accumulated Amortization—Patents account is a contra asset account to Patents.

**Copyrights**   A **copyright** gives its owner the exclusive right to publish and sell a musical, literary, or artistic work during the life of the creator plus 70 years, although the useful life of most copyrights is much shorter. The costs of a copyright are amortized over its useful life. The only identifiable cost of many copyrights is the fee paid to the Copyright Office of the federal government or international agency granting the copyright. If this fee is immaterial, it is charged directly to an expense account, but if the identifiable costs of a copyright are material, they are capitalized (recorded in an asset account) and periodically amortized by debiting an account called Amortization Expense—Copyrights.

**Leaseholds**   Property is rented under a contract called a **lease.** The property's owner, called the **lessor,** grants the lease. The one who secures the right to possess and use the property is called the **lessee.** A **leasehold** refers to the rights the lessor grants to the lessee under the terms of the lease. A leasehold is an intangible asset for the lessee.

Certain leases require no advance payment from the lessee but require monthly rent payments. In this case, we do not set up a Leasehold account. Instead, the monthly payments are debited to a Rent Expense account. If a long-term lease requires the lessee to pay the final period's rent in advance when the lease is signed, the lessee records this advance payment with a debit to the Leasehold account. Since the advance payment is not used until the final period, the Leasehold account balance remains intact until that final period when its balance is transferred to Rent Expense. (Some long-term leases give the lessee essentially the same rights as a purchaser. This results in a tangible asset and a liability reported by the lessee. Chapter 11 describes these so-called *capital leases*.)

A long-term lease can increase in value when current rental rates for similar property rise while the required payments under the lease remain constant. This increase in value of a lease is not reported on the lessee's balance sheet. However, if the property is subleased and the new tenant makes a cash payment to the original lessee for the rights under the old lease, the new tenant debits this payment to a Leasehold account, which is amortized to Rent Expense over the remaining life of the lease.

**Leasehold Improvements**   A lessee sometimes pays for alterations or improvements to the leased property such as partitions, painting, and storefronts. These alterations and improvements are called **leasehold improvements,** and the lessee debits these costs to a Leasehold Improvements account. Since leasehold improvements become part of the property and revert to the lessor at the end of the lease, the lessee amortizes these costs over the life of the lease or the life of the improvements, whichever is shorter. The amortization entry debits Amortization Expense—Leasehold Improvements and credits Accumulated Amortization—Leasehold Improvements.

**Franchises and Licenses**   **Franchises** and **licenses** are rights that a company or government grants an entity to deliver a product or service under specified conditions. Many organizations grant franchise and license rights—**McDonald's, Pizza Hut,** and **Major League Baseball** are just a few examples. The costs of franchises and licenses are debited to a Franchises and Licenses asset account and are amortized over the lives of the agreements.

**Trademarks and Trade Names**   Companies often adopt unique symbols or select unique names and brands in marketing their products. A **trademark** or **trade (brand) name** is a symbol, name, phrase, or jingle identified with a company, product, or service. Examples are Nike swoosh, Marlboro Man, Big Mac, Coca-Cola, and Corvette. Ownership and exclusive right to use a trademark or trade name is often established by showing that one company used it before another. Ownership is best established by registering a trademark or trade name with the government's Patent Office. The cost of developing, maintaining, or enhancing the value of a trademark or trade name (such as advertising) is charged to expense when incurred. If a trademark or trade name is purchased, however, its cost is debited to an asset account and then amortized over its expected useful life.

**Goodwill**   **Goodwill** has a specific meaning in accounting. Goodwill is the amount by which a company's value exceeds the value of its individual assets and liabilities. This usually implies that the company as a whole has certain valuable attributes not measured among its individual assets and liabilities. These can include superior management, skilled workforce, good supplier or customer relations, quality products or services, good location, or other competitive advantages.

To keep accounting information from being too subjective, goodwill is not recorded unless an entire company or business segment is purchased. Purchased goodwill is measured by taking the purchase price of the company and subtracting the market value of its individual net assets (excluding goodwill). For instance, **Yahoo!** paid nearly $3.0 billion to acquire **GeoCities**; about $2.8 of the $3.0 billion was for goodwill and other intangibles.

Goodwill is measured as the excess of the cost of an acquired entity over the value of the acquired net assets. Goodwill is recorded as an asset, and it is *not* amortized. Instead, the FASB (*SFAS 142*) requires that goodwill be annually tested for impairment. If the book value of goodwill does not exceed its fair (market) value, goodwill is not impaired. However, if the book value of goodwill does exceed its fair value, an impairment loss is recorded equal to that excess. (Details of this test are in advanced courses.)

**Point:** Accounting for goodwill is different for financial accounting and tax accounting. The IRS requires the amortization of goodwill over a period not to exceed 15 years.

## Quick Check

**13.** Give an example of a natural resource and of an intangible asset.

**14.** A company pays $650,000 for an ore deposit. The deposit is estimated to have 325,000 tons of ore that will be mined over the next 10 years. During the first year, it mined, processed, and sold 91,000 tons. What is that year's depletion expense?

**15.** On January 6, 2005, a company pays $120,000 for a patent with a remaining 17-year legal life to produce a toy expected to be marketable for three years. Prepare entries to record its acquisition and the December 31, 2005, amortization entry.

Answers—p. 335

<table>
<tr><td>**Total Asset Turnover**</td><td>**Decision Analysis**</td></tr>
</table>

A company's assets are important in determining its ability to generate sales and earn income. Managers devote much attention to deciding what assets a company acquires, how much it invests in assets, and how to use assets most efficiently and effectively. One important measure of a company's ability to use its assets is **total asset turnover,** defined in Exhibit 8.20.

A2 Compute total asset turnover and apply it to analyze a company's use of assets.

$$\text{Total asset turnover} = \frac{\text{Net sales}}{\text{Average total assets}}$$

**Exhibit 8.20**

Total Asset Turnover

The numerator reflects the net amounts earned from the sale of products and services. The denominator reflects the average total resources devoted to operating the company and generating sales.

To illustrate, let's look at total asset turnover in Exhibit 8.21 for two competing companies: **Coors** and **Anheuser-Busch**.

**Exhibit 8.21**

Analysis Using Total Asset Turnover

| Company | Figure ($ in millions) | 2002 | 2001 | 2000 | 1999 |
|---|---|---|---|---|---|
| **Coors** | Net sales .................. | $ 3,776 | $ 2,429 | $ 2,414 | $ 2,236 |
| | Average total assets .......... | $ 3,019 | $ 1,684 | $ 1,588 | $ 1,503 |
| | Total asset turnover ........ | 1.25 | 1.44 | 1.52 | 1.49 |
| **Anheuser-Busch** | Net sales .................. | $13,566 | $12,912 | $12,499 | $11,895 |
| | Average total assets .......... | $14,032 | $13,547 | $12,914 | $12,593 |
| | Total asset turnover ........ | 0.97 | 0.95 | 0.97 | 0.94 |

To show how we use total asset turnover, let's look at Coors. We express Coors's use of assets in generating net sales by saying "it turned its assets over 1.25 times during 2002." This means that each $1.00 of assets produced $1.25 of net sales. Is a total asset turnover of 1.25 good or bad? It is safe to say that all companies desire a high total asset turnover. Like many ratio analyses, however, a company's total asset turnover must be interpreted in comparison with that of prior years and of its competitors. Interpreting the total asset turnover also requires an understanding of the company's operations. Some operations are capital intensive, meaning that a relatively large amount is invested in assets to generate sales. This suggests a relatively lower total asset turnover. Other companies' operations are labor intensive, meaning that they generate sales more by the efforts of people than the use of assets. In that case, we expect a higher total asset turnover. Companies with low total

**Point:** A measure of **plant asset useful life** equals the plant asset cost divided by depreciation expense.

**Point:** A measure of **plant asset age** is estimated by dividing accumulated depreciation by depreciation expense. Older plant assets can signal needed asset replacements; it may also signal use of less efficient assets.

## Decision Maker

**Environmentalist**   A paper manufacturer claims it cannot afford more environmental controls. It points to its low total asset turnover of 1.9 and argues that it cannot compete with companies whose total asset turnover is much higher. Examples cited are food stores (5.5) and auto dealers (3.8). How do you respond?

Answer—p. 334

asset turnover require higher profit margins (examples are hotels and real estate); companies with high total asset turnover can succeed with lower profit margins; examples are food stores and toy merchandisers. Coors's turnover recently declined, but it is superior to that for Anheuser-Busch. Total asset turnover for Coors's competitors, available in industry publications such as Dun & Bradstreet, is generally in the range of 1.0 to 1.2 over this same period. Overall, Coors appears to be competitive and doing slightly better than its competitors on total asset turnover.

# Demonstration Problem

On July 14, 2004, Tulsa Company pays $600,000 to acquire a fully equipped factory. The purchase involves the following assets:

| Asset | Appraised Value | Salvage Value | Useful Life | Depreciation Method |
|---|---|---|---|---|
| Land ................. | $160,000 | | | Not depreciated |
| Land improvements ....... | 80,000 | $    0 | 10 years | Straight-line |
| Building ............... | 320,000 | 100,000 | 10 years | Double-declining-balance |
| Machinery ............. | 240,000 | 20,000 | 10,000 units | Units-of-production* |
| Total ................. | $800,000 | | | |

* The machinery is used to produce 700 units in 2004 and 1,800 units in 2005.

### Required

1. Allocate the total $600,000 purchase cost among the separate assets.
2. Compute the 2004 (six months) and 2005 depreciation expense for each asset and compute total depreciation expense for both years.
3. On the first day of 2006, Tulsa exchanged the machinery that was acquired on July 14, 2004, and $5,000 cash for similar machinery with a $210,000 market value. Journalize the exchange of these similar assets.
4. On the last day of calendar year 2006, Tulsa discarded machinery that had been on its books for five years. The machinery's original cost was $12,000 (estimated life of five years) and its salvage value was $2,000. No depreciation had been recorded for the fifth year when the disposal occurred. Journalize the fifth year of depreciation (straight-line method) and the asset's disposal.
5. At the beginning of year 2006, Tulsa purchased a patent for $100,000 cash. The company estimated the patent's useful life to be 10 years. Journalize the patent acquisition and its amortization for the year 2006.
6. Late in the year 2006, Tulsa acquired an ore deposit for $600,000 cash. It added roads and built mine shafts for an additional cost of $80,000. Salvage value of the mine is estimated to be $20,000. The company estimated 330,000 tons of available ore. In year 2006, Tulsa mined and sold 10,000 tons of ore. Journalize the mine's acquisition and its first year's depletion.

## Planning the Solution

- Complete a three-column table showing the following amounts for each asset: appraised value, percent of total value, and apportioned cost.
- Using allocated costs, compute depreciation for 2004 (only one-half year) and 2005 (full year) for each asset. Summarize those computations in a table showing total depreciation for each year.
- Remember that gains on exchanges of similar assets are not recognized. Make a journal entry to add the acquired machinery to the books and to remove the old machinery, along with its accumulated depreciation, and to record the cash given in the exchange.
- Remember that depreciation must be recorded up-to-date before discarding an asset. Calculate and record depreciation expense for the fifth year using the straight-line method. Since salvage value

is not received at the end of a discarded asset's life, the amount of any salvage value becomes a loss on disposal. Record the loss on the disposal as well as the removal of the discarded asset and its related accumulated depreciation.

- Record the patent (an intangible asset) at its purchase price. Use straight-line amortization over its useful life to calculate amortization expense.
- Record the ore deposit (a natural resource asset) at its cost, including any added costs to ready the mine for use. Calculate depletion per ton using the depletion formula. Multiply the depletion per ton by the amount of tons mined and sold to calculate depletion expense for the year.

## Solution to Demonstration Problem

**1.** Allocation of the total cost of $600,000 among the separate assets:

| Asset | Appraised Value | Percent of Total Value | Apportioned Cost |
|---|---|---|---|
| Land ................. | $160,000 | 20% | $120,000 ($600,000 × 20%) |
| Land improvements ....... | 80,000 | 10 | 60,000 ($600,000 × 10%) |
| Building .............. | 320,000 | 40 | 240,000 ($600,000 × 40%) |
| Machinery ............. | 240,000 | 30 | 180,000 ($600,000 × 30%) |
| Total ................. | $800,000 | 100% | $ 600,000 |

**2.** Depreciation for each asset. (*Note:* Land is not depreciated.)

**Land Improvements**

| | |
|---|---|
| Cost ....................................... | $ 60,000 |
| Salvage value ..................................... | 0 |
| Depreciable cost .............................. | $ 60,000 |
| Useful life ..................................... | 10 years |
| Annual depreciation expense ($60,000/10 years) .......... | $ 6,000 |
| **2004 depreciation ($6,000 × 6/12)** ................. | $ 3,000 |
| **2005 depreciation** ............................ | $ 6,000 |

**Building**

Straight-line rate = 100%/10 years = 10%
Double-declining-balance rate = 10% × 2 = 20%

| | |
|---|---|
| **2004 depreciation ($240,000 × 20% × 6/12)** ........... | $ 24,000 |
| **2005 depreciation [($240,000 − $24,000) × 20%]** ....... | $ 43,200 |

**Machinery**

| | |
|---|---|
| Cost ....................................... | $100,000 |
| Salvage value ..................................... | 20,000 |
| Depreciable cost .............................. | $160,000 |
| Total expected units of production .................... | 10,000 units |
| Depreciation per unit ($160,000/10,000 units) ........... | $ 16 |
| **2004 depreciation ($16 × 700 units)** ................. | $ 11,200 |
| **2005 depreciation ($16 × 1,800 units)** ............... | $ 28,800 |

Total depreciation expense:

| | 2004 | 2005 |
|---|---|---|
| Land improvements ....... | $ 3,000 | $ 6,000 |
| Building .............. | 24,000 | 43,200 |
| Machinery ............. | 11,200 | 28,800 |
| Total ................. | $38,200 | $78,000 |

**3.** Record the exchange of similar assets (machinery) with a gain on the exchange: The book value on the exchange date is $180,000 (cost) − $40,000 (accumulated depreciation). The book value of the machinery given up in the exchange ($140,000) plus the $5,000 cash paid is less than the $210,000 value of the machine acquired. The entry to record this exchange of similar assets does not recognize the $65,000 gain on exchange:

| | | |
|---|---|---|
| Machinery (new) ........................................ | 145,000* | |
| Accumulated Depreciation—Machinery (old) ................. | 40,000 | |
|      Machinery (old) ...................................... | | 180,000 |
|      Cash ................................................ | | 5,000 |
| *To record exchange of similar assets.* | | |

\* Market value of the acquired asset of $210,000 minus $65,000 gain.

**4.** Record the depreciation up to date on the discarded asset:

| | | |
|---|---|---|
| Depreciation Expense—Machinery ........................ | 2,000 | |
|      Accumulated Depreciation—Machinery ................... | | 2,000 |
| *To record depreciation on date of disposal: ($12,000 − $2,000)/5* | | |

Record the removal of the discarded asset and its loss on disposal:

| | | |
|---|---|---|
| Accumulated Depreciation—Machinery ...................... | 10,000 | |
| Loss on Disposal of Machinery ............................ | 2,000 | |
|      Machinery ........................................... | | 12,000 |
| *To record the discarding of machinery with a $2,000 book value.* | | |

**5.**

| | | |
|---|---|---|
| Patent ................................................. | 100,000 | |
|      Cash ................................................ | | 100,000 |
| *To record patent acquisition.* | | |

| | | |
|---|---|---|
| Amortization Expense—Patent ........................... | 10,000 | |
|      Accumulated Amortization—Patent ..................... | | 10,000 |
| *To record amortization expense: $100,000/10 years = $10,000.* | | |

**6.**

| | | |
|---|---|---|
| Ore Deposit ............................................ | 680,000 | |
|      Cash ................................................ | | 680,000 |
| *To record ore deposit acquisition and its related costs.* | | |

| | | |
|---|---|---|
| Depletion Expense—Ore Deposit ......................... | 20,000 | |
|      Accumulated Depletion—Ore Deposit ................... | | 20,000 |
| *To record depletion expense: ($680,000 − $20,000)/330,000 tons = $2 per ton. 10,000 tons mined and sold × $2 = $20,000 depletion.* | | |

# APPENDIX

# Goodwill Estimation

A company has goodwill when its expected future income is greater than the normal income for its industry (competitors). To illustrate, consider the information in Exhibit 8A.1 for two competing companies, Z2 and Burton, of roughly equal size in the snowboard industry.

| | Z2 | Burton |
|---|---|---|
| Net assets* (excluding goodwill) . . . . . . . . . . . . . . . . | $190,000 | $190,000 |
| Normal return on net assets in the industry . . . . . . . | 10% | 10% |
| Normal net income . . . . . . . . . . . . . . . . . . . . . . . . | 19,000 | 19,000 |
| Expected net income . . . . . . . . . . . . . . . . . . . . . . | 24,000 | 19,000 |
| **Expected net income above normal** . . . . . . . . . | **$ 5,000** | **$      0** |

**Exhibit 8A.1**

Data for Goodwill Illustration

\* Net assets (also called *equity*) equal total assets minus total liabilities.

The expected net income for Z2 is $24,000. This is $5,000 higher than the $19,000 industry norm based on the 10% return on net assets (equity) for its competitors. This implies that Z2 has goodwill that yields above normal net income. In contrast, Burton's expected income of $19,000 equals the norm for this industry. This implies zero goodwill for Burton. This means that Z2 buyers are willing to pay more than just the value of its net assets—specifically, to acquire its goodwill asset.

In accounting, goodwill is recorded when an entire company or business segment is purchased. The buyer and seller can estimate goodwill in more than one way. For instance, how do we value Z2's $5,000 per year above normal net income? One method is to value goodwill at some *multiple* of above normal net income. If we choose a multiple of 6, our goodwill estimate for Z2 is 6 × $5,000, or $30,000. Another method is to assume the $5,000 above normal net income continues indefinitely (often called *capitalizing*). This is like an *annuity*. For example, if we assume a 16% discount (interest) rate, the goodwill estimate is $5,000/16%, or $31,250. Whatever method we choose, the value of goodwill is confirmed only by the price the seller is willing to accept and the buyer is willing to pay.

## Summary

**C1** **Describe plant assets and issues in accounting for them.**
Plant assets are tangible assets used in the operations of a company and have a useful life of more than one accounting period. Plant assets are set apart from other tangible assets by two important features: use in operations and useful lives longer than one period. The four main accounting issues with plant assets are (1) computing their costs, (2) allocating their costs to the periods they benefit, (3) accounting for subsequent expenditures, and (4) recording their disposal.

**C2** **Explain depreciation and the factors affecting its computation.** *Depreciation* is the process of allocating to expense the cost of a plant asset over the accounting periods that benefit from its use. Depreciation does not measure the decline in a plant asset's market value or its physical deterioration. Three factors determine depreciation: cost, salvage value, and useful life. Salvage value is an estimate of the asset's value at the end of its benefit period. Useful (service) life is the length of time an asset is productively used.

**C3** **Explain depreciation for partial years and changes in estimates.** Partial-year depreciation is often required because assets are bought and sold throughout the year. Depreciation is revised when changes in estimates such as salvage value and useful life occur. If the useful life of a plant asset changes, for instance, the remaining cost to be depreciated is spread over the remaining (revised) useful life of the asset.

**A1** **Compare and analyze alternative depreciation methods.** The amount of depreciation expense per period is usually different for different methods, yet total depreciation expense over an asset's life is the same for all methods. Each method starts with the same total cost and ends with the same salvage value. The difference is in the pattern of depreciation expense over the asset's life. Common methods are straight-line, double-declining-balance, and units-of-production.

**A2** **Compute total asset turnover and apply it to analyze a company's use of assets.** Total asset turnover measures a company's ability to use its assets to generate sales. It is defined as net sales divided by average total assets. While all companies desire a high total asset turnover, it must be interpreted in comparison with that for prior years and its competitors.

**P1** **Apply the cost principle to compute the cost of plant assets.** Plant assets are recorded at cost when purchased. Cost includes all normal and reasonable expenditures necessary to get the asset in place and ready for its intended use. The cost of a lump-sum purchase is allocated among its individual assets.

**P2** **Compute and record depreciation using the straight-line, units-of-production, and declining-balance methods.** The straight-line method divides cost less salvage value by the asset's useful life to determine depreciation expense per period. The units-of-production method divides cost less salvage value by the estimated number of units the asset will produce over its life to determine depreciation per unit. The declining-balance method multiplies the asset's beginning-of-period book value by a factor that is often double the straight-line rate.

**P3** **Distinguish between revenue and capital expenditures, and account for them.** Revenue expenditures expire in the current period and are debited to expense accounts and matched with current revenues. Ordinary repairs are an example of revenue expenditures. Capital expenditures benefit future periods and are debited to asset accounts. Examples of capital expenditures are extraordinary repairs and betterments.

**P4  Account for asset disposal through discarding, selling, or exchanging an asset.** When a plant asset is discarded, sold, or exchanged, its cost and accumulated depreciation are removed from the accounts. Any cash proceeds from discarding or selling an asset are recorded and compared to the asset's book value to determine gain or loss. When similar assets are exchanged, losses are recognized but gains are not. When gains are not recognized, the new asset account is debited for the book value of the old asset plus any cash (assets) paid.

**P5  Account for natural resource assets and their depletion.** The cost of a natural resource is recorded in a noncurrent asset account. Depletion of a natural resource is recorded by

allocating its cost to depletion expense using the units-of-production method. Depletion is credited to an Accumulated Depletion account.

**P6  Account for intangible assets.** An intangible asset is recorded at the cost incurred to purchase it. The cost of an intangible asset with a definite useful life is allocated to expense using the straight-line method, which and is called *amortization*. Goodwill and intangible assets with an indefinite useful life are not amortized—they are annually tested for impairment. Intangible assets include patents, copyrights, leaseholds, goodwill, and trademarks.

---

## Guidance Answers to **Decision Maker** and **Decision Ethics**

**Controller**   The president's instructions may reflect an honest and reasonable prediction of the future. Since the company is struggling financially, the president may have concluded that the normal pattern of replacing assets every three years cannot continue. Perhaps the strategy is to avoid costs of frequent replacements and stretch use of equipment a few years longer until financial conditions improve. However, if you believe the president's decision is unprincipled, you might confront the president with your opinion that it is unethical to change the estimate to increase income. Another possibility is to wait and see whether the auditor will prohibit this change in estimate. In either case, you should insist that the statements be based on reasonable estimates.

**Entrepreneur**   Treating an expense as a capital expenditure means that reported expenses will be lower and income higher in the short run. This is so because a capital expenditure is not expensed

immediately but is spread over the asset's useful life. Treating an expense as a capital expenditure also means that asset and equity totals are reported at larger amounts in the short run. This continues until the asset is fully depreciated. Your friend is probably trying to help, but the suggestion is misguided. Only an expenditure benefiting future periods is a capital expenditure.

**Environmentalist**   The paper manufacturer's comparison of its total asset turnover with food stores and auto dealers is misdirected. These other industries' turnovers are higher because their profit margins are lower (about 2%). Profit margins for the paper industry are usually 3% to 3.5%. You need to collect data from competitors in the paper industry to show that a 1.9 total asset turnover is about the norm for this industry. You might also want to collect data on this company's revenues and expenses, along with compensation data for its high-ranking officers and employees.

---

## Guidance Answers to **Quick Checks**

**I. a.** Supplies—current assets
  **b.** Office equipment—plant assets
  **c.** Inventory—current assets
  **d.** Land for future expansion—long-term investments
  **e.** Trucks used in operations—plant assets

**2. a.** Land     **b.** Land Improvements

**3.** $700,000 + $49,000 − $21,000 + $3,500 + $3,000 + $2,500 = $737,000

**4. a.** Straight-line with 7-year life: ($77,000/7) = $11,000
  **b.** Straight-line with 10-year life: ($77,000/10) = $7,700

**5.** Depreciation is a process of allocating the cost of plant assets to the accounting periods that benefit from the assets' use.

**6. a.** Book value using straight-line depreciation:
   $96,000 − [($96,000 − $8,000)/5] = $78,400
  **b.** Book value using units of production:
   $96,000 − [($96,000 − $8,000) × (10,000/100,000)]
   = $87,200

**7.** ($3,800 − $200)/3 = $1,200 (original depreciation per year)
  $1,200 × 2 = $2,400 (accumulated depreciation)
  ($3,800 − $2,400)/2 = $700 (revised depreciation)

**8.**

| | | |
|---|---|---|
| Machinery . . . . . . . . . . . . . . . . . . . . . . . . . . . | 12,000 | |
| Cash . . . . . . . . . . . . . . . . . . . . . . . . . . . . | | 12,000 |

**9.** A revenue expenditure benefits only the current period and should be charged to expense in the current period. A capital expenditure yields benefits that extend beyond the end of the current period and should be charged to an asset.

**10.** A betterment involves modifying an existing plant asset to make it more efficient, usually by replacing part of the asset with an improved or superior part. The cost of a betterment is debited to the asset account.

**11.**

| | | |
|---|---|---|
| Depreciation Expense . . . . . . . . . . . . . . . . . . | 3,500 | |
| Accumulated Depreciation . . . . . . . . . . . . | | 3,500 |
| | | |
| Cash . . . . . . . . . . . . . . . . . . . . . . . . . . . . . | 32,000 | |
| Accumulated Depreciation . . . . . . . . . . . . . . . | 10,500 | |
| Gain on Sale of Equipment . . . . . . . . . . . | | 500 |
| Equipment . . . . . . . . . . . . . . . . . . . . . . | | 42,000 |

**12.**

(a)

| | |
|---|---|
| Equipment . . . . . . . . . . . . . . . . . . . . . . | 45,000 |
| Loss on Exchange of Assets . . . . . . . . . . | 3,600 |
| Accumulated Depreciation—Equipment . . . | 23,400 |
|     Equipment . . . . . . . . . . . . . . . . . . . . | 30,000 |
|     Cash ($45,000 − $3,000) . . . . . . . . . | 42,000 |

(b)

| | |
|---|---|
| Equipment* . . . . . . . . . . . . . . . . . . . . . . | 44,600 |
| Accumulated Depreciation—Equipment . . . | 23,400 |
|     Equipment . . . . . . . . . . . . . . . . . . . . | 30,000 |
|     Cash ($45,000 − $7,000) . . . . . . . . . | 38,000 |

\* Includes $400 unrecognized gain.

**13.** Examples of natural resources are timberlands, mineral deposits, and oil reserves. Examples of intangible assets are patents, copyrights, leaseholds, leasehold improvements, goodwill, trademarks, and licenses.

**14.** ($650,000/325,000 tons) × 91,000 tons = $182,000

**15.**

| | | | |
|---|---|---|---|
| Jan. 6 | Patents . . . . . . . . . . . . . . . . . . . | 120,000 | |
| |     Cash . . . . . . . . . . . . . . . . . . | | 120,000 |
| Dec. 31 | Amortization Expense . . . . . . . . . . | 40,000* | |
| |     Accumulated | | |
| |       Amortization Patents . . . . | | 40,000 |

\* $120,000/3 years = $40,000.

## Key Terms

Key Terms are available at the book's Website for learning and testing in an online Flashcard Format.

Accelerated depreciation method (p. 316)
Amortization (p. 326)
Betterments (p. 321)
Book value (p. 315)
Capital expenditures (p. 320)
Change in an accounting estimate (p. 319)
Copyright (p. 327)
Cost (p. 311)
Declining-balance method (p. 316)
Depletion (p. 325)
Depreciation (p. 313)
Extraordinary repairs (p. 321)
Franchises (p. 328)

Goodwill (p. 328)
Impairment (p. 327)
Inadequacy (p. 313)
Indefinite useful life (p. 326)
Intangible assets (p. 326)
Land improvements (p. 312)
Lease (p. 328)
Leasehold (p. 328)
Leasehold improvements (p. 328)
Lessee (p. 328)
Lessor (p. 328)
Licenses (p. 328)
Modified Accelerated Cost Recovery System (MACRS) (p. 318)

Natural resources (p. 325)
Obsolescence (p. 313)
Ordinary repairs (p. 321)
Patent (p. 327)
Plant assets (p. 310)
Revenue expenditures (p. 320)
Salvage value (p. 313)
Straight-line depreciation (p. 314)
Total asset turnover (p. 329)
Trademark or trade (brand) name (p. 328)
Units-of-production depreciation (p. 315)
Useful life (p. 313)

## Personal Interactive Quiz

Personal Interactive Quizzes A and B are available at the book's Website to reinforce and assess your learning.

*Superscript letter* <sup>A</sup> *denotes assignments based on Appendix 8A.*

## Discussion Questions

**1.** What is the general rule for costs included in a plant asset?

**2.** What characteristics of a plant asset make it different from other assets?

**3.** What is the balance sheet classification for land that is held for future expansion? Why is such land not classified as a plant asset?

**4.** What is different between land and land improvements?

**5.** Why is the Modified Accelerated Cost Recovery System not generally accepted for financial accounting purposes?

**6.** Does the balance in the Accumulated Depreciation—Machinery account represent funds to replace the machinery when it wears out? If not, what does it represent?

**7.** What accounting principle justifies charging low-cost plant asset purchases immediately to an expense account?

**Exercise 8-5**

Depreciation methods

P2

**Check**   (3) $6,768

Feng Company installs a computerized manufacturing machine in its factory at the beginning of the year at a cost of $42,300. The machine's useful life is estimated at 10 years, or 363,000 units of product, with a $6,000 salvage value. During its second year, the machine produces 35,000 units of product. Determine the machine's second-year depreciation under the (1) straight-line, (2) units-of-production, and (3) double-declining-balance methods.

---

**Exercise 8-6**

Depreciation methods; partial year depreciation   C3

On April 1, 2004, Stone's Backhoe Co. purchases a trencher for $250,000. The machine is expected to last five years and have a salvage value of $25,000. Compute depreciation expense for year 2005 using the (1) straight-line and (2) double-declining-balance methods.

---

**Exercise 8-7**

Revising depreciation

C3

**Check**   (2) $3,400

Summit Fitness Club uses straight-line depreciation for a machine costing $21,750, with an estimated four-year life and a $2,250 salvage value. At the beginning of the third year, Summit determines that the machine has three more years of remaining useful life, after which it will have an estimated $1,800 salvage value. Compute (1) the machine's book value at the end of its second year and (2) the amount of depreciation for each of the final three years given the revised estimates.

---

**Exercise 8-8**

Income effects of depreciation methods

A1

**Check**   (2) Year 3 NI, $53,328

Mulan Enterprises pays $235,200 for equipment that will last five years and have a $52,500 salvage value. By using the machine in its operations for five years, the company expects to earn $85,500 annually, after deducting all expenses except depreciation. Prepare a table showing income before depreciation, depreciation expense, and net (pretax) income for each year and for the total five-year period, assuming (1) straight-line depreciation and (2) double-declining-balance depreciation.

---

**Exercise 8-9**

Extraordinary repairs; plant asset age

P3

**Check**   (3) $207,450

Passat Company owns a building that appears on its prior year-end balance sheet at its original $561,000 cost less $420,750 accumulated depreciation. The building is depreciated on a straight-line basis assuming a 20-year life and no salvage value. During the first week in January of the current calendar year, major structural repairs are completed on the building at a $67,200 cost. The repairs extend its useful life for 7 years beyond the 20 years originally estimated.

1. Determine the building's age (plant asset age) as of the prior year-end balance sheet date.
2. Prepare the entry to record the cost of the structural repairs that are paid in cash.
3. Determine the book value of the building immediately after the repairs are recorded.
4. Prepare the entry to record the current calendar year's depreciation.

---

**Exercise 8-10**

Ordinary repairs, extraordinary repairs and betterments

P3

Patterson Company pays $262,500 for equipment expected to last four years and have a $30,000 salvage value. Prepare journal entries to record the following costs related to the equipment:

1. During the second year of the equipment's life, $21,000 cash is paid for a new component expected to increase the equipment's productivity by 10% a year.
2. During the third year, $5,250 cash is paid for normal repairs necessary to keep the equipment in good working order.
3. During the fourth year, $13,950 is paid for repairs expected to increase the useful life of the equipment from four to five years.

---

**Exercise 8-11**

Exchanging similar assets

P4

**Check**   (2) $14,500

Jericho Construction trades in an old tractor for a new tractor, receiving a $28,000 trade-in allowance and paying the remaining $82,000 in cash. The old tractor had cost $95,000, and straight-line accumulated depreciation of $52,500 had been recorded to date under the assumption that it would last eight years and have a $11,000 salvage value. Answer the following questions:

1. What is the book value of the old tractor at the time of exchange?
2. What is the loss on this similar asset exchange?
3. What amount should be recorded (debited) in the asset account for the new tractor?

On January 2, 2005, Atlantic Co. disposes of a machine costing $42,000 with accumulated depreciation of $22,625. Prepare the entries to record the disposal under each of the following separate assumptions:

**1.** Machine is sold for $16,250 cash.

**2.** Machine is traded in on a similar but newer machine having a $58,500 cash price. A $20,000 trade-in allowance is received, and the balance is paid in cash.

**3.** Machine is traded in on a similar but newer machine having a $58,500 cash price. A $15,000 trade-in allowance is received, and the balance is paid in cash.

**Exercise 8-**
Recording plant a
P4

**Check**  (2) Dr. Machinery, $5

---

Finesse Co. purchases and installs a machine on January 1, 2004, at a total cost of $92,750. Straight-line depreciation is taken each year for four years assuming a seven-year life and no salvage value. The machine is disposed of on July 1, 2008, during its fifth year of service. Prepare entries to record the partial year's depreciation on July 1, 2008, and to record the disposal under the following separate assumptions: (1) the machine is sold for $35,000 cash and (2) Finesse receives an insurance settlement of $30,000 resulting from the total destruction of the machine in a fire.

**Exercise 8-13**
Partial year depreciation; disposal of plant asset
P4

---

On April 2, 2005, Idaho Mining Co. pays $3,633,750 for an ore deposit containing 1,425,000 tons. The company installs machinery in the mine costing $171,000, with an estimated seven-year life and no salvage value. The machinery will be abandoned when the ore is completely mined. Idaho began mining on May 1, 2005, and mined and sold 156,200 tons of ore during the remaining eight months of 2005. Prepare the December 31, 2005, entries to record both the ore deposit depletion and the mining machinery depreciation. Mining machinery depreciation should be in proportion to the mine's depletion.

**Exercise 8-14**
Depletion of natural resources
P2  P5

---

Busch Gallery purchases the copyright on an oil painting for $236,700 on January 1, 2005. The copyright legally protects its owner for 19 more years. However, the company plans to market and sell prints of the original for only 12 years. Prepare entries to record the purchase of the copyright on January 1, 2005, and its annual amortization on December 31, 2005.

**Exercise 8-15**
Amortization of intangible assets
P6

---

Corey Alt has devoted years to developing a profitable business that earns an attractive return. Alt is now considering selling the business and is attempting to estimate its goodwill. The value of the business's net assets (excluding goodwill) is $437,000, and in a typical year net income is about $85,000. Most businesses of this type are expected to earn a return of about 10% on their net assets. Estimate the value of this business's goodwill for the following separate cases assuming it is (1) equal to 10 times the amount that net income is above normal and (2) computed by capitalizing at a rate of 8% the amount that net income is above normal.

**Exercise 8-16<sup>A</sup>**
Goodwill estimation
P6

**Check**  (2) $516,250

---

Refer to the statement of cash flows for **Harley-Davidson** in Appendix A for the fiscal year ended December 31, 2002, to answer the following:

**1.** What amount of cash is used to purchase property and equipment?
**2.** How much depreciation and amortization are recorded?
**3.** What total amount of net cash is used in investing activities?

**Exercise 8-17**
Cash flows related to assets
C1
**Harley-Davidson**

---

Joy Co. reports net sales of $4,862,000 for 2004 and $7,542,000 for 2005. End-of-year balances for total assets are 2003, $1,586,000; 2004, $1,700,000; and 2005, $1,882,000. (*a*) Compute Joy's total asset turnover for 2004 and 2005. (*b*) Comment on Joy's efficiency in using its assets if its competitors average a total asset turnover of 3.0.

**Exercise 8-18**
Evaluating efficient use of assets
A2

...avier Construction negotiates a lump-sum purchase of several assets from a company that is going ...t of business. The purchase is completed on January 1, 2005, at a total cash price of $787,500 for ...uilding, land, land improvements, and six vehicles. The estimated market values of the assets are ...lding, $408,000; land, $289,000; land improvements, $42,500; and four vehicles, $110,500. The ...pany's fiscal year ends on December 31.

**...uired**

...epare a table to allocate the lump-sum purchase price to the separate assets purchased (round ...rcents to the nearest 1%). Prepare the journal entry to record the purchase.

**2.** Compute the depreciation expense for year 2005 on the building using the straight-line method, assuming a 15-year life and a $25,650 salvage value.

**3.** Compute the depreciation expense for year 2005 on the land improvements assuming a five-year life and double-declining-balance depreciation.

*Analysis Component*

**4.** Defend or refute this statement: Accelerated depreciation results in payment of less taxes over the asset's life.

(3) $15,750

---

## Problem 8-2A
Asset cost allocation; straight-line depreciation

C1  C2  P1  P2

mhhe.com/wild3e

In January 2005, Keona Co. pays $2,800,000 for a tract of land with two buildings on it. It plans to demolish Building 1 and build a new store in its place. Building 2 will be a company office; it is appraised at $641,300, with a useful life of 20 years and an $80,000 salvage value. A lighted parking lot near Building 1 has improvements (Land Improvements 1) valued at $408,100 that are expected to last another 14 years with no salvage value. Without the buildings and improvements, the tract of land is valued at $1,865,600. Keona also incurs the following additional costs:

| | |
|---|---:|
| Cost to demolish Building 1 | $ 422,600 |
| Cost of additional land grading | 167,200 |
| Cost to construct new building (Building 3), having a useful life of 25 years and a $390,100 salvage value | 2,019,000 |
| Cost of new land improvements (Land Improvements 2) near Building 2 having a 20-year useful life and no salvage value | 158,000 |

**Required**

**Check** (1) Land costs, $2,381,800; Building 2 costs, $616,000

**1.** Prepare a table with the following column headings: Land, Building 2, Building 3, Land Improvements 1, and Land Improvements 2. Allocate the costs incurred by Keona to the appropriate columns and total each column (round percents to the nearest 1%).

**2.** Prepare a single journal entry to record all the incurred costs assuming they are paid in cash on January 1, 2005.

(3) Depr.—Land Improv. 1 and 2, $28,000 and $7,900

**3.** Using the straight-line method, prepare the December 31 adjusting entries to record depreciation for the 12 months of 2005 when these assets were in use.

---

## Problem 8-3A
Computing and revising depreciation; revenue and capital expenditures

C3  P1  P3

**Check**  Dec. 31, 2004, Dr. Depr. Expense—Equip., $60,238

Clarion Contractors completed the following transactions and events involving the purchase and operation of equipment in its business:

**2004**

Jan.  1   Paid $255,440 cash plus $15,200 in sales tax and $2,500 in transportation (FOB shipping point) for a new loader. The loader is estimated to have a four-year life and a $34,740 salvage value. Loader costs are recorded in the Equipment account.

Jan.  3   Paid $3,660 to enclose the cab and install air conditioning in the loader to enable operations under harsher conditions. This increased the estimated salvage value of the loader by another $1,110.

Dec. 31   Recorded annual straight-line depreciation on the loader.

**2005**

Jan.  1   Paid $4,500 to overhaul the loader's engine, which increased the loader's estimated useful life by two years.

Feb. 17   Paid $920 to repair the loader after the operator backs it into a tree.

Dec. 31   Recorded annual straight-line depreciation on the loader.

**Check**   Dec. 31, 2005, Dr. Depr. Expense—Equip., $37,042

**Required**

Prepare journal entries to record these transactions and events.

---

Chen Company completed the following transactions and events involving its delivery trucks:

**2004**

Jan.  1   Paid $19,415 cash plus $1,165 in sales tax for a new delivery truck estimated to have a five-year life and a $3,000 salvage value. Delivery truck costs are recorded in the Trucks account.

Dec. 31   Recorded annual straight-line depreciation on the truck.

**2005**

Dec. 31   Due to new information obtained earlier in the year, the truck's estimated useful life was changed from five to four years, and the estimated salvage value was increased to $3,500. Recorded annual straight-line depreciation on the truck.

**2006**

Dec. 31   Recorded annual straight-line depreciation on the truck.

Dec. 31   Sold the truck for $6,200 cash.

**Problem 8-4A**
Computing and revising depreciation; selling plant assets

C3   P2   P4

**Check**   Dec. 31, 2005, Dr. Depr. Expense—Trucks, $4,521

Dec. 31, 2006, Dr. Loss on Disposal of Trucks, $1,822

**Required**

Prepare journal entries to record these transactions and events.

---

**Part 1.** A machine costing $210,000 with a four-year life and an estimated $20,000 salvage value is installed in Calhoon Company's factory on January 1. The factory manager estimates the machine will produce 475,000 units of product during its life. It actually produces the following units: year 1, 121,400; year 2, 122,400; year 3, 119,600; and year 4, 118,200. The total number of units produced by the end of year 4 exceeds the original estimate—this difference was not predicted. (The machine must not be depreciated below its estimated salvage value.)

**Problem 8-5A**
Depreciation methods; disposal of plant asset

C3   P1   P2   P4

**Required**

Prepare a table with the following column headings and compute depreciation for each year (and total depreciation of all years combined) for the machine under each depreciation method.

| Year | Straight-Line | Units-of-Production | Double-Declining-Balance |
|------|---------------|---------------------|--------------------------|
|      |               |                     |                          |

**Check**   Year 4: Units-of-Production Depreciation, $44,640; DDB Depreciation, $6,250

**Part 2.** Calhoon purchases a used machine for $167,000 cash on January 2 and readies it for use the next day at a $3,420 cost. On January 3, it is installed on a required operating platform costing $1,080, and it is readied for operations. The company predicts the machine will be used for six years and have a $14,600 salvage value. Depreciation is to be charged on a straight-line basis. On December 31, at the end of its fifth year in operations, it is disposed of.

**Required**

**a.** Prepare journal entries to record the machine's purchase and the costs to ready and install it. Cash is paid for all costs incurred.

**b.** Prepare journal entries to record depreciation of the machine at December 31 of its first year in operations and at December 31 in the year of its disposal.

**c.** Prepare journal entries to record the machine's disposal under each of the following separate assumptions: (i) it is sold for $13,500 cash; (ii) it is sold for $45,000 cash; and (iii) it is destroyed in a fire and the insurance company pays $24,000 cash to settle the loss claim.

(b) Depr. Exp., $26,150

(iii) Dr. Loss from Fire, $16,750

## Problem 8-6A

Intangible assets and natural resources

A1   P5   P6

**Check**   Dr. Rent Expense for:
(d) $9,250, (f) $35,000

**Part 1.** On July 1, 2000, Sweetman Company signed a contract to lease space in a building for 15 years. The lease contract calls for annual (prepaid) rental payments of $70,000 on each July 1 throughout the life of the lease and for the lessee to pay for all additions and improvements to the leased property. On June 25, 2005, Sweetman decides to sublease the space to Kirk & Associates for the remaining 10 years of the lease—Kirk pays $185,000 to Sweetman for the right to sublease and it agrees to assume the obligation to pay the $70,000 annual rent to the building owner beginning July 1, 2005. After taking possession of the leased space, Kirk pays for improving the office portion of the leased space at a $129,840 cost. The improvements are paid for on July 5, 2005, and are estimated to have a useful life equal to the 16 years remaining in the life of the building.

**Required**

Prepare entries for Kirk to record (a) its payment to Sweetman for the right to sublease the building space, (b) its payment of the 2005 annual rent to the building owner, and (c) its payment for the office improvements. Prepare Kirk's year-end adjusting entries required at December 31, 2005, to (d) amortize the $185,000 cost of the sublease, (e) amortize the office improvements, and (f) record rent expense.

**Part 2.** On July 23 of the current year, Dakota Mining Co. pays $4,836,000 for land estimated to contain 7,800,000 tons of recoverable ore. It installs machinery costing $390,000 that has a 10-year life and no salvage value and is capable of mining the ore deposit in eight years. The machinery is paid for on July 25, seven days before mining operations begin. The company removes and sells 400,000 tons of ore during its first five months of operations. Depreciation of the machinery is in proportion to the mine's depletion as the machinery will be abandoned after the ore is mined.

**Required**

*Preparation Component*

(c) Depletion, $248,000;
(d) Depreciation, $20,000

Prepare entries to record (a) the purchase of the land, (b) the cost and installation of machinery, (c) the first five months' depletion assuming the land has a net salvage value of zero after the ore is mined, and (d) the first five months' depreciation on machinery.

*Analysis Component*

Describe both the similarities and differences in amortization, depletion, and depreciation.

## Problem 8-7A[A]

Goodwill estimation and analysis

P6

mhhe.com/wild3e

Rent-Center, an equipment rental business, has the following balance sheet on December 31, 2005:

| **Assets** | | |
| --- | --- | --- |
| Cash ................................ | | $ 93,930 |
| Equipment ........................... | $678,800 | |
| Accumulated depreciation—Equipment ....... | 271,500 | 407,300 |
| Buildings ............................. | 340,000 | |
| Accumulated depreciation—Buildings ......... | 182,400 | 157,600 |
| Land ................................ | | 93,000 |
| Total assets .......................... | | $751,830 |
| | | |
| **Liabilities and Equity** | | |
| Accounts payable ...................... | | $ 18,650 |
| Long-term note payable .................. | | 337,250 |
| Total equity .......................... | | 395,930 |
| Total liabilities and equity ................ | | $751,830 |

Normal annual net income averages 20% of equity in this industry. Rent-Center regularly expects to earn $100,000 annually. The balance sheet amounts are reasonable estimates of market values for both assets (except goodwill) and liabilities. In negotiations to sell the business, Rent-Center proposes to measure goodwill by capitalizing at a rate of 15% the amount of above-normal net income. The potential buyer thinks that goodwill should be valued at five times the amount of above-normal net income.

**Required**

**Check**   (1) $138,760
          (2) $104,070

**1.** Compute the amount of goodwill as proposed by Rent-Center.

**2.** Compute the amount of goodwill as proposed by the potential buyer.

**3.** The buyer purchases the business for the net asset amount (assets less liabilities) reported on the December 31, 2005, balance sheet plus the amount proposed by Rent-Center for goodwill. What is the buyer's purchase price?

**4.** If the buyer earns $100,225 of net income in its first year after acquiring the business under the terms in part 3, what rate of return does the buyer earn on this investment for the first year? Explain how goodwill impacts the buyer's net income computation.

**Check**   (4) 18.7%

---

Niemeyer Company negotiates a lump-sum purchase of several assets from a contractor who is relocating. The purchase is completed on January 1, 2005, at a total cash price of $1,610,000 for a building, land, land improvements, and six trucks. The estimated market values of the assets are building, $784,800; land, $540,640; land improvements, $226,720; and three trucks, $191,840. The company's fiscal year ends on December 31.

**PROBLEM SET B**

**Problem 8-1B**
Plant asset costs; depreciation methods

C1  C2  A1  P1  P2

**Required**

**1.** Prepare a table to allocate the lump-sum purchase price to the separate assets purchased (round percents to the nearest 1%). Prepare the journal entry to record the purchase.

**2.** Compute the depreciation expense for year 2005 on the building using the straight-line method, assuming a 12-year life and a $100,500 salvage value.

**Check**   (2) $52,000

**3.** Compute the depreciation expense for year 2005 on the land improvements assuming a 10-year life and double-declining-balance depreciation.

(3) $41,860

*Analysis Component*

**4.** Defend or refute this statement: Accelerated depreciation results in payment of more taxes over the asset's life.

---

In January 2005, InTech pays $1,350,000 for a tract of land with two buildings. It plans to demolish Building A and build a new shop in its place. Building B will be a company office; it is appraised at $472,770, with a useful life of 15 years and a $90,000 salvage value. A lighted parking lot near Building B has improvements (Land Improvements B) valued at $125,145 that are expected to last another six years with no salvage value. Without the buildings and improvements, the tract of land is valued at $792,585. InTech also incurs the following additional costs:

**Problem 8-2B**
Asset cost allocation; straight-line depreciation

C1  C2  P1  P2

| | |
|---|---:|
| Cost to demolish Building A . . . . . . . . . . . . . . . . . . . . . . . . . . . . . . . . . . . . . . | $ 117,000 |
| Cost of additional land grading . . . . . . . . . . . . . . . . . . . . . . . . . . . . . . . . . . . | 172,500 |
| Cost to construct new building (Building C), having a useful life of 20 years and a $295,500 salvage value . . . . . . . . . . . . . . . . . . . . . . . . . . . . . . . . . | 1,356,000 |
| Cost of new land improvements (Land Improvements C) near building C, having a 10-year useful life and no salvage value . . . . . . . . . . . . . . . . . . . . . . . . | 101,250 |

**Required**

**1.** Prepare a table with the following column headings: Land, Building B, Building C, Land Improvements B, and Land Improvements C. Allocate the costs incurred by InTech to the appropriate columns and total each column (round percents to the nearest 1%).

**Check**   (1) Land costs, $1,059,000; Building B costs, $459,000

**2.** Prepare a single journal entry to record all incurred costs assuming they are paid in cash on January 1, 2005.

**3.** Using the straight-line method, prepare the December 31 adjusting entries to record depreciation for the 12 months of 2005 when these assets were in use.

(3) Depr.—Land Improv. B and C, $20,250 and $10,125

---

Xpress Delivery Service completed the following transactions and events involving the purchase and operation of equipment for its business:

**Problem 8-3B**
Computing and revising depreciation; revenue and capital expenditures

C3  P1  P3

*2004*

Jan.  1   Paid $24,950 cash plus $1,950 in sales tax for a new delivery van that was estimated to have a five-year life and a $3,400 salvage value. Van costs are recorded in the Equipment account.

Jan.  3   Paid $1,550 to install sorting racks in the van for more accurate and quicker delivery of packages. This increases the estimated salvage value of the van by another $200.

Dec. 31   Recorded annual straight-line depreciation on the van.

**Check**   Dec. 31, 2004, Dr. Depr. Expense—Equip., $4,970

**2005**

Jan.  1  Paid $1,970 to overhaul the van's engine, which increased the van's estimated useful life by two years.
May 10  Paid $600 to repair the van after the driver backed it into a loading dock.
Dec. 31  Record annual straight-line depreciation on the van.

**Required**

Prepare journal entries to record these transactions and events.

---

## Problem 8-4B
Computing and revising depreciation; selling plant assets

C3  P2  P4

Field Instruments completed the following transactions and events involving its machinery:

**2004**

Jan.  1  Paid $106,600 cash plus $6,400 in sales tax for a new machine. The machine is estimated to have a six-year life and a $9,800 salvage value.
Dec. 31  Recorded annual straight-line depreciation on the machinery.

**2005**

Dec. 31  Due to new information obtained earlier in the year, the machine's estimated useful life was changed from six to four years, and the estimated salvage value was increased to $13,050. Recorded annual straight-line depreciation on the machinery.

**2006**

Dec. 31  Recorded annual straight-line depreciation on the machinery.
Dec. 31  Sold the machine for $25,240 cash.

**Required**

Prepare journal entries to record these transactions and events.

---

## Problem 8-5B
Depreciation methods; disposal of plant assets

C3  P1  P2  P4

**Part 1.** On January 2, Gannon Co. purchases and installs a new machine costing $312,000 with a five-year life and an estimated $28,000 salvage value. Management estimates the machine will produce 1,136,000 units of product during its life. Actual production of units is as follows: year 1, 245,600; year 2, 230,400; year 3, 227,000; year 4, 232,600; and year 5, 211,200. The total number of units produced by the end of year 5 exceeds the original estimate—this difference was not predicted. (The machine must not be depreciated below its estimated salvage value.)

**Required**

Prepare a table with the following column headings and compute depreciation for each year (and total depreciation of all years combined) for the machine under each depreciation method.

| Year | Straight-Line | Units-of-Production | Double-Declining-Balance |
|------|---------------|---------------------|--------------------------|
|      |               |                     |                          |

**Part 2.** On January 1, Gannon purchases a used machine for $130,000 and readies it for use the next day at a cost of $3,390. On January 4, it is mounted on a required operating platform costing $4,800, and it is readied for operations. Management estimates the machine will be used for seven years and have an $18,000 salvage value. Depreciation is to be charged on a straight-line basis. On December 31, at the end of its sixth year of use, the machine is disposed of.

**Required**

**a.** Prepare journal entries to record the machine's purchase and the costs to ready and install it. Cash is paid for all costs incurred.

**b.** Prepare journal entries to record depreciation of the machine at December 31 of its first year in operations and at December 31 in the year of its disposal.

**c.** Prepare journal entries to record the machine's disposal under each of the following separate assumptions: (i) it is sold for $30,000 cash; (ii) it is sold for $50,000 cash; and (iii) it is destroyed in a fire and the insurance company pays $20,000 cash to settle the loss claim.

**Part 1.** On January 1, 2000, Liberty Co. entered into a 12-year lease on a building. The lease contract requires (1) annual (prepaid) rental payments of $26,400 each January 1 throughout the life of the lease and (2) for the lessee to pay for all additions and improvements to the leased property. On January 1, 2007, Liberty decides to sublease the space to Moberly Co. for the remaining five years of the lease—Moberly pays $30,000 to Liberty for the right to sublease and agrees to assume the obligation to pay the $26,400 annual rent to the building owner beginning January 1, 2007. After taking possession of the leased space, Moberly pays for improving the office portion of the leased space at an $18,000 cost. The improvements are paid for on January 3, 2007, and are estimated to have a useful life equal to the 13 years remaining in the life of the building.

**Problem 8-6B**

Intangible assets and natural resources

A1   P5   P6

**Required**

Prepare entries for Moberly to record (*a*) its payment to Liberty for the right to sublease the building space, (*b*) its payment of the 2007 annual rent to the building owner, and (*c*) its payment for the office improvements. Prepare Moberly's year-end adjusting entries required on December 31, 2007, to (*d*) amortize the $30,000 cost of the sublease, (*e*) amortize the office improvements, and (*f*) record rent expense.

**Check**   Dr. Rent Expense: (*d*) $6,000, (*f*) $26,400

**Part 2.** On February 19 of the current year, Rock Chalk Co. pays $4,450,000 for land estimated to contain 5 million tons of recoverable ore. It installs machinery costing $200,000 that has a 16-year life and no salvage value and is capable of mining the ore deposit in 12 years. The machinery is paid for on March 21, eleven days before mining operations begin. The company removes and sells 352,000 tons of ore during its first nine months of operations. Depreciation of the machinery is in proportion to the mine's depletion as the machinery will be abandoned after the ore is mined.

**Required**

*Preparation Component*

Prepare entries to record (*a*) the purchase of the land, (*b*) the cost and installation of machinery, (*c*) the first nine months' depletion assuming the land has a net salvage value of zero after the ore is mined, and (*d*) the first nine months' depreciation on machinery.

(*c*) Depletion, $313,280;
(*d*) Depreciation, $14,080

*Analysis Component*

Describe both the similarities and differences in amortization, depletion, and depreciation.

Pack Casual Wear has the following balance sheet on December 31, 2005:

**Problem 8-7B**[A]

Goodwill estimation and analysis

P6

| Assets | | |
|---|---:|---:|
| Cash .................................. | | $  138,700 |
| Merchandise inventory ................... | | 607,950 |
| Buildings ............................. | $451,500 | |
| Accumulated depreciation—Buildings ....... | 210,800 | 240,700 |
| Land ................................. | | 192,400 |
| Total assets .......................... | | $1,179,750 |
| | | |
| **Liabilities and Equity** | | |
| Accounts payable ...................... | | $   98,325 |
| Long-term note payable ................. | | 414,050 |
| Total equity .......................... | | 667,375 |
| Total liabilities and equity .............. | | $1,179,750 |

Normal annual net income averages 32% of equity in this industry. Pack regularly expects to earn $230,000 annually. The balance sheet amounts are reasonable estimates of market values for both assets (except goodwill) and liabilities. In negotiations to sell the business, Pack proposes to measure goodwill by capitalizing at a rate of 10% the amount of above-normal net income. The potential buyer believes that goodwill should be valued at eight times the amount of above-normal net income.

**Required**

1. Compute the amount of goodwill as proposed by Pack.

2. Compute the amount of goodwill as proposed by the potential buyer.

3. The buyer purchases the business for the net asset amount (assets less liabilities) reported on the December 31, 2005, balance sheet plus the amount proposed by Pack for goodwill. What is the buyer's purchase price?

4. If the buyer earns $200,175 of net income in its first year after acquiring the business under the terms in part 3, what rate of return does the buyer earn on this investment for the first year? Is the goodwill asset amortized or not? Explain.

# PROBLEM SET C

Problem Set C is available at the book's Website to further reinforce and assess your learning.

# SERIAL PROBLEM

Success Systems

*(This serial problem began in Chapter 1 and continues through most of the book. If previous chapter segments were not completed, the serial problem can begin at this point. It is helpful, but not necessary, for you to use the Working Papers that accompany the book.)*

Selected ledger account balances for Success Systems follow.

| | For the Three Months Ended December 31, 2004 | For the Three Months Ended March 31, 2005 |
|---|---|---|
| Office equipment . . . . . . . . . . . . . . . | $ 8,000 | $ 8,000 |
| Accumulated depreciation— Office equipment . . . . . . . . . . . . . . | 400 | 800 |
| Computer equipment . . . . . . . . . . . . . | 20,000 | 20,000 |
| Accumulated depreciation— Computer equipment . . . . . . . . . . . | 1,250 | 2,500 |
| Total revenue . . . . . . . . . . . . . . . . . . | 31,284 | 43,853 |
| Total assets . . . . . . . . . . . . . . . . . . . | 93,248 | 129,909 |

**Required**

1. Assume that Success Systems does not acquire additional office equipment or computer equipment in 2005. Compute the amounts for the year ended December 31, 2005, for Depreciation Expense—Office Equipment and for Depreciation Expense—Computer Equipment (assume use of the straight-line method).

2. What is the book value of both the Office Equipment account and the Computer Equipment account as of December 31, 2005?

3. Compute the 3-month total asset turnover for Success Systems as of March 31, 2005. Use total revenue for the numerator and average the December 31, 2004, total assets and the March 31, 2005, total assets for the denominator. Interpret its total asset turnover if competitors average 2.5 for annual periods.

## BEYOND THE NUMBERS

### REPORTING IN ACTION

A1  A2

**BTN 8-1**   Refer to the financial statements of **Krispy Kreme** in Appendix A to answer the following:

1. What percent of the original cost of Krispy Kreme's property, plant, and equipment remains to be depreciated as of February 2, 2003, and February 3, 2002? Assume these assets have no salvage value.

2. Over what length(s) of time is Krispy Kreme amortizing its intangible assets?

3. What is the change in total property and equipment (before accumulated depreciation) for the year ended February 2, 2003? What is the amount of cash provided (used) by investing activities for property and equipment for the year ended February 2, 2003? What is one possible explanation for the difference between these two amounts?

4. Compute its total asset turnover for the year ended February 2, 2003.

*Roll On*

**5.** Access Krispy Kreme's financial statements for fiscal years ending after February 2, 2003, at its Website (**KrispyKreme.com**) or the SEC's EDGAR database (**www.sec.gov**). Recompute Krispy's total asset turnover for the additional years' data you collect. Comment on any differences relative to the turnover computed in part 4.

---

**BTN 8-2**   Key comparative figures ($ thousands) for **Krispy Kreme** and **Tastykake** follow:

| Key Figures | Krispy Kreme | | | Tastykake | | |
|---|---|---|---|---|---|---|
| | Current Year | One Year Prior | Two Years Prior | Current Year | One Year Prior | Two Years Prior |
| Total assets . . . . . . . . | $410,487 | $255,376 | $171,493 | $116,560 | $116,137 | $112,192 |
| Net sales  . . . . . . . . . | 491,549 | 394,354 | 300,715 | 162,263 | 166,245 | 162,877 |

**COMPARATIVE ANALYSIS**

A2

**Required**

**1.** Compute total asset turnover for the most recent two years for both Krispy Kreme and Tastykake using the data shown.

**2.** Which company is more efficient in generating net sales given the total assets it employs?

---

**BTN 8-3**   Flo Choi owns a small business and manages its accounting. Her company just finished a year in which a large amount of borrowed funds was invested in a new building addition as well as in equipment and fixture additions. Choi's banker requires her to submit semiannual financial statements so he can monitor the financial health of her business. He has warned her that if profit margins erode, he might raise the interest rate on the borrowed funds to reflect the increased loan risk from the bank's point of view. Choi knows profit margin is likely to decline this year. As she prepares year-end adjusting entries, she decides to apply the following depreciation rule: All asset additions are considered to be in use on the first day of the following month. (The previous rule assumed assets are in use on the first day of the month nearest to the purchase date.)

**ETHICS CHALLENGE**

C1   C2

**Required**

**1.** Identify decisions that managers like Choi must make in applying depreciation methods.

**2.** Is Choi's rule an ethical violation, or is it a legitimate decision in computing depreciation?

**3.** How will Choi's depreciation rule affect the profit margin of her business?

---

**BTN 8-4**   Teams are to select an industry, and each team member is to select a different company in that industry. Each team member is to acquire the financial statements (form 10-K) of the company selected—see the company's Website or the SEC's EDGAR database (**www.sec.gov**). Use the financial statements to compute total asset turnover. Communicate with teammates via a meeting, e-mail, or telephone to discuss the meaning of this ratio, how different companies compare to each other, and the industry norm. The team must prepare a one-page report that describes the ratios for each company and identifies the conclusions reached during the team's discussion.

**COMMUNICATING IN PRACTICE**

A2

---

**BTN 8-5**   Access **Adaptec's** (ticker: ADPT) 10-K report for its fiscal year ended March 31, 2002, filed on June 24, 2002, at **www.sec.gov** to answer the following.

**TAKING IT TO THE NET**

C1   P6

**Required**

**1.** Read the overview of Adaptec's business and briefly describe the types of products it produces.

**2.** On page 12 of its 10-K, what information is provided regarding the company's patents?

**3.** Does Adaptec show any patent-related revenue or expense on its consolidated statement of operations (income statement)?

mhhe.com/wild3e

## TEAMWORK IN ACTION

C2  A1  P2

**Point:** This activity can follow an overview of each method. Step 1 allows for three areas of expertise. Larger teams will have some duplication of areas, but the straight-line choice should not be duplicated. Expert teams can use the book and consult with the instructor.

**BTN 8-6**   Each team member is to become an expert on one depreciation method to facilitate teammates' understanding of that method. Follow these procedures:

**a.** Each team member is to select an area for expertise from one of the following depreciation methods: straight-line, units-of-production, or double-declining-balance.

**b.** Expert teams are to be formed from those who have selected the same area of expertise. The instructor will identify the location where each expert team meets.

**c.** Using the following data, expert teams are to collaborate and develop a presentation answering the requirements. Expert team members must write the presentation in a format they can show to their learning teams.

**Data and Requirements**  On January 8, 2004, Whitewater Riders purchases a van to transport rafters back to the point of departure at the conclusion of the rafting adventures they operate. The cost of the van is $44,000. It has an estimated salvage value of $2,000 and is expected to be used for four years and driven 60,000 miles. The van is expected to be driven 12,000 miles in 2004, 18,000 miles in 2005, 21,000 in 2006, and 10,000 in 2007.

   **1.** Compute annual depreciation expense for each year of the van's estimated useful life.

   **2.** Explain when and how annual depreciation is recorded.

   **3.** Explain the impact on income of this depreciation method versus others over the van's life.

   **4.** Identify the van's book value for each year of its life and illustrate the reporting of this amount for any one year.

**d.** Re-form original learning teams. In rotation, experts are to present to their teams the results from part *c*. Experts are to encourage and respond to questions.

## BUSINESS WEEK ACTIVITY

C1  P6

mhhe.com/wild3e

**BTN 8-7**   Read the article "How Much Is the Goodwill Worth?" in the September 16, 2002, issue of *Business Week*. (The book's Website provides a free link.)

**Required**

   **1.** Explain how goodwill is calculated in accounting terms.

   **2.** Before the accounting rules changed, how was goodwill accounted for?

   **3.** How have the accounting rules governing goodwill recently changed?

   **4.** Why is it a good idea to become familiar with accounting for goodwill?

## ENTREPRENEURIAL DECISION

A2

**BTN 8-8**   Review the chapter's opening feature involving **Queston Construction**. Assume that it generates annual sales of $3 million on an average total asset base of $1,000,000. To increase sales, Cordova proposes to expand her construction company, which would increase average total assets by $500,000. This expansion is expected to increase net sales by $2,500,000.

**Required**

   **1.** Compute the company's total asset turnover under (*a*) current conditions and (*b*) proposed conditions.

   **2.** Evaluate and comment on the merits of Cordova's proposal given your analysis in part 1. Identify any concerns you would express about the proposal.

## HITTING THE ROAD

C1  P5  P6

**BTN 8-9**   Team up with one or more classmates for this activity. Identify companies in your community or area that must account for at least one of the following assets: natural resource; patent; lease; leasehold improvement; copyright; trademark; or goodwill. You might find a company having more than one type of asset. Once you identify a company with a specific asset, describe the accounting this company uses to allocate the cost of that asset to the periods benefited from its use.

**BTN 8-10**   Grupo Bimbo, Krispy Kreme, and Tastykake are all competitors in the global marketplace. Key comparative figures (in millions) for these companies' recent annual accounting periods follow.

**GLOBAL DECISION**

A2

| Key Figures | Grupo Bimbo (millions of pesos) | | | Krispy Kreme | | Tastykake | |
|---|---|---|---|---|---|---|---|
| | Current Year | Prior Year | Two Years Prior | Current Year | Prior Year | Current Year | Prior Year |
| Total assets ........... | 31,719 | 23,781 | 25,035 | $410 | $255 | $117 | $116 |
| Net sales ............. | 41,373 | 34,968 | 32,008 | $492 | $394 | $162 | $166 |
| Total asset turnover ..... | ? | ? | — | 1.48 | 1.85 | 1.39 | 1.46 |

**Required**

1. Compute total asset turnover for the most recent two years for Grupo Bimbo using the data shown.

2. Which company of the three is most efficient in generating net sales given the total assets it employs?

"I like to be independent and to be able to control my own destiny"—André Downey

# 9 Reporting and Analyzing Current Liabilities

## A Look Back

Chapter 8 focused on long-term assets including plant assets, natural resources, and intangibles. We showed how to record their costs, allocate their costs to periods benefiting from their use, record their disposal, and assess their turnover.

## A Look at This Chapter

This chapter emphasizes current liabilities. We explain how to identify, compute, record, and report current liabilities in financial statements. We also analyze and interpret these liabilities, including those related to employee costs.

## A Look Ahead

Chapter 10 focuses on long-term liabilities. We explain how to value, record, amortize, and report these liabilities in financial statements.

# CAP

## Conceptual

**C1** Describe current and long-term liabilities and their characteristics. *(p. 352)*

**C2** Identify and describe known current liabilities. *(p. 354)*

**C3** Explain how to account for contingent liabilities. *(p. 364)*

## Analytical

**A1** Compute the times interest earned ratio and use it to analyze liabilities. *(p. 365)*

## Procedural

**P1** Prepare entries to account for short-term notes payable. *(p. 355)*

**P2** Compute and record *employee* payroll deductions and liabilities. *(p. 357)*

**P3** Compute and record *employer* payroll expenses and liabilities. *(p. 359)*

**P4** Account for estimated liabilities, including warranties and bonuses. *(p. 361)*

---

## Decision Feature

# Cleaning Up in Business

LANDOVER, MD—26-year-old André Downey saw opportunity in environmental cleanup. Downey, however, faced obstacles in funding his business because banks did not share his enthusiasm. Convinced of his eventual success, Downey obtained 10 credit cards that, in sum, provided him $100,000 for his start-up called **Environmental, Engineering & Construction, Inc. (EECinc.com).** That was 1993. Today, Downey's company projects annual revenues of more than $3 million.

"There is a lot of risk involved," admits Downey. "But if you're successful, the benefits definitely outweigh the risks." His company focuses on cleanup of environmental hazards such as black toxic mold, asbestos, and lead.

Downey's service-oriented business demands good employees and he is devoted to them. "Luckily, I have good people working for me," says Downey. "So I can go to the next level." This next level requires Downey to attend to many aspects of business, including the crucial task of managing liabilities for payroll, supplies, employee benefits, vacations, training, and taxes. Without his effective management of liabilities, especially payroll and employee benefits, his company would not be where it is today. Adds Downey, if you want your business to be successful, monitoring and controlling liabilities is a must.

This chapter focuses on measuring and analyzing current liabilities like those Downey insists must be dealt with by good business owners. To ignore them, especially those requiring payments to government agencies and to key employees, is too risky. "This way," says Downey, "if I fail, it's on me." Given his revenue projections, Downey is cleaning up with more than the environment.

[Sources: *Environmental, Engineering & Construction Website,* January 2004; *Black Enterprise,* November 2002; *Gazette Community News,* December 2002.]

Previous chapters introduced liabilities such as accounts payable, notes payable, wages payable, and unearned revenues. This chapter further explains these liabilities and additional ones such as warranties, taxes, payroll, vacation pay, and bonuses. It also describes contingent liabilities and introduces some basic long-term liabilities. The focus is on how to define, classify, measure, report, and analyze these liabilities so that this information is useful to business decision makers.

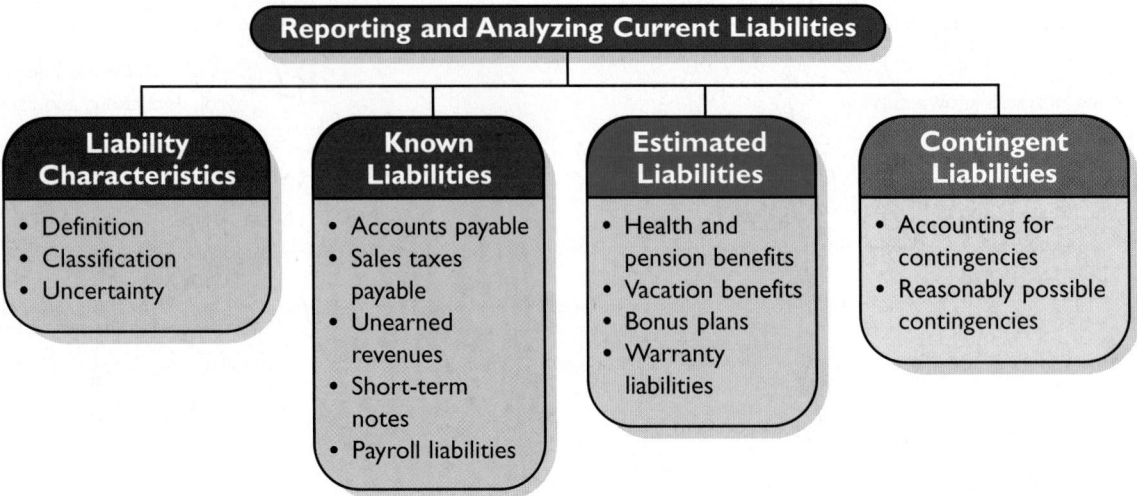

## Characteristics of Liabilities

This section discusses important characteristics of liabilities and how liabilities are classified and reported.

### Defining Liabilities

**C1**   Describe current and long-term liabilities and their characteristics.

A *liability* is a probable future payment of assets or services that a company is presently obligated to make as a result of past transactions or events. This definition includes three crucial factors:

■ A past transaction or event.
■ A present obligation.
■ A future payment of assets or services.

**Exhibit 9.1**

Characteristics of a Liability

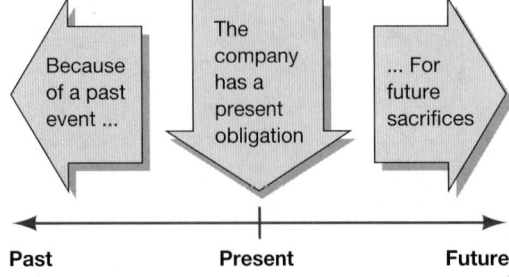

These three important elements are portrayed visually in Exhibit 9.1. Liabilities do not include all expected future payments. For example, most companies expect to pay wages to their employees in upcoming months and years, but these future payments are not liabilities because no past event such as employee work resulted in a present obligation. Instead, such liabilities arise when employees perform their work and earn the wages.

### Classifying Liabilities

Information about liabilities is more useful when the balance sheet identifies them as either current or long term. Decision makers need to know when obligations are due so they can plan for them and take appropriate action.

**Current Liabilities**  Current liabilities, also called *short-term liabilities,* are obligations due within one year or the company's operating cycle, whichever is longer. They are expected to be paid using current assets or by creating other current liabilities. Common examples of current liabilities are accounts payable, short-term notes payable, wages payable, warranty liabilities, lease liabilities, taxes payable, and unearned revenues.

Current liabilities differ across companies because they depend on the type of company operations. **Univision Communications**, for instance, reported the following current liabilities related to its Spanish-language media operations ($000s):

| | |
|---|---|
| Music copyright and artist royalties ....... | $25,611 |
| Deferred advertising revenues .......... | 4,250 |

**Harley-Davidson** reports a much different set of current liabilities. It discloses current liabilities made up of items such as warranty, recall, and dealer incentive liabilities.

**Long-Term Liabilities**  A company's obligations not expected to be paid within the longer of one year or the company's operating cycle are reported as **long-term liabilities.** They can include long-term notes payable, warranty liabilities, lease liabilities, and bonds payable. They are sometimes reported on the balance sheet in a single long-term liabilities total or in multiple categories. **Domino's Pizza**, for instance, reports long-term liabilities of $641 million. They are reported after current liabilities. A single liability also can be divided between the current and noncurrent sections if a company expects to make payments toward it in both the short and long term. Domino's reports ($ millions) long-term debt, $599; and current portion of long-term debt, $3. The second item is reported in current liabilities. We sometimes see liabilities that do not have a fixed due date but instead are payable on the creditor's demand. These are reported as current liabilities because of the possibility of payment in the near term. Exhibit 9.2 shows amounts of current liabilities and as a percent of total liabilities for selected companies.

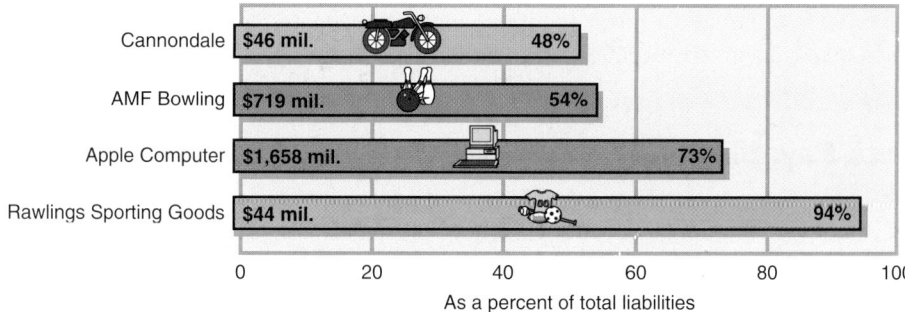

**Point:** Improper classification of liabilities can distort key ratios used in financial statement analysis and decision making.

**Global:** In some countries such as France, the balance sheet does not separate current liabilities into their own category.

**Point:** The current ratio will be overstated if a company fails to classify any portion of long-term debt due next period as a current liability.

**Exhibit 9.2**

Current Liabilities of Selected Companies

## Uncertainty in Liabilities

Accounting for liabilities involves addressing three important questions: Whom to pay? When to pay? How much to pay? Answers to these questions are often decided when a liability is incurred. For example, if a company has a $100 account payable to a specific individual, payable on March 15, the answers are clear. The company knows whom to pay, when to pay, and how much to pay. However, the answers to one or more of these questions are uncertain for some liabilities.

**Uncertainty in Whom to Pay**  Liabilities can involve uncertainty in whom to pay. For instance, a company can create a liability with a known amount when issuing a note that is payable to its holder. In this case, a specific amount is payable to the note's holder at a specified date, but the company does not know who the holder is until that date. Despite this uncertainty, the company reports this liability on its balance sheet.

**Point:** An *accrued expense* is an unpaid expense that is also a liability. This is the reason accrued expenses are also called *accrued liabilities.*

**Uncertainty in When to Pay**   A company can have an obligation of a known amount to a known creditor but not know when it must be paid. For example, a legal services firm can accept fees in advance from a client who plans to use the firm's services in the future. This means that the firm has a liability that it settles by providing services at an unknown future date. Although this uncertainty exists, the legal firm's balance sheet must report this liability. These types of obligations are reported as current liabilities because they are likely to be settled in the short term.

**Uncertainty in How Much to Pay**   A company can be aware of an obligation but not know how much will be required to settle it. For example, a company using electrical power is billed only after the meter has been read. This cost is incurred and the liability created before a bill is received. A liability to the power company is reported as an estimated amount if the balance sheet is prepared before a bill arrives.

---

### Quick Check

**1.** What is a liability? Identify its crucial characteristics.

**2.** Is every expected future payment a liability?

**3.** If a liability is payable in 15 months, is it classified as current or long term?

Answers—p. 376

---

# Known (Determinable) Liabilities

Most liabilities arise from situations with little uncertainty. They are set by agreements, contracts, or laws and are measurable. These liabilities are **known liabilities,** also called *definitely determinable liabilities.* Known liabilities include accounts payable, notes payable, payroll, sales taxes, unearned revenues, and leases. We describe how to account for these known liabilities in this section.

## Accounts Payable

**C2**   Identify and describe known current liabilities.

Accounts payable, or trade accounts payable, are amounts owed to suppliers for products or services purchased on credit. Accounting for accounts payable is primarily explained and illustrated in our discussion of merchandising activities in Chapters 4 and 5.

## Sales Taxes Payable

Nearly all states and many cities levy taxes on retail sales. Sales taxes are stated as a percent of selling prices. The seller collects sales taxes from customers when sales occur and remits these collections (often monthly) to the proper government agency. Since sellers currently owe these collections to the government, this amount is a current liability. **Home Depot,** for instance, reports sales taxes payable of $307 million in its recent annual report. To illustrate, if Home Depot sells materials on August 31 for $6,000 cash that are subject to a 5% sales tax, the revenue portion of this transaction is recorded as follows:

Assets = Liabilities + Equity
+6,300      +300      +6,000

| Aug. 31 | Cash ................................... | 6,300 | |
| | Sales ............................... | | 6,000 |
| | Sales Taxes Payable ($6,000 × 0.05) ....... | | 300 |
| | *To record cash sales and 5% sales tax.* | | |

Sales Taxes Payable is debited and Cash credited when it remits these collections to the government. Sales Taxes Payable is not an expense. It arises because laws require sellers to collect this cash from customers for the government.[1]

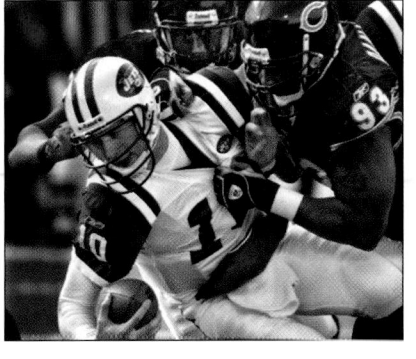

## Unearned Revenues

*Unearned revenues* (also called *deferred revenues, collections in advance,* and *prepayments*) are amounts received in advance from customers for future products or services. Advance ticket sales for sporting events or music concerts are examples. The **New York Jets**, for instance, report "deferred game revenues" from advance ticket sales in its balance sheet. To illustrate, assume the Jets sell $5 million of season tickets for 8 home games; its entry is

**Point:** To *defer* a revenue means to postpone recognition of a revenue collected in advance until it is earned. Sport teams must defer recognition of ticket sales until games are played.

| June 30 | Cash ............................... | 5,000,000 | |
| | Unearned Season Ticket Revenue ......... | | 5,000,000 |
| | *To record sale of season tickets.* | | |

Assets   =   Liabilities   +   Equity
+5,000,000    +5,000,000

When a home game is played, the Jets record revenue for that portion earned:

| Oct. 31 | Unearned Season Ticket Revenue ............ | 625,000 | |
| | Season Ticket Revenue ................ | | 625,000 |
| | *To record season ticket revenues earned.* | | |

Assets = Liabilities +   Equity
            −625,000    +625,000

Unearned Season Ticket Revenue is an unearned revenue account and is reported as a current liability. Unearned revenues also arise with airline ticket sales, magazine subscriptions, construction projects, hotel reservations, and custom orders.

## Short-Term Notes Payable

A **short-term note payable** is a written promise to pay a specified amount on a definite future date within one year or the company's operating cycle, whichever is longer. These promissory notes are negotiable (as are checks), meaning they can be transferred from party to party by endorsement. The written documentation provided by notes is helpful in resolving disputes and for pursuing legal actions involving these liabilities. Most notes payable bear interest to compensate for use of the money until payment is made. Short-term notes payable can arise from many transactions. A company that purchases merchandise on credit can sometimes extend the credit period by signing a note to replace an account payable. Such notes also can arise when money is borrowed from a bank. We describe both of these cases.

**P1** Prepare entries to account for short-term notes payable.

**Point:** Required characteristics for negotiability of a note: (1) unconditional promise, (2) in writing, (3) specific amount, and (4) definite due date.

**Note Given to Extend Credit Period**   A company can replace an account payable with a note payable. A common example is a creditor that requires the substitution of an interest-bearing note for an overdue account payable that does not bear interest. A less common situation occurs when a debtor's weak financial condition motivates the creditor to accept a note, sometimes for a lesser amount, and to close the account to ensure that this customer makes no additional credit purchases.

---

[1] Sales taxes can be computed from total sales receipts when sales taxes are not separately identified on the register. To illustrate, assume a 5% sales tax and $420 in total sales receipts (which includes sales taxes). Sales are computed as follows:

$$\text{Sales} = \text{Total sales receipts}/(1 + \text{Sales tax percentage}) = \$420/1.05 = \$400$$

Thus, the sales tax amount equals total sales receipts minus sales, or $420 − $400 = $20.

To illustrate, let's assume that on August 23, Irwin asks to extend its past-due $600 account payable to McGraw. After some negotiations, McGraw agrees to accept $100 cash and a 60-day, 12%, $500 note payable to replace the account payable. Irwin records the transaction with this entry:

Assets = Liabilities + Equity
−100        −600
            +500

| Aug. 23 | Accounts Payable—McGraw . . . . . . . . . . . . . . . | 600 | |
|---|---|---|---|
| | Cash . . . . . . . . . . . . . . . . . . . . . . . . . . . . | | 100 |
| | Notes Payable—McGraw . . . . . . . . . . . . . . | | 500 |
| | *Gave $100 cash and a 60-day, 12% note for* | | |
| | *payment on account.* | | |

Signing the note does not resolve Irwin's debt. Instead, the form of debt is changed from an account payable to a note payable. McGraw prefers the note payable over the account payable because it earns interest and it is written documentation of the debt's existence, term, and amount. When the note comes due, Irwin pays the note and interest by giving McGraw a check for $510. Irwin records that payment with this entry:

**Point:** Accounts payable are detailed in a subsidiary ledger, but notes payable are sometimes not. A file with copies of notes often serves as a subsidiary ledger.

Assets = Liabilities + Equity
−510        −500        −10

| Oct. 22 | Notes Payable—McGraw . . . . . . . . . . . . . . . . . . | 500 | |
|---|---|---|---|
| | Interest Expense . . . . . . . . . . . . . . . . . . . . . . . | 10 | |
| | Cash . . . . . . . . . . . . . . . . . . . . . . . . . . . . | | 510 |
| | *Paid note with interest ($500 × 12% × 60/360).* | | |

Interest expense is computed by multiplying the principal of the note ($500) by the annual interest rate (12%) for the fraction of the year the note is outstanding (60 days/360 days).

**Point:** Companies commonly compute interest using a 360-day year. This is known as the *banker's rule*.

**Note Given to Borrow from Bank**    A bank nearly always requires a borrower to sign a promissory note when making a loan. When the note matures, the borrower repays the note with an amount larger than the amount borrowed. The difference between the amount borrowed and the amount repaid is *interest*. This section considers a type of note whose signer promises to pay *principal* (the amount borrowed) plus interest. In this case, the *face value* of the note equals principal. Face value is the value shown on the face (front) of the note. To illustrate, assume that a company needs $2,000 for a project and borrows this money from a bank at 12% annual interest. The loan is made on September 30, 2005, and is due in 60 days. Specifically, the borrowing company signs a note with a face value equal to the amount borrowed. The note includes a statement similar to this: *"I promise to pay $2,000 plus interest at 12% within 60 days after September 30."* This simple note is shown in Exhibit 9.3.

**Point:** Cash received from long-term borrowing is reported on the statement of cash flows as a source of financing. Cash from short-term borrowing is part of operating activities. Interest incurred on a note is reported on the income statement as an expense.

**Point:** When money is borrowed from a bank, the loan is reported as an asset (receivable) on the bank's balance sheet.

## Exhibit 9.3

Note with Face Value Equal to Amount Borrowed

| **Promissory Note** | |
|---|---|
| __$2,000__ | *Sept. 30, 2005* |
| **Face Value** | **Date** |
| *Sixty days* after date, ___*I*___ promise to pay to the order of | |
| *National Bank* | |
| *Boston, MA* | |
| *Two thousand and no/100* - - - - - - - - - - - - - - - - - - - - - - - - **Dollars** | |
| **plus interest at the annual rate of** __12%__ . | |
| *Janet Lee* | |

The borrower records its receipt of cash and the new liability with this entry:

Assets = Liabilities + Equity
+2,000      +2,000

| Sept. 30 | Cash . . . . . . . . . . . . . . . . . . . . . . . . . . . . . . . . . . | 2,000 | |
|---|---|---|---|
| | Notes Payable . . . . . . . . . . . . . . . . . . . . . . . | | 2,000 |
| | *Borrowed $2,000 cash with a 60-day, 12%,* | | |
| | *$2,000 note.* | | |

When principal and interest are paid, the borrower records payment with this entry:

| Nov. 29 | Notes Payable . . . . . . . . . . . . . . . . . . . . . . . . | 2,000 | | |
|---|---|---|---|---|
| | Interest Expense . . . . . . . . . . . . . . . . . . . . . . | 40 | | |
| | Cash . . . . . . . . . . . . . . . . . . . . . . . . . . . | | 2,040 | |
| | *Paid note with interest ($2,000 × 12% × 60/360).* | | | |

Assets = Liabilities + Equity
−2,040    −2,000    −40

**End-of-period interest adjustment.** When the end of an accounting period occurs between the signing of a note payable and its maturity date, the *matching principle* requires us to record the accrued but unpaid interest on the note. To illustrate, let's return to the note in Exhibit 9.3, but assume that the company borrows $2,000 cash on December 16, 2005, instead of September 30. This 60-day note matures on February 14, 2006, and the company's fiscal year ends on December 31. Thus, we need to record interest expense for the final 15 days in December.

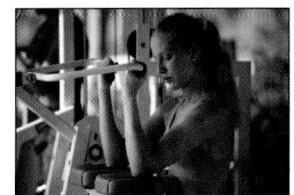

Specifically, we know that 15 days of the 60-day loan period for the $2,000, 12% note have elapsed by December 31. This means that one-fourth (15 days/60 days) of the $40 total interest is an expense of year 2005. The borrower records this expense with the following adjusting entry:

| 2005 | | | | |
|---|---|---|---|---|
| Dec. 31 | Interest Expense . . . . . . . . . . . . . . . . . . . . . . | 10 | | |
| | Interest Payable . . . . . . . . . . . . . . . . . . . . | | 10 | |
| | *To record accrued interest on note ($2,000 ×* | | | |
| | *12% × 15/360).* | | | |

Assets = Liabilities + Equity
         +10       −10

**Example:** If this note is dated December 1 instead of December 16, how much expense is recorded on December 31? *Answer:*
$2,000 × 12% × 30/360 = $20

When this note matures on February 14, the borrower must recognize 45 days of interest expense for year 2006 and remove the balances of the two liability accounts:

| 2006 | | | | |
|---|---|---|---|---|
| Feb. 14 | Interest Expense* . . . . . . . . . . . . . . . . . . . . . . | 30 | | |
| | Interest Payable | 10 | | |
| | Notes Payable . . . . . . . . . . . . . . . . . . . . . . | 2,000 | | |
| | Cash . . . . . . . . . . . . . . . . . . . . . . . . . . . | | 2,040 | |
| | *Paid note with interest. *($2,000 × 12% × 45/360)* | | | |

Assets = Liabilities + Equity
−2,040       −10      −30
             −2,000

## Payroll Liabilities

An employer incurs several expenses and liabilities from having employees. These expenses and liabilities are often large and arise from salaries and wages earned, from employee benefits, and from payroll taxes levied on the employer. **Anheuser-Busch**, for instance, reports payroll-related current liabilities of more than $280 million from "accrued salaries, wages and benefits." We discuss payroll liabilities and related accounts in this section. The appendix to this chapter describes details about payroll reports, records, and procedures.

*Employee* **Payroll Deductions** **Gross pay** is the total compensation an employee earns including wages, salaries, commissions, bonuses, and any compensation earned before deductions such as taxes. (*Wages* usually refer to payments to employees at an hourly

**P2** Compute and record *employee* payroll deductions and liabilities.

**Point:** Internal control is important for payroll accounting. Managers must monitor (1) employee hiring, (2) time-keeping, (3) payroll listings, and (4) payroll payments. Poor controls led the U.S. Army to pay nearly $10 million to deserters, fictitious soldiers, and other unauthorized entities.

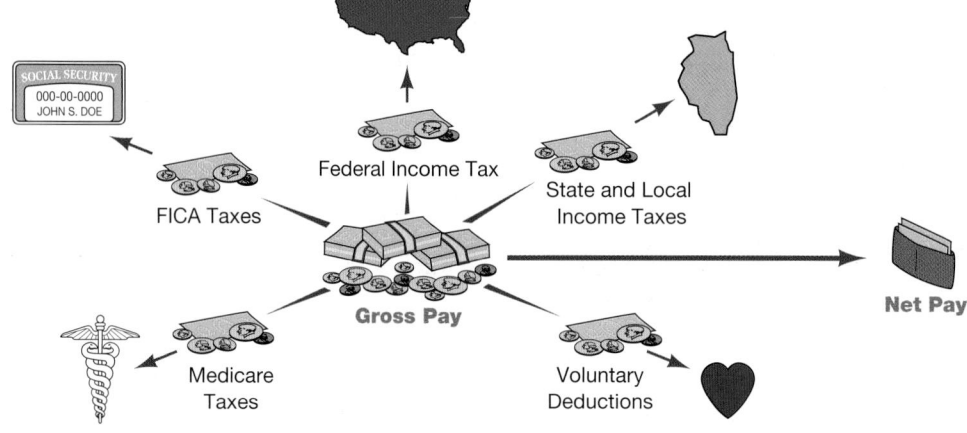

rate. *Salaries* usually refer to payments to employees at a monthly or yearly rate.) **Net pay,** also called *take-home pay,* is gross pay less all deductions. **Payroll deductions,** commonly called *withholdings,* are amounts withheld from an employee's gross pay, either required or voluntary. Required deductions result from laws and include income taxes and Social Security taxes. Voluntary deductions, at an employee's option, include pension and health contributions, union dues, and charitable giving. Exhibit 9.4 shows the typical payroll deductions of an employee. The employer withholds payroll deductions from employees' pay and is obligated to transmit this money to the designated organization. The employer records payroll deductions as current liabilities until these amounts are transmitted. This section discusses the major payroll deductions.

## Exhibit 9.4

Payroll Deductions

Topic Tackler 9-1

***Employee FICA taxes.*** The federal Social Security system provides retirement, disability, survivorship, and medical benefits to qualified workers. Laws *require* employers to withhold **Federal Insurance Contributions Act (FICA) taxes** from employees' pay to cover costs of the system. Employers usually separate FICA taxes into two groups: (1) retirement, disability, and survivorship and (2) medical. For the first group, the Social Security system provides monthly cash payments to qualified retired workers for the rest of their lives. These payments are often called *Social Security benefits.* Taxes related to this group are often called *Social Security taxes.* For the second group, the system provides monthly payments to deceased workers' surviving families and to disabled workers who qualify for assistance. These payments are commonly called *Medicare benefits;* like those in the first group, they are paid with *Medicare taxes* (part of FICA taxes).

Law requires employers to withhold FICA taxes from each employee's salary or wages on each payday. The taxes for Social Security and Medicare are computed separately. For example, for the year 2003, the amount withheld from each employee's pay for Social Security tax was 6.2% of the first $87,000 the employee earns in the calendar year, or a maximum of $5,394. The Medicare tax was 1.45% of *all* amounts the employee earns; there is no maximum limit to Medicare tax.

Employers must pay withheld taxes to the Internal Revenue Service (IRS) on specific filing dates during the year. Employers who fail to send the withheld taxes to the IRS on time can be assessed substantial penalties. Until all the taxes are sent to the IRS, they are included

**Point:** The sources of U.S. tax receipts are roughly as follows:

| | |
|---|---|
| 10% | Corporate income tax |
| 50 | Personal income tax |
| 35 | FICA and FUTA taxes |
| 5 | Other taxes |

in employers' current liabilities. For any changes in rates or with the maximum earnings level, check the IRS Website at **www.IRS.gov**.

***Employee income tax.***   Most employers are required to withhold federal income tax from each employee's paycheck. The amount withheld is computed using tables published by the IRS. The amount depends on the employee's annual earnings rate and the number of *withholding allowances* the employee claims. Allowances reduce the amount of taxes one owes the government. The more allowances one claims, the less tax the employer will withhold. Employees can claim allowances for themselves and their dependents. They also can claim additional allowances if they expect major declines in their taxable income for medical expenses. (An employee who claims more allowances than appropriate is subject to a fine.) Most states and many local governments require employers to withhold income taxes from employees' pay and to remit them promptly to the proper government agency. Until they are paid, withholdings are reported as a current liability on the employer's balance sheet.

**Point:** Part-time employees may claim "exempt from withholding" if they did not have any income tax liability in the prior year and do not expect any in the current year.

**Point:** IRS withholding tables are based on projecting weekly (or other period) pay into an annual figure.

***Employee voluntary deductions.***   Beyond Social Security, Medicare, and income taxes, employers often withhold other amounts from employees' earnings. These withholdings arise from employee requests, contracts, unions, or other agreements. They can include amounts for charitable giving, medical insurance premiums, pension contributions, and union dues. Until they are paid, such withholdings are reported as part of employers' current liabilities.

***Recording employee payroll deductions.***   Employers must accrue payroll expenses and liabilities at the end of each pay period. To illustrate, assume that an employee earns a salary of $2,000 per month. At the end of January, the employer's entry to accrue payroll expenses and liabilities for this employee is

| Jan. 31 | Salaries Expense . . . . . . . . . . . . . . . . . . . . . . . . . | 2,000 | | Assets = Liabilities + Equity |
|---|---|---|---|---|
| | FICA—Social Security Taxes Payable (6.2%) . . | | 124 | +124      −2,000 |
| | FICA—Medicare Taxes Payable (1.45%) . . . . . | | 29 | +29 |
| | Employee Federal Income Taxes Payable* . . . . | | 213 | +213 |
| | Employee Medical Insurance Payable* . . . . . . | | 85 | +85 |
| | Employee Union Dues Payable* . . . . . . . . . . | | 25 | +25 |
| | Accrued Payroll Payable . . . . . . . . . . . . . . . | | 1,524 | +1,524 |
| | *To record accrued payroll for January.* | | | |

\* Amounts taken from employer's accounting records.

Salaries Expense (debit) shows that the employee earns a gross salary of $2,000. The first five payables (credits) show the liabilities the employer owes on behalf of this employee to cover FICA taxes, income taxes, medical insurance, and union dues. The Accrued Payroll Payable account (credit) records the $1,524 net pay the employee receives from the $2,000 gross pay earned. When the employee is paid, another entry (or a series of entries) is required to record the check written and distributed (or funds transferred). The entry to record cash payment to this employee is to debit Accrued Payroll Payable and credit Cash for $1,524.

**Employer** Payroll Taxes   Employers must pay payroll taxes in addition to those required of employees. Employer taxes include FICA and unemployment taxes.

> ### Decision Insight
>
> **Check List**   Millions are lost annually to check schemes. Companies are fighting back with an internal control method called *positive pay*. Here's how it works: A company regularly (daily) sends the bank a "positive file" listing all checks written. When a check reaches the bank for payment, the bank compares the check against the positive file. This flags any forged checks and altered authentic checks.

***Employer FICA tax.***   Employers must pay FICA taxes *equal in amount to* the FICA taxes withheld from their employees. An employer's tax is credited to the same FICA Taxes Payable accounts used to record the Social Security and Medicare taxes withheld from employees. (A self-employed person must pay both the employee and employer FICA taxes.)

**P3**   Compute and record *employer* payroll expenses and liabilities.

***Federal and state unemployment taxes.***   The federal government participates with states in a joint federal and state unemployment insurance program. Each state administers its program. These programs provide unemployment benefits to qualified workers. The federal government approves state programs and pays a portion of their administrative expenses.

   ***Federal Unemployment Taxes (FUTA).***  Employers are subject to a federal unemployment tax on wages and salaries paid to their employees. For the year 2003, employers were required to pay FUTA taxes of as much as 6.2% of the first $7,000 earned by each employee. This federal tax can be reduced by a credit of up to 5.4% for taxes paid to a state program. As a result, the net federal unemployment tax is often only 0.8%.

   ***State Unemployment Taxes (SUTA).***  All states support their unemployment insurance programs by placing a payroll tax on employers. (A few states require employees to make a contribution. In the book's assignments, we assume that this tax is only on the employer.) In most states, the base rate for SUTA taxes is 5.4% of the first $7,000 paid each employee. This base rate is adjusted according to an employer's merit rating. The state assigns a **merit rating** that reflects a company's stability or instability in employing workers. A good rating reflects stability in employment and means an employer can pay less than the 5.4% base rate. A low rating reflects high turnover or seasonal hirings and layoffs. To illustrate, an employer with 50 employees each of whom earns $7,000 or more per year saves $15,400 annually if it has a merit rating of 1.0% versus 5.4%. This is computed by comparing taxes of $18,900 at the 5.4% rate to only $3,500 at the 1.0% rate.

***Recording employer payroll taxes.***   Employer payroll taxes are an added expense beyond the wages and salaries earned by employees. These taxes are often recorded in an entry separate from the one recording payroll expenses and deductions. To illustrate, assume that the $2,000 recorded salaries expense from the previous example is earned by an employee whose earnings have not yet reached $5,000 for the year. Also assume that the federal unemployment tax rate is 0.8% and the state unemployment tax rate is 5.4%. Consequently, the FICA portion of the employer's tax is $153, computed by multiplying both the 6.2% and 1.45% by the $2,000 gross pay. Moreover, state unemployment (SUTA) taxes are $108 (5.4% of the $2,000 gross pay), and federal unemployment (FUTA) taxes are $16 (0.8% of $2,000). The entry to record the employer's payroll tax expense and related liabilities is

**Example:** If the employer's merit rating in this example reduces its SUTA rate to 2.9%, what is its SUTA liability? *Answer:* SUTA payable = $2,000 × 2.9% = $58

Assets = Liabilities + Equity
   +124      −277
   +29
   +108
   +16

| Jan. 31 | Payroll Taxes Expense . . . . . . . . . . . . . . . . . . . . . | 277 | |
|---|---|---|---|
| | FICA—Social Security Taxes Payable (6.2%) . . | | 124 |
| | FICA—Medicare Taxes Payable (1.45%) . . . . . | | 29 |
| | State Unemployment Taxes Payable . . . . . . . . | | 108 |
| | Federal Unemployment Taxes Payable . . . . . . | | 16 |
| | *To record employer payroll taxes.* | | |

## Multi-Period Known Liabilities

Many known liabilities extend over multiple periods. These often include unearned revenues and notes payable. For example, if **Sports Illustrated** sells a four-year magazine subscription, it records amounts received for this subscription in an Unearned Subscription Revenues account. Amounts in this account are liabilities, but are they current or long term? They are *both.* The portion of the Unearned Subscription Revenues account that will be fulfilled in the next year is reported as a current liability. The remaining portion is reported as a long-term liability.

The same analysis applies to notes payable. For example, a borrower reports a three-year note payable as a long-term liability in the first two years it is outstanding. In the third year, the borrower reclassifies this note as a current liability since it is due within one year or the operating cycle, whichever is longer. The **current portion of long-term debt** refers to that part of long-term debt due within one year or the operating cycle, whichever is longer. Long-term debt is reported under long-term liabilities, but the *current portion due* is reported under current liabilities. To illustrate, assume that a $7,500 debt is paid in installments of $1,500 per year for five years. The $1,500 due within the year is reported as a current liability. No journal entry is necessary for this reclassification. Instead, we simply classify the amounts for debt as either current or long term when the balance sheet is prepared.

Some known liabilities are rarely reported in long-term liabilities. These include accounts payable, sales taxes, and wages and salaries.

---

**Quick Check**

4. Why does a creditor prefer a note payable to a past-due account payable?

5. A company pays its one employee $3,000 per month. This company's FUTA rate is 0.8% on the first $7,000 earned; its SUTA rate is 4.0% on the first $7,000; its Social Security tax rate is 6.2% of the first $87,000; and its Medicare tax rate is 1.45% of all amounts earned. The entry to record this company's March payroll includes what amount for total payroll taxes expense?

6. Identify whether the employer or employee or both incurs each of the following: (*a*) FICA taxes, (*b*) FUTA taxes, (*c*) SUTA taxes, and (*d*) withheld income taxes.

Answers—p. 376

---

# Estimated Liabilities

An **estimated liability** is a known obligation that is of an uncertain amount but that can be reasonably estimated. Common examples are employee benefits such as pensions, health care and vacation pay, and warranties offered by a seller. We discuss each of these in this section. Other examples of estimated liabilities include property taxes and certain contracts to provide future services.

P4   Account for estimated liabilities, including warranties and bonuses.

## Health and Pension Benefits

Many companies provide **employee benefits** beyond salaries and wages. An employer often pays all or part of medical, dental, life, and disability insurance. Many employers also contribute to *pension plans,* which are agreements by employers to provide benefits (payments) to employees after retirement. Many companies also provide medical care and insurance benefits to their retirees. When payroll taxes and charges for employee benefits are totaled, payroll cost often exceeds employees' gross earnings by 25% or more.

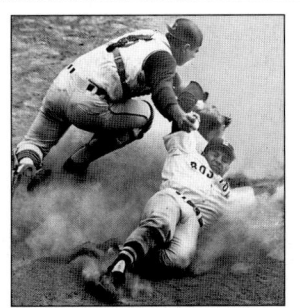

To illustrate, assume that an employer agrees to (1) pay an amount for medical insurance equal to $8,000 and (2) contribute an additional 10% of the employees' $120,000 gross salary to a retirement program. The entry to record these accrued benefits is

Assets = Liabilities + Equity<br>
       +8,000   −20,000<br>
       +12,000

| Jan. 31 | Employee Benefits Expense . . . . . . . . . . . . . . . . | 20,000 | |
|---|---|---|---|
| | Employee Medical Insurance Payable . . . . . . . | | 8,000 |
| | Employee Retirement Program Payable . . . . . | | 12,000 |
| | *To record costs of employee benefits.* | | |

## Vacation Benefits

Many employers offer paid vacation benefits, also called *paid absences*. To illustrate, assume that salaried employees earn 2 weeks' vacation per year. This benefit increases employers' payroll expenses because employees are paid for 52 weeks but work for only 50 weeks. Total annual salary is the same, but the cost per week worked is greater than the amount paid per week. For example, if an employee is paid $20,800 for 52 weeks but works only 50 weeks, the total weekly expense to the employer is $416 ($20,800/50 weeks) instead of the $400 cash paid weekly to the employee ($20,800/52 weeks). The $16 difference between these two amounts is recorded weekly as follows:

Assets = Liabilities + Equity<br>
         +16     −16

| | Vacation Benefits Expense . . . . . . . . . . . . . . . . . | 16 | |
|---|---|---|---|
| | Vacation Benefits Payable . . . . . . . . . . . . . . | | 16 |
| | *To record vacation benefits accrued.* | | |

Vacation Benefits Expense is an operating expense, and Vacation Benefits Payable is a current liability. When the employee takes a vacation, the employer reduces (debits) the Vacation Benefits Payable and credits Cash (no additional expense is recorded).

## Bonus Plans

**Global:** Bonuses are considered part of salary expense in most countries. In Japan, bonuses to members of the board of directors and to external auditors are directly charged against equity rather than treated as an expense.

Many companies offer bonuses to employees, and many of the bonuses depend on net income. To illustrate, assume that an employer offers a bonus to its employees equal to 5% of the company's annual net income (to be equally shared by all). The company's expected annual net income is $210,000. The year-end adjusting entry to record this benefit is

Assets = Liabilities + Equity<br>
      +10,000   −10,000

| Dec. 31 | Employee Bonus Expense* . . . . . . . . . . . . . . . . | 10,000 | |
|---|---|---|---|
| | Bonus Payable . . . . . . . . . . . . . . . . . . . . . . . | | 10,000 |
| | *To record expected bonus costs.* | | |

\* Bonus Expense (B) equals 5% of the quantity $210,000 minus the bonus—computed as:

$$B = 0.05\,(\$210,000 - B)$$
$$B = \$10,500 - 0.05B$$
$$1.05B = \$10,500$$
$$\mathbf{B = \$10,500/1.05 = \$10,000}$$

When the bonus is paid, Bonus Payable is debited and Cash is credited for $10,000.

## Warranty Liabilities

**Point:** Zenith recently reported $32.1 million on its balance sheet for warranties.

A **warranty** is a seller's obligation to replace or correct a product (or service) that fails to perform as expected within a specified period. Most new cars, for instance, are sold with a warranty covering parts for a specified period of time. **Ford Motor Company** reported more than $14 billion in "dealer and customer allowances and claims" in its recent annual report. To comply with the *full disclosure* and *matching principles,* the seller reports the expected warranty expense in the period when revenue from the sale of the product or service is reported. The seller reports this warranty obligation as a liability, although the existence, amount, payee, and date of future sacrifices are uncertain. This is because such warranty costs are probable and the amount can be estimated using, for instance, past experience with warranties.

To illustrate, a dealer sells a used car for $16,000 on December 1, 2005, with a maximum one-year or 12,000-mile warranty covering parts. This dealer's experience shows that warranty expense averages about 4% of a car's selling price, or $640 in this case ($16,000 × 4%). The dealer records the estimated expense and liability related to this sale with this entry:

| 2005 | | | |
|---|---|---|---|
| Dec. 1 | Warranty Expense ....................... | 640 | |
| | Estimated Warranty Liability ............. | | 640 |
| | *To record estimated warranty expense.* | | |

Assets = Liabilities − Equity
+640        −640

This entry alternatively could be made as part of end-of-period adjustments. Either way, the estimated warranty expense is reported on the 2005 income statement and the warranty liability on the 2005 balance sheet. To further extend this example, suppose the customer returns the car for warranty repairs on January 9, 2006. The dealer performs this work by replacing parts costing $200. The entry to record partial settlement of the estimated warranty liability is

**Point:** Recognition of expected warranty liabilities is necessary to comply with the matching and full disclosure principles.

| 2006 | | | |
|---|---|---|---|
| Jan. 9 | Estimated Warranty Liability ................ | 200 | |
| | Auto Parts Inventory .................. | | 200 |
| | *To record costs of warranty repairs.* | | |

Assets = Liabilities + Equity
−200        −200

This entry reduces the balance of the estimated warranty liability. Warranty expense was previously recorded in 2005, the year the car was sold with the warranty. Finally, what happens if total warranty expenses are more or less than the estimated 4%, or $640? The answer is that management should monitor actual warranty expenses to see whether the 4% rate is accurate. If experience reveals a large difference from the estimate, the rate for current and future sales should be changed. Differences are expected, but they should be small.

## Multi-Period Estimated Liabilities

Estimated liabilities can be both current and long term. For example, pension liabilities to employees are long term to workers who will not retire within the next period. For employees who are retired or will retire within the next period, a portion of pension liabilities is current. Other examples include employee health benefits and warranties. Specifically, many warranties are for 30 or 60 days in length. Estimated costs under these warranties are properly reported in current liabilities. Many other automobile warranties are for three years or 36,000 miles. A portion of these warranties is reported as long term.

# Contingent Liabilities

C3 Explain how to account for contingent liabilities.

A **contingent liability** is a potential obligation that depends on a future event arising from a past transaction or event. An example is a pending lawsuit. Here, a past transaction or event leads to a lawsuit whose result depends on the outcome of the suit. Future payment of a contingent liability depends on whether an uncertain future event occurs.

## Accounting for Contingent Liabilities

Accounting for contingent liabilities depends on the likelihood that a future event will occur and the ability to estimate the future amount owed if this event occurs. Three categories are identified (see the table in the margin):

|  | Probable | Reasonably Possible | Remote |
|---|---|---|---|
| Amount estimable | Record contingent liability | Disclose liability in notes | No action |
| Amount not estimable | Disclose liability in notes | Disclose liability in notes | No action |

(1) The future event is *probable* (likely) and the amount owed can be *reasonably estimated.* We record this amount as a liability. Examples are the estimated liabilities described earlier such as warranties, vacation pay, and income taxes.

(2) The future event is *remote* (unlikely). We do not record or disclose information on remote contingent liabilities.

(3) Likelihood of the future event is between these two extremes. That is, if the future event is *reasonably possible* (could occur), we disclose information about the contingent liability in notes to the financial statements.

This section identifies contingent liabilities that often fall in the third category—when the future event is reasonably possible. Disclosing information about contingencies in this third category is motivated by the *full-disclosure principle,* which requires information relevant to decision makers be reported.

**Point:** A contingency is an *if.* Namely, if a future event occurs, then financial consequences are likely for the entity.

## Reasonably Possible Contingent Liabilities

This section discusses common examples of reasonably possible contingent liabilities.

**Point:** A sale of a note receivable is often a contingent liability. It becomes a liability if the original signer of the note fails to pay it at maturity.

**Potential Legal Claims** Many companies are sued or at risk of being sued. The accounting issue is whether the defendant should recognize a liability on its balance sheet or disclose a contingent liability in its notes while a lawsuit is outstanding and not yet settled. The answer is that a potential claim is recorded in the accounts *only* if payment for damages is probable and the amount can be reasonably estimated. If the potential claim cannot be reasonably estimated or is less than probable but reasonably possible, it is disclosed. **Ford Motor Company,** for example, includes the following note in its recent annual report: "Various legal actions, governmental investigations and proceedings and claims are pending . . . arising out of alleged defects in our products."

### Decision Insight

**Hot Claims** Remember the infamous lawsuit against **McDonald's** that awarded an 81-year-old New Mexico woman $2.9 million—later reduced to $640,000—after she spilled hot coffee in her lap? Well, copycat litigation is booming. Companies from **Burger King** to **Starbucks** now print cautions on coffee cups, chili bowls, and so forth.

**Debt Guarantees** Sometimes a company guarantees the payment of debt owed by a supplier, customer, or another company. The guarantor usually discloses the guarantee in its financial statement notes as a contingent liability. If it is probable that the debtor will default, the guarantor needs to record and report the guarantee in its financial statements as a liability. The **Boston Celtics** report a unique guarantee when it comes to coaches and players: "Certain of the contracts provide for guaranteed payments which must be paid even if the employee [player] is injured or terminated."

### Decision Insight

**Pricing Priceless** What's it worth to see from one side of the Grand Canyon to the other? What's the cost when beaches are closed due to pollution? One method to measure these environmental liabilities is **contingent valuation,** by which people are asked to answer such questions. Regulators use their answers to levy fines and assess punitive damages.

**Other Contingencies**   Other examples of contingencies include environmental damages, possible tax assessments, insurance losses, and government investigations. **Sunoco,** for instance, reports that "federal, state and local laws . . . result in liabilities and loss contingencies. Sunoco accrues . . . cleanup costs [that] are probable and reasonably estimable. [Sunoco also] believes it is reasonably possible (i.e., less than probable but greater than remote) that additional . . . losses will be incurred." Many of Sunoco's contingencies are revealed only in notes.

**Uncertainties**   All organizations face uncertainties from future events such as natural disasters and the development of new competing products or services. These uncertainties are not contingent liabilities because they are future events *not* arising from past transactions. Accordingly, they are not disclosed.

**Point:** Auditors and managers often have different views about whether a contingency is recorded, disclosed, or omitted.

Topic Tackler 9-2

**Global:** Accounting for contingencies varies across countries. International accounting standards require disclosure only for contingent liabilities that are reasonably possible or probable.

## Quick Check

**9.** A future payment is reported as a liability on the balance sheet if payment is contingent on a future event that (*a*) is reasonably possible but the payment cannot be reasonably estimated; (*b*) is probable and the payment can be reasonably estimated; or (*c*) is not probable but the payment is known.

**10.** Under what circumstances is a future payment reported in the notes to the financial statements as a contingent liability?

Answers—p. 377

---

## Times Interest Earned Ratio                                          **Decision Analysis**

A company incurs interest expense on many of its current and long-term liabilities. Examples extend from its short-term notes and the current portion of long-term liabilities to its long-term notes and bonds. Interest expense is often viewed as a *fixed expense* because the amount of these liabilities is likely to remain in one form or another for a substantial period of time. This means that the amount of interest is unlikely to vary due to changes in sales or other operating activities. While fixed expenses can be advantageous when a company is growing, they create risk. This risk stems from the possibility that a company might be unable to pay fixed expenses if sales decline. To illustrate, consider X-Caliber's results for year 2005 and two possible outcomes for year 2006 in Exhibit 9.5.

**A1**   Compute the times interest earned ratio and use it to analyze liabilities.

Exhibit 9.5

Actual and Projected Results

| ($ thousands) | Year 2005 | Year 2006 Projections | |
| | | Sales Increase | Sales Decrease |
|---|---|---|---|
| Sales .................... | $600 | $900 | $300 |
| Expenses (75% of sales) ....... | 450 | 675 | 225 |
| Income before interest ........ | 150 | 225 | 75 |
| Interest expense (fixed) ........ | 60 | 60 | 60 |
| Net income ................ | $ 90 | $165 | $ 15 |

Expenses excluding interest are at, and expected to remain at, 75% of sales. Expenses such as these that change with sales volume are called *variable expenses.* However, interest expense is at, and expected to remain at, $60,000 per year due to its fixed nature.

The middle numerical column of Exhibit 9.5 shows that X-Caliber's income nearly doubles to $165,000 if sales increase by 50% to $900,000. In contrast, the far right column shows that income falls sharply if sales decline by 50%. These results reveal that the amount of fixed interest expense affects a company's risk of its ability to pay interest, which is numerically reflected in the **times interest earned** ratio in Exhibit 9.6.

$$\text{Times interest earned} = \frac{\text{Income before interest expense and income taxes}}{\text{Interest expense}}$$

Exhibit 9.6

Times Interest Earned

For 2005, X-Caliber's times interest earned is computed as $150,000/$60,000, or 2.5 times. This ratio suggests that X-Caliber faces low to moderate risk because its sales must decline sharply before it would be unable to cover its interest expenses. (X-Caliber is an LLC and does not pay income taxes.)

Experience shows that when times interest earned falls below 1.5 to 2.0 and remains at that level or lower for several periods, the default rate on liabilities increases sharply. This reflects increased risk for companies and their creditors. We also must interpret the times interest earned ratio in light of information about the variability of a company's income before interest. If income is stable from year to year or if it is growing, the company can afford to take on added risk by borrowing. If its income greatly varies from year to year, fixed interest expense can increase the risk that it will not earn enough income to pay interest.

### Decision Maker

**Entrepreneur**   You wish to invest in a franchise for either one of two national chains. Each franchise has an expected annual net income *after* interest and taxes of $100,000. Net income for the first franchise includes a regular fixed interest charge of $200,000. The fixed interest charge for the second franchise is $40,000. Which franchise is riskier to you if sales forecasts are not met? Does your decision change if the first franchise has more variability in its income stream?

Answer—p. 376

## Demonstration Problem

The following transactions and events took place at Kern Company during its recent calendar-year reporting period (Kern does not use reversing entries):

**a.** In September 2005, Kern sold $140,000 of merchandise covered by a 180-day warranty. Prior experience shows that costs of the warranty equal 5% of sales. Compute September's warranty expense and prepare the adjusting journal entry for the warranty liability as recorded at September 30. Also prepare the journal entry on October 8 to record a $300 cash expenditure to provide warranty service on an item sold in September.

**b.** On October 12, 2005, Kern arranged with a supplier to replace Kern's overdue $10,000 account payable by paying $2,500 cash and signing a note for the remainder. The note matures in 90 days and has a 12% interest rate. Prepare the entries recorded on October 12, December 31, and January 10, 2006, related to this transaction.

**c.** In late December, Kern learns it is facing a product liability suit filed by an unhappy customer. Kern's lawyer advises that although it will probably suffer a loss from the lawsuit, it is not possible to estimate the amount of damages at this time.

**d.** Sally Kline works for Kern. For the pay period ended November 30, her gross earnings are $3,000. Kline has $800 deducted for federal income taxes and $200 for state income taxes from each paycheck. Additionally, a $35 premium for her health care insurance and a $10 donation for the United Way are deducted. Kline pays FICA Social Security taxes at a rate of 6.2% and FICA Medicare taxes at a rate of 1.45%. She has not earned enough this year to be exempt from any FICA taxes. Journalize the payment of Kline's wages by Kern.

**e.** On November 1, Kern borrows $5,000 cash from a bank in return for a 60-day, 12%, $5,000 note. Record the note's issuance on November 1 and its repayment with interest on December 31.

**f.**[B] Kern has estimated and recorded its quarterly income tax payments. In reviewing its year-end tax adjustments, it identifies an additional $5,000 of income tax expense that should be recorded. A portion of this additional expense, $1,000, is deferrable to future years. Record this year-end income taxes expense adjusting entry.

**g.** For this calendar-year, Kern's net income is $1,000,000, its interest expense is $275,000, and its income taxes expense is $225,000. Calculate Kern's times interest earned ratio.

### Planning the Solution

- For *a*, compute the warranty expense for September and record it with an estimated liability. Record the October expenditure as a decrease in the liability.
- For *b*, eliminate the liability for the account payable and create the liability for the note payable. Compute interest expense for the 80 days that the note is outstanding in 2005 and record it as an

additional liability. Record the payment of the note, being sure to include the interest for the 10 days in 2006.

- For *c*, decide whether the company's contingent liability needs to be disclosed or accrued (recorded) according to the two necessary criteria: probable loss and reasonably estimable.
- For *d*, set up payable accounts for all items in Kline's paycheck that require deductions. After deducting all necessary items, credit the remaining amount to Accrued Payroll Payable.
- For *e*, record the issuance of the note. Calculate 60 days' interest due using the 360-day convention in the interest formula.
- For *f*, determine how much of the income taxes expense is payable in the current year and how much needs to be deferred.
- For *g*, apply and compute times interest earned.

## Solution to Demonstration Problem

**a.** Warranty expense = 5% × $140,000 = $7,000

| | | | |
|---|---|---|---|
| Sept. 30 | Warranty Expense . . . . . . . . . . . . . . . . . . . . . . . | 7,000 | |
| | Estimated Warranty Liability . . . . . . . . . . . . . | | 7,000 |
| | *To record warranty expense for the month.* | | |
| Oct. 8 | Estimated Warranty Liability. . . . . . . . . . . . . . . | 300 | |
| | Cash . . . . . . . . . . . . . . . . . . . . . . . . . . . . . | | 300 |
| | *To record the cost of the warranty service.* | | |

**b.** Interest expense for 2005 = 12% × $7,500 × 80/360 = $200

Interest expense for 2006 = 12% × $7,500 × 10/360 = $25

| | | | |
|---|---|---|---|
| Oct. 12 | Accounts Payable . . . . . . . . . . . . . . . . . . . . . . . | 10,000 | |
| | Notes Payable . . . . . . . . . . . . . . . . . . . . . . . | | 7,500 |
| | Cash. . . . . . . . . . . . . . . . . . . . . . . . . . . . . . | | 2,500 |
| | *Paid $2,500 cash and gave a 90-day, 12% note* | | |
| | *to extend the due date on the account.* | | |
| Dec. 31 | Interest Expense. . . . . . . . . . . . . . . . . . . . . . . | 200 | |
| | Interest Payable . . . . . . . . . . . . . . . . . . . . . | | 200 |
| | *To accrue interest on note payable.* | | |
| Jan. 10 | Interest Expense. . . . . . . . . . . . . . . . . . . . . . . | 25 | |
| | Interest Payable . . . . . . . . . . . . . . . . . . . . . . | 200 | |
| | Notes Payable. . . . . . . . . . . . . . . . . . . . . . . | 7,500 | |
| | Cash . . . . . . . . . . . . . . . . . . . . . . . . . . . . . | | 7,725 |
| | *Paid note with interest, including the accrued* | | |
| | *interest payable.* | | |

**c.** Disclose the pending lawsuit in the financial statement notes. Although the loss is probable, no liability can be accrued since the loss cannot be reasonably estimated.

**d.**

| | | | |
|---|---|---|---|
| Nov. 30 | Salaries Expense . . . . . . . . . . . . . . . . . . . . . . . | 3,000.00 | |
| | FICA—Social Security Taxes Payable (6.2%) . . | | 186.00 |
| | FICA—Medicare Taxes Payable (1.45%) . . . . . | | 43.50 |
| | Employee Federal Income Taxes Payable. . . . . | | 800.00 |
| | Employee State Income Taxes Payable . . . . . . | | 200.00 |
| | Employee Medical Insurance Payable . . . . . . . | | 35.00 |
| | Employee United Way Payable. . . . . . . . . . . | | 10.00 |
| | Accrued Payroll Payable . . . . . . . . . . . . . . . | | 1,725.50 |
| | *To record Kline's accrued payroll.* | | |

**e.**

| Nov. 1 | Cash .................................. | 5,000 | |
|---|---|---|---|
| | Notes Payable ...................... | | 5,000 |
| | *Borrowed cash with a 60-day, 12% note.* | | |

When the note and interest are paid 60 days later, Kern Company records this entry:

| Dec. 31 | Notes Payable......................... | 5,000 | |
|---|---|---|---|
| | Interest Expense....................... | 100 | |
| | Cash.............................. | | 5,100 |
| | *Paid note with interest ($5,000 × 12% × 60/360).* | | |

**f.**

| Dec. 31 | Income Taxes Expense.................... | 5,000 | |
|---|---|---|---|
| | Income Taxes Payable................. | | 4,000 |
| | Deferred Income Tax Liability ........... | | 1,000 |
| | *To record added income taxes expense and the deferred tax liability.* | | |

**g.** Times interest earned $= \dfrac{\$1,000,000 + \$275,000 + \$225,000}{\$275,000} = \underline{\underline{5.45 \text{ times}}}$

---

## APPENDIX

# Payroll Reports, Records, and Procedures

Understanding payroll procedures and keeping adequate payroll reports and records are essential to a company's success. This appendix focuses on payroll accounting and its reports, records, and procedures.

## Payroll Reports

Most employees and employers are required to pay local, state, and federal payroll taxes. Payroll expenses involve liabilities to individual employees, to federal and state governments, and to other organizations such as insurance companies. Beyond paying these liabilities, employers are required to prepare and submit reports explaining how they computed these payments.

**C4** Identify and describe payroll reporting.

**Reporting FICA Taxes and Income Taxes** The Federal Insurance Contributions Act (FICA) requires each employer to file an Internal Revenue Service (IRS) **Form 941,** the *Employer's Quarterly Federal Tax Return,* within one month after the end of each calendar quarter. A sample Form 941 is shown in Exhibit 9A.1 for Phoenix Sales & Service, a landscape design company. Accounting information and software are helpful in tracking payroll transactions and reporting the accumulated information on Form 941. Specifically, the employer reports total wages subject to income

| Form **941**<br>(Rev. January 2003)<br>Department of the Treasury<br>Internal Revenue Service (99) | **Employer's Quarterly Federal Tax Return**<br>▶ See separate instructions revised January 2003 for information on completing this return.<br>**Please type or print.** | | OMB No. 1545-0029 |
|---|---|---|---|

Enter state code for state in which deposits were made **only** if different from state in address to the right ▶ ☐ (see page 2 of Separate instructions).

Name (as distinguished from trade name)  
Phoenix Sales & Service

Date quarter ended  
Dec. 31, 2005

Trade name, if any

Employer identification number  
86-3214587

Address (number and street)  
1214 Mill Road  
Phoenix, AZ 85621  
USA

City, State, and ZIP code

| T | |
| FF | |
| FD | |
| FP | |
| I | |
| T | |

If address is different from prior return, check here ▶ ☐

IRS Use

1 1 1 1 1 1 1 1 1 1    2    3 3 3 3 3 3 3 3    4 4 4    5 5 5
6    7    8 8 8 8 8 8 8    9 9 9 9    10 10 10 10 10 10 10 10 10

**A** If you **do not have to file** returns in the future, check here ▶ ☐ and enter date final wages paid ▶

**B** If you are a seasonal employer, see **Seasonal employers** on page 1 of the instructions and check here ▶ ☐

| 1 | Number of employees in the pay period that includes March 12th, ▶ | 1 | | |
|---|---|---|---|---|
| 2 | Total wages and tips, plus other compensation . . . . . | | **2** | 36,599.00 |
| 3 | Total income tax withheld from wages, tips, and sick pay . . . . . | | **3** | 3,056.47 |
| 4 | Adjustment of withheld income tax for preceding quarters of **this calendar year** | | **4** | |
| 5 | Adjusted total of income tax withheld (line 3 as adjusted by line 4) . . | | **5** | 3,056.47 |
| 6 | Taxable social security wages . . . . | **6a** $ 36,599.00 | × 12.4% (.124) = | **6b** | 4,538.28 |
| | Taxable social security tips . . . . | **6c** $ | × 12.4% (.124) = | **6d** | |
| 7 | Taxable Medicare wages and tips . . . | **7a** $ 36,599.00 | × 2.9% (.029) = | **7b** | 1,061.37 |
| 8 | Total social security and Medicare taxes (add lines 6b, 6d, and 7b). **Check here if wages are not subject to social security and/or Medicare tax** . . . . . . . . ▶ ☐ | | **8** | 5,599.65 |
| 9 | Adjustment of social security and Medicare taxes (see instructions for required explanation)<br>Sick Pay $ _____ ± Fractions of Cents $ _____ ± Other $ _____ = | | **9** | |
| 10 | Adjusted total of social security and Medicare taxes (line 8 as adjusted by line 9) . . . | | **10** | 5,599.65 |
| 11 | **Total taxes** (add lines 5 and 10) . . . . . . | | **11** | 8,656.12 |
| 12 | Advance earned income credit (EIC) payments made to employees (see instructions) . . . | | **12** | |
| 13 | Net taxes (subtract line 12 from line 11). **If $2,500 or more, this must equal line 17, column (d) below (or line D of Schedule B (Form 941))** . . . . | | **13** | 8,656.12 |
| 14 | Total deposits for quarter, including overpayment applied from a prior quarter . . . . | | **14** | 8,656.12 |
| | | | **15** | |
| 15 | **Balance due** (subtract line 14 from line 13). See instructions . . . . | | | |
| 16 | **Overpayment.** If line 14 is more than line 13, enter excess here ▶ $ _____ 0.00 _____<br>and check if to be: ☐ Applied to next return **or** ☐ Refunded. | | | |

- **All filers:** If line 13 is less than $2,500, **do not** complete line 17 **or** Schedule B (Form 941).
- **Semiweekly schedule depositors:** Complete Schedule B (Form 941) and check here . . . . . ▶ ☐
- **Monthly schedule depositors:** Complete line 17, columns (a) through (d), and check here . . . . . ▶ ☒

| 17 | **Monthly Summary of Federal Tax Liability.** (Complete **Schedule B (Form 941)** Instead, if you were a semiweekly schedule depositor.) | | | |
|---|---|---|---|---|
| | (a) First month liability | (b) Second month liability | (c) Third month liability | (d) Total liability for quarter |
| | 3,079.11 | 2,049.77 | 3,527.24 | 8,656.12 |

**Third Party Designee**  
Do you want to allow another person to discuss this return with the IRS (see separate instructions)? ☐ **Yes.** Complete the following. ☒ **No.**  
Designee's name ▶  
Phone no. ▶ ( )  
Personal identification number (PIN) ▶ ☐☐☐☐☐

**Sign Here**  
Under penalties of perjury, I declare that I have examined this return, including accompanying schedules and statements, and to the best of my knowledge and belief, it is true, correct, and complete.  
Signature ▶  
Print your Name and Title ▶  
Date ▶

For Privacy Act and Paperwork Reduction Act Notice, see back of Payment Voucher.   Cat. No. 17001Z   Form **941** (Rev. 1-2003)

tax withholding on line 2 of Form 941. (For simplicity, this appendix uses *wages* to refer to both wages and salaries.) The income tax withheld is reported on lines 3 and 5. The combined amount of employee and employer FICA (Social Security) taxes for Phoenix Sales & Service is reported on line 6a (taxable Social Security wages, $36,599 × 12.4% = $4,538.28). The 12.4% is the sum of the Social Security tax withheld, computed as 6.2% tax withheld from the employee wages for the quarter plus the 6.2% tax levied on the employer. The combined amount of employee Medicare wages is reported on line 7. The 2.9% is the sum of 1.45% withheld from employee wages for the quarter plus 1.45% tax levied on the employer. Total FICA taxes are reported on lines 8 and 10 and are added to the total income taxes withheld of $3,056.47 to yield a total of $8,656.12. For this

COPYRIGHT JOHN S. PRITCHETT WWW.PRITCHETTCARTOONS.COM

Although the IRS may not be at the end of the rainbow, this cartoon reinforces the importance of taxation in all business activities and management decisions.

year, assume that income up to $87,000 is subject to Social Security tax. There is no income limit on amounts subject to Medicare tax. Congress sets annual limits on the amount owed for Social Security tax.

**Federal depository banks** are authorized to accept deposits of amounts payable to the federal government. Deposit requirements depend on the amount of tax owed. For example, when the sum of FICA taxes plus the employee income taxes is less than $500 for a quarter, the taxes can be paid when Form 941 is filed. Companies with large payrolls are often required to pay monthly or even semiweekly. If taxes owed are $100,000 or more at the end of any day, they must be paid by the end of the next banking day.

**Reporting FUTA Taxes and SUTA Taxes**    An employer's federal unemployment taxes (FUTA) are reported on an annual basis by filing an *Annual Federal Unemployment Tax Return,* IRS **Form 940.** It must be mailed on or before January 31 following the end of each tax year. Ten more days are allowed if all required tax deposits are filed on a timely basis and the full amount of tax is paid on or before January 31. FUTA payments are made quarterly to a federal depository bank if the total amount due exceeds $100. If $100 or less is due, the taxes are remitted annually. Requirements for paying and reporting state unemployment taxes (SUTA) vary depending on the laws of each state. Most states require quarterly payments and reports.

**Reporting Wages and Salaries**    Employers are required to give each employee an annual report of his or her wages subject to FICA and federal income taxes along with the amounts of these taxes withheld. This report is called a *Wage and Tax Statement,* or **Form W-2.** It must be given to employees before January 31 following the year covered by the report. Exhibit 9A.2 shows Form W-2 for one of the employees at Phoenix Sales & Service. Copies of the W-2 Form must be sent to the Social Security Administration, where the amount of the employee's wages subject to FICA taxes and FICA taxes withheld are posted to each employee's Social Security account. These posted amounts become the basis for determining an employee's retirement and survivors' benefits. The Social Security Administration also transmits to the IRS the amount of each employee's wages subject to federal income taxes and the amount of taxes withheld.

# Payroll Records

Employers must keep payroll records in addition to reporting and paying taxes. These records usually include a payroll register and an individual earnings report for each employee.

C5    Identify and describe payroll records.

**Payroll Register**    A **payroll register** usually shows the pay period dates, hours worked, gross pay, deductions, and net pay of each employee for each pay period. Exhibit 9A.3 shows a payroll register for Phoenix Sales & Service. It is organized into nine columns:

Col. 1    Employee identification (ID); Employee name; Social Security number (SS No.); Reference (check number); and Date (date check issued)
Col. 2    Pay Type (regular and overtime)
Col. 3    Pay Hours (number of hours worked as regular and overtime)
Col. 4    Gross Pay (amount of gross pay)[2]
Col. 5    FIT (federal income taxes withheld); FUTA (federal unemployment taxes)
Col. 6    SIT (state income taxes withheld); SUTA (state unemployment taxes)
Col. 7    FICA-SS_EE (social security taxes withheld, employee); FICA-SS_ER (social security taxes, employer)
Col. 8    FICA-Med_EE (medicare tax withheld, employee); FICA-Med_ER (medicare tax, employer)
Col. 9    Net pay (Gross pay less amounts withheld from employees)

---

[2] The Gross Pay column shows regular hours worked on the first line multiplied by the regular pay rate—this equals regular pay. Overtime hours multiplied by the overtime premium rate equals overtime premium pay reported on the second line. If employers are engaged in interstate commerce, federal law sets a minimum overtime rate of pay to employees. For this company, workers earn 150% of their regular rate for hours in excess of 40 per week.

| a Control number | | | |
|---|---|---|---|
| AR101 | OMB No. 1545-0008 | | |

| b Employer identification number | 1 Wages, tips, other compensation | 2 Federal income tax withheld |
|---|---|---|
| 86-3214587 | 4910.00 | 333.37 |

| c Employer's name, address, and ZIP code | 3 Social security wages | 4 Social security tax withheld |
|---|---|---|
| Phoenix Sales & Service | 4910.00 | 304.42 |
| 1214 Mill Road | 5 Medicare wages and tips | 6 Medicare tax withheld |
| Phoenix, AZ 85621 | 4910.00 | 71.20 |
| USA | 7 Social security tips | 8 Allocated tips |

| d Employee's social security number | 9 Advance EIC payment | 10 Dependent care benefits |
|---|---|---|
| 333-22-9999 | | |

| e Employee's first name and initial    Last name | 11 Nonqualified plans | 12a |
|---|---|---|
| Robert Austin | | |
| | 13 Statutory employee   Retirement plan   Third-party sick pay | 12b |
| 18 Roosevelt Blvd., Apt C | 14 Other | 12c |
| Tempe, AZ 86322 | | 12d |

| f Employee's address and ZIP code | | | | | | |
|---|---|---|---|---|---|---|
| 15 State  Employer's state ID number | 16 State wages, tips, etc. | 17 State income tax | 18 Local wages, tips, etc. | 19 Local income tax | 20 Locality name |
| AZ  13-902319 | 4910.00 | 26.68 | | | |

Form **W-2** Wage and Tax Statement   **2003**   Department of the Treasury—Internal Revenue Service

Copy 1 For State, City, or Local Tax Department

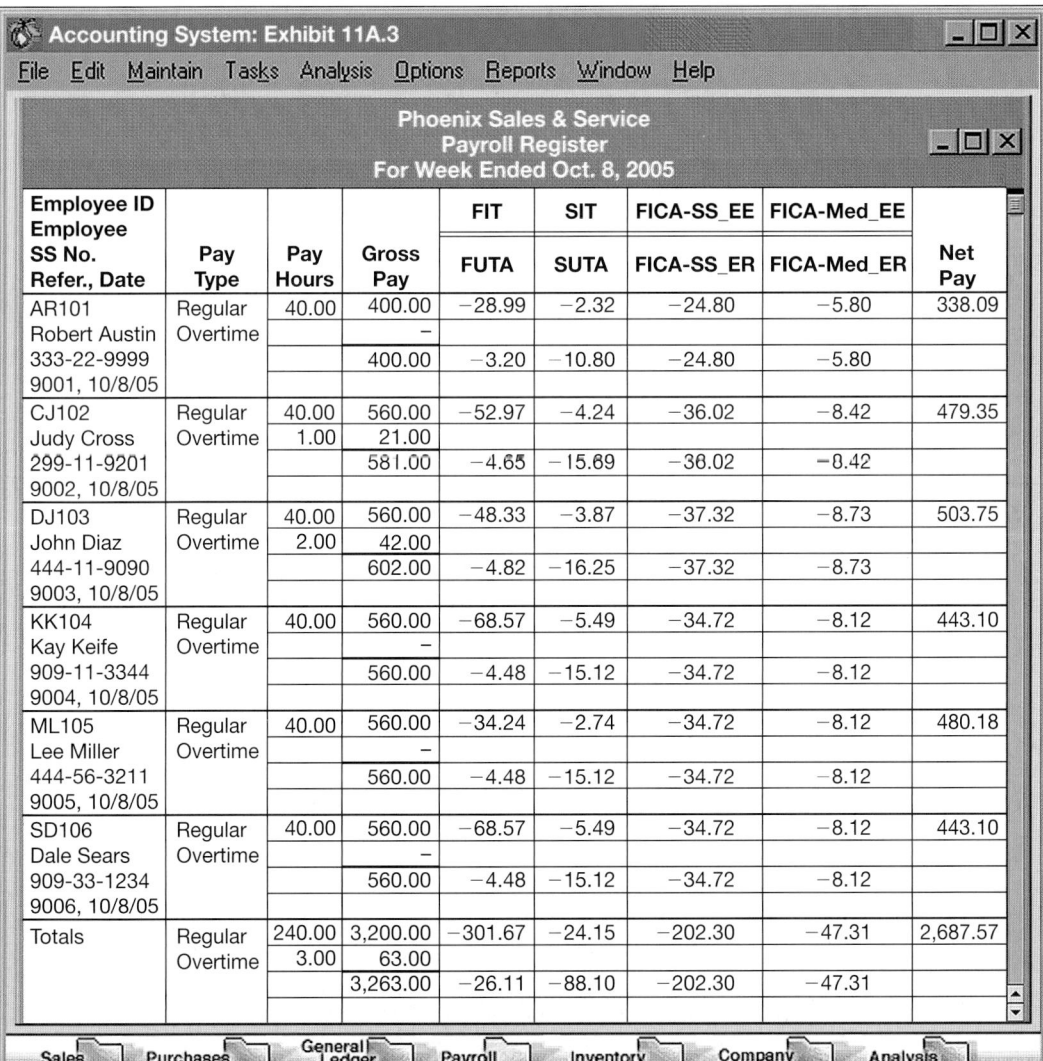

### Accounting System: Exhibit 11A.3

File  Edit  Maintain  Tasks  Analysis  Options  Reports  Window  Help

**Phoenix Sales & Service**
**Payroll Register**
**For Week Ended Oct. 8, 2005**

| Employee ID Employee SS No. Refer., Date | Pay Type | Pay Hours | Gross Pay | FIT | SIT | FICA-SS_EE | FICA-Med_EE | Net Pay |
|---|---|---|---|---|---|---|---|---|
| | | | | FUTA | SUTA | FICA-SS_ER | FICA-Med_ER | |
| AR101 | Regular | 40.00 | 400.00 | −28.99 | −2.32 | −24.80 | −5.80 | 338.09 |
| Robert Austin | Overtime | | − | | | | | |
| 333-22-9999 | | | 400.00 | −3.20 | −10.80 | −24.80 | −5.80 | |
| 9001, 10/8/05 | | | | | | | | |
| CJ102 | Regular | 40.00 | 560.00 | −52.97 | −4.24 | −36.02 | −8.42 | 479.35 |
| Judy Cross | Overtime | 1.00 | 21.00 | | | | | |
| 299-11-9201 | | | 581.00 | −4.65 | −15.69 | −36.02 | −8.42 | |
| 9002, 10/8/05 | | | | | | | | |
| DJ103 | Regular | 40.00 | 560.00 | −48.33 | −3.87 | −37.32 | −8.73 | 503.75 |
| John Diaz | Overtime | 2.00 | 42.00 | | | | | |
| 444-11-9090 | | | 602.00 | −4.82 | −16.25 | −37.32 | −8.73 | |
| 9003, 10/8/05 | | | | | | | | |
| KK104 | Regular | 40.00 | 560.00 | −68.57 | −5.49 | −34.72 | −8.12 | 443.10 |
| Kay Keife | Overtime | | − | | | | | |
| 909-11-3344 | | | 560.00 | −4.48 | −15.12 | −34.72 | −8.12 | |
| 9004, 10/8/05 | | | | | | | | |
| ML105 | Regular | 40.00 | 560.00 | −34.24 | −2.74 | −34.72 | −8.12 | 480.18 |
| Lee Miller | Overtime | | − | | | | | |
| 444-56-3211 | | | 560.00 | −4.48 | −15.12 | −34.72 | −8.12 | |
| 9005, 10/8/05 | | | | | | | | |
| SD106 | Regular | 40.00 | 560.00 | −68.57 | −5.49 | −34.72 | −8.12 | 443.10 |
| Dale Sears | Overtime | | − | | | | | |
| 909-33-1234 | | | 560.00 | −4.48 | −15.12 | −34.72 | −8.12 | |
| 9006, 10/8/05 | | | | | | | | |
| Totals | Regular | 240.00 | 3,200.00 | −301.67 | −24.15 | −202.30 | −47.31 | 2,687.57 |
| | Overtime | 3.00 | 63.00 | | | | | |
| | | | 3,263.00 | −26.11 | −88.10 | −202.30 | −47.31 | |

Sales   Purchases   General Ledger   Payroll   Inventory   Company   Analysis

Net pay for each employee is computed as gross pay minus the items on the first line of columns 5–8. The employer's payroll tax for each employee is computed as the sum of items on the third line of columns 5–8. A payroll register includes all data necessary to record payroll. In some software programs the entries to record payroll are made in a special *payroll journal.*

**Payroll Check**    Payment of payroll is usually done by check or electronic funds transfer. Exhibit 9A.4 shows a *payroll check* for a Phoenix employee. This check is accompanied with a detachable *statement of earnings* (at top) showing gross pay, deductions, and net pay.

**Exhibit 9A.4**

Check and Statement of Earnings

| EMPLOYEE NO. | EMPLOYEE NAME | | | | SOCIAL SECURITY NO. | PAY PERIOD END | CHECK DATE |
|---|---|---|---|---|---|---|---|
| AR101 | Robert Austin | | | | 333-22-9999 | 10/8/05 | 10/8/05 |

| ITEM | RATE | HOURS | TOTAL | ITEM | | THIS CHECK | YEAR TO DATE |
|---|---|---|---|---|---|---|---|
| Regular | 10.00 | 40.00 | 400.00 | Gross | | 400.00 | 400.00 |
| Overtime | 15.00 | | | Fed. Income tax | | -28.99 | -28.99 |
| | | | | FICA-Soc. Sec. | | -24.80 | -24.80 |
| | | | | FICA-Medicare | | -5.80 | -5.80 |
| | | | | State Income tax | | -2.32 | -2.32 |

| HOURS WORKED | GROSS THIS PERIOD | GROSS YEAR TO DATE | NET CHECK | CHECK No. |
|---|---|---|---|---|
| 40.00 | 400.00 | 400.00 | $338.09 | 9001 |

(Detach and retain for your records)

**PHOENIX SALES & SERVICE**           Phoenix Bank and Trust                **9001**
1214 Mill Road                        Phoenix, AZ 85621
Phoenix, AZ 85621                     3312-87044
602-555-8900

|  | CHECK NO. | DATE | AMOUNT |
|---|---|---|---|
| | 9001 | Oct 8, 2005 | *************$338.09* |

Three Hundred Thirty–Eight and 9/100 Dollars

PAY TO THE ORDER OF    Robert Austin
18 Roosevelt Blvd., Apt C
Tempe, AZ 86322

*Mary Wills*
AUTHORIZED SIGNATURE

**Employee Earnings Report**    An **employee earnings report** is a cumulative record of an employee's hours worked, gross earnings, deductions, and net pay. Payroll information on this report is taken from the payroll register. The employee earnings report for R. Austin at Phoenix Sales & Service is shown in Exhibit 9A.5.

An employee earnings report accumulates information that can show when an employee's earnings reach the tax-exempt points for FICA, FUTA, and SUTA taxes. It also gives data an employer needs to prepare Form W-2.

## Payroll Procedures

Employers must be able to compute federal income tax for payroll purposes. This section explains how we compute this tax and how to use a payroll bank account.

**P5**    Compute payroll taxes.

**Computing Federal Income Taxes**    To compute the amount of taxes withheld from each employee's wages, we need to determine both the employee's wages earned and the employee's number of *withholding allowances.* Each employee records the number of withholding allowances claimed on a withholding allowance certificate, **Form W-4,** filed with the employer. When the number of withholding allowances increases, the amount of income taxes withheld decreases.

Employers often use a **wage bracket withholding table** similar to the one shown in Exhibit 9A.6 to compute the federal income taxes withheld from each employee's gross pay. The table in

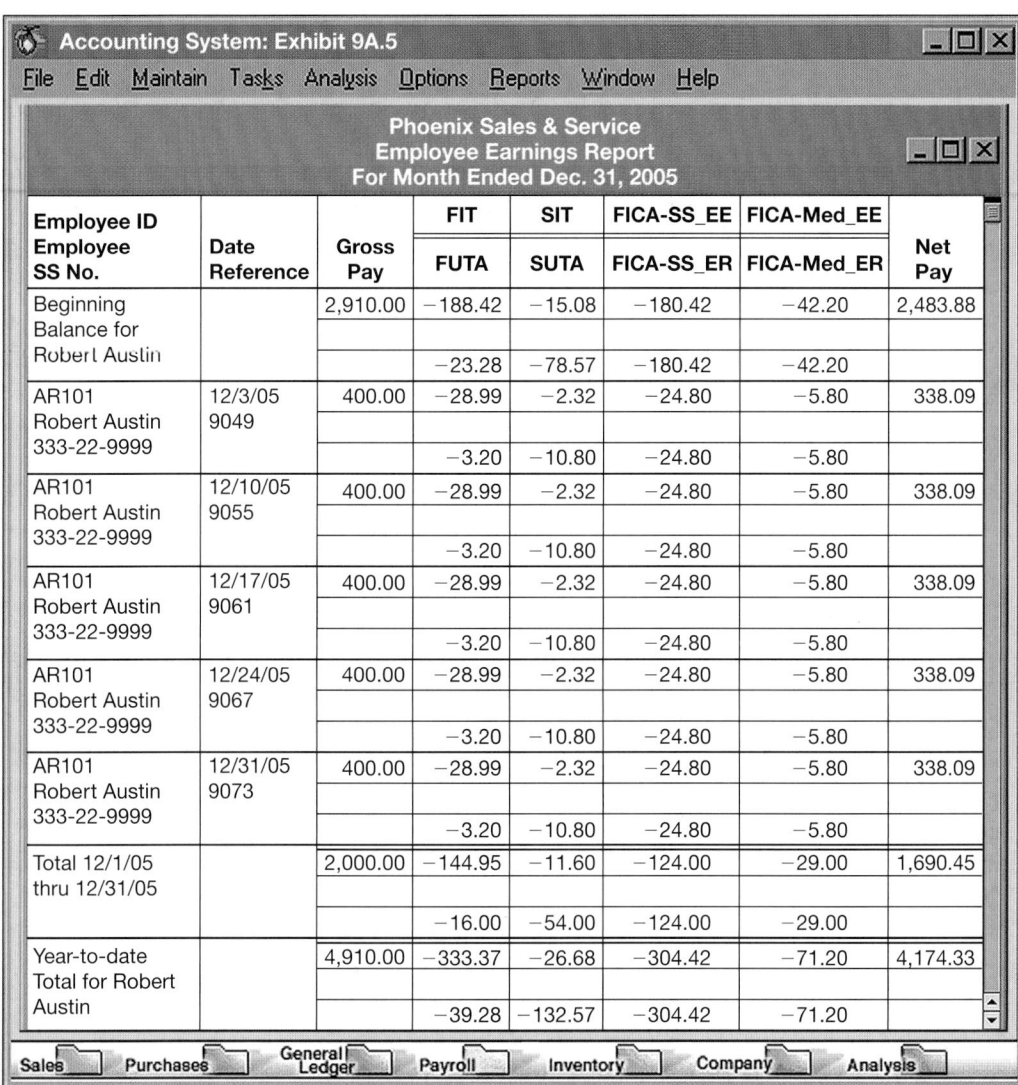

Exhibit 9A.5

Employee Earnings Report

| Accounting System: Exhibit 9A.5 |
|---|
| File   Edit   Maintain   Tasks   Analysis   Options   Reports   Window   Help |

**Phoenix Sales & Service**
**Employee Earnings Report**
**For Month Ended Dec. 31, 2005**

| Employee ID Employee SS No. | Date Reference | Gross Pay | FIT | SIT | FICA-SS_EE | FICA-Med_EE | Net Pay |
|---|---|---|---|---|---|---|---|
| | | | FUTA | SUTA | FICA-SS_ER | FICA-Med_ER | |
| Beginning Balance for Robert Austin | | 2,910.00 | −188.42 | −15.08 | −180.42 | −42.20 | 2,483.88 |
| | | | −23.28 | −78.57 | −180.42 | −42.20 | |
| AR101 Robert Austin 333-22-9999 | 12/3/05 9049 | 400.00 | −28.99 | −2.32 | −24.80 | −5.80 | 338.09 |
| | | | −3.20 | −10.80 | −24.80 | −5.80 | |
| AR101 Robert Austin 333-22-9999 | 12/10/05 9055 | 400.00 | −28.99 | −2.32 | −24.80 | −5.80 | 338.09 |
| | | | −3.20 | −10.80 | −24.80 | −5.80 | |
| AR101 Robert Austin 333-22-9999 | 12/17/05 9061 | 400.00 | −28.99 | −2.32 | −24.80 | −5.80 | 338.09 |
| | | | −3.20 | −10.80 | −24.80 | −5.80 | |
| AR101 Robert Austin 333-22-9999 | 12/24/05 9067 | 400.00 | −28.99 | −2.32 | −24.80 | −5.80 | 338.09 |
| | | | −3.20 | −10.80 | −24.80 | −5.80 | |
| AR101 Robert Austin 333-22-9999 | 12/31/05 9073 | 400.00 | −28.99 | −2.32 | −24.80 | −5.80 | 338.09 |
| | | | −3.20 | −10.80 | −24.80 | −5.80 | |
| Total 12/1/05 thru 12/31/05 | | 2,000.00 | −144.95 | −11.60 | −124.00 | −29.00 | 1,690.45 |
| | | | −16.00 | −54.00 | −124.00 | −29.00 | |
| Year-to-date Total for Robert Austin | | 4,910.00 | −333.37 | −26.68 | −304.42 | −71.20 | 4,174.33 |
| | | | −39.28 | −132.57 | −304.42 | −71.20 | |

Sales    Purchases    General Ledger    Payroll    Inventory    Company    Analysis

Exhibit 9A.6

Wage Bracket Withholding Table

**SINGLE Persons—WEEKLY Payroll Period**
(For Wages Paid in 2003)

| If the wages are – | | And the number of withholding allowances claimed is — | | | | | | | | | | |
|---|---|---|---|---|---|---|---|---|---|---|---|---|
| At least | But less than | 0 | 1 | 2 | 3 | 4 | 5 | 6 | 7 | 8 | 9 | 10 |
| | | The amount of income tax to be withheld is — | | | | | | | | | | |
| $600 | $610 | $81 | $69 | $60 | $51 | $42 | $33 | $25 | $16 | $8 | $3 | $0 |
| 610 | 620 | 83 | 70 | 61 | 53 | 44 | 35 | 26 | 17 | 9 | 4 | 0 |
| 620 | 630 | 86 | 72 | 63 | 54 | 45 | 36 | 28 | 19 | 10 | 5 | 0 |
| 630 | 640 | 89 | 73 | 64 | 55 | 47 | 38 | 29 | 20 | 12 | 6 | 0 |
| 640 | 650 | 91 | 76 | 65 | 57 | 48 | 39 | 31 | 22 | 13 | 7 | 1 |
| 650 | 660 | 94 | 78 | 67 | 59 | 60 | 41 | 32 | 23 | 15 | 8 | 2 |
| 660 | 670 | 97 | 81 | 69 | 60 | 61 | 42 | 34 | 25 | 16 | 9 | 3 |
| 670 | 680 | 99 | 84 | 70 | 62 | 63 | 44 | 35 | 26 | 18 | 10 | 4 |
| 680 | 690 | 102 | 85 | 72 | 63 | 64 | 45 | 37 | 28 | 19 | 11 | 5 |
| 690 | 700 | 103 | 89 | 73 | 65 | 65 | 47 | 38 | 29 | 21 | 12 | 6 |
| 700 | 710 | 108 | 92 | 70 | 66 | 67 | 48 | 40 | 31 | 22 | 13 | 7 |
| 710 | 720 | 110 | 94 | 79 | 69 | 69 | 60 | 41 | 32 | 24 | 15 | 8 |
| 720 | 730 | 113 | 97 | 81 | 69 | 60 | 61 | 43 | 34 | 25 | 16 | 9 |
| 730 | 740 | 116 | 100 | 84 | 71 | 62 | 63 | 44 | 35 | 27 | 18 | 10 |
| 740 | 750 | 118 | 103 | 87 | 72 | 63 | 64 | 45 | 37 | 28 | 19 | 11 |

Exhibit 9A.6 is for a single employee paid weekly. Tables are also provided for married employees and for biweekly, semimonthly, and monthly pay periods (most payroll software includes these tables). When using a wage bracket withholding table to compute federal income tax withheld from an employee's gross wages, we need to locate an employee's wage bracket within the first two columns. We then find the amount withheld by looking in the withholding allowance column for that employee.

**P6**   Record payment of payroll.

**Payroll Bank Account**    Companies with few employees often pay them with checks drawn on the company's regular bank account. Companies with many employees often use a special **payroll bank account** to pay employees. When this account is used, a company either (1) draws one check for total payroll on the regular bank account and deposits it in the payroll bank account or (2) executes an *electronic funds transfer* to the payroll bank account. Individual payroll checks are then drawn on this payroll bank account. Since only one check for the total payroll is drawn on the regular bank account each payday, use of a special payroll bank account helps with internal control. It also helps in reconciling the regular bank account. When companies use a payroll bank account, they usually include check numbers in the payroll register. The payroll register in Exhibit 9A.3 shows check numbers in column 1. For instance, Check No. 9001 is issued to Robert Austin. With this information, the payroll register serves as a supplementary record of wages earned by and paid to employees.

---

### Quick Check

**11.** What two items determine the amount deducted from an employee's wages for federal income taxes?

**12.** What amount of income tax is withheld from the salary of an employee who is single with three withholding allowances and earnings of $675 in a week? (*Hint:* Use the wage bracket withholding table in Exhibit 9A.6.)

**13.** Which of the following steps are executed when a company draws one check for total payroll and deposits it in a special payroll bank account? (*a*) Write a check to the payroll bank account for the total payroll and record it with a debit to Accrued Payroll Payable and a credit to Cash. (*b*) Deposit a check (or transfer funds) for the total payroll in the payroll bank account. (*c*) Issue individual payroll checks drawn on the payroll bank account. (*d*) All of the above.

Answers—p. 377

---

## APPENDIX

# 9B   Income Taxes

This appendix explains current liabilities involving income taxes for corporations.

**Income Tax Liabilities**    Corporations are subject to income taxes and must estimate their income tax liability when preparing financial statements. Since income tax expense is created by earning income, a liability is incurred when income is earned. This tax must be paid quarterly under federal regulations. To illustrate, consider a corporation that prepares monthly financial statements. Based on its income in January 2005, this corporation estimates that it owes income taxes of $12,100. The following adjusting entry records this estimate:

Assets = Liabilities + Equity
         +12,100    −12,100

| Jan. 31 | Income Taxes Expense ................... | 12,100 | |
| | Income Taxes Payable ................. | | 12,100 |
| | *To accrue January income taxes.* | | |

The tax liability is recorded each month until the first quarterly payment is made. If the company's estimated taxes for this first quarter total $30,000, the entry to record its payment is

| Apr. 10 | Income Taxes Payable . . . . . . . . . . . . . . . . . . . . | 30,000 | |
|---|---|---|---|
| | Cash . . . . . . . . . . . . . . . . . . . . . . . . . . . . | | 30,000 |
| | *Paid estimated quarterly income taxes based on first quarter income.* | | |

Assets = Liabilities + Equity
−30,000   −30,000

This process of accruing and then paying estimated income taxes continues through the year. When annual financial statements are prepared at year-end, the corporation knows its actual total income and the actual amount of income taxes it must pay. This information allows it to properly record income taxes expense for the fourth quarter so that the total of the four quarters' expense amounts equals the actual taxes paid to the government.

**Deferred Income Tax Liabilities**   An income tax liability for corporations can arise when the amount of income before taxes that the corporation reports on its income statement is not the same as the amount of income reported on its income tax return. This difference occurs because income tax laws and GAAP measure income differently. (Differences between tax laws and GAAP arise because Congress uses tax laws to generate receipts, stimulate the economy, and influence behavior, whereas GAAP are intended to provide financial information useful for decision making. Also, tax accounting often follows the cash basis, whereas GAAP follows the accrual basis.)

Some differences between tax laws and GAAP are temporary. *Temporary differences* arise when the tax return and the income statement report a revenue or expense in different years. As an example, companies are often able to deduct higher amounts of depreciation in the early years of an asset's life and smaller amounts in later years for tax reporting in comparison to GAAP. This means that in the early years, depreciation for tax reporting is often more than depreciation on the income statement. In later years, depreciation for tax reporting is often less than depreciation on the income statement. When temporary differences exist between taxable income on the tax return and the income before taxes on the income statement, corporations compute income taxes expense based on the income reported on the income statement. The result is that income taxes expense reported in the income statement is often different from the amount of income taxes payable to the government. This difference is the **deferred income tax liability.**

To illustrate, assume that in recording its usual quarterly income tax payments, a corporation computes $25,000 of income taxes expense. It also determines that only $21,000 is currently due and $4,000 is deferred to future years (a timing difference). The entry to record this end-of-period adjustment is

| Dec. 31 | Income Taxes Expense . . . . . . . . . . . . . . . . . . . . | 25,000 | |
|---|---|---|---|
| | Income Taxes Payable . . . . . . . . . . . . . . . . | | 21,000 |
| | Deferred Income Tax Liability . . . . . . . . . . | | 4,000 |
| | *To record tax expense and deferred tax liability.* | | |

Assets = Liabilities + Equity
+21,000   −25,000
+4,000

The credit to Income Taxes Payable reflects the amount currently due to be paid. The credit to Deferred Income Tax Liability reflects tax payments deferred until future years when the temporary difference reverses.

Temporary differences also can cause a company to pay income taxes *before* they are reported on the income statement as expense. If so, the company reports a *Deferred Income Tax Asset* on its balance sheet.

## Summary

**C1** **Describe current and long-term liabilities and their characteristics.** Liabilities are probable future payments of assets or services that past transactions or events obligate an entity to make. Current liabilities are due within one year or the operating cycle, whichever is longer. All other liabilities are long term.

**C2** **Identify and describe known current liabilities.** Known (determinable) current liabilities are set by agreements or laws and are measurable with little uncertainty. They include accounts payable, sales taxes payable, unearned revenues, notes payable, payroll liabilities, and the current portion of long-term debt.

**C3** **Explain how to account for contingent liabilities.** If an uncertain future payment depends on a probable future event and the amount can be reasonably estimated, the payment is recorded as a liability. The uncertain future payment is reported as a contingent liability (in the notes) if (*a*) the future event is reasonably possible but not probable or (*b*) the event is probable but the payment amount cannot be reasonably estimated.

**C4ᴬ** **Identify and describe payroll reporting.** Employers report FICA taxes and federal income tax withholdings using Form 941. FUTA taxes are reported on Form 940. Earnings and deductions are reported to each employee and the federal government on Form W-2.

**C5ᴬ** **Identify and describe payroll records.** An employer's payroll records include a payroll register for each pay period, payroll checks and statements of earnings, and individual employee earnings reports.

**A1** **Compute the times interest earned ratio and use it to analyze liabilities.** Times interest earned is computed by dividing a company's net income before interest expense and income taxes by the amount of interest expense. The times interest earned ratio reflects a company's ability to pay interest obligations.

**P1** **Prepare entries to account for short-term notes payable.** Short-term notes payable are current liabilities; most bear interest. When a short-term note's face value equals the amount borrowed, it identifies a rate of interest to be paid at maturity.

**P2** **Compute and record *employee* payroll deductions and liabilities.** Employee payroll deductions include FICA taxes, income taxes, and voluntary deductions such as for pensions and charities. They make up the difference between gross and net pay.

**P3** **Compute and record *employer* payroll expenses and liabilities.** An employer's payroll expenses include employees' gross earnings, any employee benefits, and the payroll taxes levied on the employer. Payroll liabilities include employees' net pay amounts, withholdings from employee wages, any employer-promised benefits, and the employer's payroll taxes.

**P4** **Account for estimated liabilities, including warranties and bonuses.** Liabilities for health and pension benefits, warranties, and bonuses are recorded with estimated amounts. These items are recognized as expenses when incurred and matched with revenues generated.

**P5ᴬ** **Compute payroll taxes.** Federal income tax deductions depend on the employee's earnings and the number of withholding allowances claimed. Wage bracket withholding tables are available for different pay periods and employee classes.

**P6ᴬ** **Record payment of payroll.** Employers with a large number of employees often use a separate payroll bank account. When this is done, the payment of employees is recorded with a transfer of cash from the regular bank account to the payroll bank account.

---

## Decision Ethics

**Web Designer** You need to be concerned about being an accomplice to unlawful payroll activities. Not paying federal and state taxes on wages earned is illegal and unethical. Such payments also will not provide the employee with Social Security and some Medicare credits. The best course of action is to request payment by check. If this fails to change the owner's payment practices, you must consider quitting this job.

**Entrepreneur** Risk is partly reflected by the times interest earned ratio. This ratio for the first franchise is 1.5 [($100,000 + $200,000)/$200,000], whereas the ratio for the second franchise is 3.5 [($100,000 + $40,000)/$40,000]. This analysis shows that the first franchise is more at risk of incurring a loss if its sales decline. The second question asks about variability of income. If income greatly varies, this increases the risk an owner will not earn sufficient income to cover interest. Since the first franchise has the greater variability, it is a riskier investment.

---

## Guidance Answers to **Quick Checks**

**1.** A liability involves a probable future payment of assets or services that an entity is presently obligated to make as a result of past transactions or events.

**2.** No, an expected future payment is not a liability unless an existing obligation was created by a past event or transaction.

**3.** In most cases, a liability due in 15 months is classified as long term. It is classified as a current liability if the company's operating cycle is 15 months or longer.

**4.** A creditor prefers a note payable instead of a past-due account payable so as to (*a*) charge interest and/or (*b*) have evidence of the debt and its terms for potential litigation or disputes.

**5.** $1,000(.008) + $1,000(.04) + $3,000(.062) + $3,000(.0145) = $277.50

**6.** (*a*) FICA taxes are incurred by both employee and employer. (*b*) FUTA taxes are incurred by the employer. (*c*) SUTA taxes are incurred by the employer. (*d*) Withheld income taxes are incurred by the employee.

**7.** (*a*)

**8.** (*a*) Warranty expense was previously estimated and recorded.

**9.** (*b*)

**10.** A future payment is reported in the notes as a contingent liability if (*a*) the uncertain future event is probable but the amount of payment cannot be reasonably estimated or (*b*) the uncertain future event is not probable but has a reasonable possibility of occurring.

**11.** An employee's gross earnings and number of withholding allowances determine the deduction for federal income taxes.

**12.** $62

**13.** (*d*)

## Key Terms

Key Terms are available at the book's Website for learning and testing in an online Flashcard Format.

**Contingent liability** (p. 364)
**Current liabilities** (p. 353)
**Current portion of long-term debt** (p. 361)
**Deferred income tax liability** (p. 375)
**Employee benefits** (p. 361)
**Employee earnings report** (p. 372)
**Estimated liability** (p. 361)
**Federal depository bank** (p. 370)
**Federal Insurance Contributions Act (FICA) Taxes** (p. 358)

**Federal Unemployment Taxes (FUTA)** (p. 360)
**Form 940** (p. 370)
**Form 941** (p. 368)
**Form W-2** (p. 370)
**Form W-4** (p. 372)
**Gross pay** (p. 357)
**Known liabilities** (p. 354)
**Long-term liabilities** (p. 353)
**Merit rating** (p. 360)

**Net pay** (p. 358)
**Payroll bank account** (p. 374)
**Payroll deductions** (p. 358)
**Payroll register** (p. 370)
**Short-term note payable** (p. 355)
**State Unemployment Taxes (SUTA)** (p. 360)
**Times interest earned** (p. 365)
**Wage bracket withholding table** (p. 372)
**Warranty** (p. 362)

## Personal Interactive Quiz

Personal Interactive Quizzes A and B are available at the book's Website to reinforce and assess your learning.

*Superscript letter* <sup>A</sup> (<sup>B</sup>) *denotes assignments based on Appendix 9A (9B).*

## Discussion Questions

**1.** What are the three important questions concerning the uncertainty of liabilities?

**2.** What is the difference between a current and a long-term liability?

**3.** What is an estimated liability?

**4.** If $894.40 is the total of a sale that includes its sales tax of 4%, what is the selling price of the item only?

**5.** What is the combined amount (in percent) of the employee and employer Social Security tax rate?

**6.** What is the current Medicare tax rate? This rate is applied to what maximum level of salary and wages?

**7.** What determines the amount deducted from an employee's wages for federal income taxes?

**8.** Which payroll taxes are the employee's responsibility and which are the employer's responsibility?

**9.** What is an employer's unemployment merit rating? How are these ratings assigned to employers?

**10.** Why are warranty liabilities usually recognized on the balance sheet as liabilities even when they are uncertain?

**11.** Suppose that a company has a facility located where disastrous weather conditions often occur. Should it report a probable loss from a future disaster as a liability on its balance sheet? Explain.

**12.**<sup>A</sup>What is a wage bracket withholding table?

**13.**[A]What amount of income tax is withheld from the salary of an employee who is single with two withholding allowances and earning $725 per week? What if the employee earned $625 and has no withholding allowances? (Use Exhibit 9A.6.)

**14.** Refer to **Krispy Kreme**'s financial statements in Appendix A. As an alternative to short-term notes, Krispy Kreme meets short-term borrowing needs through revolving lines of credit. Briefly explain how a line of credit differs from a short-term note payable.

**15.** Refer to **Tastykake**'s balance sheet in Appendix A. What accounts related to income taxes are on its balance sheet? Explain the meaning of each income tax account you identify.

**16.** Refer to **Harley-Davidson**'s balance sheet in Appendix A. Which current liability account reports its payroll-related liabilities (if any) as of December 31, 2002?

**Red numbers denote Discussion Questions that involve decision-making.**

---

*Homework Manager repeats all numerical Quick Studies on the book's Website with new numbers.* ⟶

## QUICK STUDY

**QS 9-1**
Classifying liabilities   C1

Which of the following items are normally classified as a current liability for a company that has a 15-month operating cycle?

**1.** Salaries payable.
**2.** Note payable due in 18 months.
**3.** FICA taxes payable.

**4.** Note payable maturing in 2 years.
**5.** Note payable due in 11 months.
**6.** Portion of long-term note due in 15 months.

---

**QS 9-2**
Accounting for sales taxes
C2

Gomez Computing sells merchandise for $5,000 cash on September 30 (cost of merchandise is $2,900). The sales tax law requires Gomez to collect 4% sales tax on every dollar of merchandise sold. Record the entry for the $5,000 sale and its applicable sales tax. Also record the entry that shows the remittance of the 4% tax on this sale to the state government on October 15.

---

**QS 9-3**
Unearned revenue   C2

Ticketmaster receives $4,000,000 in advance ticket sales for a four-date tour of the Rolling Stones. Record the advance ticket sales on October 31. Record the revenue earned for the first concert date of November 5, assuming it represents one-fourth of the advance ticket sales.

---

**QS 9-4**
Interest-bearing note transactions
P1

On November 7, 2005, Ortez Company borrows $150,000 cash by signing a 90-day, 8% note payable with a face value of $150,000. (1) Compute the accrued interest payable on December 31, 2005, (2) prepare the journal entry to record the accrued interest expense at December 31, 2005, and (3) prepare the journal entry to record payment of the note at maturity.

---

**QS 9-5**
Record employer payroll taxes
P2   P3

Meredith Co. has five employees, each of whom earns $2,600 per month and has been employed since January 1. FICA Social Security taxes are 6.2% of gross pay and FICA Medicare taxes are 1.45% of gross pay. FUTA taxes are 0.8% and SUTA taxes are 2.8% of the first $7,000 paid to each employee. Prepare the March 31 journal entry to record the March payroll taxes expense.

---

**QS 9-6**
Recording warranty repairs
P4

On September 11, 2004, Home Store sells a mower for $400 with a one-year warranty that covers parts. Warranty expense is estimated at 5% of sales. On July 24, 2005, the mower is brought in for repairs covered under the warranty requiring $35 in materials taken from the Repair Parts Inventory. Prepare the July 24, 2005, entry to record the warranty repairs.

---

**QS 9-7**
Accounting for bonuses   P4

Paris Company offers an annual bonus to employees if the company meets certain net income goals. Prepare the journal entry to record a $10,000 bonus owed to its workers (to be shared equally) at calendar year-end.

The following legal claims exist for Kalamazoo Co. Identify the accounting treatment for each claim as either (*a*) a liability that is recorded or (*b*) an item described in notes to its financial statements.

**1.** Kalamazoo (defendant) estimates that a pending lawsuit could result in damages of $1,000,000; it is reasonably possible that the plaintiff will win the case.

**2.** Kalamazoo faces a probable loss on a pending lawsuit; the amount is not reasonably estimable.

**3.** Kalamazoo estimates damages in a case at $2,500,000 with a high probability of losing the case.

**QS 9-8**
Accounting for contingent liabilities

C3

---

Compute the times interest earned for Dechow Company, which reports income before interest expense and income taxes of $1,575,000 and interest expense of $137,000. Interpret its times interest earned—assume that its competitors average a times interest earned of 4.0.

**QS 9-9**
Times interest earned

A1

---

Cather Corporation has made and recorded its quarterly income tax payments. After a final review of taxes for the year, the company identifies an additional $30,000 of income tax expense that should be recorded. A portion of this additional expense, $8,000, is deferred for payment in future years. Record Cather's year-end adjusting entry for income tax expense.

**QS 9-10^B**
Record deferred income tax liability

P4

---

 *Homework Manager* repeats all numerical Exercises on the book's Website with new numbers.

The following items appear on the balance sheet of a company with a two-month operating cycle. Identify the proper classification of each item as follows: *C* if it is a current liability, *L* if it is a long-term liability, or *N* if it is not a liability.

_____ **1.** Sales taxes payable.
_____ **2.** FUTA taxes payable.
_____ **3.** Accounts receivable.
_____ **4.** Accrued payroll payable.
_____ **5.** Wages payable.

_____ **6.** Notes payable (due in 6 to 12 months).
_____ **7.** Notes payable (due in 120 days).
_____ **8.** Current portion of long-term debt.
_____ **9.** Notes payable (mature in five years).
_____ **10.** Notes payable (due in 13 to 24 months).

**EXERCISES**

**Exercise 9-1**
Classifying liabilities

C1

---

Prepare any necessary adjusting entries at December 31, 2005, for Yacht Company's year-end financial statements for each of the following separate transactions and events:

**1.** During December, Yacht Company sold 3,000 units of a product that carries a 60-day warranty. December sales for this product total $120,000. The company expects 8% of the units to need warranty repairs, and it estimates the average repair cost per unit will be $15.

**2.** A disgruntled employee is suing Yacht Company. Legal advisers believe that the company will probably need to pay damages, but the amount cannot be reasonably estimated.

**3.** Employees earn vacation pay at a rate of one day per month. During December, 20 employees qualify for one vacation day each. Their average daily wage is $120 per employee.

**4.** Yacht Company guarantees the $5,000 debt of a supplier. The supplier will probably not default on the debt.

**5.** Yacht Company records an adjusting entry for $2,000,000 of previously unrecorded cash sales (costing $1,000,000) and its sales taxes at a rate of 5%.

**6.** The company earned $40,000 of $100,000 previously received in advance for services.

**Exercise 9-2**
Adjusting entries for liabilities

C2 C3 P4

---

For the year ended December 31, 2005, Winter Company has implemented an employee bonus program equal to 3% of Winter's net income, which employees will share equally. Winter's net income (prebonus) is expected to be $1,000,000, and bonus expense is deducted in computing net income.

**1.** Compute the amount of the bonus payable to the employees at year-end (use the method described in the chapter and round to the nearest dollar).

**2.** Prepare the journal entry at December 31, 2005, to record the bonus due the employees.

**3.** Prepare the journal entry at January 19, 2006, to record payment of the bonus to employees.

**Exercise 9-3**
Computing and recording bonuses C2

**Check** (1) $29,126

**Exercise 9-4**

Accounting for note payable

P1

**Check**   (2b) Interest expense, $1,880

Perfect Systems borrows $94,000 cash on May 15, 2005, by signing a 60-day, 12% note.

**1.** On what date does this note mature?

**2.** Suppose the face value of the note equals $94,000, the principal of the loan. Prepare the journal entries to record (*a*) issuance of the note and (*b*) payment of the note at maturity.

---

**Exercise 9-5**

Interest-bearing notes payable with year-end adjustments

P1

**Check**   (2) $2,250
            (3) $1,125

Kwon Co. borrows $150,000 cash on November 1, 2005, by signing a 90-day, 9% note with a face value of $150,000.

**1.** On what date does this note mature?

**2.** How much interest expense results from this note in 2005? (Assume a 360-day year.)

**3.** How much interest expense results from this note in 2006? (Assume a 360-day year.)

**4.** Prepare journal entries to record (*a*) issuance of the note, (*b*) accrual of interest at the end of 2005, and (*c*) payment of the note at maturity.

---

**Exercise 9-6**

Computing payroll taxes

P2   P3

MRI Co. has one employee, and the company is subject to the following taxes:

| Tax | Rate | Applied To |
|-----|------|------------|
| FICA—Social Security ....... | 6.20% | First $87,000 |
| FICA—Medicare .......... | 1.45 | All gross pay |
| FUTA ................. | 0.80 | First $7,000 |
| SUTA ................. | 2.90 | First $7,000 |

Compute MRI's amounts for each of these four taxes as applied to the employee's gross earnings for September under each of three separate situations (*a*), (*b*), and (*c*):

| | Gross Pay through August | Gross Pay for September |
|---|---|---|
| a. | $ 6,400 | $ 800 |
| b. | 18,200 | 2,100 |
| c. | 82,000 | 8,000 |

**Check**   (*a*) FUTA, $4.80; SUTA, $17.40

---

**Exercise 9-7**

Payroll-related journal entries

P2   P3

Using the data in situation *a* of Exercise 9-6, prepare the employer's September 30 journal entries to record (1) salary expense and its related payroll liabilities for this employee and (2) the employer's payroll taxes expense and its related liabilities. The employee's federal income taxes withheld by the employer are $135 for this pay period.

---

**Exercise 9-8**

Warranty expense and liability computations and entries

P4

**Check**   (1) $220

(4) $21

Chang Co. sold a copier costing $3,800 with a two-year parts warranty to a customer on August 16, 2005, for $5,500 cash. Chang uses the perpetual inventory system. On November 22, 2006, the copier requires on-site repairs that are completed the same day. The repairs cost $199 for materials taken from the Repair Parts Inventory. These are the only repairs required in 2006 for this copier. Based on experience, Chang expects to incur warranty costs equal to 4% of dollar sales. It records warranty expense with an adjusting entry at the end of each year.

**1.** How much warranty expense does the company report in 2005 for this copier?

**2.** How much is the estimated warranty liability for this copier as of December 31, 2005?

**3.** How much warranty expense does the company report in 2006 for this copier?

**4.** How much is the estimated warranty liability for this copier as of December 31, 2006?

**5.** Prepare journal entries to record (*a*) the copier's sale; (*b*) the adjustment on December 31, 2005, to recognize the warranty expense; and (*c*) the repairs that occur in November 2006.

Use the following information from separate companies *a* through *f* to compute times interest earned. Which company indicates the strongest ability to pay interest expense as it comes due?

| | Net Income (Loss) | Interest Expense | Income Taxes |
|---|---|---|---|
| **a.** | $140,000 | $48,000 | $ 35,000 |
| **b.** | 140,000 | 15,000 | 50,000 |
| **c.** | 140,000 | 8,000 | 70,000 |
| **d.** | 265,000 | 12,000 | 130,000 |
| **e.** | 79,000 | 12,000 | 30,000 |
| **f.** | (4,000) | 12,000 | 0 |

**Exercise 9-9**
Computing and interpreting times interest earned

A1

**Check** (b) 13.67

---

The payroll records of Clix Software show the following information about Trish Farqua, an employee, for the weekly pay period ending September 30, 2005. Farqua is single and claims one allowance. Compute her Social Security tax (6.2%), Medicare tax (1.45%), federal income tax withholding, state income tax (0.5%), and net pay for the current pay period. The state income tax is 0.5 percent on the first $9,000 earned. (Use the withholding table in Exhibit 9A.6.)

Total (gross) earnings for current pay period . . . . . . . $ 735
Cumulative earnings of previous pay periods . . . . . . . . 9,700

**Exercise 9-10^A**
Net pay and tax computations
P5

**Check** Net pay, 578.77

---

LaShonda Blake, an unmarried employee, works 48 hours in the week ended January 12. Her pay rate is $12 per hour, and her wages are subject to no deductions other than FICA—Social Security, FICA— Medicare, and federal income taxes. She claims two withholding allowances. Compute her regular pay, overtime pay (overtime premium is 50% of the regular rate for hours in excess of 40 per week), and gross pay. Then compute her FICA tax deduction (use 6.2% for the Social Security portion and 1.45% for the Medicare portion), income tax deduction (use the wage bracket withholding table of Exhibit 9A.6), total deductions, and net pay.

**Exercise 9-11^A**
Gross and net pay computation
P5  P6

**Check** Net pay, $513.26

---

Ming Corporation prepares financial statements for each month-end. As part of its accounting process, estimated income taxes are accrued each month for 30% of the current month's net income. The income taxes are paid in the first month of each quarter for the amount accrued for the prior quarter. The following information is available for the fourth quarter of year 2005. When tax computations are completed on January 20, 2006, Ming determines that the quarter's Income Taxes Payable account balance should be $29,100 on December 31, 2005 (its unadjusted balance is $23,640).

October 2005 net income . . . . . . . . . $27,900
November 2005 net income . . . . . . . 18,200
December 2005 net income . . . . . . . . 32,700

**Exercise 9-12^B**
Accounting for income taxes
P4

**1.** Determine the amount of the accounting adjustment (dated as of December 31, 2005) to produce the proper ending balance in the Income Taxes Payable account.

**Check** (1) $5,460

**2.** Prepare journal entries to record (*a*) the December 31, 2005, adjustment to the Income Taxes Payable account and (*b*) the January 20, 2006, payment of the fourth-quarter taxes.

---

Tytus Co. entered into the following transactions involving short-term liabilities in 2004 and 2005.

*2004*

Apr. 20 Purchased $38,500 of merchandise on credit from Frier, terms are 1/10, n/30. Tytus uses the perpetual inventory system.
May 19 Replaced the April 20 account payable to Frier with a 90-day, $30,000 note bearing 9% annual interest along with paying $8,500 in cash.

**PROBLEM SET A**

**Problem 9-1A**
Short-term notes payable transactions and entries

P1

mhhe.com/wild3e

July   8   Borrowed $60,000 cash from Community Bank by signing a 120-day, 10% interest-bearing note with a face value of $60,000.

____?____   Paid the amount due on the note to Frier at the maturity date.

____?____   Paid the amount due on the note to Community Bank at the maturity date.

Nov. 28   Borrowed $21,000 cash from UMB Bank by signing a 60-day, 8% interest-bearing note with a face value of $21,000.

Dec. 31   Recorded an adjusting entry for accrued interest on the note to UMB Bank.

**2005**

____?____   Paid the amount due on the note to UMB Bank at the maturity date.

**Required**

**1.** Determine the maturity date for each of the three notes described.

**2.** Determine the interest due at maturity for each of the three notes. (Assume a 360-day year.)

**3.** Determine the interest expense to be recorded in the adjusting entry at the end of 2004.

**4.** Determine the interest expense to be recorded in 2005.

**5.** Prepare journal entries for all the preceding transactions and events for years 2004–2005.

**Check**   (2) Frier, $675
            (3) $154
            (4) $126

---

### Problem 9-2A
Warranty expense and liability estimation

P4

On October 29, 2004, Lue Co. began operations by purchasing razors for resale. Lue uses the perpetual inventory method. The razors have a 90-day warranty that requires the company to replace any nonworking razor. When a razor is returned, the company discards it and mails a new one from Merchandise Inventory to the customer. The company's cost per new razor is $18 and its retail selling price is $80 in both 2004 and 2005. The manufacturer has advised the company to expect warranty costs to equal 7% of dollar sales. The following transactions and events occurred:

**2004**

Nov. 11   Sold 75 razors for $6,000 cash.
      30   Recognized warranty expense related to November sales with an adjusting entry.
Dec.   9   Replaced 15 razors that were returned under the warranty.
      16   Sold 210 razors for $16,800 cash.
      29   Replaced 30 razors that were returned under the warranty.
      31   Recognized warranty expense related to December sales with an adjusting entry.

**2005**

Jan.   5   Sold 130 razors for $10,400 cash.
      17   Replaced 50 razors that were returned under the warranty.
      31   Recognized warranty expense related to January sales with an adjusting entry.

**Required**

**1.** Prepare journal entries to record these transactions and adjustments for 2004 and 2005.

**2.** How much warranty expense is reported for November 2004 and for December 2004?

**3.** How much warranty expense is reported for January 2005?

**4.** What is the balance of the Estimated Warranty Liability account as of December 31, 2004?

**5.** What is the balance of the Estimated Warranty Liability account as of January 31, 2005?

**Check**   (3) $728
            (4) $786 Cr.
            (5) $614 Cr.

---

### Problem 9-3A
Computing and analyzing times interest earned

A1

Shown here are condensed income statements for two different companies (both are organized as LLCs and pay no income taxes):

| Ace Co. | |
|---|---|
| Sales . . . . . . . . . . . . . . . . . . . . . | $500,000 |
| Variable expenses (80%) . . . . . . . | 400,000 |
| Income before interest . . . . . . . . | 100,000 |
| Interest expense (fixed) . . . . . . . . | 30,000 |
| Net income . . . . . . . . . . . . . . | $ 70,000 |

| Deuce Co. | |
|---|---|
| Sales . . . . . . . . . . . . . . . . . . . . . | $500,000 |
| Variable expenses (60%) . . . . . . . | 300,000 |
| Income before interest . . . . . . . . | 200,000 |
| Interest expense (fixed) . . . . . . . . | 130,000 |
| Net income . . . . . . . . . . . . . . | $ 70,000 |

**Required**

1. Compute times interest earned for Ace Co.
2. Compute times interest earned for Deuce Co.
3. What happens to each company's net income if sales increase by 30%?
4. What happens to each company's net income if sales increase by 50%?
5. What happens to each company's net income if sales increase by 80%?
6. What happens to each company's net income if sales decrease by 10%?
7. What happens to each company's net income if sales decrease by 20%?
8. What happens to each company's net income if sales decrease by 40%?

*Analysis Component*

9. Comment on the results from parts 3 through 8 in relation to the fixed-cost strategies of the two companies and the ratio values you computed in parts 1 and 2.

**Check** (3) Ace net income, $100,000 (43% increase)

(6) Deuce net income, $50,000 (29% decrease)

---

Legal Stars pays its employees each week. Its employees' gross pay is subject to these taxes:

| Tax | Rate | Applied To |
|---|---|---|
| FICA—Social Security . . . . . . . . | 6.20% | First $87,000 |
| FICA—Medicare . . . . . . . . . . . | 1.45 | All gross pay |
| FUTA . . . . . . . . . . . . . . . . . . | 0.80 | First $7,000 |
| SUTA . . . . . . . . . . . . . . . . . . | 2.15 | First $7,000 |

**Problem 9-4A**
Payroll expenses, withholdings, and taxes

P2  P3

mhhe.com/wild3e

The company is preparing its payroll calculations for the week ended August 25. Payroll records show the following information for the company's four employees:

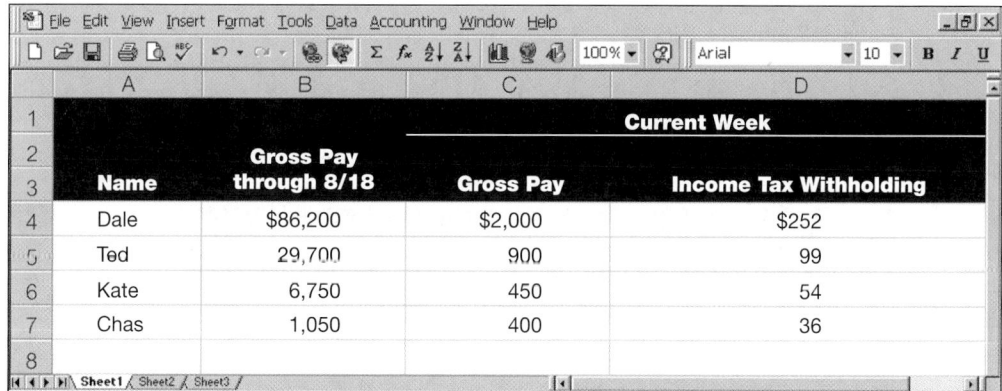

| Name | Gross Pay through 8/18 | Current Week Gross Pay | Current Week Income Tax Withholding |
|---|---|---|---|
| Dale | $86,200 | $2,000 | $252 |
| Ted | 29,700 | 900 | 99 |
| Kate | 6,750 | 450 | 54 |
| Chas | 1,050 | 400 | 36 |

In addition to gross pay, the company must pay one-half of the $32 per employee weekly health insurance; each employee pays the remaining one-half. The company also contributes an extra 8% of each employee's gross pay (at no cost to employees) to a pension fund.

**Required**

Compute the following for the week ended August 25 (round amounts to the nearest cent):

1. Each employee's FICA withholdings for Social Security.
2. Each employee's FICA withholdings for Medicare.
3. Employer's FICA taxes for Social Security.
4. Employer's FICA taxes for Medicare.
5. Employer's FUTA taxes.
6. Employer's SUTA taxes.
7. Each employee's net (take-home) pay.
8. Employer's total payroll-related expense for each employee.

**Check** (3) $158.10
(4) $54.38
(5) $5.20

(7) Total net pay, $3,032.52

## Problem 9-5A
Entries for payroll transactions

P2   P3

On January 8, the end of the first weekly pay period of the year, Royal Company's payroll register showed that its employees earned $11,380 of office salaries and $32,920 of sales salaries. Withholdings from the employees' salaries include FICA Social Security taxes at the rate of 6.2%, FICA Medicare taxes at the rate of 1.45%, $6,340 of federal income taxes, $670 of medical insurance deductions, and $420 of union dues. No employee earned more than $7,000 in this first period.

**Check**  (1) Cr. Accrued Payroll Payable, $33,481.05

(2) Dr. Payroll Taxes Expense, $5,515.35

### Required

1. Calculate FICA Social Security taxes payable and FICA Medicare taxes payable. Prepare the journal entry to record Royal Company's January 8 (employee) payroll expenses and liabilities.
2. Prepare the journal entry to record Royal's (employer) payroll taxes resulting from the January 8 payroll. Royal's merit rating reduces its state unemployment tax rate to 4.0% of the first $7,000 paid each employee. The federal unemployment tax rate is 0.8%.

## Problem 9-6A[A]
Entries for payroll transactions

P2   P3   P5   P6

Polo Company has 10 employees, each of whom earns $2,600 per month and is paid on the last day of each month. All 10 have been employed continuously at this amount since January 1. Polo uses a payroll bank account and special payroll checks to pay its employees. On March 1, the following accounts and balances exist in its general ledger:

a. FICA—Social Security Taxes Payable, $3,224; FICA—Medicare Taxes Payable, $754. (The balances of these accounts represent total liabilities for *both* the employer's and employees' FICA taxes for the February payroll only.)
b. Employees' Federal Income Taxes Payable, $3,900 (liability for February only).
c. Federal Unemployment Taxes Payable, $416 (liability for January and February together).
d. State Unemployment Taxes Payable, $2,080 (liability for January and February together).

During March and April, the company had the following payroll transactions:

Mar. 15  Issued check payable to Fleet Bank, a federal depository bank authorized to accept employers' payments of FICA taxes and employee income tax withholdings. The $7,878 check is in payment of the February FICA and employee income taxes.

**Check**  March 31: Cr. Accrued Payroll Payable, $20,111

31  Recorded the March payroll and transferred funds from the regular bank account to the payroll bank account. Issued checks payable to each employee in payment of the March payroll. The payroll register shows the following summary totals for the March pay period:

| | Salaries and Wages | | | | Federal | |
|---|---|---|---|---|---|---|
| Office Salaries | Shop Wages | Gross Pay | FICA Taxes* | Income Taxes | Net Pay |
| $10,400 | $15,600 | $26,000 | $1,612 | $3,900 | $20,111 |
| | | | $ 377 | | |

* FICA taxes are Social Security and Medicare, respectively.

March 31: Dr. Payroll Taxes Expenses, $2,853

31  Recorded the employer's payroll taxes resulting from the March payroll. The company has a merit rating that reduces its state unemployment tax rate to 4.0% of the first $7,000 paid each employee. The federal rate is 0.8%.

April 15: Cr. Cash, $7,878 (Fleet)

Apr. 15  Issued check to Fleet Bank in payment of the March FICA and employee income taxes.
15  Issued check to the State Tax Commission for the January, February, and March state unemployment taxes. Mailed the check and the first quarter tax return to the Commission.
30  Issued check payable to Fleet Bank in payment of the employer's FUTA taxes for the first quarter of the year.
30  Mailed Form 941 to the IRS, reporting the FICA taxes and the employees' federal income tax withholdings for the first quarter.

### Required

Prepare journal entries to record the transactions and events for both March and April.

Bargen Co. entered into the following transactions involving short-term liabilities in 2004 and 2005.

**PROBLEM SET B**

**Problem 9-1B**
Short-term notes payable
transactions and entries

P1

**2004**

Apr. 22   Purchased $4,000 of merchandise on credit from Quinn Products, terms are 1/10, n/30.
Bargen uses the perpetual inventory system.

May 23   Replaced the April 22 account payable to Quinn Products with a 60-day, $3,600 note bear-
ing 15% annual interest along with paying $400 in cash.

July 15   Borrowed $9,000 cash from Blackhawk Bank by signing a 120-day, 10% interest-bearing
note with a face value of $9,000.

___?___   Paid the amount due on the note to Quinn Products at maturity.

___?___   Paid the amount due on the note to Blackhawk Bank at maturity.

Dec. 6   Borrowed $16,000 cash from City Bank by signing a 45-day, 9% interest-bearing note with
a face value of $16,000.

    31   Recorded an adjusting entry for accrued interest on the note to City Bank.

**2005**

___?___   Paid the amount due on the note to City Bank at maturity.

**Required**

**1.** Determine the maturity date for each of the three notes described.

**2.** Determine the interest due at maturity for each of the three notes. (Assume a 360-day year.)

**3.** Determine the interest expense to be recorded in the adjusting entry at the end of 2004.

**4.** Determine the interest expense to be recorded in 2005.

**5.** Prepare journal entries for all the preceding transactions and events for years 2004–2005.

**Check**   (2) Quinn, $90
(3) $100
(4) $80

On November 10, 2004, Byung Co. began operations by purchasing coffee grinders for resale. Byung
uses the perpetual inventory method. The grinders have a 60-day warranty that requires the company to replace any nonworking grinder. When a grinder is returned, the company discards it and
mails a new one from Merchandise Inventory to the customer. The company's cost per new grinder
is $14 and its retail selling price is $35 in both 2004 and 2005. The manufacturer has advised the
company to expect warranty costs to equal 10% of dollar sales. The following transactions and events
occurred.

**Problem 9-2B**
Warranty expense and
liability estimation

P4

**2004**

Nov. 16   Sold 50 grinders for $1,750 cash.

    30   Recognized warranty expense related to November sales with an adjusting entry.

Dec. 12   Replaced six grinders that were returned under the warranty.

    18   Sold 150 grinders for $5,250 cash.

    28   Replaced 17 grinders that were returned under the warranty.

    31   Recognized warranty expense related to December sales with an adjusting entry.

**2005**

Jan. 7   Sold 60 grinders for $2,100 cash.

    21   Replaced 38 grinders that were returned under the warranty.

    31   Recognized warranty expense related to January sales with an adjusting entry.

**Required**

**1.** Prepare journal entries to record these transactions and adjustments for 2004 and 2005.

**2.** How much warranty expense is reported for November 2004 and for December 2004?

**3.** How much warranty expense is reported for January 2005?

**4.** What is the balance of the Estimated Warranty Liability account as of December 31, 2004?

**5.** What is the balance of the Estimated Warranty Liability account as of January 31, 2005?

**Check**   (3) $210
(4) $378 Cr.
(5) $56 Cr.

## Problem 9-3B
Computing and analyzing times interest earned

A1

Shown here are condensed income statements for two different companies (both are organized as LLCs and pay no income taxes):

| Virgo Co. | |
| --- | --- |
| Sales .................... | $120,000 |
| Variable expenses (50%) ........ | 60,000 |
| Income before interest ........ | $ 60,000 |
| Interest expense (fixed) ........ | 45,000 |
| Net income ................ | $ 15,000 |

| Zodiac Co. | |
| --- | --- |
| Sales ..................... | $120,000 |
| Variable expenses (75%) ....... | 90,000 |
| Income before interest ........ | $ 30,000 |
| Interest expense (fixed) ........ | 15,000 |
| Net income ................ | $ 15,000 |

### Required

**1.** Compute times interest earned for Virgo.

**2.** Compute times interest earned for Zodiac.

**3.** What happens to each company's net income if sales increase by 10%?

**4.** What happens to each company's net income if sales increase by 40%?

**5.** What happens to each company's net income if sales increase by 90%?

**6.** What happens to each company's net income if sales decrease by 20%?

**7.** What happens to each company's net income if sales decrease by 50%?

**8.** What happens to each company's net income if sales decrease by 80%?

*Analysis Component*

**9.** Comment on the results from parts 3 through 8 in relation to the fixed cost strategies of the two companies and the ratio values you computed in parts 1 and 2.

**Check**   (4) Virgo net income, $39,000 (160% increase)

        (6) Zodiac net income, $9,000 (40% decrease)

## Problem 9-4B
Payroll expenses, withholdings, and taxes

P2   P3

Sea Biz Company pays its employees each week. Employees' gross pay is subject to these taxes:

| Tax | Rate | Applied To |
| --- | --- | --- |
| FICA—Social Security ........ | 6.20% | First $87,000 |
| FICA—Medicare ............ | 1.45 | All gross pay |
| FUTA .................... | 0.80 | First $7,000 |
| SUTA .................... | 1.75 | First $7,000 |

The company is preparing its payroll calculations for the week ended September 30. Payroll records show the following information for the company's four employees:

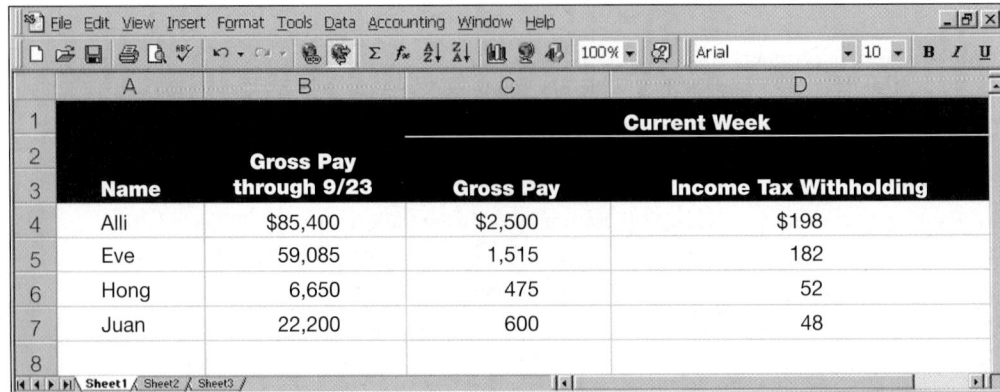

| | | Current Week | |
| --- | --- | --- | --- |
| Name | Gross Pay through 9/23 | Gross Pay | Income Tax Withholding |
| Alli | $85,400 | $2,500 | $198 |
| Eve | 59,085 | 1,515 | 182 |
| Hong | 6,650 | 475 | 52 |
| Juan | 22,200 | 600 | 48 |

In addition to gross pay, the company must pay one-half of the $44 per employee weekly health insurance; each employee pays the remaining one-half. The company also contributes an extra 5% of each employee's gross pay (at no cost to employees) to a pension fund.

**Required**

Compute the following for the week ended September 30 (round amounts to the nearest cent):

**1.** Each employee's FICA withholdings for Social Security.

**2.** Each employee's FICA withholdings for Medicare.

**3.** Employer's FICA taxes for Social Security.

**4.** Employer's FICA taxes for Medicare.

**5.** Employer's FUTA taxes.

**6.** Employer's SUTA taxes.

**7.** Each employee's net (take-home) pay.

**8.** Employer's total payroll-related expense for each employee.

**Check**  (3) $259.78
(4) $73.81
(5) $2.80

(7) Total net pay, $4,188.41

---

Palmer Company's first weekly pay period of the year ends on January 8. On that date, the column totals in Palmer's payroll register indicate its sales employees earned $69,490, its office employees earned $42,450, and its delivery employees earned $2,060. The employees are to have withheld from their wages FICA Social Security taxes at the rate of 6.2%, FICA Medicare taxes at the rate of 1.45%, $17,250 of federal income taxes, $2,320 of medical insurance deductions, and $275 of union dues. No employee earned more than $7,000 in the first pay period.

**Problem 9-5B**
Entries for payroll transactions

P2  P3

**Required**

**1.** Calculate FICA Social Security taxes payable and FICA Medicare taxes payable. Prepare the journal entry to record Palmer Company's January 8 (employee) payroll expenses and liabilities.

**2.** Prepare the journal entry to record Palmer's (employer) payroll taxes resulting from the January 8 payroll. Palmer's merit rating reduces its state unemployment tax rate to 3.4% of the first $7,000 paid each employee. The federal unemployment tax rate is 0.8%.

**Check**  (1) Cr. Accrued Payroll
Payable, $85,434
(2) Dr. Payroll Taxes
Expense, $13,509

---

JLK Company has five employees, each of whom earns $1,200 per month and is paid on the last day of each month. All five have been employed continuously at this amount since January 1. JLK uses a payroll bank account and special payroll checks to pay its employees. On June 1, the following accounts and balances exist in its general ledger:

**Problem 9-6B**<sup>A</sup>

**Problem 9-6B**[A]
Entries for payroll transactions

P2  P3  P5  P6

**a.** FICA—Social Security Taxes Payable, $744; FICA—Medicare Taxes Payable, $174. (The balances of these accounts represent total liabilities for *both* the employer's and employees' FICA taxes for the May payroll only.)

**b.** Employees' Federal Income Taxes Payable, $900 (liability for May only).

**c.** Federal Unemployment Taxes Payable, $96 (liability for April and May together).

**d.** State Unemployment Taxes Payable, $480 (liability for April and May together).

During June and July, the company had the following payroll transactions:

June 15   Issued check payable to Security Bank, a federal depository bank authorized to accept employers' payments of FICA taxes and employee income tax withholdings. The $1,818 check is in payment of the May FICA and employee income taxes.

   30   Recorded the June payroll and transferred funds from the regular bank account to the payroll bank account. Issued checks payable to each employee in payment of the June payroll. The payroll register shows the following summary totals for the June pay period:

**Check**  June 30: Cr. Accrued Payroll
Payable, $4,641

| Salaries and Wages | | | | Federal | |
| Office Salaries | Shop Wages | Gross Pay | FICA Taxes* | Income Taxes | Net Pay |
| --- | --- | --- | --- | --- | --- |
| $2,000 | $4,000 | $6,000 | $372 | $900 | $4,641 |
| | | | $ 87 | | |

\* FICA taxes are Social Security and Medicare, respectively.

**Check**   June 30: Dr. Payroll Taxes
Expenses, $699

July 15: Cr. Cash $1,818
(Security Bank)

30   Recorded the employer's payroll taxes resulting from the June payroll. The company has a merit rating that reduces its state unemployment tax rate to 4.0% of the first $7,000 paid each employee. The federal rate is 0.8%.

July 15   Issued check payable to Security Bank in payment of the June FICA and employee income taxes.

15   Issued check to the State Tax Commission for the April, May, and June state unemployment taxes. Mailed the check and the second quarter tax return to the State Tax Commission.

31   Issued check payable to Security Bank in payment of the employer's FUTA taxes for the second quarter of the year.

31   Mailed Form 941 to the IRS, reporting the FICA taxes and the employees' federal income tax withholdings for the second quarter.

**Required**

Prepare journal entries to record the transactions and events for both June and July.

# PROBLEM SET C

Problem Set C is available at the book's Website to further reinforce and assess your learning.

# SERIAL PROBLEM

Success Systems

*(This serial problem began in Chapter 1 and continues through most of the book. If previous chapter segments were not completed, the serial problem can begin at this point. It is helpful, but not necessary, for you to use the Working Papers that accompany the book.)*

Review the February 26 and March 25 transactions for Success Systems found in Chapter 4.

**Required**

1.<sup>A</sup> Assume that Sherry Adams is an unmarried employee. Her wages are subject to no deductions other than FICA Social Security taxes, FICA Medicare taxes, and federal income taxes. Her federal income taxes for this pay period total $189. Compute her net pay for the eight days' work paid on February 26.

**2.** Make the required journal entry to record the payroll payment to Sherry Adams as calculated in part 1.

**3.** Make the required journal entry to record the (employer) payroll tax expenses for the February 26 payroll. Assume Sherry Adams has not met earnings limits for FUTA and SUTA—the FUTA rate is 0.8% and the SUTA rate is 4%.

**4.** Record the entry(ies) for the merchandise sold on March 25 if a 4% sales tax rate applies.

# COMPREHENSIVE PROBLEM

Bug-Off Exterminators
(Review of Chapters 1–9)

Bug-Off Exterminators provides pest control services and sells extermination products manufactured by other companies. The following six-column table contains the company's unadjusted trial balance as of December 31, 2005.

| BUG-OFF EXTERMINATORS<br>December 31, 2005 | | | | |
|---|---|---|---|---|
| | Unadjusted<br>Trial Balance | | Adjustments | Adjusted<br>Trial Balance |
| Cash ....................... | $ 17,000 | | | |
| Accounts receivable ............ | 4,000 | | | |
| Allowance for doubtful accounts .... | | $    828 | | |
| Merchandise inventory .......... | 11,700 | | | |
| Trucks ..................... | 32,000 | | | |
| Accum. depreciation—Trucks ...... | | 0 | | |
| Equipment .................. | 45,000 | | | |
| Accum. depreciation—Equipment ... | | 12,200 | | |
| Accounts payable .............. | | 5,000 | | |

[continued on next page]

[continued from previous page]

| | | |
|---|---:|---:|
| Estimated warranty liability . . . . . . . . | | 1,400 |
| Unearned services revenue . . . . . . . . | | 0 |
| Long-term notes payable . . . . . . . . . | | 15,000 |
| Interest payable . . . . . . . . . . . . . . . | | 0 |
| Common stock . . . . . . . . . . . . . . . | | 10,000 |
| Retained earnings . . . . . . . . . . . . . | | 49,700 |
| Dividends . . . . . . . . . . . . . . . . . . | 10,000 | |
| Extermination services revenue . . . . | | 60,000 |
| Interest revenue . . . . . . . . . . . . . . | | 872 |
| Sales (of merchandise) . . . . . . . . . . | | 71,026 |
| Cost of goods sold . . . . . . . . . . . . | 46,300 | |
| Depreciation expense—Trucks . . . . . | 0 | |
| Depreciation expense—Equipment . . | 0 | |
| Wages expense . . . . . . . . . . . . . . . | 35,000 | |
| Interest expense . . . . . . . . . . . . . . | 0 | |
| Rent expense . . . . . . . . . . . . . . . . | 9,000 | |
| Bad debts expense . . . . . . . . . . . . . | 0 | |
| Miscellaneous expense . . . . . . . . . . | 1,226 | |
| Repairs expense . . . . . . . . . . . . . . | 8,000 | |
| Utilities expense . . . . . . . . . . . . . . | 6,800 | |
| Warranty expense . . . . . . . . . . . . . | 0 | |
| Totals . . . . . . . . . . . . . . . . . . . . . | $226,026 | $226,026 |

The following information applies to the company at the end of the current year:

**a.** The bank reconciliation as of December 31, 2005, includes these facts:

| | |
|---|---:|
| Balance per bank . . . . . . . . . . . . . . . . . . . . . . . . . . . . | $15,100 |
| Balance per books . . . . . . . . . . . . . . . . . . . . . . . . . . . | 17,000 |
| Outstanding checks . . . . . . . . . . . . . . . . . . . . . . . . . | 1,800 |
| Deposit in transit . . . . . . . . . . . . . . . . . . . . . . . . . . . | 2,450 |
| Interest earned (on bank account) . . . . . . . . . . . . . . . | 52 |
| Bank service charges (miscellaneous expense) . . . . . . . | 15 |

Reported on the bank statement is a canceled check that the company failed to record. (Information from the bank reconciliation allows you to determine the amount of this check, which is a payment on an account payable.)

**b.** An examination of customers' accounts shows that accounts totaling $679 should be written off as uncollectible. Using an aging of receivables, the company determines that the ending balance of the Allowance for Doubtful Accounts should be $700.

**c.** A truck is purchased and placed in service on January 1, 2005. Its cost is being depreciated with the straight-line method using these facts and estimates:

| | |
|---|---:|
| Original cost . . . . . . . . . . . . . . . | $32,000 |
| Expected salvage value . . . . . . . | 8,000 |
| Useful life (years) . . . . . . . . . . . | 4 |

**d.** Two items of equipment (a sprayer and an injector) were purchased and put into service in early January 2003. They are being depreciated with the straight-line method using these facts and estimates:

| | Sprayer | Injector |
|---|---:|---:|
| Original cost . . . . . . . . . . . . . . . | $27,000 | $18,000 |
| Expected salvage value . . . . . . . | 3,000 | 2,500 |
| Useful life (years) . . . . . . . . . . . | 8 | 5 |

**e.** On August 1, 2005, the company is paid $3,840 in advance to provide monthly service for an apartment complex for one year. The company began providing the services in August. When the cash was received, the full amount was credited to the Extermination Services Revenue account.

**f.** The company offers a warranty for the services it sells. The expected cost of providing warranty service is 2.5% of the extermination services revenue of $57,760 for 2005. No warranty expense has been recorded for 2005. All costs of servicing warranties in 2005 were properly debited to the Estimated Warranty Liability account.

**g.** The $15,000 long-term note is a 8%, five-year, interest-bearing note with interest payable annually on December 31. The note was signed with First National Bank on December 31, 2005.

**h.** The ending inventory of merchandise is counted and determined to have a cost of $11,700. Bug-Off uses a perpetual inventory system.

**Required**

**Check**  (1*a*) Cash, $15,750
(1*b*) $551 credit

(1*f*) Estim. warranty liability,
$2,844 Cr.

(2) Adjusted trial balance
totals, $238,207

(4) Net income, $9,274; Total
assets, $82,771

**1.** Use the preceding information to determine amounts for the following items:

   **a.** Correct (reconciled) ending balance of Cash, and the amount of the omitted check.

   **b.** Adjustment needed to obtain the correct ending balance of the Allowance for Doubtful Accounts.

   **c.** Depreciation expense for the truck used during year 2005.

   **d.** Depreciation expense for the two items of equipment used during year 2005.

   **e.** The adjusted 2005 ending balances of the Extermination Services Revenue and Unearned Services Revenue accounts.

   **f.** The adjusted 2005 ending balances of the accounts for Warranty Expense and Estimated Warranty Liability.

   **g.** The adjusted 2005 ending balances of the accounts for Interest Expense and Interest Payable. (Round amounts to nearest whole dollar.)

**2.** Use the results of part 1 to complete the six-column table by first entering the appropriate adjustments for items *a* through *g* and then completing the adjusted trial balance columns. (*Hint:* Item *b* requires two adjustments.)

**3.** Prepare journal entries to record the adjustments entered on the six-column table. Assume Bug-Off's adjusted balance for Merchandise Inventory matches the year-end physical count.

**4.** Prepare a single-step income statement, a statement of retained earnings (cash dividends declared during 2005 were $10,000), and a classified balance sheet.

# BEYOND THE NUMBERS

## REPORTING IN ACTION

A1 P4

**BTN 9-1**    Refer to the financial statements of **Krispy Kreme** in Appendix A to answer the following:

**1.** Compute times interest earned for the fiscal years ended 2003, 2002, and 2001. Comment on Krispy Kreme's ability to cover its interest expense for this period.

**2.** What evidence can you identify as an indication that Krispy Kreme has temporary differences between income reported on its income statement and income reported on its tax return?

*Roll On*

**3.** Access Krispy Kreme's financial statements for fiscal years ending after February 2, 2003, at its Website (**KrispyKreme.com**) or the SEC's EDGAR database (**www.sec.gov**). Compute its times interest earned for years ending after February 2, 2003, and compare your results to those in part 1.

## COMPARATIVE ANALYSIS

A1

**BTN 9-2**    Key comparative figures ($ thousands) for both **Krispy Kreme** and **Tastykake** follow:

| Key Figures | Krispy Kreme | | | Tastykake | | |
|---|---|---|---|---|---|---|
| | Current Year | One Year Prior | Two Years Prior | Current Year | One Year Prior | Two Years Prior |
| Net income ......... | $33,478 | $26,378 | $14,725 | $2,000* | $8,048* | $8,144 |
| Income taxes ........ | 21,295 | 16,168 | 9,058 | 0 | 3,775 | 4,609 |
| Interest expense ...... | 1,781 | 337 | 607 | 1,066 | 1,103 | 1,540 |

\* Net income without restructuring charges.

**Required**

1. Compute times interest earned for the three years' data shown for each company.

2. Comment on which company appears stronger in its ability to pay interest obligations if income should decline.

---

**BTN 9-3** Cannon Bly is a sales manager for an automobile dealership. He earns a bonus each year based on revenue from the number of autos sold in the year less related warranty expenses. Actual warranty expenses have varied over the prior 10 years from a low of 3% of an automobile's selling price to a high of 10%. In the past, Bly has tended to estimate warranty expenses on the high end to be conservative. He must work with the dealership's accountant at year-end to arrive at the warranty expense accrual for cars sold each year.

1. Does the warranty accrual decision create any ethical dilemma for Bly?

2. Since warranty expenses vary, what percent do you think Bly should choose for the current year? Justify your response.

**ETHICS CHALLENGE**

P4

---

**BTN 9-4** Dustin Clemens is the accounting and finance manager for a manufacturer. At year-end, he must determine how to account for the company's contingencies. His manager, Tom Pretti, objects to Clemens's proposal to recognize an expense and a liability for warranty service on units of a new product introduced in the fourth quarter. Pretti comments, "There's no way we can estimate this warranty cost. We don't owe anyone anything until a product fails and it is returned. Let's report an expense if and when we do any warranty work."

**COMMUNICATING IN PRACTICE**

C3

**Required**

Prepare a one-page memorandum for Clemens to send to Pretti defending his proposal.

---

**BTN 9-5** Access the March 12, 2003, filing of the December 31, 2002, annual 10-K report of **McDonald's Corporation** (Ticker: MCD), which is available from www.sec.gov.

**TAKING IT TO THE NET**

C1 A1

**Required**

1. Identify the current liabilities on McDonald's balance sheet as of December 31, 2002.

2. What portion (in percent) of McDonald's long-term debt matures within the next 12 months?

3. Use the consolidated statement of income for the year ended December 31, 2002, to compute McDonald's times interest earned ratio. Comment on the result.

mhhe.com/wild3e

---

**BTN 9-6** Assume that your team is in business and you must borrow $6,000 cash for short-term needs. You have been shopping banks for a loan, and you have the following two options:

**A.** Sign a $6,000, 90-day, 10% interest-bearing note dated June 1.

**B.** Sign a $6,000, 120-day, 8% interest-bearing note dated June 1.

**TEAMWORK IN ACTION**

C2 P1

**Required**

1. Discuss these two options and determine the best choice. Ensure that all teammates concur with the decision and understand the rationale.

2. Each member of the team is to prepare *one* of the following journal entries:

   **a.** Option A—at date of issuance.

   **b.** Option B—at date of issuance.

   **c.** Option A—at maturity date.

   **d.** Option B—at maturity date.

3. In rotation, each member is to explain the entry he or she prepared in part 2 to the team. Ensure that all team members concur with and understand the entries.

4. Assume that the funds are borrowed on December 1 (instead of June 1) and your business operates on a calendar-year reporting period. Each member of the team is to prepare *one* of the following entries:

    **a.** Option A—the year-end adjustment.

    **b.** Option B—the year-end adjustment.

    **c.** Option A—at maturity date.

    **d.** Option B—at maturity date.

5. In rotation, each member is to explain the entry he or she prepared in part 4 to the team. Ensure that all team members concur with and understand the entries.

---

**BUSINESS WEEK ACTIVITY**

P4

mhhe.com/wild3e

**BTN 9-7** Read the article "Bed, Board—and Big Trouble" in the October 23, 2002, online issue of *Business Week*. (This book's Website provides a free link.)

**Required**

**1.** What arrangement does the motel owner have with the long-term resident?

**2.** What risks is the motel operator exposed to by this arrangement?

**3.** How will the state of New York probably classify the tenant, and what should the motel owner do to respond to New York's probable action? Are there payroll tax implications?

---

**ENTREPRENEURIAL DECISION**

A1

**BTN 9-8** Review the chapter's opening feature involving André Downey and **Environmental, Engineering & Construction**. EEC is considering a major technological investment in a plant asset to improve its environmental cleanup process. Assume that this investment would cut variable costs from 60% of sales to 45% of sales. However, fixed interest expense would increase from $540,000 per year to $1,140,000 per year to fund the $4,800,000 plant asset investment (with zero salvage, 50-year life, and depreciated using the straight-line method). Also assume that its recent income statement (absent this potential investment) appears as follows (assume zero income taxes):

| EEC Income Statement For Year Ended January 31, 2005 | |
|---|---:|
| Sales | $3,000,000 |
| Depreciation | 60,000 |
| Variable expenses (60%) | 1,800,000 |
| Income before interest | 1,140,000 |
| Interest expense (fixed) | 540,000 |
| Net income | $ 600,000 |

**Required**

**1.** Compute EEC's times interest earned ratio at January 31, 2005.

**2.** If EEC expects sales to remain at $3,000,000, what would net income and times interest earned equal if it makes the investment?

**3.** What would net income and times interest earned equal if sales increase to $3,600,000 and the investment is (*a*) not made and (*b*) made?

**4.** What would net income and times interest earned equal if sales increase to $4,639,998 and the investment is (*a*) not made and (*b*) made?

**5.** What would net income and times interest earned equal if sales increase to $5,400,000 and the investment is (*a*) not made and (*b*) made?

**6.** Comment on the results from parts 1 through 5 and their relation to the times interest earned ratio.

---

**HITTING THE ROAD**

P2

**BTN 9-9** Check your phone book or the Social Security Administration Website (www.ssa.gov) to locate the Social Security office near you. Visit the office to request a personal earnings and estimate form. Fill out the form and mail according to the instructions. You will receive a statement from the Social Security Administration regarding your earnings history and future Social Security benefits you can receive. (*Note:* Formerly the request could be made online. The online service has been discontinued and is now under review by the Social Security Administration due to security concerns.) It is good to request an earnings and benefit statement every 5 to 10 years to make sure you have received credit for all wages earned and for which you and your employer have paid taxes into the system.

**BTN 9-10** Grupo Bimbo, Krispy Kreme, and Tastykake are all competitors in the global marketplace. Key comparative figures for Grupo Bimbo (**GrupoBimbo.com**) for the year ended December 31, 2002 (along with selected figures from Krispy Kreme and Taskykake) follows:

**GLOBAL DECISION**

A1

| Key Figures | Grupo Bimbo (millions of pesos) | | Krispy Kreme | | Tastykake | |
| --- | --- | --- | --- | --- | --- | --- |
| | Current Year | Prior Year | Current Year | Prior Year | Current Year | Prior Year |
| Net income ............... | $1,003 | $1,682 | — | — | — | — |
| Income taxes .............. | 575 | 805 | — | — | — | — |
| Interest expense ........... | 703 | 193 | — | — | — | — |
| Times interest earned ........ | ? | ? | 31.8 | 127.2 | 2.9 | 10.2 |

**Required**

1. Compute the times interest earned ratio for the most recent two years for Grupo Bimbo using the data shown.
2. Which company of the three presented provides the best coverage of interest expense?

"Being a first-time entrepreneur leading a fast-growth company is like running full speed through the dark over unfamiliar terrain"—Aaron Kennedy

# 10 Reporting and Analyzing Long-Term Liabilities

### A Look Back

Chapter 9 focused on current liabilities. It explained how liabilities are identified, computed, recorded, and reported in financial statements. Attention was directed at notes, payroll, sales taxes, warranties, employee benefits, and contingencies.

### A Look at This Chapter

This chapter describes the accounting for and analysis of bonds and notes. We explain their characteristics, payment patterns, interest computations, retirement, and reporting requirements. An appendix to this chapter introduces leases and pensions.

### A Look Ahead

Chapter 11 focuses on corporate equity transactions. We describe stock issuances, dividends, and other equity transactions. We also explain how to report and analyze income, earnings per share, and retained earnings.

# CAP

### Conceptual

**C1** Describe the types of bonds and the procedures for issuing them. *(p. 397)*

**C2** Explain the types and payment patterns of notes. *(p. 409)*

### Analytical

**A1** Compare bond financing with stock financing. *(p. 396)*

**A2** Explain collateral agreements and their effects on loan risk. *(p. 413)*

**A3** Compute the ratio of pledged assets to secured liabilities and explain its use. *(p. 413)*

### Procedural

**P1** Prepare entries to record bond issuance and bond interest expense. *(p. 399)*

**P2** Compute and record amortization of bond discount. *(p. 400)*

**P3** Compute and record amortization of bond premium. *(p. 403)*

**P4** Record the retirement of bonds. *(p. 408)*

**P5** Prepare entries to account for notes. *(p. 410)*

---

**Decision Feature**

# Using His Noodle(s) for Business Financing

BOULDER, CO—Aaron Kennedy never planned to be an entrepreneur. An evening dinner at an Asian noodle shop in New York's Greenwich Village changed all that. "All of sudden this idea hit me," says Kennedy. "There are noodle dishes all over the world. I thought, 'What if they were all on one menu? Why not bring all of these influences together and make it affordable and fast.'"

Kennedy quickly developed his global noodle concept: "high-quality food made to order." He wanted his noodles "quick and convenient, very affordable and served in a very appealing dining environment." This led to his launch of **Noodles & Company (Noodles.com).** "We're not fast food—we're casual dining," notes Kennedy.

The global noodle concept required financing to become reality. Since Kennedy lacked collateral and had no entrepreneurial experience, he approached 25 friends and family members for the $250,000 start-up financing. It was challenging, says Kennedy. He had to confront the realities of debt, interest payments, collateral agreements, and pledged assets. Moreover, he had to achieve the accounting numbers necessary to stay afloat.

With grit and determination, Kennedy obtained his financing. Six months later, he launched his first noodle shop in Denver, followed by the second in Madison, Wisconsin. "The first two restaurants nearly killed us—physically and fiscally," recalls Kennedy. Yet Noodles not only achieved the income to pay the debt with interest but also produced revenue growth for expansion. Kennedy now has taken on additional financing, which he predicts "should culminate in accelerating growth." An important new factor, says Kennedy, is Noodles' "new franchised area operator program."

Kennedy admits he is both surprised and humbled by Noodles' success but realizes that simple concepts are often the best. "Noodles are staples," Kennedy says. His task: "bring the noodles to the people." By all accounts, Kennedy has applied his noodles well.

[Sources: *Noodles & Co. Website,* January 2004; *Rocky Mountain News,* February 2002; *Augustana Magazine,* Fall 2002; *Shopping Centers Today,* December 2002; *UW Update,* Summer 2002; *Forbes,* May 2003; *Catlin Group Website,* June 2003.]

Individuals, companies, and governments issue bonds to finance their activities. In return for financing, bonds promise to repay the lender with interest. This chapter explains the basics of bonds and the accounting for their issuance and retirement. The chapter also describes long-term notes as another financing source, including interest-bearing, noninterest-bearing, and installment notes. We explain how present value concepts impact both the accounting for and reporting of bonds and notes. Appendixes to this chapter discuss present value concepts applicable to liabilities, effective interest amortization, and the accounting for leases and pensions.

**Reporting and Analyzing Long-Term Liabilities**

| **Bond Basics** | **Bond Issuances** | **Bond Retirement** | **Long-Term Notes** |
|---|---|---|---|
| • Bond financing<br>• Types of bonds<br>• Bond trading<br>• Issuance procedures | • Issuance at par<br>• Issuance at a discount<br>• Issuance at a premium<br>• Issuance between interest dates<br>• Accruing bond interest<br>• Bond pricing | • At maturity<br>• Before maturity<br>• By conversion | • Installment notes<br>• Mortgage notes and bonds |

# Basics of Bonds

This section explains the basics of bonds and a company's motivation for issuing them.

## Bond Financing

Projects that demand large amounts of money often are funded from bond issuances. (Both for-profit and nonprofit companies, as well as governmental units, such as nations, states, cities, and school districts, issue bonds.) A **bond** is its issuer's written promise to pay an amount identified as the par value of the bond with interest. The **par value of a bond,** also called the *face amount* or *face value,* is paid at a specified future date known as the bond's *maturity date.* Most bonds also require the issuer to make semiannual interest payments. The amount of interest paid each period is determined by multiplying the par value of the bond by the bond's contract rate of interest. This section explains both advantages and disadvantages of bond financing.

A1  Compare bond financing with stock financing.

**Advantages of Bonds**   There are three main advantages of bond financing:

1. *Bonds do not affect owner control.* Equity financing reflects ownership in a company, whereas bond financing does not. A person who contributes $1,000 of a company's $10,000 equity financing typically controls one-tenth of all owner decisions. A person who owns a $1,000, 11%, 20-year bond has no ownership right. This person, or bondholder, is to receive from the bond issuer 11% interest, or $110, each year the bond is outstanding and $1,000 when it matures in 20 years.

2. *Interest on bonds is tax deductible.* Bond interest payments are tax deductible for the issuer, but equity payments (distributions) to owners are not. To illustrate, assume that a corporation with no bond financing earns $15,000 in income *before* paying taxes at a 40% tax rate, which amounts to $6,000 ($15,000 × 40%) in taxes. If a portion of its financing is in bonds, however, the resulting bond interest is deducted in computing taxable income. That is, if bond interest expense is $10,000, the taxes owed would be $2,000 ([$15,000 − $10,000] × 40%), which is less than the $6,000 owed with no bond financing.

3. *Bonds can increase return on equity.* A company that earns a higher return with borrowed funds than it pays in interest on those funds increases its return on equity. This process is called *financial leverage* or *trading on the equity.*

To illustrate the third point, consider Magnum Co., which has $1 million in equity and is planning a $500,000 expansion to meet increasing demand for its product. Magnum predicts the $500,000 expansion will yield $125,000 in additional income before paying any interest. It currently earns $100,000 per year and has no interest expense. Magnum is considering three plans. Plan A is not to expand. Plan B is to expand and raise $500,000 from equity financing. Plan C is to expand and issue $500,000 of bonds that pay 10% annual interest ($50,000). Exhibit 10.1 shows how these three plans affect Magnum's net income, equity, and return on equity (net income/equity). Analysis shows that the owner(s) will earn a higher return on equity if expansion occurs. Moreover, the preferred expansion plan is to issue bonds. Projected net income under Plan C ($175,000) is smaller than under Plan B ($225,000), but the return on equity is larger because of less equity investment. Plan C has another advantage if income is taxable. This illustration reflects a general rule: *Return on equity increases when the expected rate of return from the new assets is higher than the rate of interest expense on the debt financing.*

**Point:** Financial leverage can be achieved by issuing either bonds, notes, or preferred stock.

**Example:** Compute return on equity for all three plans if Magnum currently earns $150,000 instead of $100,000. *Answer* ($ in 000s):
Plan A = 15%    ($150/$1,000)
Plan B = 18.3%  ($275/$1,500)
Plan C = 22.5%  ($225/$1,000)

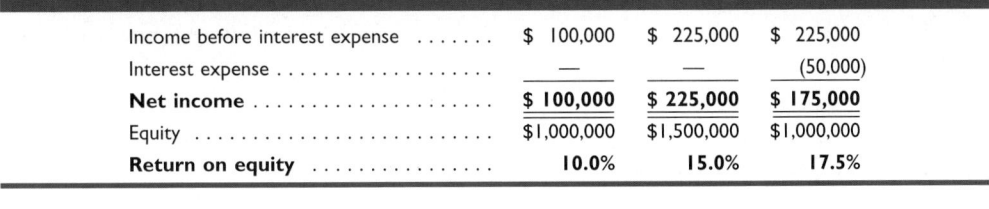

| | Plan A<br>Do Not<br>Expand | Plan B<br>Equity<br>Financing | Plan C<br>Bond<br>Financing |
|---|---|---|---|
| Income before interest expense ....... | $ 100,000 | $ 225,000 | $ 225,000 |
| Interest expense .................... | — | — | (50,000) |
| **Net income** .................... | **$ 100,000** | **$ 225,000** | **$ 175,000** |
| Equity ........................ | $1,000,000 | $1,500,000 | $1,000,000 |
| **Return on equity** ............... | **10.0%** | **15.0%** | **17.5%** |

**Exhibit 10.1**

Financing with Bonds versus Equity

**Disadvantages of Bonds** The two main disadvantages of bond financing are:

1. *Bonds can decrease return on equity.* When a company earns a lower return with the borrowed funds than it pays in interest, it decreases its return on equity. This downside risk of financial leverage is more likely to arise when a company has periods of low income or net losses.

2. *Bonds require payment of both periodic interest and the par value at maturity.* Bond payments can be especially burdensome when income and cash flow are low. Equity financing, in contrast, does not require any payments because cash withdrawals (dividends) are paid at the discretion of the owner (or board).

A company must weigh the risks and returns of the disadvantages and advantages of bond financing when deciding whether to issue bonds to finance operations.

**Point:** Debt financing is desirable when interest is tax deductible, when owner control is preferred, and when return on equity is higher than interest rate on debt.

## Types of Bonds

This section describes the more common types of bonds and their characteristics.

**C1** Describe the types of bonds and the procedures for issuing them.

**Secured and Unsecured Bonds** **Secured bonds** have specific assets of the issuer pledged (or *mortgaged*) as collateral. This arrangement gives bondholders added protection against the issuer's default. If the issuer fails to pay interest or par value, the secured bondholders can demand that the collateral be sold and the proceeds used to pay the bond obligation. **Unsecured bonds,** also called *debentures,* are backed by the issuer's general credit standing. Unsecured bonds are riskier than secured bonds. An issuer generally must be financially strong to successfully issue debentures at a favorable interest rate. *Subordinated debentures* refer to creditors whose claims on the issuer's assets are second to those of other unsecured liabilities. In a liquidation, subordinated debentures are not repaid until the claims of the more senior, unsecured liabilities have been settled.

**Secured Bond**        **Unsecured Bond**

**Term Bond**

**Serial Bond**

**Term and Serial Bonds**    **Term bonds** are scheduled for maturity on one specified date. **Serial bonds** mature at more than one date (often in series) and thus are usually repaid over a number of periods. For instance, $100,000 of serial bonds might mature at the rate of $10,000 each year from 6 to 15 years after they are issued. This involves 10 groups (or series) of bonds of $10,000 each with one series maturing after six years, another after seven years, and another each successive year until the final series is repaid. Many bonds are also **sinking fund bonds,** which to reduce the holder's risk, require the issuer to create a *sinking fund* of assets set aside at specified amounts and dates to repay the bonds at maturity.

**Registered Bond**

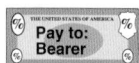

**Bearer Bond**

**Registered Bonds and Bearer Bonds**    Bonds issued in the names and addresses of their holders are **registered bonds.** The issuer makes bond payments by sending checks (or cash transfers) to these registered holders. When selling a bond to another holder, a registered holder must notify the issuer of the change. Registered bonds offer the issuer the practical advantage of not having to actually issue bond certificates, which protects holders against loss or theft of bonds.

Bonds payable to whoever holds them (the *bearer*) are called **bearer bonds** or *unregistered bonds.* Sales or exchanges might not be recorded, so the holder of a bearer bond is presumed to be its rightful owner. As a result, lost or stolen bearer bonds are difficult to replace. Many bearer bonds are also **coupon bonds.** This term reflects interest coupons that are attached to the bonds. Each coupon matures on a specific interest payment date. When each coupon matures, the holder presents it to a bank or broker for collection. At maturity, the holder follows the same process and presents the bond certificate for collection. Income tax law discourages companies from issuing coupon bonds because there is no readily available record of who actually receives the interest.

### Decision Insight

**Munis**    More than a million municipal bonds, or "munis," can be purchased, and many are tax exempt. Munis are issued by state, city, town, and county governments to pay for public projects including schools, libraries, roads, bridges, and stadiums.

**Convertible Bond**          **Callable Bond**

**Convertible and Callable Bonds**    **Convertible bonds** can be exchanged for a fixed number of shares of the issuing corporation's common stock. Convertible bonds offer bondholders the potential to participate in future increases in a stock's market value. Bondholders still receive periodic interest while the bonds are held and the par value if they hold the bond to maturity. In most cases, the bondholders decide whether and when to convert the bonds to stock. **Callable bonds** have an option exercisable by the issuer to retire them at a stated dollar amount prior to maturity.

### Decision Insight

**Quotes**    The bond quote here is interpreted (left to right) as **Bonds,** issuer name; **Rate,** contract interest rate (7%); **Mat,** matures in year 2025 when principal is paid; **Yld,** yield rate (5.9%) of bond at current price; **Vol,** daily dollar worth ($130,000) of trades (in 1,000s); **Close,** closing price (119.25) for the day as percent of par value; **Chg,** change (1.25) in closing price from prior day's close.

| Bonds | Rate | Mat | Yld | Vol | Close | Chg |
|-------|------|-----|-----|-----|-------|-----|
| IBM | 7 | 25 | 5.9 | 130 | 119¼ | +1¼ |

## Bond Trading

Bonds are securities that can be readily bought and sold. A large number of bonds trade on both the New York Exchange and the American Exchange. A bond *issue* consists of a number of bonds, usually in denominations of $1,000 or $5,000, and is sold to many different lenders. After bonds are issued, they often are bought and sold by investors, meaning that any particular bond probably has a number of owners before it matures. Since bonds are exchanged

**Point:** Issuers of coupon bonds cannot deduct the related interest expense for taxable income. This is to prevent abuse by taxpayers who own coupon bonds but fail to report interest income on their tax returns.

(bought and sold) in the market, they have a market value (price). For convenience, bond market values are expressed as a percent of their par (face) value. For example, a company's bonds might be trading at 103½, meaning they can be bought or sold for 103.5% of their par value. Bonds can also trade below par value. For instance, if a company's bonds are trading at 95, they can be bought or sold at 95% of their par value.

## Bond-Issuing Procedures

State and federal laws govern bond issuances. Bond issuers also want to ensure that they do not violate any of their existing contractual agreements when issuing bonds. Authorization of bond issuances includes the number of bonds authorized, their par value, and the contract interest rate. The legal document identifying the rights and obligations of both the bondholders and the issuer is called the **bond indenture,** which is the legal contract between the issuer and the bondholders. A bondholder may also receive a bond certificate as evidence of the company's debt. A **bond certificate,** such as that shown in Exhibit 10.2, includes specifics such as the issuer's name, the par value, the contract interest rate, and the maturity date. Many companies reduce costs by not issuing paper certificates to bondholders.

**Point:** *Indenture* refers to a bond's legal contract; *debenture* refers to an unsecured bond.

## Exhibit 10.2

Bond Certificate

The issuing company normally sells its bonds to an investment firm called an *underwriter,* which resells them to the public. An issuing company can also sell bonds directly to investors. When an underwriter sells bonds to a large number of investors, a *trustee* represents and protects the bondholders' interests. The trustee monitors the issuer to ensure that it complies with the obligations in the bond indenture. Most trustees are large banks or trust companies. The trustee writes and accepts the terms of a bond indenture before it is issued. When bonds are offered to the public, called *floating an issue,* they must be registered with the Securities and Exchange Commission (SEC). SEC registration requires the issuer to file certain financial information. Most company bonds are issued in par value units of $1,000 or $5,000. A *baby bond* has a par value of less than $1,000, such as $100.

**Point:** The *spread* between the dealer's cost and what buyers pay can be huge. Dealers are said to earn more than $25 billion in annual spread revenue. A tight oligopoly of Wall Street brokers and dealers continues to control bond prices.

**Global:** In the United Kingdom, government bonds are called *gilts*—short for gilt-edged investments.

# Bond Issuances

This section explains accounting for bond issuances at par, below par (discount), and above par (premium). It also describes how to amortize a discount or premium and record bonds issued between interest payment dates.

Topic Tackler 10-1

**P1** Prepare entries to record bond issuance and bond interest expense.

## Issuing Bonds at Par

To illustrate an issuance of bonds at par value, suppose a company receives authorization to issue $800,000 of 9%, 20-year bonds dated January 1, 2005, that mature on December 31, 2024, and pay interest semiannually on each June 30 and December 31. After accepting the bond indenture on behalf of the bondholders, the trustee can sell all or a portion of the bonds to an underwriter. If all bonds are sold at par value, the issuer records the sale as:

| 2005 | | | |
|---|---|---|---|
| Jan. 1 | Cash . . . . . . . . . . . . . . . . . . . . . . . . . . . . . . . . . . . . | 800,000 | |
| | Bonds Payable . . . . . . . . . . . . . . . . . . . . . . | | 800,000 |
| | *Sold bonds at par.* | | |

Assets  = Liabilities + Equity
+800,000   +800,000

This entry reflects increases in the issuer's cash *and* long-term liabilities.

The issuer records the first semiannual interest payment as follows:

| 2005 | | | |
|---|---|---|---|
| June 30 | Bond Interest Expense . . . . . . . . . . . . . . . . . . . . | 36,000 | |
| | Cash. . . . . . . . . . . . . . . . . . . . . . . . . . . . . . | | 36,000 |
| | *Paid semiannual interest (9% × $800,000 × ½ year).* | | |

Assets  = Liabilities +  Equity
−36,000                  −36,000

The issuer pays and records its semiannual interest obligation every six months until the bonds mature. When they mature, the issuer records its payment of principal as:

Assets = Liabilities + Equity
−800,000   −800,000

| 2024 | | | |
|---|---|---|---|
| Dec. 31 | Bonds Payable . . . . . . . . . . . . . . . . . . . . . . . . . | 800,000 | |
| | Cash. . . . . . . . . . . . . . . . . . . . . . . . . . . . . | | 800,000 |
| | *Paid bond principal at maturity.* | | |

## Bond Discount or Premium

The bond issuer pays the interest rate specified in the indenture, the **contract rate,** also referred to as the *coupon rate, stated rate,* or *nominal rate.* The annual interest paid is determined by multiplying the bond par value by the contract rate. The contract rate is usually stated on an annual basis, even if interest is paid semiannually. For example, if a company issues a $1,000, 8% bond paying interest semiannually, it pays annual interest of $80 (8% × $1,000) in two semiannual payments of $40 each.

The contract rate sets the amount of interest the issuer pays in *cash,* which is not necessarily the *bond interest expense* actually incurred by the issuer. Bond interest expense depends on the bond's market value at issuance, which is determined by market expectations of the risk of lending to the issuer. The bond's **market rate** of interest is the rate that borrowers are willing to pay and lenders are willing to accept for a particular bond and its risk level. As the risk level increases, the rate increases to compensate purchasers for the bonds' increased risk. Also, the market rate is generally higher when the time period until the bond matures is longer due to the risk of adverse events occurring over a longer time period.

Many bond issuers try to set a contract rate of interest equal to the market rate they expect as of the bond issuance date. When the contract rate and market rate are equal, a bond sells at par value, but when they are not equal, a bond does not sell at par value. Instead, it is sold at a *premium* above par value or at a *discount* below par value. Exhibit 10.3 shows the relation between the contract rate, market rate, and a bond's issue price.

**Point:** Business acquisitions are sometimes financed by issuing "junk bonds" that carry high market rates of interest but offer little security. Bondholders can suffer huge losses if the bond issuers do not generate adequate cash flows to pay interest and principal.

### Exhibit 10.3

Relation between Bond Issue Price, Contract Rate, and Market Rate

| Contract Rate Is | | Bond Sells |
|---|---|---|
| Above market rate | ➡ | At a premium |
| Equal to market rate | ➡ | At par value |
| Below market rate | ➡ | At a discount |

**Quick Check**

1. Unsecured bonds backed only by the issuer's general credit standing are called (*a*) serial bonds, (*b*) debentures, (*c*) registered bonds, or (*d*) convertible bonds.

2. How do you compute the amount of interest a bond issuer pays in cash each year?

3. When the contract rate is above the market rate, do bonds sell at a premium or a discount? Do purchasers pay more or less than the par value of the bonds?

Answers—p. 424

## Issuing Bonds at a Discount

**P2** Compute and record amortization of bond discount.

A **discount on bonds payable** occurs when a company issues bonds with a contract rate less than the market rate. This means that the issue price is less than par value. To illustrate, assume that **Fila** announces an offer to issue bonds with a $100,000 par value, an 8% annual contract rate (paid semiannually), and a five-year life. Also assume that the market rate for Fila bonds is 10%. These bonds then will sell at a discount since the contract rate is less than the market rate. The exact issue price for these bonds is 92.277 (or 92.277% of par value); we show how to compute this issue price later in the chapter. These bonds obligate the issuer to pay two separate types of future cash flows:

1. Par value of $100,000 cash at the end of the bonds' five-year life.
2. Cash interest payments of $4,000 (4% × $100,000) at the end of each semiannual period during the bonds' five-year life.

**Point:** The difference between the contract rate and the market rate of interest on a new bond issue is usually a fraction of a percent. We use a difference of 2% to emphasize the effects.

The exact pattern of cash flows for the Fila bonds is shown in Exhibit 10.4.

| | | | | | | | | $100,000 |
|---|---|---|---|---|---|---|---|---|
| $4,000 | $4,000 | $4,000 | $4,000 | | $4,000 | $4,000 | $4,000 | |
| 0 | 6 mo. | 12 mo. | 18 mo. | 24 mo. | ... | 48 mo. | 54 mo. | 60 mo. |

### Exhibit 10.4
Cash Flows for Fila Bonds

When Fila accepts $92,277 cash for its bonds on the issue date of December 31, 2005, it records the sale as follows:

| Dec. 31 | Cash . . . . . . . . . . . . . . . . . . . . . . . . . . . . . . . . | 92,277 | |
| | Discount on Bonds Payable . . . . . . . . . . . . . . . . | 7,723 | |
| | Bonds Payable . . . . . . . . . . . . . . . . . . . . . . | | 100,000 |

*Sold bonds at a discount on their issue date.*

| Assets | = Liabilities | + Equity |
|---|---|---|
| +92,277 | +100,000 | |
| | −7,723 | |

These bonds are reported in the long-term liability section of the issuer's December 31, 2005, balance sheet as shown in Exhibit 10.5. A discount is deducted from the par value of bonds to yield the **carrying (book) value of bonds.** Discount on Bonds Payable is a contra liability account.

**Point:** Book value at issuance always equals the issuer's cash amount borrowed.

| Long-term liabilities | | |
|---|---|---|
| Bonds payable, 8%, due December 31, 2010  . . . . . . . | $100,000 | |
| **Less discount on bonds payable** . . . . . . . . . . . . | **7,723** | $92,277 |

### Exhibit 10.5
Balance Sheet Presentation of Bond Discount

**Amortizing a Bond Discount**  Fila receives $92,277 for its bonds; in return it must pay bondholders $100,000 after five years (plus semiannual interest payments). The $7,723 discount is paid to bondholders at maturity and is part of the cost of using the $92,277 for five years. The upper portion of panel A in Exhibit 10.6 shows that total bond interest expense of $47,723 is the difference between the total amount repaid to bondholders ($140,000) and the amount borrowed from bondholders ($92,277). Alternatively, we can compute total bond interest expense as the sum of the 10 interest payments and the bond discount. This alternative computation is shown in the lower portion of panel A.

The total $47,723 bond interest expense must be allocated across the 10 semiannual periods in the bonds' life, and the bonds' carrying value must be updated at each balance sheet date. This is accomplished using the straight-line method (or the effective interest method in Appendix 10B). Both methods systematically reduce the bond discount to zero over the five-year life. This process is called *amortizing a bond discount.*

**Decision Maker**

**Bond Rater**  You must assign a rating to a bond that reflects its risk to bondholders. Identify factors you consider in assessing bond risk. Indicate the likely levels (relative to the norm) for the factors you identify for a bond that sells at a discount.

Answer—p. 424

**Point:** *Zero-coupon bonds* do not pay periodic interest (contract rate is zero). These bonds always sell at a discount because their 0% contract rate is always below the market rate.

**Decision Insight**

**Junk Bonds**  Junk bonds are company bonds with low credit ratings because of a higher than average likelihood of default on repayment. On the upside, the high risk of junk bonds can yield high returns if the issuer survives and repays its debt. Junk bond issuances are now running over $100 billion a year.

**Straight-Line Method**  The **straight-line method** allocates an equal portion of the total bond interest expense to each interest period. To apply the straight-line method to Fila's

## Exhibit 10.6

Interest Computation and Entry for Bonds Issued at a Discount

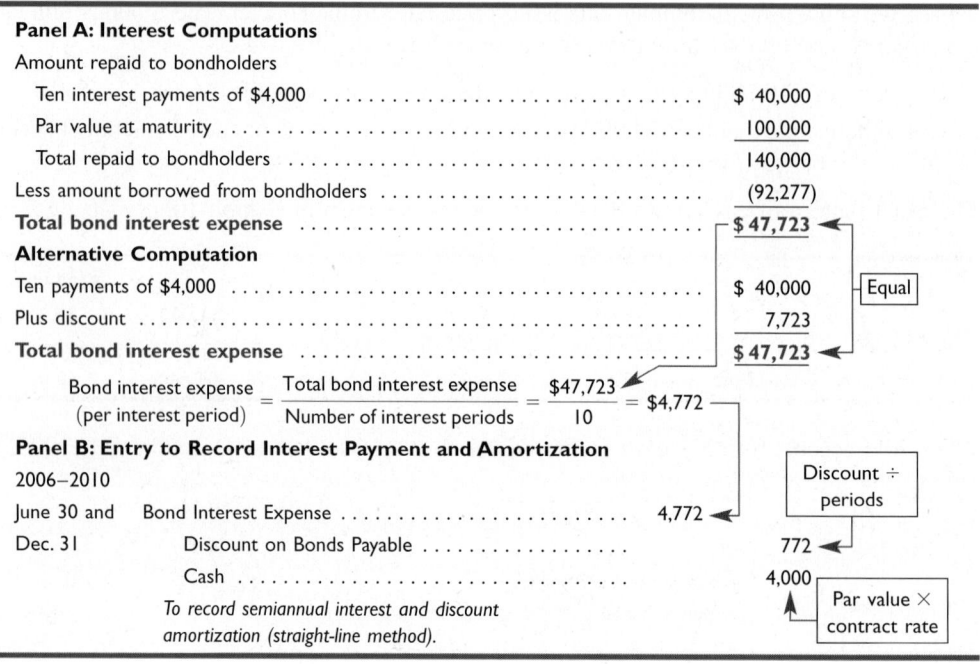

**Panel A: Interest Computations**

Amount repaid to bondholders

| | |
|---|---|
| Ten interest payments of $4,000 | $ 40,000 |
| Par value at maturity | 100,000 |
| Total repaid to bondholders | 140,000 |
| Less amount borrowed from bondholders | (92,277) |
| **Total bond interest expense** | **$ 47,723** |

**Alternative Computation**

| | |
|---|---|
| Ten payments of $4,000 | $ 40,000 |
| Plus discount | 7,723 |
| **Total bond interest expense** | **$ 47,723** |

$$\frac{\text{Bond interest expense}}{\text{(per interest period)}} = \frac{\text{Total bond interest expense}}{\text{Number of interest periods}} = \frac{\$47,723}{10} = \$4,772$$

Equal

**Panel B: Entry to Record Interest Payment and Amortization**

2006–2010

June 30 and
Dec. 31

| | | |
|---|---|---|
| Bond Interest Expense | 4,772 | |
| Discount on Bonds Payable | | 772 |
| Cash | | 4,000 |

*To record semiannual interest and discount amortization (straight-line method).*

Discount ÷ periods

Par value × contract rate

---

Topic Tackler 10-2

bonds, we divide the total bond interest expense of $47,723 by 10 (the number of semiannual periods in the bonds' life). This gives a bond interest expense of $4,772 per period (all computations, including those for assignments, are rounded to the nearest whole dollar). Alternatively, we can find this number by first dividing the $7,723 discount by 10, which yields the $772 amount of discount to be amortized each interest period. When the $772 is added to the $4,000 cash payment, the bond interest expense for each period is $4,772. Panel B of Exhibit 10.6 shows how the issuer records bond interest expense and updates the balance of the bond liability account at the end of *each* of the 10 semiannual interest periods (June 30, 2006, through December 31, 2010).

Exhibit 10.7 shows the pattern of decreases in the Discount on Bonds Payable account and the pattern of increases in the bonds' carrying value. The following points summarize the discount bonds' straight-line amortization:

## Exhibit 10.7

Straight-Line Amortization of Bond Discount

| | Semiannual Period-End | Unamortized Discount* | Carrying Value† |
|---|---|---|---|
| (0) | 12/31/2005 | $7,723 | $ 92,277 |
| (1) | 6/30/2006 | 6,951 | 93,049 |
| (2) | 12/31/2006 | 6,179 | 93,821 |
| (3) | 6/30/2007 | 5,407 | 94,593 |
| (4) | 12/31/2007 | 4,635 | 95,365 |
| (5) | 6/30/2008 | 3,863 | 96,137 |
| (6) | 12/31/2008 | 3,091 | 96,909 |
| (7) | 6/30/2009 | 2,319 | 97,681 |
| (8) | 12/31/2009 | 1,547 | 98,453 |
| (9) | 6/30/2010 | 775 | 99,225 |
| **(10)** | **12/31/2010** | **0‡** | **100,000** |

The two columns always sum to par value for a discount bond.

\* Total bond discount ($7,723) less accumulated periodic amortization ($772 per semiannual interest period).

† Bond par value ($100,000) less unamortized discount.

‡ Adjusted for rounding.

1. At issuance, the $100,000 par value consists of the $92,277 cash received by the issuer plus the $7,723 discount.

2. During the bonds' life, the (unamortized) discount decreases each period by the $772 amortization ($7,723/10), and the carrying value (par value less unamortized discount) increases each period by $772.

3. At maturity, the unamortized discount equals zero, and the carrying value equals the $100,000 par value that the issuer pays the holder.

**Global:** Some countries such as Italy report bonds and notes at their par (face) value, not at book (carrying) value.

Notice that the issuer incurs a $4,772 bond interest expense each period but pays only $4,000 cash. The $772 unpaid portion of this expense is added to the bonds' carrying value. (The total $7,723 unamortized discount is "paid" when the bonds mature; $100,000 is paid at maturity but only $92,277 was received at issuance.)

---

**Quick Check**

Five-year, 6% bonds with a $100,000 par value are issued at a price of $91,893. Interest is paid semiannually, and the bonds' market rate is 8% on the issue date. Use this information to answer the following questions:

4. Are these bonds issued at a discount or a premium? Explain your answer.

5. What is the issuer's journal entry to record the issuance of these bonds?

6. What is the amount of bond interest expense recorded at the first semiannual period using the straight-line method?

Answers—p. 424

## Issuing Bonds at a Premium

When the contract rate of bonds is higher than the market rate, the bonds sell at a price higher than par value. The amount by which the bond price exceeds par value is the **premium on bonds.** To illustrate, assume that **Adidas** issues bonds with a $100,000 par value, a 12% annual contract rate, semiannual interest payments, and a five-year life. Also assume that the market rate for Adidas bonds is 10% on the issue date. The Adidas bonds will sell at a premium because the contract rate is higher than the market rate. The exact issue price for these bonds is 107.72 (or 107.72% of par value); we show how to compute this issue price later in the chapter. These bonds obligate the issuer to pay out two separate future cash flows:

**P3**  Compute and record amortization of bond premium.

1. Par value of $100,000 cash at the end of the bonds' five-year life.
2. Cash interest payments of $6,000 (6% × $100,000) at the end of each semiannual period during the bonds' five-year life.

The exact pattern of cash flows for the Adidas bonds is shown in Exhibit 10.8.

| | | | | | | | | $100,000 |
|---|---|---|---|---|---|---|---|---|
| $6,000 | $6,000 | $6,000 | $6,000 | | $6,000 | $6,000 | $6,000 |
| 0 | 6 mo. | 12 mo. | 18 mo. | 24 mo. | ... | 48 mo. | 54 mo. | 60 mo. |

**Exhibit 10.8**

Cash Flows for Adidas Bonds

When Adidas accepts $107,720 cash for its bonds on the issue date of December 31, 2005, it records this transaction as follows:

| Dec. 31 | Cash ................................. | 107,720 | |
|---|---|---|---|
| | Premium on Bonds Payable ............. | | 7,720 |
| | Bonds Payable ...................... | | 100,000 |
| | *Sold bonds at a premium on their issue date.* | | |

| Assets | = | Liabilities | + | Equity |
|---|---|---|---|---|
| +107,720 | | +100,000 | | |
| | | +7,720 | | |

These bonds are reported in the long-term liability section of the issuer's December 31, 2005, balance sheet as shown in Exhibit 10.9. A premium is added to par value to yield the carrying (book) value of bonds. Premium on Bonds Payable is an adjunct (also called *accretion*) liability account.

| Long-term liabilities | | |
|---|---|---|
| Bonds payable, 12%, due December 31, 2010 ....... | $100,000 | |
| **Plus premium on bonds payable** ............. | **7,720** | $107,720 |

**Exhibit 10.9**

Balance Sheet Presentation of Bond Premium

**Amortizing a Bond Premium**  Adidas receives $107,720 for its bonds; in return, it pays bondholders $100,000 after five years (plus semiannual interest payments). The

$7,720 premium not repaid to issuer's bondholders at maturity goes to reduce the issuer's expense of using the $107,720 for five years. The upper portion of panel A of Exhibit 10.10 shows that total bond interest expense of $52,280 is the difference between the total amount repaid to bondholders ($160,000) and the amount borrowed from bondholders ($107,720). Alternatively, we can compute total bond interest expense as the sum of the 10 interest payments less the bond premium. The premium is subtracted because it will not be paid to bondholders when the bonds mature; see the lower portion of panel A. Total bond interest expense must be allocated over the 10 semiannual periods using the straight-line method (or the effective interest method in Appendix 10B).

**Exhibit 10.10**

Interest Computation and Entry for Bonds Issued at a Premium

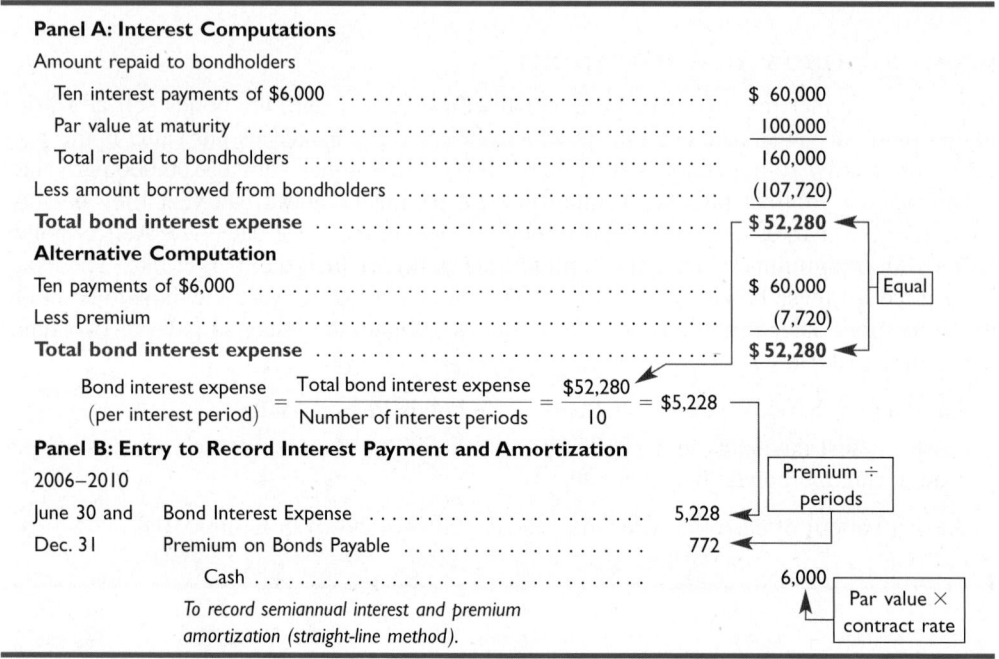

**Point:** A premium decreases Bond Interest Expense while a discount increases it.

**Exhibit 10.11**

Straight-Line Amortization of Bond Premium

| Semiannual Period-End | Unamortized Premium* | Carrying Value† |
|---|---|---|
| (0) 12/31/2005 ....... | $7,720 | $107,720 |
| (1) 6/30/2006 ....... | 6,948 | 106,948 |
| (2) 12/31/2006 ....... | 6,176 | 106,176 |
| (3) 6/30/2007 ....... | 5,404 | 105,404 |
| (4) 12/31/2007 ....... | 4,632 | 104,632 |
| (5) 6/30/2008 ....... | 3,860 | 103,860 |
| (6) 12/31/2008 ....... | 3,088 | 103,088 |
| (7) 6/30/2009 ....... | 2,316 | 102,316 |
| (8) 12/31/2009 ....... | 1,544 | 101,544 |
| (9) 6/30/2010 ....... | 772 | 100,772 |
| (10) 12/31/2010 ....... | **0** | **100,000** |

Carrying value is adjusted to par and the amortized premium to zero during the bond life.

\* Total bond premium ($7,720) less accumulated periodic amortization ($772 per semiannual interest period).

† Bond par value ($100,000) plus unamortized premium.

**Straight-Line Method**   The straight-line method allocates an equal portion of total bond interest expense to each of the bonds' semiannual interest periods. To apply this method to Adidas bonds, we divide the five years' total bond interest expense of $52,280 by 10 (the number of semiannual periods in the bonds' life). This gives a total bond interest expense of $5,228 per period. Panel B of Exhibit 10.10 shows how the issuer records bond interest expense and updates the balance of the bond liability account for *each* semiannual period (June 30, 2006, through December 31, 2010).

Exhibit 10.11 shows the pattern of decreases in the unamortized Premium on Bonds Payable account and in the bonds' carrying value. The following points summarize straight-line amortization of the premium bonds:

1. At issuance, the $100,000 par value plus the $7,720 premium equals the $107,720 cash received by the issuer.

2. During the bonds' life, the (unamortized) premium decreases each period by the $772 amortization ($7,720/10), and the carrying value decreases each period by the same $772.

3. At maturity, the unamortized premium equals zero, and the carrying value equals the $100,000 par value that the issuer pays the holder.

## Issuing Bonds between Interest Dates

An issuer can sell bonds at a date other than an interest payment date. When this occurs, the buyers normally pay the issuer the purchase price plus any interest accrued since the prior interest payment date. This accrued interest is then repaid to these buyers on the next interest payment date. To illustrate, suppose **Avia** sells $100,000 of its 9% bonds at par on March 1, 2005, sixty days after the stated issue date. The interest on Avia bonds is payable semiannually on each June 30 and December 31. Since 60 days have passed, the issuer collects accrued interest from the buyers at the time of issuance. This amount is $1,500 ($100,000 × 9% × $^{60}/_{360}$ year). This case is reflected in Exhibit 10.12.

> **Decision Insight**
>
> **Amor-tech**   Spreadsheet and accounting software such as **Excel** and **Peachtree** make amortization tables easier. Enter the bonds' par value, selling price, contract rate, and life and out comes a complete amortization table.
>
>

**Exhibit 10.12**

Accruing Interest between Interest Payment Dates

Avia records the issuance of these bonds on March 1, 2005, as follows:

| Mar. 1 | Cash ................................. | 101,500 | |
| | Interest Payable ...................... | | 1,500 |
| | Bonds Payable ....................... | | 100,000 |
| | *Sold bonds at par with accrued interest.* | | |

Assets   = Liabilities + Equity
+101,500    +100,000
                      +1,500

Note that liabilities for interest payable and bonds payable are recorded in separate accounts. When the June 30, 2005, semiannual interest date arrives, Avia pays the full semiannual interest of $4,500 ($100,000 × 9% × ½ year) to the bondholders. This payment includes the four months' interest of $3,000 earned by the bondholders from March 1 to June 30 *plus* the repayment of the 60 days' accrued interest collected by Avia when the bonds were sold. Avia records this first semiannual interest payment as follows:

**Example:** How much interest is collected from a buyer of $50,000 of Avia bonds sold at par 150 days after the contract issue date? *Answer:* $1,875 (computed as $50,000 × 9% × $^{150}/_{360}$ year)

| June 30 | Interest Payable ....................... | 1,500 | |
| | Bond Interest Expense ................... | 3,000 | |
| | Cash.............................. | | 4,500 |
| | *Paid semiannual interest on the bonds.* | | |

Assets  = Liabilities + Equity
−4,500     −1,500     −3,000

The practice of collecting and then repaying accrued interest with the next interest payment is to simplify the issuer's administrative efforts. To explain, suppose an issuer sells bonds on 15 or 20 different dates between the stated issue date and the first interest payment date. If the issuer does not collect accrued interest from buyers, it needs to pay different amounts of cash to each of them according to the time that passed after purchasing the bonds. The issuer needs to keep detailed records of buyers and the dates they bought bonds. Issuers

**Global:** In some countries such as Kuwait, Saudi Arabia, and Iran, charging explicit interest for use of money is rare due to Islamic law.

avoid this recordkeeping by having each buyer pay accrued interest at purchase. Issuers then pay the full semiannual interest to all buyers, regardless of when they bought bonds.

## Accruing Bond Interest Expense

If a bond's interest period does not coincide with the issuer's accounting period, an adjusting entry is needed to recognize bond interest expense accrued since the most recent interest payment. To illustrate, assume that the Adidas bonds described in Exhibit 10.11 are sold on the stated issue date of September 1, 2005, instead of December 31, 2005. As a result, four months' interest (and premium amortization) accrue before the end of the 2005 calendar year. Interest for this period equals $3,485, or 4/6 of the first six months' interest of $5,228. Also, the premium amortization is $515, or 4/6 of the first six months' amortization of $772. The sum of the bond interest expense and the amortization is $4,000 ($3,485 + $515), which equals 4/6 of the $6,000 cash payment due on February 28, 2006. Adidas records these effects with an adjusting entry at December 31, 2005:

**Point:** Computation of accrued bond interest may use months instead of days for simplicity purposes. For example, the accrued interest computation for the Adidas bonds is based on months.

Assets = Liabilities + Equity
       −515    −3,485
       +4,000

| Dec. 31 | Bond Interest Expense . . . . . . . . . . . . . . . . . . . . | 3,485 | |
|---|---|---|---|
| | Premium on Bonds Payable . . . . . . . . . . . . . . . . | 515 | |
| |      Interest Payable . . . . . . . . . . . . . . . . . . . . . . | | 4,000 |
| | *To record four months' accrued interest and premium amortization.* | | |

Similar entries are made on each December 31 throughout the bonds' five-year life. When the $6,000 cash payment occurs on each February 28 interest payment date, Adidas must recognize bond interest expense and amortization for January and February. It must also eliminate the interest payable liability created by the December 31 adjusting entry. For example, Adidas records its payment on February 28, 2006, as:

Assets  = Liabilities + Equity
−6,000    −4,000    −1,743
         −257

| Feb. 28 | Interest Payable . . . . . . . . . . . . . . . . . . . . . . . . | 4,000 | |
|---|---|---|---|
| | Bond Interest Expense ($5,228 × 2/6) . . . . . . . . . | 1,743 | |
| | Premium on Bonds Payable ($772 × 2/6) . . . . . . . . | 257 | |
| |      Cash . . . . . . . . . . . . . . . . . . . . . . . . . . . . . | | 6,000 |
| | *To record 2 months' interest and amortization and eliminate accrued interest liability.* | | |

The interest payments made each August 31 are recorded as usual because the entire six-month interest period is included within this company's calendar-year reporting period.

## Bond Pricing

**Point:** InvestingInBonds.com is an excellent bond research and learning source.

Prices for bonds traded on an organized exchange are often published in newspapers and through online services. This information normally includes the bond price (called *quote*), its contract rate, and its current market (called *yield*) rate. However, only a fraction of bonds are traded on organized exchanges. To compute the price of a bond, we apply present value concepts. This section explains how to use *present value concepts* to price the Fila discount bond and the Adidas premium bond described earlier.

**Present Value of a Discount Bond**    The issue price of bonds is found by computing the present value of the bonds' cash payments, discounted at the bonds' market rate. When computing the present value of the Fila bonds, we work with *semiannual* compounding periods because this is the time between interest payments; the annual market rate of 10% is considered a semiannual rate of 5%. Also, the five-year bond life is viewed as 10 semiannual periods. The price computation is twofold: (1) find the present value of the $100,000 par value paid at maturity and (2) find the present value of the series of 10 semiannual payments of $4,000 each; see Exhibit 10.4. These present values can be found by using *present value tables*. Appendix B at the end of this book shows present value tables and describes

**Point:** A bond's market value (price) at issuance equals the present value of all its future cash payments (the interest [discount] rate used is the bond's market rate).

**Point:** Many calculators provide present value functions for computation of bond prices.

their use. Table B.1 at the end of Appendix B is used for the single $100,000 maturity payment, and Table B.3 in Appendix B is used for the $4,000 series of interest payments. Specifically, we go to Table B.1, row 10, and across to the 5% column to identify the present value factor of 0.6139 for the maturity payment. Next, we go to Table B.3, row 10, and across to the 5% column, where the present value factor is 7.7217 for the series of interest payments. We compute bond price by multiplying the cash flow payments by their corresponding present value factors and adding them together; see Exhibit 10.13.

**Point:** The general approach to bond pricing is identical for discount bonds and premium bonds.

| Cash Flow | Table | Present Value Factor | Amount | Present Value |
|---|---|---|---|---|
| $100,000 par (maturity) value ....... | B.1 | 0.6139 | × $100,000 = | $ 61,390 |
| $4,000 interest payments ........... | B.3 | 7.7217 | ×    4,000 = | 30,887 |
| Price of bond ................. | | | | $92,277 |

**Exhibit 10.13**

Computing Issue Price for the Fila Discount Bonds

**Present Value of a Premium Bond**   We find the issue price of the Adidas bonds by using the market rate to compute the present value of the bonds' future cash flows. When computing the present value of these bonds, we again work with *semiannual* compounding periods because this is the time between interest payments. The annual 10% market rate is applied as a semiannual rate of 5%, and the five-year bond life is viewed as 10 semiannual periods. The computation is twofold: (1) find the present value of the $100,000 par value paid at maturity and (2) find the present value of the series of 10 payments of $6,000 each; see Exhibit 10.8. These present values can be found by using present value tables. First, go to Table B.1, row 10, and across to the 5% column where the present value factor is 0.6139 for the maturity payment. Second, go to Table B.3, row 10, and across to the 5% column, where the present value factor is 7.7217 for the series of interest payments. The bonds' price is computed by multiplying the cash flow payments by their corresponding present value factors and adding them together; see Exhibit 10.14.

**Point:** There are nearly 5 million individual U.S. bond issues, ranging from huge treasuries to tiny municipalities. This compares to about 12,000 individual U.S. stocks that are traded.

| Cash Flow | Table | Present Value Factor | Amount | Present Value |
|---|---|---|---|---|
| $100,000 par (maturity) value ........ | B.1 | 0.6139 | × $100,000 = | $ 61,390 |
| $6,000 interest payments ........... | B.3 | 7.7217 | ×    6,000 = | 46,330 |
| Price of bond ................. | | | | $107,720 |

**Exhibit 10.14**

Computing Issue Price for the Adidas Premium Bonds

## Quick Check

On December 31, 2004, a company issues 16%, 10-year bonds with a par value of $100,000. Interest is paid on June 30 and December 31. The bonds are sold to yield a 14% annual market rate at an issue price of $110,592. Use this information to answer questions 7 through 9:

7. Are these bonds issued at a discount or a premium? Explain your answer.

8. Using the straight-line method to allocate bond interest expense, the issuer records the second interest payment (on December 31, 2005) with a debit to Premium on Bonds Payable in the amount of (a) $7,470, (b) $530, (c) $8,000, or (d) $400.

9. How are these bonds reported in the long-term liability section of the issuer's balance sheet as of December 31, 2005?

10. On May 1, a company sells 9% bonds with a $500,000 par value that pay semiannual interest on each January 1 and July 1. The bonds are sold at par plus interest accrued since January 1. The issuer records the first semiannual interest payment on July 1 with (a) a debit to Interest Payable for $15,000, (b) a debit to Bond Interest Expense for $22,500, or (c) a credit to Interest Payable for $7,500.

Answers—p. 424

# Bond Retirement

This section describes the retirement of bonds (1) at maturity, (2) before maturity, and (3) by conversion to stock.

## Bond Retirement at Maturity

**P4**   Record the retirement of bonds.

The carrying value of bonds at maturity always equals par value. For example, both Exhibits 10.7 (a discount) and 10.11 (a premium) show that the carrying value of bonds at the end of their lives equals par value ($100,000). The retirement of these bonds at maturity, assuming interest is already paid and entered, is recorded as follows:

Assets   = Liabilities + Equity
−100,000    −100,000

| 2010 | | | |
|---|---|---|---|
| Dec. 31 | Bonds Payable ........................ | 100,000 | |
| | Cash ............................. | | 100,000 |
| | *To record retirement of bonds at maturity.* | | |

## Bond Retirement before Maturity

**Point:** Bond retirement is also referred to as *bond redemption.*

**Point:** Gains and losses from retiring bonds were *previously* reported as extraordinary items. New standards require that they now be judged by the "unusual and infrequent" criteria for reporting purposes.

Issuers sometimes wish to retire some or all of their bonds prior to maturity. For instance, if interest rates decline significantly, an issuer may wish to replace high-interest-paying bonds with new low-interest bonds. Two common ways to retire bonds before maturity are to (1) exercise a call option or (2) purchase them on the open market. In the first instance, an issuer can reserve the right to retire bonds early by issuing callable bonds. The bond indenture can give the issuer an option to *call* the bonds before they mature by paying the par value plus a *call premium* to bondholders. In the second case, the issuer retires bonds by repurchasing them on the open market at their current price. Whether bonds are called or repurchased, the issuer is unlikely to pay a price that exactly equals their carrying value. When a difference exists between the bonds' carrying value and the amount paid, the issuer records a gain or loss equal to the difference.

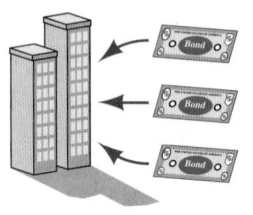

**Callable Bond**

To illustrate the accounting for retiring callable bonds, assume that a company issued callable bonds with a par value of $100,000. The call option requires the issuer to pay a call premium of $3,000 to bondholders in addition to the par value. Next, assume that after the June 30, 2005, interest payment, the bonds have a carrying value of $104,500. Then on July 1, 2005, the issuer calls these bonds and pays $103,000 to bondholders. The issuer recognizes a $1,500 gain from the difference between the bonds' carrying value of $104,500 and the retirement price of $103,000. The issuer records this bond retirement as:

Assets   = Liabilities + Equity
−103,000   −100,000   +1,500
           −4,500

| July 1 | Bonds Payable ......................... | 100,000 | |
|---|---|---|---|
| | Premium on Bonds Payable ................. | 4,500 | |
| | Gain on Bond Retirement .............. | | 1,500 |
| | Cash.............................. | | 103,000 |
| | *To record retirement of bonds before maturity.* | | |

An issuer usually must call all bonds when it exercises a call option. However, to retire as many or as few bonds as it desires, an issuer can purchase them on the open market. If it retires less than the entire class of bonds, it recognizes a gain or loss for the difference between the carrying value of those bonds retired and the amount paid to acquire them.

**Convertible Bond**

## Bond Retirement by Conversion

We described convertible bonds earlier in the chapter and explained how these bondholders have the right to convert their bonds to stock. When conversion occurs, the bonds' carrying value is transferred to equity accounts and no gain or loss is recorded. (The market prices of the bonds and stock are *not* relevant to this entry; the material in Chapter 11 is helpful in understanding this transaction.) To illustrate, assume that on January 1 the $100,000 par value bonds of **Converse**, with a carrying value of $100,000, are converted to 15,000 shares of $2 par value common stock. The entry to record this conversion is:

| Jan. 1 | Bonds Payable .......................... | 100,000 | | Assets = Liabilities + Equity |
|---|---|---|---|---|
| | Common Stock ..................... | | 30,000 | −100,000    +30,000 |
| | Contributed Capital in Excess of Par Value .. | | 70,000 | +70,000 |
| | *To record retirement of bonds by conversion.* | | | |

## Quick Check

**11.** Six years ago, a company issued $500,000 of 6%, eight-year bonds at a price of 95. The current carrying value is $493,750. The company decides to retire 50% of these bonds by buying them on the open market at a price of 102½. What is the amount of gain or loss on retirement of these bonds?

Answer—p. 424

# Long-Term Notes Payable

Like bonds, notes are issued to obtain assets such as cash. Unlike bonds, notes are typically transacted with a *single* lender such as a bank. An issuer initially records a note at its selling price; that is, the note's face value minus any discount or plus any premium. Over the note's life, the amount of interest expense allocated to each period is computed by multiplying the market rate (at issuance of the note) by the beginning-of-period note balance. The note's carrying (book) value at any time equals its face value minus any unamortized discount or plus any unamortized premium; carrying value is also computed as the present value of all remaining payments, discounted using the market rate at issuance.

## Installment Notes

An **installment note** is an obligation requiring a series of payments to the lender. Installment notes are common for franchises and other businesses when lenders and borrowers agree to spread payments over several periods. To illustrate, assume that Foghog borrows $60,000 from a bank to purchase equipment. It signs an 8% installment note requiring six annual payments of principal plus interest and it records the note's issuance as follows:

**C2**  Explain the types and payment patterns of notes.

| Dec. 31 | Cash ................................. | 60,000 | | Assets = Liabilities + Equity |
|---|---|---|---|---|
| | Notes Payable ...................... | | 60,000 | +60,000    +60,000 |
| | *Borrowed $60,000 by signing an 8%, six-year* | | | |
| | *installment note.* | | | |

Payments on an installment note normally include the accrued interest expense plus a portion of the amount borrowed (the *principal*). Two payment patterns are common: (1) accrued interest plus equal principal payments and (2) equal payments. This section describes these two patterns and how to account for them.

**Accrued Interest plus Equal Principal Payments**   The payment pattern of accrued interest plus equal amounts of principal creates cash flows that decrease in size over the note's life. This decrease occurs because each principal payment reduces the note's principal balance, yielding less interest expense for the next period.

To illustrate, assume that Foghog's $60,000, six-year, 8% note requires it to make an annual year-end payment equal to *accrued interest plus $10,000 of principal*. Exhibit 10.15 shows these payments and changes in the note balance. Column A lists the note's annual beginning balance.

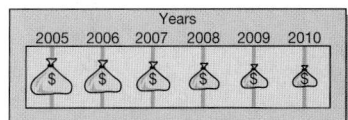

## Exhibit 10.15

Installment Note: Accrued Interest plus Equal Principal Payments

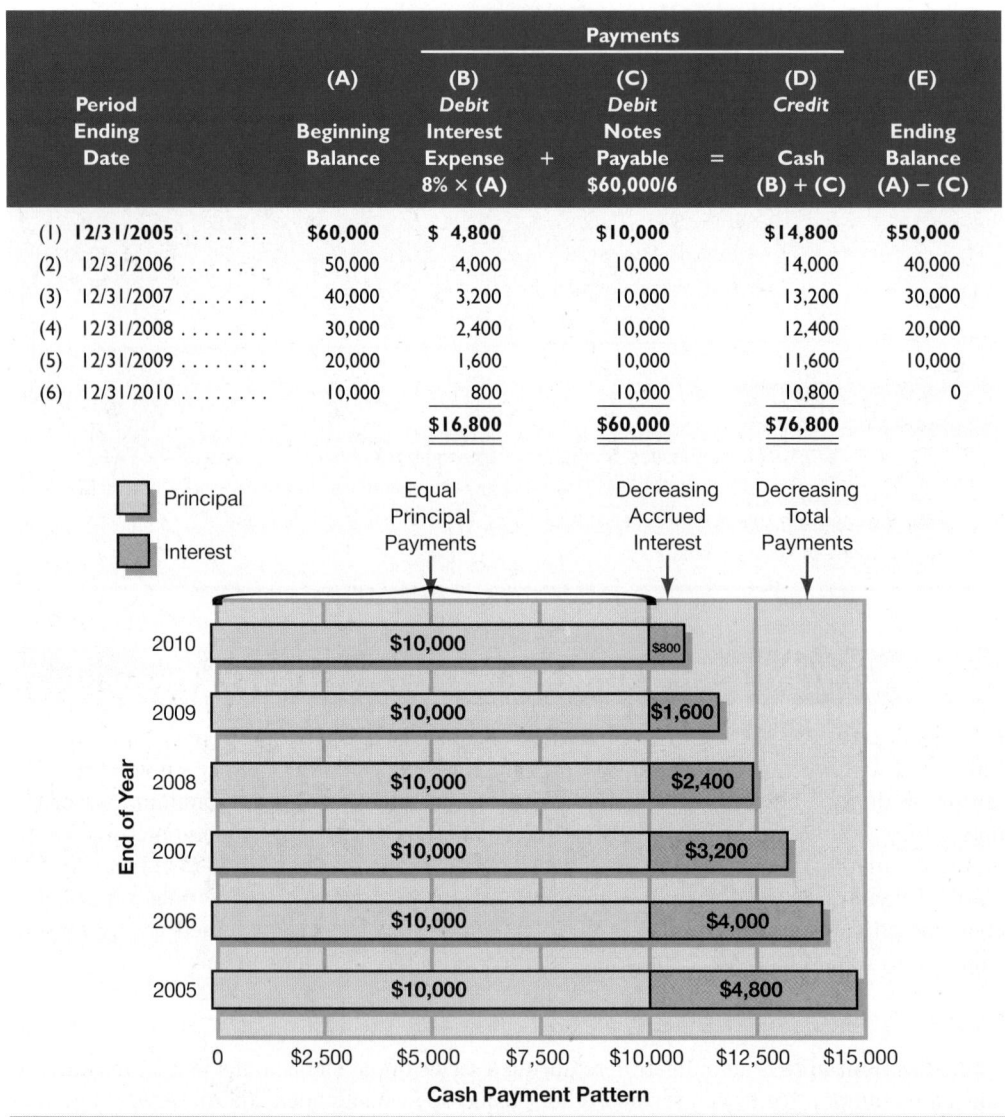

| | | (A) | (B)<br>*Debit*<br>Interest<br>Expense<br>8% × (A) | | (C)<br>*Debit*<br>Notes<br>Payable<br>$60,000/6 | | (D)<br>*Credit*<br>Cash<br>(B) + (C) | (E)<br>Ending<br>Balance<br>(A) − (C) |
|---|---|---|---|---|---|---|---|---|
| | Period<br>Ending<br>Date | Beginning<br>Balance | | + | | = | | |
| (1) | 12/31/2005 ........ | $60,000 | $ 4,800 | | $10,000 | | $14,800 | $50,000 |
| (2) | 12/31/2006 ........ | 50,000 | 4,000 | | 10,000 | | 14,000 | 40,000 |
| (3) | 12/31/2007 ........ | 40,000 | 3,200 | | 10,000 | | 13,200 | 30,000 |
| (4) | 12/31/2008 ........ | 30,000 | 2,400 | | 10,000 | | 12,400 | 20,000 |
| (5) | 12/31/2009 ........ | 20,000 | 1,600 | | 10,000 | | 11,600 | 10,000 |
| (6) | 12/31/2010 ........ | 10,000 | 800 | | 10,000 | | 10,800 | 0 |
| | | | $16,800 | | $60,000 | | $76,800 | |

**P5**   Prepare entries to account for notes.

Columns B, C, and D list each annual cash payment and its breakdown into interest and principal. Specifically, column B shows interest expense for each year at 8% of the beginning balance. Column C shows that each principal payment reduces the Notes Payable account balance by $10,000. Column D is the total annual payment. Column E shows the note's ending balance, which equals the beginning balance in column A minus the principal payment in column C. We include *debit* or *credit* in column headings to show the accounting effects. Note that the sum of debits to both interest expense and notes payable equals the credit to Cash. Also notice that total interest expense is $16,800 and total principal is $60,000, meaning cash payments for the five years total $76,800. The graph in the lower portion of Exhibit 10.15 shows the decreasing pattern in total payments, made up of decreasing accrued interest and constant principal payments. After all six payments are recorded, the balance of the Notes Payable account is zero. Foghog records its first two payments (for years 2005 and 2006) as follows:

Assets = Liabilities + Equity
−14,800   −10,000   −4,800

| 2005 | | | |
|---|---|---|---|
| Dec. 31 | Interest Expense ...................... | 4,800 | |
| | Notes Payable ...................... | 10,000 | |
| | Cash ............................ | | 14,800 |
| | *To record first installment payment.* | | |

2006

Dec. 31    Interest Expense .......................    4,000

           Notes Payable .........................   10,000

                Cash .............................             14,000

                *To record second installment payment.*

Assets  =  Liabilities  +  Equity

−14,000    −10,000      −4,000

**Equal Total Payments**   The equal total payments pattern consists of changing amounts of both interest and principal. To illustrate, assume that Foghog borrows $60,000 by signing a $60,000 note that requires six *equal payments* of $12,979 at the end of each year. (The present value of an annuity of six annual payments of $12,979, discounted at 8%, equals $60,000; we show this computation later in the section.) The $12,979 includes both interest and principal, the amounts of which change with each payment. Exhibit 10.16 shows the pattern of equal total payments and its two parts, interest and principal. Column A shows the note's beginning balance. Column B shows accrued interest for each year at 8% of the beginning note balance. Column C shows the impact on the note's principal, which equals the difference between the total payment in column D and the interest expense in column B. Column E shows the note's year-end balance.

**Point:** Most consumer notes are installment notes that require equal total payments.

**Exhibit 10.16**

Installment Note: Equal Total Payments

|  | | | Payments | | | |
|---|---|---|---|---|---|---|
| **Period Ending Date** | **(A)** Beginning Balance | **(B)** *Debit* Interest Expense 8% × (A) | + | **(C)** *Debit* Notes Payable (D) − (B) | **(D)** *Credit* Cash (computed) = | **(E)** Ending Balance (A) − (C) |
| (1)  12/31/2005 ........ | $60,000 | $ 4,800 |  | $ 8,179 | $12,979 | $51,821 |
| (2)  12/31/2006 ........ | 51,821 | 4,146 |  | 8,833 | 12,979 | 42,988 |
| (3)  12/31/2007 ........ | 42,988 | 3,439 |  | 9,540 | 12,979 | 33,448 |
| (4)  12/31/2008 ........ | 33,448 | 2,676 |  | 10,303 | 12,979 | 23,145 |
| (5)  12/31/2009 ........ | 23,145 | 1,852 |  | 11,127 | 12,979 | 12,018 |
| (6)  12/31/2010 ........ | 12,018 | 961 |  | 12,018 | 12,979 | 0 |
|  |  | $17,874 |  | $60,000 | $77,874 |  |

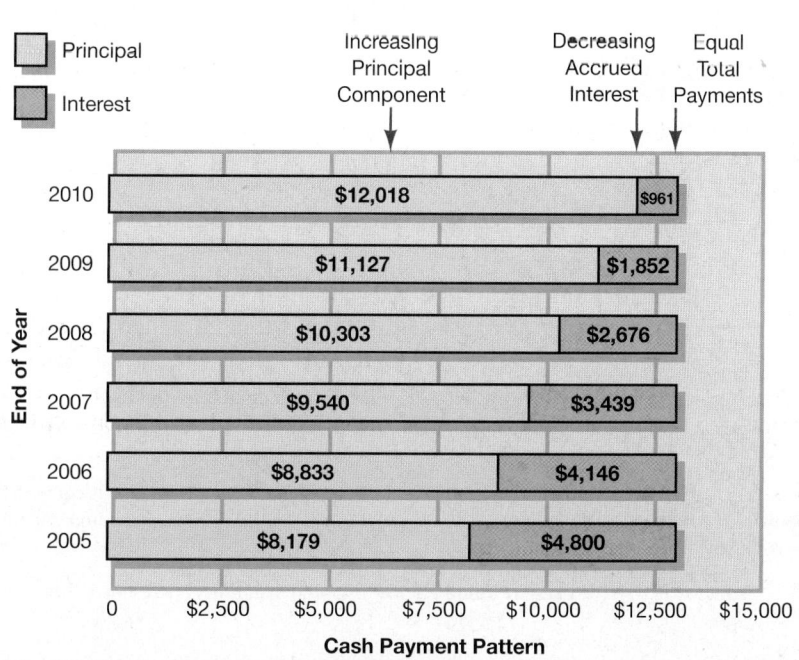

**Point:** The Truth-in-Lending Act requires lenders to provide information about loan costs including finance charges and interest rate.

Although the six cash payments are equal, accrued interest decreases each year because the principal balance of the note declines. As the amount of interest decreases each year, the portion of each payment applied to principal increases. This pattern is graphed in the lower part of Exhibit 10.16. Foghog uses the amounts in Exhibit 10.16 to record its first two payments (for years 2005 and 2006) as follows:

Assets = Liabilities + Equity
−12,979   −8,179   −4,800

| 2005 | | |
|---|---|---|
| Dec. 31 | Interest Expense ....................... | 4,800 |
| | Notes Payable ......................... | 8,179 |
| |      Cash ............................ | 12,979 |
| | *To record first installment payment.* | |

Assets = Liabilities + Equity
−12,979   −8,833   −4,146

| 2006 | | |
|---|---|---|
| Dec. 31 | Interest Expense ....................... | 4,146 |
| | Notes Payable ......................... | 8,833 |
| |      Cash ............................ | 12,979 |
| | *To record second installment payment.* | |

## Decision Insight

**Entrepreneur Aid**   Small Business Administration (SBA) provides loan programs, workshops, software, and other useful services for start-ups. It also operates an online library with facts and advice for entrepreneurs (**SBA.gov**). It reports that reliable accounting is crucial in securing financing at favorable terms.

Foghog records similar entries but with different amounts for each of the remaining four payments. After six years, the Notes Payable account balance is zero.

It is useful to compare the two payment patterns in Exhibits 10.15 and 10.16. The series of equal total payments yields more interest expense over the life of the note because the first three payments in Exhibit 10.16 are smaller and do not reduce the principal as quickly as the first three payments in Exhibit 10.15.[1]

## Mortgage Notes and Bonds

A **mortgage** is a legal agreement that helps protect a lender if a borrower fails to make required payments on bonds or notes. A mortgage gives the lender a right to be paid from the cash proceeds of the sale of a borrower's assets identified in the mortgage. A legal document, called a *mortgage contract,* describes the mortgage terms.

*Mortgage notes* carry a mortgage contract pledging title to specific assets as security for the note. Mortgage notes are especially popular in the purchase of homes and the acquisition of plant assets. Less common *mortgage bonds* are backed by the issuer's assets. Accounting for mortgage notes and bonds is similar to that for unsecured notes and bonds, except that the mortgage agreement must be disclosed. For example, **Musicland** reports that its "mortgage note payable is collateralized by land, buildings and certain fixtures."

## Decision Maker

**Entrepreneur**   You are an electronics retailer planning a holiday sale on a custom stereo system that requires no payments for two years. At the end of two years, buyers must pay the full amount. The system's suggested retail price is $4,100, but you are willing to sell it today for $3,000 cash. What is your holiday sale price if payment will not occur for two years and the market interest rate is 10%?

Answer—p. 424

**Example:** Suppose the $60,000 installment loan has an 8% interest rate with eight equal annual payments. What is the annual payment? *Answer* (using Table B.3): $60,000/5.7466 = $10,441

[1] Table B.3 in Appendix B is used to compute the dollar amount of the six payments that equal the initial note balance of $60,000 at 8% interest. We go to Table B.3, row 6, and across to the 8% column, where the present value factor is 4.6229. The dollar amount is then computed by solving this relation:

| Table | Present Value Factor | | Dollar Amount | | Present Value |
|---|---|---|---|---|---|
| B.3 | 4.6229 | × | ? | = | $60,000 |

The dollar amount is computed by dividing $60,000 by 4.6229, yielding $12,979.

## Quick Check

12. Which of the following is true for an installment note requiring a series of equal total cash payments? (*a*) Payments consist of increasing interest and decreasing principal; (*b*) Payments consist of changing amounts of principal but constant interest; or (*c*) Payments consist of decreasing interest and increasing principal.

13. How is the interest portion of an installment note payment computed?

14. When a borrower records an interest payment on an installment note, how are the balance sheet and income statement affected?

Answers—p. 424

**Global:** Countries vary in the preference given to debtholders vs. stockholders when a company is in financial distress. Some countries such as Germany, France, and Japan give preference to stockholders over debtholders.

---

# Pledged Assets to Secured Liabilities Ratio

## Decision Analysis

*Collateral agreements* can reduce the risk of loss for both bonds and notes. Unsecured bonds and notes are riskier because the issuer's obligation to pay interest and principal has the same priority as all other unsecured liabilities in the event of bankruptcy. If a company is unable to pay its debts in full, the unsecured creditors (including the holders of debentures) lose all or a portion of their balances.

**A2** Explain collateral agreements and their effects on loan risk.

A company's ability to borrow money with or without collateral agreements depends on its credit rating. In some cases, debt financing is unavailable unless the borrower can provide security to creditors with a collateral agreement. Even if unsecured loans are available, the creditors are likely to charge a higher rate of interest to compensate for the added risk. To borrow funds at a more favorable rate, many bonds and notes are secured by collateral agreements in the form of mortgages.

Notes to financial statements often describe the amounts of assets pledged as security against liabilities. Buyers (investors) of a company's secured debt obligations need to determine whether the debtor's pledged assets provide adequate security. One method to evaluate this is to compute the ratio of **pledged assets to secured liabilities** as in Exhibit 10.17.

**A3** Compute the ratio of pledged assets to secured liabilities and explain its use.

$$\text{Pledged assets to secured liabilities} = \frac{\text{Book value of pledged assets}}{\text{Book value of secured liabilities}}$$

### Exhibit 10.17

Ratio of Pledged Assets to Secured Liabilities

To illustrate, assume that a company owns assets with a book value of $230,000 pledged against loans with a balance of $100,000. The pledged assets to secured liabilities ratio is 2.3 (expressed as 2.3 to 1) and is computed as $230,000/$100,000. There are no exact guidelines for interpreting this ratio, but a 2.3 value is sufficiently high to provide secured creditors with some comfort that their loans are covered by the borrower's assets. As another example, a recent annual report of **Chock Full O'Nuts** reveals that "borrowings under the Loan Agreements . . . are collateralized by . . . accounts receivable and inventories, and substantially all of the machinery and equipment and real estate." We can use this information to compute its pledged assets to secured liabilities ratio of 20.6 ($206 million/$10 million). This ratio implies that more than $20 of collateral exists for each $1 of secured liabilities. This huge collateral commitment likely accounts for the low interest rate that Chock Full O'Nuts pays on these secured liabilities.

Pledging more assets for the benefit of secured creditors puts unsecured creditors at greater risk. Also, when using this ratio, be aware that book values of a company's net assets are unlikely to exactly reflect market values. The ratio is improved if reliable market values are used for the ratio instead of book values.

### Decision Maker

**Bond Investor**   You plan to purchase debenture bonds from one of two companies in the same industry that are similar in size and performance. The first company has $350,000 of unsecured liabilities, $575,000 of secured liabilities, and $1,265,000 in book value of pledged assets. The second company has $1,200,000 of unsecured liabilities, $800,000 of secured liabilities, and $2,000,000 in book value of pledged assets. Which company's debenture bonds are less risky based on the ratio of pledged assets to secured liabilities?

Answer—p. 424

# Demonstration Problem

Water Sports Company (WSC) patented and successfully test-marketed a new product. To expand its ability to produce and market the new product, WSC needs to raise $800,000 of financing. On January 1, 2004, the company obtained the money in two ways:

**a.** WSC signed a $400,000, 10% installment note to be repaid with five equal annual installments to be made on December 31 of 2004 through 2008.

**b.** WSC issued five-year bonds with a par value of $400,000. The bonds have a 12% annual contract rate and pay interest on June 30 and December 31. The bonds' annual market rate is 10% as of January 1, 2004.

### Required

**1.** For the installment note, (*a*) compute the size of each annual payment, (*b*) prepare an amortization table such as Exhibit 10.16, and (*c*) prepare the journal entry for the first payment.

**2.** For the bonds, (*a*) compute their issue price; (*b*) prepare the January 1, 2004, journal entry to record their issuance; (*c*) prepare an amortization table using the straight-line method; (*d*) prepare the June 30, 2004, journal entry to record the first interest payment; and (*e*) prepare a journal entry to record retiring the bonds at a $416,000 call price on January 1, 2006.

**3.**[B]Redo parts 2(*c*), 2(*d*), and 2(*e*) assuming the bonds are amortized using the effective interest method.

## Planning the Solution

* For the installment note, divide the borrowed amount by the annuity factor (from Table B.3) using the 10% rate and five payments to compute the amount of each payment. Prepare a table similar to Exhibit 10.16 and use the numbers in the table's first line for the journal entry.
* Compute the bonds' issue price by using the market rate to find the present value of their cash flows (use tables found in Appendix B). Then use this result to record the bonds' issuance. Next, prepare an amortization table like Exhibit 10.11 (and Exhibit 10B.2) and use it to get the numbers needed for the journal entry. Also use the table to find the carrying value as of the date of the bonds' retirement that you need for the journal entry.

## Solution to Demonstration Problem

### Part I: Installment Note

**a.** Annual payment = Note balance/Annuity factor = $400,000/3.7908 = $105,519 (Note: Annuity factor is for five payments and a rate of 10%.)

**b.** Amortization table follows:

| Annual Period Ending | (a) Beginning Balance | (b) Debit Interest Expense | + | (c) Debit Notes Payable | = | (d) Credit Cash | (e) Ending Balance |
|---|---|---|---|---|---|---|---|
| (1) 12/31/2004 | $400,000 | $ 40,000 | | $ 65,519 | | $105,519 | $334,481 |
| (2) 12/31/2005 | 334,481 | 33,448 | | 72,071 | | 105,519 | 262,410 |
| (3) 12/31/2006 | 262,410 | 26,241 | | 79,278 | | 105,519 | 183,132 |
| (4) 12/31/2007 | 183,132 | 18,313 | | 87,206 | | 105,519 | 95,926 |
| (5) 12/31/2008 | 95,926 | 9,593 | | 95,926 | | 105,519 | 0 |
| | | $127,595 | | $400,000 | | $527,595 | |

**c.** Journal entry for December 31, 2004, payment:

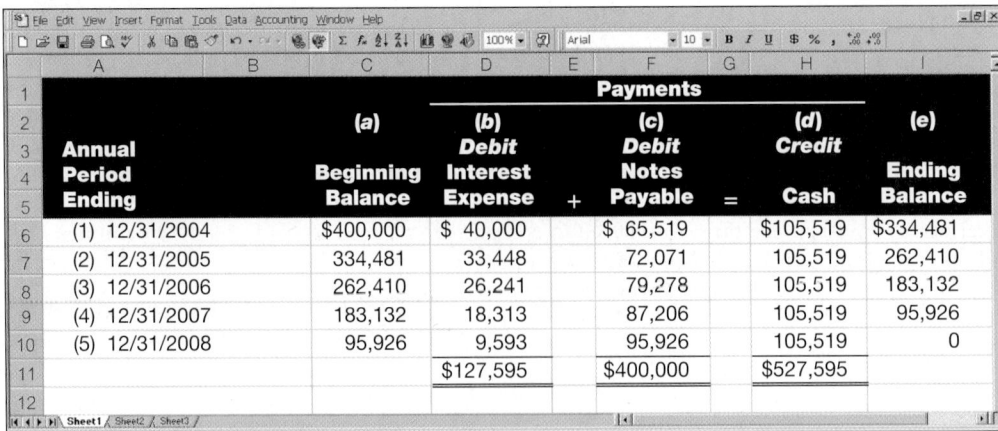

| Dec. 31 | Interest Expense | 40,000 | |
| | Notes Payable | 65,519 | |
| | Cash | | 105,519 |
| | *To record first installment payment.* | | |

## Part 2: Bonds (straight-line amortization)

**a.** Compute the bonds' issue price:

| Cash Flow | Table | Present Value Factor* | | Amount | | Present Value |
|---|---|---|---|---|---|---|
| Par (maturity) value ....... | B.1 in App. B (PV of 1) | 0.6139 | × | 400,000 | = | $245,560 |
| Interest payments ......... | B.3 in App. B (PV of annuity) | 7.7217 | × | 24,000 | = | 185,321 |
| Price of bond ........... | | | | | | $430,881 |

\* Present value factors are for 10 payments using a semiannual market rate of 5%.

**b.** Journal entry for January 1, 2004, issuance:

| Jan. 1 | Cash ................................... | 430,881 | |
|---|---|---|---|
| | Premium on Bonds Payable ............. | | 30,881 |
| | Bonds Payable ...................... | | 400,000 |
| | *Sold bonds at a premium.* | | |

**c.** Straight-line amortization table for premium bonds:

| | Semiannual Period-End | Unamortized Premium | Carrying Value |
|---|---|---|---|
| (0) | 1/1/2004 ....... | $30,881 | $430,881 |
| (1) | 6/30/2004 ....... | 27,793 | 427,793 |
| (2) | 12/31/2004 ....... | 24,705 | 424,705 |
| (3) | 6/30/2005 ....... | 21,617 | 421,617 |
| (4) | 12/31/2005 ....... | 18,529 | 418,529 |
| (5) | 6/30/2006 ....... | 15,441 | 415,441 |
| (6) | 12/31/2006 ....... | 12,353 | 412,353 |
| (7) | 6/30/2007 ....... | 9,265 | 409,265 |
| (8) | 12/31/2007 ....... | 6,177 | 406,177 |
| (9) | 6/30/2008 ....... | 3,089 | 403,089 |
| (10) | 12/31/2008 ....... | 0* | 400,000 |

\* Adjusted for rounding.

**d.** Journal entry for June 30, 2004, payment:

| June 30 | Bond Interest Expense .................... | 20,912 | |
|---|---|---|---|
| | Premium on Bonds Payable ................. | 3,088 | |
| | Cash ............................. | | 24,000 |
| | *Paid semiannual interest on bonds.* | | |

**e.** Journal entry for January 1, 2006, bond retirement:

| Jan. 1 | Bonds Payable ......................... | 400,000 | |
|---|---|---|---|
| | Premium on Bonds Payable ................. | 18,529 | |
| | Cash ............................. | | 416,000 |
| | Gain on Retirement of Bonds .......... | | 2,529 |
| | *To record bond retirement (carrying value as of Dec. 31, 2005).* | | |

## Part 3: Bonds (effective interest amortization)[B]

**c.** Effective interest amortization table for premium bonds:

| | Semiannual Interest Period | (A) Cash Interest Paid 6% × $400,000 | (B) Interest Expense 5% × Prior (E) | (C) Premium Amortization (A) − (B) | (D) Unamortized Premium Prior (D) − (C) | (E) Carrying Value $400,000 + (D) |
|---|---|---|---|---|---|---|
| (0) | 1/1/2004 | | | | $30,881 | $430,881 |
| (1) | 6/30/2004 | $ 24,000 | $ 21,544 | $ 2,456 | 28,425 | 428,425 |
| (2) | 12/31/2004 | 24,000 | 21,421 | 2,579 | 25,846 | 425,846 |
| (3) | 6/30/2005 | 24,000 | 21,292 | 2,708 | 23,138 | 423,138 |
| (4) | 12/31/2005 | 24,000 | 21,157 | 2,843 | 20,295 | 420,295 |
| (5) | 6/30/2006 | 24,000 | 21,015 | 2,985 | 17,310 | 417,310 |
| (6) | 12/31/2006 | 24,000 | 20,866 | 3,134 | 14,176 | 414,176 |
| (7) | 6/30/2007 | 24,000 | 20,709 | 3,291 | 10,885 | 410,885 |
| (8) | 12/31/2007 | 24,000 | 20,544 | 3,456 | 7,429 | 407,429 |
| (9) | 6/30/2008 | 24,000 | 20,371 | 3,629 | 3,800 | 403,800 |
| (10) | 12/31/2008 | 24,000 | 20,200* | 3,800 | 0 | 400,000 |
| | | $240,000 | $209,119 | $30,881 | | |

\* Adjusted for rounding.

**d.** Journal entry for June 30, 2004, payment:

| June 30 | Bond Interest Expense .................... | 21,544 | |
|---|---|---|---|
| | Premium on Bonds Payable ................. | 2,456 | |
| | Cash.............................. | | 24,000 |
| | *Paid semiannual interest on bonds.* | | |

**e.** Journal entry for January 1, 2006, bond retirement:

| Jan. 1 | Bonds Payable ......................... | 400,000 | |
|---|---|---|---|
| | Premium on Bonds Payable ................. | 20,295 | |
| | Cash.............................. | | 416,000 |
| | Gain on Retirement of Bonds............ | | 4,295 |
| | *To record bond retirement (carrying value as of December 31, 2005).* | | |

# APPENDIX

# Present Values of Bonds and Notes

This appendix explains how to apply present value techniques to measure a long-term liability when it is created and to assign interest expense to the periods until it is settled. Appendix B at the end of the book provides additional discussion of present value concepts.

# Present Value Concepts

The basic present value concept is that cash paid (or received) in the future has less value now than the same amount of cash paid (or received) today. To illustrate, if we must pay $1 one year from now, its present value is less than $1. To see this, assume that we borrow $0.9259 today that must be paid back in one year with 8% interest. Our interest expense for this loan is computed as $0.9259 × 8%, or $0.0741. When the $0.0741 interest is added to the $0.9259 borrowed, we get the $1 payment necessary to repay our loan with interest. This is formally computed in Exhibit 10A.1. The $0.9259 borrowed is the present value of the $1 future payment. More generally, an amount borrowed equals the present value of the future payment. (This same interpretation applies to an investment. If $0.9259 is invested at 8%, it yields $0.0741 in revenue after one year. This amounts to $1, made up of principal and interest.)

| | |
|---|---|
| **Amount borrowed** . . . . . . . . . . . | **$0.9259** |
| Interest for one year at 8% . . . . . . . | 0.0741 |
| Amount owed after 1 year . . . . . . . . | $1.0000 |

**C3** Explain and compute the present value of an amount to be paid at a future date.

**Exhibit 10A.1**

Components of a One-Year Loan

To extend this example, assume that we owe $1 two years from now instead of one year, and the 8% interest is compounded annually. *Compounded* means that interest during the second period is based on the total of the amount borrowed plus the interest accrued from the first period. The second period's interest is then computed as 8% multiplied by the sum of the amount borrowed plus interest earned in the first period. Exhibit 10A.2 shows how we compute the present value of $1 to be paid in two years. This amount is $0.8573. The first year's interest of $0.0686 is added to the principal so that the second year's interest is based on $0.9259. Total interest for this two-year period is $0.1427, computed as $0.0686 plus $0.0741.

**Point:** Benjamin Franklin is said to have described compounding as "the money, money makes, makes more money."

| | |
|---|---|
| **Amount borrowed** . . . . . . . . . . . . . . . . | **$0.8573** |
| Interest for first year ($0.8573 × 8%) . . . . . . . . | 0.0686 |
| Amount owed after 1 year . . . . . . . . . . . . . . | 0.9259 |
| Interest for second year ($0.9259 × 8%) . . . . . . . | 0.0741 |
| Amount owed after 2 years . . . . . . . . . . . . . . | $ 1.0000 |

**Exhibit 10A.2**

Components of a Two-Year Loan

# Present Value Tables

The present value of $1 that we must repay at some future date can be computed by using this formula: $1/(1 + i)^n$. The symbol $i$ is the interest rate per period and $n$ is the number of periods until the future payment must be made. Applying this formula to our two-year loan, we get $1/(1.08)^2$, or $0.8573. This is the same value shown in Exhibit 10A.2. We can use this formula to find any present value. However, a simpler method is to use a *present value table,* which lists present values computed with this formula for various interest rates and time periods. Many people find it helpful in learning present value concepts to first work with the table and then move to using a calculator.

Exhibit 10A.3 shows a present value table for a future payment of 1 for up to 10 periods at three different interest rates. Present values in this table are rounded to four decimal places. This table is drawn from the larger and more complete Table B.1 in Appendix B at the end of the book. Notice that the first value in the 8% column is 0.9259, the value we computed earlier for the present value of a $1 loan for one year at 8% (see Exhibit 10A.1). Go to the second row in the same 8% column and find the present value of 1 discounted at 8% for two years, or 0.8573. This $0.8573 is the present value of our obligation to repay $1 after two periods at 8% interest (see Exhibit 10A.2).

| | Rate | | |
|---|---|---|---|
| **Periods** | **6%** | **8%** | **10%** |
| 1 | 0.9434 | **0.9259** | 0.9091 |
| 2 | 0.8900 | **0.8573** | 0.8264 |
| 3 | 0.8396 | 0.7938 | 0.7513 |
| 4 | 0.7921 | 0.7350 | 0.6830 |
| 5 | 0.7473 | 0.6806 | 0.6209 |
| 6 | 0.7050 | 0.6302 | 0.5645 |
| 7 | 0.6651 | 0.5835 | 0.5132 |
| 8 | 0.6274 | 0.5403 | 0.4665 |
| 9 | 0.5919 | 0.5002 | 0.4241 |
| 10 | 0.5584 | 0.4632 | 0.3855 |

**Exhibit 10A.3**

Present Value of 1

**Example:** Use Exhibit 10A.3 to find the present value of $1 discounted for 2 years at 6%. *Answer:* Present value = $0.8900

# Applying a Present Value Table

To illustrate how to measure a liability using a present value table, assume that a company plans to borrow cash and repay it as follows: $2,000 after one year, $3,000 after two years, and $5,000 after three

**Exhibit 10A.4**

Present Value of a Series of
Unequal Payments

| Periods | Payments | Present Value of 1 at 10% | Present Value of Payments |
|---------|----------|---------------------------|---------------------------|
| 1 | $2,000 | 0.9091 | $ 1,818 |
| 2 | 3,000 | 0.8264 | 2,479 |
| 3 | 5,000 | 0.7513 | 3,757 |
| Present value of all payments . . . . . . | | | **$8,054** |

years. How much does this company receive to-day if the interest rate on this loan is 10%? To answer, we need to compute the present value of the three future payments, discounted at 10%. This computation is shown in Exhibit 10A.4 using present values from Exhibit 10A.3. The company can borrow $8,054 today at 10% interest in exchange for its promise to make these three payments at the scheduled dates.

## Present Value of an Annuity

**C4** Explain and compute the present value of a series of equal amounts to be paid at future dates.

The $8,054 present value for the loan in Exhibit 10A.4 equals the sum of the present values of the three payments. When payments are not equal, their combined present value is best computed by adding the individual present values as shown in Exhibit 10A.4. Sometimes payments follow an **annuity,** which is a series of *equal* payments at equal time intervals. The present value of an annuity is readily computed.

To illustrate, assume that a company must repay a 6% loan with a $5,000 payment at each year-end for the next four years. This loan amount equals the present value of the four payments discounted at 6%. Exhibit 10A.5 shows how to compute this loan's present value of $17,326 by multiplying each payment by its matching present value factor taken from Exhibit 10A.3.

**Exhibit 10A.5**

Present Value of a Series of Equal
Payments (Annuity) by
Discounting Each Payment

| Periods | Payments | Present Value of 1 at 6% | Present Value of Payments |
|---------|----------|--------------------------|---------------------------|
| 1 | $5,000 | 0.9434 | $ 4,717 |
| 2 | 5,000 | 0.8900 | 4,450 |
| 3 | 5,000 | 0.8396 | 4,198 |
| 4 | 5,000 | 0.7921 | 3,961 |
| Present value of all payments . . . . . . | | **3.4651** | **$17,326** |

However, the series of $5,000 payments is an annuity, so we can compute its present value with either of two shortcuts. First, the third column of Exhibit 10A.5 shows that the sum of the present values of 1 at 6% for periods 1 through 4 equals 3.4651. One shortcut is to multiply this total of 3.4651 by the $5,000 annual payment to get the combined present value of $17,326. It requires one multiplication instead of four.

The second shortcut uses an *annuity table* such as the one shown in Exhibit 10A.6, which is drawn from the more complete Table B.3 in Appendix B. We go directly to the annuity table to get the present value factor for a specific number of payments and interest rate. We then multiply this factor by the amount of the payment to find the present value of the annuity. Specifically, find the row for four periods and go across to the 6% column, where the factor is 3.4651. This factor equals the present value of an annuity with four payments of 1, discounted at 6%. We then multiply 3.4651 by $5,000 to get the $17,326 present value of the annuity.

**Exhibit 10A.6**

Present Value of an Annuity of 1

| Periods | Rate 6% | Rate 8% | Rate 10% |
|---------|---------|---------|----------|
| 1 | 0.9434 | 0.9259 | 0.9091 |
| 2 | 1.8334 | 1.7833 | 1.7355 |
| 3 | 2.6730 | 2.5771 | 2.4869 |
| 4 | **3.4651** | 3.3121 | 3.1699 |
| 5 | 4.2124 | 3.9927 | 3.7908 |
| 6 | 4.9173 | 4.6229 | 4.3553 |
| 7 | 5.5824 | 5.2064 | 4.8684 |
| 8 | 6.2098 | 5.7466 | 5.3349 |
| 9 | 6.8017 | 6.2469 | 5.7590 |
| 10 | 7.3601 | 6.7101 | 6.1446 |

**Example:** Use Exhibit 10A.6 to find the present value of an annuity of eight $15,000 payments with an 8% interest rate. *Answer:* Present value = $15,000 × 5.7466 = $86,199

## Compounding Periods Shorter than a Year

The present value examples all involved periods of one year. In many situations, however, interest is compounded over shorter periods. For example, the interest rate on bonds is usually stated as an annual rate but interest is often paid every six months (semiannually). This means that the present value of interest payments from such bonds must be computed using interest periods of six months.

Assume that a borrower wants to know the present value of a series of 10 *semiannual payments* of $4,000 made over five years at an *annual interest rate* of 12%. The interest rate is stated as an annual rate of 12%, but it is actually a rate of 6% per semiannual interest period. To compute the present value of this series of $4,000 payments, go to row 10 of Exhibit 10A.6 and across to the 6% column to find the factor 7.3601. The present value of this annuity is $29,440 (7.3601 × $4,000).

**Example:** If this borrower makes five semiannual payments of $8,000, what is the present value of this annuity at a 12% annual rate? *Answer:* 4.2124 × $8,000 = $33,699

*Appendix B further describes present value concepts and includes more complete present value tables and assignments.*

Answers—p. 424

## Quick Check

**15.** A company enters into an agreement to make four annual year-end payments of $1,000 each, starting one year from now. The annual interest rate is 8%. The present value of these four payments is (*a*) $2,923, (*b*) $2,940, or (*c*) $3,312.

**16.** Suppose a company has an option to pay either (*a*) $10,000 after one year or (*b*) $5,000 after six months and another $5,000 after one year. Which choice has the lower present value?

# Effective Interest Amortization

## Effective Interest Amortization of a Discount Bond

The straight-line method yields changes in the bonds' carrying value while the amount for bond interest expense remains constant. This gives the impression of a changing interest rate when users divide a constant bond interest expense over a changing carrying value. As a result, accounting standards allow use of the straight-line method only when its results do not differ materially from those obtained using the effective interest method. The **effective interest method,** or simply *interest method,* allocates total bond interest expense over the bonds' life in a way that yields a constant rate of interest. This constant rate of interest is the market rate at the issue date. Thus, bond interest expense for a period equals the carrying value of the bond at the beginning of that period multiplied by the market rate when issued.

Exhibit 10B.1 shows an effective interest amortization table for the Fila bonds (as described in Exhibit 10.4). The key difference between the effective interest and straight-line methods lies in

**Point:** The effective interest method consistently computes bond interest expense using the market rate at issuance. This rate is applied to a changing carrying value.

### Exhibit 10B.1

Effective Interest Amortization of Bond Discount

File  Edit  View  Insert  Format  Tools  Data  Accounting  Window  Help

| | Bonds: $100,000 Par Value, Semiannual Interest Payments, Five-Year Life, 4% Semiannual Contract Rate, 5% Semiannual Market Rate | | | | |
|---|---|---|---|---|---|
| | **(A)** | **(B)** | **(C)** | **(D)** | **(E)** |
| **Semiannual Interest Period-End** | **Cash Interest Paid** | **Bond Interest Expense** | **Discount Amortization** | **Unamortized Discount** | **Carrying Value** |
| (0) **12/31/2005** | | | | **$7,723** | **$ 92,277** |
| (1) **6/30/2006** | **$4,000** | **$4,614** | **$ 614** | **7,109** | **92,891** |
| (2) 12/31/2006 | 4,000 | 4,645 | 645 | 6,464 | 93,536 |
| (3) 6/30/2007 | 4,000 | 4,677 | 677 | 5,787 | 94,213 |
| (4) 12/31/2007 | 4,000 | 4,711 | 711 | 5,076 | 94,924 |
| (5) 6/30/2008 | 4,000 | 4,746 | 746 | 4,330 | 95,670 |
| (6) 12/31/2008 | 4,000 | 4,784 | 784 | 3,546 | 96,454 |
| (7) 6/30/2009 | 4,000 | 4,823 | 823 | 2,723 | 97,277 |
| (8) 12/31/2009 | 4,000 | 4,864 | 864 | 1,859 | 98,141 |
| (9) 6/30/2010 | 4,000 | 4,907 | 907 | 952 | 99,048 |
| (10) 12/31/2010 | 4,000 | 4,952 | 952 | 0 | 100,000 |
| | $40,000 | $47,723 | $7,723 | | |

Sheet1  Sheet2  Sheet3  Sheet2  Sheet3

Column (**A**) is par value ($100,000) multiplied by the semiannual contract rate (4%).
Column (**B**) is prior period's carrying value multiplied by the semiannual market rate (5%).
Column (**C**) is the difference between interest paid and bond interest expense, or [(B) − (A)].
Column (**D**) is the prior period's unamortized discount less the current period's discount amortization.
Column (**E**) is par value less unamortized discount, or [$100,000 − (D)].

**Global:** The U.S. generally requires use of the effective interest method, but some countries prefer straight-line amortization, and Brazil requires it.

computing bond interest expense. Instead of assigning an equal amount of bond interest expense to each period, the effective interest method assigns a bond interest expense amount that increases over the life of a discount bond. **Both methods allocate the *same* $47,723 of total bond interest expense to the bonds' life, but in different patterns.** Specifically, the amortization table in Exhibit 10B.1 shows that the balance of the discount (column D) is amortized until it reaches zero. Also, the bonds' carrying value (column E) changes each period until it equals par value at maturity. Compare columns D and E to the corresponding columns in Exhibit 10.7 to see the amortization patterns. Total bond interest expense is $47,723, consisting of $40,000 of semiannual cash payments and $7,723 of the original bond discount, the same for both methods.

Except for differences in amounts, journal entries recording the expense and updating the liability balance are the same under the effective interest method and the straight-line method. We can use the numbers in Exhibit 10B.1 to record each semiannual entry during the bonds' five-year life (June 30, 2006, through December 31, 2010). For instance, we record the interest payment at the end of the first semiannual period as:

Assets = Liabilities + Equity
−4,000      +614      −4,614

| | | | |
|---|---|---|---|
| **2006** | | | |
| June 30 | Bond Interest Expense . . . . . . . . . . . . . . . . . . . | 4,614 | |
| | Discount on Bonds Payable . . . . . . . . . . . . . | | 614 |
| | Cash. . . . . . . . . . . . . . . . . . . . . . . . . . . . . . | | 4,000 |

*To record semiannual interest and discount amortization (effective interest method).*

## Effective Interest Amortization of a Premium Bond

Exhibit 10B.2 shows the amortization table using the effective interest method for the Adidas bonds (as described in Exhibit 10.8). Column A lists the semiannual cash payments. Column B shows the amount of bond interest expense, computed as the 5% semiannual market rate at issuance multiplied by the beginning-of-period carrying value. The amount of cash paid in column A is larger than the bond interest expense because the cash payment is based on the higher 6% semiannual contract rate. The excess cash payment over the interest expense reduces the principal. These amounts are shown in column C. Column E shows the carrying value after deducting the amortized premium in column

**Exhibit 10B.2**

Effective Interest Amortization of Bond Premium

| | | (A) Cash Interest Paid | (B) Bond Interest Expense | (C) Premium Amortization | (D) Unamortized Premium | (E) Carrying Value |
|---|---|---|---|---|---|---|
| **Bonds: $100,000 Par Value, Semiannual Interest Payments, Five-Year Life, 6% Semiannual Contract Rate, 5% Semiannual Market Rate** | | | | | | |
| Semiannual Interest Period-End | | | | | | |
| (0) | **12/31/2005** | | | | **$7,720** | **$107,720** |
| (1) | **6/30/2006** | **$6,000** | **$5,386** | **$ 614** | 7,106 | 107,106 |
| (2) | 12/31/2006 | 6,000 | 5,355 | 645 | 6,461 | 106,461 |
| (3) | 6/30/2007 | 6,000 | 5,323 | 677 | 5,784 | 105,784 |
| (4) | 12/31/2007 | 6,000 | 5,289 | 711 | 5,073 | 105,073 |
| (5) | 6/30/2008 | 6,000 | 5,254 | 746 | 4,327 | 104,327 |
| (6) | 12/31/2008 | 6,000 | 5,216 | 784 | 3,543 | 103,543 |
| (7) | 6/30/2009 | 6,000 | 5,177 | 823 | 2,720 | 102,720 |
| (8) | 12/31/2009 | 6,000 | 5,136 | 864 | 1,856 | 101,856 |
| (9) | 6/30/2010 | 6,000 | 5,093 | 907 | 949 | 100,949 |
| (10) | 12/31/2010 | 6,000 | 5,051* | 949 | 0 | 100,000 |
| | | $60,000 | $52,280 | $7,720 | | |

Column (**A**) is par value ($100,000) multiplied by the semiannual contract rate (6%).

Column (**B**) is prior period's carrying value multiplied by the semiannual market rate (5%).

Column (**C**) is the difference between interest paid and bond interest expense, or [(A) − (B)].

Column (**D**) is the prior period's unamortized premium less the current period's premium amortization.

Column (**E**) is par value plus unamortized premium, or [$100,000 + (D)].

* Adjusted for rounding.

C from the prior period's carrying value. Column D shows the premium's reduction by periodic amortization. When the issuer makes the first semiannual interest payment, the effect of premium amortization on bond interest expense and bond liability is recorded as follows:

| 2006 | | | | |
|---|---|---|---|---|
| June 30 | Bond Interest Expense . . . . . . . . . . . . . . . . . . . | 5,386 | | |
| | Premium on Bonds Payable . . . . . . . . . . . . . . . . | 614 | | |
| | Cash . . . . . . . . . . . . . . . . . . . . . . . . . . . . | | 6,000 | |
| | *To record semiannual interest and premium* | | | |
| | *amortization (effective interest method).* | | | |

Assets = Liabilities + Equity
−6,000      −614      −5,386

Similar entries with different amounts are recorded at each payment date until the bond matures at the end of 2010. The effective interest method yields decreasing amounts of bond interest expense and increasing amounts of premium amortization over the bonds' life.

# Leases and Pensions

10C

This appendix briefly explains the accounting and analysis for both leases and pensions.

## Lease Liabilities

A **lease** is a contractual agreement between a *lessor* (asset owner) and a *lessee* (asset renter or tenant) that grants the lessee the right to use the asset for a period of time in return for cash (rent) payments. Nearly one-fourth of all equipment purchases is financed with leases. The advantages of lease financing include the lack of an immediate large cash payment and the potential to deduct rental payments in computing taxable income. From an accounting perspective, leases can be classified as either operating or capital leases.

C5 Describe the accounting for leases and pensions.

**Operating Leases**  **Operating leases** are short-term (or cancelable) leases in which the lessor retains the risks and rewards of ownership. Examples include most car and apartment rental agreements. The lessee records such lease payments as expenses; the lessor records them as revenue. The lessee does not report the leased item as an asset or a liability (it is the lessor's asset). To illustrate, if an employee of Amazon leases a car for $300 at an airport while on company business, Amazon (lessee) records this cost as:

**Point:** Home Depot's recent annual report indicates that its rental expenses from operating leases total more than $500 million.

| July 4 | Rental Expense . . . . . . . . . . . . . . . . . . . . . . . | 300 | |
|---|---|---|---|
| | Cash . . . . . . . . . . . . . . . . . . . . . . . . . . . . | | 300 |
| | *To record lease rental payment.* | | |

Assets = Liabilities + Equity
−300                    −300

**Capital Leases**  **Capital leases** are long-term (or noncancelable) leases by which the lessor transfers substantially all risks and rewards of ownership to the lessee.[2] Examples include most leases of airplanes and department store buildings. The lessee records the leased item as its own

---

[2] A *capital lease* meets any one or more of four criteria: (1) transfers title of leased asset to lessee, (2) contains a bargain purchase option, (3) has a lease term that is 75% or more of the leased asset's useful life, or (4) has a present value of lease payments that is 90% or more of the leased asset's market value.

asset along with a lease liability at the start of the lease term; the amount recorded equals the present value of all lease payments. To illustrate, assume that K2 Co. enters into a six-year lease of a building in which it will sell sporting equipment. The lease transfers all building ownership risks and rewards to K2 (the present value of its $12,979 annual lease payments is $60,000). K2 records this transaction as follows:

Assets = Liabilities + Equity
+60,000    +60,000

| 2005 | | | |
|---|---|---|---|
| Jan. 1 | Leased Asset—Building . . . . . . . . . . . . . . . . . . . | 60,000 | |
| | Lease Liability . . . . . . . . . . . . . . . . . . . . . . . | | 60,000 |
| | *To record leased asset and lease liability.* | | |

**Point:** Home Depot reports *"certain retail locations are leased under capital leases."* The net present value of its Lease Liability is about $270 million.

K2 reports the leased asset as a plant asset and the lease liability as a long-term liability. The portion of the lease liability expected to be paid in the next year is reported as a current liability.[3] At each year-end, K2 records depreciation on the leased asset (assume straight-line depreciation, six-year lease term, and no salvage value) as follows:

Assets = Liabilities + Equity
−10,000              −10,000

| | | | |
|---|---|---|---|
| Dec. 31 | Depreciation Expense—Building . . . . . . . . . . . . . | 10,000 | |
| | Accumulated Depreciation—Building. . . . . . . | | 10,000 |
| | *To record depreciation on leased asset.* | | |

K2 also accrues interest on the lease liability at each year-end. Interest expense is computed by multiplying the remaining lease liability by the interest rate on the lease. Specifically, K2 records its annual interest expense as part of its annual lease payment ($12,979) as follows (for its first year):

Assets = Liabilities + Equity
−12,979   −8,179    −4,800

| 2005 | | | |
|---|---|---|---|
| Dec. 31 | Interest Expense. . . . . . . . . . . . . . . . . . . . . . . | 4,800 | |
| | Lease Liability . . . . . . . . . . . . . . . . . . . . . . . | 8,179 | |
| | Cash. . . . . . . . . . . . . . . . . . . . . . . . . . . . | | 12,979 |
| | *To record first annual lease payment.** | | |

* These numbers are computed from a *lease payment schedule*. For simplicity, we use the same numbers from Exhibit 10.16 for this lease payment schedule—with different headings as follows:

| | (A) | Payments | | | (E) |
|---|---|---|---|---|---|
| | | (B) *Debit* | (C) *Debit* | (D) *Credit* | |
| Period Ending Date | Beginning Balance of Lease Liability | Interest on Lease + Liability 8% × (A) | Lease = Liability (D) − (B) | Cash Lease Payment | Ending Balance of Lease Liability (A) − (C) |
| 12/31/2005 . . . . . . . . . | $60,000 | $ 4,800 | $ 8,179 | $12,979 | $51,821 |
| 12/31/2006 . . . . . . . . . | 51,821 | 4,146 | 8,833 | 12,979 | 42,988 |
| 12/31/2007 . . . . . . . . . | 42,988 | 3,439 | 9,540 | 12,979 | 33,448 |
| 12/31/2008 . . . . . . . . . | 33,448 | 2,676 | 10,303 | 12,979 | 23,145 |
| 12/31/2009 . . . . . . . . . | 23,145 | 1,852 | 11,127 | 12,979 | 12,018 |
| 12/31/2010 . . . . . . . . . | 12,018 | 961 | 12,018 | 12,979 | 0 |
| | | $17,874 | $60,000 | $77,874 | |

---

[3] Most lessees try to keep leased assets and lease liabilities off their balance sheets by failing to meet any one of the four criteria of a capital lease. This is because a lease liability increases a company's total liabilities, making it more difficult to obtain additional financing. The acquisition of assets without reporting any related liabilities (or other asset outflows) on the balance sheet is called **off-balance-sheet financing.**

# Pension Liabilities

A **pension plan** is a contractual agreement between an employer and its employees for the employer to provide benefits (payments) to employees after they retire. Most employers pay the full cost of the pension, but sometimes employees pay part of the cost. An employer records its payment into a pension plan with a debit to Pension Expense and a credit to Cash. A *plan administrator* receives payments from the employer, invests them in pension assets, and makes benefit payments to *pension recipients* (retired employees). Insurance and trust companies often serve as pension plan administrators.

Many pensions are known as *defined benefit plans* that define future benefits; the employer's contributions vary, depending on assumptions about future pension assets and liabilities. Several disclosures are necessary in this case. Specifically, a pension liability is reported when the accumulated benefit obligation is *more than* the plan assets, a so-called *underfunded plan*. The accumulated benefit obligation is the present value of promised future pension payments to retirees. *Plan assets* refer to the market value of assets the plan administrator holds. A pension asset is reported when the accumulated benefit obligation is *less than* the plan assets, a so-called *overfunded plan*. An employer reports pension expense when it receives the benefits from the employees' services, which is sometimes decades before it pays pension benefits to employees. (*Other Postretirement Benefits* refer to nonpension benefits such as health care and life insurance benefits. Similar to a pension, costs of these benefits are estimated and liabilities accrued when the employees earn them.)

> **Point:** Fringe benefits are often 40% or more of salaries and wages, and pension benefits make up nearly 15% of fringe benefits.

> **Point:** Two types of pension plans are (1) *defined benefit plan*—the retirement benefit is defined and the employer estimates the contribution necessary to pay these benefits and (2) *defined contribution plan*—the pension contribution is defined and the employer and/or employee contributes amounts specified in the pension agreement.

## Summary

**C1 Describe the types of bonds and the procedures for issuing them.** Certain bonds are secured by the issuer's assets; other bonds, called *debentures,* are unsecured. Serial bonds mature at different points in time; term bonds mature at one time. Registered bonds have each bondholder's name recorded by the issuer; bearer bonds are payable to the holder. Convertible bonds are exchangeable for shares of the issuer's stock. Callable bonds can be retired by the issuer at a set price. Bonds are often issued by an underwriter and monitored by a trustee.

**C2 Explain the types and payment patterns of notes.** Notes repaid over a period of time are called *installment notes* and usually follow one of two payment patterns: (1) decreasing payments of interest plus equal amounts of principal or (2) equal total payments. Mortgage notes also are common.

**C3$^A$ Explain and compute the present value of an amount to be paid at a future date.** The basic concept of present value is that an amount of cash to be paid or received in the future is worth less than the same amount of cash to be paid or received today. Another important present value concept is that interest is compounded, meaning interest is added to the balance and used to determine interest for succeeding periods.

**C4$^A$ Explain and compute the present value of a series of equal amounts to be paid at future dates.** An annuity is a series of equal payments occurring at equal time intervals. An annuity's present value can be computed as the sum of individual present values for each payment. An alternative and preferred approach is to compute the present value of the series using the present value table for an annuity (or a calculator).

**C5$^C$ Describe the accounting for leases and pensions.** A lease is a rental agreement between the lessor and the lessee. When the lessor retains the risks and rewards of asset ownership (an *operating lease*), the lessee debits Rent Expense and credits Cash for its lease payments. When the lessor substantially transfers the risks and rewards of asset ownership to the lessee (a *capital lease*), the lessee capitalizes the leased asset and records a lease liability. Pension agreements can result in either pension assets or pension liabilities.

**A1 Compare bond financing with stock financing.** Bond financing is used to fund business activities. Advantages of bond financing versus stock include (1) no effect on owner control, (2) tax savings, and (3) increased earnings due to financial leverage. Disadvantages include (1) interest and principal payments and (2) amplification of poor performance.

**A2 Explain collateral agreements and their effects on loan risk.** Collateral agreements alter the risk of loss for creditors. Unsecured bonds and notes are riskier because the issuer's obligation to pay interest and principal has the same priority as all other unsecured liabilities in the event of bankruptcy. To borrow funds at a more favorable rate, many bonds and notes are secured by collateral agreements called *mortgages.*

**A3 Compute the ratio of pledged assets to secured liabilities and explain its use.** Both secured and unsecured creditors are concerned about the relation between the amount of assets the debtor owns and the amount of secured liabilities. Secured creditors are at less risk when the ratio of pledged assets to secured liabilities is larger, but the risks of unsecured creditors are often increased when this ratio is high because their claims to assets are secondary to secured creditors.

**P1 Prepare entries to record bond issuance and bond interest expense.** When bonds are issued at par, Cash is debited and Bonds Payable is credited for the bonds' par value. At bond interest payment dates (usually semiannual), Bond Interest Expense is debited and Cash credited; the latter for an amount equal to the bond par value multiplied by the bond contract rate.

**P2 Compute and record amortization of bond discount.** Bonds are issued at a discount when the contract rate is less than the market rate, making the issue (selling) price less than par. When this occurs, the issuer records a credit to Bonds Payable (at par) and debits both Discount on Bonds Payable and Cash. The amount of bond interest expense assigned to each period is computed using either the straight-line or effective interest method.

**P3**   **Compute and record amortization of bond premium.**
Bonds are issued at a premium when the contract rate is higher than the market rate, making the issue (selling) price greater than par. When this occurs, the issuer records a debit to Cash and credits both Premium on Bonds Payable and Bonds Payable (at par). The amount of bond interest expense assigned to each period is computed using either the straight-line or effective interest method. The Premium on Bonds Payable is allocated to reduce bond interest expense over the life of the bonds.

**P4**   **Record the retirement of bonds.** Bonds are retired at maturity with a debit to Bonds Payable and a credit to Cash at par value. The issuer can retire the bonds early by exercising

a call option or purchasing them in the market. Bondholders can also retire bonds early by exercising a conversion feature on convertible bonds. The issuer recognizes a gain or loss for the difference between the amount paid and the bond carrying value.

**P5**   **Prepare entries to account for notes.** Interest is allocated to each period in a note's life by multiplying its beginning-period carrying value by its market rate at issuance. If a note is repaid with equal payments, the payment amount is computed by dividing the borrowed amount by the present value of an annuity factor (taken from a present value table) using the market rate and the number of payments.

---

## Guidance Answers to **Decision Maker** and **Decision Ethics**

**Bond Rater**   Bonds with longer repayment periods (life) have higher risk. Also, bonds issued by companies in financial difficulties or facing higher than normal uncertainties have higher risk. Moreover, companies with higher than normal debt and large fluctuations in earnings are considered of higher risk. Discount bonds are more risky on one or more of these factors.

**Entrepreneur**   This is a "present value" question. The market interest rate (10%) and present value ($3,000) are known, but the payment required two years later is unknown. This amount ($3,630) can be computed as $3,000 × 1.10 × 1.10. Thus, the sale price is $3,630 when no payments are received for two years. Note that the $3,630 received two years from today is equivalent to $3,000 cash today.

**Bond Investor**   The ratio of pledged assets to secured liabilities for the first company is 2.2 ($1,265,000/$575,000) and for the second company is 2.5 ($2,000,000/$800,000), suggesting that secured creditors of the second company are at less risk than those of the first company. But *debenture bonds are unsecured.* Therefore, since the first company has fewer secured liabilities, it is of lower risk for unsecured debenture bonds. The first company also has fewer liabilities and, since the companies are of equal size, the first company's liabilities make up a smaller portion of total assets. Consequently, as a buyer of unsecured debenture bonds, you prefer the first company.

---

## Guidance Answers to **Quick Checks**

**1.** (*b*)

**2.** Multiply the bond's par value by its contract rate of interest.

**3.** Bonds sell at a premium when the contract rate exceeds the market rate and the purchasers pay more than their par value.

**4.** The bonds are issued at a discount, meaning that issue price is less than par value. A discount occurs because the bond contract rate (6%) is less than the market rate (8%).

**5.**

| | | |
|---|---|---|
| Cash.................................... | 91,893 | |
| Discount on Bonds Payable ............... | 8,107 | |
|     Bonds Payable ..................... | | 100,000 |

**6.** $3,811 (Total bond interest expense of $38,107 divided by 10 periods; or the $3,000 semiannual cash payment plus the $8,107 discount divided by 10 periods.)

**7.** The bonds are issued at a premium, meaning issue price is higher than par value. A premium occurs because the bonds' contract rate (16%) is higher than the market rate (14%).

**8.** (*c*) For each semiannual period: $10,592/20 periods = $530 premium amortization.

**9.**

| | | |
|---|---|---|
| Bonds payable, 16%, due 12/31/2014 ...... | $100,000 | |
| Plus premium on bonds payable ......... | 9,532* | $109,532 |

\* Original premium balance of $10,592 less $530 and $530 amortized on 6/30/2005 and 12/31/2005, respectively.

**10.** (*a*) Reflects payment of accrued interest recorded back on May 1; $500,000 × 9% × ¹⁄₁₂ = $15,000.

**11.** $9,375 loss. Computed as the difference between the repurchase price of $256,250 [50% of ($500,000 × 102.5%)] and the carrying value of $246,875 (50% of $493,750).

**12.** (*c*)

**13.** The interest portion of an installment payment equals the period's beginning loan balance multiplied by the market interest rate at the time of the note's issuance.

**14.** On the balance sheet, the account balances of the related liability (note payable) and asset (cash) accounts are decreased. On the income statement, interest expense is recorded.

**15.** (*c*) Computed as 3.3121 × $1,000 = $3,312.

**16.** The option of paying $10,000 after one year has a lower present value. It postpones paying the first $5,000 by six months. More generally, the present value of a further delayed payment is always lower than a less delayed payment.

## Key Terms

Key Terms are available at the book's Website for learning and testing in an online Flashcard Format.

Annuity (p. 418)
Bearer bonds (p. 398)
Bond (p. 396)
Bond certificate (p. 399)
Bond indenture (p. 399)
Callable bonds (p. 398)
Capital leases (p. 421)
Carrying value of bonds (p. 401)
Contract rate (p. 400)
Convertible bonds (p. 398)
Coupon bonds (p. 398)

Discount on bonds payable (p. 400)
Effective interest method (p. 419)
Installment note (p. 409)
Lease (p. 421)
Market rate (p. 400)
Mortgage (p. 412)
Off-balance-sheet financing (p. 422)
Operating leases (p. 421)
Par value of a bond (p. 396)
Pension plan (p. 423)

Pledged assets to secured liabilities (p. 413)
Premium on bonds (p. 403)
Registered bonds (p. 398)
Secured bonds (p. 397)
Serial bonds (p. 398)
Sinking fund bonds (p. 398)
Straight-line method (p. 401)
Term bonds (p. 398)
Unsecured bonds (p. 397)

## Personal Interactive Quiz

Personal Interactive Quizzes A and B are available at the book's Website to reinforce and assess your learning.

*Superscript letter* [B] *(*[C]*) denotes assignments based on Appendix 10B (10C).*

## Discussion Questions

1. What is the main difference between a bond and a share of stock?

2. What is the main difference between notes payable and bonds payable?

3. What are the duties of a trustee for bondholders?

4. What is the advantage of issuing bonds instead of obtaining financing from the company's owners?

5. What is a bond indenture? What provisions are usually included in it?

6. What are the *contract* rate and the *market* rate for bonds?

7. What factors affect the market rates for bonds?

8.[B] Does the straight-line or effective interest method produce an interest expense allocation that yields a constant rate of interest over a bond's life? Explain.

9. Why does a company that issues bonds between interest dates collect accrued interest from the bonds' purchasers?

10. If you know the par value of bonds, the contract rate, and the market rate, how do you compute the bonds' price?

11. What is the issue price of a $2,000 bond sold at 98¼? What is the issue price of a $6,000 bond sold at 101½?

12. Describe two common payment patterns for installment notes.

13. Explain why unsecured creditors are concerned when the pledged assets to secured liabilities ratio for a borrower increases.

14. What obligation does an entrepreneur (owner) have to investors that purchase bonds to finance the business?

15. Refer to **Krispy Kreme**'s annual report in Appendix A. Is there any indication that Krispy Kreme has issued bonds?

16. Refer to the statement of cash flows for **Tastykake** in Appendix A. For the year ended December 28, 2002, what is its "Net borrowings (payments) of long-term debt"?

17. Refer to the annual report for **Harley-Davidson** in Appendix A. For the year ended December 31, 2002, did it raise more cash by issuing stock or debt?

18.[C] When can a lease create both an asset and a liability for the lessee?

19.[C] Compare and contrast an operating lease with a capital lease.

20.[C] Describe the two basic types of pension plans.

*Red numbers denote Discussion Questions that involve decision-making.*

*Homework Manager repeats all numerical Quick Studies on the book's Website with new numbers.* →

## QUICK STUDY

**QS 10-1**

Bond terminology

C1

Enter the letter of the description *A* through *H* that best fits each term 1 through 8.

**A.** Records and tracks the bondholders' names.

**B.** Is unsecured; backed only by the issuer's credit standing.

**C.** Has varying maturity dates for amounts owed.

**D.** Identifies rights and responsibilities of the issuer and the bondholders.

**E.** Can be exchanged for shares of the issuer's stock.

**F.** Is unregistered; interest is paid to whoever possesses them.

**G.** Maintains a separate asset account from which bondholders are paid at maturity.

**H.** Pledges specific assets of the issuer as collateral.

**1.** _____ Debenture                  **5.** _____ Sinking fund bond

**2.** _____ Bond indenture            **6.** _____ Convertible bond

**3.** _____ Bearer bond               **7.** _____ Secured bond

**4.** _____ Registered bond           **8.** _____ Serial bond

---

**QS 10-2**

Bond computations—
straight-line

P1  P2

Alberto Company issues 8%, 10-year bonds with a par value of $350,000 and semiannual interest payments. On the issue date, the annual market rate for these bonds is 10%, which implies a selling price of 87½. The straight-line method is used to allocate interest expense.

**1.** What are the issuer's cash proceeds from issuance of these bonds?

**2.** What total amount of bond interest expense will be recognized over the life of these bonds?

**3.** What is the amount of bond interest expense recorded on the first interest payment date?

---

**QS 10-3**[B]

Bond computations—
effective interest

P1  P3

Sanchez issues 10%, 15-year bonds with a par value of $120,000 and semiannual interest payments. On the issue date, the annual market rate for these bonds is 8%, which implies a selling price of 117¼. The effective interest method is used to allocate interest expense.

**1.** What are the issuer's cash proceeds from issuance of these bonds?

**2.** What total amount of bond interest expense will be recognized over the life of these bonds?

**3.** What amount of bond interest expense is recorded on the first interest payment date?

---

**QS 10-4**

Journalize bond issuance   P1

Prepare the journal entry for the issuance of the bonds in both QS 10-2 and QS 10-3. Assume that both bonds are issued for cash on January 1, 2005.

---

**QS 10-5**

Computing bond price

P2  P3

Using the bond details in both QS 10-2 and QS 10-3, confirm that the bonds' selling prices given in each problem are approximately correct. Use the present value tables B.1 and B.3 in Appendix B.

---

**QS 10-6**

Issuing bonds between
interest dates

P1

Gooden Company plans to issue 8% bonds on January 1, 2005, with a par value of $2,000,000. The company sells $1,800,000 of the bonds on January 1, 2005. The remaining $200,000 sells at par on March 1, 2005. The bonds pay interest semiannually as of June 30 and December 31. Record the entry for the March 1 cash sale of bonds.

---

**QS 10-7**

Bond retirement by call option

P4

On July 1, 2005, Taurasi Company exercises a $5,000 call option (plus par value) on its outstanding bonds that have a carrying value of $208,000 and par value of $200,000. The company exercises the call option after the semiannual interest is paid on June 30, 2005. Record the entry to retire the bonds.

---

**QS 10-8**

Bond retirement by stock
conversion   P4

On January 1, 2005, the $1,000,000 par value bonds of Gruden Company with a carrying value of $1,000,000 are converted to 500,000 shares of $0.50 par value common stock. Record the entry for the conversion of the bonds.

---

**QS 10-9**

Computing payments for
an installment note   C2

Valdez Company borrows $170,000 cash from a bank and in return signs an installment note for five annual payments of equal amount, with the first payment due one year after the note is signed. Use Table B.3 in Appendix B to compute the amount of the annual payment for each of the following annual market rates: (*a*) 4%, (*b*) 8%, and (*c*) 12%.

Note 2 of **Collins Industries'** annual report states: "The credit facility [line] is collateralized by receivables, inventories, equipment and certain real property. Under the terms of the Agreement, the Company is required to maintain certain financial ratios and other financial conditions. The Agreement also prohibits the Company from incurring certain additional indebtedness, limits certain investments, advances or loans and restricts substantial asset sales, capital expenditures and cash dividends." What restrictions has the bank that granted the credit placed on Collins Industries?

**QS 10-10**
Interpretation of collateral agreement

A2

---

Compute the ratio of pledged assets to secured liabilities for the following two companies. Which company appears to have the riskier secured liabilities?

**QS 10-11**
Ratio of pledged assets to secured liabilities

A3

| | Xiang Co. | Xu Co. |
|---|---|---|
| Pledged assets . . . . . . . | $387,000 | $172,000 |
| Total assets . . . . . . . . . | 550,000 | 490,000 |
| Secured liabilities . . . . . | 163,000 | 158,000 |
| Unsecured liabilities . . . | 266,000 | 390,000 |

---

Lauren Wright, an employee of ETrain.com, leases a car at O'Hare airport for a three-day business trip. The rental cost is $350. Prepare the entry by ETrain.com to record Lauren's short-term car lease cost.

**QS 10-12**[C]
Recording operating leases    C5

---

Juicyfruit, Inc., signs a five-year lease for office equipment with Office Solutions. The present value of the lease payments is $20,859. Prepare the journal entry that Juicyfruit records at the inception of this capital lease.

**QS 10-13**[C]
Recording capital leases

C5

---

  ← *Homework Manager* repeats all numerical Exercises on the book's Website with new numbers.

*Round dollar amounts to the nearest whole dollar. Assume no reversing entries are used.*

## EXERCISES

On January 1, 2005, Kidman Enterprises issues bonds that have a $1,700,000 par value, mature in 20 years, and pay 9% interest semiannually on June 30 and December 31. The bonds are sold at par.

**1.** How much interest will Kidman pay (in cash) to the bondholders every six months?

**2.** Prepare journal entries to record (*a*) the issuance of bonds on January 1, 2005; (*b*) the first interest payment on June 30, 2005; and (*c*) the second interest payment on December 31, 2005.

**3.** Prepare the journal entry for issuance assuming the bonds are issued at (*a*) 98 and (*b*) 102.

**Exercise 10-1**
Recording bond issuance and interest

P1

---

ACT issues bonds with a par value of $90,000 on January 1, 2005. The annual contract rate on them is 8%, and interest is paid semiannually on June 30 and December 31. The bonds mature in three years. The annual market rate at the date of issuance is 10%, and the bonds are sold for $85,431.

**1.** What is the amount of the discount on these bonds at issuance?

**2.** How much total bond interest expense will be recognized over the life of these bonds?

**3.** Prepare an amortization table like the one in Exhibit 10.7 for these bonds; use the straight-line method to amortize the discount.

**Exercise 10-2**
Straight-line amortization of bond discount

P2

---

Welch Company issues bonds dated January 1, 2005, with a par value of $250,000. The annual contract rate on them is 9%, and interest is paid semiannually on June 30 and December 31. The bonds mature in three years. The annual market rate at the date of issuance is 12%, and the bonds are sold for $231,570.

**1.** What is the amount of the discount on these bonds at issuance?

**2.** How much total bond interest expense will be recognized over the life of these bonds?

**3.** Prepare an amortization table like the one in Exhibit 10B.1 for these bonds; use the effective interest method to amortize the discount.

**Exercise 10-3**[B]
Effective interest amortization of bond discount

P2

**Exercise 10-4**

Straight-line amortization of bond premium

P3

Prairie Dunes Company issues bonds dated January 1, 2004, with a par value of $800,000. The annual contract rate is 13%, and interest is paid semiannually on June 30 and December 31. The bonds mature in three years. The annual market rate at the date of issuance is 12%, and the bonds are sold for $819,700.

**1.** What is the amount of the premium on these bonds at issuance?

**2.** How much total bond interest expense will be recognized over the life of these bonds?

**3.** Prepare an amortization table like the one in Exhibit 10.11 for these bonds; use the straight-line method to amortize the premium.

---

**Exercise 10-5ᴮ**

Effective interest amortization of bond premium   P3

Refer to the bond details in Exercise 10-4 and prepare an amortization table like the one in Exhibit 10B.2 for these bonds using the effective interest method to amortize the premium.

---

**Exercise 10-6**

Computing bond interest and price, and recording bond issuance

P2

Check  (4) $518,465

Jester Company issues bonds with a par value of $600,000 on their stated issue date. The bonds mature in 10 years and pay 6% annual interest in semiannual payments. On the issue date, the annual market rate for the bonds is 8%.

**1.** What is the amount of each semiannual interest payment for these bonds?

**2.** How many semiannual interest payments will be made on these bonds over their life?

**3.** Use the interest rates given to determine whether the bonds are issued at par, at a discount, or at a premium.

**4.** Compute the price of the bonds as of their issue date.

**5.** Prepare the journal entry to record the bonds' issuance.

---

**Exercise 10-7**

Computing bond interest and price, and recording bond issuance

P3

Check  (4) $81,086

Metro, Inc., issues bonds with a par value of $75,000 on their stated issue date. The bonds mature in five years and pay 10% annual interest in semiannual payments. On the issue date, the annual market rate for the bonds is 8%.

**1.** What is the amount of each semiannual interest payment for these bonds?

**2.** How many semiannual interest payments will be made on these bonds over their life?

**3.** Use the interest rates given to determine whether the bonds are issued at par, at a discount, or at a premium.

**4.** Compute the price of the bonds as of their issue date.

**5.** Prepare the journal entry to record the bonds' issuance.

---

**Exercise 10-8**

Bond computations, straight-line amortization, and bond retirement

P2  P4

Check  (6) $4,095 loss

On January 1, 2004, Steadman issues $350,000 of 10%, 15-year bonds at a price of 97¾. Six years later, on January 1, 2010, Steadman retires 20% of these bonds by buying them on the open market at 104½. All interest is accounted for and paid through December 31, 2009, the day before the purchase. The straight-line method is used to amortize any bond discount.

**1.** How much does the company receive when it issues the bonds on January 1, 2004?

**2.** What is the amount of the discount on the bonds at January 1, 2004?

**3.** How much amortization of the discount is recorded on the bonds for the entire period from January 1, 2004, through December 31, 2009?

**4.** What is the carrying (book) value of the bonds as of the close of business on December 31, 2009? What is the carrying value of the 20% soon-to-be-retired bonds on this same date?

**5.** How much did the company pay on January 1, 2010, to purchase the bonds that it retired?

**6.** What is the amount of the recorded gain or loss from retiring the bonds?

**7.** Prepare the journal entry to record the bond retirement at January 1, 2010.

---

**Exercise 10-9**

Recording bond issuance with accrued interest

P1

Check  (1) $51,000

On May 1, 2005, Kidman Enterprises issues bonds dated January 1, 2005, that have a $1,700,000 par value, mature in 20 years, and pay 9% interest semiannually on June 30 and December 31. The bonds are sold at par plus four months' accrued interest.

**1.** How much accrued interest do the bond purchasers pay Kidman on May 1, 2005?

**2.** Prepare journal entries to record (*a*) the issuance of bonds on May 1, 2005; (*b*) the first interest payment on June 30, 2005; and (*c*) the second interest payment on December 31, 2005.

Simon issues four-year bonds with a $50,000 par value on June 1, 2004, at a price of $47,974. The annual contract rate is 7%, and interest is paid semiannually on November 30 and May 31.

**1.** Prepare an amortization table like the one in Exhibit 10.7 for these bonds. Use the straight-line method of interest amortization.

**2.** Prepare journal entries to record the first two interest payments and to accrue interest as of December 31, 2004.

**Exercise 10-10**
Straight-line amortization and accrued bond interest expense
P1  P2

---

On January 1, 2005, Perez borrows $25,000 cash by signing a four-year, 7% installment note that requires annual payments of accrued interest and equal amounts of principal on December 31 of each year from 2005 through 2008.

**1.** How much principal is included in each of the four annual payments?

**2.** Prepare an amortization table for this installment note like the one in Exhibit 10.15.

**Exercise 10-11**
Installment note with equal principal payments  C2  P5

**Check**  (1) $6,250

---

Use the information in Exercise 10-11 to prepare the journal entries for Perez to record the loan on January 1, 2005, and the four payments from December 31, 2005, through December 31, 2008.

**Exercise 10-12**
Installment note entries  P5

---

On January 1, 2005, Randa borrows $25,000 cash by signing a four-year, 7% installment note. The note requires four equal total payments of accrued interest and principal on December 31 of each year from 2005 through 2008.

**1.** Compute the amount of each of the four equal total payments.

**2.** Prepare an amortization table for this installment note like the one in Exhibit 10.16.

**Exercise 10-13**
Installment note with equal total payments  C2  P5

**Check**  (1) $7,381

---

Use the information in Exercise 10-13 to prepare the journal entries for Randa to record the loan on January 1, 2005, and the four payments from December 31, 2005, through December 31, 2008.

**Exercise 10-14**
Installment note entries  P5

---

An unsecured creditor of Telnet Co. is monitoring Telnet's financing activities. Two years ago, Telnet's ratio of pledged assets to secured liabilities was 1.7. One year ago, the ratio climbed to 2.3, and the most recent financial report shows the ratio is now 3.1. Describe what this trend likely indicates about the company's activities, specifically from the point of view of this unsecured creditor.

**Exercise 10-15**
Pledged assets to secured liabilities
A3

---

Indicate whether the company in each separate case 1 through 3 has entered into an operating lease or a capital lease.

**1.** The lessor retains title to the asset, and the lease term is three years on an asset that has a five-year useful life.

**2.** The title is transferred to the lessee, the lessee can purchase the asset for $1 at the end of the lease, and the lease term is five years. The leased asset has an expected useful life of six years.

**3.** The present value of the lease payments is 95% of the leased asset's market value, and the lease term is 70% of the leased asset's useful life.

**Exercise 10-16<sup>C</sup>**
Identifying capital and operating leases
C5

---

Flyer (lessee) signs a five-year capital lease for office equipment with a $20,000 annual lease payment. The present value of the five annual lease payments is $82,000, based on a 7% interest rate.

**1.** Prepare the journal entry Flyer will record at inception of the lease.

**2.** If the leased asset has a 5-year useful life with no salvage value, prepare the journal entry Flyer will record each year to recognize depreciation expense related to the leased asset.

**Exercise 10-17<sup>C</sup>**
Accounting for capital lease
C5

---

**General Motors** advertised three alternatives for a 25-month lease on a new Blazer: (1) zero dollars down and a lease payment of $1,750 per month for 25 months, (2) $5,000 down and $1,500 per month for 25 months, or (3) $38,500 down and no payments for 25 months. Use the present value Table B.3 in Appendix B to determine which is the best alternative (assume you have enough cash to accept any alternative and the annual interest rate is 12% compounded monthly).

**Exercise 10-18<sup>C</sup>**
Analyzing lease options
C3  C4  C5

## PROBLEM SET A

*Round dollar amounts to the nearest whole dollar. Assume no reversing entries are used.*

### Problem 10-1A
Computing bond price and recording issuance

P1  P2  P3

**Check**  (1) Premium, $2,718

(3) Discount, $2,294

Stowers Research issues bonds dated January 1, 2005, that pay interest semiannually on June 30 and December 31. The bonds have a $20,000 par value, an annual contract rate of 10%, and mature in 10 years.

**Required**

For each of the following three separate situations, (*a*) determine the bonds' issue price on January 1, 2005, and (*b*) prepare the journal entry to record their issuance.

**1.** Market rate at the date of issuance is 8%.

**2.** Market rate at the date of issuance is 10%.

**3.** Market rate at the date of issuance is 12%.

---

### Problem 10-2A
Straight-line amortization of both bond discount and bond premium

P1  P2  P3
mhhe.com/wild3e

**Check**  (3) $2,071,776

(4) 12/31/2005 carrying value, $1,764,460

Heathrow issues $2,000,000 of 6%, 15-year bonds dated January 1, 2004, that pay interest semiannually on June 30 and December 31. The bonds are issued at a price of $1,728,224.

**Required**

**1.** Prepare the January 1, 2004, journal entry to record the bonds' issuance.

**2.** For each semiannual period, compute (*a*) the cash payment, (*b*) the straight-line discount amortization, and (*c*) the bond interest expense.

**3.** Determine the total bond interest expense to be recognized over the bonds' life.

**4.** Prepare the first two years of an amortization table like Exhibit 10.7 using the straight-line method.

**5.** Prepare the journal entries to record the first two interest payments.

**6.** Assume that the bonds are issued at a price of $2,447,990. Repeat parts 1 through 5.

---

### Problem 10-3A
Straight-line amortization of bond premium; computing bond price

P1  P3
mhhe.com/wild3e

**Check**  (2) 6/30/2006 carrying value, $505,331

Saturn issues 6.5%, five-year bonds dated January 1, 2004, with a $500,000 par value. The bonds pay interest on June 30 and December 31 and are issued at a price of $510,666. The annual market rate is 6% on the issue date.

**Required**

**1.** Calculate the total bond interest expense over the bonds' life.

**2.** Prepare a straight-line amortization table like Exhibit 10.11 for the bonds' life.

**3.** Prepare the journal entries to record the first two interest payments.

---

### Problem 10-4A[B]
Effective interest amortization of bond premium; computing bond price   P1  P3

**Check**  (2) 6/30/2006 carrying value, $505,728

(4) $504,653

Refer to the bond details in Problem 10-3A.

**Required**

**1.** Compute the total bond interest expense over the bonds' life.

**2.** Prepare an effective interest amortization table like the one in Exhibit 10B.2 for the bonds' life.

**3.** Prepare the journal entries to record the first two interest payments.

**4.** Use the market rate at issuance to compute the present value of the remaining cash flows for these bonds as of December 31, 2006. Compare your answer with the amount shown on the amortization table as the balance for that date (from part 2) and explain your findings.

---

### Problem 10-5A
Straight-line amortization of bond discount

P1  P2

**Check**  (2) $195,639

(3) 12/31/2005 carrying value, $617,181

Patton issues $650,000 of 5%, four-year bonds dated January 1, 2004, that pay interest semiannually on June 30 and December 31. They are issued at $584,361 and their market rate is 8% at the issue date.

**Required**

**1.** Prepare the January 1, 2004, journal entry to record the bonds' issuance.

**2.** Determine the total bond interest expense to be recognized over the bonds' life.

**3.** Prepare a straight-line amortization table like the one in Exhibit 10.7 for the bonds' first two years.

**4.** Prepare the journal entries to record the first two interest payments.

*Analysis Component*

**5.** Assume the market rate on January 1, 2004, is 4% instead of 8%. Without providing numbers, describe how this change affects the amounts reported on Patton's financial statements.

---

Refer to the bond details in Problem 10-5A.

**Required**

**1.** Prepare the January 1, 2004, journal entry to record the bonds' issuance.
**2.** Determine the total bond interest expense to be recognized over the bonds' life.
**3.** Prepare an effective interest amortization table like the one in Exhibit 10B.1 for the bonds' first two years.
**4.** Prepare the journal entries to record the first two interest payments.

**Problem 10-6A**[B]

Effective interest amortization of bond discount   P1  P2

**Check**  (2) $195,639

(3) 12/31/2005 carrying value, $614,614

*eXcel*

mhhe.com/wild3e

---

McFad issues $90,000 of 11%, three-year bonds dated January 1, 2004, that pay interest semiannually on June 30 and December 31. They are issued at $92,283. Their market rate is 10% at the issue date.

**Required**

**1.** Prepare the January 1, 2004, journal entry to record the bonds' issuance.
**2.** Determine the total bond interest expense to be recognized over the bonds' life.
**3.** Prepare an effective interest amortization table like Exhibit 10B.2 for the bonds' first two years.
**4.** Prepare the journal entries to record the first two interest payments.
**5.** Prepare the journal entry to record the bonds' retirement on January 1, 2006, at 98.

*Analysis Component*

**6.** Assume that the market rate on January 1, 2004, is 12% instead of 10%. Without presenting numbers, describe how this change affects amounts reported on McFad's financial statements.

**Problem 10-7A**[B]

Effective interest amortization of bond premium; retiring bonds

P1  P3  P4

**Check**  (3) 6/30/2005 carrying value, $91,224

(5) $2,635 gain

*eXcel*

mhhe.com/wild3e

---

On November 1, 2004, Leetch Ltd. borrows $400,000 cash from a bank by signing a five-year installment note bearing 8% interest. The note requires equal total payments each year on October 31.

**Required**

**1.** Compute the total amount of each installment payment.
**2.** Complete an amortization table for this installment note similar to the one in Exhibit 10.16.
**3.** Prepare the journal entries in which Leetch (*a*) records accrued interest as of December 31, 2004 (the end of its annual reporting period), and (*b*) the first annual payment on the note.
**4.** Assume that the note does not require equal total payments but five payments of accrued interest and equal amounts of principal. Complete an amortization table for this note similar to the one in Exhibit 10.15. Prepare the journal entries to record (*a*) accrued interest as of December 31, 2004 (the end of its annual reporting period), and (*b*) the note's first annual payment.

**Problem 10-8A**

Installment notes

C2  P5

**Check**  (2) 10/31/2008 ending balance, $92,759

(4) 10/31/2007 ending balance, $160,000

---

On January 1, 2005, Wildcat Company issues at par its 11%, four-year bonds with a $135,000 par value. They are secured by a mortgage that specifies assets totaling $225,000 as collateral. Also on January 1, 2005, Athens Company issues at par its 11%, four-year bonds with a par value of $60,000. Athens secures its bonds with a mortgage that includes $150,000 of pledged assets. The December 31, 2004, balance sheet information for both companies follows:

**Problem 10-9A**

Ratio of pledged assets to secured liabilities

A2  A3

|  | Wildcat Co. | Athens Co. |
|---|---|---|
| Total assets .............. | $900,000* | $450,000† |
| Liabilities |  |  |
|   Secured ............... | $210,000 | $ 75,000 |
|   Unsecured ............. | 150,000 | 165,000 |
| Equity .................. | 540,000 | 210,000 |
| Total liabilities and equity ...... | $900,000 | $450,000 |

\* 43% are pledged. † 54% are pledged.

**Required**

**1.** Compute the ratio of pledged assets to secured liabilities for each company at January 1, 2005.

*Analysis Component*

**2.** Which company's bonds appear less risky? What other information might help to evaluate the risks of these companies' bonds?

---

## Problem 10-10A^c
Capital lease accounting

C5

Montana Company signs a five-year capital lease with Elway Company for office equipment. The annual lease payment is $20,000, and the interest rate is 8%.

**Required**

**1.** Compute the present value of Montana's five-year lease payments.

**2.** Prepare the journal entry to record Montana's capital lease at its inception.

**3.** Complete a lease payment schedule for the five years of the lease with the following headings. Assume that the beginning balance of the lease liability (present value of lease payments) is $79,854. (*Hint:* To find the amount allocated to interest in year 1, multiply the interest rate by the beginning-of-year lease liability. The amount of the annual lease payment not allocated to interest is allocated to principal. Reduce the lease liability by the amount allocated to principal to update the lease liability at each year-end.)

| Period Ending Date | Beginning Balance of Lease Liability | Interest on Lease Liability | Reduction of Lease Liability | Cash Lease Payment | Ending Balance of Lease Liability |
|---|---|---|---|---|---|
| | | | | | |

**4.** Use straight-line depreciation and prepare the journal entry to depreciate the leased asset at the end of year 1. Assume zero salvage value and a five-year life for the office equipment.

---

# PROBLEM SET B

## Problem 10-1B
Computing bond price and recording issuance

P1  P2  P3

Sedona Systems issues bonds dated January 1, 2005, that pay interest semiannually on June 30 and December 31. The bonds have a $45,000 par value, an annual contract rate of 12%, and mature in five years.

**Required**

For each of the following three separate situations, (*a*) determine the bonds' issue price on January 1, 2005, and (*b*) prepare the journal entry to record their issuance.

**1.** Market rate at the date of issuance is 10%.

**2.** Market rate at the date of issuance is 12%.

**3.** Market rate at the date of issuance is 14%.

---

## Problem 10-2B
Straight-line amortization of both bond discount and bond premium

P1  P2  P3

ParFour issues $1,700,000 of 10%, 10-year bonds dated January 1, 2004, that pay interest semiannually on June 30 and December 31. The bonds are issued at a price of $1,505,001.

**Required**

**1.** Prepare the January 1, 2004, journal entry to record the bonds' issuance.

**2.** For each semiannual period, compute (*a*) the cash payment, (*b*) the straight-line discount amortization, and (*c*) the bond interest expense.

**3.** Determine the total bond interest expense to be recognized over the bonds' life.

**4.** Prepare the first two years of an amortization table like Exhibit 10.7 using the straight-line method.

**5.** Prepare the journal entries to record the first two interest payments.

**6.** Assume that the bonds are issued at a price of $2,096,466. Repeat parts 1 through 5.

Zooba Company issues 9%, five-year bonds dated January 1, 2004, with a $160,000 par value. The bonds pay interest on June 30 and December 31 and are issued at a price of $166,494. Their annual market rate is 8% on the issue date.

**Required**

1. Calculate the total bond interest expense over the bonds' life.
2. Prepare a straight-line amortization table like Exhibit 10.11 for the bonds' life.
3. Prepare the journal entries to record the first two interest payments.

**Problem 10-3B**
Straight-line amortization of bond premium; computing bond price

P1  P3

**Check**  (2) 6/30/2006 carrying value, $163,249

---

Refer to the bond details in Problem 10-3B.

**Required**

1. Compute the total bond interest expense over the bonds' life.
2. Prepare an effective interest amortization table like the one in Exhibit 10B.2 for the bonds' life.
3. Prepare the journal entries to record the first two interest payments.
4. Use the market rate at issuance to compute the present value of the remaining cash flows for these bonds as of December 31, 2006. Compare your answer with the amount shown on the amortization table as the balance for that date (from part 2) and explain your findings.

**Problem 10-4B**[B]
Effective interest amortization of bond premium; computing bond price  P1  P3

**Check**  (2) 6/30/2006 carrying value, $163,568

(4) $162,903

---

Roney issues $120,000 of 6%, 15-year bonds dated January 1, 2004, that pay interest semiannually on June 30 and December 31. They are issued at $99,247, and their market rate is 8% at the issue date.

**Required**

1. Prepare the January 1, 2004, journal entry to record the bonds' issuance.
2. Determine the total bond interest expense to be recognized over the life of the bonds.
3. Prepare a straight-line amortization table like the one in Exhibit 10.7 for the bonds' first two years.
4. Prepare the journal entries to record the first two interest payments.

**Problem 10-5B**
Straight-line amortization of bond discount

P1  P2

**Check**  (2) $128,753

(3) 6/30/2005 carrying value, $101,323

---

Refer to the bond details in Problem 10-5B.

**Required**

1. Prepare the January 1, 2004, journal entry to record the bonds' issuance.
2. Determine the total bond interest expense to be recognized over the bonds' life.
3. Prepare an effective interest amortization table like the one in Exhibit 10B.1 for the bonds' first two years.
4. Prepare the journal entries to record the first two interest payments.

**Problem 10-6B**[B]
Effective interest amortization of bond discount

P1  P2

**Check**  (2) $128,753;

(3) 6/30/2005 carrying value, $100,402

---

Hutton issues $900,000 of 13%, four-year bonds dated January 1, 2004, that pay interest semiannually on June 30 and December 31. They are issued at $987,217, and their market rate is 10% at the issue date.

**Required**

1. Prepare the January 1, 2004, journal entry to record the bonds' issuance.
2. Determine the total bond interest expense to be recognized over the bonds' life.
3. Prepare an effective interest amortization table like the one in Exhibit 10B.2 for the bonds' first two years.
4. Prepare the journal entries to record the first two interest payments.
5. Prepare the journal entry to record the bonds' retirement on January 1, 2006, at 106.

**Problem 10-7B**[B]
Effective interest amortization of bond premium; retiring bonds

P1  P3  P4

**Check**  (3) 6/30/2005 carrying value, $958,406

(5) $6,174 loss

*Analysis Component*

6. Assume that the market rate on January 1, 2004, is 14% instead of 10%. Without presenting numbers, describe how this change affects amounts reported on Hutton's financial statements.

## Problem 10-8B

Installment notes

C2   P5

**Check** (2) 9/30/2006 ending balance, $109,673

(4) 9/30/2006 ending balance, $100,000

On October 1, 2004, Milan Enterprises borrows $300,000 cash from a bank by signing a three-year installment note bearing 10% interest. The note requires equal total payments each year on September 30.

**Required**

**1.** Compute the total amount of each installment payment.

**2.** Complete an amortization table for this installment note similar to the one in Exhibit 10.16.

**3.** Prepare the journal entries in which Milan records (*a*) accrued interest as of December 31, 2004 (the end of its annual reporting period) and (*b*) the first annual payment on the note.

**4.** Assume that the note does not require equal total payments but three payments of accrued interest and equal amounts of principal. Complete an amortization table for this note similar to the one in Exhibit 10.15. Prepare the journal entries to record (*a*) accrued interest as of December 31, 2004 (the end of its annual reporting period) and (*b*) the note's first annual payment.

## Problem 10-9B

Ratio of pledged assets to secured liabilities

A2  A3

On January 1, 2005, Hunt Company issues $45,000 of its 12%, 10-year bonds at par that are secured by a mortgage that specifies assets totaling $120,000 as collateral. Also on January 1, 2005, Hound Company issues its 12%, 10-year bonds at their par value of $150,000. Hound secures its bonds by a mortgage that includes $225,000 of pledged assets. The December 31, 2004, balance sheet information for both companies follows:

|  | Hunt Co. | Hound Co. |
|---|---|---|
| Total assets .................. | $180,000* | $750,000† |
| Liabilities |  |  |
| Secured ................... | $ 39,000 | $ 57,000 |
| Unsecured ................ | 42,000 | 505,500 |
| Equity ..................... | 99,000 | 187,500 |
| Total liabilities and equity ....... | $180,000 | $750,000 |

\* 32% are pledged. † 10% are pledged.

**Required**

**Check**  Hunt, 2.11 to 1

**1.** Compute the ratio of pledged assets to secured liabilities for each company at January 1, 2005.

*Analysis Component*

**2.** Which company's bonds appear less risky? What other information might help to evaluate the risks of these companies' bonds?

## Problem 10-10B[c]

Capital lease accounting

C5

**Check** (1) $37,908

(3) Year 3 ending balance, $17,356

Preston Company signs a five-year capital lease with Starbuck Company for office equipment. The annual lease payment is $10,000, and the interest rate is 10%.

**Required**

**1.** Compute the present value of Preston's lease payments.

**2.** Prepare the journal entry to record Preston's capital lease at its inception.

**3.** Complete a lease payment schedule for the five years of the lease with the following headings. Assume that the beginning balance of the lease liability (present value of lease payments) is $37,908. (*Hint:* To find the amount allocated to interest in year 1, multiply the interest rate by the beginning-of-year lease liability. The amount of the annual lease payment not allocated to interest is allocated to principal. Reduce the lease liability by the amount allocated to principal to update the lease liability at each year-end.)

| Period Ending Date | Beginning Balance of Lease Liability | Interest on Lease Liability | Reduction of Lease Liability | Cash Lease Payment | Ending Balance of Lease Liability |
|---|---|---|---|---|---|
|  |  |  |  |  |  |

**4.** Use straight-line depreciation and prepare the journal entry to depreciate the leased asset at the end of year 1. Assume zero salvage value and a five-year life for the office equipment.

Problem Set C is available at the book's Website to further reinforce and assess your learning.

**PROBLEM SET C**

---

*(This serial problem began in Chapter 1 and continues through most of the book. If previous chapter segments were not completed, the serial problem can begin at this point. It is helpful, but not necessary, for you to use the Working Papers that accompany the book.)*

**SERIAL PROBLEM**

Success Systems

Kay Breeze has consulted with her local banker and is considering financing an expansion of her business by obtaining a long-term bank loan. Selected account balances at March 31, 2005, for Success Systems, Inc., follow:

| | | | |
|---|---|---|---|
| Accounts receivable | $22,720 | Total assets | $129,909 |
| Merchandise inventory | 704 | Total liabilities | 875 |
| Plant assets, net | 24,700 | Total equity | 129,034 |

**Required**

**1.** The bank has offered a long-term secured note to Success Systems. This bank's loan procedures require that selected pledged assets (accounts receivable, inventory, and net plant assets) to its secured loan ratio be at least 6. As of March 31, 2005, what is the maximum amount that Success Systems could borrow from this bank?

**2.** If Success Systems borrows the maximum amount allowed from the bank, what percentage of assets would be financed (*a*) by debt, and (*b*) by equity?

---

## BEYOND THE NUMBERS

**BTN 10-1** Refer to **Krispy Kreme**'s financial statements in Appendix A to answer the following:

**1.** Does Krispy Kreme have any issued and outstanding bonds or long-term notes payable?

**2.** How much cash is paid to reduce long-term debt for the year ended February 2, 2003?

**3.** Did it have any additions to long-term debt that provided cash for year-end February 2, 2003?

**REPORTING IN ACTION**

C1 A1

*Roll On*

**4.** Access Krispy Kreme's financial statements for a year ending after February 2, 2003, from its Website (**KrispyKreme.com**) or the SEC's EDGAR database (**www.sec.gov**). Has it issued additional long-term debt since the year-end February 2, 2003? If yes, indentify the amount(s).

---

**BTN 10-2** Key comparative figures ($ thousands) for both **Krispy Kreme** and **Tastykake** follow:

**COMPARATIVE ANALYSIS**

A3

| | Krispy Kreme | | Tastykake | |
|---|---|---|---|---|
| **Key Figures** | **Current Year** | **Prior Year** | **Current Year** | **Prior Year** |
| Current receivables, net | $ 46,319 | $ 38,682 | $20,882 | $22,233 |
| Inventory | 24,365 | 16,159 | 6,777 | 8,412 |
| Property and equipment, net | 202,558 | 112,577 | 58,391 | 59,702 |
| Long-term debt (includes current portion) | 53,201 | 4,643 | 13,500 | 14,900 |

**Required**

**1.** Assume that both Krispy Kreme and Tastykake have pledged substantially all of their current receivables, inventory, and property and equipment to collateralize their long-term debt. Compute the ratio of pledged assets to secured liabilities for both companies.

**2.** Use the ratio you computed in part 1 to determine which company's long-term debt is less risky.

## ETHICS CHALLENGE

C5  A1

**BTN 10-3**   Brevard County needs a new county government building that would cost $24 million. The politicians feel that voters will not approve a municipal bond issue to fund the building since it would increase taxes. They opt to have a state bank issue $24 million of tax-exempt securities to pay for the building construction. The county then will make yearly lease payments (of principal and interest) to repay the obligation. Unlike conventional municipal bonds, the lease payments are not binding obligations on the county and, therefore, require no voter approval.

**Required**

1. Do you think the actions of the politicians and the bankers in this situation are ethical?
2. How do the tax-exempt securities used to pay for the building compare in risk to a conventional municipal bond issued by Brevard County?

## COMMUNICATING IN PRACTICE

P3

**BTN 10-4**   Your business associate mentions that she is considering investing in corporate bonds currently selling at a premium. She says that since the bonds are selling at a premium, they are highly valued and her investment will yield more than the going rate of return for the risk involved. Reply with a memorandum to confirm or correct your associate's interpretation of premium bonds.

## TAKING IT TO THE NET

C1

mhhe.com/wild3e

**BTN 10-5**   Access the March 26, 2003, filing of the 2002 calendar-year 10-K report of Coca-Cola Co. (Ticker KO) from www.sec.gov. Refer to Coca-Cola's statement of cash flows for the year ended December 31, 2002, to answer the following questions.

**Required**

1. Did the company issue any new debt in 2002? If yes, identify the amount.
2. Did the company repay any of its debt in 2002? If yes, identify the amount.
3. Did it obtain more new financing in 2002 from issuing debt or from issuing stock? List amounts.
4. The company's 10-K report shows three years of cash flow data. Does it reveal a trend of issuing more or less debt over this three-year period? Explain.

## TEAMWORK IN ACTION

P2  P3

**BTN 10-6[B]**   Break into teams and complete the following requirements related to effective interest amortization for a premium bond.

1. Each team member is to independently prepare a blank table with proper headings for amortization of a bond premium. When all have finished, compare tables and ensure all are in agreement.

*Parts 2 and 3 require use of these facts:* On January 1, 2005, BC issues $100,000, 9%, five-year bonds at 104.1. The market rate at issuance is 8%. BC pays interest semiannually on June 30 and December 31.

2. In rotation, *each* team member must explain how to complete *one* line of the bond amortization table, including all computations for his or her line. (Round amounts to the nearest dollar.) All members are to fill in their tables during this process. You need not finish the table; stop after all members have explained a line.
3. In rotation, *each* team member is to identify a separate column of the table and indicate what the final number in that column will be and explain the reasoning.
4. Reach a team consensus as to what the total bond interest expense on this bond issue will be if the bond is not retired before maturity.
5. As a team, prepare a list of similarities and differences between the amortization table just prepared and the amortization table if the bond had been issued at a discount.

**Hint:** Rotate teams to report on parts 4 and 5. Consider requiring entries for issuance and interest payments.

## BUSINESS WEEK ACTIVITY

C1

mhhe.com/wild3e

**BTN 10-7**   Read the article "Going Solo" from the November 6, 2000, issue of *Business Week*. (The book's Website provides a free link.)

**Required**

1. Summarize this article's main topic.
2. Why do you think the article refers to foreign investment as "hot money"?
3. What interest rate would you have earned if you had purchased Polish treasury bills in 2000?
4. What do emerging countries offer to lure foreigners to invest in their countries?
5. Why do foreign countries sometimes have trouble retaining foreign investment?

**BTN 10-8**   Aaron Kennedy is the entrepreneur and owner of **Noodles & Company**. Assume that Kennedy's franchise program currently has $250,000 in equity; he is considering a $100,000 expansion to meet increased demand. The $100,000 expansion will yield $16,000 in additional annual income before interest expense. Assume that Kennedy's franchise program currently earns $40,000 annual income before interest expense of $10,000, yielding a return on equity of 12% ($30,000/$250,000). To fund the expansion, Kennedy is considering the issuance of a 10-year, $100,000 note with annual interest payments (the principal due at the end of 10 years).

**ENTREPRENEURIAL DECISION**

A1

**Required**

1. Using return on equity as the decision criterion, show computations to support or reject Kennedy's expansion if interest on the $100,000 note is (*a*) 10%, (*b*) 15%, (*c*) 16%, (*d*) 17%, and (*e*) 20%.
2. What general rule do the results in part 1 illustrate?

**BTN 10-9**   Visit your city or county library. Ask the librarian to help you locate the recent financial records of your city or county government. Examine the records.

**HITTING THE ROAD**

A1

**Required**

1. Determine the amount of long-term bonds and notes currently outstanding.
2. Read the supporting information to your municipality's financial statements and record:
   **a.** Market interest rate(s) when the bonds and/or notes were issued.
   **b.** Date(s) when the bonds and/or notes will mature.
   **c.** Any rating(s) on the bonds and/or notes received from **Moody's**, **Standard & Poor's**, or another rating agency.

**BTN 10-10**   **Grupo Bimbo** (GrupoBimbo.com), **Krispy Kreme**, and **Tastykake** are competitors in the global marketplace. Selected results from these companies follow:

**GLOBAL DECISION**

A3

| Key Figures | Grupo Bimbo (millions of pesos) | | Krispy Kreme ($ thousands) | | Tastykake ($ thousands) | |
|---|---|---|---|---|---|---|
| | Current Year | Prior Year | Current Year | Prior Year | Current Year | Prior Year |
| Current receivables, net . . . . . . . . | 3,794 | 3,207 | $ 46,319 | $ 38,682 | $20,882 | $22,233 |
| Inventory . . . . . . . . . . . . . . . . | 905 | 767 | 24,365 | 16,159 | 6,777 | 8,412 |
| Property and equipment, net . . . . . . . . . . . . . . . . . . | 15,444 | 14,683 | 202,558 | 112,577 | 58,391 | 59,702 |
| Long-term debt (includes current portion) . . . . . . . . . . . | 11,466 | 5,004 | 53,201 | 4,643 | 13,500 | 14,900 |
| Pledged assets to secured liabilities . . . . . . . . . . . | ? | ? | 5.14 | 36.06 | 6.37 | 6.06 |

**Required**

1. Compute Grupo Bimbo's ratio of pledged assets to secured liabilities for the current and prior year. (Assume each company has pledged its current receivables, inventory, and net property and equipment to collateralize its long-term debt.)
2. Use the data provided and the ratios you computed in part 1 to determine which company's long-term debt is least risky.
3. Was Grupo Bimbo a net borrower or net repayer of debt in 2002?

*"Turning a profit to me is getting the dolls into the hands of kids"*—Julz Chavez

# 11

# Reporting and Analyzing Equity

## A Look Back

Chapter 10 focused on long-term liabilities—a main part of most companies' financing. We explained how to value, record, amortize, and report these liabilities in financial statements.

## A Look at This Chapter

This chapter emphasizes details of the corporate form of organization. The accounting concepts and procedures for equity transactions are explained. We also describe how to report and analyze income, earnings per share, and retained earnings.

## A Look Ahead

Chapter 12 focuses on reporting and analyzing a company's cash flows. Special emphasis is directed at the statement of cash flows—reported under the indirect method.

# CAP

## Conceptual

**C1** Identify characteristics of corporations and their organization. *(p. 440)*

**C2** Describe the components of stockholders' equity. *(p. 443)*

**C3** Explain characteristics of common and preferred stock. *(p. 447)*

**C4** Explain the form and content of a complete income statement. *(p. 456)*

**C5** Explain the items reported in retained earnings. *(p. 460)*

## Analytical

**A1** Compute earnings per share and describe this ratio's use. *(p. 458)*

**A2** Compute book value and explain its use in analysis. *(p. 462)*

**A3** Compute dividend yield and explain its use in analysis. *(p. 463)*

**A4** Compute price-earnings ratio and describe its use in analysis. *(p. 463)*

## Procedural

**P1** Record the issuance of corporate stock. *(p. 444)*

**P2** Distribute dividends between common stock and preferred stock. *(p. 447)*

**P3** Record transactions involving cash dividends. *(p. 450)*

**P4** Account for stock dividends and stock splits. *(p. 451)*

**P5** Record purchases and sales of treasury stock and the retirement of stock. *(p. 454)*

## Decision Feature

# Real Girls Invade Corporate World

 SAN FRANCISCO—The daughter of a migrant farmworker, Julz Chavez grew up with handmade toys. The oldest of 11 children, Chavez dreamed of making her own dolls—ones that looked like her. "If your skin is darker, your lips are fuller, and your body's fuller," says Chavez, "you look at the usual dolls and think 'I don't look like that.'" Three decades later, Chavez is an entrepreneur and founder of **Get Real Girl, Inc. (GetRealGirl.com),** a start-up corporation that produces ethnically diverse, active, and intelligent dolls. Skylar is Asian-American, Gabi is Brazilian, and Nakia is African-American; they travel the world with interesting stories to tell.

Chavez's road to the corporate world is a story in itself. She endured the usual moves of a migrant family working in southwestern United States. Still, she was able to graduate and land jobs as an idea person for several toy companies. The jobs frustrated Chavez. She faced the prevailing notion that girls wanted pink, "feminine" toys—like Barbie. So she took a job with Barbie's company, Mattel. "I thought, 'I'm going to change this—I'm going to go work for the biggest toy company in the world.'" Again she met resistance and finally quit to launch her own corporation.

With little money, Chavez struggled to get financial backing. Investors "wanted to see that you're successful, but without the money, you can't be successful," says Chavez. She also had to contend with corporate formation, organization form, capital stock, stock issuance, and various other accounting-related, corporate issues. Still, Chavez persisted. "I'm the outcome of that [worker] struggle to get out of the fields and into business," she says. She was determined "to make real change."

With the motto "Be your own role model," Get Real Girl produced its first dolls in 2000. "This is going to be real girls living in the real world," insists Chavez. Although she continues to confront the realities of a corporate world, such as stock distributions, dividends, and income and equity reporting, her business is making some inroads. Sales projections for next year exceed $5 million. From meager beginnings—where her parents could afford to buy her only one toy a year—Chavez is living her dream. She's also helping young children who, like the young Chavez, need dreams and role models.

[Sources: *Get Real Girl Website,* January 2004; *Entrepreneur,* April 2002; *Mercury News,* July 2002; *Sacramento Bee,* February 2002.]

**Point:** *Bylaws* are guidelines that govern the behavior of individuals employed by and managing the corporation.

**Global:** Some corporate labels are:

| Country | Label |
| --- | --- |
| United States . . . . . | Inc. |
| France . . . . . . . . . | SA |
| United Kingdom | |
| Public . . . . . . . . | PLC |
| Private . . . . . . . | LTD |
| Germany | |
| Public . . . . . . . . | AG |
| Private . . . . . . . | GmbH |
| Sweden . . . . . . . . . | AB |
| Italy . . . . . . . . . . . | SpA |

**Global:** Stockholders' access to financial information varies across countries both in scope and by level of ownership. For instance, stockholders of Mexican companies holding small percent ownership often have difficulty obtaining quality financial information.

owning or controlling votes of more than a 50% share of a corporation's stock can elect the board and control the corporation. Stockholders who do not attend stockholders' meetings must have an opportunity to delegate their voting rights to an agent by signing a **proxy,** a document that gives a designated agent the right to vote the stock.

Day-to-day direction of corporate business is delegated to executive officers appointed by the board. A corporation's chief executive officer (CEO) is often its president. Several vice presidents, who report to the president, are commonly assigned specific areas of management responsibility such as finance, production, and marketing. One person often has the dual role of chairperson of the board of directors and CEO. In this case, the president is usually designated the chief operating officer (COO).

## Stockholders of Corporations

This section explains stockholder rights, stock purchases and sales, and the role of registrar and transfer agents.

**Rights of Stockholders**  When investors buy stock, they acquire all *specific* rights the corporation's charter grants to stockholders. They also acquire *general* rights granted stockholders by the laws of the state in which the company is incorporated. When a corporation has only one class of stock, it is identified as **common stock.** State laws vary, but common stockholders usually have the general right to

1. Vote at stockholders' meetings.
2. Sell or otherwise dispose of their stock.
3. Purchase their proportional share of any common stock later issued by the corporation. This **preemptive right** protects stockholders' proportionate interest in the corporation. For example, a stockholder who owns 25% of a corporation's common stock has the first opportunity to buy 25% of any new common stock issued.
4. Receive the same dividend, if any, on each common share of the corporation.
5. Share in any assets remaining after creditors are paid when, and if, the corporation is liquidated. Each share receives the same amount of remaining liquidated assets.

Stockholders also have the right to receive timely financial reports.

**Stock Certificates and Transfer**  Investors who buy a corporation's stock, sometimes receive a *stock certificate* as proof of share ownership. Many corporations issue

## Exhibit 11.2

Stock Certificate

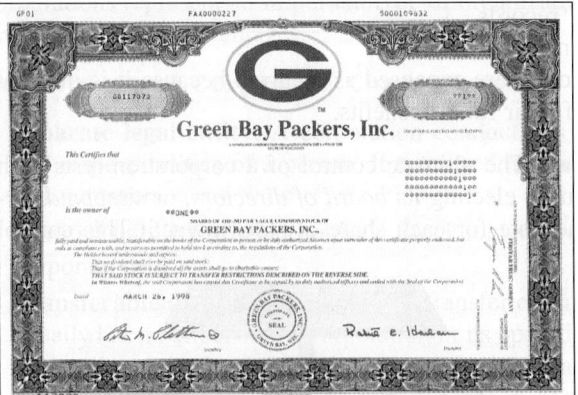

only one certificate for each block of stock purchased. A certificate can be for any number of shares. Exhibit 11.2 shows a stock certificate of the **Green Bay Packers.** A certificate shows the company name, stockholder name, number of shares, and other crucial information. Issuance of certificates is becoming less common. Instead, many stockholders maintain accounts with the corporation or their stockbrokers and never receive actual certificates.

**Registrar and Transfer Agents**  If a corporation's stock is traded on a major stock exchange, the corporation must have a registrar and a transfer agent. A *registrar* keeps stockholder records and prepares official lists of stockholders for stockholder meetings and dividend payments. A *transfer agent* assists with purchases and sales of shares by receiving and issuing certificates as necessary. Registrars and transfer agents are usually large banks or trust companies with computer facilities and staff to do this work.

# Basics of Capital Stock

**Capital stock** is a general term that refers to any shares issued to obtain capital (owner financing). This section introduces terminology and accounting for capital stock.

**Authorized Stock** **Authorized stock** is the number of shares that a corporation's charter allows it to sell. The number of authorized shares usually exceeds the number of shares issued (and outstanding), often by a large amount. (*Outstanding stock* refers to issued stock held by stockholders.) No formal journal entry is required for stock authorization. A corporation must apply to the state for a change in its charter if it wishes to issue more shares than previously authorized. A corporation discloses the number of shares authorized in the equity section of its balance sheet or notes. **Krispy Kreme**'s balance sheet in Appendix A reports 300,000 shares authorized in 2003.

**C2** Describe the components of stockholders' equity.

**Selling (Issuing) Stock** A corporation can sell stock directly or indirectly. To *sell directly,* it advertises its stock issuance to potential buyers. This type of issuance is most common with privately held corporations. To *sell indirectly,* a corporation pays a brokerage house (investment banker) to issue its stock. Some brokerage houses *underwrite* an indirect issuance of stock; that is, they buy the stock from the corporation and take all gains or losses from its resale.

**Market Value of Stock** **Market value per share** is the price at which a stock is bought and sold. Expected future earnings, dividends, growth, and other company and economic factors influence market value. Traded stocks' market values are available daily in newspapers such as *The Wall Street Journal* and online. The current market value of previously issued shares (for example, the price of stock in trades between investors) does not impact the issuing corporation's stockholders' equity.

**Classes of Stock** When all authorized shares have the same rights and characteristics, the stock is called *common stock.* A corporation is sometimes authorized to issue more than one class of stock, including preferred stock and different classes of common stock. **American Greetings**, for instance, has two types of common stock: Class A stock has 1 vote per share and Class B stock has 10 votes per share.

**Par Value Stock** **Par value stock** is a class of stock assigned a **par value,** which is an amount assigned per share by the corporation in its charter. For example, **Novell**'s common stock has a par value of $0.10. Other commonly assigned par values are $10, $5, $1 and $0.01. There is no restriction on the assigned par value. In many states, the par value of a stock establishes **minimum legal capital,** which refers to the least amount that the buyers of stock must contribute to the corporation or be subject to paying at a future date. For example, if a corporation issues 1,000 shares of $10 par value stock, the corporation's minimum legal capital in these states would be $10,000. Minimum legal capital is intended to protect a corporation's creditors. Since creditors cannot demand payment from stockholders' personal assets, their claims are limited to the corporation's assets and any minimum legal capital. At liquidation, creditor claims are paid before any amounts are distributed to stockholders.

**Point:** Managers are motivated to set a low par value when minimum legal capital or state issuance taxes are based on par value.

**Point:** Minimum legal capital was intended to protect creditors by requiring a minimum amount of net assets in the corporation. However, such net assets can be lost by unprofitable operations.

**No-Par Value Stock** **No-par value stock,** or simply *no-par stock,* is stock *not* assigned a value per share by the corporate charter. Its advantage is that it can be issued at any price without the possibility of a minimum legal capital deficiency.

## Exhibit 11.3

Equity Composition

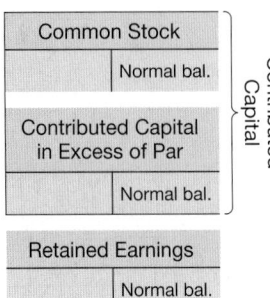

**Corporation**

**Stated Value Stock** **Stated value stock** is no-par stock to which the directors assign a "stated" value per share. Stated value per share becomes the minimum legal capital per share in this case.

**Stockholders' Equity** A corporation's equity is known as **stockholders' equity,** also called *shareholders' equity* or *corporate capital.* Stockholders' equity consists of (1) contributed (or paid-in) capital and (2) retained earnings; see Exhibit 11.3. **Contributed capital** is the total amount of cash and other assets the corporation receives from its stockholders in exchange for common stock. **Retained earnings** is the cumulative net income (and loss) retained by a corporation.

> ## Quick Check
>
> 1. Which of the following is *not* a characteristic of the corporate form of business? (*a*) Ease of capital accumulation, (*b*) Stockholder responsibility for corporate debts, (*c*) Ease in transferability of ownership rights, or (*d*) Double taxation.
> 2. Why is a corporation's income said to be taxed twice?
> 3. What is a proxy?

Answers—p. 470

# Common Stock

**P1** Record the issuance of corporate stock.

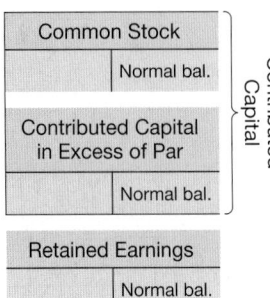

Topic Tackler 11-1

Accounting for the issuance of common stock affects only contributed capital accounts; no retained earnings accounts are affected.

## Issuing Par Value Stock

Par value stock can be issued at par, at a premium (above par), or at a discount (below par). In each case, stock can be exchanged for either cash or noncash assets.

**Issuing Par Value Stock at Par** When common stock is issued at par value, we record amounts for both the asset(s) received and the par value stock issued. To illustrate, the entry to record Dillon Snowboards' issuance of 30,000 shares of $10 par value stock for $300,000 cash on June 5, 2005, follows

| Assets | = Liabilities + | Equity |
|---|---|---|
| +300,000 | | +300,000 |

| June 5 | Cash . . . . . . . . . . . . . . . . . . . . . . . . . . . . . . . . . | 300,000 | |
|---|---|---|---|
| | Common Stock, $10 Par Value . . . . . . . . . . | | 300,000 |
| | *Issued 30,000 shares of $10 par value common stock at par.* | | |

Exhibit 11.4 shows the stockholders' equity of Dillon Snowboards at year-end 2005 (its first year of operations) after income of $65,000 and no dividend payments.

**Issuing Par Value Stock at a Premium** A **premium on stock** occurs when a corporation sells its stock for more than par (or stated) value. To illustrate, if Dillon Snowboards issues its $10 par value common stock at $12 per share, its stock is sold at a $2 per share premium. The premium, known as **contributed capital in excess of par value,** is reported as part of equity; it is not revenue and is not listed on the income statement. The entry to

**Stockholders' Equity**

Contributed capital

    Common Stock—$10 par value; 50,000 shares authorized;

        30,000 shares issued and outstanding ................................... $300,000

Retained earnings ......................................................... 65,000

Total stockholders' equity ............................................... $365,000

**Exhibit 11.4**

Stockholders' Equity for Stock Issued at Par

record Dillon Snowboards' issuance of 30,000 shares of $10 par value stock for $12 per share on June 5, 2005, follows

| June 5 | Cash ................................. | 360,000 | |
| |     Common Stock, $10 Par Value ........... | | 300,000 |
| |     **Contributed Capital in Excess of** | | |
| |       **Par Value, Common Stock** .......... | | **60,000** |
| |     *Sold and issued 30,000 shares of $10 par* | | |
| |     *value common stock at $12 per share.* | | |

Assets  = Liabilities +  Equity
+360,000                 +300,000
                          +60,000

The Contributed Capital in Excess of Par Value account is added to the par value of the stock in the equity section of the balance sheet as shown in Exhibit 11.5.

**Point:** The *Contributed Capital* terminology is interchangeable with *Paid-In Capital.*

**Stockholders' Equity**

Contributed capital

    Common Stock—$10 par value; 50,000 shares authorized;

        30,000 shares issued and outstanding ......................... $300,000

    **Contributed capital in excess of par value, common stock** ....... <u>60,000</u>

Total contributed capital ......................................... $360,000

Retained earnings ................................................. 65,000

Total stockholders' equity ........................................ $425,000

**Exhibit 11.5**

Stockholders' Equity for Stock Issued at a Premium

**Issuing Par Value Stock at a Discount**   A **discount on stock** occurs when a corporation sells its stock for less than par (or stated) value. Most states prohibit the issuance of stock at a discount. In states that allow stock to be issued at a discount, its buyers usually become contingently liable to creditors for the discount. If stock is issued at a discount, the amount by which issue price is less than par is debited to a *Discount on Common Stock* account, a contra to the common stock account, and its balance is subtracted from the par value of stock in the equity section of the balance sheet. This discount is not an expense and does not appear on the income statement.

**Point:** Retained earnings can be negative, reflecting accumulated losses. Amazon.com had an accumulated deficit of $3 billion at the start of 2003.

## Issuing No-Par Value Stock

When no-par stock is issued and is not assigned a stated value, the amount the corporation receives becomes legal capital and is recorded as Common Stock. This means that the entire proceeds are credited to a no-par stock account. To illustrate, a corporation records its issue of 1,000 shares of no-par stock for $40 cash per share as follows:

| Oct. 20 | Cash ................................. | 40,000 | |
| |     Common Stock, No-Par Value ........... | | 40,000 |
| |     *Issued 1,000 shares of no-par value common stock* | | |
| |     *at $40 per share.* | | |

Assets  = Liabilities +  Equity
+40,000                  +40,000

**Frequency of Stock Types**

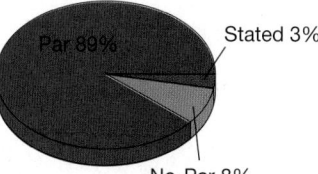

Par 89%
Stated 3%
No-Par 8%

## Issuing Stated Value Stock

When no-par stock is issued and assigned a stated value, its stated value becomes legal capital and is credited to a stated value stock account. Assuming that stated value stock is issued at an amount in excess of stated value (the usual case), the excess is credited to

Contributed Capital in Excess of Stated Value, Common Stock, which is reported in the contributed capital part of the stockholders' equity section. To illustrate, a corporation that issues 1,000 shares of no-par common stock having a stated value of $40 per share in return for $50 cash per share records this as follows:

Assets = Liabilities + Equity
+50,000          +40,000
                 +10,000

| Oct. 20 | Cash | 50,000 | |
|---|---|---|---|
| | Common Stock, $40 Stated Value | | 40,000 |
| | Contributed Capital in Excess of Stated Value, Common Stock | | 10,000 |
| | *Issued 1,000 shares of $40 per share stated value stock at $50 per share.* | | |

## Issuing Stock for Noncash Assets

A corporation can receive assets other than cash in exchange for its stock. (It can also assume liabilities on the assets received such as a mortgage on property received.) The corporation records the assets received at their market values as of the date of the transaction. The stock given in exchange is recorded at its par (or stated) value with any excess recorded in the Contributed Capital in Excess of Par (or Stated) Value account. (If no-par stock is issued, the stock is recorded at the assets' market value.) To illustrate, the entry to record receipt of land valued at $105,000 in return for issuance of 4,000 shares of $20 par value common stock is

Assets = Liabilities + Equity
+105,000          +80,000
                  +25,000

| June 10 | Land | 105,000 | |
|---|---|---|---|
| | Common Stock, $20 Par Value | | 80,000 |
| | Contributed Capital in Excess of Par Value, Common Stock | | 25,000 |
| | *Exchanged 4,000 shares of $20 par value common stock for land.* | | |

A corporation sometimes gives shares of its stock to promoters in exchange for their services in organizing the corporation, which the corporation records as **Organization Expenses.** The entry to record receipt of services valued at $12,000 in organizing the corporation in return for 600 shares of $15 par value common stock is

Assets = Liabilities + Equity
              −12,000
              +9,000
              +3,000

| June 5 | Organization Expenses | 12,000 | |
|---|---|---|---|
| | Common Stock, $15 Par Value | | 9,000 |
| | Contributed Capital in Excess of Par Value, Common Stock | | 3,000 |
| | *Gave promoters 600 shares of $15 par value common stock in exchange for their services.* | | |

Corporations sometimes issue stock through a **stock subscription,** which is the sale of stock to investors who agree to buy a certain number of shares at specified future dates and prices. The usual case occurs when a new corporation is formed and the organizers want commitments for both immediate and future financing needs.

### Quick Check

4. A company issues 7,000 shares of its $10 par value common stock in exchange for equipment valued at $105,000. The entry to record this transaction includes a credit to (*a*) Contributed Capital in Excess of Par Value, Common Stock, for $35,000. (*b*) Retained Earnings for $35,000. (*c*) Common Stock, $10 Par Value, for $105,000.

5. What is a premium on stock?

6. Who is intended to be protected by minimum legal capital?

# Preferred Stock

A corporation can issue two basic kinds of stock, common and preferred. **Preferred stock** has special rights that give it priority (or senior status) over common stock in one or more areas. Special rights typically include a preference for receiving dividends and for the distribution of assets if the corporation is liquidated.

Preferred stock carries all rights of common stock unless the corporate charter nullifies them. Most preferred stock, for instance, does not confer the right to vote. Exhibit 11.6 shows that preferred stock is issued by about one-fourth of large corporations. All corporations issue common stock.

No Preferred Stock 73%

Issued Preferred Stock 27%

**Exhibit 11.6**

Corporations and Preferred Stock

## Issuance of Preferred Stock

Preferred stock usually has a par value. Like common stock, it can be sold at a price different from par. Preferred stock is recorded in its own separate contributed capital accounts. To illustrate, if Dillon Snowboards issues 50 shares of $100 par value preferred stock for $6,000 cash on July 1, 2005, the entry is

**C3**  Explain characteristics of common and preferred stock.

| July 1 | Cash ................................. | 6,000 | |
| | Preferred Stock, $100 Par Value .......... | | 5,000 |
| | Contributed Capital in Excess of Par Value, | | |
| | Preferred Stock .................... | | 1,000 |
| | *Issued preferred stock for cash.* | | |

Assets = Liabilities + Equity
+6,000                    +5,000
                          +1,000

The preferred stock accounts are included as part of contributed capital. The equity section of the year-end balance sheet for Dillon Snowboards, including preferred stock, is shown in Exhibit 11.7. (This exhibit assumes that common stock was issued at par.) Note that issuing no-par preferred stock is similar to issuing no-par common stock. Also, the entries for issuing preferred stock for noncash assets are similar to those for common stock.

**Exhibit 11.7**

Stockholders' Equity with Common and Preferred Stock

| **Stockholders' Equity** | | |
| --- | --- | --- |
| Contributed capital | | |
| Common stock—$10 par value; 50,000 shares authorized; | | |
| 30,000 shares issued and outstanding ......................... | $300,000 | |
| Preferred stock—$100 par value; 1,000 shares authorized; | | |
| 50 shares issued and outstanding ...................... | 5,000 | |
| Contributed capital in excess of par value, preferred stock ....... | 1,000 | |
| Total contributed capital ...................................... | | $306,000 |
| Retained earnings ........................................... | | 65,000 |
| Total stockholders' equity ..................................... | | $371,000 |

## Dividend Preference of Preferred Stock

Preferred stock usually carries a preference for dividends, meaning that preferred stockholders are allocated their dividends before any dividends are allocated to common stockholders. The dividends allocated to preferred stockholders are usually expressed as a dollar amount per share or a percent applied to par value. A preference for dividends does *not* ensure dividends. If the directors do not declare a dividend, neither the preferred nor the common stockholders receive one.

**P2**  Distribute dividends between common stock and preferred stock.

**Cumulative or Noncumulative Dividend**  Most preferred stocks carry a cumulative dividend right. **Cumulative preferred stock** has a right to be paid both the current and all prior periods' unpaid dividends before any dividend is paid to common stockholders. When preferred stock is cumulative and the directors either do not declare a dividend to preferred stockholders or declare one that does not cover the total amount of cumulative

**Point:** Dividend preference does not imply that preferred stockholders receive more dividends than common stockholders, nor does it guarantee a dividend.

dividend, the unpaid dividend amount is called **dividend in arrears.** Accumulation of dividends in arrears on cumulative preferred stock does not guarantee they will be paid. **Noncumulative preferred stock** confers no right to prior periods' unpaid dividends if they were not declared in those prior periods.

To illustrate the difference between cumulative and noncumulative preferred stock, assume that a corporation's outstanding stock includes (1) 1,000 shares of $100 par, 9% preferred stock—yielding $9,000 per year in potential dividends, and (2) 4,000 shares of $50 par value common stock. During 2004, the first year of operations, the directors declare cash dividends of $5,000. In year 2005, they declare cash dividends of $42,000. See Exhibit 11.8 for the allocation of dividends for these two years. Note that allocation of year 2005 dividends depends on whether the preferred stock is noncumulative or cumulative. With noncumulative preferred, the preferred stockholders never receive the $4,000 skipped in 2004. If the preferred stock is cumulative, the $4,000 in arrears is paid in 2005 before any other dividends are paid.

**Example:** What dividends do cumulative preferred stockholders receive in 2005 if the corporation paid only $2,000 of dividends in 2004? How does this affect dividends to common stockholders in 2005? *Answers:* $16,000 ($7,000 dividends in arrears, plus $9,000 current preferred dividends). Dividends to common stockholders decrease to $26,000.

## Exhibit 11.8

Allocation of Dividends (noncumulative vs. cumulative preferred stock)

| | Preferred | Common |
|---|---|---|
| **Preferred Stock Is Noncumulative** | | |
| Year 2004 . . . . . . . . . . . . . . . . . . . . . . . . . . . . . . | $ 5,000 | $      0 |
| Year 2005 | | |
|    Step 1: Current year's preferred dividend  . . . . . . . | $ 9,000 | |
|    Step 2: Remainder to common . . . . . . . . . . . . . . | | $33,000 |
| **Preferred Stock Is Cumulative** | | |
| Year 2004 . . . . . . . . . . . . . . . . . . . . . . . . . . . . . . | $ 5,000 | $      0 |
| Year 2005 | | |
|    Step 1: Dividend in arrears . . . . . . . . . . . . . . . . . . | $ 4,000 | |
|    Step 2: Current year's preferred dividend  . . . . . . . | 9,000 | |
|    Step 3: Remainder to common . . . . . . . . . . . . . . | | $29,000 |
| Totals for year 2005 . . . . . . . . . . . . . . . . . . . . . | $13,000 | $29,000 |

A liability for a dividend does not exist until the directors declare a dividend. If a preferred dividend date passes and the corporation's board fails to declare the dividend on its cumulative preferred stock, the dividend in arrears is not a liability. The *full-disclosure principle* requires a corporation to report (usually in a note) the amount of preferred dividends in arrears as of the balance sheet date.

**Participating or Nonparticipating Dividend**  **Nonparticipating preferred stock** has a feature that limits dividends to a maximum amount each year. This maximum is often stated as a percent of the stock's par value or as a specific dollar amount per share. Once preferred stockholders receive this amount, the common stockholders receive any and all additional dividends. **Participating preferred stock** has a feature allowing preferred stockholders to share with common stockholders in any dividends paid in excess of the percent or dollar amount stated on the preferred stock. This participation feature does not apply until common stockholders receive dividends equal to the preferred stock's dividend percent. Many corporations are authorized to issue participating preferred stock but rarely do, and most managers never expect to issue it.[1]

---

[1] Participating preferred stock is usually authorized as a defense against a possible corporate *takeover* by an "unfriendly" investor (or a group of investors) who intends to buy enough voting common stock to gain control. Taking a term from spy novels, the financial world refers to this type of plan as a *poison pill* that a company swallows if enemy investors threaten its capture. A poison pill usually works as follows: A corporation's common stockholders on a given date are granted the right to purchase a large amount of participating preferred stock at a very low price. This right to purchase preferred shares is *not* transferable. If an unfriendly investor buys a large block of common shares (whose right to purchase participating preferred shares does *not* transfer to this buyer), the board can issue preferred shares at a low price to the remaining common shareholders who retained the right to purchase. Future dividends are then divided between the newly issued participating preferred shares and the common shares. This usually transfers value from common shares to preferred shares, causing the unfriendly investor's common stock to lose much of its value and reduces the potential benefit of a hostile takeover.

## Convertible Preferred Stock

Preferred stock is more attractive to investors if it carries a right to exchange preferred shares for a fixed number of common shares. **Convertible preferred stock** gives holders the option to exchange their preferred shares for common shares at a specified rate. When a company prospers and its common stock increases in value, convertible preferred stockholders can share in this success by converting their preferred stock into more valuable common stock.

## Callable Preferred Stock

**Callable preferred stock** gives the issuing corporation the right to purchase (retire) this stock from its holders at specified future prices and dates. Many issues of preferred stock are callable. The amount paid to call and retire a preferred share is its **call price,** or *redemption value,* and is set when the stock is issued. The call price normally includes the stock's par value plus a premium giving holders additional return on their investment. When the issuing corporation calls and retires a preferred stock, the terms of the agreement often require it to pay the call price *and* any dividends in arrears.

**Point:** The issuing corporation has the right, or option, to retire its callable preferred stock.

## Reasons for Issuing Preferred Stock

Corporations issue preferred stock for several reasons. One is to raise capital without sacrificing control. For example, suppose a company's organizers have $100,000 cash to invest and organize a corporation that needs $200,000 of capital to start. If they sell $200,000 worth of common stock (with $100,000 to the organizers), they would have only 50% control and would need to negotiate extensively with other stockholders in making policy. However, if they issue $100,000 worth of common stock to themselves and sell outsiders $100,000 of 8%, cumulative preferred stock with no voting rights, they retain control.

A second reason to issue preferred stock is to boost the return earned by common stockholders. To illustrate, suppose a corporation's organizers expect to earn an annual after-tax income of $24,000 on an investment of $200,000. If they sell and issue $200,000 worth of common stock, the $24,000 income produces a 12% return on the $200,000 of common stockholders' equity. However, if they issue $100,000 of 8% preferred stock to outsiders and $100,000 of common stock to themselves, their own return increases to 16% per year, as shown in Exhibit 11.9.

| | |
|---|---|
| Net (after-tax) income . . . . . . . . . . . . . . . . . . . . . . . . . . . . . | $24,000 |
| Less preferred dividends at 8% . . . . . . . . . . . . . . . . . . . . . . . | (8,000) |
| Balance to common stockholders | $16,000 |
| Return to common stockholders ($16,000/$100,000) . . . . . . . | 16% |

### Exhibit 11.9

Return to Common Stockholders When Preferred Stock Is Issued

Common stockholders earn 16% instead of 12% because assets contributed by preferred stockholders are invested to earn $12,000 while the preferred dividend is only $8,000. Use of preferred stock to increase return to common stockholders is an example of **financial leverage** (also called *trading on the equity*). As a general rule, when the dividend rate on preferred stock is less than the rate the corporation earns on its assets, the effect of issuing preferred stock is to increase (or *lever*) the rate earned by common stockholders.

Other reasons for issuing preferred stock include its appeal to some investors who believe that the corporation's common stock is too risky or that the expected return on common stock is too low.

**Point:** Financial leverage also occurs when debt is issued and the interest rate paid on it is less than the rate earned from using the assets the creditors lend the company.

**Decision Maker**

**Concert Organizer**  Assume that you alter your business strategy from organizing concerts targeted at under 1,000 people to those targeted at between 5,000 to 20,000 people. You also incorporate because of increased risk of lawsuits and a desire to issue stock for financing. It is important that you control the company for decisions on whom to schedule. What types of stock do you offer?

Answer—p. 469

---

### Quick Check

7. In what ways does preferred stock often have priority over common stock?

8. Increasing the return to common stockholders by issuing preferred stock is an example of (*a*) Financial leverage. (*b*) Cumulative earnings. (*c*) Dividend in arrears.

9. A corporation has issued and outstanding (i) 9,000 shares of $50 par value, 10% cumulative, nonparticipating preferred stock and (ii) 27,000 shares of $10 par value common stock. No dividends have been declared for the two prior years. During the current year, the corporation declares $288,000 in dividends. The amount paid to common shareholders is (*a*) $243,000. (*b*) $153,000. (*c*) $135,000.

Answers—p. 470

---

# Dividends

**P3** Record transactions involving cash dividends.

This section describes both cash and stock dividend transactions.

## Cash Dividends

The decision to pay cash dividends rests with the board of directors and involves more than evaluating the amounts of retained earnings and cash. The directors, for instance, may decide to keep the cash to invest in the corporation's growth, to meet emergencies, to take advantage of unexpected opportunities, or to pay off debt. Alternatively, many corporations pay cash dividends to their stockholders at regular dates. These cash flows provide a return to investors and almost always affect the stock's market value.

**Percent of Corporations Paying Dividends**

**Accounting for Cash Dividends** Dividend payment involves three important dates: declaration, record, and payment. **Date of declaration** is the date the directors vote to declare and pay a dividend. This creates a legal liability of the corporation to its stockholders. **Date of record** is the future date specified by the directors for identifying those stockholders listed in the corporation's records to receive dividends. The date of record usually follows the date of declaration by at least two weeks. Persons who own stock on the date of record receive dividends. **Date of payment** is the date when the corporation makes payment; it follows the date of record by enough time to allow the corporation to arrange checks, money transfers, or other means to pay dividends.

**Point:** A cash dividend reduces a company's assets (and its working capital).

To illustrate, the entry to record a January 9 declaration of a $1 per share cash dividend by the directors of Z-Tech, Inc., with 5,000 outstanding shares is

Assets = Liabilities + Equity
+5,000 −5,000

**Date of Declaration**

| Jan. 9 | Retained Earnings ...................... | 5,000 | |
| | Common Dividend Payable............. | | 5,000 |
| | *Declared $1 per common share cash dividend.*[2] | | |

Topic Tackler 11-2

Common Dividend Payable is a current liability. The date of record for the Z-Tech dividend is January 22. *No formal journal entry is needed on the date of record.* The February 1 date of payment requires an entry to record both the settlement of the liability and the reduction of the cash balance, as follows:

Assets = Liabilities + Equity
−5,000 −5,000

**Date of Payment**

| Feb. 1 | Common Dividend Payable ................ | 5,000 | |
| | Cash............................... | | 5,000 |
| | *Paid $1 per common share cash dividend.* | | |

---

[2] An alternative entry is to debit Dividends instead of Retained Earnings. The balance in Dividends is then closed to Retained Earnings at the end of the reporting period. The effect is the same: Retained Earnings is decreased and a Dividend Payable is increased. For simplicity, all assignments use the Retained Earnings account to record dividend declarations.

**Deficits and Cash Dividends**   A corporation with a debit (abnormal) balance for retained earnings is said to have a **retained earnings deficit,** which arises when a company incurs cumulative losses and/or pays more dividends than total earnings from current and prior years. A deficit is reported as a deduction on the balance sheet, as shown in Exhibit 11.10. Most states prohibit a corporation with a deficit from paying a cash dividend to its stockholders. This legal restriction is designed to protect creditors by preventing distribution of assets to stockholders when the company may be in financial difficulty.

**Point:** It is often said a dividend is a distribution of retained earnings, but it is more precise to describe a dividend as a distribution of assets to satisfy stockholder claims.

**Point:** The Retained Earnings Deficit account is also called *Accumulated Deficit.*

| | |
|---|---:|
| Common stock—$10 par value, 5,000 shares authorized, issued, and outstanding ....... | $50,000 |
| Retained earnings deficit ............................................................ | (6,000) |
| Total stockholders' equity ........................................................... | $44,000 |

**Exhibit 11.10**

Stockholders' Equity with a Deficit

Some state laws allow cash dividends to be paid by returning a portion of the capital contributed by stockholders. This type of dividend is called a **liquidating cash dividend,** or simply *liquidating dividend,* because it returns a part of the original investment back to the stockholders. This requires a debit entry to one of the contributed capital accounts instead of Retained Earnings at the declaration date.

**Decision Insight**

**Where's the Money**   Cash dividends have declined as a percent of stock prices. More companies are instead buying back shares, paying down debt, or expanding business when they have extra cash.

**Quick Check**

10. What type of an account is the Common Dividend Payable account?
11. What three crucial dates are involved in the process of paying a cash dividend?
12. When does a dividend become a company's legal obligation?

Answers—p. 470

## Stock Dividends

A **stock dividend,** declared by a corporation's directors, is a distribution of additional shares of the corporation's own stock to its stockholders without the receipt of any payment in return. Stock dividends and cash dividends are different. A stock dividend does not reduce assets and equity but instead transfers a portion of equity from retained earnings to contributed capital.

**P4**   Account for stock dividends and stock splits.

**Reasons for Stock Dividends**   Stock dividends exist for at least two reasons. First, directors are said to use stock dividends to keep the market price of the stock affordable. For example, if a corporation continues to earn income but does not issue cash dividends, the price of its common stock likely increases. The price of such a stock may become so high that it discourages some investors from buying the stock (especially in lots of 100 and 1,000). When a corporation has a stock dividend, it increases the number of outstanding shares and lowers the per share stock price. Another reason for a stock dividend is to provide evidence of management's confidence that the company is doing well and will continue to do well.

**Point:** Berkshire Hathaway has not declared a cash dividend since 1967. Its recent stock price was about $75,000 per share.

**Accounting for Stock Dividends**   A stock dividend affects the components of equity by transferring part of retained earnings to contributed capital accounts, sometimes described as *capitalizing* retained earnings. Accounting for a stock dividend depends on whether it is a small or large stock dividend. A **small stock dividend** is a distribution of 25% or less of previously outstanding shares. It is recorded by capitalizing retained earnings for an amount equal to the market value of the shares to be distributed. A **large stock dividend** is a distribution of more than 25% of previously outstanding shares. A large stock dividend is recorded by capitalizing retained earnings for the minimum amount required by state law governing the corporation. Most states require capitalizing retained earnings equal to the par or stated value of the stock.

To illustrate stock dividends, we use the equity section of X-Quest's balance sheet shown in Exhibit 11.11 just *before* its declaration of a stock dividend on December 31.

## Exhibit 11.11

Stockholders' Equity *before* Declaring a Stock Dividend

| **Stockholders' Equity (before dividend)** | |
| --- | --- |
| Common stock—$10 par value, 15,000 shares authorized, | |
| 10,000 shares issued and outstanding . . . . . . . . . . . . . . . . . . . . . . . . . . . . | $100,000 |
| Contributed capital in excess of par value, common stock . . . . . . . . . . . . . | 8,000 |
| Total contributed capital . . . . . . . . . . . . . . . . . . . . . . . . . . . . . . . . . . . . | 108,000 |
| Retained earnings . . . . . . . . . . . . . . . . . . . . . . . . . . . . . . . . . . . . . . . . . | 35,000 |
| Total stockholders' equity . . . . . . . . . . . . . . . . . . . . . . . . . . . . . . . . . . . | $143,000 |

**Recording a small stock dividend.**   Assume that X-Quest's directors declare a 10% stock dividend on December 31. This stock dividend of 1,000 shares, computed as 10% of its 10,000 issued and outstanding shares, is to be distributed on January 20 to the stockholders of record on January 15. Since the market price of X-Quest's stock on December 31 is $15 per share, this small stock dividend declaration is recorded as follows:

**Point:** Small stock dividends are recorded at market value.

Assets = Liabilities + Equity
               −15,000
               +10,000
                +5,000

| | **Date of Declaration** | | |
| --- | --- | --- | --- |
| Dec. 31 | Retained Earnings . . . . . . . . . . . . . . . . . . . . . . . . | 15,000 | |
| | Common Stock Dividend Distributable . . . . . | | 10,000 |
| | Contributed Capital in Excess of Par Value, | | |
| | Common Stock . . . . . . . . . . . . . . . . . . . | | 5,000 |
| | *Declared a 1,000-share (10%) stock dividend.* | | |

**Point:** The term *Distributable* (not *Payable*) is used for stock dividends.

**Point:** The credit to Contributed Capital in Excess of Par Value is recorded when the stock dividend is declared. This account is not affected when stock is later distributed.

**Point:** A stock dividend is never a liability on a balance sheet because it never reduces assets.

The $10,000 credit in the declaration entry equals the par value of the shares and is recorded in a contributed capital account, *Common Stock Dividend Distributable*. Its balance exists only until the shares are issued. The $5,000 credit equals the amount by which market value exceeds par value. This amount increases the Contributed Capital in Excess of Par Value account in anticipation of the issue of shares. In general, the balance sheet changes in three ways when a stock dividend is declared. First, the amount of equity attributed to common stock increases; for X-Quest, from $100,000 to $110,000 for 1,000 additional declared shares. Second, contributed capital in excess of par increases by the excess of market value over par value for the declared shares. Third, retained earnings decreases, reflecting the transfer of amounts to both common stock and contributed capital in excess of par. The stockholders' equity of X-Quest is shown in Exhibit 11.12 *after* its 10% stock dividend is declared on December 31.

## Exhibit 11.12

Stockholders' Equity *after* Declaring a Stock Dividend

| **Stockholders' Equity (after dividend)** | |
| --- | --- |
| Common stock—$10 par value, 15,000 shares authorized, | |
| 10,000 shares issued and outstanding . . . . . . . . . . . . . . . . . . . . . . . . . . . . | $100,000 |
| **Common stock dividend distributable—1,000 shares** . . . . . . . . . . . . | **10,000** |
| **Contributed capital in excess of par value, common stock** . . . . . . . | **13,000** |
| Total contributed capital . . . . . . . . . . . . . . . . . . . . . . . . . . . . . . . . . . . . | 123,000 |
| **Retained earnings** . . . . . . . . . . . . . . . . . . . . . . . . . . . . . . . . . . . . . . . | **20,000** |
| Total stockholders' equity . . . . . . . . . . . . . . . . . . . . . . . . . . . . . . . . . . . | $143,000 |

**Point:** A stock dividend does not affect assets (or working capital).

No entry is made on the date of record for a stock dividend. On January 20, the date of payment, X-Quest distributes the new shares to stockholders and records this entry:

Assets = Liabilities + Equity
               −10,000
               +10,000

| | **Date of Payment** | | |
| --- | --- | --- | --- |
| Jan. 20 | Common Stock Dividend Distributable. . . . . . . . | 10,000 | |
| | Common Stock, $10 Par Value . . . . . . . . . . | | 10,000 |
| | *To record issuance of common stock dividend.* | | |

The combined effect of these stock dividend entries is to transfer (or capitalize) $15,000 of retained earnings to contributed capital accounts. The amount of capitalized retained earnings equals the market value of the 1,000 issued shares ($15 × 1,000 shares). Note that a stock dividend has no effect on the ownership percent of individual stockholders.

Answer—p. 469

> ### Decision Maker
>
> **Entrepreneur**  A company you cofounded and own stock in announces a 50% stock dividend. Has the value of your stock investment increased, decreased, or remained the same?

***Recording a large stock dividend.***  A corporation capitalizes retained earnings equal to the minimum amount required by state law for a large stock dividend. For most states, this amount is the par or stated value of the newly issued shares. To illustrate, suppose X-Quest's board declares a stock dividend of 30% instead of 10% on December 31. Since this dividend is more than 25%, it is treated as a large stock dividend. Thus, the par value of the 3,000 dividend shares is capitalized at the date of declaration with this entry:

**Point:** Large stock dividends are recorded at par or stated value.

### Date of Declaration

| | | | |
|---|---|---|---|
| Dec. 31 | Retained Earnings . . . . . . . . . . . . . . . . . . . . . . | 30,000 | |
| | Common Stock Dividend Distributable . . . . . | | 30,000 |
| | *Declared a 3,000-share (30%) stock dividend.* | | |

Assets = Liabilities + Equity
−30,000
+30,000

This transaction decreases retained earnings and increases contributed capital by $30,000. On the date of payment the company debits Common Stock Dividend Distributable and credits Common Stock for $30,000. Note that the effects from a large stock dividend on balance sheet accounts are similar to those for a small stock dividend except for the absence of any effect on contributed capital in excess of par.

## Stock Splits

A **stock split** is the distribution of additional shares to stockholders according to their percent ownership. When a stock split occurs, the corporation "calls in" its outstanding shares and issues more than one new share in exchange for each old share. Splits can be done in any ratio, including 2-for-1, 3-for-1, or higher. Stock splits reduce the par or stated value per share.

To illustrate, CompTec has 100,000 outstanding shares of $20 par value common stock with a current market value of $88 per share. A 2-for-1 stock split cuts par value in half as it replaces 100,000 shares of $20 par value stock with 200,000 shares of $10 par value stock. Market value is reduced from $88 per share to about $44 per share. The split does not affect any equity amounts reported on the balance sheet or any individual stockholder's percent ownership. Both the Contributed Capital and Retained Earnings accounts are unchanged by a split, and *no journal entry is made*. The only effect on the accounts is a change in the stock account description. CompTec's 2-for-1 split on its $20 par value stock means that after the split, it changes its stock account title to Common Stock, $10 Par Value. This stock's description on the balance sheet also changes to reflect the additional authorized, issued, and outstanding shares and the new par value.

**Point:** A reverse stock split is the opposite of a stock split. It increases both the market value per share and the par or stated value per share by specifying the split ratio to be less than 1-for-1, such as 1-for-2. A reverse stock split results in fewer shares.

The difference between stock splits and large stock dividends is often blurred. Many companies report stock splits in their financial statements without calling in the original shares by simply changing their par value. This type of "split" is really a large stock dividend and results in additional shares issued to stockholders by capitalizing retained earnings or transferring other contributed capital to Common Stock. This approach avoids administrative costs of splitting the stock. **Harley-Davidson** recently declared a 2-for-1 stock split executed in the form of a 100% stock dividend.

> ### Quick Check
>
> 13. How does a stock dividend impact assets and retained earnings?
> 14. What distinguishes a large stock dividend from a small stock dividend?
> 15. What amount of retained earnings is capitalized for a small stock dividend?

Answers—p. 470

## Treasury Stock

**P5**  Record purchases and sales of treasury stock and the retirement of stock.

Corporations acquire shares of their own stock for several reasons: (1) to use their shares to acquire another corporation, (2) to purchase shares to avoid a hostile takeover of the company, (3) to reissue them to employees as compensation, and (4) to maintain a strong market for their stock or to show management confidence in the current price.

A corporation's reacquired shares are called **treasury stock,** which is similar to unissued stock in several ways: (1) neither treasury stock nor unissued stock is an asset, (2) neither receives cash dividends or stock dividends, and (3) neither allows the exercise of voting rights. However, treasury stock does differ from unissued stock in one major way: The corporation can resell treasury stock at less than par without having the buyers incur a liability, provided it was originally issued at par value or higher. Treasury stock purchases also require management to exercise ethical sensitivity because funds are being paid to specific stockholders instead of all stockholders. Managers must be sure the purchase is in the best interest of all stockholders. These concerns cause companies to fully disclose treasury stock transactions.

**Corporations and Treasury Stock**

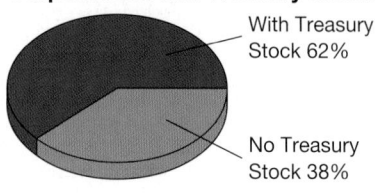

With Treasury Stock 62%

No Treasury Stock 38%

### Purchasing Treasury Stock

Purchasing treasury stock reduces the corporation's assets and equity by equal amounts. (We describe the *cost method* of accounting for treasury stock, which is the most widely used method. The *par value* method is another method explained in advanced courses.) To illustrate, Exhibit 11.13 shows Cyber Corporation's account balances *before* any treasury stock purchase (Cyber has no liabilities).

**Exhibit 11.13**

Account Balances *before* Purchasing Treasury Stock

| Assets | | Stockholders' Equity | |
|---|---|---|---|
| Cash . . . . . . . . . . . . . . | $ 30,000 | Common stock—$10 par; 10,000 shares | |
| Other assets . . . . . . . . | 95,000 | authorized, issued, and outstanding . . . . . . . . . . . | $100,000 |
| | | Retained earnings . . . . . . . . . . . . . . . . . . . . . . . . | 25,000 |
| Total assets . . . . . . . . . | $125,000 | Total stockholders' equity . . . . . . . . . . . . . . . . . . | $125,000 |

**Global:** Many countries, such as China, Japan, and Singapore, do not permit purchase of treasury stock.

Cyber then purchases 1,000 of its own shares for $11,500, which is recorded as follows:

Assets = Liabilities + Equity
−11,500              −11,500

| May 1 | Treasury Stock, Common . . . . . . . . . . . . . . . . . | 11,500 | |
|---|---|---|---|
| | Cash . . . . . . . . . . . . . . . . . . . . . . . . . . . . . . | | 11,500 |
| | Purchased 1,000 treasury shares at $11.50 per share. | | |

**Point:** Treasury stock does not carry voting or dividend rights.

This entry reduces equity through the debit to the Treasury Stock account, which is a contra equity account. Exhibit 11.14 shows account balances *after* this transaction.

**Exhibit 11.14**

Account Balances *after* Purchasing Treasury Stock

| Assets | | Stockholders' Equity | |
|---|---|---|---|
| Cash . . . . . . . . . . | $ 18,500 | Common stock—$10 par; 10,000 shares | |
| Other assets . . . . . | 95,000 | authorized and issued; 1,000 shares in treasury . . . . . | $100,000 |
| | | Retained earnings, $11,500 restricted by | |
| | | treasury stock purchase . . . . . . . . . . . . . . . . . . . . | 25,000 |
| | | **Less cost of treasury stock** . . . . . . . . . . . . . . . . . | **(11,500)** |
| Total assets . . . . . . | $113,500 | Total stockholders' equity . . . . . . . . . . . . . . . . . . . . | $113,500 |

**Point:** The Treasury Stock account is *not* an asset. This contra equity account is a subtraction in the equity section.

The treasury stock purchase reduces Cyber's cash, total assets, and total equity by $11,500 but does not reduce the balance of either the Common Stock or the Retained Earnings account. The equity reduction is reported by deducting the cost of treasury stock in the equity section. Also, two disclosures are evident. First, the stock description reveals that 1,000 issued shares are in treasury, leaving only 9,000 shares still outstanding. Second, the description for retained earnings reveals that it is partly restricted.

**Point:** A treasury stock purchase is also called a *stock buyback.*

## Reissuing Treasury Stock

Treasury stock can be reissued by selling it at cost, above cost, or below cost.

**Selling Treasury Stock at Cost**   If treasury stock is reissued at cost, the entry is the reverse of the one made to record the purchase. For instance, if on May 21 Cyber reissues 100 of the treasury shares purchased on May 1 at the same $11.50 per share cost, the entry is

| May 21 | Cash . . . . . . . . . . . . . . . . . . . . . . . . . . . . . . | 1,150 | |
|--------|------------------------------------------------------|-------|-------|
| | Treasury Stock, Common . . . . . . . . . . . . . . | | 1,150 |
| | *Received $11.50 per share for 100 treasury* | | |
| | *shares costing $11.50 per share.* | | |

Assets = Liabilities + Equity
+1,150                    +1,150

**Selling Treasury Stock *above* Cost**   If treasury stock is sold for more than cost, the amount received in excess of cost is credited to the Contributed Capital, Treasury Stock account. This account is reported as a separate item in the contributed capital section of stockholders' equity. No gain is ever reported from the sale of treasury stock. To illustrate, if Cyber receives $12 cash per share for 400 treasury shares costing $11.50 per share, the entry is

**Point:** Treasury stock does not represent ownership. A company cannot own a part of itself.

| June 3 | Cash . . . . . . . . . . . . . . . . . . . . . . . . . . . . . . | 4,800 | |
|--------|------------------------------------------------------|-------|-------|
| | Treasury Stock, Common . . . . . . . . . . . . . . | | 4,600 |
| | **Contributed Capital, Treasury Stock** . . . | | **200** |
| | *Received $12 per share for 400 treasury* | | |
| | *shares costing $11.50 per share.* | | |

Assets = Liabilities + Equity
+4,800                    +4,600
                          +200

**Selling Treasury Stock *below* Cost**   When treasury stock is sold below cost, the entry to record the sale depends on whether the Contributed Capital, Treasury Stock account has a credit balance. If it has a zero balance, the excess of cost over the sales price is debited to Retained Earnings. If the Contributed Capital, Treasury Stock account has a credit balance, it is debited for the excess of the cost over the selling price but not to exceed the balance in this account. When the credit balance in this contributed capital account is eliminated, any remaining difference between the cost and selling price is debited to Retained Earnings. To illustrate, if Cyber sells its remaining 500 shares of treasury stock at $10 per share, equity is reduced by $750 (500 shares × $1.50 per share excess of cost over selling price), as shown in this entry:

**Point:** The term *treasury stock* is believed to arise from the fact that reacquired stock is held in a corporation's treasury.

**Point:** The Contributed Capital, Treasury Stock account can have a zero or credit balance but never a debit balance.

| July 10 | Cash . . . . . . . . . . . . . . . . . . . . . . . . . . . . . . | 5,000 | |
|---------|------------------------------------------------------|-------|-------|
| | **Contributed Capital, Treasury Stock** . . . . . . . | **200** | |
| | **Retained Earnings** . . . . . . . . . . . . . . . . . . . . | **550** | |
| | Treasury Stock, Common . . . . . . . . . . . . . . | | 5,750 |
| | *Received $10 per share for 500 treasury* | | |
| | *shares costing $11.50 per share.* | | |

Assets = Liabilities + Equity
+5,000                    −200
                          −550
                          +5,750

This entry eliminates the $200 credit balance in the contributed capital account created on June 3 and then reduces the Retained Earnings balance by the remaining $550 excess of cost over selling price. A company never reports a loss (or gain) from the sale of treasury stock.

## Retiring Stock

A corporation can purchase its own stock and retire it. Retiring stock reduces the number of issued shares. Retired stock is the same as authorized and unissued shares. Purchases and retirements of stock are permissible under state law only if they do not jeopardize the interests of creditors and stockholders. When stock is purchased for retirement, we remove

**Point:** Wrigley Company recently reported that its "Directors adopted a resolution retiring the entire balance of shares of Common Stock held in the corporate treasury."

**Point:** Recording stock retirement results in canceling the equity from the original issuance of the shares.

all contributed capital amounts related to the retired shares. If the purchase price exceeds the net amount removed from contributed capital, this excess is debited to Retained Earnings. If the net amount removed from contributed capital exceeds the purchase price, this excess is credited to the Contributed Capital from Retirement of Stock account. A company's assets and equity are always reduced by the amount paid for the retiring stock.

---

### Quick Check

16. Purchase of treasury stock (a) has no effect on assets; (b) reduces total assets and total equity by equal amounts; or (c) is recorded with a debit to Retained Earnings.
17. Southern Co. purchases shares of Northern Corp. Should either company classify these shares as treasury stock?
18. How does treasury stock affect the authorized, issued, and outstanding shares?
19. When a company purchases treasury stock, (a) retained earnings are restricted by the amount paid; (b) Retained Earnings is credited; or (c) it is retired.

Answers—p. 470

---

# Reporting Income and Equity

When a company's revenue and expense transactions are from normal, continuing operations, a simple income statement is usually adequate. When a company's activities include income-related events not part of its normal, continuing operations, it must disclose information to help users understand these events and predict future performance. To meet these objectives, companies separate the income statement into continuing operations, discontinued segments, extraordinary items, changes in accounting principles, and earnings per share. For illustration, Exhibit 11.15 shows such an income statement for ComUS.

## Continuing Operations

**C4** Explain the form and content of a complete income statement.

The first major section (①) shows the revenues, expenses, and income from continuing operations. Users especially rely on this information to predict future operations. Many users view this section as the most important. Earlier chapters explained the items comprising income from continuing operations.

## Discontinued Segments

A **business segment** is a part of a company's operations that serves a particular line of business or class of customers. A segment has assets, liabilities, and financial results of operations that can be distinguished from those of other parts of the company. A company's gain or loss from selling or closing down a segment is separately reported. Section ② of Exhibit 11.15 reports both (1) income from operating the discontinued segment for the current period prior to its disposal and (2) the loss from disposing of the segment's net assets. The income tax effects of each are reported separately from the income taxes expense in section ①.

## Extraordinary Items

Section ③ reports **extraordinary gains and losses,** which are those that are *both unusual* and *infrequent.* An **unusual gain or loss** is abnormal or otherwise unrelated to the company's regular activities and environment. An **infrequent gain or loss** is not expected to recur given the company's operating environment. Reporting extraordinary items in a separate category helps users predict future performance, absent the effects of extraordinary items. Items usually considered extraordinary include (1) expropriation (taking away) of property by a foreign government, (2) condemning of property by a domestic government body, (3) prohibition against using an asset by a newly enacted law, and (4) losses and gains from an unusual and infrequent calamity ("act of God"). Items *not* considered extraordinary

Exhibit 11.15

Income Statement (all-inclusive)
for a Corporation

| ComUS Income Statement For Year Ended December 31, 2005 | | |
|---|---:|---:|
| Net sales | | $8,478,000 |
| **Operating expenses** | | |
| Cost of goods sold | $5,950,000 | |
| Depreciation expense | 35,000 | |
| Other selling, general, and administrative expenses | 515,000 | |
| Interest expense | 20,000 | |
| ① Total operating expenses | | (6,520,000) |
| **Other gains (losses)** | | |
| Loss on plant relocation | | (45,000) |
| Gain on sale of surplus land | | 72,000 |
| Income from continuing operations before taxes | | 1,985,000 |
| Income taxes expense | | (595,500) |
| Income from continuing operations | | 1,389,500 |
| **Discontinued segment** | | |
| ② Income from operating Division A (net of $180,000 taxes) | 420,000 | |
| Loss on disposal of Division A (net of $66,000 tax benefit) | (154,000) | 266,000 |
| Income before extraordinary items and cumulative effect of change in accounting principle | | 1,655,500 |
| **Extraordinary items** | | |
| ③ Gain on land expropriated by state (net of $61,200 taxes) | 142,800 | |
| Loss from earthquake damage (net of $270,000 tax benefit) | (630,000) | (487,200) |
| **Cumulative effect of a change in accounting principle** | | |
| ④ Effect on prior years' income (through Dec. 31, 2004) of changing depreciation methods (net of $24,000 taxes) | | 56,000 |
| Net income | | $1,224,300 |
| **Earnings per common share (200,000 outstanding shares)** | | |
| Income from continuing operations | | $    6.95 |
| Discontinued operations | | 1.33 |
| ⑤ Income before extraordinary items and cumulative effect of change in accounting principle | | 8.28 |
| Extraordinary items | | (2.44) |
| Cumulative effect of a change in accounting principle | | 0.28 |
| Net income (basic earnings per share) | | $    6.12 |

include (1) write-downs of inventories and write-offs of receivables, (2) gains and losses from disposing of segments, and (3) financial effects of labor strikes.

Gains and losses that are neither unusual nor infrequent are reported as part of continuing operations. Gains and losses that are *either* unusual *or* infrequent, but *not* both, are reported as part of continuing operations *but* after the normal revenues and expenses.

**Decision Maker**

**Small Business Owner**   You own an orange grove near Jacksonville, Florida. A bad frost destroys about one-half of your oranges. You are currently preparing an income statement for a bank loan. Can you claim the loss of oranges as extraordinary?

Answer—p. 469

## Changes in Accounting Principles

The *consistency principle* directs a company to apply the same accounting principles across periods, yet a company can change from one acceptable accounting principle (such as FIFO, LIFO, or straight-line) to another as long as the change improves the usefulness of

**Point:** Changes in principles are sometimes required when new accounting standards are issued.

information in its financial statements. Changes in accounting principles usually affect income in more than one way. To illustrate, ComUS purchased its only depreciable asset early in 2002 for $320,000. This asset has an eight-year life, a $40,000 salvage value, and was depreciated using double-declining-balance for 2002, 2003, and 2004. Early in 2005, ComUS decides its income statement would be more useful if depreciation is computed using straight-line. Double-declining-balance had yielded $185,000 of depreciation from 2002 through 2004, whereas if the straight-line method had been used, depreciation would have been $105,000. The cumulative effect on prior year income statements (those for 2002–2004) is to reduce depreciation expense by $80,000 and increase pretax income by $80,000. Since ComUS is subject to a 30% income tax, the after-tax effect of this change is $56,000 ($80,000 × [1 − 0.30]).

The income statement in Exhibit 11.15 shows how to report the change in an accounting principle. First, section ① reports $35,000 of depreciation using the newly adopted straight-line method. Straight-line depreciation also will be used in 2006 through 2009. Second, the income statement reports the $56,000 catch-up adjustment in section ④. This item is the cumulative effect of the change in accounting principle. Finally, a note describes the accounting change, why it is an improvement, and what income would have been under the prior method.

## Quick Check

20. Which of the following is an extraordinary item? (*a*) a settlement paid to a customer injured while using the company's product, (*b*) a loss to a plant from damages caused by a meteorite, or (*c*) a loss from selling old equipment.

21. Identify the five major sections of an income statement that are potentially reported.

22. A company using FIFO for the past 15 years decides to switch to LIFO. The effect of this event on prior years' net income is (*a*) reported as a prior period adjustment to retained earnings; (*b*) ignored because it is a change in an accounting estimate; or (*c*) reported on the current year income statement.

Answers—p. 470

## Earnings per Share

**A1**  Compute earnings per share and describe this ratio's use.

The final section of the income statement in Exhibit 11.15 reports earnings per share for each of the four subcategories of income (continuing operations, discontinued segments, extraordinary items, and the effect of accounting principle changes) when they exist. **Earnings per share,** also called *net income per share,* is the amount of income earned per each share of a company's outstanding common stock. The **basic earnings per share** formula is in Exhibit 11.16. The weighted-average common shares outstanding is explained by first considering the simple case of no changes in shares outstanding and second when shares outstanding changes.

**Point:** Earnings per share is often referred to as *EPS.*

### Exhibit 11.16

Basic Earnings per Share

$$\text{Basic earnings per share} = \frac{\text{Net income} - \text{Preferred dividends}}{\text{Weighted-average common shares outstanding}}$$

**No Changes in Common Shares Outstanding**    Assume that Quantum Co. earns $40,000 net income in 2005 and declares dividends of $7,500 on its noncumulative preferred stock. (If preferred stock is *non*cumulative, the income available [numerator] is the current period net income less any preferred dividends *declared* in that same period. If preferred stock is cumulative, the income available [numerator] is the current period net income less the preferred dividends whether declared or not.) Quantum has 5,000 common shares outstanding during all of 2005. Its basic EPS is

$$\text{Basic earnings per share} = \frac{\$40,000 - \$7,500}{5,000 \text{ shares}} = \$6.50$$

### Changes in Common Shares Outstanding (Stock Sales and Purchases)

Assume that Quantum earns $40,000 in 2005 and declares preferred dividends of $7,500. Also assume that it begins the year with 5,000 common shares outstanding, sells 4,000 additional shares on July 1, and purchases 3,000 treasury shares on November 1. Thus, 5,000 shares were outstanding for the first six months, 9,000 were outstanding for July through October (four months), and 6,000 were outstanding for the final two months. Exhibit 11.17 shows how to compute Quantum's weighted-average number of shares outstanding for 2005.

**Global:** Some countries, such as Japan and Australia, use the number of shares outstanding at the end of the period when computing EPS.

| Time Period | Outstanding Shares | | Fraction of Year | | Weighted Average |
|---|---|---|---|---|---|
| January–June .............................. | 5,000 | × | 6/12 | = | 2,500 |
| July–October .............................. | 9,000 | × | 4/12 | = | 3,000 |
| November–December ...................... | 6,000 | × | 2/12 | = | 1,000 |
| **Weighted-average shares outstanding** ....... | | | | | **6,500** |

**Exhibit 11.17**

Computing Weighted-Average Shares Outstanding

Quantum's basic EPS is

$$\text{Basic earnings per share} = \frac{\$40,000 - \$7,500}{6,500 \text{ shares}} = \$5$$

### Changes in Common Shares Outstanding (Stock Splits and Dividends)

We restate the number of shares outstanding during the period to reflect a stock split or dividend *as if it occurred at the beginning of the period.* To illustrate, use the preceding facts and assume that Quantum executed a 2-for-1 stock split on December 1, 2005. We include an additional column reflecting the effect of the split in Exhibit 11.18. The December shares already reflect the split and do not require adjustment.

| Time Period | Outstanding Shares | | Effect of Split | | Fraction of Year | | Weighted Average |
|---|---|---|---|---|---|---|---|
| January–June ............................ | 5,000 | × | 2 | × | 6/12 | = | 5,000 |
| July–October ............................ | 9,000 | × | 2 | × | 4/12 | = | 6,000 |
| November ............................... | 6,000 | × | 2 | × | 1/12 | = | 1,000 |
| December ............................... | 12,000 | × | 1 | × | 1/12 | = | 1,000 |
| **Weighted-average shares outstanding** ....... | | | | | | | **13,000** |

**Exhibit 11.18**

Computing Weighted-Average Shares Outstanding when Stock Splits (or Dividends) Occur

Quantum's basic EPS under the 2-for-1 stock split is

$$\text{Basic earnings per share} = \frac{\$40,000 - \$7,500}{13,000 \text{ shares}} = \$2.50$$

We use the same computations for stock dividends. For instance, if the 2-for-1 stock split had been a 10% stock dividend, the outstanding shares prior to the dividend are multiplied

## Decision Ethics

**Director**  The board of Intex is planning its stockholders' meeting agenda. The first item is whether to disclose a contract just signed that will increase future income. One officer argues, "The meeting should focus on actual results." After agreeing not to disclose the contract, the next item is a motion for stockholders to approve a two-year option to managers to buy shares at a price equal to the average stock price over the next 2 weeks. What action (if any) do you take?

Answer—p. 469

by 1.1 instead of 2.0 because 110% (or 1.1) of the original number of shares are now outstanding, computed as 100% + 10%.[3]

## Stock Options

The majority of corporations whose shares are publicly traded issue **stock options,** which are rights to purchase common stock at a fixed price over a specified period. As the stock's price rises above the fixed price, the option's value increases. **Starbucks** and **Home Depot** offer stock options to both full- and part-time employees. Stock options are said to motivate managers and employees to (1) focus on company performance, (2) take a long-run perspective, and (3) remain with the company. A stock option is like having an investment with no risk ("a carrot with no stick").

To illustrate, Quantum grants each of its employees the option to purchase 100 shares of its $1 par value common stock at its current market price of $50 per share anytime within the next 10 years. If the stock price rises to $70 per share, an employee can exercise the option at a gain of $20 per share (acquire a $70 stock at the $50 option price). With 100 shares, a single employee would have a total gain of $2,000, computed as $20 × 100 shares.

## Quick Check

23. FDI reports 2005 net income of $250,000 and pays preferred dividends of $70,000. On January 1, 2005, FDI had 25,000 outstanding common shares, and it purchased 5,000 treasury shares on July 1. Its 2005 basic EPS is (a) $8; (b) $9; or (c) $10.

24. How are stock splits and stock dividends treated in computing the weighted-average number of outstanding common shares?

25. What EPS figures are reported for a complex capital structure company?

Answers—p. 470

## Statement of Retained Earnings

**C5**  Explain the items reported in retained earnings.

Retained earnings generally consist of a company's cumulative net income less any net losses and dividends declared since its inception. Retained earnings are part of stockholders' claims on the company's net assets, but this does *not* imply that a certain amount of cash or other assets is available to pay stockholders. For example, **Harley-Davidson** has $2.4 billion in

---

[3] A corporation can be classified as having either a simple or complex capital structure. The term **simple capital structure** refers to a company with only common stock and nonconvertible preferred stock outstanding. The term **complex capital structure** refers to companies with dilutive securities. **Dilutive securities** include options, rights to purchase common stock, and any bonds or preferred stock that are convertible into common stock. A company with a complex capital structure must often report two EPS figures: basic and diluted. **Diluted earnings per share** is computed by adding all dilutive securities to the denominator of the basic EPS computation. It reflects the decrease in basic EPS *assuming* that all dilutive securities are converted into common shares. Since ComUS had a simple capital structure, it reported only basic EPS.

retained earnings, but only $0.3 billion in cash. This section describes events and transactions affecting retained earnings and how retained earnings are reported.

**Restrictions and Appropriations** The term **restricted retained earnings** refers to both *statutory* and *contractual* restrictions. A common statutory (or legal) restriction is to limit treasury stock purchases to the amount of retained earnings. The balance sheet in Exhibit 11.14 provides an example. A common *contractual restriction* involves loan agreements that restrict paying dividends beyond a specified amount or percent of retained earnings. Restrictions are usually described in the notes. The term **appropriated retained earnings** refers to a voluntary transfer of amounts from the Retained Earnings account to the Appropriated Retained Earnings account to inform users of special activities that require funds.

**Prior Period Adjustments** **Prior period adjustments** are corrections of material errors in prior period financial statements. These errors include arithmetic mistakes, unacceptable accounting, and missed facts. Prior period adjustments are reported in the *statement of retained earnings* (or the statement of stockholders' equity), net of any income tax effects. Prior period adjustments result in changing the beginning balance of retained earnings for events occurring prior to the earliest period reported in the current set of financial statements. To illustrate, assume that ComUS makes an error in a 2003 journal entry for the purchase of land by incorrectly debiting an expense account. When this is discovered in 2005, the statement of retained earnings includes a prior period adjustment, as shown in Exhibit 11.19. This exhibit also shows the usual format of the statement of retained earnings.

| ComUS Statement of Retained Earnings For Year Ended December 31, 2005 | |
| --- | --- |
| Retained earnings, Dec. 31, 2004, as previously reported | $4,745,000 |
| Prior period adjustment | |
| **Cost of land incorrectly expensed (net of $63,000 income taxes)** | **147,000** |
| Retained earnings, Dec. 31, 2004, as adjusted | 4,892,000 |
| Plus net income | 1,224,300 |
| Less cash dividends declared | (301,800) |
| Retained earnings, Dec. 31, 2005 | $5,814,500 |

**Exhibit 11.19**

Statement of Retained Earnings with a Prior Period Adjustment

Note that many items reported in financial statements are based on estimates. Future events are certain to reveal that some of these estimates were inaccurate even when based on the best data available at the time. These inaccuracies are *not* considered errors and are *not* reported as prior period adjustments. Instead, they are identified as **changes in accounting estimates** and are accounted for in current and future periods. To illustrate, we know that depreciation is based on estimated useful lives and salvage values. As time passes and new information becomes available, managers may need to change these estimates and the resulting depreciation expense for current and future periods.

## Statement of Stockholders' Equity

Instead of a separate statement of retained earnings, companies commonly report a statement of stockholders' equity that includes changes in retained earnings. A **statement of stockholders' equity** lists the beginning and ending balances of each equity account and describes the changes that occur during the period. The companies in Appendix A report such a statement. The usual format is to provide a column for each component of equity and use the rows to describe events occurring in the period. Exhibit 11.20 shows a condensed statement for **Outback Steakhouse.**

This cartoon reinforces the trade-off of risk (dangerous) and return (thrilling ride) when buying stock.

## Exhibit 11.20

Statement of Stockholders' Equity

| **OUTBACK STEAKHOUSE** Statement of Stockholders' Equity | | | | | |
|---|---|---|---|---|---|
| ($ thousands) | Common Stock Amount | Contributed Capital in Excess of Par | Retained Earnings | Treasury Stock | Total |
| **Balance, Dec. 31, 2001** . . . . . . . . . . . . . . | **$786** | **$220,648** | **$762,414** | **$(42,004)** | **$ 941,844** |
| Net income . . . . . . . . . . . . . . . . . . . . . . . | — | — | 156,364 | — | 156,364 |
| Issuance of Common Stock . . . . . . . . . . . . | 2 | 15,578 | — | — | 15,580 |
| Purchase of Treasury Stock . . . . . . . . . . . . | — | — | — | (81,650) | (81,650) |
| Reissuance of Treasury Stock . . . . . . . . . . . | — | — | (6,767) | 36,706 | 29,939 |
| Cash Dividends ($0.12 per share) . . . . . . . | — | — | (9,101) | — | (9,101) |
| **Balance, Dec. 31, 2002** . . . . . . . . . . . . . . | **$788** | **$236,226** | **$902,910** | **$(86,948)** | **$1,052,976** |

**Decision Analysis**          Book Value per Share, Dividend Yield, and Price-Earnings Ratio

## Book Value per Share

**A2**  Compute book value and explain its use in analysis.

**Point:** Book value per share is also referred to as *stockholders' claim to assets on a per share basis.*

*Case 1: Common Stock (Only) Outstanding.* **Book value per common share,** defined in Exhibit 11.21, is the recorded amount of stockholders' equity applicable to *common* shares on a per share basis. To illustrate, we use Dillon Snowboards' data from Exhibit 11.4. Dillon has 30,000 outstanding common shares, and the stockholders' equity applicable to common shares is $365,000. Dillon's book value per common share is $12.17, computed as $365,000 divided by 30,000 shares.

## Exhibit 11.21

Book Value per Common Share

$$\text{Book value per common share} = \frac{\text{Stockholders' equity applicable to common shares}}{\text{Number of common shares outstanding}}$$

*Case 2: Common and Preferred Stock Outstanding.* To compute book value when both common and preferred shares are outstanding, we allocate total stockholders' equity between the two types of shares. The **book value per preferred share** is computed first; its computation is shown in Exhibit 11.22.

## Exhibit 11.22

Book Value per Preferred Share

$$\text{Book value per preferred share} = \frac{\text{Stockholders' equity applicable to preferred shares}}{\text{Number of preferred shares outstanding}}$$

The stockholders' equity applicable to preferred shares equals the preferred share's call price (or par value if the preferred is not callable) plus any cumulative dividends in arrears. The remaining stockholders' equity is the portion applicable to common shares. To illustrate, consider LTD's stockholders' equity in Exhibit 11.23. Its preferred stock is callable at $108 per share, and two years of cumulative preferred dividends are in arrears.

## Exhibit 11.23

Stockholders' Equity with Preferred and Common Stock

| **Stockholders' Equity** | |
|---|---|
| Preferred stock—$100 par value, 7% cumulative, 2,000 shares authorized, 1,000 shares issued and outstanding . . . . . . . | $100,000 |
| Common stock—$25 par value, 12,000 shares authorized, 10,000 shares issued and outstanding . . . . . . . . . . . . . . . . . . . . . . | 250,000 |
| Contributed capital in excess of par value, common stock . . . . . . . . . . | 15,000 |
| Retained earnings . . . . . . . . . . . . . . . . . . . . . . . . . . . . . . . . . . . . . . | 82,000 |
| Total stockholders' equity . . . . . . . . . . . . . . . . . . . . . . . . . . . . . . . . . | $447,000 |

The book value computations are in Exhibit 11.24. Note that equity is first allocated to preferred shares before the book value of common shares is computed.

| | | | |
|---|---|---|---|
| Total stockholders' equity ................................... | | | $447,000 |
| Less equity applicable to preferred shares | | | |
| Call price (1,000 shares × $108) ........................ | $108,000 | | |
| Dividends in arrears ($100,000 × 7% × 2 years) ................ | 14,000 | (122,000) | |
| Equity applicable to common shares .................. | | | $325,000 |
| Book value per preferred share ($122,000/1,000 shares) ........ | | | $122.00 |
| Book value per common share ($325,000/10,000 shares) ....... | | | $ 32.50 |

**Exhibit 11.24**

Computing Book Value per Preferred and Common Share

Book value per share reflects the value per share if a company is liquidated at balance sheet amounts. Book value is also the starting point in many stock valuation models, merger negotiations, price setting for public utilities, and loan contracts. The main limitation in using book value is the potential difference between recorded value and market value for assets and liabilities. Investors often adjust their analysis for estimates of these differences.

**Decision Maker**

**Investor**  You are considering investing in **BMX**, whose book value per common share is $4 and price per common share on the stock exchange is $7. From this information, are BMX's net assets priced higher or lower than its recorded values?

Answer—p. 470

## Dividend Yield

Investors buy shares of a company's stock in anticipation of receiving a return from either or both cash dividends and stock price increases. Stocks that pay large dividends on a regular basis, called *income stocks,* are attractive to investors who want recurring cash flows from their investments. In contrast, some stocks pay little or no dividends but are still attractive to investors because of their expected stock price increases. The stocks of companies that distribute little or no cash but use their cash to finance expansion are called *growth stocks.* One way to help identify whether a stock is an income stock or a growth stock is to analyze its dividend yield. **Dividend yield,** defined in Exhibit 11.25, shows the annual amount of cash dividends distributed to common shares relative to their market value.

**A3**  Compute dividend yield and explain its use in analysis.

$$\text{Dividend yield} = \frac{\text{Annual cash dividends per share}}{\text{Market value per share}}$$

**Exhibit 11.25**

Dividend Yield

Dividend yield can be computed for current and prior periods using actual dividends and stock prices and for future periods using expected values. Exhibit 11.26 shows recent dividend and stock price data for **Microsoft** and **Altria Group** to compute dividend yield.

| Company | Cash Dividends per Share | Market Value per Share | Dividend Yield |
|---|---|---|---|
| Microsoft .......... | $0.08 | $25 | 0.3% |
| Altria Group ....... | 2.56 | 30 | 8.5 |

**Exhibit 11.26**

Dividend and Stock Price Information

Dividend yield is near zero for Microsoft, implying it is a growth stock. An investor in Microsoft would look for increases in stock prices (and eventual cash from the sale of stock). Altria has a dividend yield of 8.5%, implying it is an income stock for which dividends are important in assessing its value.

**Point:** The *payout ratio* equals cash dividends declared on common stock divided by net income. A low payout ratio suggests that a company is retaining earnings for future growth.

## Price-Earnings Ratio

A stock's market value is determined by its *expected* future cash flows. A comparison of a company's EPS and its market value per share reveals information about market expectations. This comparison is traditionally made using a **price-earnings** (or **PE**) **ratio,** expressed also as *price earnings, price to*

**A4**  Compute price-earnings ratio and describe its use in analysis.

**Point:** The average PE ratio of stocks in the 1950–2003 period is about 14.

*earnings,* or *PE.* Some analysts interpret this ratio as what price the market is willing to pay for a company's current earnings stream. Price-earnings ratios can differ across companies that have similar earnings because of either higher or lower expectations of future earnings. The price-earnings ratio is defined in Exhibit 11.27.

## Exhibit 11.27

Price-Earnings Ratio

$$\text{Price-earnings ratio} = \frac{\text{Market value (price) per share}}{\text{Earnings per share}}$$

**Point:** Average PE ratios for U.S. stocks have increased over the past two decades. Some analysts interpret this as a signal the market is overpriced. But higher ratios can at least partly reflect accounting changes that have reduced reported earnings.

This ratio is often computed using EPS from the most recent period. However, many users compute this ratio using *expected* EPS for the next period.

Some analysts view stocks with high PE ratios (higher than 20 to 25) as more likely to be overpriced and stocks with low PE ratios (less than 5 to 8) as more likely to be underpriced. These investors prefer to sell or avoid buying stocks with high PE ratios and to buy or hold stocks with low PE ratios. However, investment decision making is rarely so simple as to rely on a single ratio. For instance, a stock with a high PE ratio can prove to be a good investment if its earnings continue to increase beyond current expectations. Similarly, a stock with a low PE ratio can prove to be a poor investment if its earnings decline below expectations.

### Decision Maker

**Manager**   You plan to invest in one of two companies identified as having identical future prospects. One has a PE of 19 and the other a PE of 25. Which do you invest in? Does it matter if your *estimate* of PE for these two companies is 29 as opposed to 22?

Answer—p. 470

# Demonstration Problem 1

Barton Corporation began operations on January 1, 2005. The following transactions relating to stockholders' equity occurred in the first two years of the company's operations.

### 2005

Jan. 1   Authorized the issuance of 2 million shares of $5 par value common stock and 100,000 shares of $100 par value, 10% cumulative, preferred stock.

Jan. 2   Issued 200,000 shares of common stock for $12 cash per share.

Jan. 3   Issued 100,000 shares of common stock in exchange for a building valued at $820,000 and merchandise inventory valued at $380,000.

Jan. 4   Paid $10,000 cash to the company's founders for organization activities.

Jan. 5   Issued 12,000 shares of preferred stock for $110 cash per share.

### 2006

June 4   Issued 100,000 shares of common stock for $15 cash per share.

### Required

1. Prepare journal entries to record these transactions.

2. Prepare the stockholders' equity section of the balance sheet as of December 31, 2005, and December 31, 2006, based on these transactions.

3. Prepare a table showing dividend allocations and dividends per share for 2005 and 2006 assuming Barton declares the following cash dividends: 2005, $50,000, and 2006, $300,000.

4. Prepare the January 2, 2005, journal entry for Barton's issuance of 200,000 shares of common stock for $12 cash per share assuming

   a. Common stock is no-par stock without a stated value.

   b. Common stock is no-par stock with a stated value of $10 per share.

# Planning the Solution

- Record journal entries for the transactions for 2005 and 2006.
- Determine the balances for the 2005 and 2006 equity accounts for the balance sheet.
- Prepare the contributed capital portion of the 2005 and 2006 balance sheets.
- Prepare a table similar to Exhibit 11.8 showing dividend allocations for 2005 and 2006.
- Record the issuance of common stock under both specifications of no-par stock.

# Solution to Demonstration Problem 1

**1.** Journal entries:

| 2005 | | | |
|---|---|---|---|
| Jan. 2 | Cash ................................... | 2,400,000 | |
| |     Common Stock, $5 Par Value ............ | | 1,000,000 |
| |     Contributed Capital in Excess of Par Value, | | |
| |       Common Stock .................... | | 1,400,000 |
| |     *Issued 200,000 shares of common stock.* | | |
| Jan. 3 | Building ................................ | 820,000 | |
| | Merchandise Inventory .................... | 380,000 | |
| |     Common Stock, $5 Par Value ............ | | 500,000 |
| |     Contributed Capital in Excess of Par Value, | | |
| |       Common Stock .................... | | 700,000 |
| |     *Issued 100,000 shares of common stock.* | | |
| Jan. 4 | Organization Expenses .................... | 10,000 | |
| |     Cash............................... | | 10,000 |
| |     *Paid founders for organization costs.* | | |
| Jan. 5 | Cash ................................... | 1,320,000 | |
| |     Preferred Stock, $100 Par Value .......... | | 1,200,000 |
| |     Contributed Capital in Excess of Par Value, | | |
| |       Preferred Stock .................... | | 120,000 |
| |     *Issued 12,000 shares of preferred stock.* | | |
| 2006 | | | |
| June 4 | Cash ................................... | 1,500,000 | |
| |     Common Stock, $5 Par Value ............ | | 500,000 |
| |     Contributed Capital in Excess of Par Value, | | |
| |       Common Stock .................... | | 1,000,000 |
| |     *Issued 100,000 shares of common stock.* | | |

**2.** Balance sheet presentations (at December 31 year-end):

| | 2005 | 2006 |
|---|---|---|
| **Stockholders' Equity** | | |
| Contributed capital | | |
| Preferred stock—$100 par value, 10% cumulative, 100,000 shares authorized, 12,000 shares issued and outstanding ........................................ | $1,200,000 | $1,200,000 |
| Contributed capital in excess of par value, preferred stock ......... | 120,000 | 120,000 |
| Total capital contributed by preferred stockholders ............. | 1,320,000 | 1,320,000 |
| Common stock—$5 par value, 2,000,000 shares authorized, 300,000 shares issued and outstanding in 2005, and 400,000 shares issued and outstanding in 2006 ............... | 1,500,000 | 2,000,000 |
| Contributed capital in excess of par value, common stock ......... | 2,100,000 | 3,100,000 |
| Total capital contributed by common stockholders .............. | 3,600,000 | 5,100,000 |
| Total contributed capital .................................... | $4,920,000 | $6,420,000 |

**3.** Dividend allocation table:

| | Common | Preferred |
|---|---|---|
| **2005** ($50,000) | | |
| Preferred—current year (12,000 shares × $10 = $120,000) . . . . . . . . . . | $      0 | $ 50,000 |
| Common—remainder (300,000 shares outstanding) . . . . . . . . . . . . . . . | 0 | 0 |
| Total for the year . . . . . . . . . . . . . . . . . . . . . . . . . . . . . . . . . . | $      0 | $ 50,000 |
| **2006** ($300,000) | | |
| Preferred—dividend in arrears from 2005 ($120,000 − $50,000) . . . . . . . | $      0 | $ 70,000 |
| Preferred—current year . . . . . . . . . . . . . . . . . . . . . . . . . . . . . . . | 0 | 120,000 |
| Common—remainder (400,000 shares outstanding) . . . . . . . . . . . . . . . | 110,000 | 0 |
| Total for the year . . . . . . . . . . . . . . . . . . . . . . . . . . . . . . . . . . | $110,000 | $190,000 |
| Dividends per share | | |
| 2005 . . . . . . . . . . . . . . . . . . . . . . . . . . . . . . . . . . . . . . . . . . | $   0.00 | $    4.17 |
| 2006 . . . . . . . . . . . . . . . . . . . . . . . . . . . . . . . . . . . . . . . . . . | $   0.28 | $  15.83 |

**4.** Journal entries:

**a.** For 2005:

| Jan. 2 | Cash . . . . . . . . . . . . . . . . . . . . . . . . . . . . . . . . . . | 2,400,000 | |
| | Common Stock, No-Par Value . . . . . . . . . . . | | 2,400,000 |
| | *Issued 200,000 shares of no-par common* | | |
| | *stock at $12 per share.* | | |

**b.** For 2005:

| Jan. 2 | Cash . . . . . . . . . . . . . . . . . . . . . . . . . . . . . . . . . . | 2,400,000 | |
| | Common Stock, $10 Stated Value . . . . . . . . . | | 2,000,000 |
| | Contributed Capital in Excess of | | |
| | Stated Value, Common Stock . . . . . . . . . . | | 400,000 |
| | *Issued 200,000 shares of $10 stated value* | | |
| | *common stock at $12 per share.* | | |

# Demonstration Problem 2

Precision Company began year 2005 with the following balances in its stockholders' equity accounts:

| | |
|---|---|
| Common stock—$10 par, 500,000 shares authorized, | |
| 200,000 shares issued and outstanding . . . . . . . . . . . . . . . . | $2,000,000 |
| Contributed capital in excess of par, common stock . . . . . . . . . | 1,000,000 |
| Retained earnings . . . . . . . . . . . . . . . . . . . . . . . . . . . . . . . | 5,000,000 |
| Total . . . . . . . . . . . . . . . . . . . . . . . . . . . . . . . . . . . . . . . | $8,000,000 |

All outstanding common stock was issued for $15 per share when the company was created.

## Part 1

Prepare journal entries to account for the following transactions during year 2005:

Jan.  10   The board declared a $0.10 cash dividend per share to shareholders of record Jan. 28.
Feb.  15   Paid the cash dividend declared on January 10.
Mar.  31   Declared a 20% stock dividend. The market value of the stock is $18 per share.
May   1   Distributed the stock dividend declared on March 31.
July   1   Purchased 30,000 shares of treasury stock at $20 per share.
Sept.  1   Sold 20,000 treasury shares at $26 cash per share.
Dec.   1   Sold the remaining 10,000 shares of treasury stock at $7 cash per share.

## Part 2

Use the following information to prepare a complete income statement of Precision Corp. (a technology consulting company) for year 2005, including EPS results for each category of income.

| | |
|---|---|
| Cumulative effect of a change in depreciation method (net of tax benefit) . . . . . . . . . . . | $ (136,500) |
| Operating expenses related to continuing operations . . . . . . . . . . . . . . . . . . . . . . . | (2,072,500) |
| Extraordinary gain from insurance coverage of earthquake damage (net of tax) . . . . . . . | 182,000 |
| Gain on disposal of discontinued segment assets (net of tax) . . . . . . . . . . . . . . . . . . . | 29,000 |
| Gain on sale of long-term investments . . . . . . . . . . . . . . . . . . . . . . . . . . . . . . . . . . | 400,000 |
| Loss from operating discontinued segment (net of tax benefit) . . . . . . . . . . . . . . . . . . | (120,000) |
| Income taxes on income from continuing operations . . . . . . . . . . . . . . . . . . . . . . . . | (225,000) |
| Prior period adjustment for error (net of tax benefit) . . . . . . . . . . . . . . . . . . . . . . . | (75,000) |
| Net sales . . . . . . . . . . . . . . . . . . . . . . . . . . . . . . . . . . . . . . . . . . . . . . . . . . . . . | 4,140,000 |
| Loss on sale of equipment . . . . . . . . . . . . . . . . . . . . . . . . . . . . . . . . . . . . . . . . . . | (650,000) |

## Planning the Solution

- Calculate the total cash dividend to record by multiplying the cash dividend declared by the number of shares as of the date of record.
- Decide whether the stock dividend is a small or large dividend. Then analyze each event to determine the accounts affected and the appropriate amounts to be recorded.
- Based on shares of outstanding stock at the beginning of the year and the transactions during the year, compute the weighted-average number of outstanding shares for the year.
- Assign each listed item to an appropriate income statement category.
- Prepare an income statement similar to Exhibit 11.15, including EPS results.

## Solution to Demonstration Problem 2

### Part I

| | | | |
|---|---|---|---|
| Jan. 10 | Retained Earnings . . . . . . . . . . . . . . . . . . . . . . . | 20,000 | |
| | Common Dividend Payable . . . . . . . . . . . . . | | 20,000 |
| | *Declared a $0.10 per share cash dividend.* | | |
| Feb. 15 | Common Dividend Payable . . . . . . . . . . . . . . . . | 20,000 | |
| | Cash . . . . . . . . . . . . . . . . . . . . . . . . . . . . . . | | 20,000 |
| | *Paid $0.10 per share cash dividend.* | | |
| Mar. 31 | Retained Earnings . . . . . . . . . . . . . . . . . . . . . . . | 720,000 | |
| | Common Stock Dividend Distributable . . . . . | | 400,000 |
| | Contributed Capital in Excess of | | |
| | Par Value, Common Stock . . . . . . . . . . | | 320,000 |
| | *Declared a small stock dividend of 20% or* | | |
| | *40,000 shares; market value is $18 per share.* | | |
| May 1 | Common Stock Dividend Distributable . . . . . . . . | 400,000 | |
| | Common Stock . . . . . . . . . . . . . . . . . . . . . . | | 400,000 |
| | *Distributed 40,000 shares of common stock.* | | |
| July 1 | Treasury Stock, Common . . . . . . . . . . . . . . . . . | 600,000 | |
| | Cash . . . . . . . . . . . . . . . . . . . . . . . . . . . . . . | | 600,000 |
| | *Purchased 30,000 common shares at $20 per* | | |
| | *share.* | | |
| Sept. 1 | Cash . . . . . . . . . . . . . . . . . . . . . . . . . . . . . . . . | 520,000 | |
| | Treasury Stock, Common . . . . . . . . . . . . . . . | | 400,000 |
| | Contributed Capital, Treasury Stock . . . . . . . | | 120,000 |
| | *Sold 20,000 treasury shares at $26 per share.* | | |
| Dec. 1 | Cash . . . . . . . . . . . . . . . . . . . . . . . . . . . . . . . . | 70,000 | |
| | Contributed Capital, Treasury Stock . . . . . . . . . . | 120,000 | |
| | Retained Earnings . . . . . . . . . . . . . . . . . . . . . . . | 10,000 | |
| | Treasury Stock, Common . . . . . . . . . . . . . . . | | 200,000 |
| | *Sold 10,000 treasury shares at $7 per share.* | | |

## Part 2

Compute the weighted-average number of outstanding common shares:

| Time Period | Outstanding Shares | | Effect of Dividend | | Fraction of Year | | Weighted Average |
|---|---|---|---|---|---|---|---|
| January–April | 200,000 | × | 1.2 | × | 4/12 | = | 80,000 |
| May–June | 240,000* | × | 1 | × | 2/12 | = | 40,000 |
| July–August | 210,000 | × | 1 | × | 2/12 | = | 35,000 |
| September–November | 230,000 | × | 1 | × | 3/12 | = | 57,500 |
| December | 240,000 | × | 1 | × | 1/12 | = | 20,000 |
| **Weighted-average shares outstanding** | | | | | | | **232,500** |

\* 200,000 shares × 1.2 = 240,000 shares.

### PRECISION CORPORATION
### Income Statement
### For Year Ended December 31, 2005

| | | |
|---|---|---|
| Net sales | | $4,140,000 |
| Operating expenses | | (2,072,500) |
| Other gains (losses) | | |
| Gain on sale of long-term investments | | 400,000 |
| Loss on sale of equipment | | (650,000) |
| Income from continuing operations before taxes | | 1,817,500 |
| Income taxes expense | | 225,000 |
| Income from continuing operations | | 1,592,500 |
| **Discontinued segment** | | |
| Loss from operating discontinued segment (net of tax benefit) | $(120,000) | |
| Gain on disposal of discontinued segment (net of tax) | 29,000 | (91,000) |
| Income before extraordinary item and cumulative effect of a change in accounting principle | | 1,501,500 |
| **Extraordinary item** | | |
| Extraordinary gain from insurance coverage of earthquake damage (net of tax) | | 182,000 |
| **Cumulative effect of a change in accounting principle** | | |
| Cumulative effect of change in deprec. method (net of tax benefit) | | (136,500) |
| Net income | | $1,547,000 |
| **Earnings per share** (232,500 weighted-average shares) | | |
| Income from continuing operations | | $    6.85 |
| Discontinued operations | | (0.39) |
| Income before extraordinary item and cumulative effect of change in accounting principle | | 6.46 |
| Extraordinary item | | 0.78 |
| Cumulative effect of change in accounting principle | | (0.59) |
| Net income (basic earnings per share) | | $    6.65 |

## Summary

**C1** **Identify characteristics of corporations and their organization.** Corporations are legal entities whose stockholders are not liable for its debts. Stock is easily transferred, and the life of a corporation does not end with the incapacity of a stockholder. A corporation acts through its agents, who are its officers and managers. Corporations are regulated and subject to income taxes.

**C2** **Describe the components of stockholders' equity.** Authorized stock is the stock that a corporation's charter authorizes it to sell. Issued stock is the portion of authorized shares sold. Par value stock is a value per share assigned by the charter. No-par value stock is stock *not* assigned a value per share by the charter. Stated value stock is no-par stock to which the directors assign a value per share. Stockholders' equity is made up of (1) contributed capital and (2) retained earnings. Contributed capital consists of funds raised by stock issuances. Retained earnings consists of cumulative net income (losses) not distributed.

**C3 Explain characteristics of common and preferred stock.** Preferred stock has a priority (or senior status) relative to common stock in one or more areas, usually (1) dividends and (2) assets in case of liquidation. Preferred stock usually does not carry voting rights and can be convertible or callable. Convertibility permits the holder to convert preferred to common. Callability permits the issuer to buy back preferred stock under specified conditions.

**C4 Explain the form and content of a complete income statement.** An income statement has five *potential* sections: (1) continuing operations, (2) discontinued segments, (3) extraordinary items, (4) changes in accounting, and (5) earnings per share.

**C5 Explain the items reported in retained earnings.** Many companies face statutory and contractual restrictions on retained earnings. Corporations can voluntarily appropriate retained earnings to inform others about their disposition. Prior period adjustments are corrections of errors in prior financial statements.

**A1 Compute earnings per share and describe this ratio's use.** A company with a simple capital structure computes basic EPS by dividing net income less any preferred dividends by the weighted-average number of outstanding common shares. A company with a complex capital structure must usually report both basic and diluted EPS.

**A2 Compute book value and explain its use in analysis.** Book value per common share is equity applicable to common shares divided by the number of outstanding common shares. Book value per preferred share is equity applicable to preferred shares divided by the number of outstanding preferred shares.

**A3 Compute dividend yield and explain its use in analysis.** Dividend yield is the ratio of a stock's annual cash dividends per share to its market value (price) per share. Dividend yield can be compared with the yield of other companies to determine whether the stock is expected to be an income or growth stock.

**A4 Compute price-earnings ratio and describe its use in analysis.** A common stock's price-earnings (PE) ratio is computed by dividing the stock's market value (price) per share by its EPS. A stock's PE is based on expectations that can prove to be better or worse than eventual performance.

**P1 Record the issuance of corporate stock.** When stock is issued, its par or stated value is credited to the stock account and any excess is credited to a separate contributed capital account. If a stock has neither par nor stated value, the entire proceeds are credited to the stock account. Stockholders must contribute assets equal to minimum legal capital or be potentially liable for the deficiency.

**P2 Distribute dividends between common stock and preferred stock.** Preferred stockholders usually hold the right to dividend distributions before common stockholders. When preferred stock is cumulative and in arrears, the amount in arrears must be distributed to preferred before any dividends are distributed to common.

**P3 Record transactions involving cash dividends.** Cash dividends involve three events. On the date of declaration, the directors bind the company to pay the dividend. A dividend declaration reduces retained earnings and creates a current liability. On the date of record, recipients of the dividend are identified. On the date of payment, cash is paid to stockholders and the current liability is removed.

**P4 Account for stock dividends and stock splits.** Neither a stock dividend nor a stock split alters the value of the company. However, the value of each share is less due to the distribution of additional shares. The distribution of additional shares is according to individual stockholders' ownership percent. Small stock dividends ($\leq 25\%$) are recorded by capitalizing retained earnings equal to the market value of distributed shares. Large stock dividends ($>25\%$) are recorded by capitalizing retained earnings equal to the par or stated value of distributed shares. Stock splits do not yield journal entries but do yield changes in the description of stock.

**P5 Record purchases and sales of treasury stock and the retirement of stock.** When a corporation purchases its own previously issued stock, it debits the cost of these shares to Treasury Stock. Treasury stock is subtracted from equity in the balance sheet. If treasury stock is reissued, any proceeds in excess of cost are credited to Contributed Capital, Treasury Stock. If the proceeds are less than cost, they are debited to Contributed Capital, Treasury Stock to the extent a credit balance exists. Any remaining amount is debited to Retained Earnings. When stock is retired, all accounts related to the stock are removed.

---

## Guidance Answers to **Decision Maker** and **Decision Ethics**

**Concert Organizer** You have two basic options: (1) different classes of common stock or (2) common and preferred stock. Your objective is to issue to yourself stock that has all or a majority of the voting power. The other class of stock would carry limited or no voting rights. In this way, you maintain control and are able to raise the necessary funds.

**Entrepreneur** The 50% stock dividend provides you no direct income. A stock dividend often reveals management's optimistic expectations about the future and can improve a stock's marketability by making it affordable to more investors. Accordingly, a stock dividend usually reveals "good news" and because of this, it likely increases (slightly) the market value for your stock.

**Small Business Owner** The frost loss is probably not extraordinary. Jacksonville experiences enough recurring frost damage to make it difficult to argue this event is both unusual and infrequent. Still, you want to highlight the frost loss and hope the bank views this uncommon event separately from continuing operations.

**Director** This case deals with insider trading in a company's stock. The ethical conflict is between your director responsibilities to stockholders (and the public) and your interest in increasing personal wealth from the options. If information about the new contract is kept private until after the option plan is approved and the options are priced, you are likely to make more money. (*Note:* Insider trading laws may make nondisclosure in this case a crime.)

You should raise ethical and legal concerns to the board. You might also consider whether staying on the board of this company is proper since it appears there was some intent to deceive outsiders.

**Investor**  Book value reflects recorded values. BMX's book value is $4 per common share. Stock price reflects the market's expectation of net asset value (both tangible and intangible items). BMX's market value is $7 per common share. Comparing these figures suggests BMX's market value of net assets is higher than its recorded values (by an amount of $7 versus $4 per share).

**Manager**  Since one company requires a payment of $19 for each $1 of earnings, and the other requires $25, you would prefer the stock with the PE of 19; it is a better deal given identical prospects. You should make sure these companies' earnings computations are roughly the same, for example, no extraordinary items, unusual events, and so forth. Also, your PE estimates for these companies do matter. If you are willing to pay $29 for each $1 of earnings for these companies, both are solid investments because you obviously expect both to exceed current market expectations.

## Guidance Answers to **Quick Checks**

**1.** (*b*)

**2.** A corporation pays taxes on its income, and its stockholders normally pay personal income taxes (at the 15% rate or lower) on any cash dividends received from the corporation.

**3.** A proxy is a legal document used to transfer a stockholder's right to vote to another person.

**4.** (*a*)

**5.** A stock premium is an amount in excess of par (or stated) value paid by purchasers of newly issued stock.

**6.** Minimum legal capital intends to protect creditors of a corporation by obligating stockholders to some minimum level of equity financing and by constraining a corporation from excessive payments to stockholders.

**7.** Typically, preferred stock has a preference in receipt of dividends and in distribution of assets.

**8.** (*a*)

**9.** (*b*)

| | |
|---|---|
| Total cash dividend . . . . . . . . . . . . . . . . . . | $288,000 |
| To preferred shareholders . . . . . . . . . . . . . | 135,000* |
| Remainder to common shareholders . . . . . . | $153,000 |

\* 9,000 × $50 × 10% × 3 years = $135,000.

**10.** Common Dividend Payable is a current liability account.

**11.** The date of declaration, date of record, and date of payment.

**12.** A dividend is a legal liability at the date of declaration, on which date it is recorded as a liability.

**13.** A stock dividend does not transfer assets to stockholders, but it does require an amount of retained earnings to be transferred to a contributed capital account(s).

**14.** A small stock dividend is 25% or less of the previous outstanding shares. A large stock dividend is more than 25%.

**15.** Retained earnings equal to the distributable shares' market value should be capitalized for a small stock dividend.

**16.** (*b*)

**17.** No. The shares are an investment for Southern Co. and are issued and outstanding shares for Northern Corp.

**18.** Treasury stock does not affect the number of authorized or issued shares, but it reduces the outstanding shares.

**19.** (*a*)

**20.** (*b*)

**21.** The five (potentially reportable) major sections are income from continuing operations, discontinued segments, extraordinary items, cumulative effects of changes in accounting principles, and earnings per share.

**22.** (*c*)

**23.** (*a*) Weighted-average shares: $(25,000 \times 6/12) + (20,000 \times 6/12) = 22,500$. Earnings per share: $(\$250,000 - \$70,000)/22,500 = \$8$.

**24.** The number of shares previously outstanding is retroactively restated to reflect the stock split or stock dividend as if it occurred at the beginning of the period.

**25.** Basic EPS and diluted EPS.

## Key Terms

**Key Terms** are available at the book's Website for learning and testing in an online Flashcard Format.

Appropriated retained earnings (p. 461)
Authorized stock (p. 443)
Basic earnings per share (p. 458)
Book value per common share (p. 462)
Book value per preferred share (p. 462)
Business segment (p. 456)
Callable preferred stock (p. 449)
Call price (p. 449)
Capital stock (p. 443)

Changes in accounting estimates (p. 461)
Common stock (p. 442)
Complex capital structure (p. 460)
Contributed capital (p. 444)
Contributed capital in excess of par value (p. 444)
Convertible preferred stock (p. 449)
Corporation (p. 440)
Cumulative preferred stock (p. 447)

Date of declaration (p. 450)
Date of payment (p. 450)
Date of record (p. 450)
Diluted earnings per share (p. 460)
Dilutive securities (p. 460)
Discount on stock (p. 445)
Dividend in arrears (p. 448)
Dividend yield (p. 463)
Earnings per share (EPS) (p. 458)

| | | |
|---|---|---|
| **Extraordinary gains or losses** (p. 456) | **Par value** (p. 443) | **Simple capital structure** (p. 460) |
| **Financial leverage** (p. 449) | **Par value stock** (p. 443) | **Small stock dividend** (p. 451) |
| **Infrequent gain or loss** (p. 456) | **Preemptive right** (p. 442) | **Stated value stock** (p. 444) |
| **Large stock dividend** (p. 451) | **Preferred stock** (p. 447) | **Statement of stockholders' equity** (p. 461) |
| **Liquidating cash dividend** (p. 451) | **Premium on stock** (p. 444) | **Stock dividend** (p. 451) |
| **Market value per share** (p. 443) | **Price-earnings (PE) ratio** (p. 463) | **Stockholders' equity** (p. 444) |
| **Minimum legal capital** (p. 443) | **Prior period adjustment** (p. 461) | **Stock options** (p. 460) |
| **Noncumulative preferred stock** (p. 448) | **Proxy** (p. 442) | **Stock split** (p. 453) |
| **Nonparticipating preferred stock** (p. 448) | **Restricted retained earnings** (p. 461) | **Stock subscription** (p. 446) |
| **No-par value stock** (p. 444) | **Retained earnings** (p. 444) | **Treasury stock** (p. 454) |
| **Organization expenses** (p. 441) | **Retained earnings deficit** (p. 451) | **Unusual gain or loss** (p. 456) |
| **Participating preferred stock** (p. 448) | **Reverse stock split** (p. 453) | |

## Personal Interactive Quiz

Personal Interactive Quizzes A and B are available at the book's Website to reinforce and assess your learning.

## Discussion Questions

**1.** What are organization expenses? Provide examples.

**2.** How are organization expenses reported?

**3.** Who is responsible for directing a corporation's affairs?

**4.** What is the preemptive right of common stockholders?

**5.** List the general rights of common stockholders.

**6.** Why would an investor find convertible preferred stock attractive?

**7.** What is the difference between the par value and the call price of a share of preferred stock?

**8.** Identify and explain the importance of the three dates relevant to corporate dividends.

**9.** Why is the term *liquidating dividend* used to describe cash dividends debited against contributed capital accounts?

**10.** How does declaring a stock dividend affect the corporation's assets, liabilities, and total equity? What effects does the eventual distribution of the stock have?

**11.** What is the difference between a stock dividend and a stock split?

**12.** Courts have ruled that a stock dividend is not taxable income to stockholders. What justifies this decision?

**13.** How does the purchase of treasury stock affect the purchaser's assets and total equity?

**14.** Why do laws place limits on treasury stock purchases?

**15.** Where on the income statement does a company report an unusual gain not expected to occur more often than once every two years?

**16.** After taking five years of straight-line depreciation expense for an asset that was expected to have an eight-year useful life, a company decides that the asset will last six more years. Is this decision a change in accounting principles? How do the financial statements describe this change?

**17.** How are EPS results computed for a corporation with a simple capital structure?

**18.** Review the balance sheet for **Krispy Kreme** in Appendix A and determine the classes of stock that it has issued.

**19.** Refer to the balance sheet for **Tastykake** in Appendix A. What is the par value of its common stock? Suggest a rationale for the amount of par value it assigned.

**20.** Refer to the financial statements for **Tastykake** in Appendix A. How many treasury stock shares does it report as of December 28, 2002? Compute the average cost per treasury share.

**21.** Refer to the financial statements for **Harley-Davidson** in Appendix A. Was it a net seller or net purchaser of treasury stock for the fiscal year ended December 31, 2002? Explain.

*Red numbers denote Discussion Questions that involve decision-making.*

*Homework Manager* repeats all numerical Quick Studies on the book's Website with new numbers. ➜

## QUICK STUDY

**QS 11-1**
Characteristics of corporations
C1

Of the following statements, which are true for the corporate form of organization?

**1.** It is a separate legal entity.
**2.** Ownership rights cannot be easily transferred.
**3.** Owners are not agents of the corporation.
**4.** Capital is more easily accumulated than with most other forms of organization.
**5.** It has a limited life.
**6.** Owners have unlimited liability for corporate debts.
**7.** Corporate income that is distributed to shareholders is usually taxed twice.

**QS 11-2**
Issuance of common stock
P1

Prepare the journal entry to record each separate transaction. (*a*) On March 1, DVD Co. issues 44,500 shares of $4 par value common stock for $255,000 cash. (*b*) On April 1, GT Co. issues no-par value common stock for $50,000 cash. (*c*) On April 6, MTV issues 2,000 shares of $20 par value common stock for $35,000 of inventory, $135,000 of machinery, and acceptance of a $84,000 note payable.

**QS 11-3**
Dividend allocation between classes of shareholders

P2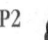

Hilton Company's stockholders' equity includes 75,000 shares of $5 par value, 8% cumulative preferred stock and 200,000 shares of $1 par value common stock. Both classes of stock have been outstanding since the company's inception. Hilton did not declare any dividends in the prior year, but it now declares and pays a $108,000 cash dividend in the current year. Determine the amount distributed to each class of stockholders for this two-year-old company.

**QS 11-4**
Accounting for cash dividends
P3

Prepare journal entries to record the following transactions for Skylar Corporation:

May 15    Declared a $48,000 cash dividend payable to common stockholders.
July 31    Paid the dividend declared on May 15.

**QS 11-5**
Accounting for small stock dividend

C2  P4

The stockholders' equity section of Catalina Company's balance sheet as of April 1 follows. On April 2, Catalina declares and distributes a 10% stock dividend. The stock's per share market value on April 2 is $25. Prepare the stockholders' equity section immediately after the stock dividend.

| | |
|---|---|
| Common stock—$5 par value, 375,000 shares authorized, 150,000 shares issued and outstanding . . . . . . . . . . . | $ 750,000 |
| Contributed capital in excess of par value, common stock . . . . . . . | 352,500 |
| Total contributed capital . . . . . . . . . . . . . . . . . . . . . . . . . . . . . . | 1,102,500 |
| Retained earnings . . . . . . . . . . . . . . . . . . . . . . . . . . . . . . . . . . | 633,000 |
| Total stockholders' equity . . . . . . . . . . . . . . . . . . . . . . . . . . . . . | $1,735,500 |

**QS 11-6**
Purchase and sale of treasury stock  P5

On May 3, Lassman Corporation purchased 3,000 shares of its own stock for $27,000 cash. On November 4, Lassman reissued 750 shares of this treasury stock for $7,080. Prepare the May 3 and November 4 journal entries to record Lassman's purchase and reissuance of treasury stock.

**QS 11-7**
Accounting for changes in estimates; error adjustments

C4  C5

Answer the following questions related to a company's activities for the current year:

**1.** A review of the notes payable files discovers that three years ago the company reported the entire amount of a payment (principal and interest) on an installment note payable as interest expense. This mistake had a material effect on the amount of income in that year. How should the correction be reported in the current year financial statements?

**2.** After using an expected useful life of seven years and no salvage value to depreciate its office equipment over the preceding three years, the company decided early this year that the equipment will last only two more years. How should the effects of this decision be reported in the current year financial statements?

**QS 11-8**
Basic earnings per share  A1

Barnes Company earned a net income of $450,000 this year. The number of common shares outstanding during the entire year was 200,000, and preferred shareholders received a $10,000 cash dividend. Compute Barnes Company's basic earnings per share.

On January 1, Vendetta Company had 100,000 shares of common stock outstanding. On February 1, it issued 20,000 additional shares of common stock. On June 1, it issued another 40,000 shares of common stock. Compute Vendetta's weighted-average shares outstanding for the calendar year.

**QS 11-9**
Weighted-average shares outstanding   A1

---

On January 1, Brazil Company had 150,000 shares of common stock outstanding. On April 1, it purchased 12,000 treasury shares and on June 2, it declared a 10% stock dividend. Compute Brazil's weighted-average shares outstanding for the calendar-year.

**QS 11-10**
Weighted-average shares outstanding   A1   P4

---

The stockholders' equity section of Axel Company's balance sheet follows. The preferred stock's call price is $30. Determine the book value per share of the common stock.

**QS 11-11**
Book value per common share

A2

| | |
|---|---:|
| Preferred stock—5% cumulative, $10 par value, 10,000 shares authorized, issued and outstanding ....... | $100,000 |
| Common stock—$5 par value, 100,000 shares authorized, 75,000 shares issued and outstanding ....... | 375,000 |
| Retained earnings ............................... | 445,000 |
| Total stockholders' equity ........................ | $920,000 |

---

Fiona Company expects to pay a $2.10 per share cash dividend this year on its common stock. The current market value of Fiona stock is $28.50 per share. Compute the expected dividend yield on the Fiona stock. Would you classify the Fiona stock as a growth or an income stock?

**QS 11-12**
Dividend yield

A3

---

Compute Fox Company's price-earnings ratio if its common stock has a market value of $30.75 per share and its EPS is $4.10. Would an analyst likely consider this stock potentially over- or underpriced?

**QS 11-13**
Price-earnings ratio   A4

---

*Homework Manager* repeats all numerical Exercises on the book's Website with new numbers.

---

Describe how each of the following characteristics of organizations applies to corporations.

1. Owner authority and control
2. Ease of formation
3. Transferability of ownership
4. Ability to raise large capital amounts
5. Duration of life
6. Owner liability
7. Legal status
8. Tax status of income

**EXERCISES**

**Exercise 11-1**
Characteristics of corporations

C1

---

Aloha Corporation issues 6,000 shares of its common stock for $144,000 cash on February 20. Prepare journal entries to record this event under each of the following separate situations:

**1.** The stock has neither par nor stated value.
**2.** The stock has a $20 par value.
**3.** The stock has a $8 stated value.

**Exercise 11-2**
Accounting for par and no-par stock issuances
P1

---

Prepare journal entries to record the following four separate issuances of stock:

**1.** Two thousand shares of no-par common stock are issued to the corporation's promoters in exchange for their efforts, estimated to be worth $30,000. The stock has no stated value.
**2.** Two thousand shares of no-par common stock are issued to the corporation's promoters in exchange for their efforts, estimated to be worth $30,000. The stock has a $1 per share stated value.
**3.** Four thousand shares of $10 par value common stock are issued for $70,000 cash.
**4.** One thousand shares of $100 par value preferred stock are issued for $120,000 cash.

**Exercise 11-3**
Recording stock issuances
P1

---

Match each description 1 through 6 with the characteristic of preferred stock that it best describes by writing the letter of the characteristic in the blank next to each description.

**A.** Callable            **B.** Convertible            **C.** Cumulative
**D.** Noncumulative      **E.** Nonparticipating       **F.** Participating

**Exercise 11-4**
Identifying characteristics of preferred stock

C2   C3

_____ **1.** Holders of the stock are not entitled to receive dividends in excess of the stated rate.

_____ **2.** Holders of the stock lose any dividends that are not declared in the current year.

_____ **3.** Holders of the stock are entitled to receive current and all past dividends before common stockholders receive any dividends.

_____ **4.** Holders of this stock can exchange it for shares of common stock.

_____ **5.** The issuing corporation can retire the stock by paying a prespecified price.

_____ **6.** Holders of the stock can receive dividends exceeding the stated rate under certain conditions.

---

**Exercise 11-5**

Dividends on common and noncumulative preferred stock

P2

Citicool's outstanding stock consists of (*a*) 40,000 shares of noncumulative 7.5% preferred stock with a $10 par value and (*b*) 100,000 shares of common stock with a $1 par value. During its first four years of operation, the corporation declared and paid the following cash dividends:

| | |
|---|---|
| 2003 ........................ | $ 10,000 |
| 2004 ........................ | 24,000 |
| 2005 ........................ | 100,000 |
| 2006 ........................ | 196,000 |

**Check**  Total paid to preferred, $94,000

Determine the amount of dividends paid each year to each of the two classes of stockholders. Also compute the total dividends paid to each class for the four years combined.

---

**Exercise 11-6**

Dividends on common and cumulative preferred stock   P2

Use the data in Exercise 11-5 to determine the amount of dividends paid each year to each of the two classes of stockholders assuming that the preferred stock is cumulative. Also determine the total dividends paid to each class for the four years combined.

---

**Exercise 11-7**

Stock dividends and splits

P4

On June 30, 2005, Scizzory Corporation's common stock is priced at $31 per share before any stock dividend or split, and the stockholders' equity section of its balance sheet appears as follows:

| | |
|---|---|
| Common stock—$10 par value, 60,000 shares authorized, 25,000 shares issued and outstanding ............ | $250,000 |
| Contributed capital in excess of par value, common stock ....... | 100,000 |
| Total contributed capital ............................... | 350,000 |
| Retained earnings ...................................... | 330,000 |
| Total stockholders' equity ............................... | $680,000 |

**1.** Assume that the company declares and immediately distributes a 100% stock dividend. This event is recorded by capitalizing retained earnings equal to the stock's par value. Answer these questions about stockholders' equity as it exists *after* issuing the new shares:

  **a.** What is the retained earnings balance?

**Check**  (1*b*) $680,000

  **b.** What is the amount of total stockholders' equity?

  **c.** How many shares are outstanding?

**2.** Assume that the company implements a 2-for-1 stock split instead of the stock dividend in part 1. Answer these questions about stockholders' equity as it exists *after* issuing the new shares:

(2*a*) $330,000

  **a.** What is the retained earnings balance?

  **b.** What is the amount of total stockholders' equity?

  **c.** How many shares are outstanding?

**3.** Explain the difference, if any, to a stockholder from receiving new shares distributed under a large stock dividend versus a stock split.

---

**Exercise 11-8**

Stock dividends and per share book values

P4

The stockholders' equity of Whiz.com at the beginning of the day on February 5 follows:

| | |
|---|---|
| Common stock—$25 par value, 150,000 shares authorized, 60,000 shares issued and outstanding ............ | $1,500,000 |
| Contributed capital in excess of par value, common stock ....... | 525,000 |
| Total contributed capital ................................ | 2,025,000 |
| Retained earnings ...................................... | 675,000 |
| Total stockholders' equity ............................... | $2,700,000 |

On February 5, the directors declare a 20% stock dividend distributable on February 28 to the February 15 stockholders of record. The stock's market value is $40 per share on February 5 before the stock dividend. The stock's market value is $34 per share on February 28.

**1.** Prepare entries to record both the dividend declaration and its distribution.

**2.** One stockholder owned 750 shares on February 5 before the dividend. Compute the book value per share and total book value of this stockholder's shares immediately before and after the stock dividend of February 5.

**Check** (2) Book value per share: before, $45.00; after, $37.50

**3.** Compute the total market value of the investor's shares in part 2 as of February 5 and February 28.

---

On October 10, the stockholders' equity of Noble Systems appears as follows:

| | |
|---|---|
| Common stock—$10 par value, 36,000 shares authorized, issued, and outstanding . . . . . . . . . . . . . . . . . . . . . . . | $360,000 |
| Contributed capital in excess of par value, common stock . . . . . . . | 108,000 |
| Total contributed capital . . . . . . . . . . . . . . . . . . . . . . . . . . . . . . | 468,000 |
| Retained earnings . . . . . . . . . . . . . . . . . . . . . . . . . . . . . . . . . . . | 432,000 |
| Total stockholders' equity . . . . . . . . . . . . . . . . . . . . . . . . . . . . . | $900,000 |

**Exercise 11-9**
Recording and reporting treasury stock transactions

P5

**1.** Prepare journal entries to record the following transactions for Noble Systems:

   **a.** Purchased 4,500 shares of its own common stock at $30 per share on October 11.

   **b.** Sold 1,200 treasury shares on November 1 for $36 cash per share.

   **c.** Sold all remaining treasury shares on November 25 for $25 cash per share.

**2.** Explain how Noble's equity section changes after the October 11 treasury stock purchase, and prepare the revised equity section of its balance sheet at that time.

**Check** (1c) Dr. Retained Earnings, $9,300

---

In 2005, Randa Merchandising, Inc., sold its interest in a chain of wholesale outlets, taking the company completely out of the wholesaling business. The company still operates its retail outlets. A listing of the major sections of an income statement follows:

**A.** Income (loss) from continuing operations

**B.** Income (loss) from operating, or gain (loss) from disposing, a discontinued segment

**C.** Extraordinary gain (loss)

**D.** Cumulative effect of a change in accounting principle

Indicate where each of the following income-related items for this company appears on its 2005 income statement by writing the letter of the appropriate section in the blank beside each item.

**Exercise 11-10**
Income statement categories

C4

| Section | Item | Debit | Credit |
|---|---|---|---|
| _____ | 1. Net sales . . . . . . . . . . . . . . . . . . . . . . . . . . . . . . . . . . . . . . . | | $2,700,000 |
| _____ | 2. Gain on state's condemnation of company property (net of tax) . . . . . . . . . . . . . . . . . . . . . . . . . . . . . . . | | 330,000 |
| _____ | 3. Cost of goods sold . . . . . . . . . . . . . . . . . . . . . . . . . . . . . . . | $1,380,000 | |
| _____ | 4. Effect of change from FIFO to LIFO (net of tax) . . . . . . . . . . . . . . | | 135,000 |
| _____ | 5. Income taxes expense . . . . . . . . . . . . . . . . . . . . . . . . . . . . . . | 207,000 | |
| _____ | 6. Depreciation expense . . . . . . . . . . . . . . . . . . . . . . . . . . . . . . | 262,500 | |
| _____ | 7. Gain on sale of wholesale business segment (net of tax) . . . . . . . . . . . . . . . . . . . . . . . . . . . . . . . | | 675,000 |
| _____ | 8. Loss from operating wholesale business segment (net of tax) . . . . . . . . . . . . . . . . . . . . . . . . . . . . . . . | 555,000 | |
| _____ | 9. Salaries expense . . . . . . . . . . . . . . . . . . . . . . . . . . . . . . . . . | 540,000 | |

**Exercise 11-11**

Income statement presentation

C4

Use the financial data for Randa Merchandising, Inc., in Exercise 11-10 to prepare its income statement for calendar year 2005. (Ignore the earnings per share section.)

**Exercise 11-12**

Reporting a change in accounting principle

C4  C5

Fast Tek put an asset costing $225,000 into service on January 1, 2004. Its predicted useful life is six years with an expected salvage value of $22,500. The company uses double-declining-balance depreciation and records $75,000 of depreciation in 2004 and $50,000 of depreciation in 2005. The scheduled depreciation expense for 2006 is $33,250. After consulting with the company's auditors, management decides to change to straight-line depreciation in 2006 without changing either the predicted useful life or salvage value. Under this new method, the annual depreciation expense for this asset is $33,750. The cumulative effect on prior year income statements (for 2004–2005) is to decrease depreciation expense by $57,500 and increase pretax income by $57,500. This company has a 35% income tax rate.

**1.** How much depreciation expense is reported on the company's income statement for this asset in 2006 and in each of the remaining years of its life?

**Check**  (2) After-tax cumulative effect, $37,375

**2.** What amount is reported on the company's 2006 income statement as the after-tax cumulative effect of the change in accounting principle?

**Exercise 11-13**

Weighted-average shares and earnings per share

A1

Nexus Company reports $1,350,000 of net income for 2005 and declares $195,000 of cash dividends on its preferred stock for 2005. At the beginning of 2005, the company had 270,000 outstanding shares of common stock. Two events change the number of outstanding common shares during 2005:

May  1   Issued 180,000 common shares for cash.
Nov.  1   Purchased 108,000 shares of its own common stock.

**1.** What amount of net income is available to common stockholders for 2005?

**Check**  (2) 372,000 shares

**2.** What is the weighted-average number of common shares outstanding for 2005?

**3.** What is the company's basic EPS for 2005?

**Exercise 11-14**

Weighted-average shares and earnings per share

A1

C4 Company reports $480,000 of net income for 2005 and declares $65,000 of cash dividends on its preferred stock for 2005. At the beginning of 2005, the company had 50,000 outstanding shares of common stock. Three events change the number of outstanding common shares during year 2005.

June  1   Issued 30,000 common shares for cash.
Sept.  1   Purchased 13,000 shares of its own common stock.
Oct.   1   Completed a 3-for-1 stock split.

**1.** What amount of net income is available to common stockholders for 2005?

**Check**  (2) 189,500 shares

**2.** What is the weighted-average number of common shares outstanding for 2005?

**3.** What is the company's basic EPS for 2005?

**Exercise 11-15**

Book value per share

A2

The equity section of Anna Corporation's balance sheet shows the following:

| | |
|---|---:|
| Preferred stock—6% cumulative, $25 par value, $30 call price, 5,000 shares issued and outstanding ............... | $125,000 |
| Common stock—$10 par value, 40,000 shares issued and outstanding ............................ | 400,000 |
| Retained earnings ................................... | 267,500 |
| Total stockholders' equity ........................... | $792,500 |

Determine the book value per share of the preferred and common stock under two separate situations:

**Check**  (1) Book value of common, $16.06

**1.** No preferred dividends are in arrears.

**2.** Three years of preferred dividends are in arrears.

Compute the dividend yield for each of these four separate companies. Which company's stock would probably *not* be classified as an income stock?

**Exercise 11-16**
Dividend yield computation and interpretation

A3

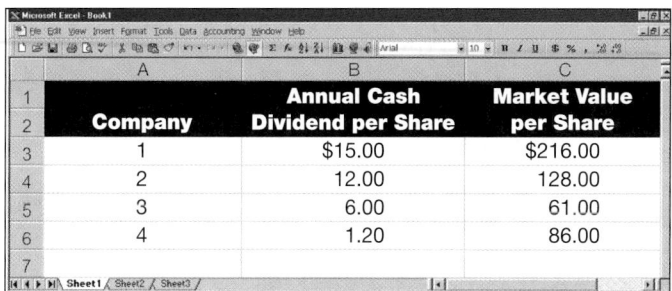

| Company | Annual Cash Dividend per Share | Market Value per Share |
|---|---|---|
| 1 | $15.00 | $216.00 |
| 2 | 12.00 | 128.00 |
| 3 | 6.00 | 61.00 |
| 4 | 1.20 | 86.00 |

Compute the price-earnings ratio for each of these four separate companies. Which stock might an analyst likely investigate as being potentially undervalued by the market?

**Exercise 11-17**
Price-earnings ratio computation and interpretation

A4

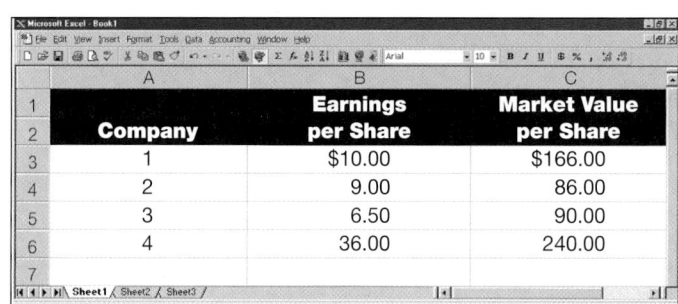

| Company | Earnings per Share | Market Value per Share |
|---|---|---|
| 1 | $10.00 | $166.00 |
| 2 | 9.00 | 86.00 |
| 3 | 6.50 | 90.00 |
| 4 | 36.00 | 240.00 |

Oxygen Co. is incorporated at the beginning of this year and engages in a number of transactions. The following journal entries impacted its stockholders' equity during its first year of operations:

**PROBLEM SET A**

**Problem 11-1A**
Stockholders' equity transactions and analysis

C2 C3 P1

| | | | |
|---|---|---|---|
| a. | Cash . . . . . . . . . . . . . . . . . . . . . . . . . . . . . . . . | 150,000 | |
| | Common Stock, $25 Par Value . . . . . . . . . . . | | 125,000 |
| | Contributed Capital in Excess of<br>Par Value, Common Stock. . . . . . . . . . . . . | | 25,000 |
| b. | Organization Expenses . . . . . . . . . . . . . . . . . . . | 75,000 | |
| | Common Stock, $25 Par Value . . . . . . . . . . . | | 62,500 |
| | Contributed Capital in Excess of<br>Par Value, Common Stock. . . . . . . . . . . . . | | 12,500 |
| c. | Cash . . . . . . . . . . . . . . . . . . . . . . . . . . . . . . . . | 21,500 | |
| | Accounts Receivable . . . . . . . . . . . . . . . . . . . . | 7,500 | |
| | Building . . . . . . . . . . . . . . . . . . . . . . . . . . . . . | 30,000 | |
| | Notes Payable . . . . . . . . . . . . . . . . . . . . . . . | | 19,000 |
| | Common Stock, $25 Par Value . . . . . . . . . . . | | 25,000 |
| | Contributed Capital in Excess of<br>Par Value, Common Stock. . . . . . . . . . . . . | | 15,000 |
| d. | Cash . . . . . . . . . . . . . . . . . . . . . . . . . . . . . . . . | 60,000 | |
| | Common Stock, $25 Par Value . . . . . . . . . . . | | 37,500 |
| | Contributed Capital in Excess of<br>Par Value, Common Stock. . . . . . . . . . . . . | | 22,500 |

**Required**

1. Explain each journal entry (*a*) through (*d*).
2. How many shares of common stock are outstanding at year-end?
3. What is the amount of minimum legal capital (based on par value) at year-end?
4. What is the total contributed capital at year-end?
5. What is the book value per share of the common stock at year-end if contributed capital plus retained earnings equals $347,500?

---

## Problem 11-2A

Cash dividends, treasury stock, and statement of retained earnings

C2　C5　P3　P5

Context Corporation reports the following components of stockholders' equity on December 31, 2005:

| | |
|---|---:|
| Common stock—$10 par value, 50,000 shares authorized, 20,000 shares issued and outstanding . . . . . . . . . . . . . . . . . . . . | $200,000 |
| Contributed capital in excess of par value, common stock . . . . . . . . | 30,000 |
| Retained earnings . . . . . . . . . . . . . . . . . . . . . . . . . . . . . . . . . . . . . | 135,000 |
| Total stockholders' equity . . . . . . . . . . . . . . . . . . . . . . . . . . . . . | $365,000 |

In year 2006, the following transactions affected its stockholders' equity accounts:

Jan.　1　Purchased 2,000 shares of its own stock at $20 cash per share.
Jan.　5　Directors declared a $2 per share cash dividend payable on Feb. 28 to the Feb. 5 stockholders of record.
Feb.　28　Paid the dividend declared on January 5.
July　6　Sold 750 of its treasury shares at $24 cash per share.
Aug.　22　Sold 1,250 of its treasury shares at $17 cash per share.
Sept.　5　Directors declared a $2 per share cash dividend payable on October 28 to the September 25 stockholders of record.
Oct.　28　Paid the dividend declared on September 5.
Dec.　31　Closed the $194,000 credit balance (from net income) in the Income Summary account to Retained Earnings.

**Required**

1. Prepare journal entries to record these transactions for 2006.
2. Prepare a statement of retained earnings for the year ended December 31, 2006.
3. Prepare the stockholders' equity section of the company's balance sheet as of December 31, 2006.

---

## Problem 11-3A

Equity analysis—journal entries and account balances

P3　P4

At September 30, the end of Excel Company's third quarter, the following stockholders' equity accounts are reported:

| | |
|---|---:|
| Common stock, $12 par value . . . . . . . . . . . . . . . . . . . . . . . . . . . . | $720,000 |
| Contributed capital in excess of par value, common stock . . . . . . . | 180,000 |
| Retained earnings . . . . . . . . . . . . . . . . . . . . . . . . . . . . . . . . . . . | 640,000 |

In the fourth quarter, the following entries related to its equity accounts are recorded:

| | | | |
|---|---|---:|---:|
| Oct. 2 | Retained Earnings . . . . . . . . . . . . . . . . . . . . . . . | 120,000 | |
| | 　　Common Dividend Payable . . . . . . . . . . . . | | 120,000 |
| Oct. 25 | Common Dividend Payable . . . . . . . . . . . . . . . . | 120,000 | |
| | 　　Cash . . . . . . . . . . . . . . . . . . . . . . . . . . . . | | 120,000 |
| Oct. 31 | Retained Earnings . . . . . . . . . . . . . . . . . . . . . . | 150,000 | |
| | 　　Common Stock Dividend Distributable . . . . | | 72,000 |
| | 　　Contributed Capital in Excess of Par Value, Common Stock . . . . . . . . . . . . | | 78,000 |
| Nov. 5 | Common Stock Dividend Distributable . . . . . . . . | 72,000 | |
| | 　　Common Stock, $12 Par Value . . . . . . . . . . | | 72,000 |

[continued on next page]

[continued from previous page]

| Dec. 1 | Memo—Change the title of the common stock account to reflect the new par value of $4. | | |
| --- | --- | --- | --- |
| Dec. 31 | Income Summary .......................... | 420,000 | |
| | Retained Earnings ..................... | | 420,000 |

## Required

**1.** Explain each journal entry.

**2.** Complete the following table showing the equity account balances at each indicated date:

| | Oct. 2 | Oct. 25 | Oct. 31 | Nov. 5 | Dec. 1 | Dec. 31 |
| --- | --- | --- | --- | --- | --- | --- |
| Common stock .................... | $____ | $____ | $____ | $____ | $____ | $____ |
| Common stock dividend distributable ..................... | ____ | ____ | ____ | ____ | ____ | ____ |
| Contributed capital in excess of par, common stock ....... | ____ | ____ | ____ | ____ | ____ | ____ |
| Retained earnings ................. | ____ | ____ | ____ | ____ | ____ | ____ |
| Total equity ..................... | $____ | $____ | $____ | $____ | $____ | $____ |

**Check**  Total equity: Oct. 2, $1,420,000; Dec. 31, $1,840,000

---

The equity sections from Salazar Group's 2005 and 2006 year-end balance sheets follow:

**Problem 11-4A**
Analysis of changes in stockholders' equity accounts

C5  P3  P4  P5

### Stockholders' Equity (December 31, 2005)

| | |
| --- | --- |
| Common stock—$4 par value, 50,000 shares authorized, 20,000 shares issued and outstanding .............. | $ 80,000 |
| Contributed capital in excess of par value, common stock ......... | 60,000 |
| Total contributed capital ............................... | 140,000 |
| Retained earnings ...................................... | 160,000 |
| Total stockholders' equity .............................. | $300,000 |

### Stockholders' Equity (December 31, 2006)

| | |
| --- | --- |
| Common stock—$4 par value, 50,000 shares authorized, 23,700 shares issued, 1,500 shares in treasury ....... | $ 94,800 |
| Contributed capital in excess of par value, common stock ......... | 89,600 |
| Total contributed capital ............................... | 184,400 |
| Retained earnings ($15,000 restricted by treasury stock) .......... | 200,000 |
| | 384,400 |
| Less cost of treasury stock ............................ | (15,000) |
| Total stockholders' equity .............................. | $369,400 |

The following transactions and events affected its equity accounts during year 2006:

| | | |
| --- | --- | --- |
| Jan. | 5 | Declared a $0.50 per share cash dividend, date of record January 10. |
| Mar. | 20 | Purchased treasury stock for cash. |
| Apr. | 5 | Declared a $0.50 per share cash dividend, date of record April 10. |
| July | 5 | Declared a $0.50 per share cash dividend, date of record July 10. |
| July | 31 | Declared a 20% stock dividend when the stock's market value is $12 per share. |
| Aug. | 14 | Issued stock dividend that was declared on July 31. |
| Oct. | 5 | Declared a $0.50 per share cash dividend, date of record October 10. |

## Required

**1.** How many common shares are outstanding on each cash dividend date?

**2.** What is the total dollar amount for each of the four cash dividends?

**3.** What is the amount of the capitalization of retained earnings for the stock dividend?

**4.** What is the per share cost of the treasury stock purchased?

**5.** How much net income did the company earn during year 2006?

**Check**  (3) $44,400

(4) $10

(5) $124,000

**Problem 11-5A**

Income statement computations and format

C4

Selected account balances from the adjusted trial balance for Chex Corporation as of its calendar year-end December 31, 2005, follow:

| | Debit | Credit |
|---|---|---|
| a. Interest revenue | | $ 12,000 |
| b. Depreciation expense—Equipment | $ 36,000 | |
| c. Loss on sale of equipment | 24,750 | |
| d. Accounts payable | | 42,000 |
| e. Other operating expenses | 97,500 | |
| f. Accumulated depreciation—Equipment | | 73,500 |
| g. Gain from settlement of lawsuit | | 42,000 |
| h. Cumulative effect of change in accounting principle (pretax) | 63,000 | |
| i. Accumulated depreciation—Buildings | | 163,500 |
| j. Loss from operating a discontinued segment (pretax) | 19,500 | |
| k. Gain on insurance recovery of tornado damage (pretax and extraordinary) | | 28,500 |
| l. Net sales | | 970,500 |
| m. Depreciation expense—Buildings | 54,000 | |
| n. Correction of overstatement of prior year's sales (pretax) | 15,000 | |
| o. Gain on sale of discontinued segment's assets (pretax) | | 33,000 |
| p. Loss from settlement of lawsuit | 24,000 | |
| q. Income taxes expense | ? | |
| r. Cost of goods sold | 487,500 | |

**Required**

Answer each of the following questions by providing supporting computations:

**1.** Assume that the company's income tax rate is 30% for all items. Identify the tax effects and after-tax amounts of the five items labeled pretax.

**2.** What is the amount of income from continuing operations before income taxes? What is the amount of the income taxes expense? What is the amount of income from continuing operations?

**Check** (3) $9,450

(4) $219,975

**3.** What is the total amount of after-tax income (loss) associated with the discontinued segment?

**4.** What is the amount of income (loss) before the extraordinary items and the cumulative effect of changes in accounting principle?

(5) $195,825

**5.** What is the amount of net income for the year?

**Problem 11-6A**

Change in accounting principle (depreciation) and its disclosure

C4

mhhe.com/wild3e

**Check** (2) 2004, $144,000

(3) 2004, $114,000

(4) After-tax cumulative effect, $89,880

On January 1, 2003, Virtuality, Inc., purchases equipment costing $600,000 with an expected salvage value of $30,000 at the end of its five-year useful life. Depreciation is allocated to 2003, 2004, and 2005 with the double-declining-balance method. Early in 2006, the company changes to the straight-line method to produce more useful financial statements and to be consistent with industry competitors.

**Required**

**1.** Do generally accepted accounting principles allow Virtuality to change depreciation methods in 2006?

**2.** Prepare a table to show the annual amount of depreciation expense allocated to 2003 through 2005 using the double-declining-balance method.

**3.** Prepare a table to show the annual amount of depreciation expense that would have been allocated to 2003 through 2005 using the straight-line method.

**4.** The cumulative effect on prior year income statements (for 2003–2005) is to decrease depreciation expense by $128,400 and increase pretax income by $128,400. The company's income tax rate is 30%. What are the pretax and after-tax cumulative effects of the accounting change?

**5.** How should the cumulative effect of the change in accounting principle be reported? Does the cumulative effect increase or decrease net income?

**6.** How much depreciation expense is reported on the company's income statement for 2006?

*Analysis Component*

(7) 2006 retained earnings understated by $44,940

**7.** Assume that Virtuality mistakenly treats the change in depreciation methods as a change in accounting estimate. Using your answers from parts 2, 3, and 4, describe the effect of this error on the 2006 financial statements.

The annual income statements for Cortez, Inc., as reported when they were initially published in 2003, 2004, and 2005 follow:

**Problem 11-7A**

Earnings per share calculation and presentation

C4   A1

mhhe.com/wild3e

| | 2003 | 2004 | 2005 |
|---|---|---|---|
| Net sales .......................... | $370,000 | $425,000 | $412,500 |
| Operating expenses ................... | 232,500 | 260,000 | 245,500 |
| Income from continuing operations ....... | 137,500 | 165,000 | 167,000 |
| Loss on discontinued segment ........... | (52,500) | — | — |
| Income before extraordinary items ........ | 85,000 | 165,000 | 167,000 |
| Extraordinary gain (loss) ............... | — | 33,000 | (70,000) |
| Net income ....................... | $ 85,000 | $198,000 | $ 97,000 |

The company also experienced changes in the number of outstanding shares from the following events:

| | |
|---|---|
| Outstanding shares on December 31, 2002 ....... | 40,000 |
| **2003** | |
| Treasury stock purchase on April 1 ............. | − 4,000 |
| Issuance of new shares on June 30 .............. | + 12,000 |
| 10% stock dividend on October 1 .............. | + 4,800 |
| Outstanding shares on December 31, 2003 ....... | 52,800 |
| **2004** | |
| Issuance of new shares on July 1 ............... | + 16,000 |
| Treasury stock purchase on November 1 ......... | − 4,800 |
| Outstanding shares on December 31, 2004 ....... | 64,000 |
| **2005** | |
| Issuance of new shares on August 1 ............. | + 20,000 |
| Treasury stock purchase on September 1 ......... | − 4,000 |
| 3-for-1 stock split on October 1 ............... | +160,000 |
| Outstanding shares on December 31, 2005 ....... | 240,000 |

**Required**

1. Compute the weighted average of the common shares outstanding for year 2003.
2. Compute the EPS component amounts to report with the year 2003 income statement for: income from continuing operations, the loss on discontinued segment, and net income.
3. Compute the weighted average of the common shares outstanding for year 2004.
4. Compute the EPS component amounts to report with the year 2004 income statement for: income from continuing operations, the extraordinary gain, and net income.
5. Compute the weighted average of the common shares outstanding for year 2005.
6. Compute the EPS component amounts to report with the year 2005 income statement for: income from continuing operations, the extraordinary loss, and net income.

*Analysis Component*

7.  Explain how you would use the EPS data from part 6 to predict EPS for 2006.

**Check**  (1) 47,300 shares

(2) EPS, $1.80

(3) 60,000 shares

(4) EPS, $3.30

Razz Corporation's common stock is currently selling on a stock exchange at $170 per share, and its current balance sheet shows the following stockholders' equity section:

**Problem 11-8A**

Computation of book values and dividend allocations

C3   A2   P2

| | |
|---|---|
| Preferred stock—5% cumulative, $___ par value, 1,000 shares authorized, issued, and outstanding .......................... | $100,000 |
| Common stock—$___ par value, 4,000 shares authorized, issued, and outstanding ....................................... | 160,000 |
| Retained earnings ....................................... | 300,000 |
| Total stockholders' equity .................................. | $560,000 |

**Required**

1. What is the current market value (price) of this corporation's common stock?

2. What are the par values of the corporation's preferred stock and its common stock?

3. If no dividends are in arrears, what are the book values per share of the preferred stock and the common stock?

4. If two years' preferred dividends are in arrears, what are the book values per share of the preferred stock and the common stock?

5. If two years' preferred dividends are in arrears and the preferred stock is callable at $110 per share, what are the book values per share of the preferred stock and the common stock?

6. If two years' preferred dividends are in arrears and the board of directors declares cash dividends of $20,000, what total amount will be paid to the preferred and to the common shareholders? What is the amount of dividends per share for the common stock?

*Analysis Component*

7. What are some factors that can contribute to a difference between the book value of common stock and its market value (price)?

---

# PROBLEM SET B

## Problem 11-1B

Stockholders' equity transactions and analysis

C2   C3   P1

Nilson Company is incorporated at the beginning of this year and engages in a number of transactions. The following journal entries impacted its stockholders' equity during its first year of operations:

| | | | |
|---|---|---:|---:|
| a. | Cash . . . . . . . . . . . . . . . . . . . . . . . . . . . . . . . . . | 60,000 | |
| | Common Stock, $1 Par Value . . . . . . . . . . . . | | 1,500 |
| | Contributed Capital in Excess of Par Value, Common Stock . . . . . . . . . . . . . | | 58,500 |
| b. | Organization Expenses . . . . . . . . . . . . . . . . . . . . | 20,000 | |
| | Common Stock, $1 Par Value . . . . . . . . . . . . | | 500 |
| | Contributed Capital in Excess of Par Value, Common Stock . . . . . . . . . . . . | | 19,500 |
| c. | Cash . . . . . . . . . . . . . . . . . . . . . . . . . . . . . . . . . | 6,650 | |
| | Accounts Receivable . . . . . . . . . . . . . . . . . . . . | 4,000 | |
| | Building . . . . . . . . . . . . . . . . . . . . . . . . . . . . . . | 12,500 | |
| | Notes Payable . . . . . . . . . . . . . . . . . . . . . . . . | | 3,150 |
| | Common Stock, $1 Par Value . . . . . . . . . . . . | | 400 |
| | Contributed Capital in Excess of Par Value, Common Stock . . . . . . . . . . . . | | 19,600 |
| d. | Cash . . . . . . . . . . . . . . . . . . . . . . . . . . . . . . . . . | 30,000 | |
| | Common Stock, $1 Par Value . . . . . . . . . . . . | | 600 |
| | Contributed Capital in Excess of Par Value, Common Stock . . . . . . . . . . . . | | 29,400 |

**Required**

1. Explain each journal entry (*a*) through (*d*).

2. How many shares of common stock are outstanding at year-end?

3. What is the amount of minimum legal capital (based on par value) at year-end?

4. What is the total contributed capital at year-end?

5. What is the book value per share of the common stock at year-end if contributed capital plus retained earnings equals $141,500?

---

## Problem 11-2B

Cash dividends, treasury stock, and statement of retained earnings

C2   C5   P3   P5

Baycore Corp. reports the following components of stockholders' equity on December 31, 2005:

| | |
|---|---:|
| Common stock—$1 par value, 160,000 shares authorized, 100,000 shares issued and outstanding . . . . . . . . . . . . . . . . . . . . | $  100,000 |
| Contributed capital in excess of par value, common stock   . . . . . . . | 700,000 |
| Retained earnings   . . . . . . . . . . . . . . . . . . . . . . . . . . . . . . . . . . | 1,080,000 |
| Total stockholders' equity   . . . . . . . . . . . . . . . . . . . . . . . . . . . | $1,880,000 |

It completed the following transactions related to stockholders' equity in year 2006:

Jan. 10  Purchased 20,000 shares of its own stock at $12 cash per share.
Mar.  2  Directors declared a $1.50 per share cash dividend payable on March 31 to the March 15 stockholders of record.
Mar. 31  Paid the dividend declared on March 2.
Nov. 11  Sold 12,000 of its treasury shares at $13 cash per share.
Nov. 25  Sold 8,000 of its treasury shares at $9.50 cash per share.
Dec.  1  Directors declared a $2.50 per share cash dividend payable on January 2, 2003, to the December 10 stockholders of record.
Dec. 31  Closed the $536,000 credit balance (from net income) in the Income Summary account to Retained Earnings.

**Required**

**1.** Prepare journal entries to record these transactions for 2006.

**2.** Prepare a statement of retained earnings for the year ended December 31, 2006.

**3.** Prepare the stockholders' equity section of the company's balance sheet as of December 31, 2006.

**Check** (2) Retained earnings, Dec. 31, 2006, $1,238,000

---

At December 31, the end of Intertec Communication's third quarter, the following stockholders' equity accounts are reported:

**Problem 11-3B**
Equity analysis—journal entries and account balances

P3  P4

| | |
|---|---|
| Common stock, $10 par value ........................... | $480,000 |
| Contributed capital in excess of par value, common stock ....... | 192,000 |
| Retained earnings ...................................... | 800,000 |

In the fourth quarter, the following entries related to its equity accounts are recorded:

| | | | |
|---|---|---|---|
| Jan. 17 | Retained Earnings ....................... | 48,000 | |
| | Common Dividend Payable ............. | | 48,000 |
| Feb.  5 | Common Dividend Payable ................. | 48,000 | |
| | Cash................................. | | 48,000 |
| Feb. 28 | Retained Earnings ....................... | 126,000 | |
| | Common Stock Dividend Distributable ..... | | 60,000 |
| | Contributed Capital in Excess of Par Value, Common Stock ............... | | 66,000 |
| Mar. 14 | Common Stock Dividend Distributable ........ | 60,000 | |
| | Common Stock, $10 Par Value ........... | | 60,000 |
| Mar. 25 | Memo—Change the title of the common stock account to reflect the new par value of $5. | | |
| Mar. 31 | Income Summary ........................ | 360,000 | |
| | Retained Earnings .................... | | 360,000 |

**Required**

**1.** Explain each journal entry.

**2.** Complete the following table showing the equity account balances at each indicated date:

| | Jan. 17 | Feb. 5 | Feb. 28 | Mar. 14 | Mar. 25 | Mar. 31 |
|---|---|---|---|---|---|---|
| Common stock .............. | $_____ | $_____ | $_____ | $_____ | $_____ | $_____ |
| Common stock dividend distributable ............... | _____ | _____ | _____ | _____ | _____ | _____ |
| Contributed capital in excess of par, common stock .... | _____ | _____ | _____ | _____ | _____ | _____ |
| Retained earnings ............. | _____ | _____ | _____ | _____ | _____ | _____ |
| Total equity ................. | $_____ | $_____ | $_____ | $_____ | $_____ | $_____ |

**Check** Total equity: Jan. 17, $1,424,000; Mar. 31, $1,784,000

## Problem 11-4B

Analysis of changes in stockholders' equity accounts

C5  P3  P4  P5

The equity sections from Jetta Corporation's 2005 and 2006 balance sheets follow:

**Stockholders' Equity (December 31, 2005)**

| | |
|---|---|
| Common stock—$20 par value, 15,000 shares authorized, 8,500 shares issued and outstanding . . . . . . . . . . . . . . . . . . . . . . | $170,000 |
| Contributed capital in excess of par value, common stock . . . . . . . . | 30,000 |
| Total contributed capital . . . . . . . . . . . . . . . . . . . . . . . . . . . . . . . | 200,000 |
| Retained earnings . . . . . . . . . . . . . . . . . . . . . . . . . . . . . . . . . . . . | 135,000 |
| Total stockholders' equity . . . . . . . . . . . . . . . . . . . . . . . . . . . . . | $335,000 |

**Stockholders' Equity (December 31, 2006)**

| | |
|---|---|
| Common stock—$20 par value, 15,000 shares authorized, 9,500 shares issued, 500 shares in treasury . . . . . . . . . . . . . . . . . | $190,000 |
| Contributed capital in excess of par value, common stock . . . . . . . . | 52,000 |
| Total contributed capital . . . . . . . . . . . . . . . . . . . . . . . . . . . . . . . | 242,000 |
| Retained earnings ($20,000 restricted by treasury stock) . . . . . . . . . | 147,600 |
| | 389,600 |
| Less cost of treasury stock . . . . . . . . . . . . . . . . . . . . . . . . . . . . . | (20,000) |
| Total stockholders' equity . . . . . . . . . . . . . . . . . . . . . . . . . . . . . | $369,600 |

The following transactions and events affected its equity accounts during year 2006:

Feb. 15  Declared a $0.40 per share cash dividend, date of record five days later.
Mar.  2  Purchased treasury stock for cash.
May 15  Declared a $0.40 per share cash dividend, date of record five days later.
Aug. 15  Declared a $0.40 per share cash dividend, date of record five days later.
Oct.  4  Declared a 12.5% stock dividend when the stock's market value is $42 per share.
Oct. 20  Issued stock dividend that was declared on October 4.
Nov. 15  Declared a $0.40 per share cash dividend, date of record five days later.

### Required

**1.** How many common shares are outstanding on each cash dividend date?
**2.** What is the total dollar amount for each of the four cash dividends?
**3.** What is the amount of the capitalization of retained earnings for the stock dividend?
**4.** What is the per share cost of the treasury stock purchased?
**5.** How much net income did the company earn during year 2006?

**Check**  (3) $42,000
(4) $40
(5) $68,000

## Problem 11-5B

Income statement computations and format  C4

Selected account balances from the adjusted trial balance for Bar Harbor Corp. as of its calendar year-end December 31, 2005, follow:

| | Debit | Credit |
|---|---|---|
| **a.** Accumulated depreciation—Buildings . . . . . . . . . . . . . . . . . . . . . . | | $ 200,000 |
| **b.** Interest revenue . . . . . . . . . . . . . . . . . . . . . . . . . . . . . . . . . . . . | | 10,000 |
| **c.** Cumulative effect of change in accounting principle (pretax) . . . . . . . . | | 46,000 |
| **d.** Net sales . . . . . . . . . . . . . . . . . . . . . . . . . . . . . . . . . . . . . . . . . | | 1,320,000 |
| **e.** Income taxes expense . . . . . . . . . . . . . . . . . . . . . . . . . . . . . . . . . | $ ? | |
| **f.** Loss on hurricane damage (pretax and extraordinary) . . . . . . . . . . . . | 32,000 | |
| **g.** Accumulated depreciation—Equipment . . . . . . . . . . . . . . . . . . . . . . | | 110,000 |
| **h.** Other operating expenses . . . . . . . . . . . . . . . . . . . . . . . . . . . . . . | 164,000 | |
| **i.** Depreciation expense—Equipment . . . . . . . . . . . . . . . . . . . . . . . . . | 50,000 | |
| **j.** Loss from settlement of lawsuit . . . . . . . . . . . . . . . . . . . . . . . . . . | 18,000 | |
| **k.** Gain from settlement of lawsuit . . . . . . . . . . . . . . . . . . . . . . . . . . | | 34,000 |

[continued on next page]

[continued from previous page]

| | |
|---|---:|
| l. Loss on sale of equipment ..................................... | 12,000 |
| m. Loss from operating a discontinued segment (pretax) .............. | 60,000 |
| n. Depreciation expense—Buildings ........................... | 78,000 |
| o. Correction of overstatement of prior year's expense (pretax) ....... | 24,000 |
| p. Cost of goods sold ....................................... | 520,000 |
| q. Loss on sale of discontinued segment's assets (pretax) ............. | 90,000 |
| r. Accounts payable ........................................ | 66,000 |

**Required**

Answer each of the following questions by providing supporting computations:

1. Assume that the company's income tax rate is 25% for all items. Identify the tax effects and after-tax amounts of the five items labeled pretax.
2. What is the amount of income from continuing operations before income taxes? What is the amount of income taxes expense? What is the amount of income from continuing operations?
3. What is the total amount of after-tax income (loss) associated with the discontinued segment?
4. What is the amount of income (loss) before the extraordinary items and the cumulative effect of changes in accounting principle?
5. What is the amount of net income for the year?

**Check**  (3) $(112,500)

(4) $279,000

(5) $289,500

---

On January 1, 2003, Belize Corp. purchases equipment costing $200,000 with an expected salvage value of zero at the end of its five-year useful life. Depreciation is allocated to 2003, 2004, and 2005 with the double-declining-balance method. Early in 2006, the company changes to the straight-line method to produce more useful financial statements and to be consistent with industry competitors.

**Problem 11-6B**
Change in accounting principle (depreciation) and its disclosure

C4

**Required**

1. Do generally accepted accounting principles allow Belize to change depreciation methods in 2006?
2. Prepare a table to show the annual amount of depreciation expense allocated to 2003 through 2005 using the double-declining-balance method.
3. Prepare a table to show the annual amount of depreciation expense that would have been allocated to 2003 through 2005 using the straight-line method.
4. The cumulative effect on prior year income statements (for 2003–2005) is to decrease depreciation expense by $36,800 and increase pretax income by $36,800. The company's income tax rate is 25%. What are the pretax and after-tax cumulative effects of the change?
5. How should the cumulative effect of the change in accounting principle be reported? Does the cumulative effect increase or decrease net income?
6. How much depreciation expense is reported on the company's income statement for 2006?

**Check**  (2) 2004, $48,000

(3) 2004, $40,000

(4) After-tax cumulative effect, $27,600

*Analysis Component*

7. Assume that Belize mistakenly treats the change in depreciation methods as a change in accounting estimate. Using your answers from parts 2, 3, and 4, describe the effect of this error on the 2006 financial statements.

(7) 2006 retained earnings understated by $13,800

---

The annual income statements for Peña, Inc., as reported when they were initially published in 2003, 2004, and 2005 follow:

**Problem 11-7B**
Earnings per share calculation and presentation

C4  A1

| | 2003 | 2004 | 2005 |
|---|---:|---:|---:|
| Net sales ......................... | $250,000 | $300,000 | $400,000 |
| Operating expenses .................. | 160,000 | 215,000 | 270,000 |
| Income from continuing operations ....... | 90,000 | 85,000 | 130,000 |
| Loss on discontinued segment .......... | (26,145) | — | — |
| Income before extraordinary items ........ | 63,855 | 85,000 | 130,000 |
| Extraordinary gain (loss) .............. | — | 14,100 | (37,125) |
| Net income ...................... | $ 63,855 | $ 99,100 | $ 92,875 |

The company also experienced changes in the number of outstanding shares from the following events:

| | |
|---|---|
| Outstanding shares on December 31, 2002 . . . . . . . | 10,000 |
| **2003** | |
| Treasury stock purchase on July 1 . . . . . . . . . . . . . . | − 1,000 |
| Issuance of new shares on September 30 . . . . . . . . | + 3,500 |
| 20% stock dividend on December 1 . . . . . . . . . . . . | + 2,500 |
| Outstanding shares on December 31, 2003 . . . . . . . | 15,000 |
| **2004** | |
| Issuance of new shares on March 31 . . . . . . . . . . . . | + 4,000 |
| Treasury stock purchase on October 1 . . . . . . . . . . | − 1,500 |
| Outstanding shares on December 31, 2004 . . . . . . . | 17,500 |
| **2005** | |
| Issuance of new shares on July 1 . . . . . . . . . . . . . . | + 3,000 |
| Treasury stock purchase on October 1 . . . . . . . . . . | − 1,750 |
| 2-for-1 stock split on November 1 . . . . . . . . . . . . . . | +18,750 |
| Outstanding shares on December 31, 2005 . . . . . . . | 37,500 |

**Required**

**Check**  (1) 12,450 shares

(2) EPS, $5.13

(3) 17,625 shares

(4) EPS, $5.62

1. Compute the weighted average of the common shares outstanding for year 2003.
2. Compute the EPS component amounts to report with the year 2003 income statement for: income from continuing operations, the loss on discontinued segment, and net income.
3. Compute the weighted average of the common shares outstanding for year 2004.
4. Compute the EPS component amounts to report with the year 2004 income statement for: income from continuing operations, the extraordinary gain, and net income.
5. Compute the weighted average of the common shares outstanding for year 2005.
6. Compute the EPS component amounts to report with the year 2005 income statement for: income from continuing operations, the extraordinary loss, and net income.

*Analysis Component*

7. Explain how you would use the EPS data from part 6 to predict EPS for 2006.

---

**Problem 11-8B**

Computation of book values and dividend allocations

C3  A2  P2

Scotch, Inc.'s common stock is currently selling on a stock exchange at $45 per share, and its current balance sheet shows the following stockholders' equity section:

| | |
|---|---|
| Preferred stock—8% cumulative, $___ par value, 1,500 shares authorized, issued, and outstanding . . . . . . . . . . . . . . . . . . . . . . . . | $ 187,500 |
| Common stock—$___ par value, 18,000 shares authorized, issued, and outstanding . . . . . . . . . . . . . . . . . . . . . . . . | 450,000 |
| Retained earnings . . . . . . . . . . . . . . . . . . . . . . . . . . . . . . . . . . . . | 562,500 |
| Total stockholders' equity . . . . . . . . . . . . . . . . . . . . . . . . . . . . . . | $1,200,000 |

**Required**

1. What is the current market value (price) of this corporation's common stock?
2. What are the par values of the corporation's preferred stock and its common stock?
3. If no dividends are in arrears, what are the book values per share of the preferred stock and the common stock?

**Check**  (4) Book value of common, $54.58

(5) Book value of common, $53.33

4. If two years' preferred dividends are in arrears, what are the book values per share of the preferred stock and the common stock?
5. If two years' preferred dividends are in arrears and the preferred stock is callable at $140 per share, what are the book values per share of the preferred stock and the common stock?

**6.** If two years' preferred dividends are in arrears and the board of directors declares cash dividends of $50,000, what total amount will be paid to the preferred and to the common shareholders? What is the amount of dividends per share for the common stock?

(6) Dividends per common share, $0.28

*Analysis Component*

**7.** Discuss why the book value of common stock is not always a good estimate of its market value.

Problem Set C is available at the book's Website to further reinforce and assess your learning.

**PROBLEM SET C**

---

**BEYOND THE NUMBERS**

**BTN 11-1**    Refer to **Krispy Kreme**'s financial statements in Appendix A to answer the following:

**1.** Has Krispy Kreme issued any preferred stock? If so, what are its features?

**2.** How many shares of common stock are issued and outstanding at the end of fiscal years 2003 and 2002? How do these numbers compare with the weighted-average common shares outstanding at the end of fiscal years 2003 and 2002?

**3.** What is the book value of its entire common stock at February 2, 2003?

**4.** What is the total amount of cash dividends paid to common stockholders for fiscal years 2003 and 2002?

**5.** Identify and compare basic EPS amounts across years 2003, 2002, and 2001. Identify and comment on any significant changes.

**6.** Does Krispy Kreme hold any treasury stock as of February 2, 2003? As of February 3, 2002?

**7.** Does Krispy Kreme report any changes in accounting principles or the occurrence of extraordinary items for fiscal years 2003 or 2002? Are there gains or losses on disposal of a business segment for fiscal years 2003 or 2002?

**REPORTING IN ACTION**

C2  C3  C4  A1  A2

*Roll On*

**8.** Access Krispy Kreme's financial statements for fiscal years ending after February 2, 2003, from its Website (**KrispyKreme.com**) or the SEC's EDGAR database (**www.sec.gov**). Has the number of common shares outstanding increased since February 2, 2003? Has Krispy Kreme increased the total amount of cash dividends paid compared to the total amount for fiscal year 2003?

**BTN 11-2**    Key comparative figures for both **Krispy Kreme** and **Tastykake** follow:

| Key Figures | Krispy Kreme | Tastykake |
|---|---|---|
| Net income (in thousands) | $ 33,478 | $ 2,000* |
| Cash dividends declared per common share | $ 0.00 | $ 0.48 |
| Common shares outstanding (in thousands) | 55,093 | 8,075 |
| Market value (price) per share | $ 30.41 | $ 9.20 |
| Equity applicable to common shares (in thousands) | $273,352 | $47,525 |

* Restructuring charges are removed from income.

**COMPARATIVE ANALYSIS**

A1  A2  A3  A4

**Required**

**1.** Compute the book value per common share for each company using these data.

**2.** Compute the basic EPS for each company using these data.

**3.** Compute the dividend yield for each company using these data. Does the dividend yield of either company characterize it as an income or growth stock? Explain.

**4.** Compute, compare, and interpret the price-earnings ratio for each company using these data.

## ETHICS CHALLENGE

C4

**BTN 11-3**   This chapter describes ComUS's change in accounting principle from the double-declining-balance depreciation method to the straight-line method. ComUS argues that its income statement computed using the straight-line method is more useful. This change in accounting principle adds $56,000 to net income for year 2005. As this company's auditor, you must review the decision to change the accounting principle. You review the equipment in question and learn that it is a piece of high-tech equipment whose risk of obsolescence in the near future is high. You also are aware that management receives year-end bonuses based on net income.

**Required**

As the auditor, would you support the change in depreciation method or ask management to continue using the double-declining-balance method? Justify your response.

## COMMUNICATING IN PRACTICE

A1   A4

**Hint:** Make a transparency of each team's memo for a class discussion.

**BTN 11-4**   Teams are to select an industry, and each team member is to select a different company in that industry. Each team member then is to acquire the selected company's financial statements (or Form 10-K) from the SEC EDGAR site (www.SEC.gov). Use these data to identify basic EPS. Use the financial press (or finance.yahoo.com/quote) to determine the market price of this stock, and then compute the price-earnings ratio. Communicate with teammates via a meeting, e-mail, or telephone to discuss the meaning of this ratio, how companies compare, and the industry norm. The team must prepare a single memorandum reporting the ratio for each company and identifying the team conclusions or consensus of opinion. The memorandum is to be duplicated and distributed to the instructor and teammates.

## TAKING IT TO THE NET

C2

mhhe.com/wild3e

**BTN 11-5**   Access the March 28, 2003, filing of the 2002 calendar-year 10-K report of HCA, Inc., (ticker HCA) from www.SEC.gov.

**Required**

1. How many classes of stock has HCA issued?
2. What are the par values of the classes of stock you identified in part 1?
3. How much cash did HCA raise in 2002 from issuing stock?
4. What total amount of cash did HCA pay in 2002 to repurchase stock?
5. What amount did HCA pay out in cash dividends for 2002?

## TEAMWORK IN ACTION

P5

**Hint:** Instructor should be sure each team accurately completes part 1 before proceeding.

**BTN 11-6**   This activity requires teamwork to reinforce understanding of accounting for treasury stock.

1. Write a brief team statement (a) generalizing what happens to a corporation's financial position when it engages in a stock "buyback" and (b) identifying reasons that a corporation would engage in this activity.
2. Assume that an entity acquires 100 shares of its $100 par value common stock at a cost of $134 cash per share. Discuss the entry to record this acquisition. Next, assign *each* team member to prepare *one* of the following entries (assume each entry applies to all shares):
   a. Reissue treasury shares at cost.
   b. Reissue treasury shares at $150 per share.
   c. Reissue treasury shares at $120 per share; assume the contributed capital account from treasury shares has a $1,500 balance.
   d. Reissue treasury shares at $120 per share; assume the contributed capital account from treasury shares has a $1,000 balance.
   e. Reissue treasury shares at $120 per share; assume the contributed capital account from treasury shares has a zero balance.
3. In sequence, each member is to present his/her entry to the team and explain the *similarities* and *differences* between that entry and the previous entry.

**BTN 11-7**   Read the commentary "So Much Cash, So Few Dividends" from the January 20, 2003, issue of *Business Week*. (The book's Website provides a free link.)

**Required**

1. Why are start-up tech companies reluctant to pay dividends to shareholders?
2. Have large tech companies historically paid dividends?
3. Do most institutional investors want tech companies to pay dividends if the tax on dividends is eliminated?
4. How have tech companies used stockpiles of cash in the past?
5. How would tech company CEOs fare if these companies start to pay dividends?

---

**BTN 11-8**   Assume that Julz Chavez's launch of **Get Real Girl** requires $312,500 of start-up capital. Chavez contributes $250,000 of personal assets in return for 5,000 shares of common stock but needs to raise another $62,500 in cash. There are two alternative plans for raising the additional cash. Plan A is to sell 1,250 shares of common stock to one or more investors for $62,500 cash. Plan B is to sell 625 shares of cumulative preferred stock to one or more investors for $62,500 cash (this preferred stock would have a $100 par value, an annual 8% dividend rate, and be issued at par).

1. If the business is expected to earn $45,000 of after-tax net income in the first year, what rate of return on beginning equity will Chavez personally earn under each alternative? Which plan will provide the higher expected return to Chavez?
2. If the business is expected to earn $10,500 of after-tax net income in the first year, what rate of return on beginning equity will Chavez personally earn under each alternative? Which plan will provide the higher expected return to Chavez?
3. Analyze and interpret the differences between the results for parts 1 and 2.

---

**BTN 11-9**   Watch 30 to 60 minutes of financial news on the CNBC television channel. Take notes on companies that are catching analysts' attention. You might hear reference to over- and undervaluation of firm and to reports about PE ratios, dividend yields, and earnings per share. Be prepared to give a brief description to the class of your observations of CNBC.

---

**BTN 11-10**   Access the annual report of **Grupo Bimbo** (GrupoBimbo.com) for the year ended December 31, 2002. Review its statements of income and its statements of changes in financial position.

**Required**

1. What is Grupo Bimbo's trend in earnings per share for the three years 2000 to 2002?
2. Has Grupo Bimbo increased or decreased its weighted-average shares outstanding from 2001 to 2002?
3. Has Grupo Bimbo increased or decreased cash dividends declared to shareholders from 2001 to 2002?

*"The most important thing I've learned is to wait out the [cash] storm"*—Chance Roth

# 12 Reporting and Analyzing Cash Flows

## A Look Back

Chapter 11 focused on corporate transactions. We described stock issuances, dividends, and other equity transactions. We also explained how to report and analyze income, earnings per share, and retained earnings.

## A Look at This Chapter

This chapter focuses on reporting and analyzing cash inflows and cash outflows. We emphasize how to prepare and interpret the statement of cash flows.

## A Look Ahead

Chapter 13 focuses on tools to help us analyze financial statements. We also describe comparative analysis and the application of ratios for financial analysis.

# CAP

### Conceptual

C1 Explain the purpose and importance of cash flow information. *(p. 492)*

C2 Distinguish among operating, investing, and financing activities. *(p. 493)*

C3 Identify and disclose noncash investing and financing activities. *(p. 494)*

C4 Describe the format of the statement of cash flows. *(p. 495)*

### Analytical

A1 Analyze the statement of cash flows. *(p. 509)*

A2 Compute and apply the cash flow on total assets ratio. *(p. 510)*

### Procedural

P1 Prepare a statement of cash flows. *(p. 496)*

P2 Compute cash flows from operating activities using the indirect method. *(p. 500)*

P3 Determine cash flows from both investing and financing activities. *(p. 505)*

## Decision Feature

# Cashing In with the Toy Biz

SAN DIEGO—Cash may not be king, but it is crucial to the king's survival. Just ask Chance Roth, the young owner of **Atomic Toys (AtomicToys.com),** an upstart toy designer, manufacturer, and distributor. He opened Atomic Toys's doors in 1999, and its revenues are projected to reach $4 million this year. Yet all was not easy; cash flow was a constant battle, especially in the beginning. While the toy biz can be wild and crazy, Roth says he had to change "from the wild-eyed, creative entrepreneur into a street smart businessman." This meant keeping a watchful eye on cash flows, especially those from operating activities. Adds Roth, "There comes a time when you realize it's not Monopoly money anymore."

Roth learned that a start-up could produce sales at the same time its cash is running short—a common and constant struggle. "We couldn't physically manufacture enough product to satisfy the demand," says Roth. "Our product was flying off the shelf." Exploding sales meant increasing cash outflows for manufacturing and distribution. Roth says he had to carefully monitor the cash flows associated with each of the operating, investing, and financing activities. With

cash under control, says Roth, "now we're poised to capitalize on that [sales] success."

Roth continues to closely scrutinize and personally oversee cash flows. "For me to take the company where it needs to go," he says, "I've got to continually step up to the plate and make it happen." Cash flow responsibility is one of those steps. This chapter focuses on cash flow: its measurement, presentation, analysis, and interpretation. It describes the importance of separately analyzing cash flows according to operating, investing, and financing activities.

Roth knows first-hand the importance of cash flow information, especially for start-ups. "It's going to be very, very difficult for at least the first two or three years," he adds. "But by just sticking it out and letting the waves crash and pound while steadily making progress," the company will win the battle of cash flows. Cash analysis demands serious attention and work. However, says Roth, "We all have to grow up sometime—even in toys!"

[Sources: *Atomic Toys Website,* January 2004; *Entrepreneur,* May 2003; *Playthings,* February, 2002 and 2003.]

Profitability is a main goal of most managers, but not the only goal. A company cannot achieve or maintain profits without carefully managing cash. Managers and other users of information pay close attention to a company's cash position and the events and transactions affecting cash. Information about cash events and transactions is reported in the statement of cash flows. This chapter explains how we prepare, analyze, and interpret a statement of cash flows. It also discusses the importance of cash flow information for predicting future performance and making managerial decisions. More generally, effectively using the statement of cash flows is crucial for managing and analyzing the operating, investing, and financing activities of businesses.

**Reporting and Analyzing Cash Flows**

| **Basics of Cash Flow Reporting** | **Cash Flows from Operating** | **Cash Flows from Investing** | **Cash Flows from Financing** |
|---|---|---|---|
| • Purpose<br>• Importance<br>• Measurement<br>• Classification<br>• Noncash activities<br>• Format<br>• Preparation | • Indirect and direct methods of reporting<br>• Application of indirect method of reporting<br>• Summary of indirect method adjustments | • Three-stage process of analysis<br>• Analysis of non-current assets<br>• Analysis of other assets | • Three-stage process of analysis<br>• Analysis of non-current liabilities<br>• Analysis of equity |

# Basics of Cash Flow Reporting

This section describes the basics of cash flow reporting, including its purpose, measurement, classification, format, and preparation.

## Purpose of the Statement of Cash Flows

**C1** Explain the purpose and importance of cash flow information.

The purpose of the **statement of cash flows** is to report all major cash receipts (inflows) and cash payments (outflows) during a period. This includes separately identifying the cash flows related to operating, investing, and financing activities. The statement of cash flows does more than simply report changes in cash. It is the detailed disclosure of individual cash flows that makes this statement useful to users. Information in this statement helps users answer questions such as these:

■ How does a company obtain its cash?

■ Where does a company spend its cash?

■ What explains the change in the cash balance?

**Point:** Internal users rely on the statement of cash flows to make investing and financing decisions. External users rely on this statement to assess the amount and timing of a company's cash flows.

The statement of cash flows addresses important questions such as these by summarizing, classifying, and reporting a company's cash inflows and cash outflows for each period.

## Importance of Cash Flows

Information about cash flows can influence decision makers in important ways. For instance, we look more favorably at a company that is financing its expenditures with cash from operations than one that does it by selling its assets. Information about cash flows helps users decide whether a company has enough cash to pay its existing debts as they mature. It is also relied upon to evaluate a company's ability to meet unexpected obligations and pursue

Topic Tackler 12-1

unexpected opportunities. External information users especially want to assess a company's ability to take advantage of new business opportunities. Internal users such as managers use cash flow information to plan day-to-day operating activities and make long-term investment decisions.

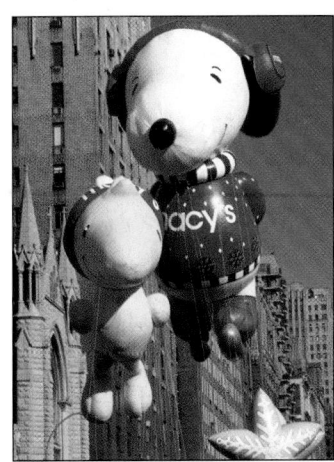

**Macy's** striking turnaround is an example of how analysis and management of cash flows can lead to improved financial stability. Several years ago Macy's obtained temporary protection from bankruptcy, at which time it desperately needed to improve its cash flows. It did so by engaging in aggressive cost-cutting measures. As a result, Macy's annual cash flow rose to $210 million, up from a negative cash flow of $38.9 million in the prior year. Macy's eventually met its financial obligations and then successfully merged with **Federated Department Stores**.

The case of **W. T. Grant Co.** is a classic example of the importance of cash flow information in predicting a company's future performance and financial strength. Grant reported net income of more than $40 million per year for three consecutive years. At that same time, it was experiencing an alarming decrease in cash provided by operations. For instance, net cash outflow was more than $90 million by the end of that three-year period. Grant soon went bankrupt. Users who relied solely on Grant's income numbers were unpleasantly surprised. This reminds us that cash flows as well as income statement and balance sheet information are crucial in making business decisions.

**Decision Insight**

**Valuation**   Some experts who value private companies do so on the basis of a multiple of operating cash flow. Medium-sized private companies usually sell for five to seven times their operating cash flows. Larger companies often can command somewhat higher multiples.

## Measurement of Cash Flows

Cash flows are defined to include both *cash* and *cash equivalents*. The statement of cash flows explains the difference between the beginning and ending balances of cash and cash equivalents. We continue to use the phrases *cash flows* and the *statement of cash flows*, but we must remember that both phrases refer to cash and cash equivalents. Recall that a cash equivalent must satisfy two criteria: (1) be readily convertible to a known amount of cash and (2) be sufficiently close to its maturity so its market value is unaffected by interest rate changes. In most cases, a debt security must be within three months of its maturity to satisfy these criteria. Companies must disclose and follow a clear policy for determining cash and cash equivalents and apply it consistently from period to period. **American Express**, for example, defines its cash equivalents as "time deposits with original maturities of 90 days or less, excluding those that are restricted by law or regulation."

Cash and Cash Equivalents

**Decision Insight**

**Know Cash**   "A lender must have a complete understanding of a borrower's cash flows to assess both the borrowing needs and repayment sources. This requires information about the major types of cash inflows and outflows. I have seen many companies, whose financial statements indicate good profitability, experience severe financial problems because the owners or managers lacked a good understanding of cash flows."   Mary E. Garza, NationsBank

## Classification of Cash Flows

Since cash and cash equivalents are combined, the statement of cash flows does not report transactions between cash and cash equivalents such as cash paid to purchase cash equivalents and cash received from selling cash equivalents. However, all other cash receipts and cash payments are classified and reported on the statement as operating, investing, or financing activities. Individual cash receipts and payments for each of these three categories are labeled to identify their originating transactions or events. A net cash inflow (source) occurs when the receipts in a category exceed the payments. A net cash outflow (use) occurs when the payments in a category exceed the receipts.

**C2**   Distinguish among operating, investing, and financing activities.

Operating Investing Financing

**Operating Activities**   **Operating activities** include those transactions and events that determine net income. Examples are the production and purchase of merchandise, the sale of goods and services to customers, and the expenditures to administer the business. Not all

**Global:** Some countries such as Saudi Arabia and Italy do not require the statement of cash flows.

items in income, such as unusual gains and losses, are operating activities (we discuss these exceptions later in the chapter). Exhibit 12.1 lists the more common cash inflows and outflows from operating activities.

## Exhibit 12.1

Cash Flows from Operating Activities

**Cash Inflows**

From customers for cash sales
From borrowers for interest
From collections on credit sales
From cash dividends received
From lawsuit settlements
From selling *trading* securities

Operating Activities

**Cash Outflows**

Operating Activities

To salaries and wages
To purchase *trading* securities
To suppliers for goods and services
To lenders for interest
To governments for taxes and fines
To charities

**Point:** Investing activities exclude transactions in trading securities.
**Point:** Common errors include misclassification of *cash dividends received* and *cash interest received* as investing activities and *cash interest paid* as financing. The FASB requires these cash flows be reported as operating activities.

**Investing Activities**    **Investing activities** generally include those transactions and events that affect long-term assets, namely, the purchase and sale of long-term assets. They also include the (1) purchase and sale of short-term investments other than cash equivalents and trading securities and (2) lending and collecting money for notes receivable. Exhibit 12.2 lists examples of cash flows from investing activities. Proceeds from collecting the principal amounts of notes deserve special mention. If the note results from sales to customers, its cash receipts are classed as operating activities whether short term or long term. If the note results from a loan to another party apart from sales, however, the cash receipts from collecting the note principal are classed as an investing activity. The FASB requires the collection of interest on loans be reported as an operating activity.

## Exhibit 12.2

Cash Flows from Investing Activities

**Cash Inflows**

From selling available-for-sale securities
From collecting principal on loans
From selling long-term productive assets
From selling (discounting) of notes
From selling held-to-maturity securities

Investing Activities

**Cash Outflows**

Investing Activities

To make loans to others
To purchase long-term productive assets
To purchase held-to-maturity securities
To purchase available-for-sale securities

**Point:** Interest payments on a loan are classified as operating activities, but payments of loan principal are financing activities.

**Financing Activities**    **Financing activities** include those transactions and events that affect long-term liabilities and equity. Examples are (1) obtaining cash from issuing debt and repaying the amounts borrowed and (2) receiving cash from or distributing cash to owners. These activities involve transactions with a company's owners and creditors. They also often involve borrowing and repaying principal amounts relating to both short- and long-term debt. Notice that payments of interest expense are classified as operating activities. Also, cash payments to settle credit purchases of merchandise, whether on account or by note, are operating activities. Exhibit 12.3 lists examples of cash flows from financing activities.

## Noncash Investing and Financing

**C3**  Identify and disclose noncash investing and financing activities.

When important investing and financing activities do not affect cash receipts or payments, they are still disclosed at the bottom of the statement of cash flows or in a note to the

Exhibit 12.3

Cash Flows from
Financing Activities

statement because of their importance and the *full-disclosure principle*. One example of such a transaction is the purchase of long-term assets using a long-term note payable. This transaction involves both investing and financing activities but does not affect any cash inflow or outflow and is not reported in any of the three sections of the statement of cash flows. This disclosure rule also extends to transactions with partial cash receipts or payments.

To illustrate, assume that Goorin purchases land for $12,000 by paying $5,000 cash and trading in used equipment with a $7,000 market value. The investing section of the statement of cash flows reports only the $5,000 cash outflow for the land purchase. The $12,000 investing transaction is only partially described in the body of the statement of cash flows, yet this information is potentially important to users because it changes the makeup of assets. Goorin could either describe the transaction in a note or include a small schedule at the bottom of its statement that lists the $12,000 land purchase along with the cash financing of $5,000 and a $7,000 trade-in of used equipment. As another example, Borg Co. acquired $900,000 of assets in exchange for $200,000 cash and a $700,000 long-term note, which is reported as follows:

**Point:** An income statement reports revenues, gains, expenses, and losses on an accrual basis. The statement of cash flows reports cash received and cash paid for operating, financing, and investing activities.

**Point:** A stock dividend transaction involving a transfer from retained earnings to common stock or a credit to contributed capital is *not* considered a noncash investing and financing activity because the company receives no consideration (asset) for shares issued.

> ### Decision Maker
>
> **Entrepreneur**   You are considering purchasing a start-up business that recently reported a $110,000 annual net loss and a $225,000 annual net cash inflow. How are these results possible?

Answer—p. 522

| | |
|---|---|
| Fair value of assets acquired . . . . . . . . . | $900,000 |
| Less cash paid . . . . . . . . . . . . . . . . . . | 200,000 |
| Liabilities incurred or assumed . . . . . . . | $700,000 |

Exhibit 12.4 lists transactions commonly disclosed as noncash investing and financing activities.

- ■ Retirement of debt by issuing equity stock.
- ■ Conversion of preferred stock to common stock.
- ■ Lease of assets in a capital lease transaction.
- ■ Purchase of long-term assets by issuing a note or bond.
- ■ Exchange of noncash assets for other noncash assets.
- ■ Purchase of noncash assets by issuing equity or debt.

Exhibit 12.4

Examples of Noncash Investing
and Financing Activities

## Format of the Statement of Cash Flows

Accounting standards require companies to include a statement of cash flows in a complete set of financial statements. This statement must report information about a company's cash receipts and cash payments during the period. Exhibit 12.5 shows the usual format. A company must report cash flows from three activities: operating, investing, and financing. The statement explains how transactions and events impact the beginning-of-period cash (and cash equivalents) balance to produce its end-of-period balance.

**C4**   Describe the format of the statement of cash flows.

## Exhibit 12.5

Format of the Statement of Cash Flows

| COMPANY NAME<br>Statement of Cash Flows<br>For *period* Ended *date* | | |
|---|---|---|
| **Cash flows from operating activities** | | |
| [List of individual inflows and outflows] | | |
| Net cash provided (used) by operating activities . . . . . . . . . . . . . . . . | $ | # |
| **Cash flows from investing activities** | | |
| [List of individual inflows and outflows] | | |
| Net cash provided (used) by investing activities . . . . . . . . . . . . . . . . | | # |
| **Cash flows from financing activities** | | |
| [List of individual inflows and outflows] | | |
| Net cash provided (used) by financing activities . . . . . . . . . . . . . . . . | | # |
| **Net increase (decrease) in cash** . . . . . . . . . . . . . . . . . . . . . . . . . . | $ | # |
| **Cash (and equivalents) balance at beginning of period** . . . . . . . | | # |
| **Cash (and equivalents) balance at end of period** . . . . . . . . . . . . | $ | # |

Note: Separate schedule or note disclosure of any "noncash investing and financing transactions" is required.

**Global:** International standards require a statement of cash flows separated into operating, investing, and financing activities.

### Quick Check

1. Does a statement of cash flows report the cash payments to purchase cash equivalents? Does it report the cash receipts from selling cash equivalents?

2. Identify the categories of cash flows reported separately on the statement of cash flows.

3. Identify the cash activity category for each transaction: (*a*) purchase equipment for cash, (*b*) cash payment of wages, (*c*) sale of common stock for cash, (*d*) receipt of cash dividends from stock investment, (*e*) cash collection from customers, (*f*) bonds issuance for cash.

Answers—p. 522

## Preparing the Statement of Cash Flows

**P1** Prepare a statement of cash flows.

Step 1: Compute net increase or decrease in cash

Step 2: Compute net cash from operating activities

Step 3: Compute net cash from investing activities

Step 4: Compute net cash from financing activities

Step 5: Prove and report beginning and ending cash balances

Preparing a statement of cash flows involves five steps: (1) compute the net increase or decrease in cash; (2) compute and report net cash provided (used) by operating activities (using either the direct or indirect method; both are explained); (3) compute and report net cash provided (used) by investing activities; (4) compute and report net cash provided (used) by financing activities; and (5) compute net cash flow by combining net cash provided (used) by operating, investing, and financing activities and then *prove it* by adding it to the beginning cash balance to show that it equals the ending cash balance. Important noncash investing and financing activities are disclosed in either a note or a separate schedule to the statement.

Computing the net increase or net decrease in cash is a simple but crucial computation. It equals the current period's cash balance minus the prior period's cash balance. This is the *bottom-line* figure for the statement of cash flows and is a check on the accuracy of one's work. The information we need to prepare a statement of cash flows comes from various sources including comparative balance sheets at the beginning and end of the period, and an income statement for the period. There are two alternative approaches to preparing the statement: (1) analyzing the Cash account and (2) analyzing noncash accounts.

**Analyzing the Cash Account** A company's cash receipts and cash payments are recorded in the Cash account in its general ledger. The Cash account is therefore a natural place to look for information about cash flows from operating, investing, and financing activities. To illustrate, review the summarized Cash T-account of Genesis, Inc., in Exhibit 12.6. Individual cash transactions are summarized in this Cash account according to the major types of cash receipts and cash payments. For instance, only the total of cash receipts from all customers is listed. Individual cash transactions underlying these totals can number in the thousands. Accounting software programs are available to provide summarized cash accounts.

Preparing a statement of cash flows from Exhibit 12.6 requires determining whether an individual cash inflow or outflow is an operating, investing, or financing activity, and then

**Exhibit 12.6**

Summarized Cash Account

listing each by activity. This yields the statement shown in Exhibit 12.7. However, preparing the statement of cash flows from an analysis of the summarized Cash account has two limitations. First, most companies have many individual cash receipts and payments, making it difficult to review them all. Accounting software minimizes this burden, but it is still a task requiring professional judgment for many transactions. Second, the Cash account does not usually carry an adequate description of each cash transaction, making assignment of all cash transactions according to activity difficult.

**Point:** View the change in cash as a *target* number that you will fully explain and prove in the statement of cash flows.

**Exhibit 12.7**

Statement of Cash Flows—
Direct Method

| GENESIS<br>Statement of Cash Flows<br>For Year Ended December 31, 2005 | | |
|---|---|---|
| Cash flows from operating activities | | |
| Cash received from customers | $570,000 | |
| Cash paid for merchandise | (319,000) | |
| Cash paid for wages and other operating expenses | (218,000) | |
| Cash paid for interest | (8,000) | |
| Cash paid for taxes | (5,000) | |
| Net cash provided by operating activities | | $20,000 |
| Cash flows from investing activities | | |
| Cash received from sale of plant assets | 12,000 | |
| Cash paid for purchase of plant assets | (10,000) | |
| Net cash provided by investing activities | | 2,000 |
| Cash flows from financing activities | | |
| Cash received from issuing stock | 15,000 | |
| Cash paid to retire bonds | (18,000) | |
| Cash paid for dividends | (14,000) | |
| Net cash used in financing activities | | (17,000) |
| Net increase in cash | | $ 5,000 |
| Cash balance at beginning of year | | 12,000 |
| Cash balance at end of year | | $17,000 |

**Analyzing Noncash Accounts**   A second approach to preparing the statement of cash flows is analyzing noncash accounts. This approach uses the fact that when a company records cash inflows and outflows with debits and credits to the Cash account (see Exhibit 12.6), it also records credits and debits in noncash accounts (reflecting double-entry accounting). Many of these noncash accounts are balance sheet accounts, for instance, from the sale of land for cash. Others are revenue and expense accounts that are closed to equity. For instance, the sale of services for cash yields a credit to Services Revenue that is closed to Retained Earnings for a corporation. In sum, *all cash transactions eventually affect noncash balance sheet accounts*. Thus, we can determine cash inflows and outflows by analyzing changes in noncash balance sheet accounts.

Exhibit 12.8 uses the accounting equation to show the relation between the Cash account and the noncash balance sheet accounts. This exhibit starts with the accounting equation at

**Global:** Some countries require a statement of funds flow instead of a statement of cash flows; *funds* are often defined as *working capital* (current assets minus current liabilities).

**Exhibit 12.8**

Relation between Cash and
Noncash Accounts

the top. It is then expanded in line (2) to separate cash from noncash asset accounts. Line (3) moves noncash asset accounts to the right-hand side of the equality where they are subtracted. This shows that cash equals the sum of the liability and equity accounts *minus* the noncash asset accounts. Line (4) points out that *changes* on one side of the accounting equation equal *changes* on the other side. It shows that we can explain changes in cash by analyzing changes in the noncash accounts consisting of liability accounts, equity accounts, and noncash assets accounts. By analyzing noncash balance sheet accounts and any related income statement accounts, we can prepare a statement of cash flows.

**Information to Prepare the Statement**   Information to prepare the statement of cash flows usually comes from three sources: (1) comparative balance sheets, (2) current income statement, and (3) additional information. Comparative balance sheets are used to compute changes in noncash accounts from the beginning to the end of the period. The current income statement is used to help compute cash flows from operating activities. Additional information often includes details on transactions and events that help explain both the cash flows and noncash investing and financing activities.

# Cash Flows from Operating

## Indirect and Direct Methods of Reporting

Cash flows provided (used) by operating activities are reported in one of two ways: the *direct method* or the *indirect method. These two different methods apply only to the operating activities section.*

The **direct method** separately lists each major item of operating cash receipts (such as cash received from customers) and each major item of operating cash payments (such as cash paid for merchandise). The cash payments are subtracted from cash receipts to determine the net cash provided (used) by operating activities. The operating activities section of Exhibit 12.7 reflects the direct method of reporting operating cash flows.

The **indirect method** reports net income and then adjusts it for items necessary to obtain net cash provided (used) by operating activities. It does *not* report individual items of cash inflows and cash outflows from operating activities. Instead, the indirect method reports the necessary adjustments to reconcile net income to net cash provided (used) by operating activities. The operating activities section for Genesis prepared under the indirect method is shown in Exhibit 12.9.

| Cash flows from operating activities | | |
|---|---|---|
| Net income | | $38,000 |
| Adjustments to reconcile net income to net cash provided by operating activities | | |
| Increase in accounts receivable | $(20,000) | |
| Increase in merchandise inventory | (14,000) | |
| Increase in prepaid expenses | (2,000) | |
| Decrease in accounts payable | (5,000) | |
| Decrease in interest payable | (1,000) | |
| Increase in income taxes payable | 10,000 | |
| Depreciation expense | 24,000 | |
| Loss on sale of plant assets | 6,000 | |
| Gain on retirement of bonds | (16,000) | |
| **Net cash provided by operating activities** | | **$20,000** |

**Exhibit 12.9**

Operating Activities Section—Indirect Method

Note that the amount of net cash provided by operating activities is *identical* under both the direct and indirect methods. This equality always exists. The difference in these methods is with the computation and presentation of this amount. The FASB recommends the direct method, but because it is not required and the indirect method is arguably easier to compute, nearly all companies report operating cash flows using the indirect method.

To illustrate, we prepare the operating activities section of the statement of cash flows for Genesis. Exhibit 12.10 shows the December 31, 2004 and 2005, balance sheets of Genesis

**Point:** To better understand the direct and indirect methods of reporting operating cash flows, identify similarities and differences between Exhibits 12.7 and 12.11.

**Exhibit 12.10**

Financial Statements

| GENESIS Balance Sheets December 31, 2005 and 2004 | | |
|---|---|---|
| | 2005 | 2004 |
| **Assets** | | |
| Current assets | | |
| Cash | $ 17,000 | $ 12,000 |
| Accounts receivable | 60,000 | 40,000 |
| Merchandise inventory | 84,000 | 70,000 |
| Prepaid expenses | 6,000 | 4,000 |
| Total current assets | 167,000 | 126,000 |
| Long-term assets | | |
| Plant assets | 250,000 | 210,000 |
| Accumulated depreciation | (60,000) | (48,000) |
| Total assets | $357,000 | $288,000 |
| **Liabilities** | | |
| Current liabilities | | |
| Accounts payable | $ 35,000 | $ 40,000 |
| Interest payable | 3,000 | 4,000 |
| Income taxes payable | 22,000 | 12,000 |
| Total current liabilities | 60,000 | 56,000 |
| Long-term bonds payable | 90,000 | 64,000 |
| Total liabilities | 150,000 | 120,000 |
| **Equity** | | |
| Common stock, $5 par | 95,000 | 80,000 |
| Retained earnings | 112,000 | 88,000 |
| Total equity | 207,000 | 168,000 |
| Total liabilities and equity | $357,000 | $288,000 |

| GENESIS Income Statement For Year Ended December 31, 2005 | | |
|---|---|---|
| Sales | | $590,000 |
| Cost of goods sold | $300,000 | |
| Wages and other operating expenses | 216,000 | |
| Interest expense | 7,000 | |
| Depreciation expense | 24,000 | (547,000) |
| | | 43,000 |
| Other gains (losses) | | |
| Gain on retirement of bonds | 16,000 | |
| Loss on sale of plant assets | (6,000) | 10,000 |
| Income before taxes | | 53,000 |
| Income taxes expense | | (15,000) |
| Net income | | $ 38,000 |

along with its 2005 income statement. We use this information to prepare a statement of cash flows that explains the $5,000 increase in cash for 2005 as reflected in its balance sheets. This $5,000 is computed as Cash of $17,000 at the end of 2005 minus Cash of $12,000 at the end of 2004. Genesis discloses additional information about 2005 transactions:

**a.** The accounts payable balances result from merchandise inventory purchases.

**b.** Purchased plant assets costing $70,000 by paying $10,000 cash and issuing $60,000 of bonds payable.

**c.** Sold plant assets with an original cost of $30,000 and accumulated depreciation of $12,000 for $12,000 cash, yielding a $6,000 loss.

**d.** Received cash of $15,000 from issuing 3,000 shares of common stock.

**e.** Paid $18,000 cash to retire bonds with a $34,000 book value, yielding a $16,000 gain.

**f.** Declared and paid cash dividends of $14,000.

> *The next section describes the indirect method. Appendix 12B describes the direct method. An instructor can choose to cover either one or both methods. Neither section depends on the other.*

Topic Tackler 12-2

**P2** Compute cash flows from operating activities using the indirect method.

## Application of the Indirect Method of Reporting

Net income is computed using accrual accounting, which recognizes revenues when earned and expenses when incurred. Revenues and expenses do not necessarily reflect the receipt and payment of cash. The indirect method of computing and reporting net cash flows from operating activities involves adjusting the net income figure to obtain the net cash provided (used) by operating activities. This includes subtracting noncash increases (credits) from net income and adding noncash charges (debits) back to net income.

To illustrate, the indirect method begins with Genesis's net income of $38,000 and adjusts it to obtain net cash provided (used) by operating activities of $20,000. Exhibit 12.11

**Exhibit 12.11**

Statement of Cash Flows—Indirect Method

| **GENESIS**<br>**Statement of Cash Flows**<br>**For Year Ended December 31, 2005** | | |
|---|---:|---:|
| Cash flows from operating activities | | |
| Net income . . . . . . . . . . . . . . . . . . . . . . . . . . . . . . | | $38,000 |
| Adjustments to reconcile net income to net cash provided by operating activities | | |
| ① Increase in accounts receivable . . . . . . . . . . . . . . | $(20,000) | |
| Increase in merchandise inventory . . . . . . . . . . . | (14,000) | |
| Increase in prepaid expenses . . . . . . . . . . . . . . . | (2,000) | |
| Decrease in accounts payable . . . . . . . . . . . . . . . | (5,000) | |
| Decrease in interest payable . . . . . . . . . . . . . . . . | (1,000) | |
| Increase in income taxes payable . . . . . . . . . . . . | 10,000 | |
| ② Depreciation expense . . . . . . . . . . . . . . . . . . . . | 24,000 | |
| ③ Loss on sale of plant assets . . . . . . . . . . . . . . . | 6,000 | |
| Gain on retirement of bonds . . . . . . . . . . . . . . . | (16,000) | |
| Net cash provided by operating activities . . . . . . . . . | | 20,000 |
| Cash flows from investing activities | | |
| Cash received from sale of plant assets . . . . . . . . . . | 12,000 | |
| Cash paid for purchase of plant assets . . . . . . . . . . . | (10,000) | |
| Net cash provided by investing activities . . . . . . . . . | | 2,000 |
| Cash flows from financing activities | | |
| Cash received from issuing stock . . . . . . . . . . . . . . . | 15,000 | |
| Cash paid to retire bonds . . . . . . . . . . . . . . . . . . . | (18,000) | |
| Cash paid for dividends . . . . . . . . . . . . . . . . . . . . | (14,000) | |
| Net cash used in financing activities . . . . . . . . . . . . | | (17,000) |
| Net increase in cash . . . . . . . . . . . . . . . . . . . . . . . | | $ 5,000 |
| Cash balance at beginning of year . . . . . . . . . . . . . . | | 12,000 |
| Cash balance at end of year . . . . . . . . . . . . . . . . . . | | $17,000 |

**Point:** Refer to Exhibit 12.10 and identify the $5,000 change in cash. This change is what the statement of cash flows explains; it serves as a check figure.

shows the results of the indirect method of reporting operating cash flows, which adjusts net income for three types of adjustments. There are adjustments ① to reflect changes in noncash current assets and current liabilities related to operating activities, ② to income statement items involving operating activities that do not affect cash inflows or outflows, and ③ to eliminate gains and losses resulting from investing and financing activities (not part of operating activities). This section describes each of these adjustments.

**Point:** *Noncash credits* refer to *revenue amounts* reported on the income statement that are *not collected in cash* this period. *Noncash charges* refer to *expense amounts* reported on the income statement that are *not paid* this period.

① **Adjustments for Changes in Current Assets and Current Liabilities**   This section describes adjustments for changes in noncash current assets and current liabilities.

*Adjustments for changes in noncash current assets.*   Changes in noncash current assets are normally the result of operating activities. Examples are sales affecting accounts receivable and asset usage affecting prepaid rent. Decreases in noncash current assets yield the following adjustment:

**Point:** Operating activities are typically those that determine income, which are often reflected in changes in current assets and current liabilities.

> **Decreases in noncash current assets are added to net income.**

To see the logic for this adjustment, consider that a decrease in a noncash current asset such as accounts receivable suggests more available cash at the end of the period compared to the beginning. This is so because a decrease in accounts receivable implies higher cash receipts than reflected in sales. We add these higher cash receipts (from decreases in noncash current assets) to net income when computing cash flow from operations.

In contrast, an increase in noncash current assets such as accounts receivable implies less cash receipts than reflected in sales. As another example, an increase in prepaid rent indicates that more cash is paid for rent than is deducted as rent expense. Increases in noncash current assets yield the following adjustment:

> **Increases in noncash current assets are subtracted from net income.**

To illustrate, these adjustments are applied to the noncash current assets in Exhibit 12.10.

*Accounts receivable.* Accounts Receivable *increase* $20,000, from a beginning balance of $40,000 to an ending balance of $60,000. This increase implies that Genesis collects less cash than is reported in sales. That is, some of these sales were in the form of accounts receivable and that amount increased during the period. To see this it is helpful to use *account analysis*. This usually involves setting up a T-account and reconstructing its major entries to compute cash receipts or payments. The following reconstructed Accounts Receivable T-account reveals the lower amount of cash receipts compared to sales:

| | Accounts Receivable | | | |
|---|---|---|---|---|
| Bal., Dec. 31, 2004 | 40,000 | | | |
| Sales | 590,000 | Cash receipts = | 570,000 | |
| Bal., Dec. 31, 2005 | 60,000 | | | |

Numbers in black are taken from Exhibit 12.10. The red number is the computed (plug) figure.

Notice that sales are $20,000 greater than the cash receipts. This $20,000—as reflected in the $20,000 increase in Accounts Receivable—is subtracted from net income when computing cash provided by operating activities (see Exhibit 12.11).

*Merchandise inventory.* Merchandise inventory *increases* by $14,000, from a $70,000 beginning balance to an $84,000 ending balance. This increase implies that Genesis had a larger amount of cash purchases than cost of goods sold. This larger amount of cash purchases is in the form of inventory, as reflected in the following account analysis:

| | Merchandise Inventory | | |
|---|---|---|---|
| Bal., Dec. 31, 2004 | 70,000 | | |
| Purchases = | 314,000 | Cost of goods sold | 300,000 |
| Bal., Dec. 31, 2005 | 84,000 | | |

The amount by which purchases exceed cost of goods sold—as reflected in the $14,000 increase in inventory—is subtracted from net income when computing cash provided by operating activities (see Exhibit 12.11).

*Prepaid expenses.* Prepaid expenses *increase* $2,000, from a $4,000 beginning balance to a $6,000 ending balance, implying that Genesis's cash payments exceed its recorded prepaid expenses. These higher cash payments increase the amount of Prepaid Expenses, as reflected in its reconstructed T-account:

| Prepaid Expenses | | | |
|---|---|---|---|
| Bal., Dec. 31, 2004 | 4,000 | | |
| **Cash payments =** | **218,000** | Wages and other operating exp. | 216,000 |
| Bal., Dec. 31, 2005 | 6,000 | | |

The amount by which cash payments exceed the recorded operating expenses—as reflected in the $2,000 increase in Prepaid Expenses—is subtracted from net income when computing cash provided by operating activities (see Exhibit 12.11).

**Adjustments for changes in current liabilities.**    Changes in current liabilities are normally the result of operating activities. An example is a purchase that affects accounts payable. Increases in current liabilities yield the following adjustment to net income when computing operating cash flows:

**Increases in current liabilities are added to net income.**

To see the logic for this adjustment, consider that an increase in the Accounts Payable account suggests that cash payments are less than the related (cost of goods sold) expense. As another example, an increase in wages payable implies that cash paid for wages is less than the recorded wages expense. Since the recorded expense is greater than the cash paid, we add the increase in wages payable to net income to compute net cash flow from operations.

Conversely, when current liabilities decrease, the following adjustment is required:

**Decreases in current liabilities are subtracted from net income.**

To illustrate, this adjustment is applied to the current liabilities in Exhibit 12.10.

*Accounts payable.* Accounts Payable *decrease* $5,000, from a beginning balance of $40,000 to an ending balance of $35,000. This decrease implies that cash payments to suppliers exceed purchases by $5,000 for the period, which is reflected in the reconstructed Accounts Payable T-account:

| Accounts Payable | | | |
|---|---|---|---|
| | | Bal., Dec. 31, 2004 | 40,000 |
| **Cash payments =** | **319,000** | Purchases | 314,000 |
| | | Bal., Dec. 31, 2005 | 35,000 |

The amount by which cash payments exceed purchases—as reflected in the $5,000 decrease in Accounts Payable—is subtracted from net income when computing cash provided by operating activities (see Exhibit 12.11).

*Interest payable.* Interest Payable *decreases* $1,000, from a $4,000 beginning balance to a $3,000 ending balance. This decrease indicates that cash paid for interest exceeds interest expense by $1,000, which is reflected in the Interest Payable T-account:

| Interest Payable | | | |
|---|---|---|---|
| | | Bal., Dec. 31, 2004 | 4,000 |
| **Cash paid for interest =** | **8,000** | Interest expense | 7,000 |
| | | Bal., Dec. 31, 2005 | 3,000 |

The amount by which cash paid exceeds recorded expense—as reflected in the $1,000 decrease in Interest Payable—is subtracted from net income (see Exhibit 12.11).

*Income taxes payable.* Income Taxes Payable *increase* $10,000, from a $12,000 beginning balance to a $22,000 ending balance. This increase implies that reported income taxes exceed the cash paid for taxes, which is reflected in the Income Taxes Payable T-account:

| Income Taxes Payable | | | |
|---|---|---|---|
| | | Bal., Dec. 31, 2004 | 12,000 |
| Cash paid for taxes = | 5,000 | Income taxes expense | 15,000 |
| | | Bal., Dec. 31, 2005 | 22,000 |

The amount by which cash paid falls short of the reported taxes expense—as reflected in the $10,000 increase in Income Taxes Payable—is added to net income when computing cash provided by operating activities (see Exhibit 12.11).

② **Adjustments for Operating Items Not Providing or Using Cash**   The income statement usually includes some expenses that do not reflect cash outflows in the period. Examples are depreciation, amortization, depletion, and bad debts expense. The indirect method for reporting operating cash flows requires that

**Expenses with no cash outflows are added back to net income.**

To see the logic of this adjustment, recall that items such as depreciation, amortization, depletion, and bad debts originate from debits to expense accounts and credits to noncash accounts. These entries have *no* cash effect, and we add them back to net income when computing net cash flows from operations. Adding them back cancels their deductions.

Similarly, when net income includes revenues that do not reflect cash inflows in the period, the indirect method for reporting operating cash flows requires that

**Revenues with no cash inflows are subtracted from net income.**

We apply these adjustments to the Genesis operating items that do not provide or use cash.

**Depreciation.**   Depreciation expense is the only Genesis operating item that has no effect on cash flows in the period. We must add back the $24,000 depreciation expense to net income when computing cash provided by operating activities. (We later explain that the cash outflow to acquire a plant asset is reported as an investing activity.)

③ **Adjustments for Nonoperating Items**   Net income often includes losses that are not part of operating activities but are part of either investing or financing activities. Examples are a loss from the sale of a plant asset and a loss from retirement of a bond payable. The indirect method for reporting operating cash flows requires that

**Nonoperating losses are added back to net income.**

To see the logic, consider that items such as a plant asset sale and a bond retirement are normally recorded by recognizing the cash, removing all plant asset or bond accounts, and recognizing any loss or gain. The cash received or paid is not part of operating activities but is part of either investing or financing activities. *No* operating cash flow effect occurs. However, because the nonoperating loss is a deduction in computing net income, we need to add it back to net income when computing cash flow from operations. Adding it back cancels the deduction.

Similarly, when net income includes gains not part of operating activities, the indirect method for reporting operating cash flows requires that

**Nonoperating gains are subtracted from net income.**

To illustrate these adjustments, we consider the nonoperating items of Genesis.

***Loss on sale of plant assets.***   Genesis reports a $6,000 loss on sale of plant assets as part of net income. This loss is a proper deduction in computing income, but it is *not part of operating activities*. Instead, a sale of plant assets is part of investing activities. Thus, the $6,000 nonoperating loss is added back to net income (see Exhibit 12.11). Adding it back cancels the loss. We later explain how to report the cash inflow from the asset sale in investing activities.

***Gain on retirement of debt.***   A $16,000 gain on retirement of debt is properly included in net income, but it is *not part of operating activities*. Thus, the $16,000 nonoperating gain is subtracted from net income to obtain net cash provided by operating activities (see Exhibit 12.11). Subtracting it cancels the recorded gain. We later describe how to report the cash outflow to retire debt.

## Summary of Adjustments for Indirect Method

Exhibit 12.12 summarizes the most common adjustments to net income when computing net cash provided (used) by operating activities under the indirect method.

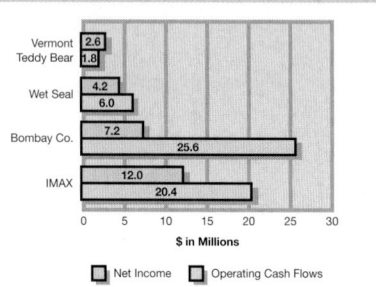
**Exhibit 12.12**

Summary of Selected Adjustments for Indirect Method

**Net Income**

+ Decrease in noncash current asset
– Increase in noncash current asset
+ Increase in current liability*
– Decrease in current liability*

    ① Adjustments for changes in current assets and current liabilities

+ Depreciation, depletion, and amortization
+ Accrued expenses
– Accrued revenues

    ② Adjustments for operating items not providing or using cash

+ Loss on disposal of long-term asset
+ Loss on retirement of debt
– Gain on disposal of long-term asset
– Gain on retirement of debt

    ③ Adjustments for nonoperating items

**Net cash provided (used) by operating activities**

\* Excludes current portion of long-term debt and any (nonsales-related) short-term notes payable—both are financing activities.

The computations in determining cash provided (used) by operating activities are different for the indirect and direct methods, but the result is identical. Both methods yield the same $20,000 figure for cash from operating activities for Genesis; see Exhibits 12.7 and 12.11.

### Quick Check

4. Determine net cash provided (used) by operating activities using the following data: net income, $74,900; decrease in accounts receivable, $4,600; increase in inventory, $11,700; decrease in accounts payable, $1,000; loss on sale of equipment, $3,400; payment of cash dividends, $21,500.

5. Why are expenses such as depreciation and amortization added to net income when cash flow from operating activities is computed by the indirect method?

6. A company reports net income of $15,000 that includes a $3,000 gain on the sale of plant assets. Why is this gain subtracted from net income in computing cash flow from operating activities using the indirect method?

# Cash Flows from Investing

The third major step in preparing the statement of cash flows is to compute and report cash flows from investing activities. We normally do this by identifying changes in (1) all noncurrent asset accounts and (2) the current accounts for both notes receivable and investments in securities (excluding trading securities). We then analyze changes in these accounts to determine their effect, if any, on cash and report the cash flow effects in the investing activities section of the statement of cash flows. *Reporting of investing activities is identical under the direct method and indirect method.*

## Three-Stage Process of Analysis

Information to compute cash flows from investing activities is usually taken from beginning and ending balance sheets and the income statement. We use a three-stage process to determine cash provided (used) by investing activities: (1) identify changes in investing-related accounts, (2) explain these changes using reconstruction analysis, and (3) report their cash flow effects.

## Analysis of Noncurrent Assets

Information about the Genesis transactions provided earlier reveals that the company both purchased and sold plant assets during the period. Both transactions are investing activities and are analyzed for their cash flow effects in this section.

**Plant Asset Transactions** The first stage in analyzing the Plant Assets account and its related Accumulated Depreciation is to identify any changes in these accounts from comparative balance sheets in Exhibit 12.10. This analysis reveals a $40,000 increase in plant assets from $210,000 to $250,000 and a $12,000 increase in accumulated depreciation from $48,000 to $60,000.

The second stage is to explain these changes. Items *b* and *c* of the additional information for Genesis (page 500) are relevant in this case. Recall that the Plant Assets account is affected by both asset purchases and sales, while its Accumulated Depreciation account is normally increased from depreciation and decreased from the removal of accumulated depreciation in asset sales. To explain changes in these accounts and to identify their cash flow effects, we prepare *reconstructed entries* from prior transactions; *they are not the actual entries by the preparer.*

To illustrate, item *b* reports that Genesis purchased plant assets of $70,000 by issuing $60,000 in bonds payable to the seller and paying $10,000 in cash. The reconstructed entry for analysis of item *b* follows:

| | | | |
|---|---|---|---|
| Reconstruction | Plant Assets . . . . . . . . . . . . . . . . . . . . . . . . . . . | 70,000 | |
| | Bonds Payable . . . . . . . . . . . . . . . . . . . . . | | 60,000 |
| | **Cash** . . . . . . . . . . . . . . . . . . . . . . . . . . | | **10,000** |

Assets = Liabilities + Equity
+70,000    +60,000
−10,000

This entry reveals a $10,000 cash outflow for plant assets and a $60,000 noncash investing and financing transaction involving bonds exchanged for plant assets.

Next, item *c* reports that Genesis sold plant assets costing $30,000 (with $12,000 of accumulated depreciation) for $12,000 cash, resulting in a $6,000 loss. The reconstructed entry for analysis of item *c* follows:

| | | | |
|---|---|---|---|
| Reconstruction | **Cash** . . . . . . . . . . . . . . . . . . . . . . . . . . . . | **12,000** | |
| | Accumulated Depreciation . . . . . . . . . . . . . . . . | 12,000 | |
| | Loss on Sale of Plant Assets . . . . . . . . . . . . . . | 6,000 | |
| | Plant Assets . . . . . . . . . . . . . . . . . . . | | 30,000 |

Assets = Liabilities + Equity
+12,000            −6,000
−30,000
+12,000

---

P3 Determine cash flows from both investing and financing activities.

**Point:** Investing activities include (1) purchasing and selling long-term assets, (2) lending and collecting on notes receivable, and (3) purchasing and selling short-term investments other than cash equivalents and trading securities.

**Point:** Financing and investing info is available in ledger accounts to help explain changes in comparative balance sheets. Post references lead to relevant entries and explanations.

This entry reveals a $12,000 cash inflow from assets sold. The $6,000 loss is computed by comparing the asset book value to the cash received and does not reflect any cash inflow or outflow. We also reconstruct the entry for Depreciation Expense using information from the income statement:

Assets = Liabilities + Equity<br>−24,000         −24,000

| Reconstruction | Depreciation Expense ..................... | 24,000 | |
| | Accumulated Depreciation ............ | | 24,000 |

This entry shows that Depreciation Expense results in no cash flow effect. These three reconstructed entries are reflected in the following plant asset and related T-accounts.

| **Plant Assets** | | | |
|---|---|---|---|
| Bal., Dec. 31, 2004 | 210,000 | | |
| **Purchase** | **70,000** | **Sale** | **30,000** |
| Bal., Dec. 31, 2005 | 250,000 | | |

| **Accumulated Depreciation—Plant Assets** | | | |
|---|---|---|---|
| | | Bal., Dec. 31, 2004 | 48,000 |
| **Sale** | **12,000** | **Depr. expense** | **24,000** |
| | | Bal., Dec. 31, 2005 | 60,000 |

This reconstruction analysis is complete in that the change in plant assets from $210,000 to $250,000 is fully explained by the $70,000 purchase and the $30,000 sale. Also, the change in accumulated depreciation from $48,000 to $60,000 is fully explained by depreciation expense of $24,000 and the removal of $12,000 in accumulated depreciation from an asset sale. (*Note:* Preparers of the statement of cash flows have the entire ledger and additional information at their disposal, but for brevity reasons only the information needed for reconstructing accounts is given.)

The third stage looks at the reconstructed entries for identification of cash flows. The two identified cash flow effects are reported in the investing section of the statement as follows (also see Exhibit 12.7 or 12.11):

**Example:** If a plant asset costing $40,000 with $37,000 of accumulated depreciation is sold at a $1,000 loss, what is the cash flow? What is the cash flow if this asset is sold at a gain of $3,000? *Answers:* +$2,000; +$6,000.

**Cash flows from investing activities**
Cash received from sale of plant assets ............ $12,000
Cash paid for purchase of plant assets ............. (10,000)

Also, the $60,000 portion of the purchase described in item *b* and financed by issuing bonds is a noncash investing and financing activity. It is reported in a note or in a separate schedule to the statement as follows:

**Noncash investing and financing activity**
Purchased plant assets with issuance of bonds ....... $60,000

## Analysis of Other Assets

Many other asset transactions (including those involving current notes receivable and investments in certain securities) are considered investing activities and can affect a company's cash flows. Since Genesis did not enter into other investing activities impacting assets, we do not need to extend our analysis to these other assets. If such transactions did exist, we would analyze them using the same three-stage process illustrated for plant assets.

## Quick Check

**7.** Equipment costing $80,000 with accumulated depreciation of $30,000 is sold at a loss of $10,000. What is the cash receipt from this sale? In what section of the statement of cash flows is this transaction reported?

Answer—p. 522

# Cash Flows from Financing

The fourth major step in preparing the statement of cash flows is to compute and report cash flows from financing activities. We normally do this by identifying changes in all noncurrent liability accounts (including the current portion of any notes and bonds) and the equity accounts. These accounts include long-term debt, notes payable, bonds payable, common stock, and retained earnings. Changes in these accounts are then analyzed using available information to determine their effect, if any, on cash. Results are reported in the financing activities section of the statement. *Reporting of financing activities is identical under the direct method and indirect method.*

## Three-Stage Process of Analysis

We again use a three-stage process to determine cash provided (used) by financing activities: (1) identify changes in financing-related accounts, (2) explain these changes using reconstruction analysis, and (3) report their cash flow effects.

## Analysis of Noncurrent Liabilities

Information about Genesis provided earlier reveals two transactions involving noncurrent liabilities. We analyzed one of those, the $60,000 issuance of bonds payable to purchase plant assets. This transaction is reported as a significant noncash investing and financing activity in a note or a separate schedule to the statement of cash flows. The other remaining transaction involving noncurrent liabilities is the cash retirement of bonds payable.

**Point:** Financing activities generally refer to changes in the noncurrent liability and the equity accounts. Examples are (1) receiving cash from issuing debt or repaying amounts borrowed and (2) receiving cash from or distributing cash to owners.

**Bonds Payable Transactions**   The first stage in analysis of bonds is to review the comparative balance sheets from Exhibit 12.10. This analysis reveals an increase in bonds payable from $64,000 to $90,000.

The second stage explains this change. Item *e* of the additional information for Genesis (page 500) reports that bonds with a carrying value of $34,000 are retired for $18,000 cash, resulting in a $16,000 gain. The reconstructed entry for analysis of item *e* follows:

| Reconstruction | Bonds Payable ......................... | 34,000 | | Assets | = Liabilities + | Equity |
|---|---|---|---|---|---|---|
| | Gain on retirement of debt ............ | | 16,000 | −18,000 | −34,000 | +16,000 |
| | **Cash** ............................ | | **18,000** | | | |

This entry reveals an $18,000 cash outflow for retirement of bonds and a $16,000 gain from comparing the bonds payable carrying value to the cash received. This gain does not reflect any cash inflow or outflow. Also, item *b* of the additional information reports that Genesis purchased plant assets costing $70,000 by issuing $60,000 in bonds payable to the seller and paying $10,000 in cash. We reconstructed this entry when analyzing investing activities: It showed a $60,000 increase to bonds payable that is reported as a noncash investing and financing transaction. The Bonds Payable account reflects (and is fully explained by) these reconstructed entries as follows:

| Bonds Payable | | | |
|---|---|---|---|
| | | Bal., Dec. 31, 2004 | 64,000 |
| **Retired bonds** | **34,000** | **Issued bonds** | **60,000** |
| | | Bal., Dec. 31, 2005 | 90,000 |

The third stage is to report the cash flow effect of the bond retirement in the financing section of the statement as follows (also see Exhibit 12.7 or 12.11):

**Cash flows from financing activities**
Cash paid to retire bonds ............... $(18,000)

## Analysis of Equity

The Genesis information reveals two transactions involving equity accounts. The first is the issuance of common stock for cash. The second is the declaration and payment of cash dividends. We analyze both.

**Common Stock Transactions**  The first stage in analyzing common stock is to review the comparative balance sheets from Exhibit 12.10, which reveals an increase in common stock from $80,000 to $95,000.

The second stage explains this change. Item *d* of the additional information (page 500) reports that 3,000 shares of common stock are issued at par for $5 per share. The reconstructed entry for analysis of item *d* follows:

Assets = Liabilities + Equity
+15,000                +15,000

| Reconstruction | **Cash** ................................. | **15,000** | |
|---|---|---|---|
| | Common Stock ..................... | | 15,000 |

This entry reveals a $15,000 cash inflow from stock issuance and is reflected in (and explains) the Common Stock account as follows:

| Common Stock | | |
|---|---|---|
| | Bal., Dec. 31, 2004 | 80,000 |
| | **Issued stock** | **15,000** |
| | Bal., Dec. 31, 2005 | 95,000 |

The third stage discloses the cash flow effect from stock issuance in the financing section of the statement as follows (also see Exhibit 12.7 or 12.11):

**Cash flows from financing activities**
Cash received from issuing stock ........... $15,000

**Retained Earnings Transactions**  The first stage in analyzing the Retained Earnings account is to review the comparative balance sheets from Exhibit 12.10. This reveals an increase in retained earnings from $88,000 to $112,000.

The second stage explains this change. Item *f* of the additional information (page 500) reports that cash dividends of $14,000 are paid. The reconstructed entry follows:

Assets = Liabilities + Equity
−14,000                −14,000

| Reconstruction | Retained Earnings ...................... | 14,000 | |
|---|---|---|---|
| | **Cash** .............................. | | **14,000** |

This entry reveals a $14,000 cash outflow for cash dividends. Also note that the Retained Earnings account is impacted by net income of $38,000. (Net income was analyzed under the operating section of the statement of cash flows.) The reconstructed Retained Earnings account follows:

| Retained Earnings | | | | |
|---|---|---|---|---|
| | | | Bal., Dec. 31, 2004 | 88,000 |
| **Cash dividend** | **14,000** | | **Net income** | **38,000** |
| | | | Bal., Dec. 31, 2005 | 112,000 |

The third stage reports the cash flow effect from the cash dividend in the financing section of the statement as follows (also see Exhibit 12.7 or 12.11):

**Cash flows from financing activities**

Cash paid for dividends . . . . . . . . . . . . . . . . . . $(14,000)

**Point:** Financing activities not affecting cash flow include *declaration* of a cash dividend, *declaration* of a stock dividend, payment of a stock dividend, and a stock split.

We now have identified and explained all of the Genesis cash inflows and cash outflows and one noncash investing and financing transaction. Specifically, our analysis has reconciled changes in all noncash balance sheet accounts.

**Global:** There are no requirements to separate domestic and international cash flows, leading some users to ask "Where in the world is cash flow?"

## Proving Cash Balances

The fifth and final step in preparing the statement is to report the beginning and ending cash balances and prove that the *net change in cash* is explained by operating, investing, and financing cash flows. This step is shown here for Genesis.

| | |
|---|---:|
| Net cash provided by operating activities . . . . . . . | $20,000 |
| Net cash provided by investing activities . . . . . . . . | 2,000 |
| Net cash used in financing activities . . . . . . . . . . | (17,000) |
| **Net increase in cash** . . . . . . . . . . . . . . . . . . . . | **$ 5,000** |
| Cash balance at beginning of 2005 . . . . . . . . . . . | 12,000 |
| Cash balance at end of 2005 . . . . . . . . . . . . . . . | $ 17,000 |

**Point:** The following ratio helps assess whether a company's operating cash flow is adequate to meet long-term obligations:
**Cash coverage of debt** = Cash flow from operations divided by noncurrent liabilities.
A low ratio suggests a higher risk of insolvency; a high ratio suggests a greater ability to meet long-term obligations.

The preceding table shows that the $5,000 net increase in cash, from $12,000 at the beginning of the period to $17,000 at the end, is reconciled by net cash flows from operating ($20,000 inflow), investing ($2,000 inflow), and financing ($17,000 outflow) activities. This is formally reported at the bottom of the statement of cash flows as shown in both Exhibits 12.7 and 12.11.

**Decision Maker**

**Reporter** Management is in labor contract negotiations and grants you an interview. It highlights a recent $600,000 net loss that involves a $930,000 extraordinary loss and a total net cash outflow of $550,000 (which includes net cash outflows of $850,000 for investing activities and $350,000 for financing activities). What is your assessment of this company?

Answer—p. 522

---

**Cash Flow Analysis**      **Decision Analysis**

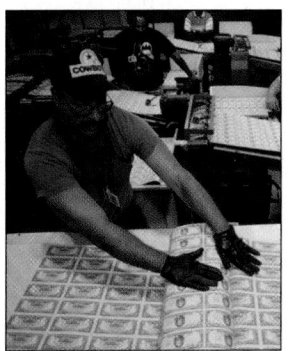

## Analyzing Cash Sources and Uses

Most managers stress the importance of understanding and predicting cash flows for business decisions. Creditors evaluate a company's ability to generate cash before deciding whether to lend money. Investors also assess cash inflows and outflows before buying and selling stock. Information in the statement of cash flows helps address these and other questions such as (1) How much cash is generated from or used in operations? (2) What expenditures are made with cash from operations? (3) What is the source of cash for debt payments? (4) What is the source of cash for distributions to owners? (5) How is the increase in investing activities financed? (6) What is the source of cash for new plant assets? (7) Why is cash flow from operations different from income? (8) How is cash from financing used?

**A1**   Analyze the statement of cash flows.

**Decision Insight**

**Free Cash** Cash-based valuation of a company is theoretically equal to earnings-based valuation, but it usually yields a different value due to practical limitations. One limitation is the measurement of cash flows that are "free" for distribution to shareholders. These *free cash flows* are defined as cash flows available to shareholders after operating asset reinvestments and debt payments. Growth and financial flexibility depend on adequate free cash flow.

To effectively answer these questions, it is important to separately analyze investing, financing, and operating activities. To illustrate, consider data from three different companies in Exhibit 12.13. These companies operate in the same industry and have been in business for several years.

**Exhibit 12.13**

Cash Flows of Competing
Companies

| ($ in thousands) | BMX | ATV | Trex |
|---|---|---|---|
| Cash provided (used) by operating activities ....... | $90,000 | $40,000 | $(24,000) |
| Cash provided (used) by investing activities | | | |
| Proceeds from sale of plant assets ............. | | | 26,000 |
| Purchase of plant assets .................... | (48,000) | (25,000) | |
| Cash provided (used) by financing activities | | | |
| Proceeds from issuance of debt .............. | | | 13,000 |
| Repayment of debt ........................ | (27,000) | | |
| Net increase (decrease) in cash ............... | $15,000 | $15,000 | $ 15,000 |

Each company generates an identical $15,000 net increase in cash, but its sources and uses of cash flows are very different. BMX's operating activities provide net cash flows of $90,000, allowing it to purchase plant assets of $48,000 and repay $27,000 of its debt. ATV's operating activities provide $40,000 of cash flows, limiting its purchase of plant assets to $25,000. Trex's $15,000 net cash increase is due to selling plant assets and incurring additional debt. Its operating activities yield a net cash outflow of $24,000. Overall, analysis of these cash flows reveals that BMX is more capable of generating future cash flows than is ATV or Trex.

## Cash Flow on Total Assets

**A2** Compute and apply the cash flow on total assets ratio.

Cash flow information has limitations, but it can help measure a company's ability to meet its obligations, pay dividends, expand operations, and obtain financing. Users often compute and analyze a cash-based ratio similar to return on total assets except that its numerator is net cash flows from operating activities. The **cash flow on total assets** ratio is in Exhibit 12.14.

**Exhibit 12.14**

Cash Flow on Total Assets

$$\text{Cash flow on total assets} = \frac{\text{Cash flow from operations}}{\text{Average total assets}}$$

**Exhibit 12.15**

Nike's Cash Flow on Total Assets

| Year | Cash Flow on Total Assets | Return on Total Assets |
|---|---|---|
| 2002 ....... | 17.6% | 10.8% |
| 2001 ....... | 11.2 | 10.1 |
| 2000 ....... | 12.6 | 10.4 |
| 1999 ....... | 17.7 | 8.5 |
| 1998 ....... | 9.6 | 7.4 |
| 1997 ....... | 6.9 | 17.1 |

This ratio reflects actual cash flows and is not affected by accounting income recognition and measurement. It can help business decision makers estimate the amount and timing of cash flows when planning and analyzing operating activities.

To illustrate, the 2002 cash flow on total assets ratio for **Nike** is 17.6%—see Exhibit 12.15. Is a 17.6% ratio good or bad? To answer this question, we compare this ratio with the ratios of prior years (we could also compare its ratio with those of its competitors and the market). Nike's cash flow on total assets ratio for several prior years is in the second column of Exhibit 12.15. Results show that its 17.6% return is higher than all but one of the prior years' returns.

As an indicator of *earnings quality,* some analysts compare the cash flow on total assets ratio to the return on total assets ratio. Nike's return on total assets is provided in the third column of Exhibit 12.15. Nike's cash flow on total assets ratio exceeds its return on total assets in five of the six years, leading these analysts to infer that Nike's earnings quality is high for that period because more earnings are realized in the form of cash.

### Decision Insight

**Cash Ratios**   Analysts use various other cash-based ratios:

$$(1)\ \text{Cash coverage of growth} = \frac{\text{Operating cash flow}}{\text{Cash outflow for plant assets}}$$

a low ratio (less than 1) implies cash inadequacy to meet asset growth, whereas a high ratio implies cash adequacy for asset growth.

$$(2)\ \text{Operating cash flow to sales} = \frac{\text{Operating cash flow}}{\text{Net sales}}$$

when this ratio substantially and consistently differs from the operating income to net sales ratio, the risk of accounting improprieties increases.

# Demonstration Problem

Umlauf's comparative balance sheets, income statement, and additional information follow.

**UMLAUF COMPANY**
**Balance Sheets**
**December 31, 2005 and 2004**

| Assets | 2005 | 2004 |
|---|---|---|
| Cash .......................... | $ 43,050 | $ 23,925 |
| Accounts receivable ................. | 34,125 | 39,825 |
| Merchandise inventory .............. | 156,000 | 146,475 |
| Prepaid expenses ................... | 3,600 | 1,650 |
| Equipment ...................... | 135,825 | 146,700 |
| Accum. depreciation—Equipment ........ | (61,950) | (47,550) |
| Total assets ..................... | $310,650 | $311,025 |
| **Liabilities and Equity** | | |
| Accounts payable ................. | $ 28,800 | $ 33,750 |
| Income taxes payable .............. | 5,100 | 4,425 |
| Dividends payable ................. | 0 | 4,500 |
| Bonds payable .................... | 0 | 37,500 |
| Common stock, $10 par ............. | 168,750 | 168,750 |
| Retained earnings ................. | 108,000 | 62,100 |
| Total liabilities and equity ............ | $310,650 | $311,025 |

**UMLAUF COMPANY**
**Income Statement**
**For Year Ended December 31, 2005**

| | | |
|---|---|---|
| Sales .......................... | | $446,100 |
| Cost of goods sold ................. | $222,300 | |
| Other operating expenses ............ | 120,300 | |
| Depreciation expense .............. | 25,500 | (368,100) |
| | | 78,000 |
| Other gains (losses) | | |
| Loss on sale of equipment ......... | 3,300 | |
| Loss on retirement of bonds ........ | 825 | (4,125) |
| Income before taxes ............... | | 73,875 |
| Income taxes expense .............. | | (13,725) |
| Net income ..................... | | $ 60,150 |

## Additional Information

**a.** Equipment costing $21,375 with accumulated depreciation of $11,100 is sold for cash.

**b.** Equipment purchases are for cash.

**c.** Accumulated Depreciation is affected by depreciation expense and the sale of equipment.

**d.** The balance of Retained Earnings is affected by dividend declarations and net income.

**e.** All sales are made on credit.

**f.** All merchandise inventory purchases are on credit.

**g.** Accounts Payable balances result from merchandise inventory purchases.

**h.** Prepaid expenses relate to "other operating expenses."

## Required

**1.** Prepare a statement of cash flows using the indirect method for year 2005.

**2.**ᴰ Prepare a statement of cash flows using the direct method for year 2005.

## Planning the Solution

- Prepare two blank statements of cash flows with sections for operating, investing, and financing activities using the (1) indirect method format and (2) direct method format.

- Compute the cash paid for equipment and the cash received from the sale of equipment using the additional information provided along with the amount for depreciation expense and the change in the balances of equipment and accumulated depreciation. Use T-accounts to help chart the effects of the sale and purchase of equipment on the balances of the Equipment account and the Accumulated Depreciation account.

- Calculate the effect of net income on the change in the Retained Earnings account balance. Assign the difference between the change in retained earnings and the amount of net income to dividends declared. Adjust the dividends declared amount for the change in the Dividends Payable balance.

- Compute cash received from customers, cash paid for merchandise, cash paid for other operating expenses, and cash paid for taxes as illustrated in the chapter.

- Enter the cash effects of reconstruction entries to the appropriate section(s) of the statement.

- Total each section of the statement, determine the total net change in cash, and add it to the beginning balance to get the ending balance of cash.

# Solution to Demonstration Problem

Supporting computations for cash receipts and cash payments:

| | | |
|---|---|---:|
| (1) | *Cost of equipment sold . . . . . . . . . . . . . . . . . . . . . . . . | $ 21,375 |
| | Accumulated depreciation of equipment sold . . . . . . . . . . | (11,100) |
| | Book value of equipment sold . . . . . . . . . . . . . . . . . . . . | 10,275 |
| | Loss on sale of equipment . . . . . . . . . . . . . . . . . . . . . . | (3,300) |
| | Cash received from sale of equipment . . . . . . . . . . . . . . | $ 6,975 |
| | Cost of equipment sold . . . . . . . . . . . . . . . . . . . . . . . | $ 21,375 |
| | Less decrease in the equipment account balance . . . . . . . | (10,875) |
| | Cash paid for new equipment . . . . . . . . . . . . . . . . . . . . | $ 10,500 |
| (2) | Loss on retirement of bonds . . . . . . . . . . . . . . . . . . . . . | $ 825 |
| | Carrying value of bonds retired . . . . . . . . . . . . . . . . . . | 37,500 |
| | Cash paid to retire bonds . . . . . . . . . . . . . . . . . . . . . . | $ 38,325 |
| (3) | Net income . . . . . . . . . . . . . . . . . . . . . . . . . . . . . . . | $ 60,150 |
| | Less increase in retained earnings . . . . . . . . . . . . . . . . | 45,900 |
| | Dividends declared . . . . . . . . . . . . . . . . . . . . . . . . . . | 14,250 |
| | Plus decrease in dividends payable . . . . . . . . . . . . . . . . | 4,500 |
| | Cash paid for dividends . . . . . . . . . . . . . . . . . . . . . . . | $ 18,750 |
| (4)B | Sales . . . . . . . . . . . . . . . . . . . . . . . . . . . . . . . . . . . | $ 446,100 |
| | Add decrease in accounts receivable . . . . . . . . . . . . . . . | 5,700 |
| | Cash received from customers . . . . . . . . . . . . . . . . . . . | $451,800 |
| (5)B | Cost of goods sold . . . . . . . . . . . . . . . . . . . . . . . . . . | $ 222,300 |
| | Plus increase in merchandise inventory . . . . . . . . . . . . . | 9,525 |
| | Purchases . . . . . . . . . . . . . . . . . . . . . . . . . . . . . . . . | 231,825 |
| | Plus decrease in accounts payable . . . . . . . . . . . . . . . . | 4,950 |
| | Cash paid for merchandise . . . . . . . . . . . . . . . . . . . . . | $236,775 |
| (6)B | Other operating expenses . . . . . . . . . . . . . . . . . . . . . . | $ 120,300 |
| | Plus increase in prepaid expenses . . . . . . . . . . . . . . . . | 1,950 |
| | Cash paid for other operating expenses . . . . . . . . . . . . | $122,250 |
| (7)B | Income taxes expense . . . . . . . . . . . . . . . . . . . . . . . . | $ 13,725 |
| | Less increase in income taxes payable . . . . . . . . . . . . . | (675) |
| | Cash paid for income taxes . . . . . . . . . . . . . . . . . . . . . | $ 13,050 |

\* Supporting T-account analysis for part 1:

| Equipment | | | | | Accumulated Depreciation—Equipment | | | |
|---|---|---|---|---|---|---|---|---|
| Bal., Dec. 31, 2004 | 146,700 | | | | | | Bal., Dec. 31, 2004 | 47,550 |
| Cash purchase | 10,500 | Sale | 21,375 | Sale | 11,100 | Depr. expense | | 25,500 |
| Bal., Dec. 31, 2005 | 135,825 | | | | | | Bal., Dec. 31, 2005 | 61,950 |

**UMLAUF COMPANY**
**Statement of Cash Flows (Indirect Method)**
**For Year Ended December 31, 2005**

| | |
|---|---:|
| Cash flows from operating activities | |
| Cash flows from operating activities | |
| Net income . . . . . . . . . . . . . . . . . . . . . . . . . . . . . | $60,150 |
| Adjustments to reconcile net income to net cash provided by operating activities | |
| Decrease in accounts receivable . . . . . . . . . . . . . . | 5,700 |
| Increase in merchandise inventory . . . . . . . . . . . . . | (9,525) |
| Increase in prepaid expenses . . . . . . . . . . . . . . . . | (1,950) |
| Decrease in accounts payable . . . . . . . . . . . . . . . | (4,950) |
| Increase in income taxes payable . . . . . . . . . . . . . | 675 |
| Depreciation expense . . . . . . . . . . . . . . . . . . . . . | 25,500 |

[continued on next page]

[continued from previous page]

| | | |
|---|---:|---:|
| Loss on sale of plant assets | 3,300 | |
| Loss on retirement of bonds | 825 | |
| Net cash provided by operating activities | | $79,725 |
| Cash flows from investing activities | | |
| Cash received from sale of equipment | 6,975 | |
| Cash paid for equipment | (10,500) | |
| Net cash used in investing activities | | (3,525) |
| Cash flows from financing activities | | |
| Cash paid to retire bonds payable | (38,325) | |
| Cash paid for dividends | (18,750) | |
| Net cash used in financing activities | | (57,075) |
| Net increase in cash | | $19,125 |
| Cash balance at beginning of year | | 23,925 |
| Cash balance at end of year | | $43,050 |

**UMLAUF COMPANY**
**Statement of Cash Flows (Direct Method)**
**For Year Ended December 31, 2005**

| | | |
|---|---:|---:|
| Cash flows from operating activities | | |
| Cash received from customers | $451,800 | |
| Cash paid for merchandise | (236,775) | |
| Cash paid for other operating expenses | (122,250) | |
| Cash paid for income taxes | (13,050) | |
| Net cash provided by operating activities | | $79,725 |
| Cash flows from investing activities | | |
| Cash received from sale of equipment | 6,975 | |
| Cash paid for equipment | (10,500) | |
| Net cash used in investing activities | | (3,525) |
| Cash flows from financing activities | | |
| Cash paid to retire bonds payable | (38,325) | |
| Cash paid for dividends | (18,750) | |
| Net cash used in financing activities | | (57,075) |
| Net increase in cash | | $19,125 |
| Cash balance at beginning of year | | 23,925 |
| Cash balance at end of year | | $43,050 |

# Spreadsheet Preparation of the Statement of Cash Flows

# 12A

This appendix explains how to use a spreadsheet to prepare the statement of cash flows under the indirect method.

## Preparing the Indirect Method Spreadsheet

Analyzing noncash accounts can be challenging when a company has a large number of accounts and many operating, investing, and financing transactions. A *spreadsheet,* also called *work sheet* or *working paper,* can help us organize the information needed to prepare a statement of cash flows. A spreadsheet also makes it easier to check the accuracy of our work. To illustrate, we return to the comparative balance

**P4** Illustrate spreadsheet use in preparing a statement of cash flows.

sheets and income statement shown in Exhibit 12.10. Information needed for the spreadsheet in preparing the statement of cash flows along with identifying letters *a* through *m* follow:

**a.** Net income is $38,000.

**b.** Accounts receivable increase by $20,000.

**c.** Merchandise inventory increases by $14,000.

**d.** Prepaid expenses increase by $2,000.

**e.** Accounts payable decrease by $5,000.

**f.** Interest payable decreases by $1,000.

**g.** Income taxes payable increase by $10,000.

**h.** Depreciation expense is $24,000.

**i.** Plant assets costing $30,000 with accumulated depreciation of $12,000 are sold for $12,000 cash. This yields a loss on sale of assets of $6,000.

**j.** Bonds with a book value of $34,000 are retired with a cash payment of $18,000, yielding a $16,000 gain on retirement.

**k.** Plant assets costing $70,000 are purchased with a cash payment of $10,000 and an issuance of bonds payable for $60,000.

**l.** Issued 3,000 shares of common stock for $15,000 cash.

**m.** Paid cash dividends of $14,000.

Exhibit 12A.1 shows the indirect method spreadsheet for Genesis. We enter both beginning and ending balance sheet amounts on the spreadsheet. We also enter information in the Analysis of Changes columns (keyed to the additional information items *a* through *m*) to explain changes in the accounts and determine the cash flows for operating, investing, and financing activities. Information about noncash investing and financing activities is reported near the bottom.

## Entering the Analysis of Changes on the Spreadsheet

The following sequence of procedures is used to complete the spreadsheet after the beginning and ending balances of the balance sheet accounts are entered:

① Enter net income as the first item in the Statement of Cash Flows section for computing operating cash inflow (debit) and as a credit to Retained Earnings.

② In the Statement of Cash Flows section, adjustments to net income are entered as debits if they increase cash flows and as credits if they decrease cash flows. Applying this same rule, adjust net income for the change in each noncash current asset and current liability account related to operating activities. For each adjustment to net income, the offsetting debit or credit must help reconcile the beginning and ending balances of a current asset or current liability account.

③ Enter adjustments to net income for income statement items not providing or using cash in the period. For each adjustment, the offsetting debit or credit must help reconcile a noncash balance sheet account.

④ Adjust net income to eliminate any gains or losses from investing and financing activities. Because the cash from a gain must be excluded from operating activities, the gain is entered as a credit in the operating activities section. Losses are entered as debits. For each adjustment, the related debit and/or credit must help reconcile balance sheet accounts and involve reconstructed entries to show the cash flow from investing or financing activities.

⑤ After reviewing any unreconciled balance sheet accounts and related information, enter the remaining reconciling entries for investing and financing activities. Examples are purchases of plant assets, issuances of long-term debt, stock issuances, and dividend payments. Some of these may require entries in the noncash investing and financing section of the spreadsheet (reconciled).

⑥ Check accuracy by totaling the Analysis of Changes columns and by determining that the change in each balance sheet account has been explained (reconciled).

We illustrate these steps in Exhibit 12A.1 for Genesis:

**Point:** Analysis of the changes on the spreadsheet are summarized as:

1. Cash flows from operating activities generally affect net income, current assets, and current liabilities.

2. Cash flows from investing activities generally affect noncurrent asset accounts.

3. Cash flows from financing activities generally affect noncurrent liability and equity accounts.

| Step | Entries |
|---|---|
| ① . . . . . . . . | (*a*) |
| ② . . . . . . . . | (*b*) through (*g*) |
| ③ . . . . . . . . | (*h*) |
| ④ . . . . . . . . | (*i*) through (*j*) |
| ⑤ . . . . . . . . | (*k*) through (*m*) |

```
File  Edit  View  Insert  Format  Tools  Data  Accounting  Window  Help                    _ 8 x
```

|  | A | B | C | D | E | F | G |
|---|---|---|---|---|---|---|---|
| 1 | | **GENESIS** | | | | | |
| 2 | | **Spreadsheet for Statement of Cash Flows–Indirect Method** | | | | | |
| 3 | | **For Year Ended December 31, 2005** | | | | | |
| 5 | | | | **Analysis of Changes** | | | |
| 6 | | **Dec. 31,** | | | | | **Dec. 31,** |
| 7 | | **2004** | | **Debit** | | **Credit** | **2005** |
| 8 | **Balance Sheet—Debits** | | | | | | |
| 9 | Cash | $ 12,000 | | | | | $ 17,000 |
| 10 | Accounts receivable | 40,000 | *(b)* | $ 20,000 | | | 60,000 |
| 11 | Merchandise inventory | 70,000 | *(c)* | 14,000 | | | 84,000 |
| 12 | Prepaid expenses | 4,000 | *(d)* | 2,000 | | | 6,000 |
| 13 | Plant assets | 210,000 | *(k1)* | 70,000 | *(i)* | $ 30,000 | 250,000 |
| 14 | | $336,000 | | | | | $417,000 |
| 16 | **Balance Sheet—Credits** | | | | | | |
| 17 | Accumulated depreciation | $ 48,000 | *(i)* | 12,000 | *(h)* | 24,000 | $ 60,000 |
| 18 | Accounts payable | 40,000 | *(e)* | 5,000 | | | 35,000 |
| 19 | Interest payable | 4,000 | *(f)* | 1,000 | | | 3,000 |
| 20 | Income taxes payable | 12,000 | | | *(g)* | 10,000 | 22,000 |
| 21 | Bonds payable | 64,000 | *(j)* | 34,000 | *(k2)* | 60,000 | 90,000 |
| 22 | Common stock, $5 par value | 80,000 | | | *(l)* | 15,000 | 95,000 |
| 23 | Retained earnings | 88,000 | *(m)* | 14,000 | *(a)* | 38,000 | 112,000 |
| 24 | | $336,000 | | | | | $417,000 |
| 26 | **Statement of Cash Flows** | | | | | | |
| 27 | Operating activities | | | | | | |
| 28 | Net income | | *(a)* | 38,000 | | | |
| 29 | Increase in accounts receivable | | | | *(b)* | 20,000 | |
| 30 | Increase in merchandise inventory | | | | *(c)* | 14,000 | |
| 31 | Increase in prepaid expenses | | | | *(d)* | 2,000 | |
| 32 | Decrease in accounts payable | | | | *(e)* | 5,000 | |
| 33 | Decrease in interest payable | | | | *(f)* | 1,000 | |
| 34 | Increase in income taxes payable | | *(g)* | 10,000 | | | |
| 35 | Depreciation expense | | *(h)* | 24,000 | | | |
| 36 | Loss on sale of plant assets | | *(i)* | 6,000 | | | |
| 37 | Gain on retirement of bonds | | | | *(j)* | 16,000 | |
| 38 | Investing activities | | | | | | |
| 39 | Receipts from sale of plant assets | | *(i)* | 12,000 | | | |
| 40 | Payment for purchase of plant assets | | | | *(k1)* | 10,000 | |
| 41 | Financing activities | | | | | | |
| 42 | Payment to retire bonds | | | | *(j)* | 18,000 | |
| 43 | Receipts from issuing stock | | *(l)* | 15,000 | | | |
| 44 | Payment of cash dividends | | | | *(m)* | 14,000 | |
| 45 | | | | | | | |
| 46 | **Noncash Investing and Financing Activities** | | | | | | |
| 47 | Purchase of plant assets with bonds | | *(k2)* | 60,000 | *(k1)* | 60,000 | |
| 48 | | | | $337,000 | | $337,000 | |

```
Sheet1 / Sheet2 / Sheet3 /
```

Since adjustments *i, j,* and *k* are more challenging, we show them in the following debit and credit format. These entries are for purposes of our understanding; they are *not* the entries actually made in the journals. Changes in the Cash account are identified as sources or uses of cash.

| | | | |
|---|---|---|---|
| *i.* | Loss from sale of plant assets.......................... | 6,000 | |
| | Accumulated depreciation ........................... | 12,000 | |
| | Receipt from sale of plant assets **(source of cash)**.......... | 12,000 | |
| | Plant assets ..................................... | | 30,000 |
| | *To describe sale of plant assets.* | | |

[continued on next page]

[continued from previous page]

| | | | |
|---|---|---|---|
| j. | Bonds payable . . . . . . . . . . . . . . . . . . . . . . . . . . . . . . . . . . . . . . | 34,000 | |
| | Payments to retire bonds **(use of cash)** . . . . . . . . . . . . . | | 18,000 |
| | Gain on retirement of bonds . . . . . . . . . . . . . . . . . . . . . . | | 16,000 |
| | *To describe retirement of bonds.* | | |
| k1. | Plant assets . . . . . . . . . . . . . . . . . . . . . . . . . . . . . . . . . . . . . . | 70,000 | |
| | Payment to purchase plant assets **(use of cash)** . . . . . . . | | 10,000 |
| | Purchase of plant assets financed by bonds . . . . . . . . . . . . | | 60,000 |
| | *To describe purchase of plant assets.* | | |
| k2. | Purchase of plant assets financed by bonds . . . . . . . . . . . . . . | 60,000 | |
| | Bonds payable . . . . . . . . . . . . . . . . . . . . . . . . . . . . . . . . | | 60,000 |
| | *To issue bonds for purchase of assets.* | | |

## APPENDIX

# 12B  Direct Method of Reporting Operating Cash Flows

**P5** Compute cash flows from operating activities using the direct method.

We compute cash flows from operating activities under the direct method by adjusting accrual-based income statement items to the cash basis. The usual approach is to adjust income statement accounts related to operating activities for changes in their related balance sheet accounts as follows:

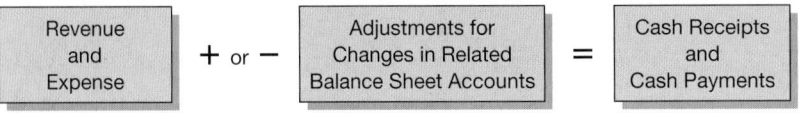

| Revenue and Expense | + or − | Adjustments for Changes in Related Balance Sheet Accounts | = | Cash Receipts and Cash Payments |

**Global:** Some countries such as Australia require the direct method of reporting.

The framework for reporting cash receipts and cash payments for the operating section of the cash flow statement under the direct method is as in Exhibit 12B.1. We consider cash receipts first and then cash payments.

## Exhibit 12B.1

Major Classes of Operating Cash Flows

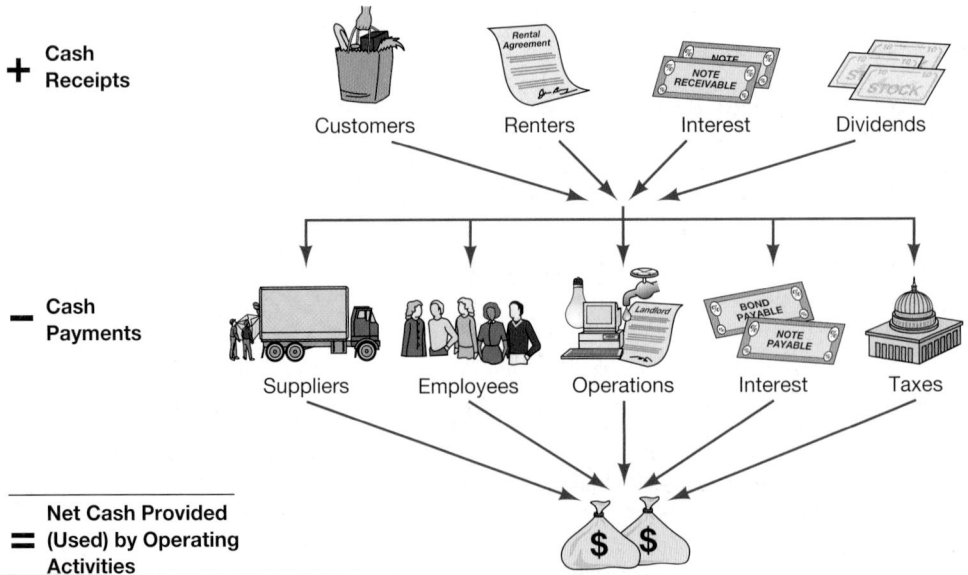

**+ Cash Receipts**

Customers     Renters     Interest     Dividends

**− Cash Payments**

Suppliers     Employees     Operations     Interest     Taxes

**= Net Cash Provided (Used) by Operating Activities**

# Operating Cash Receipts

A review of Exhibit 12.10 and the additional information reported by Genesis suggests only one potential cash receipt: sales to customers. This section, therefore, starts with sales to customers as reported on the income statement and then adjusts it as necessary to obtain cash received from customers to report on the statement of cash flows.

**Cash Received from Customers**   If all sales are for cash, the amount received from customers equals the sales reported on the income statement. When some or all sales are on account, however, we must adjust the amount of sales for the change in Accounts Receivable. It is often helpful to use *account analysis* to do this. This usually involves setting up a T-account and reconstructing its major entries, with emphasis on cash receipts and payments. To illustrate, we use a T-account that includes accounts receivable balances for Genesis on December 31, 2004 and 2005. The beginning balance is $40,000 and the ending balance is $60,000. Next, the income statement shows sales of $590,000, which we enter on the debit side of this account. We now can reconstruct the Accounts Receivable account to determine the amount of cash received from customers as follows:

| Accounts Receivable | | | |
|---|---|---|---|
| Bal., Dec. 31, 2004 | 40,000 | | |
| Sales | 590,000 | Cash receipts = | 570,000 |
| Bal., Dec. 31, 2005 | 60,000 | | |

This T-account shows that the Accounts Receivable balance begins at $40,000 and increases to $630,000 from sales of $590,000, yet its ending balance is only $60,000. This implies that cash receipts from customers are $570,000, computed as $40,000 + $590,000 − [?] = $60,000. This computation can be rearranged to express cash received as equal to sales of $590,000 minus a $20,000 increase in accounts receivable. This computation is summarized as a general rule in Exhibit 12B.2. The statement of cash flows in Exhibit 12.7 reports the $570,000 cash received from customers as a cash inflow from operating activities.

$$\text{Cash received from customers} = \text{Sales} - \begin{cases} + \text{ Decrease in accounts receivable} \\ \text{or} \\ - \text{ Increase in accounts receivable} \end{cases}$$

**Exhibit 12B.2**

Formula to Compute Cash Received from Customers—Direct Method

**Other Cash Receipts**   While Genesis's cash receipts are limited to collections from customers, we often see other types of cash receipts, most commonly cash receipts involving rent, interest, and dividends. We compute cash received from these items by subtracting an increase in their respective receivable or adding a decrease. For instance, if rent receivable increases in the period, cash received from renters is less than rent revenue reported on the income statement. If rent receivable decreases, cash received is more than reported rent revenue. The same logic applies to interest and dividends. The formulas for these computations are summarized later in this appendix.

# Operating Cash Payments

A review of Exhibit 12.10 and the additional Genesis information shows four operating expenses: cost of goods sold; wages and other operating expenses; interest expense; and taxes expense. We analyze each expense to compute its cash amounts for the statement of cash flows. (We then examine depreciation and the other losses and gains.)

**Cash Paid for Merchandise**   We compute cash paid for merchandise by analyzing both cost of goods sold and merchandise inventory. If all merchandise purchases are for cash and the ending balance of Merchandise Inventory is unchanged from the beginning balance, the amount of cash paid for merchandise equals cost of goods sold—an uncommon situation. Instead, there normally is some change in the Merchandise Inventory balance. Also, some or all merchandise purchases are often made on credit, and this yields changes in the Accounts Payable balance. When the balances of both Merchandise Inventory and Accounts Payable change, we must adjust the cost of goods sold for changes in both accounts to compute cash paid for merchandise. This is a two-step adjustment.

First, we use the change in the account balance of Merchandise Inventory, along with the cost of goods sold amount, to compute cost of purchases for the period. An increase in merchandise inventory implies that we bought more than we sold, and we add this inventory increase to cost of goods sold to compute cost of purchases. A decrease in merchandise inventory implies that we bought less than we sold, and we subtract the inventory decrease from cost of goods sold to compute purchases. We illustrate the *first step* by reconstructing the Merchandise Inventory account of Genesis:

| Merchandise Inventory | | | |
|---|---|---|---|
| Bal., Dec. 31, 2004 | 70,000 | | |
| **Purchases =** | **314,000** | Cost of goods sold | 300,000 |
| Bal., Dec. 31, 2005 | 84,000 | | |

The beginning balance is $70,000, and the ending balance is $84,000. The income statement shows that cost of goods sold is $300,000, which we enter on the credit side of this account. With this information, we determine the amount for cost of purchases to be $314,000. This computation can be rearranged to express cost of purchases as equal to cost of goods sold of $300,000 plus the $14,000 increase in inventory.

The second step uses the change in the balance of Accounts Payable, and the amount of cost of purchases, to compute cash paid for merchandise. A decrease in accounts payable implies that we paid for more goods than we acquired this period, and we would then add the accounts payable decrease to cost of purchases to compute cash paid for merchandise. An increase in accounts payable implies that we paid for less than the amount of goods acquired, and we would subtract the accounts payable increase from purchases to compute cash paid for merchandise. The *second step* is applied to Genesis by reconstructing its Accounts Payable account:

| Accounts Payable | | | |
|---|---|---|---|
| | | Bal., Dec. 31, 2004 | 40,000 |
| **Cash payments =** | **319,000** | Purchases | 314,000 |
| | | Bal., Dec. 31, 2005 | 35,000 |

**Example:** If the ending balances of Inventory and Accounts Payable are $60,000 and $50,000, respectively (instead of $84,000 and $35,000), what is cash paid for merchandise? *Answer:* $280,000

Its beginning balance of $40,000 plus purchases of $314,000 minus an ending balance of $35,000 yields cash paid of $319,000 (or $40,000 + $314,000 − [?] = $35,000). Alternatively, we can express cash paid for merchandise as equal to purchases of $314,000 plus the $5,000 decrease in accounts payable. The $319,000 cash paid for merchandise is reported on the statement of cash flows in Exhibit 12.7 as a cash outflow under operating activities.

We summarize this two-step adjustment to cost of goods sold to compute cash paid for merchandise inventory in Exhibit 12B.3.

**Exhibit 12B.3**

Two Steps to Compute Cash Paid for Merchandise—Direct Method

### Cash Paid for Wages and Operating Expenses (excluding depreciation)

The income statement of Genesis shows wages and other operating expenses of $216,000 (see Exhibit 12.10). To compute cash paid for wages and other operating expenses, we adjust this amount for any changes in their related balance sheet accounts. We begin by looking for any prepaid expenses and accrued liabilities related to wages and other operating expenses in the balance sheets of Genesis in

Exhibit 12.10. The balance sheets show prepaid expenses but no accrued liabilities. Thus, the adjustment is limited to the change in prepaid expenses. The amount of adjustment is computed by assuming that all cash paid for wages and other operating expenses is initially debited to Prepaid Expenses. This assumption allows us to reconstruct the Prepaid Expenses account:

| Prepaid Expenses | | | |
|---|---|---|---|
| Bal., Dec. 31, 2004 | 4,000 | | |
| Cash payments = | 218,000 | Wages and other operating exp. | 216,000 |
| Bal., Dec. 31, 2005 | 6,000 | | |

Prepaid Expenses increase by $2,000 in the period, meaning that cash paid for wages and other operating expenses exceeds the reported expense by $2,000. Alternatively, we can express cash paid for wages and other operating expenses as equal to its reported expenses of $216,000 plus the $2,000 increase in prepaid expenses.[1]

Exhibit 12B.4 summarizes the adjustments to wages (including salaries) and other operating expenses. The Genesis balance sheet did not report accrued liabilities, but we include them in the formula to explain the adjustment to cash when they do exist. A decrease in accrued liabilities implies that we paid cash for more goods or services than received this period, so we add the decrease in accrued liabilities to the expense amount to obtain cash paid for these goods or services. An increase in accrued liabilities implies that we paid cash for less than what was acquired, so we subtract this increase in accrued liabilities from the expense amount to get cash paid.

**Point:** A decrease in prepaid expenses implies that reported expenses include an amount(s) that did not require a cash outflow in the period.

$$\begin{array}{c}\text{Cash paid for}\\\text{wages and other}\\\text{operating expenses}\end{array} = \begin{array}{c}\text{Wages and}\\\text{other}\\\text{operating}\\\text{expenses}\end{array} \left[\begin{array}{c}+\ \text{Increase in prepaid}\\\text{expenses}\\\text{or}\\-\ \text{Decrease in prepaid}\\\text{expenses}\end{array}\right.\left.\begin{array}{c}+\ \text{Decrease in accrued}\\\text{liabilities}\\\text{or}\\-\ \text{Increase in accrued}\\\text{liabilities}\end{array}\right]$$

**Exhibit 12B.4**

Formula to Compute Cash Paid for Wages and Operating Expenses—Direct Method

**Cash Paid for Interest and Income Taxes**  Computing operating cash flows for interest and taxes is similar to that for operating expenses. Both require adjustments to their amounts reported on the income statement for changes in their related balance sheet accounts. We begin with the Genesis income statement showing interest expense of $7,000 and income taxes expense of $15,000. To compute the cash paid, we adjust interest expense for the change in interest payable and then the income taxes expense for the change in income taxes payable. These computations involve reconstructing both liability accounts:

| Interest Payable | | | |
|---|---|---|---|
| | | Bal., Dec. 31, 2004 | 4,000 |
| Cash paid for interest = | 8,000 | Interest expense | 7,000 |
| | | Bal., Dec. 31, 2005 | 3,000 |

| Income Taxes Payable | | | |
|---|---|---|---|
| | | Bal., Dec. 31, 2004 | 12,000 |
| Cash paid for taxes = | 5,000 | Income taxes expense | 15,000 |
| | | Bal., Dec. 31, 2005 | 22,000 |

These accounts reveal cash paid for interest of $8,000 and cash paid for income taxes of $5,000. The formulas to compute these amounts are in Exhibit 12B.5. Both of these cash payments are reported as operating cash outflows on the statement of cash flows in Exhibit 12.7.

---

[1] The assumption that all cash payments for wages and operating expenses are initially debited to Prepaid Expenses is not necessary for our analysis to hold. If cash payments are debited directly to the expense account, the total amount of cash paid for wages and other operating expenses still equals the $216,000 expense plus the $2,000 increase in Prepaid Expenses (which arise from end-of-period adjusting entries).

## Exhibit 12B.5

Formulas to Compute Cash Paid for Both Interest and Taxes—Direct Method

$$\text{Cash paid for interest} = \text{Interest expense} \begin{bmatrix} + \text{ Decrease in interest payable} \\ \text{or} \\ - \text{ Increase in interest payable} \end{bmatrix}$$

$$\text{Cash paid for taxes} = \text{Income taxes expenses} \begin{bmatrix} + \text{ Decrease in incomes taxes payable} \\ \text{or} \\ - \text{ Increase in incomes taxes payable} \end{bmatrix}$$

**Analysis of Additional Expenses, Gains, and Losses** Genesis has three additional items reported on its income statement: depreciation, loss on sale of assets, and gain on retirement of debt. We must consider each for its potential cash effects.

**Depreciation Expense** Depreciation expense is $24,000. It is often called a *noncash expense* because depreciation has no cash flows. Depreciation expense is an allocation of an asset's depreciable cost. The cash outflow with a plant asset is reported as part of investing activities when it is paid for. Thus, depreciation expense is *never* reported on a statement of cash flows using the direct method, nor is depletion or amortization expense.

**Loss on Sale of Assets** Sales of assets frequently result in gains and losses reported as part of net income, but the amount of recorded gain or loss does *not* reflect any cash flows in these transactions. Asset sales result in cash inflow equal to the cash amount received, regardless of whether the asset was sold at a gain or a loss. This cash inflow is reported under investing activities. Thus, the loss or gain on a sale of assets is *never* reported on a statement of cash flows using the direct method.

**Point:** The direct method is usually viewed as *user friendly* because less accounting knowledge is required to understand and use it.

**Gain on Retirement of Debt** Retirement of debt usually yields a gain or loss reported as part of net income, but that gain or loss does *not* reflect cash flow in this transaction. Debt retirement results in cash outflow equal to the cash paid to settle the debt, regardless of whether the debt is retired at a gain or loss. This cash outflow is reported under financing activities; the loss or gain from retirement of debt is *never* reported on a statement of cash flows using the direct method.

## Summary of Adjustments for Direct Method

Exhibit 12B.6 summarizes common adjustments for net income to yield net cash provided (used) by operating activities under the direct method.

## Exhibit 12B.6

Summary of Selected Adjustments for Direct Method

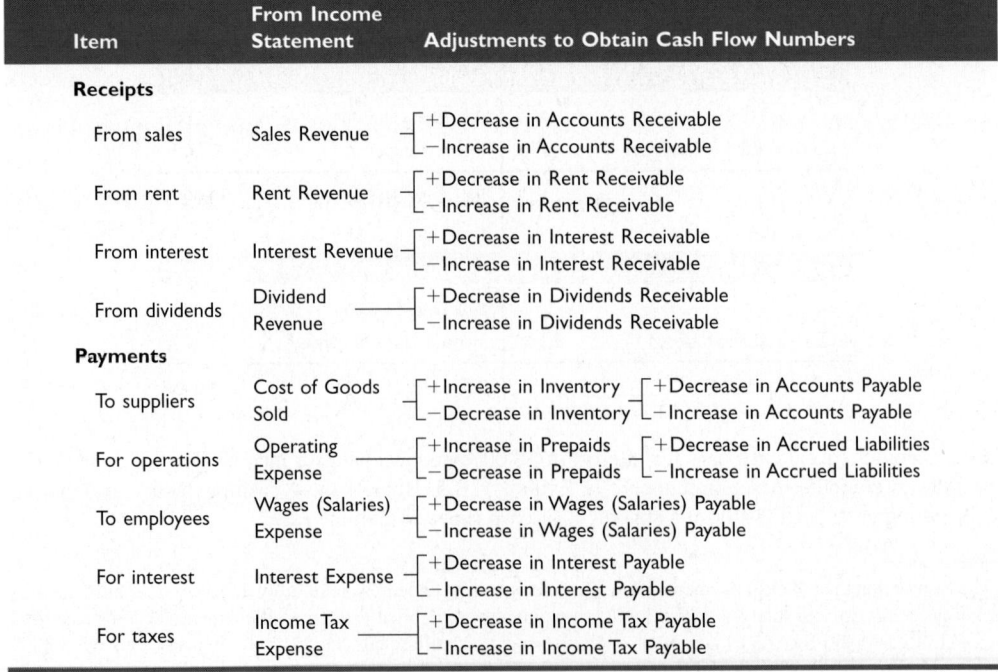

| Item | From Income Statement | Adjustments to Obtain Cash Flow Numbers |
|---|---|---|
| **Receipts** | | |
| From sales | Sales Revenue | [ +Decrease in Accounts Receivable / −Increase in Accounts Receivable |
| From rent | Rent Revenue | [ +Decrease in Rent Receivable / −Increase in Rent Receivable |
| From interest | Interest Revenue | [ +Decrease in Interest Receivable / −Increase in Interest Receivable |
| From dividends | Dividend Revenue | [ +Decrease in Dividends Receivable / −Increase in Dividends Receivable |
| **Payments** | | |
| To suppliers | Cost of Goods Sold | [ +Increase in Inventory / −Decrease in Inventory   [ +Decrease in Accounts Payable / −Increase in Accounts Payable |
| For operations | Operating Expense | [ +Increase in Prepaids / −Decrease in Prepaids   [ +Decrease in Accrued Liabilities / −Increase in Accrued Liabilities |
| To employees | Wages (Salaries) Expense | [ +Decrease in Wages (Salaries) Payable / −Increase in Wages (Salaries) Payable |
| For interest | Interest Expense | [ +Decrease in Interest Payable / −Increase in Interest Payable |
| For taxes | Income Tax Expense | [ +Decrease in Income Tax Payable / −Increase in Income Tax Payable |

# Direct Method Format of Operating Activities Section

Exhibit 12.7 shows the Genesis statement of cash flows using the direct method. Major items of cash inflows and cash outflows are listed separately in the operating activities section. The format requires that operating cash outflows be subtracted from operating cash inflows to get net cash provided (used) by operating activities. The FASB recommends that the operating activities section of the statement of cash flows be reported using the direct method, which is considered more useful to financial statement users. *However, the FASB requires a reconciliation of net income to net cash provided (used) by operating activities when the direct method is used* (which can be reported in the notes). This reconciliation is similar to preparation of the operating activities section of the statement of cash flows using the indirect method.

**Point:** Some preparers argue that it is easier to prepare a statement of cash flows using the indirect method. This likely explains its greater frequency in financial statements.

## Decision Insight

**B-Cash**   The NBA's **Boston Celtics** report operating cash flows using the direct method. The team's operating activities section from its recent statement of cash flows is shown here ($ in 000s). For this same period, its operating income is $22,953 (in 000s).

| | |
|---|---:|
| Basketball regular season receipts | |
| Ticket sales . . . . . . . . . . . . . . . . . . . . . | $35,270 |
| Television and radio broadcast fees . . . . . | 36,373 |
| Other, advertising & playoff receipts . . . . | 22,493 |
| Costs and expenses | |
| Basketball season/playoff expenditures . . | (68,415) |
| General and administrative expenses . . . | (5,124) |
| Selling and promotional expenses . . . . . . | (5,012) |
| Other expenses and revenues . . . . . . . . | (4,167) |
| Net cash flows from operations . . . . . . . | $11,418 |

## Quick Check

8. Net sales in a period are $590,000, beginning accounts receivable are $120,000, and ending accounts receivable are $90,000. What cash amount is collected from customers in the period?

9. The Merchandise Inventory account balance decreases in the period from a beginning balance of $32,000 to an ending balance of $28,000. Cost of goods sold for the period is $168,000. If the Accounts Payable balance increases $2,400 in the period, what is the cash amount paid for merchandise inventory?

10. Wages and other operating expenses total $112,000. Beginning-of-period prepaid expenses totaled $1,200, and its ending balance is $4,200. The end-of-period wages payable equal $5,600, whereas there were no accrued liabilities at period-end. How much cash is paid for wages and other operating expenses?

Answers—p. 522

## Summary

**C1   Explain the purpose and importance of cash flow information.** The main purpose of the statement of cash flows is to report the major cash receipts and cash payments for a period. This includes identifying cash flows as relating to either operating, investing, or financing activities. Most business decisions involve evaluating activities that provide or use cash.

**C2   Distinguish among operating, investing, and financing activities.** Operating activities include transactions and events that determine net income. Investing activities include transactions and events that mainly affect long-term assets. Financing activities include transactions and events that mainly affect long-term liabilities and equity.

**C3   Identify and disclose noncash investing and financing activities.** Noncash investing and financing activities must be disclosed either in a note or a separate schedule to the statement of cash flows. Examples are the retirement of debt by issuing equity and the exchange of a note payable for plant assets.

**C4   Describe the format of the statement of cash flows.** The statement of cash flows separates cash receipts and payments into operating, investing, or financing activities.

**A1   Analyze the statement of cash flows.** To understand and predict cash flows, users stress identification of the sources and uses of cash flows by operating, investing, and financing activities. Emphasis is on operating cash flows since they derive from continuing operations.

**A2** **Compute and apply the cash flow on total assets ratio.** The cash flow on total assets ratio is defined as operating cash flows divided by average total assets. Analysis of current and past values for this ratio can reflect a company's ability to yield regular and positive cash flows. It is also viewed as a measure of earnings quality.

**P1** **Prepare a statement of cash flows.** Preparation of a statement of cash flows involves five steps: (1) Compute the net increase or decrease in cash; (2) compute net cash provided (used) by operating activities (*using either the direct or indirect method*); (3) compute net cash provided (used) by investing activities; (4) compute net cash provided (used) by financing activities; and (5) report the beginning and ending cash balance and prove that it is explained by net cash flows. Noncash investing and financing activities are also disclosed.

**P2** **Compute cash flows from operating activities using the indirect method.** The indirect method for reporting net cash provided (used) by operating activities starts with net income and then adjusts it for three items: (1) changes in noncash current assets and current liabilities related to operating activities, (2) revenues and expenses not providing (using) cash, and (3) gains and losses from investing and financing activities.

**P3** **Determine cash flows from both investing and financing activities.** Cash flows from both investing and financing activities are determined by identifying the cash flow effects of transactions and events affecting each balance sheet account related to these activities. All cash flows from these activities are identified when we can explain changes in these accounts from the beginning to the end of the period.

**P4^A** **Illustrate spreadsheet use in preparing a statement of cash flows.** A spreadsheet is a useful tool in preparing a statement of cash flows. Six key steps (see appendix) are applied when using the spreadsheet to prepare the statement.

**P5^B** **Compute cash flows from operating activities using the direct method.** The direct method for reporting net cash provided (used) by operating activities lists major operating cash inflows less cash outflows to yield net cash inflow or outflow from operations.

## Guidance Answers to **Decision Maker**

**Entrepreneur**   Several factors might explain an increase in net cash flows when a net loss is reported, including (1) early recognition of expenses relative to revenues generated (such as research and development), (2) cash advances on long-term sales contracts not yet recognized in income, (3) issuances of debt or equity for cash to finance expansion, (4) cash sale of assets, (5) delay of cash payments, and (6) cash prepayment on sales. Analysis needs to focus on the components of both the net loss and the net cash flows and their implications for future performance.

**Reporter**   Your initial reaction based on the company's $600,000 loss with a $550,000 decrease in net cash flows is not positive. However, closer scrutiny reveals a more positive picture of this company's performance. Cash flow from operating activities is $650,000, computed as [?] − $850,000 − $350,000 = $(550,000). You also note that net income *before* the extraordinary loss is $330,000, computed as [?] − $930,000 = $(600,000).

## Guidance Answers to **Quick Checks**

1. No to both. The statement of cash flows reports changes in the sum of cash plus cash equivalents. It does not report transfers between cash and cash equivalents.

2. The three categories of cash inflows and outflows are operating activities, investing activities, and financing activities.

3. **a.** Investing      **c.** Financing      **e.** Operating
   **b.** Operating      **d.** Operating      **f.** Financing

4. $74,900 + $4,600 − $11,700 − $1,000 + $3,400 = $70,200

5. Expenses such as depreciation and amortization do not require current cash outflows. Therefore, adding these expenses back to net income eliminates these noncash items from the net income number, converting it to a cash basis.

6. A gain on the sale of plant assets is subtracted from net income because a sale of plant assets is not an operating activity; it is an investing activity for the amount of cash received from its sale. Also, such a gain yields no cash effects.

7. $80,000 − $30,000 − $10,000 = $40,000 cash receipt. The $40,000 cash receipt is reported as an investing activity.

8. $590,000 + ($120,000 − $90,000) = $620,000

9. $168,000 − ($32,000 − $28,000) − $2,400 = $161,600

10. $112,000 + ($4,200 − $1,200) − $5,600 = $109,400

## Key Terms

Key Terms are available at the book's Website for learning and testing in an online Flashcard Format.

**Cash flow on total assets** (p. 510)          **Indirect method** (p. 498)          **Operating activities** (p. 493)
**Direct method** (p. 498)                      **Investing activities** (p. 494)     **Statement of cash flows** (p. 492)
**Financing activities** (p. 494)

## Personal Interactive Quiz

Personal Interactive Quizzes A and B are available at the book's Website to reinforce and assess your learning.

*Superscript letter* <sup>A</sup>(<sup>B</sup>) *denotes assignments based on Appendix 12A (12B).*

## Discussion Questions

**1.** When a statement of cash flows is prepared using the direct method, what are some of the operating cash flows?

**2.** What is the direct method of reporting cash flows from operating activities?

**3.** What is the indirect method of reporting cash flows from operating activities?

**4.** What are some investing activities reported on the statement of cash flows?

**5.** What are some financing activities reported on the statement of cash flows?

**6.** Where on the statement of cash flows is the payment of cash dividends reported?

**7.** Assume that a company purchases land for $100,000, paying $20,000 cash and borrowing the remainder with a long-term note payable. How should this transaction be reported on a statement of cash flows?

**8.** On June 3, a company borrows $50,000 cash by giving its bank a 160-day, interest-bearing note. On the statement of cash flows, where should this be reported?

**9.** If a company reports positive net income for the year, can it show a net cash outflow from operating activities? Explain.

**10.** Is depreciation a source of cash flow?

**11.** Refer to **Krispy Kreme**'s statement of cash flows in Appendix A. (*a*) Which method is used  to compute its net cash provided by operating activities? (*b*) While its balance sheet shows an increase in receivables from fiscal years 2002 to 2003, why is this increase in receivables subtracted when computing net cash provided by operating activities for fiscal year 2003?

**12.** Refer to **Tastykake**'s statement of cash flows in Appendix A. What are its cash flows from  financing activities for 2002? List items and amounts.

**13.** Refer to **Harley-Davidson**'s statement of cash flows in Appendix A. What investing activities result in cash outflows for the year ended January 31, 2002? List items and amounts.      **Harley-Davidson**

*Red numbers denote Discussion Questions that involve decision-making.*

---

*Homework Manager repeats all numerical Quick Studies on the book's Website with new numbers.*

The statement of cash flows is one of the four primary financial statements.

**1.** Describe the content and layout of a statement of cash flows, including its three sections.

**2.** List at least three transactions classified as investing activities in a statement of cash flows.

**3.** List at least three transactions classified as financing activities in a statement of cash flows.

**4.** List at least three transactions classified as significant noncash financing and investing activities in the statement of cash flows.

**QUICK STUDY**

**QS 12-1**
Statement of cash flows

C1  C2  C3

---

Classify the following cash flows as operating, investing, or financing activities:

**1.** Sold long-term investments for cash.

**2.** Received cash payments from customers.

**3.** Paid cash for wages and salaries.

**4.** Purchased inventories for cash.

**5.** Paid cash dividends.

**6.** Issued common stock for cash.

**7.** Received cash interest on a note.

**8.** Paid cash interest on outstanding bonds.

**9.** Received cash from sale of land at a loss.

**10.** Paid cash for property taxes on building.

**QS 12-2**
Transaction classification by activity

C2

---

Use the following balance sheets and income statement to answer QS 12-3 through QS 12-8. Use the indirect method to prepare the cash provided (used) from operating activities section only of the statement of cash flows.

**QS 12-3**
Computing cash from operations (indirect)  P2

**ORWELL, INC.**
**Comparative Balance Sheets**
**December 31, 2005**

|  | 2005 | 2004 |
|---|---|---|
| **Assets** | | |
| Cash ............................ | $ 95,800 | $ 25,000 |
| Accounts receivable (net) ............ | 42,000 | 52,000 |
| Inventory ....................... | 86,800 | 96,800 |
| Prepaid expenses ................. | 6,400 | 5,200 |
| Furniture ...................... | 110,000 | 120,000 |
| Accum. depreciation—Furniture ....... | (18,000) | (10,000) |
| Total assets .................... | $323,000 | $289,000 |
| **Liabilities and Equity** | | |
| Accounts payable ................. | $ 16,000 | $ 22,000 |
| Wages payable ................... | 10,000 | 6,000 |
| Income taxes payable .............. | 2,400 | 3,600 |
| Notes payable (long-term) ........... | 30,000 | 70,000 |
| Common stock, $5 par value .......... | 230,000 | 180,000 |
| Retained earnings ................ | 34,600 | 7,400 |
| Total liabilities and equity ........... | $323,000 | $289,000 |

**ORWELL, INC.**
**Income Statement**
**For Year Ended December 31, 2005**

| | | |
|---|---|---|
| Sales ..................... | | $468,000 |
| Cost of goods sold .......... | | 312,000 |
| Gross profit ............... | | 156,000 |
| Operating expenses | | |
|   Depreciation expense ....... | $38,600 | |
|   Other expenses ........... | 57,000 | 95,600 |
| Income before taxes ......... | | 60,400 |
| Income taxes expense ........ | | 24,600 |
| Net income ............... | | $ 35,800 |

---

**QS 12-4**
Computing cash
from asset sales   P3

Refer to the data in QS 12-3. Furniture costing $54,000 is sold at its book value in 2005. Acquisitions of furniture total $44,000 cash, on which no depreciation is necessary because it is acquired at year-end. What is the cash inflow related to the sale of furniture?

---

**QS 12-5**
Computing financing
cash outflows   P3

Refer to the data in QS 12-3. (1) Assume that all common stock is issued for cash. What amount of cash dividends is paid during 2005? (2) Assume that no additional notes payable are issued in 2005. What cash amount is paid to reduce the notes payable balance in 2005?

---

**QS 12-6<sup>B</sup>**
Computing cash received
from customers   P5

Refer to the data in QS 12-3.
**1.** How much cash is received from sales to customers for year 2005?
**2.** What is the net increase or decrease in cash for year 2005?

---

**QS 12-7<sup>B</sup>**
Computing operating
cash outflows   P5

Refer to the data in QS 12-3. (1) How much cash is paid to acquire merchandise inventory during year 2005? (2) How much cash is paid for operating expenses during year 2005?

---

**QS 12-8<sup>B</sup>**
Computing cash from
operations (direct)   P5

Refer to the data in QS 12-3. Use the direct method to prepare the cash provided (used) from operating activities section only of the statement of cash flows.

---

**QS 12-9**
Analyses of sources
and uses of cash   A1   A2

Financial data from three competitors in the same industry follow.
**1.** Which of the three competitors is in the strongest position as shown by its statement of cash flows?
**2.** Analyze and discuss the strength of Z-Best's cash flow on total assets ratio to that of Lopez.

| ($ in thousands) | Z-Best | Lopez | Ahmed |
|---|---|---|---|
| Cash provided (used) by operating activities | $ 80,000 | $ 70,000 | $ (34,000) |
| Cash provided (used) by investing activities | | | |
|    Proceeds from sale of operating assets | | | 36,000 |
|    Purchase of operating assets | (38,000) | (35,000) | |
| Cash provided (used) by financing activities | | | |
|    Proceeds from issuance of debt | | | 33,000 |
|    Repayment of debt | (7,000) | | |
| Net increase (decrease) in cash | $ 35,000 | $ 35,000 | $ 35,000 |
| Average total assets | $ 800,000 | $ 650,000 | $ 400,000 |

When a spreadsheet for a statement of cash flows is prepared, all changes in noncash balance sheet accounts are fully explained on the spreadsheet. Explain how we use these noncash balance sheet accounts to fully account for cash flows on a spreadsheet.

**QS 12-10ᴬ**
Noncash accounts
on a spreadsheet   P4

 *Homework Manager repeats all numerical Exercises on the book's Website with new numbers.*

Rasheed Company reports net income of $390,000 for the year ended December 31, 2005. It also reports $70,000 depreciation expense and a $10,000 gain on the sale of machinery. Its comparative balance sheets reveal a $30,000 increase in accounts receivable, $16,000 increase in accounts payable, $8,000 decrease in prepaid expenses, and $12,000 decrease in wages payable.

**Required**

Prepare only the operating activities section of the statement of cash flows for 2005 using the *indirect method.*

## EXERCISES

**Exercise 12-1**
Cash flow from
operations (indirect)

P2

The following transactions and events occurred during the year. Assuming that this company uses the *indirect method* to report cash provided by operating activities, indicate where each item would appear on its statement of cash flows by placing an *x* in the appropriate column.

**Exercise 12-2**
Cash flow classification
(indirect)   C2  C3  P2

| | Statement of Cash Flows | | | Noncash Investing and Financing Activities | Not Reported on Statement or in Notes |
|---|---|---|---|---|---|
| | Operating Activities | Investing Activities | Financing Activities | | |
| *a.* Paid cash to purchase inventory. . . . . . . . . . . . . . . | ___ | ___ | ___ | ___ | ___ |
| *b.* Purchased land by issuing common stock. . . . . . . . | ___ | ___ | ___ | ___ | ___ |
| *c.* Accounts receivable decreased in the year. . . . . . . | ___ | ___ | ___ | ___ | ___ |
| *d.* Sold equipment for cash, yielding a loss. . . . . . . . | ___ | ___ | ___ | ___ | ___ |
| *e.* Recorded depreciation expense. . . . . . . . . . . . . . | ___ | ___ | ___ | ___ | ___ |
| *f.* Income taxes payable increased in the year. . . . . . . | ___ | ___ | ___ | ___ | ___ |
| *g.* Declared and paid a cash dividend. . . . . . . . . . . . | ___ | ___ | ___ | ___ | ___ |

The following transactions and events occurred during the year. Assuming that this company uses the *direct method* to report cash provided by operating activities, indicate where each item would appear on the statement of cash flows by placing an *x* in the appropriate column.

**Exercise 12-3ᴮ**
Cash flow classification
(direct)   C2  C3  P5

| | Statement of Cash Flows | | | Noncash Investing and Financing Activities | Not Reported on Statement or in Note |
|---|---|---|---|---|---|
| | Operating Activities | Investing Activities | Financing Activities | | |
| a. Retired long-term bonds payable by issuing common stock.. . . . . . . . . . . . . . . | ____ | ____ | ____ | ____ | ____ |
| b. Recorded depreciation expense. . . . . . . . . . . . | ____ | ____ | ____ | ____ | ____ |
| c. Paid cash dividend that was declared in a prior period.. . . . . . . . . . . . . . . . . . . . | ____ | ____ | ____ | ____ | ____ |
| d. Sold inventory for cash.. . . . . . . . . . . . . . . . | ____ | ____ | ____ | ____ | ____ |
| e. Borrowed cash from bank by signing a 9-month note payable. . . . . . . . . . | ____ | ____ | ____ | ____ | ____ |
| f. Paid cash to purchase a patent. . . . . . . . . . . . | ____ | ____ | ____ | ____ | ____ |
| g. Accepted six-month note receivable in exchange for plant assets. . . . . . . . . . . . . | ____ | ____ | ____ | ____ | ____ |

---

**Exercise 12-4<sup>B</sup>**

Computation of cash flows (direct)

P5

For each of the following three separate cases, use the information provided about the calendar-year 2005 operations of Sahim Company to compute the required cash flow information:

**Case A:** Compute cash received from customers:

| | |
|---|---|
| Sales . . . . . . . . . . . . . . . . . . . . . . . . . . . . . | $510,000 |
| Accounts receivable, December 31, 2004 . . . . . . . . | 25,200 |
| Accounts receivable, December 31, 2005 . . . . . . . . | 34,800 |

**Case B:** Compute cash paid for rent:

| | |
|---|---|
| Rent expense . . . . . . . . . . . . . . . . . . . . . . . . . . | $140,800 |
| Rent payable, December 31, 2004 . . . . . . . . . . . . . | 8,800 |
| Rent payable, December 31, 2005 . . . . . . . . . . . . . | 7,200 |

**Case C:** Compute cash paid for merchandise:

| | |
|---|---|
| Cost of goods sold . . . . . . . . . . . . . . . . . . . . . . | $528,000 |
| Merchandise inventory, December 31, 2004 . . . . . . . | 159,600 |
| Accounts payable, December 31, 2004 . . . . . . . . . . | 67,800 |
| Merchandise inventory, December 31, 2005 . . . . . . . | 131,400 |
| Accounts payable, December 31, 2005 . . . . . . . . . . | 84,000 |

---

**Exercise 12-5<sup>B</sup>**

Preparation of statement of cash flows (direct) and supporting note

C2   C3   C4   P1

Use the following information about the cash flows of Kansas Company to prepare a complete statement of cash flows (*direct method*) for the year ended December 31, 2005. Use a note disclosure for any noncash investing and financing activities.

| | |
|---|---|
| Cash and cash equivalents balance, December 31, 2004 . . . . . . . . . . . . . . . . . . . . . . . . . | $ 25,000 |
| Cash and cash equivalents balance, December 31, 2005 . . . . . . . . . . . . . . . . . . . . . . . . . | 70,000 |
| Cash received as interest . . . . . . . . . . . . . . . . . . . . . . . . | 2,500 |
| Cash paid for salaries . . . . . . . . . . . . . . . . . . . . . . . . . . . | 72,500 |
| Bonds payable retired by issuing common stock (no gain or loss on retirement) . . . . . . . | 187,500 |
| Cash paid to retire long-term notes payable . . . . . . . . . . . . . | 125,000 |
| Cash received from sale of equipment . . . . . . . . . . . . . . . . . | 61,250 |
| Cash received in exchange for six-month note payable . . . . . . . . . . . . . . . . . . . . . . . . . | 25,000 |
| Land purchased by issuing long-term note payable . . . . . . . . . | 106,250 |
| Cash paid for store equipment . . . . . . . . . . . . . . . . . . . . . . | 23,750 |
| Cash dividends paid . . . . . . . . . . . . . . . . . . . . . . . . . . . . | 15,000 |
| Cash paid for other expenses . . . . . . . . . . . . . . . . . . . . . . | 40,000 |
| Cash received from customers . . . . . . . . . . . . . . . . . . . . . . | 485,000 |
| Cash paid for merchandise . . . . . . . . . . . . . . . . . . . . . . . . | 252,500 |

---

**Exercise 12-6**

Cash flows from operating activities (indirect)

P2

Use the following income statement and information about changes in noncash current assets and current liabilities to prepare only the cash flows from operating activities section of the statement of cash flows using the *indirect* method:

| BECKHAM COMPANY | |
|---|---|
| **Income Statement** | |
| **For Year Ended December 31, 2005** | |
| Sales . . . . . . . . . . . . . . . . . . . . . . . . . . . . . . . | $1,818,000 |
| Cost of goods sold . . . . . . . . . . . . . . . . . . . | 891,000 |
| Gross profit . . . . . . . . . . . . . . . . . . . . . . . . | 927,000 |

[continued on next page]

[continued from previous page]

| Operating expenses | | |
|---|---|---|
| Salaries expense .................... | $248,535 | |
| Depreciation expense ................ | 43,200 | |
| Rent expense ....................... | 48,600 | |
| Amortization expenses—Patents ....... | 5,400 | |
| Utilities expense ................... | 19,125 | 364,860 |
| | | 562,140 |
| Gain on sale of equipment ............. | | 7,200 |
| Net income ........................ | | $ 569,340 |

Changes in current asset and current liability accounts for the year that relate to operations follow:

| Accounts receivable ......... | $40,500 increase | Accounts payable ....... | $13,500 decrease |
|---|---|---|---|
| Merchandise inventory ....... | 27,000 increase | Salaries payable ......... | 4,500 decrease |

---

Refer to the information about Beckham Company in Exercise 12-6. Use the *direct method* to prepare only the cash provided (used) by operating activities section of the statement of cash flows.

**Exercise 12-7[B]**
Cash flows from operating activities (direct)   P5

---

Roney Company's calendar-year 2005 income statement shows the following: Net Income, $364,000; Depreciation Expense, $45,000; Amortization Expense, $8,200; Gain on Sale of Plant Assets, $7,000. An examination of the company's current assets and current liabilities reveals the following changes (all from operating activities): Accounts Receivable decrease, $18,100; Merchandise Inventory decrease, $52,000; Prepaid Expenses increase, $3,700; Accounts Payable decrease, $9,200; Other Payables increase, $1,400. Use the *indirect method* to compute cash flow from operating activities.

**Exercise 12-8**
Cash flows from operating activities (indirect)

P2

---

Use the financial statements and additional information shown to (1) prepare a statement of cash flows for the year ended June 30, 2005, using the *indirect method,* and (2) compute the cash flow on total assets ratio for Gecko, Inc., for its fiscal year 2005.

**Exercise 12-9**
Preparation of statement of cash flows (indirect)

C2   A2   P1   P2   P3

---

**GECKO INC.**
**Income Statement**
**For Year Ended June 30, 2005**

| | | |
|---|---|---|
| Sales ........................ | | $668,000 |
| Cost of goods sold .............. | | 412,000 |
| Gross profit ................... | | 256,000 |
| Operating expenses | | |
| Depreciation expense .......... | $58,600 | |
| Other expenses .............. | 67,000 | |
| Total operating expenses ......... | | 125,600 |
| | | 130,400 |
| Other gains (losses) | | |
| Gain on sale of equipment ....... | | 2,000 |
| Income before taxes ............. | | 132,400 |
| Income taxes expense ........... | | 45,640 |
| Net income ................... | | $ 86,760 |

**GECKO INC.**
**Comparative Balance Sheets**
**June 30, 2005**

| | 2005 | 2004 |
|---|---|---|
| **Assets** | | |
| Cash ........................ | $ 85,800 | $ 45,000 |
| Accounts receivable (net) .......... | 70,000 | 52,000 |
| Inventory .................... | 66,800 | 96,800 |
| Prepaid expenses .............. | 5,400 | 5,200 |
| Equipment .................... | 130,000 | 120,000 |
| Accum. depreciation—Equip. ........ | (28,000) | (10,000) |
| Total assets ................... | $330,000 | $309,000 |
| | | |
| **Liabilities and Equity** | | |
| Accounts payable ............... | $ 26,000 | $ 32,000 |
| Wages payable ................. | 7,000 | 16,000 |
| Income taxes payable ............ | 2,400 | 3,600 |
| Notes payable (long term) ........ | 40,000 | 70,000 |
| Common stock, $5 par value ....... | 230,000 | 180,000 |
| Retained earnings ............... | 24,600 | 7,400 |
| Total liabilities and equity .......... | $330,000 | $309,000 |

**Additional Information**

**a.** A $30,000 note payable is retired at its carrying (book) value in exchange for cash.

**b.** The only changes affecting retained earnings are net income and cash dividends paid.

**c.** New equipment is acquired for $58,600 cash.

**d.** Received cash for the sale of equipment that had cost $48,600, yielding a $2,000 gain.

**e.** Prepaid Expenses and Wages Payable relate to Other Expenses on the income statement.

**f.** All purchases and sales of merchandise inventory are on credit.

**Exercise 12-10<sup>B</sup>**

Refer to the data in Exercise 12-9. Using the *direct method,* prepare the statement of cash flows for the year ended June 30, 2005.

Preparation of statement of cash flows (direct)   C2   P1   P3   P5

**Exercise 12-11<sup>B</sup>**

Preparation of statement of cash flows (direct) from Cash T-account

C2   A1   P1   P3   P5

The following summarized Cash T-account reflects the total debits and total credits to the Cash account of Texas Corporation for calendar year 2005. (1) Use this information to prepare a complete statement of cash flows for year 2005. The cash provided (used) by operating activities should be reported using the *direct method.* (2) Refer to the statement of cash flows prepared for part 1 to answer the following questions *a* through *d*: (*a*) Which section—operating, investing, or financing—shows the largest cash (i) inflow and (ii) outflow? (*b*) What is the largest individual item among the investing cash outflows? (*c*) Are the cash proceeds larger from issuing notes or issuing stock? (*d*) Does the company have a net cash inflow or outflow from borrowing activities?

**Accounting System:**

File  Edit  Maintain  Tasks  Analysis  Options  Reports  Window  Help

**Cash**

| | | | |
|---|---|---|---|
| Balance, Dec. 31, 2004 ................. | 135,200 | | |
| Receipts from customers ............... | 6,000,000 | Payments for merchandise ...................... | 1,590,000 |
| Receipts from dividends ................ | 208,400 | Payments for wages ............................... | 550,000 |
| Receipts from land sale ................. | 220,000 | Payments for rent ................................. | 320,000 |
| Receipts from machinery sale ....... | 710,000 | Payments for interest ............................. | 218,000 |
| Receipts from issuing stock .......... | 1,540,000 | Payments for taxes ................................ | 450,000 |
| Receipts from borrowing .............. | 2,600,000 | Payments for machinery .......................... | 2,236,000 |
| | | Payments for long-term investments ........ | 2,260,000 |
| | | Payments for note payable ...................... | 386,000 |
| | | Payments for dividends ........................... | 500,000 |
| | | Payments for treasury stock .................... | 218,000 |
| Balance, Dec. 31, 2005 ................. | $        ? | | |

Sales   Purchases   General Ledger   Payroll   Inventory   Company   Analysis

---

# PROBLEM SET A

**Problem 12-1A**

Statement of cash flows (indirect method)

C2   C3   A1   P1   P2   P3

Kazaam Company, a merchandiser, recently completed its calendar-year 2005 operations. For the year, (1) all sales are credit sales, (2) all credits to Accounts Receivable reflect cash receipts from customers, (3) all purchases of inventory are on credit, (4) all debits to Accounts Payable reflect cash payments for inventory, and (5) Other Expenses are paid in advance and are initially debited to Prepaid Expenses. Kazaam's balance sheets and income statement follow:

**KAZAAM COMPANY**
**Comparative Balance Sheets**
**December 31, 2005**

| | 2005 | 2004 |
|---|---|---|
| **Assets** | | |
| Cash ........................... | $ 53,875 | $ 76,625 |
| Accounts receivable ................ | 65,000 | 49,625 |
| Merchandise inventory .............. | 273,750 | 252,500 |
| Prepaid expenses .................. | 5,375 | 6,250 |
| Equipment ....................... | 159,500 | 110,000 |
| Accum. depreciation—Equipment ....... | (34,625) | (44,000) |
| Total assets ..................... | $522,875 | $451,000 |
| **Liabilities and Equity** | | |
| Accounts payable .................. | $ 88,125 | $116,625 |
| Short-term notes payable ............ | 10,000 | 6,250 |
| Long-term notes payable ............ | 93,750 | 53,750 |
| Common stock, $5 par value ......... | 168,750 | 156,250 |
| Contributed capital in excess | | |
| of par, common stock ............. | 32,500 | 0 |
| Retained earnings .................. | 129,750 | 118,125 |
| Total liabilities and equity ........... | $522,875 | $451,000 |

**KAZAAM COMPANY**
**Income Statement**
**For Year Ended December 31, 2005**

| | | |
|---|---|---|
| Sales ........................ | | $496,250 |
| Cost of goods sold ............. | | 250,000 |
| Gross profit ..................... | | 246,250 |
| Operating expenses | | |
| Depreciation expense ........... | $ 18,750 | |
| Other expenses .............. | 136,500 | 155,250 |
| Other gains (losses) | | |
| Loss on sale of equipment ....... | | 5,125 |
| Income before taxes .............. | | $ 85,875 |
| Income taxes expense ............ | | 12,125 |
| Net income ................... | | $ 73,750 |

## Additional Information on Year 2005 Transactions

**a.** The loss on the cash sale of equipment is $5,125 (details in *b*).

**b.** Sold equipment costing $46,875, with accumulated depreciation of $28,125, for $13,625 cash.

**c.** Purchased equipment costing $96,375 by paying $25,000 cash and signing a long-term note payable for the balance.

**d.** Borrowed $3,750 cash by signing a short-term note payable.

**e.** Paid $31,375 cash to reduce the long-term notes payable.

**f.** Issued 2,500 shares of common stock for $18 cash per share.

**g.** Declared and paid cash dividends of $62,125.

## Required

**1.** Prepare a complete statement of cash flows; report its operating activities using the *indirect method.* Disclose any noncash investing and financing activities in a note.

*Analysis Component*

**2.** Analyze and discuss the statement of cash flows prepared in part 1, giving special attention to the wisdom of the cash dividend payment.

**Check**   Cash from operating activities, $33,375

---

Refer to Kazaam Company's financial statements and related information in Problem 12-1A.

## Required

Prepare a complete statement of cash flows; report its operating activities according to the *direct method.* Disclose any noncash investing and financing activities in a note.

**Problem 12-2A**[B]
Statement of cash flows (direct method)   C3   P1   P3   P5

**Check**   Cash used in financing activities, $(44,750)

---

Refer to the information reported about Kazaam Company in Problem 12-1A.

## Required

Prepare a complete statement of cash flows using a spreadsheet as in Exhibit 12A.1; report its operating activities using the indirect method. Identify the debits and credits in the Analysis of Changes columns with letters that correspond to the following list of transactions and events:

**a.** Net income is $73,750.

**b.** Accounts receivable increased.

**c.** Merchandise inventory increased.

**d.** Prepaid expenses decreased.

**e.** Accounts payable decreased.

**f.** Depreciation expense is $18,750.

**g.** Sold equipment costing $46,875, with accumulated depreciation of $28,125, for $13,625 cash. This yielded a loss of $5,125.

**h.** Purchased equipment costing $96,375 by paying $25,000 cash and **(i.)** by signing a long-term note payable for the balance.

**j.** Borrowed $3,750 cash by signing a short-term note payable.

**k.** Paid $31,375 cash to reduce the long-term notes payable.

**l.** Issued 2,500 shares of common stock for $18 cash per share.

**m.** Declared and paid cash dividends of $62,125.

**Problem 12-3A**[A]
Cash flows spreadsheet (indirect method)

P1   P2   P3   P4

**Check**   Analysis of Changes column totals, $515,375

---

Galley Corp., a merchandiser, recently completed its 2005 operations. For the year, (1) all sales are credit sales, (2) all credits to Accounts Receivable reflect cash receipts from customers, (3) all purchases of inventory are on credit, (4) all debits to Accounts Payable reflect cash payments for inventory, (5) Other Expenses are all cash expenses, and (6) any change in Income Taxes Payable reflects the accrual and cash payment of taxes. Galley's balance sheets and income statement follow:

**Problem 12-4A**
Statement of cash flows (indirect method)   C3   P1   P2   P3

**GALLEY CORPORATION**
**Income Statement**
**For Year Ended December 31, 2005**

| | | |
|---|---:|---:|
| Sales | | $1,992,000 |
| Cost of goods sold | | 1,194,000 |
| Gross profit | | 798,000 |
| Operating expenses | | |
| Depreciation expense | $ 54,000 | |
| Other expenses | 501,000 | 555,000 |
| Income before taxes | | 243,000 |
| Income taxes expense | | 42,000 |
| Net income | | $ 201,000 |

**GALLEY CORPORATION**
**Comparative Balance Sheets**
**December 31, 2005**

| | 2005 | 2004 |
|---|---:|---:|
| **Assets** | | |
| Cash | $ 174,000 | $117,000 |
| Accounts receivable | 93,000 | 81,000 |
| Merchandise inventory | 609,000 | 534,000 |
| Equipment | 333,000 | 297,000 |
| Accum. depreciation—Equipment | (156,000) | (102,000) |
| Total assets | $1,053,000 | $927,000 |
| **Liabilities and Equity** | | |
| Accounts payable | $ 69,000 | $ 96,000 |
| Income taxes payable | 27,000 | 24,000 |
| Common stock, $2 par value | 582,000 | 558,000 |
| Contributed capital in excess of par value, common stock | 198,000 | 162,000 |
| Retained earnings | 177,000 | 87,000 |
| Total liabilities and equity | $1,053,000 | $927,000 |

### Additional Information on Year 2005 Transactions

**a.** Purchased equipment for $36,000 cash.

**b.** Issued 12,000 shares of common stock for $5 cash per share.

**c.** Declared and paid $111,000 in cash dividends.

### Required

**Check** Cash from operating activities, $144,000

Prepare a complete statement of cash flows; report its cash inflows and cash outflows from operating activities according to the *indirect method*.

---

**Problem 12-5A**[B]
Statement of cash flows
(direct method)   P1   P3   P5

mhhe.com/wild3e

**Check** Cash used in financing activities, $(51,000)

Refer to Galley Corporation's financial statements and related information in Problem 12-4A.

### Required

Prepare a complete statement of cash flows; report its cash flows from operating activities according to the *direct method*.

---

**Problem 12-6A**[A]
Cash flows spreadsheet
(indirect method)

P1   P2   P3   P4

mhhe.com/wild3e

**Check** Analysis of Changes column totals, $579,000

Refer to the information reported about Galley Corporation in Problem 12-4A.

### Required

Prepare a complete statement of cash flows using a spreadsheet as in Exhibit 12A.1; report operating activities under the indirect method. Identify the debits and credits in the Analysis of Changes columns with letters that correspond to the following list of transactions and events:

**a.** Net income is $201,000.

**b.** Accounts receivable increased.

**c.** Merchandise inventory increased.

**d.** Accounts payable decreased.

**e.** Income taxes payable increased.

**f.** Depreciation expense is $54,000.

**g.** Purchased equipment for $36,000 cash.

**h.** Issued 12,000 shares at $5 cash per share.

**i.** Declared and paid $111,000 of cash dividends.

Kite Corporation, a merchandiser, recently completed its calendar-year 2005 operations. For the year, (1) all sales are credit sales, (2) all credits to Accounts Receivable reflect cash receipts from customers, (3) all purchases of inventory are on credit, (4) all debits to Accounts Payable reflect cash payments for inventory, and (5) Other Expenses are paid in advance and are initially debited to Prepaid Expenses. Kite's balance sheets and income statement follow:

**PROBLEM SET B**

**Problem 12-1B**
Statement of cash flows (indirect method)

C2  C3  A1  P1  P2  P3

### KITE CORPORATION
### Comparative Balance Sheets
### December 31, 2005

| | 2005 | 2004 |
|---|---|---|
| **Assets** | | |
| Cash | $136,500 | $ 71,550 |
| Accounts receivable | 74,100 | 90,750 |
| Merchandise inventory | 454,500 | 490,200 |
| Prepaid expenses | 17,100 | 19,200 |
| Equipment | 278,250 | 216,000 |
| Accum. depreciation—Equipment | (108,750) | (93,000) |
| Total assets | $851,700 | $794,700 |
| **Liabilities and Equity** | | |
| Accounts payable | $117,450 | $123,450 |
| Short-term notes payable | 17,250 | 11,250 |
| Long-term notes payable | 112,500 | 82,500 |
| Common stock, $5 par | 465,000 | 450,000 |
| Contributed capital in excess of par, common stock | 18,000 | 0 |
| Retained earnings | 121,500 | 127,500 |
| Total liabilities and equity | $851,700 | $794,700 |

### KITE CORPORATION
### Income Statement
### For Year Ended December 31, 2005

| | | |
|---|---|---|
| Sales | | $1,083,000 |
| Cost of goods sold | | 585,000 |
| Gross profit | | 498,000 |
| Operating expenses | | |
| Depreciation expense | $ 36,600 | |
| Other expenses | 392,850 | |
| Total operating expenses | | 429,450 |
| | | 68,550 |
| Other gains (losses) | | |
| Loss on sale of equipment | | 2,100 |
| Income before taxes | | 66,450 |
| Income taxes expense | | 9,450 |
| Net income | | $ 57,000 |

### Additional Information on Year 2005 Transactions

**a.** The loss on the cash sale of equipment is $2,100 (details in *b*).

**b.** Sold equipment costing $51,000, with accumulated depreciation of $20,850, for $28,050 cash.

**c.** Purchased equipment costing $113,250 by paying $38,250 cash and signing a long-term note payable for the balance.

**d.** Borrowed $6,000 cash by signing a short-term note payable.

**e.** Paid $45,000 cash to reduce the long-term notes payable.

**f.** Issued 3,000 shares of common stock for $11 cash per share.

**g.** Declared and paid cash dividends of $63,000.

### Required

**1.** Prepare a complete statement of cash flows; report its operating activities using the *indirect method*. Disclose any noncash investing and financing activities in a note.

*Analysis Component*

**2.** Analyze and discuss the statement of cash flows prepared in part 1, giving special attention to the wisdom of the cash dividend payment.

**Check** Cash from operating activities, $144,150

---

Refer to Kite Corporation's financial statements and related information in Problem 12-1B.

### Required

Prepare a complete statement of cash flows; report its operating activities according to the *direct method*. Disclose any noncash investing and financing activities in a note.

**Problem 12-2B**[B]
Statement of cash flows (direct method)  C3  P1  P3  P5

**Check** Cash used in financing activities, $(69,000)

## Problem 12-3B[A]
Cash flows spreadsheet
(indirect method)

P1  P2  P3  P4

Refer to the information reported about Kite Corporation in Problem 12-1B.

**Required**

Prepare a complete statement of cash flows using a spreadsheet as in Exhibit 12A.1; report its operating activities using the *indirect method*. Identify the debits and credits in the Analysis of Changes columns with letters that correspond to the following list of transactions and events:

**a.** Net income is $57,000.

**b.** Accounts receivable decreased.

**c.** Merchandise inventory decreased.

**d.** Prepaid expenses decreased.

**e.** Accounts payable decreased.

**f.** Depreciation expense is $36,600.

**g.** Sold equipment costing $51,000, with accumulated depreciation of $20,850, for $28,050 cash. This yielded a loss of $2,100.

**h.** Purchased equipment costing $113,250 by paying $38,250 cash and **(i.)** by signing a long-term note payable for the balance.

**j.** Borrowed $6,000 cash by signing a short-term note payable.

**k.** Paid $45,000 cash to reduce the long-term notes payable.

**l.** Issued 3,000 shares of common stock for $11 cash per share.

**Check** Analysis of Changes column totals, $540,300

**m.** Declared and paid cash dividends of $63,000.

## Problem 12-4B
Statement of cash flows
(indirect method)

C3  P1  P2  P3

Taurasi Co., a merchandiser, recently completed its 2005 operations. For the year, (1) all sales are credit sales, (2) all credits to Accounts Receivable reflect cash receipts from customers, (3) all purchases of inventory are on credit, (4) all debits to Accounts Payable reflect cash payments for inventory, (5) Other Expenses are cash expenses, and (6) any change in Income Taxes Payable reflects the accrual and cash payment of taxes. Taurasi's balance sheets and income statement follow:

**TAURASI COMPANY**
**Comparative Balance Sheets**
**December 31, 2005**

|  | 2005 | 2004 |
|---|---|---|
| **Assets** |  |  |
| Cash | $ 53,925 | $ 31,800 |
| Accounts receivable | 19,425 | 23,250 |
| Merchandise inventory | 175,350 | 139,875 |
| Equipment | 105,450 | 76,500 |
| Accum. depreciation—Equipment | (48,300) | (30,600) |
| Total assets | $305,850 | $240,825 |
| **Liabilities and Equity** |  |  |
| Accounts payable | $ 38,475 | $ 35,625 |
| Income taxes payable | 4,500 | 6,750 |
| Common stock, $5 par value | 165,000 | 150,000 |
| Contributed capital in excess of par, common stock | 42,000 | 15,000 |
| Retained earnings | 55,875 | 33,450 |
| Total liabilities and equity | $305,850 | $240,825 |

**TAURASI COMPANY**
**Income Statement**
**For Year Ended December 31, 2005**

| | | |
|---|---|---|
| Sales | | $609,750 |
| Cost of goods sold | | 279,000 |
| Gross profit | | 330,750 |
| Operating expenses | | |
| Depreciation expense | $ 17,700 | |
| Other expenses | 179,775 | 197,475 |
| Income before taxes | | 133,275 |
| Income taxes expense | | 44,850 |
| Net income | | $ 88,425 |

**Additional Information on Year 2005 Transactions**

**a.** Purchased equipment for $28,950 cash.

**b.** Issued 3,000 shares of common stock for $14 cash per share.

**c.** Declared and paid $66,000 of cash dividends.

**Required**

**Check** Cash from operating activities, $75,075

Prepare a complete statement of cash flows; report its cash inflows and cash outflows from operating activities according to the *indirect method*.

Refer to Taurasi Company's financial statements and related information in Problem 12-4B.

**Required**

Prepare a complete statement of cash flows; report its cash flows from operating activities according to the *direct method*.

**Problem 12-5B**[B]
Statement of cash flows
(direct method)   P1  P3  P5

**Check**   Cash used by financing activities, $(24,000)

Refer to the information reported about Taurasi Company in Problem 12-4B.

**Required**

Prepare a complete statement of cash flows using a spreadsheet as in Exhibit 12A.1; report operating activities under the *indirect method*. Identify the debits and credits in the Analysis of Changes columns with letters that correspond to the following list of transactions and events:

**a.** Net income is $88,425.

**b.** Accounts receivable decreased.

**c.** Merchandise inventory increased.

**d.** Accounts payable increased.

**e.** Income taxes payable decreased.

**f.** Depreciation expense is $17,700.

**g.** Purchased equipment for $28,950 cash.

**h.** Issued 3,000 shares at $14 cash per share.

**i.** Declared and paid $66,000 of cash dividends.

**Problem 12-6B**[A]
Cash flows spreadsheet
(indirect method)

P1  P2  P3  P4

**Check**   Analysis of Changes column totals, $287,475

Problem Set C is available at the book's Website to reinforce and assess your learning.

**PROBLEM SET C**

*(This serial problem began in Chapter 1 and continues through most of the book. If previous chapter segments were not completed, the serial problem can begin at this point. It is helpful, but not necessary, for you to use the Working Papers that accompany the book.)*

Kay Breeze, owner of Success Systems, decides to prepare a statement of cash flows for her business. (Although the serial problem allowed for various changes in earlier chapters, we will prepare the statement of cash flows using the following financial data.)

**SERIAL PROBLEM**

Success Systems

| SUCCESS SYSTEMS Comparative Balance Sheets December 31, 2004 and March 31, 2005 | | |
|---|---|---|
| | **2005** | **2004** |
| **Assets** | | |
| Cash . . . . . . . . . . . . . . . . . . . . . . . . | $ 77,845 | $58,160 |
| Accounts receivable . . . . . . . . . . . . . . . . . . | 22,720 | 5,668 |
| Merchandise Inventory . . . . . . . . . . . . . . . . | 704 | 0 |
| Computer supplies . . . . . . . . . . . . . . . . | 2,005 | 580 |
| Prepaid insurance . . . . . . . . . . . . . . . . | 1,110 | 1,665 |
| Prepaid rent . . . . . . . . . . . . . . . . . . | 825 | 825 |
| Office equipment . . . . . . . . . . . . . . . . . . | 8,000 | 8,000 |
| Accumulated depreciation—Office equipment . . . . . . . . . . . . . . . . . . . | (800) | (400) |
| Computer equipment . . . . . . . . . . . . . . | 20,000 | 20,000 |
| Accumulated depreciation— Computer equipment . . . . . . . . . . . . . . | (2,500) | (1,250) |
| Total assets . . . . . . . . . . . . . . . . . . . . . | $129,909 | $93,248 |
| **Liabilities** | | |
| Accounts payable . . . . . . . . . . . . . . . . . . | $    0 | $ 1,100 |
| Wages payable . . . . . . . . . . . . . . . . . . . | 875 | 500 |
| Unearned computer service revenue . . . . . . . | 0 | 1,500 |
| **Equity** | | |
| Common stock . . . . . . . . . . . . . . . . . . . | 108,000 | 83,000 |
| Retained earnings . . . . . . . . . . . . . . . . | 21,034 | 7,148 |
| Total liabilities and equity . . . . . . . . . . . . . . | $129,909 | $93,248 |

| SUCCESS SYSTEMS Income Statement For Three Months Ended March 31, 2005 | | |
|---|---|---|
| Computer services revenue . . . . . . . . . | | $25,160 |
| Net sales . . . . . . . . . . . . . . . . . . . . . | | 18,693 |
| Total revenue . . . . . . . . . . . . . . . . . . | | 43,853 |
| Cost of goods sold . . . . . . . . . . . . . . | $14,052 | |
| Depreciation expense— Office equipment . . . . . . . . . . . . | 400 | |
| Depreciation expense— Computer equipment . . . . . . . . . . | 1,250 | |
| Wages expense . . . . . . . . . . . . . . . | 3,250 | |
| Insurance expense . . . . . . . . . . . . . | 555 | |
| Rent expense . . . . . . . . . . . . . . . . | 2,475 | |
| Computer supplies expense . . . . . . . . | 1,305 | |
| Advertising expense . . . . . . . . . . . . | 600 | |
| Mileage expense . . . . . . . . . . . . . . | 320 | |
| Repairs expense—Computer . . . . . . . | 960 | |
| Total expenses . . . . . . . . . . . . . . . | | 25,167 |
| Net income . . . . . . . . . . . . . . . . . . | | $18,686 |

**Required**

Prepare a statement of cash flows for Success Systems using the *indirect method* for the three months ended March 31, 2005. Recall that the owner Kay Breeze contributed $25,000 to the business in exchange for additional stock in the first quarter of 2005 and received $4,800 in cash dividends.

## BEYOND THE NUMBERS

### REPORTING IN ACTION

C4  A1

**BTN 12-1**  Refer to **Krispy Kreme**'s financial statements in Appendix A to answer the following:

1. Is Krispy Kreme's statement of cash flows prepared under the direct method or the indirect method?
2. For each fiscal year 2003, 2002, and 2001, is the amount of cash provided by operating activities more or less than the cash paid for dividends?
3. What is the largest amount in reconciling the difference between net income and cash flow from operating activities in 2003? In 2002? In 2001?
4. Identify the largest cash flows for investing and for financing activities in 2003 and in 2002.

*Roll On*

5. Obtain Krispy Kreme's financial statements for a fiscal year ending after February 2, 2003, from either its Website (**KrispyKreme.com**) or the SEC's EDGAR database (**www.sec.gov**). Since February 2, 2003, what are Krispy Kreme's largest cash outflows and cash inflows in the investing and in the financing sections of its statement of cash flow?

### COMPARATIVE ANALYSIS

A1  A2

**BTN 12-2**  Key comparative figures ($ thousands) for **Krispy Kreme** and **Tastykake** follow:

| Key Figures | Krispy Kreme | | | Tastykake | | |
|---|---|---|---|---|---|---|
| | Current Year | 1 Year Prior | 2 Years Prior | Current Year | 1 Year Prior | 2 Years Prior |
| Operating cash flows ....... | $ 51,036 | $ 36,210 | $ 32,112 | $ 10,115 | $ 10,905 | $ 13,199 |
| Total assets ............. | 410,487 | 255,376 | 171,493 | 116,560 | 116,136 | 112,192 |

**Required**

1. Compute the recent two years' cash flow on total assets ratios for both Krispy Kreme and Tastykake.
2. What does the cash flow on total assets ratio measure?
3. Which company has the higher cash flow on total assets ratio for the periods shown?
4. Does the cash flow on total assets ratio reflect on the quality of earnings? Explain.

### ETHICS CHALLENGE

C1  C2  A1

**BTN 12-3**  Lisa Gish is preparing for a meeting with her banker. Her business is finishing its fourth year of operations. In the first year, it had negative cash flows from operations. In the second and third years, cash flows from operations was positive. However, inventory costs rose significantly in year 4, and cash flows from operations will probably be down 25%. Gish wants to secure a line of credit from her banker as a financing buffer. From experience, she knows the banker will scrutinize operating cash flows for years 1 through 4 and will want a projected number for year 5. Gish knows that a steady progression upward in operating cash flows for years 1 through 4 will help her case. She decides to use her discretion as owner and considers several business actions that will turn her operating cash flow in year 4 from a decrease to an increase over year 3.

**Required**

1. Identify two business actions Gish might take to improve cash flows from operations.
2. Comment on the ethics and possible consequences of Gish's decision to pursue these actions.

**BTN 12-4** Your friend, Jessica Willard, recently completed the second year of her business and just received annual financial statements from her accountant. Willard finds the income statement and balance sheet informative but does not understand the statement of cash flows. She says the first section is especially confusing because it contains a lot of additions and subtractions that do not make sense to her. Willard adds, "The income statement tells me the business is more profitable than last year and that's most important. If I want to know how cash changes, I can look at comparative balance sheets."

**COMMUNICATING IN PRACTICE**

C1  C4

**Required**

Write a half-page memorandum to your friend explaining the purpose of the statement of cash flows. Speculate as to why the first section is so confusing and how it might be rectified.

**BTN 12-5** Access the April 22, 2003, filing of the 10-K report (for fiscal year ending February 1, 2003) of **J. Crew Group, Inc.**, at **www.sec.gov**.

**TAKING IT TO THE NET**

A1

mhhe.com/wild3e

**Required**

**1.** Does J. Crew use the direct or indirect method to construct its consolidated statement of cash flows?

**2.** For the fiscal year ended February 1, 2003, what is the largest item recorded in reconciling the net loss to cash flow provided by operations?

**3.** In recent years J. Crew has recorded several net losses. Has the company been more successful in generating operating cash flows over this time period than in generating net income?

**4.** In the year ended February 1, 2003, what was the largest cash outflow for investing activities and for financing activities?

**5.** What items does J. Crew report as supplementary cash flow information?

**6.** Does J. Crew report any noncash financing activities?

**BTN 12-6** Team members are to coordinate and independently answer one question within each of the following three sections. Team members should then report to the team and confirm or correct teammates' answers.

**1.** Answer *one* of the following questions about the statement of cash flows:

   **a.** What are this statement's reporting objectives?

   **b.** What two methods are used to prepare it? Identify similarities and differences between them.

   **c.** What steps are followed to prepare the statement?

   **d.** What types of analyses are often made from this statement's information?

**2.** Identify and explain the adjustment from net income to obtain cash flows from operating activities using the indirect method for *one* of the following items:

   **a.** Noncash operating revenues and expenses.

   **b.** Nonoperating gains and losses.

   **c.** Increases and decreases in noncash current assets.

   **d.** Increases and decreases in current liabilities.

**3.** [B]Identify and explain the formula for computing cash flows from operating activities using the direct method for *one* of the following items:

   **a.** Cash receipts from sales to customers.

   **b.** Cash paid for merchandise inventory.

   **c.** Cash paid for wages and operating expenses.

   **d.** Cash paid for interest and taxes.

**TEAMWORK IN ACTION**

C1  C4  A1  P2  P5

**Note:** For teams of more than four, some pairing within teams is necessary. Use as an in-class activity or as an assignment. If used in class, specify a time limit on each part. Conclude with reports to the entire class, using team rotation. Each team can prepare responses on a transparency.

*"What goes on at The Motley Fool every day is similar to what goes on in a library"*—Tom Gardner (on left; David Gardner on right)

# 13

# Analyzing and Interpreting Financial Statements

## A Look Back

Chapter 12 focused on reporting and analyzing cash inflows and cash outflows. We explained how to prepare, analyze, and interpret the statement of cash flows.

## A Look at This Chapter

This chapter emphasizes the analysis and interpretation of financial statement information. We learn to apply horizontal, vertical, and ratio analyses to better understand company performance and financial condition.

## A Look Ahead

Chapter 14 introduces us to managerial accounting. We discuss its purposes, concepts, and roles in helping managers gather and organize information for decision making. We also explain basic management principles.

# CAP

### Conceptual

**C1** Explain the purpose of analysis. *(p. 540)*

**C2** Identify the building blocks of analysis. *(p. 541)*

**C3** Describe standards for comparisons in analysis. *(p. 542)*

**C4** Identify the tools of analysis. *(p. 542)*

### Analytical

**A1** Summarize and report results of analysis. *(p. 560)*

### Procedural

**P1** Explain and apply methods of horizontal analysis. *(p. 543)*

**P2** Describe and apply methods of vertical analysis. *(p. 547)*

**P3** Define and apply ratio analysis. *(p. 551)*

---

## Decision Feature

# Fool's Gold

ALEXANDRIA, VA—A few years ago, with less than $10,000 in start-up money, then 28-year-old David Gardner and his 26-year-old brother, Tom, launched **The Motley Fool (Fool.com).** The name derives from Elizabethan drama (Shakespeare's *As You Like It*), in which only the fool could tell the king the truth without getting his head lopped off. The Gardners view themselves as modern-day fools "dedicated to educating, amusing, and enriching individuals in the search of the truth," according to their Website. The truth to which they refer involves the financial world. Their site argues that "the financial world preys on ignorance and fear." According to Tom Gardner, "There is a great need in the general populace for financial information." Given their huge success—Website, radio shows, newspaper columns, online store, investment newsletters, and international expansion—few can argue.

Still, there is a concern that individuals fail to fully exploit the available information in financial statements. The Motley Fool's bulletin board often finds "discussions" that could be readily resolved with reference to reliable accounting data. This suggests that more "educating and enriching" of individuals is required. This chapter takes that challenge. It introduces horizontal and vertical analyses—tools that reveal crucial trends and insights from financial information. It also summarizes and expands on ratio analysis—tools that reveal insights into a company's financial condition and performance. With knowledge from this chapter, along with The Motley Fool's guidance on investing, individuals will be in a much stronger position to succeed in the financial world.

[Sources: *Motley Fool Website*, January 2004; *Entrepreneur*, July 1997; *What to Do With Your Money Now*, June 2002.]

This chapter shows how to use information in financial statements to evaluate a company's financial performance and condition. We describe the purpose of financial statement analysis, its basic building blocks, the information available, standards for comparisons, and tools of analysis. The chapter emphasizes three major analysis tools: horizontal analysis, vertical analysis, and ratio analysis. We illustrate the application of each of these tools using **Krispy Kreme**'s financial statements. We also introduce comparative analysis using **Tastykake**'s financial statements. This chapter expands and organizes the ratio analyses introduced at the end of each of the prior chapters.

## Analyzing and Interpreting Financial Statements

### Basics of Analysis

- Purpose
- Building blocks
- Information
- Standards for comparisons
- Tools

### Horizontal Analysis

- Comparative balance sheets
- Comparative income statements
- Trend analysis

### Vertical Analysis

- Common-size balance sheet
- Common-size income statement
- Common-size graphics

### Ratio Analysis

- Liquidity and efficiency
- Solvency
- Profitability
- Market prospects
- Ratio summary

# Basics of Analysis

**Financial statement analysis** applies analytical tools to general-purpose financial statements and related data for making business decisions. It involves transforming accounting data into more useful information. Financial statement analysis reduces our reliance on hunches, guesses, and intuition as well as our uncertainty in decision making. It does not lessen the need for expert judgment; instead, it provides us an effective and systematic basis for making business decisions. This section describes the purpose of financial statement analysis, its information sources, the use of comparisons, and some issues in computations.

## Purpose of Analysis

**C1** Explain the purpose of analysis.

Internal users of accounting information are those involved in strategically managing and operating the company. They include managers, officers, internal auditors, consultants, budget directors, and market researchers. The purpose of financial statement analysis for these users is to provide strategic information to improve company efficiency and effectiveness in providing products and services.

**Point:** Financial statement analysis tools are also used for personal financial investment decisions.

External users of accounting information are *not* directly involved in running the company. They include shareholders, lenders, directors, customers, suppliers, regulators, lawyers, brokers, and the press. External users rely on financial statement analysis to make better and more informed decisions in pursuing their own goals.

We can identify other uses of financial statement analysis. Shareholders and creditors assess company prospects to make investing and lending decisions. A board of directors analyzes financial statements in monitoring management's decisions. Employees and unions use financial statements in labor negotiations. Suppliers use financial statement information in establishing credit terms. Customers analyze financial statements in deciding whether to establish supply relationships. Public utilities set customer rates by analyzing financial statements. Auditors use financial statements in assessing the "fair presentation" of their clients' financial reports. Analyst services such as **Dun & Bradstreet**, **Moody's**, and **Standard & Poor's** use financial statements in making buy-sell recommendations and in setting credit ratings. The common goal of these users is to evaluate company performance and financial

**Point:** Financial statement analysis is a topic on the CPA, CMA, CIA, and CFA exams.

condition. This includes evaluating (1) past and current performance, (2) current financial position, and (3) future performance and risk.

## Building Blocks of Analysis

Financial statement analysis focuses on one or more elements of a company's financial condition or performance. Our analysis emphasizes four areas of inquiry—with varying degrees of importance. These four areas are described and illustrated in this chapter and are considered the *building blocks* of financial statement analysis:

**C2**    Identify the building blocks of analysis.

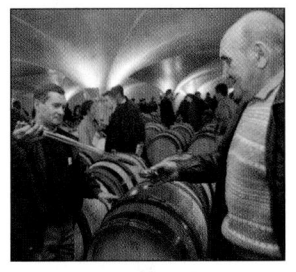

- **Liquidity** and **efficiency**—ability to meet short-term obligations and to efficiently generate revenues.
- **Solvency**—ability to generate future revenues and meet long-term obligations.
- **Profitability**—ability to provide financial rewards sufficient to attract and retain financing.
- **Market prospects**—ability to generate positive market expectations.

Applying the building blocks of financial statement analysis involves determining (1) the objectives of analysis and (2) the relative emphasis among the building blocks. We distinguish among these four building blocks to emphasize the different aspects of a company's financial condition or performance, yet we must remember that these areas of analysis are interrelated. For instance, a company's operating performance is affected by the availability of financing and short-term liquidity conditions. Similarly, a company's credit standing is not limited to satisfactory short-term liquidity but depends also on its profitability and efficiency in using assets. Early in our analysis, we need to determine the relative emphasis of each building block. Emphasis and analysis can later change as a result of evidence collected.

### Decision Insight

**Chips and Brokers**   The term *blue chips* refers to stock of big, profitable companies. The term comes from poker: The most valuable chips are blue. *Brokers* execute orders to buy or sell stock. The term comes from wine retailers—individuals who broach (break) wine casks.

## Information for Analysis

Some users, such as managers and regulatory authorities, are able to receive special financial reports prepared to meet their analysis needs. However, most users must rely on **general-purpose financial statements** that include the (1) income statement, (2) balance sheet, (3) statement of stockholders' (owner's) equity (or statement of retained earnings), (4) statement of cash flows, and (5) notes to these statements.

   **Financial reporting** refers to the communication of financial information useful for making investment, credit, and other business decisions. Financial reporting includes not only general-purpose financial statements but also information from SEC 10-K or other filings, press releases, shareholders' meetings, forecasts, management letters, auditors' reports, and Webcasts.

   Management's Discussion and Analysis (MD&A) is one example of useful information outside traditional financial statements. **Krispy Kreme**'s MD&A (available at **KrispyKreme.com**), for example, begins with critical accounting policies. It then discusses operating activities and results. The next major part examines liquidity and capital resources—roughly equivalent to investing and financing activities. The final part explains its market risks, including its exposure to currency changes, interest rates, and commodity price changes. The MD&A is an excellent starting point in understanding a company's business activities.

**Point:** Decision makers rely on financial statement analysis to help them better understand the financial position and profitability of a business. This includes estimates of the amount, timing, and uncertainty of future cash inflows and outflows.

### Decision Insight

**Analysis Online**   Many Websites offer free access and screening of companies by key numbers such as earnings, sales, and book value. For instance, **Standard & Poor's** has information for more than 10,000 stocks (**StandardPoor.com**).

## Standards for Comparisons

**C3** Describe standards for comparisons in analysis.

When interpreting measures from financial statement analysis, we need to decide whether the measures indicate good, bad, or average performance. To make such judgments, we need standards (benchmarks) for comparisons that include the following:

- *Intracompany*—The company under analysis can provide standards for comparisons based on its own prior performance and relations between its financial items. **Krispy Kreme**'s current net income, for instance, can be compared with its prior years' net income and in relation to its revenues or total assets.
- *Competitor*—One or more direct competitors of the company being analyzed can provide standards for comparisons. **Coca-Cola**'s profit margin, for instance, can be compared with **PepsiCo**'s profit margin.
- *Industry*—Industry statistics can provide standards of comparisons. Such statistics are available from services such as **Dun & Bradstreet, Standard & Poor's**, and **Moody's**.
- *Guidelines (rules of thumb)*—General standards of comparisons can develop from experience. Examples are the 2:1 level for the current ratio or 1:1 level for the acid-test ratio. Guidelines, or rules of thumb, must be carefully applied because context is crucial.

**Point:** Each chapter's *Reporting in Action* problems engage students in *intracompany* analysis, whereas *Comparative Analysis* problems require competitor analysis (Krispy Kreme vs. Tastykake).

All of these comparison standards are useful when properly applied, yet measures taken from a selected competitor or group of competitors are often best. Intracompany and industry measures are also important. Guidelines or rules of thumb should be applied with care, and then only if they seem reasonable given past experience and industry norms.

### Quick Check

1. Who are the intended users of general-purpose financial statements?
2. General-purpose financial statements consist of what information?
3. Which of the following is *least* useful as a basis for comparison when analyzing ratios?
   (a) Company results from a different economic setting. (b) Standards from past experience. (c) Rule-of-thumb standards. (d) Industry averages.
4. What is the preferred basis of comparison for ratio analysis?

Answers—p. 564

## Tools of Analysis

**C4** Identify the tools of analysis.

Three of the most common tools of financial statement analysis are

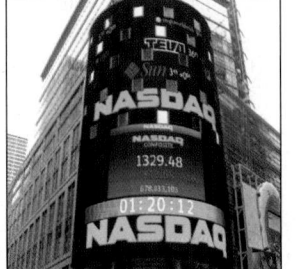

1. **Horizontal analysis**—Comparison of a company's financial condition and performance across time.
2. **Vertical analysis**—Comparison of a company's financial condition and performance to a base amount.
3. **Ratio analysis**—Measurement of key relations between financial statement items.

The remainder of this chapter describes these analysis tools and how to apply them.

## Horizontal Analysis

Analysis of any single financial number is of limited value. Instead, much of financial statement analysis involves identifying and describing relations between numbers, groups of numbers, and changes in those numbers. Horizontal analysis refers to examination of financial statement data *across time*. [The term *horizontal analysis*

arises from the left-to-right (or right-to-left) movement of our eyes as we review comparative financial statements across time.]

## Comparative Statements

Comparing amounts for two or more successive periods often helps in analyzing financial statements. **Comparative financial statements** facilitate this comparison by showing financial amounts in side-by-side columns on a single statement, called a *comparative format*. Using figures from **Krispy Kreme**'s financial statements, this section explains how to compute dollar changes and percent changes for comparative statements.

**Computation of Dollar Changes and Percent Changes**   Comparing financial statements over relatively short time periods—two to three years—is often done by analyzing changes in line items. A change analysis usually includes analyzing absolute dollar amount changes and percent changes. Both analyses are relevant because dollar changes can yield large percent changes inconsistent with their importance. For instance, a 50% change from a base figure of $100 is less important than the same percent change from a base amount of $100,000 in the same statement. Reference to dollar amounts is necessary to retain a proper perspective and to assess the importance of changes. We compute the *dollar change* for a financial statement item as follows:

$$\text{Dollar change} = \text{Analysis period amount} - \text{Base period amount}$$

*Analysis period* is the point or period of time for the financial statements under analysis, and *base period* is the point or period of time for the financial statements used for comparison purposes. The prior year is commonly used as a base period. We compute the *percent change* by dividing the dollar change by the base period amount and then multiplying this quantity by 100 as follows:

$$\text{Percent change (\%)} = \frac{\text{Analysis period amount} - \text{Base period amount}}{\text{Base period amount}} \times 100$$

We can always compute a dollar change, but we must be aware of a few rules in working with percent changes. To illustrate, look at four separate cases in this chart:

| Case | Analysis Period | Base Period | Change Analysis Dollar | Change Analysis Percent |
|------|----------------|-------------|--------|---------|
| A | $ 1,500 | $(4,500) | $ 6,000 | — |
| B | (1,000) | 2,000 | (3,000) | — |
| C | 8,000 | — | 8,000 | — |
| D | 0 | 10,000 | (10,000) | (100%) |

When a negative amount appears in the base period and a positive amount in the analysis period (or vice versa), we cannot compute a meaningful percent change; see cases A and B. Also, when no value is in the base period, no percent change is computable; see case C. Finally, when an item has a value in the base period and zero in the analysis period, the decrease is 100 percent; see case D.

It is common when using horizontal analysis to compare amounts to either average or median values from prior periods (average and median values smooth out erratic or unusual fluctuations).[1] We also commonly round percents and ratios to one or two decimal places,

---

[1] *Median* is the middle value in a group of numbers. For instance, if five prior years' incomes are (in 000s) $15, $19, $18, $20, and $22, the median value is $19. When there are two middle numbers, we can take their average. For instance, if four prior years' sales are (in 000s) $84, $91, $96, and $93, the median is $92 (computed as the average of $91 and $93).

but practice on this matter is not uniform. Computations are as detailed as necessary, which is judged by whether rounding potentially affects users' decisions. Computations should not be excessively detailed so that important relations are lost among a mountain of decimal points and digits.

**Comparative Balance Sheets**   Comparative balance sheets consist of balance sheet amounts from two or more balance sheet dates arranged side by side. Its usefulness is often improved by showing each item's dollar change and percent change to highlight large changes.

Analysis of comparative financial statements begins by focusing on items that show large dollar or percent changes. We then try to identify the reasons for these changes and, if possible, determine whether they are favorable or unfavorable. We also follow up on items with small changes when we expected the changes to be large.

Exhibit 13.1 shows comparative balance sheets for Krispy Kreme. A few items stand out. Nearly all asset categories substantially increase, which is probably not surprising because Krispy Kreme is a growth company. At least part of the increase in liquid assets is from more than $44,000 raised from borrowings this period; see the financing activities section

**Point:** Spreadsheet programs can help with horizontal, vertical, and ratio analyses, including graphical depictions of financial relations. The key is using this information effectively for business decisions.

**Point:** Business consultants use comparative statement analysis to provide management advice.

## Exhibit 13.1
Comparative Balance Sheets

| **KRISPY KREME**<br>**Comparative Balance Sheets**<br>**February 2, 2003, and February 3, 2002** | | | | |
|---|---|---|---|---|
| (in thousands) | 2002 | 2003 | Dollar<br>Change | Percent<br>Change |
| **Assets** | | | | |
| Current assets | | | | |
| Cash and cash equivalents . . . . . . . . . . . . . . . . . . . | $ 21,904 | $ 32,203 | $ 10,299 | 47.0% |
| Short-term investments . . . . . . . . . . . . . . . . . . . . . | 15,292 | 22,976 | 7,684 | 50.2 |
| Accounts receivable, net . . . . . . . . . . . . . . . . . . . | 26,894 | 34,373 | 7,479 | 27.8 |
| Inventories . . . . . . . . . . . . . . . . . . . . . . . . . . . . | 16,159 | 24,365 | 8,206 | 50.8 |
| Prepaid expenses . . . . . . . . . . . . . . . . . . . . . . . | 2,591 | 3,478 | 887 | 34.2 |
| Other current assets . . . . . . . . . . . . . . . . . . . . . | 18,929 | 23,733 | 4,804 | 25.4 |
| Total current assets . . . . . . . . . . . . . . . . . . . . | 101,769 | 141,128 | 39,359 | 38.7 |
| Property and equipment, net . . . . . . . . . . . . . . . . | 112,577 | 202,558 | 89,981 | 79.9 |
| Long-term investments . . . . . . . . . . . . . . . . . . . . | 12,700 | 4,344 | (8,356) | (65.8) |
| Intangible assets . . . . . . . . . . . . . . . . . . . . . . . . | 16,621 | 48,703 | 32,082 | 193.0 |
| Other long-term assets . . . . . . . . . . . . . . . . . . . | 11,709 | 13,754 | 2,045 | 17.5 |
| Total assets . . . . . . . . . . . . . . . . . . . . . . . . . . | $255,376 | $410,487 | $155,111 | 60.7 |
| **Liabilities** | | | | |
| Current liabilities | | | | |
| Accounts payable . . . . . . . . . . . . . . . . . . . . . . . | $ 12,095 | $ 14,055 | 1,960 | 16.2 |
| Accrued expenses . . . . . . . . . . . . . . . . . . . . . . . | 26,729 | 20,981 | (5,748) | (21.5) |
| Current maturities of long-term debt . . . . . . . . . . | 731 | 3,301 | 2,570 | 351.6 |
| Other current liabilities . . . . . . . . . . . . . . . . . . . | 12,978 | 21,350 | 8,372 | 64.5 |
| Total current liabilities . . . . . . . . . . . . . . . . . | 52,533 | 59,687 | 7,154 | 13.6 |
| Long-term debt, net of current portion . . . . . . . . | 3,912 | 49,900 | 45,988 | 1175.6 |
| Other long-term liabilities . . . . . . . . . . . . . . . . . | 8,773 | 22,355 | 13,582 | 154.8 |
| Total long-term liabilities . . . . . . . . . . . . . . . . | 12,685 | 72,255 | 59,570 | 469.6 |
| **Shareholders' Equity** | | | | |
| Common stock . . . . . . . . . . . . . . . . . . . . . . . | 121,052 | 173,112 | 52,060 | 43.0 |
| Accumulated other comprehensive<br>income (loss) . . . . . . . . . . . . . . . . . . . . . . . | 456 | (1,486) | (1,942) | — |
| Retained earnings . . . . . . . . . . . . . . . . . . . . . . | 68,925 | 102,403 | 33,478 | 48.6 |
| Other equity . . . . . . . . . . . . . . . . . . . . . . . . . | (275) | 4,516 | 4,791 | — |
| Total shareholders' equity* . . . . . . . . . . . . . . . . | 190,158 | 278,545 | 88,387 | 46.5 |
| Total liabilities and shareholders' equity . . . . . . . . . | $255,376 | $410,487 | 155,111 | 60.7 |

\* Includes any minority interest.

of the statement of cash flows. Of course, this substantial asset growth (60.7%) must be accompanied by future income to validate Krispy Kreme's growth strategy.

We likewise see substantial increases on the financing side, the most notable ones being long-term debt and stock issuances totaling about $98,000. Much of this is reflected in the $90,000 increase in property and equipment. Again, we must monitor this increase in investing and financing activities to be sure they are reflected in increased operating performance.

**Comparative Income Statements**   Comparative income statements are prepared similarly to comparative balance sheets. Amounts for two or more periods are placed side by side, with additional columns for dollar and percent changes. Exhibit 13.2 shows Krispy Kreme's comparative income statements.

**Exhibit 13.2**

Comparative Income Statements

| KRISPY KREME<br>Comparative Income Statements<br>For Years Ended February 2, 2003, and February 3, 2002 | | | | |
| --- | --- | --- | --- | --- |
| (in thousands, except per share data) | 2002 | 2003 | Dollar<br>Change | Percent<br>Change |
| Total revenues | $394,354 | $491,549 | $97,195 | 24.6% |
| Operating expenses (cost of sales) | 316,946 | 381,489 | 64,543 | 20.4 |
| General and administrative expenses | 27,562 | 28,897 | 1,335 | 4.8 |
| Depreciation and amortization expenses | 7,959 | 12,271 | 4,312 | 54.2 |
| Arbitration award | — | 9,075 | 9,075 | 100.0 |
| Income from operations | 41,887 | 59,817 | 17,930 | 42.8 |
| Interest income | 2,980 | 1,966 | (1,014) | (34.0) |
| Interest expense | (337) | (1,781) | (1,444) | (428.5) |
| Other losses | (1,749) | (4,295) | (2,546) | (145.6) |
| Loss on sale of property and equipment | (235) | (934) | (699) | (297.4) |
| Income before income taxes | 42,546 | 54,773 | 12,227 | 28.7 |
| Provision for income taxes | 16,168 | 21,295 | 5,127 | 31.7 |
| Net income | $ 26,378 | $ 33,478 | 7,100 | 26.9 |
| Basic earnings per share | $ 0.49 | $ 0.61 | 0.12 | 24.5 |
| Diluted earnings per share | $ 0.45 | $ 0.56 | 0.11 | 24.4 |

Krispy Kreme has substantial revenue growth of 24.6% in 2003. This finding helps support management's growth strategy as revealed in the comparative balance sheets. Equally impressive is its ability to control cost of sales and general and administrative expenses, which increased only 20.4% and 4.8%, respectively. Krispy Kreme is achieving asset growth and greater returns on that growth. The substantial increase in interest expense is not surprising given the huge increase in debt financing. A net income growth of 26.9% on revenue growth of 24.6% is impressive.

**Point:** Percent change can also be computed by dividing the current period by the prior period and subtracting 1.0. For example, the 24.6% revenue increase of Exhibit 13.2 is computed as: ($491,549/$394,354) − 1.

## Trend Analysis

*Trend analysis,* also called *trend percent analysis* or *index number trend analysis,* is a form of horizontal analysis that can reveal patterns in data across successive periods. It involves computing trend percents for a series of financial numbers and is a variation on the use of percent changes. The difference is that trend analysis does not subtract the base period amount in the numerator. To compute trend percents, we do the following:

1. Select a *base period* and assign each item in the base period a weight of 100%.
2. Express financial numbers as a percent of their base period number.

Specifically, a *trend percent,* also called an *index number,* is computed as follows:

**Point:** *Index* refers to the comparison of the analysis period to the base period. Percents determined for each period are called *index numbers.*

$$\text{Trend percent (\%)} = \frac{\text{Analysis period amount}}{\text{Base period amount}} \times 100$$

To illustrate trend analysis, we use the selected Krispy Kreme data in Exhibit 13.3.

## Exhibit 13.3

Revenues and Expenses

| (in thousands) | 1999 | 2000 | 2001 | 2002 | 2003 |
|---|---|---|---|---|---|
| Total revenues | $180,880 | $220,243 | $300,715 | $394,354 | $491,549 |
| Operating expenses (cost of sales) | 159,941 | 190,003 | 250,690 | 316,946 | 381,489 |
| General and administrative expenses | 10,897 | 14,856 | 20,061 | 27,562 | 28,897 |

These data are from Krispy Kreme's *Selected Financial Data* section in Appendix A. The base period is 1999 and the trend percent is computed in each subsequent year by dividing that year's amount by its 1999 amount. For instance, the revenue trend percent for 2003 is 271.8%, computed as $491,549/$180,880. The trend percents—using the data from Exhibit 13.3—are shown in Exhibit 13.4.

## Exhibit 13.4

Trend Percents of Revenues and Expenses

| (in thousands) | 1999 | 2000 | 2001 | 2002 | 2003 |
|---|---|---|---|---|---|
| Total revenues | 100% | 121.8% | 166.3% | 218.0% | 271.8% |
| Operating expenses (cost of sales) | 100% | 118.8 | 156.7 | 198.2 | 238.5 |
| General and administrative expenses | 100% | 136.3 | 184.1 | 252.9 | 265.2 |

**Point:** Trend analysis expresses a percent of base, not a percent of change.

## Exhibit 13.5

Trend Percent Lines for Revenues and Expenses

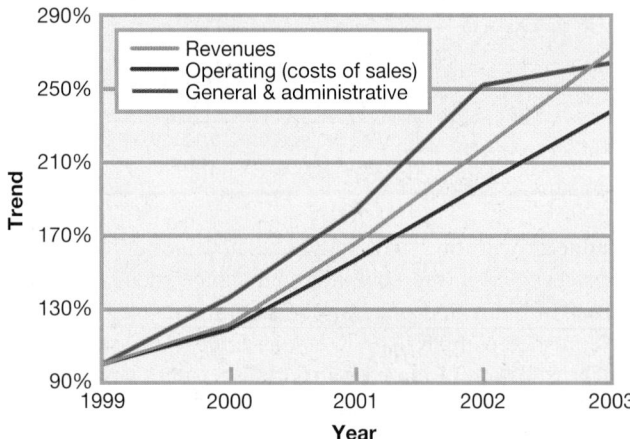

Graphical depictions often aid analysis of trend percents. Exhibit 13.5 shows the trend percents from Exhibit 13.4 in a *line graph,* which can help us identify trends and detect changes in direction or magnitude. It reveals that the trend line for revenues consistently exceeds that for operating expenses. Moreover, the magnitude of that difference has consistently grown. This result bodes well for Krispy Kreme because its operating expenses are by far its largest cost, and the company shows an ability to control these expenses as it rapidly expands. The line graph also reveals a consistent increase in each of these accounts, which is typical of high growth companies. The trend line for general and administrative expenses is troubling because it exceeds the revenue trend line in all years except one. The good news is that the most recent year is the exception, which may show management's willingness to confront and limit such costs.

## Exhibit 13.6

Trend Percent Lines—Krispy Kreme vs. Tastykake

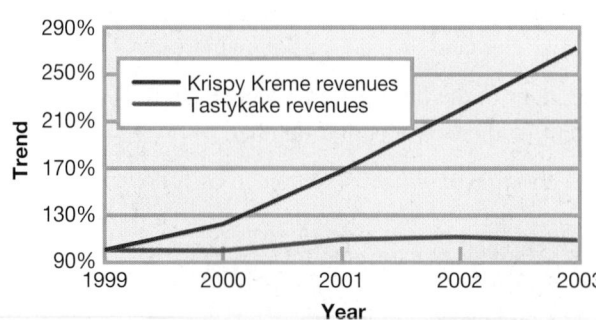

Exhibit 13.6 compares **Krispy Kreme**'s revenue trend line to that of **Tastykake** for this same period. Krispy Kreme's revenues sharply increased over this time period while those of Tastykake slightly increased. These data indicate that Krispy Kreme's products have met with considerable consumer acceptance.

Trend analysis of financial statement items can include comparisons of relations between items on different financial statements. For instance, Exhibit 13.7 compares Krispy Kreme's revenues and total assets. The rate of increase in total assets (439.9%) is greater than the increase in revenues (271.8%). Is this result favorable or not? It suggests that Krispy Kreme was less efficient in using its assets in 2003. Management apparently is expecting future years' revenues to compensate for this asset growth.

| | 1999 | 2003 | Trend Percent (1999 vs. 2003) |
|---|---|---|---|
| Total revenues ....... | $180,880 | $491,549 | 271.8% |
| Total assets ......... | 93,312 | 410,487 | 439.9 |

Exhibit 13.7

Revenue and Asset Data for Krispy Kreme

Overall we must remember that an important role of financial statement analysis is identifying questions and areas of interest, which often direct us to important factors bearing on a company's future. Accordingly, financial statement analysis should be seen as a continuous process of refining our understanding and expectations of company performance and financial condition.

**Decision Maker**

**Auditor** Your tests reveal a 3% increase in sales from $200,000 to $206,000 and a 4% decrease in expenses from $190,000 to $182,400. Both changes are within your "reasonableness" criterion of ±5%, and thus you don't pursue additional tests. The audit partner in charge questions your lack of follow-up and mentions the *joint relation* between sales and expenses. To what is the partner referring?

Answer—p. 563

## Vertical Analysis

Vertical analysis is a tool to evaluate individual financial statement items or a group of items in terms of a specific base amount. We usually define a key aggregate figure as the base, which for an income statement is usually revenue and for a balance sheet is usually total assets. This section explains vertical analysis and applies it to **Krispy Kreme**. [The term *vertical analysis* arises from the up-down (or down-up) movement of our eyes as we review common-size financial statements. Vertical analysis is also called *common-size analysis*.]

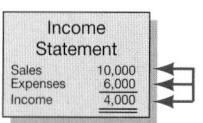

### Common-Size Statements

The comparative statements in Exhibits 13.1 and 13.2 show the change in each item over time, but they do not emphasize the relative importance of each item. We use **common-size financial statements** to reveal changes in the relative importance of each financial statement item. All individual amounts in common-size statements are redefined in terms of common-size percents. A *common-size percent* is measured by dividing each individual financial statement amount under analysis by its base amount:

**P2** Describe and apply methods of vertical analysis.

$$\text{Common-size percent (\%)} = \frac{\text{Analysis amount}}{\text{Base amount}} \times 100$$

**Common-Size Balance Sheets** Common-size statements express each item as a percent of a *base amount,* which for a common-size balance sheet is usually total assets. The base amount is assigned a value of 100%. (This implies that the total amount of liabilities plus equity equals 100% since this amount equals total assets.) We then compute a common-size percent for each asset, liability, and equity item using total assets as the base amount. When we present a company's successive balance sheets in this way, changes in the mixture of assets, liabilities, and equity are apparent.

Exhibit 13.8 shows common-size comparative balance sheets for Krispy Kreme. Some relations that stand out on both a magnitude and percent basis include (1) a decrease in accounts receivable from 10.5% to 8.4%; (2) an increase in property and equipment from

**Point:** The *base* amount in common-size analysis is an *aggregate* amount from the same period's financial statement.

**Point:** Common-size statements often are used to compare two or more companies in the same industry.

## Exhibit 13.8

Common-Size Comparative
Balance Sheets

| KRISPY KREME Common-Size Comparative Balance Sheets February 2, 2003, and February 3, 2002 | | | Common-Size Percents* | |
|---|---|---|---|---|
| ($ thousands) | 2002 | 2003 | 2002 | 2003 |
| **Assets** | | | | |
| Current assets | | | | |
| Cash and cash equivalents ..................... | $ 21,904 | $ 32,203 | 8.6% | 7.8% |
| Short-term investments ..................... | 15,292 | 22,976 | 6.0 | 5.6 |
| Accounts receivable, net ................... | 26,894 | 34,373 | 10.5 | 8.4 |
| Inventories ......................... | 16,159 | 24,365 | 6.3 | 5.9 |
| Prepaid expenses ...................... | 2,591 | 3,478 | 1.0 | 0.8 |
| Other current assets .................... | 18,929 | 23,733 | 7.4 | 5.8 |
| Total current assets .................... | 101,769 | 141,128 | 39.9 | 34.4 |
| Property and equipment, net ............... | 112,577 | 202,558 | 44.1 | 49.3 |
| Long-term investments ................... | 12,700 | 4,344 | 5.0 | 1.1 |
| Intangible assets ...................... | 16,621 | 48,703 | 6.5 | 11.9 |
| Other long-term assets .................. | 11,709 | 13,754 | 4.6 | 3.4 |
| Total assets ........................... | $255,376 | $410,487 | 100.0% | 100.0% |
| **Liabilities** | | | | |
| Current liabilities | | | | |
| Accounts payable ...................... | $ 12,095 | $ 14,055 | 4.7% | 3.4% |
| Accrued expenses ..................... | 26,729 | 20,981 | 10.5 | 5.1 |
| Current maturities of long-term debt .......... | 731 | 3,301 | 0.3 | 0.8 |
| Other current liabilities ................... | 12,978 | 21,350 | 5.1 | 5.2 |
| Total current liabilities ................. | 52,533 | 59,687 | 20.6 | 14.5 |
| Long-term debt, net of current portion ......... | 3,912 | 49,900 | 1.5 | 12.2 |
| Other long-term liabilities ................. | 8,773 | 22,355 | 3.4 | 5.4 |
| Total long-term liabilities ................ | 12,685 | 72,255 | 5.0 | 17.6 |
| **Shareholders' Equity** | | | | |
| Common stock ....................... | 121,052 | 173,112 | 47.4 | 42.2 |
| Accumulated other comprehensive income (loss) ....................... | 456 | (1,486) | 0.2 | (0.0) |
| Retained earnings ...................... | 68,925 | 102,403 | 27.0 | 24.9 |
| Other equity ......................... | (275) | 4,516 | (0.1) | 1.1 |
| Total shareholders' equity** ................. | 190,158 | 278,545 | 74.5 | 67.9 |
| Total liabilities and shareholders' equity ........ | $255,376 | $410,487 | 100.0% | 100.0% |

* Percents are rounded to tenths and thus may not exactly sum to totals and subtotals.   ** Includes minority interest.

44.1% to 49.3%; (3) an increase in intangible assets from 6.5% to 11.9%; (4) a decrease in accrued expenses from 10.5% to 5.1%; and (5) an increase in long-term debt from 1.5% to 12.2%. These changes are characteristic of a successful growth company. The concern, if any, is whether Krispy Kreme can continue to generate sufficient revenues and income to support its asset buildup and its increased financing.

**Common-Size Income Statements**   Analysis also benefits from use of a common-size income statement. Revenues is usually the base amount, which is assigned a value of 100%. Each common-size income statement item appears as a percent of revenues. If we think of the 100% revenues amount as representing one sales dollar, the remaining items show how each revenue dollar is distributed among costs, expenses, and income.

Exhibit 13.9 shows common-size comparative income statements for each dollar of Krispy Kreme's revenues. Operating expenses (cost of sales) decreased from 80.4% to 77.6% of revenues, and so have general and administrative expenses, from 7.0% to 5.9%. This implies that management is effectively controlling costs and/or the company is reaping growth

**Point:** Common-size statements are also useful in comparing firms that report in different currencies.

**Global:** International companies sometimes disclose "convenience" financial statements, which are statements translated in other languages and currencies. However, these statements rarely adjust for differences in accounting principles across countries.

| (\$ thousands) | 2002 | 2003 | 2002 | 2003 |
|---|---|---|---|---|
| **KRISPY KREME** | | | | |
| **Common-Size Comparative Income Statements** | | | | |
| **For Years Ended February 2, 2003, and February 3, 2002** | | | **Common-Size Percents*** | |
| Total revenues | \$394,354 | \$491,549 | 100.0% | 100.0% |
| Operating expenses (cost of sales) | 316,946 | 381,489 | 80.4 | 77.6 |
| General and administrative expenses | 27,562 | 28,897 | 7.0 | 5.9 |
| Depreciation and amortization expenses | 7,959 | 12,271 | 2.0 | 2.5 |
| Arbitration award | — | 9,075 | — | 1.8 |
| Income from operations | 41,887 | 59,817 | 10.6 | 12.2 |
| Interest income | 2,980 | 1,966 | 0.8 | 0.4 |
| Interest expense | (337) | (1,781) | (0.1) | (0.4) |
| Other losses | (1,749) | (4,295) | (0.4) | (0.9) |
| Loss on sale of property and equipment | (235) | (934) | (0.1) | (0.2) |
| Income before income taxes | 42,546 | 54,773 | 10.8 | 11.1 |
| Provision for income taxes | 16,168 | 21,295 | 4.1 | 4.3 |
| Net income | \$ 26,378 | \$ 33,478 | 6.7 | 6.8 |

**Exhibit 13.9**

Common-Size Comparative Income Statements

\* Percents are rounded to tenths and thus may not exactly sum totals and subtotals.

benefits, so-called *economies of scale*. Conversely, depreciation and amortization along with interest expense have increased as a percent of revenues; again, such results are expected for a growth company. This shows that common-size percents for successive income statements can uncover potentially important changes in a company's expenses. Evidence of no changes, especially when changes are expected, is also informative.

## Common-Size Graphics

Two of the most common tools of common-size analysis are trend analysis of common-size statements and graphical analysis. The trend analysis of common-size statements is similar to that of comparative statements discussed under vertical analysis. It is not illustrated here because the only difference is the substitution of common-size percents for trend percents. Instead, this section discusses graphical analysis of common-size statements.

An income statement readily lends itself to common-size graphical analysis. This is so because revenues affect nearly every item in an income statement. Exhibit 13.10 shows Krispy Kreme's 2003 common-size income statement in graphical form. This pie chart highlights the contribution of each component of revenues.

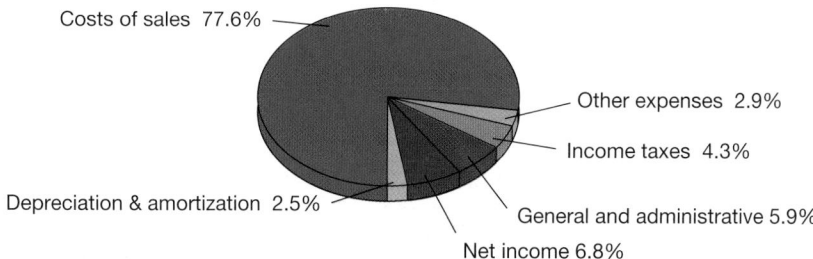

**Exhibit 13.10**

Common-Size Graphic of Income Statement

Exhibit 13.11 previews more complex graphical analyses available and the insights they provide. The data for this exhibit are taken from **Krispy Kreme**'s *Business Segment* footnote. Krispy Kreme has three reportable segments. The *Company Store Operations* segment refers to stores primarily operated by Krispy Kreme. *Franchise Operations* refers to royalties and fees from franchisees. The *KKM&D* segment supplies product mix, equipment, coffee, and other items to both company-owned and franchisee-owned stores.

## Exhibit 13.11

Revenue and Operating Income
Breakdown by Segment

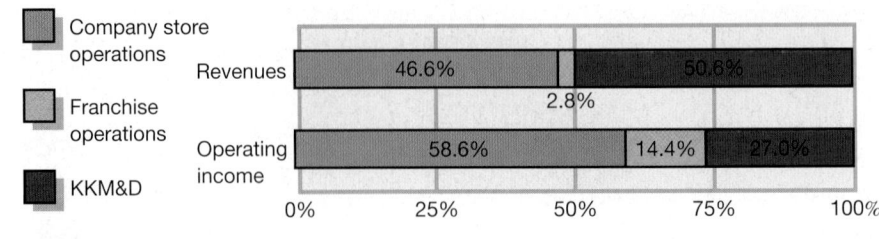

## Exhibit 13.12

Common-Size Graphic of
Asset Components

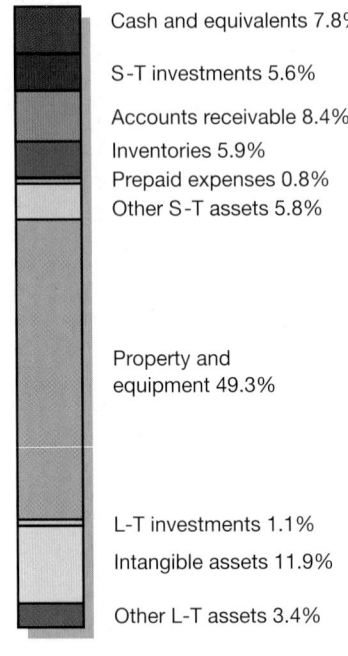

The upper bar in Exhibit 13.11 shows the percent of revenues from each segment. The two major revenue sources are Company Stores (46.6%) and KKM&D (50.6%). The lower bar shows the percent of operating income from each segment. Note that although Franchise Operations provide only 2.8% of revenues, they provide 14.4% of operating income. In contrast, KKM&D provides 50.6% of revenues but only 27.0% of operating income. This type of information can help users in determining strategic analyses and actions.

Graphical analysis is also useful in identifying (1) sources of financing including the distribution among current liabilities, noncurrent liabilities, and equity capital and (2) focuses of investing activities, including the distribution among current and noncurrent assets. As illustrative, Exhibit 13.12 shows a common-size graphical display of Krispy Kreme's assets. Common-size balance sheet analysis can be extended to examine the composition of these subgroups. For instance, in assessing liquidity of current assets, knowing what proportion of current assets consists of inventories is usually important, and not simply what proportion inventories are of total assets.

Common-size financial statements are also useful in comparing different companies. Exhibit 13.13 shows common-size graphics of both Krispy Kreme and Tastykake on financing sources. This graphic highlights the much larger percent of debt financing for Tastykake than for Krispy Kreme. Comparison of a company's common-size statements with competitors' or industry common-size statistics alerts us to differences in the structure or distribution of its financial statements but not to their dollar magnitude.

## Exhibit 13.13

Common-Size Graphic of
Financing Sources—
Competitor Analysis

---

### Quick Check

**5.** Which of the following is true for common-size comparative statements? (*a*) Each item is expressed as a percent of a base amount. (*b*) Total assets often are assigned a value of 100%. (*c*) Amounts from successive periods are placed side by side. (*d*) All are true. (*e*) None is true.

**6.** What is the difference between the percents shown on a comparative income statement and those shown on a common-size comparative income statement?

**7.** Trend percents are (*a*) shown on comparative income statements and balance sheets, (*b*) shown on common-size comparative statements, or (*c*) also called *index numbers*.

Answers—p. 564

# Ratio Analysis

Ratios are among the more widely used tools of financial analysis because they provide clues to and symptoms of underlying conditions. A ratio can help us uncover conditions and trends difficult to detect by inspecting individual components making up the ratio. Ratios, like other analysis tools, are usually future oriented; that is, they are often adjusted for their probable future trend and magnitude, and their usefulness depends on skillful interpretation.

A ratio expresses a mathematical relation between two quantities. It can be expressed as a percent, rate, or proportion. For instance, a change in an account balance from $100 to $250 can be expressed as (1) 150%, (2) 2.5 times, or (3) 2.5 to 1 (or 2.5:1). Computation of a ratio is a simple arithmetic operation, but its interpretation is not. To be meaningful, a ratio must refer to an economically important relation. For example, a direct and crucial relation exists between an item's sales price and its cost. Accordingly, the ratio of cost of goods sold to sales is meaningful. In contrast, no obvious relation exists between freight costs and the balance of long-term investments.

This section describes an important set of financial ratios and its application. The selected ratios are organized into the four building blocks of financial statement analysis: (1) liquidity and efficiency, (2) solvency, (3) profitability, and (4) market prospects. All of these ratios were explained at relevant points in prior chapters. The purpose here is to organize and apply them under a summary framework. We use four common standards for comparisons: intracompany, competitor, industry, and guidelines. Our analysis of **Krispy Kreme** uses three of the four standards in varying degrees: intracompany, competitor (**Tastykake**), and guideline comparisons. Since no obvious industry comparison is available for Krispy Kreme, we do not use industry standards as we normally would. For instance, constructing industry standards using Dunkin' Donuts, Tim Hortons, Lamar's Donuts, Winchell's Donut Houses, Donut Connection, and Mister Donut would be useful, but because all are either privately held, a subsidiary, or a non-U.S. company and do not publish statements readily comparable to those of Krispy Kreme, this is not done.

**P3** Define and apply ratio analysis.

Topic Tackler 13-2

**Point:** Some sources for industry norms are *Annual Statement Studies* by Robert Morris Associates, *Industry Norms & Key Business Ratios* by Dun & Bradstreet, *Standard & Poor's Industry Surveys,* and MarketGuide.com.

## Liquidity and Efficiency

*Liquidity* refers to the availability of resources to meet short-term cash requirements. It is affected by the timing of cash inflows and outflows along with prospects for future performance. Analysis of liquidity is aimed at a company's funding requirements. *Efficiency* refers to how productive a company is in using its assets. Efficiency is usually measured relative to how much revenue is generated from a certain level of assets.

Both liquidity and efficiency are important and complementary. If a company fails to meet its current obligations, its continued existence is doubtful. Viewed in this light, all other measures of analysis are of secondary importance. Although accounting measurements assume the company's continued existence, our analysis must always assess the validity of this assumption using liquidity measures. Moreover, inefficient use of assets can cause liquidity problems. A lack of liquidity often precedes lower profitability and fewer opportunities. It can foretell a loss of owner control or of investment. To a company's creditors, lack of liquidity can yield delays in collecting interest and principal payments or the loss of amounts due them. A company's customers and suppliers of goods and services also are affected by short-term liquidity problems. Implications include a company's inability to execute contracts and potential damage to important customer and supplier relationships. This section describes and illustrates key ratios relevant to assessing liquidity and efficiency.

**Working Capital and Current Ratio**   The amount of current assets less current liabilities is called **working capital,** or *net working capital*. A company needs adequate working capital to meet current debts, to carry sufficient inventories, and to take advantage of cash discounts. A company that runs low on working capital is less likely to meet current obligations or to continue operating. When evaluating a company's working capital, we must

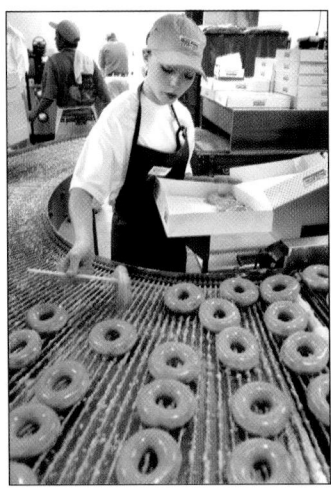

**Tastykake**
Day's sales uncollected = 47.0

If the beginning and ending inventories for the year do not represent the usual inventory amount, an average of quarterly or monthly inventories can be used. Krispy Kreme's inventory turnover of 18.8 is slightly higher than Tastykake's 14.6. A company with a high turnover requires a smaller investment in inventory than one producing the same sales with a lower turnover. Inventory turnover can be too high, however, if the inventory a company keeps is so small that it restricts sales volume.

**Days' Sales Uncollected**   Accounts receivable turnover provides insight into how frequently a company collects its accounts. Days' sales uncollected is one measure of this activity, which is defined in Chapter 6 as:

$$\text{Days' sales uncollected} = \frac{\text{Accounts receivable}}{\text{Net sales}} \times 365$$

Any short-term notes receivable from customers are normally included in the numerator. Krispy Kreme's 2003 days' sales uncollected follows:

$$\frac{\$34,373}{\$491,549} \times 365 = 25.5 \text{ days}$$

Tastykake's days' sales uncollected of 47.0 days is larger than the 25.5 days for Krispy Kreme. Days' sales uncollected is more meaningful if we know the company credit terms. A rough guideline states that days' sales uncollected should not exceed $1\frac{1}{3}$ times the days in its (1) credit period, if discounts are not offered or (2) discount period, if favorable discounts are offered.

**Days' Sales in Inventory**   Chapter 5 explained how *days' sales in inventory* is a useful measure in evaluating inventory liquidity. Days' sales in inventory is linked to inventory in a way that days' sales uncollected is linked to receivables. We compute days' sales in inventory as follows:

$$\text{Days' sales in inventory} = \frac{\text{Ending inventory}}{\text{Cost of goods sold}} \times 365$$

Krispy Kreme's days' sales in inventory for 2003 follows:

**Tastykake**
Days' sales in inventory = 22.2

$$\frac{\$24,365}{\$381,489} \times 365 = 23.3 \text{ days}$$

If the products in Krispy Kreme's inventory are in demand by customers, this formula estimates that its inventory will be converted into receivables (or cash) in 23.3 days. If all of Krispy Kreme's sales were credit sales, the conversion of inventory to receivables in 23.3 days *plus* the conversion of receivables to cash in 25.5 days implies that inventory will be converted to cash in about 48.8 days (23.3 + 25.5).

**Total Asset Turnover**   *Total asset turnover* reflects a company's ability to use its assets to generate sales and is an important indication of operating efficiency. We explained in Chapter 8 the computation of this ratio as follows:

$$\text{Total asset turnover} = \frac{\text{Net sales}}{\text{Average total assets}}$$

Krispy Kreme's total asset turnover for 2003 follows and is better than Tastykake's.

**Tastykake**
Total asset turnover = 1.39

$$\frac{\$491,549}{(\$410,487 + \$255,376)/2} = 1.48 \text{ times}$$

## Quick Check

8. Information from Paff Co. at Dec. 31, 2005, follows: cash, $820,000; accounts receivable, $240,000; inventories, $470,000; plant assets, $910,000; accounts payable, $350,000; and income taxes payable, $180,000. Compute its (a) current ratio and (b) acid-test ratio.

9. On Dec. 31, 2004, Paff Company (question 8) had accounts receivable of $290,000 and inventories of $530,000. During 2005, net sales amounted to $2,500,000 and cost of goods sold was $750,000. Compute (a) accounts receivable turnover, (b) days' sales uncollected, (c) inventory turnover, and (d) days' sales in inventory.

Answers—p. 564

## Solvency

*Solvency* refers to a company's long-run financial viability and its ability to cover long-term obligations. All of a company's business activities—financing, investing, and operating—affect its solvency. Analysis of solvency is long term and uses less precise but more encompassing measures than liquidity. One of the most important components of solvency analysis is the composition of a company's capital structure. *Capital structure* refers to a company's financing sources. It ranges from relatively permanent equity financing to riskier or more temporary short-term financing. Assets represent security for financiers, ranging from loans secured by specific assets to the assets available as general security to unsecured creditors. This section describes the tools of solvency analysis. Our analysis focuses on a company's ability to both meet its obligations and provide security to its creditors *over the long run.* Indicators of this ability include *debt* and *equity* ratios, the relation between *pledged assets and secured liabilities,* and the company's capacity to earn sufficient income to *pay fixed interest charges.*

**Debt and Equity Ratios**  One element of solvency analysis is to assess the portion of a company's assets contributed by its owners and the portion contributed by creditors. This relation is reflected in the debt ratio described in Chapter 2. The *debt ratio* expresses total liabilities as a percent of total assets. The **equity ratio** provides complementary information by expressing total equity as a percent of total assets. **Krispy Kreme**'s debt and equity ratios are computed here:

**Point:** For analysis purposes, Minority Interest is usually added to equity.

| ($ thousands) | 2003 | Ratios | |
|---|---|---|---|
| Total liabilities . . . . . . . . . . . . . . . . | $131,942 | 32.1% | [Debt ratio] |
| Total equity . . . . . . . . . . . . . . . . | 278,545 | 67.9 | [Equity ratio] |
| Total liabilities and equity . . . . . . . | $410,487 | 100.0% | |

**Tastykake**
Debt ratio = 59.2%
Equity ratio = 40.8%

Krispy Kreme's financial statements reflect less debt than equity. A company is considered less risky if its capital structure (equity and long-term debt) contains more equity. One risk factor is the required payment for interest and principal when debt is outstanding. Another factor is the greater the stockholder financing, the more losses a company can absorb through equity before the assets become inadequate to satisfy creditors' claims. From the stockholders' point of view, if a company earns a return on borrowed capital that is higher than the cost of borrowing, the difference represents increased income to stockholders. The inclusion of debt is described as *financial leverage* because debt can have the effect of increasing the return to stockholders. Companies are said to be highly leveraged if a large portion of their assets is financed by debt.

**Point:** Bank examiners from the FDIC and other regulatory agencies use debt and equity ratios to monitor compliance with regulatory capital requirements imposed on banks and S&Ls.

**Pledged Assets to Secured Liabilities**  We explained in Chapter 10 how to use the ratio of pledged assets to secured liabilities to evaluate the risk of nonpayment faced by secured creditors. This ratio also is relevant to unsecured creditors because of what it implies about the remaining assets available. We compute the ratio as follows:

$$\text{Pledged assets to secured liabilities} = \frac{\textbf{Book value of pledged assets}}{\textbf{Book value of secured liabilities}}$$

The information needed to compute this ratio is sometimes not reported in financial statements. However, persons who have the ability to obtain information directly from the company, such as bankers and lenders, nearly always examine this ratio. A generally agreed minimum value for this ratio is about 2:1 (from a secured creditor perspective), but the ratio needs careful interpretation because it is based on the *book value* of pledged assets. Book values are not necessarily intended to reflect amounts to be received from assets in event of liquidation. Also, a company's long-run earning ability is equally important. Creditors prefer that a debtor be able to pay with cash generated by operating activities rather than with cash obtained by liquidating assets.

Krispy Kreme's note 7 (*Debt*) describes several of its secured and unsecured liabilities. A complete analysis would involve assessing these details, which is left for advanced courses.

**Point:** The times interest earned ratio and the debt and equity ratios are of special interest to bank lending officers.

**Times Interest Earned**   The amount of income before deductions for interest expense and income taxes is the amount available to pay interest expense. Chapter 9 explained that the following *times interest earned* ratio reflects the creditors' risk of loan repayments with interest:

$$\text{Times interest earned} = \frac{\text{Income before interest expense and income taxes}}{\text{Interest expense}}$$

### Decision Insight

**Bears and Bulls**  A *bear market* is a declining market. The phrase comes from bear-skin jobbers who often sold the skins before the bears were caught. The term *bear* was then used to describe investors who sold shares they did not own in anticipation of a price decline. A *bull market* is a rising market. This phrase comes from the once popular sport of bear and bull baiting. The term *bull* came to mean the opposite of *bear*.

The larger this ratio, the less risky is the company for creditors. One guideline says that creditors are reasonably safe if the company earns its fixed interest expense two or more times each year. Krispy Kreme's times interest earned ratio follows; its value suggests that its creditors have little risk of nonrepayment.

$$\frac{\$33,478 + \$21,295 + \$1,781}{\$1,781} = 31.8$$

**Tastykake**
Times interest earned = 2.9*

\* Excludes restructuring

## Profitability

We are especially interested in a company's ability to use its assets efficiently to produce profits (and positive cash flows). *Profitability* refers to a company's ability to generate an adequate return on invested capital. Return is judged by assessing earnings relative to the level and sources of financing. Profitability is also relevant to solvency. This section describes key profitability measures and their importance to financial statement analysis.

**Profit Margin**   A company's operating efficiency and profitability can be expressed by two components. The first is *profit margin,* which Chapter 3 explained reflects a company's ability to earn net income from sales. It is measured by expressing net income as a percent of sales (*sales* and *revenues* are similar terms). **Krispy Kreme**'s profit margin follows:

**Tastykake**
Profit margin = 1.2%*

\* Excludes restructuring

$$\text{Profit margin} = \frac{\text{Net income}}{\text{Net sales}} = \frac{\$33,478}{\$491,549} = 6.8\%$$

To evaluate profit margin, we must consider the industry. For instance, an appliance company might require a profit margin between 10% and 15%; a retail supermarket might require a profit margin of 1% or 2%. The second component of operating efficiency is *total asset turnover* described earlier in this section. Both profit margin and total asset turnover make up the two basic components of operating efficiency. These ratios also reflect on management because managers are ultimately responsible for operating efficiency. The next section explains how we use both measures to analyze return on total assets.

**Return on Total Assets**  *Return on total assets* is defined as follows:

$$\text{Return on total assets} = \frac{\text{Net income}}{\text{Average total assets}}$$

Krispy Kreme's 2003 return on total assets is

$$\frac{\$33,478}{(\$410,487 + \$255,376)/2} = 10.1\%$$

**Tastykake**
**Return on total assets = 1.7%\***

\* Excludes restructuring

Krispy Kreme's 10.1% return on total assets is lower than that for many businesses but is higher than Tastykake's return of 1.7%. We need comparisons with other competitors and alternative investment opportunities, however, before drawing reliable conclusions. We also should evaluate any trend in the rate of return. The following computation shows the important relation between profit margin, total asset turnover, and return on total assets:

**Point:** Many analysts add back *Interest expense* × *(1 − Tax rate)* to net income in computing return on total assets.

$$\textbf{Profit margin} \times \textbf{Total asset turnover} = \textbf{Return on total assets}$$

or

$$\frac{\text{Net income}}{\text{Net sales}} \times \frac{\text{Net sales}}{\text{Average total assets}} = \frac{\text{Net income}}{\text{Average total assets}}$$

Both profit margin and total asset turnover contribute to overall operating efficiency, as measured by return on total assets. If we apply this formula to Krispy Kreme, we get

$$6.8\% \times 1.48 = 10.1\%$$

**Tastykake:** 1.2% × 1.39 = 1.7%

This analysis shows that Krispy Kreme's superior return on assets to that of Tastykake is the main driver of its higher profit margin.

**Return on Common Stockholders' Equity**  Perhaps the most important goal in operating a company is to earn net income for its owner(s). The *return on common stockholders' equity* measures a company's success in reaching this goal and is defined as follows:

$$\text{Return on common stockholders' equity} = \frac{\text{Net income} - \text{Preferred dividends}}{\text{Average common stockholders' equity}}$$

Krispy Kreme's 2003 return on common stockholders' equity is computed as follows:

$$\frac{\$33,478 - \$0}{(\$278,545 + \$190,158)/2} = 14.3\%$$

**Tastykake**
**Return on common stockholders' equity = 3.9%\***

\* Excludes restructuring

The denominator in this computation is the book value of common equity (including any minority interest). In the numerator, the dividends on cumulative preferred stock are subtracted whether they are declared or are in arrears. If preferred stock is noncumulative, its dividends are subtracted only if declared.

## Market Prospects

Market measures are useful for analyzing corporations with publicly traded stock. These market

---

**Decision Insight**

**Wall Street**  *Wall Street* is synonymous with financial markets, but its name comes from the street location of the original New York Stock Exchange. The street's name derives from stockades built by early settlers to protect New York from pirate attacks.

measures use stock price, which reflects the market's (public's) expectations for the company. This includes expectations of both company return and risk—as the market perceives it.

**Price-Earnings Ratio**   Computation of the *price-earnings ratio* was explained in Chapter 11 as follows:

$$\text{Price-earnings ratio} = \frac{\text{Market price per common share}}{\text{Earnings per share}}$$

**Point:** The PE ratio can be viewed as an indicator of the market's expected growth and risk for a stock. A high level of expected risk suggests a low PE ratio. A high growth rate suggests a high PE ratio.

Predicted earnings per share for the next period is often used in the denominator of this computation. Reported earnings per share for the most recent period is also commonly used. In both cases, the ratio is used as an indicator of the future growth and risk of a company's earnings as perceived by the stock's buyers and sellers.

The market price of Krispy Kreme's common stock at the start of fiscal year 2004 was $30.41. Using Krispy Kreme's $0.61 basic earnings per share, we compute its price-earnings ratio as follows (some analysts compute this ratio using the median of the low and high stock price):

**Tastykake**
**PE (year-end) = 37.1***

* Excludes restructuring

$$\frac{\$30.41}{\$0.61} = 49.9$$

**Point:** Some investors avoid stocks with high PE ratios under the belief they are "overpriced." Alternatively, some investors *sell these stocks short*—hoping for price declines.

Krispy Kreme's price-earnings ratio is higher than the norm. (Tastykake's ratio is high due to abnormally low earnings.) Krispy Kreme's high ratio reflects investors' expectations of continued growth and higher than normal earnings.

**Dividend Yield**   *Dividend yield* is used to compare the dividend-paying performance of different investment alternatives. We compute dividend yield as explained in Chapter 11 as follows:

$$\text{Dividend yield} = \frac{\text{Annual cash dividends per share}}{\text{Market price per share}}$$

Krispy Kreme's dividend yield, based on its fiscal year-end market price per share of $30.41 and its policy of zero cash dividends per share, is computed as follows:

**Tastykake**
**Dividend yield = 5.2%**

$$\frac{\$0.00}{\$30.41} = 0.0\%$$

Some companies do not declare and pay dividends because they wish to reinvest the cash.

## Summary of Ratios

**Point:** Corporate PE ratios and dividend yields are found in daily stock market quotations listed in *The Wall Street Journal, Investor's Business Daily,* or other business publications and Web services.

Exhibit 13.16 summarizes the major financial statement analysis ratios illustrated in this chapter and throughout the book. This summary includes each ratio's title, its formula, and the purpose for which it is commonly used.

### Quick Check

10. Which ratio best reflects a company's ability to meet immediate interest payments? (*a*) Debt ratio. (*b*) Equity ratio. (*c*) Times interest earned.
11. Which ratio best measures a company's success in earning net income for its owner(s)?
    (*a*) Profit margin. (*b*) Return on common stockholders' equity. (*c*) Price-earnings ratio.
    (*d*) Dividend yield.
12. If a company has net sales of $8,500,000, net income of $945,000, and total asset turnover of 1.8 times, what is its return on total assets?

## Exhibit 13.16

Financial Statement Analysis Ratios*

| Ratio | Formula | Measure of |
|---|---|---|
| **Liquidity and Efficiency** | | |
| Current ratio | $= \dfrac{\text{Current assets}}{\text{Current liabilities}}$ | Short-term debt-paying ability |
| Acid-test ratio | $= \dfrac{\text{Cash} + \text{Short-term investments} + \text{Current receivables}}{\text{Current liabilities}}$ | Immediate short-term debt-paying ability |
| Accounts receivable turnover | $= \dfrac{\text{Net sales}}{\text{Average accounts receivable}}$ | Efficiency of collection |
| Inventory turnover | $= \dfrac{\text{Cost of goods sold}}{\text{Average inventory}}$ | Efficiency of inventory management |
| Days' sales uncollected | $= \dfrac{\text{Accounts receivable}}{\text{Net sales}} \times 365$ | Liquidity of receivables |
| Days' sales in inventory | $= \dfrac{\text{Ending inventory}}{\text{Cost of goods sold}} \times 365$ | Liquidity of inventory |
| Total asset turnover | $= \dfrac{\text{Net sales}}{\text{Average total assets}}$ | Efficiency of assets in producing sales |
| **Solvency** | | |
| Debt ratio | $= \dfrac{\text{Total liabilities}}{\text{Total assets}}$ | Creditor financing and leverage |
| Equity ratio | $= \dfrac{\text{Total equity}}{\text{Total assets}}$ | Owner financing |
| Pledged assets to secured liabilities | $= \dfrac{\text{Book value of pledged assets}}{\text{Book value of secured liabilities}}$ | Protection to secured creditors |
| Times interest earned | $= \dfrac{\text{Income before interest expense and income taxes}}{\text{Interest expense}}$ | Protection in meeting interest payments |
| **Profitability** | | |
| Profit margin ratio | $= \dfrac{\text{Net income}}{\text{Net sales}}$ | Net income in each sales dollar |
| Gross margin ratio | $= \dfrac{\text{Net sales} - \text{Cost of goods sold}}{\text{Net sales}}$ | Gross margin in each sales dollar |
| Return on total assets | $= \dfrac{\text{Net income}}{\text{Average total assets}}$ | Overall profitability of assets |
| Return on common stockholders' equity | $= \dfrac{\text{Net income} - \text{Preferred dividends}}{\text{Average common stockholders' equity}}$ | Profitability of owner investment |
| Book value per common share | $= \dfrac{\text{Shareholders' equity applicable to common shares}}{\text{Number of common shares outstanding}}$ | Liquidation at reported amounts |
| Basic earnings per share | $= \dfrac{\text{Net income} - \text{Preferred dividends}}{\text{Weighted-average common shares outstanding}}$ | Net income per common share |
| **Market Prospects** | | |
| Price-earnings ratio | $= \dfrac{\text{Market price per common share}}{\text{Earnings per share}}$ | Market value relative to earnings |
| Dividend yield | $= \dfrac{\text{Annual cash dividends per share}}{\text{Market price per share}}$ | Cash return per common share |

* Additional ratios also examined in previous chapters included credit risk ratio; plant asset useful life; plant asset age; days' cash expense coverage; cash coverage of growth; cash coverage of debt; free cash flow; cash flow on total assets; and payout ratio. Many of these are defined on the back inside cover of the book.

| Decision Analysis | Analysis Reporting |
|---|---|

**A1**   Summarize and report results of analysis.

Understanding the purpose of financial statement analysis is crucial to the usefulness of any analysis. This understanding leads to efficiency of effort, effectiveness in application, and relevance in focus. The purpose of most financial statement analyses is to reduce uncertainty in business decisions through a rigorous and sound evaluation. A *financial statement analysis report* helps by directly addressing the building blocks of analysis and by identifying weaknesses in inference by requiring explanation: It forces us to organize our reasoning and to verify its flow and logic. A report also serves as a communication link with readers, and the writing process reinforces our judgments and vice versa. Finally, the report helps us (re)evaluate evidence and refine conclusions on key building blocks. A good analysis report usually consists of six sections:

1. **Executive summary**—brief focus on important analysis results and conclusions.
2. **Analysis overview**—background on the company, its industry, and its economic setting.
3. **Evidential matter**—financial statements and information used in the analysis, including ratios, trends, comparisons, statistics, and all analytical measures assembled; often organized under the building blocks of analysis.
4. **Assumptions**—identification of important assumptions regarding a company's industry and economic environment, and other important assumptions for estimates.
5. **Key factors**—list of important favorable and unfavorable factors, both quantitative and qualitative, for company performance; usually organized by areas of analysis.
6. **Inferences**—forecasts, estimates, interpretations, and conclusions drawing on all sections of the report.

We must remember that the user dictates relevance, meaning that the analysis report should include a brief table of contents to help readers focus on those areas most relevant to their decisions. All irrelevant matter must be eliminated. For example, decades-old details of obscure transactions and detailed miscues of the analysis are irrelevant. Ambiguities and qualifications to avoid responsibility or hedging inferences must be eliminated. Finally, writing is important. Mistakes in grammar and errors of fact compromise the report's credibility.

### Decision Insight

**Short Selling**   *Short selling* refers to selling stock before you buy it. Here's an example: You borrow 100 shares of Nike stock, sell them in the market at $40 each, and receive money from their sale. You then wait. You hope that Nike's stock price falls to, say, $35 each and you can replace the borrowed stock for less money than you sold it for, reaping a profit of $5 each less any transaction costs.

## Demonstration Problem

Use the following financial statements of Precision Co. to complete these requirements:

1. Prepare comparative income statements showing the percent increase or decrease for year 2006 in comparison to year 2005.
2. Prepare common-size comparative balance sheets for years 2006 and 2005.
3. Compute the following ratios as of December 31, 2006, or for the year ended December 31, 2006, and identify its building block category for financial statement analysis:

   a. Current ratio                            g. Pledged assets to secured liabilities
   b. Acid-test ratio                          h. Times interest earned
   c. Accounts receivable turnover             i. Profit margin ratio
   d. Days' sales uncollected                  j. Total asset turnover
   e. Inventory turnover                       k. Return on total assets
   f. Debt ratio                               l. Return on common stockholders' equity

### PRECISION COMPANY
### Comparative Income Statements
### For Years Ended December 31, 2006 and 2005

| | 2006 | 2005 |
|---|---|---|
| Sales ......................... | $2,486,000 | $2,075,000 |
| Cost of goods sold ............. | 1,523,000 | 1,222,000 |
| Gross profit .................. | 963,000 | 853,000 |
| Operating expenses | | |
| Advertising expense ........... | 145,000 | 100,000 |
| Sales salaries expense .......... | 240,000 | 280,000 |
| Office salaries expense ......... | 165,000 | 200,000 |
| Insurance expense ............ | 100,000 | 45,000 |
| Supplies expense ............. | 26,000 | 35,000 |
| Depreciation expense .......... | 85,000 | 75,000 |
| Miscellaneous expenses ........ | 17,000 | 15,000 |
| Total operating expenses ....... | 778,000 | 750,000 |
| Operating income .............. | 185,000 | 103,000 |
| Interest expense .............. | 44,000 | 46,000 |
| Income before taxes ........... | 141,000 | 57,000 |
| Income taxes ................. | 47,000 | 19,000 |
| Net income .................. | $ 94,000 | $ 38,000 |
| Earnings per share ............. | $ 0.99 | $ 0.40 |

### PRECISION COMPANY
### Comparative Balance Sheets
### December 31, 2006 and 2005

| | 2006 | 2005 |
|---|---|---|
| **Assets** | | |
| Current assets | | |
| Cash ...................... | $ 79,000 | $ 42,000 |
| Short-term investments .......... | 65,000 | 96,000 |
| Accounts receivable, net ......... | 120,000 | 100,000 |
| Merchandise inventory .......... | 250,000 | 265,000 |
| Total current assets ............ | 514,000 | 503,000 |
| Plant assets | | |
| Store equipment, net ........... | 400,000 | 350,000 |
| Office equipment, net .......... | 45,000 | 50,000 |
| Buildings, net ................ | 625,000 | 675,000 |
| Land ...................... | 100,000 | 100,000 |
| Total plant assets ............. | 1,170,000 | 1,175,000 |
| Total assets ................. | $1,684,000 | $1,678,000 |
| **Liabilities** | | |
| Current liabilities | | |
| Accounts payable ............. | $ 164,000 | $ 190,000 |
| Short-term notes payable ....... | 75,000 | 90,000 |
| Taxes payable ................ | 26,000 | 12,000 |
| Total current liabilities .......... | 265,000 | 292,000 |
| Long-term liabilities | | |
| Notes payable (secured by | | |
| mortgage on buildings) ........ | 400,000 | 420,000 |
| Total liabilities ................ | 665,000 | 712,000 |
| **Stockholders' Equity** | | |
| Common stock, $5 par value ....... | 475,000 | 475,000 |
| Retained earnings ............... | 544,000 | 491,000 |
| Total stockholders' equity ......... | 1,019,000 | 966,000 |
| Total liabilities and equity ......... | $1,684,000 | $1,678,000 |

## Planning the Solution

- Set up a four-column income statement; enter the 2006 and 2005 amounts in the first two columns and then enter the dollar change in the third column and the percent change from 2005 in the fourth column.
- Set up a four-column balance sheet; enter the 2006 and 2005 year-end amounts in the first two columns and then compute and enter the amount of each item as a percent of total assets.
- Compute the required ratios using the data provided. Use the average of beginning and ending amounts when appropriate (see Exhibit 13.16 for definitions).

## Solution to Demonstration Problem

1.

### PRECISION COMPANY
### Comparative Income Statements
### For Years Ended December 31, 2006 and 2005

| | | | Increase (Decrease) in 2006 | |
|---|---|---|---|---|
| | 2006 | 2005 | Amount | Percent |
| Sales ....................... | $2,486,000 | $2,075,000 | $411,000 | 19.8% |
| Cost of goods sold ............. | 1,523,000 | 1,222,000 | 301,000 | 24.6 |
| Gross profit .................. | 963,000 | 853,000 | 110,000 | 12.9 |
| Operating expenses | | | | |
| Advertising expense ........... | 145,000 | 100,000 | 45,000 | 45.0 |
| Sales salaries expense .......... | 240,000 | 280,000 | (40,000) | (14.3) |
| Office salaries expense ......... | 165,000 | 200,000 | (35,000) | (17.5) |

[continued on next page]

[continued from previous page]

| | | | | |
|---|---|---|---|---|
| Insurance expense | 100,000 | 45,000 | **55,000** | 122.2 |
| Supplies expense | 26,000 | 35,000 | **(9,000)** | (25.7) |
| Depreciation expense | 85,000 | 75,000 | **10,000** | 13.3 |
| Miscellaneous expenses | 17,000 | 15,000 | **2,000** | 13.3 |
| Total operating expenses | 778,000 | 750,000 | **28,000** | 3.7 |
| Operating income | 185,000 | 103,000 | **82,000** | 79.6 |
| Interest expense | 44,000 | 46,000 | **(2,000)** | (4.3) |
| Income before taxes | 141,000 | 57,000 | **84,000** | 147.4 |
| Income taxes | 47,000 | 19,000 | **28,000** | 147.4 |
| Net income | $  94,000 | $  38,000 | **$ 56,000** | 147.4 |
| Earnings per share | $     0.99 | $     0.40 | **$   0.59** | 147.5 |

**2.**

| PRECISION COMPANY<br>Common-Size Comparative Balance Sheets<br>December 31, 2006 and 2005 | | | | |
|---|---|---|---|---|
| | **December 31** | | **Common-Size Percents** | |
| | **2006** | **2005** | **2006*** | **2005*** |
| **Assets** | | | | |
| Current assets | | | | |
| Cash | $   79,000 | $   42,000 | 4.7% | 2.5% |
| Short-term investments | 65,000 | 96,000 | 3.9 | 5.7 |
| Accounts receivable, net | 120,000 | 100,000 | 7.1 | 6.0 |
| Merchandise inventory | 250,000 | 265,000 | 14.8 | 15.8 |
| Total current assets | 514,000 | 503,000 | 30.5 | 30.0 |
| **Plant Assets** | | | | |
| Store equipment, net | 400,000 | 350,000 | 23.8 | 20.9 |
| Office equipment, net | 45,000 | 50,000 | 2.7 | 3.0 |
| Buildings, net | 625,000 | 675,000 | 37.1 | 40.2 |
| Land | 100,000 | 100,000 | 5.9 | 6.0 |
| Total plant assets | 1,170,000 | 1,175,000 | 69.5 | 70.0 |
| Total assets | $1,684,000 | $1,678,000 | 100.0 | 100.0 |
| **Liabilities** | | | | |
| Current liabilities | | | | |
| Accounts payable | $  164,000 | $  190,000 | 9.7% | 11.3% |
| Short-term notes payable | 75,000 | 90,000 | 4.5 | 5.4 |
| Taxes payable | 26,000 | 12,000 | 1.5 | 0.7 |
| Total current liabilities | 265,000 | 292,000 | 15.7 | 17.4 |
| Long-term liabilities | | | | |
| Notes payable (secured by<br>mortgage on buildings) | 400,000 | 420,000 | 23.8 | 25.0 |
| Total liabilities | 665,000 | 712,000 | 39.5 | 42.4 |
| **Stockholders' Equity** | | | | |
| Common stock, $5 par value | 475,000 | 475,000 | 28.2 | 28.3 |
| Retained earnings | 544,000 | 491,000 | 32.3 | 29.3 |
| Total stockholders' equity | 1,019,000 | 966,000 | 60.5 | 57.6 |
| Total liabilities and equity | $1,684,000 | $1,678,000 | 100.0 | 100.0 |

\* Columns do not always exactly add to 100 due to rounding.

**3. Ratios for 2006:**

   **a.** Current ratio: $514,000/$265,000 = 1.9:1 (liquidity and efficiency)

   **b.** Acid-test ratio: ($79,000 + $65,000 + $120,000)/$265,000 = 1.0:1 (liquidity and efficiency)

   **c.** Average receivables: ($120,000 + $100,000)/2 = $110,000
      Accounts receivable turnover: $2,486,000/$110,000 = 22.6 times (liquidity and efficiency)

   **d.** Days' sales uncollected: ($120,000/$2,486,000) × 365 = 17.6 days (liquidity and efficiency)

   **e.** Average inventory: ($250,000 + $265,000)/2 = $257,500
      Inventory turnover: $1,523,000/$257,500 = 5.9 times (liquidity and efficiency)

  **f.** Debt ratio: $665,000/$1,684,000 = 39.5\%$ (solvency)

  **g.** Pledged assets to secured liabilities: $625,000/$400,000 = 1.56{:}1$ (solvency)

  **h.** Times interest earned: $185,000/$44,000 = 4.2$ times (solvency)

  **i.** Profit margin ratio: $94,000/$2,486,000 = 3.8\%$ (profitability)

  **j.** Average total assets: $(\$1,684,000 + \$1,678,000)/2 = \$1,681,000$
     Total asset turnover: $2,486,000/$1,681,000 = 1.48$ times (liquidity and efficiency)

  **k.** Return on total assets: $94,000/$1,681,000 = 5.6\%$ or $3.8\% \times 1.48 = 5.6\%$ (profitability)

  **l.** Average total common equity: $(\$1,019,000 + \$966,000)/2 = \$992,500$
     Return on common stockholders' equity: $94,000/$992,500 = 9.5\%$ (profitability)

## Summary

**C1 Explain the purpose of analysis.** The purpose of financial statement analysis is to help users make better business decisions. Internal users want information to improve company efficiency and effectiveness in providing products and services. External users want information to make better and more informed decisions in pursuing their goals. The common goals of all users are to evaluate a company's (1) past and current performance, (2) current financial position, and (3) future performance and risk.

**C2 Identify the building blocks of analysis.** Financial statement analysis focuses on four "building blocks" of analysis: (1) liquidity and efficiency—ability to meet short-term obligations and efficiently generate revenues; (2) solvency—ability to generate future revenues and meet long-term obligations; (3) profitability—ability to provide financial rewards sufficient to attract and retain financing; and (4) market prospects—ability to generate positive market expectations.

**C3 Describe standards for comparisons in analysis.** Standards for comparisons include (1) intracompany—prior performance and relations between financial items for the company under analysis; (2) competitor—one or more direct competitors of the company; (3) industry—industry statistics; and (4) guidelines (rules of thumb)—general standards developed from past experiences and personal judgments.

**C4 Identify the tools of analysis.** The three most common tools of financial statement analysis are (1) horizontal analysis—comparing a company's financial condition and performance across time; (2) vertical analysis—comparing a company's financial condition and performance to a base amount such as revenues or total assets; and (3) ratio analysis—using and quantifying key relations among financial statement items.

**A1 Summarize and report results of analysis.** A financial statement analysis report is often organized around the building blocks of analysis. A good report separates interpretations and conclusions of analysis from the information underlying them. An analysis report often consists of six sections: (1) executive summary, (2) analysis overview, (3) evidential matter, (4) assumptions, (5) key factors, and (6) inferences.

**P1 Explain and apply methods of horizontal analysis.** Horizontal analysis is a tool to evaluate changes in data across time. Two important tools of horizontal analysis are comparative statements and trend analysis. Comparative statements show amounts for two or more successive periods, often with changes disclosed in both absolute and percent terms. Trend analysis is used to reveal important changes occurring from one period to the next.

**P2 Describe and apply methods of vertical analysis.** Vertical analysis is a tool to evaluate each financial statement item or group of items in terms of a base amount. Two tools of vertical analysis are common-size statements and graphical analyses. Each item in common-size statements is expressed as a percent of a base amount. For the balance sheet, the base amount is usually total assets, and for the income statement, it is usually sales.

**P3 Define and apply ratio analysis.** Ratio analysis provides clues to and symptoms of underlying conditions. Ratios, properly interpreted, identify areas requiring further investigation. A ratio expresses a mathematical relation between two quantities such as a percent, rate, or proportion. Ratios can be organized into the building blocks of analysis: (1) liquidity and efficiency, (2) solvency, (3) profitability, and (4) market prospects.

## Guidance Answers to **Decision Maker**

**Auditor** The *joint relation* referred to is the combined increase in sales and the decrease in expenses yielding more than a 5% increase in income. Both *individual* accounts (sales and expenses) yield percent changes within the ±5% acceptable range. However, a joint analysis suggests a different picture. For example, consider a joint analysis using the profit margin ratio. The client's profit margin is 11.46% ($206,000 − $182,400/$206,000) for the current year compared with 5.0% ($200,000 − $190,000/$200,000) for the prior year—yielding a 129% increase in profit margin! This is what concerns the partner, and it suggests expanding audit tests to verify or refute the client's figures.

**Banker** Your decision on the loan application is positive for at least two reasons. First, the current ratio suggests a strong ability to meet short-term obligations. Second, current assets of $160,000 and a current ratio of 4:1 imply current liabilities of $40,000 (one-fourth of current assets) and a working capital excess of $120,000. This working capital excess is 60% of the loan amount. However, if the application is for a 10-year loan, our decision is less optimistic. The current ratio and working capital suggest a good safety margin, but indications of inefficiency in operations exist. In particular, a 4:1 current ratio is more than double its key competitors' ratio. This is characteristic of inefficient asset use.

## Guidance Answers to **Quick Checks**

**1.** General-purpose financial statements are intended for a variety of users interested in a company's financial condition and performance—users without the power to require specialized financial reports to meet their specific needs.

**2.** General-purpose financial statements include the income statement, balance sheet, statement of stockholders' (owner's) equity, and statement of cash flows plus the notes related to these statements.

**3.** *a*

**4.** Data from one or more direct competitors are usually preferred for comparative purposes.

**5.** *d*

**6.** Percents on comparative income statements show the increase or decrease in each item from one period to the next. On common-size comparative income statements, each item is shown as a percent of net sales for that period.

**7.** *c*

**8.** (*a*) ($820,000 + $240,000 + $470,000)/
  ($350,000 + $180,000) = 2.9 to 1.
  (*b*) ($820,000 + $240,000)/($350,000 + $180,000) = 2:1.

**9.** (*a*) $2,500,000/[($290,000 + $240,000)/2] = 9.43 times.
  (*b*) ($240,000/$2,500,000) × 365 = 35 days.
  (*c*) $750,000/[($530,000 + $470,000)/2] = 1.5 times.
  (*d*) ($470,000/$750,000) × 365 = 228.7 days.

**10.** *c*

**11.** *b*

**12.** $\text{Profit margin} \times \dfrac{\text{Total asset}}{\text{turnover}} = \dfrac{\text{Return on}}{\text{total assets}}$

$$\dfrac{\$945,000}{\$8,500,000} \times 1.8 = 20\%$$

## Key Terms

Key Terms are available at the book's Website for learning and testing in an online Flashcard Format.

**Common-size financial statement** (p. 547)
**Comparative financial statements** (p. 543)
**Efficiency** (p. 541)
**Equity ratio** (p. 555)
**Financial reporting** (p. 541)
**Financial statement analysis** (p. 540)

**General-purpose financial statements** (p. 541)
**Horizontal analysis** (p. 542)
**Liquidity** (p. 541)
**Market prospects** (p. 541)

**Profitability** (p. 541)
**Ratio analysis** (p. 542)
**Solvency** (p. 541)
**Vertical analysis** (p. 542)
**Working capital** (p. 551)

## Personal Interactive Quiz

Personal Interactive Quizzes A and B are available at the book's Website to reinforce and assess your learning.

## Discussion Questions

**1.** What is the difference between comparative financial statements and common-size comparative statements?

**2.** Which items are usually assigned a 100% value on (*a*) a common-size balance sheet and (*b*) a common-size income statement?

**3.** Explain the difference between financial reporting and financial statements.

**4.** What three factors would influence your evaluation as to whether a company's current ratio is good or bad?

**5.** Suggest several reasons that a 2:1 current ratio may not be adequate for a particular company.

**6.** Why is working capital given special attention in the process of analyzing balance sheets?

**7.** What does the number of days' sales uncollected indicate?

**8.** What does a relatively high accounts receivable turnover indicate about a company's short-term liquidity?

**9.** Why is a company's capital structure, as measured by debt and equity ratios, important to financial statement analysts?

**10.** How does inventory turnover provide information about a company's short-term liquidity?

**11.** What ratios would you compute to evaluate management performance?

**12.** Why must the ratio of pledged assets to secured liabilities be interpreted with caution?

**13.** Why would a company's return on total assets be different from its return on common stockholders' equity?

**14.** Use **Krispy Kreme**'s financial statements in Appendix A to compute its return on total assets for the years ended February 2, 2003, and February 3, 2002. Total assets at January 28, 2001, were $171,493 (in thousands).

**15.** Refer to **Tastykake**'s financial statements in Appendix A to compute its equity ratio as of December 28, 2002, and December 29, 2001.

**16.** Refer to **Harley-Davidson**'s financial statements in Appendix A. Compute its profit margin for the fiscal year ended December 31, 2002. **Harley-Davidson**

 *Red numbers denote Discussion Questions that involve decision-making.*

---

*Homework Manager repeats all numerical Quick Studies on the book's Website with new numbers.*

---

Which of the following items (1) through (9) are part of financial reporting but are *not* included as part of general-purpose financial statements? (1) stock price information and analysis, (2) statement of cash flows, (3) management discussion and analysis of financial performance, (4) income statement, (5) company news releases, (6) balance sheet, (7) financial statement notes, (8) statement of shareholders' equity, (9) prospectus.

**QUICK STUDY**

**QS 13-1**
Financial reporting C1

---

What are four possible standards of comparison used to analyze financial statement ratios? Which of these is generally considered to be the most useful? Which one is least likely to provide a good basis for comparison?

**QS 13-2**
Standard of comparison C3

---

Compute the annual dollar changes and percent changes for each of the following accounts:

**QS 13-3**
Horizontal analysis

P1

| | 2005 | 2004 |
|---|---|---|
| Short-term investments ....... | $217,800 | $165,000 |
| Accounts receivable .......... | 42,120 | 48,000 |
| Notes payable ............. | 57,000 | 0 |

---

Use the following information for Saturn Corporation to determine (1) the 2004 and 2005 common-size percents for cost of goods sold using net sales as the base and (2) the 2004 and 2005 trend percents for net sales using 2004 as the base year.

**QS 13-4**
Common-size and trend percents

P1  P2

| ($ thousands) | 2005 | 2004 |
|---|---|---|
| Net sales .............. | $201,600 | $114,800 |
| Cost of goods sold ....... | 109,200 | 60,200 |

---

Match the ratio to the building block of financial statement analysis to which it best relates.

**A.** Liquidity and efficiency      **C.** Profitability
**B.** Solvency                      **D.** Market prospects

**QS 13-5**
Building blocks of analysis

C2  C4  P3

**1.** _____ Gross margin ratio       **6.** _____ Book value per common share
**2.** _____ Acid-test ratio          **7.** _____ Days' sales in inventory
**3.** _____ Equity ratio             **8.** _____ Accounts receivable turnover
**4.** _____ Return on total assets   **9.** _____ Pledged assets to secured liabilities
**5.** _____ Dividend yield          **10.** _____ Times interest earned

---

**1.** Which two ratios are key components in measuring a company's operating efficiency? Which ratio summarizes these two components?

**2.** Which two short-term liquidity ratios measure how frequently a company collects its accounts?

**3.** What measure reflects the difference between current assets and current liabilities?

**QS 13-6**
Identifying financial ratios

C4  P3

**QS 13-7**
Ratio interpretation

P3

For each ratio listed, identify whether the change in ratio value from 2004 to 2005 is usually regarded as favorable or unfavorable.

| Ratio | 2005 | 2004 | Ratio | 2005 | 2004 |
|---|---|---|---|---|---|
| 1. Profit margin | 8% | 6% | 5. Accounts receivable turnover | 5.4 | 6.6 |
| 2. Debt ratio | 45% | 40% | 6. Basic earnings per share | $1.24 | $1.20 |
| 3. Gross margin | 33% | 45% | 7. Inventory turnover | 3.5 | 3.3 |
| 4. Acid-test ratio | 0.99 | 1.10 | 8. Dividend yield | 1% | 0.8% |

*Homework Manager repeats all numerical Exercises on the book's Website with new numbers.* →

# EXERCISES

**Exercise 13-1**
Computation and analysis of trend percents

P1

Compute trend percents for the following financial items, using 2003 as the base year. State whether the situation as revealed by the trends appears to be favorable or unfavorable for each item.

| | 2007 | 2006 | 2005 | 2004 | 2003 |
|---|---|---|---|---|---|
| Sales ................. | $283,880 | $271,800 | $253,680 | $235,560 | $151,000 |
| Cost of goods sold ........ | 129,200 | 123,080 | 116,280 | 107,440 | 68,000 |
| Accounts receivable ....... | 19,100 | 18,300 | 17,400 | 16,200 | 10,000 |

**Exercise 13-2**
Determination of income effects from common-size and trend percents

P1  P2

Common-size and trend percents for Aziz Company's sales, cost of goods sold, and expenses follow. Determine whether net income increased, decreased, or remained unchanged in this three-year period.

| | Common-Size Percents | | | Trend Percents | | |
|---|---|---|---|---|---|---|
| | 2006 | 2005 | 2004 | 2006 | 2005 | 2004 |
| Sales ................. | 100.0% | 100.0% | 100.0% | 104.4% | 103.2% | 100.0% |
| Cost of goods sold ....... | 62.4 | 60.9 | 58.1 | 102.0 | 108.1 | 100.0 |
| Total expenses ........... | 14.3 | 13.8 | 14.1 | 105.9 | 101.0 | 100.0 |

**Exercise 13-3**
Common-size percent computation and interpretation

P2

Express the following comparative income statements in common-size percents and assess whether or not this company's situation has improved in the most recent year.

| GERALDO CORPORATION | | |
|---|---|---|
| Comparative Income Statements | | |
| For Years Ended December 31, 2005 and 2004 | | |
| | 2005 | 2004 |
| Sales ................. | $720,000 | $535,000 |
| Cost of goods sold ........ | 475,200 | 280,340 |
| Gross profit ............. | 244,800 | 254,660 |
| Operating expenses ....... | 151,200 | 103,790 |
| Net income ............. | $ 93,600 | $150,870 |

**Exercise 13-4**
Analysis of short-term financial condition

A1  P3

The following information is available for Silverado Company and Titan Company, similar firms operating in the same industry. Write a half-page report comparing Silverado and Titan using the available information. Your discussion should include their ability to meet current obligations and to use current assets efficiently.

| | Silverado | | | Titan | | |
|---|---|---|---|---|---|---|
| | **2006** | **2005** | **2004** | **2006** | **2005** | **2004** |
| Current ratio | 1.6 | 1.7 | 2.0 | 3.1 | 2.6 | 1.8 |
| Acid-test ratio | 0.9 | 1.0 | 1.1 | 2.7 | 2.4 | 1.5 |
| Accounts receivable turnover | 29.5 | 24.2 | 28.2 | 15.4 | 14.2 | 15.0 |
| Merchandise inventory turnover | 23.2 | 20.9 | 16.1 | 13.5 | 12.0 | 11.6 |
| Working capital | $60,000 | $48,000 | $42,000 | $121,000 | $93,000 | $68,000 |

**Team Project:** Assume that the two companies apply for a one-year loan from the team. Identify additional information the companies must provide before the team can make a loan decision.

Rolf Company and Kent Company are similar firms that operate in the same industry. Kent began operations in 2005 and Rolf in 2002. In 2007, both companies pay 7% interest on their debt to creditors. The following additional information is available:

**Exercise 13-5**
Analysis of efficiency and financial leverage

A1   P3

| | Rolf Company | | | Kent Company | | |
|---|---|---|---|---|---|---|
| | **2007** | **2006** | **2005** | **2007** | **2006** | **2005** |
| Total asset turnover ......... | 3.0 | 2.7 | 2.9 | 1.6 | 1.4 | 1.1 |
| Return on total assets ....... | 8.9% | 9.5% | 8.7% | 5.8% | 5.5% | 5.2% |
| Profit margin ratio .......... | 2.3% | 2.4% | 2.2% | 2.7% | 2.9% | 2.8% |
| Sales ................... | $400,000 | $370,000 | $386,000 | $200,000 | $160,000 | $100,000 |

Write a half-page report comparing Rolf and Kent using the available information. Your analysis should include their ability to use assets efficiently to produce profits. Also comment on their success in employing financial leverage in 2007.

Sexton Company's year-end balance sheets follow. Express the balance sheets in common-size percents. Round amounts to the nearest one-tenth of a percent. Analyze and comment on the results.

**Exercise 13-6**
Common-size percents

P2

| | **2006** | **2005** | **2004** |
|---|---|---|---|
| Cash ...................... | $ 30,800 | $ 35,625 | $ 36,800 |
| Accounts receivable, net ............. | 88,500 | 62,500 | 49,200 |
| Merchandise inventory ............... | 111,500 | 82,500 | 53,000 |
| Prepaid expenses .................. | 9,700 | 9,375 | 4,000 |
| Plant assets, net .................. | 277,500 | 255,000 | 229,500 |
| Total assets ..................... | $518,000 | $445,000 | $372,500 |
| Accounts payable ................. | $128,900 | $ 75,250 | $ 49,250 |
| Long-term notes payable secured by | | | |
|    mortgages on plant assets ........... | 97,500 | 102,500 | 82,500 |
| Common stock, $10 par value .......... | 162,500 | 162,500 | 162,500 |
| Retained earnings .................. | 129,100 | 104,750 | 78,250 |
| Total liabilities and equity .............. | $518,000 | $445,000 | $372,500 |

Refer to Sexton Company's balance sheet accounts in Exercise 13-6. Analyze its year-end short-term liquidity position at the end of 2006, 2005, and 2004 by computing (1) the current ratio and (2) the acid-test ratio. Comment on the ratio results.

**Exercise 13-7**
Liquidity analysis

P3

**Exercise 13-8**

Liquidity analysis and interpretation

P3

Refer to the Sexton Company information in Exercise 13-6. The company's income statements for the years ended December 31, 2006 and 2005, follow. Assume that all sales are on credit and then compute: (1) days' sales uncollected, (2) accounts receivable turnover, (3) inventory turnover, and (4) days' sales in inventory. Comment on the changes in the ratios from 2005 to 2006.

|  | 2006 | | 2005 | |
| --- | --- | --- | --- | --- |
| Sales ....................... | | $672,500 | | $530,000 |
| Cost of goods sold ............ | $410,225 | | $344,500 | |
| Other operating expenses ....... | 208,550 | | 133,980 | |
| Interest expense .............. | 11,100 | | 12,300 | |
| Income taxes ................. | 8,525 | | 7,845 | |
| Total costs and expenses ........ | | 638,400 | | 498,625 |
| Net income .................. | | $ 34,100 | | $ 31,375 |
| Earnings per share ............ | | $    2.10 | | $    1.93 |

**Exercise 13-9**

Risk and capital structure analysis

P3

Refer to the Sexton Company information in Exercises 13-6 and 13-8. Compare the company's long-term risk and capital structure positions at the end of 2006 and 2005 by computing these ratios: (1) debt and equity ratios, (2) pledged assets to secured liabilities, and (3) times interest earned. Comment on these ratio results.

**Exercise 13-10**

Efficiency and profitability analysis   P3

Refer to Sexton Company's financial information in Exercises 13-6 and 13-8. Evaluate the company's efficiency and profitability by computing the following for 2006 and 2005: (1) profit margin ratio, (2) total asset turnover, and (3) return on total assets. Comment on these ratio results.

**Exercise 13-11**

Profitability analysis

P3

Refer to Sexton Company's financial information in Exercises 13-6 and 13-8. Additional information about the company follows. To help evaluate the company's profitability, compute and interpret the following ratios for 2006 and 2005: (1) return on common stockholders' equity, (2) price-earnings ratio on December 31, and (3) dividend yield.

| | |
| --- | --- |
| Common stock market price, December 31, 2006 ....... | $15.00 |
| Common stock market price, December 31, 2005 ....... | 14.00 |
| Annual cash dividends per share in 2006 .............. | 0.30 |
| Annual cash dividends per share in 2005 .............. | 0.15 |

## PROBLEM SET A

**Problem 13-1A**

Ratios, common-size statements, and trend percents

P1   P2   P3

mhhe.com/wild3e

Selected comparative financial statements of Bennington Company follow:

| BENNINGTON COMPANY | | | |
| --- | --- | --- | --- |
| Comparative Income Statements | | | |
| For Years Ended December 31, 2006, 2005, and 2004 | | | |
| | 2006 | 2005 | 2004 |
| Sales ..................... | $444,000 | $340,000 | $236,000 |
| Cost of goods sold .......... | 267,288 | 212,500 | 151,040 |
| Gross profit ............... | 176,712 | 127,500 | 84,960 |
| Selling expenses ............ | 62,694 | 46,920 | 31,152 |
| Administrative expenses ....... | 40,137 | 29,920 | 19,470 |
| Total expenses ............. | 102,831 | 76,840 | 50,622 |
| Income before taxes ......... | 73,881 | 50,660 | 34,338 |
| Income taxes .............. | 13,764 | 10,370 | 6,962 |
| Net income ................ | $ 60,117 | $ 40,290 | $ 27,376 |

| BENNINGTON COMPANY Comparative Balance Sheets December 31, 2006, 2005, and 2004 | | | |
| --- | --- | --- | --- |
| | **2006** | **2005** | **2004** |
| **Assets** | | | |
| Current assets .............. | $ 48,480 | $ 37,924 | $ 50,648 |
| Long-term investments ......... | 0 | 500 | 3,720 |
| Plant assets, net .............. | 90,000 | 96,000 | 57,000 |
| Total assets ................. | $138,480 | $134,424 | $111,368 |
| **Liabilities and Equity** | | | |
| Current liabilities .............. | $ 20,200 | $ 19,960 | $ 19,480 |
| Common stock .............. | 72,000 | 72,000 | 54,000 |
| Other contributed capital ....... | 9,000 | 9,000 | 6,000 |
| Retained earnings ............. | 37,280 | 33,464 | 31,888 |
| Total liabilities and equity ........ | $138,480 | $134,424 | $111,368 |

**Required**

**1.** Compute each year's current ratio.

**2.** Express the income statement data in common-size percents.

**3.** Express the balance sheet data in trend percents with 2004 as the base year.

*Analysis Component*

**4.** Comment on any significant relations revealed by the ratios and percents computed.

**Check**   (3) 2006, Total assets trend, 124.34%

Selected comparative financial statements of Sugu Company follow:

**Problem 13-2A**
Calculation and analysis of trend percents

A1  P1

| SUGU COMPANY Comparative Income Statements ($000) For Years Ended December 31, 2006–2000 | | | | | | | |
| --- | --- | --- | --- | --- | --- | --- | --- |
| | **2006** | **2005** | **2004** | **2003** | **2002** | **2001** | **2000** |
| Sales ................. | $1,594 | $1,396 | $1,270 | $1,164 | $1,086 | $1,010 | $828 |
| Cost of goods sold ........ | 1,146 | 932 | 802 | 702 | 652 | 610 | 486 |
| Gross profit ............. | 448 | 464 | 468 | 462 | 434 | 400 | 342 |
| Operating expenses ....... | 340 | 266 | 244 | 180 | 156 | 154 | 128 |
| Net income ............. | $ 108 | $ 198 | $ 224 | $ 282 | $ 278 | $ 246 | $214 |

| SUGU COMPANY Comparative Balance Sheets ($000) December 31, 2006–2000 | | | | | | | |
| --- | --- | --- | --- | --- | --- | --- | --- |
| | **2006** | **2005** | **2004** | **2003** | **2002** | **2001** | **2000** |
| **Assets** | | | | | | | |
| Cash ..................... | $ 68 | $ 88 | $ 92 | $ 94 | $ 98 | $ 96 | $ 99 |
| Accounts receivable, net ........ | 480 | 504 | 456 | 350 | 308 | 292 | 206 |
| Merchandise inventory .......... | 1,738 | 1,264 | 1,104 | 932 | 836 | 710 | 515 |
| Other current assets .......... | 46 | 42 | 24 | 44 | 38 | 38 | 19 |
| Long-term investments ......... | 0 | 0 | 0 | 136 | 136 | 136 | 136 |
| Plant assets, net .............. | 2,120 | 2,114 | 1,852 | 1,044 | 1,078 | 960 | 825 |
| Total assets ................. | $4,452 | $4,012 | $3,528 | $2,600 | $2,494 | $2,232 | $1,800 |
| **Liabilities and Equity** | | | | | | | |
| Current liabilities .............. | $1,120 | $ 942 | $ 618 | $ 514 | $ 446 | $ 422 | $ 272 |
| Long-term liabilities ........... | 1,194 | 1,040 | 1,012 | 470 | 480 | 520 | 390 |
| Common stock .............. | 1,000 | 1,000 | 1,000 | 840 | 840 | 640 | 640 |
| Other contributed capital ....... | 250 | 250 | 250 | 180 | 180 | 160 | 160 |
| Retained earnings ............. | 888 | 780 | 648 | 596 | 548 | 490 | 338 |
| Total liabilities and equity ........ | $4,452 | $4,012 | $3,528 | $2,600 | $2,494 | $2,232 | $1,800 |

**Required**

**Check**   (1) 2006, Total assets trend, 247.3%

**1.** Compute trend percents for all components of both statements using 2000 as the base year.

*Analysis Component*

**2.** Analyze and comment on the financial statements and trend percents from part 1.

---

## Problem 13-3A

Transactions, working capital, and liquidity ratios

P3

mhhe.com/wild3e

**Check**   May 22: Current ratio, 2.12; Acid-test, 1.04

May 29: Current ratio, 1.82; Working capital, $320,000

Park Corporation began the month of May with $650,000 of current assets, a current ratio of 2.50:1, and an acid-test ratio of 1.10:1. During the month, it completed the following transactions (the company uses a perpetual inventory system):

May  2   Purchased $75,000 of merchandise inventory on credit.
     8   Sold merchandise inventory that cost $58,000 for $103,000 cash.
    10   Collected $19,000 cash on an account receivable.
    15   Paid $21,000 cash to settle an account payable.
    17   Wrote off a $3,000 bad debt against the Allowance for Doubtful Accounts account.
    22   Declared a $1 per share cash dividend on the 40,000 shares of outstanding common stock.
    26   Paid the dividend declared on May 22.
    27   Borrowed $75,000 cash by giving the bank a 30-day, 10% note.
    28   Borrowed $90,000 cash by signing a long-term secured note.
    29   Used the $165,000 cash proceeds from the notes to buy new machinery.

**Required**

Prepare a table showing Park's (1) current ratio, (2) acid-test ratio, and (3) working capital after each transaction. Round ratios to hundredths.

---

## Problem 13-4A

Calculation of financial statement ratios

P3

mhhe.com/wild3e

Selected year-end financial statements of McCord Corporation follow. (*Note:* All sales are on credit; selected balance sheet amounts at December 31, 2004, were inventory, $32,400; total assets, $182,400; common stock, $90,000; and retained earnings, $31,300.)

| McCORD CORPORATION Income Statement For Year Ended December 31, 2005 | |
|---|---:|
| Sales | $348,600 |
| Cost of goods sold | 229,150 |
| Gross profit | 119,450 |
| Operating expenses | 52,500 |
| Interest expense | 3,100 |
| Income before taxes | 63,850 |
| Income taxes | 15,800 |
| Net income | $ 48,050 |

| McCORD CORPORATION Balance Sheet December 31, 2005 | | | |
|---|---:|---|---:|
| **Assets** | | **Liabilities and Equity** | |
| Cash | $ 9,000 | Accounts payable | $ 16,500 |
| Short-term investments | 7,400 | Accrued wages payable | 2,200 |
| Accounts receivable, net | 28,200 | Income taxes payable | 2,300 |
| Notes receivable (trade)* | 3,500 | Long-term note payable, secured | |
| Merchandise inventory | 31,150 | by mortgage on plant assets | 62,400 |
| Prepaid expenses | 1,650 | Common stock, $1 par value | 90,000 |
| Plant assets, net | 152,300 | Retained earnings | 59,800 |
| Total assets | $233,200 | Total liabilities and equity | $233,200 |

* These are short-term notes receivable arising from customer (trade) sales.

## Required

Compute the following: (1) current ratio, (2) acid-test ratio, (3) days' sales uncollected, (4) inventory turnover, (5) days' sales in inventory, (6) ratio of pledged assets to secured liabilities, (7) times interest earned, (8) profit margin ratio, (9) total asset turnover, (10) return on total assets, and (11) return on common stockholders' equity.

**Check** Acid-test ratio, 2.3 to 1; Inventory turnover, 7.2

---

Summary information from the financial statements of two companies competing in the same industry follows:

**Problem 13-5A**
Comparative ratio analysis  A1  P3

| | Ryan Company | Priest Company | | Ryan Company | Priest Company |
|---|---|---|---|---|---|
| **Data from the current year-end balance sheets** | | | **Data from the current year's income statement** | | |
| **Assets** | | | Sales ......................... | $660,000 | $780,200 |
| Cash ........................... | $ 18,500 | $ 33,000 | Cost of goods sold ................. | 485,100 | 532,500 |
| Accounts receivable, net ............. | 36,400 | 56,400 | Interest expense ................... | 6,900 | 11,000 |
| Current notes receivable (trade) ....... | 8,100 | 6,200 | Income tax expense ................. | 12,800 | 19,300 |
| Merchandise inventory .............. | 83,440 | 131,500 | Net income ...................... | 67,770 | 105,000 |
| Prepaid expenses .................. | 4,000 | 5,950 | Basic earnings per share ............. | 1.94 | 2.56 |
| Plant assets, net ................... | 284,000 | 303,400 | | | |
| Total assets ...................... | $434,440 | $536,450 | | | |
| | | | **Beginning-of-year balance sheet data** | | |
| **Liabilities and Equity** | | | Accounts receivable, net ............. | $ 28,800 | $ 53,200 |
| Current liabilities .................. | $ 60,340 | $ 92,300 | Current notes receivable (trade) ....... | 0 | 0 |
| Long-term notes payable ............. | 79,800 | 100,000 | Merchandise inventory .............. | 54,600 | 106,400 |
| Common stock, $5 par value .......... | 175,000 | 205,000 | Total assets ...................... | 388,000 | 372,500 |
| Retained earnings ................. | 119,300 | 139,150 | Common stock, $5 par value .......... | 175,000 | 205,000 |
| Total liabilities and equity ........... | $434,440 | $536,450 | Retained earnings ................. | 94,300 | 90,600 |

## Required

1. For both companies compute the (a) current ratio, (b) acid-test ratio, (c) accounts (including notes) receivable turnover, (d) inventory turnover, (e) days' sales in inventory, and (f) days' sales uncollected. Identify the company you consider to be the better short-term credit risk and explain why.

   **Check** (1) Priest: Accounts receivable turnover, 13.5; Inventory turnover, 4.5

2. For both companies compute the (a) profit margin ratio, (b) total asset turnover, (c) return on total assets, and (d) return on common stockholders' equity. Assuming that each company paid cash dividends of $1.50 per share and each company's stock can be purchased at $25 per share, compute their (e) price-earnings ratios and (f) dividend yields. Identify which company's stock you would recommend as the better investment and explain why.

   (2) Ryan: Profit margin, 10.3%; PE, 12.9

---

Selected comparative financial statements of Sawgrass Corporation follow:

## PROBLEM SET B

**Problem 13-1B**
Ratios, common-size statements, and trend percents

P1  P2  P3

| SAWGRASS CORPORATION Comparative Income Statements For Years Ended December 31, 2006, 2005, and 2004 | | | |
|---|---|---|---|
| | 2006 | 2005 | 2004 |
| Sales ..................... | $199,800 | $167,000 | $144,800 |
| Cost of goods sold ........... | 109,890 | 87,175 | 67,200 |
| Gross profit ................ | 89,910 | 79,825 | 77,600 |
| Selling expenses ............. | 23,680 | 20,790 | 19,000 |
| Administrative expenses ....... | 17,760 | 15,610 | 16,700 |
| Total expenses ............. | 41,440 | 36,400 | 35,700 |
| Income before taxes .......... | 48,470 | 43,425 | 41,900 |
| Income taxes ............... | 5,050 | 4,910 | 4,300 |
| Net income ............... | $ 43,420 | $ 38,515 | $ 37,600 |

| SAWGRASS CORPORATION Comparative Balance Sheets December 31, 2006, 2005, and 2004 | | | |
|---|---|---|---|
| | **2006** | **2005** | **2004** |
| **Assets** | | | |
| Current assets .............. | $ 55,860 | $ 33,660 | $ 37,300 |
| Long-term investments ......... | 0 | 2,700 | 11,600 |
| Plant assets, net .............. | 113,810 | 114,660 | 80,000 |
| Total assets ................. | $169,670 | $151,020 | $128,900 |
| **Liabilities and Equity** | | | |
| Current liabilities .............. | $ 23,370 | $ 20,180 | $ 17,500 |
| Common stock .............. | 47,500 | 47,500 | 38,000 |
| Other contributed capital ....... | 14,850 | 14,850 | 12,300 |
| Retained earnings ............ | 83,950 | 68,490 | 61,100 |
| Total liabilities and equity ........ | $169,670 | $151,020 | $128,900 |

**Required**

1. Compute each year's current ratio.

2. Express the income statement data in common-size percents.

**Check**  (3) 2006, Total assets trend, 131.63%

3. Express the balance sheet data in trend percents with 2004 as the base year.

*Analysis Component*

4. Comment on any significant relations revealed by the ratios and percents computed.

---

**Problem 13-2B**

Calculation and analysis of trend percents

A1  P1

Selected comparative financial statements of Deuce Company follow:

| DEUCE COMPANY Comparative Income Statements ($000) For Years Ended December 31, 2006–2000 | | | | | | | |
|---|---|---|---|---|---|---|---|
| | **2006** | **2005** | **2004** | **2003** | **2002** | **2001** | **2000** |
| Sales ................. | $660 | $710 | $730 | $780 | $840 | $870 | $960 |
| Cost of goods sold ........ | 376 | 390 | 394 | 414 | 440 | 450 | 480 |
| Gross profit ............. | 284 | 320 | 336 | 366 | 400 | 420 | 480 |
| Operating expenses ....... | 184 | 204 | 212 | 226 | 240 | 244 | 250 |
| Net income ............. | $100 | $116 | $124 | $140 | $160 | $176 | $230 |

| DEUCE COMPANY Comparative Balance Sheets ($000) December 31, 2006–2000 | | | | | | | |
|---|---|---|---|---|---|---|---|
| | **2006** | **2005** | **2004** | **2003** | **2002** | **2001** | **2000** |
| **Assets** | | | | | | | |
| Cash .................... | $ 34 | $ 36 | $ 42 | $ 44 | $ 50 | $ 52 | $ 58 |
| Accounts receivable, net ........ | 120 | 126 | 130 | 134 | 140 | 144 | 150 |
| Merchandise inventory .......... | 156 | 162 | 168 | 170 | 176 | 180 | 198 |
| Other current assets ........... | 24 | 24 | 26 | 28 | 28 | 30 | 30 |
| Long-term investments ......... | 26 | 20 | 16 | 100 | 100 | 100 | 100 |
| Plant assets, net .............. | 410 | 414 | 420 | 312 | 320 | 328 | 354 |
| Total assets .................. | $770 | $782 | $802 | $788 | $814 | $834 | $890 |
| **Liabilities and Equity** | | | | | | | |
| Current liabilities .............. | $138 | $146 | $176 | $180 | $200 | $250 | $270 |
| Long-term liabilities ............ | 82 | 110 | 132 | 138 | 184 | 204 | 250 |
| Common stock .............. | 150 | 150 | 150 | 150 | 150 | 150 | 150 |
| Other contributed capital ....... | 60 | 60 | 60 | 60 | 60 | 60 | 60 |
| Retained earnings ............. | 340 | 316 | 284 | 260 | 220 | 170 | 160 |
| Total liabilities and equity ........ | $770 | $782 | $802 | $788 | $814 | $834 | $890 |

**Required**

**1.** Compute trend percents for all components of both statements using 2000 as the base year.

*Analysis Component*

**2.** Analyze and comment on the financial statements and trend percents from part 1.

**Check**  (1) 2006, Total assets trend, 86.5%

---

Ready Corporation began the month of June with $280,000 of current assets, a current ratio of 2.80:1, and an acid-test ratio of 1.20:1. During the month, it completed the following transactions (the company uses a perpetual inventory system):

June 1  Sold merchandise inventory that cost $62,000 for $101,000 cash.
     3  Collected $78,000 cash on an account receivable.
     5  Purchased $130,000 of merchandise inventory on credit.
     7  Borrowed $90,000 cash by giving the bank a 60-day, 10% note.
    10  Borrowed $180,000 cash by signing a long-term secured note.
    12  Purchased machinery for $280,000 cash.
    15  Declared a $1 per share cash dividend on the 60,000 shares of outstanding common stock.
    19  Wrote off a $7,000 bad debt against the Allowance for Doubtful Accounts account.
    22  Paid $11,000 cash to settle an account payable.
    30  Paid the dividend declared on June 15.

**Problem 13-3B**
Transactions, working capital, and liquidity ratios

P3

**Check**  June 1: Current ratio, 3.19; Acid-test, 2.21

June 30: Working capital, $59,000; Current ratio, 1.19

**Required**

Prepare a table showing the company's (1) current ratio, (2) acid-test ratio, and (3) working capital after each transaction. Round ratios to hundredths.

---

Selected year-end financial statements of Overland Corporation follow. (*Note:* All sales are on credit; selected balance sheet amounts at December 31, 2004, were inventory, $16,400; total assets, $95,900; common stock, $41,500; and retained earnings, $19,800.)

**Problem 13-4B**
Calculation of financial statement ratios

P3

| OVERLAND CORPORATION |
| :-- |
| **Income Statement** |
| **For Year Ended December 31, 2005** |

| | |
| :-- | --: |
| Sales | $215,500 |
| Cost of goods sold | 136,100 |
| Gross profit | 79,400 |
| Operating expenses | 50,200 |
| Interest expense | 1,200 |
| Income before taxes | 28,000 |
| Income taxes | 2,200 |
| Net Income | $ 25,800 |

| OVERLAND CORPORATION |
| :-- |
| **Balance Sheet** |
| **December 31, 2005** |

| Assets | | Liabilities and Equity | |
| :-- | --: | :-- | --: |
| Cash | $ 5,100 | Accounts payable | $ 10,500 |
| Short-term investments | 5,900 | Accrued wages payable | 2,300 |
| Accounts receivable, net | 11,100 | Income taxes payable | 1,600 |
| Notes receivable (trade)* | 2,000 | Long-term note payable, secured | |
| Merchandise inventory | 12,500 | by mortgage on plant assets | 25,000 |
| Prepaid expenses | 1,000 | Common stock, $5 par value | 41,000 |
| Plant assets, net | 72,900 | Retained earnings | 30,100 |
| Total assets | $110,500 | Total liabilities and equity | $110,500 |

* These are short-term notes receivable arising from customer (trade) sales.

**Required**

Compute the following: (1) current ratio, (2) acid-test ratio, (3) days' sales uncollected, (4) inventory turnover, (5) days' sales in inventory, (6) ratio of pledged assets to secured liabilities, (7) times interest earned, (8) profit margin ratio, (9) total asset turnover, (10) return on total assets, and (11) return on common stockholders' equity.

**Check**  Acid-test ratio, 1.7 to 1; Inventory turnover, 9.4

## Problem 13-5B

Comparative
ratio analysis    A1   P3

Summary information from the financial statements of two companies competing in the same industry follows:

| | Loud Company | Clear Company | | Loud Company | Clear Company |
|---|---|---|---|---|---|
| **Data from the current year-end balance sheets** | | | **Data from the current year's income statement** | | |
| **Assets** | | | Sales .......................... | $395,600 | $669,500 |
| Cash .......................... | $ 22,000 | $ 38,500 | Cost of goods sold ................ | 292,600 | 482,000 |
| Accounts receivable, net ............ | 79,100 | 72,500 | Interest expense .................. | 7,900 | 12,400 |
| Current notes receivable (trade) ....... | 13,600 | 11,000 | Income tax expense ................ | 7,700 | 14,300 |
| Merchandise inventory ............... | 88,800 | 84,000 | Net income ....................... | 35,850 | 63,700 |
| Prepaid expenses .................. | 11,700 | 12,100 | Basic earnings per share ............. | 1.33 | 2.23 |
| Plant assets, net ................... | 178,900 | 254,300 | | | |
| Total assets ..................... | $394,100 | $472,400 | | | |
| | | | **Beginning-of-year balance sheet data** | | |
| **Liabilities and Equity** | | | Accounts receivable, net .............. | $ 74,200 | $ 75,300 |
| Current liabilities .................. | $ 92,500 | $ 99,000 | Current notes receivable (trade) ........ | 0 | 0 |
| Long-term notes payable ............. | 95,000 | 95,300 | Merchandise inventory ............... | 107,100 | 82,500 |
| Common stock, $5 par value .......... | 135,000 | 143,000 | Total assets ..................... | 385,400 | 445,000 |
| Retained earnings ................. | 71,600 | 135,100 | Common stock, $5 par value .......... | 135,000 | 143,000 |
| Total liabilities and equity ............. | $394,100 | $472,400 | Retained earnings ................. | 51,100 | 111,700 |

**Required**

1. For both companies compute the (*a*) current ratio, (*b*) acid-test ratio, (*c*) accounts (including notes) receivable turnover, (*d*) inventory turnover, (*e*) days' sales in inventory, and (*f*) days' sales uncollected. Identify the company you consider to be the better short-term credit risk and explain why.

2. For both companies compute the (*a*) profit margin ratio, (*b*) total asset turnover, (*c*) return on total assets, and (*d*) return on common stockholders' equity. Assuming that each company paid cash dividends of $3.00 per share and each company's stock can be purchased at $25 per share, compute their (*e*) price-earnings ratios and (*f*) dividend yields. Identify which company's stock you would recommend as the better investment and explain why.

## PROBLEM SET C

Problem Set C is available at the book's Website to reinforce and assess your learning.

## SERIAL PROBLEM

Success Systems

*(This serial problem began in Chapter 1 and continues through most of the book. If previous chapter segments were not completed, the serial problem can begin at this point. It is helpful, but not necessary, for you to use the Working Papers that accompany the book.)*

Use the following selected data from Success Systems's income statement for the three months ended March 31, 2005, and from its March 31, 2005, balance sheet to complete the requirements below: computer services revenue, $25,160; net (goods) sales, $18,693; total revenue, $43,853; cost of goods sold, $14,052; net income, $18,686; quick assets, $100,565; current assets, $105,209; total assets, $129,909; current liabilities, $20,875; total liabilities, $20,875; and total equity, $109,034.

**Required**

1. Compute the gross margin ratio (both with and without services revenue) and net profit margin ratio.
2. Compute the current ratio and acid-test ratio.
3. Compute the debt ratio and equity ratio.
4. What percent of its assets are current? What percent are long term?

**BTN 13-1**   Refer to **Krispy Kreme**'s financial statements in Appendix A to answer the following:

1. Using 2001 as the base year, compute trend percents for 2001, 2002, and 2003 for revenues, operating expenses (cost of sales), general and administrative expenses, income taxes, and net income. (Round to the nearest whole percent.)

2. Compute common-size percents for 2003 and 2002 for the following categories of assets: (*a*) total current assets, (*b*) property and equipment, net, (*c*) intangible assets, and (*d*) accrued expenses. (Round to the nearest tenth of a percent.)

3. Comment on any significant changes across the years for the income statement trends computed in part 1 and the balance sheet percents computed in part 2.

*Roll On*

4. Access Krispy Kreme's financial statements for fiscal years ending after February 2, 2003, from Krispy Kreme's Website (**KrispyKreme.com**) or the SEC database (**www.SEC.gov**). Update your work for parts 1, 2, and 3 using the new information accessed.

**REPORTING IN ACTION**

A1  P1  P2

---

**BTN 13-2**   Key comparative figures ($ thousands) for both **Krispy Kreme** and **Tastykake** follow:

| Key Figures | Krispy Kreme | Tastykake |
|---|---|---|
| Cash and equivalents | $ 32,203 | $    282 |
| Accounts receivable, net | 34,373 | 20,882 |
| Inventories | 24,365 | 6,777 |
| Retained earnings | 102,403 | 26,622 |
| Operating expenses (Krispy Kreme) | 381,489 | — |
| Costs of sales (Tastykake) | — | 111,187 |
| Revenues (Krispy Kreme) | 491,549 | — |
| Net sales (Tastykake) | — | 162,263 |
| Total assets | 410,487 | 116,560 |

**COMPARATIVE ANALYSIS**

C3  P2

**Required**

1. Compute common-size percents for both companies using the data provided.
2. Which company retains a higher portion of cumulative net income in the company?
3. Which company has a higher gross margin ratio on sales?
4. Which company holds a higher percent of its total assets as inventory?

---

**BTN 13-3**   As Beacon Company controller, you are responsible for informing the board of directors about its financial activities. At the board meeting, you present the following:

**ETHICS CHALLENGE**

A1

| | 2006 | 2005 | 2004 |
|---|---|---|---|
| Sales trend percent | 147.0% | 135.0% | 100.0% |
| Selling expenses to sales | 10.1% | 14.0% | 15.6% |
| Sales to plant assets ratio | 3.8 to 1 | 3.6 to 1 | 3.3 to 1 |
| Current ratio | 2.9 to 1 | 2.7 to 1 | 2.4 to 1 |
| Acid-test ratio | 1.1 to 1 | 1.4 to 1 | 1.5 to 1 |
| Inventory turnover | 7.8 times | 9.0 times | 10.2 times |
| Accounts receivable turnover | 7.0 times | 7.7 times | 8.5 times |
| Total asset turnover | 2.9 times | 2.9 times | 3.3 times |
| Return on total assets | 10.4% | 11.0% | 13.2% |
| Return on stockholders' equity | 10.7% | 11.5% | 14.1% |
| Profit margin ratio | 3.6% | 3.8% | 4.0% |

After the meeting, the company's CEO holds a press conference with analysts in which she mentions these ratios:

|  | 2006 | 2005 | 2004 |
|---|---|---|---|
| Sales trend percent . . . . . . . . . . . . | 147.0% | 135.0% | 100.0% |
| Selling expenses to sales . . . . . . . . | 10.1% | 14.0% | 15.6% |
| Sales to plant assets ratio . . . . . . . . | 3.8 to 1 | 3.6 to 1 | 3.3 to 1 |
| Current ratio . . . . . . . . . . . . . . . | 2.9 to 1 | 2.7 to 1 | 2.4 to 1 |

**Required**

**1.** Why do you think the CEO decided to report 4 ratios instead of the 11 prepared?

**2.** Comment on the possible consequences of the CEO's reporting of the ratios.

## COMMUNICATING IN PRACTICE

C2  A1  P3

**BTN 13-4**   Each team is to select a different industry, and each team member is to select a different company in that industry and acquire its financial statements. Use those statements to analyze the company, including at least one ratio from each of the four building blocks of analysis. When necessary, use the financial press to determine the market price of its stock. Communicate with teammates via a meeting, e-mail, or telephone to discuss how different companies compare to each other and to industry norms. The team is to prepare a single one-page memorandum reporting on its analysis and the conclusions reached.

## TAKING IT TO THE NET

C4  P3

mhhe.com/wild3e

**BTN 13-5**   Access the March 21, 2003, filing of the 2002 10-K report of **Yahoo! Inc.** (ticker YHOO) at **www.sec.gov** to complete the following requirements.

**Required**

Compute or locate the following profitability ratios of Yahoo! for its fiscal years ending December 31, 2002 *and* 2001. Interpret its profitability using these ratio results.

**1.** Profit margin ratio

**2.** Gross profit ratio

**3.** Return on total assets (*Note:* Total assets in 2000 were $2,269,576,000.)

**4.** Return on common stockholders' equity (*Note:* Total shareholders' equity in 2000 was $1,896,914,000.)

**5.** Basic earnings per share

## TEAMWORK IN ACTION

C2  P1  P2  P3

**BTN 13-6**   A team approach to learning financial statement analysis is often useful.

**Required**

**1.** Each team should write a description of horizontal and vertical analysis that all team members agree with and understand. Illustrate each description with an example.

**2.** *Each* member of the team is to select *one* of the following categories of ratio analysis. Explain what the ratios in that category measure. Choose one ratio from the category selected, present its formula, and explain what it measures.

   **a.** Liquidity and efficiency    **c.** Profitability

   **b.** Solvency    **d.** Market prospects

**3.** Each team member is to present his or her notes from part 2 to teammates. Team members are to confirm or correct other teammates' presentation.

**Hint:** Pairing within teams may be necessary for part 2. Use as an in-class activity or as an assignment. Consider presentations to the entire class using team rotation with transparencies.

## BUSINESS WEEK ACTIVITY

C1  C4

mhhe.com/wild3e

**BTN 13-7**   Read the article "Eyes Peeled for Those 'Big Red Flags'" in the September 24, 2002, issue of *Business Week*. (The book's Website provides a free link.)

**Required**

**1.** What does it mean to short sell a stock?

**2.** What strategies for short selling does Tom Taulli (the interviewee) advise?

**3.** What items does Taulli pay particular attention to on the balance sheet of a company that he might short sell?

**4.** If you are 100% correct in your financial analysis of a stock, are you guaranteed to make money short selling?

**5.** Does Taulli find the PE ratio very valuable as a factor to consider when shorting stocks?

---

**BTN 13-8**   Assume that David and Tom Gardner of **The Motley Fool** (**Fool.com**) have impressed you since you first heard of their rather improbable rise to prominence in financial circles. You learn of a staff opening at The Motley Fool and decide to apply for it. Your resume is successfully screened from the thousands received and you advance to the interview process. You learn that the interview consists of analyzing the following financial facts and answering analysis questions. (*Note:* The data are taken from a small merchandiser in outdoor recreational equipment.)

**ENTREPRENEURIAL DECISION**

A1  P1  P2  P3

|                                      | 2005      | 2004      | 2003      |
|--------------------------------------|-----------|-----------|-----------|
| Sales trend percents                 | 137.0%    | 125.0%    | 100.0%    |
| Selling expenses to sales            | 9.8%      | 13.7%     | 15.3%     |
| Sales to plant assets ratio          | 3.5 to 1  | 3.3 to 1  | 3.0 to 1  |
| Current ratio                        | 2.6 to 1  | 2.4 to 1  | 2.1 to 1  |
| Acid-test ratio                      | 0.8 to 1  | 1.1 to 1  | 1.2 to 1  |
| Merchandise inventory turnover       | 7.5 times | 8.7 times | 9.9 times |
| Accounts receivable turnover         | 6.7 times | 7.4 times | 8.2 times |
| Total asset turnover                 | 2.6 times | 2.6 times | 3.0 times |
| Return on total assets               | 8.8%      | 9.4%      | 11.1%     |
| Return on equity                     | 9.75%     | 11.50%    | 12.25%    |
| Profit margin ratio                  | 3.3%      | 3.5%      | 3.7%      |

**Required**

Use these data to answer each of the following questions with explanations:

**1.** Is it becoming easier for the company to meet its current liabilities on time and to take advantage of any available cash discounts?

**2.** Is the company collecting its accounts receivable more rapidly?

**3.** Is the company's investment in accounts receivable decreasing?

**4.** Is the company's investment in plant assets increasing?

**5.** Is the owner's investment becoming more profitable?

**6.** Did the dollar amount of selling expenses decrease during the three-year period?

---

**BTN 13-9**   You are to devise an investment strategy to enable you to accumulate $1,000,000 by age 65. Start by making some assumptions about your salary. Next compute the percent of your salary that you will be able to save each year. If you will receive any lump-sum monies, include those amounts in your calculations. Historically, stocks have delivered average annual returns of 10–11%. Given this history, you should probably not assume that you will earn above 10% on the money you invest. It is not necessary to specify exactly what types of assets you will buy for your investments; just assume a rate you expect to earn. Use the future value tables in Appendix B to calculate how your savings will grow. Experiment a bit with your figures to see how much less you have to save if you start at, for example, age 25 versus age 35 or 40. (For this assignment, do not include inflation in your calculations.)

**HITTING THE ROAD**

C1  P3

---

**BTN 13-10**   **Krispy Kreme**, **Tastykake**, and **Grupo Bimbo** are competitors in the global market-place. Visit the Grupo Bimbo Website (**GrupoBimbo.com**) and access its most recent annual report.

**GLOBAL DECISION**

A1

**Required**

Review Grupo Bimbo's Website and skim through its annual report. Compare its annual report to one of its U.S. competitor's reports (Krispy Kreme or Tastykake) presented in Appendix A. Identify five ways that the Mexican company's report or its Website differs from that of its U.S. competitors.

*"I wanted to have a chip company that kids from the hood could relate to"*—James Lindsay

# 14

# Managerial Accounting Concepts and Principles

## A Look Back

Chapter 13 described the analysis and interpretation of financial statement information. We applied horizontal, vertical, and ratio analyses to better understand company performance and financial condition.

## A Look at This Chapter

We begin our study of managerial accounting by explaining its purpose and describing its major characteristics. We also discuss cost concepts and describe how they help managers to gather and organize information they need for making decisions. The reporting of manufacturing activities is also discussed.

## A Look Ahead

Chapters 15 through 21 discuss information that managers need to make informed decisions and how they obtain that information. We explain the types of decisions managers must make and how managerial accounting helps with these decisions. The first of these chapters, Chapter 15, considers how we measure costs assigned to certain types of processes.

# CAP

## Conceptual

**C1** Explain the purpose of managerial accounting. *(p. 580)*

**C2** Describe major characteristics of managerial accounting. *(p. 581)*

**C3** Describe the lean business model. *(p. 583)*

**C4** Describe accounting concepts useful in classifying costs. *(p. 585)*

**C5** Define product and period costs and explain how they impact financial statements. *(p. 586)*

**C6** Explain how the balance sheets for manufacturing and merchandising companies differ. *(p. 588)*

**C7** Explain how income statements for manufacturing and merchandising companies differ. *(p. 589)*

**C8** Explain manufacturing activities and the flow of manufacturing costs. *(p. 592)*

## Analytical

**A1** Compute unit contribution margin and describe what it reveals about a company's cost structure. *(p. 595)*

## Procedural

**P1** Compute cost of goods sold for a manufacturer. *(p. 590)*

**P2** Prepare a manufacturing statement and explain its purpose and links to financial statements. *(p. 593)*

---

## Decision Feature

# Rap Snacks for Hip-Hop Kids

PHILADELPHIA—James "Fly" Lindsay and his three sisters were raised by their mother in North Philadelphia. "We were poor," says Lindsay, "but we were rich in the values that she set forth." One of those values was education—Lindsay was the first in his family to attend college—and another was the commitment to community. "You have everyone taking away, but you have to give back," says Lindsay. He especially saw the dollars spent on food yet noted "that dollar is not going back into our communities."

Lindsay decided to take matters into his own hands. With $40,000 collected from family and friends, he launched **Rap Snacks [RapSnacks.com]**, a maker of snack foods. In the beginning, its snacks featured "M.C. Potato," a cartoon spud wearing a backward baseball cap—but nothing to distinguish them from similar snack foods. With a renewed "customer orientation" and first-hand knowledge of urban youth, Lindsay altered his packaging. He decided to sell his snacks with rappers on the wrappers to target urban youth immersed in hip-hop culture. The wrappers, importantly, were designed to instill a craving for success, commitment, and entrepreneurship, says Lindsay. The snack wrappers featured hip-hop artists such as

Warren G, Lil' Romeo, and Big Tymers paired with positive messages telling buyers to "respect yourself" and "stay in school."

Rap Snacks also promoted an entrepreneurial training program for urban youth. Lindsay says that urban youth need to learn about business and how it can help a community. Basic managerial principles and concepts, product and period costs, unit contribution margin, and manufacturing statements are like another language to most urban youth. Lindsay struggles to change that and more. "You can make money," says Lindsay, "but also have a social responsibility to where you came from." Investing in urban youth is a priority, says Lindsay. Specifically, he wants to convey the knowledge of managerial principles and concepts and the belief that urban youth can be successful. Understanding manufacturing activities and cost flows is not easy, says Lindsay, but the costs of not understanding are more severe. "It feels good to make a difference," says Lindsay, "and set an example for the kids."

[Sources: *Rap Snacks Website*, January 2004; *Entrepreneur*, July 2003; *Philadelphia Inquirer*, October 2002; *Gannett News Service*, January 2003; *Source*, June 2001; *Maxim*, March 2002.]

Managerial accounting, like financial accounting, provides information to help users make better decisions. However, managerial accounting and financial accounting differ in important ways, which this chapter explains. This chapter also compares the accounting and reporting practices used by manufacturing and merchandising companies. Both types of companies earn revenues by selling products. A merchandising company sells products without changing their condition. A manufacturing

company buys raw materials and turns them into finished products for sale to customers. A service company earns revenues by providing services rather than products. The skills, tools, and techniques developed for measuring a manufacturing company's activities apply to service companies as well. The chapter concludes by explaining the flow of manufacturing activities and preparing the manufacturing statement.

**Managerial Accounting Concepts and Principles**

**Managerial Accounting Basics**
- Purpose of managerial accounting
- Nature of managerial accounting
- Managerial decision making
- Focus on managerial accounting

**Managerial Cost Concepts**
- Types of cost classifications
- Identification of cost classifications
- Cost concepts for service companies

**Reporting Manufacturing Activities**
- Balance sheet
- Income statement
- Flow of activities
- Manufacturing statement

# Managerial Accounting Basics

The previous chapters focused on a financial accounting system whose main purpose is to prepare general-purpose financial statements. However, this information is incomplete for internal decision makers who manage organizations. For this purpose, a managerial accounting system is required. **Managerial accounting** is an activity that provides financial and nonfinancial information to an organization's managers and other internal decision makers. This section explains the purpose of managerial accounting (also called *management accounting*) and compares it with financial accounting.

## Purpose of Managerial Accounting

**C1** Explain the purpose of managerial accounting.

The purpose of both managerial accounting and financial accounting is providing useful information to decision makers. They do this by collecting, managing, and reporting information in demand by their users. Both areas of accounting also share the common practice of reporting monetary information; although managerial accounting includes the reporting of nonmonetary information. They even report some of the same information. For instance, a company's financial statements contain information useful for both its managers (insiders) and other persons interested in the company (outsiders).

The remainder of this book looks carefully at managerial accounting information, how accounting professionals gather it, and how managers use it. We consider the concepts and procedures used to determine the costs of products and services as well as topics such as budgeting, break-even analysis, product costing, profit planning, and cost analysis. Information about the costs of products and services is important for many decisions that managers make. These decisions include predicting the future costs of a product or service. Predicted costs are used in product pricing, profitability analysis, and in deciding whether to make or buy a product or component. More generally, much of managerial accounting involves gathering information about costs for planning and control decisions.

**Planning** is the process of setting goals and making plans to achieve them. Companies formulate long-term strategic plans that usually span a 5- to 10-year horizon and then refine them with medium-term and short-term plans. Strategic plans usually set a firm's long-term direction by developing a road map for the future based on potential opportunities such as new products, new markets, and capital investments. A strategic plan's goals and objectives are often broadly defined given its long-term orientation. Medium- and short-term plans are more operational in nature. They translate the strategic plan into actions. These plans are more concrete and consist of better defined objectives and goals. A short-term plan often covers a one-year period that, when translated in monetary terms, is known as a budget (see Chapter 19).

**Control** is the process of monitoring planning decisions and evaluating an organization's activities and employees. It includes the measurement and evaluation of actions, processes, and outcomes. Feedback provided by the control function allows managers to revise their plans. Measurement of actions and processes also allows managers to take corrective actions to avoid undesirable outcomes. For example, managers periodically compare actual results with planned results using a process called *variance analysis* (see Chapter 20). Exhibit 14.1 portrays the important management functions of planning and control.

**Point:** Costs are important to managers because they impact both the financial position and profitability of a business. Managerial accounting assists in analysis, planning, and control of costs.

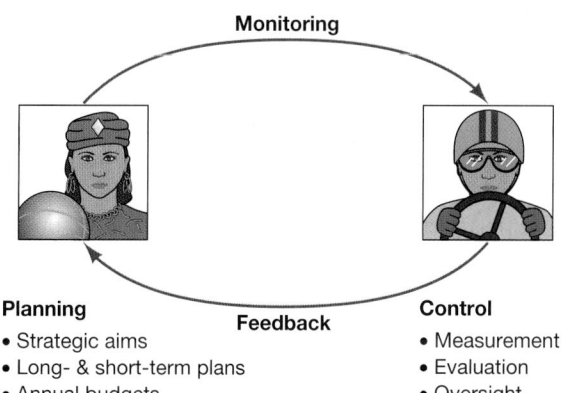

**Exhibit 14.1**

Planning and Control

Managers use information, including that of costs, to plan and control business activities. In later chapters, we explain how managers also use this information to direct and improve business operations.

## Nature of Managerial Accounting

Managerial accounting has its own special characteristics. To understand these characteristics, we compare managerial accounting to financial accounting; they differ in at least seven important ways. These differences are summarized in Exhibit 14.2. This section discusses each of these characteristics.

**C2** Describe major characteristics of managerial accounting.

**Exhibit 14.2**

Major Differences between Managerial Accounting and Financial Accounting

| | Financial Accounting | Managerial Accounting |
|---|---|---|
| 1. Users and decision makers | Investors, creditors, and other users external to the organization | Managers, employees, and decision makers internal to the organization |
| 2. Purpose of information | Assist external users in making investment, credit, and other decisions | Assist managers in making planning and control decisions |
| 3. Flexibility of practice | Structured and often controlled by GAAP | Relatively flexible (no GAAP) |
| 4. Timeliness of information | Often available only after an audit is complete | Available quickly without the need to wait for an audit |
| 5. Time dimension | Historical information with some predictions | Many projections and estimates; historical information also presented |
| 6. Focus of information | Emphasis on whole organization | Emphasis on an organization's projects, processes, and subdivisions |
| 7. Nature of information | Monetary information | Mostly monetary; but also nonmonetary information |

**Point:** It is desirable to accumulate information for management reports in a database separate from financial accounting records.

**Users and Decision Makers** Companies accumulate, process, and report financial accounting and managerial accounting information for different groups of decision makers. Financial accounting information is primarily provided to external users including investors, creditors, analysts, and regulators. External users rarely have a major role in managing a company's daily activities. Managerial accounting information is primarily provided to internal users who are responsible for making and implementing decisions about a company's business activities.

**Purpose of Information** Investors, creditors, and other external users of financial accounting information must often decide whether to invest in or lend to a company. If they have already done so, they must decide whether to continue owning the company or carrying the loan. Internal decision makers must plan a company's future. They seek to take advantage of opportunities or to overcome obstacles. They also try to control activities and ensure their effective and efficient implementation. Managerial accounting information helps these internal users make both planning and control decisions.

**Point:** The *Institute of Management Accountants* issues statements that govern the practice of managerial accounting. Accountants who pass a qualifying exam are awarded the CMA.

**Flexibility of Practice** External users compare companies by using financial reports and need protection against false or misleading information. Accordingly, financial accounting relies on accepted principles that are enforced through an extensive set of rules and guidelines, or GAAP. Internal users need managerial accounting information for planning and controlling their company's activities rather than for external comparisons. They require different types of information depending on the activity. This makes standardizing managerial accounting systems across companies difficult. Instead, managerial accounting systems are flexible. The design of a company's managerial accounting system largely depends on the nature of the business and the arrangement of its internal operations. Managers can decide for themselves what information they want and how they want it reported. Even within a single company, different managers often design their own systems to meet their special needs. This flexibility allows managers to modify their systems quickly in response to changes in the environment. The important question a manager must ask is whether the information being collected and reported is useful for planning, decision-making, and control purposes.

**Point:** Financial statements are usually issued several weeks after the period-end. GAAP requires the reporting of important events that occur while the statements are being prepared. These events are called *subsequent events*.

**Point:** Independent auditors test the integrity of managerial accounting records when they are used in preparing financial statements.

**Timeliness of Information** Formal financial statements reporting past transactions and events are not immediately available to outside parties. Independent certified public accountants often must *audit* a company's financial statements before it provides them to external users. Thus, because audits often take several weeks to complete, financial reports to outsiders usually are not available until well after the period-end. However, managers can quickly obtain managerial accounting information. External auditors need not review it. Estimates and projections are acceptable. To get information quickly, managers often accept less precision in reports. As an example, an early internal report to management prepared right after the year-end could report net income for the year between $4.2 and $4.8 million. An audited income statement could later show net income for the year at $4.6 million. The internal report is not precise, but its information can be more useful because it is available earlier.

*Internal auditing* plays an important role in managerial accounting. Internal auditors evaluate the flow of information not only inside but also outside the company. Managers are responsible for preventing and detecting fraudulent activities in their companies.

**Time Dimension** To protect external users from false expectations, financial reports deal primarily with results of both past activities and current conditions. While some predictions such as service lives and salvage values of plant assets

---

### Decision Ethics

**Production Supervisor** You invite three friends to a restaurant. When the dinner check arrives, David, a self-employed entrepreneur, picks it up saying, "Here, let me pay. I'll deduct it as a business expense on my tax return. It won't cost me as much." Denise, a salesperson, takes the check from David's hand and says, "I'll put this on my company's credit card. It won't cost us anything." Derek, a factory manager for a company, laughs and says, "Neither of you understands. I'll put this on my company's credit card and call it overhead on a cost-plus contract my company has with the government." (*A cost-plus contract means the company receives its costs plus a percent of those costs.*) Adds Derek, "That way, my company pays for dinner *and* makes a profit." Who should pay the bill?

Answer—p. 601

are necessary, financial accounting avoids predictions whenever possible. Managerial accounting regularly includes predictions of conditions and events. As an example, one important managerial accounting report is a budget, which predicts revenues, expenses, and other items. If managerial accounting reports were restricted to the past and present, managers would be less able to plan activities and less effective in managing and evaluating current activities.

**Focus of Information** Companies often organize into divisions and departments, but investors rarely can buy shares in one division or department. Nor do creditors lend money to a company's single division or department. Instead, they own shares in or make loans to the entire company. Financial accounting focuses primarily on a company as a whole as depicted in Exhibit 14.3. The focus of managerial accounting is different. While top-level managers are responsible for managing the whole company, most other managers are responsible for much smaller sets of activities. These middle-level and lower-level managers need managerial accounting reports dealing with specific activities, projects, and subdivisions for which they are responsible. For instance, division sales managers are directly responsible only for the results achieved in their divisions. Accordingly, division sales managers need information about results achieved in their own divisions to improve their performance. This information includes the level of success achieved by each individual or department in each division as depicted in Exhibit 14.4.

**Nature of Information** Both financial and managerial accounting systems report monetary information. Managerial accounting systems also report considerable nonmonetary information. Monetary information is an important part of managerial decisions, and nonmonetary information plays a crucial role, especially when monetary effects are difficult to measure. Common examples of nonmonetary information are the quality and delivery criteria of purchasing decisions.

**Exhibit 14.3**

Focus of External Reports

**Exhibit 14.4**

Focus of Internal Reports

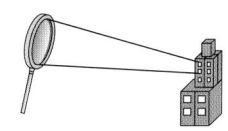

**Point:** To apply these concepts, work QS 14-2.

## Managerial Decision Making

The previous section emphasized differences between financial and managerial accounting, but they are not entirely separate. Similar information is useful to both external and internal users. For instance, information about costs of manufacturing products is useful to all users in making decisions. Also, both financial and managerial accounting affect peoples' actions. For example, **Harley-Davidson**'s design of a sales compensation plan affects the behavior of its salesforce. It also must estimate the dual effects of promotion and sales compensation plans on buying patterns of customers. These estimates impact the equipment purchase decisions for manufacturing and can affect the supplier selection criteria established by purchasing. Thus, financial and managerial accounting systems do more than measure; they also affect people's decisions and actions.

> **Decision Maker**
>
> **Division Manager** At a recent managers' meeting, you are asked to explore the manufacturing of a component that your division has been purchasing from an outside supplier for several years. What information do you collect to evaluate these two alternative sources?
>
> Answer—p. 601

## Focus on Managerial Accounting

We have explained the importance of managerial accounting for internal decision making. Although the analytical tools and techniques of managerial accounting have always been useful, their relevance and importance continue to increase. This is so because of changes in the business environment. This section describes some of these changes and their impact on managerial accounting.

**C3** Describe the lean business model.

**Lean Business Model** Two important factors have encouraged companies to be more effective and efficient in running their operations. First, there is an increased emphasis on *customers* as the most important constituent of a business. Customers expect to derive a certain value for the money they spend to buy products and services. Specifically, they expect that their suppliers will offer them the right service (or product) at the right time and the right price. This implies that companies accept the notion of **customer orientation,** which means that employees understand the changing needs and wants of their customers and align their management and operating practices accordingly.

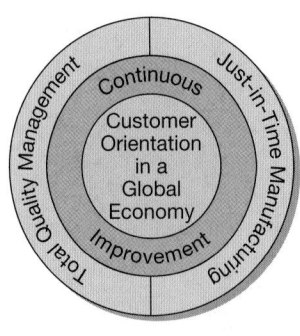

Second, our *global economy* expands competitive boundaries, thereby providing customers more choices. The global economy also produces changes in business activities. One notable case that reflects these changes in customer demand and global competition is auto manufacturing. The top three Japanese auto manufacturers (**Honda, Nissan,** and **Toyota**) once controlled more than 40% of the U.S. auto market. Customers perceived that Japanese auto manufacturers provided value not available from other manufacturers. Many European and North American auto manufacturers responded to this challenge and regained much of the lost market share.

Companies must be alert to these and other factors. Many companies have responded by adopting the **lean business model,** whose goal is to *eliminate waste* while "satisfying the customer" and "providing a positive return" to the company.

**Point:** Many industries, in addition to the automobile industry, can benefit from a JIT system.

**Lean Practices**   **Continuous improvement** rejects the notions of "good enough" or "acceptable" and challenges employees and managers to continuously experiment with new and improved business practices. This has led companies to adopt practices such as total quality management (TQM) and just-in-time (JIT) manufacturing. The philosophy underlying both practices is continuous improvement; the difference is in the focus.

**Point:** Goals of a TQM process include reduced waste, better inventory control, fewer defects, and continuous improvement. Just-in-time concepts have similar goals.

**Total quality management** focuses on quality improvement and applies this standard to all aspects of business activities. In doing so, managers and employees seek to uncover waste in business activities including accounting activities such as payroll and disbursements. To encourage an emphasis on quality, the U.S. Congress established the Malcolm Baldridge National Quality Award (MBQNA). Entrants must conduct a thorough analysis and evaluation of their business using guidelines from the Baldrige committee. **Ritz Carlton Hotel Company, L.L.C** is a recent recipient of the Baldrige award in the service category. The company applies a core set of values, collectively called *The Gold Standards,* to improve customer service.

**Point:** The time between buying raw materials and selling the finished goods is called *throughput time.*

**Just-in-time manufacturing** is a system that acquires inventory and produces only when needed. An important aspect of JIT is that companies manufacture products only after they receive an order (a *demand-pull* system) and then deliver the customer's requirements on time. This means that processes must be aligned to eliminate any delays and inefficiencies including inferior inputs and outputs. Companies must also establish good relations and communications with their suppliers. On the downside, JIT is more susceptible to disruption than tra-

### Decision Insight

**Global Lean**   Toyota Motor Corporation in Japan pioneered lean manufacturing, and it has since spread to other manufacturers throughout the world. The goals include improvements in quality, reliability, inventory turnover, productivity, exports, and—above all—sales and income.

ditional systems. As one recent example, several **General Motors** plants were temporarily shut down due to a strike at an assembly division; the plants supplied components *just in time* to the assembly division.

**Implications for Managerial Accounting**   Adopting the lean business model can be challenging because to foster its implementation, all systems and procedures that a company follows must be realigned. Managerial accounting has an important role to play by providing accurate cost and performance information. Companies must understand the nature and sources of cost and must develop systems that capture costs accurately. Developing such a system is important to measuring the "value" provided to customers. The price that customers pay for acquiring goods and services is an important determinant of value. In turn, the costs a company incurs are key determinants of price. All else being equal, the better a company is at controlling its costs, the better its performance.

### Decision Insight

**Balanced Scorecard**   The *balanced scorecard* aids continuous improvement by augmenting financial measures with information on the "drivers" (indicators) of future financial performance along four dimensions: (1) *financial*—profitability and risk, (2) *customer*—value creation and product and service differentiation, (3) *internal business processes*—businesses activities that create customer and owner satisfaction, and (4) *learning and growth*—organizational change, innovation, and growth.

Answers—p. 601

# Managerial Cost Concepts

## Types of Cost Classifications

An organization incurs many different types of costs that are classified differently, depending on management needs (different costs for different purposes). Specifically, we can classify costs on the basis of their (1) behavior, (2) traceability, (3) controllability, (4) relevance, and (5) function. This section explains each concept for assigning costs to products and services.

**C4** Describe accounting concepts useful in classifying costs.

**Classification by Behavior**    At a basic level, a cost can be classified as fixed or variable. A **fixed cost** does not change with changes in the volume of activity (within a range of activity known as an activity's *relevant range*). For example, straight-line depreciation on equipment is a fixed cost. A **variable cost** changes in proportion to changes in the volume of activity. Sales commissions computed as a percent of sales revenue are variable costs. Additional examples of fixed and variable costs for a bike manufacturer are provided in Exhibit 14.5. When cost items are combined, total cost can be fixed, variable, or mixed. *Mixed* refers to a combination of fixed and variable costs. Equipment rental often includes a fixed cost for some minimum amount and a variable cost based on amount of usage. Classification of costs by behavior is helpful in cost-volume-profit analyses and short-term decision making. We discuss these in Chapters 18 and 21.

Topic Tackler 14-1

## Exhibit 14.5
Fixed and Variable Costs

**Fixed Cost:** Rent for Rocky Mountain Bikes' building is $22,000, and doesn't change with the number of bikes produced.

**Variable Cost:** Cost of bicycle tires is variable with the number of bikes produced—this cost is $15 per pair.

**Classification by Traceability**    A cost is often traced to a **cost object,** which is a product, process, department, or customer to which costs are assigned. When a cost is traceable to a cost object, it is classified as a direct cost. **Direct costs** are incurred for the benefit of one specific cost object. For example, if a product is a cost object, its material and labor costs are usually directly traceable. **Indirect costs** are incurred for the benefit of more than one cost object. An example of an indirect traceable cost is a maintenance plan that benefits two or more departments. Exhibit 14.6 identifies examples of both direct and indirect costs for the maintenance department in

## Exhibit 14.6
Direct and Indirect Costs

**Direct Costs**
- Salaries of maintenance department employees
- Equipment purchased by maintenance department
- Materials purchased by maintenance department
- Maintenance department equipment depreciation

**Indirect Costs**
- Factory accounting
- Factory administration
- Factory rent
- Factory managers' salary
- Factory light and heat
- Factory internal audit
- Factory intranet

## Exhibit 14.7

Controllability of Costs

**Senior Manager**
Controls costs of
investment in land,
buildings, and
equipment.

**Supervisor**
Controls daily
expenses such as
supplies, maintenance,
and overtime.

**Point:** Opportunity costs are not recorded by the accounting system.

**C5**   Define product and period costs and explain how they impact financial statements.

**Point:** Only costs of production and purchases are classed as product costs.

**Point:** Product costs are either in the income statement as part of cost of goods sold or in the balance sheet as inventory. Period costs appear only on the income statement under operating expenses. See Exhibit 14.8.

a manufacturing plant. Classification of costs by traceability is useful for cost allocation. This is discussed in Chapter 17.

**Classification by Controllability**   A cost can be defined as **controllable** or **not controllable.** Whether a cost is controllable or not depends on the employee's responsibilities, as shown in Exhibit 14.7. This is referred to as *hierarchical levels* in management, or *pecking order.* For example, investments in machinery are controllable by upper-level managers but not lower-level managers. Many daily operating expenses such as overtime often are controllable by lower-level managers. Classification of costs by controllability is especially useful for assigning responsibility to and evaluating managers.

**Classification by Relevance**   A cost can be classified by relevance by identifying it as either a sunk cost or an out-of-pocket cost. A **sunk cost** has already been incurred and cannot be avoided or changed. It is irrelevant to future decisions. One example is the cost of a company's office equipment previously purchased. An **out-of-pocket cost** requires a future outlay of cash and is relevant for decision making. Future purchases of equipment involve out-of-pocket costs. A discussion of relevant costs must also consider opportunity costs. An **opportunity cost** is the potential benefit lost by choosing a specific action from two or more alternatives. One example is a student giving up wages from a job to attend evening classes. Consideration of opportunity cost is important when, for example, an insurance company must decide whether to outsource its payroll function or maintain it internally. This is discussed in Chapter 21.

**Classification by Function**   Another cost classification (for manufacturers) is capitalization as inventory or to expense as incurred. Costs capitalized as inventory are called **product costs,** which refer to expenditures necessary and integral to finished products. They include direct materials, direct labor, and overhead costs. Product costs pertain to activities carried out to manufacture the product. Costs expensed are called **period costs,** which refer to expenditures identified more with a time period than with finished products. They include selling and general administrative expenses. Period costs pertain to activities that are not part of the manufacturing process. A distinction between product and period costs is important because period costs are expensed in the income statement and product costs are assigned to inventory on the balance sheet. An ability to understand and identify product costs and period costs is crucial to using and interpreting a *manufacturing statement* described later in this chapter.

Exhibit 14.8 shows the different effects of product and period costs. Period costs flow directly to the current income statement as expenses. They are not reported as assets. Product costs are first assigned to inventory. Their final treatment depends on when inventory is sold or disposed of. Product costs assigned to finished goods that are sold in year 2005 are reported on the 2005 income statement as part of cost of goods sold. Product costs assigned to unsold inventory are carried forward on the balance sheet at the end of year 2005. If this inventory is sold in year 2006, product costs assigned to it are reported as part of cost of goods sold in that year's income statement.

The difference between period and product costs explains why the year 2005 income statement does not report operating expenses related to either factory workers' wages or

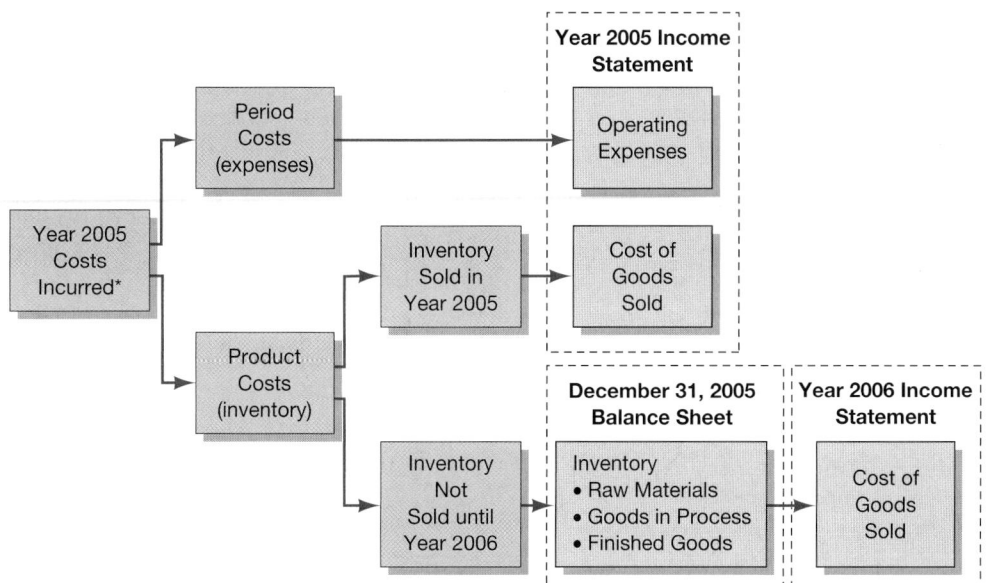

Exhibit 14.8

Period and Product Costs in
Financial Statements

\* This diagram excludes costs to acquire assets other than inventory.

depreciation on factory buildings and equipment. Instead, both costs are combined with the cost of raw materials to compute the product cost of finished goods. A portion of these manufacturing costs (related to the goods sold) is reported in the year 2005 income statement as part of Cost of Goods Sold. The other portion is reported on the balance sheet at the end of that year as part of Inventory. The portion assigned to inventory could be included in any or all of raw materials, goods in process, or finished goods inventories.

**Point:** For a team approach to identifying period and product costs, see *Teamwork in Action* in the *Beyond the Numbers* section.

**Point:** To apply these concepts, work Exercise 14-6.

## Identification of Cost Classification

It is important to understand that a cost can be classified using any one (or combination) of the five different means described here. To do this we must understand costs and operations. Specifically, for the five classifications, we must be able to identify the *activity* for behavior, *cost object* for traceability, *management hierarchical level* for controllability, *opportunity cost* for relevance, and *benefit period* for function. Factory rent, for instance, can be classified as a product cost; it is fixed with respect to number of units produced, it is indirect with respect to the product, and it is not controllable by a production supervisor. Potential multiple classifications are shown in Exhibit 14.9 using different cost items incurred in manufacturing mountain bikes. The finished bike is the cost object. Proper allocation of these costs and the managerial decisions based on cost data depend on a correct cost classification.

**Point:** All expenses of service companies are period costs because these companies do not have inventory.

| Cost Item | By Behavior | By Traceability | By Function |
|---|---|---|---|
| Bicycle tires . . . . . . . . . . . . . . . . . . | Variable | Direct | Product |
| Wages of assembly worker\* . . . . . . . | Variable | Direct | Product |
| Advertising . . . . . . . . . . . . . . . . . . . | Fixed | Indirect | Period |
| Production manager's salary . . . . . . . . | Fixed | Indirect | Product |
| Office depreciation . . . . . . . . . . . . . | Fixed | Indirect | Period |

Exhibit 14.9

Examples of Multiple
Cost Classifications

\* Although an assembly worker's wages are classified as variable costs, their actual behavior depends on how workers are paid and whether their wages are based on a union contract (such as piece rate or monthly wages).

## Cost Concepts for Service Companies

The cost concepts described are generally applicable to service organizations. For example, consider **Delta Air Lines**. Its cost of food for passengers is a variable cost based on number

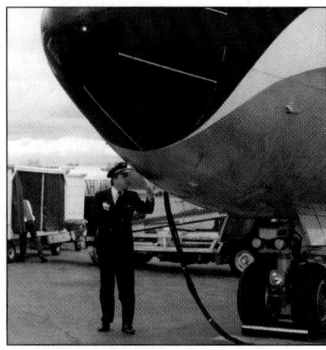

**Service Costs**

• Food and beverages
• Cleaning fees
• Pilot salaries
• Attendant salaries
• Fuel costs
• Travel agent fees
• Ground crew salaries

Answers—p. 602

of passengers. The cost of leasing an aircraft is fixed with respect to number of passengers. We can also trace a flight crew's salary to a specific flight whereas we likely cannot trace wages for the ground crew to a specific flight. Classification by function (such as product versus period costs) is not relevant to service companies because services are not inventoried. Instead, costs incurred by a service firm are expensed in the reporting period when incurred.

Managers in service companies must understand and apply cost concepts. They seek and rely on accurate cost estimates for many decisions. For example, an airline manager must often decide between canceling or rerouting flights. The manager must also be able to estimate costs saved by canceling a flight versus rerouting. Knowledge of fixed costs is equally important. We explain more about the cost requirements for these and other managerial decisions in Chapter 21.

---

## Quick Check

**5.** Which type of cost behavior increases total costs when volume of activity increases?

**6.** How could traceability of costs improve managerial decisions?

---

# Reporting Manufacturing Activities

Companies with manufacturing activities differ from both merchandising and service companies. The main difference between merchandising and manufacturing companies is that merchandisers buy goods ready for sale while manufacturers produce goods from materials and labor. **Payless** is an example of a merchandising company. It buys and sells shoes without physically changing them. **Nike** is primarily a manufacturer of shoes and apparel. It purchases materials such as leather, cloth, dye, plastic, rubber, glue, and laces and then uses employees' labor to convert these materials to products. **Delta Air Lines** is a service company that transports people and items.

Much of our focus in this book has been on the business activities of merchandising and service companies. We described their activities and how to account for them. Manufacturing activities differ from both selling merchandise and providing services. Also, the financial statements for manufacturing companies differ slightly. This section considers some of these differences and compares them to accounting for a merchandising company.

## Manufacturer's Balance Sheet

**C6** Explain how the balance sheets for manufacturing and merchandising companies differ.

Manufacturers carry several unique assets and usually have three inventories instead of the single inventory that merchandisers carry. Exhibit 14.10 shows three different inventories in the current asset section of the balance sheet for Rocky Mountain Bikes, a manufacturer. The three inventories are raw materials, goods in process, and finished goods.

**Point:** Reducing the size of inventories saves storage costs and frees money for other uses.

**Raw Materials Inventory**  **Raw materials inventory** refers to the goods a company acquires to use in making products. It uses raw materials in two ways: directly and indirectly. Most raw materials physically become part of a product and are identified with specific units or batches of a product. Raw materials used directly in a product are called *direct materials*. Other materials used to support production processes are sometimes not as clearly identified with specific units or batches of product. These materials are called **indirect materials** because they are not clearly identified with specific product units or batches. Items used as indirect materials often appear on a balance sheet as factory supplies or are included in raw materials. Some direct materials are classified as indirect materials when their costs are low (insignificant). Examples include screws and nuts used in assembling mountain bikes and

**Inventories of Rocky Mountain Bikes**

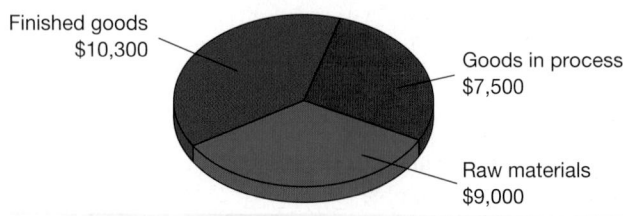

Finished goods $10,300
Goods in process $7,500
Raw materials $9,000

## Exhibit 14.10

Balance Sheet for a Manufacturer

| | ROCKY MOUNTAIN BIKES | | | |
|---|---|---|---|---|
| | Balance Sheet | | | |
| | December 31, 2005 | | | |

| **Assets** | | **Liabilities and Equity** | |
|---|---|---|---|
| Current assets | | Current liabilities | |
| Cash | $ 11,000 | Accounts payable | $ 14,000 |
| Accounts receivable, net | 30,150 | Wages payable | 540 |
| **Raw materials inventory** | **9,000** | Interest payable | 2,000 |
| **Goods in process inventory** | **7,500** | Income taxes payable | 32,600 |
| **Finished goods inventory** | **10,300** | Total current liabilities | 49,140 |
| Factory supplies | 350 | Long-term liabilities | |
| Prepaid insurance | 300 | Long-term notes payable | 50,000 |
| Total current assets | 68,600 | Total liabilities | 99,140 |
| Plant assets | | | |
| Small tools | 1,100 | Stockholders' equity | |
| Delivery equipment, net | 5,000 | Common stock, $5 par | 100,000 |
| Office equipment, net | 1,300 | Retained earnings | 49,760 |
| Factory machinery, net | 65,500 | Total stockholders' equity | 149,760 |
| Factory building, net | 86,700 | Total liabilities and equity | $248,900 |
| Land | 9,500 | | |
| Total plant assets | 169,100 | | |
| Intangible assets (patents) | 11,200 | | |
| Total assets | $248,900 | | |

staples and glue used in manufacturing shoes. Using the *materiality principle,* individually tracing the costs of each of these materials and classifying them separately as direct materials does not make much economic sense. For instance, keeping detailed records of the amount of glue used to manufacture one shoe is not cost beneficial.

**Goods in Process Inventory**    Another inventory held by manufacturers is **goods in process inventory,** also called *work in process inventory.* It consists of products in the process of being manufactured but not yet complete. The amount of goods in process inventory depends on the type of production process. If the time required to produce a unit of product is short, the goods in process inventory is likely small, but if weeks or months are needed to produce a unit, the goods in process inventory is usually larger.

**Finished Goods Inventory**    A third inventory owned by a manufacturer is **finished goods inventory,** which consists of completed products ready for sale. This inventory is similar to merchandise inventory owned by a merchandising company. Manufacturers also often own unique plant assets such as small tools, factory buildings, factory equipment, and patents to manufacture products. The balance sheet in Exhibit 14.10 shows that Rocky Mountain Bikes owns all of these assets. Some manufacturers invest millions or even billions of dollars in production facilities and patents. **Caterpillar**'s recent balance sheet shows a $7 billion net investment in land, buildings, machinery and equipment, much of which involves production facilities.

## Manufacturer's Income Statement

The main difference between the income statement of a manufacturer and that of a merchandiser involves the items making up cost of goods sold. Exhibit 14.11 compares the components of cost of goods sold for a manufacturer and a merchandiser. A merchandiser adds its cost of goods purchased to beginning merchandise inventory and then subtracts

**C7**  Explain how income statements for manufacturing and merchandising companies differ.

## Exhibit 14.11

Cost of Goods Sold Computation

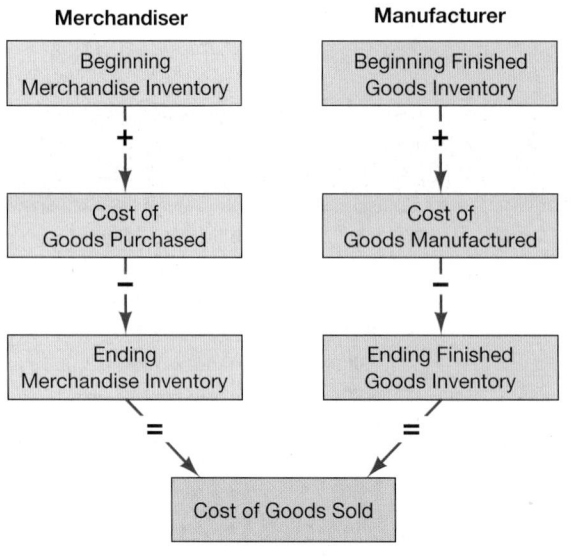

**Merchandiser**

Beginning Merchandise Inventory

+

Cost of Goods Purchased

−

Ending Merchandise Inventory

=

**Manufacturer**

Beginning Finished Goods Inventory

+

Cost of Goods Manufactured

−

Ending Finished Goods Inventory

=

Cost of Goods Sold

**P1** Compute cost of goods sold for a manufacturer.

ending merchandise inventory to get cost of goods sold. A manufacturer adds its cost of goods manufactured to beginning finished goods inventory and then subtracts ending finished goods inventory to get cost of goods sold.

A merchandiser often uses the term *merchandise* inventory; a manufacturer often uses the term *finished goods* inventory. A manufacturer's inventories of raw materials and goods in process are not included in finished goods because they are not available for sale. A manufacturer also shows cost of goods *manufactured* instead of cost of goods *purchased*. This difference occurs because a manufacturer produces its goods instead of purchasing them ready for sale. We show later in this chapter how to derive cost of goods manufactured from the manufacturing statement.

The Cost of Goods Sold section for both a merchandiser (Tele-Mart) and a manufacturer (Rocky Mountain Bikes) is shown in Exhibit 14.12 to highlight these differences. The remaining income statement sections are similar.

## Exhibit 14.12

Cost of Goods Sold for a Merchandiser and Manufacturer

| Merchandising Company | | Manufacturing Company | |
|---|---:|---|---:|
| Cost of goods sold | | Cost of goods sold | |
| **Beginning *merchandise* inventory** ......... | $ 14,200 | **Beginning *finished goods* inventory** ......... | $ 11,200 |
| **Cost of merchandise *purchased*** .......... | 234,150 | **Cost of goods *manufactured*** ............. | 170,500 |
| Goods available for sale .................. | 248,350 | Goods available for sale .................. | 181,700 |
| **Less ending *merchandise* inventory** ....... | 12,100 | **Less ending *finished goods* inventory** ....... | 10,300 |
| Cost of goods sold ..................... | $236,250 | Cost of goods sold ..................... | $171,400 |

\* Cost of goods manufactured is reported in the income statement of Exhibit 14.14.

Topic Tackler 14-2

Although the cost of goods sold computations are similar, the numbers in these computations reflect different activities. A merchandiser's cost of goods purchased is the cost of buying products to be sold. A manufacturer's cost of goods manufactured is the sum of direct materials, direct labor, and factory overhead costs incurred in producing products. The remainder of this section further explains these three manufacturing costs and describes prime and conversion costs.

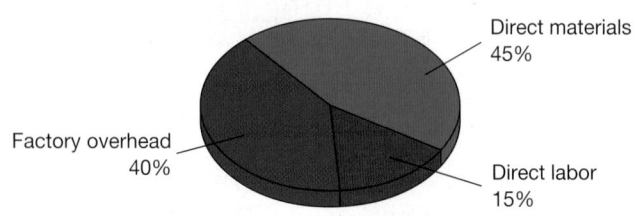

**Typical Manufacturing Costs in Today's Products**

Direct materials 45%

Direct labor 15%

Factory overhead 40%

**Direct Materials** **Direct materials** are tangible components of a finished product. **Direct material costs** are the expenditures for direct materials that are separately and readily traced through the manufacturing process to finished goods. Examples of direct materials in manufacturing a mountain bike include its tires, seat, frame, pedals, brakes, cables, gears, and handlebars. The chart in the margin shows that direct materials generally make up about 45% of manufacturing costs in today's products, but this amount varies across industries and companies.

**Direct Labor** **Direct labor** refers to the efforts of employees who physically convert materials to finished product. **Direct labor costs** are the wages and salaries for direct labor that are separately and readily traced through the manufacturing process to finished goods. Examples of direct labor in manufacturing a mountain bike include operators directly involved in converting raw materials into finished products (welding, painting, forming) and assembly workers who attach materials such as tires, seats, pedals, and brakes to the bike frames. Costs of other workers on the assembly line who assist direct laborers are classified as **indirect labor costs. Indirect labor** refers to manufacturing workers' efforts not linked to specific units or batches of the product.

**Point:** Indirect labor costs are part of factory overhead.

**Factory Overhead** **Factory overhead** involves components or activities that support the manufacturing process but are not direct materials or direct labor. **Factory overhead costs** are the expenditures for factory overhead that cannot be separately or readily traced to finished goods. These costs include indirect materials and indirect labor, costs not directly traceable to the product. Overtime paid to direct laborers is also included in overhead because overtime is due to delays, interruptions, or constraints not necessarily identifiable to a specific product or batches of product. Factory overhead costs also include maintenance of the mountain bike factory, supervision of its employees, repairing manufacturing equipment, factory utilities (water, gas, electricity), production manager's salary, factory rent, depreciation on factory buildings and equipment, factory insurance, property taxes on factory buildings and equipment, and factory accounting and legal services. Factory overhead does *not* include selling and administrative expenses because they are not incurred in manufacturing products. These expenses are called *period costs* and are recorded as expenses on the income statement when incurred.

**Point:** Factory overhead is also called *manufacturing overhead.*

**Prime and Conversion Costs** Direct material costs and direct labor costs are also called **prime costs**—expenditures directly associated with the manufacture of finished goods. Direct labor costs and overhead costs are called **conversion costs**—expenditures incurred in the process of converting raw materials to finished goods. Direct labor costs are considered both prime costs and conversion costs. Exhibit 14.13 conveys the relation between prime and conversion costs and their components of direct material, direct labor, and factory overhead.

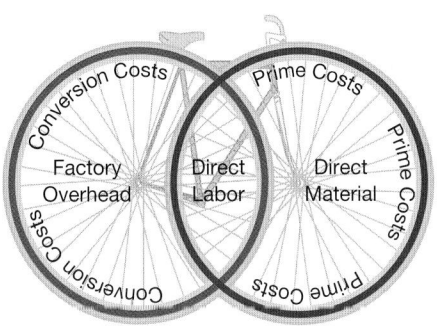

## Exhibit 14.13

Prime and Conversion Costs and Their Components

**Point:** Prime costs = Direct materials + Direct labor.
Conversion costs = Direct labor + Factory overhead.

**Reporting Performance** Exhibit 14.14 shows the income statement for Rocky Mountain Bikes. Its operating expenses include sales salaries, office salaries, and depreciation of delivery and office equipment. Operating expenses do not include manufacturing costs such as factory workers' wages and depreciation of production equipment and the factory buildings. These manufacturing costs are reported as part of cost of goods manufactured and included in cost of goods sold. We explained why and how this is done in the section Classification by Function.

**Point:** Manufacturers treat costs such as depreciation and rent as product costs if they are related to manufacturing.

Answers—p. 602

**Quick Check**

7. What are the three types of inventory on a manufacturing company's balance sheet?
8. How does cost of goods sold differ for merchandising versus manufacturing companies?

## Exhibit 14.14

Income Statement for a Manufacturer

### ROCKY MOUNTAIN BIKES
### Income Statement
### For Year Ended December 31, 2005

| | | |
|---|---:|---:|
| Sales | | $310,000 |
| Cost of goods sold | | |
| Finished goods inventory, Dec. 31, 2004 | $ 11,200 | |
| **Cost of goods manufactured** | **170,500** | |
| Goods available for sale | 181,700 | |
| Less finished goods inventory, Dec. 31, 2005 | 10,300 | |
| Cost of goods sold | | 171,400 |
| Gross profit | | 138,600 |
| Operating expenses | | |
| Selling expenses | | |
| Sales salaries expense | 18,000 | |
| Advertising expense | 5,500 | |
| Delivery wages expense | 12,000 | |
| Shipping supplies expense | 250 | |
| Insurance expense—Delivery equipment | 300 | |
| Depreciation expense—Delivery equipment | 2,100 | |
| Total selling expenses | | 38,150 |
| General and administrative expenses | | |
| Office salaries expense | 15,700 | |
| Miscellaneous expense | 200 | |
| Bad debts expense | 1,550 | |
| Office supplies expense | 100 | |
| Depreciation expense—Office equipment | 200 | |
| Interest expense | 4,000 | |
| Total general and administrative expenses | | 21,750 |
| Total operating expenses | | 59,900 |
| Income before income taxes | | 78,700 |
| Income taxes expense | | 32,600 |
| Net income | | $ 46,100 |
| Net income per common share (20,000 shares) | | $ 2.31 |

## Flow of Manufacturing Activities

**C8** Explain manufacturing activities and the flow of manufacturing costs.

To understand manufacturing and its reports, we must first understand the flow of manufacturing activities and costs. Exhibit 14.15 shows the flow of manufacturing activities for a manufacturer. This exhibit has three important sections: *materials activity, production activity,* and *sales activity.* We explain each activity in this section.

**Materials Activity**    The far left side of Exhibit 14.15 shows the flow of raw materials. Manufacturers usually start a period with some beginning raw materials inventory carried over from the previous period. The company then acquires additional raw materials in the current period. Adding these purchases to beginning inventory gives total raw materials available for use in production. These raw materials are then either used in production in the current period or remain in inventory at the end of the period for use in future periods.

**Production Activity**    The middle section of Exhibit 14.15 describes production activity. Four factors come together in production: beginning goods in process inventory, direct materials, direct labor, and overhead. Beginning goods in process inventory consists of partly assembled products from the previous period. Production activity results in products that are either finished or remain unfinished. The cost of finished products makes up the cost of goods

**Point:** Knowledge of managerial accounting provides us a means of measuring manufacturing costs and is a sound foundation for studying advanced business topics.

**Point:** The series of activities that add value to a company's products or services is called a **value chain.**

## Exhibit 14.15

Activities and Cost Flows in Manufacturing

manufactured for the current period. Unfinished products are identified as ending goods in process inventory. The cost of unfinished products consists of direct materials, direct labor, and factory overhead, and is reported on the current period's balance sheet. The costs of both finished goods manufactured and goods in process are *product costs.*

**Sales Activity**   The company's sales activity is portrayed in the far right side of Exhibit 14.15. Newly completed units are combined with beginning finished goods inventory to make up total finished goods available for sale in the current period. The cost of finished products sold is reported on the income statement as cost of goods sold. The cost of products not sold is reported on the current period's balance sheet as ending finished goods inventory.

## Manufacturing Statement

A company's manufacturing activities are described in a **manufacturing statement**, also called the *schedule of manufacturing activities* or the *schedule of cost of goods manufactured.* The manufacturing statement summarizes the types and amounts of costs incurred in a company's manufacturing process. Exhibit 14.16 shows the manufacturing statement for Rocky Mountain Bikes. The statement is divided into four parts: *direct materials, direct labor, overhead,* and *computation of cost of goods manufactured.* We describe each of these parts in this section.

**P2**  Prepare a manufacturing statement and explain its purpose and links to financial statements.

① The manufacturing statement begins by computing direct materials used. We start by adding beginning raw materials inventory of $8,000 to the current period's purchases of $86,500. This yields $94,500 of total raw materials available for use. A physical count of inventory shows $9,000 of ending raw materials inventory. This implies a total cost of raw materials used during the period of $85,500 ($94,500 total raw materials available for use − $9,000 ending inventory). (*Note:* All raw materials are direct materials for Rocky Mountain Bikes.)

② The second part of the manufacturing statement reports direct labor costs. Rocky Mountain Bikes had total direct labor costs of $60,000 for the period. This amount includes payroll taxes and fringe benefits.

Exhibit 14.16

Manufacturing Statement

| ROCKY MOUNTAIN BIKES | | |
|---|---|---|
| **Manufacturing Statement** | | |
| **For Year Ended December 31, 2005** | | |

|  | | | |
|---|---|---|---|
| **Direct materials** | | | |
| Raw materials inventory, Dec. 31, 2004 . . . . . . . . . . . . | | $ 8,000 | |
| Raw materials purchases . . . . . . . . . . . . . . . . . . . . . | | 86,500 | |
| Raw materials available for use . . . . . . . . . . . . . . . . | | 94,500 | |
| Less raw materials inventory, Dec. 31, 2005 . . . . . . . . | | 9,000 | |
| Direct materials used . . . . . . . . . . . . . . . . . . . . . . . | | | $ 85,500 |
| **Direct labor** . . . . . . . . . . . . . . . . . . . . . . . . . . . . | | | 60,000 |
| **Factory overhead** | | | |
| Indirect labor . . . . . . . . . . . . . . . . . . . . . . . . . . . . . | | 9,000 | |
| Factory supervision . . . . . . . . . . . . . . . . . . . . . . . | | 6,000 | |
| Factory utilities . . . . . . . . . . . . . . . . . . . . . . . . . . | | 2,600 | |
| Repairs—Factory equipment . . . . . . . . . . . . . . . . . . | | 2,500 | |
| Property taxes—Factory building . . . . . . . . . . . . . . | | 1,900 | |
| Factory supplies used . . . . . . . . . . . . . . . . . . . . . . | | 600 | |
| Factory insurance expired . . . . . . . . . . . . . . . . . . . | | 1,100 | |
| Small tools written off . . . . . . . . . . . . . . . . . . . . . | | 200 | |
| Depreciation expense—Factory equipment . . . . . . . . | | 3,500 | |
| Depreciation expense—Factory building . . . . . . . . . . | | 1,800 | |
| Amortization expense—Patents . . . . . . . . . . . . . . . | | 800 | |
| Total factory overhead . . . . . . . . . . . . . . . . . . . . . . | | | 30,000 |
| Total manufacturing costs . . . . . . . . . . . . . . . . . . . . . | | | 175,500 |
| Add goods in process inventory, Dec. 31, 2004 . . . . . . . . | | | 2,500 |
| Total cost of goods in process . . . . . . . . . . . . . . . . . . | | | 178,000 |
| Less goods in process inventory, Dec. 31, 2005 . . . . . . . | | | 7,500 |
| **Cost of goods manufactured** . . . . . . . . . . . . . . . . . | | | $170,500 |

①  Direct materials section

②  Direct labor

③  Factory overhead section

④  Cost of goods manufactured section

**Point:** Direct material and direct labor costs increase with increases in production volume and are called *variable costs.* Overhead can be both variable and fixed. When overhead costs vary with production, they are called *variable overhead.* When overhead costs don't vary with production, they are called *fixed overhead.*

**Point:** Manufacturers sometimes report variable and fixed overhead separately in the manufacturing statement to provide more information to managers about cost behavior.

③ The third part of the manufacturing statement reports overhead costs. The statement lists each important factory overhead item and its cost. Total factory overhead cost for the period is $30,000. Some companies report only *total* factory overhead on the manufacturing statement and attach a separate schedule listing individual overhead costs.

④ The final section of the manufacturing statement computes and reports the *cost of goods manufactured.* (Total manufacturing costs for the period are $175,500 [$85,500 + $60,000 + $30,000], the sum of direct materials used and direct labor and overhead costs incurred.) This amount is first added to beginning goods in process inventory. This gives the total goods in process inventory of $178,000 ($175,500 + $2,500). We then compute the current period's cost of goods manufactured of $170,500 by taking the $178,000 total goods in process and subtracting the $7,500 cost of ending goods in process inventory that consists of direct materials, direct labor, and factory overhead. The cost of goods manufactured amount is also called *net cost of goods manufactured* or *cost of goods completed.* Exhibit 14.14 shows that this item and amount are listed in the Cost of Goods Sold section of Rocky Mountain Bikes' income statement.

A managerial accounting system records costs and reports them in various reports that eventually determine financial statements. Exhibit 14.17 shows how overhead costs flow through the system: from an initial listing of specific costs, to a section of the manufacturing statement, to the reporting on the income statement.

Management uses information in the manufacturing statement to plan and control the company's manufacturing activities. To provide timely information for decision making, the statement is often prepared monthly, weekly, or even daily. The manufacturing statement

## Exhibit 14.17

Overhead Cost Flows across Accounting Reports

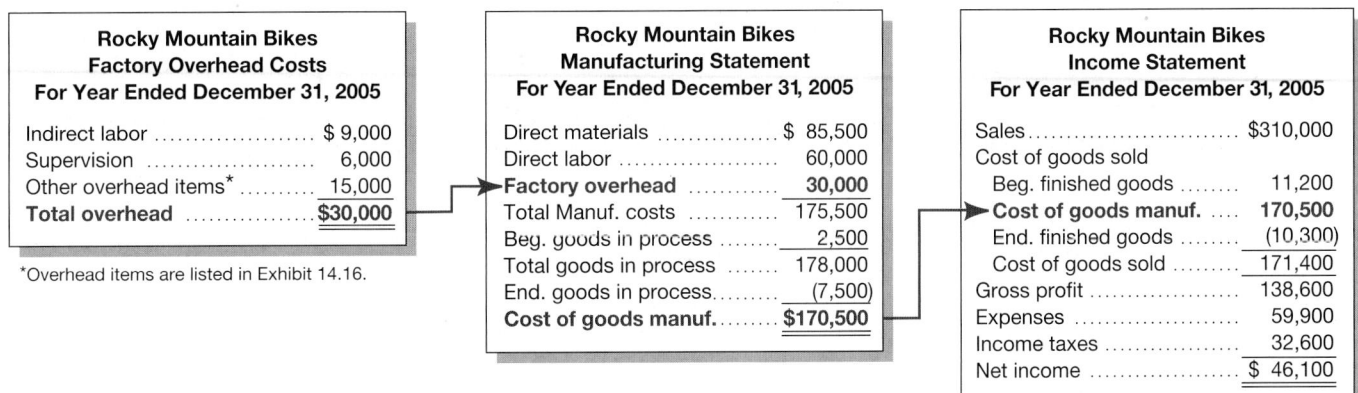

| Rocky Mountain Bikes Factory Overhead Costs For Year Ended December 31, 2005 | |
|---|---|
| Indirect labor | $ 9,000 |
| Supervision | 6,000 |
| Other overhead items* | 15,000 |
| Total overhead | $30,000 |

*Overhead items are listed in Exhibit 14.16.

| Rocky Mountain Bikes Manufacturing Statement For Year Ended December 31, 2005 | |
|---|---|
| Direct materials | $ 85,500 |
| Direct labor | 60,000 |
| **Factory overhead** | 30,000 |
| Total Manuf. costs | 175,500 |
| Beg. goods in process | 2,500 |
| Total goods in process | 178,000 |
| End. goods in process | (7,500) |
| **Cost of goods manuf.** | **$170,500** |

| Rocky Mountain Bikes Income Statement For Year Ended December 31, 2005 | |
|---|---|
| Sales | $310,000 |
| Cost of goods sold | |
| Beg. finished goods | 11,200 |
| **Cost of goods manuf.** | 170,500 |
| End. finished goods | (10,300) |
| Cost of goods sold | 171,400 |
| Gross profit | 138,600 |
| Expenses | 59,900 |
| Income taxes | 32,600 |
| Net income | $ 46,100 |

contains information useful to external users but is not a general-purpose financial statement. Companies rarely publish the manufacturing statement because managers view this information as proprietary and potentially harmful to them if released to competitors.

**Point:** To apply these concepts, work Exercise 14-11.

### Quick Check

9. A manufacturing statement (*a*) computes cost of goods manufactured for the period, (*b*) computes cost of goods sold for the period, or (*c*) reports operating expenses incurred for the period.

10. Are companies required to report a manufacturing statement?

11. How are both beginning and ending goods in process inventories reported on a manufacturing statement?

Answers—p. 602

---

## Unit Contribution Margin                          Decision Analysis

We explained in this chapter how managers classify costs by behavior. This usually refers to costs as being fixed or variable with respect to volume of activity. In manufacturing companies, volume of activity usually refers to the number of units produced. We then classify a cost as either fixed or variable, depending on whether total cost changes as the number of units produced changes. Once we separate costs by behavior, we can then compute a product's contribution margin. **Unit contribution margin,** or *contribution margin per unit,* is the amount a product's unit selling price exceeds its total unit variable cost. This excess amount contributes to covering fixed costs and generating profits on a per unit basis. Exhibit 14.18 shows the unit contribution margin formula.

**A1** Compute unit contribution margin and describe what it reveals about a company's cost structure.

> **Unit contribution margin = Sales price per unit − Total variable cost per unit**

**Exhibit 14.18**

Unit Contribution Margin

Users often use contribution margin in the form of a **contribution margin ratio,** which is the percent of a unit's selling price that exceeds total unit variable cost. It can be interpreted as the percent of each sales dollar that remains after deducting total unit variable cost. Exhibit 14.19 shows the formula for the contribution margin ratio.

$$\text{Contribution margin ratio} = \frac{\text{Unit contribution margin}}{\text{Sales price per unit}}$$

**Exhibit 14.19**

Contribution Margin Ratio

Contribution Margin    Variable Costs
56¢                     44¢

We use Rocky Mountain Bikes' Tracker® product to show the usefulness of these measures. The selling price of a Tracker mountain bike is $450, and the variable costs of its manufacturing and marketing are $200. The contribution margin per bike is computed as $250 ($450 − $200). This measure is useful to managers in determining the money contributed by the sale of each Tracker bike to both (1) fixed costs and (2) net income. Specifically, each sale of a Tracker bike yields a $250 contribution margin to cover fixed costs of Rocky Mountain Bikes. Once fixed costs are covered, net income is left.

We also compute the Tracker mountain bike's contribution margin ratio as 55.55% ($250/$450). This information is useful to managers working with estimates of sales in dollars. Specifically, approximately 56¢ (or 55.55%) of each sales dollar is available as contribution to fixed costs and profits. The contribution margin ratio is also useful in cost-volume-profit (CVP) analysis, a method we use to assess the volume of activity necessary to achieve different performance levels (including income, loss, and breakeven points). We explain CVP analysis in Chapter 18.

## Decision Maker

**Sales Manager**   You are evaluating orders from two customers but can accept only one of the orders because of your company's limited capacity. The first order is for 100 units of a product with a contribution margin ratio of 60% and a selling price of $1,000. The second order is for 500 units of a product with a contribution margin ratio of 20% and a selling price of $800. The incremental fixed costs are the same for both orders. Which order do you accept?

Answer—p. 601

# Demonstration Problem 1: Cost Behavior

Understanding the classification and assignment of costs is important. Consider the following company, **Chip Making Systems,** that manufactures computer chips. It incurs the following costs in manufacturing chips and in operating the company:

1.  Plastic board used to mount the chip, $3.50 each.
2.  Assembly worker pay of $15 per hour to attach chips to plastic board.
3.  Salary for factory maintenance workers who maintain factory equipment.
4.  Factory supervisor pay of $55,000 per year to supervise employees.
5.  Real estate taxes paid on the factory, $14,500.
6.  Real estate taxes paid on the company office, $6,000.
7.  Depreciation costs on machinery used by workers, $30,000.
8.  Salary paid to the chief financial officer, $95,000.
9.  Advertising costs of $7,800 paid to promote products.
10. Salespersons' commissions of $0.50 for each assembled chip sold.
11. CMS could rent the manufacturing plant to store medical records for six local hospitals instead of producing and assembling chips.

Classify each cost in the following table according to the categories listed across the top. A cost can be classified under more than one category. The plastic board used to mount chips, for instance, is classified as a direct material product cost and as a direct unit cost.

| Cost | Period Costs | Product Costs | | | Unit Cost Classification | | Sunk Cost | Opportunity Cost |
|---|---|---|---|---|---|---|---|---|
| | Selling and Administrative | Direct Material (prime cost) | Direct Labor (prime and conversion) | Factory Overhead (conversion cost) | Direct | Indirect | | |
| 1. Plastic board used to mount the chip, $3.50 each | | ✔ | | | ✔ | | | |

## Solution to Demonstration Problem 1

| | | Period Costs | Product Costs | | | Unit Cost Classification | | Sunk Cost | Opportunity Cost |
|---|---|---|---|---|---|---|---|---|---|
| Cost* | | Selling and Administrative | Direct Material (prime cost) | Direct Labor (prime and conversion) | Factory Overhead (conversion cost) | Direct | Indirect | | |
| 1. | | | ✔ | | | ✔ | | | |
| 2. | | | | ✔ | | ✔ | | | |
| 3. | | | | | ✔ | | ✔ | | |
| 4. | | | | | ✔ | | ✔ | | |
| 5. | | | | | ✔ | | ✔ | | |
| 6. | | ✔ | | | | | | | |
| 7. | | | | | ✔ | | ✔ | ✔ | |
| 8. | | ✔ | | | | | | | |
| 9. | | ✔ | | | | | | | |
| 10. | | ✔ | | | | | | | |
| 11. | | | | | | | | | ✔ |

* Costs 1 through 11 refer to the 11 cost items described at the beginning of the problem.

## Demonstration Problem 2: Reporting for Manufacturers

A manufacturing company's balance sheet and income statement differ from those for a merchandising or service company.

**Required**

1. Fill in the [BLANKS] on the partial balance sheets for both the manufacturing company and the merchandising company. Explain why a different presentation is required.

*Manufacturing Company*

| CHIP MAKING SYSTEMS Partial Balance Sheet December 31, 2005 | |
|---|---|
| Current assets | |
| Cash .................. | $10,000 |
| [BLANK] .............. | 8,000 |
| [BLANK] .............. | 5,000 |
| [BLANK] .............. | 7,000 |
| Supplies ............... | 500 |
| Prepaid insurance ......... | 500 |
| Total current assets ....... | $31,000 |

*Merchandising Company*

| PAYLESS SHOE OUTLET Partial Balance Sheet December 31, 2005 | |
|---|---|
| Current assets | |
| Cash .................. | $ 5,000 |
| [BLANK] .............. | 12,000 |
| Supplies ............... | 500 |
| Prepaid insurance ........ | 500 |
| Total current assets ....... | $18,000 |

2. Fill in the [BLANKS] on the income statements for the manufacturing company and the merchandising company. Explain why a different presentation is required.

*Manufacturing Company*

| CHIP MAKING SYSTEMS Partial Income Statement For Year Ended December 31, 2005 | |
|---|---|
| Sales | $200,000 |
| Cost of goods sold | |
| Finished goods inventory, Dec. 31, 2004 | 10,000 |
| [BLANK] | 120,000 |
| Goods available for sale | 130,000 |
| Finished goods inventory, Dec. 31, 2005 | (7,000) |
| Cost of goods sold | 123,000 |
| Gross profit | $ 77,000 |

*Merchandising Company*

| PAYLESS SHOE OUTLET Partial Income Statement For Year Ended December 31, 2005 | |
|---|---|
| Sales | $190,000 |
| Cost of goods sold | |
| Merchandise inventory, Dec. 31, 2004 | 8,000 |
| [BLANK] | 108,000 |
| Net purchases | 116,000 |
| Merchandise inventory, Dec. 31, 2005 | (12,000) |
| Cost of goods sold | 104,000 |
| Gross profit | $ 86,000 |

**3.** The manufacturer's cost of goods manufactured is the sum of (a) _____, (b) _____, and (c) _____ costs incurred in producing the product.

## Solution to Demonstration Problem 2

**1.** Inventories for a manufacturer and for a merchandiser.

*Manufacturing Company*

| CHIP MAKING SYSTEMS Partial Balance Sheet December 31, 2005 | |
|---|---|
| Current assets | |
| Cash | $10,000 |
| **Raw materials inventory** | 8,000 |
| **Goods in process inventory** | 5,000 |
| **Finished goods inventory** | 7,000 |
| Supplies | 500 |
| Prepaid insurance | 500 |
| Total current assets | $31,000 |

*Merchandising Company*

| PAYLESS SHOE OUTLET Partial Balance Sheet December 31, 2005 | |
|---|---|
| Current assets | |
| Cash | $ 5,000 |
| **Merchandise inventory** | 12,000 |
| Supplies | 500 |
| Prepaid insurance | 500 |
| Total current assets | $18,000 |

*Explanation:* A manufacturing company must control and measure three types of inventories: raw materials, goods in process, and finished goods. In the sequence of making a product, the raw materials move into production—called *goods in process inventory*—and then to finished goods. All raw materials and goods in process inventory at the end of each accounting period are considered current assets. All unsold finished inventory is considered a current asset at the end of each accounting period. The merchandising company must control and measure only one type of inventory, purchased goods.

**2.** Cost of goods sold for a manufacturer and for a merchandiser.

*Manufacturing Company*

| CHIP MAKING SYSTEMS Partial Income Statement For Year Ended December 31, 2005 | |
|---|---|
| Sales | $ 200,000 |
| Cost of goods sold | |
| Finished goods inventory, Dec. 31, 2004 | 10,000 |
| **Cost of goods manufactured** | 120,000 |
| Goods available for sale | 130,000 |
| Finished goods inventory, Dec. 31, 2005 | (7,000) |
| Cost of goods sold | 123,000 |
| Gross profit | $ 77,000 |

*Merchandising Company*

| PAYLESS SHOE OUTLET Partial Income Statement For Year Ended December 31, 2005 | |
|---|---|
| Sales | $ 190,000 |
| Cost of goods sold | |
| Merchandise inventory, Dec. 31, 2004 | 8,000 |
| **Cost of purchases** | 108,000 |
| Net purchases | 116,000 |
| Merchandise inventory, Dec. 31, 2005 | (12,000) |
| Cost of goods sold | 104,000 |
| Gross profit | $ 86,000 |

*Explanation:* Manufacturing and merchandising companies use different reporting terms. In particular, the terms *finished goods* and *cost of goods manufactured* are used to reflect the production of goods, yet the concepts and techniques of reporting cost of goods sold for a manufacturing company and merchandising company are similar.

3. A manufacturer's cost of goods manufactured is the sum of (a) *direct material,* (b) *direct labor,* and (c) *factory overhead* costs incurred in producing the product.

## Demonstration Problem 3: Manufacturing Statement

The following account balances and other information are from SUNN Corporation's accounting records for year-end December 31, 2005. Use this information to prepare (1) a table listing factory overhead costs, (2) a manufacturing statement (show only the total factory overhead cost), and (3) an income statement.

| | | | |
|---|---|---|---|
| Advertising expense | $ 85,000 | Goods in process inventory, Dec. 31, 2004 ....... | $ 8,000 |
| Amortization expense—Patents ............... | 16,000 | Goods in process inventory, Dec. 31, 2005 ........ | 9,000 |
| Bad debts expense ........................ | 28,000 | Income taxes ............................. | 53,400 |
| Depreciation expense—Office equipment ........ | 37,000 | Indirect labor ........................... | 26,000 |
| Depreciation expense—Factory building .......... | 133,000 | Interest expense ......................... | 25,000 |
| Depreciation expense—Factory equipment ....... | 78,000 | Miscellaneous expense .................... | 55,000 |
| Direct labor ............................. | 250,000 | Property taxes on factory equipment ........... | 14,000 |
| Factory insurance expired ................... | 62,000 | Raw materials inventory, Dec. 31, 2004 .......... | 60,000 |
| Factory supervision ....................... | 74,000 | Raw materials inventory, Dec. 31, 2005 .......... | 78,000 |
| Factory supplies used ..................... | 21,000 | Raw materials purchases .................... | 313,000 |
| Factory utilities .......................... | 115,000 | Repairs expense—Factory equipment ........... | 31,000 |
| Finished goods inventory, Dec. 31, 2004 .......... | 15,000 | Salaries expense ......................... | 150,000 |
| Finished goods inventory, Dec. 31, 2005 .......... | 12,500 | Sales .................................. | 1,630,000 |

## Planning the Solution

- Analyze the account balances and select those that are part of factory overhead costs.
- Arrange these costs in a table that lists factory overhead costs for the year.
- Analyze the remaining costs and select those related to production activity for the year; selected costs should include the materials and goods in process inventories and direct labor.
- Prepare a manufacturing statement for the year showing the calculation of the cost of materials used in production, the cost of direct labor, and the total factory overhead cost. When presenting overhead cost on this statement, report only total overhead cost from the table of overhead costs for the year. Show the costs of beginning and ending goods in process inventory to determine cost of goods manufactured
- Organize the remaining revenue and expense items into the income statement for the year. Combine cost of goods manufactured from the manufacturing statement with the finished goods inventory amounts to compute cost of goods sold for the year.

## Solution to Demonstration Problem 3

| SUNN CORPORATION Factory Overhead Costs For Year Ended December 31, 2005 | |
|---|---|
| Amortization expense—Patents ............... | $ 16,000 |
| Depreciation expense—Factory building .......... | 133,000 |
| Depreciation expense—Factory equipment ....... | 78,000 |
| Factory insurance expired ................... | 62,000 |
| Factory supervision ....................... | 74,000 |
| Factory supplies used ..................... | 21,000 |

| SUNN CORPORATION Manufacturing Statement For Year Ended December 31, 2005 | | |
|---|---|---|
| Direct materials | | |
| Raw materials inventory, Dec. 31, 2004 ............ | $ 60,000 | |
| Raw materials purchase ...................... | 313,000 | |
| Raw materials available for use .................. | 373,000 | |
| Less raw materials inventory, Dec. 31, 2005 ......... | 78,000 | |
| Direct materials used ........................ | 295,000 | |

[continued on next page]

[continued from previous page]

| | |
|---|---|
| Factory utilities ............................. | 115,000 |
| Indirect labor ............................. | 26,000 |
| Property taxes on factory equipment ........... | 14,000 |
| Repairs expense—Factory equipment ........... | 31,000 |
| Total factory overhead ..................... | $570,000 |

| | |
|---|---|
| Direct labor .................................... | 250,000 |
| Factory overhead ............................. | 570,000 |
| Total manufacturing costs ..................... | 1,115,000 |
| Goods in process inventory, Dec. 31, 2004 ........... | 8,000 |
| Total cost of goods in process ..................... | 1,123,000 |
| Less goods in process inventory, Dec. 31, 2005 ........ | 9,000 |
| Cost of goods manufactured ..................... | $1,114,000 |

**SUNN CORPORATION**
**Income Statement**
**For Year Ended December 31, 2005**

| | | |
|---|---|---|
| Sales ...................................... | | $1,630,000 |
| Cost of goods sold | | |
| Finished goods inventory, Dec. 31, 2004 ........... | $ 15,000 | |
| Cost of goods manufactured ................... | 1,114,000 | |
| Goods available for sale ..................... | 1,129,000 | |
| Less finished goods inventory, Dec. 31, 2005 ....... | 12,500 | |
| Cost of goods sold ...................... | | 1,116,500 |
| Gross profit .............................. | | 513,500 |
| Operating expenses | | |
| Advertising expense ....................... | 85,000 | |
| Bad debts expense ........................ | 28,000 | |
| Depreciation expense—Office equipment ......... | 37,000 | |
| Interest expense ......................... | 25,000 | |
| Miscellaneous expense ..................... | 55,000 | |
| Salaries expense ......................... | 150,000 | |
| Total operating expenses .................... | | 380,000 |
| Income before income taxes .................... | | 133,500 |
| Income taxes ............................. | | 53,400 |
| Net income ............................... | | $ 80,100 |

## Summary

**C1** **Explain the purpose of managerial accounting.** The purpose of managerial accounting is to provide useful information to management and other internal decision makers. It does this by collecting, managing, and reporting both monetary and nonmonetary information in a manner useful to internal users.

**C2** **Describe major characteristics of managerial accounting.** Major characteristics of managerial accounting include (1) focus on internal decision makers, (2) emphasis on planning and control, (3) flexibility, (4) timeliness, (5) reliance on forecasts and estimates, (6) focus on segments and projects, and (7) reporting both monetary and nonmonetary information.

**C3** **Describe the lean business model.** The main purpose of the lean business model is the elimination of waste. Concepts such as total quality management and just-in-time production often aid in effective application of the model.

**C4** **Describe accounting concepts useful in classifying costs.** We can classify costs on the basis of their (1) behavior—fixed vs. variable, (2) traceability—direct vs. indirect, (3) controllability—controllable vs. uncontrollable,

(4) relevance—sunk vs. out of pocket, and (5) function—product vs. period. A cost can be classified in more than one way, depending on the purpose for which the cost is being determined. These classifications help to understand cost patterns, analyze performance, and plan operations.

**C5** **Define product and period costs and explain how they impact financial statements.** Costs that are capitalized because they are expected to have future value are called *product costs;* costs that are expensed are called *period costs.* This classification is important because it affects the amount of costs expensed in the income statement and the amount of costs assigned to inventory on the balance sheet. Product costs are commonly made up of direct materials, direct labor, and overhead. Period costs include selling and administrative expenses.

**C6** **Explain how the balance sheets for manufacturing and merchandising companies differ.** The main difference is that manufacturers usually carry three inventories—raw materials, goods in process, and finished goods—instead of one inventory that merchandisers carry.

**C7** **Explain how income statements for manufacturing and merchandising companies differ.** The main difference between income statements of manufacturers and merchandisers is the items making up cost of goods sold. A merchandiser adds beginning merchandise inventory to cost of goods purchased and then subtracts ending merchandise inventory to get cost of goods sold. A manufacturer adds beginning finished goods inventory to cost of goods manufactured and then subtracts ending finished goods inventory to get cost of goods sold.

**C8** **Explain manufacturing activities and the flow of manufacturing costs.** Manufacturing activities consist of materials, production, and sales activities. The materials activity consists of the purchase and issuance of materials to production. The production activity consists of converting materials into finished goods. At this stage in the process, the materials, labor, and overhead costs have been incurred and the manufacturing statement is prepared. The sales activity consists of selling some or all of finished goods available for sale. At this stage, the cost of goods sold is determined.

**A1** **Compute unit contribution margin and describe what it reveals about a company's cost structure.** Unit contribution margin is a product's sales price less its total variable costs. Contribution margin ratio is a product's unit contribution margin divided by its sales price. Unit contribution margin is the amount received from each sale that contributes to fixed costs and income. The contribution margin ratio reveals what portion of each sales dollar is available as contribution to fixed costs and income.

**P1** **Compute cost of goods sold for a manufacturer.** A manufacturer adds beginning finished goods inventory to cost of goods manufactured and then subtracts ending finished goods inventory to get cost of goods sold.

**P2** **Prepare a manufacturing statement and explain its purpose and links to financial statements.** The manufacturing statement reports computation of cost of goods manufactured for the period. It begins by showing the period's costs for direct materials, direct labor, and overhead and then adjusts these numbers for the beginning and ending inventories of the goods in process to yield cost of goods manufactured.

## Guidance Answers to **Decision Maker** and **Decision Ethics**

**Production Supervisor** It appears that all three friends want to pay the bill with someone else's money. David is using money belonging to the tax authorities, Denise is taking money from her company, and Derek is defrauding the government. To prevent such practices, companies have internal audit mechanisms. Many companies also adopt ethical codes of conduct to help guide employees. We must recognize that some entertainment expenses are justifiable and even encouraged. For example, the tax law allows certain deductions for entertainment that have a business purpose. Corporate policies also sometimes allow and encourage reimbursable spending for social activities, and government contracts can include entertainment as allowable costs. Nevertheless, without further details, payment for this bill should be made from personal accounts.

**Division Manager** You need information pertaining to the costs of making it in-house: direct materials, direct labor, and overhead. You also need information about investments in machinery required to make the component. Regarding the possibility of continuing to buy from the outside, you need information about costs of the outside purchase: price of components, costs to place the order, and costs to receive and store components. You must also consider nonfinancial factors such as quality of components currently supplied and the quality of in-house production.

**Entrepreneur** Tracing all costs directly to cost objects is always desirable, but you need to be able to do so in an economically feasible manner. In this case, you are able to trace 90% of the

assembly department's direct costs. It may not be economical to spend more money on a new software to trace the final 10% of costs. You need to make a cost-benefit trade-off. If the software offers benefits beyond tracing the remaining 10% of the assembly department's costs, your decision should consider this.

**Purchase Manager** Opportunity costs relate to the potential quality and delivery benefits given up by not choosing supplier (A). Selecting supplier (B) might involve future costs of poor-quality seats (inspection, repairs, and returns). Also, potential delivery delays could interrupt work and increase manufacturing costs. Your company could also incur sales losses if the product quality of supplier (B) is low. As purchase manager, you are responsible for these costs and must consider them in making your decision.

**Sales Manager** The contribution margin for the first order is $600 per unit (60% of $1,000); the contribution margin per unit for the second order is $160 (20% of $800). You are likely tempted to accept the first order based on its high contribution margin per unit, but you must compute total contribution margin based on the number of units sold for each order. Total contribution margin is $60,000 ($600 per unit × 100 units) and $80,000 ($160 per unit × 500 units) for the two orders, respectively. The second order provides the largest return in absolute dollars and is the order you would accept. Another factor to consider in your selection is the potential for a long-term relationship with these customers including repeat sales and growth.

## Guidance Answers to **Quick Checks**

**1.** *d*

**2.** Financial accounting information is intended for users external to an organization such as investors, creditors, and government authorities. Managerial accounting focuses on providing information to managers, officers, and other decision makers within the organization.

**3.** No, GAAP do not control the practice of managerial accounting. Unlike external users, the internal users need managerial accounting information for planning and controlling business activities rather than for external comparison. Different types of information are required, depending on the activity. Therefore it is difficult to standardize managerial accounting.

**4.** Under TQM, all managers and employees should strive toward higher standards in their work and in the products and services they offer to customers.

**5.** Variable costs increase when volume of activity increases.

**6.** By being able to trace costs to cost objects (say, to products and departments), managers better understand the total costs associated with a cost object. This is useful when managers consider making changes to the cost object (such as when dropping the product or expanding the department).

**7.** Raw materials inventory, goods in process inventory, and finished goods inventory.

**8.** The cost of goods sold for merchandising companies includes all costs of acquiring the merchandise; the cost of goods sold for manufacturing companies includes the three costs of manufacturing: direct materials, direct labor, and overhead.

**9.** *a*

**10.** No; companies rarely report a manufacturing statement.

**11.** Beginning goods in process inventory is added to total manufacturing costs to yield total goods in process. Ending goods in process inventory is subtracted from total goods in process to yield cost of goods manufactured for the period.

## Key Terms

Key Terms are available at the book's Website for learning and testing in an online Flashcard Format.

**Continuous improvement** (p. 584)
**Contribution margin ratio** (p. 595)
**Control** (p. 581)
**Controllable or not controllable cost** (p. 586)
**Conversion costs** (p. 591)
**Cost object** (p. 585)
**Customer orientation** (p. 583)
**Direct costs** (p. 585)
**Direct labor** (p. 591)
**Direct labor costs** (p. 591)
**Direct material** (p. 590)
**Direct material costs** (p. 590)

**Factory overhead** (p. 591)
**Factory overhead costs** (p. 591)
**Finished goods inventory** (p. 589)
**Fixed cost** (p. 585)
**Goods in process inventory** (p. 589)
**Indirect costs** (p. 585)
**Indirect labor** (p. 591)
**Indirect labor costs** (p. 591)
**Indirect material** (p. 588)
**Just-in-time (JIT) manufacturing** (p. 584)
**Lean business model** (p. 584)
**Managerial accounting** (p. 580)
**Manufacturing statement** (p. 593)

**Opportunity cost** (p. 586)
**Out-of-pocket cost** (p. 586)
**Period costs** (p. 586)
**Planning** (p. 580)
**Prime costs** (p. 591)
**Product costs** (p. 586)
**Raw materials inventory** (p. 588)
**Sunk cost** (p. 586)
**Total quality management (TQM)** (p. 584)
**Unit contribution margin** (p. 595)
**Value chain** (p. 592)
**Variable cost** (p. 585)

## Personal Interactive Quiz

Personal Interactive Quizzes A and B are available at the book's Website to reinforce and assess your learning.

## Discussion Questions

**1.** Discuss the managerial accountant's role in business planning, control, and decision making.

**2.** Distinguish between managerial and financial accounting on
  **a.** Users and decision makers
  **b.** Purpose of information
  **c.** Flexibility of practice
  **d.** Time dimension
  **e.** Focus of information

**3.** Identify the usual changes that a company must make when it adopts a customer orientation.

**4.** Distinguish between direct material and indirect material.

**5.** Distinguish between direct labor and indirect labor.

**6.** Distinguish between factory overhead and selling and administrative overhead.

**7.** What product cost is listed as both a prime cost and a conversion cost?

**8.** Assume that you tour **Tastykake**'s factory where it makes its line of bakery items. List three direct costs and three indirect costs you are likely to see.

**9.** Should we evaluate a manager's performance on the basis of controllable or noncontrollable costs? Why?

**10.** Explain why knowledge of cost behavior is useful in product performance evaluation.

**11.** Explain why product costs are capitalized but period costs are expensed in the current accounting period.

**12.** Explain how business activities and inventories for a manufacturing company, a merchandising company, and a service company differ.

**13.** Why does managerial accounting often involve working with numerous predictions and estimates?

**14.** How do an income statement and a balance sheet for a manufacturing company and a merchandising company differ?

**15.** Refer to Appendix A and identify **Krispy Kreme**'s five inventory components (see its note 4) and reconcile this total to the amount reported on its balance sheet.

**16.** Besides inventories, what other assets often appear on manufacturers' balance sheets but not on merchandisers' balance sheets?

**17.** Why does a manufacturing company require three different inventory categories?

**18.** Manufacturing activities of a company are described in the _____. This statement summarizes the types and

amounts of costs incurred in a company's manufacturing _____.

**19.** What are the three categories of manufacturing costs?

**20.** List several examples of factory overhead.

**21.** List the four components of a manufacturing statement and provide specific examples of each for **Harley-Davidson**. **Harley-Davidson**

**22.** Prepare a proper title for the annual "manufacturing" statement of **Harley-Davidson**. Does the date match the balance sheet or income statement? Why? **Harley-Davidson**

**23.** Describe the relations among the income statement, the manufacturing statement, and a detailed listing of factory overhead costs.

**24.** Define and describe *unit contribution margin*.

**25.** Define and explain the *contribution margin ratio*.

**26.** Describe the contribution margin ratio in layperson's terms.

**27.** Why is the contribution margin ratio a useful measure for **Krispy Kreme** in deciding what products to manufacture?

---

**Red numbers denote Discussion Questions that involve decision-making.**

---

*Homework Manager repeats all numerical Quick Studies on the book's Website with new numbers.*

---

Managerial accounting (choose one):

**1.** Must follow generally accepted accounting principles.

**2.** Provides information to aid management in planning and controlling business activities.

**3.** Is directed at reporting aggregate data on the company as a whole.

**4.** Provides information that is widely available to all interested parties.

**QUICK STUDY**

**QS 14-1**
Managerial accounting defined

C1

---

Identify whether each description most likely applies to managerial or financial accounting:

**1.** _____ Its primary focus is on the organization as a whole.

**2.** _____ Its principles and practices are very flexible.

**3.** _____ It is directed at external users in making investment, credit, and other decisions.

**4.** _____ Its primary users are company managers.

**5.** _____ Its information is often available only after an audit is complete.

**QS 14-2**
Managerial accounting versus financial accounting

C2

---

Match each lean business concept with its best description by entering its letter in the blank:

**1.** _____ Customer orientation

**2.** _____ Total quality management

**3.** _____ Just-in-time manufacturing

**4.** _____ Continuous improvements

**A.** Inventory is acquired or produced only as needed.

**B.** Flexible product designs can be modified to accommodate customer choices.

**C.** Every manager and employee constantly looks for ways to improve company operations.

**D.** Focuses on quality throughout the production process.

**QS 14-3**
Lean business concepts

C3

---

Which of these statements is true regarding fixed and variable costs?

**1.** Fixed costs increase and variable costs decrease in total as activity volume decreases.

**2.** Fixed costs stay the same and variable costs increase in total as activity volume increases.

**3.** Both fixed and variable costs increase as activity volume increases.

**4.** Both fixed and variable costs stay the same in total as activity volume increases.

**QS 14-4**
Fixed and variable costs

C4

**QS 14-5**
Product and period costs
C5

Which of these statements is true regarding product and period costs?

**1.** Sales commission is a product cost and factory rent is a period cost.

**2.** Factory wages is a product cost and direct material is a period cost.

**3.** Factory maintenance is a product cost and sales commission is a period cost.

**4.** Sales commission is a product cost and depreciation on factory equipment is a product cost.

---

**QS 14-6**
Inventory reporting for
manufacturers
C6

Three inventory categories are reported on a manufacturing company's balance sheet: (a) raw materials, (b) goods in process, and (c) finished goods. Identify the usual order in which these inventory items are reported on a balance sheet.

**1.** (a)(b)(c)     **2.** (b)(a)(c)     **3.** (b)(c)(a)     **4.** (c)(b)(a)

---

**QS 14-7**
Cost of goods sold   P1

A company has year-end cost of goods manufactured of $5,000, beginning finished goods inventory of $700, and ending finished goods inventory of $850. Its cost of goods sold is

**1.** $4,250     **2.** $4,000     **3.** $4,850     **4.** $6,550

---

**QS 14-8**
Manufacturing flows identified
C8

Identify the usual sequence of manufacturing activities by filling in the blank (1, 2, or 3) corresponding to its order: _____ Production activities; _____ Sales activities; _____ Materials activities.

---

**QS 14-9**
Cost of goods manufactured
P2

Prepare the manufacturing statement for Triton Company using the following information.

| | |
|---|---|
| Direct materials . . . . . . . . . . . . . . . . . . . | $192,500 |
| Direct labor . . . . . . . . . . . . . . . . . . . . . | 65,150 |
| Factory overhead costs . . . . . . . . . . . . . . | 26,000 |
| Goods in process, Dec. 31, 2004 . . . . . . . | 159,600 |
| Goods in process, Dec. 31, 2005 . . . . . . . | 144,750 |

---

**QS 14-10**
Contribution margin
ratio  A1

Compute and interpret the contribution margin ratio using the following data: sales, $6,000; total variable cost, $4,000.

---

**QS 14-11**
Cost of goods sold
P1

Compute cost of goods sold for year 2005 using the following information.

| | |
|---|---|
| Finished goods inventory, Dec. 31, 2004 . . . . . . . . . . | $321,500 |
| Goods in process inventory, Dec. 31, 2004 . . . . . . . | 74,550 |
| Goods in process inventory, Dec. 31, 2005 . . . . . . . | 81,200 |
| Cost of goods manufactured, year 2005 . . . . . . . . . . | 972,345 |
| Finished goods inventory, Dec. 31, 2005 . . . . . . . . . . | 297,200 |

*Homework Manager repeats all numerical Exercises on the book's Website with new numbers.*

---

# EXERCISES

**Exercise 14-1**
Sources of accounting
information

C1

Both managerial accounting and financial accounting provide useful information to decision makers. Indicate in this chart the most likely source of information for each business decision (a decision can require major input from both sources):

| Business Decision | Primary Information Source | |
|---|---|---|
| | Managerial | Financial |
| Estimate product cost for a new line of basketball shoes . . . . . . . . . . | ____ | ____ |
| Plan the budget for next quarter . . . . . . . . . . . . . . . . . . . . . . . . . . . | ____ | ____ |
| Report financial performance to the board of directors . . . . . . . . . . . . | ____ | ____ |
| Measure profitability of all individual stores . . . . . . . . . . . . . . . . . . . . | ____ | ____ |
| Prepare financial reports according to GAAP . . . . . . . . . . . . . . . . . . . | ____ | ____ |
| Determine amount of dividends to pay common stockholders . . . . . . . | ____ | ____ |
| Determine location and size for a new plant . . . . . . . . . . . . . . . . . . . | ____ | ____ |
| Evaluate a purchasing department's performance . . . . . . . . . . . . . . . . | ____ | ____ |

Complete the following statements by filling in the blanks:

**1.** _____ is the process of setting goals and making plans to achieve them.

**2.** _____ _____ usually covers a period of 5 to 10 years.

**3.** _____ _____ usually covers a period of one year.

**4.** _____ is the process of monitoring planning decisions and evaluating an organization's activities and employees.

**Exercise 14-2**
Planning and control descriptions
C1

---

In the following chart, compare financial accounting and managerial accounting by describing how each differs for the items listed. Be specific in your responses.

**Exercise 14-3**
Characteristics of financial accounting and managerial accounting
C2

|  | Financial Accounting | Managerial Accounting |
|---|---|---|
| 1. Users and decision makers . . . . . . . . | ____ | ____ |
| 2. Purpose of information . . . . . . . . . . | ____ | ____ |
| 3. Flexibility of practice . . . . . . . . . . . . | ____ | ____ |
| 4. Timeliness of information . . . . . . . . | ____ | ____ |
| 5. Time dimension . . . . . . . . . . . . . . | ____ | ____ |
| 6. Focus of information . . . . . . . . . . . | ____ | ____ |
| 7. Nature of information . . . . . . . . . . . | ____ | ____ |

---

Customer orientation means that a company's managers and employees respond to customers' changing wants and needs. You are to stop at a restaurant, hotel, or other local business in your area and pick up a customer response card. (1) On the right hand side of a sheet of paper, write the usual competitive forces: time, quality, cost, and flexibility of service. Attach the customer response card to the left side of the sheet. Draw arrows linking questions on the customer response card to the competitive forces. (2) Identify how the response card provides information to management and employees to better meet competitive forces. Be prepared to form small groups to compare and contrast customer response cards across the types of businesses.

**Exercise 14-4**
Customer orientation in practice
C3

---

Following are three separate events affecting the managerial accounting systems for different companies. Match the management concept(s) that the company is likely to adopt for the event identified. There is some overlap in the meaning of customer orientation and total quality management and, therefore, some responses can include more than one concept.

**Exercise 14-5**
Management concepts
C3

| Event | Management Concept |
|---|---|
| _____ 1. The company starts measuring inventory turnover and discontinues elaborate inventory records. Its new focus is to pull inventory through the system. | a. Total quality management (TQM) |
| _____ 2. The company starts reporting measures on customer complaints and product returns from customers. | b. Just-in-time (JIT) system<br>c. Continuous improvement (CI) |
| _____ 3. The company starts reporting measures such as the percent of defective products and the number of units scrapped. | d. Customer orientation (CO) |

---

**Johnson & Johnson,** a manufacturing company, incurs the following costs. (1) Classify each cost as either a product or a period cost. If a product cost, identify it as a prime and/or conversion cost. (2) Classify each cost as either a direct cost or an indirect cost using the product as the cost object.

**Exercise 14-6**
Cost analysis and identification
C4  C5

| Cost | Product Cost | | Period Cost | Direct Cost | Indirect Cost |
|---|---|---|---|---|---|
|  | Prime | Conversion | | | |
| Direct materials used . . . . . . . . . . . . . . . . . . | ____ | ____ | ____ | ____ | ____ |
| State and federal income taxes . . . . . . . . . . . . | ____ | ____ | ____ | ____ | ____ |
| Payroll taxes for production supervisor . . . . . . | ____ | ____ | ____ | ____ | ____ |
| Amortization of patents on factory machine . . . | ____ | ____ | ____ | ____ | ____ |

[continued on next page]

[continued from previous page]

| | | | | |
|---|---|---|---|---|
| Accident insurance on factory workers ...... | ___ | ___ | ___ | ___ |
| Wages to assembly workers ............. | ___ | ___ | ___ | ___ |
| Factory utilities ........................ | ___ | ___ | ___ | ___ |
| Small tools used ...................... | ___ | ___ | ___ | ___ |
| Bad debts expense .................... | ___ | ___ | ___ | ___ |
| Depreciation—Factory building ........... | ___ | ___ | ___ | ___ |
| Advertising .......................... | ___ | ___ | ___ | ___ |
| Office supplies used ................... | ___ | ___ | ___ | ___ |

**Exercise 14-7**

Cost classifications    C4

(1) Identify each of the five cost classifications discussed in the chapter. (2) List two purposes of identifying these separate cost classifications.

**Exercise 14-8**

Cost analysis and classification

C4

Listed here are product costs for the production of soccer balls. (1) Classify each cost (a) as either fixed or variable and (b) as either direct or indirect. (2) What pattern do you see regarding the relation between costs classified by behavior and costs classified by traceability?

| | Cost by Behavior | | Cost by Traceability | |
|---|---|---|---|---|
| **Product Cost** | **Variable** | **Fixed** | **Direct** | **Indirect** |
| Leather cover for soccer balls ............. | ___ | ___ | ___ | ___ |
| Lace to hold leather together ............. | ___ | ___ | ___ | ___ |
| Wages of assembly workers .............. | ___ | ___ | ___ | ___ |
| Taxes on factory ...................... | ___ | ___ | ___ | ___ |
| Annual flat fee paid for office security ........ | ___ | ___ | ___ | ___ |
| Coolants for machinery ................. | ___ | ___ | ___ | ___ |
| Machinery depreciation ................. | ___ | ___ | ___ | ___ |

**Exercise 14-9**

Balance sheet identification and preparation

C6

Current assets for two different companies at calendar year-end 2005 are listed here. One is a manufacturer, Roller Blades Mfg., and the other, Sun Fresh Foods, is a grocery distribution company. (1) Identify which set of numbers relates to the manufacturer and which to the merchandiser. (2) Prepare the current asset section for each company from this information. Discuss why the current asset section for these two companies is different.

| Account | Company 1 | Company 2 |
|---|---|---|
| Cash ...................... | $ 9,000 | $ 7,000 |
| Raw materials inventory .......... | — | 44,000 |
| Merchandise inventory ........... | 47,000 | — |
| Goods in process inventory ....... | — | 32,000 |
| Finished goods inventory .......... | — | 52,000 |
| Accounts receivable, net .......... | 64,000 | 77,000 |
| Prepaid expenses .............. | 3,500 | 700 |

**Exercise 14-10**

Cost of goods sold computation

C7   P1

Compute cost of goods sold for each of these two companies for the year ended December 31, 2005:

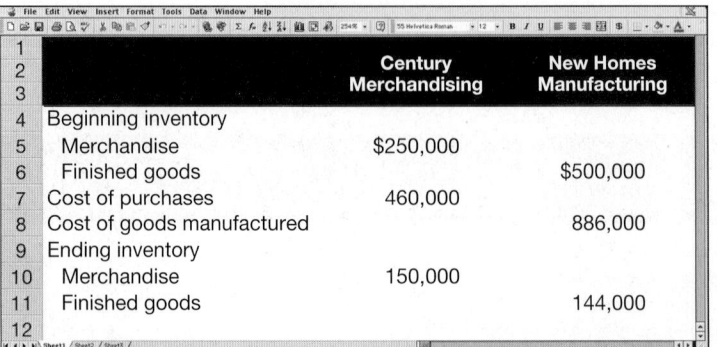

| | Century Merchandising | New Homes Manufacturing |
|---|---|---|
| Beginning inventory | | |
| Merchandise | $250,000 | |
| Finished goods | | $500,000 |
| Cost of purchases | 460,000 | |
| Cost of goods manufactured | | 886,000 |
| Ending inventory | | |
| Merchandise | 150,000 | |
| Finished goods | | 144,000 |

**Check**   Century COGS, $560,000

Using the following data, compute (1) the cost of goods manufactured and (2) the cost of goods sold for both Canyon Company and Crossings Company.

**Exercise 14-11**
Cost of goods manufactured and cost of goods sold computation
P1   P2

| | Canyon Company | Crossings Company |
|---|---|---|
| Beginning finished goods inventory ......... | $14,000 | $18,450 |
| Beginning goods in process inventory ....... | 16,500 | 21,950 |
| Beginning raw materials inventory .......... | 9,250 | 11,000 |
| Rental cost on factory equipment .......... | 29,000 | 24,750 |
| Direct labor ........................ | 21,000 | 37,000 |
| Ending finished goods inventory ........... | 19,650 | 15,300 |
| Ending goods in process inventory ......... | 24,000 | 18,000 |
| Ending raw materials inventory ............ | 7,300 | 9,200 |
| Factory utilities ...................... | 11,000 | 14,000 |
| Factory supplies used .................. | 10,200 | 5,200 |
| General and administrative expenses ........ | 23,000 | 45,000 |
| Indirect labor ....................... | 3,250 | 9,660 |
| Repairs—Factory equipment .............. | 6,780 | 3,500 |
| Raw materials purchases ................ | 35,000 | 54,000 |
| Sales salaries ....................... | 52,000 | 48,000 |

**Check**   Canyon COGS, $105,030

---

For each of the following account balances for a manufacturing company, place a ✔ in the appropriate column indicating that it appears on the balance sheet, the income statement, the manufacturing statement, and/or a detailed listing of factory overhead costs. Assume that the income statement shows the calculation of cost of goods sold and the manufacturing statement shows only the total amount of factory overhead. (*An account balance can appear on more than one report.*)

**Exercise 14-12**
Components of accounting reports
C8   P2

| | Account | Balance Sheet | Income Statement | Manufacturing Statement | Overhead Report |
|---|---|---|---|---|---|
| 4 | Accounts receivable | | | | |
| 5 | Computer supplies used in office | | | | |
| 6 | Beginning finished goods inventory | | | | |
| 7 | Beginning goods in process inventory | | | | |
| 8 | Beginning raw materials inventory | | | | |
| 9 | Cash | | | | |
| 10 | Depreciation expense—Factory building | | | | |
| 11 | Depreciation expense—Factory equipment | | | | |
| 12 | Depreciation expense—Office building | | | | |
| 13 | Depreciation expense—Office equipment | | | | |
| 14 | Direct labor | | | | |
| 15 | Ending finished goods inventory | | | | |
| 16 | Ending goods in process inventory | | | | |
| 17 | Ending raw materials inventory | | | | |
| 18 | Factory maintenance wages | | | | |
| 19 | Computer supplies used in factory | | | | |
| 20 | Income taxes | | | | |
| 21 | Insurance on factory building | | | | |
| 22 | Rent cost on office building | | | | |
| 23 | Office supplies used | | | | |
| 24 | Property taxes on factory building | | | | |
| 25 | Raw materials purchases | | | | |
| 26 | Sales | | | | |

---

Given the following selected account balances of Randa Company, prepare its manufacturing statement in proper form for the year ended on December 31, 2005. Include a listing of the individual overhead account balances in this statement.

**Exercise 14-13**
Manufacturing statement preparation   P2

| Sales ................................... | $1,252,000 |
|---|---|
| Raw materials inventory, Dec. 31, 2004 .......... | 39,000 |
| Goods in process inventory, Dec. 31, 2004 ....... | 55,900 |
| Finished goods inventory, Dec. 31, 2004 .......... | 64,750 |
| Raw materials purchases ..................... | 177,600 |
| Direct labor ............................. | 227,000 |
| Factory computer supplies used .............. | 19,840 |
| Indirect labor .......................... | 49,000 |
| Repairs—Factory equipment ................. | 7,250 |
| Rent cost of factory building ................. | 59,000 |
| Advertising expenses ...................... | 96,000 |
| General and administrative expenses ........... | 131,300 |
| Raw materials inventory, Dec. 31, 2005 .......... | 44,700 |
| Goods in process inventory, Dec. 31, 2005 ....... | 43,500 |
| Finished goods inventory, Dec. 31, 2005 .......... | 69,300 |

**Check**   Cost of goods manufactured,
$546,390

---

**Exercise 14-14**

Income statement
preparation   P2

Use the information in Exercise 14-13 to prepare an income statement for Randa Company (a manufacturer). Assume that its cost of goods manufactured is $546,390.

---

**Exercise 14-15**

Cost flows in manufacturing

C8   P2

The following chart shows how costs flow through a business as a product is manufactured. Some boxes in the flowchart show cost amount. Compute the cost amounts for boxes that contain question marks.

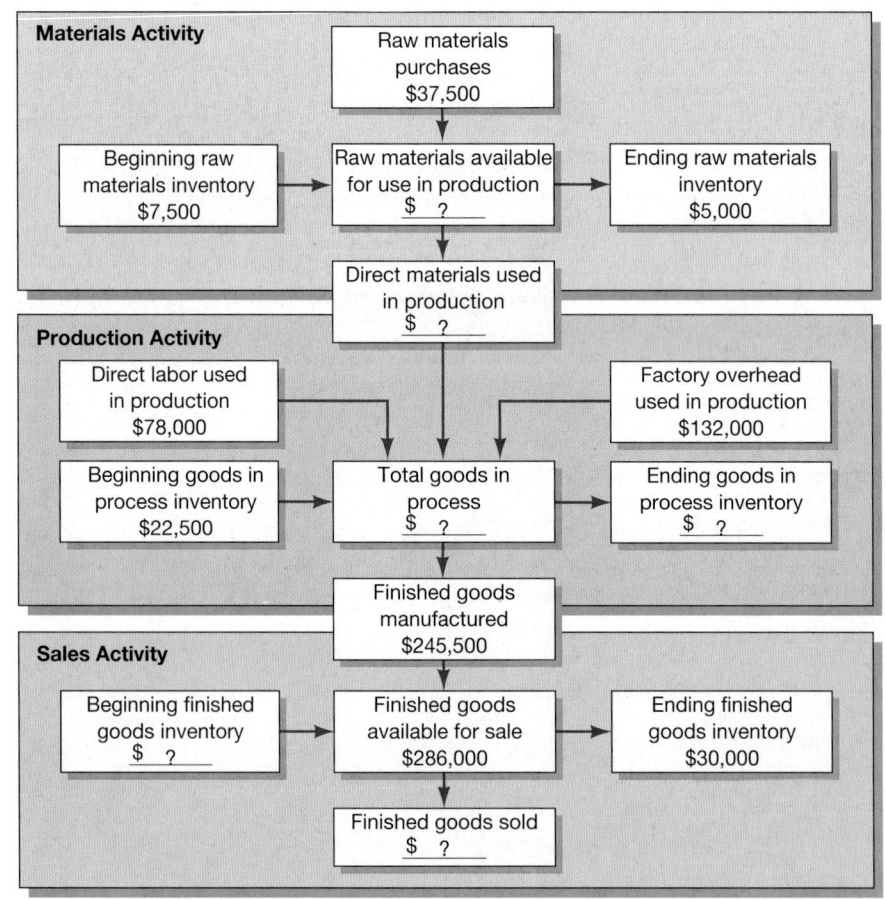

---

## PROBLEM SET A

**Problem 14-1A**

Managerial accountant's role

C1   C3

This chapter discusses the purposes of managerial accounting and the current business environment. You are to look through the *automobile* section of your local newspaper; the Sunday paper is often best. Review advertisements of sport utility vehicles and note how many manufacturers offer these products and the factors on which they compete.

**Required**

Discuss the potential contributions and responsibilities of the managerial accounting professional in helping an automobile manufacturer succeed. (*Hint:* Think about information and estimates that a managerial accountant might provide new entrants into the sports utility market.)

A trip through a drive-up window of any leading fast-food restaurant is useful in understanding concepts such as total quality management (TQM), just-in-time (JIT), and continuous improvement (CI). Each restaurant can be viewed as a small manufacturing center. List two fast-food restaurants you are familiar with in the first column of the following table (e.g., McDonald's, Taco Bell, Burger King, and KFC). Record in the table how each company is putting each of these lean business concepts into action, both favorably and unfavorably.

**Problem 14-2A**

Lean business concepts

C3

| Restaurant | TQM | JIT | CI |
|---|---|---|---|
| 1. | | | |
| 2. | | | |

Listed here are the total costs associated with the production of 1,000 drum sets manufactured by NeatBeat. The drum sets sell for $300 each.

**Problem 14-3A**

Cost computation, classification, and analysis; contribution margin income statement

C4  A1

| Costs | Cost by Behavior | | Cost by Function | |
|---|---|---|---|---|
| | Variable | Fixed | Product | Period |
| Plastic for casing—$12,000 . . . . . . . . . . . . . . . . . . . . . . . | $12,000 | | $12,000 | |
| Wages of assembly workers—$60,000 . . . . . . . . . . . . . . . . | | | | |
| Property taxes on factory—$4,500 . . . . . . . . . . . . . . . . . . | | | | |
| Accounting staff salaries—$45,000 . . . . . . . . . . . . . . . . . . | | | | |
| Drum stands (1,000 stands outsourced)—$25,000 . . . . . . . . | | | | |
| Rent cost of equipment for sales staff—$7,000 . . . . . . . . . | | | | |
| Upper management salaries—$100,000 . . . . . . . . . . . . . . . | | | | |
| Annual flat fee for maintenance service—$9,000 . . . . . . . . . | | | | |
| Sales commissions—$10 per unit . . . . . . . . . . . . . . . . . . . | | | | |
| Machinery depreciation—$10,000 . . . . . . . . . . . . . . . . . . . | | | | |

**Required**

1. Classify each cost and its amount as (a) either fixed or variable and (b) either product or period (the first cost is completed as an example).

2. Compute the (a) contribution margin and (b) contribution margin ratio by filling in the boxes in the following report:

| NeatBeat |
|---|
| **Contribution Margin Income Statement** |
| **For Year Ended December 31, 2005** |

| | | | | |
|---|---|---|---|---|
| Sales ($300 × 1,000) . . . . . . | $☐ | | | 100% |
| Variable costs | | | | |
| Plastic for casing . . . . . . . . | $☐ | | | |
| Assembly worker wages . . | ☐ | | | |
| Drum stands . . . . . . . . . . | ☐ | | | |
| Sales commissions . . . . . . . | ☐ | ☐ | | 36% |
| Contribution margin . . . . . . . | $☐ | Contribution margin ratio* | ☐% | |

**Check**  Total variable cost, $107,000

\* Contribution margin ratio = Contribution margin/Sales.

*Analysis Component*

3. Interpret the contribution margin and the contribution margin ratio.

**Problem 14-4A**
Cost classification
and explanation

C4   C5

Assume that you must make a presentation to the marketing staff explaining the difference between product and period costs. Your supervisor tells you the marketing staff would also like clarification regarding prime and conversion costs and an explanation of how these terms fit with product and period cost. You are told that many on the staff are unable to classify costs in their merchandising activities.

**Required**

Prepare a one-page memorandum to your supervisor outlining your presentation to the marketing staff.

---

**Problem 14-5A**
Opportunity cost
estimation and application

C1   C4

Refer to *Decision Maker,* **Purchase Manager,** in this chapter. Assume that you are the motorcycle manufacturer's managerial accountant. The purchasing manager asks you about preparing an estimate of the related costs for buying motorcycle seats from supplier (B). She tells you this estimate is needed because unless dollar estimates are attached to nonfinancial factors, such as lost production time, her supervisor will not give it full attention. The purchasing manager also shows you this information:

- Production output is 3,000 motorcycles per year based on 250 production days a year.
- Production time per day is 8 hours at a cost of $2,000 per hour to run the production line.
- Lost production time due to poor quality is 1%.
- Satisfied customers purchase, on average, three motorcycles during a lifetime.
- Satisfied customers recommend the product, on average, to 10 other people.
- Marketing predicts that using seat (B) will result in 10 lost customers per year from repeat business and referrals.
- Average contribution margin per motorcycle is $3,000.

**Required**

Estimate the costs (including opportunity costs) of buying motorcycle seats from supplier (B). This problem requires you to think creatively and make reasonable estimates and, therefore, there could be more than one correct answer. (*Hint:* Reread the answer to *Decision Maker* and compare the cost savings for buying from supplier [B] to the sum of lost customer revenue from repeat business and referrals and the cost of lost production time.)

**Check**   Cost of lost production time, $40,000

---

**Problem 14-6A**
Ending inventory computation
and evaluation

C3   C6

Shepler's Boot Company makes specialty boots for the rodeo circuit. On December 31, 2004, the company had (a) 500 pairs of boots in finished goods inventory and (b) 1,500 heels at a cost of $5 each in raw materials inventory. During 2005, the company purchased 50,000 additional heels at $5 each and manufactured 20,000 pairs of boots.

**Required**

**Check**   (1) Ending (heel) inventory, $57,500 (11,500 units)

**1.** Determine the unit and dollar amounts of raw materials inventory in heels at December 31, 2005.

*Analysis Component*

**2.** Write a one-half page memorandum to the production manager explaining why a just-in-time inventory system for heels should be considered. Include the amount of working capital that can be reduced at December 31, 2005, if the ending heel raw material inventory is cut in half.

---

**Problem 14-7A**
Inventory computation
and reporting

C4   C7   P1

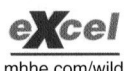
mhhe.com/wild

Shown here are the annual financial data at December 31, 2005, taken from two different companies.

|  | Pinnacle Retail | Slope Board Manufacturing |
|---|---|---|
| Beginning inventory |  |  |
| Merchandise ................ | $150,000 |  |
| Finished goods .............. |  | $300,000 |
| Cost of purchases ............. | 250,000 |  |
| Cost of goods manufactured ....... |  | 586,000 |
| Ending inventory |  |  |
| Merchandise ................ | 100,000 |  |
| Finished goods .............. |  | 200,000 |

**Required**

1. Compute the cost of goods sold section of the income statement at December 31, 2005, for each company. Include proper title and format in the solution.
2. Write a half-page memorandum to your instructor (a) identifying the inventory accounts and (b) describing where each is reported on the income statement and balance sheet for both companies.

**Check** (1) Slope Board's cost of goods sold, $686,000

---

The following calendar year-end information is taken from the December 31, 2005, adjusted trial balance and other records of Plaza Company.

**Problem 14-8A**

Manufacturing and income statements; inventory analysis   P2

| | | | |
|---|---|---|---|
| Advertising expense | $ 30,750 | Direct labor | 677,480 |
| Depreciation expense—Office equipment | 9,250 | Income taxes expense | 235,725 |
| Depreciation expense—Selling equipment | 10,600 | Indirect labor | 58,875 |
| Depreciation expense—Factory equipment | 35,550 | Miscellaneous production costs | 10,425 |
| Factory supervision | 104,600 | Office salaries expense | 65,000 |
| Factory supplies used | 9,350 | Raw materials purchases | 927,000 |
| Factory utilities | 35,000 | Rent expense—Office space | 24,000 |
| Inventories | | Rent expense—Selling space | 28,100 |
| Raw materials, December 31, 2004 | 168,850 | Rent expense—Factory building | 78,800 |
| Raw materials, December 31, 2005 | 184,000 | Maintenance expense—Factory equipment | 37,400 |
| Goods in process, December 31, 2004 | 17,700 | Sales | 4,527,000 |
| Goods in process, December 31, 2005 | 21,380 | Sales discounts | 64,500 |
| Finished goods, December 31, 2004 | 169,350 | Sales salaries expense | 394,560 |
| Finished goods, December 31, 2005 | 138,490 | | |

**Required**

1. Prepare the company's 2005 manufacturing statement.
2. Prepare the company's 2005 income statement that reports separate categories for (a) selling expenses and (b) general and administrative expenses.

**Check** (1) Cost of goods manufactured, $1,955,650

*Analysis Component*

3. Compute the (a) inventory turnover and (b) days' sales in inventory for both its raw materials inventory and its finished goods inventory (see Chapter 5). Discuss some possible reasons for differences between these ratios for the two types of inventories.

---

King grocery chain, a market leader, wants to increase sales to its existing customers by creating a customer orientation to better meet buyer needs and wants. Assume that King hires you as a consultant to analyze its operations and suggest improvements. King's goal is to increase its contribution margin by $40,000.

**Problem 14-9A**

Sales and costs estimation; contribution margin analysis

C3   A1

**Required**

1. To increase King's sales and contribution margin from existing customers, offer three improvements that you have observed in other stores and believe would be successful here.
2. What level of increase in sales is necessary for King to increase contribution margin by $40,000? (*Hint:* With each suggestion in part [1], identify the expected sales dollars and the contribution margin ratio to meet the $40,000 increase in contribution margin.)

---

This chapter discusses the purposes of managerial accounting and the current business environment. You are to look through the *home electronics* section of your local newspaper; the Sunday paper is often best. Review advertisements of home electronics and note how many manufacturers offer these products and the factors on which they compete.

**PROBLEM SET B**

**Problem 14-1B**

Managerial accountant's role

C1   C3

**Required**

Discuss the potential contributions and responsibilities of the managerial accounting professional in helping a home electronics manufacturer succeed. (*Hint:* Think about information and estimates that a managerial accountant might provide new entrants into the home electronics market.)

**Problem 14-2B**

Lean business concepts

C3

A trip to the photography store is useful in understanding concepts such as total quality management (TQM), just-in-time (JIT), and continuous improvement (CI). List two photography stores you are familiar with in the first column of the following table. Record in the table how each store is putting each of these lean business concepts into action, both favorably and unfavorably. (*Hint:* To prepare a response to this question, you may want to watch how film is processed and prints prepared within 1 hour.)

| Photography Store | TQM | JIT | CI |
|---|---|---|---|
| 1. | | | |
| 2. | | | |

---

**Problem 14-3B**

Cost computation, classification, and analysis; contribution margin income statement

C4  A1

Listed here are the total costs associated with the production of 12,000 CDs manufactured by Hip-Hop. The CDs sell for $15 each.

| | | Cost by Behavior | | Cost by Function | |
|---|---|---|---|---|---|
| **Costs** | | **Variable** | **Fixed** | **Product** | **Period** |
| Plastic for CDs—$1,000 . . . . . . . . . . . . . . . . . . . . | | $1,000 | | $1,000 | |
| Wages of assembly workers—$20,000 . . . . . . . . . . . . . | | | | | |
| Rent cost of factory—$4,500 . . . . . . . . . . . . . . . . . | | | | | |
| Systems staff salaries—$10,000 . . . . . . . . . . . . . . . . | | | | | |
| Labeling (12,000 outsourced)—$2,500 . . . . . . . . . . . . | | | | | |
| Rent cost of office equipment—$700 . . . . . . . . . . . . . | | | | | |
| Upper management salaries—$100,000 . . . . . . . . . . . . | | | | | |
| Annual fixed fee for cleaning service—$3,000 . . . . . . . . | | | | | |
| Sales commissions—$0.50 per CD . . . . . . . . . . . . . . | | | | | |
| Machinery depreciation—$15,000 . . . . . . . . . . . . . . . | | | | | |

**Required**

**1.** Classify each cost and its amount as (a) either fixed or variable and (b) either product or period.

**2.** Compute the (a) contribution margin and (b) contribution margin ratio by filling in the boxes in the following report:

| HIP-HOP | | | |
|---|---|---|---|
| **Contribution Margin Income Statement** | | | |
| **For Year Ended December 31, 2005** | | | |
| Sales ($15 × 12,000) . . . . . . | $☐ | | 100% |
| Variable costs | | | |
| Plastic for CDs . . . . . . . . . | $☐ | | |
| Assembly worker wages . . | ☐ | | |
| Labels outsourced . . . . . . | ☐ | | |
| Sales commissions . . . . . . | ☐ | ☐ | 16% |
| Contribution margin . . . . . . . | $☐ | Contribution margin ratio* ☐% | |

**Check**   Total variable cost, $29,500

\* Contribution margin ratio = Contribution margin/Sales.

*Analysis Component*

**3.** Interpret the contribution margin and the contribution margin ratio.

---

**Problem 14-4B**

Cost classification and explanation

C4  C5

Assume that you must make a presentation to a client explaining the difference between prime and conversion costs. The client makes and sells cookies for 50,000 customers per week. The client tells you that her sales staff also would like a clarification regarding product and period costs. She tells you that most of the staff lack training in managerial accounting.

**Required**

Prepare a one-page memorandum to your client outlining your planned presentation to her sales staff.

Refer to *Decision Maker,* **Purchase Manager,** in this chapter. Assume that you are the motorcycle manufacturer's managerial accountant. The purchasing manager asks you about preparing an estimate of the related costs for buying motorcycle seats from supplier (B). She tells you this estimate is needed because unless dollar estimates are attached to nonfinancial factors such as lost production time, her supervisor will not give it full attention. The purchasing manager also shows you this information:

- Production output is 2,000 motorcycles per year based on 250 production days a year.
- Production time per day is 8 hours at a cost of $500 per hour to run the production line.
- Lost production time due to poor quality is 1%.
- Satisfied customers purchase, on average, three motorcycles during a lifetime.
- Satisfied customers recommend the product, on average, to four other people.
- Marketing predicts that using seat (B) will result in eight lost customers per year from repeat business and referrals.
- Average contribution margin per motorcycle is $4,000.

**Required**

Estimate the costs (including opportunity costs) of buying motorcycle seats from supplier (B). This problem requires you to think creatively and make reasonable estimates and, therefore, there could be more than one correct answer. (*Hint:* Reread the answer to *Decision Maker,* and compare the cost savings for buying from supplier [B] to the sum of lost customer revenue from repeat business and referrals and the cost of lost production time.)

**Problem 14-5B**
Opportunity cost estimation and application

C1   C4

**Check**    Cost of lost customer revenue, $32,000

---

Icey Edges makes specialty skates for the ice skating circuit. On December 31, 2004, the company had (a) 1,500 skates in finished goods inventory and (b) 2,000 blades at a cost of $15 each in raw materials inventory. During 2005, Icey Edges purchased 45,000 additional blades at $15 each and manufactured 20,000 pairs of skates.

**Required**

**1.** Determine the unit and dollar amounts of raw materials inventory in blades at December 31, 2005.

*Analysis Component*

**2.** Write a one-half page memorandum to the production manager explaining why a just-in-time inventory system for blades should be considered. Include the amount of working capital that can be reduced at December 31, 2005, if the ending blade raw material inventory is cut in half.

**Problem 14-6B**
Ending inventory computation and evaluation

C3   C6

**Check**    (1) Ending (blade) inventory, $105,000 (7,000 units)

---

Shown here are the annual financial data at December 31, 2005, taken from two different companies.

| | Cardinal Drug Retail | Nandina Manufacturing |
|---|---|---|
| Beginning inventory | | |
|    Merchandise | $ 50,000 | |
|    Finished goods | | $200,000 |
| Cost of purchases | 350,000 | |
| Cost of goods manufactured | | 686,000 |
| Ending inventory | | |
|    Merchandise | 25,000 | |
|    Finished goods | | 300,000 |

**Problem 14-7B**
Inventory computation and reporting

C4   C7   P1

**Required**

**1.** Compute the cost of goods sold section of the income statement at December 31, 2005, for each company. Include proper title and format in the solution.

**2.** Write a half-page memorandum to your instructor (a) identifying the inventory accounts and (b) identifying where each is reported on the income statement and balance sheet for both companies.

**Check**    (1) Cardinal Drug cost of goods sold, $375,000

**Problem 14-8B**

Manufacturing and income statements; analysis of inventories

P2

The following calendar year-end information is taken from the December 31, 2005, adjusted trial balance and other records of Firethorn Furniture.

| | | | |
|---|---|---|---|
| Advertising expense | $ 22,250 | Direct labor | 564,500 |
| Depreciation expense—Office equipment | 10,440 | Income taxes expense | 138,700 |
| Depreciation expense—Selling equipment | 12,125 | Indirect labor | 61,000 |
| Depreciation expense—Factory equipment | 37,400 | Miscellaneous production costs | 10,440 |
| Factory supervision | 123,500 | Office salaries expense | 72,875 |
| Factory supplies used | 8,060 | Raw materials purchases | 896,375 |
| Factory utilities | 39,500 | Rent expense—Office space | 25,625 |
| Inventories | | Rent expense—Selling space | 29,000 |
|   Raw materials, December 31, 2004 | 42,375 | Rent expense—Factory building | 95,500 |
|   Raw materials, December 31, 2005 | 72,430 | Maintenance expense—Factory equipment | 32,375 |
|   Goods in process, December 31, 2004 | 14,500 | Sales | 5,002,000 |
|   Goods in process, December 31, 2005 | 16,100 | Sales discounts | 59,375 |
|   Finished goods, December 31, 2004 | 179,200 | Sales salaries expense | 297,300 |
|   Finished goods, December 31, 2005 | 143,750 | | |

**Check** (1) Cost of goods manufactured, $1,836,995

**Required**

1. Prepare the company's 2005 manufacturing statement.

2. Prepare the company's 2005 income statement that reports separate categories for (a) selling expenses and (b) general and administrative expenses.

*Analysis Component*

3. Compute the (a) inventory turnover and (b) days' sales in inventory for both its raw materials inventory and its finished goods inventory (see Chapter 5). Discuss some possible reasons for differences between these ratios for the two types of inventories.

---

**Problem 14-9B**

Sales and costs estimation; contribution margin analysis

C3  A1

The Hole Bagel chain, a market leader, wishes to increase sales to its existing customers by creating a customer orientation to better meet buyer needs and wants. Assume that The Hole Bagel hires you as a consultant to analyze its operations and suggest improvements. The Hole Bagel's goal is to increase its contribution margin by $10,000.

**Required**

1. To increase The Hole Bagel's sales and contribution margin from existing customers, offer three improvements that you have observed in other stores and believe would be successful here.

2. What level of increase in sales is necessary for The Hole Bagel to increase contribution margin by $10,000? (*Hint:* With each suggestion in part [1], identify the expected sales dollars and contribution margin ratio to meet the $10,000 increase in contribution margin.)

---

**PROBLEM SET C**

Problem Set C is available at the book's Website to reinforce and assess your learning.

---

**SERIAL PROBLEM**

Success Systems

*(This serial problem began in Chapter 1 and continues through most of the book. If previous chapter segments were not completed, the serial problem can begin at this point. It is helpful, but not necessary, for you to use the Working Papers that accompany the book.)*

Kay Breeze, owner of Success Systems, decides to diversify her business by manufacturing computer workstation furniture.

**Required**

**1.** Classify the following manufacturing costs of Success Systems by behavior and traceability.

| | Cost by Behavior | | Cost by Traceability | |
|---|---|---|---|---|
| **Product Costs** | **Variable** | **Fixed** | **Direct** | **Indirect** |
| Laminate coverings for desktops ......... | ____ | ____ | ____ | ____ |
| Wages of desk assembler .............. | ____ | ____ | ____ | ____ |
| Taxes on assembly workshop ............ | ____ | ____ | ____ | ____ |
| Glue to assemble workstation component parts .................. | ____ | ____ | ____ | ____ |
| Depreciation on tools ................ | ____ | ____ | ____ | ____ |
| Electricity for workshop .............. | ____ | ____ | ____ | ____ |
| Monthly flat fee to clean workshop ........ | ____ | ____ | ____ | ____ |

**2.** Prepare a manufacturing statement for Success Systems for the month ended January 31, 2006. Assume the following manufacturing costs:

Direct materials: $1,925

Factory overhead: $260

Direct labor: $652

Beginning goods in process: none (December 31, 2005)

Ending goods in process: $1,596 (January 31, 2006)

Beginning finished goods inventory: none (December 31, 2005)

Ending finished goods inventory: $144 (January 31, 2006)

**3.** Prepare the costs of goods sold section of a partial income statement for Success Systems for the month ended January 31, 2006.

**Check**   COGS, $1,097

---

## BEYOND THE NUMBERS

**BTN 14-1**   Managerial accounting is more than recording, maintaining, and reporting financial results. Managerial accountants must provide managers with both financial and nonfinancial information including estimates, projections, and forecasts. Looking into the future involves risk. **Krispy Kreme**'s managers, including its managerial accountants, must notify shareholders of this risk.

**REPORTING IN ACTION**

C1   C2

**Required**

**1.** Access and read Krispy Kreme's Management Discussion and Analysis (MD&A) section in either its annual report or its 10-K for the year ended February 3, 2002 [**KrispyKreme.com**]. What risks do Krispy Kreme's shareholders face as management and employees work to position the company for long-term success?

**2.** What are the managerial accountants' responsibilities in evaluating risk?

*Roll On*

**3.** Access **Krispy Kreme**'s annual report for a fiscal year ending after February 3, 2002, from either its Website [**KrispyKreme.com**] or the SEC's EDGAR database [**www.sec.gov**]. Answer the questions in parts (1) and (2) after reading the current MD&A section. Identify any major changes.

---

**BTN 14-2**   **Krispy Kreme** and **Tastykake** are both manufacturing and merchandising companies. Answer the following questions using their financial information reported in Appendix A.

**COMPARATIVE ANALYSIS**

C3   C6

**Required**

**1.** Review each company's balance sheet and then identify and record clues indicating that each performs manufacturing operations.

**2.** Search the notes to Krispy Kreme's financial statements for evidence that it is a manufacturer. Record your evidence.

**3.** Compute inventory turnover (using ending inventory in the denominator) and the days' sales in inventory for the most recent two years reported for each company. Interpret both measures.

**4.** What likely impact would a just-in-time inventory system have on the turnover values in part 3?

## ETHICS CHALLENGE

C1  C4  C5

**BTN 14-3** Assume that you are the managerial accountant at Spinex, a manufacturer of hard drives, CDs, and diskettes. Its reporting year-end is December 31. The chief financial officer is concerned about having enough cash to pay the expected income tax bill because of poor cash flow management. On November 15, the purchasing department purchased excess inventory of CD raw materials in anticipation of rapid growth of this product beginning in January. To decrease the company's tax liability, the chief financial officer tells you to record the purchase of this inventory as part of supplies and expense it in the current year; this would decrease the company's tax liability by increasing expenses.

### Required

**1.** In which account should the purchase of CD raw materials be recorded?

**2.** How should you respond to this request by the chief financial officer?

## COMMUNICATING IN PRACTICE

**BTN 14-4** Write a one-page memorandum to a prospective college student about salary expectations for graduates in business. Compare and contrast the expected salaries for accounting (including different subfields such as public, corporate, tax, audit, and so forth), marketing, management, and finance majors. Prepare a graph showing average starting salaries (and those for experienced professionals in those fields if available). To get this information, stop by your school's career services office; libraries also have this information. The Website **JobStar.org** (click on *Salary Info*) also can get you started.

## TAKING IT TO THE NET

C1  C2

mhhe.com/wild

**BTN 14-5** Managerial accounting professionals follow a code of ethics. As a member of the Institute of Management Accountants, the managerial accountant must comply with Standards of Ethical Conduct.

### Required

Identify, print, and read the *Ethical Standards* posted at **www.IMAnet.org**. (Search using "ethical standards.")

## TEAMWORK IN ACTION

C8  P2

**BTN 14-6** The following calendar-year information is taken from the December 31, 2005, adjusted trial balance and other records of Azalea Company.

| | | | |
|---|---:|---|---:|
| Advertising expense | $ 19,125 | Direct labor | 650,750 |
| Depreciation expense—Office equipment | 8,750 | Indirect labor | 60,000 |
| Depreciation expense—Selling equipment | 10,000 | Miscellaneous production costs | 8,500 |
| Depreciation expense—Factory equipment | 32,500 | Office salaries expense | 100,875 |
| Factory supervision | 122,500 | Raw materials purchases | 872,500 |
| Factory supplies used | 15,750 | Rent expense—Office space | 21,125 |
| Factory utilities | 36,250 | Rent expense—Selling space | 25,750 |
| Inventories | | Rent expense—Factory building | 79,750 |
|   Raw materials, December 31, 2004 | 177,500 | Maintenance expense—Factory equipment | 27,875 |
|   Raw materials, December 31, 2005 | 168,125 | Sales | 3,275,000 |
|   Goods in process, December 31, 2004 | 15,875 | Sales discounts | 57,500 |
|   Goods in process, December 31, 2005 | 14,000 | Sales salaries expense | 286,250 |
|   Finished goods, December 31, 2004 | 164,375 | | |
|   Finished goods, December 31, 2005 | 129,000 | | |

**Required**

**I.** *Each* team member is to be responsible for computing **one** of the following amounts. You are not to duplicate your teammates' work. Get any necessary amounts from teammates. Each member is to explain the computation to the team in preparation for reporting to class.

| | |
|---|---|
| **a.** Materials used. | **d.** Total cost of goods in process. |
| **b.** Factory overhead. | **e.** Cost of goods manufactured. |
| **c.** Total manufacturing costs. | |

**2.** Check your cost of goods manufactured with the instructor. If it is correct, proceed to part (3).

**3.** *Each* team member is to be responsible for computing **one** of the following amounts. You are not to duplicate your teammates' work. Get any necessary amounts from teammates. Each member is to explain the computation to the team in preparation for reporting to class.

| | |
|---|---|
| **a.** Net sales. | **d.** Total operating expenses. |
| **b.** Cost of goods sold. | **e.** Net income or loss before taxes. |
| **c.** Gross profit. | |

**Point:** Provide teams with transparencies and markers for presentation purposes.

---

**BTN 14-7**    Read the article "Mattel's New Toy Story" in the November 18, 2002, issue of *Business Week*. (The book's Website provides a free link.)

**Required**

**I.** Does **Mattel** employ just-in-time inventory management practices? (Support your answer.)

**2.** Identify two or three overall product strategies of Mattel.

**3.** Identify at least four changes that Mattel CEO Robert A. Eckert is implementing at Mattel to steady the company's performance.

**BUSINESS WEEK ACTIVITY**

C1  C2  C3  C8

mhhe.com/wild

---

**BTN 14-8**    James Lindsay of **Rap Snacks** has negotiated a deal with **Universal Studios** to use the image of rappers on his snack food bags. Representing the rappers, Universal pays Lindsay an advertising fee to gain exposure for the rappers. Lindsay also sponsors a summer seminar for urban youth to convey information needed to successfully own and manage entrepreneurial businesses. Assume that he has asked you to briefly speak at this year's seminar on accounting for the advertising fees that Universal pays and Rap Snacks receives. On the cost accounting side, Lindsay encourages you to emphasize the cost behavior, cost traceability, and cost function concepts when you explain how both Rap Snacks and Universal accounts for these advertising fees.

**Required**

Identify the main revenue and cost issues you would include in the seminar talk.

**ENTREPRENEURIAL DECISION**

C1  C4

---

**BTN 14-9**    Visit your favorite fast-food restaurant. Observe its business operations.

**Required**

**I.** Describe all business activities from the time a customer arrives to the time that customer departs.

**2.** List all costs you can identify with the separate activities described in part 1.

**3.** Classify each cost from part 2 as fixed or variable, and explain your classification.

**HITTING THE ROAD**

C1  C5

---

**BTN 14-10**    **Grupo Bimbo**, **Krispy Kreme**, and **Tastykake** are competitors. Access Grupo Bimbo's annual report for the year ended December 31, 2002, at **GrupoBimbo.com**.

**Required**

**I.** Identify the footnote in which Grupo Bimbo provides the detail of its inventory balances.

**2.** Prepare a table showing dollar balances and common-size percentages (percentages of inventory item to the total inventory balance) for each inventory component for the years 2001 and 2002.

**3.** How do the types of manufacturing inventory accounted for by Grupo Bimbo differ from those explained in this chapter?

**GLOBAL DECISION**

"If the fear and uncertainty of risk are perceived as the enemy, then entrepreneurs … must counter the enemy with a set of weapons called optimism and rationalization"—Rebecca Smith

# 15

# Job Order Cost Accounting

## A Look Back

Chapter 14 introduced managerial accounting. We compared it to financial accounting and explained basic cost concepts. We also described the lean business model and the reporting of manufacturing activities, including the manufacturing statement.

## A Look at This Chapter

We begin this chapter by describing a cost accounting system. We then explain the procedures used to determine costs using a job order costing system. We conclude with a discussion of over- and underapplied overhead.

## A Look Ahead

Chapter 16 considers how to measure costs in process production companies. We explain process production, describe how to assign costs to processes, and compute and analyze the cost per equivalent unit.

# CAP

### Conceptual

**C1** Explain the cost accounting system. *(p. 620)*

**C2** Describe important features of job order manufacturing. *(p. 620)*

**C3** Explain job cost sheets and how they are used in job order cost accounting. *(p. 622)*

### Analytical

**A1** Apply job order costing in pricing services. *(p. 632)*

### Procedural

**P1** Describe and record the flow of materials costs in job order cost accounting. *(p. 623)*

**P2** Describe and record the flow of labor costs in job order cost accounting. *(p. 625)*

**P3** Describe and record the flow of overhead costs in job order cost accounting. *(p. 627)*

**P4** Determine adjustments for overapplied and underapplied factory overhead. *(p. 631)*

---

**Decision Feature**

# Woodshop instead of Home Economics

TAMPA—Rebecca Smith's interest in construction surfaced in ninth grade, the year she elected to take woodshop instead of home economics. "I've been training for this position all of my life," says Smith. "Everything I've done has been in preparation for this." "This" is **A.D. Morgan Corporation [ADMorgan.com],** a construction company founded by Smith from her home and initially funded with a $10,000 loan from her father. "To top it off," says Smith, "I was young—29 years old—and a 'girl' going into a 'man's' business."

Smith was determined to make her business a success. "I heard so many reasons why my construction start-up would fail," says Smith. "There was only one smart thing to do—prove the naysayers wrong." She worked tirelessly to secure construction projects and wore many hats: estimator, project manager, superintendent, secretary, and accountant. She was an "army of one." Success depended not only on securing business but also on maintaining cost controls and emphasizing quality work. Smith's focus on monitoring and controlling labor, materials, and overhead costs produced consistent profits and growth. Moreover, her focus on quality helped land several lucrative jobs such as those at Brevard Community College,

St. Petersburg College, Florida Atlantic University, and Poynter Institute.

Smith uses state-of-the-art job order cost accounting to track construction job costs, including the flow of materials, labor, and overhead costs. She also manages costs and prepares periodic job order cost sheets for client review. These accounting processes help A.D. Morgan avoid the pitfalls of many start-ups that fail to use cost accounting systems and experience run-away job costs. Smith also recruits top-notch personnel, which was especially crucial in the early years. "The quality of our employees was unreal," she says.

Smith still enjoys the reaction of new acquaintances when telling them she runs a construction firm. "The best part is watching their jaws drop," she says. "But I walk away knowing that it was just one more person who . . . assumed construction firms were only run by big guys with lumps of tobacco in their lips." And, by the way, who is A.D. Morgan? Turns out Smith named the company for her two golden retrievers, Addie and Morgan.

[Sources: *A.D. Morgan Website,* January 2004; *Business Week,* January 2003; *Maddux Report,* 2002; *EntreWorld.org,* January 2002.]

This chapter introduces a cost accounting system for assigning costs to the flow of goods through a production process. We then describe the details of a *job order cost accounting system*. Job order costing is frequently used by manufacturers of custom products or providers of custom services. Manufac-turers that use job order costing typically base it on a perpetual inventory system, which provides a continuous record of materials, goods in process, and finished goods inventories.

**Job Order Cost Accounting**

**Job Order Cost Accounting**
- Cost accounting system
- Job order manufacturing
- Events in job order costing

**Job Order Cost Flows and Reports**
- Materials cost flows and documents
- Labor cost flows and documents
- Overhead cost flows and documents
- Summary of cost flows

**Adjustment of Overapplied and Underapplied Overhead**
- Underapplied overhead
- Overapplied overhead

# Job Order Cost Accounting

This section describes a cost accounting system and job order manufacturing and costing.

## Cost Accounting System

**C1** Explain the cost accounting system.

An ever-increasing number of companies use a cost accounting system to generate timely and accurate inventory information. A **cost accounting system** records manufacturing activities using a *perpetual* inventory system, which continuously updates records for costs of materials, goods in process, and finished goods inventories. A cost accounting system also provides timely information about inventories and manufacturing costs per unit of product. This is especially helpful for managers' efforts to control costs and determine selling prices. (A **general accounting system** records manufacturing activities using a *periodic* inventory system. Some companies still use a general accounting system, but its use is declining as competitive forces and customer demands have increased pressures on companies to better manage inventories.)

**Point:** Cost accounting systems accumulate costs and then assign them to products or services.

**Point:** Many professional examinations including the CPA and CMA exams require knowledge of job order and process cost accounting.

The two basic types of cost accounting systems are *job order cost accounting* and *process cost accounting.* We describe job order cost accounting in this chapter. Process cost accounting is explained in Chapter 16.

## Job Order Manufacturing

**C2** Describe important features of job order manufacturing.

Topic Tackler 15-1

Many companies manufacture products individually designed to meet the needs of a specific customer. Each customized product is manufactured separately and its production is called **job order manufacturing** (also called *customized production,* which is the production of products in response to special orders). Examples are special machines, a building, custom-made jewelry, and artwork. The production activities for a customized product represent a **job.** Although we use the term *job order manufacturing,* the principle of customization is equally applicable to both manufacturing *and* service companies. Most service companies meet customers' needs by performing a custom service for a specific customer. Examples of such services include an accountant auditing a client's financial statements, an interior designer remodeling an office, a wedding consultant planning and supervising a reception, and a lawyer defending a client. Whether the setting is manufacturing or

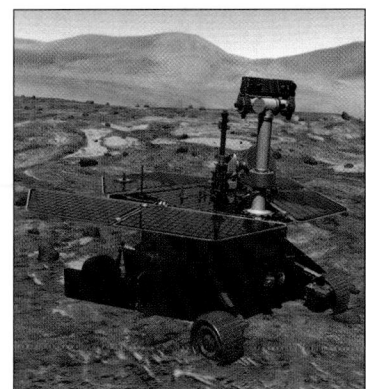

services, job order operations involve meeting the needs of customers by producing or performing custom jobs.

**Boeing**'s aerospace division is one example of a job order manufacturing system. Its primary business is twofold: (1) design, develop, and integrate space carriers and (2) provide systems engineering and integration of Department of Defense (DoD) systems. Most of its orders are customized and produced through job order manufacturing.

When a job involves producing more than one unit of a custom product, it is often called a **job lot.** Products produced as job lots could include benches for a church, imprinted T-shirts for a 10K race or company picnic, or advertising signs for a chain of stores. Although these orders involve more than one unit, the volume of production is typically low, such as 50 benches, 200 T-shirts, or 100 signs. Another feature of job order manufacturing is the diversity, often called *heterogeneity,* of the products manufactured. Namely, each customer order is likely to differ from another in some important respect. These variations can be minor or major.

## Events in Job Order Costing

The initial event in a normal job order manufacturing operation is the receipt of a customer order for a custom product. This causes the manufacturer to begin work on a job. A less common case occurs when management decides to begin work on a job before it has a signed contract. This is referred to as *jobs manufactured on speculation.*

> ### Decision Insight
>
> **Custom Design**  A Copernican revolution of sorts is underway. Managers once saw their companies as the center of a solar system orbited by suppliers and customers. Now the customer has become the center of the business universe. Companies such as **Dell Computer** encourage consumers to customize products. Soon consumers may be able to personalize almost any product, from cellular phones to appliances to furniture.

The first step in both cases is to predict the cost to complete the job. This cost depends on the product design prepared by either the customer or the manufacturer. The second step is to negotiate a sales price and decide whether to pursue the job. Some jobs are priced on a *cost-plus basis:* The customer pays the manufacturer for costs incurred on the job plus a negotiated amount or rate of profit. The third step is for the manufacturer to schedule production of the job to meet the customer's needs and to fit within its own production constraints. Preparation of this work schedule should consider workplace facilities including equipment, personnel, and supplies. Once this schedule is complete, the manufacturer can place orders for raw materials. Production occurs as materials and labor are applied to the job.

An overview of job order production activity is shown in Exhibit 15.1. This exhibit shows the March production activity of Road Warriors, which manufactures security equipped cars and trucks. The company converts any vehicle by giving it a diversity of security items such as alarms, reinforced exterior, bulletproof glass, and bomb detectors. The company began by catering to high-profile celebrities, but it now caters to anyone who desires added security in a vehicle.

Job order manufacturing for Road Warriors requires materials, labor, and overhead costs. Recall that direct materials are goods used in manufacturing that are clearly identified with a particular job. Similarly, direct labor is effort devoted to a particular job. Overhead costs support production of more than one job. Common overhead items are depreciation on factory buildings and equipment, factory supplies, supervision, maintenance, cleaning, and utilities.

Exhibit 15.1 shows that materials, labor, and overhead are added to Jobs B15, B16, B17, B18, and B19 during March. Road Warriors completed Jobs B15, B16, and B17 in March and delivered Jobs B15 and B16 to customers. At the end of March, Jobs B18 and B19 remain

> ### Decision Insight
>
> **Job Order Education**  Many companies invest in their employees, and the demand for executive education is strong. Annual spending on U.S. corporate training and education is nearby $20 billion. Moreover, annual revenues for providers of executive education continue to rise, with about 40% of revenues coming from custom programs designed for one or a group of companies.
>
>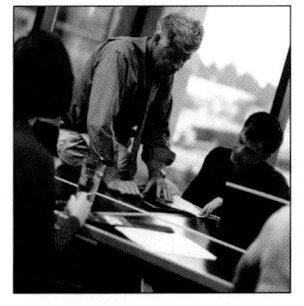

## Exhibit 15.1

Job Order Manufacturing Activities

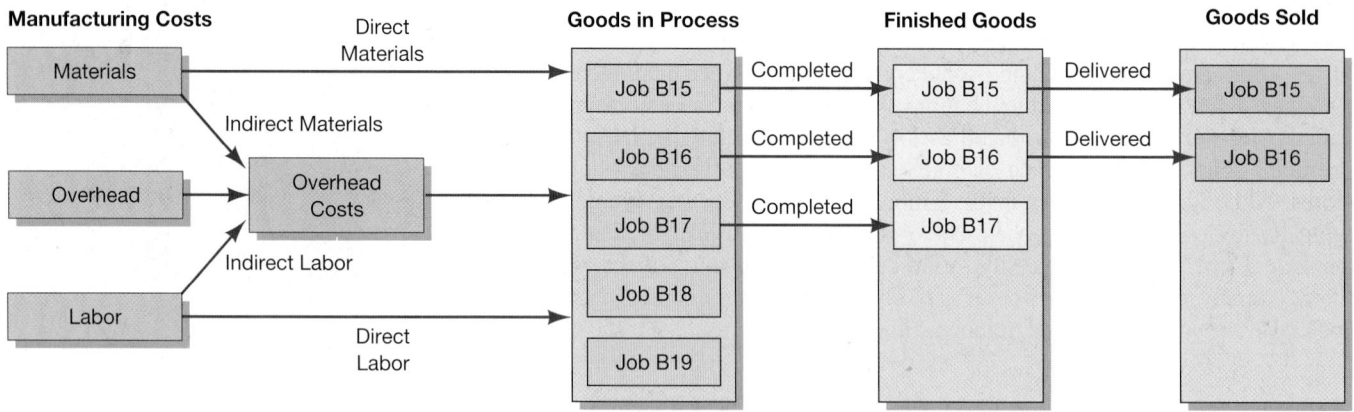

**Management Consultant** One of your tasks is to control and manage costs for a consulting company. At the end of a recent month, you find that three consulting jobs were completed and two are 60% complete. Each unfinished job is estimated to cost $10,000 and to earn a revenue of $12,000. You are unsure how to recognize goods in process inventory and record costs and revenues. Do you recognize any inventory? If so, how much? Also, how much revenue is recorded for the unfinished jobs in this month?

Answer—p. 636

**C3** Explain job cost sheets and how they are used in job order cost accounting.

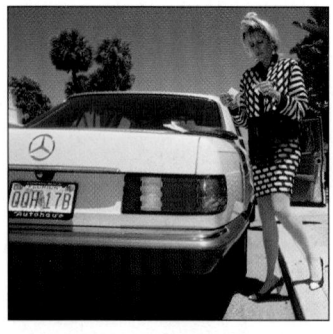

**Point:** Factory overhead consists of costs (other than direct materials and direct labor) that ensure the production activities are carried out.

in goods in process inventory and Job B17 is in finished goods inventory. Both labor and materials costs are also separated into their direct and indirect components. Their indirect amounts are added to overhead. Total overhead cost is then allocated to the various jobs.

## Job Cost Sheet

General ledger accounts usually do not provide the accounting information that managers of job order cost operations need to plan and control production activities. This is so because the needed information often requires more detailed data. Such detailed data are usually stored in subsidiary records controlled by general ledger accounts. Subsidiary records store information about raw materials, overhead costs, jobs in process, finished goods, and other items. This section describes the use of these records.

A major aim of a **job order cost accounting system** is to determine the cost of producing each job or job lot. In the case of a job lot, the system also aims to compute the cost per unit. The accounting system must include separate records for each job to accomplish this, and it must capture information about costs incurred and charge these costs to each job.

A **job cost sheet** is a separate record maintained for each job. Exhibit 15.2 shows a job cost sheet for an alarm system that Road Warriors produced for a customer. This job cost sheet identifies the customer, the job number assigned, the product, and key dates. Costs incurred on the job are immediately recorded on this sheet. When each job is complete, the supervisor enters the date of completion, records any remarks, and signs the sheet. The job cost sheet in Exhibit 15.2 classifies costs as direct materials, direct labor, or overhead. It shows that a total of $600 in direct materials is added to Job B15 on four different dates. It also shows seven entries for direct labor costs that total $1,000. Road Warriors *allocates* (also termed *applies, assigns,* or *charges*) factory overhead costs of $1,600 to this job using an allocation rate of 160% of direct labor cost (160% × $1,000)—we discuss overhead allocation later in this chapter.

While a job is being manufactured, its accumulated costs are kept in **Goods in Process Inventory.** The collection of job cost sheets for all jobs in process makes up a subsidiary ledger controlled by the Goods in Process Inventory account in the general ledger. Managers use job cost sheets to monitor costs incurred to date and to predict and control costs for each job.

Exhibit 15.2

Job Cost Sheet

**Accounting System: Exhibit 19-2**

File   Edit   Maintain   Tasks   Analysis   Options   Reports   Window   Help

**Road Warriors**                                                                    Los Angeles, California

## •Job Cost Sheet•

Customer's Name   _Carroll Connor_                                    Job No.   _B15_

Address   _1542 High Point Dr._                     City & State   _Portland, Oregon_

Job Description   _Level I Alarm System on Ford Expedition_

Date promised   _March 15_        Date started   _March 3_        Date completed   _March 11_

| Direct Materials | | | Direct Labor | | | Manufacturing Overhead | | |
|---|---|---|---|---|---|---|---|---|
| Date | Requisition | Cost | Date | Time Ticket | Cost | Date | Rate | Cost |
| 3/3/2005 | R-4698 | 100.00 | 3/3/2005 | L-3393 | 120.00 | 3/11/2005 | 160% of | 1,600.00 |
| 3/7/2005 | R-4705 | 225.00 | 3/4/2005 | L-3422 | 150.00 |  | Direct |  |
| 3/9/2005 | R-4725 | 180.00 | 3/5/2005 | L-3456 | 180.00 |  | Labor |  |
| 3/10/2005 | R-4777 | 95.00 | 3/8/2005 | L-3479 | 60.00 |  | Cost |  |
|  |  |  | 3/9/2005 | L-3501 | 90.00 |  |  |  |
|  |  |  | 3/10/2005 | L-3535 | 240.00 |  |  |  |
|  |  |  | 3/11/2005 | L-3559 | 160.00 |  |  |  |
| Total |  | 600.00 | Total |  | 1,000.00 | Total |  | 1,600.00 |

**REMARKS:** _Completed job on March 11, and shipped to customer on March 15.  Met all specifications and requirements._

**SUMMARY:**

| | |
|---|---|
| Materials | 600.00 |
| Labor | 1,000.00 |
| Overhead | 1,600.00 |
| Total cost | 3,200.00 |

Signed:   _C. Luther, Supervisor_

Sales      Purchases      General Ledger      Payroll      Inventory      Company      Analysis

When a job is finished, its job cost sheet is completed and moved from the jobs in process file to the finished jobs file. This latter file acts as a subsidiary ledger controlled by the **Finished Goods Inventory** account. When a finished job is delivered to a customer, the job cost sheet is moved to a permanent file supporting the total cost of goods sold. This permanent file contains records from both current and prior periods.

**Point:** Documents are crucial in a job order system, and the job cost sheet is a cornerstone. Understanding it aids in grasping concepts of capitalizing product costs and product cost flow.

**Point:** To apply these concepts, work QS 15-3.

## Quick Check

1. Which of these products is likely to involve job order manufacturing? (*a*) inexpensive watches, (*b*) racing bikes, or (*c*) bottled soft drinks.

2. What is the difference between a job and a job lot?

3. Which of these statements is correct? (*a*) The collection of job cost sheets for unfinished jobs makes up a subsidiary ledger controlled by the Goods in Process Inventory account, (*b*) Job cost sheets are financial statements provided to investors, or (*c*) A separate job cost sheet is maintained in the general ledger for each job in process.

4. What three costs are normally accumulated on job cost sheets?

Answers—p. 637

# Job Order Cost Flows and Reports

## Materials Cost Flows and Documents

This section focuses on the flow of materials costs and the related documents in a job order cost accounting system. We begin analysis of the flow of materials costs by examining Exhibit 15.3. When materials are first received from suppliers, the employees count and inspect them and record the items' quantity and cost on a receiving report. The receiving

Materials

**P1**   Describe and record the flow of materials costs in job order cost accounting.

**Exhibit 15.3**

Materials Cost Flows through
Subsidiary Records

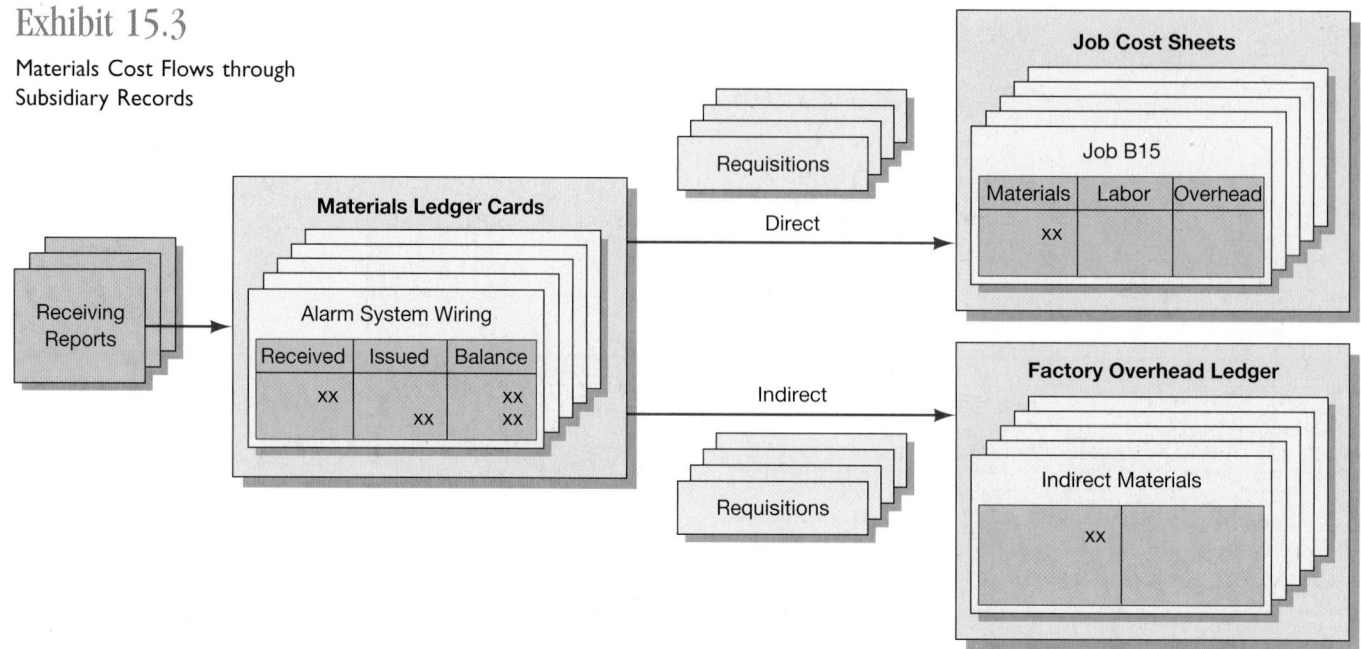

**Exhibit 15.3**

Materials Cost Flows through
Subsidiary Records

report serves as the *source document* for recording materials received in both a materials
ledger card and in the general ledger. In nearly all job order cost systems, **materials ledger
cards** (or files) are perpetual records that are updated each time units are purchased and each
time units are issued for use in production.

Exhibit 15.3 shows that materials can be requisitioned for use either on a specific job (direct materials) or as overhead (indirect materials). Cost of direct materials flows from the
materials ledger card to the job cost sheet. The cost of indirect materials flows from the materials ledger card to the Indirect Materials account in the factory overhead ledger, which is
a subsidiary ledger controlled by the Factory Overhead account in the general ledger.

Exhibit 15.4 shows a materials ledger card for material received and issued by Road
Warriors. The card identifies the item as alarm system wiring and shows the item's stock
number, its location in the storeroom, information about the maximum and minimum quantities that should be available, and the reorder quantity. For example, alarm system wiring
is issued and recorded on March 7, 2005. The job cost sheet in Exhibit 15.2 showed that
Job B15 used this wiring.

When materials are needed in production, a production manager prepares a **materials
requisition** and sends it to the materials manager. The requisition shows the job number,

**Exhibit 15.4**

Materials Ledger Card

## Road Warriors

Item _____Alarm system wiring_____    Stock No. ___M–347___    Location in Storeroom ___Bin 137___

Maximum quantity _____5 units_____    Minimum quantity ___1 unit___    Quantity to reorder ___2 units___

| | Received | | | | Issued | | | | Balance | | |
|---|---|---|---|---|---|---|---|---|---|---|---|
| Date | Receiving Report Number | Units | Unit Price | Total Price | Requi-sition Number | Units | Unit Price | Total Price | Units | Unit Price | Total Price |
| | | | | | | | | | 1 | 225.00 | 225.00 |
| 3/ 4/2005 | C-7117 | 2 | 225.00 | 450.00 | | | | | 3 | 225.00 | 675.00 |
| 3/ 7/2005 | | | | | R–4705 | 1 | 225.00 | 225.00 | 2 | 225.00 | 450.00 |

the type of material, the quantity needed, and the signature of the manager authorized to make the requisition. Exhibit 15.5 shows the materials requisition for alarm system wiring for Job B15. To see how this requisition ties to the flow of costs, compare the information on the requisition with the March 7, 2005, data in Exhibits 15.2 and 15.4.

---

## Road Warriors

### MATERIALS REQUISITION NUMBER R–4705

Job No. _____ B15 _____          Date _____ 3/7/2005 _____

Material Stock No. ___ M–347 ___          Material Description ___ Alarm system wiring ___

Quantity Requested ___ 1 ___          Requested By ___ C. Luther ___

===================================================================

Quantity Provided ___ 1 ___          Date Provided ___ 3/7/2005 ___

Filled By ___ M. Bateman ___          Material Received By ___ C. Luther ___

Remarks _____

---

**Exhibit 15.5**

Materials Requisition

The use of alarm system wiring on Job B15 yields the following entry (locate this cost item in the job cost sheet shown in Exhibit 15.2):

| Mar. 7 | Goods in Process Inventory—Job B15 . . . . . . . . . | 225 | |
| | Raw Materials Inventory—M-347 . . . . . . . . . | | 225 |
| | *To record use of material on Job B15.* | | |

Assets = Liabilities + Equity
+225
−225

This entry is posted both to its general ledger accounts and to subsidiary records. Posting to subsidiary records includes a debit to a job cost sheet and a credit to a materials ledger card. (*Note:* An entry to record use of indirect materials is the same as that for direct materials *except* the debit is to Factory Overhead. In the subsidiary factory overhead ledger, this entry is posted to Indirect Materials.)

**Point:** Requisitions are often accumulated and recorded in one entry. The frequency of entries depends on the job, the industry, and management procedures.

## Labor Cost Flows and Documents

Exhibit 15.6 shows the flow of labor costs from clock cards and the Factory Payroll account to subsidiary records of the job order cost accounting system. Recall that costs in subsidiary records give detailed information needed to manage and control operations.

Labor

**P2** Describe and record the flow of labor costs in job order cost accounting.

The flow of costs in Exhibit 15.6 begins with **clock cards.** Employees commonly use these cards to record the number of hours worked, and they serve as source documents for entries to record labor costs. Clock card data on the number of hours worked is used at the end of each pay period to determine total labor cost. This amount is then debited to the Factory Payroll account, a temporary account containing the total payroll cost (both direct and indirect). Payroll cost is later allocated to both specific jobs and overhead.

To assign labor costs to specific jobs and to overhead, we must know how each employee's time is used and its costs. Source documents called **time tickets** usually capture these data. Employees regularly fill out time tickets to report how much time they spent on each job. An employee who works on several jobs during a day completes a separate time ticket for each job. Tickets are also prepared for time charged to overhead as indirect labor. A supervisor signs an employee's time ticket to confirm its accuracy.

Exhibit 15.7 shows a time ticket reporting the time a Road Warrior employee spent working on Job B15. The employee's supervisor signed the ticket to confirm its accuracy. The hourly rate and total labor cost are computed after the time ticket is turned in. To see the effect of this time ticket on the job cost sheet, look at the entry dated March 8, 2005, in Exhibit 15.2.

**Point:** Indirect materials are included in overhead on the job cost sheet. Assigning overhead costs to products is described in the next section.

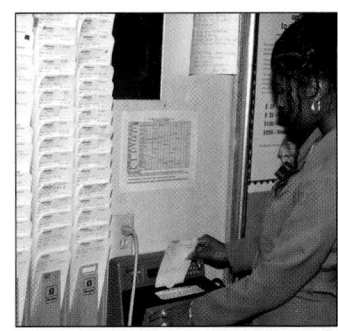

## Exhibit 15.6

Labor Cost Flows through
Subsidiary Records

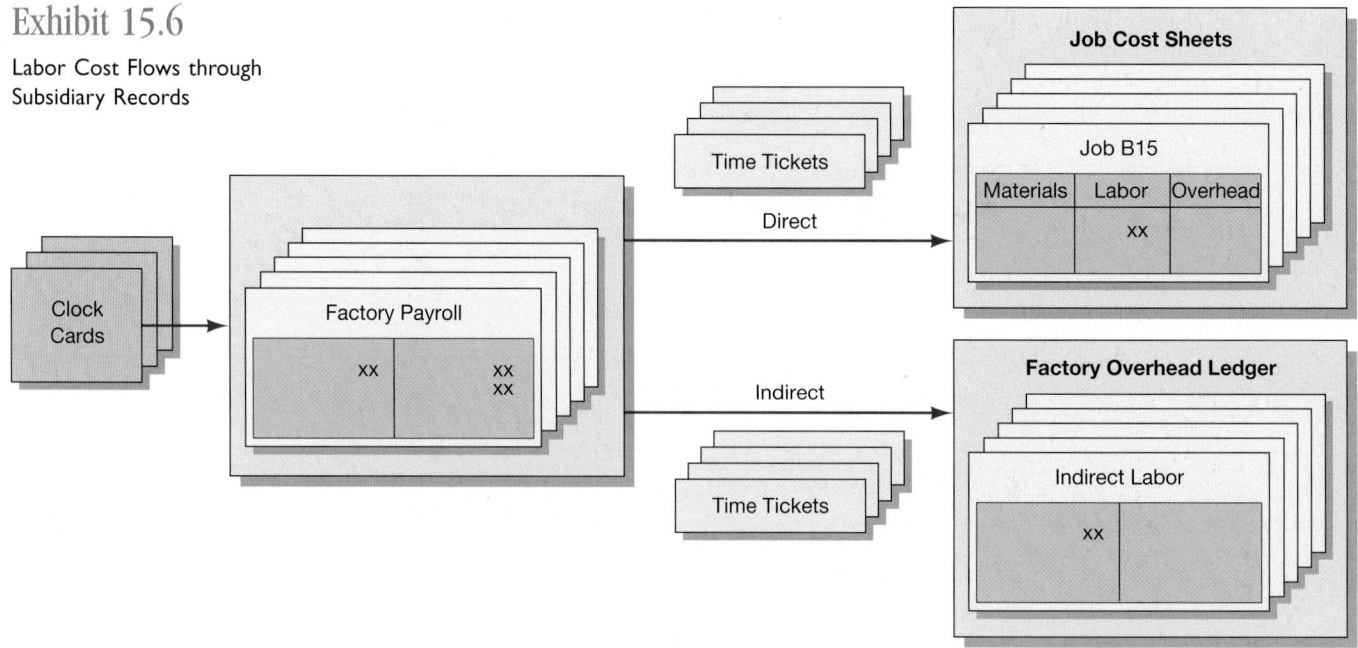

## Exhibit 15.7

Time Ticket

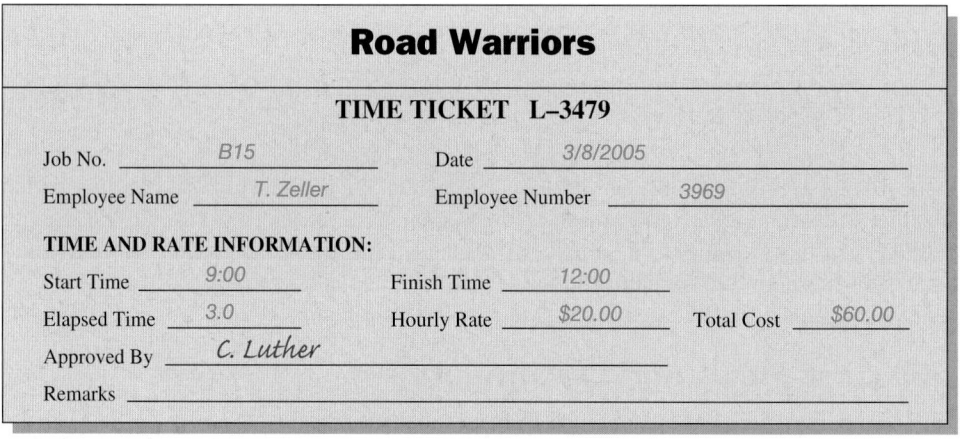

When time tickets report labor used on a specific job, this cost is recorded as direct labor. The following entry records the data from the time ticket in Exhibit 15.7:

Assets = Liabilities + Equity
+60                    +60[1]

| Mar. 8 | Goods in Process Inventory—Job B15 . . . . . . . . | 60 | |
| | Factory Payroll . . . . . . . . . . . . . . . . . . . . . . | | 60 |
| | *To record direct labor used on Job B15.* | | |

The debit in this entry is posted both to the general ledger account and to the appropriate job cost sheet. (*Note:* An entry to record indirect labor is the same as for direct labor *except* that it debits Factory Overhead and credits Factory Payroll. In the subsidiary factory overhead ledger, the debit in this entry is posted to the Indirect Labor account.)

---

[1] In the accounting equation, we treat accounts such as Factory Overhead and Factory Payroll as temporary accounts, which hold various expenses until they are allocated to balance sheet or income statement accounts.

# Overhead Cost Flows and Documents

Factory overhead (or simply overhead) cost flows are shown in Exhibit 15.8. Factory overhead includes all manufacturing costs other than direct materials and direct labor. Two sources of overhead costs are indirect materials and indirect labor. These costs are recorded from requisitions for indirect materials and time tickets for indirect labor. Two other sources of overhead are (1) vouchers authorizing payments for items such as supplies or utilities and (2) adjusting entries for costs such as depreciation.

Overhead

**P3** Describe and record the flow of overhead costs in job order cost accounting.

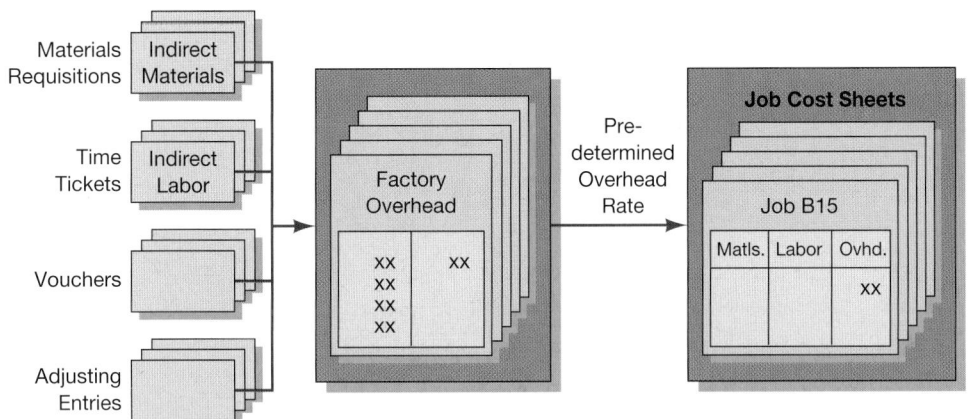

## Exhibit 15.8

Overhead Cost Flows through Subsidiary Records

Factory overhead usually includes many different costs and, thus, a separate account for each is often maintained in a subsidiary factory overhead ledger. This ledger is controlled by the Factory Overhead account in the general ledger. Factory Overhead is a temporary account that accumulates costs until they are allocated to jobs.

Recall that overhead costs are recorded with debits to the Factory Overhead account and with credits to other accounts such as Cash, Accounts Payable, and Accumulated Depreciation—Equipment. In the subsidiary factory overhead ledger, the debits are posted to their respective accounts such as Depreciation Expense—Equipment, Insurance Expense—Equipment, or Amortization Expense—Patents.

Exhibit 15.8 shows that overhead costs flow from the Factory Overhead account to job cost sheets. Because overhead is made up of costs not directly associated with specific jobs or job lots, we cannot determine the dollar amount incurred on a specific job. We know, however, that overhead costs represent a necessary part of business activities. If a job cost is to include all costs needed to complete the job, some amount of overhead must be included. Given the difficulty in determining the overhead amount for a specific job, however, we allocate overhead to individual jobs in some reasonable manner.

We generally allocate overhead by linking it to another factor used in production, such as direct labor or machine hours. The factor to which overhead costs are linked is known as the *allocation base*. A manager must think carefully about how many and which allocation bases to use. This managerial decision influences the accuracy with which overhead costs are allocated to individual jobs. In Exhibit 15.2, overhead is expressed as 160% of direct labor. We then allocated overhead by multiplying 160% by the estimated amount of direct labor on the jobs.

We cannot wait until the end of a period to allocate overhead to jobs because perpetual inventory records are part of the job order costing system (demanding immediate and up-to-date costs). Instead, we must predict overhead in advance and assign it to jobs so that a job's total costs can be estimated prior to its completion. This estimated cost is useful for managers in many decisions including setting prices. Being able to estimate overhead in advance requires a **predetermined overhead rate,** or also called *predetermined overhead allocation* (or *application*) *rate*. This rate requires an estimate of total overhead cost and an allocation factor such as total direct labor cost before the start of the period.

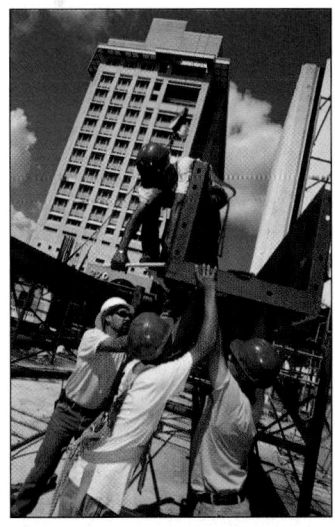

Topic Tackler 15-2

**Point:** The predetermined overhead rate is computed at the start of the period and is used throughout the period to allocate overhead to jobs.

**Point:** Predetermined overhead rates can be estimated using mathematical equations, statistical analysis, or professional experience.

**Point:** To apply these concepts, work QS 15-6 and Exercise 15-3.

Exhibit 15.9 shows the usual formula for computing a predetermined overhead rate (estimates are commonly based on annual amounts). This rate is used during the period to allocate overhead to jobs. It is common for companies to use multiple allocation factors (bases) and multiple predetermined overhead rates for different types of products and services.

## Exhibit 15.9

Predetermined Overhead Allocation Rate Formula

$$\text{Predetermined overhead rate} = \frac{\text{Estimated overhead costs}}{\div} \frac{\text{Estimated factor costs}}{}$$

**Example:** If management predicts total direct labor costs of $100,000 and total overhead costs of $200,000, what is its predetermined overhead rate? *Answer:* 200% of direct labor cost.

To illustrate, Road Warriors allocates overhead by linking it to direct labor. At the start of the current period, management predicts total direct labor costs of $125,000 and total overhead costs of $200,000. Using these estimates, management computes its predetermined overhead rate as 160% of direct labor cost ($200,000 ÷ $125,000). Specifically, reviewing the job order cost sheet in Exhibit 15.2, we see that $1,000 of direct labor went into Job B15. We then use the predetermined overhead rate of 160% to allocate $1,600 of overhead to this job. The entry to record this allocation is

| Assets = Liabilities + Equity | | | | |
|---|---|---|---|---|
| +1,600 | | +1,600 | | |

| Mar. 11 | Goods in Process Inventory—Job B15 . . . . . . . . . | 1,600 | |
|---|---|---|---|
| | Factory Overhead . . . . . . . . . . . . . . . . . . . | | 1,600 |
| | *To assign overhead to Job B15.* | | |

### Decision Ethics

**Web Consultant**   You are working on seven client engagements. Two clients reimburse your firm for actual costs plus a 10% markup. The other five pay a fixed fee for services. Your firm's costs include overhead allocated at $47 per labor hour. The managing partner of your firm instructs you to record as many labor hours as possible to the two markup engagements by transferring labor hours from the other five. What do you do?

Answer—p. 636

Since the allocation rate for overhead is estimated at the start of a period, the total amount assigned to jobs during a period rarely equals the amount actually incurred. We explain how this difference is treated later in this chapter.

## Summary of Cost Flows

We showed journal entries for charging Goods in Process Inventory (Job B15) with the cost of (1) direct materials requisitions, (2) direct labor time tickets, and (3) factory overhead. We made separate entries for each of these costs, but they are usually recorded in one entry. Specifically, materials requisitions are often collected for a day or a week and recorded with a single entry summarizing them. The same is done with labor time tickets. When summary entries are made, supporting schedules of the jobs charged and the types of materials used provide the basis for postings to subsidiary records.

**Point:** Study the flow of manufacturing costs through general ledger accounts and job cost sheets. Use Exhibit 15.11 as reinforcement.

To show all manufacturing cost flows for a period and their related entries, we again look at Road Warriors' activities. Exhibit 15.10 shows costs linked to all of Road Warriors' manufacturing activities for March. Road Warriors did not have any jobs in process at the beginning of March, but it did apply materials, labor, and overhead costs to five new jobs in March. Jobs B15 and B16 are completed and delivered to customers in March, Job B17 is completed but not delivered, and Jobs B18 and B19 are still in process. Exhibit 15.10 also shows purchases of raw materials for $2,750, labor costs incurred for $5,300, and overhead costs of $6,720.

**Point:** To apply these concepts, work Exercises 15-2 and 15-5.

### Decision Maker

**Entrepreneur**   Your division's product is facing increasing competition; competitors' prices are often lower than yours. Of the total product cost used in setting prices, 53% is factory overhead allocated using direct labor hours. You believe that product costs are distorted and wonder whether there is a better way to allocate factory overhead and to set product price. What do you suggest?

Answer—p. 637

The upper part of Exhibit 15.11 shows the flow of these costs through general ledger accounts and the end-of-month balances in key subsidiary records. Arrow lines are numbered to show the flows of costs for March. Each numbered cost flow reflects several entries made in March. The lower part of Exhibit 15.11 shows summarized job cost sheets and

## Exhibit 15.10

Job Order Costs of All Manufacturing Activities

| | | | Overhead | | Goods in | Finished | Cost of Goods |
|---|---|---|---|---|---|---|---|
| **Explanation** | **Materials** | **Labor** | **Incurred** | **Allocated** | **Process** | **Goods** | **Sold** |
| Job B15 ........................ | $ 600 | $1,000 | | $1,600 | | | $3,200 |
| Job B16 ........................ | 300 | 800 | | 1,280 | | | 2,380 |
| Job B17 ........................ | 500 | 1,100 | | 1,760 | | $3,360 | |
| Job B18 ........................ | 150 | 700 | | 1,120 | $1,970 | | |
| Job B19 ........................ | 250 | 600 | | 960 | 1,810 | | |
| Total job costs .................. | 1,800 | 4,200 | | $6,720 | $3,780 | $3,360 | $5,580 |
| Indirect materials ............... | 550 | | $ 550 | | | | |
| Indirect labor .................. | | 1,100 | 1,100 | | | | |
| Other overhead ................. | | | 5,070 | | | | |
| Total costs used in production ......... | 2,350 | $5,300 | $6,720 | | | | |
| Ending materials inventory .......... | 1,400 | | | | | | |
| Materials available ............ | 3,750 | | | | | | |
| Less beginning materials inventory ..... | (1,000) | | | | | | |
| Materials purchased .............. | $2,750 | | | | | | |

Heading above table:

**ROAD WARRIORS**
**Job Order Manufacturing Costs**
**For Month Ended March 31, 2005**

## Exhibit 15.11

Job Order Cost Flows and Ending Job Cost Sheets

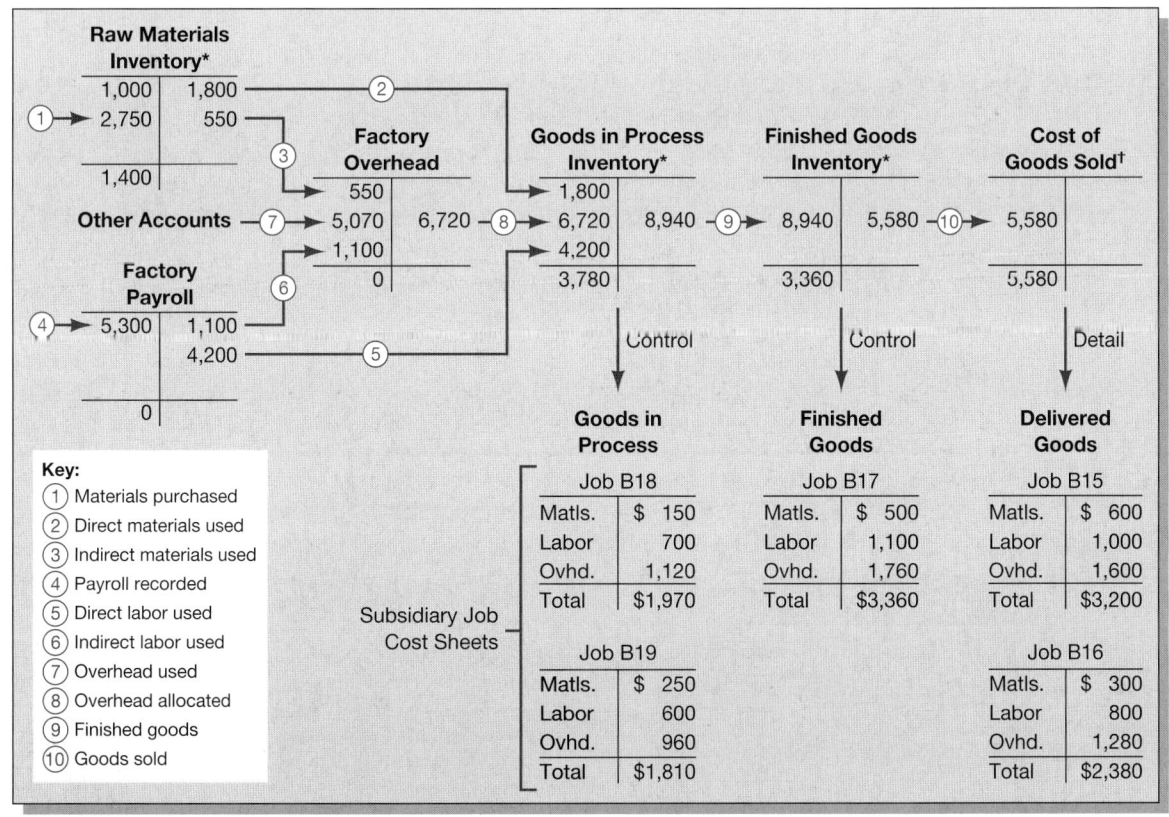

\* The ending balances in the inventory accounts are carried to the balance sheet.
†The Cost of Goods Sold balance is carried to the income statement.

their status at the end of March. The sum of costs assigned to the jobs in process ($1,970 + $1,810) equals the $3,780 balance in Goods in Process Inventory shown in Exhibit 15.10. Also, costs assigned to Job B17 equal the $3,360 balance in Finished Goods Inventory. The sum of costs assigned to Jobs B15 and B16 ($3,200 + $2,380) equals the $5,580 balance in Cost of Goods Sold.

Exhibit 15.12 shows each cost flow with a single entry summarizing the actual individual entries made in March. Each entry is numbered to link with the arrow lines in Exhibit 15.11.

**Exhibit 15.12**

Entries for Job Order
Manufacturing Costs*

| | | | |
|---|---|---|---|
| ① | Raw Materials Inventory .......................... | 2,750 | |
| |     Accounts Payable ........................... | | 2,750 |
| | *Acquired materials on credit for factory use.* | | |
| ② | Goods in Process Inventory ...................... | 1,800 | |
| |     Raw Materials Inventory ...................... | | 1,800 |
| | *To assign costs of direct materials used.* | | |
| ③ | Factory Overhead ............................. | 550 | |
| |     Raw Materials Inventory ...................... | | 550 |
| | *To record use of indirect materials.* | | |
| ④ | Factory Payroll ............................... | 5,300 | |
| |     Cash (and other accounts) ................. | | 5,300 |
| | *To record salaries and wages of factory workers (including various payroll liabilities).* | | |
| ⑤ | Goods in Process Inventory ...................... | 4,200 | |
| |     Factory Payroll ......................... | | 4,200 |
| | *To assign costs of direct labor used.* | | |
| ⑥ | Factory Overhead ............................. | 1,100 | |
| |     Factory Payroll ......................... | | 1,100 |
| | *To record indirect labor costs as overhead.* | | |
| ⑦ | Factory Overhead ............................. | 5,070 | |
| |     Cash (and other accounts) ................. | | 5,070 |
| | *To record factory overhead costs such as insurance, utilities, rent, and depreciation.* | | |
| ⑧ | Goods in Process Inventory ...................... | 6,720 | |
| |     Factory Overhead ......................... | | 6,720 |
| | *To apply overhead at 160% of direct labor.* | | |
| ⑨ | Finished Goods Inventory ....................... | 8,940 | |
| |     Goods in Process Inventory ................. | | 8,940 |
| | *To record completion of Jobs B15, B16, and B17.* | | |
| ⑩ | Cost of Goods Sold ........................... | 5,580 | |
| |     Finished Goods Inventory ................. | | 5,580 |
| | *To record sale of Jobs B15 and B16.* | | |

\* Transactions are numbered to be consistent with arrow lines in Exhibit 15.11.

**Point:** Actual overhead is debited to Factory Overhead. Allocated overhead is credited to Factory Overhead.

**Quick Check**

5. In job order cost accounting, which account is debited in recording a raw materials requisition? (*a*) Raw Materials Inventory, (*b*) Raw Materials Purchases, (*c*) Goods in Process Inventory if for a job, or (*d*) Goods in Process Inventory if they are indirect materials.

6. What are four sources of information for recording costs in the Factory Overhead account?

7. Why does job order cost accounting require a predetermined overhead rate?

8. What events result in a debit to Factory Payroll? What events result in a credit?

# Adjustment of Overapplied and Underapplied Overhead

Refer to the debits in the Factory Overhead account in Exhibit 15.11 (or Exhibit 15.12). The total cost of factory overhead incurred during March is $6,720 ($550 + $5,070 + $1,100). The $6,720 exactly equals the amount assigned to goods in process inventory (see arrow line ⑧). Therefore, the overhead incurred equals the overhead applied in March. The amount of overhead incurred rarely equals the amount of overhead applied, however, because a job order cost accounting system uses a predetermined overhead rate in applying factory overhead costs to jobs. This rate is determined using estimated amounts before the period begins, and estimates rarely equal the exact amounts actually incurred. This section explains what we do when too much or too little overhead is applied to jobs.

## Underapplied Overhead

When less overhead is applied than is actually incurred, the remaining debit balance in the Factory Overhead account at the end of the period is called **underapplied overhead.** To illustrate, assume that Road Warriors actually incurred *other overhead costs* of $5,550 instead of the $5,070 shown in Exhibit 15.11. This yields an actual total overhead cost of $7,200 in March. Since the amount of overhead applied was only $6,720, the Factory Overhead account is left with a $480 debit balance as shown in the ledger account in Exhibit 15.13.

**P4** Determine adjustments for overapplied and underapplied factory overhead.

| Factory Overhead | | | | Acct. No. 540 | |
|---|---|---|---|---|---|
| **Date** | **Explanation** | **Debit** | **Credit** | **Balance** | |
| 2005 | | | | | |
| Mar. 31 | Indirect materials cost | 550 | | 550 Dr. | |
| 31 | Indirect labor cost | 1,100 | | 1,650 Dr. | |
| 31 | Other overhead cost | 5,550 | | 7,200 Dr. | |
| 31 | Overhead costs applied to jobs | | 6,720 | 480 Dr. | |

## Exhibit 15.13

Underapplied Overhead in the Factory Overhead Ledger Account

The $480 debit balance reflects manufacturing costs not assigned to jobs. This means that the balances in Goods in Process Inventory, Finished Goods Inventory, and Cost of Goods Sold do not include all manufacturing costs incurred. When the underapplied overhead amount is immaterial, it is allocated (closed) to the Cost of Goods Sold account with the following adjusting entry:[2]

**Example:** If we do not adjust for underapplied overhead, will net income be overstated or understated? *Answer:* Overstated.

| | | | |
|---|---|---|---|
| Mar. 31 | Cost of Goods Sold . . . . . . . . . . . . . . . . . . . . . . | 480 | |
| | Factory Overhead . . . . . . . . . . . . . . . . . . | | 480 |
| | *To adjust for underapplied overhead costs.* | | |

Assets = Liabilities + Equity
−480
+480

The $480 debit (increase) to Cost of Goods Sold reduces income by $480.

---

[2] When the underapplied (or overapplied) overhead is significant, the amount is normally allocated to the Cost of Goods Sold, Finished Goods Inventory, and Goods in Process Inventory accounts. The preferred method of allocating underapplied (or overapplied) overhead in this case is one consistent with the allocation method used in the period. For Road Warriors, underapplied overhead is allocated to jobs based on direct labor. Jobs B15 and B16, which are sold, account for 42.8% of the total direct labor cost in March. Also, 26.2% of direct labor was consumed by B17, which is in Finished Goods inventory, and the remaining 31% was consumed by Jobs B18 and B19, which are in Goods in Process inventory. These percents are multiplied by $480 to compute the amount of underapplied overhead allocated to each account (for example, 42.8% of $480, or $205, is allocated to the Cost of Goods Sold account). An adjusting entry records this allocation:

| | | | |
|---|---|---|---|
| Mar. 31 | Goods in Process Inventory . . . . . . . . . . . . . . . . . . . . . | 149 | |
| | Finished Goods Inventory . . . . . . . . . . . . . . . . . . . . | 126 | |
| | Cost of Goods Sold. . . . . . . . . . . . . . . . . . . . . . . . . | 205 | |
| | Factory Overhead. . . . . . . . . . . . . . . . . . . . . . . | | 480 |
| | *To adjust for underapplied overhead costs.* | | |

## Overapplied Overhead

When the overhead applied in a period exceeds the overhead incurred, the resulting credit balance in the Factory Overhead account is called **overapplied overhead.** We treat overapplied overhead at the end of the period in the same way we treat underapplied overhead, except that we debit Factory Overhead and credit Cost of Good Sold for the amount.

### Quick Check

**9.** In a job order cost accounting system, why does the Factory Overhead account usually have an overapplied or underapplied balance at period-end?

**10.** When the Factory Overhead account has a debit balance at period-end, does this reflect overapplied or underapplied overhead?

Answers—p. 637

---

## Decision Analysis                                                Pricing for Services

**A1**  Apply job order costing in pricing services.

The chapter described job order costing mainly using a manufacturing setting. However, these concepts and procedures are applicable to a service setting. Consider AdWorld, an advertising agency that develops Web-based ads for small firms. Each of its customers has unique requirements, so costs for each individual job must be tracked separately.

AdWorld uses two types of labor: Web designers ($65 per hour) and computer staff ($50 per hour). It also incurs overhead costs that it assigns using two different predetermined overhead allocation rates: $125 per designer hour and $96 per staff hour. For each job, AdWorld must estimate the number of designer and staff hours needed. Then total costs pertaining to each job are determined using the procedures in the chapter. (*Note:* Most service firms have neither the category of materials cost nor inventory.)

To illustrate, a manufacturer of golf balls requested a quote from AdWorld for an advertising engagement. AdWorld estimates that the job will require 43 designer hours and 61 staff hours, with the following total estimated cost for this job:

| | | |
|---|---:|---:|
| **Direct Labor** | | |
| Designers (43 hours × $65) . . . . . . . . . . . . . | $ 2,795 | |
| Staff (61 hours × $50) . . . . . . . . . . . . . . . . | 3,050 | |
| Total direct labor . . . . . . . . . . . . . . . . . . . . . | | $ 5,845 |
| **Overhead** | | |
| Designer related (43 hours × $125) . . . . . . . | 5,375 | |
| Staff related (61 hours × $96) . . . . . . . . . . . | 5,856 | |
| Total overhead . . . . . . . . . . . . . . . . . . . . . . . | | 11,231 |
| Total estimated job cost . . . . . . . . . . . . . . . . | | $17,076 |

### Decision Maker

**Sales Manager**   As AdWorld's sales manager, assume that you estimate the costs pertaining to a proposed job to be $17,076. Your company's normal pricing policy is to apply a markup of 18% from total costs. Your assessment of the competition suggests that three other agencies are likely to bid for the same job, and that their quotes will range from $16,500 to $22,000. What price should you quote? What factors other than cost must you consider?

Answer—p. 637

AdWorld can use this cost information to help determine the price quote for the job (see *Decision Maker,* **Sales Manager**).

Another source of information that AdWorld must consider is the market, that is, how much competitors will quote for this job. Competitor information is often unavailable; therefore, AdWorld's managers must use estimates based on their assessment of the competitive environment.

# Demonstration Problem—Job Order Costing

The following information reflects Peak Manufacturing Company's job order manufacturing activities for May:

| | |
|---|---|
| Raw materials purchases . . . . . . . . . | $16,000 |
| Factory payroll cost . . . . . . . . . . . . | 15,400 |
| Overhead costs incurred | |
| Indirect materials . . . . . . . . . . . | 5,000 |
| Indirect labor . . . . . . . . . . . . . . | 3,500 |
| Other factory overhead . . . . . . . | 9,500 |

The predetermined overhead rate is 150% of direct labor cost. These costs are allocated to the three jobs worked on during May as follows:

| | Job 401 | Job 402 | Job 403 |
|---|---|---|---|
| Balances on April 30 | | | |
| Direct materials . . . . . . . . . | $3,600 | | |
| Direct labor . . . . . . . . . . . . | 1,700 | | |
| Applied overhead . . . . . . . . | 2,550 | | |
| Costs during May | | | |
| Direct materials . . . . . . . . . | 3,550 | $3,500 | $1,400 |
| Direct labor . . . . . . . . . . . . | 5,100 | 6,000 | 800 |
| Applied overhead . . . . . . . . | ? | ? | ? |
| Status on May 31 . . . . . . . . . . | **Finished (sold)** | **Finished (unsold)** | **In process** |

## Required

**1.** Determine the total cost of:
  **a.** The April 30 inventory of jobs in process.
  **b.** Materials used during May.
  **c.** Labor used during May.
  **d.** Factory overhead incurred and applied during May and the amount of any over- or underapplied overhead on May 31.
  **e.** Each job as of May 31, the May 31 inventories of both goods in process and finished goods, and the goods sold during May.

**2.** Prepare summarized journal entries for the month to record:
  **a.** Materials purchases (on credit), the factory payroll (paid with cash), indirect materials, indirect labor, and the other factory overhead (paid with cash).
  **b.** Assignment of direct materials, direct labor, and overhead costs to the Goods in Process Inventory account. (Use separate debit entries for each job.)
  **c.** Transfer of each completed job to the Finished Goods Inventory account.
  **d.** Cost of goods sold.
  **e.** Removal of any underapplied or overapplied overhead from the Factory Overhead account. (Assume the amount is not material.)

**3.** Prepare a manufacturing statement for May.

## Planning the Solution

- Determine the cost of the April 30 goods in process inventory by totaling the materials, labor, and applied overhead costs for Job 401.
- Compute the cost of materials used and labor by totaling the amounts assigned to jobs and to overhead.

- Compute the total overhead incurred by totaling the amounts of the three components. Compute the amount of applied overhead by multiplying the total direct labor cost by the predetermined overhead rate. Compute the underapplied or overapplied amount as the difference between the actual cost and the applied cost.
- Determine the total cost charged to each job by adding the costs incurred in April (if any) to the cost of materials, labor, and overhead applied during May.
- Group the costs of the jobs according to their completion status.
- Record the direct materials costs assigned to the three jobs, using a separate Goods in Process Inventory account for each job; do the same for the direct labor and the applied overhead.
- Transfer costs of Jobs 401 and 402 from Goods in Process Inventory to Finished Goods.
- Record the costs of Job 401 as cost of goods sold.
- Record the transfer of underapplied overhead from the Factory Overhead account to the Cost of Goods Sold account.
- On the manufacturing statement, remember to include the beginning and ending goods in process inventories and to deduct the underapplied overhead.

## Solution to Demonstration Problem

**1.** Total cost of

**a.** April 30 inventory of jobs in process (Job 401):

| | |
|---|---|
| Direct materials ........ | $3,600 |
| Direct labor ........... | 1,700 |
| Applied overhead ....... | 2,550 |
| Total cost ........... | $7,850 |

**b.** Materials used during May:

| | |
|---|---|
| Direct materials | |
| Job 401 .............. | $ 3,550 |
| Job 402 .............. | 3,500 |
| Job 403 .............. | 1,400 |
| Total direct materials ...... | 8,450 |
| Indirect materials .......... | 5,000 |
| Total materials used ....... | $13,450 |

**c.** Labor used during May:

| | |
|---|---|
| Direct labor | |
| Job 401 ............. | $ 5,100 |
| Job 402 ............. | 6,000 |
| Job 403 ............. | 800 |
| Total direct labor ....... | 11,900 |
| Indirect labor .......... | 3,500 |
| Total labor used ....... | $15,400 |

**d.** Factory overhead incurred in May:

| | |
|---|---|
| Actual overhead | |
| Indirect materials ................... | $ 5,000 |
| Indirect labor ..................... | 3,500 |
| Other factory overhead .............. | 9,500 |
| Total actual overhead ................. | 18,000 |
| Overhead applied (150% × $11,900) ....... | 17,850 |
| Underapplied overhead ................ | $ 150 |

**e.** Total cost of each job:

| | 401 | 402 | 403 |
|---|---|---|---|
| From April | | | |
| Direct materials ........ | $ 3,600 | | |
| Direct labor ........... | 1,700 | | |
| Applied overhead* ....... | 2,550 | | |
| From May | | | |
| Direct materials ........ | 3,550 | $ 3,500 | $1,400 |
| Direct labor ........... | 5,100 | 6,000 | 800 |
| Applied overhead* ....... | 7,650 | 9,000 | 1,200 |
| Total costs ............. | $24,150 | $18,500 | $3,400 |

* Equals 150% of the direct labor cost.

Total cost of the May 31 inventory of goods in process (Job 403) = $3,400

Total cost of the May 31 inventory of finished goods (Job 402) = $18,500

Total cost of goods sold during May (Job 401) = $24,150

2. Journal entries:

**a.**

| | | |
|---|---:|---:|
| Raw Materials Inventory . . . . . . . . . . . . . . . . . . . | 16,000 | |
|     Accounts Payable . . . . . . . . . . . . . . . . . . . | | 16,000 |
| *To record materials purchases.* | | |
| Factory Payroll . . . . . . . . . . . . . . . . . . . . . . . | 15,400 | |
|     Cash . . . . . . . . . . . . . . . . . . . . . . . . . . | | 15,400 |
| *To record factory payroll.* | | |
| Factory Overhead . . . . . . . . . . . . . . . . . . . . . . | 5,000 | |
|     Raw Materials Inventory . . . . . . . . . . . . . . | | 5,000 |
| *To record indirect materials.* | | |
| Factory Overhead . . . . . . . . . . . . . . . . . . . . . . | 3,500 | |
|     Factory Payroll . . . . . . . . . . . . . . . . . . . . | | 3,500 |
| *To record indirect labor.* | | |
| Factory Overhead . . . . . . . . . . . . . . . . . . . . . . | 9,500 | |
|     Cash . . . . . . . . . . . . . . . . . . . . . . . . . . | | 9,500 |
| *To record other factory overhead.* | | |

**b.** Assignment of costs to Goods in Process Inventory:

| | | |
|---|---:|---:|
| Goods in Process Inventory (Job 401) . . . . . . . . . | 3,550 | |
| Goods in Process Inventory (Job 402) . . . . . . . . . | 3,500 | |
| Goods in Process Inventory (Job 403) . . . . . . . . . | 1,400 | |
|     Raw Materials Inventory . . . . . . . . . . . . . . | | 8,450 |
| *To assign direct materials to jobs.* | | |
| Goods in Process Inventory (Job 401) . . . . . . . . . | 5,100 | |
| Goods in Process Inventory (Job 402) . . . . . . . . . | 6,000 | |
| Goods in Process Inventory (Job 403) . . . . . . . . . | 800 | |
|     Factory Payroll . . . . . . . . . . . . . . . . . . . . | | 11,900 |
| *To assign direct labor to jobs.* | | |
| Goods in Process Inventory (Job 401) . . . . . . . . . | 7,650 | |
| Goods in Process Inventory (Job 402) . . . . . . . . . | 9,000 | |
| Goods in Process Inventory (Job 403) . . . . . . . . . | 1,200 | |
|     Factory Overhead . . . . . . . . . . . . . . . . . . | | 17,850 |
| *To apply overhead to jobs.* | | |

**c.** Transfer of completed jobs to Finished Goods Inventory:

| | | |
|---|---:|---:|
| Finished Goods Inventory . . . . . . . . . . . . . . . . . | 42,650 | |
|     Goods in Process Inventory (Job 401) . . . . . | | 24,150 |
|     Goods in Process Inventory (Job 402) . . . . . | | 18,500 |
| *To record completion of jobs.* | | |

**d.**

| | | |
|---|---:|---:|
| Cost of Goods Sold . . . . . . . . . . . . . . . . . . . . . | 24,150 | |
|     Finished Goods Inventory . . . . . . . . . . . . . | | 24,150 |
| *To record sale of Job 401.* | | |

**e.**

| | | |
|---|---:|---:|
| Cost of Goods Sold . . . . . . . . . . . . . . . . . . . . . | 150 | |
|     Factory Overhead . . . . . . . . . . . . . . . . . . | | 150 |
| *To assign underapplied overhead.* | | |

**3.**

| PEAK MANUFACTURING COMPANY Manufacturing Statement For Month Ended May 31 | | |
|---|---|---|
| Direct materials | | $ 8,450 |
| Direct labor | | 11,900 |
| Factory overhead | | |
| Indirect materials | $5,000 | |
| Indirect labor | 3,500 | |
| Other factory overhead | 9,500 | 18,000 |
| Total manufacturing costs | | 38,350 |
| Add goods in process, April 30 | | 7,850 |
| Total cost of goods in process | | 46,200 |
| Less goods in process, May 31 | | 3,400 |
| Less underapplied overhead | | 150 |
| Cost of goods manufactured | | $42,650 |

Note how underapplied overhead is reported. Overapplied overhead is similarly reported, but is added.

# Summary

**C1 Explain the cost accounting system.** A cost accounting system records manufacturing activities using a perpetual inventory system, which continuously updates records for transactions and events that affect inventory costs.

**C2 Describe important features of job order manufacturing.** Certain manufacturers called *job order manufacturers* produce custom-made products for customers. These customized products are manufactured in response to a customer's orders. A job order manufacturer produces products that usually are different and, typically, manufactured in low volumes. The manufacturing systems of job order companies are flexible and are not highly standardized.

**C3 Explain job cost sheets and how they are used in job order cost accounting.** In a job order cost accounting system, the costs of producing each job are accumulated on a separate job cost sheet. Costs of direct materials, direct labor, and overhead are accumulated separately on the job cost sheet and then added to determine the total cost of a job. Job cost sheets for jobs in process, finished jobs, and jobs sold make up subsidiary records controlled by general ledger accounts.

**A1 Apply job order costing in pricing services.** Job order costing can usefully be applied to a service setting. The resulting job cost estimate can then be used to help determine a price for services.

**P1 Describe and record the flow of materials costs in job order cost accounting.** Costs of materials flow from receiving reports to materials ledger cards and then to either job cost sheets or the Indirect Materials account in the factory overhead ledger.

**P2 Describe and record the flow of labor costs in job order cost accounting.** Costs of labor flow from clock cards to the Factory Payroll account and then to either job cost sheets or the Indirect Labor account in the factory overhead ledger.

**P3 Describe and record the flow of overhead costs in job order cost accounting.** Overhead costs are accumulated in the Factory Overhead account that controls the subsidiary factory overhead ledger. Then, using a predetermined overhead rate, overhead costs are charged to jobs.

**P4 Determine adjustments for overapplied and underapplied factory overhead.** At the end of each period, the Factory Overhead account usually has a residual debit (underapplied overhead); or credit (overapplied overhead) balance. If the balance is not material, it is transferred to Cost of Goods Sold, but if it is material, it is allocated to Goods in Process Inventory, Finished Goods Inventory, and Cost of Goods Sold.

# Guidance Answers to **Decision Maker** and **Decision Ethics**

**Management Consultant** Service companies (such as this consulting firm) do not recognize goods in process inventory or finished goods inventory—an important difference between service and manufacturing companies. For the two jobs that are 60% complete, you could recognize revenues and costs at 60% of the total expected amounts. This means you could recognize revenue of $7,200 (0.60 × $12,000) and costs of $6,000 (0.60 × $10,000), yielding net income of $1,200 from each job.

**Web Consultant** The partner has a monetary incentive to *manage* the numbers and assign more costs to the two cost-plus engagements. This also would reduce costs on the fixed-price engagements. To act in such a manner is unethical. As a professional and an honest person, it is your responsibility to engage in ethical behavior. You must not comply with the partner's instructions. If the partner insists you act in an unethical manner, you should report the matter to a higher authority in the organization.

**Entrepreneur** An inadequate cost system can distort product costs. You should review overhead costs in detail. Once you know the different cost elements in overhead, you can classify them into groups such as material related, labor related, or machine related. Other groups can also be formed (we discuss this in Chapter 17). Once you have classified overhead items into groups, you can better establish overhead allocation bases and use them to compute predetermined overhead rates. These multiple rates and bases can then be used to assign overhead costs to products. This will likely improve product pricing.

**Sales Manager** The price based on AdWorld's normal pricing policy is $20,150 ($17,076 × 1.18), which is within the price range offered by competitors. One option is to apply normal pricing policy and quote a price of $20,150. On the other hand, assessing the competition, particularly in terms of their service quality and other benefits they might offer, would be useful. Although price is an input customers use to select suppliers, factors such as quality and timeliness (responsiveness) of suppliers are important. Accordingly, your price can reflect such factors.

## Guidance Answers to **Quick Checks**

**1.** *b*

**2.** A job is a special order for a custom product. A job lot consists of a quantity of identical, special-order items.

**3.** *a*

**4.** Three costs normally accumulated on a job cost sheet are direct materials, direct labor, and factory overhead.

**5.** *c*

**6.** Four sources of factory overhead are materials requisitions, time tickets, vouchers, and adjusting entries.

**7.** Since a job order cost accounting system uses perpetual inventory records, overhead costs must be assigned to jobs before the end of a period. This requires the use of a predetermined overhead rate.

**8.** Debits are recorded when wages and salaries of factory employees are paid or accrued. Credits are recorded when direct labor costs are assigned to jobs and when indirect labor costs are transferred to the Factory Overhead account.

**9.** Overapplied or underapplied overhead usually exists at the end of a period because application of overhead is based on estimates of overhead and another variable such as direct labor. Estimates rarely equal actual amounts incurred.

**10.** A debit balance reflects underapplied factory overhead.

## Key Terms

Key Terms are available at the book's Website for learning and testing in an online Flashcard Format.

**Clock card** (p. 625)
**Cost accounting system** (p. 620)
**Finished Goods Inventory** (p. 623)
**General accounting system** (p. 620)
**Goods in Process Inventory** (p. 622)
**Job** (p. 620)

**Job cost sheet** (p. 622)
**Job lot** (p. 621)
**Job order cost accounting system** (p. 622)
**Job order manufacturing** (p. 620)
**Materials ledger card** (p. 624)

**Materials requisition** (p. 624)
**Overapplied overhead** (p. 632)
**Predetermined overhead rate** (p. 627)
**Time ticket** (p. 625)
**Underapplied overhead** (p. 631)

## Personal Interactive Quiz

Personal Interactive Quizzes A and B are available at the book's Website to reinforce and assess your learning.

## Discussion Questions

**1.** Refer to **Krispy Kreme**'s financial statements and notes in Appendix A. What are the major components and amounts of its inventory for 2003?

**2.** Why must a company estimate the amount of factory overhead assigned to individual jobs or job lots?

**3.** The chapter used a percent of labor cost to assign factory overhead to jobs. Identify another factor (or base) a company might reasonably use to assign overhead costs.

**4.** What information is recorded on a job cost sheet? How do management and employees use job cost sheets?

**5.** In a job order cost accounting system, what records serve as a subsidiary ledger for Goods in Process Inventory? For Finished Goods Inventory?

**6.** What journal entry is recorded when a materials manager receives a materials requisition and then issues materials (both direct and indirect) for use in the factory?

**7.** How does the materials requisition help safeguard a company's assets?

**8.** What is the difference between a clock card and a time ticket?

**9.** What events cause debits to be recorded in the Factory Overhead account? What events cause credits to be recorded in the Factory Overhead account?

**10.** What account(s) is(are) used to eliminate overapplied or underapplied overhead from the Factory Overhead account, assuming the amount is not material?

**11.** Assume that **Tastykake** produces a batch of 1,000 snack cakes. Does it account for this as 1,000 individual jobs or as a job lot? Explain (consider costs and benefits).

**12.** Why must a company prepare a predetermined overhead rate when using job order cost accounting?

**13.** How would a hospital apply job order costing? Explain.

**14.** **Harley-Davidson** manufactures 30 luxury-model motorcycles. Does it account for these motorcycles as 30 individual jobs or as a job lot? Explain. **Harley-Davidson**

 *Red numbers denote Discussion Questions that involve decision-making.*

*Homework Manager repeats all numerical Quick Studies on the book's Website with new numbers.*

## QUICK STUDY

**QS 15-1**
Factory overhead rates   P3

FasTrack Company incurred the following manufacturing costs this period: direct labor, $484,000; direct materials, $356,000; and factory overhead, $120,000. Compute overhead cost as a percent of (1) direct labor and (2) direct materials. Round percents to the nearest whole number.

**QS 15-2**
Jobs and job lots
C2

Determine which products are most likely to be manufactured as a job and which as a job lot:

**1.** A hand-crafted table.

**2.** A 90-foot motor yacht.

**3.** Wedding dresses for a chain of stores.

**4.** A custom-designed home.

**5.** Hats imprinted with company logo.

**6.** Little League trophies.

**QS 15-3**
Job cost computation
C3

The following information is from the materials requisitions and time tickets for Job 9-1005 completed by Around-The-Bay Boats. The requisitions are identified by code numbers starting with the letter Q and the time tickets start with W:

| Date | Document | Amount |
|------|----------|--------|
| 7/1/2005 . . . . . . . . | Q-4698 | $1,350 |
| 7/1/2005 . . . . . . . . | W-3393 | 700 |
| 7/5/2005 . . . . . . . . | Q-4725 | 1,100 |
| 7/5/2005 . . . . . . . . | W-3479 | 550 |
| 7/10/2005 . . . . . . . | W-3559 | 400 |

At the start of the year, management estimated that overhead cost would equal 140% of direct labor cost for each job. Determine the total cost on the job cost sheet for Job 9-1005.

**QS 15-4**
Direct materials journal entries
P1

During the current month, a company that uses a job order cost accounting system purchases $70,000 in raw materials for cash. It then uses $22,000 of raw materials indirectly as factory supplies and uses $42,000 of raw materials as direct materials. Prepare entries to record these three transactions.

**QS 15-5**
Direct labor journal entries   P2

During the current month, a company that uses a job order cost accounting system incurred a monthly factory payroll of $120,000, paid in cash. Of this amount, $30,000 is classified as indirect labor and the remainder as direct. Prepare entries to record these transactions.

**QS 15-6**
Factory overhead journal entries
P3

During the current month, a company that uses a job order cost accounting system incurred a monthly factory payroll of $120,000, paid in cash. Of this amount, $30,000 is classified as indirect labor and the remainder as direct for the production of a job lot. Factory overhead is applied at 150% of direct labor. Prepare the entry to apply factory overhead to this job lot.

**QS 15-7**
Entry for over- or underapplied overhead   P4

Java Company allocates overhead at a rate of 140% of direct labor cost. Actual overhead cost for the current period is $745,000, and direct labor cost is $500,000. Prepare the entry to close over- or underapplied overhead to cost of goods sold.

*Homework Manager repeats all numerical Exercises on the book's Website with new numbers.*

# EXERCISES

The left column lists the titles of documents and accounts used in job order cost accounting. The right column presents short descriptions of the purposes of the documents. Match each document in the left column to its numbered description in the right column.

**Exercise 15-1**
Documents in job order cost accounting
C2  C3  P1  P2  P3

**A.** Factory Payroll account

**B.** Materials ledger card

**C.** Time ticket

**D.** Voucher

**E.** Materials requisition

**F.** Factory Overhead account

**G.** Clock card

_____ **1.** Communicates the need for materials to complete a job.

_____ **2.** Shows only total time an employee works each day.

_____ **3.** Shows amount approved for payment of an overhead or other cost.

_____ **4.** Shows amount of time an employee works on a job.

_____ **5.** Temporarily accumulates the cost of incurred overhead until the cost is assigned to specific jobs.

_____ **6.** Temporarily accumulates incurred labor costs until they are assigned to specific jobs or to overhead.

_____ **7.** Perpetual inventory record of raw materials received, used, and available for use.

---

As of the end of June, the job cost sheets at Racing Wheels, Inc., show the following total costs accumulated on three custom jobs:

**Exercise 15-2**
Analysis of cost flows
C2  P1  P2  P3

|                  | Job 102 | Job 103 | Job 104 |
|------------------|---------|---------|---------|
| Direct materials ....... | $30,000 | $66,000 | $54,000 |
| Direct labor .......... | 16,000 | 28,400 | 42,000 |
| Overhead ............ | 8,000 | 14,200 | 21,000 |

Job 102 was started in production in May and the following costs were assigned to it in May: direct materials, $12,000; direct labor, $3,600; and overhead, $1,800. Jobs 103 and 104 are started in June. Overhead cost is applied with a predetermined rate based on direct labor cost. Jobs 102 and 103 are finished in June, and Job 104 is expected to be finished in July. No raw materials are used indirectly in June. Using this information, answer the following questions:

**1.** What is the cost of the raw materials requisitioned in June for each of the three jobs?

**2.** How much direct labor cost is incurred during June for each of the three jobs?

**3.** What predetermined overhead rate is used during June?

**4.** How much total cost is transferred to finished goods during June?

**Check**  (4) $162,600

---

In December 2004, Kent Computer's management establishes the year 2005 predetermined overhead rate based on direct labor cost. The information used in setting this rate includes estimates that the company will incur $756,000 of overhead costs and $540,000 of direct labor cost in year 2005. During March 2005, Kent began and completed Job No. 13-56.

**Exercise 15-3**
Overhead rate; costs assigned to jobs
P3

**1.** What is the predetermined overhead rate for year 2005?

**2.** Use the information on the following job cost sheet to determine the total cost of the job:

**Check**  (2) $23,280

### JOB COST SHEET

**Customer's Name**   Keiser Co.                **Job No.**   13-56

**Job Description**   5 color monitors—21 inch

| Date | Direct Materials | | Direct Labor | | Overhead Costs Applied | |
|------|------------------|--------|--------------|--------|------|--------|
|      | Requisition No. | Amount | Time-Ticket No. | Amount | Rate | Amount |
| Mar. 8 | 4-129 | $5,000 | T-306 | $ 640 | | |
| Mar. 11 | 4-142 | 7,050 | T-432 | 1,280 | | |
| Mar. 18 | 4-167 | 3,550 | T-456 | 1,280 | | |
| Totals | | | | | | |

**Exercise 15-4**

Analysis of costs assigned to goods in process

P3

Lopez Company uses a job order cost accounting system that charges overhead to jobs on the basis of direct material. At year-end, the Goods in Process Inventory account shows the following:

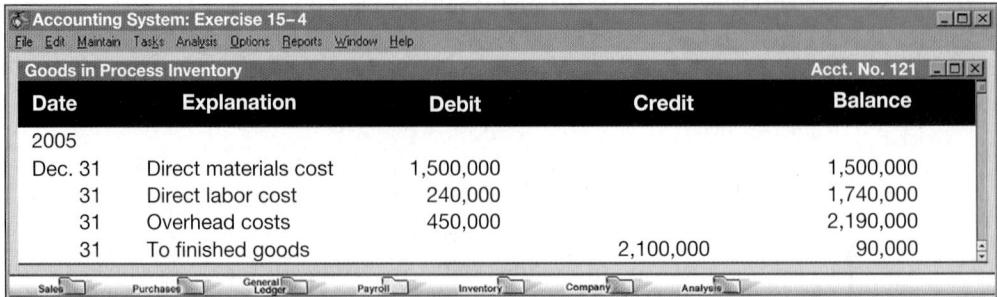

| Date | Explanation | Debit | Credit | Balance |
|------|-------------|-------|--------|---------|
| 2005 | | | | |
| Dec. 31 | Direct materials cost | 1,500,000 | | 1,500,000 |
| 31 | Direct labor cost | 240,000 | | 1,740,000 |
| 31 | Overhead costs | 450,000 | | 2,190,000 |
| 31 | To finished goods | | 2,100,000 | 90,000 |

**Check**   (2) Direct labor cost, $51,000

**1.** Determine the overhead rate used (based on direct material cost).

**2.** Only one job remained in the goods in process inventory at December 31, 2005. Its direct materials cost is $30,000. How much direct labor cost and overhead cost are assigned to it?

**Exercise 15-5**

Cost flows in a job order cost system

C3   P3

The following information is available for Lock-Down Company, which produces special-order security products and uses a job order cost accounting system:

| | April 30 | May 31 |
|---|---|---|
| Inventories | | |
| Raw materials .................................... | $40,000 | $ 50,000 |
| Goods in process .................................. | 9,600 | 19,500 |
| Finished goods .................................... | 60,000 | 33,200 |
| Activities and information for May | | |
| Raw materials purchases (paid with cash) ................... | | 189,000 |
| Factory payroll (paid with cash) ........................ | | 400,000 |
| Factory overhead | | |
| Indirect materials ................................. | | 12,000 |
| Indirect labor ................................... | | 75,000 |
| Other overhead costs .............................. | | 100,500 |
| Sales (received in cash) ............................. | | 1,200,000 |
| Predetermined overhead rate based on direct labor cost ....... | | 65% |

Compute the following amounts for the month of May:

**1.** Cost of direct materials used.      **4.** Cost of goods sold.

**2.** Cost of direct labor used.      **5.** Gross profit.

**Check**   (3) $693,350

**3.** Cost of goods manufactured.      **6.** Overapplied or underapplied overhead.

**Exercise 15-6**

Journal entries for a job order cost accounting system

P1   P2   P3   P4

Use information in Exercise 15-5 to prepare journal entries for the following events in May:

**1.** Raw materials purchases for cash.

**2.** Direct materials usage.

**3.** Indirect materials usage.

**4.** Factory payroll costs in cash.

**5.** Direct labor usage.

**6.** Indirect labor usage.

**7.** Factory overhead other than indirect materials and indirect labor (record credit to Other Accounts).

**8.** Application of overhead to goods in process.

**9.** Transfer of finished jobs to the finished goods inventory.

**10.** Sale and delivery of finished goods to customers for cash.

**11.** Allocation (closing) of overapplied or underapplied overhead to Cost of Goods Sold.

In December 2004, Ultravision established its predetermined overhead rate for movies produced during year 2005 by using the following cost predictions: overhead costs, $1,800,000, and direct labor costs, $450,000. At year end 2005, the company's records show that actual overhead costs for the year are $1,770,000. Actual direct labor cost had been assigned to jobs as follows:

| | |
|---|---:|
| Movies completed and released  . . . . . . . | $400,000 |
| Movies still in production . . . . . . . . . . . | 45,000 |
| Total actual direct labor cost  . . . . . . . . . | $445,000 |

**1.** Determine the predetermined overhead rate for year 2005.

**2.** Set up a T-account for overhead and enter the overhead costs incurred and the amounts applied to movies during the year using the predetermined overhead rate.

**3.** Determine whether overhead is overapplied or underapplied (and the amount) during the year.

**4.** Prepare the adjusting entry to allocate any over- or underapplied overhead to Cost of Goods Sold.

**Exercise 15-7**
Factory overhead computed, applied, and adjusted
P3  P4

**Check**  (3) $10,000 overapplied

In December 2004, Perez Company established its predetermined overhead rate for jobs produced during year 2005 by using the following cost predictions: overhead costs, $600,000, and direct labor costs, $500,000. At year end 2005, the company's records show that actual overhead costs for the year are $680,000. Actual direct labor cost had been assigned to jobs as follows:

| | |
|---|---:|
| Jobs completed and sold . . . . . . . . . . . . . . | $420,000 |
| Jobs in finished goods inventory  . . . . . . . . . | 84,000 |
| Jobs in goods in process inventory  . . . . . . . | 56,000 |
| Total actual direct labor cost . . . . . . . . . . . | $560,000 |

**1.** Determine the predetermined overhead rate for year 2005.

**2.** Set up a T-account for Factory Overhead and enter the overhead costs incurred and the amounts applied to jobs during the year using the predetermined overhead rate.

**3.** Determine whether overhead is overapplied or underapplied (and the amount) during the year.

**4.** Prepare the adjusting entry to allocate any over- or underapplied overhead to Cost of Goods Sold.

**5.** Prepare the adjusting entry to allocate any over- or underapplied overhead to Cost of Goods Sold, Finished Goods Inventory, and Goods in Process Inventory.

**Exercise 15-8**
Factory overhead computed, applied, and adjusted
P3  P4

**Check**  (3) $8,000 underapplied

Red Wing Company uses the relation between factory overhead and direct labor costs to assign factory overhead to its inventories of goods in process and finished goods. The company incurred the following costs during 2005: direct materials costs, $637,500; direct labor costs, $2,500,000; and factory overhead costs, $1,000,000.

**1.** Determine the company's predetermined overhead rate for year 2005.

**2.** Assuming that the company's $57,000 ending Goods in Process Inventory account for year 2005 had $18,000 of direct labor costs, determine the inventory's direct materials costs.

**3.** Assuming that the company's $337,485 ending Finished Goods Inventory account for year 2005 had $137,485 of direct materials costs, determine the inventory's direct labor costs and its overhead costs.

**Exercise 15-9**
Overhead rate calculation, allocation, and analysis
P3

**Check**  (3) $57,143 overhead costs

Vegas Company's ending Goods in Process Inventory account consists of 4,500 units of partially completed product, and its Finished Goods Inventory account consists of 11,700 units of product. The factory manager determines that Goods in Process Inventory includes direct materials cost of $10 per unit and direct labor cost of $7 per unit. Finished goods are estimated to have $12 of direct materials cost per unit and $9 of direct labor cost per unit. The company established the predetermined overhead rate using the following predictions: estimated direct labor cost, $300,000, and estimated factory overhead, $360,000. The company allocates factory overhead to its goods in process and finished goods inventories by relating overhead to direct labor cost. During the period, the company incurred these costs: direct materials, $460,000; direct labor, $277,000; and factory overhead, $332,400.

**1.** Determine the predetermined overhead rate.

**2.** Compute the total cost of the two ending inventories.

**3.** Compute cost of goods sold for the year (assume no beginning inventories).

**Exercise 15-10**
Costs allocated to ending inventories
P3

**Check**  (3) Cost of goods sold, $583,040

**Exercise 15-11**

Cost-based pricing

A1

Multiplex Corporation has requested bids from several architects to design its new corporate head-quarters. Friesen Architects is one of the firms bidding on the job. Friesen estimates that the job will require the following direct labor:

| Labor | Estimated Hours | Hourly Rate |
|-------|-----------------|-------------|
| Architects........ | 200 | $300 |
| Staff............... | 400 | 75 |
| Clerical............ | 700 | 20 |

Friesen applies overhead to jobs at 160% of direct labor cost. Friesen would like to earn at least $80,000 profit on the architectural job. Based on past experience and market research, it estimates that the competition will bid between $325,000 and $400,000 for the job.

**Check**   (1) $270,400

**1.** What is Friesen's estimated cost of the architectural job?

**2.** What bid would you suggest that Friesen submit?

# PROBLEM SET A

**Problem 15-1A**

Manufacturing costs computed and recorded; reports prepared

C3  P1  P2  P3  P4

Winfrey Co.'s March 31 inventory of raw materials is $150,000. Raw materials purchases in April are $400,000, and factory payroll cost in April is $220,000. Overhead costs incurred in April are: indirect materials, $30,000; indirect labor, $14,000; factory rent, $20,000; factory utilities, $12,000; and factory equipment depreciation, $30,000. The predetermined overhead rate is 50% of direct labor cost. Job 306 is sold for $380,000 cash in April. Costs of the three jobs worked on in April follow:

|  | Job 306 | Job 307 | Job 308 |
|--|---------|---------|---------|
| **Balances on March 31** | | | |
| Direct materials .......... | $ 14,000 | $ 18,000 | |
| Direct labor ............. | 18,000 | 16,000 | |
| Applied overhead ......... | 9,000 | 8,000 | |
| **Costs during April** | | | |
| Direct materials .......... | 100,000 | 170,000 | $ 80,000 |
| Direct labor ............. | 30,000 | 56,000 | 120,000 |
| Applied overhead ......... | ? | ? | ? |
| Status on April 30 ......... | Finished (sold) | Finished (unsold) | In process |

**Required**

**1.** Determine the total of each manufacturing cost incurred for April (direct labor, direct materials, and applied overhead), and the total cost assigned to each job (including the balances from March 31).

**2.** Prepare journal entries for the month of April to record

  **a.** Materials purchases (on credit), factory payroll (paid in cash), and actual overhead costs including indirect materials and indirect labor. (Factory rent and utilities are paid in cash.)

  **b.** Assignment of direct materials, direct labor, and applied overhead costs to the Goods in Process Inventory.

  **c.** Transfer of Jobs 306 and 307 to the Finished Goods Inventory.

  **d.** Cost of goods sold for Job 306.

  **e.** Revenue from the sale of Job 306.

**Check**   (2f) $3,000 underapplied

  **f.** Assignment of any underapplied or overapplied overhead to the Cost of Goods Sold account. (The amount is not material.)

    (3) Cost of goods
manufactured, $482,000

**3.** Prepare a manufacturing statement for April (use a single line presentation for direct materials and show the details of overhead cost).

**4.** Compute gross profit for April. Show how to present the inventories on the April 30 balance sheet.

*Analysis Component*

**5.** When the over- or underapplied overhead adjustment is made, we close Factory Overhead to Cost of Goods Sold. Discuss how this adjustment impacts business decision making regarding individual jobs or batches of jobs.

Thai Bay's computer system generated the following trial balance on December 31, 2005. The company's manager knows something is wrong with the trial balance because it does not show any balance for Goods in Process Inventory but does show balances for the Factory Payroll and Factory Overhead accounts.

**Problem 15-2A**
Source documents, journal entries, overhead, and financial reports

P1  P2  P3  P4

|  | Debit | Credit |
|---|---|---|
| Cash ........................ | $48,000 | |
| Accounts receivable ............. | 42,000 | |
| Raw materials inventory .......... | 26,000 | |
| Goods in process inventory ....... | 0 | |
| Finished goods inventory ......... | 9,000 | |
| Prepaid rent ................... | 3,000 | |
| Accounts payable .............. | | $ 10,500 |
| Notes payable ................. | | 13,500 |
| Common stock ................ | | 30,000 |
| Retained earnings .............. | | 87,000 |
| Sales ....................... | | 180,000 |
| Cost of goods sold ............. | 105,000 | |
| Factory payroll ................ | 16,000 | |
| Factory overhead .............. | 27,000 | |
| Operating expenses ............ | 45,000 | |
| Totals ..................... | $321,000 | $321,000 |

After searching various files, the manager finds six source documents that need to be processed to bring the accounting records up to date:

| | |
|---|---|
| Materials requisition 21-3010: | $4,600 direct materials to Job 402 |
| Materials requisition 21-3011: | $7,600 direct materials to Job 404 |
| Materials requisition 21-3012: | $2,100 indirect materials |
| Labor time ticket 6052: | $5,000 direct labor to Job 402 |
| Labor time ticket 6053: | $8,000 direct labor to Job 404 |
| Labor time ticket 6054: | $3,000 indirect labor |

Jobs 402 and 404 are the only units in process at year-end. The predetermined overhead rate is 200% of direct labor cost.

**Required**

1. Use information on the six source documents to prepare journal entries to assign the following costs:
   a. Direct materials costs to Goods in Process Inventory.
   b. Direct labor costs to Goods in Process Inventory.
   c. Overhead costs to Goods in Process Inventory.
   d. Indirect materials costs to the Factory Overhead account.
   e. Indirect labor costs to the Factory Overhead account.

2. Determine the revised balance of the Factory Overhead account after making the entries in part 1. Determine whether there is any under- or overapplied overhead for the year. Prepare the adjusting entry to allocate any over- or underapplied overhead to Cost of Goods Sold, assuming the amount is not material.

**Check** (2) $6,100 underapplied overhead

3. Prepare a revised trial balance.

(3) T. B. totals, $321,000

4. Prepare an income statement for year 2005 and a balance sheet as of December 31, 2005.

(4) Net income, $23,900

*Analysis Component*

5. Assume that the $2,100 on materials requisition 21-3012 should have been direct materials charged to Job 404. Without providing specific calculations, describe the impact of this error on the income statement for 2005 and the balance sheet at December 31, 2005.

**Problem 15-3A**

Source documents, journal entries, and accounts in job order cost accounting

P1  P2  P3

Woodoo Watercraft's predetermined overhead rate for year 2005 is 200% of direct labor. The company's activities related to manufacturing during May 2005 follow:

**a.** Purchased raw materials on credit, $125,000.

**b.** Paid $84,000 cash for factory wages.

**c.** Paid $11,000 cash to a computer consultant to reprogram factory equipment.

**d.** Materials requisitions record use of the following materials for the month:

| | |
|---|---|
| Job 136 . . . . . . . . . . . . . . . . | $30,000 |
| Job 137 . . . . . . . . . . . . . . . . | 20,000 |
| Job 138 . . . . . . . . . . . . . . . . | 12,000 |
| Job 139 . . . . . . . . . . . . . . . . | 14,000 |
| Job 140 . . . . . . . . . . . . . . . . | 4,000 |
| Total direct materials . . . . . . . | 80,000 |
| Indirect materials . . . . . . . . . . | 12,000 |
| Total materials used . . . . . . . . | $92,000 |

**e.** Time tickets record use of the following labor for the month:

| | |
|---|---|
| Job 136 . . . . . . . . . . . . . . . | $ 8,000 |
| Job 137 . . . . . . . . . . . . . . . | 7,000 |
| Job 138 . . . . . . . . . . . . . . . | 25,000 |
| Job 139 . . . . . . . . . . . . . . . | 26,000 |
| Job 140 . . . . . . . . . . . . . . . | 2,000 |
| Total direct labor . . . . . . . | 68,000 |
| Indirect labor . . . . . . . . . . | 16,000 |
| Total . . . . . . . . . . . . . . . | $84,000 |

**f.** Applied overhead to Jobs 136, 138, and 139.

**g.** Transferred Jobs 136, 138, and 139 to Finished Goods.

**h.** Sold Jobs 136 and 138 on credit at a total price of $340,000.

**i.** Incurred the following overhead costs during the month (credit Prepaid Insurance for expired factory insurance):

| | |
|---|---|
| Depreciation of factory building . . . . . . . . . . | $37,000 |
| Depreciation of factory equipment . . . . . . . | 21,000 |
| Expired factory insurance . . . . . . . . . . . . . | 7,000 |
| Accrued property taxes payable . . . . . . . . . | 31,000 |

**j.** Applied overhead at month-end to the Goods in Process (Jobs 137 and 140) using the predetermined overhead rate of 200% of direct labor cost.

**Required**

**1.** Prepare a job cost sheet for each job worked on during the month. Use the following simplified form:

| Job No. _____ | |
|---|---|
| Materials . . . . . . . . | $ _____ |
| Labor . . . . . . . . . . | _____ |
| Overhead . . . . . . . | _____ |
| Total cost . . . . . . . | $ _____ |

**Check**   (2f) Cr. Factory Overhead, $118,000

**2.** Prepare journal entries to record the events and transactions *a* through *j*.

**3.** Set up T-accounts for each of the following general ledger accounts, each of which started the month with a zero balance: Raw Materials Inventory; Goods in Process Inventory; Finished Goods

Inventory; Factory Payroll; Factory Overhead; Cost of Goods Sold. Then post the journal entries to these T-accounts and determine the balance of each account.

**4.** Prepare a report showing the total cost of each job in process and prove that the sum of their costs equals the Goods in Process Inventory account balance. Prepare similar reports for Finished Goods Inventory and Cost of Goods Sold.

**Check** (4) Finished Goods Inventory, $92,000

---

In December 2004, Gomez Company's manager estimated next year's total direct labor cost assuming 50 persons working an average of 2,000 hours each at an average wage rate of $15 per hour. The manager also estimated the following manufacturing overhead costs for year 2005:

**Problem 15-4A**

Overhead allocation and adjustment using a predetermined overhead rate

C3  P3  P4

mhhe.com/wild

| | |
|---|---:|
| Indirect labor . . . . . . . . . . . . . . . . . . . . . . . . . | $159,600 |
| Factory supervision . . . . . . . . . . . . . . . . . . . . . | 120,000 |
| Rent on factory building . . . . . . . . . . . . . . . . . | 70,000 |
| Factory utilities . . . . . . . . . . . . . . . . . . . . . . | 44,000 |
| Factory insurance expired . . . . . . . . . . . . . . . . | 34,000 |
| Depreciation—Factory equipment . . . . . . . . . . | 240,000 |
| Repairs expense—Factory equipment . . . . . . . . | 30,000 |
| Factory supplies used . . . . . . . . . . . . . . . . . . | 34,400 |
| Miscellaneous production costs . . . . . . . . . . . . | 18,000 |
| Total estimated overhead costs . . . . . . . . . . . | $750,000 |

At the end of 2005, records show the company incurred $725,000 of actual overhead costs. It completed and sold five jobs with the following direct labor costs: Job 201, $354,000; Job 202, $330,000; Job 203, $175,000; Job 204, $420,000; and Job 205, $184,000. In addition, Job 206 is in process at the end of 2005 and had been charged $10,000 for direct labor. No jobs were in process at the end of 2004. The company's predetermined overhead rate is based on direct labor cost.

**Required**

**1.** Determine the following:

 **a.** Predetermined overhead rate for year 2005.

 **b.** Total overhead cost applied to each of the six jobs during year 2005.

 **c.** Over- or underapplied overhead at year-end 2005.

**2.** Assuming that any over- or underapplied overhead is not material, prepare the adjusting entry to allocate any over- or underapplied overhead to Cost of Goods Sold at the end of year 2005.

**Check** (1c) $11,500 overapplied

(2) Dr. Factory Overhead $11,500

---

*If the working papers that accompany this book are not available, do not attempt to solve this problem.* Sagrillo Company manufactures variations of its product, a technopress, in response to custom orders from its customers. On May 1, the company had no inventories of goods in process or finished goods but held the following raw materials.

**Problem 15-5A**

Manufacturing transactions; subsidiary records; and source documents

P1  P2  P3  P4

| | | | |
|---|---|---|---:|
| Material M  . . . . . . . | 120 units @ $200 = | $24,000 |
| Material R . . . . . . . . | 80 units @   160 = | 12,800 |
| Paint . . . . . . . . . . . | 44 units @    72 = | 3,168 |
| Total cost  . . . . . . . | | $39,968 |

On May 4, the company began working on two technopresses: Job 102 for Global Company and Job 103 for Rolf Company.

**Required**

Follow the instructions in this list of activities and complete the materials provided in the working papers.

**a.** Purchased raw materials on credit and recorded the following information from receiving reports and invoices:

Receiving Report No. 426, Material M, 150 units at $200 each.
Receiving Report No. 427, Material R, 70 units at $160 each.

*Instructions:* Record these purchases with a single journal entry and post it to general ledger T-accounts, using the transaction letter *a* to identify the entry. Enter the receiving report information on the materials ledger cards.

**b.** Requisitioned the following raw materials for production:

> Requisition No. 35, for Job 102, 80 units of Material M.
> Requisition No. 36, for Job 102, 60 units of Material R.
> Requisition No. 37, for Job 103, 40 units of Material M.
> Requisition No. 38, for Job 103, 30 units of Material R.
> Requisition No. 39, for 12 units of paint.

*Instructions:* Enter amounts for direct materials requisitions on the materials ledger cards and the job cost sheets. Enter the indirect material amount on the materials ledger card and record a debit to the Indirect Materials account in the subsidiary factory overhead ledger. Do not record a journal entry at this time.

**c.** Received the following employee time tickets for work in May:

> Time tickets Nos. 1 to 10 for direct labor on Job 102, $40,000.
> Time tickets Nos. 11 to 30 for direct labor on Job 103, $32,000.
> Time tickets Nos. 31 to 36 for equipment repairs, $12,000.

*Instructions:* Record direct labor from the time tickets on the job cost sheets and then debit indirect labor to the Indirect Labor account in the subsidiary factory overhead ledger. Do not record a journal entry at this time.

**d.** Paid cash for the following items during the month: factory payroll, $84,000, and miscellaneous overhead items, $36,000.

*Instructions:* Record these payments with journal entries and then post them to the general ledger accounts. Also record a debit in the Miscellaneous Overhead account in the subsidiary factory overhead ledger.

**e.** Finished Job 102 and transferred it to the warehouse. The company assigns overhead to each job with a predetermined overhead rate equal to 70% of direct labor cost.

*Instructions:* Enter the allocated overhead on the cost sheet for Job 102, fill in the cost summary section of the cost sheet, and then mark the cost sheet "Finished." Prepare a journal entry to record the job's completion and its transfer to Finished Goods and then post it to the general ledger accounts.

**f.** Delivered Job 102 and accepted the customer's promise to pay $290,000 within 30 days.

*Instructions:* Prepare journal entries to record the sale of Job 102 and the cost of goods sold. Post them to the general ledger accounts.

**g.** Applied overhead to Job 103 based on the job's direct labor to date.

*Instructions:* Enter overhead on the job cost sheet but do not make a journal entry at this time.

**Check**  (h) Dr. Goods in Process Inventory, $38,400

**h.** Recorded the total direct and indirect materials costs as reported on all the requisitions for the month.

*Instructions:* Prepare a journal entry to record these costs and post it to general ledger accounts.

**i.** Recorded the total direct and indirect labor costs as reported on all time tickets for the month.

*Instructions:* Prepare a journal entry to record these costs and post it to general ledger accounts.

**j.** Recorded the total overhead costs applied to jobs.

**Check**  Balance in Factory Overhead, $1,536 Cr., overapplied

*Instructions:* Prepare a journal entry to record the allocation of these overhead costs and post it to general ledger accounts.

---

## PROBLEM SET B

### Problem 15-1B
Manufacturing costs computed and recorded; reports prepared

C3  P1  P2  P3  P4

Pak Co.'s August 31 inventory of raw materials is $16,000. Raw materials purchases in September are $60,000, and factory payroll cost in September is $68,000. Overhead costs incurred in September are: indirect materials, $6,000; indirect labor, $4,000; factory rent, $24,000; factory utilities, $22,000; and factory equipment depreciation, $25,000. The predetermined overhead rate is 130% of direct labor cost. Job 114 is sold for $100,000 cash in September. Costs for the three jobs worked on in September follow:

| | Job 114 | Job 115 | Job 116 |
|---|---|---|---|
| **Balances on August 31** | | | |
| Direct materials . . . . . . . . . . . . | $ 4,000 | $ 6,000 | |
| Direct labor . . . . . . . . . . . . . . | 2,000 | 2,200 | |
| Applied overhead . . . . . . . . . . | 2,600 | 2,860 | |
| **Costs during September** | | | |
| Direct materials . . . . . . . . . . . . | 10,000 | 30,000 | $16,000 |
| Direct labor . . . . . . . . . . . . . . | 16,000 | 28,000 | 20,000 |
| Applied overhead . . . . . . . . . . . | ? | ? | ? |
| Status on September 30 . . . . . . . . | Finished (sold) | Finished (unsold) | In process |

## Required

**1.** Determine the total of each manufacturing cost incurred for September (direct labor, direct materials, and applied overhead), and the total cost assigned to each job (including the balances from August 31).

**2.** Prepare journal entries for the month of September to record

   **a.** Materials purchases (on credit), factory payroll (paid in cash), and actual overhead costs including indirect materials and indirect labor. (Factory rent and utilities are paid in cash.)

   **b.** Assignment of direct materials, direct labor, and applied overhead costs to Goods in Process Inventory.

   **c.** Transfer of Jobs 114 and 115 to the Finished Goods Inventory.

   **d.** Cost of Job 114 in the Cost of Goods Sold account.

   **e.** Revenue from the sale of Job 114.

   **f.** Assignment of any underapplied or overapplied overhead to the Cost of Goods Sold account. (The amount is not material.)

**Check**  (2f) $2,200 overapplied

**3.** Prepare a manufacturing statement for September (use a single line presentation for direct materials and show the details of overhead cost).

(3) Cost of goods manufactured, $160,860

**4.** Compute gross profit for September. Show how to present the inventories on the September 30 balance sheet.

### Analysis Component

**5.** When the over- or underapplied overhead adjustment is made, we close Factory Overhead to Cost of Goods Sold. Discuss how this adjustment impacts business decision making regarding individual jobs or batches of jobs.

---

Metro's computer system generated the following trial balance on December 31, 2005. The company's manager knows that the trial balance is wrong because it does not show any balance for Goods in Process Inventory but does show balances for the Factory Payroll and Factory Overhead accounts.

**Problem 15-2B**
Source documents, journal entries, overhead, and financial reports

P1  P2  P3  P4

| | Debit | Credit |
|---|---|---|
| Cash . . . . . . . . . . . . . . . . . . . . . . | $ 40,000 | |
| Accounts receivable . . . . . . . . . . . . | 80,000 | |
| Raw materials inventory . . . . . . . . . | 24,000 | |
| Goods in process inventory . . . . . . . | 0 | |
| Finished goods inventory . . . . . . . . . | 50,000 | |
| Prepaid rent . . . . . . . . . . . . . . . . . | 4,000 | |
| Accounts payable . . . . . . . . . . . . . . | | $ 16,000 |
| Notes payable . . . . . . . . . . . . . . . . | | 30,000 |
| Common stock . . . . . . . . . . . . . . . | | 60,000 |
| Retained earnings . . . . . . . . . . . . . | | 33,800 |
| Sales . . . . . . . . . . . . . . . . . . . . . | | 250,000 |
| Cost of goods sold . . . . . . . . . . . . . | 140,000 | |
| Factory payroll . . . . . . . . . . . . . . . | 20,000 | |
| Factory overhead . . . . . . . . . . . . . . | 9,800 | |
| Operating expenses . . . . . . . . . . . . | 22,000 | |
| Totals . . . . . . . . . . . . . . . . . . . . . | $389,800 | $389,800 |

After searching various files, the manager finds six source documents that need to be processed to bring the accounting records up to date:

| | |
|---|---|
| Materials requisition 94-231: | $ 5,000 direct materials to Job 603 |
| Materials requisition 94-232: | $ 8,000 direct materials to Job 604 |
| Materials requisition 94-233: | $ 1,500 indirect materials |
| Labor time ticket 765: | $ 6,000 direct labor to Job 603 |
| Labor time ticket 766: | $12,000 direct labor to Job 604 |
| Labor time ticket 777: | $ 2,000 indirect labor |

Jobs 603 and 604 are the only units in process at year-end. The predetermined overhead rate is 80% of direct labor cost.

**Required**

1. Use information on the six source documents to prepare journal entries to assign the following costs:
    a. Direct materials costs to Goods in Process Inventory.
    b. Direct labor costs to Goods in Process Inventory.
    c. Overhead costs to Goods in Process Inventory.
    d. Indirect materials costs to the Factory Overhead account.
    e. Indirect labor costs to the Factory Overhead account.

**Check** (2) $1,100 overapplied overhead

2. Determine the revised balance of the Factory Overhead account after making the entries in part 1. Determine whether there is under- or overapplied overhead for the year. Prepare the adjusting entry to allocate any over- or underapplied overhead to Cost of Goods Sold, assuming the amount is not material.

(3) T. B. totals, $389,800

3. Prepare a revised trial balance.

(4) Net income, $89,100

4. Prepare an income statement for year 2005 and a balance sheet as of December 31, 2005.

*Analysis Component*

5. Assume that the $1,500 indirect materials on materials requisition 94-233 should have been direct materials charged to Job 604. Without providing specific calculations, describe the impact of this error on the income statement for 2005 and the balance sheet at December 31, 2005.

---

**Problem 15-3B**
Source documents, journal entries, and accounts in job order cost accounting

P1  P2  P3

Troupe Company's predetermined overhead rate is 90% of direct labor. The company's activities related to manufacturing during September 2005 follow:

a. Purchased raw materials on credit, $57,000.
b. Paid $99,750 cash for factory wages.
c. Paid $11,250 cash for miscellaneous factory overhead costs.
d. Materials requisitions record use of the following materials for the month:

| | |
|---|---|
| Job 487 . . . . . . . . . . . . . . . . | $13,500 |
| Job 488 . . . . . . . . . . . . . . . . | 9,000 |
| Job 489 . . . . . . . . . . . . . . . . | 12,000 |
| Job 490 . . . . . . . . . . . . . . . . | 10,500 |
| Job 491 . . . . . . . . . . . . . . . . | 1,500 |
| Total direct materials . . . . . . . | 46,500 |
| Indirect materials . . . . . . . . . | 3,750 |
| Total materials used . . . . . . . . | $50,250 |

e. Time tickets record use of the following labor for the month:

| | |
|---|---|
| Job 487 . . . . . . . . . . . . . . | $16,500 |
| Job 488 . . . . . . . . . . . . . . | 19,500 |
| Job 489 . . . . . . . . . . . . . . | 25,500 |
| Job 490 . . . . . . . . . . . . . . | 18,000 |
| Job 491 . . . . . . . . . . . . . . | 7,500 |
| Total direct labor . . . . . . . | 87,000 |
| Indirect labor . . . . . . . . . | 12,750 |
| Total . . . . . . . . . . . . . . . | $99,750 |

**f.** Allocated overhead to Jobs 487, 489, and 490.

**g.** Transferred Jobs 487, 489, and 490 to Finished Goods.

**h.** Sold Jobs 487 and 489 on credit for a total price of $225,000.

**i.** Incurred the following overhead costs during the month (credit Prepaid Insurance for expired factory insurance):

| | |
|---|---|
| Depreciation of factory building . . . . . . . . . . | $24,750 |
| Depreciation of factory equipment . . . . . . . | 18,750 |
| Expired factory insurance . . . . . . . . . . . . . | 2,250 |
| Accrued property taxes payable . . . . . . . . . | 5,250 |

**j.** Applied overhead at month-end to the Goods in Process (Jobs 488 and 491) using the predetermined overhead rate of 90% of direct labor cost.

**Required**

**1.** Prepare a job cost sheet for each job worked on during the month. Use the following simplified form:

| Job No. _____ | |
|---|---|
| Materials . . . . . . . . | $_____ |
| Labor . . . . . . . . . . | _____ |
| Overhead . . . . . . . | _____ |
| Total cost . . . . . . . | $_____ |

**2.** Prepare journal entries to record the events and transactions *a* through *j*.

**3.** Set up T-accounts for each of the following general ledger accounts, each of which started the month with a zero balance: Raw Materials Inventory, Goods in Process Inventory, Finished Goods Inventory, Factory Payroll, Factory Overhead, Cost of Goods Sold. Then post the journal entries to these T-accounts and determine the balance of each account.

**4.** Prepare a report showing the total cost of each job in process and prove that the sum of their costs equals the Goods in Process Inventory account balance. Prepare similar reports for Finished Goods Inventory and Cost of Goods Sold.

**Check** (2f) Cr. Factory Overhead, $54,000

(4) Finished Goods Inventory, $44,700

---

In December 2004, Monk Company's manager estimated next year's total direct labor cost assuming 40 persons working an average of 1,500 hours each at an average wage rate of $50 per hour. The manager also estimated the following manufacturing overhead costs for year 2005.

**Problem 15-4B**
Overhead allocation and adjustment using a predetermined overhead rate

C3 P3 P4

| | |
|---|---|
| Indirect labor . . . . . . . . . . . . . . . . . . . . . . . | $ 540,000 |
| Factory supervision . . . . . . . . . . . . . . . . . . . | 450,000 |
| Rent on factory building . . . . . . . . . . . . . . . | 360,000 |
| Factory utilities . . . . . . . . . . . . . . . . . . . . . . | 200,000 |
| Factory insurance expired . . . . . . . . . . . . . . | 60,000 |
| Depreciation—Factory equipment . . . . . . . . . | 300,000 |
| Repairs expense—Factory equipment . . . . . . . | 180,000 |
| Factory supplies used . . . . . . . . . . . . . . . . . | 110,000 |
| Miscellaneous production costs . . . . . . . . . . . | 200,000 |
| Total estimated overhead costs . . . . . . . . . . . | $2,400,000 |

At the end of 2005, records show the company incurred $2,200,000 of actual overhead costs. It completed and sold five jobs with the following direct labor costs: Job 625, $300,000; Job 626, $225,000; Job 627, $975,000; Job 628, $240,000; and Job 629, $375,000. In addition, Job 630 is in process at the end of 2005 and had been charged $75,000 for direct labor. No jobs were in process at the end of 2004. The company's predetermined overhead rate is based on direct labor cost.

**Required**

1. Determine the following:

    **a.** Predetermined overhead rate for year 2005.

    **b.** Total overhead cost applied to each of the six jobs during year 2005.

    **c.** Over- or underapplied overhead at year-end 2005.

2. Assuming that any over- or underapplied overhead is not material, prepare the adjusting entry to allocate any over- or underapplied overhead to Cost of Goods Sold at the end of year 2005.

---

**Problem 15-5B**

Manufacturing transactions; subsidiary records; and source documents

P1  P2  P3  P4

*If the working papers that accompany this book are not available, do not attempt to solve this problem.* Sim Company manufactures variations of its product, a megatron, in response to custom orders from its customers. On June 1, the company had no inventories of goods in process or finished goods but held the following raw materials:

| | | |
|---|---|---|
| Material M  ....... | 150 units @ $ 40 = | $ 6,000 |
| Material R ........ | 50 units @  160 = | 8,000 |
| Paint ........... | 20 units @   20 = | 400 |
| Total cost  ....... | | $14,400 |

On June 3, the company began working on two megatrons: Job 450 for Olivas Company and Job 451 for Ireland, Inc.

**Required**

Follow instructions in this list of activities and complete the materials provided in the working papers.

**a.** Purchased raw materials on credit and recorded the following information from receiving reports and invoices:

> Receiving Report No. 20, Material M, 150 units at $40 each.
> Receiving Report No. 21, Material R, 200 units at $160 each.

*Instructions:* Record these purchases with a single journal entry and post it to general ledger T-accounts, using the transaction letter *a* to identify the entry. Enter the receiving report information on the materials ledger cards.

**b.** Requisitioned the following raw materials for production:

> Requisition No. 223, for Job 450, 60 units of Material M.
> Requisition No. 224, for Job 450, 100 units of Material R.
> Requisition No. 225, for Job 451, 30 units of Material M.
> Requisition No. 226, for Job 451, 75 units of Material R.
> Requisition No. 227, for 10 units of paint.

*Instructions:* Enter amounts for direct materials requisitions on the materials ledger cards and the job cost sheets. Enter the indirect material amount on the materials ledger card and record a debit to the Indirect Materials account in the subsidiary factory overhead ledger. Do not record a journal entry at this time.

**c.** Received the following employee time tickets for work in June:

> Time tickets Nos. 1 to 10 for direct labor on Job 450, $24,000.
> Time tickets Nos. 11 to 20 for direct labor on Job 451, $20,000.
> Time tickets Nos. 21 to 24 for equipment repairs, $4,000.

*Instructions:* Record direct labor from the time tickets on the job cost sheets and then debit indirect labor to the Indirect Labor account in the subsidiary factory overhead ledger. Do not record a journal entry at this time.

**d.** Paid cash for the following items during the month: factory payroll, $48,000, and miscellaneous overhead items, $47,000.

*Instructions:* Record these payments with journal entries and post them to the general ledger accounts. Also record a debit in the Miscellaneous Overhead account in the subsidiary factory overhead ledger.

**e.** Finished Job 450 and transferred it to the warehouse. The company assigns overhead to each job with a predetermined overhead rate equal to 120% of direct labor cost.

*Instructions:* Enter the allocated overhead on the cost sheet for Job 450, fill in the cost summary section of the cost sheet, and then mark the cost sheet "Finished." Prepare a journal entry to record the job's completion and its transfer to Finished Goods and then post it to the general ledger accounts.

**f.** Delivered Job 450 and accepted the customer's promise to pay $130,000 within 30 days.

*Instructions:* Prepare journal entries to record the sale of Job 450 and the cost of goods sold. Post them to the general ledger accounts.

**g.** Applied overhead cost to Job 451 based on the job's direct labor used to date.

*Instructions:* Enter overhead on the job cost sheet but do not make a journal entry at this time.

**h.** Recorded the total direct and indirect materials costs as reported on all the requisitions for the month.

*Instructions:* Prepare a journal entry to record these costs and post it to general ledger accounts.

**Check** (h) Dr. Goods in Process Inventory, $31,600

**i.** Recorded the total direct and indirect labor costs as reported on all time tickets for the month.

*Instructions:* Prepare a journal entry to record these costs and post it to general ledger accounts.

**j.** Recorded the total overhead costs applied to jobs.

*Instructions:* Prepare a journal entry to record the allocation of these overhead costs and post it to general ledger accounts.

**Check** Balance in Factory Overhead, $1,600 Cr., overapplied

---

Problem Set C is available at the book's Website to reinforce and assess your learning.

## PROBLEM SET C

---

*(This serial problem began in Chapter 1 and continues through most of the book. If previous chapter segments were not completed, the serial problem can begin at this point. It is helpful, but not necessary, for you to use the Working Papers that accompany the book.)*

## SERIAL PROBLEM

Success Systems

The computer workstation furniture manufacturing that Kay Breeze started in January 2006 is progressing well. As of the end of June, Success Systems' job cost sheets show these total costs accumulated on three furniture jobs:

|  | Job 6.02 | Job 6.03 | Job 6.04 |
|---|---|---|---|
| Direct materials ....... | $1,500 | $3,300 | $2,700 |
| Direct labor .......... | 800 | 1,420 | 2,100 |
| Overhead ........... | 400 | 710 | 1,050 |

Job 6.02 was started in production in May, and these costs were assigned to it in May: direct materials, $600; direct labor, $180; and overhead, $90. Jobs 6.03 and 6.04 were started in June. Overhead cost is applied with a predetermined rate based on direct labor costs. Jobs 6.02 and 6.03 are finished in June, and Job 6.04 is expected to be finished in July. No raw materials are used indirectly in June.

### Required

**1.** What is the cost of the raw materials used in June for each of the three jobs and in total?

**Check** (1) Total cost, $6,900

**2.** How much total direct labor cost is incurred in June?

**3.** What predetermined overhead rate is used in June?

(3) 50%

**4.** How much cost is transferred to finished goods inventory in June?

# BEYOND THE NUMBERS

## REPORTING IN ACTION

C2

**BTN 15-1**   Krispy Kreme's financial statements and notes in Appendix A provide evidence of growth potential in its domestic sales.

**Required**

**1.** Identify at least two types of costs that will predictably increase as a percent of sales with growth in domestic sales.

**2.** Explain why you believe the types of costs identified for part 1 will increase, and describe how you might assess Krispy Kreme's success with these costs. (*Hint:* You might consider the gross margin ratio.)

*Roll On*

**3.** Access Krispy Kreme's annual report for a fiscal year ending after February 2, 2003, from its Website [**KrispyKreme.com**] or the SEC's EDGAR database [**www.sec.gov**]. Review and report its growth in sales along with its cost and income levels (including its gross margin ratio).

## COMPARATIVE ANALYSIS

C1

**BTN 15-2**   Both **Krispy Kreme** and **Tastykake** want to know the impact of a just-in-time (JIT) inventory system for their operating cash flows. Review each company's statement of cash flows in Appendix A to answer the following.

**Required**

**1.** Identify the impact on operating cash flows (increase or decrease) for changes in inventory levels (increase or decrease) for both companies for each of the three most recent years.

**2.** What impact would a JIT inventory system have on both Krispy Kreme's and Tastykake's level of raw materials and their operating cash flows? Link the answer to your response for part 1.

**3.** Would the move to a JIT system have a one-time or recurring impact on operating cash flow?

## ETHICS CHALLENGE

P3

**BTN 15-3**   An accounting professional requires at least two skill sets. The first is to be technically competent. Knowing how to capture, manage, and report information is a necessary skill. Second, the ability to assess manager and employee actions and biases for accounting analysis is another skill. For instance, knowing how a person is compensated helps anticipate information biases. Draw on these skills and write a one-half page memo to the financial officer on the following practice of allocating overhead.

*Background:* Assume that your company sells portable housing to both general contractors and the government. It sells jobs to contractors on a bid basis. A contractor asks for three bids from different manufacturers. The combination of low bid and high quality wins the job. However, jobs sold to the government are bid on a cost-plus basis. This means price is determined by adding all costs plus a profit based on cost at a specified percent, such as 10%. You observe that the amount of overhead allocated to government jobs is higher than that allocated to contract jobs. These allocations concern you and motivate your memo.

## COMMUNICATING IN PRACTICE

C2   C3

**BTN 15-4**   Assume that you are preparing for a second interview with a manufacturing company. The company is impressed with your credentials but has indicated that it has several qualified applicants. You anticipate that in this second interview, you must show what you offer over other candidates. You learn the company currently uses a periodic inventory system and is not satisfied with the timeliness of its information and its inventory management. The company manufactures custom-order holiday decorations and display items. To show your abilities, you plan to recommend that it use a cost accounting system.

**Required**

In preparation for the interview, prepare notes outlining the following:

**1.** Your cost accounting system recommendation and why it is suitable for this company.

**2.** A general description of the documents that the proposed cost accounting system requires.

**3.** How the documents in part 2 facilitate the operation of the cost accounting system.

**BTN 15-5**   Most contractors work on custom jobs that usually require a job order costing system.

**Required**

Access the Website AEC.Geac.com and under *Software Solutions* and then *Construction,* click on *Job Cost Accounting.* Prepare a one-page memorandum for the CEO of a construction company providing information about the job order costing software this company offers. Would you recommend that the company purchase this software?

**TAKING IT TO THE NET**

C2

mhhe.com/wild

**BTN 15-6**   Consider the activities undertaken by a medical clinic in your area.

**Required**

**1.** Do you consider a job order cost accounting system appropriate for the clinic?
**2.** Identify as many factors as possible to lead you to conclude that it uses a job order system.

**TEAMWORK IN ACTION**

C2

**BTN 15-7**   Managing materials in the production process is a challenging and crucial task for a company. Read the article "Smart Tools" in the March 24, 2003, issue of *Business Week.*

**Required**

**1.** Identify five different types of businesses that are exploring artificial intelligence applications.
**2.** What is DARPA? How are civilian businesses using it to improve direct materials management?

**BUSINESS WEEK ACTIVITY**

C1   C2

mhhe.com/wild

**BTN 15-8**   Rebecca Smith of **A.D. Morgan Corporation** already uses state-of-the-art job order cost accounting to track construction job costs on jobs in progress. Smith is considering purchasing a cost estimator *Excel* software package to help her bid competitively for new business and allow her to incorporate technology at an earlier stage of the job management process.

**Required**

**1.** Identify five features that you believe are important for the cost estimator software to possess.
**2.** What benefits should Smith reap from using job cost estimator software?

**ENTREPRENEURIAL DECISION**

C2

**BTN 15-9**   Job order cost accounting is frequently used by builders.

**Required**

**1.** You (or your team) are to prepare a job cost sheet for a single-family home under construction. List four items of both direct materials and direct labor. Explain how you think overhead should be applied.
**2.** Contact a builder and compare your job cost sheet to this builder's job cost sheet. If possible, speak to that company's accountant. Write your findings in a short report.

**HITTING THE ROAD**

C3   P2   P3   P4

**BTN 15-10**   **Grupo Bimbo, Krispy Kreme,** and **Tastykake** are competitors in the global marketplace. Access Grupo Bimbo's annual report (**GrupoBimbo.com**) for the year ended December 31, 2002. Review its balance sheet and its statement of changes in financial position to complete the following.

**Required**

**1.** Identify the impact on net resources generated by operating activities (increase or decrease) for changes in inventory levels (increase or decrease) for Grupo Bimbo for the last two years by reviewing its statement of changes in financial position.
**2.** Would a move to a JIT system likely impact Grupo Bimbo more significantly than it would Krispy Kreme or Tastykake? Explain.

**GLOBAL DECISION**

C1

"We don't have any superstars, just a lot of people who make the routine plays"—Shawn Buchanan

# 16 Process Cost Accounting

## A Look Back

Chapter 14 introduced managerial accounting and described cost concepts and the reporting of manufacturing activities. Chapter 15 explained job order costing—an important cost accounting system for customized products and services.

## A Look at This Chapter

This chapter focuses on how to measure and account for costs in process operations. We explain process production, describe how to assign costs to processes, and compute cost per equivalent unit for a process.

## A Look Ahead

Chapter 17 describes managerial accounting reports useful in directing a company's operations. We explain how to allocate factory overhead costs to different products and describe the activity-based costing method of overhead allocation.

# CAP

| Conceptual | Analytical | Procedural |
|---|---|---|

## Conceptual

**C1** Explain process operations and the way they differ from job order operations. *(p. 656)*

**C2** Define equivalent units and explain their use in process cost accounting. *(p. 664)*

**C3** Explain the four steps in accounting for production activity in a period. *(p. 665)*

**C4** Define a process cost summary and describe its purposes. *(p. 669)*

## Analytical

**A1** Compare process cost accounting and job order cost accounting. *(p. 657)*

**A2** Explain and illustrate a hybrid costing system. *(p. 675)*

## Procedural

**P1** Record the flow of direct materials costs in process cost accounting. *(p. 660)*

**P2** Record the flow of direct labor costs in process cost accounting. *(p. 661)*

**P3** Record the flow of factory overhead costs in process cost accounting. *(p. 662)*

**P4** Compute equivalent units produced in a period. *(p. 664)*

**P5** Prepare a process cost summary. *(p. 669)*

**P6** Record the transfer of goods between departments. *(p. 669)*

**P7** Record the transfer of completed goods to Finished Goods Inventory and Cost of Goods Sold. *(p. 673)*

---

**Decision Feature**

# A Beef with the Entrepreneur

OMAHA—Shawn Buchanan never dreamed he would be working in the beef industry. "The funny thing is," says Buchanan, "the only thing I knew about meat or beef was that I enjoyed a good steak." That changed after he met Bill Hughes, owner of a beef-processing plant and the father of a player whom Buchanan coached in youth baseball. Before long, Buchanan was hooked by the beef business and took an unpaid management trainee job with Hughes's company. In return, Hughes mentored him in the business. Nearly one year later, with $500 in start-up capital, Buchanan launched **All American Meats [AllAmericanMeats.com],** a producer and distributor of beef products.

"As far as being an entrepreneur," says Buchanan, "it's in my blood—my dad had a machine shop." Still, a beef producer is quite a different animal than a machinist. Buchanan had to learn the beef-processing operations and the materials, labor, and overhead costs necessary to achieve high-quality meat products. His ability to monitor and control these costs was the difference between success and failure. "I learned how to operate and survive in a lean and mean situation," he says.

Buchanan's success extends to his ability to effectively prepare and interpret process cost summaries on his beef operations. Sales are important, but without cost controls, net income is quickly cut away. "When I go after something," he says, "I'm totally committed to it." This included his commitment to improving process operations and accounting for its various costs. "We hold a daily production meeting," says Buchanan. "We talk about what customers are saying about us, how we need to improve and other issues."

Buchanan encourages feedback on his process operations from his employees. "I want them to know that every idea is important." He even posts "idea boards" in the production area. "Any employee can write down an agenda item or idea on the board, and it gets discussed at the next meeting." One employee's idea, says Buchanan, "reduced the need from four to two employees on the production line." Such practices yield huge cost savings, and often kudos for the employee. "I'm a firm believer in the work ethic," says Buchanan. "You have to earn your stripes." And your steak.

[Sources: *All American Meats Website*, January 2004; *Entrepreneur*, November 2001; *PeerSpectives Report*, August 2002.]

The type of product or service a company offers determines its cost accounting system. Job order costing is used to account for custom products that meet the requirements of a particular customer. Not all products are manufactured in this way; many carry standard designs so that one unit is no different than any other unit. Such a system often produces large numbers of units on a continuous basis, all of which pass through similar manufacturing steps or processes. This chapter describes how to use a process cost accounting system to account for these types of products. It also explains how manufacturing costs are accumulated for each process and then assigned to units passing through those processes. This information helps to understand and estimate the cost of each process as well as find ways to reduce costs and improve processes.

## Process Cost Accounting

| Process Operations | Process Cost Accounting | Equivalent Units of Production (EUP) | Process Costing Illustration |
|---|---|---|---|
| • Comparison of job order and process operations<br>• Organization of process operations<br>• GenX Company— An Illustration | • Direct and indirect costs<br>• Accounting for materials costs<br>• Accounting for labor costs<br>• Accounting for factory overhead | • Accounting for goods in process<br>• Differences between EUP for materials and that for labor and overhead | • Physical flow of units<br>• EUP<br>• Cost per EUP<br>• Cost reconciliation<br>• Process cost summary<br>• Transfers between departments<br>• Transfers to finished goods and to cost of goods sold |

# Process Operations

**C1** Explain process operations and the way they differ from job order operations.

**Process manufacturing,** also called *process operations* or *process production,* is the mass production of products in a continuous flow of steps. This means that products pass through a series of sequential processes. Petroleum refining is a common example of process operations. Crude oil passes through a series of steps before it is processed into different grades of petroleum. **Exxon Mobil**'s oil activities reflect a process operation. An important characteristic of process operations is the high level of standardization necessary if the system is to produce large volumes of products. Process operations also extend to services. Examples include mail sorting in large post offices and order processing in large mail-order firms such as **L.L. Bean.** The common feature in these service organizations is that operations are performed in a sequential manner using a series of standardized processes.

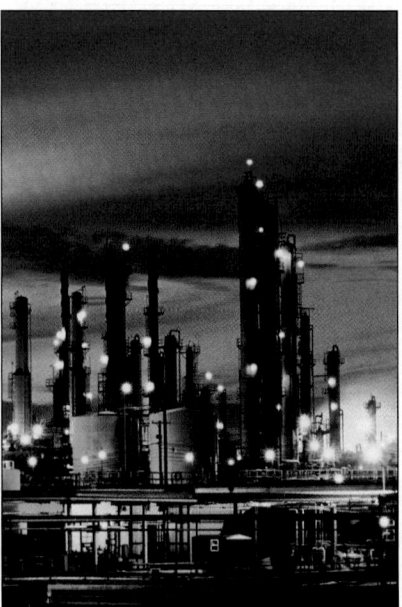

Each of these examples of products and services involves operations having a series of *processes,* or steps. Each process involves a different set of activities. A manufacturing operation that processes chemicals, for instance, might include the four steps shown in Exhibit 16.1. Understanding such processes for companies with process operations is crucial for measuring their costs.

Exhibit 16.1

Process Manufacturing
Operations: Chemicals

## Comparing Job Order and Process Operations

Job order and process operations can be considered as two ends of a continuum. Important features of both systems are shown in Exhibit 16.2. We often describe job order and process operations with manufacturing examples, but they both apply to service companies. In a job order costing system, the measurement focus is on the individual job or batch. In a process costing system, the measurement focus is on the process itself and the standardized units produced.

**A1** Compare process cost accounting and job order cost accounting.

| Job Order Systems | Process Systems |
| --- | --- |
| • Custom orders | • Repetitive operations |
| • Heterogeneous products | • Homogeneous products |
| • Low production volume | • High production volume |
| • High product flexibility | • Low product flexibility |
| • Low to medium standardization | • High standardization |

**Exhibit 16.2**

Comparing Job Order and Process Operations

## Organization of Process Operations

In a process manufacturing operation, each process is identified as a separate *production department, workstation,* or *work center.* With the exception of the first process or department, each receives the output from the prior department as a partially processed product. Depending on the nature of the process, a company applies direct labor, overhead, and, perhaps, additional direct materials to move the product toward completion. Only the final process or department in the series produces finished goods ready for sale to customers.

Exhibit 16.3 shows an operation that manufactures components of a final product in three parallel processes (each shown in sequential layout) and combines them at different production stages. In the context of parallel and sequential processes, many operations involve numerous components and related production processes.

## GenX Company— An Illustration

The GenX Company illustrates process operations. It produces Profen®, an over-the-counter pain reliever for athletes. GenX sells Profen to wholesale distributors who in turn sell it to retailers. Profen is produced in two steps. Step 1 uses a grinding process to pulverize blocks of its active ingredient, Profelene. Step 2 mixes the resulting powder with flavorings and preservatives, molds it into Profen tablets, and

**Decision Insight**

**Accounting for Health**  Many service companies use process departments to perform specific tasks for consumers. Hospitals, for instance, have radiology and physical therapy facilities with special equipment and trained employees. When patients need services, they are processed through departments to receive prescribed care. Service companies need process cost accounting information as much as manufacturers to estimate costs of providing services, to plan future operations, to control costs, and to determine charges to customers.

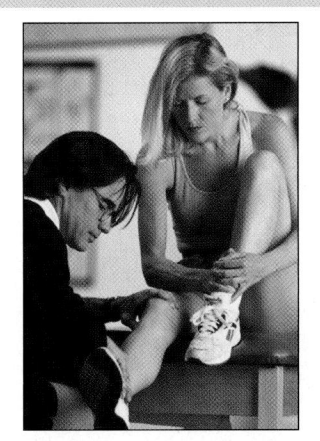

## Exhibit 16.3

Manufacturing Operations
with Parallel and
Sequential Processes

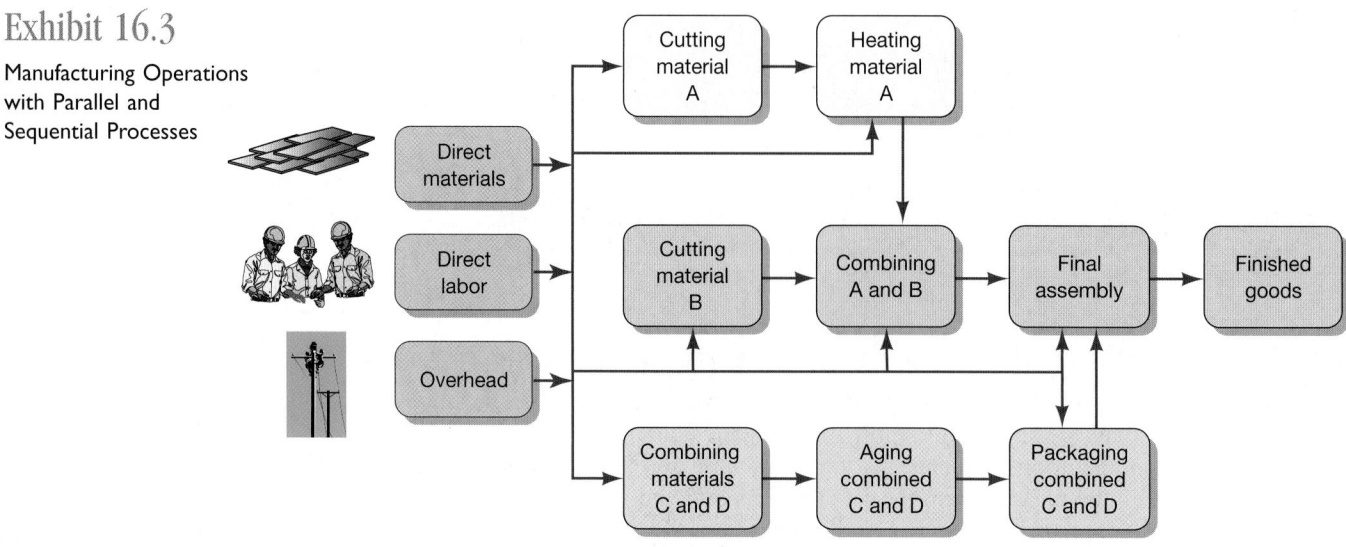

packages the tablets. Exhibit 16.4 shows a summary floor plan of the GenX factory, which
has five areas:

1. *Storeroom*—materials are received and then distributed when requisitioned.
2. *Production support offices*—used by administrative and maintenance employees who
   support manufacturing operations.
3. *Locker rooms*—workers change from street clothes into sanitized uniforms before working in the factory.
4. *Production floor*—areas divided between the grinding and mixing departments.
5. *Warehouse*—finished products are stored before being shipped to wholesalers.

**Point:** Robots, computers, and online
information are common in today's
factory.

## Exhibit 16.4

Floor Plan of GenX's Factory

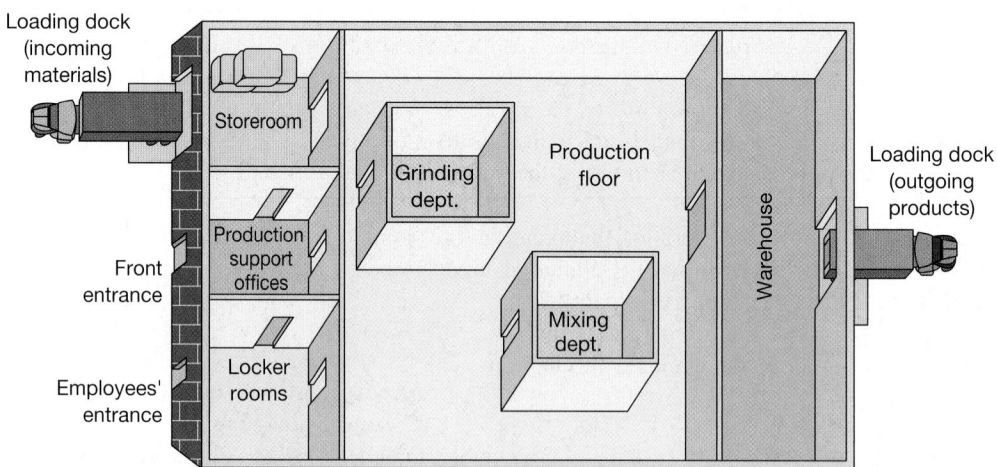

The first step in process manufacturing is to decide to produce a product. Management
determines the types and quantities of materials and labor needed and then schedules
the work for departments. Based on these plans, production begins. The flowchart in Exhibit
16.5 shows the production steps for GenX. The table in part B of the exhibit summarizes
GenX's April costs of its manufacturing processes. This includes costs at the beginning of
April and costs incurred in April and the application of those costs to the grinding and mixing departments. The following sections explain how GenX uses a process cost accounting system to compute these costs. Many of the explanations refer to this exhibit and its
numbered cost flows.

## A. Process Manufacturing Operations

Exhibit 16.5

Process Manufacturing
Operations and Costs: GenX

## B. Manufacturing Costs of Goods Transferred and Sold in April

| | Grinding Department | Mixing Department | Finished Goods |
|---|---|---|---|
| Beginning inventory | $ 4,250 | $ 3,520 | $ 6,440 |
| Direct materials | 9,900 | 2,040 | |
| Direct labor | 5,700 | 5,100 | |
| Overhead applied* | 4,275 | 1,020 | |
| Total costs—Grinding | 24,125 | | |
| Less ending inventory—Grinding | 2,725 | | |
| Transferred to Mixing | $21,400 ⟶ | 21,400 | |
| Total costs—Mixing | | 33,080 | |
| Less ending inventory—Mixing | | 3,610 | |
| Transferred to finished goods | | $29,470 ⟶ | 29,470 |
| Less ending inventory—Finished goods | | | 5,251 |
| Cost of goods sold | | | $30,659 |

* Overhead is applied to the two production departments using predetermined overhead rates based on direct labor dollars.
  Actual overhead incurred: Indirect materials, $1,195; indirect labor, $3,220; other overhead purchases and costs, $880.

# Process Cost Accounting

Process and job order manufacturing operations are similar in that both combine materials, labor, and overhead in the process of producing products. They differ in how they are organized and managed. The measurement focus in a job order costing system is on the individual job or batch, whereas in a process costing system, it is on the individual process. Regardless of the measurement focus, we are ultimately interested in determining the cost per unit of product (or service) resulting from either system.

Specifically, the **job order cost accounting system** assigns direct materials, direct labor, and overhead to jobs. The total job cost is then divided by the number of units to compute a cost per unit for that job. The **process cost accounting system** assigns direct materials, direct labor, and overhead to specific processes. The total costs associated with each process are then divided by the number of units passing through that process to determine the cost per equivalent unit (defined later in the chapter) for that process. The cost per equivalent unit for each process is summed for all processes to determine the total cost per unit of a product. The differences in the way these two systems apply materials, labor, and overhead costs are highlighted in Exhibit 16.6.

**Point:** The cost object in a job order system is the specific job; the cost object in a process costing system is the process.

## Exhibit 16.6

Comparing Job Order and
Process Cost Accounting Systems

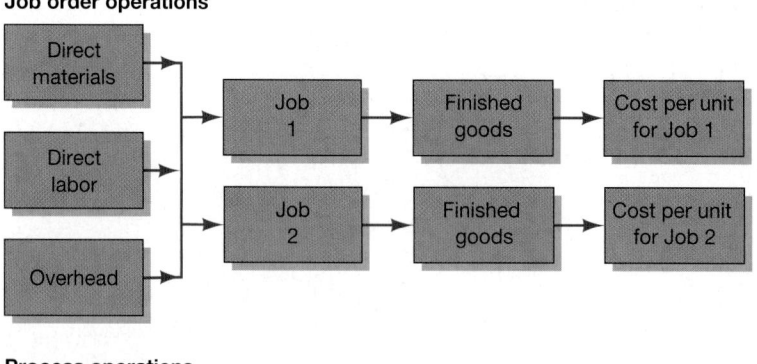

### Direct and Indirect Costs

**Point:** If a cost can be directly linked
to the cost object, it is direct; if it cannot, it is indirect.

Like job order operations, process cost accounting systems use the concepts of direct and
indirect costs. Materials and labor that are clearly linked with specific processes are assigned
to those processes as direct costs. Materials and labor not clearly linked with a specific
process are indirect costs and are assigned to overhead. Some costs classified as overhead
in a job order system may be classified as di-
rect costs in process cost accounting. For example, depreciation of a machine used entirely
by one process is a direct cost of that process.
The next three subsections explain the accounting for materials, labor, and overhead in
a process cost accounting system.

**Decision Insight**

**JIT Boon to Process Operations** Companies that adopt JIT
manufacturing often organize their production system as a series of sequential
processes. One survey found 60% of companies that converted to JIT used
process operations; this compares to only 20% before converting to JIT.

### Accounting for Materials Costs

**P1** Record the flow of direct
materials costs in process
cost accounting.

In Exhibit 16.5, arrow line ① reflects the arrival of materials at GenX's factory. These materials include Profelene, flavorings, preservatives, and packaging. They also include supplies for the production support office. GenX uses a perpetual inventory system and makes
all purchases on credit. The summary entry for receipts of raw materials in April follows
(dates in journal entries numbered ① through ⑩ are omitted because they are summary
entries, often reflecting two or more transactions or events):

Assets  = Liabilities + Equity
+14,135    +14,135

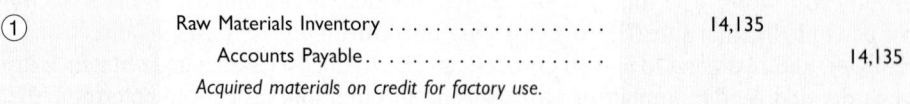

| ① | Raw Materials Inventory . . . . . . . . . . . . . . . . . . . | 14,135 | |
|---|---|---|---|
| | Accounts Payable. . . . . . . . . . . . . . . . . . . . | | 14,135 |

*Acquired materials on credit for factory use.*

Arrow line ② in Exhibit 16.5 reflects the flow of direct materials to the grinding and mixing departments, where they are used to produce Profen. Most direct materials are physically

combined into the finished product; the remaining direct materials include those used and clearly linked with a specific process. The manager of a process usually obtains materials by submitting a *materials requisition* to the materials storeroom manager. In some situations, materials move continuously from raw materials inventory through the manufacturing process. **Pepsi Bottling**, for instance, uses a process in which inventory moves continuously through the system. In these cases, a **materials consumption report** summarizes the materials used by a department during a reporting period and replaces materials requisitions. The entry to record the use of direct materials by GenX's two production departments in April follows:

| ② | Goods in Process Inventory—Grinding . . . . . . . . | 9,900 | |
| | Goods in Process Inventory—Mixing . . . . . . . . . | 2,040 | |
| |     Raw Materials Inventory . . . . . . . . . . . . . . . | | 11,940 |
| | *To assign costs of direct materials used in the grinding and mixing departments.* | | |

Assets  = Liabilities + Equity
+9,900
+2,040
−11,940

This entry transfers costs from one asset account to two other asset accounts. Use of two Goods in Process Inventory accounts allows the costs incurred by each process to be separately accumulated.

In Exhibit 16.5, the arrow line ③ reflects the flow of indirect materials from the storeroom to factory overhead. These materials are not clearly linked with either the grinding or the mixing departments but are used to support overall production activity. The following entry records the cost of indirect materials used by GenX in April:

**Example:** What types of materials might the flow of arrow line ③ in Exhibit 16.5 reflect? *Answer:* Goggles, gloves, protective clothing, recordkeeping supplies, and cleaning supplies.

| ③ | Factory Overhead . . . . . . . . . . . . . . . . . . . . . . | 1,195 | |
| |     Raw Materials Inventory . . . . . . . . . . . . . . . | | 1,195 |
| | *To record indirect materials used in April.* | | |

Assets  = Liabilities + Equity
−1,195            −1,195

After the entries for both direct and indirect materials are posted, the Raw Materials Inventory account appears as shown in Exhibit 16.7. The April 30 balance sheet reports the $5,000 Raw Materials Inventory account as a current asset.

**Exhibit 16.7**

Raw Materials Inventory

| Raw Materials Inventory | | | Acct. No. 132 | | |
| --- | --- | --- | --- | --- | --- |
| Date | | Explanation | Debit | Credit | Balance |
| 2005 | | | | | |
| Mar. | 31 | Balance | | | 4,000 |
| Apr. | 30 | Materials purchases | 14,135 | | 18,135 |
| | 30 | Direct materials usage | | 11,940 | 6,195 |
| | 30 | Indirect materials usage | | 1,195 | 5,000 |

## Accounting for Labor Costs

Exhibit 16.5 shows GenX factory payroll costs as reflected in arrow line ④. Total labor costs of $14,020 are paid in cash and are recorded in the Factory Payroll account:

**P2** Record the flow of direct labor costs in process cost accounting.

| ④ | Factory Payroll . . . . . . . . . . . . . . . . . . . . . . . . | 14,020 | |
| |     Cash . . . . . . . . . . . . . . . . . . . . . . . . . . . . | | 14,020 |
| | *To record factory wages for April.* | | |

Assets  = Liabilities + Equity
−14,020           −14,020

Time reports from the two production departments and the production support office triggered this entry. (For simplicity, we do not separately identify withholdings and additional payroll taxes for employees.) In a process operation, the direct labor of a production department (such as mixing) includes all labor used exclusively by that department. This is the case even if the labor is not applied to the product itself. If a production department in a process operation, for instance, has a full-time manager and a full-time maintenance worker, their salaries are direct labor costs of a process, not factory overhead.

Arrow line ⑤ in Exhibit 16.5 shows GenX's use of direct labor in the grinding and mixing departments. The following entry transfers April's direct labor costs from the Factory Payroll account to the two Goods in Process Inventory accounts:

Assets = Liabilities + Equity
+5,700              +10,800
+5,100

| ⑤ | Goods in Process Inventory—Grinding . . . . . . . . | 5,700 | |
|---|---|---|---|
| | Goods in Process Inventory—Mixing . . . . . . . . . . | 5,100 | |
| | Factory Payroll . . . . . . . . . . . . . . . . . . . . . . . | | 10,800 |
| | *To assign costs of direct labor used in the grinding and mixing departments.* | | |

**Point:** A department's indirect labor cost might include an allocated portion of the salary of a manager who supervises two departments. Allocation of costs between departments is discussed in Chapter 17.

Arrow line ⑥ in Exhibit 16.5 reflects GenX's indirect labor costs. These employees provide clerical, maintenance, and other services that help both the grinding *and* mixing departments produce Profen efficiently. For example, they order materials, deliver them to the factory floor, repair equipment, operate and program computers used in production, keep payroll and other production records, clean up, and move the finished goods to the warehouse. The following entry charges these indirect labor costs to factory overhead:

Assets = Liabilities + Equity
              −3,220
              +3,220

| ⑥ | Factory Overhead . . . . . . . . . . . . . . . . . . . . . . | 3,220 | |
|---|---|---|---|
| | Factory Payroll . . . . . . . . . . . . . . . . . . . . . . . | | 3,220 |
| | *To record indirect labor as overhead.* | | |

After these entries for both direct and indirect labor are posted, the Factory Payroll account appears as shown in Exhibit 16.8. The Factory Payroll account is now closed and ready to receive entries for May.

**Exhibit 16.8**

Factory Payroll

| Factory Payroll | | | | | Acct. No. 530 | | |
|---|---|---|---|---|---|---|---|
| Date | | Explanation | | | Debit | Credit | Balance |
| 2005 | | | | | | | |
| Mar. | 31 | Balance | | | | | 0 |
| Apr. | 30 | Total payroll for April | | | 14,020 | | 14,020 |
| | 30 | Direct labor costs | | | | 10,800 | 3,220 |
| | 30 | Indirect labor costs | | | | 3,220 | 0 |

## Accounting for Factory Overhead

**P3** Record the flow of factory overhead costs in process cost accounting.

Overhead costs other than indirect materials and indirect labor are reflected by arrow line ⑦ in Exhibit 16.5. These overhead items include the costs of insuring manufacturing assets, renting the factory building, using factory utilities, and depreciating equipment not directly related to a specific process. The following entry records overhead costs for April:

Assets = Liabilities + Equity
  −80      +200      −880
−250
−350

| ⑦ | Factory Overhead . . . . . . . . . . . . . . . . . . . . . . | 880 | |
|---|---|---|---|
| | Prepaid Insurance . . . . . . . . . . . . . . . . . . . . | | 80 |
| | Utilities Payable . . . . . . . . . . . . . . . . . . . . . | | 200 |
| | Cash . . . . . . . . . . . . . . . . . . . . . . . . . . . . . | | 250 |
| | Accumulated Depreciation—Factory Equipment . . . . . . . . . . . . . . . . . . . . . . | | 350 |
| | *To record overhead items incurred in April.* | | |

After this entry is posted, the Factory Overhead account balance is $5,295, comprising indirect materials of $1,195, indirect labor of $3,220, and $880 of other overhead.

Arrow line ⑧ in Exhibit 16.5 reflects the application of factory overhead to the two production departments. Factory overhead is applied to processes by relating overhead cost to another variable such as direct labor hours or machine hours used. In many situations, a single allocation basis such as direct labor hours (or a single rate for the entire plant) fails to provide useful allocations. As a result, management may use different rates for different production departments. Based on an analysis of each department's operations, GenX applies its April overhead on the basis of direct labor cost but with different predetermined rates, as shown in Exhibit 16.9.

**Point:** The time it takes to process (cycle) products through a process can also be used to allocate costs.

| Production Department | Direct Labor Cost | Predetermined Rate* | Overhead Applied |
|---|---|---|---|
| Grinding . . . . . . . . . . . | $5,700 | 75% | $4,275 |
| Mixing . . . . . . . . . . . . | 5,100 | 20 | 1,020 |
| Total . . . . . . . . . . . . . | | | $5,295 |

\* Predetermined overhead rates: Grinding department, 75% of direct labor cost; and Mixing department, 20% of direct labor cost.

### Exhibit 16.9
Applying Factory Overhead

**Example:** If grinding uses a 70% rate (instead of 75%), what balance remains in the factory overhead account after overhead is applied to both departments? *Answer:*

| | |
|---|---|
| Overhead costs | $5,295 |
| Overhead applied | 5,010 |
| Underapplied overhead | $ 285 |

GenX records its applied overhead with the following entry:

| | | | |
|---|---|---|---|
| ⑧ | Goods in Process Inventory—Grinding . . . . . . . . | 4,275 | |
| | Goods in Process Inventory—Mixing . . . . . . . . . . | 1,020 | |
| | Factory Overhead . . . . . . . . . . . . . . . . . . . | | 5,295 |
| | *Allocated overhead costs to grinding department at 75% of direct labor cost and to mixing department at 20% of direct labor cost.* | | |

Assets = Liabilities + Equity
+4,275                    +5,295
+1,020

After posting this entry, the Factory Overhead account appears as shown in Exhibit 16.10. For GenX, the amount of overhead applied equals the actual overhead incurred during April. In most cases, using a predetermined overhead rate leaves an overapplied or underapplied balance in the Factory Overhead account. At the end of the period, this overapplied or underapplied balance should be either closed to the Cost of Goods Sold account or allocated among the Cost of Goods Sold, the Goods in Process Inventory, and the Finished Goods Inventory. Procedures for this allocation are the same as that described in Chapter 15 for job order cost accounting systems.

**Decision Ethics**

**Budget Officer** You are working to identify the direct and indirect costs of a new processing department that has several machines. This department's manager instructs you to classify a majority of the costs as indirect to take advantage of the direct labor–based overhead allocation method so it will be charged a lower amount of overhead (because of its small direct labor cost). This would penalize other departments charged with higher allocations. It also will cause the performance ratings of managers in these other departments to suffer. What action do you take?

Answer—p. 680

| Factory Overhead | | | | Acct. No. 540 | | |
|---|---|---|---|---|---|---|
| Date | | Explanation | Debit | Credit | Balance |
| 2005 | | | | | |
| Mar. | 31 | Balance | | | 0 |
| Apr. | 30 | Indirect materials usage | 1,195 | | 1,195 |
| | 30 | Indirect labor costs | 3,220 | | 4,415 |
| | 30 | Other overhead costs | 880 | | 5,295 |
| | 30 | Applied to production departments | | 5,295 | 0 |

### Exhibit 16.10
Factory Overhead

**Example:** If applied overhead results in a $5,400 credit to the factory overhead account, does it yield an over- or underapplied overhead amount? *Answer:* $105 overapplied overhead

Answers—p. 680

# Equivalent Units of Production

**C2** Define equivalent units and explain their use in process cost accounting.

Topic Tackler 16-1

We explained how materials, labor, and overhead costs for a period are accumulated in separate Goods in Process Inventory accounts for each process, but we have not explained the arrow lines labeled ⑨ₐ, ⑨ᵦ, and ⑩ in Exhibit 16.5. These lines reflect the transfer of products from the grinding department to the mixing department, from the mixing department to finished goods inventory, and from finished goods inventory to cost of goods sold. To determine the costs recorded for these flows, we must first determine the cost per unit of product and then apply this result to the number of units transferred.

## Accounting for Goods in Process

If a process has *no beginning and no ending goods in process inventory,* the unit cost of goods transferred out of a process is defined as follows:

$$\frac{\text{Total cost assigned to the process (direct materials, direct labor, and overhead)}}{\text{Total number of units started and finished in the period}}$$

If a process has a beginning or ending inventory of partially processed units (or both), however, the total cost assigned to the process must be allocated to all completed and incomplete units worked on during the period. Therefore, the denominator must measure the entire production activity of the process for the period, called **equivalent units of production** (or **EUP**), a term that refers to the number of units that would be completed if all effort during a period had been applied to only those units started in that period. This measure is then used to compute the cost per equivalent unit and to assign costs to finished goods and goods in process inventory.

To illustrate, assume that GenX adds (or introduces) 100 units into the grinding process during a period. Suppose at the end of that period, the production supervisor determines that those 100 units are 60% processed. Therefore, equivalent units of production for that period total 60 units (100 units × 60%). This means that if we had introduced 60 units into the process, we would have completely processed these 60 units.

## Differences between Equivalent Units for Materials and that for Labor and Overhead

**P4** Compute the equivalent units produced in a period.

In many processes, the equivalent units of production for materials are not the same with respect to labor and overhead. To illustrate, consider the 5-step process operation shown in Exhibit 16.11.

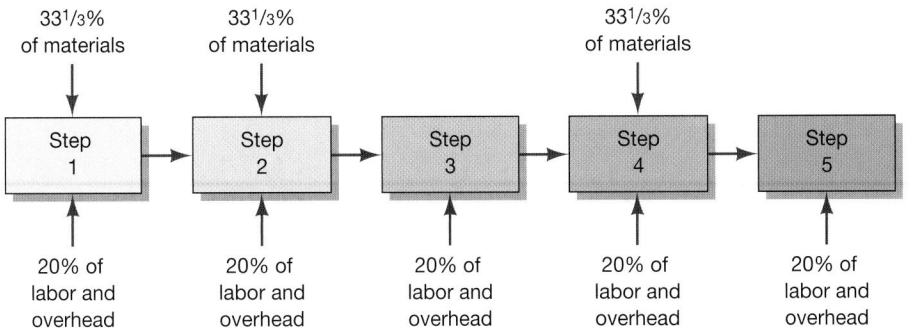

Exhibit 16.11

Process Manufacturing: An Example

This exhibit shows that one-third of the direct material cost is added at each of three steps: 1, 2, and 4. One-fifth of the direct labor cost is added at each of the five steps. One-fifth of the overhead also is added at each step because overhead is applied as a percent of direct labor for this company.

When units finish step 1, they are one-third complete with respect to materials but only one-fifth complete with respect to labor and overhead. When they finish step 2, they are two-thirds complete with respect to materials but only two-fifths complete with respect to labor and overhead. When they finish step 3, they re-main two-thirds complete with respect to materials but are now three-fifths complete with respect to labor and overhead. When they finish step 4, they are 100% complete with respect to materials (all materials have been added) but only four-fifths complete with respect to labor and overhead.

### Decision Insight

**Process Services**  Customer-interaction software is a hot item in customer-service processes. Whether in insurance, delivery, or technology services, companies are finding that this software can turn their customer-service process into an asset. How does it work? For starters, it cuts time spent on service calls because a customer describes a problem only once. It also yields a database of customer questions and complaints that gives insights into needed improvements. It also recognizes incoming phone numbers and accesses previous dealings.

As an example, if 300 units of product are started and processed through step 1 of Exhibit 16.11, they are said to be one-third complete *with respect to materials*. Expressed in terms of equivalent finished units, the processing of these 300 units is equal to finishing 100 units with respect to materials (300 units × 33⅓%). However, only one-fifth of direct labor and overhead has been applied to the 300 units at the end of step 1. This means that the equivalent units of production *with respect to labor and overhead* total 60 units (300 units × 20%).

## Process Costing Illustration

This section applies the process costing concepts and procedures to GenX.

### Accounting for First (Grinding) Department

Exhibit 16.12 shows selected information from the first (grinding) department for the month of April. In computing equivalent units, assume that each of GenX's production depart-ments processes units on a first-in, first-out basis.[1] Accounting for a department's activ-ity for a period includes four steps involving analysis of (1) physical flow, (2) equivalent units, (3) cost per equivalent unit, and (4) cost reconciliation. The next sections describe each step.

C3  Explain the four steps in accounting for production activity in a period.

---

[1] Assume a FIFO flow for all computations and assignments in this chapter unless explicitly stated differently. Weighted average and LIFO also can be used, but they are less useful for measuring how effectively costs are controlled during a period. When using a just-in-time inventory system, the different inventory methods yield similar results because inventories are immaterial.

## Exhibit 16.12

Production Data—First
(Grinding) Department

| | |
|---|---|
| Beginning inventory (March 31) | |
|     Units of product . . . . . . . . . . . . . . . . . . . . . . . . | 30,000 |
|     Percentage of completion—Direct materials . . . . . . . | 100% |
|     Percentage of completion—Direct labor . . . . . . . . . . | 33⅓% |
|     Direct materials costs . . . . . . . . . . . . . . . . . . . . . . | $ 2,780 |
|     Direct labor costs . . . . . . . . . . . . . . . . . . . . . . . . | $ 700 |
|     Factory overhead costs . . . . . . . . . . . . . . . . . . . . . | $ 770 |
| Activities during the current period | |
|     Units started this period (April) . . . . . . . . . . . . . . . | 90,000 |
|     Units transferred to mixing (during April) . . . . . . . . . | 100,000 |
|     Direct materials costs . . . . . . . . . . . . . . . . . . . . . . | $ 9,900 |
|     Direct labor costs . . . . . . . . . . . . . . . . . . . . . . . . | $ 5,700 |
|     Factory overhead costs . . . . . . . . . . . . . . . . . . . . . | $ 4,275 |
| Ending inventory (April 30) | |
|     Units of product . . . . . . . . . . . . . . . . . . . . . . . . | 20,000 |
|     Percentage of completion—Direct materials . . . . . . . | 100% |
|     Percentage of completion—Direct labor . . . . . . . . . . | 25% |

**Physical Flow of Units—First Department**   *Physical flow* is a reconciliation of (1) the physical units started in a period with (2) the physical units completed in that period. A physical flow reconciliation for GenX is shown in Exhibit 16.13 for April.

## Exhibit 16.13

Physical Flow Reconciliation—
First (Grinding) Department

| Units to Account For | | Units Accounted For | |
|---|---|---|---|
| Beginning inventory . . . . . . . . . . | 30,000 units | Units transferred from grinding to mixing . . . . . . . . . | 100,000 units |
| Units started (in April) . . . . . . . | 90,000 units | Ending inventory . . . . . . . . . . . | 20,000 units |
| Total number of units . . . . . . . . | **120,000 units** | Total number of units . . . . . . . . | **120,000 units** |

reconciled

The 100,000 units transferred from grinding to mixing during April include the 30,000 units from the beginning goods in process inventory (or simply beginning inventory) because of the FIFO assumption. The remaining 70,000 units transferred out are from units started in April. Of the total 90,000 units started in April, 70,000 of these are completed, and 20,000 remain unfinished at period-end.

**Equivalent Units of Production—First Department**   The second step is to compute *equivalent units of production* in the grinding department for direct materials, direct labor, and factory overhead for April. Overhead is applied using direct labor as the allocation base. This means that the equivalent units are the same for both labor and overhead for GenX.

***Equivalent units—Direct materials***   Direct materials (the Profelene blocks) are added at the *beginning* of the process. A unit of product is 100% complete with respect to materials as soon as it is started. This means that beginning goods in process inventory for April received all its materials in March and is not assigned any additional materials. The 70,000 units started and completed in April and the 20,000 units in ending goods in process inventory on April 30 received all of their materials in April. The grinding department's equivalent units of production for materials are computed in Exhibit 16.14.

***Equivalent units—Direct labor and factory overhead.***   Direct labor and factory overhead, both conversion costs, are assigned uniformly throughout the GenX process. Recall that beginning inventory of 30,000 units is partially completed in March. In April, additional labor and overhead are assigned to these units to complete them. Based on percent of

**Point:** To apply these concepts, work QS 16-3.

| EUP for Materials | Units of Product | | Percent Added This Period | | Equivalent Units |
|---|---|---|---|---|---|
| Beginning goods in process . . . . . . . . . . | 30,000 | × | 0% | = | 0 |
| Goods started and completed . . . . . . . | 70,000 | × | 100 | = | 70,000 |
| Ending goods in process . . . . . . . . . . . | 20,000 | × | 100 | = | 20,000 |
| Total units . . . . . . . . . . . . . . . . . . . . . | 120,000 | | | | 90,000 |

Exhibit 16.14

Equivalent Units of Production for Direct Materials—First (Grinding) Department

completion (see Exhibit 16.12), 33⅓% of labor and overhead was assigned in March. The remaining 66⅔% is assigned in April. The 70,000 units started and completed in April are assigned 100% of labor and overhead. The 20,000 partly completed units in ending inventory are assigned only 25% of labor at the end of April. Exhibit 16.15 shows these computations.

| EUP for Labor and Overhead | Units of Product | | Percent Added This Period | | Equivalent Units |
|---|---|---|---|---|---|
| Beginning goods in process . . . . . . . . . . | 30,000 | × | 66⅔% | = | 20,000 |
| Goods started and completed . . . . . . . | 70,000 | × | 100 | = | 70,000 |
| Ending goods in process . . . . . . . . . . . | 20,000 | × | 25 | = | 5,000 |
| Total units . . . . . . . . . . . . . . . . . . . . . | 120,000 | | | | 95,000 |

Exhibit 16.15

Equivalent Units of Production for Direct Labor and Overhead—First (Grinding) Department

**Example:** If ending goods in process are 20% complete, what are total equivalent units for labor and overhead for April? *Answer:* 94,000 units

A summary of April's equivalent units of production for the grinding department is shown in Exhibit 16.16.[2]

| | Equivalent Units of Production | | |
|---|---|---|---|
| EUP Summary | Direct Materials | Direct Labor* | Factory Overhead* |
| Beginning goods in process . . . . . . . . . . . . . . . . . . . . . . | 0 | 20,000 | 20,000 |
| Goods started and completed in current period . . . . . . . . | 70,000 | 70,000 | 70,000 |
| Ending goods in process . . . . . . . . . . . . . . . . . . . . . . . | 20,000 | 5,000 | 5,000 |
| Equivalent units of production for period . . . . . . . . . . . . | 90,000 | 95,000 | 95,000 |

Exhibit 16.16

Equivalent Units of Production Summary—First (Grinding) Department*

\* The columns for direct labor and factory overhead are sometimes combined and termed *conversion costs;* when this is done, these columns in all other reports should be similarly combined.

**Cost per Equivalent Unit—First Department**   The third step is to compute the *cost per equivalent unit* for direct materials, direct labor, and factory overhead as shown in Exhibit 16.17. Specifically, the $9,900 direct materials costs for April (from Exhibit 16.5) are assigned to the 90,000 equivalent units for materials, yielding a cost per equivalent unit of $0.11. The $5,700 direct labor costs and the $4,275 factory overhead costs for April (from Exhibit 16.5) are assigned to 95,000 equivalent units for direct labor and factory overhead,

| Activities during April | Direct Materials | Direct Labor | Factory Overhead |
|---|---|---|---|
| Costs assigned to grinding in current period . . . . . . . . . . | $ 9,900 | $ 5,700 | $ 4,275 |
| Equivalent units of production in current period . . . . . . . | 90,000 | 95,000 | 95,000 |
| Cost per equivalent unit for period . . . . . . . . . . . . . . . . | $ 0.11 | $ 0.06 | $ 0.045 |

Exhibit 16.17

Cost per Equivalent Unit—First (Grinding) Department

[2] Under the *weighted-average method,* the 100,000 units transferred out during April are *not* separated into their two components of 30,000 from beginning inventory and 70,000 started and completed during the month. Thus, the equivalent units for direct materials equal 120,000 [(100,000 × 100%) + (20,000 × 100%)], and for direct labor and overhead would equal 105,000 [(100,000 × 100%) + (20,000 × 25%)].

Assets = Liabilities + Equity
+21,400
−21,400

⑨ₐ Goods in Process Inventory—Mixing . . . . . . . . . . 21,400
    Goods in Process Inventory—Grinding . . . . . 21,400
*To record transfer of partially completed goods from the grinding department to the mixing department.*

## Exhibit 16.19

Process Cost Summary—First (Grinding) Department

### GENX COMPANY
### Process Cost Summary (Grinding Department)
### For Month Ended April 30, 2005

**Costs Charged to Department**

|  |  |
|---|---|
| Direct materials requisitioned . . . . . . . . . . . . . . . . . . . . . . . . . . . . . . . . . . . . . . . . . | $ 9,900 |
| Direct labor charged . . . . . . . . . . . . . . . . . . . . . . . . . . . . . . . . . . . . . . . . . . . . . . . . | 5,700 |
| ① Overhead allocated (at predetermined rate) . . . . . . . . . . . . . . . . . . . . . . . . . . . . . | 4,275 |
| Total processing costs for the period . . . . . . . . . . . . . . . . . . . . . . . . . . . . . . . . . . . | 19,875 |
| Goods in process at the beginning of the period . . . . . . . . . . . . . . . . . . . . . . . . . . | 4,250 |
| Total costs to be accounted for . . . . . . . . . . . . . . . . . . . . . . . . . . . . . . . . . . . . . . . . | **$24,125** ◄ |

|  | Units of Product | Equivalent Units — Direct Materials | Equivalent Units — Labor and Overhead |
|---|---|---|---|
| **Equivalent Unit Processing Costs** |  |  |  |
| Units processed |  |  |  |
|   Beginning goods in process . . . . . . . . . . . . . . . . . . . . . . | 30,000 | 0 | 20,000 |
|   Units started and completed . . . . . . . . . . . . . . . . . . . | 70,000 | 70,000 | 70,000 |
|   Ending goods in process . . . . . . . . . . . . . . . . . . . . . . . | 20,000 | 20,000 | 5,000 |
| ②   Total . . . . . . . . . . . . . . . . . . . . . . . . . . . . . . . . . . . . . | 120,000 | 90,000 | 95,000 |

|  |  |
|---|---|
| Total direct materials cost for the period . . . . . . . . . . . . . . . . . . . . . . . . . . . . . . . . | $9,900 |
| Direct materials cost per equivalent unit ($9,900/90,000 units) . . . . . . . . . . . . . . . . | $0.110 |
| Total direct labor cost for the period . . . . . . . . . . . . . . . . . . . . . . . . . . . . . . . . . . . | $5,700 |
| Direct labor cost per equivalent unit ($5,700/95,000 units) . . . . . . . . . . . . . . . . . . . | $0.060 |
| Total overhead cost for the period . . . . . . . . . . . . . . . . . . . . . . . . . . . . . . . . . . . . . | $4,275 |
| Overhead cost per equivalent unit ($4,275/95,000 units) . . . . . . . . . . . . . . . . . . . . | $0.045 |

| **Assignment of Costs to Output of Department** | Equivalent Units | Cost per Unit | Total Cost |
|---|---|---|---|
| Goods in process, March 31, 2005, and completed in the period |  |  |  |
|   Costs from prior period . . . . . . . . . . . . . . . . . . . . . . . |  |  | $ 4,250 |
|   Direct materials added . . . . . . . . . . . . . . . . . . . . . . . . | 0 | $0.110 | 0 |
|   Direct labor added . . . . . . . . . . . . . . . . . . . . . . . . . . | 20,000 | 0.060 | 1,200 |
|   Overhead applied . . . . . . . . . . . . . . . . . . . . . . . . . . . | 20,000 | 0.045 | 900 |
|   Total costs to process . . . . . . . . . . . . . . . . . . . . . . . . |  |  | 6,350 |
| Goods started and completed in the period |  |  |  |
|   Direct materials added . . . . . . . . . . . . . . . . . . . . . . . . | 70,000 | $0.110 | 7,700 |
| ③   Direct labor added . . . . . . . . . . . . . . . . . . . . . . . . . . | 70,000 | 0.060 | 4,200 |
|   Overhead applied . . . . . . . . . . . . . . . . . . . . . . . . . . . | 70,000 | 0.045 | 3,150 |
|   Total costs to process . . . . . . . . . . . . . . . . . . . . . . . . |  |  | 15,050 |
| Total costs transferred to next department |  |  |  |
|   (unit cost = $21,400/100,000 units = $0.214) . . . . . . . . |  |  | 21,400 |
| Goods in process, April 30, 2005 |  |  |  |
|   Direct materials added . . . . . . . . . . . . . . . . . . . . . . . . | 20,000 | $0.110 | 2,200 |
|   Direct labor added . . . . . . . . . . . . . . . . . . . . . . . . . . | 5,000 | 0.060 | 300 |
|   Overhead applied . . . . . . . . . . . . . . . . . . . . . . . . . . . | 5,000 | 0.045 | 225 |
|   Total costs to process . . . . . . . . . . . . . . . . . . . . . . . . |  |  | 2,725 |
| Total costs accounted for ($21,400 + $2,725) . . . . . . . . . . |  |  | **$24,125** ◄ |

After this entry is posted, the Goods in Process Inventory—Grinding account appears as shown in Exhibit 16.20. The $2,725 ending balance in this account equals the cost assigned to partially completed units as shown in section 3 of the process cost summary.

| Goods in Process Inventory—Grinding | | | Acct. No. 133 | | |
|---|---|---|---|---|---|
| **Date** | | **Explanation** | **Debit** | **Credit** | **Balance** |
| 2005 | | | | | |
| Mar. | 31 | Balance | | | 4,250 |
| Apr. | 30 | Direct materials usage | 9,900 | | 14,150 |
| | 30 | Direct labor costs | 5,700 | | 19,850 |
| | 30 | Applied overhead | 4,275 | | 24,125 |
| | 30 | Transfer to mixing department | | 21,400 | 2,725 |

**Exhibit 16.20**

Goods in Process Inventory—Grinding

## Accounting for Second (Mixing) Department

The mixing department begins work on Profelene when it is received from the grinding department. Most of its costs are in the form of labor for specialists mixing the compounds and laborers packaging the product. Direct labor and overhead are added at the same rate as direct materials for this department.

**Equivalent Units of Production—Second Department**   The mixing department requires only one computation of equivalent units of production because direct materials, direct labor, and overhead are used at the same rate. Exhibit 16.21 provides the data needed to compute equivalent units of production for the mixing department for April.

| | |
|---|---|
| Beginning inventory (March 31) | |
| Units of product ........................................... | 16,000 |
| Percentage of completion—Direct materials, direct labor, and overhead ....... | 25% |
| Activities during the current period | |
| Units received from grinding (in April) .............................. | 100,000 |
| Units transferred to finished goods (in April) ......................... | 101,000 |
| Ending inventory (April 30) | |
| Units of product .......................................... | 15,000 |
| Percentage of completion—Direct materials, direct labor, and overhead ....... | 33⅓% |

**Exhibit 16.21**

Production Data—Second (Mixing) Department

A total of 101,000 units is transferred from the mixing department to finished goods in the period. Based on a FIFO assumption, this implies that 16,000 of these units are from beginning goods in process inventory and another 85,000 are received and completed in the current period. Since 100,000 units are received from the grinding department this period and only 85,000 of these units are completed, this explains the 15,000 units in the ending goods in process inventory.

Exhibit 16.22 computes the mixing department's equivalent units of production for direct materials, direct labor, and overhead for the month of April. (Recall that because materials, labor, and overhead are added at the same rate in this department, only one report is needed.)

| EUP for Materials, Labor, and Overhead | Units of Product | | Percent Added This Period | | Equivalent Units |
|---|---|---|---|---|---|
| Beginning goods in process .......... | 16,000 | × | 75% | = | 12,000 |
| Goods started and completed ....... | 85,000 | × | 100 | = | 85,000 |
| Ending goods in process ............ | 15,000 | × | 33⅓ | = | 5,000 |
| Total units ..................... | 116,000 | | | | 102,000 |

**Exhibit 16.22**

Equivalent Units of Production for Materials, Labor, and Overhead—Second (Mixing) Department

Arrow line ⑩ in Exhibit 16.5 reflects the sale of finished goods. GenX sold 106,000 units of Profen in April. The beginning inventory of finished goods consists of 23,000 units with a cost of $6,440. All 23,000 units are sold in April. The remaining 83,000 units sold are from the 101,000 units completed in April. Ending finished goods inventory equals the 18,000 units remaining. Section ③ of Exhibit 16.23 shows that total cost per unit of finished goods in April is $0.2918 ($29,470/101,000 units). Using this information, we can compute cost of goods sold for April as shown in Exhibit 16.25.

**Exhibit 16.25**

Cost of Goods Sold

| | |
|---|---|
| 23,000 units from beginning inventory* . . . . . . . . . . . . . . . . . | $ 6,440 |
| 83,000 units processed in period (83,000 × $0.2918) . . . . . . . | 24,219 |
| Total cost of goods sold . . . . . . . . . . . . . . . . . . . . . . . . . | $30,659 |

\* Computations assume a FIFO inventory system.

The summary entry to record cost of goods sold for April is:

Assets = Liabilities + Equity
−30,659                  −30,659

⑩          Cost of Goods Sold . . . . . . . . . . . . . . . . . . . . . .    30,659
                Finished Goods Inventory. . . . . . . . . . . . . . .              30,659
           *To record cost of goods sold for April.*

The Finished Goods Inventory account now appears as shown in Exhibit 16.26.

**Exhibit 16.26**

Finished Goods Inventory

| Finished Goods Inventory | | | | Acct. No. 135 | | |
|---|---|---|---|---|---|---|
| Date | | Explanation | | Debit | Credit | Balance |
| 2005 | | | | | | |
| Mar. | 31 | Balance | | | | 6,440 |
| Apr. | 30 | Transfer in from mixing department | | 29,470 | | 35,910 |
| | 30 | Cost of goods sold | | | 30,659 | 5,251 |

**Summary of Cost Flows**   Exhibit 16.27 shows GenX's manufacturing cost flows for April. Each of these cost flows and the entries to record them have been explained. The flow of costs through the accounts reflects the flow of manufacturing activities and products.

## Effect of Lean Business Model on Process Operations

Adopting lean business practices often yields changes in process operations. Management concerns with throughput and just-in-time manufacturing, for instance, cause boundary lines between departments to become less distinct. In some cases, higher quality and better efficiency are obtained by entirely reorganizing production processes. For example, instead of producing different types of computers in a series of departments, a separate work center for each computer can be established in one department. When such a rearrangement occurs, the process cost accounting system is changed to account for each work center's costs.

To illustrate, when a company adopts a just-in-time inventory system, its inventories can be minimal. For example, if raw materials are

**Decision Insight**

**Lean Machine**   Attention to customer orientation has led to improved processes for companies. A manufacturer of control devices improved quality and reduced production time by forming teams to study processes and suggest improvements. Another company set up project groups to evaluate its manufacturing processes. Still another company uses statistical process control to identify problems and implement corrective actions.

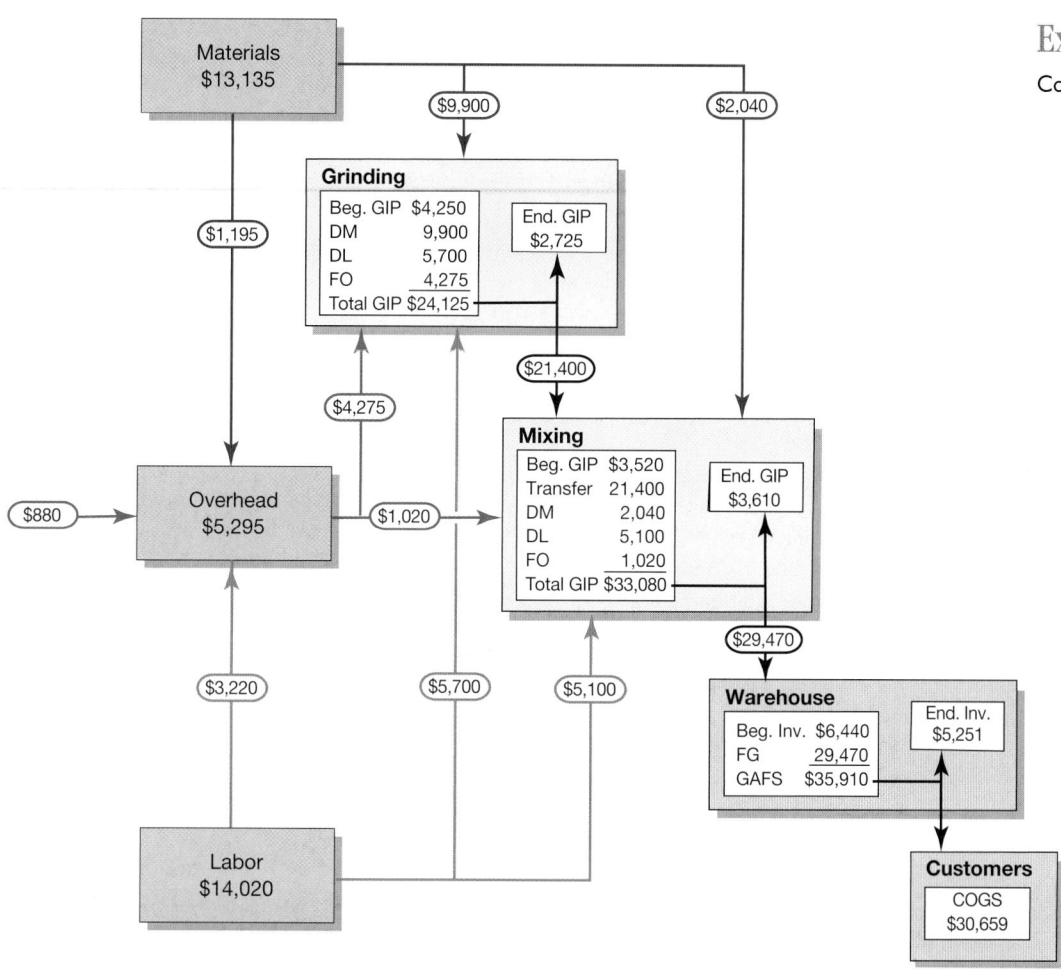

Exhibit 16.27*

Cost Flows through GenX

*Abbreviations: GIP (goods in process); DM (direct materials); DL (direct labor); FO (factory overhead); FG (finished goods); GAFS (goods available for sale); COGS (cost of goods sold).

not ordered or received until needed, a Raw Materials Inventory account may be unnecessary. Instead, materials cost is immediately debited to the Goods in Process Inventory account. Similarly, a Finished Goods Inventory account may not be needed. Instead, cost of finished goods may be immediately debited to the Cost of Goods Sold account.

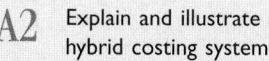

**Decision Insight**

**Best of Both**  Customer orientation demands both flexibility and standardization. Flexibility allows companies to supply products or services to a customer's specifications as in a job order setting, and standardization helps achieve efficiencies and lower costs as in a process operation. Companies that successfully combine flexibility and standardization can better satisfy customers.

## Hybrid Costing System

**Decision Analysis**

This chapter explained the process costing system and contrasted it with the job order costing system. Many organizations use a *hybrid system* that contains features of both process and job order operations. A recent survey of manufacturers revealed that a majority use hybrid systems.

To illustrate, consider a car manufacturer's assembly line. On one hand, the line resembles a process operation in that the assembly steps for each car are nearly identical. On the other hand, the specifications of most cars have several important differences. At the **Ford** Mustang plant in Michigan, each car assembled on a given day can be different from the previous car and the next car. This means that the costs of materials (subassemblies or components) for each car can differ. Accordingly, while the conversion costs (direct labor and overhead) can be accounted for using a process costing system, the component costs (direct materials) are accounted for using a job order system (separately for each car or type of car).

**A2**  Explain and illustrate a hybrid costing system.

A hybrid system of processes requires a *hybrid costing system* to properly cost products or services. In the Ford assembly plant case, the assembly costs per car are readily determined using process costing. The costs of additional components can then be added to the assembly costs to determine each car's total cost (as in job order costing). To illustrate, consider the following information for the assembly process at Ford for a recent day:

| Assembly process costs | |
|---|---|
| Direct materials | $10,600,000 |
| Direct labor | $5,800,000 |
| Factory overhead | $6,200,000 |
| Number of cars assembled | 1,000 |
| Costs of three different types of steering wheels | $240, $330, $480 |
| Costs of three different types of seats | $620, $840, $1,360 |

## Decision Ethics

**Entrepreneur**   You operate a process manufacturing company making similar products for three different customers. One customer demands 100% quality inspection of the products at your location before shipping them. The added costs of the quality inspection are spread across all customers, not just the one using the service. If you charge the added costs to that customer, the company could lose the customer and experience a loss. Moreover, your other two customers have agreed to pay 110% of full costs. What actions (if any) do you take?

Answer—p. 680

The assembly process costs $22,600 per car. Depending on the type of steering wheel and seats the customer requests, the cost of a car can range from $23,460 to $24,440 (a $980 difference).

Today companies are increasingly trying to standardize processes while attempting to meet individual customer needs. To the extent that differences among individual customers' requests are large, understanding the costs to satisfy those requests is important. Thus, monitoring and controlling both process and job order costs are important.

# Demonstration Problem

Pennsylvania Company produces a product that passes through a molding process and then through an assembly process. Information related to its manufacturing activities for July follows:

**Raw Materials**

| | |
|---|---|
| Beginning inventory . . . . . . . . . . . . . . . . . | $100,000 |
| Raw materials purchased on credit . . . . . . . . | 300,000 |
| Direct materials—Molding . . . . . . . . . . . . | (190,000) |
| Direct materials—Assembly . . . . . . . . . . . | (88,600) |
| Indirect materials used . . . . . . . . . . . . . . | (51,400) |
| Ending inventory . . . . . . . . . . . . . . . . . . | $ 70,000 |

**Factory Payroll**

| | |
|---|---|
| Direct labor—Molding . . . . . . . . . . . . . . | $ 42,000 |
| Direct labor—Assembly . . . . . . . . . . . . . | 55,375 |
| Indirect labor used . . . . . . . . . . . . . . . . | 50,625 |
| Total payroll cost (paid in cash) . . . . . . . . | $148,000 |

**Factory Overhead**

| | |
|---|---|
| Indirect materials used . . . . . . . . . . . . . . | $ 51,400 |
| Indirect labor used . . . . . . . . . . . . . . . . | 50,625 |
| Other overhead costs . . . . . . . . . . . . . . . | 71,725 |
| Total factory overhead incurred . . . . . . . . . | $173,750 |

**Factory Overhead Applied**

| | |
|---|---|
| Molding (150% of direct labor) . . . . . . . . . | $ 63,000 |
| Assembly (200% of direct labor) . . . . . . . . | 110,750 |
| Total factory overhead applied . . . . . . . . . . | $173,750 |

**Molding Department**

| | |
|---|---|
| Beginning goods in process inventory (units) . . . . . . . . . | 5,000 |
| Percentage completed—Materials . . . . . . . . . . . . . . | 100% |
| Percentage completed—Labor and overhead . . . . . . . | 60% |
| Units started and completed . . . . . . . . . . . . . . . . . . | 17,000 |
| Ending goods in process inventory (units) . . . . . . . . . . | 8,000 |
| Percentage completed—Materials . . . . . . . . . . . . . . | 100% |
| Percentage completed—Labor and overhead . . . . . . . | 25% |

Costs

| | |
|---|---|
| Beginning goods in process inventory . . . . . . . . . . . | $ 53,000 |
| Direct materials added . . . . . . . . . . . . . . . . . . . . . | 190,000 |
| Direct labor added . . . . . . . . . . . . . . . . . . . . . . . | 42,000 |
| Overhead applied (150% of direct labor) . . . . . . . . . | 63,000 |
| Total costs . . . . . . . . . . . . . . . . . . . . . . . . . . . . | $348,000 |

**Assembly Department**

| | |
|---|---|
| Beginning goods in process inventory . . . . . . . . . . . | $154,800 |
| Ending goods in process inventory . . . . . . . . . . . . . | 108,325 |

**Finished Goods Inventory**

| | |
|---|---|
| Beginning inventory . . . . . . . . . . . . . . . . . . . . . . | $ 96,400 |
| Cost transferred in from assembly . . . . . . . . . . . . . | 578,400 |
| Cost of goods sold . . . . . . . . . . . . . . . . . . . . . . . | (506,100) |
| Ending Inventory . . . . . . . . . . . . . . . . . . . . . . . . | $168,700 |

**Required**

1. Compute the equivalent units of production for the molding department for July and determine the costs per equivalent unit for direct materials, direct labor, and factory overhead.

2. Compute the cost of the units transferred from molding to assembly in July and the cost of the ending goods in process inventory for the molding department.

3. Prepare summary journal entries to record the transactions and events of July for (a) raw materials purchases, (b) direct materials usage, (c) indirect materials usage, (d) factory payroll costs, (e) direct labor usage, (f) indirect labor usage, (g) other overhead costs (credit Other Accounts), (h) application of overhead to the two departments, (i) transfer of partially completed goods from molding to assembly, (j) transfer of finished goods out of assembly, and (k) the cost of goods sold.

## Planning the Solution

- Compute the molding department's equivalent units of production and cost per unit with respect to direct materials.

- Compute the molding department's equivalent units of production with respect to direct labor and overhead and determine the cost per unit for each.

- Compute the total cost of the goods transferred to the assembly department by using the equivalent units and unit costs to determine (a) the cost of the beginning in-process inventory, (b) the materials, labor, and overhead costs added to the beginning in-process inventory, and (c) the materials, labor, and overhead costs added to the units started and completed in the month.

- Use the information to record the summary journal entries for July.

## Solution to Demonstration Problem

**1. Equivalent units of production—direct materials**

| EUP for Materials | Units of Product | | Percent Added This Period | | Equivalent Units |
|---|---|---|---|---|---|
| Beginning goods in process . . . . . . . . . . | 5,000 | × | 0% | = | 0 |
| Goods started and completed   . . . . . . . | 17,000 | × | 100 | = | 17,000 |
| Ending goods in process . . . . . . . . . . . . | 8,000 | × | 100 | = | 8,000 |
| Total units . . . . . . . . . . . . . . . . . . . . . | 30,000 | | | | **25,000** |

The direct materials used in molding total $190,000. Therefore,

Materials cost per equivalent unit = $190,000/25,000 units = $7.60 per unit

**Equivalent units of production—direct labor and overhead**

| EUP for Labor and Overhead | Units of Product | | Percent Added This Period | | Equivalent Units |
|---|---|---|---|---|---|
| Beginning goods in process . . . . . . . . . . | 5,000 | × | 40% | = | 2,000 |
| Goods started and completed   . . . . . . . | 17,000 | × | 100 | = | 17,000 |
| Ending goods in process . . . . . . . . . . . . | 8,000 | × | 25 | = | 2,000 |
| Total units . . . . . . . . . . . . . . . . . . . . . | 30,000 | | | | **21,000** |

The direct labor used in molding totals $42,000. Therefore,

Labor cost per equivalent unit = $42,000/21,000 units = $2 per unit

The overhead applied in molding totals 150% of direct labor cost. Therefore,

Overhead cost per equivalent unit = $63,000/21,000 units = $3 per unit

**2. Cost of units transferred from molding to assembly in July**

|  | Equivalent Units | Cost per Unit | Total Cost |
|---|---|---|---|
| **Beginning goods in process** | | | |
| Costs from prior month . . . . . . . . . . | | | $ 53,000 |
| Direct materials added . . . . . . . . . . . | 0 | $7.60 | 0 |
| Direct labor added . . . . . . . . . . . . . | 2,000 | 2.00 | 4,000 |
| Overhead applied . . . . . . . . . . . . . . | 2,000 | 3.00 | 6,000 |
| Total cost to process . . . . . . . . . . . | | | $ 63,000 |
| **Goods started and completed** | | | |
| Direct materials added . . . . . . . . . . | 17,000 | $7.60 | $ 129,200 |
| Direct labor added . . . . . . . . . . . . . | 17,000 | 2.00 | 34,000 |
| Overhead applied . . . . . . . . . . . . . . | 17,000 | 3.00 | 51,000 |
| Total cost to process . . . . . . . . . . . | | | 214,200 |
| **Cost of transferred units** . . . . . . . . . . . | | | **$277,200** |

**Cost of the July ending goods in process inventory for the molding department**

|  | Equivalent Units | Cost per Unit | Total Cost |
|---|---|---|---|
| Direct materials added . . . . . . . . . . . . . . . . . . . | 8,000 | $7.60 | $ 60,800 |
| Direct labor added . . . . . . . . . . . . . . . . . . . . . . | 2,000 | 2.00 | 4,000 |
| Overhead applied . . . . . . . . . . . . . . . . . . . . . . | 2,000 | 3.00 | 6,000 |
| Cost of ending goods in process inventory . . . . . . . . | | | **$70,800** |

**3.** Summary journal entries for the transactions and events in July:

| | | | |
|---|---|---|---|
| a. | Raw Materials Inventory . . . . . . . . . . . . . . . . . . . | 300,000 | |
| |     Accounts Payable. . . . . . . . . . . . . . . . . . . . | | 300,000 |
| | *To record raw materials purchases.* | | |
| b. | Goods in Process Inventory—Molding . . . . . . . . . | 190,000 | |
| | Goods in Process Inventory—Assembly . . . . . . . . | 88,600 | |
| |     Raw Materials Inventory. . . . . . . . . . . . . . . | | 278,600 |
| | *To record direct materials usage.* | | |
| c. | Factory Overhead. . . . . . . . . . . . . . . . . . . . . . . | 51,400 | |
| |     Raw Materials Inventory. . . . . . . . . . . . . . . | | 51,400 |
| | *To record indirect materials usage.* | | |
| d. | Factory Payroll . . . . . . . . . . . . . . . . . . . . . . . | 148,000 | |
| |     Cash. . . . . . . . . . . . . . . . . . . . . . . . . . . | | 148,000 |
| | *To record factory payroll costs.* | | |
| e. | Goods in Process Inventory—Molding . . . . . . . . . | 42,000 | |
| | Goods in Process Inventory—Assembly . . . . . . . . | 55,375 | |
| |     Factory Payroll . . . . . . . . . . . . . . . . . . . . | | 97,375 |
| | *To record direct labor usage.* | | |
| f. | Factory Overhead. . . . . . . . . . . . . . . . . . . . . . . | 50,625 | |
| |     Factory Payroll . . . . . . . . . . . . . . . . . . . . | | 50,625 |
| | *To record indirect labor usage.* | | |
| g. | Factory Overhead. . . . . . . . . . . . . . . . . . . . . . . | 71,725 | |
| |     Other Accounts. . . . . . . . . . . . . . . . . . . . | | 71,725 |
| | *To record other overhead costs.* | | |

[continued on next page]

[continued from previous page]

| | | | |
|---|---|---|---|
| **h.** | Goods in Process Inventory—Molding . . . . . . . . . | 63,000 | |
| | Goods in Process Inventory—Assembly . . . . . . . . | 110,750 | |
| | Factory Overhead . . . . . . . . . . . . . . . . . . . | | 173,750 |
| | *To record application of overhead.* | | |
| **i.** | Goods in Process Inventory—Assembly . . . . . . . . | 277,200 | |
| | Goods in Process Inventory—Molding . . . . . | | 277,200 |
| | *To record transfer of partially completed goods from molding to assembly.* | | |
| **j.** | Finished Goods Inventory . . . . . . . . . . . . . . . . . | 578,400 | |
| | Goods in Process Inventory—Assembly . . . . | | 578,400 |
| | *To record transfer of finished goods out of assembly.* | | |
| **k.** | Cost of Goods Sold . . . . . . . . . . . . . . . . . . . . . | 506,100 | |
| | Finished Goods Inventory . . . . . . . . . . . . . . | | 506,100 |
| | *To record cost of goods sold.* | | |

## Summary

**C1** **Explain process operations and the way they differ from job order operations.** Process operations produce large quantities of similar products or services by passing them through a series of processes, or steps, in production. Like job order operations, they combine direct materials, direct labor, and overhead in the operations. Unlike job order operations that assign the responsibility for each job to a manager, process operations assign the responsibility for each *process* to a manager.

**C2** **Define equivalent units and explain their use in process cost accounting.** Equivalent units of production measure the activity of a process as the number of units that would be completed in a period if all effort had been applied to units that were started and finished. This measure of production activity is used to compute the cost per equivalent unit and to assign costs to finished goods and goods in process inventory.

**C3** **Explain the four steps in accounting for production activity in a period.** The four steps involved in accounting for production activity in a period are (1) recording the physical flow of units, (2) computing the equivalent units of production, (3) computing the cost per equivalent unit of production, and (4) reconciling costs. The last step involves assigning costs to finished goods and goods in process inventory for the period.

**C4** **Define a process cost summary and describe its purposes.** A process cost summary reports on the activities of a production process or department for a period. It describes the costs charged to the department, the equivalent units of production for the department, and the costs assigned to the output. The report aims to (1) help managers control their departments, (2) help factory managers evaluate department managers' performances, and (3) provide cost information for financial statements.

**A1** **Compare process cost accounting and job order cost accounting.** Process and job order manufacturing operations are similar in that both combine materials, labor, and factory overhead to produce products or services. They differ in the way they are organized and managed. In job order operations, the job order cost accounting system assigns materials, labor, and over-

head to specific jobs. In process operations, the process cost accounting system assigns materials, labor, and overhead to specific processes. The total costs associated with each process are then divided by the number of units passing through that process to get cost per equivalent unit. The costs per equivalent unit for all processes are added to determine the total cost per unit of a product or service.

**A2** **Explain and illustrate a hybrid costing system.** A hybrid costing system contains features of both job order and process costing systems. Generally, certain direct materials are accounted for by individual products as in job order costing, but direct labor and overhead costs are accounted for similar to process costing.

**P1** **Record the flow of direct materials costs in process cost accounting.** Materials purchased are debited to a Raw Materials Inventory account. As direct materials are issued to processes, they are separately accumulated in a Goods in Process Inventory account for that process.

**P2** **Record the flow of direct labor costs in process cost accounting.** Direct labor costs are initially debited to the Factory Payroll account. The total amount in it is then assigned to the goods in process inventory account pertaining to each process.

**P3** **Record the flow of factory overhead costs in process cost accounting.** The different factory overhead items are first accumulated in the Factory Overhead account and are then allocated, using a predetermined overhead rate, to the different processes. The allocated amount is debited to the goods in process inventory account pertaining to each process.

**P4** **Compute equivalent units produced in a period.** To compute equivalent units, determine the number of units that would have been finished if all materials (or labor or overhead) had been used to produce units that were started and completed during the period. The costs incurred by a process are divided by its equivalent units to yield cost per unit.

**P5    Prepare a process cost summary.** A process cost summary includes the physical flow of units, equivalent units of production, costs per equivalent unit, and a cost reconciliation. It reports the units and costs to account for during the period and how they were accounted for during the period. In terms of units, the summary includes the beginning goods in process inventory and the units started during the month. These units are accounted for in terms of the goods completed and transferred out, and the ending goods in process inventory. With respect to costs, the summary includes materials, labor, and overhead costs assigned to the process during the period. It shows how these costs are assigned to goods completed and transferred out, and to ending goods in process inventory.

**P6    Record the transfer of goods between departments.** As units of product are transferred from one process to the next, the accumulated cost of those units is transferred from one goods in process account to the next. Once the goods are completed in the preceding process, they are transferred out to the next process in the sequence. Costs associated with goods completed in the preceding process are then debited to the goods in process inventory of the next process.

**P7    Record the transfer of completed goods to Finished Goods Inventory and Cost of Goods Sold.** As units complete the final process and are eventually sold, their accumulated cost is transferred to Finished Goods Inventory and finally to Cost of Goods Sold.

## Guidance Answers to **Decision Maker** and **Decision Ethics**

**Budget Officer**  By instructing you to classify a majority of costs as indirect, the manager is passing some of his department's costs to a common overhead pool that other departments will partially absorb. Since overhead costs are allocated on the basis of direct labor for this company and the new department has a relatively low direct labor cost, the new department will be assigned less overhead. Such action suggests unethical behavior by this manager. You must object to such reclassification. If this manager refuses to comply, you must inform someone in a more senior position.

**Cost Manager**  Differences between the FIFO and weighted-average methods are greatest when large work in process inventories exist and when costs fluctuate. The method used if inventories are eliminated does not matter; both produce identical costs.

**Entrepreneur**  By spreading the added quality-related costs across three customers, the entrepreneur is probably trying to remain competitive with respect to the customer that demands the 100% quality inspection. Moreover, the entrepreneur is partly covering the added costs by recovering 2/3 of them from the other two customers who are paying 110% of total costs. This act likely breaches the trust placed by the two customers in this entrepreneur's application of its costing system. The costing system should be changed, and the entrepreneur should consider renegotiating the pricing and/or quality-test agreement with this one customer (at the risk of losing this currently loss-producing customer).

## Guidance Answers to **Quick Checks**

**1.** *c*

**2.** When a company produces large quantities of similar products/ services, a process cost system is often more suitable.

**3.** *b*

**4.** The costs are direct materials, direct labor, and overhead.

**5.** A goods in process inventory account is needed for *each* production department.

**6.** *a*

**7.** Equivalent units with respect to direct labor are the number of units that would have been produced if all labor had been used on units that were started and finished during the period.

**8.**

|                              | Units of Product |   | Percent Added |   | Equivalent Units |
|------------------------------|------------------|---|---------------|---|------------------|
| Beginning Inventory ......... | 8,000 | × | 75% | = | 6,000 |
| Units started and finished ..... | 50,000 | × | 100 | = | 50,000 |
| Ending inventory ........... | 6,000 | × | 33⅓ | = | 2,000 |
| Equivalent units ............ |   |   |   |   | 58,000 |

**9.** The first section shows the costs charged to the department. The second section describes the equivalent units produced by the department. The third section shows the assignment of total costs to units worked on during the period.

**10.** The transfer decreases one Goods in Process Inventory account and increases another. This has no effect on total assets.

**11.** Equivalent unit processing cost:

$262,500/(20,000 + 70,000 + 15,000) units = $2.50.

Costs to process goods received and completed follow:

| | |
|---|---|
| Costs transferred in ................. | $225,000 |
| Total costs added (70,000 × $2.50) ....... | 175,000 |
| Total costs to process ................ | $400,000 |

## Key Terms

Key Terms are available at the book's Website for learning and testing in an online Flashcard Format.

**Equivalent units of production (EUP)**
(p. 664)
**Job order cost accounting system** (p. 659)

**Materials consumption report** (p. 661)
**Process cost accounting system** (p. 659)

**Process cost summary** (p. 669)
**Process manufacturing** (p. 656)

## Personal Interactive Quiz

Personal Interactive Quizzes A and B are available at the book's Website to reinforce and assess your learning.

*Assume FIFO inventory method is used for all assignments unless stated differently.*

## Discussion Questions

**1.** Can services be delivered by means of process operations? Support your answer with an example.

**2.** What is the main factor for a company in choosing between the job order costing and process costing accounting systems? Give two likely applications of each system.

**3.** Identify the control document for materials flow when a materials requisition slip is not used.

**4.** The focus in a job order costing system is the job or batch. Identify the main focus in process costing.

**5.** Are the journal entries that match cost flows to product flows in process costing primarily the same or much different than those in job order costing? Explain.

**6.** Explain in simple terms the notion of equivalent units of production (EUP). Why is it necessary to use EUP in process costing?

**7.** What are the two main inventory methods used in process costing? What are the differences between these methods?

**8.** Why is it possible for direct labor in process operations to include the labor of employees who do not work directly on products or services?

**9.** Assume that a company produces a single product by processing it first through a mixing department and next through a cutting department. Direct labor costs flow through what accounts in this company's process cost system?

**10.** After all labor costs for a period are allocated, what balance should remain in the Factory Payroll account?

**11.** Is it possible to have under- or overapplied overhead costs in a process cost accounting system? Explain.

**12.** Explain why equivalent units of production for both direct labor and overhead can be the same as, and why they can be different from, equivalent units for direct materials.

**13.** List the four steps in accounting for production activity in a reporting period (for process operations).

**14.** What purposes does a process cost summary serve?

**15.** Assume that **Krispy Kreme** takes a special order to produce donuts for all employees of Andrews Air Force Base. Chart Krispy Kreme's production process, assuming it has three production departments: (1) mixing and shaping, (2) baking, and (3) glazing. Begin the flowchart with delivery of raw materials and finish with shipment of the goods (see Exhibit 16.5 for guidance).

**16.** **Harley-Davidson** produces motorcycles with a multiple process production line. Starting with assembling the motor cycles from inventory parts, list some of the motorcycle manufacturing processes.

### Red numbers denote Discussion Questions that involve decision-making.

*Homework Manager repeats all numerical Quick Studies on the book's Website with new numbers.*

For each of the following products and services, indicate whether it is most likely produced in a process operation or in a job order operation:

**1.** Door hinges
**2.** Cut flower arrangements
**3.** House paints
**4.** Concrete swimming pools

**5.** Custom tailored suits
**6.** Grand pianos
**7.** Wall clocks
**8.** Sport shirts

**9.** Bolts and nuts
**10.** Folding chairs

## QUICK STUDY

**QS 16-1**

Matching of product to cost accounting system

C1

**QS 16-2**
Identifying and recording cost flows
P1  P2  P3  P7

Jeans Co. manufactures a product requiring two processes, cutting and sewing. During August, partially completed units with a cost of $287,200 are transferred from cutting to sewing. The sewing department requisitions $58,200 of direct materials and incurs direct labor of $96,000. Overhead is applied to the sewing department at 100% of direct labor. Finally, units with a cost of $102,400 are completed and transferred from sewing to finished goods. Prepare journal entries dated August 31 to record these August activities of the sewing department: (1) goods transferred from cutting to sewing, (2) direct materials used, (3) direct labor used, (4) overhead applied, and (5) goods transferred from sewing to finished goods.

**QS 16-3**
Computing equivalent units of production—FIFO
C2  P4

This information refers to units processed in Sunflower Printing's binding department in March:

|  | Units of Product | Percent of Labor Added |
|---|---|---|
| Beginning goods in process . . . . . . . . . . | 150,000 | 25% |
| Goods started and completed . . . . . . . | 340,000 | 100 |
| Ending goods in process . . . . . . . . . . . . | 120,000 | 40 |

Compute the total equivalent units of production with respect to labor for March using the FIFO inventory method.

**QS 16-4**
Computing equivalent units—weighted average   C2  P4

Refer to QS 16-3 and compute the total equivalent units of production with respect to labor for March using the weighted average inventory method.

**QS 16-5**
Computing EUP cost   C4  P5

The cost of beginning inventory plus the costs added during the period should equal the cost of units _____ plus the cost of _____.

**QS 16-6**
Hybrid costing system   A2

Explain a hybrid costing system. Identify a product or service operation that might well fit a hybrid costing system.

*Homework Manager repeats all numerical Exercises on the book's Website with new numbers.*

## EXERCISES

**Exercise 16-1**
Terminology in process cost accounting
C1  A1  P1  P2  P3

Match each of the following items A through H with the best numbered description of its purpose.

**A.** Materials consumption report
**B.** Process cost summary
**C.** Equivalent units of production
**D.** Goods in Process Inventory—Dept. A

**E.** Raw Materials Inventory account
**F.** Materials requisition
**G.** Finished Goods Inventory account
**H.** Factory Overhead account

_____ **1.** Notifies the materials manager to send materials to a production department.
_____ **2.** Holds costs of indirect materials, indirect labor, and similar costs until assigned to production.
_____ **3.** Holds costs of direct materials, direct labor, and applied overhead until products are transferred from Department A to another department.
_____ **4.** Describes the direct materials used in a production department.
_____ **5.** Standardizes partially completed units into equivalent completed units.
_____ **6.** Holds costs of finished products until sold to customers.
_____ **7.** Describes the activity and output of a production department for a period.
_____ **8.** Holds costs of materials until they are used in production or as factory overhead.

**Exercise 16-2**
Journal entries in process cost accounting
P1  P2  P3

Wooden Toy Company manufactures products with two processes: sanding and painting. Prepare journal entries to record its following production activities for January.

**1.** Purchased $40,000 of raw materials on credit.
**2.** Used $19,000 of direct materials in the sanding department and $5,000 in the painting department.
**3.** Used $20,500 of indirect materials.
**4.** Incurred total labor cost of $75,000, which is paid in cash.
**5.** Used $30,000 of direct labor in the sanding department and $24,000 in the painting department.

**6.** Used $21,000 of indirect labor.

**7.** Incurred overhead costs of $24,000 (paid in cash).

**8.** Applied overhead at 125% of direct labor in the sanding department and at 75% of direct labor in the painting department.

**Check** (8) Cr. Factory Overhead, $55,500

**9.** Transferred partially completed products with a cost of $79,900 from the sanding department to the painting department.

**10.** Transferred completed products with a cost of $145,000 from the painting department to the finished goods inventory.

**11.** Sold $300,000 of products on credit. Their accumulated cost is $150,000.

---

The following journal entries are recorded in Kiera Co.'s process cost accounting system. Kiera produces clothing items by passing them through a cutting department and an assembly department. Overhead is applied to production departments based on direct labor cost for the period. Prepare a brief explanation (including any overhead rates applied) for each journal entry *a* through *k*.

**Exercise 16-3**
Interpretation of journal entries in process cost accounting

P1  P2  P3  P6  P7

| | | | |
|---|---|---|---|
| **a.** | Raw Materials Inventory | 26,000 | |
| | Accounts Payable | | 26,000 |
| **b.** | Goods in Process Inventory—Cutting | 12,000 | |
| | Goods in Process Inventory—Assembly | 9,000 | |
| | Raw Materials Inventory | | 21,000 |
| **c.** | Goods in Process Inventory—Cutting | 8,000 | |
| | Goods in Process Inventory—Assembly | 5,000 | |
| | Factory Payroll | | 13,000 |
| **d.** | Factory Payroll | 16,000 | |
| | Cash | | 16,000 |
| **e.** | Factory Overhead | 5,000 | |
| | Cash | | 5,000 |
| **f.** | Factory Overhead | 5,000 | |
| | Raw Materials Inventory | | 5,000 |
| **g.** | Factory Overhead | 3,000 | |
| | Factory Payroll | | 3,000 |
| **h.** | Goods in Process Inventory—Cutting | 6,000 | |
| | Goods in Process Inventory—Assembly | 7,000 | |
| | Factory Overhead | | 13,000 |
| **i.** | Goods in Process Inventory—Assembly | 30,000 | |
| | Goods in Process Inventory—Cutting | | 30,000 |
| **j.** | Finished Goods Inventory | 44,000 | |
| | Goods in Process Inventory—Assembly | | 44,000 |
| **k.** | Accounts Receivable | 125,000 | |
| | Sales | | 125,000 |
| | Cost of Goods Sold | 50,000 | |
| | Finished Goods Inventory | | 50,000 |

---

Lowes Lumber produces shredded bark using a two-step process. The system begins by processing bark chips through the shredding department and then through the bagging department. The following information describes production operations for October.

**Exercise 16-4**
Recording cost flows in a process cost system

P1  P2  P3  P6  P7

| | Shredding Department | Bagging Department |
|---|---|---|
| Direct materials used | $ 40,000 | $ 460,000 |
| Direct labor used | $ 45,000 | $ 75,000 |
| Predetermined overhead rate (based on direct labor) | 120% | 200% |
| Goods transferred from shredding to bagging | $(145,000) | |
| Goods transferred from bagging to finished goods | | $(403,000) |

The company's revenue for the month totaled $900,000 from credit sales, and its cost of goods sold for the month is $300,000. Prepare summary journal entries dated October 31 to record its October production activities for (1) direct material usage, (2) direct labor usage, (3) overhead allocation, (4) goods transfer from shredding to bagging, (5) goods transfer from bagging to finished goods, and (6) sales.

**Check** (3) Cr. Factory Overhead, $204,000

---

**Exercise 16-5**
Computing equivalent units of production—FIFO

C2 P4

**Check** (2) EUP for materials, 292,800 units

During April, the production department of a process manufacturing system completed a number of units of a product and transferred them to finished goods. Of these transferred units, 50,000 were in process in the department at the beginning of April and 220,000 were started and completed in April. April's beginning inventory units were 60% complete with respect to materials and 40% complete with respect to labor. At the end of April, 66,000 additional units were in process in the department and were 80% complete with respect to materials and 30% complete with respect to labor. Compute (1) the number of units transferred to finished goods and (2) the number of equivalent units with respect to both materials used and labor used in the department for April using the FIFO method.

---

**Exercise 16-6**
Computing equivalent units of production—weighted average

C2 P4

Refer to the information in Exercise 16-5 to compute the number of equivalent units with respect to both materials used and labor used in the department for April using the weighted average method.

---

**Exercise 16-7**
Costs assigned to output and inventories—FIFO

C3 P4 P5

**Check** (2) Costs accounted for, $1,200,000

The production department described in Exercise 16-5 had $700,000 of direct materials and $500,000 of direct labor cost charged to it during April. Also, its beginning inventory included $90,000 of direct materials cost and $40,000 of direct labor. (1) Compute the direct materials cost and the direct labor cost per equivalent unit for the department—see Exhibit 16.17 for guidance. (2) Assign costs to the department's output; specifically, its beginning inventory, its goods started and completed, and its ending goods in process inventory for April using the FIFO method—see section ③ of Exhibit 16.19 for guidance.

---

**Exercise 16-8**
Costs assigned to output—weighted average C3 P4 P5

Refer to the information in Exercise 16-7 and complete its parts (1) and (2) using the weighted average method.

---

**Exercise 16-9**
Equivalent units computed

C2 P4 P5

**Check** (3) EUP for materials, 237,500 units

The production department in a process manufacturing system completed 250,000 units of product and transferred them to finished goods during a recent period. Of these units, 75,000 were in process at the beginning of the period. The other 175,000 units were started and completed during the period. At period-end, 50,000 units were in process. Compute the department's equivalent units of production with respect to direct materials under each of three separate assumptions: (1) All direct materials are added to products when processing begins. (2) Direct materials are added to products evenly throughout the process. Beginning goods in process inventory was 50% complete, and ending goods in process inventory was 70% complete. (3) One-half of direct materials is added to products when the process begins and the other half is added when the process is 75% complete as to direct labor. Beginning goods in process inventory is 40% complete as to direct labor and ending goods in process inventory is 60% complete as to direct labor.

---

**Exercise 16-10**
Flowchart of costs for a process operation P1 P2 P3 P6 P7

The flowchart on the opposite page shows the August production activity of the punching and bending departments of Utility Box Company. Use the amounts shown on the flowchart to compute the missing numbers identified by question marks.

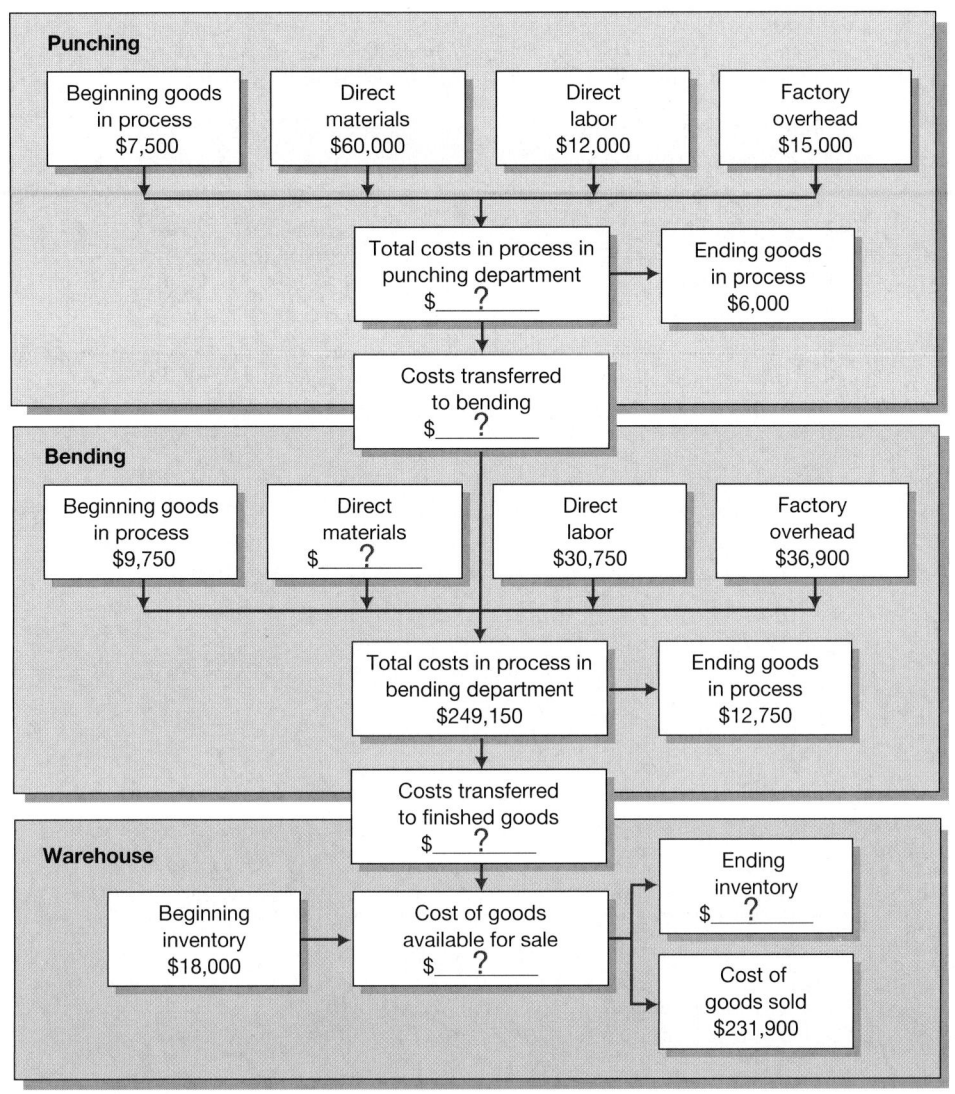

**Punching**

| Beginning goods in process $7,500 | Direct materials $60,000 | Direct labor $12,000 | Factory overhead $15,000 |

Total costs in process in punching department $___?___

Ending goods in process $6,000

Costs transferred to bending $___?___

**Bending**

| Beginning goods in process $9,750 | Direct materials $___?___ | Direct labor $30,750 | Factory overhead $36,900 |

Total costs in process in bending department $249,150

Ending goods in process $12,750

Costs transferred to finished goods $___?___

**Warehouse**

Beginning inventory $18,000

Cost of goods available for sale $___?___

Ending inventory $___?___

Cost of goods sold $231,900

---

The following partially completed process cost summary describes the July activities of Soriano Company's slicing department. Its output is sent to the canning department, which sends the finished goods to the warehouse for shipping.

**Exercise 16-11**

Completing a process cost summary

P5

### Costs Charged to the Department

| | |
|---|---|
| Direct materials requisitioned .................................... | $224,000 |
| Direct labor charged ......................................... | 39,000 |
| Overhead allocated (at 200% of direct labor) ..................... | 78,000 |
| Total processing costs for the month ........................... | 341,000 |
| Goods in process at the beginning of the month ................... | 24,000 |
| Total costs to be accounted for .............................. | $365,000 |

| | | Equivalent Units | |
|---|---|---|---|
| **Equivalent Unit Processing Costs** | **Units of Product** | **Direct Materials** | **Labor and Overhead** |
| Units processed | | | |
|   Beginning goods in process .............. | 1,600 | 0 | 1,200 |
|   Units started and completed ............. | 20,000 | 20,000 | 20,000 |
|   Ending goods in process ............... | 2,400 | 2,400 | 1,800 |
|   Total ........................... | 24,000 | 22,400 | 23,000 |

Prepare the process cost summary for the slicing department by completing both (1) the *Equivalent Unit Processing Costs* section and (2) the *Assignment of Costs to Output of Department* sections.

## PROBLEM SET A

### Problem 16-1A
Production cost flow and measurement; journal entries prepared

P1 P2 P3 P6 P7

Sullivan Company manufactures blankets by passing the products through a weaving department and a sewing department. The following information is available regarding its May inventories:

| | Beginning Inventory | Ending Inventory |
|---|---|---|
| Raw materials inventory | $ 120,000 | $ 185,000 |
| Goods in process inventory—Weaving | 300,000 | 330,000 |
| Goods in process inventory—Sewing | 570,000 | 700,000 |
| Finished goods inventory | 1,266,000 | 1,206,000 |

The following additional information describes the company's manufacturing activities for May:

| | |
|---|---|
| Raw materials purchases (on credit) | $ 500,000 |
| Factory payroll cost (paid in cash) | 3,060,000 |
| Other overhead cost (Other Accounts credited) | 156,000 |
| Materials used | |
| Direct—Weaving | $ 240,000 |
| Direct—Sewing | 75,000 |
| Indirect | 120,000 |
| Labor used | |
| Direct—Weaving | $1,200,000 |
| Direct—Sewing | 360,000 |
| Indirect | 1,500,000 |
| Overhead rates as a percent of direct labor | |
| Weaving | 80% |
| Sewing | 150% |
| Sales (on credit) | $4,000,000 |

### Required

**Check** (1c) Cost of goods sold $3,275,000

1. Compute the cost of (a) products transferred from weaving to sewing, (b) products transferred from sewing to finished goods, and (c) goods sold. (*Hint:* Prepare a table of cost flows and computations like that in part B of Exhibit 16.5.)

2. Prepare summary journal entries dated May 31 to record the following production activities during May: (a) raw materials purchases, (b) direct materials usage, (c) indirect materials usage, (d) payroll costs, (e) direct labor costs, (f) indirect labor costs, (g) other overhead costs, (h) overhead applied, (i) goods transferred from weaving to sewing, (j) goods transferred from sewing to finished goods, and (k) sale of finished goods.

### Problem 16-2A
Cost per equivalent unit; costs assigned to products

P4 P5

mhhe.com/wild

Liberty Company's product passes through several departments, the last of which is the carving department where direct labor is added evenly throughout the process. Also, one-fourth of direct materials is added at the beginning of the carving process and the remaining three-fourths is added when the process is 50% complete with respect to direct labor. During November, the carving department transferred 575,000 units of product to finished goods. Of these units, 100,000 were 40% complete with respect to labor at the beginning of the period; also, 475,000 were started and completed during the period. At the end of November, the goods in process inventory consists of 300,000 units that are 25% complete with respect to labor. The carving department's direct labor cost for November is $1,220,000, and its direct materials cost is $1,875,000.

### Required

**Check** (2) Direct labor cost per equivalent unit, $2

(3c) $375,000

1. Determine the carving department's equivalent units of production with respect to (a) direct labor and (b) direct materials.

2. Compute both the direct labor cost and the direct materials cost per equivalent unit (see Exhibit 16.17 for guidance).

3. Compute both direct labor cost and direct materials cost assigned to the (a) beginning goods in process inventory, (b) units started and completed, and (c) ending goods in process inventory (see section ③ of Exhibit 16.19 for guidance).

## Analysis Component

**4.** Liberty sells and ships all units to customers as soon as they are completed. Assume that an error is made in determining the percentage of completion for units in ending inventory. Instead of being 25% complete with respect to labor, they are actually 60% complete. Write a one-page memo to the plant manager describing how this error affects its November financial statements.

Newman Company produces large quantities of a product that pass through two processes, spinning and cutting. The following information is available on its manufacturing activities for March:

**Problem 16-3A**
Journalizing in process cost accounting; equivalent units and costs  P1  P2  P3  P4  P6  P7

| **Raw materials** | | | **Factory overhead incurred** | |
|---|---|---|---|---|
| Beginning inventory . . . . . . . . . . . . . . . . . . . . | $ 32,000 | | Indirect materials used . . . . . . . . . . . . . . . | $ 40,560 |
| Raw materials purchased (on credit) . . . . . . . | 221,120 | | Indirect labor used . . . . . . . . . . . . . . . . . | 36,320 |
| Direct materials—Spinning . . . . . . . . . . . . . . | (160,000) | | Other overhead costs . . . . . . . . . . . . . . | 91,640 |
| Direct materials—Cutting . . . . . . . . . . . . . . | (37,120) | | Total factory overhead incurred . . . . . . . | $168,520 |
| Indirect materials used . . . . . . . . . . . . . . . . | (40,560) | | | |
| Ending inventory . . . . . . . . . . . . . . . . . . . . . | $ 15,440 | | **Factory overhead applied** | |
| | | | Spinning (125% of direct labor) . . . . . . . . | $ 85,000 |
| **Factory payroll** | | | Cutting (150% of direct labor) . . . . . . . . | 83,520 |
| Direct labor—Spinning . . . . . . . . . . . . . . . . | $ 68,000 | | Total factory overhead applied . . . . . . . . | $168,520 |
| Direct labor—Cutting . . . . . . . . . . . . . . . . . | 55,680 | | | |
| Indirect labor used . . . . . . . . . . . . . . . . . . . | 36,320 | | | |
| Total payroll cost (paid in cash) . . . . . . . . . . | $160,000 | | | |

Information about the inventory in the *spinning department* follows:

| **Units** | | **Costs** | |
|---|---|---|---|
| Beginning goods in process inventory . . . . . . . . | 4,000 | Beginning goods in process inventory . . . . | $ 41,000 |
| Started and completed . . . . . . . . . . . . . . . . . . | 12,000 | Direct materials added . . . . . . . . . . . . . . | 160,000 |
| Ending goods in process inventory . . . . . . . . . . | 8,000 | Direct labor added . . . . . . . . . . . . . . . . . | 68,000 |
| **Beginning goods in process inventory** | | Overhead applied (125% of | |
| Materials—Percent complete . . . . . . . . . . . . . | 100% | direct labor) . . . . . . . . . . . . . . . . . . . . | 85,000 |
| Labor and overhead—Percent complete . . . . . . | 25% | Total costs . . . . . . . . . . . . . . . . . . . . . . | 354,000 |
| **Ending goods in process inventory** | | Costs transferred from spinning | |
| Materials—Percent complete . . . . . . . . . . . . . | 100% | to cutting department . . . . . . . . . . . . | (272,000) |
| Labor and overhead—Percent complete . . . . . . | 25% | Ending goods in process inventory . . . . . | $ 82,000 |

Information about the goods in process inventories for the *cutting department* follows: beginning goods in process inventory, $174,000; and ending goods in process inventory, $177,120. Also, information regarding finished goods follows:

| | |
|---|---|
| Beginning finished goods inventory . . . . . . . | $148,400 |
| Cost transferred in from cutting . . . . . . . . . | 445,200 |
| Cost of goods sold . . . . . . . . . . . . . . . . . . . | (530,000) |
| Ending finished goods inventory . . . . . . . . . . | $ 63,600 |

During March, 10,000 units of finished goods are sold for $120 cash each.

### Required

**1.** Prepare journal entries dated March 31 to record the following March activities: (a) raw materials purchases, (b) direct materials usage, (c) indirect materials usage, (d) payroll costs, (e) direct labor costs, (f) indirect labor costs, (g) other overhead costs—credit Other Accounts, (h) overhead applied, (i) goods transferred from spinning to cutting, (j) goods transferred from cutting to finished goods, (k) sale of finished goods.

**2.** Compute the spinning department's equivalent units of production and its cost per equivalent unit for direct materials, direct labor, and overhead for March.

**3.** Compute the cost of the ending goods in process inventory for the spinning department.

**Check** (2) Cost per equivalent unit: materials, $8; labor, $4; overhead, $5

(3) $82,000

*Analysis Component*

**4.** Newman provides incentives to its department managers by paying monthly bonuses based on their success in controlling costs per equivalent unit of production. Assume that the spinning department underestimates the percentage of completion for units in ending inventory with the result that its equivalent units of production in ending inventory for March are understated. What impact does this error have on the March bonuses paid to the managers of the spinning department and the cutting department? What impact, if any, does this error have on April bonuses?

---

**Problem 16-4A**

Process cost summary; equivalent units

P4  P5  P7

mhhe.com/wild

RSTN Co. produces its product through a single processing department. Direct materials, direct labor, and overhead are added to the product evenly throughout the process. The company uses monthly reporting periods for its process cost accounting system. The Goods in Process Inventory account appears as follows after entries for direct materials, direct labor, and overhead costs for October:

| Goods in Process Inventory | | | | Acct. No. 133 | |
|---|---|---|---|---|---|
| Date | | Explanation | Debit | Credit | Balance |
| Oct. | 1 | Balance | | | 40,800 |
| | 31 | Direct materials | 100,200 | | 141,000 |
| | 31 | Direct labor | 400,500 | | 541,500 |
| | 31 | Applied overhead | 123,000 | | 664,500 |

During October, the company finished and transferred 150,000 units of its product to finished goods. Of these units, 30,000 were in process at the beginning of the month and 120,000 were started and completed during the month. The beginning goods in process inventory was 30% complete. At the end of the month, the goods in process inventory consisted of 20,000 units that were 80% complete.

**Required**

**Check** (1) 157,000 units

(2) Total cost transferred to finished goods, $600,570

**1.** Compute the number of equivalent units of production for October.

**2.** Prepare the department's process cost summary for October.

**3.** Prepare the journal entry dated October 31 to transfer the cost of the completed units to finished goods inventory.

---

**Problem 16-5A**

Process cost summary; equivalent units; cost estimates

P4  P5  P7

Vista Co. manufactures a single product in one department. All direct materials are added at the beginning of the manufacturing process. Direct labor and overhead are added evenly throughout the process. Vista uses monthly reporting periods for its process cost accounting system. During May, the company completed and transferred 22,200 units of product to finished goods inventory. The beginning goods in process inventory consisted of 3,000 units that were 100% complete with respect to direct materials and 40% complete with respect to direct labor and overhead. The other 19,200 completed units were started during the month. Also, another 2,400 units (100% complete with respect to direct materials and 80% complete with respect to direct labor and overhead) are in process at month-end. After entries to record direct materials, direct labor, and overhead for May, the company's Goods in Process Inventory account appears as follows:

| Goods in Process Inventory | | | | Acct. No. 133 | |
|---|---|---|---|---|---|
| Date | | Explanation | Debit | Credit | Balance |
| May | 1 | Balance | | | 181,320 |
| | 31 | Direct materials | 496,800 | | 678,120 |
| | 31 | Direct labor | 1,185,600 | | 1,863,720 |
| | 31 | Applied overhead | 948,480 | | 2,812,200 |

**Required**

**Check** (1) EUP for labor and overhead, 22,920 units

(2) Cost transferred to finished goods, $2,578,230

**1.** Compute the equivalent units of production in May for direct materials and for direct labor and overhead.

**2.** Prepare the department's process cost summary for May.

**3.** Prepare the journal entry dated May 31 to transfer the cost of completed units to finished goods inventory.

*Analysis Components*

**4.** The cost accounting process depends on numerous estimates.

**a.** Identify two major estimates that determine the cost per equivalent unit.

**b.** In what direction might you anticipate a bias from management for each estimate in part 4a (assume that management compensation is based on maintaining low inventory amounts)? Explain your answer.

Dream Toys Company manufactures dolls by passing the products through a molding department and an assembly department. The following information is available regarding its June inventories:

| | Beginning Inventory | Ending Inventory |
|---|---|---|
| Raw materials inventory | $36,000 | $45,000 |
| Goods in process inventory—Molding | 12,000 | 21,000 |
| Goods in process inventory—Assembly | 66,000 | 54,000 |
| Finished goods inventory | 78,000 | 99,000 |

The following additional information describes the company's manufacturing activities for June:

| | |
|---|---|
| Raw materials purchases (on credit) | $100,000 |
| Factory payroll cost (paid in cash) | 200,000 |
| Other overhead cost (Other Accounts credited) | 50,000 |
| Materials used | |
| Direct—molding | $ 6,000 |
| Direct—assembly | 54,000 |
| Indirect | 21,000 |
| Labor used | |
| Direct—molding | $100,000 |
| Direct—assembly | 75,000 |
| Indirect | 25,000 |
| Overhead rates as a percent of direct labor | |
| Molding | 80% |
| Assembly | 75% |
| Sales (on credit) | $500,000 |

**Required**

**1.** Compute the cost of (a) products transferred from molding to assembly, (b) products transferred from assembly to finished goods, and (c) goods sold. (*Hint:* Prepare a table of cost flows and computations like that in part B of Exhibit 16.5.)

**2.** Prepare journal entries dated June 30 to record the following production activities during June: (a) raw materials purchases, (b) direct materials usage, (c) indirect materials usage, (d) payroll costs, (e) direct labor costs, (f) indirect labor costs, (g) other overhead costs, (h) overhead applied, (i) goods transferred from molding to assembly, (j) goods transferred from assembly to finished goods, and (k) sale of finished goods.

Packard Company's product passes through several departments, the last of which is the bagging department where direct materials are added evenly throughout the process. Also, one-half of the direct labor is added at the beginning of the bagging process and the other half is added when the process is 50% complete with respect to materials. During September, the bagging department transferred 40,000 units of product to finished goods. Of these units, 9,000 were 60% complete with respect to materials at the beginning of the period; also, 31,000 were started and completed during the period. At the end of September, the goods in process inventory consists of 4,000 units that are 25% complete with respect to materials. The bagging department's direct materials cost for September is $356,000, and its direct labor cost is $990,000.

**PROBLEM SET B**

**Problem 16-1B**
Production cost flow and measurement; journal entries prepared

P1  P2  P3  P6  P7

**Check**  (1c) Cost of goods sold, $353,250

**Problem 16-2B**
Cost per equivalent unit; costs assigned to products

P4  P5

**Required**

1. Determine the bagging department's equivalent units of production with respect to (a) direct labor and (b) direct materials.

2. Compute both the direct labor cost and the direct materials cost per equivalent unit (see Exhibit 16.17 for guidance).

3. Compute both direct labor cost and direct materials cost assigned to the (a) beginning goods in process inventory, (b) units started and completed, and (c) ending goods in process inventory (see section ③ of Exhibit 16.19 for guidance).

*Analysis Component*

4. Packard sells and ships all units to customers as soon as they are completed. Assume that an error is made in determining the percentage of completion for units in ending inventory. Instead of being 25% complete with respect to materials, they are actually 75% complete. Write a one-page memo to the plant manager describing how this error affects its September financial statements.

## Problem 16-3B
Journalizing in process cost accounting; equivalent units and costs

P1  P2  P3  P4

P6  P7

Sox Company produces large quantities of a product that pass through two processes, tooling and machining. The following information is available on its manufacturing activities for May:

| Raw materials | | Factory overhead incurred | |
|---|---:|---|---:|
| Beginning inventory .................... | $ 84,000 | Indirect materials used .............. | $101,600 |
| Raw materials purchased (on credit) ....... | 500,000 | Indirect labor used ................. | 46,360 |
| Direct materials—Tooling .............. | (248,200) | Other overhead costs ............... | 50,520 |
| Direct materials—Machining ............. | (178,200) | Total factory overhead incurred ........ | $198,480 |
| Indirect materials used ................ | (101,600) | | |
| Ending inventory ..................... | $ 56,000 | **Factory overhead applied** | |
| | | Tooling (40% of direct labor) .......... | $127,200 |
| **Factory payroll** | | Machining (200% of direct labor) ....... | 71,280 |
| Direct labor—Tooling ................. | $ 318,000 | Total factory overhead applied ......... | $198,480 |
| Direct labor—Machining ............... | 35,640 | | |
| Indirect labor used ................... | 46,360 | | |
| Total payroll cost (paid in cash) .......... | $ 400,000 | | |

Information about the inventory in the *tooling department* follows:

| Units | | Costs | |
|---|---:|---|---:|
| Beginning goods in process inventory ........ | 40,000 | Beginning goods in process inventory ..... | $ 99,200 |
| Started and completed .................. | 120,000 | Direct materials added .............. | 248,200 |
| Ending goods in process inventory .......... | 20,000 | Direct labor added ................. | 318,000 |
| **Beginning goods in process inventory** | | Overhead applied (40% of | |
| Materials—percent complete .............. | 80% | direct labor) .................... | 127,200 |
| Labor and overhead—Percent complete ...... | 40% | Total costs ...................... | 792,600 |
| **Ending goods in process inventory** | | Costs transferred from tooling to | |
| Materials—Percent complete ............. | 90% | machining department ............. | (720,000) |
| Labor and overhead—Percent complete ...... | 75% | Ending goods in process inventory ...... | $ 72,600 |

Information about the goods in process inventories for the *machining department* follows: beginning goods in process inventory, $249,000; and ending goods in process inventory, $229,320. Also, information regarding finished goods follows:

| | |
|---|---:|
| Beginning finished goods inventory ........ | $   36,600 |
| Cost transferred in from machining ....... | 1,024,800 |
| Cost of goods sold ................... | (1,000,400) |
| Ending finished goods inventory .......... | $   61,000 |

During May, 80,000 units of finished goods are sold for $20 cash each.

**Required**

1. Prepare journal entries dated May 31 to record the following May activities: (a) raw materials purchases, (b) direct materials usage, (c) indirect materials usage, (d) payroll costs, (e) direct labor costs, (f) indirect labor costs, (g) other overhead costs—credit Other Accounts, (h) overhead applied, (i) goods transferred from tooling to machining, (j) goods transferred from machining to finished goods, (k) sale of finished goods.

2. Compute the tooling department's equivalent units of production and its cost per equivalent unit for direct materials, direct labor, and overhead for May, assuming that all product costs are added evenly throughout the process.

3. Compute the cost of the ending goods in process inventory for the tooling department.

*Analysis Component*

4. Sox provides incentives to its department managers by paying monthly bonuses based on their success in controlling costs per equivalent unit of production. Assume that the tooling department overestimates the percentage of completion for units in ending inventory with the result that its equivalent units of production in ending inventory for May are overstated. What impact does this error have on bonuses paid to the managers of the tooling department and the machining department? What impact, if any, does this error have on these managers' June bonuses?

**Check** (2) Cost per equivalent unit: materials, $1.70; labor, $2; overhead, $0.80

(3) $72,600

---

Oxford Company produces its product through a single processing department. Direct materials, direct labor, and overhead are added to the product evenly throughout the process. The company uses monthly reporting periods for its process cost accounting system. The Goods in Process Inventory account appears as follows after entries for direct materials, direct labor, and overhead costs for November:

**Problem 16-4B**
Process cost summary; equivalent units

P4  P5  P7

| Goods in Process Inventory | | | | Acct. No. 133 |
| Date | | Explanation | Debit | Credit | Balance |
|---|---|---|---|---|---|
| Nov. | 1 | Balance | | | 70,000 |
| | 30 | Direct materials | 115,000 | | 185,000 |
| | 30 | Direct labor | 425,000 | | 610,000 |
| | 30 | Applied overhead | 600,000 | | 1,210,000 |

During November, the company finished and transferred 100,000 units of its product to finished goods. Of these units, 7,500 were in process at the beginning of the month, and 92,500 were started and completed during the month. The beginning goods in process inventory was 80% complete. At the end of the month, the goods in process inventory consisted of 12,000 units that were 25% completed.

**Required**

1. Compute the number of equivalent units of production for November.

2. Prepare the department's process cost summary for November.

3. Prepare the journal entry dated November 30 to transfer the cost of the completed units to finished goods inventory.

**Check** (1) 97,000 units

(2) Cost of goods transferred to finished goods, $1,175,440

---

Roadrunner Co. manufactures a single product in one department. Direct labor and overhead are added evenly throughout the process. Direct materials are added as needed. The company uses monthly reporting periods for its process cost accounting system. During January, Roadrunner completed and transferred 110,000 units of product to finished goods inventory. The beginning goods in process inventory consisted of 10,000 units (75% complete with respect to direct materials and 60% complete with respect to direct labor and overhead). The other 100,000 completed units were started during the month. Also, another 20,000 units (50% complete with respect to direct materials and 30% complete with respect to direct labor and overhead) are in process at month-end. After entries for direct

**Problem 16-5B**
Process cost summary; equivalent units; cost estimates

P4  P5  P7

materials, direct labor, and overhead for January, the company's Goods in Process Inventory account appears as follows:

| Goods in Process Inventory | | | | | Acct. No. 133 |
| Date | | Explanation | Debit | Credit | Balance |
|------|---|-------------|-------|--------|---------|
| Jan. | 1 | Balance | | | 20,550 |
| | 31 | Direct materials | 56,250 | | 76,800 |
| | 31 | Direct labor | 88,000 | | 164,800 |
| | 31 | Applied overhead | 220,000 | | 384,800 |

### Required

**1.** Compute the equivalent units of production for direct materials and for direct labor and overhead.

**2.** Prepare the department's process cost summary for January.

**3.** Prepare the journal entry dated January 31 to transfer the cost of completed units to finished goods inventory.

#### Analysis Components

**4.** The cost accounting process depends on several estimates.

   **a.** Identify two major estimates that affect the cost per equivalent unit.

   **b.** In what direction might you anticipate a bias from management for each estimate in part 4a (assume that management compensation is based on maintaining low inventory amounts)? Explain your answer.

## PROBLEM SET C

Problem Set C is available at the book's Website to further reinforce and assess your learning.

## COMPREHENSIVE PROBLEM

### Corked Bat Company
(Review of Chapters 2, 4, 14, 16)

Corked Bat Company manufactures baseball bats. The bats go through two processes: one cuts the wood into bats and drills a hole for the cork (department 1), and the other fills the hole with cork and stamps the company's logo on the bat (department 2). All of department 1's output is transferred to department 2. In addition to the goods in process inventories in departments 1 and 2, Corked Bat maintains inventories of raw materials and finished goods. It uses raw materials as direct materials in both departments and as indirect materials. Its factory payroll costs include direct labor for each department and indirect labor. All materials are added at the beginning of the process in each department, and direct labor and factory overhead are applied uniformly throughout each department's process.

### Required

You are to maintain records and produce measures of inventories to reflect the July events of this company. All computations of unit costs are rounded to the nearest penny and all other dollar amounts to the nearest whole dollar. Set up the following general ledger accounts and enter their June 30 balances: Raw Materials Inventory, $25,000; Goods in Process Inventory—Department 1, $65,000; Goods in Process Inventory—Department 2, $25,000; Finished Goods Inventory, $110,000; Sales, $0; Cost of Goods Sold, $0; Factory Payroll, $0; and Factory Overhead, $0.

**1.** Prepare journal entries to record the following July transactions and events:

   **a.** Purchased raw materials for $125,000 cash (the company uses a perpetual inventory system).

   **b.** Used raw materials as follows: department 1, $30,000; department 2, $22,440; and indirect materials, $10,000.

   **c.** Incurred factory payroll cost of $227,250 paid in cash (ignore taxes).

   **d.** Assigned factory payroll costs as follows: department 1, $135,000; department 2, $67,250; and indirect labor, $25,000.

   **e.** Incurred additional factory overhead costs of $80,000 paid in cash.

   **f.** Allocated factory overhead to departments 1 and 2 at 50% of direct labor costs.

**2.** Information about the July inventories for the two departments follows:

| | Department 1 | Department 2 |
|---|---|---|
| **Units** | | |
| Beginning inventory . . . . . . . . . . . . . . . . . . . . . . | 500 units | 1,000 units |
| Started and finished . . . . . . . . . . . . . . . . . . . . . | 2,000 units | 1,800 units |
| Ending inventory . . . . . . . . . . . . . . . . . . . . . . . | 1,000 units | 1,600 units |
| **Beginning inventory** | | |
| Materials—Percent complete . . . . . . . . . . . . . . . . | 100% | 100% |
| Labor and overhead—Percent complete . . . . . . . | 20% | 75% |
| **Ending inventory** | | |
| Materials—Percent complete . . . . . . . . . . . . . . . . | 100% | 100% |
| Labor and overhead—Percent complete . . . . . . . | 30% | 40% |

Use this information with that from part 1 to compute the following:

**a.** Department 1's equivalent units of production and its per unit costs for labor, materials, and overhead.

**b.** Department 2's equivalent units of production and its per unit costs for labor, materials, and overhead.

**Check** (2b) EUP for overhead, 2,690 units

**3.** Using results from part 2 and the available information, make computations and prepare journal entries to record the following:

**a.** Total costs transferred from department 1 to department 2 for July (label entry *g*).

**b.** Total costs transferred from department 2 to finished goods for July (label entry *h*).

**c.** Sale of finished goods costing $265,700 for $625,000 in cash (label entry *i*).

(3a) $265,000
(3b) $378,755

**4.** Post entries from parts 1 and 3 to the ledger accounts set up at the beginning of the problem.

**5.** Compute the amount of gross profit from the sales in July. (*Note:* Add any underapplied overhead to, or deduct any overapplied overhead from, cost of goods sold. Ignore the corresponding journal entry.)

# BEYOND THE NUMBERS

**BTN 16-1**   A company must consider the costs and benefits of reporting externally the precise estimates of the percentage complete for goods in process inventory. It must also consider whether reasonable estimates are acceptable. Review **Krispy Kreme**'s inventory (Note 4 in Appendix A) and assume that its work in process inventory value for 2003 is overstated by 10% and for 2002 is understated by 15% due to estimation errors.

**REPORTING IN ACTION**

C2

**Required**

**1.** Compute the dollar amount that work in process inventory is (a) overstated for 2003 and (b) understated for 2002. Separately consider each error and compute the impact on net income for only the year of the error (assume a 40% tax rate).

**2.** Compute the amount (in percent) that Krispy Kreme's net income increased or decreased for 2003 and for 2002 due to the estimation errors. (*Hint:* Work a simple example to see how an error in inventory impacts income.)

**3.** Are amounts in part 2 material? Explain in reference to costs and benefits of decision makers.

*Roll On*

**4.** Access Krispy Kreme's annual report for fiscal years ending after February 2, 2003, from its Website [**KrispyKreme.com**] or the SEC's EDGAR database [**www.sec.gov**]. Identify its current period work in process inventory value and assume a 10% understatement and a 40% tax rate. Recompute answers for parts 1 through 3 using this current information.

**BTN 16-2**   Leading process manufacturers such as **Krispy Kreme** and **Tastykake** usually work to maintain a high-quality and low-cost operation. One ratio routinely computed for this assessment is the cost of goods sold divided by total expenses. A decline in this ratio can mean that the company is spending too much on selling and administrative activities and not enough on production. An increase in this ratio beyond a reasonable level can mean that the company is spending too much on production or not enough on selling activities. (Assume for this analysis that total expenses equal cost of goods sold plus selling, general, and administrative expenses.)

**COMPARATIVE ANALYSIS**

C1

**Required**

1. For both Krispy Kreme and Tastykake, refer to Appendix A and compute the ratio of cost of goods sold to total expenses for their two most recent fiscal years.
2. Comment on the similarities or differences in the ratio results across both years and companies.

---

**ETHICS
CHALLENGE**

C1   C3

**BTN 16-3**   Many accounting and accounting-related professionals are skilled in financial analysis, but most are not skilled in manufacturing. This is especially the case for process manufacturing environments (for example, a bottling plant or chemical factory). To provide professional accounting and financial services, one must understand the industry, product, and processes. We have an ethical responsibility to develop this understanding before offering services to clients in these areas.

**Required**

Write a one-page action plan, in memorandum format, on how you would obtain an understanding of key business processes of a company that hires you to provide financial services. The memorandum should specify an industry, product, and one selected process and should draw on at least one reference, such as a professional journal or industry magazine.

---

**COMMUNICATING
IN PRACTICE**

A1   C1   P1   P2

**BTN 16-4**   You hire a new assistant production manager whose prior experience is with a company that produced goods to order. Your company engages in continuous production of homogeneous products that go through various manufacturing processes. Your new assistant e-mails you questioning some cost classifications on an internal report, specifically why the costs of some materials that do not actually become part of the finished product, including some labor costs not directly associated with producing the product, are classified as direct costs. Respond to this concern via memorandum.

---

**TAKING IT TO
THE NET**

C1   C3

mhhe.com/wild

**BTN 16-5**   Teamwork is essential for business success and for the effective application of accounting software. Software products must work together to be useful in providing information in support of decision making. Check the Website for **QPR Management Software [QPR.com]** and complete the following requirements.

**Required**

1. Give examples of common business processes.
2. Click on **Products** and then on **QPR Management Software.** Explain how such software is helpful to business.

---

**TEAMWORK IN
ACTION**

C1   P1   P2   P3   P6   P7

**BTN 16-6**   The purpose of this team activity is to ensure that each team member understands process operations and the related accounting entries. Find the activities and flows identified in Exhibit 16.5 with numbers ①–⑩. Pick a member of the team to start by describing activity number ① in this exhibit, then verbalizing the related journal entry, and describing how the amounts in the entry are computed. The other members of the team are to agree or disagree; discussion is to continue until all members express understanding. Rotate to the next numbered activity and next team member until all activities and entries have been discussed. If at any point a team member is uncertain about an answer, the team member may pass and get back in the rotation when he or she can contribute to the team's discussion.

---

**BUSINESS WEEK
ACTIVITY**

C1   C3

mhhe.com/wild

**BTN 16-7**   Read the article "A Mass Market of One" in the December 2, 2002, issue of *Business Week*. (The book's Website provides a free link to the article.)

**Required**

1. Provide examples of goods that have formerly been mass-produced but are now being offered on a customized basis.
2. What are some of the challenges that manufacturers have encountered in customizing goods?
3. Why did customization of goods emerge in the late 1990s but not earlier?

**BTN 16-8** Shawn Buchanan of **All American Meats** welcomes ideas for improvements from employees via the "idea boards" posted in the production area of his plant. Recently, an employee suggested that cost savings might be achieved if Buchanan outsourced selected parts of the plant's processes such as payroll.

**Required**

How should Buchanan evaluate which processes to retain and which to outsource?

**BTN 16-9** In process costing, the process is analyzed first and then a unit measure is computed in the form of equivalent units for direct materials, direct labor, overhead, and all three combined. The same analysis applies to both manufacturing and service processes.

**Required**

Visit your local **U.S. Mail** center. Look into the backroom and you will see several ongoing processes. Select one process, such as sorting, and list the costs associated with this process. Your list should include materials, labor, and overhead; be specific. Classify each cost as fixed or variable. At the bottom of your list, outline how overhead should be assigned to your identified process. The following format (with an example) is suggested:

**Point:** The class can compare and discuss the different processes studied and the answers provided.

| Cost Description | Direct Material | Direct Labor | Overhead | Variable Cost | Fixed Cost |
|---|---|---|---|---|---|
| Manual sorting ....... | | X | | X | |
| ⋮ | | | | | |
| Overhead allocation suggestions: | | | | | |

**BTN 16-10** **Grupo Bimbo**, **Krispy Kreme**, and **Tastykake** are competitors in the global marketplace. Selected data for each of these companies follow.

| | Grupo Bimbo* | | Krispy Kreme† | | Tastykake† | |
|---|---|---|---|---|---|---|
| | Current Year | Prior Year | Current Year | Prior Year | Current Year | Prior Year |
| Cost of goods sold ... | 19,155,865 | 15,707,809 | $381,489 | $316,946 | $111,187 | $103,297 |
| General, selling, and administrative expenses ........ | 19,220,603 | 15,816,046 | 28,897 | 27,562 | 44,983 | 43,236 |
| Total expenses ...... | 38,376,468 | 31,523,855 | 410,386 | 344,508 | 156,170 | 146,533 |

\* thousands of pesos
† thousands of dollars

**Required**

1. Review the discussion of the importance of the cost of goods sold divided by total expenses ratio in BTN 16-2. Compute the cost of goods sold to total expenses ratio for all three companies for the two years of data provided.
2. Comment on the similarities or differences in the ratio results across years and companies.

*"People are drawn to Jake usually with a grin or a big laugh. ... Jake rules!"*—Bert Jacobs (on left; John Jacobs on right)

# 17 Cost Allocation and Performance Measurement

### A Look Back

Chapter 16 focused on how to measure and account for costs in process operations. It explained process production, described how to assign costs to processes, and computed cost per equivalent unit for a process.

### A Look at This Chapter

This chapter describes cost allocation and activity-based costing. It identifies managerial reports useful in directing a company's activities. It also describes responsibility accounting, measuring departmental performance, and allocating common costs across departments.

### A Look Ahead

Chapter 18 looks at cost behavior and explains how its identification is useful to managers in performing cost-volume-profit analyses. It also describes break-even analysis and how to apply cost-volume-profit analysis for managerial decisions.

# CAP

## Conceptual

**C1** Explain departmentalization and the role of departmental accounting. *(p. 704)*

**C2** Distinguish between direct and indirect expenses. *(p. 705)*

**C3** Identify bases for allocating indirect expenses to departments. *(p. 706)*

**C4** Explain controllable costs and responsibility accounting. *(p. 711)*

**C5** Describe allocation of joint costs across products. *(p. 714)*

## Analytical

**A1** Analyze investment centers using return on total assets. *(p. 715)*

## Procedural

**P1** Assign overhead costs using two-stage cost allocation. *(p. 698)*

**P2** Assign overhead costs using activity-based costing. *(p. 700)*

**P3** Prepare departmental income statements. *(p. 707)*

**P4** Prepare departmental contribution reports. *(p. 710)*

# Life Is Good . . . and So Is Business

BOSTON—Bert and John Jacobs launched their T-shirt company, **Life Is Good**® **[LifeIsGood.com]**, with as Bert says, "nothing in our bank account and $78 in cash." The brothers spent early days visiting college campuses and street fairs peddling T-shirts. Although they lived and slept out of their van and made only enough to eat and pay for gas, they stayed the course. Then, as they like to say, "We created Jake, and he showed us the way!"

Jake is the smiling stick figure that now adorns their products. The brothers initially drew him on their apartment wall and then transferred the figure to a batch of T-shirts that sold out in less than an hour at a Cambridge street fair. "It scared the hell out of us," says Bert. "We looked at each other and said, 'Oh my God, what do we have here?'" What they had was a Hollywood story in the making. Within a few years, their Jake-adorned T-shirts, sweatshirts, and headwear produced annual sales exceeding $10 million.

Bert and John have also successfully merged their fun and quirky style with business. The Life Is Good factory comes with loud music, popcorn machines, free-roaming dogs, and giant murals on bright-colored walls. "We have a great team, so we encourage autonomy," says John, "and people know how to mix laughs into their day." The brothers have also successfully merged cost controls and departmental and individual responsibility into their factory. They identify and monitor costs—including direct, indirect, joint, and controllable costs—and allocate them to departments and products. The brothers know which products are selling and their contribution margins. Says John, "Consistent performance is what has enhanced and strengthened" our products.

Yet these cost management realities have not curtailed their fun-loving approach. This past year featured a factory talent show, bowling tournament, and watermelon seed-spitting contest. Our factory is "kind of like your favorite neighbor's basement," says John. "It just has a good vibe." The tight-knit factory crew works across departments and centers for the common good of both the workers and bottom-line income. "We want to make products we're proud of," says Bert, "and kind of enjoy the ride the whole time." And that ride is through the roof.

[Sources: *Life Is Good Website,* January 2004; *New Hampshire Business Review,* February 2003; *Boston Magazine,* 2003; *Improper Bostonian,* 2003.]

This chapter describes how to allocate costs shared by more than one product across those different products and how to allocate indirect costs of shared items such as utilities, advertising, and rent. The chapter also describes activity-based costing and how it traces the costs of individual activities. This knowledge helps managers better understand how to assign costs and assess company performance. The chapter also introduces additional managerial accounting reports useful in managing a company's activities and explains how and why management divides companies into departments.

## Cost Allocation and Performance Measurement

### Overhead Cost Allocation Methods

- Two-stage cost allocation
- Activity-based cost allocation
- Comparison of allocation methods

### Departmental Accounting

- Motivation for departmentalization
- Departmental evaluation
- Departmental reporting and analysis

### Departmental Expense Allocation

- Direct and indirect expenses
- Allocation of indirect expenses
- Departmental income statements
- Departmental contribution to overhead

### Responsibility Accounting

- Controllable versus direct costs
- Responsibility accounting system
- Joint costs and their allocation

# Overhead Cost Allocation Methods

**P1** Assign overhead costs using two-stage cost allocation.

**Point:** Use of a single overhead allocation rate is known as using a *plantwide rate.*

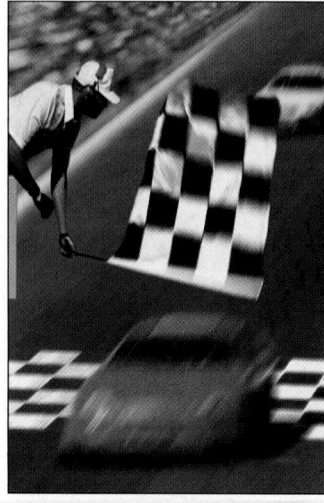

We previously explained how to assign overhead costs to jobs (and processes) by using a predetermined overhead rate per unit of an allocation base such as direct labor cost. When a single overhead rate is used on a companywide basis, all overhead is lumped together, and a predetermined overhead rate per unit of an allocation base is computed and used to assign overhead to jobs (and processes). The use of a single predetermined overhead rate suggests that this allocation process is simple. In reality, it can be complicated. This chapter explains the traditional two-stage cost allocation procedure and then introduces the activity-based cost allocation procedure.

## Two-Stage Cost Allocation

An organization incurs overhead costs in many activities. These activities can be identified with various departments, which can be broadly classified as either *operating* or *service* departments. *Operating departments* perform an organization's main functions. For example, an accounting firm's main functions usually include auditing, tax, and advisory services. Similarly, the production and selling departments of a manufacturing firm perform its main functions and serve as operating departments. *Service departments* provide support to an organization's operating departments. Examples of service departments are payroll, human resource management, accounting, and executive management. Service departments do not engage in activities that generate revenues, yet their support is crucial for the operating departments' success. In this section, we apply a two-stage cost allocation procedure to assign (1) service department costs to operating departments and (2) operating department costs, including those assigned from service departments, to the organization's output.

**Illustration of Two-Stage Cost Allocation** Exhibit 17.1 shows the two-stage cost allocation procedure. This exhibit uses data from **AutoGrand,** a custom automobile manufacturer. AutoGrand has five manufacturing-related departments: janitorial, maintenance, factory accounting, machining, and assembly. Expenses incurred by each of these departments are considered product costs. There are three service departments—janitorial,

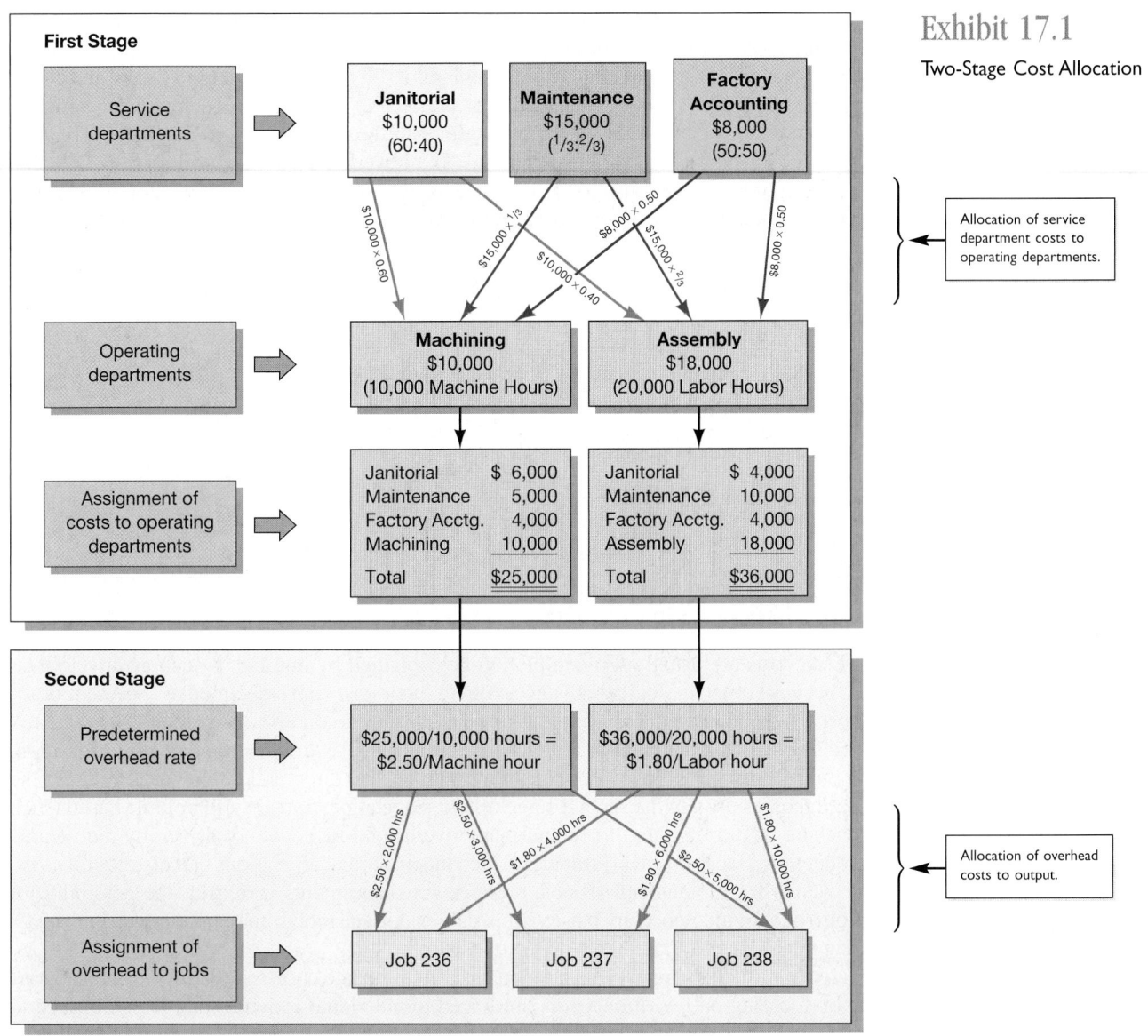

Exhibit 17.1

Two-Stage Cost Allocation

maintenance, and factory accounting; each incurs expenses of $10,000, $15,000 and $8,000, respectively. As shown in Exhibit 17.1, the first stage of the two-stage procedure involves allocating the costs of the three service departments to the two operating departments (machining and assembly). The two operating departments use the resources of these service departments.

To illustrate the first stage of cost allocation, we use the janitorial department. Its costs are allocated to machining and assembly in the ratio 60 : 40. This means that 60%, or $6,000, of janitorial costs are assigned to the machining department and 40%, or $4,000, to the assembly department. The expenses incurred by the maintenance and factory accounting departments are similarly assigned to machining and assembly. We then add the expenses directly incurred by each operating department to these assigned costs to determine the total expenses for each operating department. This yields total costs of $25,000 for machining and $36,000 for assembly.

In the second stage, predetermined overhead rates are computed for each operating department. The allocation base is machine hours for machining and labor hours for assembly. The predetermined overhead rate is $2.50 per machine hour for the machining department and $1.80 per labor hour for the assembly department. These predetermined overhead rates are then used to assign overhead to output.

**Point:** Use of a separate overhead allocation rate for each department is known as using *departmental rates.*

To illustrate this second stage, assume that three jobs were started and finished in a recent month. These jobs consumed resources as follows: Job 236—2,000 machine hours in machining and 4,000 labor hours in assembly; Job 237—3,000 machine hours and 6,000 labor hours; Job 238—5,000 machine hours and 10,000 labor hours. The overhead assigned to these three jobs is shown with the arrow lines in the bottom row of Exhibit 17.1.

Exhibit 17.2 summarizes these allocations. Total overhead allocated to Jobs 236, 237, and 238, is $12,200, $18,300, and $30,500, respectively. These allocated costs sum to $61,000, which is the total amount of overhead started with.

**Exhibit 17.2**

Assignment of Overhead Costs to Output

|  | Job 236 | Job 237 | Job 238 |
|---|---|---|---|
| **Machining** | | | |
| $2.50 × 2,000 hours . . . . . . . . . . | $ 5,000 | | |
| $2.50 × 3,000 hours . . . . . . . . . . | | $ 7,500 | |
| $2.50 × 5,000 hours . . . . . . . . . . | | | $12,500 |
| **Assembly** | | | |
| $1.80 × 4,000 hours . . . . . . . . . . | 7,200 | | |
| $1.80 × 6,000 hours . . . . . . . . . . | | 10,800 | |
| $1.80 × 10,000 hours . . . . . . . . | | | 18,000 |
| Total overhead assigned . . . . . . . | $12,200 | $18,300 | $30,500 |

## Activity-Based Cost Allocation

**P2** Assign overhead costs using activity-based costing.

**Topic Tackler 17-1**

**Point:** A recent survey found that most respondents believe that activity-based costing is worth the investment because of improved management decisions.

Overhead costs are usually too complex to be explained by one factor such as direct labor. Also, because of technological advances, direct labor costs have declined as a percent of total cost. In some companies, direct labor cost is such a small part of total cost that it is treated as overhead. Computing multiple overhead rates, as in the two-stage cost allocation, is an improvement over a single allocation rate based on direct labor. However, because the allocation bases used in the second stage of two-stage allocation are still volume based (such as machine hours), they fail to reflect many overhead cost items not driven by the volume of production or services. Unfortunately, such inappropriate allocations can distort unit costs. Moreover, when the number of jobs, products, or departments increases, the possibility of improperly assigning costs increases. This can lead managers to make poor decisions and a company's eventual failure.

**Activity-based costing (ABC)** attempts to better allocate costs to the proper users of overhead by focusing on *activities*. Costs are traced to individual activities and then allocated to cost objects. Exhibit 17.3 shows the (two-stage) activity-based cost allocation method. The first stage identifies the activities involved in processing Jobs 236, 237, and 238 and then forms activity cost *pools* by combining these activities into sets. The second stage involves computing predetermined overhead cost rates for each cost pool and then assigning costs to jobs.

We begin our explanation at the top of Exhibit 17.3. The first stage identifies individual activities, which are then pooled in a logical manner into homogenous groups, or *cost pools*. A homogenous cost pool consists of activities that belong to the same process and/or are caused by the same cost driver. A **cost driver** is a factor that causes the cost of an activity to go up or down. For example, preparing an invoice, checking it, and dispatching it are activities of the "invoicing" process and can therefore be grouped in a single cost pool. Moreover, the number of invoices processed likely drives the costs of these activities.

An **activity cost pool** is a temporary account accumulating the costs a company incurs to support an identified set of activities. Costs accumulated in an activity cost pool include the variable and fixed costs of the activities in the pool. Variable costs pertain to resources acquired as needed (such as materials); fixed costs pertain

# Exhibit 17.3

Activity-Based Cost Allocation

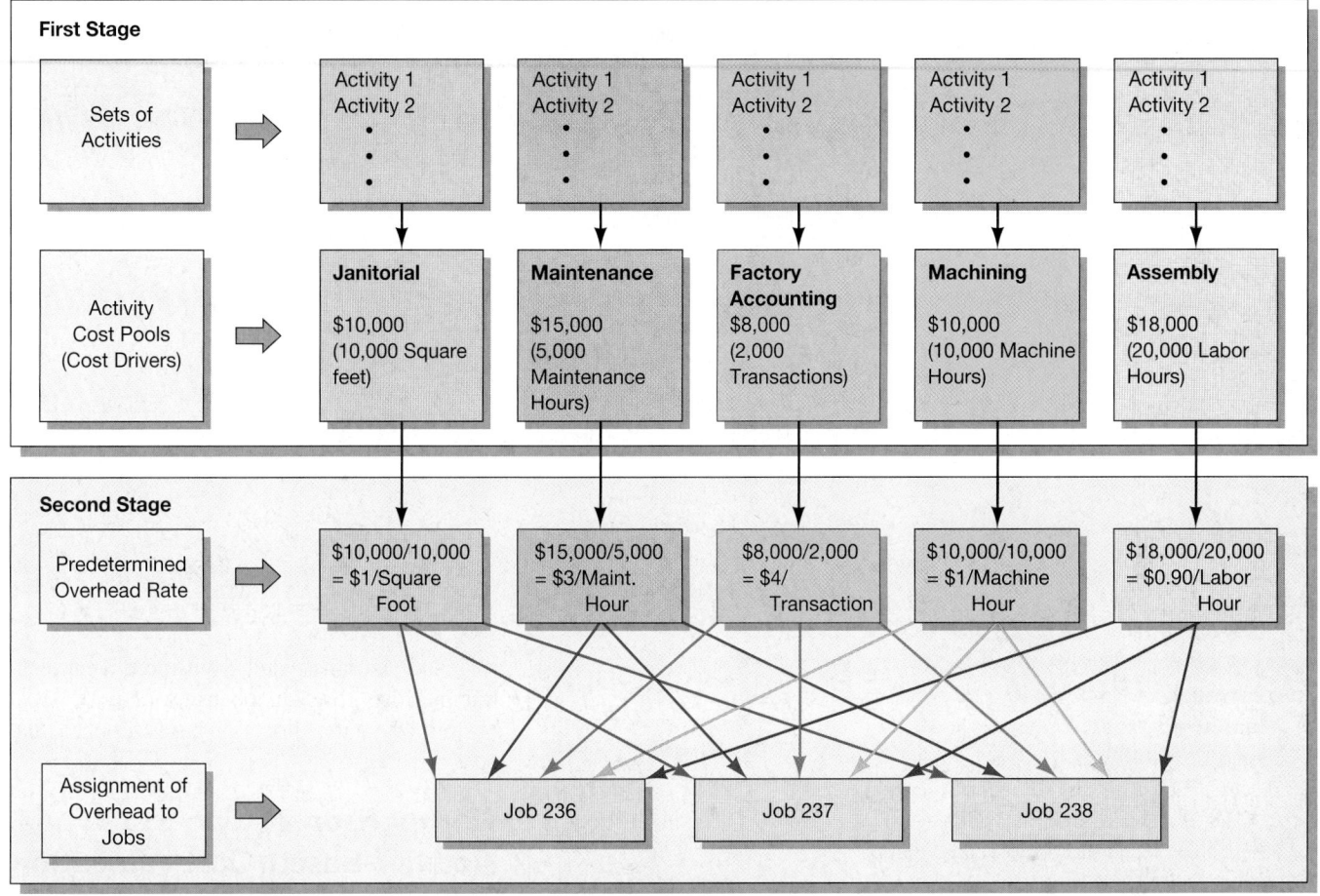

to resources acquired in advance (such as equipment). An activity cost pool account is handled like a factory overhead account.

In the second stage, after all activity costs are accumulated in an activity cost pool account, overhead rates are computed. Then, costs are allocated to cost objects (users) based on cost drivers (allocation bases).

**Point:** A cost driver is different from an allocation base. An allocation base is used as a basis for assigning overhead but need not have a cause-effect relation with the costs assigned. However, a cost driver has a cause-effect relation with the cost assigned.

**Illustration of Activity-Based Costing**    To illustrate, let's return to AutoGrand's three jobs. Assume that resources used to complete Jobs 236, 237, and 238 are shown in Exhibit 17.4.

| Resources Used | Job 236 | Job 237 | Job 238 |
|---|---|---|---|
| Square feet of space . . . . . . . . . . | 5,000 | 3,000 | 2,000 |
| Maintenance hours . . . . . . . . . . . | 2,500 | 1,500 | 1,000 |
| Number of transactions . . . . . . . | 500 | 700 | 800 |
| Machine hours . . . . . . . . . . . . . . | 2,000 | 3,000 | 5,000 |
| Direct labor hours . . . . . . . . . . . | 4,000 | 6,000 | 10,000 |

# Exhibit 17.4

Activity Resource Use

The $61,000 of total costs are assigned to these three jobs using activity-based costing as shown in Exhibit 17.5 (rates are taken from the second stage of Exhibit 17.3). Comparing Exhibits 17.2 and 17.5, we see that the costs assigned to the three jobs vary markedly depending on whether two-stage cost allocation or activity-based costing is used. Costs assigned to Job 236 go from $12,200 using two-stage cost allocation to $20,100 under activity-based costing. Costs assigned to Job 238 decline from $30,500 to $22,200. These differences in

## Exhibit 17.5

Activity-Based Assignment of Overhead to Output

| | Job 236 | Job 237 | Job 238 |
|---|---|---|---|
| **Janitorial** | | | |
| $1.00 × 5,000 sq. ft. . . . . . . . . . . . . . | $ 5,000 | | |
| $1.00 × 3,000 sq. ft. . . . . . . . . . . . . | | $ 3,000 | |
| $1.00 × 2,000 sq. ft. . . . . . . . . . . . . | | | $ 2,000 |
| **Maintenance** | | | |
| $3.00 × 2,500 maint. hrs. . . . . . . . . . | 7,500 | | |
| $3.00 × 1,500 maint. hrs. . . . . . . . . . | | 4,500 | |
| $3.00 × 1,000 maint. hrs. . . . . . . . . . | | | 3,000 |
| **Factory Accounting** | | | |
| $4.00 × 500 transactions . . . . . . . . . | 2,000 | | |
| $4.00 × 700 transactions . . . . . . . . . | | 2,800 | |
| $4.00 × 800 transactions . . . . . . . . . | | | 3,200 |
| **Machining** | | | |
| $1.00 × 2,000 machine hrs. . . . . . . . | 2,000 | | |
| $1.00 × 3,000 machine hrs. . . . . . . . | | 3,000 | |
| $1.00 × 5,000 machine hrs. . . . . . . . | | | 5,000 |
| **Assembly** | | | |
| $0.90 × 4,000 labor hrs. . . . . . . . . . . | 3,600 | | |
| $0.90 × 6,000 labor hrs. . . . . . . . . . . | | 5,400 | |
| $0.90 × 10,000 labor hrs. . . . . . . . . . | | | 9,000 |
| Total overhead assigned . . . . . . . . . . | $20,100 | $18,700 | $22,200 |

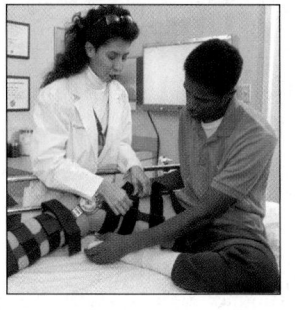

assigned amounts result from more accurately tracing costs to each job using activity-based costing where the allocation bases reflect actual cost drivers.

## Comparison of Two-Stage and Activity-Based Cost Allocation

Traditional cost systems capture overhead costs by individual department (or function) and accumulate these costs in one or more overhead accounts. Companies then assign these overhead costs using a single allocation base such as direct labor or multiple allocation bases. Unfortunately, traditional cost systems have tended to use allocation bases that are often not closely related to the way these costs are actually incurred.

In contrast, activity-based cost systems capture costs by individual activity. These activities and their costs are then accumulated into activity cost pools. A company selects a cost driver (allocation base) for each activity pool. It uses this cost driver to assign the accumulated activity costs to cost objects (such as jobs or products) benefiting from the activity.

An activity-based costing system commonly consists of more allocation bases as compared to a traditional cost system. For example, a Chicago-based manufacturer currently uses nearly 20 different activity cost drivers to assign overhead costs to its products. Also, **Perkin-Elmer**, a maker of analytical instruments, uses an activity-based cost system. The company's controller reports that at first they tried to analyze too many cost drivers. Eventually, they set up cross-functional teams able to identify the important cost drivers for each pool. Exhibit 17.6 lists examples of overhead cost pools and their usual cost drivers.

### Decision Maker

**Director of Operations**   Two department managers at your ad agency complain to you that overhead costs assigned to them are too high. Overhead is currently assigned on the basis of labor hours for artwork designers. These managers argue that overhead depends not only on the designers' hours but on many activities unrelated to these hours. What is your response?

Answer—p. 719

| Activity Cost Pool | Cost Driver |
|---|---|
| Materials purchasing | Number of purchase orders |
| Materials handling | Number of materials requisitions |
| Personnel processing | Number of employees hired or laid off |
| Equipment depreciation | Number of products produced or hours of use |
| Quality inspection | Number of units inspected |
| Indirect labor in setting up equipment | Number of setups required |
| Engineering costs for product modifications | Number of modifications (engineering change orders) |

Exhibit 17.6

Cost Pools and Cost Drivers in
Activity-Based Costing

Activity-based costing is especially effective when the same department or departments produce many different types of products. For instance, more complex products often require more help from service departments such as engineering, maintenance, and materials handling. If the same amount of direct labor is applied to the complex and simple products, a traditional overhead allocation system assigns the same overhead cost to both. With activity-based costing, however, the complex products are assigned a larger portion of overhead. The difference in overhead assigned can affect product pricing, make-or-buy, and other managerial decisions. Activity-based costing allows production managers to focus on managing activities that drive overhead cost instead of reducing allocated overhead by reducing direct labor cost.

Activity-based costing causes managers to pay closer attention to all activities. If overhead costs are accumulated in one account, attention is less likely to be directed at controlling any individual item. Activity-based costing requires managers to look at each item and encourages them to manage each cost to increase the benefit from each dollar spent. It also encourages managers to cooperate because it shows how their efforts are interrelated. This results in *activity-based management.*

**Decision Ethics**

**Accounting Officer**  You work for a company that produces expensive garments, whose production involves many complex and specialized activities. The company's general manager recently learned about activity-based costing (ABC) and requests your opinion. However, your supervisor does not want to disturb the existing cost system and instructs you to prepare a report stating that "implementation of ABC is a complicated process involving too many steps and not worth the effort." You believe ABC will actually help the company to identify sources of costs and control them. What action do you take?

Answer—p. 719

**Point:** To apply these concepts, work QS 17-3.

**Quick Check**

1. What is a cost driver?
2. When activity-based costing is used rather than traditional allocation methods, (a) managers must identify cost drivers for various items of overhead cost, (b) individual cost items in service departments are allocated directly to products or services, (c) managers can direct their attention to the activities that drive overhead cost, or (d) all of the above.

Answers—p. 719

# Departmental Accounting

Companies are divided into *departments,* also called *subunits,* when they are too large to be managed effectively as a single unit. Managerial accounting for departments has two main goals. The first is to set up a **departmental accounting system** to provide information for managers to use to evaluate the profitability or cost effectiveness of each department's activities. The second goal is to set up a **responsibility accounting system** to control costs and expenses and evaluate managers' performances by assigning costs and expenses to the managers responsible for controlling them. Departmental and responsibility accounting systems are related and share much information. We discuss departmental accounting in this and the next section. Then we describe responsibility accounting.

## Motivation for Departmentalization

**C1** Explain departmentalization and the role of departmental accounting.

Many companies are so large and complex that they are broken into separate divisions for efficiency and/or effectiveness purposes. Divisions then are usually organized into separate departments. When a company is departmentalized, each department is often placed under the direction of a manager. As a company grows, management often divides departments into new departments so that responsibilities for a department's activities do not overwhelm the manager's ability to oversee and control them. A company also creates departments to take advantage of the skills of individual managers. Departments are broadly classified as either operating or service departments.

## Departmental Evaluation

**Point:** To improve profitability, **Sears, Roebuck & Co.** eliminated several departments, including its catalog division.

Topic Tackler 17-2

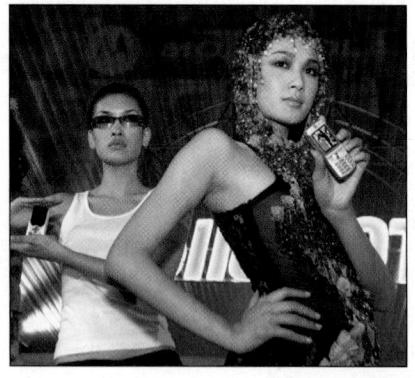

**Point:** Selling departments are often treated as *revenue centers;* their managers are responsible for maximizing sales revenues.

When a company is divided into departments, managers need to know how each department is performing. The accounting system must supply information about resources used and outputs achieved by each department. This requires a system to measure and accumulate revenue and expense information for each department whenever possible.

Departmental information is rarely distributed publicly because of its potential usefulness to competitors. Information about departments is prepared for internal managers to help control operations, appraise performance, allocate resources, and plan strategy. If a department is highly profitable, management may decide to expand its operations, or if a department is performing poorly, information about revenues or expenses can suggest useful changes.

More companies are emphasizing customer satisfaction as a main responsibility of many departments. This has led to changes in the measures reported. Increasingly, financial measurements are being supplemented with quality and customer satisfaction indexes. **Motorola**, for instance, uses two key measures: the number of defective parts per million parts produced and the percent of orders delivered on time to customers. (Note that some departments have only "internal customers.")

Financial information used to evaluate a department depends on whether it is evaluated as a profit center or a cost center. A **profit center** incurs costs and generates revenues; selling departments are often evaluated as profit centers. A **cost center** incurs costs without directly generating revenues. The manufacturing departments of a manufacturer and its service departments such as accounting, advertising, and purchasing, are all cost centers. Evaluating managers' performance depends on whether they are responsible for profit centers or cost centers. Profit center managers are judged on their abilities to generate revenues in excess of the department's costs. They are assumed to influence both revenue generation and cost incurrence. Cost center managers are judged on their abilities to control costs by keeping them within a satisfactory range under an assumption that only they influence costs.

### Decision Insight

**Nonfinancial Measures**   Survey data show that a majority of companies now report nonfinancial performance measures to management. The nonfinancial measures commonly used are cycle time, defect rate, on-time deliveries, inventory turnover, customer satisfaction, and safety. When nonfinancial measures are used with financial measures, the performance measurement system resembles a *balanced scorecard.* Also, many of these companies are implementing activity-based management as part of their performance measurement system.

## Departmental Reporting and Analysis

Companies use various measures (financial and nonfinancial) and reporting formats to evaluate their departments. The type and form of information depend on management's focus and philosophy. **Hewlett-Packard's** statement of corporate objectives, for instance, indicates that its goal is to satisfy customer needs. Its challenge is to set up managerial accounting systems to provide relevant feedback for evaluating performance in terms of its stated objectives. Also, the means used to obtain information about departments depend on how extensively a company uses computer and information technology.

When accounts are not maintained separately in the general ledger by department, a company can create departmental information by using a *departmental spreadsheet analysis*. For example, after recording sales in its usual manner, a company can compute daily total sales by department and enter these totals on a sales spreadsheet. At period-end, column totals of the spreadsheet show sales by department. The combined total of all columns equals the balance of the Sales account. A merchandiser that uses a spreadsheet analysis of department sales often uses separate spreadsheets to accumulate sales, sales returns, purchases, and purchases returns by department. If each department keeps a count of its inventory, it can also compute its gross profit (assuming it's a profit center).

**Point:** Some retailers use a point-of-sales system capturing sales data and creating documents to release inventory from the warehouse and order additional merchandise. **Wal-Mart's** sales system not only collects data for internal use but also is used by **Procter & Gamble** to plan its production and product delivery schedule to **Wal-Mart.**

**Point: Link Wood Products,** a manufacturer of lawn and garden products, records each sale by department on a spreadsheet. Daily totals are accumulated in another spreadsheet to obtain monthly totals by department.

### Quick Check

3. What is the difference between a departmental accounting system and a responsibility accounting system?

4. Service departments (a) manufacture products, (b) make sales directly to customers, (c) produce revenues, (d) assist operating departments.

5. Explain the difference between a cost center and a profit center. Cite an example of each.

Answers—p. 719

# Departmental Expense Allocation

When a company computes departmental profits, it confronts some accounting challenges that involve allocating its expenses across its operating departments.

## Direct and Indirect Expenses

**Direct expenses** are costs readily traced to a department because they are incurred for that department's sole benefit. They require no allocation across departments. For example, the salary of an employee who works in only one department is a direct expense of that one department.

**Indirect expenses** are costs that are incurred for the joint benefit of more than one department and cannot be readily traced to only one department. For example, if two or more departments share a single building, all enjoy the benefits of the expenses for rent, heat, and light. Indirect expenses are allocated across departments benefiting from them when we need information about departmental profits. Ideally, we allocate indirect expenses by using a cause-effect relation. When we cannot identify cause-effect relations, we allocate each indirect expense on a basis approximating the relative benefit each department receives. Measuring the benefit for each department from an indirect expense can be difficult or sometimes impossible.

**C2**  Distinguish between direct and indirect expenses.

**Point:** Utility expense has elements of both direct and indirect expenses.

**Illustration of Indirect Expense Allocation**   To illustrate how to allocate an indirect expense, we consider a retail store that purchases janitorial services from an outside company. Management allocates this cost across the store's three departments according to the floor space each occupies. Costs of janitorial services for a recent month are $300. Exhibit 17.7 shows the square feet of floor space each department occupies. The store computes the percent of total square feet alloted to each department and uses it to allocate the $300 cost.

| Department | Square Feet | Percent of Total | Allocated Cost |
|---|---|---|---|
| Jewelry | 2,400 | 60% | $180 |
| Watch repair | 600 | 15 | 45 |
| China and silver | 1,000 | 25 | 75 |
| Totals | 4,000 | 100% | $300 |

Exhibit 17.7

Indirect Expense Allocation

Specifically, because the jewelry department occupies 60% of the floor space, 60% of the total $300 cost is assigned to it. The same procedure is applied to the other departments. When the allocation process is complete, these and other allocated costs are deducted from the gross profit for each department to determine net income for each. One consideration in allocating costs is to motivate managers and employees to behave as desired. As a result, a cost incurred in one department might be best allocated to other departments when one of the other departments caused the cost.

## Allocation of Indirect Expenses

C3    Identify bases for
      allocating indirect
expenses to departments.

This section describes how to identify the bases used to allocate indirect expenses across departments. No standard rule identifies the best basis because expense allocation involves several factors, and the relative importance of these factors varies across departments and organizations. Judgment is required, and people do not always agree. In our discussion, note the parallels between activity-based costing and the departmental expense allocation procedures described here.

**Point:** Expense allocations cannot always avoid some arbitrariness.

**Wages and Salaries**   Employee wages and salaries can be either direct or indirect expenses. If their time is spent entirely in one department, their wages are direct expenses of that department. However, if employees work for the benefit of more than one department, their wages are indirect expenses and must be allocated across the departments benefited. An employee's contribution to a department usually depends on the number of hours worked in contributing to that department. Thus, a reasonable basis for allocating employee wages and salaries is the *relative amount of time spent in each department.* In the case of a supervisor who manages more than one department, recording the time spent in each department may not always be practical. Instead, a company can allocate the supervisor's salary to departments on the basis of the number of employees in each department—a reasonable basis if a supervisor's main task is managing people. Another basis of allocation is on sales across departments, also a reasonable basis if a supervisor's job reflects on departmental sales.

**Point:** Some companies ask supervisors to estimate time spent supervising specific departments for purposes of expense allocation.

**Rent and Related Expenses**   Rent expense for a building is reasonably allocated to a department on the basis of floor space it occupies. Location can often make some floor space more valuable than other space. Thus, the allocation method can charge departments that occupy more valuable space a higher expense per square foot. Ground floor retail space, for instance, is often more valuable than basement or upper-floor space because all customers pass departments near the entrance but fewer go beyond the first floor. When no precise measures of floor space values exist, basing allocations on data such as customer traffic and real estate assessments are helpful. When a company owns its building, its expenses for depreciation, taxes, insurance, and other related building expenses are allocated like rent expense.

**Advertising Expenses**   Effective advertising of a department's products increases its sales and customer traffic. Moreover, advertising products for some departments usually helps other departments' sales because customers also often buy unadvertised products. Thus, many stores treat advertising as an indirect expense allocated on the basis of each department's proportion of total sales. For example, a department with 10% of a store's total sales is assigned 10% of advertising expense. Another method is to analyze each advertisement to compute the Web/newspaper space or TV/radio time devoted to the products of a department and charge that department for the proportional costs of advertisements. Management must consider whether this more detailed and costly method is justified.

**Point:** To apply these concepts, work QS 17-2.

**Equipment and Machinery Depreciation**   Depreciation on equipment and machinery used only in one department is a direct expense of that department. Depreciation on equipment and machinery used by more than one department is an indirect expense to be allocated across departments. Accounting for each department's depreciation expense requires a company to keep records showing which departments use specific assets. The number of hours that a department uses equipment and machinery is a reasonable basis for allocating depreciation.

**Point:** Employee morale suffers when allocations are perceived as unfair. Thus, it is important to carefully design and explain the allocation of service department costs.

**Utilities Expenses** Utilities expenses such as heating and lighting are usually allocated on the basis of floor space occupied by departments. This practice assumes their use is uniform across departments. When this is not so, a more involved allocation can be necessary, although there is often a trade-off between the usefulness of more precise allocations and the effort to compute them.

**Service Department Expenses** To generate revenues, operating departments require support services provided by departments such as personnel, payroll, advertising, and purchasing. Such service departments are typically evaluated as cost centers because they do not produce revenues. (Evaluating them as profit centers requires the use of a system that "charges" user departments a price that then serves as the "revenue" generated by service departments.) A departmental accounting system can accumulate and report costs incurred directly by each service department for this purpose. The system then allocates a service department's expenses to operating departments benefiting from them. This is often done, for example, using traditional two-stage cost allocation (see Exhibit 17.1). Exhibit 17.8 shows some commonly used bases for allocating service department expenses to operating departments.

| Service Department | Common Allocation Bases |
| --- | --- |
| Office expenses . . . . . . . . . . . . . | Number of employees or sales in each department |
| Personnel expenses . . . . . . . . . . | Number of employees in each department |
| Payroll expenses . . . . . . . . . . . . . | Number of employees in each department |
| Advertising expenses . . . . . . . . . | Sales or amount of advertising charged directly to each department |
| Purchasing costs . . . . . . . . . . . . . | Dollar amounts of purchases or number of purchase orders processed |
| Cleaning expenses . . . . . . . . . . . | Square feet of floor space occupied |
| Maintenance expenses . . . . . . . . | Square feet of floor space occupied |

**Exhibit 17.8**

Bases for Allocating Service Department Expenses

## Departmental Income Statements

An income statement can be prepared for each operating department once expenses have been assigned to it. Its expenses include both direct expenses and its share of indirect expenses. For this purpose, compiling all expenses incurred in service departments before assigning them to operating departments is useful. We illustrate the steps to prepare departmental income statements using **A-1 Hardware** and its five departments. Two of them (office and purchasing) are service departments and the other three (hardware, housewares, and appliances) are operating (selling) departments. Allocating costs to operating departments and preparing departmental income statements involves four steps.

**P3** Prepare departmental income statements.

**Step 1** Step 1 accumulates direct expenses for each service and operating department as shown in Exhibit 17.9. Direct expenses include salaries, wages, and other expenses that each department incurs but does not share with any other department. This information is accumulated in departmental expense accounts.

| Direct Expenses | Direct Expenses | Direct Expenses | Direct Expenses | Direct Expenses |
| --- | --- | --- | --- | --- |
|  |  |  |  |  |
| General office | Purchasing | Hardware | Housewares | Appliances |

**Exhibit 17.9**

Step 1: Direct Expense Accumulation

**Step 2** Step 2 allocates indirect expenses across all departments using the allocation base identified for each expense as shown in Exhibit 17.10. Indirect expenses can include items such as depreciation, rent, advertising, and any other expenses that cannot be directly assigned to a department. Indirect expenses are recorded in expense accounts, and costs are allocated using a *departmental expense allocation spreadsheet* described in step 3.

**Exhibit 17.10**

Step 2: Indirect Expense
Allocation

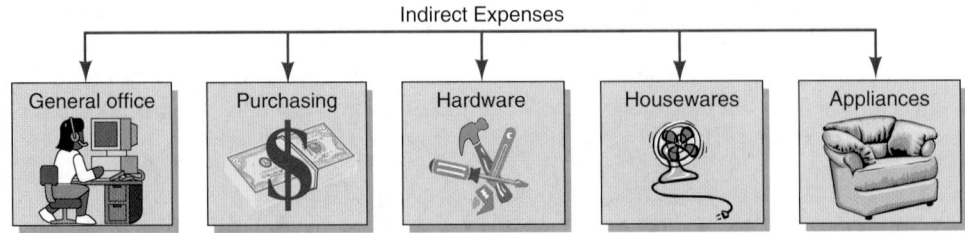

**Step 3**   Step 3 allocates expenses of the service departments (office and purchasing) to the operating departments. Exhibit 17.11 reflects the allocation of service department expenses using the allocation base(s).

**Exhibit 17.11**

Step 3: Service Department
Expense Allocation to Operating
Departments

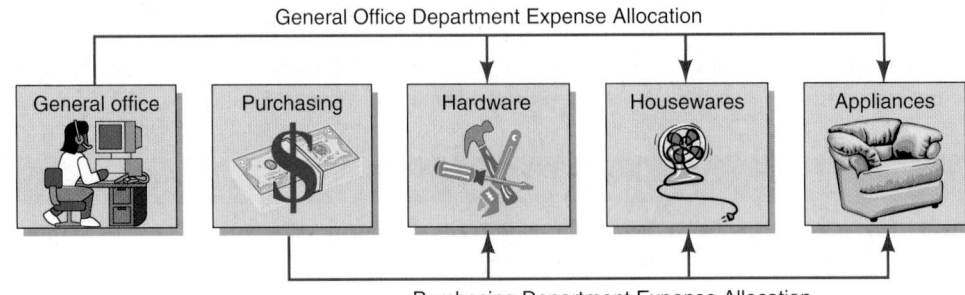

**Point:** To apply these concepts, work Exercise 17-1.

**Exhibit 17.12**

Departmental Expense
Allocation Spreadsheet

Computations for both steps 2 and 3 are commonly made using a departmental expense allocation spreadsheet as shown in Exhibit 17.12.[1] The first two sections of this spreadsheet list direct expenses and indirect expenses by department. The third section lists the service

File   Edit   View   Insert   Format   Tools   Data   Window   Help

**A-1 HARDWARE**
**Departmental Expense Allocations**
**For Year Ended December 31, 2005**

| | Allocation Base | Expense Account Balance | Allocation of Expenses to Departments | | | | |
| --- | --- | --- | --- | --- | --- | --- | --- |
| | | | General Office Dept. | Purchasing Dept. | Hardware Dept. | House-wares Dept. | Appliances Dept. |
| **Direct expenses** | | | | | | | |
| Salaries expense.................... | Payroll records ........................ | $51,900 | $13,300 | $8,200 | $15,600 | $ 7,000 | $ 7,800 |
| Depreciation—Equipment...... | Depreciation records ............. | 1,500 | 500 | 300 | 400 | 100 | 200 |
| Supplies expense.................... | Requisitions............................ | 900 | 200 | 100 | 300 | 200 | 100 |
| **Indirect expenses** | | | | | | | |
| Rent expense .......................... | Amount and value of space .. | 12,000 | 600 | 600 | 4,860 | 3,240 | 2,700 |
| Utilities expense..................... | Floor space............................. | 2,400 | 300 | 300 | 810 | 540 | 450 |
| Advertising expense............... | Sales....................................... | 1,000 | | | 500 | 300 | 200 |
| Insurance expense.................. | Value of insured assets ........ | 2,500 | 400 | 200 | 900 | 600 | 400 |
| Total department expenses ...... | | 72,200 | 15,300 | 9,700 | 23,370 | 11,980 | 11,850 |
| **Service department expenses** | | | | | | | |
| General office department..... | Sales....................................... | | 15,300 | | 7,650 | 4,590 | 3,060 |
| Purchasing department ......... | Purchase orders.................... | | | 9,700 | 3,880 | 2,630 | 3,190 |
| **Total expenses allocated to operating departments**........................ | | $72,200 | $      0 | $      0 | $34,900 | $19,200 | $18,100 |

Sheet1   Sheet2   Sheet3

[1] In some cases we allocate a service department's expenses to other service departments when they use its services. For example, expenses of a payroll office benefit all service and operating departments and can be assigned to all departments. Nearly all examples and assignment materials in this book allocate service expenses only to operating departments for simplicity.

department expenses and their allocations to operating departments. The allocation bases are identified in the second column, and total expense amounts are reported in the third column.

The departmental expense allocation spreadsheet is useful in implementing the first three steps. To illustrate, first (step 1) the three direct expenses of salaries, depreciation, and supplies are accumulated in each of the five departments.

Second (step 2), the four indirect expenses of rent, utilities, advertising, and insurance are allocated to all departments using the allocation bases identified. For example, consider rent allocation. Exhibit 17.13 lists the five departments' square footage of space occupied. The two service departments (office and purchasing) occupy 25% of the total space (3,000 sq. feet/12,000 sq. feet). However, they are located near the back of the building, which is of lower value than space near the front that is occupied by operating departments. Management esti-mates that space near the back accounts for $1,200 of the total rent expense of $12,000. Exhibit 17.14 shows how we allocate the $1,200 rent expense between these two service

**Exhibit 17.13**

Departments' Square Footages

| | |
|---|---|
| General office ....... | 1,500 sq. ft. |
| Purchasing ......... | 1,500 sq. ft. |
| Hardware ......... | 4,050 sq. ft. |
| Housewares ........ | 2,700 sq. ft. |
| Appliances ......... | 2,250 sq. ft. |
| Total ............ | 12,000 sq. ft. |

**Exhibit 17.14**

Allocating Indirect (Rent) Expense to Service Departments

| Department | Square Feet | Percent of Total | Allocated Cost |
|---|---|---|---|
| General office ........ | 1,500 | 50.0% | $ 600 |
| Purchasing ......... | 1,500 | 50.0 | 600 |
| Totals ............. | 3,000 | 100.0% | $1,200 |

departments in proportion to their square footage. We then allocate the remaining $10,800 of rent expense to the three operating departments as shown in Exhibit 17.15. We continue step 2 by allocating the $2,400 of utilities expense to all departments based on the square

**Exhibit 17.15**

Allocating Indirect (Rent) Expense to Operating Departments

| Department | Square Feet | Percent of Total | Allocated Cost |
|---|---|---|---|
| Hardware ........... | 4,050 | 45.0% | $ 4,860 |
| Housewares ........ | 2,700 | 30.0 | 3,240 |
| Appliances ......... | 2,250 | 25.0 | 2,700 |
| Totals ............. | 9,000 | 100.0% | $10,800 |

footage occupied as shown in Exhibit 17.16. The rows in Exhibit 17.12 for rent and utilities expenses show the amounts from Exhibits 17.14, 17.15, and 17.16. The allocations of the two other indirect expenses of advertising and insurance are similarly computed. Note that because advertising expense is allocated on the basis of sales and because service departments do not have sales, it is allocated only to the three operating departments.

**Exhibit 17.16**

Allocating Indirect (Utilities) Expense to All Departments

| Department | Square Feet | Percent of Total | Allocated Cost |
|---|---|---|---|
| General office ........ | 1,500 | 12.50% | $ 300 |
| Purchasing ......... | 1,500 | 12.50 | 300 |
| Hardware ........... | 4,050 | 33.75 | 810 |
| Housewares ........ | 2,700 | 22.50 | 540 |
| Appliances ......... | 2,250 | 18.75 | 450 |
| Totals ............. | 12,000 | 100.00% | $2,400 |

**Example:** If the $15,300 general office expenses in Exhibit 17.12 are allocated equally across departments, what is net income for the hardware department and for the combined company? *Answer:* Hardware income, $13,350; combined income, $19,000.

Third (step 3), total expenses of the two service departments are allocated to the three operating departments using the allocation bases shown in the final three rows of Exhibit 17.12.

**Step 4**   When the departmental expense spreadsheet is complete, the amounts in the operating department columns are used to prepare departmental income statements as shown in Exhibit 17.17. This exhibit uses the spreadsheet for its operating expenses; information on sales and cost of goods sold comes from departmental records.

## Exhibit 17.17

Departmental Income Statements

| | A-I HARDWARE | | | |
|---|---|---|---|---|
| | **Departmental Income Statements** | | | |
| | **For Year Ended December 31, 2005** | | | |
| | Hardware Department | Housewares Department | Appliances Department | Combined |
| Sales ....................... | $119,500 | $71,700 | $47,800 | $239,000 |
| Cost of goods sold ............... | 73,800 | 43,800 | 30,200 | 147,800 |
| Gross profit .................... | 45,700 | 27,900 | 17,600 | 91,200 |
| Operating expenses | | | | |
| Salaries expense ............... | 15,600 | 7,000 | 7,800 | 30,400 |
| Depreciation expense—Equipment ... | 400 | 100 | 200 | 700 |
| Supplies expense ............... | 300 | 200 | 100 | 600 |
| Rent expense .................. | 4,860 | 3,240 | 2,700 | 10,800 |
| Utilities expense ............... | 810 | 540 | 450 | 1,800 |
| Advertising expense ............. | 500 | 300 | 200 | 1,000 |
| Insurance expense .............. | 900 | 600 | 400 | 1,900 |
| Share of general office expenses ..... | 7,650 | 4,590 | 3,060 | 15,300 |
| Share of purchasing expenses ....... | 3,880 | 2,630 | 3,190 | 9,700 |
| Total operating expenses ......... | 34,900 | 19,200 | 18,100 | 72,200 |
| **Net income (loss)** .............. | **$ 10,800** | **$ 8,700** | **$ (500)** | **$ 19,000** |

## Departmental Contribution to Overhead

**P4**   Prepare departmental contribution reports.

**Point:** Net income is the same in Exhibits 17.17 and 17.18. The method of reporting indirect expenses in Exhibit 17.18 does not change total net income but does identify each department's contribution to overhead and net income.

Data from departmental income statements are not always best for evaluating each department's performance, especially when indirect expenses are a large portion of total expenses and when weaknesses in assumptions and decisions in allocating indirect expenses can markedly affect net income. In these and other cases, we might better evaluate department performance using the **departmental contribution to overhead,** which is a report of the amount of sales less *direct* expenses.[2]

The upper half of Exhibit 17.18 shows a departmental contribution to overhead as part of an expanded income statement. This format is common when reporting departmental

contributions to overhead. Using the information in Exhibits 17.17 and 17.18, we can evaluate the profitability of the three operating departments. For instance, let's compare the performance of the appliances department as described in these two exhibits. Exhibit 17.17 shows a $500 net loss resulting from this department's operations, but Exhibit 17.18 shows a $9,500 positive contribution to overhead, which is 19.9% of sales. The contribution of the appliances department is not as large as that of the other selling departments, but a $9,500 contribution to overhead is better than a $500 loss. This tells us that the appliances department is not a money loser. On the contrary, it is contributing $9,500 toward defraying total indirect expenses of $40,500.

[2] A department's contribution is said to be "to overhead" because of the practice of considering all indirect expenses as overhead. Thus, the excess of a department's sales over direct expenses is a contribution toward at least a portion of its total overhead.

Exhibit 17.18

Departmental Contribution to Overhead

| A-1 HARDWARE Income Statement Showing Departmental Contribution to Overhead For Year Ended December 31, 2005 | | | | |
| --- | --- | --- | --- | --- |
| | Hardware Department | Housewares Department | Appliances Department | Combined |
| Sales .......................... | $119,500 | $ 71,700 | $47,800 | $239,000 |
| Cost of goods sold ............... | 73,800 | 43,800 | 30,200 | 147,800 |
| Gross profit ................... | 45,700 | 27,900 | 17,600 | 91,200 |
| Direct expenses | | | | |
| Salaries expense ............... | 15,600 | 7,000 | 7,800 | 30,400 |
| Depreciation expense—Equipment .. | 400 | 100 | 200 | 700 |
| Supplies expense ............... | 300 | 200 | 100 | 600 |
| Total direct expenses ............ | 16,300 | 7,300 | 8,100 | 31,700 |
| **Departmental contributions** to overhead ................. | **$ 29,400** | **$20,600** | **$ 9,500** | **$ 59,500** |
| Indirect expenses | | | | |
| Rent expense ................... | | | | 10,800 |
| Utilities expense ................ | | | | 1,800 |
| Advertising expense ............. | | | | 1,000 |
| Insurance expense .............. | | | | 1,900 |
| General office department expense .. | | | | 15,300 |
| Purchasing department expense ..... | | | | 9,700 |
| Total indirect expenses ........... | | | | 40,500 |
| Net income .................... | | | | $ 19,000 |
| Contribution as percent of sales ...... | 24.6% | 28.7% | 19.9% | 24.9% |

## Quick Check

6. If a company has two operating (selling) departments (shoes and hats) and two service departments (payroll and advertising), which of the following statements is correct? (a) Wages incurred in the payroll department are direct expenses of the shoe department, (b) Wages incurred in the payroll department are indirect expenses of the operating departments, or (c) Advertising department expenses are allocated to the other three departments.

7. Which of the following bases can be used to allocate supervisors' salaries across operating departments? (a) Hours spent in each department, (b) number of employees in each department, (c) sales achieved in each department, or (d) any of the above, depending on which information is most relevant and accessible.

8. What three steps are used to allocate expenses to operating departments?

9. An income statement showing departmental contribution to overhead, (a) subtracts indirect expenses from each department's revenues, (b) subtracts only direct expenses from each department's revenues, or (c) shows net income for each department.

Answers—p. 719

# Responsibility Accounting

Departmental accounting reports often provide data used to evaluate a department's performance, but are they useful in assessing how well a department *manager* performs? Neither departmental income nor its contribution to overhead may be useful because many expenses can be outside a manager's control. Instead, we often evaluate a manager's performance using responsibility accounting reports that describe a department's activities in terms of **controllable costs.**[3] A cost is controllable if a manager has the power to determine or at

C4 Explain controllable costs and responsibility accounting.

---

[3] The terms *cost* and *expense* are often used interchangeably in managerial accounting, but they are not necessarily the same. *Cost* often refers to the monetary outlay to acquire some resource that can have present and future benefit. *Expense* usually refers to an expired cost. That is, as the benefit of a resource expires, a portion of its cost is written off as an expense.

## Joint Costs and Their Allocation

**C5**   Describe allocation of joint costs across products.

Most manufacturing processes involve **joint costs,** which refer to costs incurred to produce or purchase two or more products at the same time. A joint cost is like an indirect expense in the sense that more than one cost object share it. For example, a sawmill company incurs a joint cost when it buys logs that it cuts into lumber as shown in Exhibit 17.21. The joint cost includes the logs (raw material) and its cutting (conversion) into boards classified as Clear (FAS), Select, No. 1 Common, No. 2 Common, No. 3 Common, and other types of lumber and by-products.

**Exhibit 17.21**

Joint Products from Logs

**Joint Products**

Joint Cost — Cutting of Logs — Split-off Point

Clear · Select · No. 1 Common · No. 2 Common · No. 3 Common

When a joint cost is incurred, a question arises as to whether to allocate it to different products resulting from it. The answer is that when management wishes to estimate the costs of individual products, joint costs are included and must be allocated to these joint products. However, when management needs information to help decide whether to sell a product at a certain point in the production process or to process it further, the joint costs are ignored.

Financial statements prepared according to GAAP must assign joint costs to products. To do this, management must decide how to allocate joint costs across products benefiting from these costs. If some products are sold and others remain in inventory, allocating joint costs involves assigning costs to both cost of goods sold and ending inventory.

The two usual methods to allocate joint costs are the (1) *physical basis* and (2) the *value basis*. The physical basis typically involves allocating joint cost using physical characteristics such as the ratio of pounds, cubic feet, or gallons of each joint product to the total pounds, cubic feet, or gallons of all joint products flowing from the cost. This method is not preferred because the resulting cost allocations do not reflect the relative market values the joint cost generates. The preferred approach is the value basis, which allocates joint cost in proportion to the sales value of the output produced by the process at the "split-off point"; see Exhibit 17.21.

**Physical Basis Allocation of Joint Cost**   To illustrate the physical basis of allocating a joint cost, we consider a sawmill that bought logs for $30,000. When cut, these logs produce 100,000 board feet of lumber in the grades and amounts shown in Exhibit 17.22. The logs produce 20,000 board feet of No. 3 Common lumber, which is 20% of the total. With physical allocation, the No. 3 Common lumber is assigned 20% of the $30,000 cost of the logs, or $6,000 ($30,000 × 20%). Because this low-grade lumber sells for $4,000, this allocation gives a $2,000 loss from its production and sale. The physical basis for allocating joint costs does not reflect the extra value flowing into some products or the inferior value flowing into others. That is, the portion of a log that produces Clear and Select grade lumber is worth more than the portion used to produce the three grades of common lumber, but the physical basis fails to reflect this.

| Grade of Lumber | Board Feet Produced | Percent of Total | Allocated Cost | Sales Value | Gross Profit |
|---|---|---|---|---|---|
| Clear and Select . . . . . . . . . . | 10,000 | 10.0% | $ 3,000 | $12,000 | $ 9,000 |
| No. 1 Common . . . . . . . . . . . | 30,000 | 30.0 | 9,000 | 18,000 | 9,000 |
| No. 2 Common . . . . . . . . . . . | 40,000 | 40.0 | 12,000 | 16,000 | 4,000 |
| No. 3 Common . . . . . . . . . . . | 20,000 | 20.0 | 6,000 | 4,000 | (2,000) |
| Totals . . . . . . . . . . . . . . . . . | 100,000 | 100.0% | $30,000 | $50,000 | $20,000 |

**Exhibit 17.22**

Allocating Joint Costs on a Physical Basis

**Value Basis Allocation of Joint Cost**   Exhibit 17.23 illustrates the value basis method of allocation. It determines the percents of the total costs allocated to each grade by the ratio of each grade's sales value to the total sales value of $50,000 (sales value is the unit selling price multiplied by the number of units produced). The Clear and Select lumber grades receive 24% of the total cost ($12,000/$50,000) instead of the 10% portion using a physical basis. The No. 3 Common lumber receives only 8% of the total cost, or $2,400, which is much less than the $6,000 assigned to it using the physical basis.

| Grade of Lumber | Sales Value | Percent of Total | Allocated Cost | Gross Profit |
|---|---|---|---|---|
| Clear and Select . . . . . . . . . . | $12,000 | 24.0% | $ 7,200 | $ 4,800 |
| No. 1 Common . . . . . . . . . . . | 18,000 | 36.0 | 10,800 | 7,200 |
| No. 2 Common . . . . . . . . . . . | 16,000 | 32.0 | 9,600 | 6,400 |
| No. 3 Common . . . . . . . . . . . | 4,000 | 8.0 | 2,400 | 1,600 |
| Totals . . . . . . . . . . . . . . . . . | $50,000 | 100.0% | $30,000 | $20,000 |

**Exhibit 17.23**

Allocating Joint Costs on a Value Basis

**Example:** Refer to Exhibit 17.23. If the sales value of Clear and Select lumber is changed to $10,000, what is the revised ratio of the market value of No. 1 Common to the total? *Answer:* $18,000/$48,000 = 37.5%

An outcome of value basis allocation is that *each* grade produces exactly the same 40% gross profit at the split-off point. This 40% rate equals the gross profit rate from selling all the lumber made from the $30,000 logs for a combined price of $50,000.

---

## Quick Check

12. A company produces three products, B1, B2, and B3. The joint cost incurred for the current month for these products is $180,000. The following data relate to this month's production:

| Product | Units Produced | Unit Sales Value |
|---|---|---|
| B1 | 96,000 | $3.00 |
| B2 | 64,000 | 6.00 |
| B3 | 32,000 | 9.00 |

The amount of joint cost allocated to product B3 using the value basis allocation is (*a*) $30,000, (*b*) $54,000, or (*c*) $90,000.

Answer—p. 720

---

## Investment Center Return on Total Assets

## Decision Analysis

We discussed the classification of departments and divisions as profit centers or cost centers. Another way is to classify (and evaluate) a department as an **investment center.** An investment center manager is responsible for effectively using the center's assets to generate income for the center.

A measure often used to evaluate the performance of an investment center manager is the **investment center return on total assets,** also called *return on investment.* This measure is computed as a center's net income divided by the center's average total assets. To illustrate, if a center with an average investment of $1 million yields a net income of $210,000, its return on total assets is 21%.

Top management can use a center's return on total assets to assess how well its manager has utilized the center's assets to generate returns for the company. Top management can also compare performance

**A1** Analyze investment centers using return on total assets.

Topic Tackler 17-3

**Decision Maker**

**Center Manager**   Your center's usual return on total assets is 19%. You are considering two new investing opportunities for your center. The first requires a $250,000 average investment and is expected to yield annual net income of $50,000. The second requires a $1 million average investment with an expected annual net income of $175,000. Do you pursue either opportunity?

Answer—p. 719

across departments and/or divisions using this measure. Many companies establish a center's target return on total assets and reward managers based on whether they meet targets. In addition, center managers often use the center's return on total assets to decide whether to invest additional resources in the center.

# Demonstration Problem

We must prepare departmental income statements for Hacker's Haven, a computer store that has five departments. Three are operating departments (hardware, software, and repairs) and two are service departments (general office and purchasing).

| | General Office | Purchasing | Hardware | Software | Repairs |
|---|---|---|---|---|---|
| Sales . . . . . . . . . . . . . . . . . | — | — | $960,000 | $600,000 | $840,000 |
| Cost of goods sold . . . . . . . | — | — | 500,000 | 300,000 | 200,000 |
| Direct expenses | | | | | |
|   Payroll . . . . . . . . . . . . . . | $60,000 | $45,000 | 80,000 | 25,000 | 325,000 |
|   Depreciation . . . . . . . . . | 6,000 | 7,200 | 33,000 | 4,200 | 9,600 |
|   Supplies . . . . . . . . . . . . | 15,000 | 10,000 | 10,000 | 2,000 | 25,000 |

The departments incur several indirect expenses. To prepare departmental income statements, the indirect expenses must be allocated across the five departments. Then the expenses of the two service departments must be allocated to the three operating departments. Total cost amounts and the allocation bases for each indirect expense are as follows:

| Indirect Expense | Total Cost | Allocation Basis |
|---|---|---|
| Rent . . . . . . . . . . . . . . . . . . | $150,000 | Square footage occupied |
| Utilities . . . . . . . . . . . . . . . . | 50,000 | Square footage occupied |
| Advertising . . . . . . . . . . . . . | 125,000 | Dollars of sales |
| Insurance . . . . . . . . . . . . . . | 30,000 | Value of assets insured |
| Service departments | | |
|   General office . . . . . . . . . | ? | Number of employees |
|   Purchasing . . . . . . . . . . . . | ? | Dollars of cost of goods sold |

The following additional information is needed for indirect expense allocations:

| Department | Square Feet | Sales | Insured Assets | Employees | Cost of Goods Sold |
|---|---|---|---|---|---|
| General office . . . . . . . . | 500 | | $ 60,000 | | |
| Purchasing . . . . . . . . . | 500 | | 72,000 | | |
| Hardware . . . . . . . . . . | 4,000 | $ 960,000 | 330,000 | 5 | $ 500,000 |
| Software . . . . . . . . . . | 3,000 | 600,000 | 42,000 | 5 | 300,000 |
| Repairs . . . . . . . . . . . | 2,000 | 840,000 | 96,000 | 10 | 200,000 |
| Totals . . . . . . . . . . . . . | 10,000 | $2,400,000 | $600,000 | 20 | $1,000,000 |

**Required**

1. Prepare a departmental expense allocation spreadsheet for Hacker's Haven.

2. Prepare a departmental income statement reporting net income for each operating department and for all operating departments combined.

## Planning the Solution

- Set up and complete four tables to allocate the indirect expenses—one each for rent, utilities, advertising, and insurance.

- Allocate the departments' indirect expenses using a spreadsheet like the one in Exhibit 17.12. Enter the given amounts of the direct expenses for each department. Then enter the allocated amounts of the indirect expenses that you computed.

- Complete two tables for allocating the general office and purchasing department costs to the three operating departments. Enter these amounts on the spreadsheet and determine the total expenses allocated to the three operating departments.

- Prepare departmental income statements like the one in Exhibit 17.17. Show sales, cost of goods sold, gross profit, individual expenses, and net income for each of the three operating departments and for the combined company.

## Solution to Demonstration Problem

Allocations of the four indirect expenses across the five departments:

| Rent | Square Feet | Percent of Total | Allocated Cost |
|---|---|---|---|
| General office ....... | 500 | 5.0% | $  7,500 |
| Purchasing .......... | 500 | 5.0 | 7,500 |
| Hardware .......... | 4,000 | 40.0 | 60,000 |
| Software .......... | 3,000 | 30.0 | 45,000 |
| Repairs ........... | 2,000 | 20.0 | 30,000 |
| Totals ........... | 10,000 | 100.0% | $150,000 |

| Utilities | Square Feet | Percent of Total | Allocated Cost |
|---|---|---|---|
| General office ....... | 500 | 5.0% | $  2,500 |
| Purchasing .......... | 500 | 5.0 | 2,500 |
| Hardware .......... | 4,000 | 40.0 | 20,000 |
| Software .......... | 3,000 | 30.0 | 15,000 |
| Repairs ........... | 2,000 | 20.0 | 10,000 |
| Totals ........... | 10,000 | 100.0% | $50,000 |

| Advertising | Sales Dollars | Percent of Total | Allocated Cost |
|---|---|---|---|
| Hardware .......... | $ 960,000 | 40.0% | $ 50,000 |
| Software ........... | 600,000 | 25.0 | 31,250 |
| Repairs ........... | 840,000 | 35.0 | 43,750 |
| Totals ........... | $2,400,000 | 100.0% | $125,000 |

| Insurance | Assets Insured | Percent of Total | Allocated Cost |
|---|---|---|---|
| General office ....... | $ 60,000 | 10.0% | $ 3,000 |
| Purchasing .......... | 72,000 | 12.0 | 3,600 |
| Hardware .......... | 330,000 | 55.0 | 16,500 |
| Software ........... | 42,000 | 7.0 | 2,100 |
| Repairs ........... | 96,000 | 16.0 | 4,800 |
| Totals ........... | $600,000 | 100.0% | $30,000 |

1. Allocations of service department expenses to the three operating departments:

| General Office Allocations to | Employees | Percent of Total | Allocated Cost |
|---|---|---|---|
| Hardware ........... | 5 | 25.0% | $23,500 |
| Software ............ | 5 | 25.0 | 23,500 |
| Repairs ........... | 10 | 50.0 | 47,000 |
| Totals ............. | 20 | 100.0% | $94,000 |

| Purchasing Allocations to | Cost of Goods Sold | Percent of Total | Allocated Cost |
|---|---|---|---|
| Hardware ......... | $ 500,000 | 50.0% | $37,900 |
| Software .......... | 300,000 | 30.0 | 22,740 |
| Repairs ........... | 200,000 | 20.0 | 15,160 |
| Totals ........... | $1,000,000 | 100.0% | $75,800 |

**HACKER'S HAVEN**
**Departmental Expense Allocations**
**For Year Ended December 31, 2005**

| | Allocation Base | Expense Account Balance | General Office Dept. | Purchasing Dept. | Hardware Dept. | Software Dept. | Repairs Dept. |
|---|---|---|---|---|---|---|---|
| **Direct Expenses** | | | | | | | |
| Payroll | | $  535,000 | $ 60,000 | $ 45,000 | $  80,000 | $  25,000 | $ 325,000 |
| Depreciation | | 60,000 | 6,000 | 7,200 | 33,000 | 4,200 | 9,600 |
| Supplies | | 62,000 | 15,000 | 10,000 | 10,000 | 2,000 | 25,000 |
| **Indirect Expenses** | | | | | | | |
| Rent | Square ft. | 150,000 | 7,500 | 7,500 | 60,000 | 45,000 | 30,000 |
| Utilities | Square ft. | 50,000 | 2,500 | 2,500 | 20,000 | 15,000 | 10,000 |
| Advertising | Sales | 125,000 | — | — | 50,000 | 31,250 | 43,750 |
| Insurance | Assets | 30,000 | 3,000 | 3,600 | 16,500 | 2,100 | 4,800 |
| Total expenses | | 1,012,000 | 94,000 | 75,800 | 269,500 | 124,550 | 448,150 |
| **Service Department Expenses** | | | | | | | |
| General office | Employees | | 94,000 | | 23,500 | 23,500 | 47,000 |
| Purchasing | Goods sold | | | 75,800 | 37,900 | 22,740 | 15,160 |
| Total expenses allocated to operating departments | | $1,012,000 | $        0 | $        0 | $330,900 | $170,790 | $510,310 |

**2.** Departmental income statements for Hacker's Haven:

**HACKER'S HAVEN**
**Departmental Income Statements**
**For Year Ended December 31, 2005**

| | Hardware | Software | Repairs | Combined |
|---|---|---|---|---|
| Sales | $ 960,000 | $ 600,000 | $ 840,000 | $2,400,000 |
| Cost of goods sold | 500,000 | 300,000 | 200,000 | 1,000,000 |
| Gross profit | 460,000 | 300,000 | 640,000 | 1,400,000 |
| Expenses | | | | |
| Payroll | 80,000 | 25,000 | 325,000 | 430,000 |
| Depreciation | 33,000 | 4,200 | 9,600 | 46,800 |
| Supplies | 10,000 | 2,000 | 25,000 | 37,000 |
| Rent | 60,000 | 45,000 | 30,000 | 135,000 |
| Utilities | 20,000 | 15,000 | 10,000 | 45,000 |
| Advertising | 50,000 | 31,250 | 43,750 | 125,000 |
| Insurance | 16,500 | 2,100 | 4,800 | 23,400 |
| Share of general office | 23,500 | 23,500 | 47,000 | 94,000 |
| Share of purchasing | 37,900 | 22,740 | 15,160 | 75,800 |
| Total expenses | 330,900 | 170,790 | 510,310 | 1,012,000 |
| **Net income** | **$129,100** | **$129,210** | **$129,690** | **$ 388,000** |

## Summary

**C1**  **Explain departmentalization and the role of departmental accounting.** Companies are divided into departments when they are too large to be effectively managed as a single unit. Operating departments carry out an organization's main functions. Service departments support the activities of operating departments. Departmental accounting systems provide information for evaluating departmental performance.

**C2**  **Distinguish between direct and indirect expenses.** Direct expenses are traced to a specific department and are incurred for the sole benefit of that department. Indirect expenses benefit more than one department. Indirect expenses are allocated to departments when computing departmental net income.

**C3**  **Identify bases for allocating indirect expenses to departments.** Ideally, we allocate indirect expenses by using a cause-effect relation for the allocation base. When a cause-effect relation is not identifiable, each indirect expense is allocated on a basis reflecting the relative benefit received by each department.

**C4**  **Explain controllable costs and responsibility accounting.** A controllable cost is one that is influenced by a specific management level. The total expenses of operating a department often include some items a department manager does not control. Responsibility accounting systems provide information for evaluating the performance of department managers. A responsibility accounting system's performance reports for evaluating department managers should include only the expenses (and revenues) that each manager controls.

**C5**  **Describe allocation of joint costs across products.** A joint cost refers to costs incurred to produce or purchase two or more products at the same time. When income statements are prepared, joint costs are usually allocated to the resulting joint products using either a physical or value basis.

**A1**  **Analyze investment centers using return on total assets.** A measure often used to evaluate an investment center manager is the *investment center return on total assets,* also called *return on investment.* This measure is computed as the center's net income divided by the center's average total assets.

**P1**  **Assign overhead costs using two-stage cost allocation.** In the traditional two-stage cost allocation procedure, service department costs are first assigned to operating departments.

Then, in the second stage, a predetermined overhead allocation rate is computed for each operating department and is used to assign overhead to output.

**P2**  **Assign overhead costs using activity-based costing.** In activity-based costing, the costs of related activities are collected and then pooled in some logical manner into activity cost pools. After all activity costs have been accumulated in an activity cost pool account, users of the activity, termed *cost objects,* are assigned a portion of the total activity cost using a cost driver (allocation base).

**P3**  **Prepare departmental income statements.** Each profit center (department) is assigned its expenses to yield its own income statement. These costs include its direct expenses and its share of indirect expenses. The departmental income statement lists its revenues and costs of goods sold to determine gross profit. Its operating expenses (direct expenses and its indirect expenses allocated to the department) are deducted from gross profit to yield departmental net income.

**P4**  **Prepare departmental contribution reports.** The departmental contribution report is similar to the departmental income statement in terms of computing the gross profit for each department. Then the direct operating expenses for each department are deducted from gross profit to determine the contribution generated by each department. Indirect operating expenses are deducted *in total* from the company's combined contribution.

## Guidance Answers to **Decision Maker** and **Decision Ethics**

**Director of Operations**  You should collect details on overhead items and review them to see whether direct labor does indeed drive these costs. If it does not, overhead might be improperly assigned to departments. The situation also provides an opportunity to consider other overhead allocation bases, including the use of activity-based costing.

**Accounting Officer**  You should not author a report that you disagree with. You are responsible for ascertaining all the facts of ABC (implementation procedures, advantages and disadvantages, and costs). You should then approach your supervisor with these facts and suggest that you would like to modify the report to request, for example, a pilot implementation. The pilot test will allow you to further assess the suitability of ABC. Your suggestion might be rejected, at which time you may wish to speak with a more senior-level manager.

**Center Manager**  We must first realize that the two investment opportunities are not comparable on the basis of absolute dollars of income or on assets. For instance, the second investment provides a higher income in absolute dollars but requires a higher investment. Accordingly, we need to compute return on total assets for each alternative: (1) $50,000 ÷ $250,000 = 20%, and (2) $175,000 ÷ $1 million = 17.5%. Alternative 1 has the higher return and is preferred over alternative 2. Do you pursue one, both, or neither? Because alternative 1's return is higher than the center's usual return of 19%, it should be pursued, assuming its risks are acceptable. Also, since alternative 1 requires a small investment, top management is likely to be more agreeable to pursuing it. Alternative 2's return is lower than the usual 19% and is not likely to be acceptable.

## Guidance Answers to **Quick Checks**

**1.** Cost drivers are the factors that have a cause-effect relation with costs (or activities that pertain to costs).

**2.** *d*

**3.** A departmental accounting system provides information used to evaluate the performance of *departments.* A responsibility accounting system provides information used to evaluate the performance of *department managers.*

**4.** *d*

**5.** A cost center, such as a service department, incurs costs without directly generating revenues. A profit center, such as a product division, incurs costs but also generates revenues.

**6.** *b*

**7.** *d*

**8.** (1) Assign the direct expenses to each department. (2) Allocate indirect expenses to all departments. (3) Allocate the service department expenses to the operating departments.

**9.** *b*

**10.** No, because many expenses that enter into these calculations are beyond the manager's control, and managers should not be evaluated using costs they do not control.

**11.** *c*

**12.** *b*; $180,000 \times ([32,000 \times \$9]/[96,000 \times \$3 + 64,000 \times \$6 + 32,000 \times \$9]) = \underline{\$54,000}$.

## Key Terms

Key Terms are available at the book's Website for learning and testing in an online Flashcard Format.

**Activity-based costing (ABC)** (p. 700)
**Activity cost pool** (p. 700)
**Controllable costs** (p. 711)
**Cost center** (p. 704)
**Cost driver** (p. 700)
**Departmental accounting system** (p. 703)
**Departmental contribution to overhead** (p. 710)

**Direct expenses** (p. 705)
**Indirect expenses** (p. 705)
**Investment center** (p. 715)
**Investment center return on total assets** (p. 715)
**Joint cost** (p. 714)
**Profit center** (p. 704)

**Responsibility accounting budget** (p. 712)
**Responsibility accounting performance report** (p. 712)
**Responsibility accounting system** (p. 704)
**Uncontrollable costs** (p. 712)

## Personal Interactive Quiz

Personal Interactive Quizzes A and B are available at the book's Website to reinforce and assess your learning.

## Discussion Questions

**1.** Why are many companies divided into departments?

**2.** Complete the following for a traditional two-stage allocation system: In the first stage, service department costs are assigned to _____ departments. In the second stage, a predetermined overhead rate is computed for each operating department and used to assign overhead to _____.

**3.** What is the difference between operating departments and service departments?

**4.** What is activity-based costing? What is its goal?

**5.** Identify at least four common cost pools for activity-based costing in most organizations.

**6.** In activity-based costing, costs in a cost pool are allocated to _____ using predetermined overhead rates.

**7.** What company circumstances especially encourage use of activity-based costing?

**8.** What are two main goals in managerial accounting for reporting on and analyzing departments?

**9.** Is it possible to evaluate a cost center's profitability? Explain.

**10.** What is the difference between direct and indirect expenses?

**11.** Suggest a reasonable basis for allocating each of the following indirect expenses to departments: (a) salary of a supervisor who manages several departments, (b) rent, (c) heat, (d) electricity for lighting, (e) janitorial services, (f) advertising, (g) expired insurance on equipment, and (h) property taxes on equipment.

**12.** How is a department's contribution to overhead measured?

**13.** What are controllable costs?

**14.** Controllable and uncontrollable costs must be identified with a particular _____ and a definite _____ period.

**15.** Why should managers be closely involved in preparing their responsibility accounting budgets?

**16.** In responsibility accounting, who receives timely cost reports and specific cost information? Explain.

**17.** What is a joint cost? How are joint costs usually allocated among the products produced from them?

**18.** Give two examples of products with joint costs.

**19.** **Krispy Kreme** receives orders for donuts from different types of stores, such as grocery stores and convenience stores. Why is it useful to (a) collect information for each particular store category and (b) treat each category as a profit center?

**20.** **Harley-Davidson** delivers its products to locations around the world. List three controllable and three uncontrollable costs for its delivery department.

*Red numbers denote Discussion Questions that involve decision-making.*

*Homework Manager* repeats all numerical Quick Studies on the book's Website with new numbers.

## QUICK STUDY

In each blank next to the following terms, place the identifying letter of its best description.

**1.** _____ Cost center

**2.** _____ Investment center

**3.** _____ Departmental accounting system

**4.** _____ Operating department

**5.** _____ Profit center

**6.** _____ Responsibility accounting system

**7.** _____ Service department

**A.** Incurs costs without directly yielding revenues.

**B.** Provides information used to evaluate the performance of a department manager.

**C.** Holds manager responsible for revenues, costs, and investments.

**D.** Engages directly in manufacturing or in making sales directly to customers.

**E.** Does not directly manufacture products but contributes to profitability of the entire company.

**F.** Incurs costs and also generates revenues.

**G.** Provides information used to evaluate the performance of a department.

**QS 17-1**
Allocation and measurement terms

C1   C2   C3   C4   A1

---

For each of the following types of indirect expenses and service department expenses, identify one allocation basis that could be used to distribute it to the departments indicated.

**1.** Computer service expenses of production scheduling for operating departments.

**2.** Electric utility expenses of all departments.

**3.** Maintenance department expenses of the operating departments.

**4.** General office department expenses of the operating departments.

**QS 17-2**
Basis for cost allocation

C3

---

The following is taken from Rankin Co.'s internal records of its factory with two operating departments. The cost driver for indirect labor and supplies is direct labor costs, and the cost driver for the remaining overhead items is number of hours of machine use. Compute the total amount of overhead cost allocated to Operating Department 1 using activity-based costing.

**QS 17-3**
Activity-based costing and overhead cost allocation

P2

| | Direct Labor | Hours of Machine Use |
|---|---|---|
| Operating department 1 ........ | $10,400 | 2,200 |
| Operating department 2 ........ | 9,600 | 3,000 |
| Totals .................... | $20,000 | 5,200 |
| **Factory overhead costs** | | |
| Rent and utilities .................... | $ 7,100 | |
| Indirect labor ...................... | 3,700 | |
| General office expense ............... | 2,700 | |
| Depreciation—Equipment ............. | 4,500 | |
| Supplies ........................... | 300 | |
| Total factory overhead ............... | $18,300 | |

**Check** Dept. 1 allocation, $8,130

---

A company purchases a 12,000 square foot commercial building for $322,000 and spends an additional $50,000 to divide the space into two separate rental units and prepare it for rent. Unit A, which has the desirable location on the corner and contains 4,000 square feet, will be rented for $1.00 per square foot. Unit B contains 8,000 square feet and will be rented for $0.75 per square foot. How much of the joint cost should be assigned to Unit B using the value basis of allocation?

**QS 17-4**
Joint cost allocation

C5

---

Use the information in the following table to compute each department's contribution to overhead (both in dollars and as a percent). Which department contributes the highest dollar amount to total overhead? Which contributes the highest percent (as a percent of sales)?

**QS 17-5**
Departmental contribution to overhead  P4

|                              | Dept. A | Dept. B | Dept. C |
|------------------------------|---------|---------|---------|
| Sales                        | $53,000 | $170,000 | $84,000 |
| Cost of goods sold           | 34,185  | 103,700 | 49,560  |
| Gross profit                 | 18,815  | 66,300  | 34,440  |
| Total direct expenses        | 6,360   | 37,060  | 8,736   |
| Contribution to overhead     | $       | $       | $       |
| Contribution percent         | %       | %       | %       |

**QS 17-6**

Investment center analysis

A1

Compute return on assets for each of these Reebok shoe divisions (each is an investment center). Comment on the relative performance of each investment center.

| Investment Center | Net Income | Average Assets | Return on Assets |
|-------------------|------------|----------------|------------------|
| Basketball        | $4,000,000 | $20,000,000    | _____       |
| Soccer            | 1,500,000  | 15,000,000     | _____       |
| Cross-trainer     | 750,000    | 10,000,000     | _____       |

*Homework Manager repeats all numerical Exercises on the book's Website with new numbers.*

# EXERCISES

**Exercise 17-1**

Departmental expense allocations

P1   C3

Won Han Co. has four departments: materials, personnel, manufacturing, and packaging. In a recent month, the four departments incurred three shared indirect expenses. The amounts of these indirect expenses and the bases used to allocate them follow:

| Indirect Expense | Cost | Allocation Base |
|------------------|------|-----------------|
| Supervision      | $ 75,000 | Number of employees |
| Utilities        | 60,000 | Square feet occupied |
| Insurance        | 16,500 | Value of assets in use |
| Total            | $151,500 |                 |

Departmental data for the company's recent reporting period follow:

| Department    | Employees | Square Feet | Asset Values |
|---------------|-----------|-------------|--------------|
| Materials     | 18        | 27,000      | $ 6,000      |
| Personnel     | 6         | 4,500       | 1,200        |
| Manufacturing | 66        | 45,000      | 37,800       |
| Packaging     | 30        | 13,500      | 15,000       |
| Total         | 120       | 90,000      | $60,000      |

**Check**   (2) $30,900 assigned to materials

(1) Use this information to allocate each of the three indirect expenses across the four departments.
(2) Prepare a summary table that reports the indirect expenses assigned to each of the four departments.

**Exercise 17-2**

Activity-based costing of overhead

P2

Pane Company manufactures two types of glass shelving, rounded edge and squared edge, on the same production line. For the current period, the company reports the following data:

|                                        | Rounded Edge | Squared Edge | Total    |
|----------------------------------------|--------------|--------------|----------|
| Direct materials                       | $ 9,500      | $21,600      | $ 31,100 |
| Direct labor                           | 6,100        | 11,900       | 18,000   |
| Overhead (300% of direct labor cost)   | 18,300       | 35,700       | 54,000   |
| Total cost                             | $33,900      | $69,200      | $103,100 |
| Quantity produced                      | 10,500 ft.   | 14,100 ft.   |          |
| Average cost per ft.                   | $ 3.23       | $ 4.91       |          |

Pane's controller wishes to apply activity-based costing (ABC) to the $54,000 of overhead costs incurred by the two product lines to see whether cost per foot would change significantly from that recorded above. She has collected the following information:

| Overhead Cost Category (Activity Cost Pool) | Cost |
|---|---|
| Supervision | $ 2,160 |
| Depreciation of machinery | 28,840 |
| Assembly line preparation | 23,000 |
| Total overhead | $54,000 |

She has also collected the following information about the cost drivers for each category (cost pool) and the amount of each driver used by the two product lines:

| Overhead Cost Category (Activity Cost Pool) | Driver | Usage | | |
|---|---|---|---|---|
| | | Rounded Edge | Squared Edge | Total |
| Supervision | Direct labor cost($) | $6,100 | $11,900 | $18,000 |
| Depreciation of machinery | Machine hours | 300 hours | 700 hours | 1,000 hours |
| Assembly line preparation | Setups (number) | 31 times | 94 times | 125 times |

Use this information to (1) assign these three overhead cost pools to each of the two products using ABC, (2) determine average cost per foot for each of the two products using ABC, and (3) compare the average cost per foot under ABC with the average cost per foot under the current method for each product. For part 3, explain why a difference between the two cost allocation methods exists.

**Check**  (2) Rounded edge, $2.92; Squared edge, $5.14

---

Auto Market pays $128,000 rent each year for its two-story building. The space in this building is occupied by five departments as specified here:

| | |
|---|---|
| Paint department | 1,390 square feet of first-floor space |
| Engine department | 3,410 square feet of first-floor space |
| Window department | 2,040 square feet of second-floor space |
| Electrical department | 960 square feet of second-floor space |
| Accessory department | 1,800 square feet of second-floor space |

**Exercise 17-3**
Rent expense allocated to departments

P1  C3

The company allocates 65% of total rent expense to the first floor and 35% to the second floor and then allocates rent expense for each floor to the departments occupying that floor on the basis of space occupied. Determine the rent expense to be allocated to each department. (Round percents to the nearest one-tenth and dollar amounts to the nearest whole dollar.)

**Check**  Paint dept., $24,128

---

Overroad Cycle Shop has two service departments (advertising and administration) and two operating departments (cycles and clothing). During 2005, the departments had the following direct expenses and occupied the following amount of floor space:

**Exercise 17-4**
Departmental expense allocation spreadsheet

C3  P1

| Department | Direct Expenses | Square Feet |
|---|---|---|
| Advertising | $ 16,000 | 1,088 |
| Administrative | 18,500 | 1,152 |
| Cycles | 101,600 | 6,336 |
| Clothing | 11,900 | 4,224 |

The advertising department developed and distributed 100 advertisements during the year. Of these, 76 promoted cycles and 24 promoted clothing. The store sold $300,000 of merchandise during the year. Of this amount, $225,000 is from the cycles department, and $75,000 is from the clothing department. The utilities expense of $64,000 is an indirect expense to all departments. Prepare a departmental expense allocation spreadsheet for Overroad Cycle Shop. The spreadsheet should assign

The building has 4,000 square feet on each floor. In prior periods, the accounting manager merely divided the $64,000 occupancy cost by 8,000 square feet to find an average cost of $8 per square foot and then charged each department a building occupancy cost equal to this rate times the number of square feet that it occupied.

Laura Diaz manages a first-floor department that occupies 1,000 square feet, and Lauren Wright manages a second-floor department that occupies 1,800 square feet of floor space. In discussing the departmental reports, they question whether using the same rate per square foot for all departments makes sense because the first-floor space is more valuable. The two managers also check a recent real estate study of average local rental costs for similar space that shows first-floor space worth $30 per square foot and second-floor space worth $20 per square foot (excluding costs for heating, lighting, and maintenance).

**Required**

**1.** Allocate all occupancy costs to the Diaz and Wright departments using the current allocation method.

**Check**   (2) Total occupancy cost to
Diaz, $9,330

**2.** Allocate the depreciation, interest, and taxes occupancy costs to the Diaz and Wright departments in proportion to the relative market values of the floor space. Allocate the heating, lighting, and maintenance costs to the Diaz and Wright departments in proportion to the square feet occupied (ignoring floor space market values).

*Analysis Component*

**3.** Which allocation method would you prefer if you were a manager of a second-floor department? Explain.

---

**Problem 17-2A**

Activity-based costing

P2

We Care is an outpatient surgical clinic that was profitable for many years, but Medicare has cut its reimbursements by as much as 50%. As a result, the clinic wants to better understand its costs. It decides to prepare an activity-based cost analysis, including an estimate of the average cost of both general surgery and orthopedic surgery. The clinic's three cost centers and their cost drivers follow:

| Cost Center | Cost | Cost Driver | Driver Quantity |
|---|---|---|---|
| Professional salaries .............. | $1,500,000 | Professional hours ......... | 10,000 |
| Patient services and supplies ....... | 25,000 | Number of patients ........ | 500 |
| Building cost ................... | 150,000 | Square feet .............. | 1,500 |

The two main surgical units and their related data follow:

| Service | Hours | Square Feet* | Patients |
|---|---|---|---|
| General surgery .......... | 2,500 | 500 | 400 |
| Orthopedic surgery ....... | 7,500 | 1,000 | 100 |

\* Orthopedic surgery requires more space for patients, supplies, and equipment.

**Required**

**1.** Compute the cost per cost driver for each of the three cost centers.

**Check**   (2) Average cost of general
(orthopedic) surgery, $1,113 ($12,300)
per patient

**2.** Use the results from part 1 to allocate costs from each of the three cost centers to both the general surgery and the orthopedic surgery units. Compute total cost and average cost per patient for both the general surgery and the orthopedic surgery units.

*Analysis Component*

**3.** Without providing computations, would the average cost of general surgery be higher or lower if all center costs were allocated based on the number of patients? Explain.

Time-To-See Co. began operations in January 2005 with two operating (selling) departments and one service (office) department. Its departmental income statements follow:

| TIME-TO-SEE Co. Departmental Income Statements For Year Ended December 31, 2005 | | | |
|---|---|---|---|
| | **Clock** | **Mirror** | **Combined** |
| Sales .................................. | $122,500 | $52,500 | $175,000 |
| Cost of goods sold ..................... | 60,000 | 32,000 | 92,000 |
| Gross profit .......................... | 62,500 | 20,500 | 83,000 |
| Direct expenses | | | |
| Sales salaries ......................... | 20,000 | 7,000 | 27,000 |
| Advertising ......................... | 1,200 | 500 | 1,700 |
| Store supplies used ................... | 900 | 400 | 1,300 |
| Depreciation—Equipment ............... | 1,500 | 300 | 1,800 |
| Total direct expenses ................. | 23,600 | 8,200 | 31,800 |
| Allocated expenses | | | |
| Rent expense ...................... | 7,020 | 3,780 | 10,800 |
| Utilities expense ..................... | 2,600 | 1,400 | 4,000 |
| Share of office department expenses ....... | 10,500 | 4,500 | 15,000 |
| Total allocated expenses ............... | 20,120 | 9,680 | 29,800 |
| Total expenses ....................... | 43,720 | 17,880 | 61,600 |
| Net income ......................... | $ 18,780 | $ 2,620 | $ 21,400 |

Time-To-See plans to open a third department in January 2006 that will sell paintings. Management predicts that the new department will generate $35,000 in sales with a 55% gross profit margin and will require the following direct expenses: sales salaries, $8,000; advertising, $800; store supplies, $500; and equipment depreciation, $200. It will fit the new department into the current rented space by taking some square footage from the other two departments. When opened the new painting department will fill one-fifth of the space presently used by the clock department and one-sixth used by the mirror department. Management does not predict any increase in utilities costs, which are allocated to the departments in proportion to occupied space (or rent expense). The company allocates office department expenses to the operating departments in proportion to their sales. It expects the painting department to increase total office department expenses by $7,000. Since the painting department will bring new customers into the store, management expects sales in both the clock and mirror departments to increase by 7%. No changes for those departments' gross profit percents or their direct expenses are expected except for store supplies used, which will increase in proportion to sales.

**Required**

Prepare departmental income statements that show the company's predicted results of operations for calendar year 2006 for the three operating (selling) departments and their combined totals. (Round percents to the nearest one-tenth and dollar amounts to the nearest whole dollar.)

**Problem 17-3A**

Departmental income statements; forecasts

P3

mhhe.com/wild

**Check**   2006 forecasted combined net income (sales), $29,869 ($222,250)

Becky Hofer, the plant manager of Travel Far's Indiana plant, is responsible for all of that plant's costs other than her own salary. The plant has two operating departments and one service department. The camper and trailer operating departments manufacture different products and have their own managers. The office department, which Hofer also manages, provides services equally to the two operating departments. A budget is prepared for each operating department and the office department. The company's responsibility accounting system must assemble information to present budgeted and actual costs in performance reports for each operating department manager and the plant manager. Each performance report includes only those costs that a particular operating department manager can control: raw materials, wages, supplies used, and equipment depreciation. The plant manager is responsible for the department managers' salaries, utilities, building rent, office salaries other than her own, and other office costs plus all costs controlled by the two operating department managers. The annual

**Problem 17-4A**

Responsibility accounting performance reports; controllable and budgeted costs

C4   P4

departmental budgets and actual costs for the two operating departments follow:

| | Budget | | | Actual | | |
|---|---|---|---|---|---|---|
| | Campers | Trailers | Combined | Campers | Trailers | Combined |
| Raw materials ......... | $160,000 | $250,000 | $ 410,000 | $159,400 | $246,500 | $ 405,900 |
| Employee wages ....... | 99,000 | 191,000 | 290,000 | 102,300 | 193,700 | 296,000 |
| Dept. manager salary .... | 40,000 | 44,000 | 84,000 | 41,000 | 47,000 | 88,000 |
| Supplies used .......... | 34,000 | 83,000 | 117,000 | 31,900 | 84,600 | 116,500 |
| Depreciation—Equip. ..... | 58,000 | 110,000 | 168,000 | 58,000 | 110,000 | 168,000 |
| Utilities .............. | 2,800 | 4,200 | 7,000 | 2,700 | 3,800 | 6,500 |
| Building rent .......... | 5,000 | 8,000 | 13,000 | 4,800 | 7,200 | 12,000 |
| Office department costs .. | 56,000 | 56,000 | 112,000 | 54,450 | 54,450 | 108,900 |
| Totals .............. | $454,800 | $746,200 | $1,201,000 | $454,550 | $747,250 | $1,201,800 |

The office department's annual budget and its actual costs follow:

| | Budget | Actual |
|---|---|---|
| Plant manager salary ....... | $ 60,000 | $ 62,000 |
| Other office salaries ........ | 30,000 | 27,700 |
| Other office costs ......... | 22,000 | 19,200 |
| Totals ................. | $112,000 | $108,900 |

### Required

**1.** Prepare responsibility accounting performance reports like those in Exhibit 17.20 that list costs controlled by the following:

**Check**   (a) $600 total over budget

**a.** Manager of the camper department.

**b.** Manager of the trailer department.

(c) Indiana plant controllable costs, $1,200 total under budget

**c.** Manager of the Indiana plant.

In each report, include the budgeted and actual costs and show the amount that each actual cost is over or under the budgeted amount.

### Analysis Component

**2.** Did the plant manager or the operating department managers better manage costs? Explain.

---

**Problem 17-5A**
Allocation of joint costs

C5

Bloom Orchards produced a good crop of peaches this year. After preparing the following income statement, Bloom believes it should have given its No. 3 peaches to charity and saved its efforts.

| BLOOM ORCHARDS Income Statement For Year Ended December 31, 2005 | | | | |
|---|---|---|---|---|
| | No. 1 | No. 2 | No. 3 | Combined |
| Sales (by grade) | | | | |
| No. 1: 300,000 lbs. @ $1.50/lb ............. | $450,000 | | | |
| No. 2: 300,000 lbs. @ $1.00/lb ............. | | $300,000 | | |
| No. 3: 750,000 lbs. @ $0.20/lb ............. | | | $ 150,000 | |
| Total sales ............................ | | | | $900,000 |
| Costs | | | | |
| Tree pruning and care @ $0.20/lb .......... | 60,000 | 60,000 | 150,000 | 270,000 |
| Picking, sorting, and grading @ $0.12/lb ....... | 36,000 | 36,000 | 90,000 | 162,000 |
| Delivery costs @ $0.03/lb ................ | 9,000 | 9,000 | 22,500 | 40,500 |
| Total costs ......................... | 105,000 | 105,000 | 262,500 | 472,500 |
| Net income (loss) ...................... | $345,000 | $195,000 | $(112,500) | $427,500 |

In preparing this statement, Bloom allocated joint costs among the grades on a physical basis as an equal amount per pound. Bloom's delivery cost records show that $30,000 of the $40,500 relates to crating the No. 1 and No. 2 peaches and hauling them to the buyer. The remaining $10,500 of delivery costs is for crating the No. 3 peaches and hauling them to the cannery.

### Required

1. Prepare reports showing cost allocations on a sales value basis to the three grades of peaches. Separate the delivery costs into the amounts directly identifiable with each grade. Then allocate any shared delivery costs on the basis of the relative sales value of each grade. (Round percents to the nearest one-tenth and dollar amounts to the nearest whole dollar.)

2. Using your answers to part 1, prepare an income statement using the joint costs allocated on a sales value basis.

### Analysis Component

3. Do you think delivery costs fit the definition of a joint cost? Explain.

**Check** (1) $89,910 tree pruning and care costs allocated to No. 2

(2) Net income from No. 1 & No. 2 peaches, $216,000 & $144,144

---

Dixon's has several departments that occupy all floors of a two-story building that includes a basement floor. Dixon rented this building under a long-term lease negotiated when rental rates were low. The departmental accounting system has a single account, Building Occupancy Cost, in its ledger. The types and amounts of occupancy costs recorded in this account for the current period follow:

| | |
|---|---|
| Building rent . . . . . . . . . . . . . . | $300,000 |
| Lighting expense . . . . . . . . . . . | 24,000 |
| Cleaning expense . . . . . . . . . . | 16,000 |
| Total occupancy cost . . . . . . . | $340,000 |

The building has 7,500 square feet on each of the upper two floors but only 5,000 square feet in the basement. In prior periods, the accounting manager merely divided the $340,000 occupancy cost by 20,000 square feet to find an average cost of $17 per square foot and then charged each department a building occupancy cost equal to this rate times the number of square feet that it occupies.

Alex Ferrero manages a department that occupies 2,000 square feet of basement floor space. In discussing the departmental reports with other managers, he questions whether using the same rate per square foot for all departments makes sense because different floor space has different values. Ferrero checked a recent real estate report of average local rental costs for similar space that shows first-floor space worth $40 per square foot, second-floor space worth $20 per square foot, and basement space worth $10 per square foot (excluding costs for lighting and cleaning).

### Required

1. Allocate all occupancy costs to Ferrero's department using the current allocation method.

2. Allocate the building rent cost to Ferrero's department in proportion to the relative market value of the floor space. Allocate to Ferrero's department the lighting and heating costs in proportion to the square feet occupied (ignoring floor space market values).

### Analysis Component

3. Which allocation method would you prefer if you were a manager of a basement department?

## PROBLEM SET B

### Problem 17-1B
Allocation of building occupancy costs to departments

C3 P1

**Check** (2) Total costs allocated to Ferrero, $16,000

---

Prairie Landscaping has enjoyed profits for many years, but new competition has cut service revenue by as much as 30%. As a result, the company wants to better understand its costs. It decides to prepare an activity-based cost analysis, including an estimate of the average cost of both general landscaping services and custom design landscaping services. The company's three cost centers and their cost drivers follow:

### Problem 17-2B
Activity-based costing

P2

| Cost Center | Cost | Cost Driver | Driver Quantity |
|---|---|---|---|
| Professional salaries . . . . . . . | $500,000 | Professional hours . . . . . . . . . . | 10,000 |
| Customer supplies . . . . . . . . | 125,000 | Number of customers . . . . . . . | 500 |
| Building cost . . . . . . . . . . . . | 150,000 | Square feet . . . . . . . . . . . . . . | 1,500 |

The two main landscaping units and their related data follow:

| Service | Hours | Square Feet* | Customers |
|---|---|---|---|
| General landscaping . . . . . . . . . . . . | 2,500 | 500 | 400 |
| Custom design landscaping . . . . . . . | 7,500 | 1,000 | 100 |

\* Custom design landscaping requires more space for equipment, supplies, and planning.

### Required

**Check**  (2) Average cost of general (custom) landscaping, $687.50 ($5,000) per customer

**1.** Compute the cost per cost driver for each of the three cost centers.

**2.** Use the results from part 1 to allocate costs from each of the three cost centers to both the general landscaping and the custom design landscaping units. Compute total cost and average cost per customer for both the general landscaping and the custom design landscaping units.

### Analysis Component

**3.** Without providing computations, would the average cost of general landscaping be higher or lower if all center costs were allocated based on the number of customers? Explain.

**Problem 17-3B**
Departmental income statements; forecasts

P3

Hollywood Entertainment began operations in January 2005 with two operating (selling) departments and one service (office) department. Its departmental income statements follow:

| **HOLLYWOOD ENTERTAINMENT**<br>**Departmental Income Statements**<br>**For Year Ended December 31, 2005** | | | |
|---|---|---|---|
| | **Movies** | **Video Games** | **Combined** |
| Sales . . . . . . . . . . . . . . . . . . . . . . . . . . . . | $540,000 | $180,000 | $720,000 |
| Cost of goods sold . . . . . . . . . . . . . . . . . . . . | 378,000 | 138,600 | 516,600 |
| Gross profit . . . . . . . . . . . . . . . . . . . . . . . | 162,000 | 41,400 | 203,400 |
| Direct expenses | | | |
| Sales salaries . . . . . . . . . . . . . . . . . . . . . | 35,000 | 14,000 | 49,000 |
| Advertising . . . . . . . . . . . . . . . . . . . . . | 10,500 | 5,500 | 16,000 |
| Store supplies used . . . . . . . . . . . . . . . . | 3,300 | 700 | 4,000 |
| Depreciation—Equipment . . . . . . . . . . . . . . | 4,200 | 2,800 | 7,000 |
| Total direct expenses . . . . . . . . . . . . . . . . | 53,000 | 23,000 | 76,000 |
| Allocated expenses | | | |
| Rent expense . . . . . . . . . . . . . . . . . . . . . | 29,520 | 6,480 | 36,000 |
| Utilities expense . . . . . . . . . . . . . . . . . . | 4,100 | 900 | 5,000 |
| Share of office department expenses . . . . . . . | 39,000 | 14,000 | 53,000 |
| Total allocated expenses . . . . . . . . . . . . . . | 72,620 | 21,380 | 94,000 |
| Total expenses . . . . . . . . . . . . . . . . . . . . . | 125,620 | 44,380 | 170,000 |
| Net income (loss) . . . . . . . . . . . . . . . . . . . . | $ 36,380 | $ (2,980) | $ 33,400 |

Hollywood plans to open a third department in January 2006 that will sell compact discs. Management predicts that the new department will generate $250,000 in sales with a 35% gross profit margin and will require the following direct expenses: sales salaries, $18,000; advertising, $10,000; store supplies, $1,500; and equipment depreciation, $1,000. The company will fit the new department into the current rented space by taking some square footage from the other two departments. When opened, the new compact disc department will fill one-fourth of the space presently used by the movie department and one-third of the space used by the video game department. Management does not predict any increase in utilities costs, which are allocated to the departments in proportion to occupied space (or rent expense). The company allocates office department expenses to the operating departments in proportion to their sales. It expects the compact disc department to increase total office department expenses by $8,000. Since the compact disc department will bring new customers into the store, management expects sales in both the movie and video game departments to increase by 10%.

No changes for those departments' gross profit percents or for their direct expenses are expected, except for store supplies used, which will increase in proportion to sales.

**Required**

Prepare departmental income statements that show the company's predicted results of operations for calendar year 2006 for the three operating (selling) departments and their combined totals. (Round percents to the nearest one-tenth and dollar amounts to the nearest whole dollar.)

**Check** 2006 forecasted movies net income (sales), $64,885 ($594,000)

Ann Braun, the plant manager of SOS Co.'s Chicago plant, is responsible for all of that plant's costs other than her own salary. The plant has two operating departments and one service department. The refrigerator and dishwasher operating departments manufacture different products and have their own managers. The office department, which Braun also manages, provides services equally to the two operating departments. A monthly budget is prepared for each operating department and the office department. The company's responsibility accounting system must assemble information to present budgeted and actual costs in performance reports for each operating department manager and the plant manager. Each performance report includes only those costs that a particular operating department manager can control: raw materials, wages, supplies used, and equipment depreciation. The plant manager is responsible for the department managers' salaries, utilities, building rent, office salaries other than her own, and other office costs plus all costs controlled by the two operating department managers. The April departmental budgets and actual costs for the two operating departments follow:

**Problem 17-4B**
Responsibility accounting performance reports; controllable and budgeted costs

C4  P4

| | **Budget** | | | **Actual** | | |
|---|---|---|---|---|---|---|
| | **Refrigerators** | **Dishwashers** | **Combined** | **Refrigerators** | **Dishwashers** | **Combined** |
| Raw materials . . . . . . . . . . . . . . | $400,000 | $200,000 | $ 600,000 | $375,000 | $200,000 | $ 575,000 |
| Employee wages . . . . . . . . . . . . | 172,000 | 80,000 | 252,000 | 174,700 | 76,800 | 251,500 |
| Dept. manager salary . . . . . . . . . . | 55,000 | 49,000 | 104,000 | 55,000 | 46,500 | 101,500 |
| Supplies used . . . . . . . . . . . . . . | 15,000 | 9,000 | 24,000 | 14,000 | 10,000 | 24,000 |
| Depreciation—Equip. . . . . . . . . . | 53,000 | 37,000 | 90,000 | 53,000 | 37,000 | 90,000 |
| Utilities . . . . . . . . . . . . . . . . . . . | 30,000 | 18,000 | 48,000 | 34,500 | 20,700 | 55,200 |
| Building rent . . . . . . . . . . . . . . . | 63,000 | 17,000 | 80,000 | 61,000 | 15,000 | 76,000 |
| Office department costs . . . . . . . | 70,500 | 70,500 | 141,000 | 75,000 | 75,000 | 150,000 |
| Totals . . . . . . . . . . . . . . . . . . . . | $858,500 | $480,500 | $1,339,000 | $842,200 | $481,000 | $1,323,200 |

The office department's budget and its actual costs for April follow:

| | **Budget** | **Actual** |
|---|---|---|
| Plant manager salary . . . . . . . | $ 80,000 | $ 85,000 |
| Other office salaries . . . . . . . . | 40,000 | 35,200 |
| Other office costs . . . . . . . . . | 21,000 | 29,800 |
| Totals . . . . . . . . . . . . . . . . . | $141,000 | $150,000 |

**Required**

**1.** Prepare responsibility accounting performance reports like those in Exhibit 17.20 that list costs controlled by the following:

   **a.** Manager of the refrigerator department.

   **b.** Manager of the dishwasher department.

   **c.** Manager of the Chicago plant.

In each report, include the budgeted and actual costs for the month and show the amount by which each actual cost is over or under the budgeted amount.

**Check** (a) $23,300 total under budget

(c) Chicago plant controllable costs, $20,800 total under budget

*Analysis Component*

**2.** Did the plant manager or the operating department managers better manage costs? Explain.

**Problem 17-5B**
Allocation of joint costs

C5

Sarah and Stew Salsa own and operate a tomato grove. After preparing the following income statement, Sarah believes they should have offered the No. 3 tomatoes to the public for free and saved themselves time and money.

| SARAH AND STEW SALSA<br>Income Statement<br>For Year Ended December 31, 2005 | | | | |
| --- | --- | --- | --- | --- |
| | No. 1 | No. 2 | No. 3 | Combined |
| Sales (by grade) | | | | |
| No. 1: 400,000 lbs. @ $1.50/lb ....................... | $600,000 | | | |
| No. 2: 300,000 lbs. @ $1.00/lb ....................... | | $300,000 | | |
| No. 3: 100,000 lbs. @ $0.30/lb ....................... | | | $ 30,000 | |
| Total sales ....................................... | | | | $930,000 |
| Costs | | | | |
| Land preparation, seeding, and cultivating @ $0.50/lb ....... | 200,000 | 150,000 | 50,000 | 400,000 |
| Harvesting, sorting, and grading @ $0.02/lb .............. | 8,000 | 6,000 | 2,000 | 16,000 |
| Delivery costs @ $0.01/lb .......................... | 4,000 | 3,000 | 1,000 | 8,000 |
| Total costs ...................................... | 212,000 | 159,000 | 53,000 | 424,000 |
| Net income (loss) ................................. | $388,000 | $141,000 | $(23,000) | $506,000 |

In preparing this statement, Sarah and Stew allocated joint costs among the grades on a physical basis as an equal amount per pound. Also, their delivery cost records show that $7,000 of the $8,000 relates to crating the No. 1 and No. 2 tomatoes and hauling them to the buyer. The remaining $1,000 of delivery costs is for crating the No. 3 tomatoes and hauling them to the cannery.

**Required**

**Check** (1) $512 harvesting, sorting and grading costs allocated to No. 3

1. Prepare reports showing cost allocations on a sales value basis to the three grades of tomatoes. Separate the delivery costs into the amounts directly identifiable with each grade. Then allocate any shared delivery costs on the basis of the relative sales value of each grade. (Round percents to the nearest one-tenth and dollar amounts to the nearest whole dollar.)

(2) Net income from No. 1 & No. 2 tomatoes, $327,011 & $163,301

2. Using your answers to part 1, prepare an income statement using the joint costs allocated on a sales value basis.

*Analysis Component*

3. Do you think delivery costs fit the definition of a joint cost? Explain.

**PROBLEM SET C**

Problem Set C is available at the book's Website to further reinforce and assess your learning.

---

**BEYOND THE NUMBERS**

**REPORTING IN ACTION**

C4

**BTN 17-1**   A careful review of **Krispy Kreme**'s financial statements in Appendix A offers clues to its growth in revenues. In particular, you should read its note 14.

**Required**

1. Compute the growth (in percent) for Krispy Kreme's revenues using 2001 as the base for 2002 and 2002 as the base for 2003. Do this for each of the three business segments listed in its note and for total revenue.

2. Which business segment in part 1 is growing the fastest for Krispy Kreme?

3. How can Krispy Kreme's managers use this information?

*Roll On*

**4.** Access Krispy Kreme's annual report for a fiscal year ending after February 2, 2003, from its Website [**KrispyKreme.com**] or the SEC's EDGAR database [**www.sec.gov**]. Compute its growth in revenues by business segment and for total revenue for the most recent reporting period(s). Compare results to those from part 1. What growth patterns, if any, do you observe?

---

**BTN 17-2** **Krispy Kreme** and **Tastykake** compete in several markets. The most common competitive markets for these two companies are likely grocery stores and convenience stores.

**COMPARATIVE ANALYSIS**

P3

**Required**

**1.** Design a three-tier responsibility accounting organizational chart assuming that you have available internal information for both companies. Use Exhibit 17.19 as an example. The goal of this assignment is to design a reporting framework for the companies; numbers are not required. Limit your reporting framework to sales activity only.

**2.** Explain why it is important to have similar performance reports when comparing performance within a company (and across different companies). Be specific in your response.

---

**BTN 17-3** Senior Security Co. offers a range of security services for senior citizens. Each type of service is considered within a separate department. Gary Pinkel, the overall manager, is compensated partly on the basis of departmental performance by staying within the quarterly cost budget. He often revises operations to make sure departments stay within budget. Says Pinkel, "I will not go over budget even if it means slightly compromising the level and quality of service. These are minor compromises that don't significantly affect my clients, at least in the short term."

**ETHICS CHALLENGE**

P3

**Required**

**1.** Is there an ethical concern in this situation? If so, which parties are affected? Explain.

**2.** Can Gary Pinkel take action to eliminate or reduce any ethical concerns? Explain.

**3.** What is Senior Security's ethical responsibility in offering professional services?

---

**BTN 17-4** Home Station is a national home improvement chain with more than 100 stores throughout the country. The manager of each store receives a salary plus a bonus equal to a percent of the store's net income for the reporting period. The following net income calculation is on the Denver store manager's performance report for the recent monthly period:

**COMMUNICATING IN PRACTICE**

C4 C5 P3

| | |
|---|---:|
| Sales .................... | $5,000,000 |
| Cost of goods sold ......... | 1,600,000 |
| Wages expense ............. | 1,000,000 |
| Utilities expense ........... | 400,000 |
| Home office expense ........ | 150,000 |
| Net income ............... | $1,850,000 |
| Manager's bonus (0.5%) ...... | $ 9,250 |

In previous periods, the bonus had also been 0.5%, but the performance report had not included any charges for the home office expense, which is now assigned to each store as a percent of its sales.

**Required**

Assume that you are the national office manager. Write a one-half page memorandum to your store managers explaining why home office expense is in the new performance report.

**TAKING IT TO THE NET**

A1

mhhe.com/wild

**BTN 17-5**   This chapter described and used spreadsheets to prepare various managerial reports (see Exhibit 17-12). You can download from Websites various tutorials showing how spreadsheets are used in managerial accounting and other business applications.

**Required**

1. Check out the Website **Lacher.com**. Scroll down and open its table of contents. Select "Business Solutions Tutorials" and identify and list three tutorials for review.
2. Describe in a one-half page memorandum to your instructor how the applications described in each tutorial are helpful in business and managerial decision making.

**TEAMWORK IN ACTION**

C1  C2

**BTN 17-6**   Activity-based costing (ABC) is increasingly popular as a useful managerial tool to (1) measure the cost of resources consumed and (2) assign cost to products and services. This managerial tool has been available to accounting and business decision makers for more than 25 years.

**Required**

Break into teams and identify at least three likely reasons that activity-based costing has gained popularity in recent years. Be prepared to present your answers in a class discussion. (*Hint:* What changes have occurred in products and services over the past 25 years?)

**BUSINESS WEEK ACTIVITY**

C4

mhhe.com/wild

**BTN 17-7**   Read the article "The Measure of Your Management" in the April 23, 2003, issue of *Business Week*. (The book's Website provides free access to the article.)

**Required**

1. At **TriNet**, what activity indicators are closely monitored?
2. How does TriNet use its *set measuring system* to monitor executive performance?
3. What benefits does TriNet feel its set measuring system provides to the company as a whole?

**ENTREPRENEURIAL DECISION**

C1  C2  C3

**BTN 17-8**   Bert and John Jacobs of **Life Is Good** have come a long way from their start-up's initial cash balance of $78. As the business grew, the Jacobs began to understand how effective organizational structure can improve managerial control. Assume that Life Is Good recently created three departments (cutting, sewing, and screening) to produce the T-shirts. The Jacobs are not sure how to determine the costs associated with each department's activity, particularly because several costs are common across the entire business.

**Required**

1. As a consultant to the Jacobs, how would you suggest they address the cost allocation issue?
2. What type of costing system would you implement to monitor each department's performance? Explain.

**HITTING THE ROAD**

P3

**BTN 17-9**   Visit a local movie theater and check out both its concession area and its showing areas. The manager of a theater must confront questions such as:

- How much return do we earn on concessions?
- What types of movies generate the greatest sales?
- What types of movies generate the greatest net income?

**Required**

Assume that you are the new accounting manager for a 16-screen movie theater. You are to set up a responsibility accounting reporting framework for the theater.

1. Recommend how to segment the different departments of a movie theater for responsibility reporting.
2. Propose an expense allocation system for heat, rent, insurance, and maintenance costs of the theater.

**BTN 17-10**    Key segment data of **Grupo Bimbo** (<u>GrupoBimbo.com</u>) follows.

| Segment | Net Sales | | Operating Income | |
|---|---|---|---|---|
| | 2002 | 2001 | 2002 | 2001 |
| Mexico ............. | 27,964 | 26,297 | 3,207 | 3,612 |
| United States ........ | 10,810 | 6,238 | 30 | (53) |
| Latin America ........ | 2,599 | 2,433 | (240) | (115) |
| Totals ............. | 41,373 | 34,968 | 2,997 | 3,444 |

In millions of pesos in accordance with generally accepted accounting standards
in Mexico.

**Required**

**1.** Compute the growth (in percent) for Grupo Bimbo's total net sales from year 2001 to 2002.

**2.** Compute the growth (in percent) for each segment's net sales from 2001 to 2002.

**3.** Which segment's net sales grew the fastest?

**4.** Which segment was most profitable?

**5.** How can Grupo Bimbo's managers use this information?

*"I began to dream up sweet/spice concoctions, and that was the start of it all!"*—Katrina Markoff

# 18 Cost-Volume-Profit Analysis

## A Look Back

Chapter 17 focused on cost allocation, activity-based costing, and performance measurement. We identified several managerial reports useful in measuring and analyzing the activities of a company, its departments, and its managers.

## A Look at This Chapter

This chapter shows how information on both costs and sales behavior is useful to managers in performing cost-volume-profit analysis. This analysis is an important part of successful management and sound business decisions.

## A Look Ahead

Chapter 19 introduces and describes the budgeting process and its importance to management. It also explains the master budget and its usefulness to the planning of future company activities.

# CAP

## Conceptual

**C1** Describe different types of cost behavior in relation to production and sales volume. (p. 738)

**C2** Identify assumptions in cost-volume-profit analysis and explain their impact. (p. 746)

**C3** Describe several applications of cost-volume-profit analysis. (p. 747)

## Analytical

**A1** Compare the scatter diagram, high-low, and regression methods of estimating costs. (p. 743)

**A2** Analyze changes in sales using the degree of operating leverage. (p. 751)

## Procedural

**P1** Determine cost estimates using three different methods. (p. 741)

**P2** Compute the break-even point for a single product company. (p. 744)

**P3** Graph costs and sales for a single product company. (p. 745)

**P4** Compute break-even point for a multiproduct company. (p. 750)

---

**Decision Feature**

# Sweet and Spice and . . . Culinary Adventures

CHICAGO—"My heritage is Macedonian," says Katrina Markoff, "and my love of cooking has been with me from childhood. I began to think why not combine international spices and chocolate?" It is no surprise that Markoff created a chocolate confectionary company, **Vosges Haut Chocolat [VosgesChocolate.com],** with an "East-meets-West" feel. "I noticed a lack of creativity in chocolate," says Markoff. "They were all gold boxes with chocolate that tasted lousy and raspberry and strawberry filling."

Markoff's chocolates are far from the norm. With ingredients such as wasabi, balsamic vinegar, jasmine flower, curry, and anise, you won't confuse her chocolate with that of Hershey. "When I tell people stories about the ingredients," says Markoff, "they tend to slow down and pay attention to what they're putting in their mouths."

Markoff is also a businessperson. Her use of exotic spices, seasonings, and chocolates is combined with a keen business sense. "I couldn't help it," says Markoff, "my mother is an entrepreneur." That business sense mixed with her culinary skills gives her unique insights on how materials and labor costs relate to sales volume and profits. She not only achieves the break-even level but also markedly exceeds it, with this year's sales projected to exceed $2 million. Markoff also tracks the individual products in her multiproduct offerings. "Best sellers include Naga, Black Pearl, and Absinthe," she notes. Such results foretell even further growth. "I'd like to just keep expanding," Markoff says.

Cost management is crucial to Markoff's past and future success. She personally inspects and purchases each spice, flower, and chocolate used. "Right now, I'm trying out a Jamaican-style truffle, flavored with rum and allspice." Once new products meet her culinary standards, they are appropriately priced to reflect expected costs and sales volume. "Vosges is very expensive and is not something that can be everywhere," says Markoff.

"We want people to experience chocolate through the use of their senses—all six!" exclaims Markoff. One of her newer products is the Aztec collection that combines chocolate with spices of the vanilla bean, ancho chili pepper, Ceylon cinnamon, and cashews. Adds Markoff, both chocolate and spices have a long history as aphrodisiacs. Now we're cooking!

[Sources: *Vosges Haut Chocolat Website,* January 2004; *Entrepreneur,* November 2002; *Chicago Business,* November 2002; *Victoria,* February 2003; *Recipes Today Website,* 2003.]

This chapter describes different types of costs and shows how changes in a company's operating volume affect these costs. The chapter also analyzes a company's costs and sales to understand how different operating strategies affect profit or loss. Managers use this type of analysis to forecast what will happen if changes are made to costs, sales volume, selling prices, or product mix. They then use these forecasts to select the best business strategy for the company.

## Cost-Volume-Profit Analysis

### Identifying Cost Behavior

- Fixed costs
- Variable costs
- Mixed costs
- Step-wise costs
- Curvilinear costs

### Measuring Cost Behavior

- Scatter diagrams
- High-low method
- Least-squares regression
- Comparison of cost estimation methods

### Using Break-Even Analysis

- Computing break-even point
- Preparing a cost-volume-profit chart
- Making assumptions in cost-volume-profit analysis

### Applying Cost-Volume-Profit Analysis

- Computing income from sales and costs
- Computing sales for a target income
- Computing margin of safety
- Using sensitivity analysis
- Computing multiproduct break-even point

# Identifying Cost Behavior

**Point:** *Profit* is another term for *income*.

Planning a company's future activities and events is a crucial phase in successful management. One of the first steps in planning is to predict the volume of activity, the costs to be incurred, sales to be made, and profit to be received. An important tool to help managers carry out this step is **cost-volume-profit (CVP) analysis,** which helps them predict how changes in costs and sales levels affect income. In its basic form, CVP analysis involves computing the sales level at which a company neither earns an income nor incurs a loss, called the *break-even point.* For this reason, this basic form of cost-volume-profit analysis is often called *break-even analysis.* Managers use variations of CVP analysis to answer questions such as these:

- What sales volume is needed to earn a target income?
- What is the change in income if selling prices decline and sales volume increases?
- How much does income increase if we install a new machine to reduce labor costs?
- What is the income effect if we change the sales mix of our products or services?

Topic Tackler 18-1

Consequently, cost-volume-profit analysis is useful in a wide range of business decisions.

Conventional cost-volume-profit analysis requires management to classify all costs as either *fixed* or *variable* with respect to production or sales volume. The remainder of this section discusses the concepts of fixed and variable cost behavior as they relate to CVP analysis.

**C1** Describe different types of cost behavior in relation to production and sales volume.

## Fixed Costs

A *fixed cost* remains unchanged in amount when the volume of activity varies from period to period within a relevant range. For example, $5,000 in monthly rent paid for a factory building remains the same whether the factory operates with a single eight-hour shift or around the clock with three shifts. This means that rent cost is the same each month at any level of output from zero to the plant's full productive capacity. Notice that while *total* fixed cost does not change as the level of production changes the fixed cost *per unit* of output decreases as volume increases. For instance, if 20 units are produced when monthly rent is $5,000, the average rent cost per unit is $250 (computed as $5,000/20 units). When production increases to 100 units per month, the average cost per unit decreases to $50 (computed as $5,000/100 units). The average cost decreases to $10 per unit if production increases to 500 units per month. Common examples of fixed costs include depreciation, property taxes, office salaries, and many service department costs.

> **Decision Insight**
>
> **Cost Driven** Fixed costs were a driving force behind the **Daimler-Benz** and **Chrysler** merger. The auto business has huge fixed costs, mainly in plant and equipment. This means that with higher sales volume, fixed costs can be spread over more units. This yields lower fixed costs (and price) per auto.
>
>

When production volume and costs are graphed, units of product are usually plotted on the *horizontal axis* and dollars of cost are plotted on the *vertical axis*. Fixed costs then are represented as a horizontal line because they remain constant at all levels of production. To illustrate, the graph in Exhibit 18.1 shows that fixed costs remain at $32,000 at all production levels up to the company's monthly capacity of 2,000 units of output. The *relevant range* for fixed costs in Exhibit 18.1 is 0 to 2,000 units. If the relevant range changes (that is, production capacity extends beyond this range), the amount of fixed costs will likely change.

**Exhibit 18.1**

Relations of Fixed and Variable Costs to Volume

## Variable Costs

A *variable cost* changes in proportion to changes in volume of activity. The direct material cost of a product is one example of a variable cost. If one unit of product requires material costing $20, total material costs are $200 when 10 units of product are manufactured, $400 for 20 units, $600 for 30 units, and so on. Notice that variable cost *per unit* remains constant but the *total* amount of variable cost changes with the level of production. In addition to direct material, common variable costs include direct labor (if employees are paid per unit), sales commissions, shipping costs, and some overhead costs.

When variable costs are plotted on a graph of cost and volume, they appear as a straight line starting at the zero cost level. This straight line is upward (positive) sloping. The line rises as volume of activity increases. A variable cost line using a $20 per unit cost is graphed in Exhibit 18.1.

## Mixed Costs

A **mixed cost** includes both fixed and variable cost components. For example, compensation for sales representatives often includes a fixed monthly salary and a variable commission based on sales. The total cost line in Exhibit 18.1 is a mixed cost. Like a fixed cost, it is greater than zero when volume is zero, but unlike a fixed cost, it increases steadily in proportion to increases in volume. The mixed cost line in Exhibit 18.1 starts on the vertical axis at the $32,000 fixed cost point. Thus, at the zero volume level, total cost equals the fixed costs. As the activity level increases, the mixed cost line increases at an amount equal to the variable cost per unit. This line is highest when volume of activity is at 2,000 units (the end point of the relevant range). In CVP analysis, mixed costs are often separated into fixed and variable components. The fixed component is added to other fixed costs, and the variable component is added to other variable costs.

## Step-Wise Costs

A **step-wise cost** reflects a step pattern in costs. Salaries of production supervisors often behave in a step-wise manner in that their salaries are fixed within a *relevant range* of the current production volume. However, if production volume expands significantly (for example, with the addition of another shift), additional supervisors must be hired. This means that the total cost for supervisory salaries goes up by a lump-sum amount. Similarly, if volume takes another significant step up, supervisory salaries will increase by another lump sum. This behavior reflects a step-wise cost, also known as *stair-step costs,* which is graphed in Exhibit 18.2. See how it is flat within ranges (steps). Then, when volume significantly changes, it shifts to another level for that range (step).

## Exhibit 18.2

Step-Wise and Curvilinear Costs

In a conventional CVP analysis, a step-wise cost is usually treated as either a fixed cost or a variable cost. This treatment involves manager judgment and depends on the width of the range and the expected volume. To illustrate, suppose after the production of every 25 snowboards, an operator lubricates the finishing machine. The cost of this lubricant reflects a step-wise pattern. Also, suppose that after the production of every 1,000 units, the snowboard cutting tool is replaced. Again, this is a step-wise cost. Note that the range of 25 snowboards is much narrower than the range of 1,000 snowboards. Some managers might treat the lubricant cost as a variable cost and the cutting tool cost as a fixed cost.

**Point:** Computer spreadsheets are important and effective tools for CVP analysis and for analyzing alternative "what-if" strategies.

## Curvilinear Costs

A variable cost, as explained, is a *linear* cost; that is, it increases at a constant rate as volume of activity increases. A **curvilinear cost,** also called *nonlinear cost,* increases at a nonconstant rate as volume increases. When graphed, curvilinear costs appear as a curved line. Exhibit 18.2 shows a curvilinear cost beginning at zero when production is zero and then increasing at different rates.

An example of a curvilinear cost is total direct labor cost when workers are paid by the hour. At low to medium levels of production, adding more employees allows each of them to specialize by doing certain tasks repeatedly instead of doing several different tasks. This

**Point:** To apply these concepts, work QS 18-1 and QS 18-2.

often yields additional units of output at lower costs. A point is eventually reached at which adding more employees creates inefficiencies. For instance, a large crew demands more time and effort in communicating and coordinating their efforts. While adding employees in this case increases output, the labor cost per unit increases, and the total labor cost goes up at a steeper slope. This pattern is seen in Exhibit 18.2 where the curvilinear cost curve starts at zero, rises, flattens out, and then increases at a faster rate as output nears the maximum.

**Point:** Cost-volume-profit analysis helped Rod Canion, Jim Harris, and Bill Murto raise start-up capital of $20 million to launch **Compaq Computer.** They showed that break-even volumes were attainable within the first year.

## Quick Check

1. Which of the following statements is typically true? (*a*) Variable cost per unit increases as volume increases, (*b*) fixed cost per unit decreases as volume increases, or (*c*) a curvilinear cost includes both fixed and variable elements.

2. Describe the behavior of a fixed cost.

3. If cost per unit of activity remains constant (fixed), why is it called a variable cost?

Answers—p. 754

# Measuring Cost Behavior

Identifying and measuring cost behavior requires careful analysis and judgment. An important part of this process is to identify costs that can be classified as either fixed or variable, which often requires analysis of past cost behavior. Three methods are commonly used to analyze past costs: scatter diagrams, high-low method, and least-squares regression. Each method is discussed in this section using the sales and cost data shown in Exhibit 18.3, which is taken from a start-up company, which uses sales volume (in dollars) as the activity base in estimating cost behavior.

**P1**   Determine cost estimates using three different methods.

## Scatter Diagrams

**Scatter diagrams** display past cost data in graphical form. In preparing a scatter diagram, sales volume ($) is plotted on the horizontal axis and cost is plotted on the vertical axis. Each individual point on a scatter diagram reflects the cost and sales levels for a prior period. In Exhibit 18.4, the prior 12 months' cost and sales figures are graphed. Each point reflects total costs incurred and sales volume for one of those months. For instance, the point labeled March had sales of $25,000 and costs of $25,000.

Exhibit 18.3

Data for Estimating Cost Behavior

| Month | Sales Volume ($) | Total Cost ($) |
|---|---|---|
| January . . . . . | $17,500 | $20,500 |
| February . . . . | 27,500 | 21,500 |
| March . . . . . . | 25,000 | 25,000 |
| April . . . . . . . | 35,000 | 21,500 |
| May . . . . . . . | 47,500 | 25,500 |
| June . . . . . . . | 22,500 | 18,500 |
| July . . . . . . . . | 30,000 | 23,500 |
| August . . . . . | 52,500 | 28,500 |
| September . . | 37,500 | 26,000 |
| October . . . . | 57,500 | 26,000 |
| November . . | 62,500 | 31,000 |
| December . . . | 67,500 | 29,000 |

Exhibit 18.4

Scatter Diagram

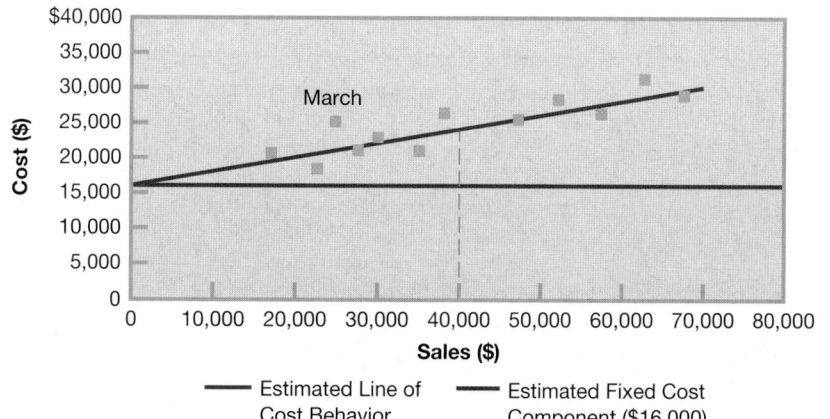

The **estimated line of cost behavior** is drawn on a scatter diagram to reflect the relation between cost and sales volume. This line best visually "fits" the points in a scatter diagram. Fitting this line demands judgment. The line drawn in Exhibit 18.4 intersects the vertical axis at approximately $16,000, which reflects fixed cost. To compute variable cost per unit, or the slope, we perform three steps. First, we select any two points on the horizontal axis (sales), say $0 and $40,000. Second, we draw a vertical line from each of these points to intersect the estimated line of cost behavior. The point on the vertical axis (cost) corresponding to the $40,000 sales point that intersects the estimated line is roughly $24,000. Similarly, the cost corresponding to zero sales is $16,000 (the fixed cost point). Third, we compute the slope of the line, or variable cost, as the change in cost divided by the change in sales. Exhibit 18.5 shows this computation.

## Exhibit 18.5

Variable Cost per Unit
(Scatter Diagram)

$$\frac{\text{Change in cost}}{\text{Change in sales}} = \frac{\$24,000 - \$16,000}{\$40,000 - \$0} = \frac{\$8,000}{\$40,000} = \$0.20 \text{ per sales dollar}$$

Variable cost is $0.20 per sales dollar. Thus, the cost equation that management will use to estimate costs for different sales levels is **$16,000 plus $0.20 per sales dollar**.

## High-Low Method

The **high-low method** is a way to estimate the cost equation by graphically connecting the two cost amounts at the highest and lowest sales volumes. In our case, the lowest sales volume is $17,500, and the highest is $67,500. The costs corresponding to these sales volumes are $20,500 and $29,000, respectively (see data in Exhibit 18.3). The estimated line of cost behavior for the high-low method is then drawn by connecting these two points on the scatter diagram corresponding to the lowest and highest sales volumes as follows:

If we extend this line to the vertical axis, it intersects the vertical axis at a cost of about $17,525, which is the fixed cost. The variable cost per unit is determined as the change in cost divided by the change in sales and uses the data from the high and low sales volumes. This results in a slope, or variable cost per sales dollar, of $0.17 as computed in Exhibit 18.6.

## Exhibit 18.6

Variable Cost per Unit
(High-Low Method)

$$\frac{\text{Change in cost}}{\text{Change in sales}} = \frac{\$29,000 - \$20,500}{\$67,500 - \$17,500} = \frac{\$8,500}{\$50,000} = \$0.17 \text{ per sales dollar}$$

Thus, the cost equation used to estimate costs at different sales levels is **$17,525 plus $0.17 per sales dollar**. This cost equation differs slightly from that determined from the scatter diagram method. Note that a deficiency of the high-low method is that it ignores all sales points except the highest and lowest. The result is less precision because the high-low method uses the most extreme points rather than the more usual conditions likely to recur.

## Least-Squares Regression

**Least-squares regression** is a statistical method for identifying cost behavior. For our purposes, we use the cost equation estimated from this method but leave the computational details for more advanced courses. Such computations for least-squares regression are readily done using most spreadsheet programs and calculators.

The regression cost equation for the data presented in Exhibit 18.3 is **$16,947 plus $0.19 per sales dollar**; that is, fixed cost is estimated as $16,947 and variable cost at $0.19 per sales dollar. Both costs are reflected in the following graph:

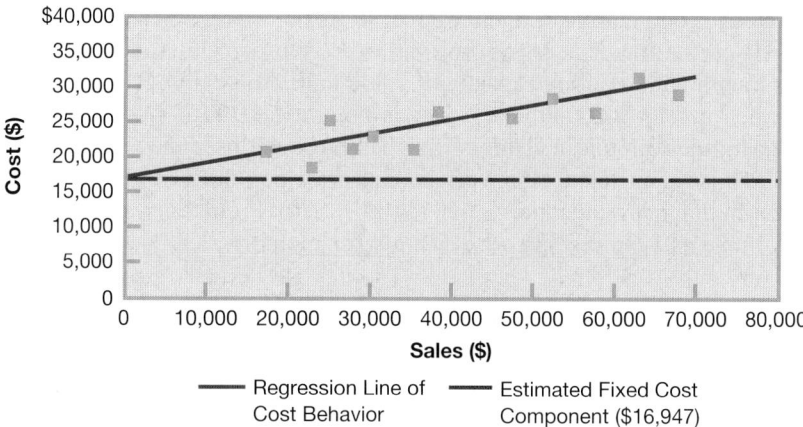

## Comparison of Cost Estimation Methods

The three cost estimation methods result in slightly different estimates of fixed and variable costs as summarized in Exhibit 18.7. Estimates from the scatter diagram are based on a visual fit of the cost line and are subject to interpretation. Estimates from the high-low method use only two sets of values corresponding to the lowest and highest sales volumes. Estimates from least-squares regression use a statistical technique and all available data points.

A1  Compare the scatter diagram, high-low, and regression methods of estimating costs.

| Estimation Method | Fixed Cost | Variable Cost |
|---|---|---|
| Scatter diagram | $16,000 | $0.20 per sales dollar |
| High-low method | 17,525 | 0.17 per sales dollar |
| Least-squares regression | 16,947 | 0.19 per sales dollar |

Exhibit 18.7

Comparison of Cost Estimation Methods

We must remember that all three methods use *past data*. Thus, cost estimates resulting from these methods are only as good as the data used for estimation. Managers must establish that the data are reliable in deriving cost estimates for future costs.

## Quick Check

4. Which of the following methods is likely to yield the most precise estimated line of cost behavior? (*a*) high-low, (*b*) least-squares regression, or (*c*) scatter diagram.
5. What is the primary weakness of the high-low method?
6. Using conventional CVP analysis, a mixed cost should be (*a*) disregarded, (*b*) treated as a fixed cost, or (*c*) separated into fixed and variable components.

Answers—p. 754

# Using Break-Even Analysis

**P2** Compute break-even point for a single product company.

Topic Tackler 18-2

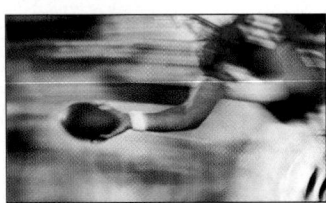

Break-even analysis is a special case of cost-volume-profit analysis. This section describes break-even analysis by computing the break-even point and preparing a CVP (or break-even) chart.

## Computing Break-Even Point

The **break-even point** is the sales level at which a company neither earns a profit nor incurs a loss. The concept of breakeven is applicable to nearly all organizations, activities, and events. One of the most important items of information when launching a project is whether it will break even, that is, whether sales will at least cover total costs. The break-even point can be expressed in either units or dollars of sales.

To illustrate the computation of break-even analysis, let's look at **Rydell,** which sells footballs for $100 per unit and incurs $70 of variable costs per unit sold. Its fixed costs are $24,000 per month with monthly capacity of 1,800 units (footballs). Rydell breaks even for the month when it sells 800 footballs (sales volume of $80,000). We compute this break-even point using the formula in Exhibit 18.8. This formula uses the **contribution margin per unit,** which is the difference between selling price per unit and variable cost per unit. Rydell's contribution margin per unit is $30 ($100 − $70). From this we can compute break-even sales volume as $24,000/$30, or 800 units per month.

## Exhibit 18.8

Formula for Computing Break-Even Sales (in units)[1]

**Point:** The break-even point is where total expenses equal total sales and the profit is zero.

$$\text{Break-even point in units} = \frac{\text{Fixed costs}}{\text{Contribution margin per unit}}$$

At a price of $100 per unit, monthly sales of 800 units yields sales dollars of $80,000 (called *break-even sales dollars*). This $80,000 break-even sales can be computed directly using the formula in Exhibit 18.9. The **contribution margin ratio** is the proportion of a unit's selling price that exceeds its unit variable cost, which is defined as contribution margin per unit divided by unit selling price.

## Exhibit 18.9

Formula for Computing Break-Even Sales (in dollars)[2]

**Point:** While a company may operate at a level in excess of its break-even point, management may decide to stop operating because it is not earning a reasonable return on investment.

$$\text{Break-even point in dollars} = \frac{\text{Fixed costs}}{\text{Contribution margin ratio}}$$

Rydell's contribution margin ratio is 30%, computed as $30/$100. Break-even sales dollars are then computed as $24,000/0.30, or $80,000 of monthly sales. To verify that Rydell's break-even point equals $80,000 (or 800 units), we prepare a simplified income statement in Exhibit 18.10. It shows that the $80,000 revenue from sales of 800 units exactly equals the sum of variable and fixed costs.

---

[1] To obtain this formula, we define $S$ = Sales in units; $R$ = Revenue per unit; $F$ = Fixed costs per period; $V$ = Variable cost per unit; $S \times R$ = Dollar sales; $S \times V$ = Total variable cost; and contribution margin per unit = $R - V$. At breakeven, net income is zero, so therefore,

$$\text{Sales} = \text{Fixed costs} + \text{Variable costs}$$
$$(S \times R) = F + (S \times V)$$
$$(S \times R) - (S \times V) = F$$
$$S \times (R - V) = F$$
$$S = F/(R - V)$$
$$S = F/\text{Contribution margin per unit}$$

[2] To obtain this formula, recall that: Contribution margin ratio = $(R - V)/R$. Then, at breakeven,

$$S = F/(R - V) \text{ [from footnote 1]}$$
$$S \times R = (F \times R)/(R - V)$$
$$S \times R = F \times [R/(R - V)]$$
$$S \times R = F/[(R - V)/R]$$
$$S \times R = F/\text{Contribution margin ratio}$$

The statement in Exhibit 18.10 is called a *contribution margin income statement.* It differs in format from a conventional income statement in two ways. First, it separately classifies costs and expenses as variable or fixed. Second, it reports contribution margin (Sales − Variable costs). The contribution margin income statement format is used in this chapter's assignment materials because of its usefulness in CVP analysis.

**Point:** A *contribution margin income statement* groups variable and fixed expenses separately and reports the contribution margin.

| RYDELL COMPANY<br>Contribution Margin Income Statement (at Breakeven)<br>For Month Ended January 31, 2005 | |
| --- | --- |
| Sales (800 units @ $100 each) . . . . . . . . . . . . . | $80,000 |
| Variable costs (800 units @ $70 each) . . . . . . . | 56,000 |
| **Contribution margin** . . . . . . . . . . . . . . . . . . | 24,000 |
| Fixed costs . . . . . . . . . . . . . . . . . . . . . . . . . . . | 24,000 |
| **Net income** . . . . . . . . . . . . . . . . . . . . . . . . | $    0 |

**Exhibit 18.10**

Contribution Margin Income Statement for Break-Even Sales

## Preparing a Cost-Volume-Profit Chart

Exhibit 18.11 is a graph of Rydell's cost-volume-profit relations. This graph is called a **cost-volume-profit (CVP) chart,** or a *break-even chart* or a *break-even graph.* The horizontal axis is the number of units sold and the vertical axis is dollars of sales and costs. The lines in the chart depict both sales and costs at different output levels.

**P3**  Graph costs and sales for a single product company.

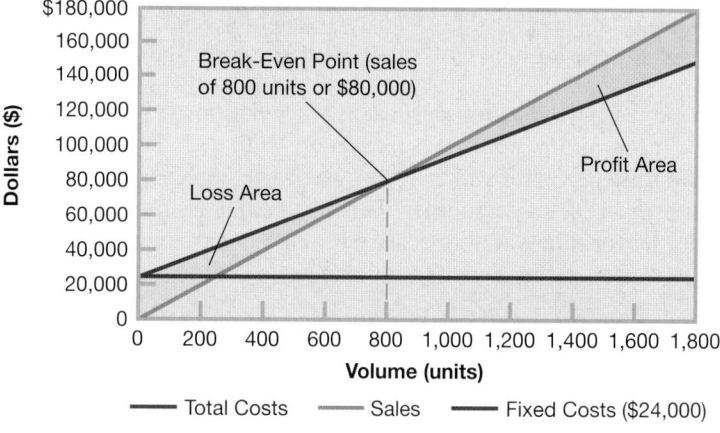

**Exhibit 18.11**

Cost-Volume-Profit Chart

We follow three steps to prepare a CVP chart, which can also be drawn with computer programs that convert numeric data to graphs:

1. Plot fixed costs on the vertical axis ($24,000 for Rydell). Draw a horizontal line at this level to show that fixed costs remain unchanged regardless of sales volume (drawing this fixed cost line is not essential to the chart).

2. Draw the total (variable plus fixed) costs line for a relevant range of sales levels. This line starts at the fixed costs level on the vertical axis because total costs equal fixed costs at zero sales. The slope of the total cost line equals the variable cost per unit ($70). To draw the line, compute the total costs for any sales level, and connect this point with the vertical axis intercept ($24,000). Do not draw this line beyond the productive capacity for the planning period (1,800 units for Rydell).

3. Draw the sales line. Start at the origin (zero units and zero dollars of sales) and make the slope of this line equal to the selling price per unit ($100). To sketch the line, compute dollar sales for any sales level and connect this point with the origin. Do not extend this line beyond the productive capacity. Total sales will be at the highest level at maximum capacity.

The total costs line and the sales line intersect at 800 units in Exhibit 18.11, which is the break-even point, the point where total dollar sales of $80,000 equals the sum of both fixed and variable costs ($80,000).

**Point:** A contribution margin income statement is also referred to as a *variable costing income statement.* This differs from the traditional **absorption costing** approach where product costs are assigned to units sold and to units in ending inventory. Recall that variable costing expenses all product costs. Thus, income for the two approaches differs depending on the level of finished goods inventory; the lower is inventory, the more similar the two approaches.

**Example:** In Exhibit 18.11, the sales line intersects the total cost line at 800 units. At what point would the two lines intersect if selling price is increased by 20% to $120 per unit? *Answer:* $24,000/ ($120 − $70) = 480 units

On either side of the break-even point, the vertical distance between the sales line and the total costs line at any specific volume measures the profit or loss expected at that point. At volume levels to the left of the break-even point, this vertical distance is the amount of the expected loss because the total costs line is above the total sales line. At volume levels to the right of the break-even point, the vertical distance represents the expected profit because the total sales line is above the total costs line.

## Making Assumptions in Cost-Volume-Profit Analysis

**C2** Identify assumptions in cost-volume-profit analysis and explain their impact.

Cost-volume-profit analysis assumes that relations can normally be expressed as simple lines similar to those in Exhibits 18.1 and 18.11. Such assumptions allow users to answer several important questions, but the usefulness of the answers depends on the validity of three assumptions: (1) constant selling price per unit, (2) constant variable costs per unit, and (3) constant total fixed costs. These assumptions are not always realistic, but they do not necessarily limit the usefulness of CVP analysis as a way to better understand costs and sales. This section discusses these assumptions and other issues for CVP analysis.

**Point:** CVP analysis can be very useful for business decision making even when its assumptions are not strictly met.

**Working with Assumptions** The behavior of individual costs and sales often is not perfectly consistent with CVP assumptions. If the expected costs and sales behavior differ from the assumptions, the results of CVP analysis can be limited. Still, we can perform useful analyses in spite of limitations with these assumptions for several reasons.

*Summing costs can offset individual deviations.* Deviations from assumptions with individual costs are often minor when these costs are summed. That is, individual variable cost items may not be perfectly variable, but when we sum these variable costs, their individual deviations can offset each other. This means the assumption of variable cost behavior can be proper for total variable costs. Similarly, an assumption that total fixed costs are constant can be proper even when individual fixed cost items are not exactly constant.

**Point:** To apply these concepts, work QS 18-7.

*CVP is applied to a relevant range of operations.* Sales, variable costs, and fixed costs often are reasonably reflected in straight lines on a graph when the assumptions are applied over a relevant range. The **relevant range of operations** is the normal operating range for a business. Except for unusually difficult or prosperous times, management typically plans for operations within a range of volume neither close to zero nor at maximum capacity. The relevant range excludes extremely high and low operating levels that are unlikely to occur. The validity of assuming that a specific cost is fixed or variable is more acceptable when operations are within the relevant range. As shown in Exhibit 18.2, a curvilinear cost can be treated as variable and linear if the relevant range covers volumes where it has a nearly constant slope. Management must plan according to the normal relevant range of activity. If the normal range of activity changes, some costs might need reclassification.

*CVP analysis yields estimates.* CVP analysis yields approximate answers to questions about costs, volumes, and profits. These answers do not have to be precise because the analysis makes rough estimates about the future. As long as managers understand that CVP analysis gives estimates, it can be a useful tool for starting the planning process. Other qualitative factors also must be considered.

**Example:** If selling price declines, what happens to the break-even point? *Answer:* It increases.

**Working with Output Measures** CVP analysis usually describes the level of activity in terms of *sales volume*, which can be expressed in terms of either units sold or dollar sales. However, other measures of output exist. For instance, a manufacturer can use the number of units produced as a measure of output. Also, to simplify analysis, we sometimes assume that production level is the same as the sales level. That is, inventory levels are ignored. This often is justified by arguing that CVP analysis provides only approximations.

**7.** Fixed cost divided by the contribution margin ratio yields the (*a*) break-even point in dollars, (*b*) contribution margin per unit, or (*c*) break-even point in units.

**8.** A company sells a product for $90 per unit with variable costs of $54 per unit. What is the contribution margin ratio?

**9.** Refer to Quick Check (8). If fixed costs for the period are $90,000, what is the break-even point in dollars?

**10.** What three basic assumptions are used in CVP analysis?

Answers—p. 754

# Applying Cost-Volume-Profit Analysis

Managers consider a variety of strategies in planning business operations. Cost-volume-profit analysis is useful in helping managers evaluate the likely effects of these strategies, which is the focus of this section.

## Computing Income from Sales and Costs

An important question managers often need an answer to is "What is the predicted income from a predicted level of sales?" To answer this, we look at four variables in CVP analysis. These variables and their relations to income (pretax) are shown in Exhibit 18.12. We use these relations to compute expected income from predicted sales and cost levels.

**C3** Describe several applications of cost-volume-profit analysis.

$$\text{Income (pretax)} = \text{Sales} - \text{Variable costs} - \text{Fixed costs}$$

**Exhibit 18.12**

Income Relations in CVP Analysis

To illustrate, let's assume that Rydell's management expects to sell 1,500 units this month. What is the amount of income if this sales level is achieved? At this level, sales are $150,000 (1,500 units × $100). Also, Rydell's fixed costs are $24,000 per month, its variable costs per unit are $70, and its total variable costs for 1,500 units are $105,000 (1,500 units × $70). Following Exhibit 18.12, we compute Rydell's expected income in Exhibit 18.13.

$$\text{Income (pretax)} = [1{,}500 \text{ units} \times \$100] - [1{,}500 \text{ units} \times \$70] - \$24{,}000$$
$$= \$21{,}000$$

**Exhibit 18.13**

Computing Expected Income from Expected Sales

The $21,000 income does not include the effects of income taxes. To find the amount of *after-tax* income from selling 1,500 units, management must apply the proper tax rate to the $21,000. If the tax rate is 25%, income tax is $5,250 and net income is $15,750. Management then assesses whether this net income is an adequate return on assets invested. Management should also consider whether sales and income can be increased by raising or lowering prices. CVP analysis is a good tool for addressing these kinds of "what-if" questions.

## Computing Sales for a Target Income

Many companies' annual plans are based on certain income targets (sometimes called *budgets*). Rydell's income target for this year is to increase income by 10% over the prior year. When prior year income is known, Rydell easily computes its target income. CVP analysis helps to determine the sales level needed to achieve the target income. Computing this sales level is important because planning for the year is then based on this level. We use the formula shown in Exhibit 18.14 to compute sales for a target *after-tax* income.

"How many units must I sell to earn $50,000?"

## Exhibit 18.14

Computing Sales (dollars) for a Target After-Tax Income[3]

$$\text{Dollar sales at target after-tax income} = \frac{\text{Fixed costs} + \text{Target after-tax income} + \text{Income taxes}}{\text{Contribution margin ratio}} \quad or = \frac{\text{Fixed costs} + \text{Target pretax income}}{\text{Contribution margin ratio}}$$

**Example:** If variable costs decline, what happens to the break-even point? *Answer:* It decreases.

To illustrate, Rydell has monthly fixed costs of $24,000 and a 30% contribution margin ratio. Assume that it sets a target monthly after-tax income of $9,000 when the tax rate is 25%. This means the pretax income is targeted at $12,000 [$9,000/(1 − 0.25)] with a tax expense of $3,000. Using the formula in Exhibit 18.14, we find that $120,000 of sales is needed to produce a $9,000 after-tax income as shown in Exhibit 18.15.

## Exhibit 18.15

Rydell's Dollar Sales for a Target Income

$$\text{Dollar sales at target after-tax income} = \frac{\$24,000 + \$9,000 + \$3,000}{30\%} = \$120,000$$

We can alternatively compute *unit sales* instead of dollar sales. To do this, we substitute *contribution margin per unit* for the contribution margin ratio in the denominator. This gives the number of units to sell to reach the target after-tax income. Exhibit 18.16 illustrates this for Rydell. The two computations in Exhibits 18.15 and 18.16 are equivalent because sales of 1,200 units at $100 per unit equals $120,000 of sales.

## Exhibit 18.16

Computing Sales (units) for a Target After-Tax Income

$$\text{Unit sales at target after-tax income} = \frac{\text{Fixed costs} + \text{Target after-tax income} + \text{Income taxes}}{\text{Contribution margin per unit}} \quad or = \frac{\text{Fixed costs} + \text{Target pretax income}}{\text{Contribution margin per unit}}$$

$$= \frac{\$24,000 + \$9,000 + \$3,000}{\$30} = 1,200 \text{ units}$$

**Point:** If a company is not subject to taxes, then substitute *pretax income* for *after-tax income* and delete *income taxes* in both Exhibits 18.14 and 18.16.

## Computing the Margin of Safety

All companies wish to sell more than the break-even number of units. The excess of expected sales over the break-even sales level is called a company's **margin of safety,** the amount that sales can drop before the company incurs a loss. It can be expressed in units, dollars, or even as a percent of the predicted level of sales. To illustrate, if Rydell's expected sales are $100,000, the margin of safety is $20,000, above break-even sales of $80,000. As a percent, the margin of safety is 20% of expected sales as shown in Exhibit 18.17.

### Decision Ethics

**Supervisor** You are part of a team debating a new product. Different sales projections have a range of income levels. One member suggests picking numbers yielding favorable income because any estimate is "as good as any other." Another member points to a scatter diagram of 20 months' production on a comparable product and suggests dropping unfavorable data points for cost estimation. Your task is to conduct a cost-volume-profit analysis to reflect these suggestions. What do you do?

Answer—p. 754

---

[3] To obtain this formula, we define $S$ = Sales in units; $R$ = Revenue per unit; $F$ = Fixed costs per period; $V$ = Variable cost per unit; $N$ = Target net income; $T$ = Income taxes; $S \times R$ = Dollar sales; $S \times V$ = Total variable cost; and the Contribution margin ratio = $(R - V)/R$. The after-tax target net income is then defined as:

$$(S \times R) - F - (S \times V) - T = N$$
$$(S \times R) - (S \times V) = F + N + T$$
$$S \times (R - V) = F + N + T$$
$$S = (F + N + T)/(R - V)$$
$$S \times R = [(F + N + T) \times R]/(R - V)$$
$$S \times R = (F + N + T) \times [R/(R - V)]$$
$$S \times R = (F + N + T)/[(R - V)/R]$$
$$S \times R = (F + N + T)/\text{Contribution margin ratio}$$

$$\text{Margin of safety (in percent)} = \frac{\text{Expected sales} - \text{Break-even sales}}{\text{Expected sales}}$$

$$= \frac{\$100,000 - \$80,000}{\$100,000} = 20\%$$

**Exhibit 18.17**

Computing Margin of Safety (in percent)

Management must assess whether the margin of safety is adequate in light of factors such as sales variability, competition, consumer tastes, and economic conditions.

## Using Sensitivity Analysis

Knowing the effects of changing some estimates used in CVP analysis is often useful because they are *estimates,* not actual values. For instance, we might want to know what happens if we reduce a product's selling price to increase sales. Or we might want to know what happens to income if we automate a currently manual process. We can use CVP analysis to predict income if we can describe how these changes affect a company's fixed costs, variable costs, selling price, and volume.

To illustrate, assume that Rydell Company is looking into buying a new machine that would increase monthly fixed costs from $24,000 to $30,000 but decrease variable costs from $70 per unit to $60 per unit. The machine is used to produce output whose selling price will remain unchanged at $100. This results in increases in both the unit contribution margin and the contribution margin ratio. The revised contribution margin per unit is $40 ($100 − $60), and the revised contribution margin ratio is 40% of selling price ($40/$100). Using CVP analysis, Rydell's revised break-even point in dollars would be $75,000 as computed in Exhibit 18.18.

> **Decision Insight**
>
> **Eco-CVP**  Ford Escape, Toyota Prius, and Honda Insight are hybrids powered by a small gas engine and an electric motor. Many promise to save owners $500 a year in fuel costs relative to comparables and they generate less carbon dioxide and other greenhouse gases. Are these models economically feasible? Analysts estimate that **Ford** can break even with its Escape when a $3,000 premium is paid over comparable gas-based models.

**Example:** If fixed costs decline, what happens to the break-even point? *Answer:* It decreases.

$$\text{Revised break-even point in dollars} = \frac{\text{Revised fixed costs}}{\text{Revised contribution margin ratio}} = \frac{\$30,000}{40\%} = \$75,000$$

**Exhibit 18.18**

Revising Breakeven When Changes Occur

The revised fixed costs and the revised contribution margin ratio can also be used to address other issues including computation of (1) expected income for a given sales level and (2) the sales level needed to earn a target income. Another use of sensitivity analysis is to generate different sets of revenue and cost estimates that are *optimistic, pessimistic,* and *most likely.* Different CVP analyses based on these estimates provide different scenarios that management can analyze and use in planning business strategy.

**Point:** Price competition led paging companies to give business to resellers—companies that lease services at a discount and then resell to subscribers. **Paging Network** charged some resellers under $1 per month, less than a third of what is needed to break even. Its CEO now admits the low-price strategy was flawed.

> ## Quick Check
>
> 11. A firm has fixed costs of $50,000 and a 25% contribution margin ratio. What dollar sales are necessary to achieve an after-tax net income of $120,000 if the tax rate is 20%? (a) $800,000, (b) $680,000, or (c) $600,000.
>
> 12. If the contribution margin ratio decreases from 50% to 25%, what can be said about unit sales needed to achieve the same target income level?
>
> 13. What is a company's margin of safety?

Answers—p. 754

## Computing Multiproduct Break-Even Point

P4 Compute break-even point for a multiproduct company.

To this point, we have looked only at cases where the company sells a single product or service. This was to keep the basic CVP analysis simple. However, many companies sell multiple products or services, and we can modify the CVP analysis for use in these cases. An important assumption in a multiproduct setting is that the sales mix of different products is known and remains constant during the planning period. **Sales mix** is the ratio (proportion) of the sales volumes for the various products. For instance, if a company normally sells 10,000 footballs, 5,000 softballs, and 4,000 basketballs per month, its sales mix can be expressed as 10:5:4 for footballs, softballs, and basketballs.

To apply multiproduct CVP analysis, we need to estimate the break-even point by using a **composite unit,** which consists of a specific number of units of each product in proportion to their expected sales mix. Multiproduct CVP analysis treats this composite unit as a single product. To illustrate, let's look at **Hair-Today,** a styling salon that offers three cuts: basic, ultra, and budget in the ratio of 4 basic units to 2 ultra units to 1 budget unit (expressed as 4:2:1). Management wants to estimate its break-even point for next year. Unit selling prices for these three cuts are basic, $10; ultra, $16; and budget, $8. Using the 4:2:1 sales mix, the selling price of a composite unit of the three products is computed as follows:

| | |
|---|---:|
| 4 units of basic @ $10 per unit . . . . . . . . | $40 |
| 2 units of ultra @ $16 per unit . . . . . . . . | 32 |
| 1 unit of budget @ $8 per unit . . . . . . . . | 8 |
| Selling price of a composite unit . . . . . . . | **$80** |

**Point:** Selling prices and variable costs are usually expressed in per unit amounts. Fixed costs are usually expressed in total amounts.

Hair-Today's fixed costs are $96,000 per year, and its variable costs of the three products are basic, $6.50; ultra, $9.00; and budget, $4.00. Variable costs for a composite unit of these products follow:

| | |
|---|---:|
| 4 units of basic @ $6.50 per unit . . . . . . . . | $26 |
| 2 units of ultra @ $9.00 per unit . . . . . . . . . | 18 |
| 1 unit of budget @ $4.00 per unit . . . . . . . . | 4 |
| Variable costs of a composite unit . . . . . . . . | **$48** |

**Point:** To apply these concepts, work QS 18-9.

Hair-Today's $32 contribution margin for a composite unit is computed by subtracting the variable costs of a composite unit ($48) from its selling price ($80). We then use the contribution margin to determine Hair-Today's break-even point in composite units in Exhibit 18.19.

## Exhibit 18.19

Break-Even Point in Composite Units

$$\text{Break-even point in composite units} = \frac{\text{Fixed costs}}{\text{Contribution margin per composite unit}}$$

$$= \frac{\$96,000}{\$32} = 3,000 \text{ composite units}$$

**Point:** The break-even point in dollars for Exhibit 18.19 is: $96,000/($32/$80) = $240,000.

This computation implies that Hair-Today breaks even when it sells 3,000 composite units. To determine how many units of each product it must sell to break even, we multiply the number of units of each product in the composite by 3,000:

| | | | |
|---|---|---|---|
| Basic: | 4 × 3,000 | . . . . . . . | 12,000 units |
| Ultra: | 2 × 3,000 | . . . . . . . | 6,000 units |
| Budget: | 1 × 3,000 | . . . . . . . | 3,000 units |

Exhibit 18.20 verifies these results by showing Hair-Today's sales and costs at this break-even point using a contribution margin income statement.

| HAIR-TODAY Forecasted Contribution Margin Income Statement (at Breakeven) | | | | |
|---|---|---|---|---|
| | Basic | Ultra | Budget | Combined |
| Sales | | | | |
| Basic (12,000 @ $10) . . . . . . . . . | $120,000 | | | |
| Ultra (6,000 @ $16) . . . . . . . . . . | | $96,000 | | |
| Budget (3,000 @ $8) . . . . . . . . . | | | $24,000 | |
| Total sales . . . . . . . . . . . . . . . . | | | | $240,000 |
| Variable costs | | | | |
| Basic (12,000 @ $6.50) . . . . . . . . | 78,000 | | | |
| Ultra (6,000 @ $9) . . . . . . . . . . . | | 54,000 | | |
| Budget (3,000 @ $4) . . . . . . . . . | | | 12,000 | |
| Total variable costs . . . . . . . . . . | | | | 144,000 |
| Contribution margin . . . . . . . . . . . | $ 42,000 | $42,000 | $12,000 | 96,000 |
| Fixed costs . . . . . . . . . . . . . . . . . | | | | 96,000 |
| Net income . . . . . . . . . . . . . . . . | | | | $ 0 |

**Exhibit 18.20**

Multiproduct Break-Even Income Statement

A CVP analysis using composite units can be used to answer a variety of planning questions. Once a product mix is set, all answers are based on the assumption that the mix remains constant at all relevant sales levels as other factors in the analysis do. We also can vary the sales mix to see what happens under alternative strategies.

**Decision Maker**

**Entrepreneur** A CVP analysis indicates that your start-up, which markets electronic products, will break even with the current sales mix and price levels. You have a target income in mind. What analysis might you perform to assess likelihood for achieving this income?

Answer—p. 754

**Quick Check**

14. The sales mix of a company's two products, X and Y, is 2:1. Unit variable costs for both products are $2, and unit sales price is $5 for X and $4 for Y. What is the contribution margin per composite unit? (a) $5, (b) $10, or (c) $8.

15. What additional assumption about sales mix must be made in doing a conventional CVP analysis for a company that produces and sells more than one product?

Answers—p. 754

## Degree of Operating Leverage

**Decision Analysis**

CVP analysis is especially useful when management begins the planning process and wishes to predict outcomes of alternative strategies. These strategies can involve changes in selling prices, fixed costs, variable costs, sales volume, and product mix. Managers are interested in seeing the effects of changes in some or all of these factors.

**A2** Analyze changes in sales using the degree of operating leverage.

One goal of all managers is to get maximum benefits from their fixed costs. Managers would like to use 100% of their output capacity so that fixed costs are spread over the largest number of units. This would decrease fixed cost per unit and increase income. The extent, or relative size, of fixed costs in the total cost structure is known as **operating leverage.** Companies having a higher proportion of fixed costs in their total cost structure are said to have higher operating leverage. An example of this is a company that chooses to automate its processes instead of using direct labor, increasing its fixed costs and lowering its variable costs. A useful managerial measure to help assess the effect of changes in the level of sales on income is the **degree of operating leverage (DOL)** defined as:

**DOL = Total contribution margin (in dollars)/Pretax income**

One tool useful in assessing the effect of changes in sales on income is the degree of operating leverage, or DOL. DOL is the ratio of the contribution margin divided by pretax income. This ratio can be used to determine the expected percent change in income given a percent change in sales.

**P1  Determine cost estimates using three different methods.** Three different methods used to estimate costs are the scatter diagram, the high-low method, and least-squares regression. All three methods use past data to estimate costs.

**P2  Compute break-even point for a single product company.** A company's break-even point for a period is the sales volume at which total revenues equal total costs. To compute a break-even point in terms of sales units, we divide total fixed costs by the contribution margin per unit. To compute a

break-even point in terms of sales dollars, divide total fixed costs by the contribution margin ratio.

**P3  Graph costs and sales for a single product company.** The costs and sales for a company can be graphically illustrated using a CVP chart. In this chart, the horizontal axis represents the number of units sold and the vertical axis represents dollars of sales or costs. Straight lines are used to depict both costs and sales on the CVP chart.

**P4  Compute break-even point for a multiproduct company.** CVP analysis can be applied to a multiproduct company by expressing sales volume in terms of composite units. A composite unit consists of a specific number of units of each product in proportion to their expected sales mix. Multiproduct CVP analysis treats this composite unit as a single product.

## Guidance Answers to **Decision Maker** and **Decision Ethics**

**Operations Manager**  Without the availability of past data, none of the three methods described in the chapter can be used to measure cost behavior. Instead, the manager must investigate whether data from similar manufacturers can be accessed. This is likely difficult due to the sensitive nature of such data. In the absence of data, the manager should develop a list of the different production inputs and identify input-output relations. This provides guidance to the manager in measuring cost behavior. After several months, actual cost data will be available for analysis.

**Supervisor**  Your dilemma is whether to go along with the suggestions to "manage" the numbers to make the project look like it will achieve sufficient profits. You should not succumb to these suggestions. Many people will likely be affected negatively if you manage the predicted numbers and the project eventually is unprofitable.

Moreover, if it does fail, an investigation would likely reveal that data in the proposal were "fixed" to make it look good. Probably the only benefit from managing the numbers is the short-term payoff of pleasing those who proposed the product. One way to deal with this dilemma is to prepare several analyses showing results under different assumptions and then let senior management make the decision.

**Entrepreneur**  You must first compute the level of sales required to achieve the desired net income. Then you must conduct sensitivity analysis by varying the price, sales mix, and cost estimates. Results from the sensitivity analysis provide information you can use to assess the possibility of reaching the target sales level. For instance, you might have to pursue aggressive marketing strategies to push the high-margin products, or you might have to cut prices to increase sales and profits, or another strategy might emerge.

## Guidance Answers to **Quick Checks**

**1.** *b*

**2.** A fixed cost remains unchanged in total amount regardless of output levels. However, fixed *cost per unit* declines with increased output.

**3.** Such a cost is considered variable because the *total* cost changes in proportion to volume changes.

**4.** *b*

**5.** The high-low method ignores all costs and sales (activity-base) volume data points except the costs corresponding to the highest and lowest (most extreme) sales (activity-basc) volume.

**6.** *c*

**7.** *a*

**8.** ($90 − $54)/$90 = 40%

**9.** $90,000/40% = $225,000

**10.** Three basic CVP assumptions are that (1) selling price per unit is constant, (2) variable costs per unit are constant, and (3) total fixed costs are constant.

**11.** a; Two steps are required for explanation:
  (1) Pretax income = $120,000/(1 − 0.20) = $150,000

$$(2) \quad \frac{\$50,000 + \$120,000 + (\$150,000 \times 20\%)}{25\%} = \$800,000$$

**12.** If the contribution margin ratio decreases from 50% to 25%, unit sales would have to double.

**13.** A company's margin of safety is the excess of the predicted sales level over its break-even sales level.

**14.** *c*; Selling price of a composite unit:

| | |
|---|---|
| 2 units of X @ $5 per unit . . . . . . . . . . . | $10 |
| 1 unit of Y @ $4 per unit . . . . . . . . . . . . | 4 |
| Selling price of a composite unit . . . . . . . | $14 |

Variable costs of a composite unit:

| | |
|---|---|
| 2 units of X @ $2 per unit . . . . . . . . . . . | $4 |
| 1 unit of Y @ $2 per unit . . . . . . . . . . . . | 2 |
| Variable costs of a composite unit . . . . . . | $6 |

Therefore, contribution margin per composite unit is $8.

**15.** It must be assumed that the sales mix remains unchanged at all sales levels in the relevant range.

## Key Terms

Key Terms are available at the book's Website for learning and testing in an online Flashcard Format.

Break-even point (p. 744)
Composite unit (p. 750)
Contribution margin per unit (p. 744)
Contribution margin ratio (p. 744)
Cost-volume-profit (CVP) analysis (p. 738)
Cost-volume-profit (CVP) chart (p. 745)

Curvilinear cost (p. 740)
Degree of operating leverage (DOL) (p. 751)
Estimated line of cost behavior (p. 742)
High-low method (p. 742)
Least-squares regression (p. 743)
Margin of safety (p. 748)

Mixed cost (p. 739)
Operating leverage (p. 751)
Relevant range of operations (p. 746)
Sales mix (p. 750)
Scatter diagram (p. 741)
Step-wise cost (p. 740)

## Personal Interactive Quiz

Personal Interactive Quizzes A and B are available at the book's Website to reinforce and assess your learning.

## Discussion Questions

**1.** How is cost-volume-profit analysis useful?

**2.** What is a variable cost? Identify two variable costs.

**3.** When output volume increases, do variable costs per unit increase, decrease, or stay the same within the relevant range of activity? Explain.

**4.** When output volume increases, do fixed costs per unit increase, decrease, or stay the same within the relevant range of activity? Explain.

**5.** How do step-wise costs and curvilinear costs differ?

**6.** In performing CVP analysis for a manufacturing company, what simplifying assumption is usually made about the volume of production and the volume of sales?

**7.** What two arguments tend to justify classifying all costs as either fixed or variable even though individual costs might not behave perfectly consistently with these classifications?

**8.** How does assuming that operating activity occurs within a relevant range affect cost-volume-profit analysis?

**9.** List three methods to measure cost behavior.

**10.** How is a scatter diagram used to identify and measure the behavior of a company's costs?

**11.** In cost-volume-profit analysis, what is the estimated profit at the break-even point?

**12.** Assume that a straight line on a CVP chart intersects the vertical axis at the level of fixed costs and has a positive slope that rises with each additional unit of volume by the amount of the variable costs per unit. What does this line represent?

**13.** Why are fixed costs depicted as a horizontal line on a CVP chart?

**14.** Each of two similar companies has sales of $20,000 and total costs of $15,000 for a month. Company A's total costs include $10,000 of variable costs and $5,000 of fixed costs. If Company B's total costs include $4,000 of variable costs and $11,000 of fixed costs, which company will enjoy more profit if sales double?

**15.** _____ of _____ reflects expected sales in excess of the level of break-even sales.

**16.** **Krispy Kreme** produced donuts for sale during the Olympic games. Identify some of the variable and fixed product costs associated with that production. [*Hint:* Limit costs to product costs.]

**17.** Should **Tastykake** use single product or multi-product break-even analysis? Explain.

**18.** **Harley-Davidson** is thinking of expanding sales of its most popular motorcycle model by 65%. Do you expect its variable and fixed costs for this model to stay within the relevant range? Explain.

### Red numbers denote Discussion Questions that involve decision-making.

*Homework Manager* repeats all numerical Quick Studies on the book's Website with new numbers.

Determine whether each of the following is best described as a fixed, variable, or mixed cost with respect to product units:

**1.** Factory supervisor's salary.
**2.** Taxes on factory building.
**3.** Rubber used to manufacture athletic shoes.
**4.** Maintenance of factory machinery.
**5.** Packaging expense.
**6.** Wages of an assembly-line worker paid on the basis of acceptable units produced.

## QUICK STUDY

**QS 18-1**
Cost behavior identification

C1

**QS 18-2**

Cost behavior identification

C1

Listed here are four series of separate costs measured at various volume levels. Examine each series and identify whether it is best described as a fixed, variable, step-wise, or curvilinear cost. (It may help to graph the cost series.)

| Volume (Units) | Series 1 | Series 2 | Series 3 | Series 4 |
|---|---|---|---|---|
| 0 | $ 0 | $900 | $ 400 | $200 |
| 100 | 400 | 900 | 400 | 210 |
| 200 | 800 | 900 | 400 | 240 |
| 300 | 1,200 | 900 | 800 | 290 |
| 400 | 1,600 | 900 | 800 | 380 |
| 500 | 2,000 | 900 | 1,200 | 500 |
| 600 | 2,400 | 900 | 1,200 | 640 |

**QS 18-3**

Cost behavior estimation

C1   P1

This scatter diagram reflects past maintenance hours and their corresponding maintenance costs.

1. Draw an estimated line of cost behavior.
2. Estimate the fixed and variable components of maintenance costs.

**QS 18-4**

Contribution margin per
unit and break-even units   P2

MCU Phone Company sells its cordless phone for $100 per unit. Fixed costs total $180,000, and variable costs are $40 per unit. Determine (1) contribution margin per unit and (2) break-even point in units.

**QS 18-5**

Contribution margin ratio
and break-even dollars   P2

Refer to QS 18-4. Determine (1) contribution margin ratio and (2) break-even point in dollars.

**QS 18-6**

CVP analysis and target income

C3   P2

Refer to QS 18-4. Assume that MCU Phone Co. is subject to a 30% income tax rate. Compute the units of product that must be sold to earn after-tax income of $140,000.

**QS 18-7**

CVP assumptions

C2

Which one of the following is an assumption that underlies cost-volume-profit analysis?
1. Selling price per unit must change in proportion to the number of units sold.
2. All costs have approximately the same relevant range.
3. For costs classified as variable, the costs per unit of output must change constantly.
4. For costs classified as fixed, the costs per unit of output must remain constant.

**QS 18-8**

Operating leverage analysis   A2

A high proportion of Company A's total costs are variable with respect to units sold; a high proportion of Company B's total costs are fixed with respect to units sold. Which company is likely to have a higher degree of operating leverage (DOL)? Explain.

Hot Pager Company manufactures and sells two products, green beepers and gold beepers, in the ratio of 5:3. Fixed costs are $85,000, and the contribution margin per composite unit is $170. What number of both green and gold beepers is sold at the break-even point?

**QS 18-9**
Multiproduct break-even
P4

---

🖑 ✏️ *Homework Manager repeats all numerical Exercises on the book's Website with new numbers.*

---

A company reports the following information about its sales and its cost of sales. Each unit of its product sells for $500. Use these data to prepare a scatter diagram. Draw an estimated line of cost behavior and determine whether the cost appears to be variable, fixed, or mixed.

| Period | Sales | Cost of Sales |
|---|---|---|
| 1 . . . . . . . . . . . | $15,000 | $10,100 |
| 2 . . . . . . . . . . . | 11,500 | 7,500 |
| 3 . . . . . . . . . . . | 10,500 | 7,000 |
| 4 . . . . . . . . . . . | 7,500 | 5,500 |
| 5 . . . . . . . . . . . | 9,000 | 6,000 |
| 6 . . . . . . . . . . . | 12,500 | 9,500 |

**EXERCISES**

**Exercise 18-1**
Measurement of cost behavior using a scatter diagram
P1

---

Following are five graphs representing various cost behaviors. (1) Identify whether the cost behavior in each graph is mixed, step-wise, fixed, variable, or curvilinear. (2) Identify the graph (by number) that best illustrates each cost behavior: (a) Factory policy requires one supervisor for every 30 factory workers; (b) real estate taxes on factory; (c) electricity charge that includes the standard monthly charge plus a charge for each kilowatt hour; (d) commissions to salespersons; and (e) costs of hourly paid workers that provide substantial gains in efficiency when a few workers are added but gradually smaller gains in efficiency when more workers are added.

**Exercise 18-2**
Cost behavior in graphs
C1

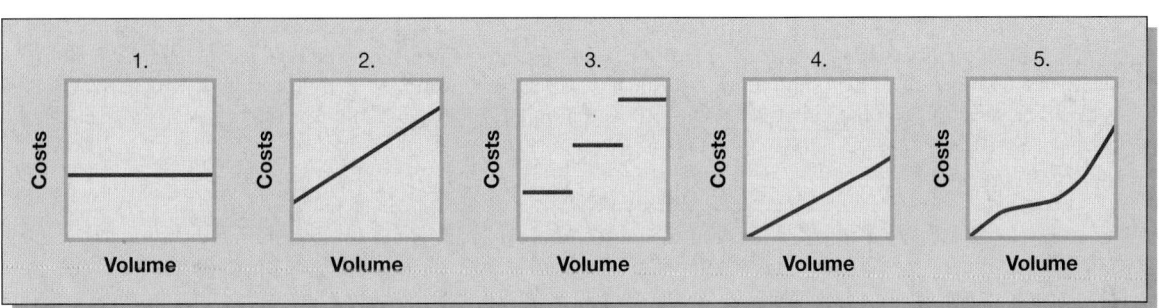

---

The left column lists several categories of costs. The right column presents short definitions of those costs. In the blank space beside each of the numbers in the right column, write the letter of the cost best described by the definition.

**A.** Total cost
**B.** Mixed cost
**C.** Variable cost
**D.** Curvilinear cost
**E.** Step-wise cost
**F.** Fixed cost

_____ **1.** This cost remains constant over all volume levels within the productive capacity for the planning period.

_____ **2.** This cost increases in direct proportion to increases in volume; its amount is constant for each unit produced.

_____ **3.** This cost is the combined amount of all the other costs.

_____ **4.** This cost remains constant over a limited range of volume; when it reaches the end of its limited range, it changes by a lump sum and remains at that level until it exceeds another limited range.

_____ **5.** This cost has a component that remains the same over all volume levels and another component that increases in direct proportion to increases in volume.

_____ **6.** This cost increases when volume increases, but the increase is not constant for each unit produced.

**Exercise 18-3**
Cost behavior defined
C1

## Exercise 18-4

Cost behavior identification

C1

Following are five series of costs *A* through *E* measured at various volume levels. Examine each series and identify which is fixed, variable, mixed, step-wise, or curvilinear.

| | Volume (Units) | Series A | Series B | Series C | Series D | Series E |
|---|---|---|---|---|---|---|
| 1 | 0 | $     0 | $2,500 | $     0 | $2,000 | $4,000 |
| 2 | 200 | 3,600 | 3,100 | 6,000 | 2,000 | 4,000 |
| 3 | 400 | 7,200 | 3,700 | 6,600 | 4,000 | 4,000 |
| 4 | 600 | 10,800 | 4,300 | 7,200 | 4,000 | 4,000 |
| 5 | 800 | 14,400 | 4,900 | 8,200 | 6,000 | 4,000 |
| 6 | 1,000 | 18,000 | 5,500 | 9,600 | 6,000 | 4,000 |
| 7 | 1,200 | 21,600 | 6,100 | 13,500 | 8,000 | 4,000 |

## Exercise 18-5

Scatter diagram and measurement of cost behavior

P1

Use the following information about sales and costs to prepare a scatter diagram. Draw a cost line that reflects the behavior displayed by this cost. Determine whether the cost is variable, step-wise, fixed, mixed, or curvilinear.

| Period | Sales | Costs | Period | Sales | Costs |
|---|---|---|---|---|---|
| 1 | $760 | $590 | 9 | $580 | $390 |
| 2 | 800 | 560 | 10 | 320 | 240 |
| 3 | 200 | 230 | 11 | 240 | 230 |
| 4 | 400 | 400 | 12 | 720 | 550 |
| 5 | 480 | 390 | 13 | 280 | 260 |
| 6 | 620 | 550 | 14 | 440 | 410 |
| 7 | 680 | 590 | 15 | 380 | 260 |
| 8 | 540 | 430 | | | |

## Exercise 18-6

Predicting sales and variable costs using contribution margin

C3

Orlando Company management predicts that it will incur fixed costs of $250,000 and earn pretax income of $350,000 in the next period. Its expected contribution margin ratio is 60%. Use this information to compute the amounts of (1) total dollar sales and (2) total variable costs.

## Exercise 18-7

Contribution margin, break-even, and CVP chart   P2   P3

Apollo Company manufactures a single product that sells for $168 per unit and whose total variable costs are $126 per unit. The company's annual fixed costs are $630,000. (1) Use this information to compute the company's (a) contribution margin, (b) contribution margin ratio, (c) break-even point in units, and (d) break-even point in dollars of sales. (2) Draw a CVP chart for the company.

## Exercise 18-8

Income reporting and break-even analysis   C3

Refer to Exercise 18-7. (1) Prepare a contribution margin income statement for Apollo Company showing sales, variable costs, and fixed costs at the break-even point. (2) If Apollo's fixed costs increase by $135,000, what amount of sales (in dollars) is needed to break even?

## Exercise 18-9

Computing sales to achieve target income

C3

Apollo Company management (in Exercise 18-7) targets an annual after-tax income of $840,000. The company is subject to a 20% income tax rate. Assume that fixed costs remain at $630,000. Compute the (1) unit sales to earn the target after-tax net income and (2) dollar sales to earn the target after-tax net income.

## Exercise 18-10

Forecasted income statement

C3

Apollo Company sales manager (in Exercise 18-7) predicts that annual sales of the company's product will soon reach 40,000 units and its price will increase to $200 per unit. According to the production manager, the variable costs are expected to increase to $140 per unit but fixed costs will remain at $630,000. The income tax rate is 20%. What amounts of pretax and after-tax income can the company expect to earn from these predicted changes? (*Hint:* Prepare a forecasted contribution margin income statement as in Exhibit 18.20.)

**Check**   Forecast income, $1,416,000

Greenspan Company management predicts $500,000 of variable costs, $800,000 of fixed costs, and a pretax income of $100,000 in the next period. Management also predicts that the contribution margin per unit will be $60. Use this information to compute the (1) total expected dollar sales for next period and (2) number of units expected to be sold next period.

**Exercise 18-11**
Predicting unit and dollar sales
C3

---

Cinquante Company expects to sell 100,000 units of its product next year, which would generate total sales of $12 million. Management predicts that pretax net income for next year will be $3,000,000 and that the contribution margin per unit will be $40. (1) Use this information to compute next year's total expected (a) variable costs and (b) fixed costs. (2) Prepare a CVP chart from this information.

**Exercise 18-12**
Computation of variable and fixed costs; CVP chart   P3

---

Company A is a manufacturer with current sales of $1,000,000 and a 65% contribution margin. Its fixed costs equal $500,000. Company B is a consulting firm with current service revenues of $1,000,000 and a 25% contribution margin. Its fixed costs equal $100,000. Compute the degree of operating leverage (DOL) for each company. Identify which company benefits more from a 20% increase in sales and explain why.

**Exercise 18-13**
Operating leverage computed and applied
A2

---

Home Builders sells windows and doors in the ratio of 8:2 (windows:doors). The selling price of each window is $100 and of each door is $250. The variable cost of a window is $62.50 and of a door is $175. Fixed costs are $450,000. Use this information to determine the (1) selling price per composite unit, (2) variable costs per composite unit, (3) break-even point in composite units, and (4) number of units of each product that will be sold at the break-even point.

**Exercise 18-14**
CVP analysis using composite units   P4

**Check**   (3) 1,000 units

---

Edge Equipment Co. manufactures and markets a number of rope products. Management is considering the future of Product XT, a special rope for hang gliding, that has not been as profitable as planned. Since Product XT is manufactured and marketed independently of the other products, its total costs can be precisely measured. Next year's plans call for a $150 selling price per 100 yards of XT rope. Its fixed costs for the year are expected to be $200,000, up to a maximum capacity of 550,000 yards. Forecasted variable costs are $100 per 100 yards of XT rope.

**PROBLEM SET A**

**Problem 18-1A**
CVP analysis and charting

P2   P3

mhhe.com/wild

**Check**   (1) Break-even sales, 4,000 units or $600,000

**Required**

1. Estimate Product XT's break-even point in terms of (a) sales units and (b) sales dollars.
2. Prepare a CVP chart for Product XT like that in Exhibit 18.11. Use 550,000 yards as the maximum number of sales units on the horizontal axis of the graph, and $900,000 as the maximum dollar amount on the vertical axis.
3. Prepare a contribution margin income statement showing sales, variable costs, and fixed costs for Product XT at the break-even point.

---

Lazra Co.'s monthly sales and cost data for its operating activities of the past year follow. Management wants to use these data to predict future fixed and variable costs.

**Problem 18-2A**
Scatter diagram and cost behavior estimation
P1

| Period | Sales | Total Cost |
|---|---|---|
| 1 ........... | $160,000 | $ 80,000 |
| 2 ........... | 80,000 | 50,000 |
| 3 ........... | 140,000 | 110,000 |
| 4 ........... | 100,000 | 50,000 |
| 5 ........... | 150,000 | 115,000 |
| 6 ........... | 100,000 | 60,000 |
| 7 ........... | 170,000 | 110,000 |
| 8 ........... | 140,000 | 80,000 |
| 9 ........... | 10,000 | 40,000 |
| 10 ........... | 80,000 | 70,000 |
| 11 ........... | 50,000 | 50,000 |
| 12 ........... | 55,000 | 40,000 |

**Required**

1. Prepare a scatter diagram for these data with sales volume (in $) plotted on the horizontal axis and total cost plotted on the vertical axis.

2. Estimate the line of cost behavior by a visual inspection and draw it on the scatter diagram. (Assume a linear relation, which means that you should draw a straight cost line on the graph.)

3. Using the estimated line of cost behavior from part 2 and the assumption that the future will be like the past, predict the monthly fixed costs. Also predict variable costs *per sales dollar*.

4. Use the estimated line of cost behavior and results from part 3 to predict future total costs when sales volume is (a) $100,000 and (b) $150,000.

---

**Problem 18-3A**

Break-even analysis; income targeting and forecasting

C3   P2

Jetson Co. sold 20,000 units of its only product and incurred a $50,000 loss (ignoring taxes) for the current year as shown below. During a planning session for year 2006's activities, the production manager notes that variable costs can be reduced 50% by installing a machine that automates several operations. To obtain these savings, the company must increase its annual fixed costs by $150,000. The maximum output capacity of the company is 40,000 units per year.

| JETSON COMPANY | |
| --- | --- |
| **Contribution Margin Income Statement** | |
| **For Year Ended December 31, 2005** | |
| Sales . . . . . . . . . . . . . . . . . . | $750,000 |
| Variable costs . . . . . . . . . . . . | 600,000 |
| Contribution margin . . . . . . . | 150,000 |
| Fixed costs . . . . . . . . . . . . . | 200,000 |
| Net loss . . . . . . . . . . . . . . . | $ (50,000) |

**Required**

1. Compute the break-even point in dollar sales for year 2005.

2. Compute the predicted break-even point in dollar sales for year 2006 assuming the machine is installed and there is no change in unit sales price.

3. Prepare a forecasted contribution margin income statement for 2006 that shows the expected results with the machine installed. Assume that the unit sales price and the number of units sold will not change and no income taxes.

4. Compute the sales level required in both dollars and units to earn $140,000 of after-tax income in 2006 with the machine installed and no change in unit sales price. Assume that the income tax rate is 30%. (*Hint:* Use procedures in Exhibits 18.14 and 18.16.)

5. Prepare a forecasted contribution margin income statement that shows the results at the sales level computed in part 4. Assume an income tax rate of 30%.

---

**Problem 18-4A**

Break-even analysis, different cost structures, and income calculations

C3

Letter Co. produces and sells two products, T and O. It manufactures these products in separate factories and markets them through different channels. They have no shared costs. This year, Letter sold 50,000 units of each product. Sales and costs for each product follow.

| | Product T | Product O |
| --- | --- | --- |
| Sales . . . . . . . . . . . . . . . . . . . . . . | $800,000 | $800,000 |
| Variable costs . . . . . . . . . . . . . . | 560,000 | 100,000 |
| Contribution margin . . . . . . . . . | 240,000 | 700,000 |
| Fixed costs . . . . . . . . . . . . . . . . | 100,000 | 560,000 |
| Income before taxes . . . . . . . . . | 140,000 | 140,000 |
| Income taxes (32% rate) . . . . . . | 44,800 | 44,800 |
| Net income . . . . . . . . . . . . . . . . | $ 95,200 | $ 95,200 |

**Required**

1. Compute the break-even point in dollar sales for each product.

2. Assume that the company expects sales of each product to decline to 33,000 units next year with no change in unit sales price. Prepare forecasted financial results for next year following the format of the contribution margin income statement as shown above with columns for each of the two products (assume a 32% tax rate). Also, assume that any loss before taxes yields a 32% tax savings.

3. Assume that the company expects sales of each product to increase to 64,000 units next year with no change in unit sales price. Prepare forecasted financial results for next year following the format of the contribution margin income statement as shown above with columns for each of the two products (assume a 32% tax rate).

*Analysis Component*

4. If sales greatly decrease, which product would experience a greater loss? Explain.

5. Describe some factors that might have created the different cost structures for these two products.

**Check**  (2) After-tax income: T, $39,712; O, $(66,640)

(3) After-tax income: T, $140,896; O, $228,480

---

This year Cairo Company sold 35,000 units of its only product for $16 per unit. Manufacturing and selling the product required $120,000 of fixed manufacturing costs and $180,000 of fixed selling and administrative costs. Its per unit variable costs were as follows:

**Problem 18-5A**
Analysis of price, cost, and volume changes for contribution margin and net income

C3  P2

mhhe.com/wild

| | |
|---|---|
| Material ..................................... | $4.00 |
| Direct labor (paid on the basis of completed units) ....... | 3.00 |
| Variable overhead costs .......................... | 0.40 |
| Variable selling and administrative costs .............. | 0.20 |

Next year the company will use new material that is easier to work. The new material will reduce material costs by 60% and direct labor costs by 40% and will not affect product quality or marketability. Management is considering an increase in the unit sales price to reduce the number of units sold because the factory's output is nearing its annual output capacity of 40,000 units. Two plans are being considered. Under plan 1, the company will keep the price at the current level and sell the same volume as last year. This plan will increase income because of the reduced costs from using the new material. Under plan 2, the company will increase price by 25%. This plan will decrease unit sales volume by 10%. Under both plans 1 and 2, the total fixed costs and the variable costs per unit for overhead and for selling and administrative costs will remain the same.

**Required**

1. Compute the break-even point in dollar sales for both (a) plan 1 and (b) plan 2.

2. Prepare a forecasted contribution margin income statement with two columns showing the expected results of plan 1 and plan 2. The statements should report sales, total variable costs, contribution margin, total fixed costs, income before taxes, income taxes (30% rate), and net income.

**Check**  (1) Breakeven: Plan 1, $400,000; Plan 2, $375,000

(2) Net income: Plan 1, $84,000; Plan 2, $142,800

---

National Co. manufactures and sells three products: red, white, and blue. Their unit sales prices are red, $55; white, $85; and blue, $110. The per unit variable costs to manufacture and sell these products are red, $40; white, $60; and blue, $80. Their sales mix is reflected in a ratio of 5:4:2 (red:white:blue). Annual fixed costs shared by all three products are $150,000. One type of raw material has been used to manufacture all three products. The company has developed a new material of equal quality for less cost. The new material would reduce variable costs per unit as follows: red, by $10; white, by $20; and blue, by $10. However, the new material requires new equipment, which will increase annual fixed costs by $20,000. (Round answers to whole composite unit.)

**Problem 18-6A**
Break-even analysis with composite units

P4  C3

**Required**

1. If it continues to use the old material, determine the company's break-even point in both sales units and sales dollars of each individual product.

2. If it uses the new material, determine the company's new break-even point in both sales units and sales dollars of each individual product.

**Check**  (1) Old plan breakeven, 639 composite units

(2) New plan breakeven, 442 composite units

*Analysis Component*

3. What insight does this analysis offer management for long-term planning?

## PROBLEM SET B

### Problem 18-1B
CVP analysis and charting

P2   P3

Jammin Co. manufactures and markets a number of products. Management is considering the future of one product, electronic keyboards, that has not been as profitable as planned. Since this product is manufactured and marketed independently of the other products, its total costs can be precisely measured. Next year's plans call for a $225 selling price per unit. The fixed costs for the year are expected to be $30,000, up to a maximum capacity of 700 units. Forecasted variable costs are $150 per unit.

**Required**

**Check** (1) Break-even sales, 400 units or $90,000

1. Estimate the keyboards' break-even point in terms of (a) sales units and (b) sales dollars.
2. Prepare a CVP chart for keyboards like that in Exhibit 18.11. Use 700 keyboards as the maximum number of sales units on the horizontal axis of the graph, and $180,000 as the maximum dollar amount on the vertical axis.
3. Prepare a contribution margin income statement showing sales, variable costs, and fixed costs for keyboards at the break-even point.

### Problem 18-2B
Scatter diagram and cost behavior estimation

P1

Koto Co.'s monthly sales and costs data for its operating activities of the past year follow. Management wants to use these data to predict future fixed and variable costs.

| Period | Sales | Total Costs |
|--------|-------|-------------|
| 1 | $390 | $194 |
| 2 | 250 | 174 |
| 3 | 210 | 146 |
| 4 | 310 | 178 |
| 5 | 190 | 162 |
| 6 | 430 | 220 |
| 7 | 290 | 186 |
| 8 | 370 | 210 |
| 9 | 270 | 170 |
| 10 | 170 | 130 |
| 11 | 350 | 190 |
| 12 | 230 | 158 |

**Required**

1. Prepare a scatter diagram for these data with sales volume (in $) plotted on the horizontal axis and total costs plotted on the vertical axis.
2. Estimate the line of cost behavior by a visual inspection and draw it on the scatter diagram. (Assume a linear relation, which means that you should draw a straight cost line on the graph.)

**Check** (3) Variable costs, $0.30 per sales dollar; Fixed costs, $90

3. Use the estimated line of cost behavior from part 2 and the assumption that the future will be like the past, to predict the monthly fixed costs. Also predict variable costs *per sales dollar*.
4. Use the estimated line of cost behavior and results from part 3 to predict future total costs when sales volume is (a) $150 and (b) $250.

### Problem 18-3B
Break-even analysis; income targeting and forecasting

C3   P2

Caruso Co. sold 40,000 units of its only product and incurred a $100,000 loss (ignoring taxes) for the current year as shown below.

| CARUSO COMPANY<br>Contribution Margin Income Statement<br>For Year Ended December 31, 2005 | |
|---|---|
| Sales | $1,500,000 |
| Variable costs | 1,200,000 |
| Contribution margin | 300,000 |
| Fixed costs | 400,000 |
| Net loss | $ (100,000) |

During a planning session for year 2006's activities, the production manager notes that variable costs can be reduced 50% by installing a machine that automates several operations. To obtain these savings, the company must increase its annual fixed costs by $300,000. The maximum output capacity of the company is 80,000 units per year.

**Required**

1. Compute the break-even point in dollar sales for year 2005.

2. Compute the predicted break-even point in dollar sales for year 2006 assuming the machine is installed and no change in unit sales price. (Round the change in variable costs to a whole number.)

3. Prepare a forecasted contribution margin income statement for 2006 that shows the expected results with the machine installed. Assume that the unit sales price and the number of units sold will not change and no income taxes.

4. Compute the sales level required in both dollars and units to earn $280,000 of after-tax income in 2006 with the machine installed and no change in unit sales price. Assume that the income tax rate is 30%. (*Hint:* Use procedures in Exhibits 18.14 and 18.16.)

5. Prepare a forecasted contribution margin income statement that shows the results at the sales level computed in part 4. Assume an income tax rate of 30%.

**Check**   (3) Net income, $200,000

(4) Required sales, $1,833,333 or 48,889 units

(5) Net income, $280,000

---

Dominico Co. produces and sells two products, BB and TT. It manufactures these products in separate factories and markets them through different channels. They have no shared costs. This year, Dominico Co. sold 120,000 units of each product. Sales and costs for each product follow.

**Problem 18-4B**
Break-even analysis, different cost structures, and income calculations

C3

| | Product BB | Product TT |
|---|---|---|
| Sales ..................... | $3,000,000 | $3,000,000 |
| Variable costs .............. | 1,800,000 | 600,000 |
| Contribution margin .......... | 1,200,000 | 2,400,000 |
| Fixed costs ................. | 600,000 | 1,800,000 |
| Income before taxes .......... | 600,000 | 600,000 |
| Income taxes (35% rate) ....... | 210,000 | 210,000 |
| Net income ................. | $ 390,000 | $ 390,000 |

**Required**

1. Compute the break-even point in dollar sales for each product.

2. Assume that the company expects sales of each product to decline to 104,000 units next year with no change in unit sales price. Prepare forecasted financial results for next year following the format of the contribution margin income statement as shown above with columns for each of the two products (assume a 35% tax rate).

3. Assume that the company expects sales of each product to increase to 190,000 units next year with no change in unit sales price. Prepare forecasted financial results for next year following the format of the contribution margin income statement as shown above with columns for each of the two products (assume a 35% tax rate).

**Check**   (2) After-tax income: BB, $286,000; TT, $182,000

(3) After-tax income: BB, $845,000; TT, $1,300,000

*Analysis Component*

4. If sales greatly increase, which product would experience a greater increase in profit? Explain.

5. Describe some factors that might have created the different cost structures for these two products.

---

This year Jostens Company earned a disappointing 4.2% after-tax return on sales from marketing 100,000 units of its only product. The company buys its product in bulk and repackages it for resale at the price of $25 per unit. Jostens incurred the following costs this year:

**Problem 18-5B**
Analysis of price, cost, and volume changes for contribution margin and net income

C3  P2

| | |
|---|---|
| Total variable unit costs ........... | $1,000,000 |
| Total variable packaging costs ....... | $ 100,000 |
| Fixed costs .................... | $1,250,000 |
| Income tax rate ................ | 30% |

The marketing manager claims that next year's results will be the same as this year's unless some changes are made. The manager predicts the company can increase the number of units sold by 80% if it reduces the selling price by 20% and upgrades the packaging. This change would increase variable packaging costs by 25%. Increased sales would allow the company to take advantage of a 20% quantity purchase discount on the cost of the bulk product. Neither the packaging change nor the volume discount would affect fixed costs, which provide an annual output capacity of 200,000 units.

**Required**

1. Compute the break-even point in dollar sales under the (a) existing business strategy and (b) new strategy that alters both unit sales price and variable costs.

2. Prepare a forecasted contribution margin income statement with two columns showing the expected results of (a) the existing strategy and (b) changing to the new strategy. The statements should report sales, total variable costs (unit and packaging), contribution margin, fixed costs, income before taxes, income taxes, and net income. Also determine the after-tax return on sales for these two strategies.

---

**Problem 18-6B**

Break-even analysis with composite units

P4  C3

Texon Co. manufactures and sells three products: product 1, product 2, and product 3. Their unit sales prices are product 1, $40; product 2, $30; and product 3, $14. The per unit variable costs to manufacture and sell these products are product 1, $30; product 2, $20; and product 3, $8. Their sales mix is reflected in a ratio of 6:3:5. Annual fixed costs shared by all three products are $200,000. One type of raw material has been used to manufacture products 1 and 2. The company has developed a new material of equal quality for less cost. The new material would reduce variable costs per unit as follows: product 1 by $10, and product 2, by $5. However, the new material requires new equipment, which will increase annual fixed costs by $50,000.

**Required**

1. If it continues to use the old material, determine the company's break-even point in both sales units and sales dollars of each individual product.

2. If it uses the new material, determine the company's new break-even point in both sales units and sales dollars of each individual product.

*Analysis Component*

3. What insight does this analysis offer management for long-term planning?

---

# PROBLEM SET C

Problem Set C is available at the book's Website to further reinforce and assess your learning.

---

# SERIAL PROBLEM

Success Systems

*(This serial problem began in Chapter 1 and continues through most of the book. If previous chapter segments were not completed, the serial problem can begin at this point. It is helpful, but not necessary, for you to use the Working Papers that accompany the book.)*

Success Systems sells upscale modular desk units and office chairs in the ratio of 2:1 (desk unit: chair). The selling price is $2,500 per desk unit and $1,000 per chair. The variable cost is $1,500 per desk unit and $500 per chair. Fixed costs are $60,000.

**Required**

1. Compute the selling price per composite unit.
2. Compute the variable costs per composite unit.

3. Compute the break-even point in composite units.
4. Compute the number of units of each product that would be sold at the break-even point.

**BTN 18-1** **Krispy Kreme** has expanded its product line from the original hot glazed yeast-raised donut to 19 varieties of donuts. Assume that you are to head Krispy Kreme's new product, special blended "America's Cup of Coffee," to be sold through its chain of stores. You have permission to use all existing resources, such as its purchasing department, legal department, and buildings and equipment, to get the coffee to market.

### REPORTING IN ACTION

C1

**Required**

**1.** What costs, variable or fixed, are your most immediate concern? Explain.

**2.** Identify the coffee's direct costs and where they are primarily reflected in the financial reports.

**3.** Assume that the contribution margin per package of coffee is 60% and you anticipate coffee sales of $5 million this year. Explain why gross margin on the income statement will not fully reflect your success. (*Hint:* Consider the difference between gross margin and contribution margin.)

**BTN 18-2** Both **Krispy Kreme** and **Tastykake** make baked goods, but one company is usually more profitable than the other with its products. We know that each company makes decisions about purchasing plant assets and that the fixed costs along with the variable costs of manufacturing and selling determine the break-even point and profitability of these companies.

### COMPARATIVE ANALYSIS

P2 C3 A2

**Required**

**1.** Using the following data, compute the total cost per each dozen (or unit) of baked goods for Krispy Kreme and Tastykake. (Assume that sales volume equals production volume.)

| | Krispy Kreme | Tastykake |
|---|---|---|
| Estimated sales units and price ......... | 10,000 units @ $6/unit | 10,000 units @ $6/unit |
| Direct material per unit .............. | $1.00/unit | $1.00/unit |
| Direct labor per unit ................ | $3.00/unit | $3.40/unit |
| Factory rent per month .............. | $ 3,000 | $ 1,000 |
| Factory equipment (depreciation) ....... | $ 5,000 | $ 6,000 |

**2.** Compare Krispy Kreme and Tastykake using the results from your analysis of part 1 to explain why one company is more profitable than the other.

**3.** If sales decline to very low levels, which company will yield the higher net income (computations are unnecessary)?

**BTN 18-3** Labor costs of an auto repair mechanic are seldom based on actual hours worked. Instead, the amount paid a mechanic is based on an industry average of time estimated to complete a repair job. The repair shop bills the customer for the industry average amount of time at the repair center's billable cost per hour. This means a customer can pay, for example, $120 for two hours of work on a car when the actual time worked was only one hour. Many experienced mechanics can complete repair jobs well under the industry average. The average data are compiled by engineering studies and surveys conducted in the auto repair business. Assume that you are asked to complete such a survey for a repair center. The survey calls for objective input, and many questions require detailed cost data and analysis. The mechanics and owners know you have the survey and encourage you to complete it in a way that increases the average billable cost per hour for repair work.

### ETHICS CHALLENGE

C1

**Required**

Write a one-page memorandum to the mechanics and owners that describes the direct labor analysis you will undertake in completing this survey.

**BTN 18-4** Several important assumptions underlie CVP analysis. Assumptions often help simplify and focus our analysis of sales and costs. A common application of CVP analysis is as a tool to forecast sales, costs, and income.

### COMMUNICATING IN PRACTICE

C2

**Required**

Assume that you are actively searching for a job. Prepare a one-half page report identifying (1) three assumptions relating to your expected revenue (salary) and (2) three assumptions relating to your expected costs for the first year of your new job. Be prepared to discuss your assumptions in class.

---

**TAKING IT TO THE NET**

C1  C3

mhhe.com/wild

**BTN 18-5**  Access and review the entrepreneurial information at **Business Owner's Toolkit** [Toolkit.cch.com]. Access and review its *Initial Cash Requirements Worksheet* for a business start-up [Toolkit.cch.com/tools/CashNe_m.asp] or similar worksheets related to controls of cash and costs.

**Required**

Write a one-half page report that describes the information and resources available at the Business Owner's Toolkit to help the owner of a start-up business to control and monitor its costs.

---

**TEAMWORK IN ACTION**

C2

**BTN 18-6**  A local movie theater owner explains to you that ticket sales on weekends and evenings are strong, but attendance during the weekdays, Monday through Thursday, is poor. The owner proposes to offer a contract to the local grade school to show educational materials at the theater for a set charge per student during school hours. The owner asks your help to prepare a CVP analysis listing the cost and sales projections for the proposal. The owner must propose to the school's administration a charge per child. At a minimum, the charge per child needs to be sufficient for the theater to break even.

**Required**

Your team is to prepare two separate lists of questions that enable you to complete a reliable CVP analysis of this situation. One list is to be answered by the school's administration, the other by the owner of the movie theater.

---

**BUSINESS WEEK ACTIVITY**

C3

**BTN 18-7**  Read the article "Cooking Up a Global Empire" in the May 19, 2003, issue of *Business Week*. (The book's Website provides free access to the article.)

**Required**

**1.** What does the term *haute cuisine* mean?

**2.** What percent of haute cuisine restaurants fail?

**3.** Why is it so difficult for haute cuisine restaurants to break even or earn a profit?

**4.** What formula has **Chef Ducasse** found to make haute cuisine profitable?

---

**ENTREPRENEURIAL DECISION**

C1

**BTN 18-8**  Katrina Markoff of **Vosges Haut Chocolat** has always packaged her chocolates with only one exotic flavor per box. She now is considering offering a new variety box to allow her customers to sample each flavor. Markoff is concerned that offering the variety box in addition to the individually packaged flavors could change costs.

**Required**

**1.** What information do you recommend that Markoff collect to help address her concern?

**2.** What managerial accounting tools might be especially useful to her in this situation?

---

**HITTING THE ROAD**

P4

**BTN 18-9**  Multiproduct break-even analysis is often viewed differently when actually applied in practice. You are to visit a local fast-food restaurant and count the number of items on the menu. To apply multiproduct break-even analysis to the restaurant, similar menu items must often be fit into groups. A reasonable approach is to classify menu items into approximately five groups, for example, drink group. We then estimate average selling price and average variable cost to compute average contribution margin. (*Hint:* The contribution margin ratio on drinks is about 90%.)

**Required**

1. Prepare a one-year multiproduct break-even analysis for the restaurant you visit. Begin by establishing groups. Next, estimate each group's volume and contribution margin. These estimates are necessary to compute each group's contribution margin. Assume that annual fixed costs in total are $500,000 per year. (*Hint:* You must develop your own estimates on volume and contribution margin for each group to obtain the break-even point and sales.)

2. Prepare a one-page report on the results of your analysis. Comment on the volume of sales necessary to break even at a fast-food restaurant.

**BTN 18-10**   Access and review **Grupo Bimbo**'s Website (**GrupoBimbo.com**) to answer the following questions:

1. Do you believe that Grupo Bimbo managers use single product CVP analysis or multiproduct break-even point analysis? Explain.

2. Identify at least seven products as part of Grupo Bimbo's sales mix.

3. On January 21, 2003, Grupo Bimbo added variety to its existing sales mix by entering into an exclusive distributor agreement with what world-famous company?

**GLOBAL DECISION**

C3

*"The way you grow a large company is by growing it a little bit each year, the next thing you know, it's a huge amount"*—John Chuang (far left)

# 19

# Master Budgets and Planning

### A Look Back

Chapter 18 looked at cost behavior and described its relevance for managers in performing cost-volume-profit analysis. That chapter also explained and illustrated the application of cost-volume-profit analysis.

### A Look at This Chapter

This chapter explains the importance of budgeting and describes the master budget and its preparation. It also discusses the value of the master budget to the planning of future business activities.

### A Look Ahead

Chapter 20 focuses on flexible budgets, standard costs, and variance reporting. It explains the usefulness of these procedures and reports for business decisions.

# CAP

**Conceptual**

C1 Describe the importance and benefits of budgeting. *(p. 770)*

C2 Explain the process of budget administration. *(p. 772)*

C3 Describe a master budget and the process of preparing it. *(p. 774)*

**Analytical**

A1 Analyze expense planning using activity-based budgeting. *(p. 783)*

**Procedural**

P1 Prepare each component of a master budget and link each to the budgeting process. *(p. 776)*

P2 Link both operating and capital expenditures budgets to budgeted financial statements. *(p. 780)*

# Big Budgets and Bigger Plans

BOSTON—John Chuang, Mia Wenjen, and Steve Kapner started with a PC in their college dorm room. "We formed a business doing typesetting work," says Chuang. "We soon became known ... as people who knew how to do desktop publishing." The phone rang off the hook. In spite of what Wenjen says was a college term of "serious grade point average tankage and serious parent freakage," the three pushed forward. Their start-up survived and is now called **Aquent** **[Aquent.com]**, which helps its clients with staffing, consulting, outsourcing, and technology.

The three friends always had big plans and even bigger dreams. "We had a sign on our dorm room that read 'Worldwide Headquarters,'" says Chuang. With those plans and dreams came budgets. However, in the early stages, Wenjen admits that their budgeting process and planning were not ideal. We would hire someone, says Wenjen, and then say "you're going to be getting a budget ... one big number of money to spend. Spend it how you see fit, but be smart about it." She would then add, "Spend on things that grow the business."

The friends now more seriously attend to master budgets and the budgeting process. They say budgets help formalize business expectations and objectives. Budgets also help direct employees and put everyone on the same page. "Every manager, for example, has the ability to make monetary decisions without going through various levels of approvals," says Chuang. To make such a system successful requires trust, an understanding of the process, and knowledge of how decisions impact the budgeted financial statements.

The three friends continue to expand their business. Master budgets and planning are an important part of their expansion decisions. "With each new unit we create," says Chuang, "we examine the marketplace first to see if the market has a need for our service and can sustain it." This includes analysis of plans and budgets of both costs and revenues. This approach, says Chuang, has been successful; the company "performs very well." Still, the three want more. "We have a long way to go," adds Chuang. "We're just getting started!"

[Sources: *Aquent Website*, January 2004; *Asian Business News*, Summer 2002; *Staffing Today Website*, February 2002; *Asian American Supersite—Goldsea 100*, 2003.]

After management applies cost-volume-profit analysis or other techniques in devising a strategy for future periods, it then seeks to turn this strategy into action plans. These action plans include financial details that are compiled in a master budget. The budgeting process serves several purposes, including motivating employees and effectively communicating with them. The budget process also helps coordinate a company's activities toward common goals and is useful in evaluating actual results and management performance. In this chapter, we explain how to prepare a master budget and use it as a formal plan of a company's future activities. The ability to prepare this type of formal plan is of enormous help in starting and operating a company. Such planning gives managers a glimpse into the future, and it can help translate ideas into actions.

## Budget Process

### Strategic Budgeting

Most companies prepare long-term strategic plans spanning 5 to 10 years. They then fine-tune them in preparing medium-term and short-term plans. Strategic plans usually set a company's long-term direction. They provide a road map for the future about potential opportunities such as new products, markets, and investments. The strategic plan can be inexact, given its long-term focus. Medium- and short-term plans are more operational and translate strategic plans into actions. These action plans are fairly concrete and consist of defined objectives and goals.

**C1** Describe the importance and benefits of budgeting.

Short-term plans are usually called *budgets* and typically cover a one-year period. A **budget** is a formal statement of a company's future plans. It is usually expressed in monetary terms because the economic or financial aspects of the business are the primary factors driving management's decisions. All managers should be involved in **budgeting,** the process of planning future business actions and expressing them as formal plans. Managers who plan carefully and formalize plans in a budgeting process increase the likelihood of both personal and company success. (Although most firms prepare annual budgets, it is not unusual for organizations to prepare three-year and five-year budgets that are revised at least annually.)

The relevant focus of a budgetary analysis is the future. Management must focus on future transactions and events and the opportunities available. A focus on the future is important because the pressures of daily operating problems often divert management's attention and take precedence over planning. A good budgeting system counteracts this tendency by formalizing the planning process and demanding relevant input. Budgeting makes planning an explicit management responsibility.

### Benchmarking Budgets

The control function requires management to evaluate (benchmark) business operations against some norm. Evaluation involves comparing actual results against one of two usual alternatives: (1) past performance or (2) expected performance.

An evaluation assists management in identifying problems and taking corrective actions if necessary. Evaluation using expected, or budgeted, performance is potentially superior to using past performance to decide whether actual results trigger a need for corrective actions. This is so because past performance is often an inferior standard for evaluation because it fails to consider several changes that can affect current and future activities. Changes in economic conditions, shifts in competitive advantages within the industry, new product developments, increased or decreased advertising, and other factors reduce the usefulness of comparisons with past results. In hi-tech industries, for instance, increasing competition, technological advances, and other innovations often reduce the usefulness of performance comparisons across years.

Budgeted performance is computed after careful analysis and research that attempts to anticipate and adjust for changes in important company, industry, and economic factors. Therefore, budgets usually provide management an effective control and monitoring system.

**Point:** Managers can evaluate performance by preparing reports that compare actual results to budgeted plans.

## Budgeting and Human Behavior

Budgeting provides standards for evaluating performance and can affect the attitudes of employees evaluated by them. It can be used to create a positive effect on employees' attitudes, but it can also create negative effects if not properly applied. Budgeted levels of performance, for instance, must be realistic to avoid discouraging employees. Personnel who will be evaluated should be consulted and involved in preparing the budget to increase their commitment to meeting it. Performance evaluations must allow the affected employees to explain the reasons for apparent performance deficiencies.

The budgeting process has three important guidelines: (1) Employees affected by a budget should be consulted when it is prepared (*participatory budgeting*), (2) goals reflected in a budget should be attainable, and (3) evaluations should be made carefully with opportunities to explain any failures. Budgeting can be a positive motivating force when these guidelines are followed. Budgeted performance levels can provide goals for employees to attain or even exceed as they carry out their responsibilities. This is especially important in organizations that consider the annual budget a "sacred" document.

**Point:** The practice of involving employees in the budgeting process is known as *participatory budgeting*.

> **Decision Insight**
>
> **Budgets Exposed** When companies go public and trade their securities on an organized exchange, management usually develops specific future plans and budgets. For this purpose, companies often develop detailed six- to twelve-month budgets and less-detailed budgets spanning 2 to 5 years.

## Budgeting as a Management Tool

An important management objective in large companies is to ensure that activities of all departments contribute to meeting the company's overall goals. This requires coordination. Budgeting provides a way to achieve this coordination.

We describe later in this chapter that a company's budget, or operating plan, is based on its objectives. This operating plan starts with the sales budget, which drives all other budgets including production, materials, labor, and overhead. The budgeting process coordinates the activities of these various departments to meet the company's overall goals.

## Budgeting Communication

Managers of small companies can adequately explain business plans directly to employees through conversations and other informal communications. However, conversations can create uncertainty and confusion if not supported by clear documentation of the plans. A written budget is preferred and can inform employees in all types of organizations about management's plans. The budget can also communicate management's specific action plans for the employees in the budget period.

> **Decision Ethics**
>
> **Budget Staffer** You learn that your company's earnings for the current period will be far below the budgeted amount reported in the press. You also know that one of your superiors, who is also aware of the earnings shortfall, has accepted a management position with a competitor. This superior is selling her shares of the company. Does this situation present ethical concerns for you?

Answer—p. 791

## Budget Administration

### Budget Committee

C2    Explain the process of budget administration.

The task of preparing a budget should not be the sole responsibility of any one department. Similarly, the budget should not be simply handed down as top management's final word. Instead, budget figures and budget estimates developed through a *bottom-up* process usu-

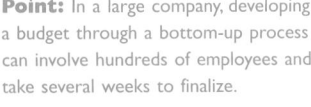

ally are more useful. This includes, for instance, involving the sales department in preparing sales estimates. Likewise, the production department should have initial responsibility for preparing its own expense budget. Without active employee involvement in preparing budget figures, there is a risk these employees will feel that the numbers fail to reflect their special problems and needs.

Most budgets should be developed by a bottom-up process, but the budgeting system requires central guidance. This guidance is supplied by a budget committee of department heads and other executives responsible for seeing that budgeted amounts are realistic and coordinated. If a department submits initial budget figures not reflecting efficient performance, the budget committee should return them with explanatory comments on how to improve them. Then the originating department must either adjust its proposals or explain why they are acceptable. Communication between the originating department and the budget committee should continue as needed to ensure that both parties accept the budget as reasonable, attainable, and desirable.

**Point:** In a large company, developing a budget through a bottom-up process can involve hundreds of employees and take several weeks to finalize.

The concept of continuous improvement applies to budgeting as well as production. **BP** streamlined its monthly budget report from a one-inch-thick stack of monthly control reports to a tidy, two-page flash report on monthly earnings and key production statistics. The key to this efficiency gain was the integration of new budgeting and cost allocation processes with its strategic planning process. BP's controller explained the new role of the finance department with respect to the budgetary control process as follows: "there's less of an attitude that finance's job is to control. People really have come to see that our job is to help attain business objectives."

### Budget Reporting

The budget period usually coincides with the accounting period. Most companies prepare at least an annual budget, which reflects the objectives for the next year. To provide specific guidance, the annual budget usually is separated into quarterly or monthly budgets. These short-term budgets allow management to periodically evaluate performance and take needed corrective action.

Managers can compare actual results to budgeted amounts in a report such as that shown in Exhibit 19.1. This report shows actual amounts, budgeted amounts, and their differences. A difference is called a *variance*. Management examines variances to identify areas for improvement and corrective action.

### Budget Timing

The time period required for the annual budgeting process can vary considerably. For example, budgeting for 2006 can begin as early as January 2005 or as late as December 2005. Large, complex organizations usually require a longer time to prepare their budgets than do smaller organizations. This is so because considerable effort is required to coordinate the different units (departments) within large organizations.

Many companies apply **continuous budgeting** by preparing **rolling budgets.** As each monthly or quarterly budget period goes by, these companies revise their entire set of budgets for the months or quarters remaining and add new monthly or quarterly budgets to replace the ones that have lapsed. At any point in time, monthly or quarterly budgets are

| **ECCENTRIC MUSIC**<br>**Income Statement with Variations from Budget**<br>**For Month Ended April 30, 2005** | | | |
|---|---|---|---|
| | **Actual** | **Budget** | **Variance** |
| Net sales ................................. | $60,500 | $57,150 | $+3,350 |
| Cost of goods sold ......................... | 41,350 | 39,100 | +2,250 |
| Gross profit ............................... | 19,150 | 18,050 | +1,100 |
| Operating expenses | | | |
| Selling expenses | | | |
| Sales salaries ........................... | 6,250 | 6,000 | +250 |
| Advertising .............................. | 900 | 800 | +100 |
| Store supplies .......................... | 550 | 500 | +50 |
| Depreciation—Store equipment .............. | 1,600 | 1,600 | |
| Total selling expenses .................... | 9,300 | 8,900 | +400 |
| General and administrative expenses | | | |
| Office salaries .......................... | 2,000 | 2,000 | |
| Office supplies used ..................... | 165 | 150 | +15 |
| Rent .................................... | 1,100 | 1,100 | |
| Insurance ............................... | 200 | 200 | |
| Depreciation—Office equipment .............. | 100 | 100 | |
| Total general and administrative expenses ....... | 3,565 | 3,550 | +15 |
| Total operating expenses .................... | 12,865 | 12,450 | +415 |
| Net income ............................... | $ 6,285 | $ 5,600 | $ +685 |

**Exhibit 19.1**

Comparing Actual Performance with Budgeted Performance

available for the next 12 months or four quarters. Exhibit 19.2 shows rolling budgets prepared at the end of five consecutive periods. The first set (at top) is prepared in December 2004 and covers the four calendar quarters of 2005. In March 2005, the company prepares another rolling budget for the next four quarters through March 2006. This same process is repeated every three months. As a result, management is continuously planning ahead.

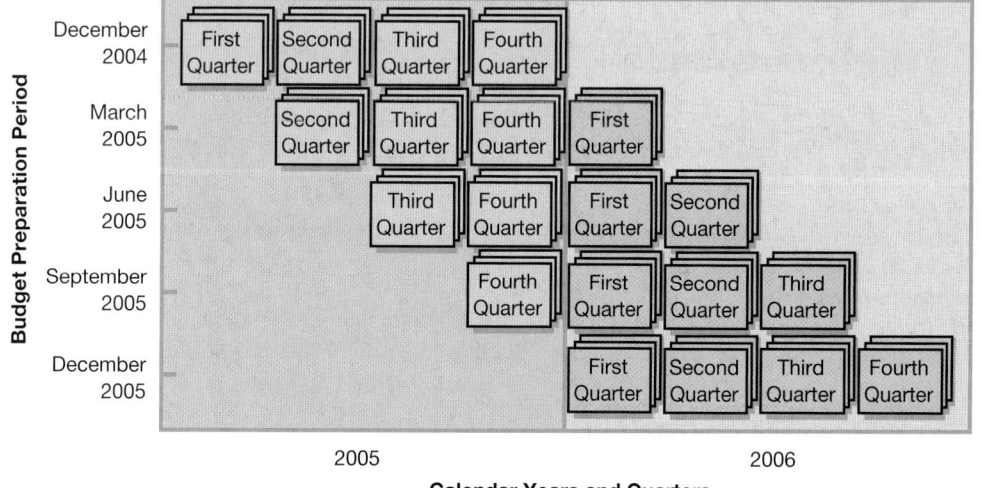

**Exhibit 19.2**

Rolling Budgets

Exhibit 19.2 reflects an annual budget composed of four quarters prepared four times per year using the most recent information available. For example, the budget for the fourth quarter of 2005 is prepared in December 2004 and revised in March, June, and September of 2005. When continuous budgeting is not used, the fourth-quarter budget is nine months old and perhaps out of date when applied.

### Decision Insight

**Budget Calendar**   Many companies use long-range operating budgets. For large companies, three groups usually determine or influence the budgets: creditors, directors, and management. All three are interested in the companies' future cash flows and earnings. The annual budget process often begins six months or more before the budget is due to the board of directors. A typical budget calendar, shown here, provides insight into the budget process during this period.

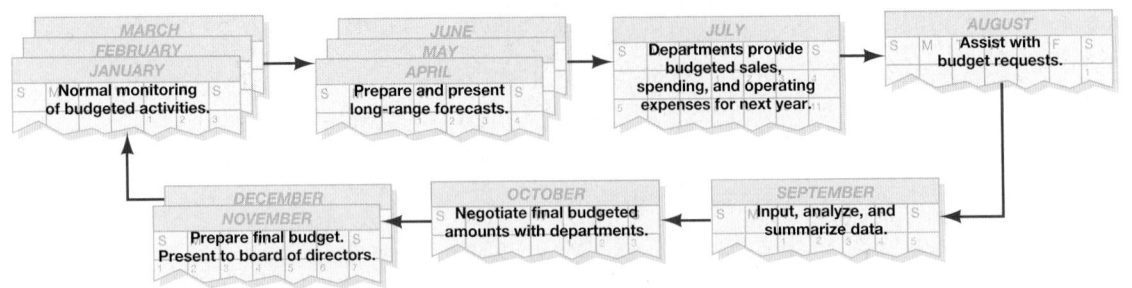

### Quick Check

1. What are the major benefits of budgeting?
2. What is the main responsibility of the budget committee?
3. What is the usual time period covered by a budget?
4. What are rolling budgets?

Answers—p. 791

## Master Budget

**C3**   Describe a master budget and the process of preparing it.

A **master budget** is a formal, comprehensive plan for a company's future. It contains several individual budgets that are linked with each other to form a coordinated plan.

### Master Budget Components

The master budget typically includes individual budgets for sales, purchases, production, various expenses, capital expenditures, and cash. Managers often express the expected financial results of these planned activities with both a budgeted income statement for the budget period and a budgeted balance sheet for the end of the budget period. The usual number and types of budgets included in a master budget depend on the company's size and complexity. A master budget should include, at a minimum, the budgets listed in Exhibit 19.3. In addition to these individual budgets, managers often include supporting calculations and additional tables with the master budget.

### Decision Insight

**Budgeting Targets**   Budgeting is a crucial part of any acquisitions or takeover analyses. Analysis begins by projecting annual sales volume and prices. It then estimates cost of sales, expenses, and income for the next several years. By computing the present value of this projected income stream, buyers determine an offer price.

## Exhibit 19.3

Basic Components of a Master Budget

- **Operating budgets**
  - *Sales budget*
  - For merchandisers add: *Merchandise purchases budget* (units to be purchased)
  - For manufacturers add: *Production budget* (units to be produced)
                            *Manufacturing budget* (manufacturing costs)
  - *Selling expense budget*
  - *General and administrative expense budget*
- **Capital expenditures budget** (expenditures for plant assets)
- **Financial budgets**
  - *Cash budget* (cash receipts and disbursements)
  - *Budgeted income statement*
  - *Budgeted balance sheet*

Some budgets require the input of other budgets. For example, the merchandise purchases budget cannot be prepared until the sales budget has been prepared because the number of units to be purchased depends on how many units are expected to be sold. As a result, we often must sequentially prepare budgets within the master budget.

A typical sequence for a quarterly budget consists of the five steps in Exhibit 19.4. Any stage in this budgeting process might reveal undesirable outcomes, so changes often must be made to prior budgets by repeating the previous steps. For instance, an early version of the cash budget could show an insufficient amount of cash unless cash outlays are reduced. This could yield a reduction in planned equipment purchases. A preliminary budgeted balance sheet could also reveal too much debt from an ambitious capital expenditures budget. Findings such as these often result in revised plans and budgets.

Topic Tackler 19-1

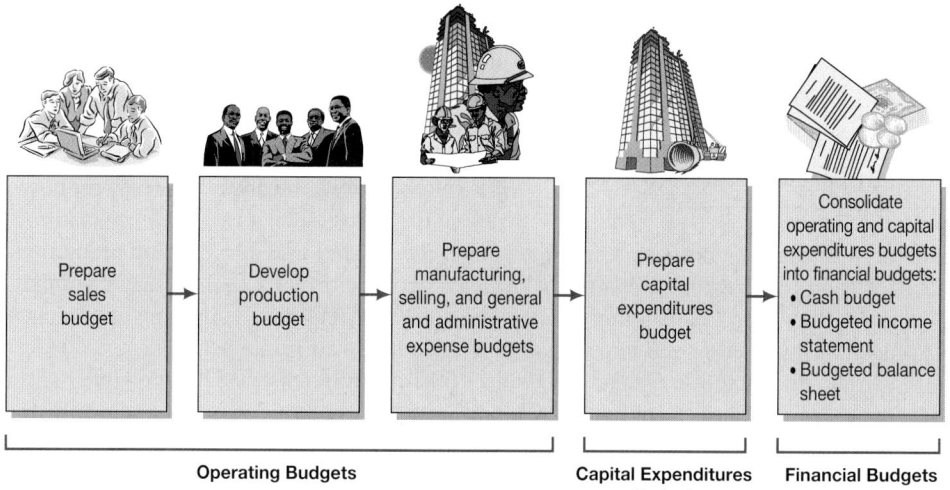

**Exhibit 19.4**

Master Budget Sequence

The remainder of this section explains how Hockey Den (HD), a retailer of youth hockey sticks, prepares its master budget. Its master budget includes operating, capital expenditures, and cash budgets for each month in each quarter. It also includes a budgeted income statement for each quarter and a budgeted balance sheet as of the last day of each quarter. We show how HD prepares budgets for October, November, and December 2005. Exhibit 19.5 presents HD's balance sheet at the start of this budgeting period, which we often refer to as we prepare the component budgets.

**Exhibit 19.5**

Balance Sheet Prior to the Budgeting Periods

| HOCKEY DEN<br>Balance Sheet<br>September 30, 2005 | | |
|---|---|---|
| **Assets** | | |
| Cash | | $ 20,000 |
| Accounts receivable | | 42,000 |
| Inventory (900 units @ $60) | | 54,000 |
| Equipment* | $200,000 | |
| Less accumulated depreciation | 36,000 | 164,000 |
| Total assets | | $280,000 |
| **Liabilities and Equity** | | |
| Liabilities | | |
| Accounts payable | $ 58,200 | |
| Income taxes payable (due 10/31/2005) | 20,000 | |
| Note payable to bank | 10,000 | $ 88,200 |
| Stockholders' equity | | |
| Common stock | 150,000 | |
| Retained earnings | 41,800 | 191,800 |
| Total liabilities and equity | | $280,000 |

* Equipment is depreciated on a straight-line basis over 10 years (salvage value is $20,000).

## P1 Prepare each component of a master budget and link each to the budgeting process.

# Operating Budgets

This section explains HD's preparation of operating budgets. Its operating budgets consist of the sales budget, merchandise purchases budget, selling expense budget, and general and administrative expense budget. HD does not prepare production and manufacturing budgets because it is a merchandiser. (The preparation of production budgets and manufacturing budgets is described in Appendix 19A.)

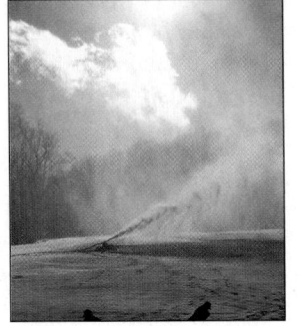

**Sales Budget**   The first step in preparing the master budget is planning the **sales budget,** which shows the planned sales units and the expected dollars from these sales. The sales budget is the starting point in the budgeting process because plans for most departments are linked to sales.

The sales budget should emerge from a careful analysis of forecasted economic and market conditions, business capacity, proposed selling expenses (such as advertising), and predictions of unit sales. A company's sales personnel are usually asked to develop predictions of sales for each territory and department because people normally feel a greater commitment to goals they help set. Another advantage to this participatory budgeting approach is that it draws on knowledge and experience of people involved in the activity.

**Example:** Assume a company's sales force receives a bonus when sales exceed the budgeted amount. How would this arrangement affect the bottom-up process of sales forecasts? *Answer:* Sales reps may understate their budgeted sales.

To illustrate, in September 2005, HD sold 700 hockey sticks at $100 per unit. After considering sales predictions and market conditions, HD prepares its sales budget for the next quarter (three months) plus one extra month (see Exhibit 19.6). The sales budget includes January 2006 because the purchasing department relies on estimated January sales to decide on December 2005 inventory purchases. The sales budget in Exhibit 19.6 includes forecasts of both unit sales and unit prices. Some sales budgets are expressed only in total sales dollars, but most are more detailed. Management finds it useful to know budgeted units and unit prices for many different products, regions, departments, and sales representatives.

## Exhibit 19.6

Sales Budget for Planned Unit and Dollar Sales

| HOCKEY DEN<br>Monthly Sales Budget<br>October 2005–January 2006 | Budgeted<br>Unit Sales | Budgeted<br>Unit Price | Budgeted<br>Total Sales |
|---|---|---|---|
| September 2005 (actual) . . . . . . . | 700 | $100 | $ 70,000 |
| October 2005 . . . . . . . . . . . . . . | 1,000 | $100 | $100,000 |
| November 2005 . . . . . . . . . . . . | 800 | 100 | 80,000 |
| December 2005 . . . . . . . . . . . . . | 1,400 | 100 | 140,000 |
| Total for the quarter . . . . . . . . . | 3,200 | 100 | $320,000 |
| January 2006 . . . . . . . . . . . . . . | 900 | 100 | $ 90,000 |

**Merchandise Purchases Budget**   Companies use various methods to help managers make inventory purchasing decisions. These methods recognize that the number of units added to inventory depends on budgeted sales volume. Whether a company manufactures or purchases the product it sells, budgeted future sales volume is the primary factor in most inventory management decisions. A company must also consider its inventory system and other factors that we discuss next.

Answer—p. 791

***Just-in-time inventory systems.***   Managers of *just-in-time* (JIT) inventory systems use sales budgets for short periods (often as few as one or two days) to order just enough merchandise or materials to satisfy the immediate sales demand. This keeps the amount of inventory to a minimum (or zero in an ideal situation). A JIT system minimizes the costs of maintaining inventory, but it is practical only if customers are content to order in advance or if managers can accurately determine short-term sales demand. Suppliers also must be able and willing to ship small quantities regularly and promptly.

***Safety stock inventory systems.***   Market conditions and manufacturing processes for some products do not allow use of a just-in-time system. Companies in these cases maintain sufficient inventory to reduce the risk and cost of running short. This practice requires enough purchases to satisfy the budgeted sales amounts and to maintain a **safety stock,** a quantity of inventory that provides protection against lost sales caused by unfulfilled demands from customers or delays in shipments from suppliers.

***Merchandise purchases budget preparation.***   A merchandiser usually expresses a **merchandise purchases budget** in both units and dollars. Exhibit 19.7 shows the general layout for this budget in equation form. If this formula is expressed in units and only one product is involved, we can compute the number of dollars of inventory to be purchased for the budget by multiplying the units to be purchased by the cost per unit.

**Point:** Accurate estimates of future sales are crucial in a JIT system.

Topic Tackler 19-2

## Exhibit 19.7

Formula for a Merchandise Purchases Budget

To illustrate, after assessing the cost of keeping inventory along with the risk and cost of inventory shortages, HD decided that the number of units in its inventory at each month-end should equal 90% of next month's predicted sales. For example, inventory at the end of October should equal 90% of budgeted November sales, and the November ending inventory should equal 90% of budgeted December sales, and so on. Also, HD's suppliers expect the September 2005 per unit cost of $60 to remain unchanged through January 2006. This information along with knowledge of 900 units in inventory at September 30 (see Exhibit 19.5) allows the company to prepare the merchandise purchases budget shown in Exhibit 19.8.

**Example:** Assume Hockey Den adopts a JIT system in purchasing merchandise. How will its sales budget differ from its merchandise purchases budget? *Answer:* The two budgets will be similar because future inventory should be near zero.

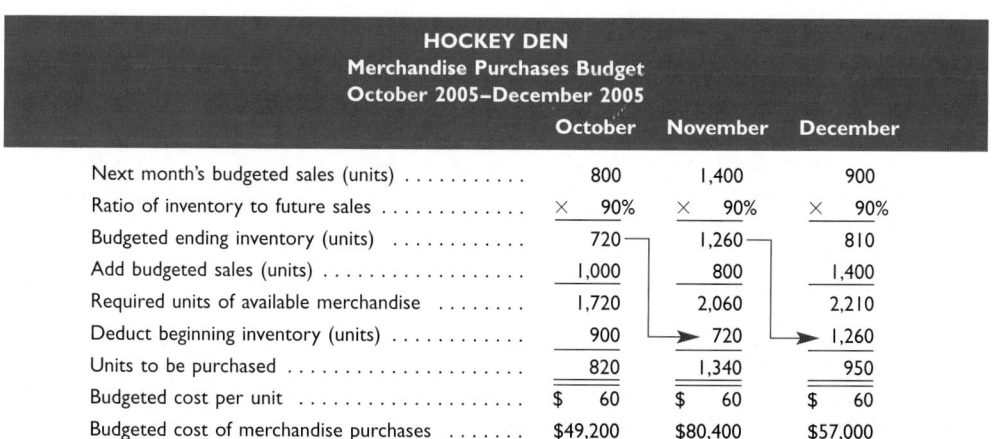

## Exhibit 19.8

Merchandise Purchases Budget

| HOCKEY DEN Merchandise Purchases Budget October 2005–December 2005 | | | |
| --- | --- | --- | --- |
| | October | November | December |
| Next month's budgeted sales (units) | 800 | 1,400 | 900 |
| Ratio of inventory to future sales | × 90% | × 90% | × 90% |
| Budgeted ending inventory (units) | 720 | 1,260 | 810 |
| Add budgeted sales (units) | 1,000 | 800 | 1,400 |
| Required units of available merchandise | 1,720 | 2,060 | 2,210 |
| Deduct beginning inventory (units) | 900 | 720 | 1,260 |
| Units to be purchased | 820 | 1,340 | 950 |
| Budgeted cost per unit | $  60 | $  60 | $  60 |
| Budgeted cost of merchandise purchases | $49,200 | $80,400 | $57,000 |

The first three lines of HD's merchandise purchases budget determine the required ending inventories (in units). Budgeted unit sales are then added to the desired ending inventory to give the required units of available merchandise. We then subtract beginning inventory to determine the budgeted number of units to be purchased. The last line is the budgeted cost of the purchases, computed by multiplying the number of units to be purchased by the predicted cost per unit.

**Example:** If ending inventory in Exhibit 19.8 is required to equal 80% of next month's predicted sales, how many units must be purchased each month? *Answer:* Budgeted ending inventory: Oct. = 640 units; Nov. = 1,120 units; Dec. = 720 units. Required purchases: Oct. = 740 units; Nov. = 1,280 units; Dec. = 1,000 units.

We already indicated that some budgeting systems describe only the total dollars of budgeted sales. Likewise, a system can express a merchandise purchases budget only in terms of the total cost of merchandise to be purchased, omitting the number of units to be purchased. This method assumes a constant relation between sales and cost of goods sold. HD, for instance, might assume the expected cost of goods sold to be 60% of sales, computed from the budgeted unit cost of $60 and the budgeted sales price of $100. However, it still must consider the effects of changes in beginning and ending inventories in determining the amounts to be purchased.

**Point:** To apply these concepts, work Exercise 19-1.

**Selling Expense Budget**   The **selling expense budget** is a plan listing the types and amounts of selling expenses expected during the budget period. Its initial responsibility usually rests with the vice president of marketing or an equivalent sales manager. The selling expense budget is normally created to provide sufficient selling expenses to meet sales goals reflected in the sales budget. Predicted selling expenses are based on both the sales budget and the experience of previous periods. After some or all of the master budget is prepared, management might decide that projected sales volume is inadequate. If so, subsequent adjustments in the sales budget can require corresponding adjustments in the selling expense budget.

To illustrate, HD's selling expense budget is in Exhibit 19.9. The firm's selling expenses consist of commissions paid to sales personnel and a $2,000 monthly salary paid to the sales manager. Sales commissions equal 10% of total sales and are paid in the month sales occur. Sales commissions are variable with respect to sales volume, but the sales manager's salary is fixed. No advertising expenses are budgeted for this particular quarter.

### Decision Insight

**Goals and Budgets**   France Telecom failed to properly budget and coordinate its efforts for World Cup ticket sales. According to the company, it assigned 60 of its operators to take orders for the few thousand tickets available to U.K. citizens. In the first 60 minutes after the phone lines opened, **British Telecom** logged an amazing four million call attempts. The odds of a U.K. soccer fan getting through to the ticket hotline were around one in two million.

**Exhibit 19.9**

Selling Expense Budget

| HOCKEY DEN Selling Expense Budget October 2005–December 2005 | | | | |
| --- | --- | --- | --- | --- |
| | October | November | December | Total |
| Budgeted sales .............. | $100,000 | $80,000 | $140,000 | $320,000 |
| Sales commission percent ....... | × 10% | × 10% | × 10% | × 10% |
| Sales commissions ............ | 10,000 | 8,000 | 14,000 | 32,000 |
| Salary for sales manager ........ | 2,000 | 2,000 | 2,000 | 6,000 |
| Total selling expenses .......... | $ 12,000 | $10,000 | $ 16,000 | $ 38,000 |

**Example:** If sales commissions in Exhibit 19.9 are increased, which budgets are affected? *Answer:* Selling expenses budget, cash budget, and budgeted income statement.

**General and Administrative Expense Budget**   The **general and administrative expense budget** plans the predicted operating expenses not included in the selling expenses budget. General and administrative expenses can be either variable or fixed with respect to sales volume. The office manager responsible for general administration often is responsible for preparing the initial general and administrative expense budget.

Interest expense and income tax expense are often classified as general and administrative expenses in published income statements, but normally cannot be planned at this stage of the budgeting process. The prediction of interest expense follows the preparation of the cash budget and the decisions regarding debt. The predicted income tax expense depends on the budgeted amount of pretax income. Both interest and income taxes are usually beyond the control of the office manager. As a result, they are not used in comparison to the budget to evaluate that person's performance.

Exhibit 19.10 shows HD's general and administrative expense budget. It includes salaries of $54,000 per year, or $4,500 per month (paid each month when they are earned). Using information in Exhibit 19.5, the depreciation on equipment is computed as $18,000 per year [($200,000 − $20,000)/10 years], or $1,500 per month ($18,000/12 months).

| HOCKEY DEN<br>General and Administrative Expense Budget<br>October 2005–December 2005 | | | | |
|---|---|---|---|---|
| | October | November | December | Total |
| Administrative salaries ..................... | $4,500 | $4,500 | $4,500 | $13,500 |
| Depreciation of equipment ................ | 1,500 | 1,500 | 1,500 | 4,500 |
| Total general and administrative expenses ....... | $6,000 | $6,000 | $6,000 | $18,000 |

**Exhibit 19.10**

General and Administrative Expense Budget

**Example:** In Exhibit 19.10, how would a rental agreement of $5,000 per month plus 1% of sales affect the general and administrative expense budget? (Budgeted sales are in Exhibit 19.6.) *Answer: Rent expense:* Oct. = $6,000; Nov. = $5,800; Dec. = $6,400; Total = 18,200; *Revised total general and administrative expenses:* Oct. = $12,000; Nov. = $11,800; Dec. = $12,400; Total = $36,200.

## Quick Check

5. What is a master budget?

6. A master budget (*a*) always includes a manufacturing budget specifying the units to be produced, (*b*) is prepared with a process starting with the operating budgets and continues with the capital expenditures budget, and then financial budgets, or (*c*) is prepared with a process ending with the sales budget.

7. What are the three primary categories of budgets in the master budget?

8. In preparing monthly budgets for the third quarter, a company budgeted sales of 120 units for July and 140 units for August. Management wants each month's ending inventory to be 60% of next month's sales. The June 30 inventory consists of 50 units. How many units of product for July acquisition should the merchandise purchases budget specify for the third quarter? (*a*) 84, (*b*) 120, (*c*) 154, or (*d*) 204.

9. How do the operating budgets for merchandisers and manufacturers differ?

10. How does a just-in-time inventory system differ from a safety stock system?

Answers—p. 791

## Capital Expenditures Budget

The **capital expenditures budget** lists dollar amounts to be both received from plant asset disposals and spent to purchase additional plant assets to carry out the budgeted business activities. It is usually prepared after the operating budgets. Since a company's plant assets determine its productive capacity, this budget is usually affected by long-range plans for the business. Yet the process of preparing a sales or purchases budget can reveal that the company requires more (or less) capacity, which implies more (or less) plant assets.

*Capital budgeting* is the process of evaluating and planning for capital (plant asset) expenditures. This is an important management task because these expenditures often involve long-run commitments of large amounts, affect predicted cash flows, and impact future debt and equity financing. This means that the capital expenditures budget is often linked with management's evaluation of the company's ability to take on more debt. We describe capital budgeting in Chapter 21.

Hockey Den does not anticipate disposal of any plant assets through December 2005, but it does plan to acquire additional equipment for $25,000 cash near the end of December 2005. This is the only budgeted capital expenditure from October 2005 through January 2006. Thus, no separate budget is shown. The cash budget in Exhibit 19.11 reflects this $25,000 planned expenditure.

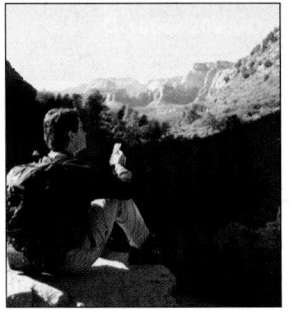

balance to $372, far below the $20,000 minimum. The company expects to borrow $19,628
in that month to reach the minimum desired
ending balance.

**Budgeted Income Statement**  One of
the final steps in preparing the master budget
is to summarize the income effects. The **budgeted income statement** is a managerial accounting report showing predicted amounts of
sales and expenses for the budget period.
Information needed for preparing a budgeted
income statement is primarily taken from al-
ready prepared budgets. The volume of information summarized in the budgeted income
statement is so large for some companies that they often use spreadsheets to accumulate the
budgeted transactions and classify them by their effects on income. We condense HD's budgeted income statement and show it in Exhibit 19.14. All information in this exhibit is taken
from earlier budgets. Also, we now can predict the amount of income tax expense for the
quarter, computed as 40% of the budgeted pretax income. This amount is included in the
cash budget and/or the budgeted balance sheet as necessary.

**Exhibit 19.14**

Budgeted Income Statement

| HOCKEY DEN<br>Budgeted Income Statement<br>For Three Months Ended December 31, 2005 | | |
|---|---|---|
| Sales (Exhibit 19.6, 3,200 units @ $100) . . . . . . . . . . . | | $320,000 |
| Cost of goods sold (3,200 units @ $60) . . . . . . . . . . | | 192,000 |
| Gross profit . . . . . . . . . . . . . . . . . . . . . . . . . . . . . . | | 128,000 |
| Operating expenses | | |
| Sales commissions (Exhibit 19.9) . . . . . . . . . . . . . . | $32,000 | |
| Sales salaries (Exhibit 19.9) . . . . . . . . . . . . . . . . . | 6,000 | |
| Administrative salaries (Exhibit 19.10) . . . . . . . . . . | 13,500 | |
| Depreciation on equipment (Exhibit 19.10) . . . . . . . | 4,500 | |
| Interest expense (Exhibit 19.11) . . . . . . . . . . . . . . | 328 | 56,328 |
| Income before income taxes . . . . . . . . . . . . . . . . . . . | | 71,672 |
| Income tax expense ($71,672 × 40%) . . . . . . . . . . . . | | 28,669 |
| Net income . . . . . . . . . . . . . . . . . . . . . . . . . . . . . . | | $ 43,003 |

**Point:** Lending institutions often
require potential borrowers to provide
cash budgets, budgeted income statements, and budgeted balance sheets, as
well as data on past performance.

**Point:** To apply these concepts,
work Exercise 19-4.

**Budgeted Balance Sheet**  The final step in preparing the master budget is summarizing the company's financial position. The **budgeted balance sheet** shows predicted
amounts for the company's assets, liabilities, and equity as of the end of the budget
period. HD's budgeted balance sheet in Exhibit 19.15 is prepared using information
from the other budgets. The sources of amounts are reported in the notes to the budgeted
balance sheet.[1]

---

[1] An eight-column spreadsheet, or work sheet, can be used to prepare a budgeted balance sheet (and income
statement). The first two columns show the ending balance sheet amounts from the period prior to the budget
period. The budgeted transactions and adjustments are entered in the third and fourth columns in the same manner as adjustments are entered on an ordinary work sheet. After all budgeted transactions and adjustments have
been entered, the amounts in the first two columns are combined with the budget amounts in the third and fourth
columns and sorted to the proper Income Statement (fifth and sixth columns) and Balance Sheet columns (sev-
enth and eighth columns). Amounts in these columns are used to prepare the budgeted income statement and
balance sheet.

Exhibit 19.15

Budgeted Balance Sheet

| HOCKEY DEN Budgeted Balance Sheet December 31, 2005 | | |
|---|---|---|
| **Assets** | | |
| Cash[a] . . . . . . . . . . . . . . . . . . . . . . . . . . | | $ 20,000 |
| Accounts receivable[b] . . . . . . . . . . . . . . | | 84,000 |
| Inventory (810 unit @ $60)[c] . . . . . . . . | | 48,600 |
| Equipment[d] . . . . . . . . . . . . . . . . . . . . . | $225,000 | |
| Less accumulated depreciation[e] . . . . . . . | 40,500 | 184,500 |
| Total assets . . . . . . . . . . . . . . . . . . . . . | | $337,100 |
| **Liabilities and Equity** | | |
| Liabilities | | |
| Accounts payable[f] . . . . . . . . . . . . . . | $ 57,000 | |
| Income taxes payable[g] . . . . . . . . . . . | 28,669 | |
| Bank loan payable[h] . . . . . . . . . . . . . . | 19,628 | $105,297 |
| Stockholders' equity | | |
| Common stock[i] . . . . . . . . . . . . . . . . | 150,000 | |
| Retained earnings[j] . . . . . . . . . . . . . . | 81,803 | 231,803 |
| Total liabilities and equity . . . . . . . . . . . | | $337,100 |

[a] Ending balance for December from the cash budget in Exhibit 19.11.

[b] 60% of $140,000 sales budgeted for December from the sales budget in Exhibit 19.6.

[c] 810 units in budgeted December ending inventory at the budgeted cost of $60 per unit (from the purchases budget in Exhibit 19.8).

[d] September 30 balance of $200,000 from the beginning balance sheet in Exhibit 19.5 plus $25,000 cost of new equipment from the cash budget in Exhibit 19.11.

[e] September 30 balance of $36,000 from the beginning balance sheet in Exhibit 19.5 plus $4,500 expense from the general and administrative expense budget in Exhibit 19.10.

[f] Budgeted cost of purchases for December from the purchases budget in Exhibit 19.8.

[g] Income tax expense from the budgeted income statement for the fourth quarter in Exhibit 19.14.

[h] Budgeted December 31 balance from the cash budget in Exhibit 19.11.

[i] Unchanged from the beginning balance sheet in Exhibit 19.5.

[j] September 30 balance of $41,800 from the beginning balance sheet in Exhibit 19.5 plus budgeted net income of $43,003 from the budgeted income statement in Exhibit 19.14 minus budgeted cash dividends of $3,000 from the cash budget in Exhibit 19.11.

## Quick Check

11. In preparing a budgeted balance sheet, (a) plant assets are determined by analyzing the capital expenditures budget and the balance sheet from the beginning of the budget period, (b) liabilities are determined by analyzing the general and administrative expense budget, or (c) retained earnings are determined from information contained in the cash budget and the balance sheet from the beginning of the budget period.

12. What sequence is followed in preparing the budgets that constitute the master budget?

Answers—p. 791

## Activity-Based Budgeting

**Decision Analysis**

**Activity-based budgeting (ABB)** is a budget system based on expected activities. Knowledge of expected activities and their levels for the budget period enables management to plan for resources required to perform the activities. To illustrate, we consider the budget of a company's accounting department. Traditional budgeting systems list items such as salaries, supplies, equipment, and utilities. Such an itemized budget informs management of the use of the funds budgeted (for example, salaries), but management cannot assess the basis for increases or decreases in budgeted amounts as compared to prior periods. Accordingly, management often makes across-the-board cuts or increases. In contrast, ABB requires management to list activities performed by, say, the accounting department such as auditing, tax reporting, financial reporting, and cost accounting. Exhibit 19.16 contrasts a

**A1** Analyze expense planning using activity-based budgeting.

## Exhibit 19.16

Activity-Based Budgeting versus
Traditional Budgeting (for an
accounting department)

| Activity-Based Budget | | Traditional Budget | |
|---|---|---|---|
| Auditing | $ 58,000 | Salaries | $152,000 |
| Tax reporting | 71,000 | Supplies | 22,000 |
| Financial reporting | 63,000 | Depreciation | 36,000 |
| Cost accounting | 32,000 | Utilities | 14,000 |
| Total | $224,000 | Total | $224,000 |

traditional budget with an activity-based budget for a company's accounting department. An understanding of the resources required to perform the activities, the costs associated with these resources,
and the way resource use changes with changes in activity levels allows management to better assess how expenses will change to accommodate changes in activity levels. Moreover, by knowing the relation between activities and costs, management can attempt to reduce costs by eliminating nonvalue-added activities.

### Decision Maker

**Environmental Manager**   You hold the new position of environmental control manager for a chemical company. You are asked to develop a budget for your job and identify job responsibilities. How do you proceed?

Answer—p. 791

# Demonstration Problem

Wild Wood Co's management asks you to prepare its master budget using the following information. The budget is to cover the months of April, May, and June 2005.

### WILD WOOD COMPANY
### Balance Sheet
### March 31, 2005

| Assets | | | Liabilities and Equity | |
|---|---|---|---|---|
| Cash | | $ 50,000 | Accounts payable | $156,000 |
| Accounts receivable | | 175,000 | Short-term notes payable | 12,000 |
| Inventory | | 126,000 | Total current liabilities | 168,000 |
| Total current assets | | 351,000 | Long-term note payable | 200,000 |
| Equipment | $480,000 | | Total liabilities | 368,000 |
| Accumulated depreciation | (90,000) | 390,000 | Common stock | 235,000 |
| | | | Retained earnings | 138,000 |
| | | | Total stockholders' equity | 373,000 |
| Total assets | | $741,000 | Total liabilities and equity | $741,000 |

### Additional Information

a. Sales for March total 10,000 units. Each month's sales are expected to exceed the prior month's results by 5%. The product's selling price is $25 per unit.

b. Company policy calls for a given month's ending inventory to equal 80% of the next month's expected unit sales. The March 31 inventory is 8,400 units, which complies with the policy. The purchase price is $15 per unit.

c. Sales representatives' commissions are 12.5% of sales and are paid in the month of the sales. The sales manager's monthly salary will be $3,500 in April and $4,000 per month thereafter.

d. Monthly general and administrative expenses include $8,000 administrative salaries, $5,000 depreciation, and 0.9% monthly interest on the long-term note payable.

e. The company expects 30% of sales to be for cash and the remaining 70% on credit. Receivables are collected in full in the month following the sale (none is collected in the month of the sale).

f. All merchandise purchases are on credit, and no payables arise from any other transactions. One month's purchases are fully paid in the next month.

g. The minimum ending cash balance for all months is $50,000. If necessary, the company borrows enough cash using a short-term note to reach the minimum. Short-term notes require an interest payment of 1% at each month-end (before any repayment). If the ending cash balance exceeds the minimum, the excess will be applied to repaying the short-term notes payable balance.

**h.** Dividends of $100,000 are to be declared and paid in May.

**i.** No cash payments for income taxes are to be made during the second calendar quarter. Income taxes will be assessed at 35% in the quarter.

**j.** Equipment purchases of $55,000 are scheduled for June.

### Required

Prepare the following budgets and other financial information as required:

1. Sales budget, including budgeted sales for July.
2. Purchases budget, the budgeted cost of goods sold for each month and quarter, and the cost of the June 30 budgeted inventory.
3. Selling expense budget.
4. General and administrative expense budget.
5. Expected cash receipts from customers and the expected June 30 balance of accounts receivable.
6. Expected cash payments for purchases and the expected June 30 balance of accounts payable.
7. Cash budget.
8. Budgeted income statement.
9. Budgeted statement of retained earnings.
10. Budgeted balance sheet.

## Planning the Solution

- The sales budget shows expected sales for each month in the quarter. Start by multiplying March sales by 105% and then do the same for the remaining months. July's sales are needed for the purchases budget. To complete the budget, multiply the expected unit sales by the selling price of $25 per unit.

- Use these results and the 80% inventory policy to budget the size of ending inventory for April, May, and June. Add the budgeted sales to these numbers and subtract the actual or expected beginning inventory for each month. The result is the number of units to be purchased each month. Multiply these numbers by the per unit cost of $15. Find the budgeted cost of goods sold by multiplying the unit sales in each month by the $15 cost per unit. Compute the cost of the June 30 ending inventory by multiplying the expected units available at that date by the $15 cost per unit.

- The selling expense budget has only two items. Find the amount of the sales representatives' commissions by multiplying the expected dollar sales in each month by the 12.5% commission rate. Then include the sales manager's salary of $3,500 in April and $4,000 in May and June.

- The general and administrative expense budget should show three items. Administrative salaries are fixed at $8,000 per month, and depreciation is $5,000 per month. Budget the monthly interest expense on the long-term note by multiplying its $200,000 balance by the 0.9% monthly interest rate.

- Determine the amounts of cash sales in each month by multiplying the budgeted sales by 30%. Add to this amount the credit sales of the prior month (computed as 70% of prior month's sales). April's cash receipts from collecting receivables equals the March 31 balance of $175,000. The expected June 30 accounts receivable balance equals 70% of June's total budgeted sales.

- Determine expected cash payments on accounts payable for each month by making them equal to the merchandise purchases in the prior month. The payments for April equal the March 31 balance of accounts payable shown on the beginning balance sheet. The June 30 balance of accounts payable equals merchandise purchases for June.

- Prepare the cash budget by combining the given information and the amounts of cash receipts and cash payments on account that you computed. Complete the cash budget for each month by either borrowing enough to raise the preliminary balance to the minimum or paying off short-term debt as much as the balance allows without falling below the minimum. Show the ending balance of the short-term note in the budget.

- Prepare the budgeted income statement by combining the budgeted items for all three months. Determine the income before income taxes and multiply it by the 35% rate to find the quarter's income tax expense.

- The budgeted statement of retained earnings should show the March 31 balance plus the quarter's net income minus the quarter's dividends.

- The budgeted balance sheet includes updated balances for all items that appear in the beginning balance sheet and an additional liability for unpaid income taxes. Amounts for all asset, liability, and equity accounts can be found either in the budgets, other calculations, or by adding amounts found there to the beginning balances.

## Solution to Demonstration Problem

**1.** Sales budget

|  | April | May | June | July |
|---|---|---|---|---|
| Prior month's sales . . . . . . . . | 10,000 | ►10,500 | ►11,025 | ►11,576 |
| Plus 5% growth . . . . . . . . . . | 500 | 525 | 551 | 579 |
| Projected unit . . . . . . . . . . | 10,500 | 11,025 | 11,576 | 12,155 |

|  | April | May | June | Quarter |
|---|---|---|---|---|
| Projected unit sales . . . . . . . | 10,500◄ | 11,025◄ | 11,576◄ |  |
| Selling price per unit . . . . . . | × $25 | × $25 | × $25 |  |
| Projected sales . . . . . . . . . . | $262,500 | $275,625 | $289,400 | $827,525 |

**2.** Purchases budget

|  | April | May | June | Quarter |
|---|---|---|---|---|
| Next month's unit sales (part 1) . . . . . . . | 11,025 | 11,576 | 12,155 |  |
| Ending inventory percent . . . . . . . . . . . . | × 80% | × 80% | × 80% |  |
| Desired ending inventory . . . . . . . . . . . | 8,820 | 9,261 | 9,724 |  |
| This month's unit sales (part 1) . . . . . . . | 10,500 | 11,025 | 11,576 |  |
| Units to be available . . . . . . . . . . . . . . | 19,320 | 20,286 | 21,300 |  |
| Less beginning inventory . . . . . . . . . . . | 8,400 | 8,820 | 9,261 |  |
| Units to be purchased . . . . . . . . . . . . . | 10,920 | 11,466 | 12,039 |  |
| Budgeted cost per unit . . . . . . . . . . . . . | × $15 | × $15 | × $15 |  |
| Projected purchases . . . . . . . . . . . . . . | $163,800 | $171,990 | $180,585 | $516,375 |

Budgeted cost of goods sold

|  | April | May | June | Quarter |
|---|---|---|---|---|
| This month's unit sales (part 1) . . . . . . . | 10,500 | 11,025 | 11,576 |  |
| Budgeted cost per unit . . . . . . . . . . . . . | × $15 | × $15 | × $15 |  |
| Projected cost of goods sold . . . . . . . . . | $157,500 | $165,375 | $173,640 | $496,515 |

Budgeted inventory for June 30

| Units (part 2) . . . . . . . | 9,724 |
|---|---|
| Cost per unit . . . . . . . | × $15 |
| Total . . . . . . . . . . . . . | $145,860 |

**3.** Selling expense budget

|  | April | May | June | Quarter |
|---|---|---|---|---|
| Budgeted sales (part 1) . . . . . . . . . . . . . | $262,500 | $275,625 | $289,400 | $827,525 |
| Commission percent . . . . . . . . . . . . . . . | × 12.5% | × 12.5% | × 12.5% | × 12.5% |
| Sales commissions . . . . . . . . . . . . . . . . | 32,813 | 34,453 | 36,175 | 103,441 |
| Manager's salary . . . . . . . . . . . . . . . . . | 3,500 | 4,000 | 4,000 | 11,500 |
| Projected selling expenses . . . . . . . . . . . | $ 36,313 | $ 38,453 | $ 40,175 | $114,941 |

**4.** General and administrative expense budget

|  | April | May | June | Quarter |
|---|---|---|---|---|
| Administrative salaries ...................... | $ 8,000 | $ 8,000 | $ 8,000 | $24,000 |
| Depreciation ............................. | 5,000 | 5,000 | 5,000 | 15,000 |
| Interest on long-term note payable (0.9% × $200,000) ................. | 1,800 | 1,800 | 1,800 | 5,400 |
| Projected expenses ....................... | $14,800 | $14,800 | $14,800 | $44,400 |

**5.** Expected cash receipts from customers

|  | April | May | June | Quarter |
|---|---|---|---|---|
| Budgeted sales (part 1) ..................... | $262,500 | $275,625 | $289,400 |  |
| Ending accounts receivable (70%) .............. | $183,750 | $192,938 | $202,580 |  |
| Cash receipts |  |  |  |  |
| Cash sales (30%) ....................... | $ 78,750 | $ 82,687 | $ 86,820 | $248,257 |
| Collections of prior month's receivables ....... | 175,000 | 183,750 | 192,938 | 551,688 |
| Total cash to be collected ................... | $253,750 | $266,437 | $279,758 | $799,945 |

**6.** Expected cash payments to suppliers

|  | April | May | June | Quarter |
|---|---|---|---|---|
| Cash payments (equal to prior month's purchases) ............................ | $156,000 | $163,800 | $171,990 | $491,790 |
| Expected June 30 balance of accounts payable (June purchases) .................. |  |  | $180,585 |  |

**7.** Cash budget

|  | April | May | June |
|---|---|---|---|
| Beginning cash balance ................... | $ 50,000 | $ 89,517 | $ 50,000 |
| Cash receipts (part 5) .................... | 253,750 | 266,437 | 279,758 |
| Total cash available .................... | 303,750 | 355,954 | 329,758 |
| Cash payments |  |  |  |
| Payments for merchandise (part 6) ........ | 156,000 | 163,800 | 171,990 |
| Sales commissions (part 3) .............. | 32,813 | 34,453 | 36,175 |
| Salaries |  |  |  |
| Sales (part 3) ....................... | 3,500 | 4,000 | 4,000 |
| Administrative (part 4) ............... | 8,000 | 8,000 | 8,000 |
| Interest on long-term note (part 4) ....... | 1,800 | 1,800 | 1,800 |
| Dividends ......................... |  | 100,000 |  |
| Equipment purchase .................... |  |  | 55,000 |
| Interest on short-term notes |  |  |  |
| April ($12,000 × 1.0%) .............. | 120 |  |  |
| June ($6,099 × 1.0%) ................ |  |  | 61 |
| Total cash payments .................. | 202,233 | 312,053 | 277,026 |
| Preliminary balance ................... | 101,517 | 43,901 | 52,732 |
| Additional loan ...................... |  | 6,099 |  |
| Loan repayment ...................... | (12,000) |  | (2,732) |
| Ending cash balance .................. | $ 89,517 | $ 50,000 | $ 50,000 |
| Ending short-term notes .............. | $    0 | $ 6,099 | $ 3,367 |

8.

### WILD WOOD COMPANY
### Budgeted Income Statement
### For Quarter Ended June 30, 2005

| | | |
|---|---|---|
| Sales (part 1) | | $ 827,525 |
| Cost of goods sold (part 2) | | 496,515 |
| Gross profit | | 331,010 |
| Operating expenses | | |
| Sales commissions (part 3) | $103,441 | |
| Sales salaries (part 3) | 11,500 | |
| Administrative salaries (part 4) | 24,000 | |
| Depreciation (part 4) | 15,000 | |
| Interest on long-term note (part 4) | 5,400 | |
| Interest on short-term notes (part 7) | 181 | |
| Total operating expenses | | 159,522 |
| Income before income taxes | | 171,488 |
| Income taxes (35%) | | 60,021 |
| Net income | | $ 111,467 |

9.

### WILD WOOD COMPANY
### Budgeted Statement of Retained Earnings
### For Quarter Ended June 30, 2005

| | |
|---|---|
| Beginning retained earnings (given) | $138,000 |
| Net income (part 8) | 111,467 |
| | 249,467 |
| Less cash dividends (given) | 100,000 |
| Ending retained earnings | $149,467 |

10.

### WILD WOOD COMPANY
### Budgeted Balance Sheet
### June 30, 2005

**Assets**

| | | |
|---|---|---|
| Cash (part 7) | | $ 50,000 |
| Accounts receivable (part 5) | | 202,580 |
| Inventory (part 2) | | 145,860 |
| Total current assets | | 398,440 |
| Equipment (given plus purchase) | $535,000 | |
| Less accumulated depreciation (given plus expense) | 105,000 | 430,000 |
| Total assets | | $828,440 |

**Liabilities and Equity**

| | |
|---|---|
| Accounts payable (part 6) | $180,585 |
| Short-term notes payable (part 7) | 3,367 |
| Income taxes payable (part 8) | 60,021 |
| Total current liabilities | 243,973 |
| Long-term note payable (given) | 200,000 |
| Total liabilities | 443,973 |
| Common stock (given) | 235,000 |
| Retained earnings (part 9) | 149,467 |
| Total stockholders' equity | 384,467 |
| Total liabilities and equity | $828,440 |

# Production and Manufacturing Budgets

# 19A

Unlike a merchandising company, a manufacturer must prepare a **production budget** instead of a merchandise purchases budget. A production budget, which shows the number of units to be produced each month, is similar to merchandise purchases budgets except that the number of units to be purchased each month (as shown in Exhibit 19.8) is replaced by the number of units to be manufactured each month. A production budget does not show costs; it is *always expressed in units of product.* Exhibit 19A.1 shows the production budget for **Toronto Sticks Company** (**TSC**), a manufacturer of hockey sticks. TSC is an exclusive supplier of hockey sticks to Hockey Den, meaning that TSC uses HD's budgeted sales figures (Exhibit 19.6) to determine its production and manufacturing budgets.

**P3** Prepare production and manufacturing budgets.

| TSC Production Budget October 2005–December 2005 | | | |
|---|---|---|---|
| | October | November | December |
| Next month's budgeted sales (units) .......... | 800 | 1,400 | 900 |
| Ratio of inventory to future sales ............. | × 90% | × 90% | × 90% |
| Budgeted ending inventory (units) ............ | 720 | 1,260 | 810 |
| Add budgeted sales for the month (units) ....... | 1,000 | 800 | 1,400 |
| Required units of available production .......... | 1,720 | 2,060 | 2,210 |
| Deduct beginning inventory (units) ............. | (900) | (720) | (1,260) |
| Units to be produced ...................... | 820 | 1,340 | 950 |

Exhibit 19A.1

Production Budget

A **manufacturing budget** shows the budgeted costs for direct materials, direct labor, and overhead. It is based on the budgeted production volume from the production budget. The manufacturing budget for most companies consists of three individual budgets: direct materials budget, direct labor budget, and overhead budget. Exhibits 19A.2–19A.4 show these three manufacturing budgets for TSC. These budgets yield the total expected cost of goods to be manufactured in the budget period.

The *direct materials budget* is driven by the budgeted materials needed to satisfy each month's production requirement. To this we must add the desired ending inventory requirements. The desired ending inventory of direct materials as shown in Exhibit 19A.2 is 50% of next month's budgeted materials requirements of wood. For instance, in October 2005, an ending inventory of 335 units of material is desired (50% of November's 670 units). The desired ending inventory for December 2005

| TSC Direct Materials Budget October 2005–December 2005 | | | |
|---|---|---|---|
| | October | November | December |
| Budget production (units) ................. | 820 | 1,340 | 950 |
| Materials requirements per unit ............. | × 0.5 | × 0.5 | × 0.5 |
| Materials needed for production (units) ....... | 410 | 670 | 475 |
| Add budgeted ending inventory (units) ........ | 335 | 237.5 | 225 |
| Total materials requirements (units) .......... | 745 | 907.5 | 700 |
| Deduct beginning inventory (units) ........... | (205) | (335) | (237.5) |
| Materials to be purchased (units) ............ | 540 | 572.5 | 462.5 |
| Material price per unit .................... | $ 20 | $ 20 | $ 20 |
| Total cost of direct materials purchases ........ | $10,800 | $11,450 | $9,250 |

Exhibit 19A.2

Direct Materials Budget

is 225 units, computed from the direct material requirement of 450 units for a production level of 900 units in January 2006. The total materials requirements are computed by adding the desired ending inventory figures to that month's budgeted production material requirements. For October 2005, the total materials requirement is 745 units (335 + 410). From the total materials requirement, we then subtract the units of materials available in beginning inventory. For October 2005, the materials available from September 2005 are computed as 50% of October's materials requirements to satisfy production, or 205 units (50% of 410). Therefore, direct materials purchases in October 2005 are budgeted at 540 units (745 − 205). See Exhibit 19A.2.

TSC's *direct labor budget* is shown in Exhibit 19A.3. About 15 minutes of labor time is required to produce one unit. Labor is paid at the rate of $12 per hour. Budgeted labor hours are computed by multiplying the budgeted production level for each month by one-quarter (0.25) of an hour. Direct labor cost is then computed by multiplying budgeted labor hours by the labor rate of $12 per hour.

**Exhibit 19A.3**

Direct Labor Budget

| | | | |
|---|---|---|---|
| **TSC** | | | |
| **Direct Labor Budget** | | | |
| **October 2005–December 2005** | | | |
| | October | November | December |
| Budgeted production (units) . . . . . . . . . . . . . . | 820 | 1,340 | 950 |
| Labor requirements per unit (hours) . . . . . . . | × 0.25 | × 0.25 | × 0.25 |
| Total labor hours needed . . . . . . . . . . . . . . . | 205 | 335 | 237.5 |
| Labor rate (per hour) . . . . . . . . . . . . . . . . . | $ 12 | $ 12 | $ 12 |
| Labor dollars . . . . . . . . . . . . . . . . . . . . . . . | $2,460 | $4,020 | $2,850 |

TSC's *factory overhead budget* is shown in Exhibit 19A.4. The variable portion of overhead is assigned at the rate of $2.50 per unit of production. The fixed portion stays constant at $1,500 per month. The budget in Exhibit 19A.4 is in condensed form; most overhead budgets are more detailed, listing each overhead cost item.

**Exhibit 19A.4**

Factory Overhead Budget

| | | | |
|---|---|---|---|
| **TSC** | | | |
| **Factory Overhead Budget** | | | |
| **October 2005–December 2005** | | | |
| | October | November | December |
| Budgeted production (units) . . . . . . . . . . . . . . | 820 | 1,340 | 950 |
| Variable factory overhead rate . . . . . . . . . . . . | × $2.50 | × $2.50 | × $2.50 |
| Budgeted variable overhead . . . . . . . . . . . . . . | 2,050 | 3,350 | 2,375 |
| Budgeted fixed overhead . . . . . . . . . . . . . . . | 1,500 | 1,500 | 1,500 |
| Budgeted total overhead . . . . . . . . . . . . . . . | $3,550 | $4,850 | $3,875 |

## Summary

**C1 Describe the importance and benefits of budgeting.**
Planning is a management responsibility of critical importance to business success. Budgeting is the process management uses to formalize its plans. Budgeting promotes management analysis and focuses its attention on the future. Budgeting also provides a basis for evaluating performance, serves as a source of motivation, is a means of coordinating activities, and communicates management's plans and instructions to employees.

**C2 Explain the process of budget administration.** Budgeting is a detailed activity that requires administration. At least three aspects are important: budget committee, budget reporting, and budget timing. A budget committee oversees the budget preparation. The budget period pertains to the time period for which the budget is prepared such as a year or month.

**C3 Describe a master budget and the process of preparing it.** A master budget is a formal overall plan for a company. It consists of plans for business operations and capital expenditures, plus the financial results of those activities. The budgeting process begins with a sales budget. Based on expected sales volume, companies can budget purchases, selling expenses, and administrative expenses. Next, the capital expenditures budget is prepared, followed by the cash budget and budgeted financial statements. Manufacturers also must budget production quantities, materials purchases, labor costs, and overhead.

**A1 Analyze expense planning using activity-based budgeting.** Activity-based budgeting requires management to identify activities performed by departments, plan necessary activity levels, identify resources required to perform these activities, and budget the resources.

P1   **Prepare each component of a master budget and link each to the budgeting process.** The term *master budget* refers to a collection of individual component budgets. Each component budget is designed to guide persons responsible for activities covered by that component. A master budget must reflect the components of a company and their interaction in pursuit of company goals.

P2   **Link both operating and capital expenditures budgets to budgeted financial statements.** The operating budgets, capital expenditures budget, and cash budget contain much of the in-

formation to prepare a budgeted income statement for the budget period and a budgeted balance sheet at the end of the budget period. Budgeted financial statements show the expected financial consequences of the planned activities described in the budgets.

P3[A]   **Prepare production and manufacturing budgets.** A manufacturer must prepare a *production budget* instead of a purchases budget. A *manufacturing budget* shows the budgeted production costs for direct materials, direct labor, and overhead.

## Guidance Answers to **Decision Maker** and **Decision Ethics**

**Budget Staffer**   Your superior's actions appear unethical because she is using private information for personal gain. As a budget staffer, you are low in the company's hierarchical structure and probably unable to confront this superior directly. You should inform an individual with a position of authority within the organization about your concerns.

**Entrepreneur**   You must deal with two issues. First, because fashions and designs frequently change, you cannot heavily rely on previous budgets. As a result, you must carefully analyze the market to understand what designs are in vogue. This will help you plan the product mix and estimate demand. The second issue is the

budgeting period. An annual sales budget may be unreliable because tastes can quickly change. Your best bet might be to prepare monthly and quarterly sales budgets that you continuously monitor and revise.

**Environmental Manager**   You are unlikely to have data on this new position to use in preparing your budget. In this situation, you can use activity-based budgeting. This requires developing a list of activities to conduct, the resources required to perform these activities, and the expenses associated with these resources. You should challenge yourself to be absolutely certain that the listed activities are necessary and that the listed resources are required.

## Guidance Answers to **Quick Checks**

1. Major benefits include promoting a focus on the future; providing a basis for evaluating performance; providing a source of motivation; coordinating the departments of a business; and communicating plans and instructions.

2. The budget committee's responsibility is to provide guidance to ensure that budget figures are realistic and coordinated.

3. Budget periods usually coincide with accounting periods and therefore cover a month, quarter, or a year. Budgets can also be prepared for longer time periods, such as five years.

4. Rolling budgets are budgets that are periodically revised in the ongoing process of continuous budgeting.

5. A master budget is a comprehensive or overall plan for the company that is generally expressed in monetary terms.

6. *b*

7. The master budget includes operating budgets, the capital expenditures budget, and financial budgets.

8. *c*; Computed as $(60\% \times 140) + 120 - 50 = 154$.

9. Merchandisers prepare merchandise purchases budgets; manufacturers prepare production and manufacturing budgets.

10. A just-in-time system keeps the level of inventory to a minimum and orders merchandise or materials to meet immediate sales demand. A safety stock system maintains an inventory that is large enough to meet sales demands plus an amount to satisfy unexpected sales demands and an amount to cover delayed shipments from suppliers.

11. *a*

12. (a) Operating budgets (such as sales, selling expense, and administrative budgets), (b) capital expenditures budget, (c) financial budgets: cash budget, budgeted income statement, and budgeted balance sheet.

## Key Terms

Key Terms are available at the book's Website for learning and testing in an online Flashcard Format.

**Activity-based budgeting (ABB)** (p. 783)      **Cash budget** (p. 780)                  **Merchandise purchases budget** (p. 777)
**Budget** (p. 770)                              **Continuous budgeting** (p. 772)         **Production budget** (p. 789)
**Budgeted balance sheet** (p. 782)              **General and administrative expense**    **Rolling budgets** (p. 772)
**Budgeted income statement** (p. 782)           **budget** (p. 778)                       **Safety stock** (p. 777)
**Budgeting** (p. 770)                           **Manufacturing budget** (p. 789)         **Sales budget** (p. 776)
**Capital expenditures budget** (p. 779)         **Master budget** (p. 774)                **Selling expense budget** (p. 778)

## Exercise 19-3

Preparation of a cash budget

C3  P2

Use the following information to prepare the July cash budget for Sanchez Co. It should show expected cash receipts and cash disbursements for the month and the cash balance expected on July 31.

**a.** Beginning cash balance on July 1: $50,000.

**b.** Cash receipts from sales: 30% is collected in the month of sale, 50% in the next month, and 20% in the second month after sale (uncollectible accounts are negligible and can be ignored). Sales amounts are: May (actual), $1,720,000; June (actual), $1,200,000; and July (budgeted), $1,400,000.

**c.** Payments on merchandise purchases: 60% in the month of purchase and 40% in the month following purchase. Purchases amounts are: June (actual), $430,000; and July (budgeted), $600,000.

**d.** Budgeted cash disbursements for salaries in July: $211,000.

**e.** Budgeted depreciation expense for July: $12,000.

**f.** Other cash expenses budgeted for July: $150,000.

**g.** Accrued income taxes due in July: $80,000.

**h.** Bank loan interest due in July: $6,600.

## Exercise 19-4

Preparing a budgeted income statement and balance sheet

C3  P2

Use the information in Exercise 19-3 and the following additional information to prepare a budgeted income statement for the month of July and a budgeted balance sheet for July 31:

**a.** Cost of goods sold is 44% of sales.

**b.** Inventory at the end of June is $80,000 and at the end of July is $64,000.

**c.** Salaries payable on June 30 are $50,000 and are expected to be $40,000 on July 31.

**d.** The equipment account balance is $1,600,000 on July 31. On June 30, the accumulated depreciation on equipment is $280,000.

**e.** The $6,600 cash payment of interest represents the 1% monthly expense on a bank loan of $660,000.

**f.** Income taxes payable on July 31 are $124,320, and the income tax rate applicable to the company is 30%.

**g.** The only other balance sheet accounts are: Common Stock, with a balance of $600,000 on June 30; and Retained Earnings, with a balance of $1,072,000 on June 30.

## Exercise 19-5

Computing budgeted cash payments for purchases

C3  P2

Powerdyne Company's cost of goods sold is consistently 60% of sales. The company plans to carry ending merchandise inventory for each month equal to 40% of the next month's budgeted cost of goods sold. All merchandise is purchased on credit, and 50% of the purchases made during a month is paid for in that month. Another 35% is paid for during the first month after purchase, and the remaining 15% is paid for during the second month after purchase. Expected sales are: August (actual), $150,000; September (actual), $350,000; October (estimated), $200,000; November (estimated), $300,000. Use this information to determine October's expected cash payments for purchases. (*Hint:* Use the layout of Exhibit 19.8, but revised for the facts given here.)

## Exercise 19-6

Computing budgeted purchases and costs of goods sold

C3  P1  P2

Sand Dollar Company purchases all merchandise on credit. It recently budgeted the following month-end accounts payable balances and merchandise inventory balances. Cash payments on accounts payable during each month are expected to be: May, $1,300,000; June, $1,450,000; July, $1,350,000; and August, $1,400,000. Use the available information to compute the budgeted amounts of (1) merchandise purchases for June, July, and August, and (2) cost of goods sold for June, July, and August.

| | Accounts Payable | Merchandise Inventory |
|---|---|---|
| May 31 . . . . . . . . . . | $120,000 | $250,000 |
| June 30 . . . . . . . . . | 170,000 | 400,000 |
| July 31 . . . . . . . . . . | 200,000 | 300,000 |
| August 31 . . . . . . . | 160,000 | 330,000 |

## Exercise 19-7

Computing budgeted accounts payable and purchases  P1  P2

Sound Check, a merchandising company specializing in home computer speakers, budgets its monthly cost of goods sold to equal 70% of sales. Its inventory policy calls for ending inventory in each month to equal 25% of the next month's budgeted cost of goods sold. All purchases are on credit, and 20% of the purchases in a month is paid for in the same month. Another 50% is paid for during the first month after purchase, and the remaining 30% is paid for in the second month after purchase. The following sales budgets are set: July, $300,000; August, $240,000; September, $270,000; October, $240,000; and November, $210,000. Compute the following: (1) budgeted merchandise purchases for July, August, September, and October; (2) budgeted payments on accounts payable for September and October; and (3) budgeted ending balances of accounts payable for September and October.

**Check**  July purchases, $199,500; Sept. payments on accts. pay., $183,225

---

Nascar Company manufactures an innovative automobile transmission for electric cars. Management predicts that ending inventory for the first quarter will be 37,500 units. The following unit sales of the transmissions are expected during the rest of the year: second quarter, 225,000 units; third quarter, 262,500 units; and fourth quarter, 237,500 units. Company policy calls for the ending inventory of a quarter to equal 20% of the next quarter's budgeted sales. Prepare a production budget for both the second and third quarters that shows the number of transmissions to manufacture.

**Exercise 19-8A**
Preparing production budgets (for two periods)   P3

**Check**  Second quarter production, 240,000

---

Pinsetter's Supply is a merchandiser of three different products. The company's February 28 inventories are footwear, 15,500 units; sports equipment, 70,000 units; and apparel, 40,000 units. Management believes that excessive inventories have accumulated for all three products. As a result, a new policy dictates that ending inventory in any month should equal 40% of the expected unit sales for the following month. Expected sales in units for March, April, May, and June follow:

# PROBLEM SET A

**Problem 19-1A**
Preparation and analysis of merchandise purchases budgets

C3   P1

mhhe.com/wild

| | Budgeted Sales in Units | | | |
| --- | --- | --- | --- | --- |
| | March | April | May | June |
| Footwear ............. | 10,000 | 20,000 | 30,000 | 33,000 |
| Sports equipment ....... | 66,000 | 85,000 | 90,000 | 80,000 |
| Apparel ............... | 36,000 | 30,000 | 30,000 | 18,000 |

**Required**

**1.** Prepare a merchandise purchases budget (in units) for each product for each of the months of March, April, and May.

*Analysis Component*

**2.** The purchases budgets in part 1 should reflect fewer purchases of all three products in March compared to those in April and May. What factor caused fewer purchases to be planned? Suggest business conditions that would cause this factor to both occur and impact the company in this way.

**Check**  (1) March budgeted purchases: Footwear, 2,500; Sports equip., 30,000; Apparel, 8,000

---

During the last week of August, Apache Arts Company's owner approaches the bank for an $80,000 loan to be made on September 2 and repaid on November 30 with annual interest of 12%, for an interest cost of $2,400. The owner plans to increase the store's inventory by $60,000 during September and needs the loan to pay for inventory acquisitions. The bank's loan officer needs more information about Apache Arts' ability to repay the loan and asks the owner to forecast the store's November 30 cash position. On September 1, Apache Arts is expected to have a $3,000 cash balance, $135,000 of accounts receivable, and $100,000 of accounts payable. Its budgeted sales, merchandise purchases, and various cash disbursements for the next three months follow:

**Problem 19-2A**
Preparation of cash budgets (for three periods)

C3   P2

mhhe.com/wild

| | | September | October | November |
| --- | --- | --- | --- | --- |
| 1 | **Budgeted Figures\*** | **September** | **October** | **November** |
| 2 | Sales ........................................... | $220,000 | $300,000 | $380,000 |
| 3 | Merchandise purchases .............. | 210,000 | 180,000 | 220,000 |
| 4 | Cash disbursements | | | |
| 5 | Payroll ..................................... | 16,000 | 17,000 | 18,000 |
| 6 | Rent ........................................ | 6,000 | 6,000 | 6,000 |
| 7 | Other cash expenses .............. | 64,000 | 8,000 | 7,000 |
| 8 | Repayment of bank loan ......... | | | 80,000 |
| 9 | Interest on the bank loan ......... | | | 2,400 |
| 10 | | | | |

\* Operations began in August; August sales were $180,000 and purchases were $100,000.

To prepare a master budget for January, February, and March of 2006, management gathers the following information:

a. Simid Sports' single product is purchased for $30 per unit and resold for $55 per unit. The expected inventory level of 2,500 units on December 31, 2005, is more than management's desired level for 2006, which is 20% of the next month's expected sales (in units). Expected sales are: January, 3,500 units; February, 4,500 units; March, 5,500 units; and April, 5,000 units.

b. Cash sales and credit sales represent 25% and 75%, respectively, of total sales. Of the credit sales, 60% is collected in the first month after the month of sale and 40% in the second month after the month of sale. For the December 31, 2005, accounts receivable balance, $62,500 is collected in January and the remaining $200,000 is collected in February.

c. Merchandise purchases are paid for as follows: 20% in the first month after the month of purchase and 80% in the second month after the month of purchase. For the December 31, 2005, accounts payable balance, $40,000 is paid in January and the remaining $140,000 is paid in February.

d. Sales commissions equal to 20% of sales are paid each month. Sales salaries (excluding commissions) are $30,000 per year.

e. General and administrative salaries are $72,000 per year. Maintenance expense equals $1,000 per month and is paid in cash.

f. Equipment reported in the December 31, 2005, balance sheet was purchased in January 2005. It is being depreciated over eight years under the straight-line method with no salvage value. The following amounts for new equipment purchases are planned in the coming quarter: January, $18,000; February, $48,000; and March, $14,400. This equipment will be depreciated under the straight-line method over eight years with no salvage value. A full month's depreciation is taken for the month in which equipment is purchased.

g. The company plans to acquire land at the end of March at a cost of $75,000, which will be paid with cash on the last day of the month.

h. Simid Sports has a working arrangement with its bank to obtain additional loans as needed. The interest rate is 12% per year, and interest is paid at each month-end based on the beginning balance. Partial or full payments on these loans can be made on the last day of the month. The company has agreed to maintain a minimum ending cash balance of $12,500 in each month.

i. The income tax rate for the company is 40%. Income taxes on the first quarter's income will not be paid until April 15.

### Required

Prepare a master budget for each of the first three months of 2006; include the following component budgets (show supporting calculations as needed, and round amounts to the nearest dollar):

**Check**  (2) Budgeted purchases: January, $57,000; February, $141,000

(3) Budgeted selling expenses: January, $41,000; February, $52,000

(6) Ending cash bal.: January, $15,050; February, $105,150

(8) Budgeted total assets at March 31, $784,325

1. Monthly sales budgets (showing both budgeted unit sales and dollar sales).
2. Monthly merchandise purchases budgets.
3. Monthly selling expense budgets.
4. Monthly general and administrative expense budgets.
5. Monthly capital expenditures budgets.
6. Monthly cash budgets.
7. Budgeted income statement for the entire first quarter (not for each month).
8. Budgeted balance sheet as of March 31, 2006.

---

### Problem 19-6A<sup>A</sup>

Preparing production and direct materials budgets

C3  P3

**Check**  (1) Units manuf., 117,000;
(2) Cost of carbon fiber purchases, $2,748,000

Diamond Slope Company produces snow skis. Each ski requires 2 pounds of carbon fiber. The company's management predicts that 7,000 skis and 10,000 pounds of carbon fiber will be in inventory on June 30 of the current year and that 120,000 skis will be sold during the next (third) quarter. Management wants to end the third quarter with 4,000 skis and 5,000 pounds of carbon fiber in inventory. Carbon fiber can be purchased for $12 per pound.

### Required

1. Prepare the third-quarter production budget for skis.
2. Prepare the third-quarter direct materials (carbon fiber) budget; include the dollar cost of purchases.

H2O Sports Corp. is a merchandiser of three different products. The company's March 31 inventories are water skis, 40,000 units; tow ropes, 90,000 units; and life jackets, 250,000 units. Management believes that excessive inventories have accumulated for all three products. As a result, a new policy dictates that ending inventory in any month should equal 10% of the expected unit sales for the following month. Expected sales in units for April, May, June, and July follow:

**PROBLEM SET B**

**Problem 19-1B**
Preparation and analysis of merchandise purchases budgets

C3   P1

| | Budgeted Sales in Units | | | |
|---|---|---|---|---|
| | **April** | **May** | **June** | **July** |
| Water skis . . . . . . . . | 70,000 | 90,000 | 130,000 | 140,000 |
| Tow ropes . . . . . . . . | 100,000 | 90,000 | 110,000 | 100,000 |
| Life jackets . . . . . . . | 300,000 | 260,000 | 310,000 | 260,000 |

**Required**

**1.** Prepare a merchandise purchases budget (in units) for each product for each of the months of April, May, and June.

*Analysis Component*

**2.** The purchases budgets in part 1 should reflect fewer purchases of all three products in April compared to those in May and June. What factor caused fewer purchases to be planned? Suggest business conditions that would cause this factor to both occur and affect the company as it has.

**Check** (1) April budgeted purchases: Water skis, 39,000; Tow ropes, 19,000; Life jackets, 76,000

---

During the last week of March, Siro Stereo's owner approaches the bank for a $125,000 loan to be made on April 1 and repaid on June 30 with annual interest of 10%, for an interest cost of $3,125. The owner plans to increase the store's inventory by $100,000 in April and needs the loan to pay for inventory acquisitions. The bank's loan officer needs more information about Siro Stereo's ability to repay the loan and asks the owner to forecast the store's June 30 cash position. On April 1, Siro Stereo is expected to have a $12,000 cash balance, $121,500 of accounts receivable, and $90,000 of accounts payable. Its budgeted sales, merchandise purchases, and various cash disbursements for the next three months follow:

**Problem 19-2B**
Preparation of cash budgets (for three periods)

C3   P2

File  Edit  View  Insert  Format  Tools  Data  Window  Help

| | **Budgeted Figures\*** | **April** | **May** | **June** |
|---|---|---|---|---|
| 1 | | | | |
| 2 | Sales . . . . . . . . . . . . . . . . . . . . . . . . . . . | $350,000 | $500,000 | $550,000 |
| 3 | Merchandise purchases . . . . . . . . . . . . . | 250,000 | 200,000 | 190,000 |
| 4 | Cash disbursements | | | |
| 5 | Payroll . . . . . . . . . . . . . . . . . . . . . . . . . | 22,500 | 30,000 | 37,500 |
| 6 | Rent . . . . . . . . . . . . . . . . . . . . . . . . . . | 12,000 | 12,000 | 12,000 |
| 7 | Other cash expenses . . . . . . . . . . . . . | 9,000 | 13,500 | 16,500 |
| 8 | Repayment of bank loan . . . . . . . . . | | | 125,000 |
| 9 | Interest on the bank loan . . . . . . . . . | | | 3,125 |
| 10 | | | | |

\* Operations began in March; March sales were $135,000 and purchases were $90,000.

The budgeted April merchandise purchases include the inventory increase. All sales are on account. Company experience is that 10% of credit sales is collected in the month of the sale, 60% in the month following the sale, 25% in the second month, 3% in the third, and the remainder is uncollectible. Applying these percents to the March credit sales, for example, shows that $81,000 of the $135,000 will be collected in April, $33,750 in May, and $4,050 in June. All merchandise is purchased on credit; 80% of the balance is paid in the month following a purchase and the remaining 20% is paid in the second month. For example, of the $90,000 March purchases, $72,000 will be paid in April and $18,000 in May.

**Required**

Prepare a cash budget for April, May, and June for Siro Stereo. Show supporting calculations as needed.

**Check** Budgeted cash balance: April, $137,500; May, $157,750; June, $200,175

## Problem 19-3B

Preparation and analysis of cash budgets with supporting inventory and purchases budgets

C3  P2

LaRocca Company sells its product for $20 per unit. Its actual and projected sales follow:

|  | Units | Dollars |
|---|---|---|
| January (actual) . . . . . . . . . | 18,000 | $360,000 |
| February (actual) . . . . . . . . | 27,000 | 540,000 |
| March (budgeted) . . . . . . . | 15,000 | 300,000 |
| April (budgeted) . . . . . . . . | 27,000 | 540,000 |
| May (budgeted) . . . . . . . . . | 33,000 | 660,000 |

All sales are on credit. Recent experience shows that 40% of credit sales is collected in the month of the sale, 30% in the month after the sale, 25% in the second month after the sale, and 5% proves to be uncollectible. The product's purchase price is $12 per unit. All purchases are payable within 21 days. Thus, 30% of purchases made in a month is paid in that month and the other 70% is paid in the next month. LaRocca has a policy to maintain an ending monthly inventory of 30% of the next month's unit sales plus a safety stock of 300 units. The January 31 and February 28 actual inventory levels are consistent with this policy. Selling and administrative expenses for the year are $1,440,000 and are paid evenly throughout the year in cash. The company's minimum cash balance for month-end is $45,000. This minimum is maintained, if necessary, by borrowing cash from the bank. If the balance exceeds $45,000, the company repays as much of the loan as it can without going below the minimum. This type of loan carries an annual 12% interest rate. At February 28, the loan balance is $12,000, and the company's cash balance is $45,000.

### Required

**Check** (1) Cash collections: March, $372,000; April, $441,000

1. Prepare a table that shows the computation of cash collections of its credit sales (accounts receivable) in each of the months of March and April.

2. Prepare a table showing the computations of budgeted ending inventories (units) for January, February, March, and April.

(3) Budgeted purchases: February, $280,800; March, $223,200

3. Prepare the merchandise purchases budget for February, March, and April. Report calculations in units and then show the dollar amount of purchases for each month.

4. Prepare a table showing the computation of cash payments on product purchases for March and April.

(5) Ending cash balance: March, $45,000; April, $82,204

5. Prepare a cash budget for March and April, including any loan activity and interest expense. Compute the loan balance at the end of each month.

### Analysis Component

6. Refer to your answer to part 5. LaRocca's cash budget indicates the company must borrow additional funds at the end of March. Suggest some reasons that knowing this information in February would be helpful to management.

## Problem 19-4B

Preparation and analysis of budgeted income statements

C3  P2

Computa-Cations buys its product for $20 and sells it for $50 per unit. The sales staff receives a 10% commission on the sale of each unit. Its June income statement follows:

| COMPUTA-CATIONS COMPANY<br>Income Statement<br>For Month Ended June 30, 2005 | |
|---|---|
| Sales . . . . . . . . . . . . . . . . . . . . . . . | $1,000,000 |
| Cost of goods sold . . . . . . . . . . . . | 400,000 |
| Gross profit . . . . . . . . . . . . . . . . | 600,000 |
| Expenses | |
| Sales commissions (10%) . . . . . . . | 100,000 |
| Advertising . . . . . . . . . . . . . . . | 100,000 |
| Store rent . . . . . . . . . . . . . . . . | 10,000 |
| Administrative salaries . . . . . . . . | 20,000 |
| Depreciation . . . . . . . . . . . . . . | 12,000 |
| Other expenses . . . . . . . . . . . . | 24,000 |
| Total expenses . . . . . . . . . . . . | 266,000 |
| Net income . . . . . . . . . . . . . . . . | $ 334,000 |

Management expects June's results to be repeated in July, August, and September without any changes in strategy. Management, however, has another plan. It believes that unit sales will increase at a rate of 10% *each* month for the next three months (beginning with July) if the item's selling price is reduced to $45 per unit and advertising expenses are increased by 20% and remain at that level for all three months. The cost of its product will remain at $20 per unit, the sales staff will continue to earn a 10% commission, and the remaining expenses will stay the same.

### Required

**1.** Prepare budgeted income statements for each of the months of July, August, and September that show the expected results from implementing the proposed changes. Use a three-column format, with one column for each month.

**Check** Budgeted net income: July, $265,000; August, $310,100; September, $359,710

### Analysis Component

**2.** Use the budgeted income statements from part 1 to recommend whether management should implement the proposed plan. Explain.

---

Near the end of 2005, the management of Oasis Corp., a merchandising company, prepared the following estimated balance sheet for December 31, 2005:

**Problem 19-5B**
Preparation of a complete master budget

C2  C3  P1  P2

**OASIS CORPORATION**
**Estimated Balance Sheet**
**December 31, 2005**

#### Assets

| | | |
|---|---:|---:|
| Cash | | $ 160,000 |
| Accounts receivable | | 400,000 |
| Inventory | | 180,000 |
| Total current assets | | 740,000 |
| Equipment | $1,200,000 | |
| Less accumulated depreciation | 120,000 | 1,080,000 |
| Total assets | | $1,820,000 |

#### Liabilities and Equity

| | | |
|---|---:|---:|
| Accounts payable | $ 300,000 | |
| Bank loan payable | 20,000 | |
| Taxes payable (due 3/15/2006) | 200,000 | |
| Total liabilities | | $ 520,000 |
| Common stock | 1,500,000 | |
| Retained earnings (deficit) | (200,000) | |
| Total stockholders' equity | | 1,300,000 |
| Total liabilities and equity | | $1,820,000 |

To prepare a master budget for January, February, and March of 2006, management gathers the following information:

**a.** Oasis Corp.'s single product is purchased for $10 per unit and resold for $24 per unit. The expected inventory level of 18,000 units on December 31, 2005, is more than management's desired level for 2006, which is 40% of the next month's expected sales (in units). Expected sales are: January, 30,000 units; February, 24,000 units; March, 40,000 units; and April, 50,000 units.

**b.** Cash sales and credit sales represent 40% and 60%, respectively, of total sales. Of the credit sales, 70% is collected in the first month after the month of sale and 30% in the second month after the month of sale. For the $400,000 accounts receivable balance at December 31, 2005, $280,000 is collected in January 2006 and the remaining $120,000 is collected in February 2006.

**c.** Merchandise purchases are paid for as follows: 80% in the first month after the month of purchase and 20% in the second month after the month of purchase. For the $300,000 accounts payable balance at December 31, 2005, $240,000 is paid in January 2006 and the remaining $60,000 is paid in February 2006.

**d.** Sales commissions equal to 10% of sales are paid each month. Sales salaries (excluding commissions) are $288,000 per year.

**e.** General and administrative salaries are $336,000 per year. Maintenance expense equals $6,000 per month and is paid in cash.

**f.** Equipment reported in the December 31, 2005, balance sheet was purchased in January 2005. It is being depreciated over 10 years under the straight-line method with no salvage value. The following amounts for new equipment purchases are planned in the coming quarter: January, $240,000; February, $120,000; and March, $96,000. This equipment will be depreciated using the straight-line method over 10 years with no salvage value. A full month's depreciation is taken for the month in which equipment is purchased.

**g.** The company plans to acquire land at the end of March at a cost of $232,000, which will be paid with cash on the last day of the month.

**h.** Oasis Corp. has a working arrangement with its bank to obtain additional loans as needed. The interest rate is 12% per year, and interest is paid at each month-end based on the beginning balance. Partial or full payments on these loans can be made on the last day of the month. Oasis has agreed to maintain a minimum ending cash balance of $160,000 in each month.

**i.** The income tax rate for the company is 30%. Income taxes on the first quarter's income will not be paid until April 15.

**Required**

Prepare a master budget for each of the first three months of 2006; include the following component budgets (show supporting calculations as needed, and round amounts to the nearest dollar):

**1.** Monthly sales budgets (showing both budgeted unit sales and dollar sales).

**2.** Monthly merchandise purchases budgets.

**3.** Monthly selling expense budgets.

**4.** Monthly general and administrative expense budgets.

**5.** Monthly capital expenditures budgets.

**6.** Monthly cash budgets.

**7.** Budgeted income statement for the entire first quarter (not for each month).

**8.** Budgeted balance sheet as of March 31, 2006.

**Check** (2) Budgeted purchases: January, $216,000; February, $304,000;

(3) Budgeted selling expenses: January, $96,000; February, $81,600

(6) Ending cash bal.: January, $160,000; February, $281,578

(8) Budgeted total assets at March 31, $2,768,880

---

**Problem 19-6B**[A]

Preparing production and direct materials budgets

C3   P3

RBI Company produces baseball bats. Each bat requires 4 pounds of aluminum alloy. Management predicts that 10,000 bats and 28,000 pounds of aluminum alloy will be in inventory on March 31 of the current year and that 100,000 bats will be sold during this year's second quarter. Management wants to end the second quarter with 3,000 finished bats and 2,000 pounds of aluminum alloy in inventory. Aluminum alloy can be purchased for $3 per pound.

**Required**

**1.** Prepare the second-quarter production budget for bats.

**2.** Prepare the second-quarter direct materials (aluminum alloy) budget; include the dollar cost of purchases.

**Check** (1) Units manuf., 93,000; (2) Cost of aluminum purchases, $1,038,000

---

# PROBLEM SET C

Problem Set C is available at the book's Website to further reinforce and assess your learning.

---

# SERIAL PROBLEM

Success Systems

*(This serial problem began in Chapter 1 and continues through most of the book. If previous chapter segments were not completed, the serial problem can begin at this point. It is helpful, but not necessary, for you to use the Working Papers that accompany the book.)*

Kay Breeze expects second quarter 2006 sales of her new line of computer furniture to be the same as the first quarter's sales (reported below) without any changes in strategy. Monthly sales averaged 20 desk units (sales price of $2,500) and 10 chairs (sales price of $1,000).

| SUCCESS SYSTEMS Segment Income Statement* For the Quarter Ended March 31, 2006 | |
|---|---|
| Sales† . . . . . . . . . . . . . . . . . . . . . | $180,000 |
| Cost of goods sold‡ . . . . . . . . . | 105,000 |
| Gross profit . . . . . . . . . . . . . . . | 75,000 |
| Expenses | |
| Sales commissions (10%) . . . . . . . | 18,000 |
| Advertising expenses . . . . . . . . . . | 12,000 |
| Other fixed expenses . . . . . . . . . | 15,000 |
| Total expenses . . . . . . . . . . . . . | 45,000 |
| Net income . . . . . . . . . . . . . . . | $ 30,000 |

\* Reflects revenue and expense activity only related to the computer furniture segment.

† Revenue: (60 desks × $2,500) + (30 chairs × $1,000) = $150,000 + $30,000 = $180,000

‡ Cost of goods sold: (60 desks × $1,500) + (30 chairs × $500) = $90,000 + $15,000 = $105,000

Breeze believes that sales will increase each month for the next three months (April, 22 desks, 11 chairs; May, 24 desks, 12 chairs; June, 26 desks, 13 chairs) *if* selling prices are reduced to $2,250 for desks and $750 for chairs and advertising expenses are increased by 25% and remain at that level for all three months. The products' cost will remain at $1,500 for desks and $500 for chairs. The sales staff will continue to earn a 10% commission, and the fixed costs per month will remain at $5,000.

### Required

**1.** Prepare budgeted income statements for each of the months of April, May, and June that show the expected results from implementing the proposed changes. Use a three-column format, with one column for each month.

**2.** Use the budgeted income statements from part 1 to recommend whether Breeze should implement the proposed changes. Explain.

**Check**   (1) Budgeted income: April, $3,475; May, $4,700

---

## BEYOND THE NUMBERS

**BTN 19-1**   Financial statements often serve as a starting point in formulating the budget. You are assigned to review **Krispy Kreme**'s financial statements to determine its cash paid for dividends in the current year and the budgeted cash needed to pay its next year's dividend.

**REPORTING IN ACTION**

P2   C2   C3

### Required

**1.** Which financial statement(s) reports the amount of (a) cash dividends paid and (b) annual cash dividends declared? Explain where on the statement(s) this information is reported.

**2.** Indicate the amount of cash dividends (a) paid in the year ended February 2, 2003, and (b) to be paid (budgeted for) next year under the assumption that annual cash dividends equal 25% of the prior year's net income.

*Roll On*

**3.** Access Krispy Kreme's financial statements for a fiscal year ending after February 2, 2003, from either its Website [KrispyKreme.com] or the SEC's EDGAR database [www.SEC.gov]. Compare your answer for part 2 with actual cash dividends paid for the year ended February 2, 2003. Compute the error, if any, in your estimate. Speculate as to why dividends were higher or lower than budgeted.

## COMPARATIVE ANALYSIS

P2

**BTN 19-2**   One source of cash savings for a company is improved management of inventory. To illustrate, assume that **Krispy Kreme** and **Tastykake** both have $250,000 per month in sales in the Virginia area, and both forecast this level of sales per month for the next 24 months. Also assume that both Krispy Kreme and Tastykake have a 20% contribution margin and equal fixed costs, and that cost per dozen of baked goods is the only variable cost. Assume that the main difference between Krispy Kreme and Tastykake is the distribution system. Krispy Kreme bakes onsite without preservatives and requires ending inventory of only 10% of next month's sales of nonperishable items (for example, coffee) in inventory at each month-end. However, Tastykake's retail outlets are mostly off-site from the factory. Tastykake is building an improved distribution system and requires 40% of next month's sales in inventory at each month-end.

### Required

1. Compute the amount by which Tastykake can reduce its inventory level if it can match Krispy Kreme's system of maintaining an inventory equal to 10% of next month's sales. (*Hint:* Focus on the facts given and only on the Virginia area.)

2. Explain how the analysis in part 1 that shows ending inventory levels for both the 40% and 10% required inventory policies can help justify a just-in-time inventory system. You can assume a 15% interest cost for resources that are tied up in ending inventory.

## ETHICS CHALLENGE

C1  C2

**BTN 19-3**   Both the budget process and budgets themselves can impact management actions, both positively and negatively. For instance, a common practice among not-for-profit organizations and government agencies is for management to spend any amounts remaining in a budget at the end of the budget period, a practice often called "use it or lose it." The view is that if a department manager does not spend the budgeted amount, top management will reduce next year's budget by the amount not spent. To avoid losing budget dollars, department managers often spend all budgeted amounts regardless of the value added to products or services. All of us pay for the costs associated with this budget system.

### Required

Write a one-half page report to a local not-for-profit organization or government agency offering a solution to the "use it or lose it" budgeting problem.

## COMMUNICATING IN PRACTICE

P1

**BTN 19-4**   The sales budget is usually the first and most crucial of the component budgets in a master budget because all other budgets usually rely on it for planning purposes.

### Required

Assume that your company's sales staff provides information on expected sales and selling prices for items making up the sales budget. Prepare a one-page memorandum to your supervisor outlining concerns with the sales staff's input in the sales budget when its compensation is at least partly tied to these budgets. More generally, explain the importance of assessing any potential bias in information provided to the budget process.

## TAKING IT TO THE NET

C2  P1  P2

mhhe.com/wild

**BTN 19-5**   Access an e-budgets Website at **HelmsmanGroup.com** (by **FRx Corporation**). Review the information at this site; click on the link *CFO Tour* and examine the information provided.

### Required

1. Assume the role of a senior manager in a large, multidivision company. What are the benefits of using e-budgets?

2. As a senior manager, what concerns do you have with the concept and application of e-budgets?

## TEAMWORK IN ACTION

A1

**BTN 19-6**   Your team is to prepare a budget report outlining the costs of attending college (full-time) for the next two semesters (30 hours) or three quarters (45 hours). This budget's focus is solely on attending college; do not include personal items in the team's budget. Your budget must include tuition, books, supplies, club fees, food, housing, and all costs associated with travel to and from college. This budgeting exercise is similar to the initial phase in activity-based budgeting. Include a list of any assumptions you use in completing the budget. Be prepared to present your budget in class.

**BTN 19-7**   Read the article "A Wrong Turn for Pro Cycling" in the June 23, 2003, issue of *Business Week*. (This book's Website provides free access to this article.)

**Required**

1. Which corporate budget is the subject of this article?
2. Would Krispy Kreme or Tastykake be potential good fits for pro cycle sponsoring given the types of companies that have sponsored teams in the past? Explain.
3. Is sponsoring a pro cycling team ever a good investment? Explain.

**BTN 19-8**   Chuang, Wenjen, and Kapner are continually in an expansion mode with their entrepreneurial business, **Aquent**. Their vision for expansion will require outside financing. Assume that the three Aquent owners call on a financial institution for backing and have been asked by the bankers for a detailed business plan.

**Required**

1. What should Aquent's business plan include?
2. How can budgeting help the three owners effectively develop and operate their business?

**BTN 19-9**   To help understand the factors impacting a sales budget, you are to visit three businesses with the same ownership or franchise membership. Record the selling prices of two identical products at each location, such as regular and premium gas sold at Texaco stations. You are likely to find a difference in prices for at least one of the three locations you visit.

**Required**

1. Identify at least three external factors that must be considered when setting the sales budget. (*Note:* There is a difference between internal and external factors that impact the sales budget.)
2. What factors might explain any differences identified in the prices of the businesses you visited?

**BTN 19-10**   Access **Grupo Bimbo**'s income statement (<u>GrupoBimbo.com</u>) for the year ended December 31, 2002.

**Required**

1. Is Grupo Bimbo's selling expense budget likely to be an important budget in its master budgeting process? Explain.
2. Identify three types of expenses that would be reported as distribution and selling expenses on Grupo Bimbo's income statement.
3. Who likely has the initial responsibility for Grupo Bimbo's selling expense budget? Explain.

SCOTTeVEST™ *SPORT LITE*

*"All my friends told me it was ridiculous"*—Scott Jordan

# 20

# Flexible Budgets and Standard Costs

## A Look Back

Chapter 19 explained the importance of budgeting. It also described the master budget and its component budgets as well as their usefulness for planning and monitoring company activities.

## A Look at This Chapter

This chapter describes flexible budgets, variance analysis, and standard costs. It explains how each is used for purposes of better controlling and monitoring business activities.

## A Look Ahead

Chapter 21 focuses on capital budgeting decisions. It explains and illustrates several procedures used in evaluating short-term managerial decisions.

# CAP

### Conceptual

**C1** Define *standard costs* and explain their computation and uses. *(p. 813)*

**C2** Describe variances and what they reveal about performance. *(p. 815)*

**C3** Explain how standard cost information is useful for management by exception. *(p. 824)*

### Analytical

**A1** Compare fixed and flexible budgets. *(p. 810)*

**A2** Analyze changes in sales from expected amounts. *(p. 826)*

### Procedural

**P1** Prepare a flexible budget and interpret a flexible budget performance report. *(p. 811)*

**P2** Compute materials and labor variances. *(p. 816)*

**P3** Compute overhead variances. *(p. 820)*

**P4** Prepare journal entries for standard costs and account for price and quantity variances. *(p. 824)*

---

**Decision Feature**

# Vested Interest in Geek Chic

CHICAGO—Success for clothing and accessory companies usually depends on the current fad. Scott Jordan has taken a different tack, however. Jordan, a former corporate lawyer, created **Technology Enabled Clothing, LLC [TechnologyEnabledClothing.com]** and **SCOTTeVEST, LLC,** which focus on functionality. "I couldn't carry all of my electronic gadgets," says Jordan. "So the idea of technology-enabled clothing came to me." This led to another problem, he says: "The difficult part was finding a way to use the gadgets while on the go."

Jordan then assembled an expert design team to fit conduits throughout a garment that did not look "geeky." The result was *SCOTTeVEST,* a stylish, lightweight jacket with zip off sleeves, which comes in different versions, colors, and styles. Says Jordan, "I view our product as the convergence of apparel, luggage, and technology." On the first day the Website went live, he says, "I got 50,000 hits and more than 100 orders. I didn't even have a manufacturer lined up!"

The realities of business quickly became apparent. Jordan admits that he didn't have "any real management experience—so that was

the tough part, having to learn about business and management from scratch." He persisted and quickly learned the importance of cost analysis and variances, flexible and fixed budgets, and performance reports. He also learned to keep tabs on sales variances because production pricing is one key to his successful performance. Complicating Jordan's analysis was the garment industry. "We had trouble to get a retailer to stock our goods," he admits. "They're so risk averse."

The company has outperformed Jordan's most optimistic budget goals. Disneyland even helped by including his vest in its "Tomorrow Land" exhibit. "We continue to create new and improved versions," says Jordan. With budgeted sales projections of $5 million for his two-year-old company, he has seemingly grasped business principles.

"I'm told the president got one [eVEST] with the presidential seal on it," exclaims Jordan. Now, that's one big *seal of approval!*

[Sources: *Technology Enabled Clothing Website,* January 2004; *Entrepreneur,* February 2003; *The Wall Street Journal,* January 2003; *Business Week,* September 2002; *Computer User,* January 2003.]

Budgeting helps organize and formalize management's planning activities. This chapter extends the study of budgeting to look more closely at the use of budgets to evaluate performance. Evaluations are important for controlling and monitoring business activities. This chapter also describes and illustrates the use of standard costs and variance analyses. These managerial tools are useful for both evaluating and controlling organizations and for the planning of future activities.

## Section 1—Flexible Budgets

This section introduces fixed budgets and fixed budget performance reports. It then introduces flexible budgets and flexible budget performance reports and illustrates their advantages.

## Budgetary Process

A master budget reflects management's planned objectives for a future period. The preparation of a master budget is based on a predicted level of activity such as sales volume for the budget period. This section discusses the effects on the usefulness of budget reports when the actual level of activity differs from the predicted level.

### Budgetary Control and Reporting

**Budgetary control** refers to management's use of budgets to monitor and control a company's operations. This includes using budgets to see that planned objectives are met. **Budget reports** contain relevant information that compares actual results to planned activities. This comparison is motivated by a need to both monitor performance and control activities. Budget reports are sometimes viewed as progress reports, or *report cards,* on management's performance in achieving planned objectives. These reports can be prepared at any time and for any period. Three common periods for a budget report are a month, quarter, and year.

**Point:** Budget reports are often used as a base to determine bonuses of managers.

The budgetary control process involves at least four steps: (1) develop the budget from planned objectives, (2) compare actual results to budgeted amounts and analyze any differences, (3) take corrective and strategic actions, and (4) establish new planned objectives and prepare a new budget. Exhibit 20.1 shows this continual process of budgetary control. Budget

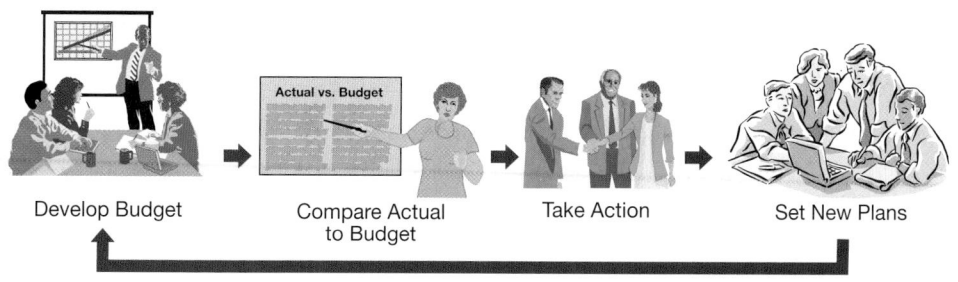

Exhibit 20.1

Process of Budgetary Control

Develop Budget → Compare Actual to Budget → Take Action → Set New Plans

reports and related documents are effective tools for managers to obtain the greatest benefits from this budgetary process.

## Fixed Budget Performance Report

In a fixed budgetary control system, the master budget is based on a single prediction for sales volume or other activity level. The budgeted amount for each cost essentially assumes that a specific (or *fixed*) amount of sales will occur. A **fixed budget,** also called *static budget,* is based on a single predicted amount of sales or other measure of activity.

One benefit of a budget is its usefulness in comparing actual results with planned activities. Information useful for analysis is often presented for comparison in a performance report. As shown in Exhibit 20.2, a **fixed budget performance report** for Optel compares actual results for January 2005 with the results expected under its fixed budget that predicted 10,000 (composite) units of sales. Optel manufactures inexpensive eyeglasses, frames, contact lens, and related supplies. For this report, its production volume equals sales volume (its inventory level did not change).

Exhibit 20.2

Fixed Budget
Performance Report

| OPTEL Fixed Budget Performance Report For Month Ended January 31, 2005 | Fixed Budget | Actual Results | Variances* |
|---|---|---|---|
| Sales (in units) ......................... | 10,000 | 12,000 | |
| Sales (in dollars) ...................... | $100,000 | $125,000 | $25,000 F |
| Cost of goods sold | | | |
| Direct materials ..................... | 10,000 | 13,000 | 3,000 U |
| Direct labor ...................... | 15,000 | 20,000 | 5,000 U |
| Overhead | | | |
| Factory supplies ................... | 2,000 | 2,100 | 100 U |
| Utilities ........................ | 3,000 | 4,000 | 1,000 U |
| Depreciation—Machinery ............. | 8,000 | 8,000 | 0 |
| Supervisory salaries ................ | 11,000 | 11,000 | 0 |
| Selling expenses | | | |
| Sales commissions ................... | 9,000 | 10,800 | 1,800 U |
| Shipping expenses ................... | 4,000 | 4,300 | 300 U |
| General and administrative expenses | | | |
| Office supplies ...................... | 5,000 | 5,200 | 200 U |
| Insurance expenses ................. | 1,000 | 1,200 | 200 U |
| Depreciation—Office equipment ........ | 7,000 | 7,000 | 0 |
| Administrative salaries .............. | 13,000 | 13,000 | 0 |
| Total expenses ...................... | 88,000 | 99,600 | 11,600 U |
| Income from operations ............... | $ 12,000 | $ 25,400 | $13,400 F |

* F = Favorable variance; and U = Unfavorable variance.

This type of performance report designates differences between budgeted and actual results as variances. We see the letters *F* and *U* located beside the numbers in the third number column of this report. Their meanings are as follows:

*F* = **Favorable variance**   When compared to budget, the actual cost or revenue contributes to a *higher* income. That is, actual revenue is higher than budgeted revenue, or actual cost is lower than budgeted cost.

**Example:** How is it that the favorable sales variance in Exhibit 20.2 is linked with so many unfavorable cost and expense variances? *Answer:* Costs have increased with the increase in sales.

*U* = **Unfavorable variance**   When compared to budget, the actual cost or revenue contributes to a *lower* income; actual revenue is lower than budgeted revenue, or actual cost is higher than budgeted cost.

This convention is common in practice and is used throughout this chapter.

## Budget Reports for Evaluation

A primary use of budget reports is as a tool for management to monitor and control operations. Evaluation by Optel management is likely to focus on a variety of questions that might include these:

- Why is actual income from operations $13,400 higher than budgeted?
- Are amounts paid for each expense item too high?
- Is manufacturing using too much direct material?
- Is manufacturing using too much direct labor?

The performance report in Exhibit 20.2 provides little help in answering these questions because actual sales volume is 2,000 units higher than budgeted. A manager does not know if this higher level of sales activity is the cause of variations in total dollar sales and expenses or if other factors have influenced these amounts. This inability of fixed budget reports to adjust for changes in activity levels is a major limitation of a fixed budget performance report. That is, it fails to show whether actual costs are out of line due to a change in actual sales volume or some other factor.

**Decision Insight**

**Natural Budget**   Budget reporting and evaluation are used at the **Environmental Protection Agency (EPA)**. It regularly prepares performance plans and budget requests that describe performance goals, measure outcomes, and analyze variances.

# Flexible Budget Reports

## Purpose of Flexible Budgets

A1   Compare fixed and flexible budgets.

Topic Tackler 20-1

To help address limitations with the fixed budget performance report, particularly from the effects of changes in sales volume, management can use a flexible budget. A **flexible budget,** also called a *variable budget,* is a report based on predicted amounts of revenues and expenses corresponding to the actual level of output. Unlike fixed budgets, a flexible budget is prepared after a period's activities are complete. A flexible budget can be viewed as a fixed budget prepared at the activity level corresponding to the actual level of activity.

A flexible budget's primary purpose is to help managers evaluate past performance. It is especially useful for such an evaluation because it reflects budgeted revenues and costs based on the actual level of activity. Thus, comparisons of actual results with budgeted performance are more likely to identify the causes of any differences. This can help managers focus attention on real problem areas and implement corrective actions. This is in contrast to a fixed budget, whose primary purpose is to assist managers in planning future activities and whose numbers are based on a single predicted amount of budgeted sales or production.

## Preparation of Flexible Budgets

A flexible budget is designed to reveal the effects of volume of activity on revenues and costs. To prepare a flexible budget, management relies on the distinctions between fixed and variable costs. Recall that the cost per unit of activity remains constant for variable costs so that the total amount of a variable cost changes in direct proportion to a change in activity level. The total amount of fixed cost remains unchanged regardless of changes in the level of activity within a relevant (normal) operating range. (Assume that costs can be reasonably classified as variable or fixed within a relevant range.)

When we create the numbers constituting a flexible budget, we express each variable cost as either a constant amount per unit of sales or as a percent of a sales dollar. In the case of a fixed cost, we express its budgeted amount as the total amount expected to occur at any sales volume within the relevant range.

Exhibit 20.3 shows a set of flexible budgets for Optel in January 2005. Seven of its expenses are classified as variable costs. Its remaining five expenses are fixed costs. These classifications result from management's investigation of each expense. Variable and fixed expense categories are *not* the same for every company, and we must avoid drawing conclusions from specific cases. For example, depending on the nature of a company's operations, office supplies expense can be either fixed or variable with respect to sales.

P1 Prepare a flexible budget and interpret a flexible budget performance report.

**Point:** Usefulness of a flexible budget depends on valid classification of variable and fixed costs. Some costs are mixed and must be analyzed to determine their variable and fixed portions.
**Point:** To apply these concepts, work Exercise 20-2.

## Exhibit 20.3

Flexible Budgets

| **OPTEL** Flexible Budgets For Month Ended January 31, 2005 | Variable Amount per Unit | Total Fixed Cost | Flexible Budget for Unit Sales of 10,000 | Flexible Budget for Unit Sales of 12,000 | Flexible Budget for Unit Sales of 14,000 |
|---|---|---|---|---|---|
| Sales ........................... | $10.00 | | $100,000 | $120,000 | $140,000 |
| **Variable costs** | | | | | |
| Direct materials ................... | 1.00 | | 10,000 | 12,000 | 14,000 |
| Direct labor ...................... | 1.50 | | 15,000 | 18,000 | 21,000 |
| Factory supplies ................... | 0.20 | | 2,000 | 2,400 | 2,800 |
| Utilities ......................... | 0.30 | | 3,000 | 3,600 | 4,200 |
| Sales commissions ................. | 0.90 | | 9,000 | 10,800 | 12,600 |
| Shipping expenses ................. | 0.40 | | 4,000 | 4,800 | 5,600 |
| Office supplies ................... | 0.50 | | 5,000 | 6,000 | 7,000 |
| Total variable costs ............... | 4.80 | | 48,000 | 57,600 | 67,200 |
| Contribution margin ............... | $ 5.20 | | $ 52,000 | $ 62,400 | $ 72,800 |
| **Fixed costs** | | | | | |
| Depreciation—Machinery ............ | | $ 8,000 | 8,000 | 8,000 | 8,000 |
| Supervisory salaries ............... | | 11,000 | 11,000 | 11,000 | 11,000 |
| Insurance expense ................. | | 1,000 | 1,000 | 1,000 | 1,000 |
| Depreciation—Office equipment ....... | | 7,000 | 7,000 | 7,000 | 7,000 |
| Administrative salaries .............. | | 13,000 | 13,000 | 13,000 | 13,000 |
| Total fixed costs .................. | | $40,000 | 40,000 | 40,000 | 40,000 |
| Income from operations .............. | | | $ 12,000 | $ 22,400 | $ 32,800 |

The layout for the flexible budgets in Exhibit 20.3 begins with sales followed by variable costs and then fixed costs. Both the expected individual and total variable costs are reported and then subtracted from sales. The difference between sales and variable costs equals contribution margin. The expected amounts of fixed costs are listed next, followed by the expected income from operations before taxes.

**Example:** Using Exhibit 20.3, what is the budgeted income from operations for unit sales of (a) 11,000 and (b) 13,000? *Answers:* $17,200 for unit sales of 11,000. $27,600 for unit sales of 13,000.

The first and second number columns of Exhibit 20.3 show the flexible budget amounts for variable costs per unit and each fixed cost for any volume of sales in the relevant range. The third, fourth, and fifth columns show the flexible budget amounts computed for three different sales volumes. For instance, the third column's flexible budget is based on 10,000 units. These numbers are the same as those in the fixed budget of Exhibit 20.2 because the expected volumes are the same for these two budgets.

**Point:** Flexible budgeting allows a budget to be prepared at the *actual* output level. Performance reports are then prepared comparing the flexible budget to actual revenues and costs.

**Point:** A flexible budget yields an "apples to apples" comparison because budgeted activity levels are the same as the actual.

Recall that Optel's actual sales volume for January is 12,000 units. This sales volume is 2,000 units more than the 10,000 units originally predicted in the master budget. When differences between actual and predicted volume arise, the usefulness of a flexible budget is apparent. For instance, compare the flexible budget for 10,000 units in the third column (which is the same as the fixed budget in Exhibit 20.2) with the flexible budget for 12,000 units in the fourth column. The higher levels for both sales and variable costs reflect nothing more than the increase in sales activity. Any budget analysis comparing actual with planned results that ignores this information is less useful to management.

To illustrate, when we evaluate Optel's performance, we need to prepare a flexible budget showing actual and budgeted values at 12,000 units. As part of a complete profitability analysis, managers could compare the actual income of $25,400 (from Exhibit 20.2) with the $22,400 income expected at the actual sales volume of 12,000 units (from Exhibit 20.3). This results in a total income variance of $3,000 to be explained and interpreted. This variance is markedly different from the $13,400 variance identified in Exhibit 20.2 using a fixed budget. After receiving the flexible budget based on January's actual volume, management must determine what caused this $3,000 difference. The next section describes a flexible budget performance report that provides guidance in this analysis.

## Flexible Budget Performance Report

**Point:** To apply these concepts, work QS 20-1.

A **flexible budget performance report** lists differences between actual performance and budgeted performance based on actual sales volume or other activity level. This report helps direct management's attention to those costs or revenues that differ substantially from budgeted amounts. Exhibit 20.4 shows Optel's flexible budget performance report for January. We prepare this report after the actual volume is known to be 12,000 units. This report shows a $5,000 favorable variance in total dollar sales. Because actual and budgeted volumes are both 12,000 units, the $5,000 sales variance must have resulted from a higher than expected selling price. Further analysis of the facts surrounding this $5,000 sales variance reveals a favorable sales variance per unit of nearly $0.42 as shown here:

| | |
|---|---|
| Actual average price per unit (rounded to cents) . . . . . . . | $125,000/12,000 = $10.42 |
| Budgeted price per unit . . . . . . . . . . . . . . . . . . . . . . . . . | $120,000/12,000 = 10.00 |
| Favorable sales variance per unit . . . . . . . . . . . . . . . . . | $5,000/12,000 = $ 0.42 |

**Decision Maker**

**Entrepreneur** The heads of both strategic consulting and tax consulting divisions of your financial services firm complain to you about the unfavorable variances on their performance reports. "We worked on more consulting assignments than planned. It's not surprising our costs are higher than expected. To top it off, this report characterizes our work as *poor!*" How do you respond?

Answer—p. 832

The other variances in Exhibit 20.4 also direct management's attention to areas where corrective actions can help control Optel's operations. Each expense variance is analyzed as the sales variance was. We can think of each expense as the joint result of using a given number of units and paying a specific price per unit.

More generally, each variance in Exhibit 20.4 is due in part to a difference between *actual price* per unit of input and *budgeted price* per unit of input. This is a **price variance.** Each variance also can be due in part to a difference between *actual quantity* of input used and *budgeted quantity* of input. This is a **quantity variance.** We explain more about this breakdown, known as **variance analysis,** later in the standard costs section.

| OPTEL Flexible Budget Performance Report For Month Ended January 31, 2005 | Flexible Budget | Actual Results | Variances* |
|---|---|---|---|
| Sales (12,000 units) . . . . . . . . . . . . . . . . . . | $120,000 | $125,000 | $5,000 F |
| **Variable costs** | | | |
| Direct materials . . . . . . . . . . . . . . . . . . . | 12,000 | 13,000 | 1,000 U |
| Direct labor . . . . . . . . . . . . . . . . . . . . . | 18,000 | 20,000 | 2,000 U |
| Factory supplies . . . . . . . . . . . . . . . . . . . | 2,400 | 2,100 | 300 F |
| Utilities . . . . . . . . . . . . . . . . . . . . . . . . . | 3,600 | 4,000 | 400 U |
| Sales commissions . . . . . . . . . . . . . . . . . | 10,800 | 10,800 | 0 |
| Shipping expenses . . . . . . . . . . . . . . . . . | 4,800 | 4,300 | 500 F |
| Office supplies . . . . . . . . . . . . . . . . . . . . | 6,000 | 5,200 | 800 F |
| Total variable costs . . . . . . . . . . . . . . | 57,600 | 59,400 | 1,800 U |
| Contribution margin . . . . . . . . . . . . . . . . . | 62,400 | 65,600 | 3,200 F |
| **Fixed costs** | | | |
| Depreciation—Machinery . . . . . . . . . . . . | 8,000 | 8,000 | 0 |
| Supervisory salaries . . . . . . . . . . . . . . . . | 11,000 | 11,000 | 0 |
| Insurance expense . . . . . . . . . . . . . . . . . | 1,000 | 1,200 | 200 U |
| Depreciation—Office equipment . . . . . . . | 7,000 | 7,000 | 0 |
| Administrative salaries . . . . . . . . . . . . . . | 13,000 | 13,000 | 0 |
| Total fixed costs . . . . . . . . . . . . . . . . | 40,000 | 40,200 | 200 U |
| Income from operations . . . . . . . . . . . . . . | $ 22,400 | $ 25,400 | $3,000 F |

**Exhibit 20.4**

Flexible Budget Performance Report

\* F = Favorable variance; and U = Unfavorable variance.

---

### Quick Check

**1.** A flexible budget (a) shows fixed costs as constant amounts of cost per unit of activity, (b) shows variable costs as constant amounts of cost per unit of activity, or (c) is prepared based on one expected amount of budgeted sales or production.

**2.** What is the initial step in preparing a flexible budget?

**3.** What is the main difference between a fixed and a flexible budget?

**4.** What is contribution margin?

Answers—p. 832

# Section 2—Standard Costs

**Standard costs** are preset costs for delivering a product or service under normal conditions. These costs are established by personnel, engineering, and accounting studies using past experiences and data. Management uses these costs to assess the reasonableness of actual costs incurred for producing the product or service. When actual costs vary from standard costs, management follows up to identify potential problems and take corrective actions.

Standard costs are often used in preparing budgets because they are the anticipated costs incurred under normal conditions. Terms such as *standard materials cost, standard labor cost,* and *standard overhead cost* are often used to refer to amounts budgeted for direct materials, direct labor, and overhead.

**C1** Define *standard costs* and explain their computation and uses.

**Point:** Since standard costs are often budgeted costs, they can be used to prepare both fixed budgets and flexible budgets.

# Materials and Labor Standards

This section explains how to set materials and labor standards and how to prepare a standard cost card.

## Identifying Standard Costs

**Point:** Business practice often uses the word *budget* when speaking of total values and *standard* when discussing per unit values.

Managerial accountants, engineers, personnel administrators, and other managers combine their efforts to set standard costs. To identify standards for direct labor costs, we can conduct time and motion studies for each labor operation in the process of providing a product or service. From these studies, management can learn the best way to perform the operation and then sets the standard labor time required for the operation under normal conditions. Similarly, standards for materials are set by studying the quantity, grade, and cost of each material used. Standards for overhead costs are explained later in the chapter.

Regardless of the care used in setting standard costs and in revising them as conditions change, actual costs frequently differ from standard costs, often as a result of one or more factors. For instance, the actual quantity of material used can differ from the standard, or the price paid per unit of material can differ from the standard. Quantity and price differences from standard amounts can also occur for labor. That is, the actual labor time and actual labor rate can vary from what was expected. The same analysis applies to overhead costs.

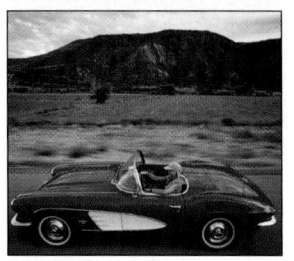

## Setting Standard Costs

**Example:** What factors might be considered when deciding whether to revise standard costs? *Answer:* Changes in the processes and/or resources needed to carry out the processes.

**Point:** Companies promoting continuous improvement strive to achieve ideal standards by eliminating inefficiencies and waste.

To illustrate the setting of a standard cost, we consider a professional league baseball bat manufactured by ProBat. Its engineers have determined that manufacturing one bat requires 0.90 kgs. of high-grade wood. They also expect some loss of material as part of the process because of inefficiencies and waste. This results in adding an *allowance* of 0.10 kgs., making the standard requirement 1.0 kg. of wood for each bat.

The 0.90 kgs. portion is called an *ideal standard;* it is the quantity of material required if the process is 100% efficient without any loss or waste. Reality suggests that some loss of material usually occurs with any process. The standard of 1.0 kg. is known as the *practical standard,* the quantity of material required under normal application of the process.

High-grade wood can be purchased at a standard price of $25 per kg. The purchasing department sets this price as the expected price for the budget period. To determine this price, the purchasing department considers factors such as the quality of materials, future economic conditions, supply factors (shortages and excesses), and any available discounts. The engineers also decide that two hours of labor time (after including allowances) are required to manufacture a bat. The wage rate is $20 per hour (better than average skilled labor is required). ProBat assigns all overhead at the rate of $10 per labor hour. The standard costs of direct materials, direct labor, and overhead for one bat are as shown in Exhibit 20.5 in what is called a *standard cost card.* These cost amounts are then used to prepare manufacturing budgets for a budgeted level of production.

## Exhibit 20.5

Standard Cost Card

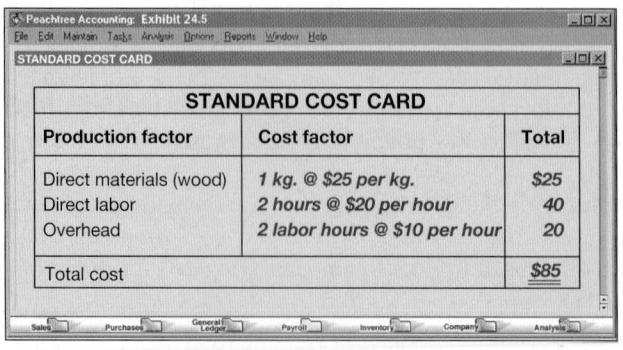

| STANDARD COST CARD | | |
|---|---|---|
| **Production factor** | **Cost factor** | **Total** |
| Direct materials (wood) | 1 kg. @ $25 per kg. | $25 |
| Direct labor | 2 hours @ $20 per hour | 40 |
| Overhead | 2 labor hours @ $10 per hour | 20 |
| Total cost | | $85 |

# Cost Variances

A **cost variance,** also simply called a *variance,* is the difference between actual and standard costs. A cost variance can be favorable or unfavorable. A variance from standard cost is considered favorable if actual cost is less than standard cost. It is considered unfavorable if actual cost is more than standard cost.[1] This section discusses variance analysis.

**C2** Describe variances and what they reveal about performance.

## Cost Variance Analysis

Variances are usually identified in performance reports. When a variance occurs, management wants to determine the factors causing it. This often involves analysis, evaluation, and explanation. The results of these efforts should enable management to assign responsibility for the variance and then to take actions to correct the situation.

To illustrate, Optel's standard materials cost for producing 12,000 units of its product is $12,000. Its actual materials cost for January proved to be $13,000. The $1,000 unfavorable variance raises questions that call for answers that, in turn, can lead to changes to correct the situation and eliminate this variance in the next period. A performance report often identifies the existence of a problem, but we must follow up with further investigation to see what can be done to improve future performance.

Exhibit 20.6 shows the flow of events in the effective management of variance analysis. It shows four steps: (1) preparing a standard cost performance report, (2) computing and analyzing variances, (3) identifying questions and their explanations, and (4) taking corrective and strategic actions. These variance analysis steps are interrelated and are frequently applied in good organizations.

Prepare Reports          Analyze Variances          Questions and Answers          Take Action

**Exhibit 20.6**

Variance Analysis

## Cost Variance Computation

Management needs information about the factors causing a cost variance, but first it must properly compute the variance. In its most simple form, a cost variance (CV) is computed as the difference between actual cost (AC) and standard cost (SC) as shown in Exhibit 20.7.

> **Cost Variance** (CV) = **Actual Cost** (AC) − **Standard Cost** (SC)
>
> where:
>
> **Actual Cost** (AC) = **Actual Quantity** (AQ) × **Actual Price** (AP)
> **Standard Cost** (SC) = **Standard Quantity** (SQ) × **Standard Price** (SP)

**Exhibit 20.7**

Cost Variance Formulas

A cost variance is further defined by its components. Actual quantity (AQ) is the input (material or labor) used to manufacture the quantity of output. Standard quantity (SQ) is the expected input for the quantity of output. Actual price (AP) is the amount paid to acquire the input (material or labor), and standard price (SP) is the expected price.

---

[1] Short-term favorable variances can sometimes lead to long-term unfavorable variances. For instance, if management spends less than the budgeted amount on maintenance or insurance, the performance report would show a favorable variance. Cutting these expenses can lead to major losses in the long run if machinery wears out prematurely or insurance coverage proves inadequate.

Two main factors cause a cost variance: (1) the difference between actual price and standard price results in a *price* (or rate) *variance* and (2) the difference between actual quantity and standard quantity results in a *quantity* (or usage or efficiency) *variance*. To assess the impacts of these two factors on a cost variance, we use the formula in Exhibit 20.8.

## Exhibit 20.8

Price Variance and Quantity Variance Formulas

These formulas identify the sources of the cost variance. Managers sometimes find it useful to apply an alternative (but equivalent) computation for the price and quantity variances as shown in Exhibit 20.9.

## Exhibit 20.9

Alternative Price Variance and Quantity Variance Formulas

**Price Variance (PV) = [Actual Price (AP) − Standard Price (SP)] × Actual Quantity (AQ)**

**Quantity Variance (QV) = [Actual Quantity (AQ) − Standard Quantity (SQ)] × Standard Price (SP)**

The results from applying the formulas in Exhibits 20.8 and 20.9 are identical.

## Materials and Labor Variances

**P2** Compute materials and labor variances.

We illustrate the computation of the materials and labor cost variances using data from **G-Max,** a company that makes specialty golf equipment and accessories for individual customers. This company has set the following standard quantities and prices for materials and labor per unit for one of its hand-crafted golf clubheads:

| | |
|---|---|
| Direct materials (1 lb. per unit at $1 per lb.) . . . . . . . | $1.00 |
| Direct labor (1 hr. per unit at $8 per hr.) . . . . . . . . . | 8.00 |
| Total standard direct cost per unit . . . . . . . . . . . . . . | $9.00 |

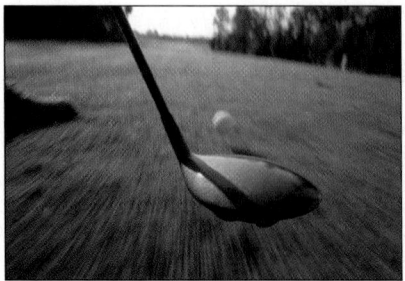

**Materials Cost Variances** During May 2005, G-Max budgeted to produce 4,000 clubheads (units). It actually produced only 3,500 units. It used 3,600 pounds of direct materials (titanium) costing $1.05 per pound, meaning its total materials cost was $3,780. This information allows us to compute both actual and standard direct materials costs for G-Max's 3,500 units and its direct materials cost variance:

| | | |
|---|---|---|
| Actual cost . . . . . . . . . . . . . . . . . . . . . . . . . . . . . | 3,600 lbs. @ $1.05 per lb. | = $3,780 |
| Standard cost . . . . . . . . . . . . . . . . . . . . . . . . . . . | 3,500 lbs. @ $1.00 per lb. | = 3,500 |
| Direct materials cost variance (unfavorable) . . . . . . . | | = $ 280 |

The materials price and quantity variances for these G-Max clubheads are computed and shown in Exhibit 20.10.

| Actual Cost | AQ × SP | Standard Cost |
|---|---|---|
| AQ × AP | 3,600 lbs. × $1.00 | SQ × SP |
| 3,600 lbs. × $1.05 | $3,600 | 3,500 lbs. × $1.00 |
| $3,780 | | $3,500 |

$180 U — Price Variance

$100 U — Quantity Variance

$280 U — Total Direct Materials Variance

**Exhibit 20.10**

Materials Price and Quantity Variances

The $180 unfavorable price variance results from paying 5 cents more than the standard price, computed as 3,600 lbs. × $0.05. The $100 unfavorable quantity variance is due to using 100 lbs. more materials than the standard quantity, computed as 100 lbs. × $1. The total direct materials variance is $280 and is unfavorable. This information allows management to ask the responsible individuals for explanations and corrective actions.

The purchasing department is usually responsible for the price paid for materials. Responsibility for explaining the price variance in this case rests with the purchasing manager if a price higher than standard caused the variance. The production department is usually responsible for the amount of material used and in this case is responsible for explaining why the process used more than the standard amount of materials.

Variance analysis presents challenges. For instance, the production department could have used more than the standard amount of material because its quality did not meet specifications and led to excessive waste. In this case, the purchasing manager is responsible for explaining why inferior materials were acquired. However, the production manager is responsible for explaining what happened if analysis shows that waste was due to inefficiencies, not poor quality material.

In evaluating price variances, managers must recognize that a favorable price variance can indicate a problem with poor product quality. **Redhook Ale**, a micro brewery in the Pacific Northwest, can probably save 10% to 15% in material prices by buying six-row barley malt instead of the better two-row from Washington's Yakima valley. Attention to quality, however, has helped Redhook Ale become the only craft brewer to be "kosher" certified. Redhook's purchasing activities are judged on both the quality of the materials and the purchase price variance. This stand on quality has helped Redhook report increases in both sales and gross margin.

**Labor Cost Variances**  Labor cost for a specific product or service depends on the number of hours worked (quantity) and the wage rate paid to employees (price). When actual amounts for a task differ from standard, the labor cost variance can be divided into a rate (price) variance and an efficiency (quantity) variance.

To illustrate, G-Max's direct labor standard for 3,500 units of its hand-crafted clubheads is one hour per unit, or 3,500 hours at $8 per hour. Since only 3,400 hours at $8.30 per hour were actually used to complete the units, the actual and standard labor costs are

**Example:** Identify at least two factors that might have caused the $100 unfavorable quantity variance and the $180 unfavorable price variance in Exhibit 20.10. *Answer:* Poor quality materials or untrained workers for the former; poor price negotiation or higher quality materials for the latter.

**Example:** Give an example of a manufacturing situation in which a favorable price variance for material might be the cause of an unfavorable quantity variance. *Answer:* Buying cheap materials.

| | | |
|---|---|---|
| Actual cost . . . . . . . . . . . . . . . . . . . . . . . . . . | 3,400 hrs. @ $8.30 per hr. | = $28,220 |
| Standard cost . . . . . . . . . . . . . . . . . . . . . . . | 3,500 hrs. @ $8.00 per hr. | = 28,000 |
| Direct labor cost variance (unfavorable) . . . . . . . | | = $ 220 |

This analysis shows that actual cost is merely $220 over the standard and suggests no immediate concern. Computing both the labor rate and efficiency variances reveals a different picture, however, as shown in Exhibit 20.11.

**Exhibit 20.11**

Labor Rate and
Efficiency Variances*

\* AH is actual direct labor hours; AR is actual wage rate; SH is standard direct labor hours allowed for actual output; SR is standard wage rate.

**Example:** Compute the rate variance and the efficiency variance for Exhibit 20.11 if 3,700 actual hours are used at an actual price of $7.50 per hour. *Answer:* $1,850 favorable labor rate variance and $1,600 unfavorable labor efficiency variance.

**Point:** To apply these concepts, work Exercise 20-5.

The analysis in Exhibit 20.11 shows that an $800 favorable efficiency variance results from using 100 fewer direct labor hours than standard for the units produced, but this favorable variance is more than offset by a wage rate that is $0.30 higher than standard. The personnel administrator or possibly the production manager needs to explain why the wage rate is higher than expected. The production manager should also explain how the labor hours were reduced. If this experience can be repeated and transferred to other departments, more savings are possible.

One possible explanation of these labor rate and efficiency variances is the use of workers with different skill levels. If this is the reason, senior management must discuss the implications with the production manager who has the responsibility to assign workers to tasks with the appropriate skill level. In this case, an investigation might show that higher skilled workers were used to produce 3,500 units of hand-crafted clubheads. As a result, fewer labor hours might be required for the work, but the wage rate paid these workers is higher than standard because of their greater skills. The effect of this strategy is a higher than standard total cost, which would require actions to remedy the situation or adjust the standard.

### Decision Maker

**Human Resource Manager**   You receive the manufacturing variance report for June and discover a large unfavorable labor efficiency (quantity) variance. What factors do you investigate to identify its possible causes?

Answer—p. 832

### Quick Check

**5.** A standard cost (*a*) changes in direct proportion to changes in the level of activity, (*b*) is an amount incurred at the actual level of production for the period, or (*c*) is an amount incurred under normal conditions to provide a product or service.

**6.** What is a cost variance?

**7.** The following information is available for York Company:

| | |
|---|---|
| Actual direct labor hours per unit .......... | 2.5 hours |
| Standard direct labor hours per unit ........ | 2.0 hours |
| Actual production (units) ................ | 2,500 units |
| Budgeted production (units) .............. | 3,000 units |
| Actual rate per hour .................... | $3.10 |
| Standard rate per hour .................. | $3.00 |

The labor efficiency variance is (*a*) $3,750 U, (*b*) $3,750 F, or (*c*) $3,875 U.

**8.** Refer to Quick Check 7; the labor rate variance is (*a*) $625 F or (*b*) $625 U.

**9.** If a material quantity variance is favorable and a material price variance is unfavorable, can the total material cost variance be favorable?

Answers—p. 832

# Overhead Standards and Variances

When standard costs are used, a predetermined overhead rate is used to assign standard overhead costs to products or services produced. This predetermined rate is often based on some overhead allocation base (such as standard labor cost, standard labor hours, or standard machine hours).

## Setting Overhead Standards

Standard overhead costs are the amounts expected to occur at a certain activity level. Unlike direct materials and direct labor, overhead includes fixed costs and variable costs. This results in the average overhead cost per unit changing as the predicted volume changes. Since standard costs are also budgeted costs, they must be established before the reporting period begins. Standard overhead costs are therefore average per unit costs based on the predicted activity level.

To establish the standard overhead cost rate, management uses the same cost structure it used to construct a flexible budget at the end of a period. This cost structure identifies the different overhead cost components and classifies them as variable or fixed. To get the standard overhead rate, management selects a level of activity (volume) and predicts total overhead cost. It then divides this total by the allocation base to get the standard rate. Standard direct labor hours expected to be used to produce the predicted volume is a common allocation base and is used in this section.

**Point:** Managers consider the types of overhead costs when choosing the basis for assigning overhead costs to products.

To illustrate, Exhibit 20.12 shows the overhead cost structure used to develop G-Max's flexible overhead budgets for May 2005. The predetermined standard overhead rate for May is set before the month begins. The first two number columns list the per unit amounts of variable costs and the monthly amounts of fixed costs. The four rightmost columns show the costs expected to occur at four different levels of activity. The predetermined overhead rate per labor hour is smaller as volume of activity increases because fixed costs remain constant.

G-Max managers predicted an 80% activity level for May, or a production volume of 4,000 clubheads. At this volume, they budget $8,000 as the May total overhead. This choice implies a $2 per unit (labor hour) average overhead cost ($8,000/4,000 units). Since G-Max has a standard of one direct labor hour per unit, the predetermined standard overhead rate for May is $2 per standard direct labor hour. The variable overhead rate remains constant at $1 per direct labor hour regardless of the budgeted production level. The fixed overhead rate changes according to the budgeted production volume. For instance, for the predicted level of 4,000 units of production, the fixed rate is $1 per hour ($4,000 fixed costs/4,000 units). For a production level of 5,000 units, however, the fixed rate is $0.80 per hour.

**Point:** Variable costs per unit remain constant, but fixed costs per unit decline with increases in volume. This means the average total overhead cost per unit declines with increases in volume.

When choosing the predicted activity level, management considers many factors. The level can be set as high as 100% of capacity, but this is rare. Factors causing the activity level to be less than full capacity include difficulties in scheduling work, equipment under repair or maintenance, and insufficient product demand. Good long-run management practices often call for some plant capacity in excess of current operating needs to allow for special opportunities and demand changes.

## Exhibit 20.12

Flexible Overhead Budgets

| | | | G-MAX Flexible Overhead Budgets For Month Ended May 31, 2005 | | | | |
| | | | Flexible Budget | | | | |
| | Variable Amount per Unit | Total Fixed Cost | Flexible Budget at 70% Capacity | Flexible Budget at 80% Capacity | Flexible Budget at 90% Capacity | Flexible Budget at 100% Capacity |
|---|---|---|---|---|---|---|
| Production (in units) .......................... | I unit | | 3,500 | 4,000 | 4,500 | 5,000 |
| Factory overhead | | | | | | |
| Variable costs | | | | | | |
| Indirect labor ......................... | $0.40/unit | | $1,400 | $1,600 | $1,800 | $2,000 |
| Indirect materials ...................... | 0.30/unit | | 1,050 | 1,200 | 1,350 | 1,500 |
| Power and lights ....................... | 0.20/unit | | 700 | 800 | 900 | 1,000 |
| Maintenance ......................... | 0.10/unit | | 350 | 400 | 450 | 500 |
| Total variable overhead costs .............. | $1.00/unit | | 3,500 | 4,000 | 4,500 | 5,000 |
| Fixed costs (per month) | | | | | | |
| Building rent .......................... | | $1,000 | 1,000 | 1,000 | 1,000 | 1,000 |
| Depreciation—Machinery ............... | | 1,200 | 1,200 | 1,200 | 1,200 | 1,200 |
| Supervisory salaries .................... | | 1,800 | 1,800 | 1,800 | 1,800 | 1,800 |
| Total fixed overhead costs ............... | | $4,000 | 4,000 | 4,000 | 4,000 | 4,000 |
| Total factory overhead ................... | | | $7,500 | $8,000 | $8,500 | $9,000 |
| Standard direct labor hours ................. | I hr./unit | | 3,500 hrs. | 4,000 hrs. | 4,500 hrs. | 5,000 hrs. |
| Predetermined overhead rate per standard direct labor hour ...................... | | | $ 2.14 | $ 2.00 | $ 1.89 | $ 1.80 |

**P3**  Compute overhead variances.

## Exhibit 20.13

Overhead Cost Variance

## Using Overhead Cost Variance Analysis

When standard costs are used, the cost accounting system applies overhead to the good units produced using the predetermined standard overhead rate. At period-end, the difference between the total overhead cost applied to products and the total overhead cost actually incurred is called an **overhead cost variance,** which is defined in Exhibit 20.13.

> **Overhead cost variance (OCV) = Actual overhead incurred (AOI) − Standard overhead applied (SOA)**

To help identify factors causing the overhead cost variance, managers analyze this variance separately for variable and fixed overhead. The results provide information useful for taking strategic actions to improve company performance. Similar to analysis of direct materials and direct labor variances, both the variable and fixed overhead variances can be separated into useful components as shown in Exhibit 20.14.

A **spending variance** occurs when management pays an amount different than the standard price to acquire an item. For instance, the actual wage rate paid to indirect labor might be higher than the standard rate. Similarly, actual supervisory salaries might be different than expected. Spending variances such as these cause management to investigate the reasons that the amount paid differs from the standard. Both variable and fixed overhead costs can yield their own spending variances. Analyzing variable overhead includes computing an **efficiency variance,** which occurs when standard direct labor hours (the allocation base) expected for actual production differ from the actual direct labor hours used.

Exhibit 20.14

Variable and Fixed
Overhead Variances

**Variable Overhead Variance***

| Actual Overhead | | Applied Overhead |
|---|---|---|
| AH × AVR | AH × SVR | SH × SVR |

Spending Variance          Efficiency Variance

Variable Overhead Variance

\* AH = actual direct labor hours; AVR = actual variable overhead rate; SH = standard direct labor hours; SVR = standard variable overhead rate.

**Fixed Overhead Variance**

| Actual Overhead | Budgeted Overhead | Applied Overhead |
|---|---|---|

Spending Variance          Volume Variance

Fixed Overhead Variance

This efficiency variance reflects on the cost-effectiveness in using the overhead allocation base (such as direct labor).

A **volume variance** occurs when a difference occurs between the actual volume of production and the standard volume of production. The budgeted fixed overhead amount is the same regardless of the volume of production (within the relevant range). This budgeted amount is computed based on standard direct labor hours that the budgeted production volume allows. The applied overhead is based, however, on the standard direct labor hours allowed for the actual volume of production. A difference between budgeted and actual production volumes results in a difference in the standard direct labor hours allowed for these two production levels. This situation yields a volume variance different from zero.

We can combine the variable overhead spending variance, the fixed overhead spending variance, and the variable overhead efficiency variance to get **controllable variance;** see Exhibit 20.15. The controllable variance is so named because it refers to activities usually under management control.

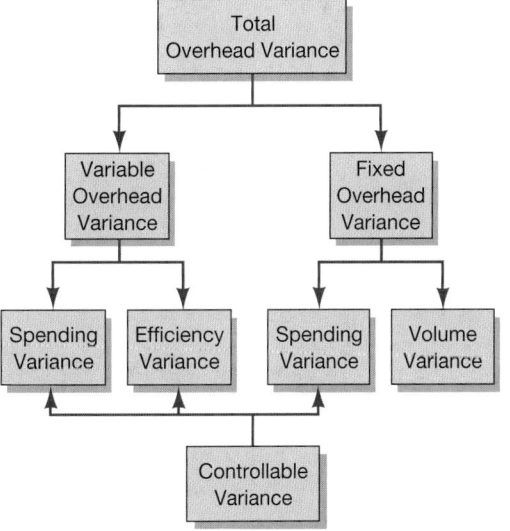

Exhibit 20.15

Framework for Understanding
Total Overhead Variance

## Computing Overhead Cost Variances

To illustrate how to compute overhead cost variances, return to the G-Max data. We know that it actually produced 3,500 units when 4,000 units were budgeted. Additional G-Max data show that actual overhead cost incurred is $7,650 (variable portion of $3,650; fixed portion of $4,000). Using this information, we can compute overhead variances for both variable and fixed overhead.

**Variable Overhead Cost Variances**   Recall that G-Max applies overhead based on direct labor hours as the allocation base. We know that it used 3,400 direct labor hours to produce 3,500 units. This compares favorably to the standard requirement of 3,500 direct labor hours at one labor hour per unit. We compute and separate G-Max's variable overhead cost variances as shown in Exhibit 20.16.

**Exhibit 20.16**

Computing Variable Overhead Cost Variances

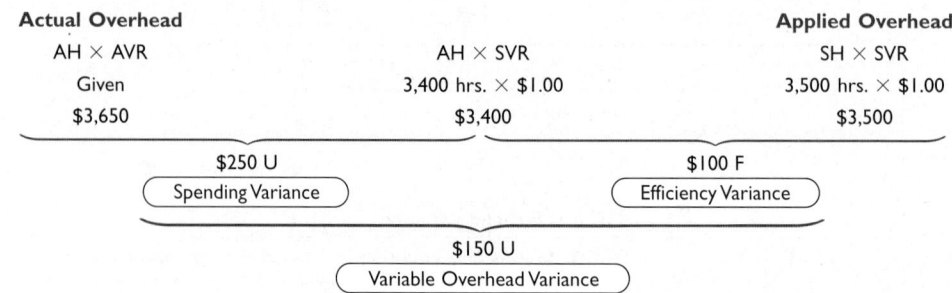

The $3,650 actual variable overhead from G-Max's cost records is used to compute the actual variable overhead rate of $1.07 per direct labor hour ($3,650/3,400 direct labor hours). This reveals that, on average, G-Max incurred $0.07 more per direct labor hour in variable overhead than the standard rate. The middle column of Exhibit 20.16 is computed by multiplying the 3,400 actual direct labor hours by the $1 standard rate per direct labor hour. The applied overhead is computed by multiplying the 3,500 standard hours allowed for actual production by the $1 standard rate per direct labor hour.

**Fixed Overhead Cost Variances**    G-Max reports that it incurred $4,000 in actual fixed overhead ; this amount equals the budgeted fixed overhead for May (see Exhibit 20.12). G-Max's budgeted fixed overhead application rate is $1 per hour ($4,000/4,000 direct labor hours), but the actual production level is only 3,500 units. Using this information, we can compute the fixed overhead cost variances shown in Exhibit 20.17. The applied fixed overhead is computed by multiplying 3,500 standard hours allowed for the actual production by the $1 fixed overhead allocation rate. Exhibit 20.17 reveals that the fixed overhead spending variance is zero and the volume variance is $500. The volume variance occurs because 500 fewer units are produced than budgeted; namely, 80% of the manufacturing capacity is budgeted but only 70% is used.

**Exhibit 20.17**

Computing Fixed Overhead Cost Variances

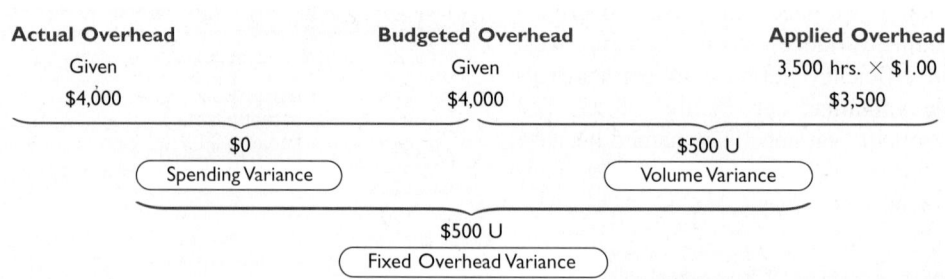

We show this volume variance graphically in Exhibit 20.18. The upward-sloping line reflects the amount of fixed overhead costs applied to the units produced in May using the predetermined fixed overhead rate. The uppermost horizontal line reflects the $4,000 of total fixed costs budgeted for May. These two lines cross at the planned operating volume of 4,000 units. When unit volume is 3,500 units, the overhead-costs-applied line falls $500 below the budgeted fixed overhead line. This shortfall is the volume variance.

An unfavorable volume variance implies that the company did not reach its predicted operating level. Management needs to know why the actual level of performance differs

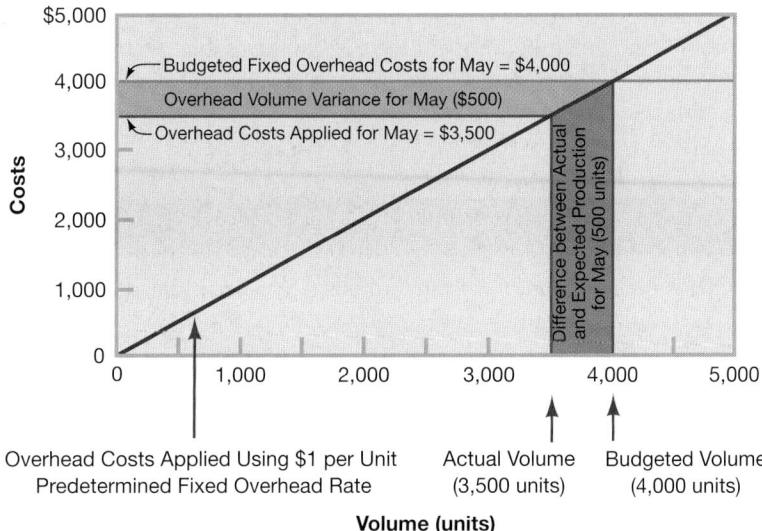

**Exhibit 20.18**

Fixed Overhead Volume Variance

from the expected level. The main purpose of the volume variance is to identify what portion of the total variance is caused by failing to meet the expected volume level. This information permits management to focus on the controllable variance.

A complete overhead variance report provides managers information about specific overhead costs and how they differ from budgeted amounts. Exhibit 20.19 shows G-Max's overhead variance report for May. It reveals that (1) fixed costs and maintenance cost were incurred as expected, (2) costs for indirect labor and power and lights were higher than expected, and (3) indirect materials cost was less than expected.

Using information from Exhibits 20.16 and 20.17, we can compute the total controllable overhead variance as $150 unfavorable ($250 U + $100 F + $0). This amount is also readily

**Exhibit 20.19**

Overhead Variance Report

| G-MAX<br>Overhead Variance Report<br>For Month Ended May 31, 2005 | | | |
|---|---|---|---|
| **Volume Variance** | | | |
| Expected production level . . . . . . . . . . | 80% of capacity | | |
| Production level achieved . . . . . . . . . . . | 70% of capacity | | |
| Volume variance . . . . . . . . . . . . . . . . . . | **$500 (unfavorable)** | | |
| | **Flexible<br>Budget** | **Actual<br>Results** | **Variances*** |
| **Controllable Variance** | | | |
| Variable overhead costs | | | |
| Indirect labor . . . . . . . . . . . . . . . . . . | $1,400 | $1,525 | $125 U |
| Indirect materials . . . . . . . . . . . . . . . | 1,050 | 1,025 | 25 F |
| Power and lights . . . . . . . . . . . . . . . . | 700 | 750 | 50 U |
| Maintenance . . . . . . . . . . . . . . . . . . . | 350 | 350 | 0 |
| Total variable overhead costs . . . . . . . | 3,500 | 3,650 | 150 U† |
| Fixed overhead costs | | | |
| Building rent . . . . . . . . . . . . . . . . . . | 1,000 | 1,000 | 0 |
| Depreciation—Machinery . . . . . . . . . . | 1,200 | 1,200 | 0 |
| Supervisory salaries . . . . . . . . . . . . . | 1,800 | 1,800 | 0 |
| Total fixed overhead costs . . . . . . . . . | 4,000 | 4,000 | 0‡ |
| Total overhead costs . . . . . . . . . . . . . . | $7,500 | $7,650 | $150 U |

* F = Favorable variance; and U = Unfavorable variance.

† Total variable overhead (spending and efficiency) variance.

‡ Fixed overhead spending variance.

available from Exhibit 20.19. The overhead variance report shows the total volume variance as $500 unfavorable (shown at the top) and the $150 unfavorable controllable variance. The sum of the controllable variance and the volume variance equals the total (fixed and variable) overhead variance of $650 unfavorable.

# Extensions of Standard Costs

This section extends the application of standard costs for control purposes, for service companies, and for accounting systems.

## Standard Costs for Control

**C3**  Explain how standard cost information is useful for management by exception.

To control business activities, top management must be able to affect the actions of lower-level managers responsible for the company's revenues and costs. After preparing a budget and establishing standard costs, management should take actions to gain control when actual costs differ from standard or budgeted amounts.

Reports such as the ones illustrated in this chapter call management's attention to variances from business plans and other standards. When managers use these reports to focus on problem areas, the budgeting process contributes to the control function. In using budgeted performance reports, practice of management by exception is often useful. **Management by exception** means that managers focus attention on the most significant variances and give less attention to areas where performance is reasonably close to the standard. This practice leads management to concentrate on the exceptional or irregular situations. Management by exception is especially useful when directed at controllable items.

## Standard Costs for Services

Many managers use standard costs and variance analysis to investigate manufacturing costs. Many managers also recognize that standard costs and variances can help them control *non* manufacturing costs. Companies providing services instead of products can benefit from the use of standard costs. Application of standard costs and variances can be readily adapted to nonmanufacturing situations. To illustrate, many service providers use standard costs to help control expenses. First, they use standard costs as a basis for budgeting all services. Second, they use periodic performance reports to compare actual results to standards. Third, they use these reports to identify significant variances within specific areas of responsibility. Fourth, they implement the appropriate control procedures.

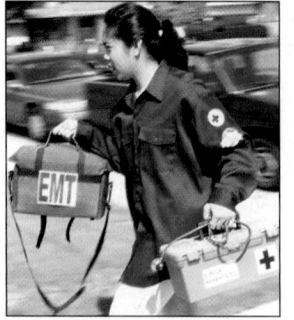

## Standard Cost Accounting System

**P4**  Prepare journal entries for standard costs and account for price and quantity variances.

We have shown how companies use standard costs in management reports. Most standard cost systems also record these costs and variances in accounts. This practice simplifies recordkeeping and helps in preparing reports. Although we do not need knowledge of standard cost accounting practices to understand standard costs and their use, we must know how to interpret the accounts in which standard costs and variances are recorded. The entries in this section briefly illustrate the important aspects of this process for G-Max's standard costs and variances for May.

The first of these entries records standard materials cost incurred in May in the Goods in Process Inventory account. This part of the entry is similar to the usual accounting entry, but the amount of the debit equals the standard cost ($3,500) instead of the actual cost ($3,780). This entry credits Raw Materials Inventory for actual cost. The difference between standard and actual costs is recorded with debits to two separate materials variance accounts (recall Exhibit 20.10). Both the materials price and quantity variances are recorded as debits because they reflect additional costs higher than the standard cost (if actual costs were less than the standard, they are recorded as credits). This treatment (debit) reflects their unfavorable effect because they represent higher costs and lower income.

| May 31 | Goods in Process Inventory . . . . . . . . . . . . . . . . | 3,500 | | Assets | = Liabilities + | Equity |
|---|---|---|---|---|---|---|
| | **Direct Materials Price Variance\*** . . . . . . . . . . | 180 | | +3,500 | | −100 |
| | **Direct Materials Quantity Variance** . . . . . . . | 100 | | −3,780 | | −180 |
| | Raw Materials Inventory . . . . . . . . . . . . . . . | | 3,780 | | | |
| | *To charge production for standard quantity of* | | | | | |
| | *materials used (3,500 lbs.) at the standard* | | | | | |
| | *price ($1 per lb.), and to record material price* | | | | | |
| | *and material quantity variances.* | | | | | |

\* Many companies record the materials price variance when materials are purchased. For simplicity, we record both the materials price and quantity variances when materials are issued to production.

The second entry debits Goods in Process Inventory for the standard labor cost of the goods manufactured during May ($28,000). Actual labor cost ($28,220) is recorded with a credit to the Factory Payroll account. The difference between standard and actual labor costs is explained by two variances (see Exhibit 20.11). The direct labor rate variance is unfavorable and is debited to that account. The direct labor efficiency variance is favorable and is credited. The direct labor efficiency variance is favorable because it represents a lower cost and a higher net income.

| May 31 | Goods in Process Inventory . . . . . . . . . . . . . . . . | 28,000 | | Assets | = Liabilities + | Equity |
|---|---|---|---|---|---|---|
| | **Direct Labor Rate Variance** . . . . . . . . . . . . . | 1,020 | | +28,000 | | +28,220 |
| | **Direct Labor Efficiency Variance** . . . . . . | | 800 | | | − 1,020 |
| | Factory Payroll . . . . . . . . . . . . . . . . . . . . . | | 28,220 | | | + 800 |
| | *To charge production with 3,500 standard* | | | | | |
| | *hours of direct labor at the standard $8 per* | | | | | |
| | *hour rate, and to record the labor rate and* | | | | | |
| | *efficiency variances.* | | | | | |

The entry to assign standard predetermined overhead to the cost of goods manufactured must debit the $7,000 predetermined amount to the Goods in Process Inventory account. The $7,650 actual overhead costs are debited to the Factory Overhead account. Thus, when Factory Overhead is applied to Goods in Process Inventory, the amount applied is debited to the Goods in Process Inventory account and credited to the Factory Overhead account. To account for the difference between actual and standard costs, the entry includes a $250 debit to the Variable Overhead Spending Variance, a $100 credit to the Variable Overhead Efficiency Variance, and a $500 debit to the Volume Variance (recall Exhibits 20.16 and 20.17). An alternative (simpler) approach, shown here, is to record the difference with a $150 debit to the Controllable Variance account and a $500 debit to the Volume Variance account (recall from Exhibit 20.15 that controllable variance is the sum of both variable overhead variances and the fixed overhead spending variance).

Assets = Liabilities + Equity
+7,000                  +7,650
                          − 150
                          − 500

| May 31 | Goods in Process Inventory. . . . . . . . . . . . . . . . | 7,000 | |
|---|---|---|---|
| | **Controllable Variance** . . . . . . . . . . . . . . . . . . . | **150** | |
| | **Volume Variance** . . . . . . . . . . . . . . . . . . . . . . . | **500** | |
| | Factory Overhead . . . . . . . . . . . . . . . . . . . . | | 7,650 |

*To apply overhead at the standard rate of
$2 per standard direct labor hour (3,500 hours),
and to record overhead variances.*

**Point:** To apply these concepts, work Exercises 20-8 and 20-9.

The balances of these six different variance accounts accumulate until the end of the accounting period. As a result, the unfavorable variances of some months offset the favorable variances of others.

These variance account balances, which reflect results of the period's various transactions and events, are closed at period-end. If the variances are *material,* they are added to or subtracted from the balances of the Goods in Process Inventory, the Finished Goods Inventory, and the Cost of Goods Sold accounts. If the amounts are *immaterial,* they are added to or subtracted from the balance of the Cost of Goods Sold account. This process is similar to that shown in Chapter 15 for eliminating an underapplied or overapplied balance in the Factory Overhead account. (*Note:* These variance balances, which represent differences between actual and standard costs, must be added to or subtracted from the materials, labor, and overhead costs recorded. In this way, the recorded costs equal the actual costs incurred in the period; a company must use actual costs in external financial statements prepared in accordance with generally accepted accounting principles.)

## Quick Check

10. Under what conditions is an overhead volume variance considered favorable?

11. To use management by exception with standard costs, a company (*a*) must record standard costs in its accounting, (*b*) should compute variances from flexible budget amounts to allow management to focus its attention on significant differences between actual and budgeted results, or (*c*) should analyze only variances for direct materials and direct labor.

12. A company uses a standard cost accounting system. Prepare the journal entry to record these direct materials variances:

| | |
|---|---|
| Direct materials cost actually incurred . . . . . . . . . . . . . | $73,200 |
| Direct materials quantity variance (favorable) . . . . . . . . | 3,800 |
| Direct materials price variance (unfavorable) . . . . . . . . | 1,300 |

13. If standard costs are recorded in the manufacturing accounts, how are recorded variances treated at the end of an accounting period?

Answers—p. 832

---

## Decision Analysis                                                    Sales Variances

**A2** Analyze changes in sales from expected amounts.

This chapter explained the computation and analysis of cost variances. A similar variance analysis can be applied to sales. To illustrate, consider the following sales data from G-Max for two of its golf products, fluorescent Excel balls and Big Bert® drivers.

| | Budgeted | Actual |
|---|---|---|
| Sales of Excel golf balls (units) . . . . . . . . . | 1,000 | 1,100 |
| Sales price per Excel golf ball . . . . . . . . . . | $ 10 | $ 10.50 |
| Sales of Big Bert® drivers (units) . . . . . . . . | 150 | 140 |
| Sales price per Big Bert® driver . . . . . . . . | $ 200 | $ 190 |

Using this information, we compute both the *sales price variance* and the *sales volume variance* as shown in Exhibit 20.20. The total sales price variance is $850 unfavorable, and the total sales volume variance is $1,000 unfavorable. Neither variance implies anything positive about these two products. Further analysis of these total sales variances reveals that both the sales price and sales volume variances for Excel golf balls are favorable, meaning that both the unfavorable total sales price variance and the unfavorable total sales volume variance are due to the Big Bert driver.

**Exhibit 20.20**

Computing Sales Variances

| Excel Golf Balls | Actual Results | Flexible Budget | Fixed Budget |
|---|---|---|---|
| Sales units (balls) | 1,100 | 1,100 | 1,000 |
| Sales dollars (balls) | $11,550 | $11,000 | $10,000 |

$550 F — Sales Price Variance        $1,000 F — Sales Volume Variance

| Big Bert® Drivers | | | |
|---|---|---|---|
| Sales units (drivers) | 140 | 140 | 150 |
| Sales dollars (drivers) | $26,600 | $28,000 | $30,000 |

$1,400 U — Sales Price Variance        $2,000 U — Sales Volume Variance

| Total | $850 U | | $1,000 U |
|---|---|---|---|

Managers use sales variances for planning and control purposes. The sales variance information is used to plan future actions to avoid unfavorable variances. G-Max sold 90 total combined units (both balls and drivers) more than planned, but these 90 units were not sold in the proportion budgeted. G-Max sold fewer than the budgeted quantity of the higher priced driver, which contributed to the unfavorable total sales variances. Managers use such detail to question what caused the company to sell more golf balls and fewer drivers. Managers also use this information to evaluate and even reward their salespeople. Extra compensation is paid to salespeople who contribute to a higher profit margin. Finally, with multiple products, the sales volume variance can be separated into a *sales mix variance* and a *sales quantity variance*. The sales mix variance is the difference between the actual and budgeted sales mix of the products. The sales quantity variance is the difference between the total actual and total budgeted quantity of units sold.

**Decision Maker**

**Sales Manager**   The current performance report reveals a large favorable sales volume variance but an unfavorable sales price variance. You did not expect to see a large increase in sales volume. What steps do you take to analyze this situation?

Answer—p. 832

# Demonstration Problem

Pacific Company provides the following information about its budgeted and actual results for June 2005. Although the expected June volume was 25,000 units produced and sold, the company actually produced and sold 27,000 units as detailed here:

| | Budget (25,000 units) | Actual (27,000 units) |
|---|---|---|
| Selling price | $5.00 per unit | $5.23 per unit |
| Variable costs (per unit) | | |
| Direct materials | 1.24 per unit | 1.12 per unit |
| Direct labor | 1.50 per unit | 1.40 per unit |
| Factory supplies* | 0.25 per unit | 0.37 per unit |
| Utilities* | 0.50 per unit | 0.60 per unit |
| Selling costs | 0.40 per unit | 0.34 per unit |

[continued on next page]

[continued from previous page]

Fixed costs (per month)

| | | |
|---|---|---|
| Depreciation—Machinery* . . . . . . . . . . . . . . | $3,750 | $3,710 |
| Depreciation—Building* . . . . . . . . . . . . . . . | 2,500 | 2,500 |
| General liability insurance . . . . . . . . . . . . . . | 1,200 | 1,250 |
| Property taxes on office equipment . . . . . . . | 500 | 485 |
| Other administrative expense . . . . . . . . . . . | 750 | 900 |

\* Indicates factory overhead item; $0.75 per unit or $3 per direct labor hour for variable overhead, and
$0.25 per unit or $1 per direct labor hour for fixed overhead.

## Standard costs based on expected output of 25,000 units

| | Per Unit of Output | Quantity to Be Used | Total Cost |
|---|---|---|---|
| Direct materials, 4 oz. @ $0.31/oz. . . . . . . . . | $1.24/unit | 100,000 oz. | $31,000 |
| Direct labor, 0.25 hrs. @ $6.00/hr. . . . . . . . . | 1.50/unit | 6,250 hrs. | 37,500 |
| Overhead . . . . . . . . . . . . . . . . . . . . . . . . | 1.00/unit | | 25,000 |

## Actual costs incurred to produce 27,000 units

| | Per Unit of Output | Quantity Used | Total Cost |
|---|---|---|---|
| Direct materials, 4 oz. @ $0.28/oz. . . . . . . . . | $1.12/unit | 108,000 oz. | $30,240 |
| Direct labor, 0.20 hrs. @ $7.00/hr. . . . . . . . . | 1.40/unit | 5,400 hrs. | 37,800 |
| Overhead . . . . . . . . . . . . . . . . . . . . . . . . | 1.20/unit | | 32,400 |

## Standard costs based on expected output of 27,000 units

| | Per Unit of Output | Quantity to Be Used | Total Cost |
|---|---|---|---|
| Direct materials, 4 oz. @ $0.31/oz. . . . . . . . . | $1.24/unit | 108,000 oz. | $33,480 |
| Direct labor, 0.25 hrs. @ $6.00/hr. . . . . . . . . | 1.50/unit | 6,750 hrs. | 40,500 |
| Overhead . . . . . . . . . . . . . . . . . . . . . . . . | | | 26,500 |

## Required

**1.** Prepare June flexible budgets showing expected sales, costs, and net income assuming 20,000, 25,000, and 30,000 units of output produced and sold.

**2.** Prepare a flexible budget performance report that compares actual results with the amounts budgeted if the actual volume had been expected.

**3.** Apply variance analysis for direct materials, for direct labor, and for overhead.

## Planning the Solution

- Prepare a table showing the expected results at the three specified levels of output. Compute the variable costs by multiplying the per unit variable costs by the expected volumes. Include fixed costs at the given amounts. Combine the amounts in the table to show total variable costs, contribution margin, total fixed costs, and income from operations.

- Prepare a table showing the actual results and the amounts that should be incurred at 27,000 units. Show any differences in the third column and label them with an *F* for favorable if they increase income or a *U* for unfavorable if they decrease income.

- Using the chapter's format, compute these total variances and the individual variances requested:
  - Total materials variance (including the direct materials quantity variance and the direct materials price variance).

- Total direct labor variance (including the direct labor efficiency variance and rate variance).
- Total overhead variance (including both variable and fixed overhead variances and their component variances).

## Solution to Demonstration Problem

**1.**

### PACIFIC COMPANY
### Flexible Budgets
### For Month Ended June 30, 2005

| | Flexible Budget | | Flexible Budget for Unit Sales of 20,000 | Flexible Budget for Unit Sales of 25,000 | Flexible Budget for Unit Sales of 30,000 |
|---|---|---|---|---|---|
| | Variable Amount per Unit | Total Fixed Cost | | | |
| Sales ......................... | $5.00 | | $100,000 | $125,000 | $150,000 |
| **Variable costs** | | | | | |
| Direct materials ................. | 1.24 | | 24,800 | 31,000 | 37,200 |
| Direct labor ..................... | 1.50 | | 30,000 | 37,500 | 45,000 |
| Factory supplies ................. | 0.25 | | 5,000 | 6,250 | 7,500 |
| Utilities .......................... | 0.50 | | 10,000 | 12,500 | 15,000 |
| Selling costs .................... | 0.40 | | 8,000 | 10,000 | 12,000 |
| Total variable costs ............. | 3.89 | | 77,800 | 97,250 | 116,700 |
| Contribution margin ............... | $1.11 | | 22,200 | 27,750 | 33,300 |
| **Fixed costs** | | | | | |
| Depreciation—Machinery ........... | | $3,750 | 3,750 | 3,750 | 3,750 |
| Depreciation—Building ............ | | 2,500 | 2,500 | 2,500 | 2,500 |
| General liability insurance .......... | | 1,200 | 1,200 | 1,200 | 1,200 |
| Property taxes on office equipment .... | | 500 | 500 | 500 | 500 |
| Other administrative expense ......... | | 750 | 750 | 750 | 750 |
| Total fixed costs ................. | | $8,700 | 8,700 | 8,700 | 8,700 |
| Income from operations ............. | | | $ 13,500 | $ 19,050 | $ 24,600 |

**2.**

### PACIFIC COMPANY
### Flexible Budget Performance Report
### For Month Ended June 30, 2005

| | Flexible Budget | Actual Results | Variance* |
|---|---|---|---|
| Sales (27,000 units) ................... | $135,000 | $141,210 | $6,210 F |
| **Variable costs** | | | |
| Direct materials ..................... | 33,480 | 30,240 | 3,240 F |
| Direct labor ......................... | 40,500 | 37,800 | 2,700 F |
| Factory supplies ..................... | 6,750 | 9,990 | 3,240 U |
| Utilities ............................ | 13,500 | 16,200 | 2,700 U |
| Selling costs ....................... | 10,800 | 9,180 | 1,620 F |
| Total variable costs .................. | 105,030 | 103,410 | 1,620 F |
| Contribution margin ................... | 29,970 | 37,800 | 7,830 F |
| **Fixed costs** | | | |
| Depreciation—Machinery .............. | 3,750 | 3,710 | 40 F |
| Depreciation—Building ................ | 2,500 | 2,500 | 0 |
| General liability insurance ............. | 1,200 | 1,250 | 50 U |
| Property taxes on office equipment ........ | 500 | 485 | 15 F |
| Other administrative expense ........... | 750 | 900 | 150 U |
| Total fixed costs .................... | 8,700 | 8,845 | 145 U |
| Income from operations ................ | $ 21,270 | $ 28,955 | $7,685 F |

* F = Favorable variance; and U = Unfavorable variance.

**3.** Variance analysis of materials, labor, and overhead costs.

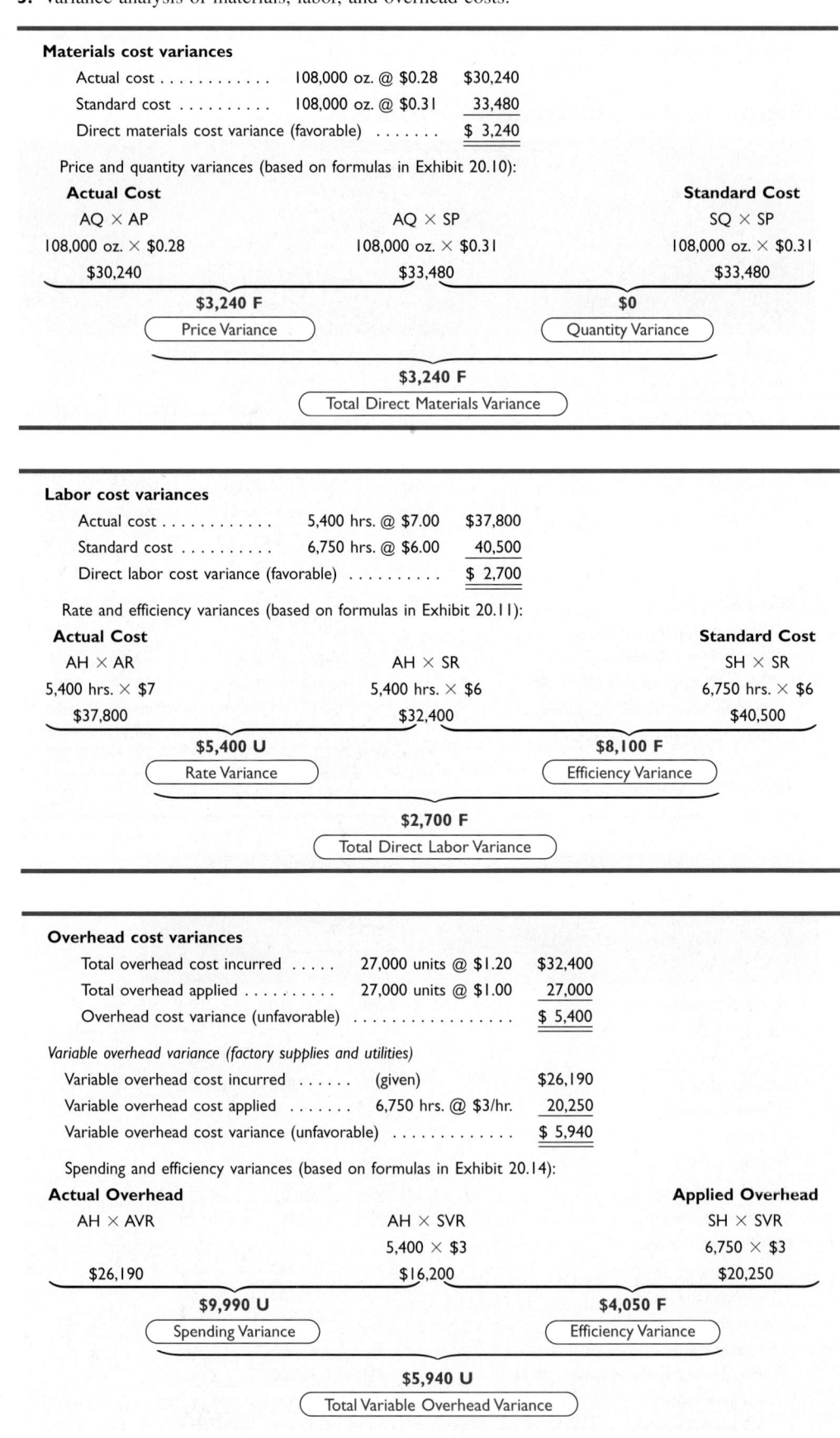

**Materials cost variances**

| | | |
|---|---|---|
| Actual cost . . . . . . . . . . . | 108,000 oz. @ $0.28 | $30,240 |
| Standard cost . . . . . . . . . | 108,000 oz. @ $0.31 | 33,480 |
| Direct materials cost variance (favorable) . . . . . . . | | $ 3,240 |

Price and quantity variances (based on formulas in Exhibit 20.10):

| **Actual Cost** | | **Standard Cost** |
|---|---|---|
| AQ × AP | AQ × SP | SQ × SP |
| 108,000 oz. × $0.28 | 108,000 oz. × $0.31 | 108,000 oz. × $0.31 |
| $30,240 | $33,480 | $33,480 |

$3,240 F    Price Variance

$0    Quantity Variance

$3,240 F    Total Direct Materials Variance

**Labor cost variances**

| | | |
|---|---|---|
| Actual cost . . . . . . . . . . . | 5,400 hrs. @ $7.00 | $37,800 |
| Standard cost . . . . . . . . . | 6,750 hrs. @ $6.00 | 40,500 |
| Direct labor cost variance (favorable) . . . . . . . . . | | $ 2,700 |

Rate and efficiency variances (based on formulas in Exhibit 20.11):

| **Actual Cost** | | **Standard Cost** |
|---|---|---|
| AH × AR | AH × SR | SH × SR |
| 5,400 hrs. × $7 | 5,400 hrs. × $6 | 6,750 hrs. × $6 |
| $37,800 | $32,400 | $40,500 |

$5,400 U    Rate Variance

$8,100 F    Efficiency Variance

$2,700 F    Total Direct Labor Variance

**Overhead cost variances**

| | | |
|---|---|---|
| Total overhead cost incurred . . . . . | 27,000 units @ $1.20 | $32,400 |
| Total overhead applied . . . . . . . . . | 27,000 units @ $1.00 | 27,000 |
| Overhead cost variance (unfavorable) . . . . . . . . . . . . . . . . | | $ 5,400 |

*Variable overhead variance (factory supplies and utilities)*

| | | |
|---|---|---|
| Variable overhead cost incurred . . . . . . | (given) | $26,190 |
| Variable overhead cost applied . . . . . . . | 6,750 hrs. @ $3/hr. | 20,250 |
| Variable overhead cost variance (unfavorable) . . . . . . . . . . . . | | $ 5,940 |

Spending and efficiency variances (based on formulas in Exhibit 20.14):

| **Actual Overhead** | | **Applied Overhead** |
|---|---|---|
| AH × AVR | AH × SVR | SH × SVR |
| | 5,400 × $3 | 6,750 × $3 |
| $26,190 | $16,200 | $20,250 |

$9,990 U    Spending Variance

$4,050 F    Efficiency Variance

$5,940 U    Total Variable Overhead Variance

[continued on next page]

[continued from previous page]

*Fixed overhead (depreciation on machinery and building)*

| | | |
|---|---|---|
| Fixed overhead cost incurred ........ | (given) | $ 6,210 |
| Fixed overhead cost applied ........ | 6,750 hrs. @ $1/hr. | 6,750 |
| Fixed overhead cost variance (favorable) ................ | | $   540 |

Spending and volume variances (based on formulas in Exhibit 20.14):

| **Actual Overhead** | **Budgeted Overhead** | **Applied Overhead** |
|---|---|---|
| | | 6,750 × $1 |
| $6,210 | $6,250 | $6,750 |

$40 F
Spending Variance

$500 F
Volume Variance

$540 F
Total Fixed Overhead Variance

We can also compute

**Controllable variance:**  $5,900 U (both spending variances plus efficiency variance)

**Volume variance:**          500 F (identified as above)

# Summary

**C1  Define standard costs and explain their computation and uses.** Standard costs are the normal costs that should be incurred to produce a product or perform a service. They should be based on a careful examination of the processes used to produce a product or perform a service as well as the quantities and prices that should be incurred in carrying out those processes. On a performance report, standard costs (which are flexible budget amounts) are compared to actual costs, and the differences are presented as variances.

**C2  Describe variances and what they reveal about performance.** Management can use variances to monitor and control activities. Total cost variances can be broken into price and quantity variances to direct management's attention to those responsible for quantities used and prices paid.

**C3  Explain how standard cost information is useful for management by exception.** Standard cost accounting provides management information about costs that differ from budgeted (expected) amounts. Performance reports disclose the costs or areas of operations that have significant variances from budgeted amounts. This allows managers to focus attention on the exceptions and less attention on areas proceeding normally.

**A1  Compare fixed and flexible budgets.** A fixed budget shows the revenues and costs expected to occur at a specified volume level. If actual volume is at some other level, the amounts in the fixed budget do not provide a reasonable basis for evaluating actual performance. A flexible budget expresses variable costs in per unit terms so that it can be used to develop budgeted amounts for any volume level within the relevant range. Thus, managers compute budgeted amounts for evaluation after a period for the volume that actually occurred.

**A2  Analyze changes in sales from expected amounts.** Actual sales can differ from budgeted sales, and managers can in-

vestigate this difference by computing both the sales price and sales volume variances. The *sales price variance* refers to that portion of total variance resulting from a difference between actual and budgeted selling prices. The *sales volume variance* refers to that portion of total variance resulting from a difference between actual and budgeted sales quantities.

**P1  Prepare a flexible budget and interpret a flexible budget performance report.** To prepare a flexible budget, we express each variable cost as a constant amount per unit of sales (or as a percent of sales dollar). In contrast, the budgeted amount of each fixed cost is expressed as a total amount expected to occur at any sales volume within the relevant range. The flexible budget is then determined using these computations and amounts for fixed and variable costs at the expected sales volume.

**P2  Compute materials and labor variances.** Materials and labor variances are due to differences between the actual costs incurred and the budgeted costs. The price (or rate) variance is computed by comparing the actual cost with the flexible budget amount that should have been incurred to acquire the actual quantity of resources. The quantity (or efficiency) variance is computed by comparing the flexible budget amount that should have been incurred to acquire the actual quantity of resources with the flexible budget amount that should have been incurred to acquire the standard quantity of resources.

**P3  Compute overhead variances.** Overhead variances are due to differences between the actual overhead costs incurred and the overhead applied to production. An overhead spending variance arises when the actual amount incurred differs from the budgeted amount of overhead. An overhead efficiency (or volume) variance arises when the flexible overhead budget amount differs from the overhead applied to production. It is important to realize that overhead is assigned using an overhead allocation base, meaning that an efficiency variance (in the case of variable overhead) is a result of the overhead application base being used more or less efficiently than planned.

P4  **Prepare journal entries for standard costs and account for price and quantity variances.** When a company records standard costs in its accounts, the standard costs of materials, labor, and overhead are debited to the Goods in Process Inventory account. Based on an analysis of the material, labor, and overhead costs, each quantity variance, price variance, volume variance, and controllable variance is recorded in a separate account. At period-end, if the variances are material, they are allocated among the balances of the Goods in Process Inventory, Finished Goods Inventory, and Cost of Goods Sold accounts. If they are not material, they are simply debited or credited to the Cost of Goods Sold account.

## Guidance Answers to **Decision Maker** and **Decision Ethics**

**Entrepreneur**  From the complaints, this performance report appears to compare actual results with a fixed budget. This comparison is useful in determining whether the amount of work actually performed was more or less than planned, but it is not useful in determining whether the divisions were more or less efficient than planned. If the two consulting divisions worked on more assignments than expected, some costs will certainly increase. Therefore, you should prepare a flexible budget using the actual number of consulting assignments and then compare actual performance to the flexible budget.

**Human Resource Manager**  As HR manager, you should investigate the causes for any labor-related variances although you may not be responsible for them. An unfavorable labor efficiency variance occurs because more labor hours than standard were used during the period. There are at least three possible reasons for this: (1) materials quality could be poor, resulting in more labor consumption due to rework, (2) unplanned interruptions (strike, breakdowns, accidents) could have occurred during the period, and (3) the production manager could have used a different labor mix to expedite orders. This new labor mix could have consisted of a larger proportion of untrained labor, which resulted in more labor hours.

**Internal Auditor**  Although the manager's actions might not be unethical, this action is undesirable. The internal auditor should report this behavior, possibly recommending that for the purchase of such discretionary items, the manager must provide budgetary requests using an activity-based budgeting process. The internal auditor would then be given full authority to verify this budget request.

**Sales Manager**  The unfavorable sales price variance suggests that actual prices were lower than budgeted prices. As the sales manager, you want to know the reasons for a lower than expected price. Perhaps your salespeople lowered the price of certain products by offering quantity discounts. You then might want to know what prompted them to offer the quantity discounts (perhaps competitors were offering discounts). You want to break the sales volume variance into both the sales mix and sales quantity variances. You could find that although the sales quantity variance is favorable, the sales mix variance is not. Then you need to investigate why actual sales mix differs from budgeted sales mix.

## Guidance Answers to **Quick Checks**

**1.** *b*

**2.** The first step is classifying each cost as variable or fixed.

**3.** A fixed budget is prepared using an expected volume of sales or production. A flexible budget is prepared using the actual volume of activity.

**4.** Contribution margin equals sales less variable costs.

**5.** *c*

**6.** It is the difference between actual cost and standard cost.

**7.** *a*; Total actual hours: 2,500 × 2.5 = 6,250

Total standard hours: 2,500 × 2.0 = 5,000

Efficiency variance = (6,250 − 5,000) × $3.00
= $3,750 U

**8.** *b*; Rate variance = ($3.10 − $3.00) × 6,250 = $625 U

**9.** Yes, this will occur when the materials quantity variance is more than the materials price variance.

**10.** The overhead volume variance is favorable when the actual operating level is higher than the expected level.

**11.** *b*

**12.**

| | | |
|---|---|---|
| Goods in Process Inventory . . . . . . . . . . | 75,700 | |
| Direct Materials Price Variance . . . . . . . . . | 1,300 | |
| Direct Materials Quantity Variance . . . . . | | 3,800 |
| Raw Materials Inventory . . . . . . . . . . . | | 73,200 |

**13.** If the variances are material, they should be prorated among the Goods in Process Inventory, Finished Goods Inventory, and Cost of Goods Sold accounts. If they are not material, they can be closed to Cost of Goods Sold.

## Key Terms

Key Terms are available at the book's Website for learning and testing in an online Flashcard Format.

Budgetary control (p. 808)
Budget report (p. 808)
Controllable variance (p. 821)
Cost variance (p. 815)
Efficiency variance (p. 820)
Favorable variance (p. 810)
Fixed budget (p. 809)

Fixed budget performance report (p. 809)
Flexible budget (p. 810)
Flexible budget performance report (p. 812)
Management by exception (p. 824)
Overhead cost variance (p. 820)
Price variance (p. 812)

Quantity variance (p. 812)
Spending variance (p. 820)
Standard costs (p. 813)
Unfavorable variance (p. 810)
Variance analysis (p. 812)
Volume variance (p. 821)

## Personal Interactive Quiz

Personal Interactive Quizzes A and B are available at the book's Website to reinforce and assess your learning.

## Discussion Questions

**1.** What limits the usefulness to managers of fixed budget performance reports?

**2.** Identify the main purpose of a flexible budget for managers.

**3.** Prepare a flexible budget performance report title (in proper form) for Spalding Company for the calendar year 2005. Why is a proper title important for this or any report?

**4.** What type of analysis does a flexible budget performance report help management perform?

**5.** In what sense can a variable cost be considered constant?

**6.** What department is usually responsible for a direct labor rate variance? What department is usually responsible for a direct labor efficiency variance? Explain.

**7.** What is a price variance? What is a quantity variance?

**8.** What is the purpose of using standard costs?

**9.** In an analysis of fixed overhead cost variances, what is the volume variance?

**10.** What is the predetermined standard overhead rate? How is it computed?

**11.** In general, variance analysis is said to provide information about _____ and _____ variances.

**12.** In an analysis of overhead cost variances, what is the controllable variance and what causes it?

**13.** What is the relation among standard costs, flexible budgets, variance analysis, and management by exception?

**14. Krispy Kreme** has a standard cost for a special type of donut. List several factors that might cause the actual cost incurred to vary from the standard cost.

**15.** Assume that **Tastykake**'s overhead costs consist only of variable costs and its actual sales volume is 10% higher than its budgeted sales volume. What type of volume variance would it experience?

**16.** Assume that **Harley-Davidson** is budgeted to **Harley-Davidson** operate at 80% of capacity but actually operates at 75% of capacity. What effect will the 5% deviation have on the controllable variance? The volume variance?

*Red numbers denote Discussion Questions that involve decision-making.*

---

*Homework Manager repeats all numerical Quick Studies on the book's Website with new numbers.*

Santana Company reports the following selected financial results for May. For the level of production achieved in May, the budgeted amounts would be: sales, $650,000; variable costs, $375,000; and fixed costs, $150,000. Prepare a flexible budget performance report for May.

| | |
|---|---|
| Sales (150,000 units) ....... | $637,500 |
| Variable costs ............ | 356,250 |
| Fixed costs ............. | 150,000 |

## QUICK STUDY

**QS 20-1**
Flexible budget
performance report

P1

**QS 20-2**
Labor cost variances
C2  P2

Reflection Company's output for the current period results in a $40,000 unfavorable direct labor rate variance and a $20,000 unfavorable direct labor efficiency variance. Production for the current period was assigned an $800,000 standard direct labor cost. What is the actual total direct labor cost for the current period?

**QS 20-3**
Materials cost variances
C2  P2

Jacomo Company's output for the current period was assigned a $300,000 standard direct materials cost. The direct materials variances included a $24,000 favorable price variance and a $4,000 favorable quantity variance. What is the actual total direct materials cost for the current period?

**QS 20-4**
Materials cost variances
C2  P2

For the current period, Kawaga Company's manufacturing operations yield a $4,000 favorable price variance on its direct materials usage. The actual price per pound of material is $77; the standard price is $77.50. How many pounds of material are used in the current period?

**QS 20-5**
Management by exception
C3

Managers use *management by exception* for control purposes. (1) Describe the concept of management by exception. (2) Explain how standard costs help managers apply this concept to monitor and control costs.

**QS 20-6**
Overhead cost variances
P3

Hewitt Company's output for the current period yields a $30,000 favorable overhead volume variance and a $50,400 unfavorable overhead controllable variance. Standard overhead charged to production for the period is $225,000. What is the actual total overhead cost incurred for the period?

**QS 20-7**
Preparing overhead entries   P4

Refer to the information in QS 20-6. Hewitt records standard costs in its accounts. Prepare the journal entry to charge overhead costs to the Goods in Process Inventory account and to record any variances.

**QS 20-8**
Computing sales price and
volume variances
A2

VanWay, Inc., specializes in selling used SUVs. During the first six months of 2005, the dealership sold 100 SUVs at an average price of $10,000 each. The budget for the first six months of 2005 was to sell 90 SUVs at an average price of $10,500 each. Compute the dealership's sales price variance and sales volume variance for the first six months of 2005.

*Homework Manager repeats all numerical Exercises on the book's Website with new numbers.*

# EXERCISES

**Exercise 20-1**
Preparation of
flexible budgets
P1

Mesa Company's fixed budget for the first quarter of calendar year 2005 reveals the following. Prepare flexible budgets following the format of Exhibit 20.3 that show variable costs per unit, fixed costs, and three different flexible budgets for sales volumes of 7,500, 10,000, and 12,500 units.

| | | |
|---|---:|---:|
| Sales (10,000 units) . . . . . . . . . . . . . . . | | $3,000,000 |
| Cost of goods sold | | |
|     Direct materials . . . . . . . . . . . . . . . | $320,000 | |
|     Direct labor . . . . . . . . . . . . . . . . . . | 680,000 | |
|     Production supplies . . . . . . . . . . . . . . | 264,000 | |
|     Plant manager salary . . . . . . . . . . . . | 60,000 | 1,324,000 |
| Gross profit . . . . . . . . . . . . . . . . . . . . | | 1,676,000 |
| Selling expenses | | |
|     Sales commissions . . . . . . . . . . . . . . | 120,000 | |
|     Packaging . . . . . . . . . . . . . . . . . . . | 210,000 | |
|     Advertising . . . . . . . . . . . . . . . . . . . | 100,000 | 430,000 |
| Administrative expenses | | |
|     Administrative salaries . . . . . . . . . . . | 80,000 | |
|     Depreciation—Office equip. . . . . . . . | 30,000 | |
|     Insurance . . . . . . . . . . . . . . . . . . . | 18,000 | |
|     Office rent . . . . . . . . . . . . . . . . . . . | 24,000 | 152,000 |
| Income from operations . . . . . . . . . . . | | $1,094,000 |

**Check**  Income (at 7,500 units),
$742,500

KMAR Company manufactures and sells mountain bikes. It normally operates eight hours a day, five days a week. Using this information, classify each of the following costs as fixed or variable. If additional information would affect your decision, describe the information.

**a.** Incoming shipping expenses
**b.** Office supplies
**c.** Depreciation on tools
**d.** Taxes on property
**e.** Pension cost
**f.** Gas used for heating

**g.** Bike frames
**h.** Direct labor
**i.** Screws for assembly
**j.** Repair expense for tools
**k.** Management salaries

**Exercise 20-2**
Classification of costs as fixed or variable

P1

---

Daytec Company's fixed budget performance report for June follows. The $440,000 budgeted expenses include $300,000 variable expenses and $140,000 fixed expenses. Actual expenses include $130,000 fixed expenses. Prepare a flexible budget performance report that shows any variances between budgeted results and actual results. List fixed and variable expenses separately.

| | Fixed Budget | Actual Results | Variances |
|---|---|---|---|
| Sales (in units) . . . . . . . . . . . . . . | 6,000 | 4,800 | |
| Sales (in dollars) . . . . . . . . . . . . | $480,000 | $422,400 | $57,600 U |
| Total expenses . . . . . . . . . . . . . . | 440,000 | 394,000 | 46,000 F |
| Income from operations . . . . . . . | $ 40,000 | $ 28,400 | $11,600 U |

**Exercise 20-3**
Preparation of a flexible budget performance report

A1

**Check**  Income variance, $24,400 F

---

Cimarron Company's fixed budget performance report for July follows. The $630,000 budgeted expenses include $588,000 variable expenses and $42,000 fixed expenses. Actual expenses include $54,000 fixed expenses. Prepare a flexible budget performance report showing any variances between budgeted and actual results. List fixed and variable expenses separately.

| | Fixed Budget | Actual Results | Variances |
|---|---|---|---|
| Sales (in units) . . . . . . . . . . . . . . | 8,400 | 10,800 | |
| Sales (in dollars) . . . . . . . . . . . . | $840,000 | $1,080,000 | $240,000 F |
| Total expenses . . . . . . . . . . . . . . | 630,000 | 756,000 | 126,000 U |
| Income from operations . . . . . . . | $210,000 | $ 324,000 | $114,000 F |

**Exercise 20-4**
Preparation of a flexible budget performance report

A1

**Check**  Income variance, $42,000 F

---

After evaluating Zero Company's manufacturing process, management decides to establish standards of 1.5 hours of direct labor per unit of product and $11 per hour for the labor rate. During October, the company uses 3,780 hours of direct labor at a $45,360 total cost to produce 2,700 units of product. In November, the company uses 4,480 hours of direct labor at a $47,040 total cost to produce 2,800 units of product. (1) Compute the rate variance, the efficiency variance, and the total direct labor cost variance for each of these two months. (2) Interpret the October direct labor variances.

**Exercise 20-5**
Computation and interpretation of labor variances

C2  P2

---

Sonic Company set the following standard costs for one unit of its product for 2005:

| | |
|---|---|
| Direct material (20 lbs. @ $2.50 per lb.) . . . . . . . . . . . . . . . | $ 50.00 |
| Direct labor (15 hrs. @ $8.00 per hr.) . . . . . . . . . . . . . . . . . | 120.00 |
| Factory variable overhead (15 hrs. @ $2.50 per hr.) . . . . . . . . | 37.50 |
| Factory fixed overhead (15 hrs. @ $0.50 per hr.) . . . . . . . . . | 7.50 |
| Standard cost . . . . . . . . . . . . . . . . . . . . . . . . . . . . . . . . | $215.00 |

**Exercise 20-6**
Computation and interpretation of overhead variances

C2  P3

The $3.00 ($2.50 + $0.50) total overhead rate per direct labor hour is based on an expected operating level equal to 75% of the factory's capacity of 50,000 units per month. The following monthly flexible budget information is also available:

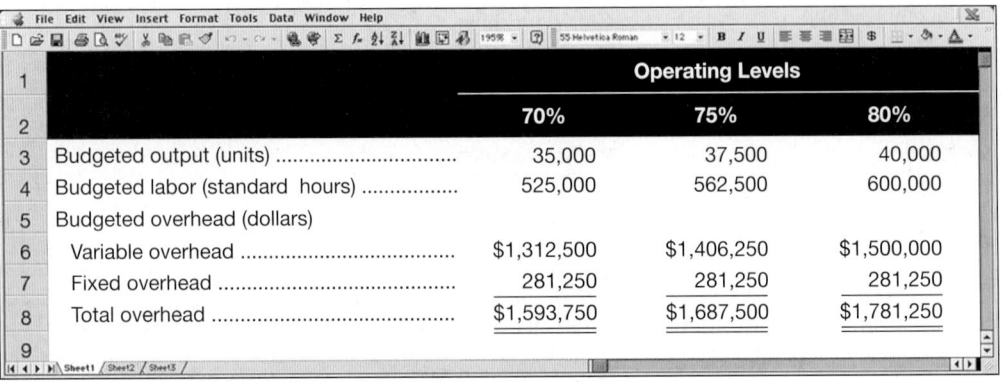

| | Operating Levels | | |
|---|---|---|---|
| | 70% | 75% | 80% |
| Budgeted output (units) ................................ | 35,000 | 37,500 | 40,000 |
| Budgeted labor (standard hours) ................. | 525,000 | 562,500 | 600,000 |
| Budgeted overhead (dollars) | | | |
| Variable overhead ..................................... | $1,312,500 | $1,406,250 | $1,500,000 |
| Fixed overhead ......................................... | 281,250 | 281,250 | 281,250 |
| Total overhead ......................................... | $1,593,750 | $1,687,500 | $1,781,250 |

During the current month, the company operated at 70% of capacity, employees worked 500,000 hours, and the following actual overhead costs are incurred:

| | |
|---|---|
| Variable overhead costs  ....... | $1,267,500 |
| Fixed overhead costs  ......... | 285,000 |
| Total overhead costs ......... | $1,552,500 |

**Check**  (2) Variable overhead:
Spending, $17,500 U; Efficiency, $62,500 F

(1) Show how the company computed its predetermined overhead application rate per hour for total overhead, variable overhead, and fixed overhead. (2) Compute and interpret the variable overhead spending and efficiency variances. (3) Compute and interpret the fixed overhead spending and volume variances.

---

## Exercise 20-7
Computation and interpretation of materials variances

C2 P2

BTS Company made 6,000 bookshelves using 88,000 board feet of wood costing $607,200. The company's direct materials standards for one bookshelf are 16 board feet of wood at $7 per board foot. (1) Compute the direct materials variances incurred in manufacturing these bookshelves. (2) Interpret the direct materials variances.

---

## Exercise 20-8
Materials variances recorded and closed

C3 P4

Refer to Exercise 20-7. BTS Company records standard costs in its accounts and its material variances in separate accounts when it assigns materials costs to the Goods in Process Inventory account. (1) Show the journal entry that both charges the direct materials costs to the Goods in Process Inventory account and records the materials variances in their proper accounts. (2) Assume that BTS's material variances are the only variances accumulated in the accounting period and that they are immaterial. Prepare the adjusting journal entry to close the variance accounts at period-end. (3) Identify the variance that should be investigated according to the management by exception concept. Explain.

---

## Exercise 20-9
Computation of volume and controllable overhead variances

P3

**Check**  (3) $27,000 U

Earth Company expects to operate at 80% of its productive capacity of 25,000 units per month. At this planned level, the company expects to use 40,000 standard hours of direct labor. Overhead is allocated to products using a predetermined standard rate based on direct labor hours. At the 80% capacity level, the total budgeted cost includes $40,000 fixed overhead cost and $280,000 variable overhead cost. In the current month, the company incurred $340,000 actual overhead and 39,000 actual labor hours while producing 19,500 units. Compute the (1) total overhead variance, (2) overhead volume variance, and (3) overhead controllable variance.

---

## Exercise 20-10
Computing and interpreting sales variances   A2

Comp Wiz sells computers. During May 2005, it sold 500 computers at a $900 average price each. The May 2005 budget included sales of 550 computers at an average price of $850 each. (1) Compute the sales price variance and the sales volume variance for May 2005. (2) Interpret the findings.

Tuna Company set the following standard unit costs for its single product:

| | |
|---|---|
| Direct materials (25 lbs. @ $4 per lb.) . . . . . . . . . . . . . . . . | $100.00 |
| Direct labor (6 hrs. @ $8 per hr.) . . . . . . . . . . . . . . . . . . . | 48.00 |
| Factory overhead—Variable (6 hrs. @ $5 per hr.) . . . . . . . . | 30.00 |
| Factory overhead—Fixed (6 hrs. @ $7 per hr.) . . . . . . . . . | 42.00 |
| Total standard cost . . . . . . . . . . . . . . . . . . . . . . . . . . . . . | $220.00 |

The predetermined overhead rate is based on a planned operating volume of 80% of the productive capacity of 60,000 units per quarter. The following flexible budget information is available:

| | Operating Levels | | |
|---|---|---|---|
| | **70%** | **80%** | **90%** |
| Production in units . . . . . . . . . . . . . . | 42,000 | 48,000 | 54,000 |
| Standard direct labor hours . . . . . . . . | 252,000 | 288,000 | 324,000 |
| Budgeted overhead | | | |
| Fixed factory overhead . . . . . . . . . | $2,016,000 | $2,016,000 | $2,016,000 |
| Variable factory overhead . . . . . . . | $1,260,000 | $1,440,000 | $1,620,000 |

During the current quarter, the company operated at 70% of capacity and produced 42,000 units of product; actual direct labor totaled 250,000 hours. Units produced are assigned the following standard costs:

| | |
|---|---|
| Direct materials (1,050,000 lbs. @ $4 per lb.) . . . . . . . . . | $4,200,000 |
| Direct labor (252,000 hrs. @ $8 per hr.) . . . . . . . . . . . . . | 2,016,000 |
| Factory overhead (252,000 hrs. @ $12 per hr.) . . . . . . . . | 3,024,000 |
| Total standard cost . . . . . . . . . . . . . . . . . . . . . . . . . . . . | $9,240,000 |

Actual costs incurred during the current quarter follow:

| | |
|---|---|
| Direct materials (1,000,000 lbs. @ $4.25) . . . . . . . . . . . . | $4,250,000 |
| Direct labor (250,000 hrs. @ $7.75) . . . . . . . . . . . . . . . . | 1,937,500 |
| Fixed factory overhead costs . . . . . . . . . . . . . . . . . . . . . | 1,960,000 |
| Variable factory overhead costs . . . . . . . . . . . . . . . . . . . | 1,200,000 |
| Total actual costs . . . . . . . . . . . . . . . . . . . . . . . . . . . . . | $9,347,500 |

**Required**

**1.** Compute the direct materials cost variance, including its price and quantity variances.

**2.** Compute the direct labor variance including its rate and efficiency variances.

**3.** Compute these variances: (a) variable overhead spending and efficiency, (b) fixed overhead spending and volume, and (c) total overhead controllable.

Pebco Company's 2005 master budget included the following fixed budget performance report. It is based on an expected production and sales volume of 20,000 units.

| PEBCO COMPANY | | |
|---|---|---|
| **Fixed Budget Performance Report** | | |
| **For Year Ended December 31, 2005** | | |
| Sales . . . . . . . . . . . . . . . . . . . . . . . . . . . . . . . . | | $3,000,000 |
| Cost of goods sold | | |
| Direct materials . . . . . . . . . . . . . . . . . . . . . | $1,200,000 | |
| Direct labor . . . . . . . . . . . . . . . . . . . . . . . | 260,000 | |
| Machinery repairs (variable cost) . . . . . . . . | 57,000 | |
| Depreciation—Plant equipment . . . . . . . . . | 250,000 | |
| Utilities ($50,000 is variable) . . . . . . . . . . | 200,000 | |
| Plant management salaries . . . . . . . . . . . . | 140,000 | 2,107,000 |
| Gross profit . . . . . . . . . . . . . . . . . . . . . . . . | | 893,000 |

[continued on next page]

---

**PROBLEM SET A**

**Problem 20-1A**
Computation of materials, labor, and overhead variances

C2  P2  P3

e**X**cel
mhhe.com/wild

**Check** (1) Materials variances: Price, $250,000 U; Quantity, $200,000 F.
(2) Labor variances: Rate, $62,500 F; Efficiency, $16,000 F

**Problem 20-2A**
Preparation and analysis of a flexible budget

P1  A1

[continued from previous page]

| | | |
|---|---:|---:|
| Selling expenses | | |
| Packaging | 80,000 | |
| Shipping | 116,000 | |
| Sales salary (fixed annual amount) | 160,000 | 356,000 |
| General and administrative expenses | | |
| Advertising expense | 81,000 | |
| Salaries | 241,000 | |
| Entertainment expense | 90,000 | 412,000 |
| Income from operations | | $ 125,000 |

## Required

**1.** Classify all items listed in the fixed budget as variable or fixed. Also determine their amounts per unit or their amounts for the year, as appropriate.

**Check**   (2) Budgeted income at 24,000 units, $372,400

**2.** Prepare flexible budgets (see Exhibit 20.3) for the company at sales volumes of 18,000 and 24,000 units.

**3.** The company's business conditions are improving. One possible result is a sales volume of approximately 28,000 units. The company president is confident that this volume is within the relevant range of existing capacity. How much would operating income increase over the 2005 budgeted amount of $125,000 if this level is reached without increasing capacity?

(4) Potential operating loss, $(246,100)

**4.** An unfavorable change in business is remotely possible; in this case, production and sales volume for 2005 could fall to 14,000 units. How much income (or loss) from operations would occur if sales volume falls to this level?

## Problem 20-3A
Preparation and analysis of a flexible budget performance report

P1   A2

mhhe.com/wild

Refer to information in Problem 20-2A. Pebco Company's actual income statement for 2005 follows:

| PEBCO COMPANY Statement of Income from Operations For Year Ended December 31, 2005 | | |
|---|---:|---:|
| Sales (24,000 units) | | $3,648,000 |
| Cost of goods sold | | |
| Direct materials | $1,400,000 | |
| Direct labor | 360,000 | |
| Machinery repairs (variable cost) | 60,000 | |
| Depreciation—Plant equipment | 250,000 | |
| Utilities (fixed cost is $154,000) | 218,000 | |
| Plant management salaries | 155,000 | 2,443,000 |
| Gross profit | | 1,205,000 |
| Selling expenses | | |
| Packaging | 90,000 | |
| Shipping | 124,000 | |
| Sales salary (annual) | 162,000 | 376,000 |
| General and administrative expenses | | |
| Advertising expense | 104,000 | |
| Salaries | 232,000 | |
| Entertainment expense | 100,000 | 436,000 |
| Income from operations | | $ 393,000 |

## Required

**Check**   (1) Variances: Fixed costs, $45,000 U; Income, $20,600 F

**1.** Prepare a flexible budget performance report for 2005.

### Analysis Component

**2.** Analyze and interpret both the (a) sales variance and (b) direct materials variance.

Kwikeze Company set the following standard costs for one unit of its product:

**Problem 20-4A**
Flexible budget preparation;
computation of materials, labor,
and overhead variances; and
overhead variance report

P1  P2  P3  C2

| | |
|---|---|
| Direct materials (4.5 lbs. @ $6 per lb.) . . . . . . . | $27.00 |
| Direct labor (1.5 hrs. @ $12 per hr.) . . . . . . . . . | 18.00 |
| Overhead (1.5 hrs. @ $16 per hr.) . . . . . . . . . . | 24.00 |
| Total standard cost . . . . . . . . . . . . . . . . . . . . . | $69.00 |

The predetermined overhead rate ($16 per direct labor hour) is based on expected volume of 75% of the factory's capacity of 20,000 units per month. Following are the company's budgeted overhead costs per month at the 75% level:

| Overhead Budget (75% capacity) | | |
|---|---|---|
| Variable overhead costs | | |
| Indirect materials . . . . . . . . . . . . . . . . | $22,500 | |
| Indirect labor . . . . . . . . . . . . . . . . . . | 90,000 | |
| Power . . . . . . . . . . . . . . . . . . . . . . | 22,500 | |
| Repairs and maintenance . . . . . . . . . . . | 45,000 | |
| Total variable overhead costs . . . . . . . | | $180,000 |
| Fixed overhead costs | | |
| Depreciation—Building . . . . . . . . . . . . | 24,000 | |
| Depreciation—Machinery . . . . . . . . . . | 72,000 | |
| Taxes and insurance . . . . . . . . . . . . . . | 18,000 | |
| Supervision . . . . . . . . . . . . . . . . . . . | 66,000 | |
| Total fixed overhead costs . . . . . . . . . | | 180,000 |
| Total overhead costs . . . . . . . . . . . . . . | | $360,000 |

The company incurred the following actual costs when it operated at 75% of capacity in October:

| | | |
|---|---|---|
| Direct materials (69,000 lbs. @ $6.10 per lb.) . . . . . . . . | | $ 420,900 |
| Direct labor (22,800 hrs. @ $12.30 per hr.) . . . . . . . . . | | 280,440 |
| Overhead costs | | |
| Indirect materials . . . . . . . . . . . . . . . . . . . . . . . | $21,600 | |
| Indirect labor . . . . . . . . . . . . . . . . . . . . . . . . . | 82,260 | |
| Power . . . . . . . . . . . . . . . . . . . . . . . . . . . . . | 23,100 | |
| Repairs and maintenance . . . . . . . . . . . . . . . . . | 46,800 | |
| Depreciation—Building . . . . . . . . . . . . . . . . . . | 24,000 | |
| Depreciation—Machinery . . . . . . . . . . . . . . . . . | 75,000 | |
| Taxes and insurance . . . . . . . . . . . . . . . . . . . . | 16,500 | |
| Supervision . . . . . . . . . . . . . . . . . . . . . . . . . | 66,000 | 355,260 |
| Total costs . . . . . . . . . . . . . . . . . . . . . . . . . . | | $1,056,600 |

## Required

**1.** Examine the monthly overhead budget to (a) determine the costs per unit for each variable overhead item and its total per unit costs, and (b) identify the total fixed costs per month.

**2.** Prepare flexible overhead budgets (as in Exhibit 20.12) for October showing the amounts of each variable and fixed cost at the 65%, 75%, and 85% capacity levels.

**3.** Compute the direct materials cost variance, including its price and quantity variances.

**4.** Compute the direct labor cost variance, including its rate and efficiency variances.

**5.** Compute the (a) variable overhead spending and efficiency variances, (b) fixed overhead spending and volume variances, and (c) total overhead controllable variance.

**6.** Prepare a detailed overhead variance report (as in Exhibit 20.19) that shows the variances for individual items of overhead.

**Check** (2) Budgeted total overhead
at 13,000 units, $336,000.

(3) Materials variances: Price,
$6,900 U; Quantity, $9,000 U.

(4) Labor variances: Rate,
$6,840 U; Efficiency, $3,600 U

**Problem 20-5A**

Materials, labor, and overhead variances; and overhead variance report

C2  P2  P3

Kudos Company has set the following standard costs per unit for the product it manufactures:

| | |
|---|---|
| Direct materials (10 lbs. @ $3 per lb.) . . . . . . . | $30.00 |
| Direct labor (4 hrs. @ $6 per hr.) . . . . . . . . . | 24.00 |
| Overhead (4 hrs. @ $2.50 per hr.) . . . . . . . . . | 10.00 |
| Total standard cost . . . . . . . . . . . . . . . . . . . | $64.00 |

The predetermined overhead rate is based on a planned operating volume of 80% of the productive capacity of 10,000 units per month. The following flexible budget information is available:

| | Operating Levels | | |
|---|---|---|---|
| | 70% | 80% | 90% |
| Production in units . . . . . . . . . . . . . . | 7,000 | 8,000 | 9,000 |
| Standard direct labor hours . . . . . . . . . | 28,000 | 32,000 | 36,000 |
| Budgeted overhead | | | |
| Variable overhead costs | | | |
| Indirect materials . . . . . . . . . . . . | $ 8,750 | $ 10,000 | $11,250 |
| Indirect labor . . . . . . . . . . . . . . . | 14,000 | 16,000 | 18,000 |
| Power . . . . . . . . . . . . . . . . . . . | 3,500 | 4,000 | 4,500 |
| Maintenance . . . . . . . . . . . . . . . | 1,750 | 2,000 | 2,250 |
| Total variable costs . . . . . . . . . . | 28,000 | 32,000 | 36,000 |
| Fixed overhead costs | | | |
| Rent of factory building . . . . . . . . | 12,000 | 12,000 | 12,000 |
| Depreciation—Machinery . . . . . . . | 20,000 | 20,000 | 20,000 |
| Supervisory salaries . . . . . . . . . . . | 16,000 | 16,000 | 16,000 |
| Total fixed costs . . . . . . . . . . . . | 48,000 | 48,000 | 48,000 |
| Total overhead costs . . . . . . . . . . . | $76,000 | $ 80,000 | $84,000 |

During May, the company operated at 90% of capacity and produced 9,000 units, incurring the following actual costs:

| | | |
|---|---|---|
| Direct materials (92,000 lbs. @ $2.95 per lb.) . . . . . . . . | | $271,400 |
| Direct labor (37,600 hrs. @ $6.05 per hr.) . . . . . . . . . . | | 227,480 |
| Overhead costs | | |
| Indirect materials . . . . . . . . . . . . . . . . . . . . . . . . . | $10,000 | |
| Indirect labor . . . . . . . . . . . . . . . . . . . . . . . . . . . | 16,000 | |
| Power . . . . . . . . . . . . . . . . . . . . . . . . . . . . . . . . | 4,500 | |
| Maintenance . . . . . . . . . . . . . . . . . . . . . . . . . . . . | 3,000 | |
| Rent of factory building . . . . . . . . . . . . . . . . . . . . | 12,000 | |
| Depreciation—Machinery . . . . . . . . . . . . . . . . . . . . | 19,200 | |
| Supervisory salaries . . . . . . . . . . . . . . . . . . . . . . . | 17,000 | 81,700 |
| Total costs . . . . . . . . . . . . . . . . . . . . . . . . . . . . . | | $580,580 |

**Check**  (1) Materials variances: Price, $4,600 F; Quantity, $6,000 U. (2) Labor variances: Rate, $1,880 U; Efficiency, $9,600 U.

**Required**

1. Compute the direct materials variance, including its price and quantity variances.

2. Compute the direct labor variance, including its rate and efficiency variances.

3. Compute these variances: (a) variable overhead spending and efficiency, (b) fixed overhead spending and volume, and (c) total overhead controllable.

4. Prepare a detailed overhead variance report (as in Exhibit 20.19) that shows the variances for individual items of overhead.

**Problem 20-6A**

Materials, labor, and overhead variances recorded and analyzed

C3  P4

Loretto Company's standard cost accounting system recorded this information from its December operations.

| | |
|---|---|
| Standard direct materials cost . . . . . . . . . . . . . . . . . . . . . | $130,000 |
| Direct materials quantity variance (unfavorable) . . . . . . . | 5,000 |
| Direct materials price variance (favorable) . . . . . . . . . . . | 1,500 |
| Actual direct labor cost . . . . . . . . . . . . . . . . . . . . . . . . . | 65,000 |

[continued on next page]

[continued from previous page]

| | |
|---|---:|
| Direct labor efficiency variance (favorable) ........... | 7,000 |
| Direct labor rate variance (unfavorable) ............. | 500 |
| Actual overhead cost ............................ | 250,000 |
| Volume variance (unfavorable) .................. | 12,000 |
| Controllable variance (unfavorable) ............... | 8,000 |

## Required

**1.** Prepare December 30 journal entries to record the company's costs and variances for the month.

*Analysis Component*

**2.** Identify the areas that would attract the attention of a manager who uses management by exception. Explain what action(s) the manager should consider.

**Check** (1) Dr. Goods in Process Inventory (for overhead), $230,000

---

Sabates Company set the following standard unit costs for its single product:

| | |
|---|---:|
| Direct materials (5 lbs. @ $10 per lb.) ............... | $ 50.00 |
| Direct labor (3 hrs. @ $15 per hr.) .................. | 45.00 |
| Factory overhead—Variable (3 hrs. @ $5 per hr.) ........ | 15.00 |
| Factory overhead—Fixed (3 hrs. @ $3 per hr.) ......... | 9.00 |
| Total standard cost ............................. | $119.00 |

## PROBLEM SET B

### Problem 20-1B
Computation of materials, labor, and overhead variances

C2 P2 P3

The predetermined overhead rate is based on a planned operating volume of 90% of the productive capacity of 100,000 units per quarter. The following flexible budget information is available:

| | Operating Levels | | |
|---|---|---|---|
| | **80%** | **90%** | **100%** |
| Production in units .............. | 32,000 | 36,000 | 40,000 |
| Standard direct labor hours ........ | 96,000 | 108,000 | 120,000 |
| Budgeted overhead | | | |
| Fixed factory overhead ......... | $324,000 | $324,000 | $324,000 |
| Variable factory overhead ....... | 480,000 | 540,000 | 600,000 |

During the current quarter, the company operated at 80% of capacity and produced 32,000 units of product; direct labor hours worked were 100,000. Units produced are assigned the following standard costs:

| | |
|---|---:|
| Direct materials (160,000 lbs. @ $10 per lb.) ......... | $1,600,000 |
| Direct labor (96,000 hrs. @ $15 per hr.) ............. | 1,440,000 |
| Factory overhead (96,000 hrs. @ $8.00 per hr.) ........ | 768,000 |
| Total standard cost ........................... | $3,808,000 |

Actual costs incurred during the current quarter follow:

| | |
|---|---:|
| Direct materials (155,000 lbs. @ $10.20) ........ | $1,581,000 |
| Direct labor (100,000 hrs. @ $14.00) .......... | 1,400,000 |
| Fixed factory overhead costs ................ | 370,000 |
| Variable factory overhead costs .............. | 480,000 |
| Total actual costs ......................... | $3,831,000 |

## Required

**1.** Compute the direct materials cost variance, including its price and quantity variances.

**2.** Compute the direct labor variance, including its rate and efficiency variances.

**3.** Compute these variances: (a) variable overhead spending and efficiency, (b) fixed overhead spending and volume, and (c) total overhead controllable.

**Check** (1) Materials variances: Price, $31,000 U; Quantity, $50,000 F. (2) Labor variances: Rate, $100,000 F; Efficiency, $60,000 U

**Problem 20-2B**
Preparation and analysis of a flexible budget

P1　A1

Razorback Company's 2005 master budget included the following fixed budget performance report. It is based on an expected production and sales volume of 10,000 units.

**RAZORBACK COMPANY**
**Fixed Budget Performance Report**
**For Year Ended December 31, 2005**

| | | |
|---|---:|---:|
| Sales | | $250,000 |
| Cost of goods sold | | |
| Direct materials | $100,000 | |
| Direct labor | 20,000 | |
| Machinery repairs (variable cost) | 3,000 | |
| Depreciation—Machinery | 11,920 | |
| Utilities (80% is variable cost) | 8,000 | |
| Plant manager salaries | 6,000 | 148,920 |
| Gross profit | | 101,080 |
| Selling expenses | | |
| Packaging | 9,000 | |
| Shipping | 30,000 | |
| Sales salary (fixed annual amount) | 18,000 | 57,000 |
| General and administrative expenses | | |
| Advertising | 4,000 | |
| Salaries | 9,360 | |
| Entertainment expense | 10,000 | 23,360 |
| Income from operations | | $ 20,720 |

**Required**

1. Classify all items listed in the fixed budget as variable or fixed. Also determine their amounts per unit or their amounts for the year, as appropriate.

**Check** (2) Budgeted income at 12,000 units, $37,040

2. Prepare flexible budgets (see Exhibit 20.3) for the company at sales volumes of 8,000 and 12,000 units.

3. The company's business conditions are improving. One possible result is a sales volume of approximately 14,400 units. The company president is confident that this volume is within the relevant range of existing capacity. How much would operating income increase over the 2005 budgeted amount of $20,720 if this level is reached without increasing capacity?

(4) Potential operating loss, $(20,080)

4. An unfavorable change in business is remotely possible; in this case, production and sales volume for 2005 could fall to 5,000 units. How much income (or loss) from operations would occur if sales volume falls to this level?

**Problem 20-3B**
Preparation and analysis of a flexible budget performance report

P1　A2

Refer to information in Problem 20-2B. Razorback Company's actual income statement for 2005 follows:

**RAZORBACK COMPANY**
**Statement of Income from Operations**
**For Year Ended December 31, 2005**

| | | |
|---|---:|---:|
| Sales (12,000 units) | | $288,000 |
| Cost of goods sold | | |
| Direct materials | $95,000 | |
| Direct labor | 16,000 | |
| Machinery repairs (variable cost) | 3,300 | |
| Depreciation—Machinery | 11,920 | |
| Utilities (variable cost, $7,160) | 8,520 | |
| Plant manager salaries | 6,720 | 141,460 |
| Gross profit | | 146,540 |
| Selling expenses | | |
| Packaging | 10,800 | |
| Shipping | 37,200 | |
| Sales salary (annual) | 19,200 | 67,200 |
| General and administrative expenses | | |
| Advertising expense | 4,200 | |
| Salaries | 9,360 | |
| Entertainment expense | 10,000 | 23,560 |
| Income from operations | | $ 55,780 |

**Required**

**1.** Prepare a flexible budget performance report for 2005.

*Analysis Component*

**2.** Analyze and interpret both the (a) sales variance and (b) direct materials variance.

**Check** (1) Variances: Fixed costs, $1,880 U; Income, $18,740 F

---

Sunburst Company set the following standard costs for one unit of its product:

**Problem 20-4B**
Flexible budget preparation; computation of materials, labor, and overhead variances; and overhead variance report

P1 P2 P3 C2

| | |
|---|---|
| Direct materials (48 kgs. @ $4 per kg.) ....... | $192.00 |
| Direct labor (12 hrs. @ $9 per hr.) .......... | 108.00 |
| Overhead (12 hrs. @ $4.50 per hr.) .......... | 54.00 |
| Total standard cost ..................... | $354.00 |

The predetermined overhead rate ($4.50 per direct labor hour) is based on an expected volume of 50% of the factory's capacity of 10,000 units per month. Following are the company's budgeted overhead costs per month at the 50% level:

| Overhead Budget (50% capacity) | | |
|---|---|---|
| Variable overhead costs | | |
| Indirect materials ................ | $40,000 | |
| Indirect labor .................. | 80,000 | |
| Power ...................... | 20,000 | |
| Repairs and maintenance .......... | 30,000 | |
| Total variable overhead costs ....... | | $170,000 |
| Fixed overhead costs | | |
| Depreciation—Building ........... | 20,000 | |
| Depreciation—Machinery .......... | 30,000 | |
| Taxes and insurance ............. | 10,000 | |
| Supervision ................... | 40,000 | |
| Total fixed overhead costs ......... | | 100,000 |
| Total overhead costs ............. | | $270,000 |

The company incurred the following actual costs when it operated at 40% of capacity in December:

| | | |
|---|---|---|
| Direct materials (196,000 kgs. @ $4.00) ........ | | $ 784,000 |
| Direct labor (46,000 hrs. @ $9.15) ........... | | 420,900 |
| Overhead costs | | |
| Indirect materials ..................... | $30,000 | |
| Indirect labor ....................... | 66,000 | |
| Power ........................... | 15,600 | |
| Repairs and maintenance ................ | 21,000 | |
| Depreciation—Building ................. | 20,000 | |
| Depreciation—Machinery ................ | 30,000 | |
| Taxes and insurance .................. | 9,600 | |
| Supervision ........................ | 39,600 | 231,800 |
| Total costs ........................ | | $1,436,700 |

**Required**

**1.** Examine the monthly overhead budget to (a) determine the costs per unit for each variable overhead item and its total per unit costs, and (b) identify the total fixed costs per month.

**2.** Prepare flexible overhead budgets (as in Exhibit 20.12) for December showing the amounts of each variable and fixed cost at the 40%, 50%, and 60% capacity levels.

**3.** Compute the direct materials cost variance, including its price and quantity variances.

**4.** Compute the direct labor cost variance, including its rate and efficiency variances.

**5.** Compute the (a) variable overhead spending and efficiency variances, (b) fixed overhead spending and volume variances, and (c) total overhead controllable variance.

**6.** Prepare a detailed overhead variance report (as in Exhibit 20.19) that shows the variances for individual items of overhead.

**Check** (2) Budgeted total overhead at 6,000 units, $304,000;

(3) Materials variances: Price, $0; Quantity, $16,000 U

(4) Labor variances: Rate, $6,900 U; Efficiency, $18,000 F

## Problem 20-5B

Materials, labor, and overhead variances; and overhead variance report

C2  P2  P3

Carlsbad Company has set the following standard costs per unit for the product it manufactures:

| | |
|---|---:|
| Direct materials (40 oz. @ $0.75 per oz.) . . . . . . . . | $ 30.00 |
| Direct labor (2 hr. @ $20 per hr.) . . . . . . . . . . . . | 40.00 |
| Overhead (2 hr. @ $53.50 per hr.) . . . . . . . . . . | 107.00 |
| Total standard cost . . . . . . . . . . . . . . . . . . . . . | $177.00 |

The predetermined overhead rate is based on a planned operating volume of 60% of the productive capacity of 3,000 units per month. The following flexible budget information is available:

| | Operating Levels | | |
|---|---:|---:|---:|
| | 50% | 60% | 70% |
| Production in units . . . . . . . . . . . . . . . | 1,500 | 1,800 | 2,100 |
| Standard direct labor hours . . . . . . . . . | 3,000 | 3,600 | 4,200 |
| Budgeted overhead | | | |
| Variable overhead costs | | | |
| Indirect materials . . . . . . . . . . . . . | $ 18,000 | $21,600 | $25,200 |
| Indirect labor . . . . . . . . . . . . . . . | 10,500 | 12,600 | 14,700 |
| Power . . . . . . . . . . . . . . . . . . . . | 7,500 | 9,000 | 10,500 |
| Maintenance . . . . . . . . . . . . . . . | 4,500 | 5,400 | 6,300 |
| Total variable costs . . . . . . . . . . . | 40,500 | 48,600 | 56,700 |
| Fixed overhead costs | | | |
| Rent of factory building . . . . . . . . . | 48,000 | 48,000 | 48,000 |
| Depreciation—Machinery . . . . . . . | 44,000 | 44,000 | 44,000 |
| Taxes and insurance . . . . . . . . . . . | 20,000 | 20,000 | 20,000 |
| Supervisory salaries . . . . . . . . . . . | 32,000 | 32,000 | 32,000 |
| Total fixed costs . . . . . . . . . . . . | 144,000 | 144,000 | 144,000 |
| Total overhead costs . . . . . . . . . . . | $184,500 | $192,600 | $200,700 |

During March, the company operated at 70% of capacity and produced 2,100 units, incurring the following actual costs:

| | | |
|---|---:|---:|
| Direct materials (88,000 ozs. @ $0.70 per oz.) . . . . . . . | | $ 61,600 |
| Direct labor (4,000 hrs. @ $19.50 per hr.) . . . . . . . . . | | 78,000 |
| Overhead costs | | |
| Indirect materials . . . . . . . . . . . . . . . . . . . . . . . | $23,600 | |
| Indirect labor . . . . . . . . . . . . . . . . . . . . . . . . . | 14,800 | |
| Power . . . . . . . . . . . . . . . . . . . . . . . . . . . . . | 10,000 | |
| Maintenance . . . . . . . . . . . . . . . . . . . . . . . . . | 3,200 | |
| Rent of factory building . . . . . . . . . . . . . . . . . . . | 48,000 | |
| Depreciation—Machinery . . . . . . . . . . . . . . . . . . | 44,000 | |
| Taxes and insurance . . . . . . . . . . . . . . . . . . . . | 24,000 | |
| Supervisory salaries . . . . . . . . . . . . . . . . . . . . | 31,600 | 199,200 |
| Total costs . . . . . . . . . . . . . . . . . . . . . . . . . . | | $338,800 |

**Check**  (1) Materials variances: Price, $4,400 F; Quantity, $3,000 U.

(2) Labor variances: Rate, $2,000 F; Efficiency, $4,000 F

### Required

1. Compute the direct materials cost variance, including its price and quantity variances.

2. Compute the direct labor variance, including its rate and efficiency variances.

**3.** Compute these variances: (a) variable overhead spending and efficiency, (b) fixed overhead spending and volume, and (c) total overhead controllable.

**4.** Prepare a detailed overhead variance report (as in Exhibit 20.19) that shows the variances for individual items of overhead.

Kincaid Company's standard cost accounting system recorded this information from its June operations:

| | |
|---|---|
| Standard direct materials cost . . . . . . . . . . . . . . . . . . . . | $220,500 |
| Direct materials quantity variance (favorable) . . . . . . . | 20,250 |
| Direct materials price variance (favorable) . . . . . . . . . . | 14,500 |
| Actual direct labor cost . . . . . . . . . . . . . . . . . . . . . . . . | 335,000 |
| Direct labor efficiency variance (favorable) . . . . . . . . . . | 26,700 |
| Direct labor rate variance (unfavorable) . . . . . . . . . . . . | 3,500 |
| Actual overhead cost . . . . . . . . . . . . . . . . . . . . . . . . . . | 359,000 |
| Volume variance (unfavorable) . . . . . . . . . . . . . . . . . . | 1,650 |
| Controllable variance (unfavorable) . . . . . . . . . . . . . . | 32,500 |

**Problem 20-6B**
Materials, labor, and overhead variances recorded and analyzed

C3   P4

**Required**

**1.** Prepare journal entries dated June 30 to record the company's costs and variances for the month.

**Check**  (1) Dr. Goods in Process Inventory (for overhead), $324,850

*Analysis Component*

**2.** Identify the areas that would attract the attention of a manager who uses management by exception. Describe what action(s) the manager should consider.

Problem Set C is available at the book's Website to further reinforce and assess your learning.

# PROBLEM SET C

*(This serial problem began in Chapter 1 and continues through most of the book. If previous chapter segments were not completed, the serial problem can begin at this point. It is helpful, but not necessary, for you to use the Working Papers that accompany the book.)*

# SERIAL PROBLEM

Success Systems

Success Systems' second quarter 2006 fixed budget performance report for its computer furniture operations follows. The $174,900 budgeted expenses include $159,900 variable expenses and $15,000 fixed expenses. The actual expenses include $18,000 fixed expenses. Prepare a flexible budget performance report that shows any variances between budgeted results and actual results. List fixed and variable expenses separately.

| | Fixed Budget | Actual Results | Variances |
|---|---|---|---|
| Desk sales (in units) . . . . . . . . . . | 72 | 90 | |
| Chair sales (in units) . . . . . . . . . . | 36 | 45 | |
| Desk sales (in dollars) . . . . . . . . . | $162,000 | $207,000 | $45,000 F |
| Chair sales (in dollars) . . . . . . . . . | $ 27,000 | $ 33,750 | $ 6,750 F |
| Total expenses . . . . . . . . . . . . . . | $174,900 | $162,300 | $12,600 F |
| Income from operations . . . . . . . | $ 14,100 | $ 78,450 | $64,350 F |

**Check**  Variances: Fixed expenses, $3,000 U

## BEYOND THE NUMBERS

**REPORTING IN ACTION**

C1

**BTN 20-1** Analysis of flexible budgets and standard costs emphasizes the importance of a similar unit of measure for meaningful comparisons and evaluations. When **Krispy Kreme** compiles its financial reports in compliance with GAAP, it applies the same unit of measurement, U.S. dollars, for most measures of business operations. One issue for Krispy Kreme is how best to adjust account values for its subsidiaries that compile financial reports in currencies other than the U.S. dollar.

**Required**

1. Read Krispy Kreme's Note 2 in Appendix A and identify the financial statement where it reports foreign currency translation.
2. Record the annual amount of its foreign currency translation adjustment and its ending balance for the three fiscal years 2001–2003.

*Roll On*

3. Access Krispy Kreme's financial statements for a fiscal year ending after February 2, 2003, from either its Website [**KrispyKreme.com**] or the SEC's EDGAR database [**www.sec.gov**]. (a) Identify its foreign currency translation adjustment. (b) Does this adjustment increase or decrease net income? Explain.

**COMPARATIVE ANALYSIS**

A2

**BTN 20-2** The usefulness of budgets, variances, and related analyses often depends on the accuracy of management's estimates of future sales activity.

**Required**

1. Identify and record the prior three years' sales (in dollars) for both **Krispy Kreme** and **Tastykake** using their financial statements in Appendix A.
2. Using the data in part 1, predict both companies' sales activity for the next two to three years. (If possible, compare your predictions to actual sales figures for these years.)

**ETHICS CHALLENGE**

C1

**BTN 20-3** Setting materials, labor, and overhead standards is challenging. If standards are set too low, companies might purchase inferior products and employees might not work to their full potential. If standards are set too high, companies could be unable to offer a quality product at a profitable rate and employees could be overworked. The ethical challenge is to set a high but reasonable standard. Assume that as a manager, you are asked to set the standard materials price and quantity for the new 1,000 CKB Mega-Max chip, a technically advanced product. To properly set the price and quantity standards, you assemble a team of specialists to provide input.

**Required**

Identify four types of specialists that you would assemble to provide information to help set the materials price and quantity standards. Briefly explain why you chose each individual.

**COMMUNICATING IN PRACTICE**

P4 C2

**BTN 20-4** The reason we use the words *favorable* and *unfavorable* when evaluating variances is made clear when we look at the closing of accounts. To see this, consider that (1) all variance accounts are closed at the end of each period (temporary accounts), (2) a favorable variance is always a credit balance, and (3) an unfavorable variance is always a debit balance. Write a one-half page memorandum to your instructor with three parts that answer the three following requirements. (Assume that variance accounts are closed to Cost of Goods Sold.)

**Required**

1. Does Cost of Goods Sold increase or decrease when closing a favorable variance? Does gross margin increase or decrease when a favorable variance is closed to Cost of Goods Sold? Explain.
2. Does Cost of Goods Sold increase or decrease when closing an unfavorable variance? Does gross margin increase or decrease when an unfavorable variance is closed to Cost of Goods Sold? Explain.
3. Explain the meaning of a favorable variance and an unfavorable variance.

**BTN 20-5** Access **Hoover's Online** Website (**Hoovers.com**) or other Websites such as **BestPracticeDatabase.com** and **SMThacker.Co.UK** to search for and read information about *benchmarking* to complete the requirements.

**TAKING IT TO THE NET**
C1

mhhe.com/wild

**Required**

**1.** Write a one-paragraph explanation (in layperson's terms) of benchmarking.

**2.** How does standard costing relate to benchmarking?

---

**BTN 20-6** Many service industries link labor rate and time (quantity) standards with their processes. One example is the standard time to board an aircraft. The reason time plays such an important role in the service industry is that it is viewed as a competitive advantage: best service in the shortest amount of time. Although the labor rate component is difficult to observe, the time component of a service delivery standard is often readily apparent, for example, "Lunch will be served in less than five minutes, or it is free."

**TEAMWORK IN ACTION**
C2

**Required**

Break into teams and select two service industries for your analysis. Identify and describe all the time elements each industry uses to create a competitive advantage.

---

**BTN 20-7** Read the article "Doing a Job on Labor" in the October 30, 2002, issue of *Business Week*. (The book's Website provides free access to the article.)

*BUSINESS WEEK ACTIVITY*
C2

mhhe.com/wild

**Required**

**1.** Identify two ways that Internet use has impacted labor markets.

**2.** How might Internet hiring impact labor markets in Europe and other international locations?

**3.** Does the Internet impact union/member communications? Explain.

---

**BTN 20-8** Entrepreneur Scott Jordan of **Technology Enabled Clothing** has implemented a costing system with standard costs for direct materials, direct labor, and overhead costs. Two comments frequently are mentioned in relation to standard costing and variance analysis: "Variances are not explanations" and "Management's goal is not to minimize variances."

**ENTREPRENEURIAL DECISION**
C1 C2

**Required**

Write Scott Jordan a short memo interpreting these two comments.

---

**BTN 20-9** Training employees to use standard amounts of materials in production is common. Typically, large companies invest in this training but small organizations do not. One can observe these different practices in a trip to two different pizza businesses. Visit both a local pizza business and a national pizza chain business and then complete the following.

**HITTING THE ROAD**
C1

**Required**

**1.** Observe and record the number of raw material items used to make a typical cheese pizza. Also observe how the person making the pizza applies each item when preparing the pizza.

**2.** Record any differences in how items are applied between the two businesses.

**3.** Estimate which business is more profitable from your observations. Explain.

---

**BTN 20-10** Access the annual report of **Grupo Bimbo** (at **GrupoBimbo.com**) for the year ended December 31, 2002. The usefulness of its budgets, variances, and related analyses depends on the accuracy of management's estimates of future sales activity.

**GLOBAL DECISION**

**Required**

**1.** Identify and record the prior two years' sales (in pesos) for Grupo Bimbo from its income statement.

**2.** Using the data in part 1, predict sales activity for Grupo Bimbo for the next two years. Explain your prediction process.

*"We're taking advantage of the revolution in consumer electronics and communications, and that has not been done in the medical field"*—Corinna Lathan

# 21

# Capital Budgeting and Managerial Decisions

## A Look Back

Chapter 20 discussed flexible budgets, variance analysis, and standard costs. It explained how management uses each to control and monitor business activities.

## A Look at This Chapter

This chapter focuses on evaluating capital budgeting decisions. It also explains several tools and procedures used in making and evaluating short-term managerial decisions.

# CAP

## Conceptual

**C1** Explain the importance of capital budgeting. *(p. 850)*

**C2** Describe the selection of a hurdle rate for an investment. *(p. 858)*

**C3** Describe the importance of relevant costs for short-term decisions. *(p. 861)*

## Analytical

**A1** Evaluate short-term managerial decisions using relevant costs. *(p. 861)*

**A2** Analyze a capital investment project using break-even time. *(p. 868)*

## Procedural

**P1** Compute payback period and describe its use. *(p. 851)*

**P2** Compute accounting rate of return and explain its use. *(p. 853)*

**P3** Compute net present value and describe its use. *(p. 855)*

**P4** Compute internal rate of return and explain its use. *(p. 857)*

---

**Decision Feature**

# Therapist, Technician, Teacher . . . and Entrepreneur

COLLEGE PARK, MD—"No one knows how to categorize **AnthroTronix**," says Corinna Lathan, its founder. "That's kind of the story of my life: 'What are you?'" Lathan is an entrepreneur. Her company **[AnthroTronix.com]** develops practical applications from research in virtual reality, robotics, and telecommunications. Her personal focus is on interactive, rehabilitative technologies for children with disabilities. "I was appalled at the lack of technology available for kids with disabilities," says Lathan. "I saw a huge opportunity in rehabilitation."

Lathan's pet project, CosmoBot, is a twenty first century version of a short C-3PO. Wearing an ordinary-looking glove or cap embedded with sensors, a child can direct the robot to perform various movements and activities. "This is absolutely revolutionary in the world of rehab," says Lathan. The robot can be programmed to respond to voice commands, to record a child's movements, and to download new software from the Internet. Plans are to sell an enhanced CosmoBot model to clinics and therapists for $2,500 and a home model to individuals for $500. "I'm interested in problem solving . . . using technology," says Lathan. "How can you enable . . .

a person with a disability to complete an activity of daily living?" That's her goal.

To achieve this goal, Lathan must overcome business realities such as making capital budgeting and managerial decisions. She has several projects in the works and a diverse client base, including companies in the rehabilitation and entertainment fields as well as private and government defense agencies. She also confronts financing requirements and the realities of hurdle rates, payback periods, rates of returns, net present values, and break-even time. "Because there's nothing out there like this, it's a real battle with venture capitalists," says Lathan. The key for her is to identify the successful projects from those that are not.

In spite of these tough capital budgeting and managerial decisions, Lathan loves what she's doing. "I love working with new technologies and new applications. I'm designing robotic technology to motivate children to increase their progress with physical and educational therapy programs." Many would say the payback on Lathan's investment is priceless.

[Sources: *AnthroTronix Website,* January 2004; *Inc. Magazine,* September 2002; *Daily Record,* June and September 2002; *Washington City Paper,* October 2001; *Technology Review,* June 2002.]

Making business decisions involves choosing between alternative courses of action. Many factors affect business decisions, yet analysis typically focuses on finding the alternative that offers the highest return on investment or the greatest reduction in costs. Some decisions are based on little more than an intuitive understanding of the situation because available information is too limited to allow a more systematic analysis.

In other cases, intangible factors such as convenience, prestige, and environmental considerations are more important than strictly quantitative factors. In all situations, managers can reach a sounder decision if they identify the consequences of alternative choices in financial terms. This chapter explains several methods of analysis that can help managers make business decisions.

# Section 1—Capital Budgeting

**C1** Explain the importance of capital budgeting.

The capital expenditures budget is management's plan for acquiring and selling plant assets. **Capital budgeting** is the process of analyzing alternative long-term investments and deciding which assets to acquire or sell. These decisions can involve developing a new product or process, buying a new machine or a new building, or acquiring an entire company. An objective for these decisions is to earn a satisfactory return on investment.

Capital budgeting decisions require careful analysis because they are usually the most difficult and risky decisions that managers make. These decisions are difficult because they require predicting events that will not occur until well into the future. Many of these predictions are tentative and potentially unreliable. Specifically, a capital budgeting decision is risky because (1) the outcome is uncertain, (2) large amounts of money are usually involved, (3) the investment involves a long-term commitment, and (4) the decision could be difficult or impossible to reverse, no matter how poor it turns out to be. Risk is especially high for investments in technology due to innovations and uncertainty.

Managers use several methods to evaluate capital budgeting decisions. Nearly all of these methods involve predicting cash inflows and cash outflows of proposed investments, assessing the risk of and returns on those flows, and then choosing the investments to make. Management often restates future cash flows in terms of their present value. This approach applies the time value of money: A dollar today is worth more than a dollar tomorrow. Similarly, a dollar tomorrow is worth less than a dollar today. The process of restating future cash flows in terms of their present value is called *discounting*. The time value of money is important when evaluating capital investments, but managers sometimes apply evaluation methods that ignore present value. This section describes four methods for comparing alternative investments.

**Point:** The nature of capital spending has changed with the business environment. Budgets for information technology have increased from about 25% of corporate capital spending 20 years ago to an estimated 35% today.

# Methods Not Using Time Value of Money

All investments, whether they involve the purchase of a machine or another long-term asset, are expected to produce net cash flows. *Net cash flow* is cash inflows minus cash outflows. Sometimes managers perform simple analyses of the financial feasibility of an investment's net cash flow without using the time value of money. This section explains two of the most common methods in this category: (1) payback period and (2) accounting rate of return.

## Payback Period

An investment's **payback period (PBP)** is the expected time period to recover the initial investment amount. Managers prefer investing in assets with shorter payback periods to reduce the risk of an unprofitable investment over the long run. Acquiring assets with short payback periods reduces a company's risk from potentially inaccurate long-term predictions of future cash flows.

**P1** Compute payback period and describe its use.

**Computing Payback Period with Even Cash Flows**   To illustrate use of the payback period for an investment with even cash flows,[1] we look at data from FasTrac, a manufacturer of exercise equipment and supplies. It is considering several different capital investments, one of which is to purchase a machine to use in manufacturing a new product. This machine costs $16,000 and is expected to have an eight-year life with no salvage value. Management predicts this machine will produce 1,000 units of product each year and that the new product will be sold for $30 per unit. Exhibit 21.1 shows the expected annual net cash flows for this asset over its life as well as the expected annual revenues and expenses (including depreciation and income taxes) from investing in the machine.

### Decision Insight

**Telecom Decisions**   Profits of telecoms are dropping as too much capital investment chases too little revenue. Telecoms' success depends on keeping up with technology. Communications gear is evolving at a rate that is dizzying, even when compared to the computer industry. Consequently, managers of telecoms often demand short payback periods and large expected net cash flows to compensate for the investment risk.

**Exhibit 21.1**

Cash Flow Analysis

| FASTRAC Cash Flow Analysis—New Machinery January 15, 2005 | Expected Accrual Figures | Expected Net Cash Flows |
|---|---|---|
| Annual sales of new product | $30,000 | $30,000 |
| Deduct annual expenses | | |
| Cost of materials, labor, and overhead (except depr.) | 15,500 | 15,500 |
| Depreciation—Machinery | 2,000 | |
| Additional selling and administrative expenses | 9,500 | 9,500 |
| Annual pretax accrual income | 3,000 | |
| Income taxes (30%) | 900 | 900 |
| Annual net income | $ 2,100 | |
| **Annual net cash flow** | | **$ 4,100** |

The amount of net cash flow from the machinery is computed by subtracting expected cash outflows from expected cash inflows. The cash flows column of Exhibit 21.1 excludes all noncash revenues and expenses. Depreciation is FasTrac's, only noncash item. Alternatively,

**Point:** Annual net cash flow in Exhibit 21.1 equals net income plus depreciation (a noncash expense).

---

[1] *Even cash flows* refers to cash flows that are the same each and every year. *Uneven cash flows* refers to cash flows that are not all equal in amount.

managers can adjust the projected net income for revenue and expense items that do not affect cash flows. For FasTrac, this means taking the $2,100 net income and adding back the $2,000 depreciation.

The formula for computing the payback period of an investment that yields even net cash flows is in Exhibit 21.2.

## Exhibit 21.2

Payback Period Formula with Even Cash Flows

$$\text{Payback period} = \frac{\text{Cost of investment}}{\text{Annual net cash flow}}$$

The payback period reflects the amount of time for the investment to generate enough net cash flow to return (or pay back) the cash initially invested to purchase it. FasTrac's payback period for this machine is just under four years:

$$\text{Payback period} = \frac{\$16,000}{\$4,100} = 3.9 \text{ years}$$

**Example:** If an alternative machine (with different technology) yields a payback period of 3.5 years, which one do you choose? *Answer:* The alternative (3.5 is less than 3.9).

**Point:** To apply these concepts, work Exercise 21-1.

The initial investment is fully recovered in 3.9 years, or just before reaching the halfway point of this machine's useful life of eight years.

**Computing Payback Period with Uneven Cash Flows**  Computing the payback period in the prior section assumed even net cash flows. What happens if the net cash flows are uneven? In this case, the payback period is computed using the *cumulative total of net cash flows*. The word *cumulative* refers to the addition of each period's net cash flows as we progress through time. To illustrate, consider data for another investment that FasTrac is considering. This machine is predicted to generate uneven net cash flows over the next eight years. The relevant data and payback period computation are shown in Exhibit 21.3.

## Exhibit 21.3

Payback Period Calculation with Uneven Cash Flows

| Period* | Expected Net Cash Flows | Cumulative Net Cash Flows |
|---|---|---|
| Year 0 ......... | $(16,000) | $(16,000) |
| Year 1 ......... | 3,000 | (13,000) |
| Year 2 ......... | 4,000 | (9,000) |
| Year 3 ......... | 4,000 | (5,000) |
| Year 4 ......... | 4,000 | (1,000) |
| Year 5 ......... | 5,000 | 4,000 |
| Year 6 ......... | 3,000 | 7,000 |
| Year 7 ......... | 2,000 | 9,000 |
| Year 8 ......... | 2,000 | 11,000 |
| | | **Payback period = 4.2 years** |

\* All cash inflows and outflows occur uniformly during the year.

**Example:** Find the payback period in Exhibit 21.3 if net cash flows for the first 4 years are:
Year 1 = $6,000; Year 2 = $5,000;
Year 3 = $4,000; Year 4 = $3,000.
*Answer:* 3.33 years

Year 0 refers to the period of initial investment in which the $16,000 cash outflow occurs at the end of year 0 to acquire the machinery. By the end of year 1, the cumulative net cash flow is reduced to $(13,000), computed as the $(16,000) initial cash outflow plus year 1's $3,000 cash inflow. This process continues throughout the asset's life. The cumulative net cash flow amount changes from negative to positive in year 5. Specifically, at the end of year 4, the cumulative net cash flow is $(1,000). As soon as FasTrac receives net cash inflow of $1,000 during the fifth year, it has fully recovered the investment. If we assume that cash flows are received uniformly *within* each year, receipt of the $1,000 occurs about one-fifth of the way through the year. This is computed as $1,000 divided by year 5's total net cash flow of $5,000, or 0.20. This yields a payback period of 4.2 years, computed as 4 years plus 0.20 of year 5.

**Point:** To apply these concepts, work Exercise 21-2.

**Using the Payback Period**  Companies desire a short payback period to increase return and reduce risk. The more quickly a company receives cash, the sooner it is available for other uses and the less time it is at risk of loss. A shorter payback period also improves the company's ability to respond to unanticipated changes and lowers its risk of having to keep an unprofitable investment.

Payback period should never be the only consideration in evaluating investments. This is so because it ignores at least two important factors. First, it fails to reflect differences in the timing of net cash flows within the payback period. In Exhibit 21.3, FasTrac's net cash flows in the first five years were $3,000, $4,000, $4,000, $4,000, and $5,000. If another investment had predicted cash flows of $9,000, $3,000, $2,000, $1,800, and $1,000 in these five years, its payback period would also be 4.2 years, but this second alternative could be more desirable because it provides cash more quickly. The second important factor is that the payback period ignores *all* cash flows after the point where its costs are fully recovered. For example, one investment might pay back its cost in 3 years but stop producing cash after 4 years. A second investment might require 5 years to pay back its cost yet continue to produce net cash flows for another 15 years. A focus on only the payback period would mistakenly lead management to choose the first investment over the second.

**Point:** To apply these concepts, work QS 21-1.

## Quick Check

1. Capital budgeting is (a) concerned with analyzing alternative sources of capital, including debt and equity, (b) an important activity for companies when considering what assets to acquire or sell, or (c) best done by intuitive assessments of the value of assets and their usefulness.

2. Why are capital budgeting decisions often difficult?

3. A company is considering purchasing equipment costing $75,000. Future annual net cash flows from this equipment are $30,000, $25,000, $15,000, $10,000, and $5,000. The payback period is (a) 4 years, (b) 3.5 years, or (c) 3 years.

4. If depreciation is an expense, why is it added back to an investment's net income to compute the net cash flow from that investment?

5. If two investments have the same payback period, are they equally desirable? Explain.

Answers—p. 872

## Accounting Rate of Return

The **accounting rate of return,** also called *return on average investment,* is computed by dividing a project's after-tax net income by the average amount invested in it. To illustrate, we return to FasTrac's $16,000 machinery investment described in Exhibit 21.1. We first compute (1) the after-tax net income and (2) the average amount invested. The $2,100 after-tax net income is already available from Exhibit 21.1. To compute the average amount invested, we assume that net cash flows are received evenly throughout each year. Thus, the average investment for each year is computed as the average of its beginning and ending book values. If FasTrac's $16,000 machine is depreciated $2,000 each year, the average amount invested in the machine for each year is computed as shown in Exhibit 21.4. The average for any year is the average of the beginning and ending book values.

**P2**  Compute accounting rate of return and explain its use.

| | Beginning Book Value | Annual Depreciation | Ending Book Value | Average Book Value |
|---|---|---|---|---|
| Year 1 ....... | $16,000 | $2,000 | $14,000 | $15,000 |
| Year 2 ....... | 14,000 | 2,000 | 12,000 | 13,000 |
| Year 3 ....... | 12,000 | 2,000 | 10,000 | 11,000 |
| Year 4 ....... | 10,000 | 2,000 | 8,000 | 9,000 |
| Year 5 ....... | 8,000 | 2,000 | 6,000 | 7,000 |
| Year 6 ....... | 6,000 | 2,000 | 4,000 | 5,000 |
| Year 7 ....... | 4,000 | 2,000 | 2,000 | 3,000 |
| Year 8 ....... | 2,000 | 2,000 | 0 | 1,000 |
| Years 1—8 .................................................. | | | | **$ 8,000** |

**Exhibit 21.4**

Computing Average Amount Invested

Next we need the average book value for the asset's entire life. This amount is computed by taking the average of the individual yearly averages. This average equals $8,000, computed as $64,000 (the sum of the individual years' averages) divided by eight years (see last column of Exhibit 21.4).

**Point:** General formula for *annual average investment* is the sum of individual years' average book values divided by the number of years of the planned investment.

If a company uses straight-line depreciation, we can find the average amount invested by using the formula in Exhibit 21.5. Because FasTrac uses straight-line depreciation, its average amount invested for the eight years equals the sum of the book value at the beginning of the asset's investment period and the book value at the end of its investment period, divided by 2, as shown in Exhibit 21.5.

**Exhibit 21.5**

Computing Average Amount Invested under Straight-Line Depreciation

$$\text{Annual average investment} = \frac{\text{Beginning book value} + \text{Ending book value}}{2}$$
(straight-line case only)

$$= \frac{\$16{,}000 + \$0}{2} = \$8{,}000$$

Note that if an investment carries a salvage value, the average amount invested when using straight-line depreciation is computed as (Beginning book value + Salvage value)/2.

Once we determine the after-tax net income and the average amount invested, the accounting rate of return on the investment can be computed as Annual after-tax net income/ Average amount invested, as shown in Exhibit 21.6.

**Exhibit 21.6**

Accounting Rate of Return Formula

$$\text{Accounting rate of return} = \frac{\text{Annual after-tax net income}}{\text{Annual average investment}}$$

This yields an accounting rate of return of 26.25% ($2,100/$8,000). FasTrac management must decide whether a 26.25% accounting rate of return is satisfactory. To make this decision, we must factor in the investment's risk. For instance, we cannot say an investment with a 26.25% return is preferred over one with a lower return unless we recognize any differences in risk. Thus, an investment's return is satisfactory or unsatisfactory only when it is related to returns from other investments with similar lives and risk.

When accounting rate of return is used to choose among capital investments, the one with the least risk, the shortest payback period, and the highest return for the longest time period is often identified as the best. However, use of accounting rate of return to evaluate investment opportunities is limited because it bases the amount invested on book values (not predicted market values) in future periods. Accounting rate of return is also limited when an asset's net incomes are expected to vary from year to year. This requires computing the rate using *average* annual net incomes, yet this accounting rate of return fails to distinguish between two investments with the same average annual net income but different amounts of income in early years versus later years or different levels of income variability.

**Point:** To apply these concepts, work QS 21-4 and Exercise 21-4.

---

### Quick Check

**6.** The following data relate to a company's decision on whether to purchase a machine:

| | |
|---|---|
| Cost . . . . . . . . . . . . . . . . . . . . . . . . | $180,000 |
| Salvage value . . . . . . . . . . . . . . . . . . | 15,000 |
| Annual after-tax net income . . . . . . . | 40,000 |

The machine's accounting rate of return, assuming even receipt of its net cash flows during the year and use of straight-line depreciation, is (a) 22%, (b) 41%, or (c) 21%.

**7.** Is a 15% accounting rate of return for a machine a good rate?

Answers—p. 872

---

# Methods Using Time Value of Money

This section describes two methods that help managers with capital budgeting decisions and that use the time value of money: (1) net present value and (2) internal rate of return. *(To apply these methods, you need a basic understanding of the concept of present value. An*

*expanded explanation of present value concepts is in Appendix B near the end of the book.
You can use the present value tables at the end of Appendix B to solve many of this chapter's assignments that use the time value of money.)*

**P3** Compute net present value and describe its use.

Topic Tackler 21-1

## Net Present Value

Net present value analysis applies the time value of money to future cash inflows and cash outflows so management can evaluate a project's benefits and costs at one point in time. Specifically, **net present value (NPV)** is computed by discounting the future net cash flows from the investment at the project's required rate of return and then subtracting the initial amount invested.

To illustrate, let's return to FasTrac's proposed machinery purchase described in Exhibit 21.1. Does this machine provide a satisfactory return while recovering the amount invested? Recall that the machine requires a $16,000 investment and is expected to provide $4,100 annual net cash inflows for the next eight years. If we assume that net cash flows from this machine are received at each year-end and that FasTrac requires a 12% annual return, net present value can be computed as in Exhibit 21.7.

**Point:** The assumption of end-of-year cash flows simplifies computations and is common in practice.

| | Net Cash Flows* | Present Value of 1 at 12%† | Present Value of Net Cash Flows |
|---|---|---|---|
| Year 1 | $ 4,100 | 0.8929 | $ 3,661 |
| Year 2 | 4,100 | 0.7972 | 3,269 |
| Year 3 | 4,100 | 0.7118 | 2,918 |
| Year 4 | 4,100 | 0.6355 | 2,606 |
| Year 5 | 4,100 | 0.5674 | 2,326 |
| Year 6 | 4,100 | 0.5066 | 2,077 |
| Year 7 | 4,100 | 0.4523 | 1,854 |
| Year 8 | 4,100 | 0.4039 | 1,656 |
| Totals | $32,800 | | $20,367 |
| Amount invested | | | (16,000) |
| Net present value | | | $ 4,367 |

### Exhibit 21.7
Net Present Value Calculation with Equal Cash Flows

\* Cash flows occur at the end of each year.

† Present value of 1 factors are taken from Table B.1 in Appendix B.

The first number column of Exhibit 21.7 shows the annual net cash flows. Present value of 1 factors, also called *discount factors,* are shown in the second column. Taken from Table B.1 in Appendix B, they assume that net cash flows are received at each year-end. *(To simplify present value computations and for assignment material at the end of this chapter, we assume that net cash flows are received at each year-end.)* Annual net cash flows from the first column of Exhibit 21.7 are multiplied by the discount factors in the second column to give present values shown in the third column. The last three lines of this exhibit show the final NPV computations. The asset's $16,000 initial cost is deducted from the $20,367 total present value of all future net cash flows to give this asset's NPV of $4,367. The machine is thus expected to (1) recover its cost, (2) provide a 12% compounded return, and (3) generate $4,367 above cost. We summarize this analysis by saying the present value of this machine's future net cash flows to FasTrac exceeds the $16,000 investment by $4,367.

**Point:** The amount invested includes all costs that must be incurred to get the asset in its proper location and ready for use.

**Example:** What is the net present value in Exhibit 21.7 if a 10% return is applied? *Answer:* $5,873

**Net Present Value Decision Rule**  The decision rule in applying NPV is as follows: When an asset's expected cash flows are discounted at the required rate and yield a *positive* net present value, the asset should be acquired. This decision rule is reflected in the graphic at the right. When comparing several investment opportunities of about the same cost and same risk, we prefer the one with the highest positive net present value.

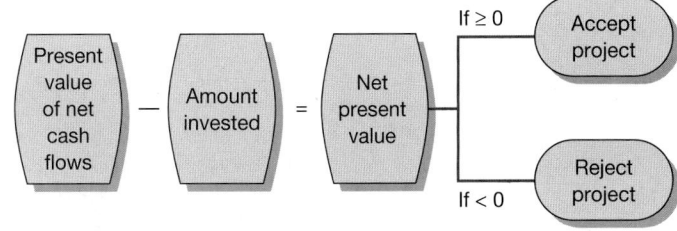

**Example:** Why does the net present value of an investment increase when a lower discount rate is used? *Answer:* Time value of money.

### Decision Ethics

**Systems Manager**    Top management recently adopted a new policy requiring all proposals for purchases in excess of $5,000 to be submitted with cash flow predictions to the financial analysis group for capital budget analysis and approval. As systems manager, you want to upgrade your department's computers at a $25,000 cost. You are considering submitting several orders all under $5,000 to avoid the proposal process. You believe the computers will increase profits and wish to avoid a delay. What do you do?

Answer—p. 872

**Point:** To apply these concepts, work Exercise 21-7.

**Simplifying Computations**    The computations in Exhibit 21.7 use separate present value of 1 factors for each of the eight years. Each year's net cash flow is multiplied by its present value of 1 factor to determine its present value. The individual present values for each of the eight net cash flows are added to give the asset's total present value. This computation can be simplified in two ways if annual net cash flows are equal in amount. One way is to add the eight annual present value of 1 factors for a total of 4.9676 and multiply this amount by the annual $4,100 net cash flow to get the $20,367 total present value of net cash flows.[2] A second simplification is to use a calculator with compound interest functions or a spreadsheet program. Whatever procedure you use, it is important to understand the concepts behind these computations.

**Uneven Cash Flows**    Net present value analysis can also be applied when net cash flows are uneven (unequal). To illustrate, assume that FasTrac can choose only one capital investment from among projects A, B, and C. Each project requires the same $12,000 initial investment. Future net cash flows for each project are shown in the first three number columns of Exhibit 21.8.

## Exhibit 21.8

Net Present Value Calculation with Uneven Cash Flows

| | Net Cash Flows | | | Present Value of 1 at 10% | Present Value of Net Cash Flows | | |
|---|---|---|---|---|---|---|---|
| | **A** | **B** | **C** | | **A** | **B** | **C** |
| Year 1 .............. | $ 5,000 | $ 8,000 | $ 1,000 | 0.9091 | $ 4,546 | $ 7,273 | $   909 |
| Year 2 .............. | 5,000 | 5,000 | 5,000 | 0.8264 | 4,132 | 4,132 | 4,132 |
| Year 3 .............. | 5,000 | 2,000 | 9,000 | 0.7513 | 3,757 | 1,503 | 6,762 |
| Totals .............. | $15,000 | $15,000 | $15,000 | | 12,435 | 12,908 | 11,803 |
| Amount invested ...... | | | | | (12,000) | (12,000) | (12,000) |
| **Net present value**  ... | | | | | **$   435** | **$   908** | **$ (197)** |

**Example:** If 12% is the required return in Exhibit 21.8, which project is preferred? *Answer:* Project B. Net present values are: A = $10; B = $553; C = $(715).

**Example:** Will the rankings of Projects A, B, and C change with the use of different discount rates, assuming the same rate is used for all projects? *Answer:* No; only the NPV amounts will change.

**Point:** Projects with higher cash flows in earlier years generally yield higher net present values.

The three projects in Exhibit 21.8 have the same expected total net cash flows of $15,000. Project A is expected to produce equal amounts of $5,000 each year. Project B is expected to produce a larger amount in the first year. Project C is expected to produce a larger amount in the third year. The fourth column of Exhibit 21.8 shows the present value of 1 factors from Table B.1 assuming 10% required return.

Computations in the right-most columns show that Project A has a $435 positive NPV. Project B has the largest NPV of $908 because it brings in cash more quickly. Project C has a $(197) *negative* NPV because its larger cash inflows are delayed. If FasTrac requires a 10% return, it should reject Project C because its NPV implies a return *under* 10%. If only one project can be accepted, project B appears best because it yields the highest NPV.

**Salvage Value and Accelerated Depreciation**    FasTrac predicted the $16,000 machine to have zero salvage value at the end of its useful life (recall Exhibit 21.1). In many

---

[2] We can simplify this computation even further using Table B.3, which gives the present value of 1 to be received periodically for a number of periods. To determine the present value of these eight annual receipts discounted at 12%, go down the 12% column of Table B.3 to the factor on the eighth line. This cumulative discount factor, also known as an *annuity* factor, is 4.9676. We then compute the $20,367 present value for these eight annual $4,100 receipts, computed as 4.9676 × $4,100.

cases, assets are expected to have salvage values. If so, this amount is an additional net cash inflow received at the end of the final year of the asset's life. All other computations remain the same.

Depreciation computations also affect net present value analysis. FasTrac computes depreciation using the straight-line method. Accelerated depreciation is also commonly used, especially for income tax reports. Accelerated depreciation produces larger depreciation deductions in the early years of an asset's life and smaller deductions in later years. This pattern results in smaller income tax payments in early years and larger payments in later years. Accelerated depreciation does not change the basics of a present value analysis, but it can change the result. Using accelerated depreciation for tax reporting affects the NPV of an asset's cash flows because it produces larger net cash inflows in the early years of the asset's life and smaller ones in later years. Being able to use accelerated depreciation for tax reporting always makes an investment more desirable because early cash flows are more valuable than later ones.

**Example:** When is it appropriate to use different discount rates for different projects? *Answer:* When risk levels are different.

**Use of Net Present Value** In deciding whether to proceed with a capital investment project, we approve the proposal if the NPV is positive but reject it if the NPV is negative. When considering several projects of similar investment amounts and risk levels, we can compare the different projects' NPVs and rank them on the basis of their NPVs. However, if the amount invested differs substantially across projects, the NPV is of limited value for comparison purposes. To illustrate, suppose that Project X requires a $1 million investment and provides a $100,000 NPV. Project Y requires an investment of only $100,000 and returns a $75,000 NPV. Ranking on the basis of NPV puts Project X ahead of Y, yet X's NPV is only 10% of the initial investment whereas Y's NPV is 75% of its investment. We must also remember that when reviewing projects with different risks, we computed the NPV of individual projects using different discount rates. The higher the risk, the higher the discount rate.

## Internal Rate of Return

Another means to evaluate capital investments is to use the **internal rate of return,** which equals the rate that yields an NPV of zero for an investment. This means that if we compute the total present value of a project's net cash flows using the IRR as the discount rate and then subtract the initial investment from this total present value, we get a zero NPV.

To illustrate, we use the data for FasTrac's Project A from Exhibit 21.8 to compute its IRR. Exhibit 21.9 shows the two-step process in computing IRR.

**P4** Compute internal rate of return and explain its use.

**Step 1:** Compute the present value factor for the investment project.

$$\text{Present value factor} = \frac{\textbf{Amount invested}}{\textbf{Net cash flows}} = \frac{\$12,000}{\$5,000} = 2.4000$$

**Step 2: Identify the discount rate (IRR) yielding the present value factor**

Search Table B.3 for a present value factor of 2.4000 in the three-year row (equaling the 3-year project duration). The 12% discount rate yields a present value factor of 2.4018. This implies that the IRR is approximately 12%.*

Exhibit 21.9

Computing Internal Rate of Return (with even cash flows)

\* Since the present value factor of 2.4000 is not exactly equal to the 12% factor of 2.4018, we can more precisely estimate the IRR as follows:

| Discount rate | Present Value Factor from Table B.3 |
|---|---|
| 12% | 2.4018 |
| 15% | 2.2832 |
| | 0.1186 = difference |

$$\text{Then, IRR} = 12\% + \left[ (15\% - 12\%) \times \frac{2.4018 - 2.4000}{0.1186} \right] = \underline{\underline{12.05\%}}$$

When cash flows are equal, as with Project A, we compute the present value factor (as shown in Exhibit 21.9) by dividing the initial investment by its annual net cash flows. We then use an annuity table to determine the discount rate equal to this present value factor. For FasTrac's Project A, we look across the three-period row of Table B.3 and find that the discount rate corresponding to the present value factor of 2.4000 roughly equals the 2.4018 value for the 12% rate. This row is reproduced here:

*Present Value of an Annuity of 1 for Three Periods*

| | Rate | | | | |
|---|---|---|---|---|---|
| Periods | 1% | 5% | 10% | 12% | 15% |
| 3 .......... | 2.9410 | 2.7232 | 2.4869 | 2.4018 | 2.2832 |

The 12% rate is the Project's IRR. A more precise IRR estimate can be computed following the procedure shown in the note to Exhibit 21.9. Spreadsheet software and calculators can also compute this IRR.

**Decision Insight**

**Fun-IRR**  Many theme parks use both financial and nonfinancial criteria to evaluate their investments in new rides and activities. The use of IRR is a major part of this evaluation. This requires good estimates of future cash inflows and outflows. It also requires risk assessments of the uncertainty of the future cash flows.

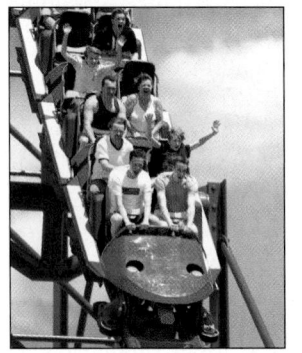

**Uneven Cash Flows**  If net cash flows are uneven, we must use trial and error to compute the IRR. We do this by selecting any reasonable discount rate and computing the NPV. If the amount is positive (negative), we recompute the NPV using a higher (lower) discount rate. We continue these steps until we reach a point where two consecutive computations result in NPVs having different signs (positive and negative). Because the NPV is zero using IRR, we know that the IRR lies between these two discount rates. We can then estimate its value. Spreadsheet programs and calculators can do these computations for us.

**C2** Describe the selection of a hurdle rate for an investment.

**Use of Internal Rate of Return**  When we use the IRR to evaluate a project, we compare it to a predetermined **hurdle rate,** which is a minimum acceptable rate of return and is applied as follows:

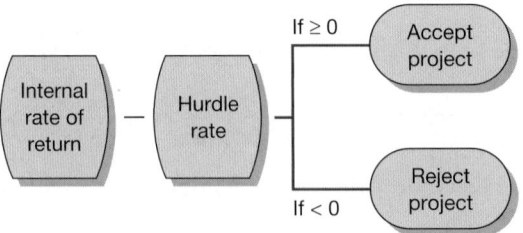

**Example:** How can management evaluate the risk of an investment? *Answer:* It must assess the uncertainty of future cash flows.

**Point:** To apply these concepts, work Exercise 21-7.

Top management selects the hurdle rate to use in evaluating capital investments. Financial formulas aid in this selection, but the choice of a minimum rate is subjective and left to management. For projects financed from borrowed funds, the hurdle rate must exceed the interest rate paid on these funds. The return on an investment must cover its interest and provide an additional profit to reward the company for its risk. For instance, if money is borrowed at 10%, an average risk investment often requires an after-tax return of 15% (or 5% above the borrowing rate). Remember that lower-risk investments require a lower rate of return compared with higher-risk investments.

If the project is internally financed, the hurdle rate is often based on actual returns from comparable projects. If the IRR is higher than the hurdle rate, the project is accepted. Multiple projects are often ranked by the extent to which their IRR exceeds the hurdle rate. The hurdle rate for individual projects is often different, depending on the risk involved. IRR is not subject to the limitations of NPV when comparing projects with different amounts invested because the IRR is expressed as a percent rather than as an absolute dollar value in NPV.

## Decision Maker

**Entrepreneur** For a new product being developed, you use a 12% discount rate to compute its NPV. Your banker, with whom you share your analysis, expresses concern that your discount rate is too low. How do you respond?

Answer—p. 872

## Comparison of Capital Budgeting Methods

We explained four methods that managers use to evaluate capital investment projects. How do these methods compare with each other? Exhibit 21.10 addresses that question. Note that neither the payback period nor the accounting rate of return considers the time value of money. On the other hand, both the net present value and the internal rate of return do.

### Exhibit 21.10

Comparing Capital Budgeting Methods

| | Payback Period | Accounting Rate of Return | Net Present Value | Internal Rate of Return |
|---|---|---|---|---|
| **Measurement basis** | ■ Cash flows | ■ Accrual income | ■ Cash flows<br>■ Profitability | ■ Cash flows<br>■ Profitability |
| **Measurement unit** | ■ Years | ■ Percent | ■ Dollars | ■ Percent |
| **Strengths** | ■ Easy to understand | ■ Easy to understand | ■ Reflects time value of money | ■ Reflects time value of money |
| | ■ Allows comparison of projects | ■ Allows comparison of projects | ■ Reflects varying risks over project's life | ■ Allows comparisons of dissimilar projects |
| **Limitations** | ■ Ignores time value of money | ■ Ignores time value of money | ■ Difficult to compare dissimilar projects | ■ Ignores varying risks over life of project |
| | ■ Ignores cash flows after payback period | ■ Ignores annual rates over life of project | | |

The payback period is probably the simplest method. It gives managers an estimate of how soon they will recover their initial investment. Managers sometimes use this method when they have limited cash to invest and a number of projects to choose from. The accounting rate of return yields a percent measure computed using accrual income instead of cash flows. The accounting rate of return is an average rate for the entire investment period. Net present value considers all estimated net cash flows for the project's expected life. It can be applied to even and uneven cash flows and can reflect changes in the level of risk over a project's life. Since it yields a dollar measure, comparing projects of unequal sizes is more difficult. The internal rate of return considers all cash flows from a project. It is readily computed when the cash flows are even but requires some trial and error estimation when cash flows are uneven. Because the IRR is a percent measure, it is readily used to compare projects with different investment amounts. However, IRR does not reflect changes in risk over a project's life.

## Decision Insight

### And the Winner Is . . .

How do we choose among the methods for evaluating capital investments? Management surveys consistently show the internal rate of return (IRR) as the most popular method followed by the payback period and net present value (NPV). Few companies use the accounting rate of return (ARR), but nearly all use more than one method.

### Quick Check

8. A company can invest in only one of two projects, A or B. Each project requires a $20,000 investment and is expected to generate end-of-period, annual cash flows as follows:

|  | Year 1 | Year 2 | Year 3 | Total |
|---|---|---|---|---|
| Project A ......... | $12,000 | $8,500 | $4,000 | $24,500 |
| Project B ......... | 4,500 | 8,500 | 13,000 | 26,000 |

Assuming a discount rate of 10%, which project has the higher net present value?

9. Two investment alternatives are expected to generate annual cash flows with the same net present value (assuming the same discount rate applied to each). Using this information, can you conclude that the two alternatives are equally desirable?

10. When two investment alternatives have the same total expected cash flows but differ in the timing of those flows, which method of evaluating those investments is superior, (a) accounting rate of return or (b) net present value?

Answers—p. 872

# Section 2—Managerial Decisions

This section focuses on the use of accounting information to make several important managerial decisions. It emphasizes the use of quantitative measures to help managers make business decisions. Most of these involve short-term decisions. Methods for long-term managerial decisions are described in the first section of this chapter and in several other chapters of this book.

## Decisions and Information

This section explains how managers make decisions and the information relevant to these decisions.

### Decision Making

Managerial decision making involves five steps: (1) define the decision task, (2) identify alternative courses of action, (3) collect relevant information and evaluate each alternative, (4) select the preferred course of action, and (5) analyze and assess decisions made. These five steps are illustrated in Exhibit 21.11.

**Exhibit 21.11**

Managerial Decision Making

| Define Task and Goal | Identify Alternative Actions | Collect Relevant Information | Select Course of Action | Analyze and Assess Decision |

Both managerial and financial accounting information play an important role in most management decisions. The accounting system is expected to provide primarily *financial* information such as performance reports and budget analyses for decision making. *Nonfinancial* information is also relevant, however; it includes information on environmental effects, political sensitivities, and social responsibility.

# Relevant Costs

Most financial measures of revenues and costs from cost accounting systems are based on historical costs. Although historical costs are important and useful for many tasks such as product pricing and the control and monitoring of business activities, we sometimes find that an analysis of *relevant costs,* or *avoidable costs,* is especially useful for certain managerial decisions. Three types of costs are pertinent to our discussion of relevant costs: sunk costs, out-of-pocket costs, and opportunity costs.

A *sunk cost* arises from a past decision and cannot be avoided or changed; it is irrelevant to future decisions. An example is the cost of computer equipment previously purchased by a company. Most of a company's allocated costs, including fixed overhead items such as depreciation and administrative expenses, are sunk costs.

An *out-of-pocket cost* requires a future outlay of cash and is relevant for current and future decision making. These costs are usually the direct result of management's decisions. For instance, future purchases of computer equipment involve out-of-pocket costs.

An *opportunity cost* is the potential benefit lost by taking a specific action when two or more alternative choices are available. An example is a student giving up wages from a job to attend summer school. Companies continually must choose from alternative courses of action. For instance, a company making standardized products might be approached by a customer to supply a special (nonstandard) product. A decision to accept or reject the special order must consider not only the profit to be made from the special order but also the profit given up by devoting time and resources to this order instead of pursuing an alternative project. The profit given up is an opportunity cost. Consideration of opportunity costs is important. The implications extend to internal resource allocation decisions. For instance, a computer manufacturer must decide between internally manufacturing a chip versus buying it externally. In another case, management of a multidivisional company must decide whether to continue operating or close a particular division.

Besides relevant costs, management must also consider the relevant benefits associated with a decision. **Relevant benefits** refer to the additional or *incremental* revenue generated by selecting a particular course of action over another. For instance, a student must decide the relevant benefits of taking one course over another. In sum, both relevant costs and relevant benefits are crucial to managerial decision making.

**C3** Describe the importance of relevant costs for short-term decisions.

**Example:** Depreciation and amortization are allocations of the original cost of plant and intangible assets. Are they out-of-pocket costs? *Answer:* No; they are sunk costs.

**Point:** Opportunity costs are not entered in accounting records. This does not reduce their relevance for managerial decisions.

# Managerial Decision Scenarios

Managers experience many different scenarios that require analyzing alternative actions and making a decision. We describe several different types of decision scenarios in this section. We set these tasks in the context of FasTrac, the exercise supplies and equipment manufacturer introduced earlier. *We treat each of these decision tasks as separate from each other.*

## Additional Business

FasTrac is operating at its normal level of 80% of full capacity. At this level, it produces and sells approximately 100,000 units of product annually. Its per unit and annual total costs are shown in Exhibit 21.12.

**A1** Evaluate short-term managerial decisions using relevant costs.

## Exhibit 21.12

Selected Operating Income Data

| | Per Unit | Annual Total |
|---|---|---|
| Sales (100,000 units) . . . . . . . . . . . | $10.00 | $1,000,000 |
| Direct materials . . . . . . . . . . . . . . | (3.50) | (350,000) |
| Direct labor . . . . . . . . . . . . . . . . | (2.20) | (220,000) |
| Overhead . . . . . . . . . . . . . . . . . . | (1.10) | (110,000) |
| Selling expenses . . . . . . . . . . . . . . | (1.40) | (140,000) |
| Administrative expenses . . . . . . . . | (0.80) | (80,000) |
| Total costs and expenses . . . . . . . | (9.00) | (900,000) |
| Operating income . . . . . . . . . . . | $ 1.00 | $ 100,000 |

A current buyer of FasTrac's products wants to purchase additional units of its product and export them to another country. This buyer offers to buy 10,000 units of the product at $8.50 per unit, or $1.50 less than the current price. The offer price is low, but FasTrac is considering the proposal because this sale would be several times larger than any single previous sale. Also, the units will be exported, so this new business will not affect current sales.

To determine whether to accept or reject this order, management needs to know whether accepting the offer will increase net income. The analysis in Exhibit 21.13 shows that if management relies on per unit historical costs, it would reject the sale because it yields a loss. However, historical costs are *not* relevant to this decision. Instead, the relevant costs are the additional costs called **incremental costs.** These costs, also called *differential costs,* are the additional costs incurred if a company pursues a certain course of action. FasTrac's incremental costs are those related to the added volume that this new order would bring.

**Exhibit 21.13**

Analysis of Additional Business Using Historical Costs

| | Per Unit | Total |
|---|---|---|
| Sales (10,000 additional units) | $ 8.50 | $ 85,000 |
| Direct materials | (3.50) | (35,000) |
| Direct labor | (2.20) | (22,000) |
| Overhead | (1.10) | (11,000) |
| Selling expenses | (1.40) | (14,000) |
| Administrative expenses | (0.80) | (8,000) |
| Total costs and expenses | (9.00) | (90,000) |
| Operating loss | $(0.50) | $ (5,000) |

To make its decision, FasTrac must analyze the costs of this new business in a different manner. The following information regarding the order is available:

- Manufacturing 10,000 additional units requires direct materials of $3.50 per unit and direct labor of $2.20 per unit (same as for all other units).
- Manufacturing 10,000 additional units adds $5,000 of incremental overhead costs for power, packaging, and indirect labor (all variable costs).
- Incremental commissions and selling expenses from this sale of 10,000 additional units would be $2,000 (all variable costs).
- Incremental administrative expenses of $1,000 for clerical efforts are needed (all fixed costs) with the sale of 10,000 additional units.

We use this information, as shown in Exhibit 21.14, to assess how accepting this new business will affect FasTrac's income.

**Exhibit 21.14**

Analysis of Additional Business Using Relevant Costs

| | Current Business | Additional Business | Combined |
|---|---|---|---|
| Sales | $1,000,000 | $ 85,000 | $1,085,000 |
| Direct materials | (350,000) | (35,000) | (385,000) |
| Direct labor | (220,000) | (22,000) | (242,000) |
| Overhead | (110,000) | (5,000) | (115,000) |
| Selling expenses | (140,000) | (2,000) | (142,000) |
| Administrative expense | (80,000) | (1,000) | (81,000) |
| Total costs and expenses | (900,000) | (65,000) | (965,000) |
| Operating income | $ 100,000 | $ 20,000 | $ 120,000 |

**Example:** Exhibit 21.14 uses quantitative information. Suggest some qualitative factors to be considered when deciding whether to accept this project. *Answer:* (1) Impact on relationships with other customers and (2) Improved relationship with customer buying additional units.

The analysis of relevant costs in Exhibit 21.14 suggests that the additional business be accepted. It would provide $85,000 of added revenue while incurring only $65,000 of added costs. This would yield $20,000 of additional pretax income, or a pretax profit margin of 23.5%. More generally, FasTrac would increase its income with any price that exceeded $6.50 per unit ($65,000 incremental cost/10,000 additional units).

An analysis of the incremental costs pertaining to the additional volume is always relevant for this type of decision. We must proceed cautiously, however, when the additional volume approaches or exceeds the factory's existing available capacity. If the additional volume requires the company to expand its capacity by obtaining more equipment, more space, or more personnel, the incremental costs could quickly exceed the incremental revenue. Another cautionary note is the effect on existing sales. All new units of the extra business will be sold outside FasTrac's normal domestic sales channels. If accepting additional business would cause existing sales to decline, this information must be included in our analysis. The contribution margin lost from a decline in sales is an opportunity cost. If future cash flows over several time periods are affected, their net present value also must be computed and used in this analysis.

**Point:** To apply these concepts, work Exercise 21-8.

The key point is that management must not blindly use historical costs, especially allocated overhead costs. Instead, the accounting system needs to provide information about the incremental costs to be incurred if the additional business is accepted.

> ### Decision Maker
>
> **Partner**  You are a partner in a small accounting firm that specializes in keeping the books and preparing taxes for clients such as doctors and lawyers. A local restaurant is interested in obtaining these services from your firm. Identify factors that are relevant in deciding whether to accept the engagement.

Answer—p. 872

## Make or Buy

The managerial decision to make or buy a component for one of its current products is commonplace and depends on incremental costs. To illustrate, FasTrac has excess productive capacity it can use to manufacture Part 417, a component of the main product it sells. The part is currently purchased and delivered to the plant at a cost of $1.20 per unit. FasTrac estimates that making Part 417 would cost $0.45 for direct materials, $0.50 for direct labor, and an undetermined amount for overhead. The task is to determine how much overhead to add to these costs so we can decide whether to make or buy Part 417. If FasTrac's normal predetermined overhead application rate is 100% of direct labor cost, we might be tempted to conclude that overhead cost is $0.50 per unit, computed as 100% of the $0.50 direct labor cost. We would then mistakenly conclude that total cost is $1.45 ($0.45 of materials + $0.50 of labor + $0.50 of overhead). A wrong decision in this case would be to conclude that the company is better off buying the part at $1.20 each than making it for $1.45 each.

Topic Tackler 21-2

Instead, as we explained earlier, only incremental overhead costs are relevant in this situation. Thus, we must compute an *incremental overhead rate.* Incremental overhead costs might include, for example, additional power for operating machines, extra supplies, added cleanup costs, materials handling, and quality control. We can prepare a per unit analysis in this case as shown in Exhibit 21.15.

We can see that if incremental overhead costs are less than $0.25 per unit, the total cost of making the component is less than the purchase price of $1.20 and FasTrac should make the part. FasTrac's decision rule in this case is that any amount of overhead less than $0.25 per unit yields a total cost for Part 417 that is less than the $1.20 purchase price. FasTrac must consider sev-

| | Make | Buy |
|---|---|---|
| Direct materials ......... | $0.45 | — |
| Direct labor ........... | 0.50 | — |
| **Overhead costs** ....... | [?] | — |
| Purchase price ......... | — | $1.20 |
| **Total incremental costs** .. | **$0.95 + [?]** | **$1.20** |

### Exhibit 21.15

Make or Buy Analysis

eral factors in the make or buy decision, including product quality, timeliness of delivery (especially in a just-in-time setting), reactions of customers and suppliers, and other intangibles such as employee morale and workload. It must also consider whether making the part requires incremental fixed costs to expand plant capacity. When these added factors are considered, small cost differences may not matter.

**Point:** To apply these concepts, work QS 21-6.

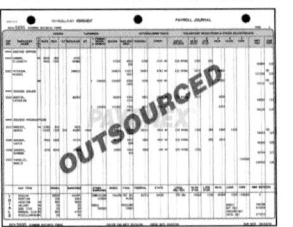

## Scrap or Rework

Managers often must make a decision on whether to scrap or rework products in process. Remember that costs already incurred in manufacturing the units of a product that do not meet quality standards are sunk costs that have been incurred and cannot be changed. Sunk costs are irrelevant in any decision on whether to sell the substandard units as scrap or to rework them to meet quality standards.

To illustrate, assume that FasTrac has 10,000 defective units of a product that have already cost $1 per unit to manufacture. These units can be sold as is (as scrap) for $0.40 each, or they can be reworked for $0.80 per unit and then sold for their full price of $1.50 each. Should FasTrac sell the units as scrap or rework them?

To make this decision, management must recognize that the already incurred manufacturing costs of $1 per unit are sunk (unavoidable). These costs are *entirely irrelevant* to the decision. In addition, we must be certain that all costs of reworking defects, including interfering with normal operations, are accounted for in our analysis. For instance, reworking the defects means that FasTrac is unable to manufacture 10,000 *new* units with an incremental cost of $1 per unit and a selling price of $1.50 per unit, meaning it incurs an opportunity cost equal to the lost $5,000 net return from making and selling 10,000 new units. This opportunity cost is the difference between the $15,000 revenue (10,000 units × $1.50) from selling these new units and their $10,000 manufacturing costs (10,000 units × $1). Our analysis is reflected in Exhibit 21.16.

**Exhibit 21.16**

Scrap or Rework Analysis

| | Scrap | Rework |
|---|---|---|
| Sale of scrapped/reworked units | $ 4,000 | $ 15,000 |
| Less costs to rework defects | | (8,000) |
| **Less opportunity cost of not making new units** | | **(5,000)** |
| **Incremental net income** | **$4,000** | **$ 2,000** |

The analysis yields a $2,000 difference in favor of scrapping the defects, yielding a total incremental net income of $4,000. If we had failed to include the opportunity costs of $5,000, the rework option would have shown an income of $7,000 instead of $2,000, mistakenly making the reworking appear more favorable than scrapping.

**Quick Check**

11. A company receives a special order for 200 units that requires stamping the buyer's name on each unit, yielding an additional fixed cost of $400 to its normal costs. Without the order, the company is operating at 75% of capacity and produces 7,500 units of product at the following costs:

| | |
|---|---|
| Direct materials | $37,500 |
| Direct labor | 60,000 |
| Overhead (30% variable) | 20,000 |
| Selling expenses (60% variable) | 25,000 |

The special order will not affect normal unit sales and will not increase fixed overhead and selling expenses. Variable selling expenses on the special order are reduced to one-half the normal amount. The price per unit necessary to earn $1,000 on this order is (*a*) $14.80, (*b*) $15.80, (*c*) $19.80, (*d*) $20.80, or (*e*) $21.80.

12. What are the incremental costs of accepting additional business?

## Sell or Process

The managerial decision to sell partially completed products as is or to process them further for sale depends significantly on relevant costs. To illustrate, suppose that FasTrac has 40,000 units of partially finished Product Q. It has already spent $0.75 per unit to manufacture these 40,000 units

| Product | Price | Units | Revenues |
|---|---|---|---|
| Product X . . . . . | $4.00 | 10,000 | $ 40,000 |
| Product Y . . . . . | 6.00 | 22,000 | 132,000 |
| Product Z . . . . . | 8.00 | 6,000 | 48,000 |
| Spoilage . . . . . . . | — | 2,000 | 0 |
| Totals . . . . . . . . | | 40,000 | $220,000 |

*Exhibit 21.17*

Revenues from Processing Further

at a $30,000 total cost. FasTrac can sell the 40,000 units to another manufacturer as raw material for $50,000. Alternatively, it can process them further and produce finished products X, Y, and Z at an incremental cost of $2 per unit. The added processing yields the products and revenues shown in Exhibit 21.17. FasTrac must decide whether the added revenues from selling finished products X, Y, and Z exceed the costs of finishing them.

**Point:** To apply these concepts, work Exercise 21-10.

Exhibit 21.18 shows the two-step analysis for this decision. First, FasTrac computes its incremental revenue from further processing Q into products X, Y, and Z. This amount is the difference between the $220,000 revenue from the further processed products and the $50,000 FasTrac will give up by not selling Q as is (a $50,000 opportunity cost). Second,

| | |
|---|---|
| Revenue if processed . . . . . . . . . . | $220,000 |
| Revenue if sold as is . . . . . . . . . . . | (50,000) |
| Incremental revenue . . . . . . . . . . . | 170,000 |
| Cost if processed . . . . . . . . . . . . . | (80,000) |
| **Incremental net income** . . . . . . . | **$ 90,000** |

*Exhibit 21.18*

Sell or Process Analysis

FasTrac computes its incremental costs from further processing Q into X, Y, and Z. This amount is $80,000 (40,000 units × $2 incremental cost). The analysis shows that FasTrac can earn incremental net income of $90,000 from a decision to further process Q. (Notice that the earlier incurred $30,000 manufacturing cost for the 40,000 units of Product Q does not appear in Exhibit 21.18 because it is a sunk cost and as such is irrelevant to the decision.)

**Example:** Does the decision change if incremental costs in Exhibit 21.18 increase to $4 per unit and the opportunity cost increases to $95,000? *Answer:* Yes. There is now an incremental net loss of $35,000.

## Quick Check

13. A company has already incurred a $1,000 cost in partially producing its four products. Their selling prices when partially and fully processed follow with additional costs necessary to finish these partially processed units:

| Product | Unfinished Selling Price | Finished Selling Price | Further Processing Costs |
|---|---|---|---|
| Alpha . . . . . . . . . . . | $300 | $600 | $150 |
| Beta . . . . . . . . . . . . | 450 | 900 | 300 |
| Gamma . . . . . . . . . | 275 | 425 | 125 |
| Delta . . . . . . . . . . . | 150 | 210 | 75 |

Which product(s) should *not* be processed further, (a) Alpha, (b) Beta, (c) Gamma, or (d) Delta?

14. Under what conditions is a sunk cost relevant to decision making?

Answers—p. 872

## Sales Mix Selection

When a company sells a mix of products, some are likely to be more profitable than others. Management is often wise to concentrate sales efforts on more profitable products. If production facilities or other factors are limited, an increase in the production and sale of one product usually requires reducing the production and sale of others. In this case, management must identify the most profitable combination, or *sales mix* of products. To identify the best sales mix, management must know the contribution

### Decision Insight

The **Estee Lauder Companies** must continuously monitor and manage the sales mix of its enormous product list. Selling its products in more than 130 countries and territories further complicates this decision process. The contribution margin of each product is crucial to its product mix strategy.

margin of each product, the facilities required to produce each product, any constraints on these facilities, and its markets.

To illustrate, assume that FasTrac makes and sells two products, A and B. The same machines are used to produce both products. A and B have the following selling prices and variable costs per unit:

| | Product A | Product B |
|---|---|---|
| Selling price per unit . . . . . . . . . . . . . . | $5.00 | $7.50 |
| Variable costs per unit . . . . . . . . . . . . | 3.50 | 5.50 |
| Contribution margin per unit . . . . . . . | $1.50 | $2.00 |

The variable costs are included in the analysis because they are the incremental costs of producing these products within the existing capacity of 100,000 machine hours per month. We consider three separate cases.

*Case 1:* Assume that (1) each product requires 1 machine hour per unit for production and (2) the markets for these products are unlimited. Under these conditions, FasTrac should produce as much of Product B as it can because of its larger contribution margin of $2 per unit. At full capacity, FasTrac would produce $200,000 of total contribution margin per month, computed as $2 per unit times 100,000 machine hours.

*Case 2:* Assume that (1) Product A requires 1 machine hour per unit, (2) Product B requires 2 machine hours per unit, and (3) the markets for these products are unlimited. Under these conditions, FasTrac should produce as much of Product A as it can because it has a contribution margin of $1.50 per machine hour compared with only $1 per machine hour for Product B. Exhibit 21.19 shows the relevant analysis.

## Exhibit 21.19

Sales Mix Analysis

| | Product A | Product B |
|---|---|---|
| Selling price per unit . . . . . . . . . . . . . . . . . . . . . . . | $5.00 | $7.50 |
| Variable costs per unit . . . . . . . . . . . . . . . . . . . . . | 3.50 | 5.50 |
| Contribution margin per unit . . . . . . . . . . . . . . . . | $1.50 | $2.00 |
| Machine hours per unit . . . . . . . . . . . . . . . . . . . . . | 1.0 | 2.0 |
| **Contribution margin per machine hour** . . . . . . . | **$1.50** | **$1.00** |

At its full capacity of 100,000 machine hours, FasTrac would produce 100,000 units of Product A, yielding $150,000 of total contribution margin per month. In contrast, if it uses all 100,000 hours to produce Product B, only 50,000 units would be produced yielding a contribution margin of $100,000. These results suggest that when a company faces excess demand and limited capacity, only the most profitable product per input should be manufactured.

*Case 3:* The need for a mix of different products arises when market demand is not sufficient to allow a company to sell all that it produces. For instance, assume that (1) Product A requires 1 machine hour per unit, (2) Product B requires 2 machine hours per unit, and (3) the market for Product A is limited to 80,000 units. Under these conditions, FasTrac should produce no more than 80,000 units of Product A. This would leave another 20,000 machine hours of capacity for making Product B. FasTrac should use this spare capacity to produce 10,000 units of Product B. This sales mix would maximize FasTrac's total contribution margin per month at an amount of $140,000.

## Segment Elimination

When a segment such as a department or division is performing poorly, management must consider eliminating it. Segment information on either net income (loss) or its contribution to overhead is not sufficient for this decision. Instead, we must look at the segment's avoidable expenses and unavoidable expenses. **Avoidable expenses,** also called *escapable expenses,* are amounts the company would not incur if it eliminated the segment. **Unavoidable**

**Example:** For Case 2, if Product B's variable costs per unit increase to $6, Product A's variable costs per unit decrease to $3, and the same machine hours per unit are used, which product should FasTrac produce? *Answer:* Product A. Its contribution margin of $2 per machine hour is higher than B's $.75 per machine hour.

**Point:** To apply these concepts, work QS 21-5.

**Point:** A method called *linear programming* is useful for finding the optimal sales mix for several products subject to many market and production constraints. This method is described in advanced courses.

**expenses,** also called *inescapable expenses,* are amounts that would continue even if the segment is eliminated.

To illustrate, FasTrac considers eliminating its treadmill division because its $48,300 total expenses are higher than its $47,800 sales. Classification of this division's operating expenses into avoidable or unavoidable expenses is shown in Exhibit 21.20.

| | Total | Avoidable Expenses | Unavoidable Expenses |
|---|---|---|---|
| Cost of goods sold | $ 30,000 | $ 30,000 | — |
| Direct expenses | | | |
| Salaries expense | 7,900 | 7,900 | — |
| Depreciation expense—Equipment | 200 | — | $  200 |
| Indirect expenses | | | |
| Rent and utilities expense | 3,150 | — | 3,150 |
| Advertising expense | 400 | 400 | — |
| Insurance expense | 400 | 300 | 100 |
| Service department costs | | | |
| Share of office department expenses | 3,060 | 2,200 | 860 |
| Share of purchasing expenses | 3,190 | 1,000 | 2,190 |
| Total | $48,300 | $41,800 | $6,500 |

**Exhibit 21.20**

Classification of Segment Operating Expenses for Analysis

FasTrac's analysis shows that it can avoid $41,800 expenses if it eliminates the treadmill division. Because this division's sales are $47,800, eliminating it will cause FasTrac to lose $6,000 of income. *Our decision rule is that a segment is a candidate for elimination if its revenues are less than its avoidable expenses.* Avoidable expenses can be viewed as the costs to generate this segment's revenues.

When considering elimination of a segment, we must assess its impact on other segments. A segment could be unprofitable on its own, but it might still contribute to other segments' revenues and profits. It is possible then to continue a segment even when its revenues are less than its avoidable expenses. Similarly, a profitable segment might be discontinued if its space, assets, or staff can be more profitably used by expanding existing segments or by creating new ones. Our decision to keep or eliminate a segment requires a more complex analysis than simply looking at a segment's performance report. Such reports provide useful information, but they do not provide all the information necessary for this decision.

**Example:** How can insurance be classified as either avoidable or unavoidable? *Answer:* Depends on whether the assets insured can be removed and the premiums canceled.

**Example:** Give an example of a segment that a company might profitably use to attract customers even though it might incur a loss. *Answer:* Warranty and post-sales services.

**Point:** To apply these concepts, work Exercise 21-11.

## Qualitative Decision Factors

Managers must consider qualitative factors in making managerial decisions. Consider a decision on whether to buy a component from an outside supplier or continue to make it. Several qualitative decision factors must be considered. For example, the quality, delivery, and reputation of the proposed supplier are important. The effects from deciding not to make the component can include potential layoffs and impaired worker morale. Consider another situation in which a company is considering a one-time sale to a new customer at a special low price. Qualitative factors to consider in this situation include the effects of a low price on the company's image and the threat that regular customers might demand a similar price. The company must also consider whether this customer is really a one-time customer. If not, can it continue to offer this low price in the long run? Clearly, management cannot rely solely on financial data to make such decisions.

### Quick Check

**15.** What is the difference between avoidable and unavoidable expenses?

**16.** A segment is a candidate for elimination if (*a*) its revenues are less than its avoidable expenses, (*b*) it has a net loss, (*c*) its unavoidable expenses are higher than its revenues.

Answers—p. 872

## Decision Analysis                                          Break-Even Time

**A2** Analyze a capital investment project using break-even time.

The first section of this chapter explained several methods to evaluate capital investments. Break-even time of an investment project is a variation of the payback period method that overcomes the limitation of not using the time value of money. **Break-even time (BET)** is a time-based measure used to evaluate a capital investment's acceptability. Its computation yields a measure of expected time, reflecting the time period until the *present value* of the net cash flows from an investment equals the initial cost of the investment. In basic terms, break-even time is computed by restating future cash flows in terms of present values and then determining the payback period using these present values.

To illustrate, we return to the FasTrac case described in Exhibit 21.1 involving a $16,000 investment in machinery. The annual net cash flows from this investment are projected at $4,100 for eight years. Exhibit 21.21 shows the computation of break-even time for this investment decision.

**Exhibit 21.21**

Break-Even Time Analysis*

| Year | Cash Flows | Present Value of 1 at 10% | Present Value of Cash Flows | Cumulative Present Value of Cash Flows |
|------|-----------|--------------------------|----------------------------|----------------------------------------|
| 0 . . . . . . . . . | $(16,000) | 1.0000 | $(16,000) | $(16,000) |
| 1 . . . . . . . . . | 4,100 | 0.9091 | 3,727 | (12,273) |
| 2 . . . . . . . . . | 4,100 | 0.8264 | 3,388 | (8,885) |
| 3 . . . . . . . . . | 4,100 | 0.7513 | 3,080 | (5,805) |
| 4 . . . . . . . . . | 4,100 | 0.6830 | 2,800 | (3,005) |
| 5 . . . . . . . . . | 4,100 | 0.6209 | 2,546 | **(459)** |
| 6 . . . . . . . . . | 4,100 | 0.5645 | 2,314 | **1,855** |
| 7 . . . . . . . . . | 4,100 | 0.5132 | 2,104 | 3,959 |
| 8 . . . . . . . . . | 4,100 | 0.4665 | 1,913 | 5,872 |

\* The time of analysis is the start of year 1 (same as end of year 0). All cash flows occur at the end of each year.

The right-most column of this exhibit shows that break-even time is between 5 and 6 years, or about 5.2 years. This is the time the project takes to break even after considering the time value of money (recall that the payback period computed without considering the time value of money was 3.9 years). We interpret this as cash flows earned after 5.2 years contribute to a positive net present value that, in this case, eventually amounts to $5,872.

Break-even time is a useful measure for managers because it identifies the point in time when they can expect the cash flows to begin to yield net positive returns. Managers expect a positive net present value from an investment if break-even time is less than the investment's estimated life. The method allows managers to compare and rank alternative investments, giving the project with the shortest break-even time the highest rank.

### Decision Maker

**Investment Manager**   As the investment manager, management asks you to evaluate three alternative investments. Investment recovery time is crucial because cash is scarce. The time value of money is also important. Which capital budgeting method(s) do you choose to evaluate the investments?

Answers—p. 872

## Demonstration Problem

Determine the appropriate action in each of the following managerial decision situations.

1. Packer Company is operating at 80% of its manufacturing capacity of 100,000 product units per year. A chain store has offered to buy an additional 10,000 units at $22 each and sell them to customers so as not to compete with Packer Co. The following data are available:

| Costs at 80% Capacity | Per Unit | Total |
|-----------------------|----------|-------|
| Direct materials . . . . . . . . . . . . . . . . | $ 8.00 | $ 640,000 |
| Direct labor . . . . . . . . . . . . . . . . . . . | 7.00 | 560,000 |
| Overhead (fixed and variable) . . . . . . . | 12.50 | 1,000,000 |
| Totals . . . . . . . . . . . . . . . . . . . . . . . | $27.50 | $2,200,000 |

In producing 10,000 additional units, fixed overhead costs would remain at their current level but incremental variable overhead costs of $3 per unit would be incurred. Should the company accept or reject this order?

2. Green Company uses Part JR3 in manufacturing its products. It has always purchased this part from a supplier for $40 each. It recently upgraded its own manufacturing capabilities and has enough excess capacity (including trained workers) to begin manufacturing Part JR3 instead of buying it. The company prepares the following cost projections of making the part, assuming that overhead is allocated to the part at the normal predetermined rate of 200% of direct labor cost.

| | |
|---|---:|
| Direct materials | $11 |
| Direct labor | 15 |
| Overhead (fixed and variable) (200% of direct labor) | 30 |
| Total | $56 |

The required volume of output to produce the part will not require any incremental fixed overhead. Incremental variable overhead cost will be $17 per unit. Should the company make or buy this part?

3. Gold Company's manufacturing process causes a relatively large number of defective parts to be produced. The defective parts can be (a) sold for scrap, (b) melted to recover the recycled metal for reuse, or (c) reworked to be good units. Reworking defective parts reduces the output of other good units because no excess capacity exists. Each unit reworked means that one new unit cannot be produced. The following information reflects 500 defective parts currently available:

| | |
|---|---:|
| Proceeds of selling as scrap | $2,500 |
| Additional cost of melting down defective parts | 400 |
| Cost of purchases avoided by using recycled metal from defects | 4,800 |
| Cost to rework 500 defective parts | |
|   Direct materials | 0 |
|   Direct labor | 1,500 |
|   Incremental overhead | 1,750 |
| Cost to produce 500 new parts | |
|   Direct materials | 6,000 |
|   Direct labor | 5,000 |
|   Incremental overhead | 3,200 |
| Selling price per good unit | 40 |

Should the company melt the parts, sell them as scrap, or rework them?

4. White Company can invest in one of two projects, TD1 or TD2. Each project requires an initial investment of $100,000 and produces the year-end cash inflows shown in the following table. Use net present values to determine which project, if any, should be chosen. Assume that the company requires a 10% return from its investments.

| | Net Cash Flows | |
|---|---:|---:|
| | **TD1** | **TD2** |
| Year 1 | $ 20,000 | $ 40,000 |
| Year 2 | 30,000 | 40,000 |
| Year 3 | 70,000 | 40,000 |
| Totals | $120,000 | $120,000 |

## Planning the Solution

- Determine whether Packer Company should accept the additional business by finding the incremental costs of materials, labor, and overhead that will be incurred if the order is accepted. Omit fixed costs that the order will not increase. If the incremental revenue exceeds the incremental cost, accept the order.
- Determine whether Green Company should make or buy the component by finding the incremental cost of making each unit. If the incremental cost exceeds the purchase price, the component should be purchased. If the incremental cost is less than the purchase price, make the component.

- Determine whether Gold Company should sell the defective parts, melt them down and recycle the metal, or rework them. To compare the three choices, examine all costs incurred and benefits received from the alternatives in working with the 500 defective units versus the production of 500 new units. For the scrapping alternative, include the costs of producing 500 new units and subtract the $2,500 proceeds from selling the old ones. For the melting alternative, include the costs of melting the defective units, add the net cost of new materials in excess over those obtained from recycling, and add the direct labor and overhead costs. For the reworking alternative, add the costs of direct labor and incremental overhead. Select the alternative that has the lowest cost. The cost assigned to the 500 defective units is sunk and not relevant in choosing among the three alternatives.

- Compute White Company's net present value of each investment using a 10% discount rate.

## Solution to Demonstration Problem

1. This decision involves accepting additional business. Since current unit costs are $27.50, it appears initially as if the offer to sell for $22 should be rejected, but the $27.50 cost includes fixed costs. When the analysis includes only *incremental* costs, the per unit cost is as shown in the following table. The offer should be accepted because it will produce $4 of additional profit per unit (computed as $22 price less $18 incremental cost), which yields a total profit of $40,000 for the 10,000 additional units.

| | |
|---|---:|
| Direct materials | $ 8.00 |
| Direct labor | 7.00 |
| Variable overhead (given) | 3.00 |
| Total incremental cost | $18.00 |

2. For this make or buy decision, the analysis must not include the $13 nonincremental overhead per unit ($30 − $17). When only the $17 incremental overhead is included, the relevant unit cost of manufacturing the part is shown in the following table. It would be better to continue buying the part for $40 instead of making it for $43.

| | |
|---|---:|
| Direct materials | $11.00 |
| Direct labor | 15.00 |
| Variable overhead | 17.00 |
| Total incremental cost | $43.00 |

3. The goal of this scrap or rework decision is to identify the alternative that produces the greatest net benefit to the company. To compare the alternatives, we determine the net cost of obtaining 500 marketable units as follows:

| Incremental Cost to Produce 500 Marketable Units | Sell as Is | Melt and Recycle | Rework Units |
|---|---:|---:|---:|
| Direct materials | | | |
| New materials | $ 6,000 | $6,000 | |
| Recycled metal materials | | (4,800) | |
| Net materials cost | | 1,200 | |
| Melting costs | | 400 | |
| Total direct materials cost | 6,000 | 1,600 | |
| Direct labor | 5,000 | 5,000 | $1,500 |
| Incremental overhead | 3,200 | 3,200 | 1,750 |
| Cost to produce 500 marketable units | 14,200 | 9,800 | 3,250 |
| Less proceeds of selling defects as scrap | (2,500) | | |
| Opportunity costs* | | | 5,800 |
| Net cost | $11,700 | $9,800 | $9,050 |

* The $5,800 opportunity cost is the lost contribution margin from not being able to produce and sell 500 units because of reworking, computed as ($40 − $28.40) × 500 units.

The incremental cost of 500 marketable parts is smallest if the defects are reworked.

**4. TD1:**

| | Net Cash Flows | Present Value of 1 at 10% | Present Value of Net Cash Flows |
|---|---|---|---|
| Year 1 .................. | $ 20,000 | 0.9091 | $ 18,182 |
| Year 2 .................. | 30,000 | 0.8264 | 24,792 |
| Year 3 .................. | 70,000 | 0.7513 | 52,591 |
| Totals .................. | $120,000 | | 95,565 |
| Amount invested .......... | | | (100,000) |
| **Net present value** ....... | | | **$ (4,435)** |

**TD2:**

| | Net Cash Flows | Present Value of 1 at 10% | Present Value of Net Cash Flows |
|---|---|---|---|
| Year 1 .................. | $ 40,000 | 0.9091 | $ 36,364 |
| Year 2 .................. | 40,000 | 0.8264 | 33,056 |
| Year 3 .................. | 40,000 | 0.7513 | 30,052 |
| Totals .................. | $120,000 | | 99,472 |
| Amount invested .......... | | | (100,000) |
| **Net present value** ....... | | | **$ (528)** |

White Co. should not invest in either project. Both are expected to yield a negative net present value, and it should invest only in positive net present value projects.

## Summary

**C1 Explain the importance of capital budgeting.** Capital budgeting is the process of analyzing alternative investments and deciding which assets to acquire or sell. It involves predicting the cash flows to be received from the alternatives, evaluating their merits, and then choosing which ones to pursue.

**C2 Describe the selection of a hurdle rate for an investment.** Top management should select the hurdle (discount) rate to use in evaluating capital investments. The required hurdle rate should be at least higher than the interest rate on money borrowed because the return on an investment must cover the interest and provide an additional profit to reward the company for risk.

**C3 Describe the importance of relevant costs for short-term decisions.** A company must rely on relevant costs pertaining to alternative courses of action rather than historical costs. Out-of-pocket expenses and opportunity costs are relevant because these are avoidable; sunk costs are irrelevant because they result from past decisions and are therefore unavoidable. Managers must also consider the relevant benefits associated with alternative decisions.

**A1 Evaluate short-term managerial decisions using relevant costs.** Relevant costs are useful in making decisions such as to accept additional business, make or buy, and sell as is or process further. For example, the relevant factors in deciding whether to produce and sell additional units of product are incremental costs and incremental revenues from the additional volume.

**A2 Analyze a capital investment project using break-even time.** Break-even time (BET) is a method for evaluating capital investments by restating future cash flows in terms of their present values (discounting the cash flows) and then calculating the payback period using these present values of cash flows.

**P1 Compute payback period and describe its use.** One way to compare potential investments is to compute and compare their payback periods. The payback period is an estimate of the expected time before the cumulative net cash inflow from the investment equals its initial cost. A payback period analysis fails to reflect risk of the cash flows, differences in the timing of cash flows within the payback period, and cash flows that occur after the payback period.

**P2 Compute accounting rate of return and explain its use.** A project's accounting rate of return is computed by dividing the expected annual after-tax net income by the average amount of investment in the project. When the net cash flows are received evenly throughout each period and straight-line depreciation is used, the average investment is computed as the average of the investment's initial book value and its salvage value.

**P3 Compute net present value and describe its use.** An investment's net present value is determined by predicting the future cash flows it is expected to generate, discounting them at a rate that represents an acceptable return, and then by subtracting the investment's initial cost from the sum of the present values. This technique can deal with any pattern of expected cash flows and applies a superior concept of return on investment.

**P4 Compute internal rate of return and explain its use.** The internal rate of return (IRR) is the discount rate that results in a zero net present value. When the cash flows are equal, we can compute the present value factor corresponding to the IRR by dividing the initial investment by the annual cash flows. We then use the annuity tables to determine the discount rate corresponding to this present value factor.

## Guidance Answers to **Decision Maker** and **Decision Ethics**

**Systems Manager**  Your dilemma is whether to abide by rules designed to prevent abuse or to bend them to acquire an investment that you believe will benefit the firm. You should not pursue the latter action because breaking up the order into small components is dishonest and there are consequences of being caught at a later stage. Develop a proposal for the entire package and then do all you can to expedite its processing, particularly by pointing out its benefits. When faced with controls that are not working, there is rarely a reason to overcome its shortcomings by dishonesty. A direct assault on those limitations is more sensible and ethical.

**Entrepreneur**  The banker is probably concerned because new products are risky and should therefore be evaluated using a higher rate of return. You should conduct a thorough technical analysis and obtain detailed market data and information about any similar products available in the market. These factors might provide sufficient information to support the use of a lower return. You must convince yourself that the risk level is consistent with the discount rate used.

You should also be confident that your company has the capacity and the resources to handle the new product.

**Partner**  You should identify the differences between existing clients and this potential client. A key difference is that the restaurant business has additional inventory components (groceries, vegetables, meats, etc.) and is likely to have a higher proportion of depreciable assets. These differences imply that the partner must spend more hours auditing the records and understanding the business, regulations, and standards that pertain to the restaurant business. Such differences suggest that the partner must use a different "formula" for quoting a price to this potential client vis-à-vis current clients.

**Investment Manager**  You should probably focus on either the payback period or break-even time because both the time value of money and recovery time are important. Break-even time method is superior because it accounts for the time value of money, which is an important consideration in this decision.

## Guidance Answers to **Quick Checks**

**1.** *b*

**2.** A capital budgeting decision is difficult because (1) the outcome is uncertain, (2) large amounts of money are usually involved, (3) a long-term commitment is required, and (4) the decision could be difficult or impossible to reverse.

**3.** *b*

**4.** Depreciation expense is subtracted from revenues in computing net income but does not use cash and should be added back to net income to compute net cash flows.

**5.** Not necessarily. One investment can continue to generate cash flows beyond the payback period for a longer time period than the other. The timing of their cash flows within the payback period also can differ.

**6.** *b*; Annual average investment = ($180,000 + $15,000)/2
= $97,500
Accounting rate of return = $40,000/$97,500 = 41%

**7.** For this determination, we need to compare it to the returns expected from alternative investments with similar risk.

**8.** Project A has the higher net present value as shown:

| Year | Present Value of 1 at 10% | Project A Net Cash Flows | Project A Present Value of Net Cash Flows | Project B Net Cash Flows | Project B Present Value of Net Cash Flows |
|------|------|------|------|------|------|
| 1 | 0.9091 | $12,000 | $10,909 | $ 4,500 | $ 4,091 |
| 2 | 0.8264 | 8,500 | 7,024 | 8,500 | 7,024 |
| 3 | 0.7513 | 4,000 | 3,005 | 13,000 | 9,767 |
| Totals | | $24,500 | $20,938 | $26,000 | $20,882 |
| Amount invested | | | (20,000) | | (20,000) |
| **Net present value** | | | $  938 | | $  882 |

**9.** No, the information is too limited to draw that conclusion. For example, one investment could be riskier than the other, or one could require a substantially larger initial investment.

**10.** *b*

**11.** *e*; Variable costs per unit for this order of 200 units follow:

| | |
|---|---|
| Direct materials ($37,500/7,500) . . . . . . . . . . . . . . . . . . . . . . . . | $ 5.00 |
| Direct labor ($60,000/7,500) . . . . . . . . . . . . . . . . . . . . . . . . . . . | 8.00 |
| Variable overhead [(0.30 × $20,000)/7,500] . . . . . . . . . . . . . . . . | 0.80 |
| Variable selling expenses [(0.60 × $25,000 × 0.5)/7,500] . . . . . . . | 1.00 |
| Total variable costs per unit . . . . . . . . . . . . . . . . . . . . . . . . . . . | $14.80 |

Cost to produce special order: (200 × $14.80) + $400
= $3,360.
Price per unit to earn $1,000: ($3,360 + $1,000)/200 = 21.80.

**12.** They are the additional (new) costs of accepting new business.

**13.** *d*;

| | Incremental benefits | | Incremental costs |
|---|---|---|---|
| Alpha | $300 ($600 − $300) | > | $150 (given) |
| Beta | $450 ($900 − $450) | > | $300 (given) |
| Gamma | $150 ($425 − $275) | > | $125 (given) |
| Delta | $ 60 ($210 − $150) | < | $ 75 (given) |

**14.** A sunk cost is *never* relevant because it results from a past decision and is already incurred.

**15.** Avoidable expenses are ones a company will not incur by eliminating a segment; unavoidable expenses will continue even after a segment is eliminated.

**16.** *a*

## Key Terms

Key Terms are available at the book's Website for learning and testing in an online Flashcard Format.

**Accounting rate of return** (p. 853)
**Avoidable expense** (p. 866)
**Break-even time (BET)** (p. 868)
**Capital budgeting** (p. 850)

**Hurdle rate** (p. 858)
**Incremental cost** (p. 862)
**Internal rate of return (IRR)** (p. 857)
**Net present value (NPV)** (p. 855)

**Payback period (PBP)** (p. 851)
**Relevant benefits** (p. 861)
**Unavoidable expense** (p. 866)

## Personal Interactive Quiz

Personal Interactive Quizzes A and B are available at the book's Website to reinforce and assess your learning.

## Discussion Questions

**1.** What is capital budgeting?

**2.** Identify four reasons that capital budgeting decisions by managers are risky.

**3.** Capital budgeting decisions require careful analysis because they are generally the _____ _____ and _____ decisions that management faces.

**4.** Identify two disadvantages of using the payback period for comparing investments.

**5.** Why is an investment more attractive to management if it has a shorter payback period?

**6.** What is the average amount invested in a machine during its predicted five-year life if it costs $200,000 and has a $20,000 salvage value? Assume that net income is received evenly throughout each year and straight-line depreciation is used.

**7.** If the present value of the expected net cash flows from a machine, discounted at 10%, exceeds the amount to be invested, what can you say about the investment's expected rate of return? What can you say about the expected rate of return if the present value of the net cash flows, discounted at 10%, is less than the investment amount?

**8.** Why is the present value of $100 that you expect to receive one year from today worth less than $100 received today? What is the present value of $100 that you expect to receive one year from today, discounted at 12%?

**9.** Why should managers set the required rate of return higher than the rate at which money can be borrowed when making a typical capital budgeting decision?

**10.** Why does the use of the accelerated depreciation method (instead of straight line) for income tax reporting increase an investment's value?

**11.** What is an out-of-pocket cost? What is an opportunity cost? Are opportunity costs recorded in the accounting records?

**12.** Why are sunk costs irrelevant in deciding whether to sell a product in its present condition or to make it into a new product through additional processing?

**13.** Identify the incremental costs incurred by **Krispy Kreme** for shipping one additional dozen donuts to a convenience store along with the store's normal order of 6 dozen donuts.

**14.** **Tastykake** is considering purchasing five new ovens for its factory. Identify three methods management can use to evaluate whether to purchase the new ovens.

**15.** Assume that **Harley-Davidson** manufactures and sells 500,000 units of a memorabilia product at $30 per unit in domestic markets. It costs $20 per unit to manufacture ($13 variable cost per unit, $7 fixed cost per unit). Can you describe a situation under which the company is willing to sell an additional 25,000 units of the product in an international market at $15 per unit?

*Red numbers denote Discussion Questions that involve decision-making.*

*Homework Manager repeats all numerical Quick Studies on the book's Website with new numbers.*

Ortega Company is considering two alternative investments. The payback period is 4.5 years for Investment A and 5 years for Investment B. (1) If management relies on the payback period, which investment is preferred? (2) Why might Ortega's analysis of these two alternatives lead to the selection of B over A?

**QUICK STUDY**

**QS 21-1**
Analyzing payback periods   P1

**QS 21-2**

Payback period   P1

Rivera Company is considering an investment that requires immediate payment of $18,000 and provides expected cash inflows of $6,000 annually for four years. What is the investment's payback period?

---

**QS 21-3**

Computation of
net present value   P3

If VHS Company invests $100,000 today, it can expect to receive $20,000 at the end of each year for the next seven years plus an extra $12,000 at the end of the seventh year. What is the net present value of this investment assuming a required 10% return on investments?

---

**QS 21-4**

Computation of
accounting rate of return   P2

Cardinal Company is considering an investment expected to generate an average net income after taxes of $1,300 for three years. The investment costs $30,000 and has an estimated $4,000 salvage value. Compute the accounting rate of return for this investment.

---

**QS 21-5**

Selection of sales mix

C3   A1

Memory Lane Company can sell all units of computer memory X and Y that it can produce, but it has limited production capacity. It can produce two units of X per hour *or* three units of Y per hour, and it has 8,000 production hours available. Contribution margin is $10 for Product X and $8 for Product Y. What is the most profitable sales mix for Memory Lane Company?

---

**QS 21-6**

Analysis of incremental costs

C3   A1

Mo-Kan Company incurs a $6 per unit cost for Product A, which it currently manufactures and sells for $9 per unit. Instead of manufacturing and selling this product, Mo-Kan can purchase Product B for $5 per unit and sell it for $8 per unit. If it does so, unit sales would remain unchanged and $5 of the $6 per unit costs assigned to Product A would be eliminated. Should Mo-Kan continue to manufacture Product A or purchase Product B for resale?

---

**QS 21-7**

Computation of break-even time

A2

Soles, a shoe manufacturer, is evaluating the costs and benefits of new equipment that would custom fit each pair of athletic shoes. The customer would have his or her foot scanned by digital computer equipment; this information would be used to cut the raw materials to provide the customer a perfect fit. The new equipment costs $100,000 and is expected to generate an additional $35,000 in cash flows for five years. A bank will make a $100,000 loan to Soles at a 10% interest rate for this equipment's purchase. Use the following table to determine the break-even time for this equipment.

| Year | Cash Flows* | Present Value of 1 at 10% | Present Value of Cash Flows | Cumulative Present Value of Cash Flows |
|------|-------------|---------------------------|-----------------------------|----------------------------------------|
| 0 | $(100,000) | 1.0000 | | |
| 1 | 35,000 | 0.9091 | | |
| 2 | 35,000 | 0.8264 | | |
| 3 | 35,000 | 0.7513 | | |
| 4 | 35,000 | 0.6830 | | |
| 5 | 35,000 | 0.6209 | | |

\* All cash flows occur at year-end.

*Homework Manager repeats all numerical Exercises on the book's Website with new numbers.*

---

# EXERCISES

**Exercise 21-1**

Payback period computation;
even cash flows

P1

Compute the payback period for each of these two separate investments:

**a.** A new operating system for an existing machine is expected to cost $260,000 and have a useful life of five years. The system yields an incremental after-tax income of $75,000 each year after deducting its straight-line depreciation. The predicted salvage value of the system is $10,000.

**b.** A machine costs $190,000, has a $10,000 salvage value, is expected to last nine years, and will generate an after-tax income of $30,000 per year after straight-line depreciation.

Wenro Company is considering the purchase of an asset for $90,000. It is expected to produce the following net cash flows. The cash flows occur evenly throughout each year. Compute the payback period for this investment.

| | Year 1 | Year 2 | Year 3 | Year 4 | Year 5 | Total |
|---|---|---|---|---|---|---|
| Net cash flows ........ | $30,000 | $20,000 | $30,000 | $60,000 | $19,000 | $159,000 |

**Exercise 21-2**
Payback period computation; uneven cash flows

P1

**Check**   3.167 years

A machine can be purchased for $300,000 and used for 5 years, yielding the following net incomes. In projecting net incomes, double-declining balance depreciation is applied, using a 5-year life and a $50,000 salvage value. Compute the machine's payback period. Ignore taxes.

| | Year 1 | Year 2 | Year 3 | Year 4 | Year 5 |
|---|---|---|---|---|---|
| Net incomes ....... | $20,000 | $50,000 | $100,000 | $75,000 | $200,000 |

**Exercise 21-3**
Payback period computation; declining-balance depreciation

P1

**Check**   2.265 years

A machine costs $500,000 and is expected to yield an after-tax net income of $15,000 each year. Management predicts this machine has a 10-year service life and a $100,000 salvage value. Compute this machine's accounting rate of return.

**Exercise 21-4**
Accounting rate of return   P2

K2B Co. is considering the purchase of equipment that would allow the company to add a new product to its line. The equipment is expected to cost $240,000 with a 12-year life and no salvage value. It will be depreciated on a straight-line basis. The company expects to sell 96,000 units of the equipment's product each year. The expected annual income related to this equipment follows. Compute the (1) payback period and (2) accounting rate of return for this equipment.

**Exercise 21-5**
Payback period and accounting rate of return on investment

P1   P2

| | |
|---|---|
| Sales ........................................ | $150,000 |
| Costs | |
| Materials, labor, and overhead (except depreciation) ....... | 80,000 |
| Depreciation on new equipment .................... | 20,000 |
| Selling and administrative expenses .................... | 15,000 |
| Total costs and expenses ........................... | 115,000 |
| Pretax income ..................................... | 35,000 |
| Income taxes (30%) ............................... | 10,500 |
| Net income ...................................... | $ 24,500 |

**Check**   (1) 5.39 years (2) 20.42%

After evaluating the risk of the investment described in Exercise 21-5, K2B Co. concludes that it must earn at least an 8% return on this investment. Compute the net present value of this investment.

**Exercise 21-6**
Computing net present value   P3

Kase Company can invest in each of three cheese-making projects: C1, C2, and C3. Each project requires an initial investment of $190,000 and would yield the following annual cash flows:

| | C1 | C2 | C3 |
|---|---|---|---|
| Year 1 ........ | $ 10,000 | $ 80,000 | $150,000 |
| Year 2 ........ | 90,000 | 80,000 | 50,000 |
| Year 3 ........ | 140,000 | 80,000 | 40,000 |
| Totals ........ | $240,000 | $240,000 | $240,000 |

**Exercise 21-7**
Computation and interpretation of net present value and internal rate of return

P3   P4

(1) Assuming that the company requires a 12% return from its investments, use net present value to determine which projects, if any, should be acquired. (2) Using the answer from part 1, explain whether the internal rate of return is higher or lower than 12% for project C2? (3) Compute the internal rate of return for project C2.

**Check**   (3) IRR = 13%

**Exercise 21-8**

Decision to accept additional business or not

C3  A1

Feist Co. expects to sell 200,000 units of its product in the next period with the following results:

| | |
|---|---:|
| Sales (200,000 units) . . . . . . . . . . . . | $3,000,000 |
| Costs and expenses | |
|    Direct materials . . . . . . . . . . . . . | 400,000 |
|    Direct labor . . . . . . . . . . . . . . . | 800,000 |
|    Overhead . . . . . . . . . . . . . . . . . | 200,000 |
|    Selling expenses . . . . . . . . . . . . | 300,000 |
|    Administrative expenses . . . . . . . | 514,000 |
| Total costs and expenses . . . . . . . . . | 2,214,000 |
| Net income . . . . . . . . . . . . . . . . . | $ 786,000 |

The company has an opportunity to sell 20,000 additional units at $12 per unit. The additional sales would not affect its current expected sales. Direct materials and labor costs would be the same for the additional units as they are for the regular units. However, the additional volume would create the following incremental costs: (1) total overhead would increase by 15% and (2) administrative expenses would increase by $86,000. Prepare an analysis to determine whether the company should accept or reject the offer to sell additional units at the reduced price of $12 per unit.

**Check**  Income increase, $4,000

---

**Exercise 21-9**

Make or buy decision

C3  A1

**Check**  $10,000 increased costs to buy

Santos Company currently manufactures one of its crucial parts at a cost of $3.40 per unit. This cost is based on a normal production rate of 50,000 units per year. Variable costs are $1.50 per unit, fixed costs related to making this part are $50,000 per year, and allocated fixed costs are $45,000 per year. Allocated fixed costs are unavoidable whether the company makes or buys the part. Santos is considering buying the part from a supplier for a quoted price of $2.70 per unit guaranteed for a three-year period. Should the company continue to manufacture the part, or should it buy the part from the outside supplier? Support your answer with analyses.

---

**Exercise 21-10**

Sell or process decision

C3  A1

Cantrell Company has already manufactured 20,000 units of Product A at a cost of $20 per unit. The 20,000 units can be sold at this stage for $500,000. Alternatively, it can be further processed at a $300,000 total additional cost and be converted into 4,000 units of Product B and 8,000 units of Product C. Per unit selling price for Product B is $75 and for Product C is $50. Prepare an analysis that shows whether the 20,000 units of Product A should be processed further or not.

---

**Exercise 21-11**

Analysis of income effects from eliminating departments

C3  A1

Suresh Co. expects its five departments to yield the following income for next year:

File  Edit  View  Insert  Format  Tools  Data  Window  Help

| | Dept. M | Dept. N | Dept. O | Dept. P | Dept. T |
|---|---|---|---|---|---|
| 1 | | | | | |
| 2  Sales . . . . . . . . . . . . . . . | $31,500 | $17,500 | $28,000 | $21,000 | $14,000 |
| 3  Expenses | | | | | |
| 4    Avoidable . . . . . . . . . . . | 4,900 | 18,200 | 11,200 | 7,000 | 18,900 |
| 5    Unavoidable . . . . . . . . . | 25,900 | 6,300 | 2,100 | 14,700 | 4,900 |
| 6    Total expenses . . . . . . . . | 30,800 | 24,500 | 13,300 | 21,700 | 23,800 |
| 7  Net income (loss) . . . . . . . | $  700 | $ (7,000) | $14,700 | $  (700) | $ (9,800) |
| 8 | | | | | |

Sheet1 / Sheet2 / Sheet3

**Check**  Total income (loss): (2) $(10,500), (3) $3,500

Recompute and prepare the departmental income statements (including a combined total column) for the company under each of the following separate scenarios: Management (1) does not eliminate any department, (2) eliminates departments with expected net losses, and (3) eliminates departments with sales dollars that are less than avoidable expenses. Explain your answers to parts 2 and 3.

---

**Exercise 21-12**

Sales mix determination and analysis

C3  A1

Bethel Company owns a machine that can produce two specialized products. Production time for Product TLX is two units per hour and for Product MTV is five units per hour. The machine's capacity is 2,200 hours per year. Both products are sold to a single customer who has agreed to buy all of the company's output up to a maximum of 3,750 units of Product TLX and 2,000 units of Product

MTV. Selling prices and variable costs per unit to produce the products follow. Determine (1) the company's most profitable sales mix and (2) the contribution margin that results from that sales mix.

|  | Product TLX | Product MTV |
|---|---|---|
| Selling price per unit . . . . . . . . . | $12.50 | $7.50 |
| Variable costs per unit . . . . . . . . | 3.75 | 4.50 |

**Check** (2) $37,688

---

This chapter explained two methods to evaluate investments using recovery time, the payback period and break-even time (BET). Refer to QS 21-7 and (1) compute the recovery time for both the payback period and break-even time, (2) discuss the advantage(s) of break-even time over the payback period, and (3) list two conditions under which payback period and break-even time are similar.

**Exercise 21-13**
Comparison of payback and BET

P1   A2

---

Elite Company is planning to add a new product to its line. To manufacture this product, the company needs to buy a new machine at a $300,000 cost with an expected four-year life and a $20,000 salvage value. All sales are for cash, and all costs are out of pocket except for depreciation on the new machine. Additional information includes the following:

| | |
|---|---|
| Expected annual sales of new product . . . . . . . . . . . . . . . . . . . . . . . . . . | $1,150,000 |
| Expected annual costs of new product | |
| Direct materials . . . . . . . . . . . . . . . . . . . . . . . . . . . . . . . . . . . . . . . | 300,000 |
| Direct labor . . . . . . . . . . . . . . . . . . . . . . . . . . . . . . . . . . . . . . . . . . | 420,000 |
| Overhead excluding straight-line depreciation on new machine . . . . . . . . | 210,000 |
| Selling and administrative expenses . . . . . . . . . . . . . . . . . . . . . . . . . . | 100,000 |
| Income taxes . . . . . . . . . . . . . . . . . . . . . . . . . . . . . . . . . . . . . . . . . | 30% |

**PROBLEM SET A**

**Problem 21-1A**
Computation of payback period, accounting rate of return, and net present value

P1   P2   P3

mhhe.com/wild

**Required**

1. Compute straight-line depreciation for each year of this new machine's life.
2. Determine expected net income and net cash flow for each year of this machine's life.
3. Compute this machine's payback period, assuming that cash flows occur evenly throughout each year.
4. Compute this machine's accounting rate of return, assuming that income is earned evenly throughout each year.
5. Compute the net present value for this machine using a discount rate of 7% and assuming that cash flows occur at each year-end. (*Hint:* Salvage value is a cash inflow at the end of the asset's life.)

**Check** (4) 21.88%

(5) $70,915

---

Pleasant Company has an opportunity to invest in one of two new projects. Project Y requires a $700,000 investment for new machinery with a four-year life and no salvage value. Project Z requires a $700,000 investment for new machinery with a three-year life and no salvage value. The two projects yield the following predicted annual results. The company uses straight-line depreciation, and cash flows occur evenly throughout each year.

**Problem 21-2A**
Analysis and computation of payback period, accounting rate of return, and net present value

P1   P2   P3

| | Project Y | Project Z |
|---|---|---|
| Sales . . . . . . . . . . . . . . . . . . . . . . . . . . . | $700,000 | $560,000 |
| Expenses | | |
| Direct materials . . . . . . . . . . . . . . . . . . . . | 98,000 | 70,000 |
| Direct labor . . . . . . . . . . . . . . . . . . . . . . . | 140,000 | 84,000 |
| Overhead including depreciation . . . . . . . . . | 252,000 | 252,000 |
| Selling and administrative expenses . . . . . . . | 50,000 | 50,000 |
| Total expenses . . . . . . . . . . . . . . . . . . . . . | 540,000 | 456,000 |
| Pretax income . . . . . . . . . . . . . . . . . . . . . | 160,000 | 104,000 |
| Income taxes (30%) . . . . . . . . . . . . . . . . . | 48,000 | 31,200 |
| Net income . . . . . . . . . . . . . . . . . . . . . . . | $112,000 | $ 72,800 |

**Required**

1. Compute each project's annual expected net cash flows.

2. Determine each project's payback period.

3. Compute each project's accounting rate of return.

4. Determine each project's net present value using 8% as the discount rate. For part 4 only, assume that cash flows occur at each year-end.

*Analysis Component*

5. Identify the project you would recommend to management and explain your choice.

---

**Problem 21-3A**
Computation of cash flows
and net present values with
alternative depreciation
methods

P3

Angiletta Corporation is considering a new project requiring a $30,000 investment in test equipment with no salvage value. The project would produce $12,000 of pretax income before depreciation at the end of each of the next six years. The company's income tax rate is 40%. In compiling its tax return and computing its income tax payments, the company can choose between the two alternative depreciation schedules shown in the table.

|  | Straight-Line Depreciation | MACRS Depreciation* |
|---|---|---|
| Year 1 ........ | $ 3,000 | $ 6,000 |
| Year 2 ........ | 6,000 | 9,600 |
| Year 3 ........ | 6,000 | 5,760 |
| Year 4 ........ | 6,000 | 3,456 |
| Year 5 ........ | 6,000 | 3,456 |
| Year 6 ........ | 3,000 | 1,728 |
| Totals ........ | $30,000 | $30,000 |

\* The modified accelerated cost recovery system (MACRS) for
depreciation is discussed in Chapter 8.

**Required**

1. Prepare a five-column table that reports amounts (assuming use of straight-line depreciation) for each of the following for each of the six years: (a) pretax income before depreciation, (b) straight-line depreciation expense, (c) taxable income, (d) income taxes, and (e) net cash flow. Net cash flow equals the amount of income before depreciation minus the income taxes.

2. Prepare a five-column table that reports amounts (assuming use of MACRS depreciation) for each of the following for each of the six years: (a) pretax income before depreciation, (b) MACRS depreciation expense, (c) taxable income, (d) income taxes, and (e) net cash flow. Net cash flow equals the income amount before depreciation minus the income taxes.

3. Compute the net present value of the investment if straight-line depreciation is used. Use 10% as the discount rate.

4. Compute the net present value of the investment if MACRS depreciation is used. Use 10% as the discount rate.

*Analysis Component*

5. Explain why the MACRS depreciation method increases this project's net present value.

---

**Problem 21-4A**
Analysis of income effects of
additional business

C3   A1

mhhe.com/wild

Cayman Products manufactures and sells to wholesalers approximately 300,000 packages per year of underwater markers at $4 per package. Annual costs for the production and sale of this quantity are shown in the table.

| | |
|---|---|
| Direct materials ............. | $384,000 |
| Direct labor ................ | 96,000 |
| Overhead ................ | 288,000 |
| Selling expenses ............. | 120,000 |
| Administrative expenses ........ | 80,000 |
| Total costs and expenses ....... | $968,000 |

A new wholesaler has offered to buy 50,000 packages for $3.44 each. These markers would be marketed under the wholesaler's name and would not affect Cayman Products' sales through its normal channels. A study of the costs of this additional business reveals the following:

- Direct materials costs are 100% variable.
- Per unit direct labor costs for the additional units would be 50% higher than normal because their production would require overtime pay at one-and-one-half times the usual labor rate.
- 25% of the normal annual overhead costs are fixed at any production level from 250,000 to 400,000 units. The remaining 75% of the annual overhead cost is variable with volume.
- Accepting the new business would involve no additional selling expenses.
- Accepting the new business would increase administrative expenses by a $4,000 fixed amount.

**Required**

Prepare a three-column comparative income statement that shows the following:

**1.** Annual operating income without the special order (column 1).

**2.** Annual operating income received from the new business only (column 2).

**3.** Combined annual operating income from normal business and the new business (column 3).

**Check** Operating income:
(1) $232,000, (2) $44,000

---

Ortiz Company is able to produce two products, G and B, with the same machine in its factory. The following information is known:

**Problem 21-5A**
Analysis of sales mix strategies

C3 A1

| | Product G | Product B |
|---|---|---|
| Selling price per unit . . . . . . . . . . . . . . . . . | $120 | $160 |
| Variable costs per unit . . . . . . . . . . . . . . . | 40 | 90 |
| Contribution margin per unit . . . . . . . . . . | $ 80 | $ 70 |
| Machine hours to produce 1 unit . . . . . . . | 0.8 hours | 2.0 hours |
| Maximum unit sales per month . . . . . . . . . | 400 units | 350 units |

Ortiz presently operates the machine for a single eight-hour shift for 22 working days each month. Management is thinking about operating the machine for two shifts, which will increase its productivity by another eight hours per day for 22 days per month. This change would require $6,500 additional fixed costs per month.

**Required**

**1.** Determine the contribution margin per machine hour that each product generates.

**2.** How many units of Product G and Product B should the company produce if it continues to operate with only one shift? How much total contribution margin does this mix produce each month?

**3.** If the company adds another shift, how many units of Product G and Product B should it produce? How much total contribution margin would this mix produce each month? Should the company add the new shift? Explain.

**Check** Units of Product G: (2) 220, (3) 400, (4) 440

**4.** Suppose that the company determines that it can increase Product G's maximum sales to 440 units per month by spending $2,000 per month in marketing efforts. Should the company pursue this strategy and the double shift? Explain.

---

Home Decor Company's management is trying to decide whether to eliminate Department 200, which has produced losses or low profits for several years. The company's 2005 departmental income statement shows the following:

**Problem 21-6A**
Analysis of possible elimination of a department

C3 A1

| HOME DECOR COMPANY<br>Departmental Income Statements<br>For Year Ended December 31, 2005 | | | |
|---|---|---|---|
| | Dept. 100 | Dept. 200 | Combined |
| Sales . . . . . . . . . . . . . . . . . . . . . . . . . . . | $872,000 | $580,000 | $1,452,000 |
| Cost of goods sold . . . . . . . . . . . . . . . . . | 524,000 | 414,000 | 938,000 |
| Gross profit . . . . . . . . . . . . . . . . . . . . . | 348,000 | 166,000 | 514,000 |
| Operating expenses | | | |
| Direct expenses | | | |
| Advertising . . . . . . . . . . . . . . . . . . . . | 34,000 | 24,000 | 58,000 |
| Store supplies used . . . . . . . . . . . . . . . | 8,000 | 7,600 | 15,600 |
| Depreciation—Store equipment . . . . . . . . | 10,000 | 6,600 | 16,600 |
| Total direct expenses . . . . . . . . . . . . . . | 52,000 | 38,200 | 90,200 |

[continued on next page]

[continued from previous page]

| Allocated expenses | | | |
|---|---:|---:|---:|
| Sales salaries | 130,000 | 78,000 | 208,000 |
| Rent expense | 18,880 | 9,440 | 28,320 |
| Bad debts expense | 19,800 | 16,200 | 36,000 |
| Office salary | 37,440 | 24,960 | 62,400 |
| Insurance expense | 4,000 | 2,200 | 6,200 |
| Miscellaneous office expenses | 4,800 | 3,200 | 8,000 |
| Total allocated expenses | 214,920 | 134,000 | 348,920 |
| Total expenses | 266,920 | 172,200 | 439,120 |
| Net income (loss) | $ 81,080 | $ (6,200) | $ 74,880 |

In analyzing whether to eliminate Department 200, management considers the following:

**a.** The company has one office worker who earns $1,200 per week, or $62,400 per year, and four salesclerks who each earn $1,000 per week, or $52,000 per year.

**b.** The full salaries of two salesclerks are charged to Department 100. The full salary of one sales clerk is charged to Department 200. The salary of the fourth clerk, who works half-time in both departments, is divided evenly between the two departments.

**c.** Eliminating Department 200 would avoid the sales salaries and the office salary currently allocated to it. However, management prefers another plan. Two salesclerks have indicated that they will be quitting soon. Management believes that their work can be done by the other two clerks if the one office worker works in sales half-time. Eliminating Department 200 will allow this shift of duties. If this change is implemented, half the office worker's salary would be reported as sales salaries and half would be reported as office salary.

**d.** The store building is rented under a long-term lease that cannot be changed. Therefore, Department 100 will use the space and equipment currently used by Department 200.

**e.** Closing Department 200 will eliminate its expenses for advertising, bad debts, and store supplies; 70% of the insurance expense allocated to it to cover its merchandise inventory; and 25% of the miscellaneous office expenses presently allocated to it.

**Required**

**Check**   (1) Total expenses:
(a) $1,377,120, (b) $568,140

**1.** Prepare a three-column report that lists items and amounts for (a) the company's total expenses (including cost of goods sold)—in column 1, (b) the expenses that would be eliminated by closing Department 200—in column 2, and (c) the expenses that will continue—in column 3.

(2) Forecasted net income
without Department 200, $63,020

**2.** Prepare a forecasted annual income statement for the company reflecting the elimination of Department 200 assuming that it will not affect Department 100's sales and gross profit. The statement should reflect the reassignment of the office worker to one-half time as a salesclerk.

*Analysis Component*

**3.** Reconcile the company's combined net income with the forecasted net income assuming that Department 200 is eliminated (list both items and amounts). Analyze the reconciliation and explain why you think the department should or should not be eliminated.

# PROBLEM SET B

## Problem 21-1B
Computation of payback period, accounting rate of return, and net present value

P1  P2  P3

Concorde Company is planning to add a new product to its line. To manufacture this product, the company needs to buy a new machine at a $100,000 cost with an expected five-year life and a $25,000 salvage value. All sales are for cash and all costs are out of pocket, except for depreciation on the new machine. Additional information includes the following:

| | |
|---|---:|
| Expected annual sales of new product | $350,000 |
| Expected annual costs of new product | |
| Direct materials | 150,000 |
| Direct labor | 50,000 |
| Overhead excluding straight-line depreciation on new machine | 100,000 |
| Selling and administrative expenses | 23,000 |
| Income taxes | 20% |

**Required**

1. Compute straight-line depreciation for each year of this new machine's life.

2. Determine expected net income and net cash flow for each year of this machine's life.

3. Compute this machine's payback period, assuming that cash flows occur evenly throughout each year.

4. Compute this machine's accounting rate of return, assuming that income is earned evenly throughout each year.

**Check** (4) 15.36%

5. Compute the net present value for this machine using a discount rate of 12% and assuming that cash flows occur at each year-end. (*Hint:* Salvage value is a cash inflow at the end of the asset's life.)

(5) $2,862

---

Micelli Company has an opportunity to invest in one of two projects. Project A requires a $480,000 investment for new machinery with a three-year life and no salvage value. Project B also requires a $480,000 investment for new machinery with a four-year life and no salvage value. The two projects yield the following predicted annual results. The company uses straight-line depreciation, and cash flows occur evenly throughout each year.

**Problem 21-2B**

Analysis and computation of payback period, accounting rate of return, and net present value

P1  P2  P3

|  | Project A | Project B |
|---|---|---|
| Sales ............................. | $750,000 | $800,000 |
| Expenses |  |  |
| Direct materials ..................... | 125,000 | 250,000 |
| Direct labor ........................ | 130,000 | 80,000 |
| Overhead including depreciation ......... | 330,000 | 276,000 |
| Selling and administrative expenses ....... | 120,000 | 120,000 |
| Total expenses ....................... | 705,000 | 726,000 |
| Pretax income ....................... | 45,000 | 74,000 |
| Income taxes (30%) .................. | 13,500 | 22,200 |
| Net income .......................... | $ 31,500 | $ 51,800 |

**Required**

1. Compute each project's annual expected net cash flows.

2. Determine each project's payback period.

3. Compute each project's accounting rate of return.

4. Determine each project's net present value using 10% as the discount rate. For part 4 only, assume that cash flows occur at each year-end.

**Check** For Project A: (2) 2.5 years, (3) 13.1%, (4) $(3,759)

*Analysis Component*

5. Identify the project you would recommend to management and explain your choice.

---

Cologne Corporation is considering a new project requiring a $25,000 investment in an asset having no salvage value. The project would produce $15,000 of pretax income before depreciation at the end of each of the next six years. The company's income tax rate is 30%. In compiling its tax return and computing its income tax payments, the company can choose between two alternative depreciation schedules as shown in the table.

**Problem 21-3B**

Computation of cash flows and net present values with alternative depreciation methods

P3

|  | Straight-Line Depreciation | MACRS Depreciation* |
|---|---|---|
| Year 1 ..... | $ 2,500 | $ 5,000 |
| Year 2 ..... | 5,000 | 8,000 |
| Year 3 ..... | 5,000 | 4,800 |
| Year 4 ..... | 5,000 | 2,880 |
| Year 5 ..... | 5,000 | 2,880 |
| Year 6 ..... | 2,500 | 1,440 |
| Totals ..... | $25,000 | $25,000 |

\* The modified accelerated cost recovery system (MACRS) for depreciation is discussed in Chapter 8.

**Required**

1. Prepare a five-column table that reports amounts (assuming use of straight-line depreciation) for each of the following items for each of the six years: (a) pretax income before depreciation, (b) straight-line depreciation expense, (c) taxable income, (d) income taxes, and (e) net cash flow. Net cash flow equals the amount of income before depreciation minus the income taxes.

2. Prepare a five-column table that reports amounts (assuming use of MACRS depreciation) for each of the following items for each of the six years: (a) income before depreciation, (b) MACRS depreciation expense, (c) taxable income, (d) income taxes, and (e) net cash flow. Net cash flow equals the amount of income before depreciation minus the income taxes.

**Check** Net present value:
(3) $19,437, (4) $19,914

3. Compute the net present value of the investment if straight-line depreciation is used. Use 15% as the discount rate.

4. Compute the net present value of the investment if MACRS depreciation is used. Use 15% as the discount rate.

*Analysis Component*

5. Explain why the MACRS depreciation method increases the net present value of this project.

---

**Problem 21-4B**
Analysis of income effects of additional business

C3　A1

Windtrax Company manufactures and sells to local wholesalers approximately 200,000 units per month at a sales price of $1 per unit. Monthly costs for the production and sale of this quantity follow.

| | |
|---|---:|
| Direct materials . . . . . . . . . . . . . . | $ 30,000 |
| Direct labor . . . . . . . . . . . . . . . . | 12,000 |
| Overhead . . . . . . . . . . . . . . . . . | 50,000 |
| Selling expenses . . . . . . . . . . . . . | 7,500 |
| Administrative expenses . . . . . . . . | 31,500 |
| Total costs and expenses . . . . . . . | $131,000 |

A new out-of-state distributor has offered to buy 20,000 units next month for $0.80 each. These units would be marketed in other states and would not affect Windtrax's sales through its normal channels. A study of the costs of this new business reveals the following:

- Direct materials costs are 100% variable.
- Per unit direct labor costs for the additional units would be 100% higher than normal because their production would require double overtime pay to meet the distributor's deadline.
- Eighty percent of the normal annual overhead costs are fixed at any production level from 120,000 to 300,000 units. The remaining 20% is variable with volume.
- Accepting the new business would involve no additional selling expenses.
- Accepting the new business would increase administrative expenses by a $750 fixed amount.

**Required**

Prepare a three-column comparative income statement that shows the following:

**Check** Operating income:
(1) $69,000, (2) $8,850

1. Monthly operating income without the special order (column 1).
2. Monthly operating income received from the new business only (column 2).
3. Combined monthly operating income from normal business and the new business (column 3).

---

**Problem 21-5B**
Analysis of sales mix strategies

C3　A1

Digits Company is able to produce two products, 22 and 44, with the same machine in its factory. The following information is known:

| | Product 22 | Product 44 |
|---|---:|---:|
| Selling price per unit . . . . . . . . . . . . . . . | $175 | $200 |
| Variable costs per unit . . . . . . . . . . . . . . | 100 | 150 |
| Contribution margin per unit . . . . . . . . . | $ 75 | $ 50 |
| Machine hours to produce 1 unit . . . . . . . | 0.8 hours | 0.5 hours |
| Maximum unit sales per month . . . . . . . . | 525 units | 450 units |

Digits presently operates the machine for a single eight-hour shift for 23 working days each month. Management is thinking about operating the machine for two shifts, which will increase its productivity by another eight hours per day for 23 days per month. This change would require $5,000 additional fixed costs per month.

**Required**

1. Determine the contribution margin per machine hour that each product generates.

2. How many units of Product 22 and Product 44 should the company produce if it continues to operate with only one shift? How much total contribution margin does this mix produce each month?

3. If the company adds another shift, how many units of Product 22 and Product 44 should it produce? How much total contribution margin would this mix produce each month? Should the company add the new shift? Explain.

4. Suppose that the company determines that it can increase Product 44's maximum sales to 500 units per month by spending $500 per month in marketing efforts. Should the company pursue this strategy and the double shift? Explain.

**Check** Units of Product 44: (2) 368, (3) 450, (4) 500

---

Turftime Company's management is trying to decide whether to eliminate Department Z, which has produced low profits or losses for several years. The company's 2005 departmental income statement shows the following:

**Problem 21-6B**
Analysis of possible elimination of a department

C3 A1

| TURFTIME COMPANY Departmental Income Statements For Year Ended December 31, 2005 | | | |
|---|---|---|---|
| | **Dept. A** | **Dept. Z** | **Combined** |
| Sales | $350,000 | $87,500 | $437,500 |
| Cost of goods sold | 230,650 | 62,550 | 293,200 |
| Gross profit | 119,350 | 24,950 | 144,300 |
| Operating expenses | | | |
| Direct expenses | | | |
| Advertising | 13,500 | 1,500 | 15,000 |
| Store supplies used | 2,800 | 700 | 3,500 |
| Depreciation—Store equipment | 7,000 | 3,500 | 10,500 |
| Total direct expenses | 23,300 | 5,700 | 29,000 |
| Allocated expenses | | | |
| Sales salaries | 35,100 | 11,700 | 46,800 |
| Rent expense | 11,040 | 2,760 | 13,800 |
| Bad debts expense | 10,500 | 2,000 | 12,500 |
| Office salary | 10,400 | 2,600 | 13,000 |
| Insurance expense | 2,100 | 700 | 2,800 |
| Miscellaneous office expenses | 850 | 1,250 | 2,100 |
| Total allocated expenses | 69,990 | 21,010 | 91,000 |
| Total expenses | 93,290 | 26,710 | 120,000 |
| Net income (loss) | $ 26,060 | $ (1,760) | $ 24,300 |

In analyzing whether to eliminate Department Z, management considers the following items:

**a.** The company has one office worker who earns $250 per week or $13,000 per year and four salesclerks who each earn $225 per week or $11,700 per year.

**b.** The full salaries of three salesclerks are charged to Department A. The full salary of one salesclerk is charged to Department Z.

**c.** Eliminating Department Z would avoid the sales salaries and the office salary currently allocated to it. However, management prefers another plan. Two salesclerks have indicated that they will be quitting soon. Management believes that their work can be done by the two remaining clerks if the one office worker works in sales half time. Eliminating Department Z will allow this shift of duties. If this change is implemented, half the office worker's salary would be reported as sales salaries and half would be reported as office salary.

**d.** The store building is rented under a long-term lease that cannot be changed. Therefore, Department A will use the space and equipment currently used by Department Z.

**e.** Closing Department Z will eliminate its expenses for advertising, bad debts, and store supplies; 65% of the insurance expense allocated to it to cover its merchandise inventory; and 30% of the miscellaneous office expenses presently allocated to it.

### Required

**Check**  (1) Total expenses:
(a) $413,200, (b) $90,980

          (2) Forecasted net income
without Department Z, $27,780

**1.** Prepare a three-column report that lists items and amounts for (a) the company's total expenses (including cost of goods sold)—in column 1, (b) the expenses that would be eliminated by closing Department Z—in column 2, and (c) the expenses that will continue—in column 3.

**2.** Prepare a forecasted annual income statement for the company reflecting the elimination of Department Z assuming that it will not affect Department A's sales and gross profit. The statement should reflect the reassignment of the office worker to one-half time as a salesclerk.

### Analysis Component

**3.** Reconcile the company's combined net income with the forecasted net income assuming that Department Z is eliminated (list both items and amounts). Analyze the reconciliation and explain why you think the department should or should not be eliminated.

## PROBLEM SET C

Problem Set C is available at the book's Website to further reinforce and assess your learning.

## SERIAL PROBLEM

Success Systems

Kay Breeze is considering the purchase of equipment for Success Systems that would allow the company to add a new product to its computer furniture line. The equipment is expected to cost $120,000 and to have a six-year life and no salvage value. It will be depreciated on a straight-line basis. Success Systems expects to sell 50 units of the equipment's product each year. The expected annual income related to this equipment follows:

| | |
|---|---:|
| Sales | $150,000 |
| Costs | |
| Materials, labor, and overhead (except depreciation) | 80,000 |
| Depreciation on new equipment | 20,000 |
| Selling and administrative expenses | 15,000 |
| Total costs and expenses | 115,000 |
| Pretax income | 35,000 |
| Income taxes (30%) | 10,500 |
| Net income | $ 24,500 |

### Required

Compute the (1) payback period and (2) accounting rate of return for this equipment.

## BEYOND THE NUMBERS

### REPORTING IN ACTION

C1  A1  P3

**BTN 21-1**    Advertising is an important component of product mix decisions because it helps drive product sales. In 2003 **Krispy Kreme**'s stores in the Kansas City area ran a unique promotion associated with the performance of the **Kansas City Royals** major league baseball team. If the Royals scored 12 hits (not runs) in a home game, each person with a ticket stub for that game could redeem it for a free dozen Krispy Kreme donuts at a local Krispy Kreme store.

**Required**

1. Can you compute Krispy Kreme's incremental product cost for this advertisement? Explain.

2. Assume that the average attendance for home games at Royals stadium is 20,000 fans. How many dozen donuts must Krispy Kreme give away every time the Royals score 12 hits if 5% of fans redeem ticket stubs? Explain.

3. What would Krispy Kreme's total promotional cost be if the Royals score 12 hits in 15 home games? Assume the same attendance and redemption rates as in part 2, and that the cost to produce one dozen donuts is $2 per dozen. Explain.

4. What does Krispy Kreme potentially gain by this unique promotion? What behavior does management hope results from people redeeming ticket stubs for free donuts?

*Roll On*

5. Do research on the Internet to determine whether Krispy Kreme extended this promotion to the 2004 (or later) baseball season. Offer possible reasons that such a popular promotion would be discontinued or continued.

---

**BTN 21-2**  **Krispy Kreme** and **Tastykake** sell several different products; most are profitable but some are not. Teams of employees in each company make advertising, investment, and product mix decisions. A certain portion of advertising for both companies is on a local basis to a target audience.

**COMPARATIVE ANALYSIS**

C3

**Required**

1. Find one major advertisement of a product or group of products for each company in your local newspaper. Contact the newspaper and ask the approximate cost of this ad space (for example, cost of one page or one-half page of advertising).

2. Estimate how many products this advertisement must sell to justify its cost. Begin by taking the product's sales price advertised for each company and assume a 20% contribution margin.

3. Prepare a one-half page memorandum explaining the importance of effective advertising when making a product mix decision. Be prepared to present your ideas in class.

---

**BTN 21-3**  A consultant commented that "too often the numbers look good but feel bad." This comment stems from estimation error common to capital budgeting proposals that relate to future cash flows. Three reasons for this error often exist. First, reliably predicting cash flows several years into the future is very difficult. Second, the present value of cash flows many years into the future (say, beyond 10 years) is often very small. Third, it is difficult for personal biases and expectations not to unduly influence present value computations.

**ETHICS CHALLENGE**

P3

**Required**

1. Compute the present value of $100 to be received in 10 years assuming a 12% discount rate.

2. Why is understanding the three reasons mentioned for estimation errors important when evaluating investment projects? Link this response to your answer for part 1.

---

**BTN 21-4**  Payback period, accounting rate of return, net present value, and internal rate of return are common methods to evaluate capital investment opportunities. Assume that your manager asks you to identify the type of measurement basis and unit that each method offers and to list the advantages and disadvantages of each. Present your response in memorandum format of less than one page.

**COMMUNICATING IN PRACTICE**

P1  P2  P3  P4

---

**BTN 21-5**  Capital budgeting is an important issue for every organization, particularly as it relates to an organization's future. The United States set up a commission to study capital budgeting at the federal government level. Access the report of *The President's Commission to Study Capital Budgeting* from the following Website: **http://Clinton2.nara.gov/pcscb**.

**TAKING IT TO THE NET**

mhhe.com/wild

**Required**

1. Does the commission's concept of *capital* for federal government differ from that used by the private sector?

2. Are the investment analysis techniques explained in the chapter relevant to the government?

## TEAMWORK IN ACTION

P1   P3

**BTN 21-6** Break into teams and identify four reasons that an international airline such as **Southwest, Northwest,** or **American** would invest in a project when its direct analysis using both payback period and net present value indicate it to be a poor investment. (*Hint:* Think about qualitative factors.) Provide an example of an investment project supporting your answer.

## BUSINESS WEEK ACTIVITY

C1

mhhe.com/wild

**BTN 21-7** Read the article "An MBA: Is It Still Worth It?" in the October 21, 2002, issue of *Business Week*. (The book's Website provides free access to the article.)

**Required**

1. Describe how deciding to obtain graduate education is similar to a capital budgeting decision.
2. Explain the calculation used by Professor Jens Stephan in the article to determine the payback on an investment in an MBA degree.
3. How long will it take for an average 2002 MBA graduate to break even on the investment in graduate business education?
4. Do European or U.S. MBA graduates have a shorter payback period on their investment in education?
5. What is the annual return on investment over a 10-year period for an average MBA graduate?

## ENTREPRENEURIAL DECISION

A1

mhhe.com/wild

**BTN 21-8** In the chapter's opening feature, Corinna Lathan of **AnthroTronix** says she hopes to produce and sell two models of CosmoBot. The selling price of the enhanced model available to clinics and therapists is $2,500. The selling price of the home model to individuals is $500. Assume that AnthroTronix can sell all units of both CosmoBot models that it can produce but that it has limited production capacity. Specifically, it estimates that it can produce two units of the enhanced model per hour or, alternatively, four units of the home model per hour. The company has 2,080 production hours available. Contribution margin is $500 for the enhanced model and $400 for the home model.

**Required**

What is the most profitable sales mix for AnthroTronix? Explain.

## HITTING THE ROAD

C1   P3

**BTN 21-9** Visit or call a local auto dealership and inquire about leasing a car. Ask about the down payment and the required monthly payments. You will likely find the salesperson does not discuss the cost to purchase this car but focuses on the affordability of the monthly payments. This chapter gives you the tools to compute the cost of this car using the lease payment schedule in present dollars and to estimate the profit from leasing for an auto dealership.

**Required**

1. Compare the cost of leasing the car to buying it in present dollars using the information from the dealership you contact. (Assume you will make a final payment at the end of the lease and then own the car.)
2. Is it more costly to lease or buy the car? Support your answer with computations.

## GLOBAL DECISION

C1

**BTN 21-10** Access **Grupo Bimbo**'s 2002 annual report from its Website <u>GrupoBimbo.com</u>. Read the message from its Chief Executive Officer Daniel M. Servitje near the beginning of the report.

**Required**

1. What tool did Grupo Bimbo provide to its entire sales force to improve productivity?
2. Did Grupo Bimbo close any of its plants in 2002 to improve operating efficiency?
3. Identify two new products that Grupo Bimbo added to its product mix in 2002.
4. In what markets did Grupo Bimbo increase its sales volume in 2002?
5. What does it identify as its most outstanding promotional and advertising activity in 2002?

# Financial Statement Information

This appendix includes financial information for (1) **Krispy Kreme**, (2) **Tastykake**, and (3) **Harley-Davidson**. This information is taken from their annual reports. An **annual report** is a summary of a company's financial results for the year along with its current financial condition and future plans. This report is directed to external users of financial information, but it also affects the actions and decisions of internal users.

A company uses an annual report to showcase itself and its products. Many annual reports include attractive photos, diagrams, and illustrations related to the company. The primary objective of annual reports, however, is the *financial section,* which communicates much information about a company, with most data drawn from the accounting information system. The layout of an annual report's financial section is fairly established and typically includes the following:

- Letter to Shareholders
- Financial History and Highlights
- Management Discussion and Analysis
- Management's Report
- Report of Independent Accountants (Auditor's Report)
- Financial Statements
- Notes to Financial Statements
- List of Directors and Officers

This appendix provides the financial statements for Krispy Kreme (plus selected notes), Tastykake, and Harley-Davidson. The appendix is organized as follows:

- **Krispy Kreme A-2** through **A-17**
- **Tastykake A-18** through **A-24**
- **Harley-Davidson A-25** through **A-30**

Many assignments at the end of each chapter refer to information in this appendix. We encourage readers to spend time with these assignments; they are especially useful in showing the relevance and diversity of financial accounting and reporting.

---

*Special note:* The SEC maintains the EDGAR (**E**lectronic **D**ata **G**athering, **A**nalysis, and **R**etrieval) database at **www.sec.gov.** The **Form 10-K** is the annual report form for most companies. It provides electronically accessible information. The **Form 10-KSB** is the annual report form filed by "small businesses." It requires slightly less information than the Form 10-K. One of these forms must be filed within 90 days after the company's fiscal year-end. (Forms 10-K405, 10-KT, 10-KT405, and 10-KSB405 are slight variations of the usual form due to certain regulations or rules.)

---

KRISPY KREME

KRISPY KREME
2003 ANNUAL REPORT

## SELECTED FINANCIAL DATA

The following table shows selected financial data for Krispy Kreme. The selected historical statement of operations data for each of the years ended, and the selected historical balance sheet data as of January 31, 1999, January 30, 2000, January 28, 2001, February 3, 2002 and February 2, 2003 have been derived from our audited consolidated financial statements. Please note that our fiscal year ended February 3, 2002 contained 53 weeks.

Systemwide sales include the sales by both our company and franchised stores and exclude the sales by our KKM&D business segment and the royalties and fees received from our franchised stores. Our consolidated financial statements appearing elsewhere in this annual report exclude franchised store sales and include royalties and fees received from our franchisees. The consolidated financial statements also include the results of Freedom Rings, LLC, the area developer in Philadelphia, and Golden Gate Doughnuts, LLC, the area developer in Northern California, in which Krispy Kreme has a majority ownership interest, as well as the results of Glazed Investments, LLC, the area developer in Colorado, Minnesota and Wisconsin, for periods subsequent to August 22, 2002, the date the Company acquired a controlling interest in this area developer.

You should read the following selected financial data in conjunction with "Management's Discussion and Analysis of Financial Condition and Results of Operations," the consolidated financial statements and accompanying notes and the other financial data included elsewhere herein. All references to per share amounts and any other reference to shares in "Selected Financial Data," unless otherwise noted, have been adjusted to reflect a two-for-one stock split paid on March 19, 2001 to shareholders of record as of March 5, 2001 and a two-for-one stock split paid on June 14, 2001 to shareholders of record as of May 29, 2001. Unless otherwise specified, references in this annual report to "Krispy Kreme," the "Company," "we," "us" or "our" refer to Krispy Kreme Doughnuts, Inc. and its subsidiaries.

IN THOUSANDS, EXCEPT PER SHARE DATA AND STORE NUMBERS

| YEAR ENDED | Jan. 31, 1999 | Jan. 30, 2000 | Jan. 28, 2001 | Feb. 3, 2002 | Feb. 2, 2003 |
|---|---|---|---|---|---|
| **Statement of Operations Data:** | | | | | |
| Total revenues | $180,880 | $220,243 | $300,715 | $394,354 | $491,549 |
| Operating expenses | 159,941 | 190,003 | 250,690 | 316,946 | 381,489 |
| General and administrative expenses | 10,897 | 14,856 | 20,061 | 27,562 | 28,897 |
| Depreciation and amortization expenses | 4,278 | 4,546 | 6,457 | 7,959 | 12,271 |
| Arbitration award | — | — | — | — | 9,075 |
| Provision for restructuring | 9,466 | — | — | — | — |
| Income (loss) from operations | (3,702) | 10,838 | 23,507 | 41,887 | 59,817 |
| Interest expense (income), net, and other | 1,577 | 1,232 | (1,698) | (2,408) | 749 |
| Equity loss in joint ventures | — | — | 706 | 602 | 2,008 |
| Minority interest | — | — | 716 | 1,147 | 2,287 |
| Income (loss) before income taxes | (5,279) | 9,606 | 23,783 | 42,546 | 54,773 |
| Provision (benefit) for income taxes | (2,112) | 3,650 | 9,058 | 16,168 | 21,295 |
| Net income (loss) | $ (3,167) | $ 5,956 | $ 14,725 | $ 26,378 | $ 33,478 |
| Net income (loss) per share: | | | | | |
|   Basic | $ (.09) | $ .16 | $ .30 | $ .49 | $ .61 |
|   Diluted | (.09) | .15 | .27 | .45 | .56 |
| Shares used in calculation of net income (loss) per share: | | | | | |
|   Basic | 32,996 | 37,360 | 49,184 | 53,703 | 55,093 |
|   Diluted | 32,996 | 39,280 | 53,656 | 58,443 | 59,492 |
| Cash dividends declared per common share | $ .04 | $ — | $ — | $ — | $ — |
| **Operating Data (Unaudited):** | | | | | |
| Systemwide sales | $240,316 | $318,854 | $448,129 | $621,665 | $778,573 |
| Number of stores at end of period: | | | | | |
|   Company | 61 | 58 | 63 | 75 | 99 |
|   Franchised | 70 | 86 | 111 | 143 | 177 |
|   Systemwide | 131 | 144 | 174 | 218 | 276 |
| Average weekly sales per store: | | | | | |
|   Company | $ 47 | $ 54 | $ 69 | $ 72 | $ 76 |
|   Franchised | 28 | 38 | 43 | 53 | 58 |
| **Balance Sheet Data (at end of period):** | | | | | |
| Working capital | $ 8,387 | $ 11,452 | $ 29,443 | $ 49,236 | $ 81,441 |
| Total assets | 93,312 | 104,958 | 171,493 | 255,376 | 410,487 |
| Long-term debt, including current maturities | 21,020 | 22,902 | — | 4,643 | 60,489 |
| Total shareholders' equity | 42,247 | 47,755 | 125,679 | 187,667 | 273,352 |

**KRISPY KREME**

**KRISPY KREME DOUGHNUTS, INC.**
**REPORT OF INDEPENDENT ACCOUNTANTS**

### To the Board of Directors and Shareholders of Krispy Kreme Doughnuts, Inc.

In our opinion, the accompanying consolidated balance sheets and the related consolidated statements of operations, of shareholders' equity and of cash flows present fairly, in all material respects, the financial position of Krispy Kreme Doughnuts, Inc. and its subsidiaries (the Company) at February 3, 2002 and February 2, 2003, and the results of their operations and their cash flows for each of the three years in the period ended February 2, 2003, in conformity with accounting principles generally accepted in the United States of America. These financial statements are the responsibility of the Company's management; our responsibility is to express an opinion on these financial statements based on our audits. We conducted our audits of these statements in accordance with auditing standards generally accepted in the United States of America, which require that we plan and perform the audit to obtain reasonable assurance about whether the financial statements are free of material misstatement. An audit includes examining, on a test basis, evidence supporting the amounts and disclosures in the financial statements, assessing the accounting principles used and significant estimates made by management, and evaluating the overall financial statement presentation. We believe that our audits provide a reasonable basis for the opinion expressed above.

As discussed in Note 2 to the consolidated financial statements, effective February 4, 2002, the Company changed its method of accounting for goodwill and other intangible assets to conform to Statement of Financial Accounting Standards No. 142, "Goodwill and Other Intangible Assets."

Greensboro, North Carolina
March 13, 2003

---

**KRISPY KREME DOUGHNUTS, INC.**
**CONSOLIDATED STATEMENTS OF OPERATIONS**

In Thousands, Except Per Share Amounts

| YEAR ENDED | Jan. 28, 2001 | Feb. 3, 2002 | Feb. 2, 2003 |
|---|---|---|---|
| Total revenues | $300,715 | $394,354 | $491,549 |
| Operating expenses* | 250,690 | 316,946 | 381,489 |
| General and administrative expenses | 20,061 | 27,562 | 28,897 |
| Depreciation and amortization expenses | 6,457 | 7,959 | 12,271 |
| Arbitration award (Note 18) | — | — | 9,075 |
| Income from operations | 23,507 | 41,887 | 59,817 |
| Interest income | 2,325 | 2,980 | 1,966 |
| Interest expense | (607) | (337) | (1,781) |
| Equity loss in joint ventures | (706) | (602) | (2,008) |
| Minority interest | (716) | (1,147) | (2,287) |
| Loss on sale of property and equipment | (20) | (235) | (934) |
| Income before income taxes | 23,783 | 42,546 | 54,773 |
| Provision for income taxes | 9,058 | 16,168 | 21,295 |
| Net income | $ 14,725 | $ 26,378 | $ 33,478 |
| Basic earnings per share | $    0.30 | $    0.49 | $    0.61 |
| Diluted earnings per share | $    0.27 | $    0.45 | $    0.56 |

\* Operating expenses consist entirely of cost of goods sold.

*The accompanying notes are an integral part of these consolidated financial statements.*

**KRISPY KREME DOUGHNUTS, INC.**
**CONSOLIDATED BALANCE SHEETS**

| | | IN THOUSANDS |
| --- | --- | --- |
| | **Feb. 3, 2002** | **Feb. 2, 2003** |
| **ASSETS** | | |
| **Current Assets:** | | |
| Cash and cash equivalents | $ 21,904 | $ 32,203 |
| Short-term investments | 15,292 | 22,976 |
| Accounts receivable, less allowance for doubtful accounts of $1,182 (2002) and $1,453 (2003) | 26,894 | 34,373 |
| Accounts receivable, affiliates | 9,017 | 11,062 |
| Other receivables | 2,771 | 884 |
| Inventories | 16,159 | 24,365 |
| Prepaid expenses | 2,591 | 3,478 |
| Income taxes refundable | 2,534 | 1,963 |
| Deferred income taxes | 4,607 | 9,824 |
| Total current assets | 101,769 | 141,128 |
| Property and equipment, net | 112,577 | 202,558 |
| Long-term investments | 12,700 | 4,344 |
| Investments in unconsolidated joint ventures | 3,400 | 6,871 |
| Intangible assets | 16,621 | 48,703 |
| Other assets | 8,309 | 6,883 |
| Total assets | $255,376 | $410,487 |
| **LIABILITIES AND SHAREHOLDERS' EQUITY** | | |
| **Current Liabilities:** | | |
| Accounts payable | $ 12,095 | $ 14,055 |
| Book overdraft | 9,107 | 11,375 |
| Accrued expenses | 26,729 | 20,981 |
| Arbitration award | — | 9,075 |
| Revolving line of credit | 3,871 | — |
| Current maturities of long-term debt | 731 | 3,301 |
| Short-term debt — related party | — | 900 |
| Total current liabilities | 52,533 | 59,687 |
| Deferred income taxes | 3,930 | 9,849 |
| Long-term debt, net of current portion | 3,912 | 49,900 |
| Revolving lines of credit | — | 7,288 |
| Other long-term obligations | 4,843 | 5,218 |
| Total long-term liabilities | 12,685 | 72,255 |
| Commitments and contingencies | | |
| Minority interest | 2,491 | 5,193 |
| **Shareholders' Equity:** | | |
| Preferred stock, no par value, 10,000 shares authorized; none issued and outstanding | — | — |
| Common stock, no par value, shares authorized — 100,000 (2002) and 300,000 (2003); issued and outstanding — 54,271 (2002) and 56,295 (2003) | 121,052 | 173,112 |
| Unearned compensation | (186) | (119) |
| Notes receivable, employees | (2,580) | (558) |
| Nonqualified employee benefit plan assets | (138) | (339) |
| Nonqualified employee benefit plan liability | 138 | 339 |
| Accumulated other comprehensive income (loss) | 456 | (1,486) |
| Retained earnings | 68,925 | 102,403 |
| Total shareholders' equity | 187,667 | 273,352 |
| Total liabilities and shareholders' equity | $255,376 | $410,487 |

*The accompanying notes are an integral part of these consolidated financial statements.*

**KRISPY KREME DOUGHNUTS, INC.**
**CONSOLIDATED STATEMENTS OF SHAREHOLDERS' EQUITY**

| | KRISPY KREME DOUGHNUT CORPORATION | | | KRISPY KREME DOUGHNUTS, INC. | | | |
|---|---|---|---|---|---|---|---|
| | Common Shares | Common Stock | Additional Paid-In Capital | Preferred Shares | Preferred Stock | Common Shares | Common Stock |
| **Balance at January 30, 2000** | 467 | $ 4,670 | $ 10,805 | — | $ — | — | $ — |
| Comprehensive income: | | | | | | | |
| Net income for the year ended January 28, 2001 | | | | | | | |
| Unrealized holding gain, net | | | | | | | |
| Total comprehensive income | | | | | | | |
| Proceeds from public offering | | | | | | 13,800 | 65,637 |
| Conversion of Krispy Kreme Doughnut Corporation shares to Krispy Kreme Doughnuts, Inc. shares | (467) | (4,670) | (10,805) | | | 37,360 | 15,475 |
| Cash dividend to shareholders | | | | | | | |
| Issuance of shares to employee stock ownership plan | | | | | | 580 | 3,039 |
| Contribution to the nonqualified employee benefit plan | | | | | | | |
| Liability under the nonqualified employee benefit plan | | | | | | | |
| Issuance of restricted common shares | | | | | | 12 | 210 |
| Exercise of stock options, including tax benefit of $595 | | | | | | 80 | 699 |
| Amortization of restricted common shares | | | | | | | |
| Collection of notes receivable | | | | | | | |
| **Balance at January 28, 2001** | — | $ — | $ — | — | $ — | 51,832 | $ 85,060 |
| Comprehensive income: | | | | | | | |
| Net income for the year ended February 3, 2002 | | | | | | | |
| Unrealized holding loss, net | | | | | | | |
| Foreign currency translation adjustment, net | | | | | | | |
| Total comprehensive income | | | | | | | |
| Proceeds from public offering | | | | | | 1,086 | 17,202 |
| Exercise of stock options, including tax benefit of $9,772 | | | | | | 1,183 | 13,678 |
| Issuance of shares in conjunction with acquisition of franchise market | | | | | | 115 | 4,183 |
| Adjustment of nonqualified employee benefit plan investments | | | | | | | |
| Issuance of restricted common shares | | | | | | 1 | 50 |
| Amortization of restricted common shares | | | | | | | |
| Issuance of stock for notes receivable | | | | | | 54 | 879 |
| Collection of notes receivable | | | | | | | |
| **Balance at February 3, 2002** | — | $ — | $ — | — | $ — | 54,271 | $121,052 |
| Comprehensive income: | | | | | | | |
| Net income for the year ended February 2, 2003 | | | | | | | |
| Unrealized holding loss, net of tax benefit of $241 | | | | | | | |
| Foreign currency translation adjustment, net of tax expense of $7 | | | | | | | |
| Unrealized loss from cash flow hedge, net of tax benefit of $982 | | | | | | | |
| Total comprehensive income | | | | | | | |
| Exercise of stock options, including tax benefit of $13,795 | | | | | | 1,187 | 20,935 |
| Issuance of shares in conjunction with acquisition of franchise markets | | | | | | 837 | 30,975 |
| Adjustment of nonqualified employee benefit plan investments | | | | | | | |
| Amortization of restricted common shares | | | | | | | |
| Issuance of stock options in exchange for services | | | | | | | 150 |
| Collection of notes receivable | | | | | | | |
| **Balance at February 2, 2003** | — | $ — | $ — | — | $ — | 56,295 | $173,112 |

*The accompanying notes are an integral part of these consolidated financial statements.*

IN THOUSANDS

| Unearned Compensation | Notes Receivable, Employees | Nonqualified Employee Benefit Plan Assets | Nonqualified Employee Benefit Plan Liability | Accumulated Other Comprehensive Income (Loss) | Retained Earnings | Total |
|---|---|---|---|---|---|---|
| $  — | $(2,547) | $  — | $  — | $  — | $ 34,827 | $ 47,755 |
|  |  |  |  |  | 14,725 | 14,725 |
|  |  |  |  | 609 |  | 609 |
|  |  |  |  |  |  | 15,334 |
|  |  |  |  |  |  | 65,637 |
|  |  |  |  |  |  | — |
|  |  |  |  |  | (7,005) | (7,005) |
|  |  |  |  |  |  | 3,039 |
|  |  | (126) |  |  |  | (126) |
|  |  |  | 126 |  |  | 126 |
| (210) |  |  |  |  |  | — |
|  |  |  |  |  |  | 699 |
| 22 |  |  |  |  |  | 22 |
|  | 198 |  |  |  |  | 198 |
| $(188) | $(2,349) | $(126) | $126 | $  609 | $ 42,547 | $125,679 |
|  |  |  |  |  | 26,378 | 26,378 |
|  |  |  |  | (111) |  | (111) |
|  |  |  |  | (42) |  | (42) |
|  |  |  |  |  |  | 26,225 |
|  |  |  |  |  |  | 17,202 |
|  |  |  |  |  |  | 13,678 |
|  |  |  |  |  |  | 4,183 |
|  |  | (12) | 12 |  |  | — |
| (50) |  |  |  |  |  | — |
| 52 |  |  |  |  |  | 52 |
|  | (879) |  |  |  |  | — |
|  | 648 |  |  |  |  | 648 |
| $(186) | $(2,580) | $(138) | $138 | $  456 | $ 68,925 | $187,667 |
|  |  |  |  |  | 33,478 | 33,478 |
|  |  |  |  | (385) |  | (385) |
|  |  |  |  | 11 |  | 11 |
|  |  |  |  | (1,568) |  | (1,568) |
|  |  |  |  |  |  | 31,536 |
|  |  |  |  |  |  | 20,935 |
|  |  |  |  |  |  | 30,975 |
|  |  | (201) | 201 |  |  | — |
| 67 |  |  |  |  |  | 67 |
|  |  |  |  |  |  | 150 |
|  | 2,022 |  |  |  |  | 2,022 |
| $(119) | $  (558) | $(339) | $339 | $ (1,486) | $102,403 | $273,352 |

**KRISPY KREME DOUGHNUTS, INC..**
**CONSOLIDATED STATEMENTS OF CASH FLOWS**

IN THOUSANDS

| YEAR ENDED | Jan. 28, 2001 | Feb. 3, 2002 | Feb. 2, 2003 |
|---|---|---|---|
| **Cash Flow From Operating Activities:** | | | |
| Net income | $ 14,725 | $ 26,378 | $ 33,478 |
| Items not requiring cash: | | | |
| Depreciation and amortization | 6,457 | 7,959 | 12,271 |
| Deferred income taxes | 1,668 | 2,553 | 1,632 |
| Loss on disposal of property and equipment, net | 20 | 235 | 934 |
| Compensation expense related to restricted stock awards | 22 | 52 | 67 |
| Tax benefit from exercise of nonqualified stock options | 595 | 9,772 | 13,795 |
| Provision for store closings and impairment | 318 | — | — |
| Minority interest | 716 | 1,147 | 2,287 |
| Equity loss in joint ventures | 706 | 602 | 2,008 |
| Change in assets and liabilities: | | | |
| Receivables | (3,434) | (13,317) | (7,390) |
| Inventories | (2,052) | (3,977) | (7,866) |
| Prepaid expenses | 1,239 | (682) | (331) |
| Income taxes, net | 902 | (2,575) | 571 |
| Accounts payable | 2,279 | 3,884 | (33) |
| Accrued expenses | 7,966 | 4,096 | (9,296) |
| Arbitration award | — | — | 9,075 |
| Other long-term obligations | (15) | 83 | (166) |
| Net cash provided by operating activities | 32,112 | 36,210 | 51,036 |
| **Cash Flow From Investing Activities:** | | | |
| Purchase of property and equipment | (25,655) | (37,310) | (83,196) |
| Proceeds from disposal of property and equipment | 1,419 | 3,196 | 701 |
| Proceeds from disposal of assets held for sale | — | — | 1,435 |
| Acquisition of franchise markets, net of cash acquired | — | (20,571) | (4,965) |
| Investments in unconsolidated joint ventures | (4,465) | (1,218) | (7,869) |
| Purchases of investments | (41,375) | (10,128) | (32,739) |
| Proceeds from investments | 6,004 | 18,005 | 33,097 |
| Increase in other assets | (3,216) | (4,237) | (1,038) |
| Net cash used for investing activities | (67,288) | (52,263) | (94,574) |
| **Cash Flow From Financing Activities:** | | | |
| Borrowings of long-term debt | — | 4,643 | 44,234 |
| Repayment of long-term debt | (3,600) | — | (2,170) |
| Net (repayments) borrowings from revolving line of credit | (15,775) | 345 | (121) |
| Repayment of short-term debt — related party | — | — | (500) |
| Debt issue costs | — | — | (194) |
| Proceeds from exercise of stock options | 104 | 3,906 | 7,140 |
| Proceeds from stock offering | 65,637 | 17,202 | — |
| Book overdraft | (941) | 3,960 | 2,268 |
| Collection of notes receivable | 198 | 648 | 3,612 |
| Minority interest | 401 | 227 | (432) |
| Cash dividends paid | (7,005) | — | — |
| Net cash provided by financing activities | 39,019 | 30,931 | 53,837 |
| Net increase in cash and cash equivalents | 3,843 | 14,878 | 10,299 |
| Cash and cash equivalents at beginning of year | 3,183 | 7,026 | 21,904 |
| Cash and cash equivalents at end of year | $ 7,026 | $ 21,904 | $ 32,203 |
| Supplemental schedule of non-cash investing and financing activities: | | | |
| Issuance of stock in conjunction with acquisition of franchise markets | $ — | $ 4,183 | $ 8,727 |
| Issuance of stock in conjunction with acquisition of additional interest in area developer franchisee | — | — | 22,248 |
| Unrealized gain (loss) on investments | 609 | (111) | (385) |
| Issuance of stock options in exchange for services | — | — | 150 |
| Issuance of stock to Krispy Kreme Profit-Sharing Stock Ownership Plan | 3,039 | — | — |
| Issuance of restricted common shares | 210 | 50 | — |
| Issuance of stock in exchange for employee notes receivable | — | 879 | — |

*The accompanying notes are an integral part of these consolidated financial statements.*

**KRISPY KREME DOUGHNUTS, INC.**
**SELECTED** NOTES TO CONSOLIDATED FINANCIAL STATEMENTS

## 1. ORGANIZATION AND PURPOSE

Krispy Kreme Doughnuts, Inc. was incorporated in North Carolina on December 2, 1999 as a wholly-owned subsidiary of Krispy Kreme Doughnut Corporation ("KKDC"). Pursuant to a plan of merger approved by shareholders on November 10, 1999, the shareholders of KKDC became shareholders of Krispy Kreme Doughnuts, Inc. on April 4, 2000. Each shareholder received 80 shares of Krispy Kreme Doughnuts, Inc. common stock and $15 in cash for each share of KKDC common stock they held. As a result of the merger, KKDC became a wholly owned subsidiary of Krispy Kreme Doughnuts, Inc. Krispy Kreme Doughnuts, Inc. closed a public offering of its common stock on April 10, 2000.

All consolidated financial statements prior to the merger are those of KKDC and all consolidated financial statements after the merger are those of Krispy Kreme Doughnuts, Inc.

## 2. NATURE OF BUSINESS AND SIGNIFICANT ACCOUNTING POLICIES

**Nature of Business.**   Krispy Kreme Doughnuts, Inc. and its subsidiaries (the "Company") are engaged principally in the sale of doughnuts and related items through Company-owned stores. The Company also derives revenue from franchise and development fees and the collection of royalties from franchisees. Additionally, the Company sells doughnut-making equipment, mix, coffee and other ingredients and supplies used in operating a doughnut store to Company-owned and franchised stores.

The significant accounting policies followed by the Company in preparing the accompanying consolidated financial statements are as follows:

**Basis of Consolidation.**   The consolidated financial statements include the accounts of the Company and its wholly-owned subsidiaries. All significant intercompany accounts and transactions are eliminated in consolidation. Generally, investments greater than 50 percent in affiliates for which the Company maintains control are also consolidated and the portion not owned by the Company is shown as a minority interest. As of February 2, 2003, the Company consolidated the accounts of three joint ventures which the Company controlled: Freedom Rings, LLC ("Freedom Rings"), the joint venture with the rights to develop stores in the Philadelphia market; Glazed Investments, LLC ("Glazed Investments"), the joint venture with the rights to develop stores in Colorado, Minnesota and Wisconsin; and Golden Gate Doughnuts, LLC ("Golden Gate"), the joint venture with the rights to develop stores in Northern California. Generally, investments in 20- to 50-percent owned affiliates for which the Company has the ability to exercise significant influence over operating and financial policies are accounted for by the equity method of accounting, whereby the investment is carried at the cost of acquisition, plus the Company's equity in undistributed earnings or losses since acquisition, less any distributions received by the Company. Accordingly, the Company's share of the net earnings of these companies is included in consolidated net income. Investments in less than 20-percent owned affiliates are accounted for by the cost method of accounting.

**Fiscal Year.**   The Company's fiscal year is based on a fifty-two/fifty-three week year. The fiscal year ends on the Sunday closest to the last day in January. The years ended January 28, 2001, February 3, 2002 and February 2, 2003 contained 52, 53 and 52 weeks, respectively.

**Cash and Cash Equivalents.**   The Company considers cash on hand, deposits in banks, and all highly liquid debt instruments with a maturity of three months or less at date of acquisition to be cash and cash equivalents.

**Inventories.**   Inventories are recorded at the lower of average cost (first-in, first-out) or market.

**Investments.**   Investments consist of United States Treasury notes, mortgage-backed government securities, corporate debt securities, municipal securities and certificates of deposit and are included in short-term and long-term investments in the accompanying consolidated balance sheets. Certificates of deposit are carried at cost which approximates fair value. All other marketable securities are stated at market value as determined by the most recently traded price of each security at the balance sheet date.

Management determines the appropriate classification of its investments in marketable securities at the time of the purchase and reevaluates such determination at each balance sheet date. At February 2, 2003, all marketable securities are classified as available-for-sale. Available-for-sale securities are carried at fair value with the unrealized gains and losses reported as a separate component of shareholders' equity in accumulated other comprehensive income (loss). The cost of investments sold is determined on the specific identification or the first-in, first-out method.

**Property and Equipment.**   Property and equipment are stated at cost less accumulated depreciation. Major renewals and betterments are charged to the property accounts while replacements, maintenance and repairs which do not improve or extend the lives of the respective assets are expensed currently. Interest is capitalized on major capital expenditures during the period of construction.

Depreciation of property and equipment is provided on the straight-line method over the estimated useful lives: Buildings — 15 to 35 years; Machinery and equipment — 3 to 15 years; Leasehold improvements — lesser of useful lives of assets or lease term.

**Intangible Assets.** In July 2001, the Financial Accounting Standards Board ("FASB") issued Statement of Financial Accounting Standards ("SFAS") No. 141, "Business Combinations," and SFAS No. 142, "Goodwill and Other Intangible Assets." These pronouncements provide guidance on accounting for the acquisition of businesses and other intangible assets, including goodwill, which arise from such activities. SFAS No. 141 affirms that only the purchase method of accounting may be applied to a business combination and provides guidance on the allocation of purchase price to the assets acquired. SFAS No. 141 applies to all business combinations initiated after June 30, 2001. Under SFAS No. 142, goodwill and intangible assets that have indefinite useful lives are no longer amortized but are reviewed at least annually for impairment. SFAS No. 142 is effective for the Company's fiscal 2003, although goodwill and intangible assets acquired after June 30, 2001 were subject immediately to the non-amortization provisions of SFAS No. 142. The Company has evaluated its intangible assets, which at February 2, 2003 consist of goodwill recorded in connection with a business acquisition ($201,000) and the value assigned to reacquired franchise rights in connection with the acquisition of rights to certain markets from franchisees ($48,502,000), and determined that all such assets have indefinite lives and, as a result, are not subject to amortization provisions. For the fiscal year ended February 3, 2002, the Company recorded an expense of $100,000 to amortize intangible assets related to an acquisition completed prior to June 30, 2001. The Company completed impairment analyses of its intangible assets in fiscal 2003 and found no instances of impairment.

**Use of Estimates in Preparation of Financial Statements.** The preparation of financial statements in conformity with generally accepted accounting principles requires management to make estimates and assumptions that affect the reported amounts of assets and liabilities and disclosure of contingent assets and liabilities at the date of the financial statements and the reported amounts of revenues and expenses during the reporting period. Actual results could differ from those estimates.

**Revenue Recognition.** A summary of the revenue recognition policies for each segment of the Company (see Note 14) is as follows:

- Company Store Operations revenue is derived from the sale of doughnuts and related items to on-premises and off-premises customers. Revenue is recognized at the time of sale for on-premises sales. For off-premises sales, revenue is recognized at the time of delivery.

- Franchise Operations revenue is derived from: (1) development and franchise fees from the opening of new stores; and (2) royalties charged to franchisees based on sales. Development and franchise fees are charged for certain new stores and are deferred until the store is opened and the Company has performed substantially all of the initial services it is required to provide. The royalties recognized in each period are based on the sales in that period.

- KKM&D revenue is derived from the sale of doughnut-making equipment, mix, coffee and other supplies needed to operate a doughnut store to Company-owned and franchised stores. Revenue is recognized at the time the title and the risk of loss pass to the customer, generally upon delivery of the goods. Revenue from Company-owned stores and consolidated joint venture stores is eliminated in consolidation.

**Income Taxes.** The Company uses the asset and liability method to account for income taxes, which requires the recognition of deferred tax assets and liabilities for the expected future tax consequences of temporary differences between tax bases and financial reporting bases for assets and liabilities.

**Fair Value Of Financial Instruments.** Cash, accounts receivable, accounts payable, accrued liabilities and debt are reflected in the financial statements at carrying amounts which approximate fair value.

**Advertising Costs.** All costs associated with advertising and promoting products are expensed in the period incurred.

**Store Opening Costs.** All costs, both direct and indirect, incurred to open either Company or franchise stores are expensed in the period incurred. Direct costs to open stores amounted to $464,000, $551,000 and $845,000 in fiscal 2001, 2002 and 2003, respectively.

**Asset Impairment.** When a store is identified as underperforming or when a decision is made to close a store, the Company makes an assessment of the potential impairment of the related assets. The assessment is based upon a comparison of the carrying amount of the assets, primarily property and equipment, to the estimated undiscounted cash flows expected to be generated from those assets. To estimate cash flows, management projects the net cash flows anticipated from continuing operation of the store until its closing as well as cash flows anticipated from disposal of the related assets, if any. If the carrying amount of the assets exceeds the sum of the undiscounted cash flows, the Company records an impairment charge measured as the excess of the carrying value over the fair value of the assets. The resulting net book value of the assets less estimated net realizable value at disposition, is depreciated over the remaining term that the store will continue in operation.

**Comprehensive Income.** SFAS No. 130, "Reporting Comprehensive Income," requires that certain items such as foreign currency translation adjustments, unrealized gains and losses on certain investments in debt and equity securities and minimum pension liability adjustments be presented as separate components of shareholders' equity. SFAS No. 130 defines these as items of other comprehensive income which must be reported in a financial statement displayed with the same prominence as other financial statements. Accumulated other comprehensive income (loss), as reflected in the consolidated statements of shareholders' equity, was comprised of net unrealized holding gains on marketable securities of $498,000 at February 3, 2002 and $113,000 at February 2, 2003 and foreign currency translation adjustment, net, of $42,000 at February 3, 2002 and $31,000 at February 2, 2003. At February 2, 2003, accumulated other comprehensive income (loss) also included the unrealized loss from a cash flow hedge, net of related tax benefits, of $1,568,000. Total comprehensive income for fiscal 2001, 2002 and 2003 was $15,334,000, $26,225,000 and $31,536,000, respectively.

**Foreign Currency Translation.**    For all non-U.S. joint ventures, the functional currency is the local currency. Assets and liabilities of those operations are translated into U.S. dollars using exchange rates at the balance sheet date. Revenue and expenses are translated using the average exchange rates for the reporting period. Translation adjustments are deferred in accumulated other comprehensive income (loss), a separate component of shareholders' equity.

## 3. INVESTMENTS

The following table provides certain information about investments at February 3, 2002 and February 2, 2003.

IN THOUSANDS

|  | Amortized Cost | Gross Unrealized Holding Gains | Gross Unrealized Holding Losses | Fair Value |
|---|---|---|---|---|
| **February 3, 2002** |  |  |  |  |
| U.S. government notes | $ 9,049 | $ — | $ (17) | $ 9,032 |
| Federal government agencies | 10,959 | 442 | (166) | 11,235 |
| Corporate debt securities | 6,475 | 317 | (88) | 6,704 |
| Other bonds | 1,043 | — | (22) | 1,021 |
| Total | $27,526 | $759 | $(293) | $27,992 |
| **February 2, 2003** |  |  |  |  |
| U.S. government notes | $16,657 | $152 | $ (97) | $16,712 |
| Federal government agencies | 7,485 | 289 | (197) | 7,577 |
| Corporate debt securities | 1,000 | 76 | (45) | 1,031 |
| Certificate of deposit | 2,000 | — | — | 2,000 |
| Total | $27,142 | $517 | $(339) | $27,320 |

Maturities of investments were as follows at February 2, 2003:

IN THOUSANDS

|  | Amortized Cost | Fair Value |
|---|---|---|
| Due within one year | $22,844 | $22,976 |
| Due after one year through five years | 4,298 | 4,344 |
| Total | $27,142 | $27,320 |

## KRISPY KREME

## 4. INVENTORIES

**The components of inventories are as follows:**

IN THOUSANDS

| | Distribution Center | Equipment Department | Mix Department | Company Stores | Total |
|---|---|---|---|---|---|
| **February 3, 2002** | | | | | |
| Raw materials | $ — | $3,060 | $ 788 | $1,826 | $ 5,674 |
| Work in progress | — | 28 | — | — | 28 |
| Finished goods | 1,318 | 2,867 | 95 | — | 4,280 |
| Purchased merchandise | 5,503 | — | — | 613 | 6,116 |
| Manufacturing supplies | — | — | 61 | — | 61 |
| Totals | $ 6,821 | $5,955 | $ 944 | $2,439 | $16,159 |
| **February 2, 2003** | | | | | |
| Raw materials | $ — | $3,828 | $1,069 | $1,922 | $ 6,819 |
| Work in progress | — | 234 | — | — | 234 |
| Finished goods | 2,222 | 3,616 | 172 | — | 6,010 |
| Purchased merchandise | 10,191 | — | — | 966 | 11,157 |
| Manufacturing supplies | — | — | 145 | — | 145 |
| Totals | $12,413 | $7,678 | $1,386 | $2,888 | $24,365 |

## 5. PROPERTY AND EQUIPMENT

**Property and equipment consists of the following:**

IN THOUSANDS

| | Feb. 3, 2002 | Feb. 2, 2003 |
|---|---|---|
| Land | $ 14,823 | $ 24,741 |
| Buildings | 39,566 | 88,641 |
| Machinery and equipment | 86,683 | 118,332 |
| Leasehold improvements | 13,463 | 19,522 |
| Construction in progress | 1,949 | 1,534 |
| | 156,484 | 252,770 |
| Less: accumulated depreciation | 43,907 | 50,212 |
| Property and equipment, net | $112,577 | $202,558 |

Depreciation expense was $6,141,000, $7,398,000 and $11,570,000 for fiscal 2001, fiscal 2002 and fiscal 2003, respectively.

## 6. ACCRUED EXPENSES

**Accrued expenses consist of the following:**

IN THOUSANDS

| | Feb. 3, 2002 | Feb. 2, 2003 |
|---|---|---|
| Insurance | $ 4,891 | $ 6,150 |
| Salaries, wages and incentive compensation | 11,686 | 6,034 |
| Deferred revenue | 2,082 | 1,485 |
| Taxes, other than income | 1,632 | 1,865 |
| Other | 6,438 | 5,447 |
| Total | $ 26,729 | $ 20,981 |

## 7. DEBT

**The Company's debt, including debt of consolidated joint ventures, consists of the following:**

| | | IN THOUSANDS |
|---|---|---|
| | Feb. 3, 2002 | Feb. 2, 2003 |
| Krispy Kreme Doughnut Corporation: | | |
| $40 million revolving line of credit | $ — | $ — |
| Golden Gate: | | |
| $6.75 million revolving line of credit | 3,871 | 4,750 |
| Freedom Rings: | | |
| $5 million revolving line of credit | — | 2,538 |
| Revolving lines of credit | $ 3,871 | $ 7,288 |
| Glazed Investments: | | |
| Short-term debt — related party | $ — | $ 900 |
| Krispy Kreme Doughnut Corporation: | | |
| $33 million term loan | $ — | $ 31,763 |
| Golden Gate: | | |
| $4.5 million term loan | 4,418 | 3,926 |
| $3 million term loan | — | 2,976 |
| Glazed Investments: | | |
| Real Estate and Equipment loans | — | 14,400 |
| Subordinated notes | — | 136 |
| Freedom Rings: | | |
| Other debt | 225 | — |
| | 4,643 | 53,201 |
| Current maturities of long-term debt | (731) | (3,301) |
| Long-term debt, net of current portion | $ 3,912 | $ 49,900 |

### $40 Million Revolving Line of Credit

On December 29, 1999, the Company entered into an unsecured loan agreement ("Agreement") with a bank to increase borrowing availability and extend the maturity of its revolving line of credit. The Agreement provides a $40 million revolving line of credit and expires on June 30, 2004.

Under the terms of the Agreement, interest on the revolving line of credit is charged, at the Company's option, at either the lender's prime rate less 110 basis points or at the one-month LIBOR plus 100 basis points. There was no interest, fee or other charge for the unadvanced portion of the line of credit until July 1, 2002 at which time the Company began paying a fee of 0.10% on the unadvanced portion. No amounts were outstanding on the revolving line of credit at February 3, 2002 or February 2, 2003. The amount available under the revolving line of credit is reduced by letters of credit, amounts outstanding under certain loans made by the bank to franchisees which are guaranteed by the Company and certain amounts available or outstanding in connection with credit cards issued by the lender on behalf of the Company and was $31,695,000 at February 2, 2003. Outstanding letters of credit, primarily for insurance purposes, totaled $6,626,000, amounts outstanding under the loans guaranteed by the Company totaled $152,000 and amounts available in connection with credit cards issued by the lender totaled $1,527,000 at February 2, 2003.

The Agreement contains provisions that, among other requirements, restrict capital expenditures, require the maintenance of certain financial ratios, place various restrictions on the sale of properties, restrict the Company's ability to enter into collateral repurchase agreements and guarantees, restrict the payment of dividends and require compliance with other customary financial and nonfinancial covenants. At February 2, 2003, the Company was in compliance with each of these covenants.

### 8. LEASE COMMITMENTS

The Company conducts some of its operations from leased facilities and, additionally, leases certain equipment under operating leases. Generally, these leases have initial terms of 5 to 18 years and contain provisions for renewal options of 5 to 10 years.

**At February 2, 2003, future minimum annual rental commitments, gross, under noncancelable operating leases, including lease commitments of consolidated joint ventures, are as follows:**

|  | In Thousands |
|---|---|
| **FISCAL YEAR ENDING IN** | **Amount** |
| 2004 | $10,969 |
| 2005 | 9,187 |
| 2006 | 6,707 |
| 2007 | 5,018 |
| 2008 | 5,433 |
| Thereafter | 32,397 |
|  | $69,711 |

Rental expense, net of rental income, totaled $8,540,000 in fiscal 2001, $10,576,000 in fiscal 2002 and $13,169,000 in fiscal 2003.

## 9. INCOME TAXES

**The components of the provision for federal and state income taxes are summarized as follows:**

|  |  |  | In Thousands |
|---|---|---|---|
| **YEAR ENDED** | **Jan. 28, 2001** | **Feb. 3, 2002** | **Feb. 2, 2003** |
| Currently payable | $7,390 | $13,615 | $19,663 |
| Deferred | 1,668 | 2,553 | 1,632 |
|  | $9,058 | $16,168 | $21,295 |

**A reconciliation of the statutory federal income tax rate with the company's effective rate is as follows:**

|  |  |  | In Thousands |
|---|---|---|---|
| **YEAR ENDED** | **Jan. 28, 2001** | **Feb. 3, 2002** | **Feb. 2, 2003** |
| Federal taxes at statutory rate | $8,321 | $14,891 | $19,170 |
| State taxes, net of federal benefit | 673 | 1,158 | 1,405 |
| Other | 64 | 119 | 720 |
|  | $9,058 | $16,168 | $21,295 |

Income tax payments, net of refunds, were $5,894,000 in fiscal 2001, $6,616,000 in fiscal 2002 and $5,298,000 in fiscal 2003. The income tax payments in fiscal 2002 and fiscal 2003 were lower than the current provision due to the income tax benefit of stock option exercises of $9,772,000 and $13,795,000 during fiscal 2002 and fiscal 2003, respectively.

**The net current and non-current components of deferred income taxes recognized in the balance sheet are as follows:**

|  |  | In Thousands |
|---|---|---|
|  | **Feb. 3, 2002** | **Feb. 2, 2003** |
| Net current assets | $ 4,607 | $ 9,824 |
| Net non-current liabilities | (3,930) | (9,849) |
|  | $   677 | $   (25) |

**The tax effects of the significant temporary differences which comprise the deferred tax assets and liabilities are as follows:**

|  | | In Thousands |
|---|---|---|
|  | Feb. 3, 2002 | Feb. 2, 2003 |
| **ASSETS** | | |
| Compensation deferred (unpaid) | $ 676 | $ 663 |
| Insurance | 1,859 | 2,368 |
| Other long-term obligations | 659 | 395 |
| Accrued restructuring expenses | 1,183 | 501 |
| Deferred revenue | 791 | 1,165 |
| Accounts receivable | 449 | 556 |
| Inventory | 436 | 278 |
| Charitable contributions carryforward | — | 714 |
| Gain/loss on hedging transactions | — | 982 |
| Accrued litigation | — | 3,494 |
| Accrued payroll | — | 1,018 |
| State tax credit carryforwards | — | 179 |
| State NOL carryforwards | 2,524 | 2,463 |
| Other | 676 | 687 |
| Gross deferred tax assets | 9,253 | 15,463 |
| **LIABILITIES** | | |
| Property and equipment | 5,589 | 11,628 |
| Goodwill | 198 | 1,037 |
| Prepaid expenses | 265 | 360 |
| Gross deferred tax liabilities | 6,052 | 13,025 |
| Valuation allowance — State NOL carryforwards | (2,524) | (2,463) |
| Net asset/(liability) | $ 677 | $ (25) |

At February 2, 2003, the Company has recorded a valuation allowance against the state NOL carryforwards of $2,463,000. If these carryforwards are realized in the future, $2,232,000 of the tax benefit would be recorded as an addition to common stock as this portion of the carryforwards were a result of the tax benefits of stock option exercises in fiscal 2002 and 2003.

The Company records deferred tax assets reflecting the benefit of future deductible amounts. Realization of these assets is dependent on generating sufficient future taxable income and the ability to carryback losses to previous years in which there was taxable income. Although realization is not assured, management believes it is more likely than not that all of the deferred tax assets, for which a valuation allowance has not been established, will be realized. The amount of the deferred tax assets considered realizable, however, could be reduced in the near term if estimates of future taxable income are reduced.

## 10. EARNINGS PER SHARE

The computation of basic earnings per share is based on the weighted average number of common shares outstanding during the period. The computation of diluted earnings per share reflects the potential dilution that would occur if stock options were exercised and the dilution from the issuance of restricted shares. The treasury stock method is used to calculate dilutive shares. This reduces the gross number of dilutive shares by the number of shares purchasable from the proceeds of the options assumed to be exercised, the proceeds of the tax benefits recognized by the Company in conjunction with nonqualified stock plans and from the amounts of unearned compensation associated with the restricted shares.

**The following table sets forth the computation of basic and diluted earnings per share:**

|  | | | In Thousands, Except Share Amounts |
|---|---|---|---|
| YEAR ENDED | Jan. 28, 2001 | Feb. 3, 2002 | Feb. 2, 2003 |
| Numerator: | | | |
| Net income | $ 14,725 | $ 26,378 | $ 33,478 |
| Denominator: | | | |
| Basic earnings per share — weighted average shares | 49,183,916 | 53,702,916 | 55,092,542 |
| Effect of dilutive securities: | | | |
| Stock options | 4,471,576 | 4,734,371 | 4,395,864 |
| Restricted stock | — | 5,698 | 3,967 |
| Diluted earnings per share — adjusted weighted average shares | 53,655,492 | 58,442,985 | 59,492,373 |

## 14. BUSINESS SEGMENT INFORMATION

The Company has three reportable business segments. The Company Store Operations segment is comprised of the operating activities of the stores owned by the Company and those in consolidated joint ventures. These stores sell doughnuts and complementary products through both on-premises and off-premises sales. The majority of the ingredients and materials used by Company Store Operations is purchased from the KKM&D business segment.

The Franchise Operations segment represents the results of the Company's franchise program. Under the terms of the franchise agreements, the licensed operators pay royalties and fees to the Company in return for the use of the Krispy Kreme name. Expenses for this business segment include costs incurred to recruit new franchisees and to open, monitor and aid in the performance of these stores and direct general and administrative expenses.

The KKM&D segment supplies mix, equipment, coffee and other items to both Company and franchisee-owned stores. All intercompany transactions between the KKM&D business segment and Company stores and consolidated joint venture stores are eliminated in consolidation.

Segment information for total assets and capital expenditures is not presented as such information is not used in measuring segment performance or allocating resources among segments.

Segment operating income is income before general corporate expenses and income taxes.

**Information about the Company's operations by business segment is as follows:**

| | | | IN THOUSANDS |
|---|---|---|---|
| YEAR ENDED | Jan. 28, 2001 | Feb. 3, 2002 | Feb. 2, 2003 |
| Revenues: | | | |
| Company Store Operations | $ 213,677 | $ 266,209 | $ 319,592 |
| Franchise Operations | 9,445 | 14,008 | 19,304 |
| KKM&D | 201,406 | 269,396 | 347,642 |
| Intercompany sales eliminations | (123,813) | (155,259) | (194,989) |
| Total revenues | $ 300,715 | $ 394,354 | $ 491,549 |
| Operating income: | | | |
| Company Store Operations | $ 27,370 | $ 42,932 | $ 58,214 |
| Franchise Operations | 5,730 | 9,040 | 14,319 |
| KKM&D | 11,712 | 18,999 | 26,843 |
| Unallocated general and administrative expenses | (21,305) | (29,084) | (30,484) |
| Arbitration award | — | — | (9,075) |
| Total operating income | $ 23,507 | $ 41,887 | $ 59,817 |
| Depreciation and Amortization Expenses: | | | |
| Company Store Operations | $ 4,838 | $ 5,859 | $ 8,854 |
| Franchise Operations | 72 | 72 | 108 |
| KKM&D | 303 | 507 | 1,723 |
| Corporate administration | 1,244 | 1,521 | 1,586 |
| Total depreciation and amortization expenses | $ 6,457 | $ 7,959 | $ 12,271 |

## 16. COMMITMENTS AND CONTINGENCIES

In order to assist certain associate and franchise operators in obtaining third-party financing, the Company from time-to-time enters into collateral repurchase agreements involving both Company stock and doughnut-making equipment. The Company's contingent liability related to these agreements was approximately $70,000 at February 3, 2002. The Company was not contingently liable under any such agreements at February 2, 2003. Additionally, primarily for the purpose of providing financing guarantees in a percentage equivalent to the Company's ownership percentage in various joint venture investments, the Company has guaranteed certain leases and loans from third-party financial institutions on behalf of franchise operators. The Company's contingent liability related to these guarantees was approximately $3,805,000 at February 3, 2002 and $7,652,000 at February 2, 2003. Of the total guaranteed amount of $7,652,000 at February 2, 2003, $6,450,000 are for franchisees in which we have an ownership interest and $1,202,000 are for franchisees in which we have no ownership interest. The expirations of these guarantees for the five fiscal years ending after February 2, 2003 are $2,903,000, $498,000, $517,000, $357,000 and $355,000, respectively.

Because the Company enters into long-term contracts with its suppliers, in the event that any of these relationships terminate unexpectedly, even where it has multiple suppliers for the same ingredient, the Company's ability to obtain adequate quantities of the same high quality ingredient at the same competitive price could be negatively impacted.

## COMPANY PROFILE

Krispy Kreme is a leading branded specialty retailer of premium quality doughnuts which are made throughout the day in our stores. We opened our first store in 1937, and there were 276 Krispy Kreme stores, consisting of 99 company-owned and 177 franchised stores, as of February 2, 2003. Our principal business is the high volume production and sale of over 20 varieties of premium quality doughnuts, including our signature Hot Original Glazed. We have established Krispy Kreme as a leading consumer brand with a loyal customer base through our longstanding commitment to quality and consistency. Our place in American society was recognized in 1997 with the induction of Krispy Kreme artifacts into the Smithsonian Institution's National Museum of American History. We differentiate ourselves by combining quality ingredients, vertical integration and a unique retail experience featuring our stores' fully displayed production process, or doughnut-making theater.

Krispy Kreme has been a publicly held company since April 5, 2000. Our stock is listed on the New York Stock Exchange with shares trading under the ticker symbol KKD.

| BOARD OF DIRECTORS | OFFICERS |
|---|---|
| SCOTT A. LIVENGOOD<br>Krispy Kreme Doughnuts, Inc.<br>Chairman of the Board,<br>President and Chief Executive Officer | SCOTT A. LIVENGOOD<br>Chairman of the Board,<br>President and Chief Executive Officer |
| ERSKINE BOWLES<br>Senior Advisor<br>Carousel Capital | JOHN W. TATE<br>Chief Operating Officer |
| MARY DAVIS HOLT<br>Senior Executive Vice President<br>of Time Life Inc. | RANDY S. CASSTEVENS<br>Chief Financial Officer and Treasurer |
| WILLIAM T. LYNCH JR.<br>Liam Holdings LLC, President<br>and Chief Executive Officer<br>Retired Chief Executive Officer of<br>Leo Burnett Company | R. FRANK MURPHY<br>Executive Vice President,<br>General Counsel and Secretary |
| JOHN N. (JACK) McALEER<br>Krispy Kreme Doughnuts, Inc.<br>Vice Chairman of the Board<br>and Executive Vice President<br>of Concept Development | JOHN N. (JACK) McALEER<br>Vice Chairman of the Board<br>and Executive Vice President<br>of Concept Development |
| JAMES H. MORGAN<br>Chairman of Morgan, Semones and Associates<br>and former Chairman and Chief Executive<br>Officer of Wachovia Securities, Inc. | STEPHEN E. GORMAN<br>Executive Vice President<br>of Operations Support |
| DR. SU HUA NEWTON<br>Co-owner Newton Vineyard | STEVE A. MARTIN<br>Executive Vice President,<br>Dean of the Learning Institute |
| ROBERT L. STRICKLAND<br>Chairman Emeritus of<br>Lowe's Companies, Inc. | PHILIP R.S. WAUGH JR.<br>Executive Vice President<br>of Worldwide Development |
| TOGO D. WEST JR.<br>Of Counsel, Covington and Burling | |

KRISPY KREME

TASTYKAKE

# FIVE YEAR SELECTED FINANCIAL DATA

All amounts presented are in thousands except for per share amounts.

| | 2002(a) | 2001(b) | 2000 | 1999(c) | 1998 |
|---|---|---|---|---|---|
| **Operating Results** | | | | | |
| Gross sales | $255,504 | $255,336 | $249,691 | $226,350 | $228,453 |
| Net sales (d) | 162,263 | 166,245 | 162,877 | 148,830 | 149,054 |
| Net income (loss) | (4,341) | 6,320 | 8,144 | 4,703 | 5,729 |
| **Per Share Amounts** | | | | | |
| Net income: | | | | | |
| Basic | $(.54) | $.79 | $1.04 | $.60 | $.73 |
| Diluted | (.54) | .78 | 1.04 | .60 | .72 |
| Cash dividends | .48 | .48 | .48 | .48 | .48 |
| Shareholders' equity | 5.86 | 6.84 | 6.40 | 5.81 | 5.67 |
| **Financial Position** | | | | | |
| Working capital | $16,788 | $18,284 | $15,474 | $14,406 | $15,830 |
| Total assets | 116,560 | 116,137 | 112,192 | 111,753 | 101,744 |
| Long-term obligations | 12,486 | 14,603 | 16,843 | 21,060 | 13,761 |
| Shareholders' equity | 47,525 | 55,065 | 50,174 | 45,422 | 44,357 |
| Shares of common stock | | | | | |
| Outstanding | 8,104 | 8,052 | 7,845 | 7,823 | 7,822 |
| **Statistical Information** | | | | | |
| Capital expenditures | $5,359 | $7,314 | $8,116 | $14,038 | $11,328 |
| Depreciation | 6,807 | 7,204 | 7,759 | 7,016 | 6,650 |
| Average common shares | | | | | |
| Outstanding: | | | | | |
| Basic | 8,075 | 7,998 | 7,837 | 7,824 | 7,808 |
| Diluted | 8,159 | 8,140 | 7,861 | 7,865 | 7,953 |

(a) During the second quarter of 2002, the company incurred a $1,405 restructure charge related to its decision to close six thrift stores and to eliminate certain manufacturing and administrative positions.

During the fourth quarter of 2002, the company incurred a $4,936 restructure charge related to the closing of the remaining twelve thrift stores and the specific arrangements made with senior executives who departed the company in the fourth quarter of 2002.

Also, during the fourth quarter of 2002, the company recorded additional pension expense in the amount of $4,656 in connection with the company's method of immediately recognizing gains and losses that fall outside the pension corridor.

(b) During the fourth quarter of 2001, the company incurred a $1,728 restructure charge related to its decision to close its Dutch Mill Baking Company production facility and two company thrift stores.

(c) During 1999 the company incurred a route restructure charge of $950. Also included is an after-tax charge of $205 that is the cumulative effect of an accounting change that required the write-off of start-up costs. Long-term obligations reflect the renewal of a capital lease with the trustees of the company pension plan.

(d) For comparative purposes net sales for 2001, 2000, 1999 and 1998 have been reclassified to reflect changes in accounting for thrift stores and cooperative advertising. The change was an increase of $1,637 for 2001 and a decrease of $1,406, $1,832 and $1,675, for 2000, 1999 and 1998 respectively.

TASTYKAKE

# TASTYKAKE

## CONSOLIDATED FINANCIAL STATEMENTS
### Tasty Baking Company and Subsidiaries

**Consolidated Statements of Operations and Retained Earnings**

| | | 52 Weeks Ended Dec. 28, 2002 | 52 Weeks Ended Dec. 29, 2001(a) | 53 Weeks Ended Dec. 30, 2000(a) |
|---|---|---|---|---|
| **Operations** | | | | |
| **Gross sales** | $ | 255,503,818 | $ 255,335,587 | $ 249,690,639 |
| Less discounts and allowances | | (93,240,612) | (89,090,607) | (86,813,226) |
| Net sales | | 162,263,206 | 166,244,980 | 162,877,413 |
| **Costs and expenses:** | | | | |
| Cost of sales | | 111,187,357 | 103,297,040 | 105,036,081 |
| Depreciation | | 6,807,369 | 7,203,688 | 7,759,345 |
| Selling, general and administrative | | 44,982,205 | 43,236,117 | 35,959,008 |
| Restructure charges | | 6,340,810 | 1,727,844 | — |
| Interest expense | | 1,066,250 | 1,102,777 | 1,540,242 |
| Provision for doubtful accounts | | 958,365 | 772,372 | 1,250,385 |
| Other income, net | | (1,165,548) | (1,189,606) | (1,420,557) |
| | | 170,176,808 | 156,150,232 | 150,124,504 |
| Income (loss) before provision for income taxes | | (7,913,602) | 10,094,748 | 12,752,909 |
| **Provision for (benefit from) income taxes:** | | | | |
| Federal | | (11,432) | 3,284,796 | 2,562,171 |
| State | | (315,262) | (89,526) | (269,625) |
| Deferred | | (3,246,179) | 579,276 | 2,316,823 |
| | | (3,572,873) | 3,774,546 | 4,609,369 |
| **Net income (loss)** | | (4,340,729) | 6,320,202 | 8,143,540 |
| **Retained Earnings** | | | | |
| Balance, beginning of year | | 34,838,636 | 32,351,894 | 27,968,811 |
| Cash dividends paid on common shares ($.48 per share in 2002, 2001 and 2000) | | (3,875,855) | (3,833,460) | (3,760,457) |
| Balance, end of year | $ | 26,622,052 | $ 34,838,636 | $ 32,351,894 |
| **Per share of common stock:** | | | | |
| **Net income:** | | | | |
| Basic | $ | (.54) | $ .79 | $ 1.04 |
| Diluted | $ | (.54) | $ .78 | $ 1.04 |

(a) 2001 and 2000 have been reclassified for comparative purposes to reflect the changes in accounting for thrift stores and cooperative advertising.

See accompanying notes to consolidated financial statements.

**Consolidated Statements of Cash Flows**

| | 52 Weeks Ended Dec. 28, 2002 | 52 Weeks Ended Dec. 29, 2001 | 53 Weeks Ended Dec. 30, 2000 |
|---|---|---|---|
| **Cash flows from (used for) operating activities** | | | |
| Net income (loss) | $ (4,340,729) | $ 6,320,202 | $ 8,143,540 |
| Adjustments to reconcile net income to net cash provided by operating activities: | | | |
| Depreciation | 6,807,369 | 7,203,688 | 7,759,345 |
| Restructure charges, net of cash expenditures | 5,133,794 | 850,879 | — |
| Conditional stock grant | — | 804,759 | 319,016 |
| Provision for doubtful accounts | 958,365 | 772,372 | 1,250,385 |
| Pension expense | 5,456,000 | (216,770) | (2,318,000) |
| Deferred taxes | (3,246,179) | 579,276 | 2,316,823 |
| Other | (547,841) | (420,277) | (154,683) |
| Changes in assets and liabilities: | | | |
| Decrease (increase) in receivables | 393,451 | (2,233,932) | (2,339,505) |
| Decrease (increase) in inventories | 1,634,632 | (2,481,235) | (1,424,770) |
| Increase in prepayments and other | (1,839,688) | (197,658) | (948,500) |
| Increase (decrease) in accrued payroll, accrued income taxes, accounts payable and other current liabilities | (294,575) | (76,690) | 594,924 |
| **Net cash from operating activities** | 10,114,599 | 10,904,614 | 13,198,575 |
| **Cash flows from (used for) investing activities** | | | |
| Proceeds from owner/operator loan repayments | 3,987,420 | 3,494,763 | 4,065,144 |
| Purchase of property, plant and equipment | (5,359,051) | (7,313,982) | (8,116,213) |
| Loans to owner/operators | (3,881,472) | (4,043,379) | (3,038,759) |
| Other | (46,359) | 46,131 | 40,402 |
| **Net cash used for investing activities** | (5,299,462) | (7,816,467) | (7,049,426) |
| **Cash flows from (used for) financing activities** | | | |
| Dividends paid | (3,875,855) | (3,833,460) | (3,760,457) |
| Payment of long-term debt | (2,117,092) | (3,216,821) | (10,196,240) |
| Net increase in short-term debt | 600,000 | 1,700,000 | 1,450,000 |
| Additional long-term debt | — | 1,000,000 | 6,000,000 |
| Net proceeds from sale of common stock | 492,275 | 1,318,112 | (36,704) |
| **Net cash used for financing activities** | (4,900,672) | (3,032,169) | (6,543,401) |
| **Net increase (decrease) in cash** | (85,535) | 55,978 | (394,252) |
| Cash, beginning of year | 367,220 | 311,242 | 705,494 |
| Cash, end of year | $ 281,685 | $ 367,220 | $ 311,242 |
| **Supplemental cash flow information** | | | |
| **Cash paid during the year for:** | | | |
| Interest | $ 1,084,322 | $ 1,231,521 | $ 1,750,990 |
| Income taxes | $ 1,011,650 | $ 3,065,069 | $ 4,819,057 |

*See accompanying notes to consolidated financial statements.*

**TASTYKAKE**

TASTYKAKE

**Consolidated Balance Sheets**

| | | Dec. 28, 2002 | Dec. 29, 2001 |
|---|---|---:|---:|
| **Assets** | | | |
| **Current Assets:** | | | |
| Cash | $ | 281,685 | $ 367,220 |
| Receivables, less allowance of $3,606,117 and $3,751,854, respectively | | 20,881,597 | 22,233,413 |
| Inventories | | 6,777,152 | 8,411,784 |
| Deferred income taxes | | 5,213,847 | 3,055,410 |
| Prepayments and other | | 2,941,033 | 1,101,345 |
| Total current assets | | 36,095,314 | 35,169,172 |
| **Property, plant and equipment:** | | | |
| Land | | 1,097,987 | 1,097,987 |
| Buildings and improvements | | 37,831,789 | 37,103,226 |
| Machinery and equipment | | 148,990,425 | 146,023,373 |
| | | 187,920,201 | 184,224,586 |
| Less accumulated depreciation and amortization | | 129,528,979 | 124,522,610 |
| | | 58,391,222 | 59,701,976 |
| **Other assets:** | | | |
| Long-term receivables from owner/operators | | 10,095,101 | 10,201,049 |
| Deferred income taxes | | 8,229,612 | 7,381,934 |
| Spare parts inventory | | 3,698,780 | 3,632,687 |
| Miscellaneous | | 50,001 | 50,001 |
| | | 22,073,494 | 21,265,671 |
| | $ | 116,560,030 | $ 116,136,819 |

*See accompanying notes to consolidated financial statements.*

TASTYKAKE

|  | | Dec. 28, 2002 | Dec. 29, 2001 |
|---|---|---|---|
| **Liabilities** | | | |
| **Current Liabilities:** | | | |
| Current obligations under capital leases | $ | 175,715 | $ 239,593 |
| Notes payable, banks | | 4,500,000 | 3,900,000 |
| Accounts payable | | 6,074,193 | 5,306,976 |
| Accrued payroll and employee benefits | | 5,158,820 | 6,208,889 |
| Reserve for restructures | | 2,417,178 | 850,879 |
| Other | | 981,459 | 378,982 |
| Total current liabilities | | 19,307,365 | 16,885,319 |
| Long-term debt | | 9,000,000 | 11,000,000 |
| Long-term obligations under capital leases, less current portion | | 3,486,218 | 3,603,310 |
| Reserve for restructures-less current portion | | 3,567,495 | — |
| Accrued pensions and other liabilities | | 15,923,020 | 11,506,969 |
| Postretirement benefits other than pensions | | 17,750,696 | 18,076,719 |
| Total liabilities | | 69,034,794 | 61,072,317 |
| **Shareholders' Equity** | | | |
| Common stock, par value $.50 per share, and entitled to one vote per share: | | | |
| Authorized 15,000,000 shares, issued 9,116,483 shares | | 4,558,243 | 4,558,243 |
| Capital in excess of par value of stock | | 29,432,917 | 29,388,567 |
| Retained earnings | | 26,622,052 | 34,838,636 |
| | | 60,613,212 | 68,785,446 |
| **Less:** | | | |
| Treasury stock, at cost: | | | |
| 1,012,798 shares and 1,064,539 shares, respectively | | 12,538,632 | 13,167,082 |
| Management Stock Purchase Plan receivables and deferrals | | 549,344 | 553,862 |
| | | 47,525,236 | 55,064,502 |
| | $ | 116,560,030 | $ 116,136,819 |

*See accompanying notes to consolidated financial statements.*

TASTYKAKE

## Consolidated Statements of Changes in Capital Accounts

| | Dec. 28, 2002 | | Dec. 29, 2001 | | Dec. 30, 2000 | |
|---|---|---|---|---|---|---|
| | Shares | Amount | Shares | Amount | Shares | Amount |
| **Common Stock:** | | | | | | |
| Balance, beginning of year | 9,116,483 | $ 4,558,243 | 9,116,483 | $ 4,558,243 | 9,116,483 | $ 4,558,243 |
| Balance, end of year | 9,116,483 | $ 4,558,243 | 9,116,483 | $ 4,558,243 | 9,116,483 | $ 4,558,243 |
| **Capital in Excess of Par Value of Stock:** | | | | | | |
| Balance, beginning of year | | $ 29,388,567 | | $ 29,742,434 | | $ 29,778,768 |
| Issuances: | | | | | | |
| Management Stock Purchase Plan | | 16,975 | | 53,766 | | (4,211) |
| Stock Option Plan | | (24,777) | | (599,642) | | – |
| Conditional Stock Grant | | – | | (11,535) | | (35,573) |
| Tax benefits related to Management Stock Purchase Plan and Stock Option Plan | | 52,152 | | 203,544 | | 3,450 |
| Balance, end of year | | $ 29,432,917 | | $ 29,388,567 | | $ 29,742,434 |
| **Treasury Stock:** | | | | | | |
| Balance, beginning of year | 1,064,539 | $ 13,167,082 | 1,271,171 | $ 16,106,361 | 1,293,135 | $ 16,408,808 |
| Management Stock Purchase Plan: | | | | | | |
| Reissued | (11,900) | (159,117) | (20,345) | (270,021) | (1,400) | (20,048) |
| Reacquired | 7,634 | 128,490 | 5,775 | 64,790 | 2,365 | 35,488 |
| Net shares reissued in connection with: | | | | | | |
| Stock Option Plan | (47,475) | (597,823) | (155,820) | (2,141,247) | – | – |
| Conditional Stock Grant | – | – | (36,242) | (592,801) | (22,929) | (317,887) |
| Balance, end of year | 1,012,798 | $ 12,538,632 | 1,064,539 | $ 13,167,082 | 1,271,171 | $ 16,106,361 |
| **Management Stock Purchase Plan Receivables and Deferrals:** | | | | | | |
| Balance, beginning of year | | $ 553,862 | | $ 372,532 | | $ 475,470 |
| Common stock issued | | 176,092 | | 323,787 | | 15,837 |
| Common stock repurchased | | (98,861) | | (60,083) | | (29,904) |
| Note payments and amortization of deferred compensation | | (81,749) | | (82,374) | | (88,871) |
| Balance, end of year | | $ 549,344 | | $ 553,862 | | $ 372,532 |

*See accompanying notes to consolidated financial statements.*

# Harley-Davidson

CONSOLIDATED STATEMENTS *of* INCOME

*(In thousands, except per share amounts)*

| Years ended December 31, | 2002 | 2001 | 2000 |
|---|---|---|---|
| Net revenue | $4,090,970 | $3,406,786 | $2,943,346 |
| Cost of goods sold | 2,673,129 | 2,253,815 | 1,979,572 |
| Gross profit | 1,417,841 | 1,152,971 | 963,774 |
| | | | |
| Financial services income | 211,500 | 181,545 | 140,135 |
| Financial services expense | 107,273 | 120,272 | 102,957 |
| Operating income from financial services | 104,227 | 61,273 | 37,178 |
| | | | |
| Selling, administrative and engineering expense | (639,366) | (551,743) | (485,980) |
| Income from operations | 882,702 | 662,501 | 514,972 |
| Gain on sale of credit card business | — | — | 18,915 |
| Interest income, net | 16,541 | 17,478 | 17,583 |
| Other, net | (13,416) | (6,524) | (2,914) |
| Income before provision for income taxes | 885,827 | 673,455 | 548,556 |
| Provision for income taxes | 305,610 | 235,709 | 200,843 |
| Net income | $  580,217 | $  437,746 | $  347,713 |
| | | | |
| Basic earnings per common share | $1.92 | $1.45 | $1.15 |
| Diluted earnings per common share | $1.90 | $1.43 | $1.13 |
| Cash dividends per common share | $ .14 | $ .12 | $ .10 |

*The accompanying notes are an integral part of the consolidated financial statements.*

REPORT *of* ERNST & YOUNG LLP, INDEPENDENT AUDITORS

..........................

We have audited the accompanying consolidated balance sheets of Harley-Davidson, Inc. as of December 31, 2002 and 2001, and the related consolidated statements of income, shareholders' equity and cash flows for each of the three years in the period ended December 31, 2002. These financial statements are the responsibility of the Company's management. Our responsibility is to express an opinion on these financial statements based on our audits.

We conducted our audits in accordance with auditing standards generally accepted in the United States. Those standards require that we plan and perform the audit to obtain reasonable assurance about whether the financial statements are free of material misstatement. An audit includes examining, on a test basis, evidence supporting the amounts and disclosures in the financial statements. An audit also includes assessing the accounting principles used and significant estimates made by management, as well as evaluating the overall financial statement presentation. We believe that our audits provide a reasonable basis for our opinion.

In our opinion, the consolidated financial statements referred to above present fairly, in all material respects, the consolidated financial position of Harley-Davidson, Inc. at December 31, 2002 and 2001, and the consolidated results of its operations and its cash flows for each of the three years in the period ended December 31, 2002, in conformity with accounting principles generally accepted in the United States.

As discussed in Note 1 to the consolidated financial statements, on January 1, 2002, the Company changed its method of accounting for goodwill.

Milwaukee, Wisconsin
January 16, 2003

*Ernst & Young LLP*

HARLEY-DAVIDSON

CONSOLIDATED BALANCE SHEETS

*(In thousands, except share amounts)*

| December 31, | 2002 | 2001 |
|---|---|---|
| **ASSETS** | | |
| Current assets: | | |
| Cash and cash equivalents | $ 280,928 | $ 439,438 |
| Marketable securities | 514,800 | 196,011 |
| Accounts receivable, net | 108,694 | 118,843 |
| Current portion of finance receivables, net | 855,771 | 656,421 |
| Inventories | 218,156 | 181,115 |
| Deferred income taxes | 41,430 | 38,993 |
| Prepaid expenses & other current assets | 46,807 | 34,443 |
| Total current assets | 2,066,586 | 1,665,264 |
| | | |
| Finance receivables, net | 589,809 | 379,335 |
| Property, plant, and equipment, net | 1,032,596 | 891,820 |
| Goodwill, net | 49,930 | 49,711 |
| Other assets | 122,296 | 132,365 |
| | $3,861,217 | $3,118,495 |
| | | |
| **LIABILITIES *and* SHAREHOLDERS' EQUITY** | | |
| Current liabilities: | | |
| Accounts payable | $ 226,977 | $ 194,683 |
| Accrued expenses and other liabilities | 380,496 | 304,376 |
| Current portion of finance debt | 382,579 | 217,051 |
| Total current liabilities | 990,052 | 716,110 |
| | | |
| Finance debt | 380,000 | 380,000 |
| Other long-term liabilities | 123,353 | 158,374 |
| Postretirement health care benefits | 105,419 | 89,912 |
| Deferred income taxes | 29,478 | 17,816 |
| Commitments and contingencies (Note 7) | | |
| | | |
| Shareholders' equity: | | |
| Series A Junior participating preferred stock, none issued | — | — |
| Common stock, 325,298,404 and 324,340,432 shares issued in 2002 and 2001, respectively | 3,254 | 3,242 |
| Additional paid-in capital | 386,284 | 359,165 |
| Retained earnings | 2,372,095 | 1,833,335 |
| Accumulated other comprehensive loss | (46,266) | (13,728) |
| | 2,715,367 | 2,182,014 |
| Less: | | |
| Treasury stock (22,636,295 and 21,550,923 shares in 2002 and 2001, respectively), at cost | (482,360) | (425,546) |
| Unearned compensation | (92) | (185) |
| Total shareholders' equity | 2,232,915 | 1,756,283 |
| | $3,861,217 | $3,118,495 |

*The accompanying notes are an integral part of the consolidated financial statements.*

HARLEY-DAVIDSON

CONSOLIDATED STATEMENTS *of* SHAREHOLDERS' EQUITY

*(In thousands, except share amounts)*

| | Common Stock | |
| --- | --- | --- |
| | Issued Shares | Balance |
| **BALANCE DECEMBER 31, 1999** | **318,586,144** | **$3,184** |
| Comprehensive income: | | |
|   Net income | — | — |
|   Other comprehensive income (loss): | | |
|     Foreign currency translation adjustment | — | — |
|     Change in net unrealized gains on investment in retained | | |
|      securitization interests, net of taxes of $(3,759) | — | — |
|     Minimum pension liability adjustment, net of tax benefit of $120 | — | — |
| Comprehensive income | | |
| Dividends | — | — |
| Repurchase of common stock | — | — |
| Amortization of unearned compensation | — | — |
| Exercise of stock options | 2,599,423 | 26 |
| Tax benefit of stock options | — | — |
| **BALANCE DECEMBER 31, 2000** | **321,185,567** | **$3,210** |
| Comprehensive income: | | |
|   Net income | — | — |
|   Other comprehensive income (loss): | | |
|     Foreign currency translation adjustment | — | — |
|     Change in net unrealized gains on investment in retained | | |
|      securitization interests, net of taxes of $(6,117) | — | — |
|     Change in net unrealized gains on derivative financial instruments, | | |
|      net of taxes of $(407) | — | — |
|     Minimum pension liability adjustment, net of tax benefit of $11,515 | — | — |
| Comprehensive income | | |
| Dividends | — | — |
| Repurchase of common stock | — | — |
| Amortization of unearned compensation | — | — |
| Exercise of stock options | 3,154,865 | 32 |
| Tax benefit of stock options | — | — |
| **BALANCE DECEMBER 31, 2001** | **324,340,432** | **$3,242** |
| Comprehensive income: | | |
|   Net income | — | — |
|   Other comprehensive income (loss): | | |
|     Foreign currency translation adjustment | — | — |
|     Change in net unrealized gains on investment in retained | | |
|      securitization interests, net of taxes of $(6,113) | — | — |
|     Change in net unrealized losses on derivative financial instruments, | | |
|      net of tax benefit of $5,929 | — | — |
|     Change in net unrealized gains on marketable securities, net of taxes of $(377) | — | — |
|     Minimum pension liability adjustment, net of tax benefit of $29,896 | — | — |
| Comprehensive income | | |
| Dividends | — | — |
| Repurchase of common stock | — | — |
| Amortization of unearned compensation | — | — |
| Exercise of stock options | 957,972 | 12 |
| Tax benefit of stock options | — | — |
| **BALANCE DECEMBER 31, 2002** | **325,298,404** | **$3,254** |

*The accompanying notes are an integral part of the consolidated financial statements.*

CONSOLIDATED STATEMENTS *of* SHAREHOLDERS' EQUITY

| Additional Paid-In Capital | Retained Earnings | Other Comprehensive Income (Loss) | Treasury Balance | Unearned Compensation | Total |
|---|---|---|---|---|---|
| $234,948 | $ 1,113,376 | $ (2,067) | $ (187,992) | $(369) | $1,161,080 |
| — | 347,713 | — | — | — | 347,713 |
| — | — | (4,383) | — | — | (4,383) |
| — | — | 6,981 | — | — | 6,981 |
| — | — | (223) | — | — | (223) |
| | | | | | 350,088 |
| — | (30,072) | — | — | — | (30,072) |
| — | — | — | (126,002) | — | (126,002) |
| — | — | — | — | 93 | 93 |
| 14,566 | — | — | — | — | 14,592 |
| 35,876 | — | — | — | — | 35,876 |
| $285,390 | $ 1,431,017 | $ 308 | $(313,994) | $(276) | $1,405,655 |
| — | 437,746 | — | — | — | 437,746 |
| — | — | (6,143) | — | — | (6,143) |
| — | — | 11,115 | — | — | 11,115 |
| — | — | 668 | — | — | 668 |
| — | — | (19,676) | — | — | (19,676) |
| | | | | | 423,710 |
| — | (35,428) | — | — | — | (35,428) |
| — | — | — | (111,552) | — | (111,552) |
| — | — | — | — | 91 | 91 |
| 28,807 | — | — | — | — | 28,839 |
| 44,968 | — | — | — | — | 44,968 |
| $ 359,165 | $ 1,833,335 | $ (13,728) | $(425,546) | $(185) | $1,756,283 |
| — | 580,217 | — | — | — | 580,217 |
| — | — | 14,545 | — | — | 14,545 |
| — | — | 11,108 | — | — | 11,108 |
| — | — | (9,824) | — | — | (9,824) |
| — | — | 618 | — | — | 618 |
| — | — | (48,985) | — | — | (48,985) |
| | | | | | 547,679 |
| — | (41,457) | — | — | — | (41,457) |
| — | — | — | (56,814) | — | (56,814) |
| — | — | — | — | 93 | 93 |
| 12,667 | — | — | — | — | 12,679 |
| 14,452 | — | — | — | — | 14,452 |
| $386,284 | $2,372,095 | $(46,266) | $(482,360) | $ (92) | $2,232,915 |

CONSOLIDATED STATEMENTS *of* CASH FLOWS

*(In thousands)*

| Years ended December 31, | 2002 | 2001 | 2000 |
|---|---|---|---|
| Cash flows from operating activities: | | | |
| Net income | $ 580,217 | $ 437,746 | $ 347,713 |
| Adjustments to reconcile net income to net cash provided by operating activities: | | | |
| Depreciation and amortization | 175,778 | 153,061 | 133,348 |
| Gain on sale of credit card business | — | — | (18,915) |
| Tax benefit from the exercise of stock options | 14,452 | 44,968 | 35,876 |
| Provision for finance credit losses | 6,167 | 22,178 | 9,919 |
| Deferred income taxes | 38,560 | (3,539) | 1,363 |
| Long-term employee benefits | 57,124 | 40,882 | 17,433 |
| Contributions to pension plans | (153,636) | (19,294) | (12,802) |
| Other | 7,057 | 3,045 | 1,800 |
| Net changes in current assets and current liabilities | 53,827 | 77,761 | 49,609 |
| Total adjustments | 199,329 | 319,062 | 217,631 |
| Net cash provided by operating activities | 779,546 | 756,808 | 565,344 |
| | | | |
| Cash flows from investing activities: | | | |
| Capital expenditures | (323,866) | (290,381) | (203,611) |
| Finance receivables acquired or originated | (5,611,217) | (4,387,371) | (3,556,195) |
| Finance receivables collected | 3,933,125 | 3,123,941 | 2,727,746 |
| Finance receivables sold | 1,279,324 | 987,676 | 723,928 |
| Net proceeds from sale of credit card business | — | — | 170,146 |
| Purchase of marketable securities | (1,508,285) | (247,989) | — |
| Sales and redemptions of marketable securities | 1,190,114 | 51,978 | — |
| Purchase of Italian distributor | — | (1,873) | (18,777) |
| Other, net | 22,813 | (7,488) | (14,124) |
| Net cash used in investing activities | (1,017,992) | (771,507) | (170,887) |
| | | | |
| Cash flows from financing activities: | | | |
| Net increase (decrease) in finance debt | 165,528 | 152,542 | (16,654) |
| Dividends paid | (41,457) | (35,428) | (30,072) |
| Purchase of common stock for treasury | (56,814) | (111,552) | (126,002) |
| Issuance of common stock under employee stock option plans | 12,679 | 28,839 | 14,592 |
| Net cash provided by (used in) financing activities | 79,936 | 34,401 | (158,136) |
| | | | |
| Net (decrease) increase in cash and cash equivalents | (158,510) | 19,702 | 236,321 |
| | | | |
| Cash and cash equivalents: | | | |
| At beginning of year | 439,438 | 419,736 | 183,415 |
| At end of year | $ 280,928 | $ 439,438 | $ 419,736 |

*The accompanying notes are an integral part of the consolidated financial statements.*

# Applying Present and Future Values in Accounting

## CAP

**Conceptual**

**C1** Describe the earning of interest and the concepts of present and future values. (p. B-2)

**Procedural**

**P1** Apply present value concepts to a single amount by using interest tables. (p. B-3)

**P2** Apply future value concepts to a single amount by using interest tables. (p. B-5)

**P3** Apply present value concepts to an annuity by using interest tables. (p. B-6)

**P4** Apply future value concepts to an annuity by using interest tables. (p. B-7)

The concepts of present and future values are important to modern business activity. The purpose of this appendix is to explain, illustrate, and compute present and future values. This appendix applies these concepts with reference to both business and everyday activities.

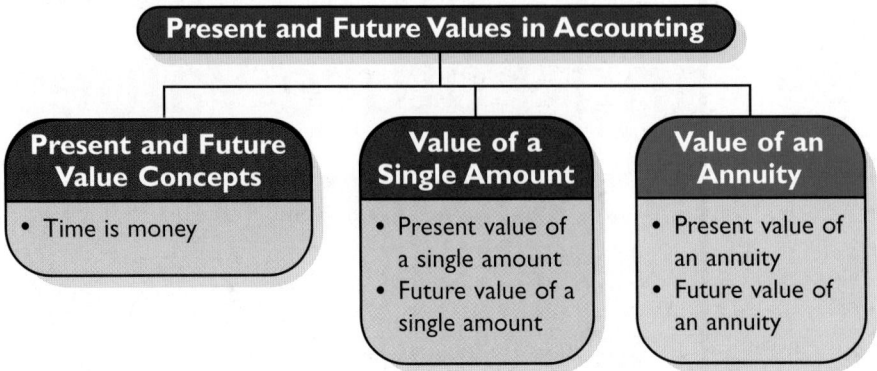

# Present and Future Value Concepts

**C1** Describe the earning of interest and the concepts of present and future values.

The old saying "Time is money" reflects the notion that as time passes, the values of our assets and liabilities change. This change is due to *interest*, which is a borrower's payment to the owner of an asset for its use. The most common example of interest is a savings account asset. As we keep a balance of cash in the account, it earns interest that the financial institution pays us. An example of a liability is a car loan. As we carry the balance of the loan, we accumulate interest costs on it. We must ultimately repay this loan with interest.

Present and future value computations enable us to measure or estimate the interest component of holding assets or liabilities over time. The present value computation is important when we want to know the value of future-day assets *today*. The future value computation is important when we want to know the value of present-day assets *at a future date*. The first section focuses on the present value of a single amount. The second section focuses on the future value of a single amount. Then both the present and future values of a series of amounts (called an *annuity*) are defined and explained.

# Present Value of a Single Amount

We graphically express the present value, called *p*, of a single future amount, called *f*, that is received or paid at a future date in Exhibit B.1.

**Exhibit B.1**

Present Value of a Single Amount Diagram

The formula to compute the present value of a single amount is shown in Exhibit B.2, where $p$ = present value; $f$ = future value; $i$ = rate of interest per period; and $n$ = number of periods. (Interest is also called the *discount*, and an interest rate is also called the *discount rate*.)

**Exhibit B.2**

Present Value of a Single Amount Formula

$$p = \frac{f}{(1 + i)^n}$$

To illustrate present value concepts, assume that we need $220 one period from today. We want to know how much we must invest now, for one period, at an interest rate of 10% to provide for this $220. For this illustration, the $p$, or present value, is the unknown amount— the specifics are shown graphically as follows:

Conceptually, we know $p$ must be less than $220. This is obvious from the answer to this question: Would we rather have $220 today or $220 at some future date? If we had $220 today, we could invest it and see it grow to something more than $220 in the future. Therefore, we would prefer the $220 today. This means that if we were promised $220 in the future, we would take less than $220 today. But how much less? To answer that question, we compute an estimate of the present value of the $220 to be received one period from now using the formula in Exhibit B.2 as follows:

$$p = \frac{f}{(1 + i)^n} = \frac{\$220}{(1 + 0.10)^1} = \$200$$

We interpret this result to say that given an interest rate of 10%, we are indifferent between $200 today or $220 at the end of one period.

We can also use this formula to compute the present value for *any number of periods.* To illustrate, consider a payment of $242 at the end of two periods at 10% interest. The present value of this $242 to be received two periods from now is computed as follows:

$$p = \frac{f}{(1 + i)^n} = \frac{\$242}{(1 + 0.10)^2} = \$200$$

Together, these results tell us we are indifferent between $200 today, or $220 one period from today, or $242 two periods from today given a 10% interest rate per period.

The number of periods ($n$) in the present value formula does not have to be expressed in years. Any period of time such as a day, a month, a quarter, or a year can be used. Whatever period is used, the interest rate ($i$) must be compounded for the same period. This means that if a situation expresses $n$ in months and $i$ equals 12% per year, then $i$ is transformed into interest earned per month (or 1%). In this case, interest is said to be *compounded monthly.*

A present value table helps us with present value computations. It gives us present values (factors) for a variety of both interest rates ($i$) and periods ($n$). Each present value in a present value table assumes that the future value ($f$) equals 1. When the future value ($f$) is different from 1, we simply multiply the present value ($p$) from the table by that future value to give us the estimate. The formula used to construct a table of present values for a single future amount of 1 is shown in Exhibit B.3.

$$p = \frac{1}{(1 + i)^n}$$

## Exhibit B.3

Present Value of 1 Formula

This formula is identical to that in Exhibit B.2 except that $f$ equals 1. Table B.1 at the end of this appendix is such a present value table. It is often called a **present value of 1 table**. A present value table involves three factors: $p$, $i$, and $n$. Knowing two of these three factors allows us to compute the third. (A fourth is $f$, but as already explained, we need only multiply the 1 used in the formula by $f$.) To illustrate the use of a present value table, consider three cases.

**P1** Apply present value concepts to a single amount by using interest tables.

**Case 1** (solve for $p$ when knowing $i$ and $n$). To show how we use a present value table, let's look again at how we estimate the present value of $220 (the $f$ value) at the end of one period ($n = 1$) where the interest rate ($i$) is 10%. To solve this case, we go to the present value table (Table B.1) and look in the row for 1 period and in the column for 10% interest. Here we find a present value ($p$) of 0.9091 based on a future value of 1. This means, for instance, that $1 to be received one period from today at 10% interest is worth $0.9091 today. Since the future value in this case is not $1 but $220, we multiply the 0.9091 by $220 to get an answer of $200.

**Case 2** (solve for $n$ when knowing $p$ and $i$). To illustrate, assume a $100,000 future value ($f$) that is worth $13,000 today ($p$) using an interest rate of 12% ($i$) but where $n$ is unknown. In particular, we want to know how many periods ($n$) there are between the present value and the future value. To put this in context, it would fit a situation in which we want to retire with $100,000 but currently have only $13,000 that is earning a 12% return. How long will it be before we can retire? To answer this, we go to Table B.1 and look in the 12% interest column. Here we find a column of present values ($p$) based on a future value of 1. To use the present value table for this solution, we must divide $13,000 ($p$) by $100,000 ($f$), which equals 0.1300. This is necessary because *a present value table defines* f *equal to 1, and* p *as a fraction of 1.* We look for a value nearest to 0.1300 ($p$), which we find in the row for 18 periods ($n$). This means that the present value of $100,000 at the end of 18 periods at 12% interest is $13,000 or, alternatively stated, we must work 18 more years.

**Case 3** (solve for $i$ when knowing $p$ and $n$). In this case, we have, say, a $120,000 future value ($f$) worth $60,000 today ($p$) when there are nine periods ($n$) between the present and future values, but the interest rate is unknown. As an example, suppose we want to retire with $120,000, but we have only $60,000 and hope to retire in nine years. What interest rate must we earn to retire with $120,000 in nine years? To answer this, we go to the present value table (Table B.1) and look in the row for nine periods. To use the present value table, we must divide $60,000 ($p$) by $120,000 ($f$), which equals 0.5000. Recall that this step is necessary because a present value table defines $f$ equal to 1 and $p$ as a fraction of 1. We look for a value in the row for nine periods that is nearest to 0.5000 ($p$), which we find in the column for 8% interest ($i$). This means that the present value of $120,000 at the end of nine periods at 8% interest is $60,000 or, in our example, we must earn 8% annual interest to retire in nine years.

> ### Decision Insight
>
> **Keep That Job**   Lottery winners often never work again. Kenny Dukes, a recent Georgia lottery winner, doesn't have that option. He is serving parole for burglary charges, and Georgia requires its parolees to be employed (or in school). Dukes had to choose between $31 million in 30 annual payments or $16 million in one lump sum ($10.6 million after-tax); he chose the latter.

> ### Quick Check
>
> 1. A company is considering an investment expected to yield $70,000 after six years. If this company demands an 8% return, how much is it willing to pay for this investment?

Answer—p. B-8

# Future Value of a Single Amount

We must modify the formula for the present value of a single amount to obtain the formula for the future value of a single amount. In particular, we multiply both sides of the equation in Exhibit B.2 by $(1 + i)^n$ to get the result shown in Exhibit B.4.

## Exhibit B.4

Future Value of a Single
Amount Formula

$$f = p \times (1 + i)^n$$

The future value ($f$) is defined in terms of $p$, $i$, and $n$. We can use this formula to determine that $200 ($p$) invested for 1 ($n$) period at an interest rate of 10% ($i$) yields a future value of $220 as follows:

$$f = p \times (1 + i)^n$$
$$= \$200 \times (1 + 0.10)^1$$
$$= \$220$$

This formula can also be used to compute the future value of an amount for *any number of periods* into the future. To illustrate, assume that $200 is invested for three periods at 10%. The future value of this $200 is $266.20, computed as follows:

$$f = p \times (1 + i)^n$$
$$= \$200 \times (1 + 0.10)^3$$
$$= \$266.20$$

A future value table makes it easier for us to compute future values ($f$) for many different combinations of interest rates ($i$) and time periods ($n$). Each future value in a future value table assumes the present value ($p$) is 1. As with a present value table, if the future amount is something other than 1, we simply multiply our answer by that amount. The formula used to construct a table of future values (factors) for a single amount of 1 is in Exhibit B.5.

**P2**    Apply future value concepts to a single amount by using interest tables.

$$f = (1 + i)^n$$

Exhibit B.5

Future Value of 1 Formula

Table B.2 at the end of this appendix shows a table of future values for a current amount of 1. This type of table is called a **future value of 1 table**.

There are some important relations between Tables B.1 and B.2. In Table B.2, for the row where $n = 0$, the future value is 1 for each interest rate. This is so because no interest is earned when time does not pass. Also notice that Tables B.1 and B.2 report the same information but in a different manner. In particular, one table is simply the *inverse* of the other. To illustrate this inverse relation, let's say we invest $100 annually for a period of five years at 12% per year. How much do we expect to have after five years? We can answer this question using Table B.2 by finding the future value ($f$) of 1, for five periods from now, compounded at 12%. From that table we find $f = 1.7623$. If we start with $100, the amount it accumulates to after five years is $176.23 ($100 $\times$ 1.7623). We can alternatively use Table B.1. Here we find that the present value ($p$) of 1, discounted five periods at 12%, is 0.5674. Recall the inverse relation between present value and future value. This means that $p = 1/f$ (or equivalently, $f = 1/p$). We can compute the future value of $100 invested for five periods at 12% as follows: $f = \$100 \times (1/0.5674) = \$176.24$.

A future value table involves three factors: $f$, $i$, and $n$. Knowing two of these three factors allows us to compute the third. To illustrate, consider these three possible cases.

**Case 1** (solve for $f$ when knowing $i$ and $n$). Our preceding example fits this case. We found that $100 invested for five periods at 12% interest accumulates to $176.24.

**Case 2** (solve for $n$ when knowing $f$ and $i$). In this case, we have, say, $2,000 ($p$) and we want to know how many periods ($n$) it will take to accumulate to $3,000 ($f$) at 7% ($i$) interest. To answer this, we go to the future value table (Table B.2) and look in the 7% interest column. Here we find a column of future values ($f$) based on a present value of 1. To use a future value table, we must divide $3,000 ($f$) by $2,000 ($p$), which equals 1.500. This is necessary because *a future value table defines* p *equal to 1, and* f *as a multiple of 1.* We look for a value nearest to 1.50 ($f$), which we find in the row for six periods ($n$). This means that $2,000 invested for six periods at 7% interest accumulates to $3,000.

**Case 3** (solve for $i$ when knowing $f$ and $n$). In this case, we have, say, $2,001 ($p$) and in nine years ($n$), we want to have $4,000 ($f$). What rate of interest must we earn to accomplish this? To answer that, we go to Table B.2 and search in the row for nine periods. To use a future value table, we must divide $4,000 ($f$) by $2,001 ($p$), which equals 1.9990. Recall that this is necessary because a future value table defines $p$ equal to 1 and $f$ as a multiple of 1. We look for a value nearest to 1.9990 ($f$), which we find in the column for 8% interest ($i$). This means that $2,001 invested for nine periods at 8% interest accumulates to $4,000.

2. Assume that you win a $150,000 cash sweepstakes. You decide to deposit this cash in an account earning 8% annual interest, and you plan to quit your job when the account equals $555,000. How many years will it be before you can quit working?

Answer—p. B-8

# Present Value of an Annuity

An *annuity* is a series of equal payments occurring at equal intervals. One example is a series of three annual payments of $100 each. An *ordinary annuity* is defined as equal end-of-period payments at equal intervals. An ordinary annuity of $100 for 3 periods and its present value ($p$) are illustrated in Exhibit B.6.

**Exhibit B.6**

Present Value of an Ordinary Annuity Diagram

| | $100 | $100 | $100 | |
| --- | --- | --- | --- | --- |
| $p$ | | | | Time |
| Today | Future ($n = 1$) | Future ($n = 2$) | Future ($n = 3$) | |

**P3** Apply present value concepts to an annuity by using interest tables.

One way to compute the present value of an ordinary annuity is to find the present value of each payment using our present value formula from Exhibit B.3. We then add each of the three present values. To illustrate, let's look at three $100 payments at the end of each of the next three periods with an interest rate of 15%. Our present value computations are

$$p = \frac{\$100}{(1 + 0.15)^1} + \frac{\$100}{(1 + 0.15)^2} + \frac{\$100}{(1 + 0.15)^3} = \$228.32$$

This computation is identical to computing the present value of each payment (from Table B.1) and taking their sum or, alternatively, adding the values from Table B.1 for each of the three payments and multiplying their sum by the $100 annuity payment.

A more direct way is to use a present value of annuity table. Table B.3 at the end of this appendix is one such table. This table is called a **present value of an annuity of 1 table**. If we look at Table B.3 where $n = 3$ and $i = 15\%$, we see the present value is 2.2832. This means that the present value of an annuity of 1 for three periods, with a 15% interest rate, equals 2.2832.

A present value of an annuity formula is used to construct Table B.3. It can also be constructed by adding the amounts in a present value of 1 table. To illustrate, we use Table B.1 and B.3 to confirm this relation for the prior example:

| From Table B.1 | | From Table B.3 | |
| --- | --- | --- | --- |
| $i = 15\%, n = 1$ ....... | 0.8696 | | |
| $i = 15\%, n = 2$ ....... | 0.7561 | | |
| $i = 15\%, n = 3$ ....... | 0.6575 | | |
| Total ............. | 2.2832 | $i = 15\%, n = 3$ ....... | 2.2832 |

We can also use business calculators or spreadsheet programs to find the present value of an annuity.

**Quick Check**

3. A company is considering an investment paying $10,000 every six months for three years. The first payment would be received in six months. If this company requires an 8% annual return, what is the maximum amount it is willing to pay for this investment?

Answer—p. B-8

# Future Value of an Annuity

The future value of an *ordinary annuity* is the accumulated value of each annuity payment with interest as of the date of the final payment. To illustrate, let's consider the earlier annuity of three annual payments of $100. Exhibit B.7 shows the point in time for the future value ($f$). The first payment is made two periods prior to the point when future value is determined, and the final payment occurs on the future value date.

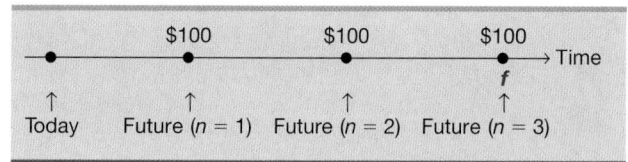

**Exhibit B.7**

Future Value of an Ordinary Annuity Diagram

One way to compute the future value of an annuity is to use the formula to find the future value of *each* payment and add them. If we assume an interest rate of 15%, our calculation is

$$f = \$100 \times (1 + 0.15)^2 + \$100 \times (1 + 0.15)^1 + \$100 \times (1 + 0.15)^0 = \$347.25$$

This is identical to using Table B.2 and summing the future values of each payment, or by adding the future values of the three payments of 1 and multiplying the sum by $100.

A more direct way is to use a table showing future values of annuities. Such a table is called a **future value of an annuity of 1 table**. Table B.4 at the end of this appendix is one such table. Note that in Table B.4 when $n = 1$, the future values equal 1 ($f = 1$) for all rates of interest. This is so because such an annuity consists of only one payment and the future value is determined on the date of that payment—no time passes between the payment and its future value. The future value of an annuity formula is used to construct Table B.4. We can also construct it by adding the amounts from a future value of 1 table. To illustrate, we use Tables B.2 and B.4 to confirm this relation for the prior example:

**P4**  Apply future value concepts to an annuity by using interest tables.

| From Table B.2 | | From Table B.4 | |
|---|---|---|---|
| $i = 15\%, n = 0$ ....... | 1.0000 | | |
| $i = 15\%, n = 1$ ....... | 1.1500 | | |
| $i = 15\%, n = 2$ ....... | 1.3225 | | |
| Total ............. | 3.4725 | $i = 15\%, n = 3$ ....... | 3.4725 |

Note that the future value in Table B.2 is 1.0000 when $n = 0$, but the future value in Table B.4 is 1.0000 when $n = 1$. Is this a contradiction? No. When $n = 0$ in Table B.2, the future value is determined on the date when a single payment occurs. This means that no interest is earned because no time has passed, and the future value equals the payment. Table B.4 describes annuities with equal payments occurring at the end of each period. When $n = 1$, the annuity has one payment, and its future value equals 1 on the date of its final and only payment. Again, no time passes from the payment and its future value date.

---

### Quick Check

**4.** A company invests $45,000 per year for five years at 12% annual interest. Compute the value of this annuity investment at the end of five years.

Answer—p. B-8

---

## Summary

**C1** **Describe the earning of interest and the concepts of present and future values.** Interest is payment by a borrower to the owner of an asset for its use. Present and future value computations are a way for us to estimate the interest component of holding assets or liabilities over a period of time.

**P1** **Apply present value concepts to a single amount by using interest tables.** The present value of a single amount received at a future date is the amount that can be invested now at the specified interest rate to yield that future value.

**P2** **Apply future value concepts to a single amount by using interest tables.** The future value of a single amount

invested at a specified rate of interest is the amount that would accumulate by the future date.

**P3** **Apply present value concepts to an annuity by using interest tables.** The present value of an annuity is the amount that can be invested now at the specified interest rate to yield that series of equal periodic payments.

**P4** **Apply future value concepts to an annuity by using interest tables.** The future value of an annuity invested at a specific rate of interest is the amount that would accumulate by the date of the final payment.

---

## Guidance Answers to **Quick Checks**

**1.** $70,000 \times 0.6302 = $44,114 (use Table B.1, $i = 8\%$, $n = 6$).

**2.** $555,000/$150,000 = 3.7000; Table B.2 shows this value is not achieved until after 17 years at 8% interest.

**3.** $10,000 \times 5.2421 = $52,421 (use Table B.3, $i = 4\%$, $n = 6$).

**4.** $45,000 \times 6.3528 = $285,876 (use Table B.4, $i = 12\%$, $n = 5$).

---

*Homework Manager repeats all numerical Quick Studies on the book's Website with new numbers.*

---

## QUICK STUDY

**QS B-1**

Identifying interest rates in tables

C1

Assume that you must make future value estimates using the *future value of 1 table* (Table B.2). Which interest rate column do you use when working with the following rates?

**1.** 8% compounded quarterly

**2.** 12% compounded annually

**3.** 6% compounded semiannually

**4.** 12% compounded monthly

---

**QS B-2**

Interest rate on an investment    P1

Ken Francis is offered the possibility of investing $2,745 today and in return to receive $10,000 after 15 years. What is the annual rate of interest for this investment? (Use Table B.1.)

---

**QS B-3**

Number of periods of an investment    P1

Megan Brink is offered the possibility of investing $6,651 today at 6% interest per year in a desire to accumulate $10,000. How many years must Brink wait to accumulate $10,000? (Use Table B.1.)

---

**QS B-4**

Present value of an amount    P1

Flaherty is considering an investment that, if paid for immediately, is expected to return $140,000 five years from now. If Flaherty demands a 9% return, how much is she willing to pay for this investment?

CII, Inc., invests $630,000 in a project expected to earn a 12% annual rate of return. The earnings will be reinvested in the project each year until the entire investment is liquidated 10 years later. What will the cash proceeds be when the project is liquidated?

**QS B-5**
Future value
of an amount    P2

Beene Distributing is considering a project that will return $150,000 annually at the end of each year for six years. If Beene demands an annual return of 7% and pays for the project immediately, how much is it willing to pay for the project?

**QS B-6**
Present value
of an annuity    P3

Claire Fitch is planning to begin an individual retirement program in which she will invest $1,500 at the end of each year. Fitch plans to retire after making 30 annual investments in the program earning a return of 10%. What is the value of the program on the date of the last payment?

**QS B-7**
Future value
of an annuity    P4

🖳    ↤ **Homework Manager** repeats all numerical Exercises on the book's Website with new numbers.

Bill Thompson expects to invest $10,000 at 12% and, at the end of a certain period, receive $96,463. How many years will it be before Thompson receives the payment? (Use Table B.2.)

**EXERCISES**

**Exercise B-1**
Number of periods
of an investment    P2

Ed Summers expects to invest $10,000 for 25 years, after which he wants to receive $108,347. What rate of interest must Summers earn? (Use Table B.2.)

**Exercise B-2**
Interest rate on
an investment    P2

Jones expects an immediate investment of $57,466 to return $10,000 annually for eight years, with the first payment to be received one year from now. What rate of interest must Jones earn? (Use Table B.3.)

**Exercise B-3**
Interest rate on
an investment    P3

Keith Riggins expects an investment of $82,014 to return $10,000 annually for several years. If Riggins earns a return of 10%, how many annual payments will he receive? (Use Table B.3.)

**Exercise B-4**
Number of periods
of an investment    P3

Algoe expects to invest $1,000 annually for 40 years to yield an accumulated value of $154,762 on the date of the last investment. For this to occur, what rate of interest must Algoe earn? (Use Table B.4.)

**Exercise B-5**
Interest rate on
an investment    P4

Kate Beckwith expects to invest $10,000 annually that will earn 8%. How many annual investments must Beckwith make to accumulate $303,243 on the date of the last investment? (Use Table B.4.)

**Exercise B-6**
Number of periods
of an investment    P4

Sam Weber finances a new automobile by paying $6,500 cash and agreeing to make 40 monthly payments of $500 each, the first payment to be made one month after the purchase. The loan bears interest at an annual rate of 12%. What is the cost of the automobile?

**Exercise B-7**
Present value
of an annuity    P3

Spiller Corp. plans to issue 10%, 15-year, $500,000 par value bonds payable that pay interest semiannually on June 30 and December 31. The bonds are dated December 31, 2005, and are issued on that date. If the market rate of interest for the bonds is 8% on the date of issue, what will be the total cash proceeds from the bond issue?

**Exercise B-8**
Present value of bonds
P1    P3

McAdams Company expects to earn 10% per year on an investment that will pay $606,773 six years from now. Use Table B.1 to compute the present value of this investment.

**Exercise B-9**
Present value
of an amount    P1

---

**Exercise B-10**
Present value of
an amount and
of an annuity   P1   P3

Compute the amount that can be borrowed under each of the following circumstances:

**1.** A promise to repay $90,000 seven years from now at an interest rate of 6%.

**2.** An agreement made on February 1, 2005, to make three separate payments of $20,000 on February 1 of 2006, 2007, and 2008. The annual interest rate is 10%.

---

**Exercise B-11**
Present value
of an amount   P1

On January 1, 2005, a company agrees to pay $20,000 in three years. If the annual interest rate is 10%, determine how much cash the company can borrow with this agreement.

---

**Exercise B-12**
Present value
of an amount   P1

Find the amount of money that can be borrowed today with each of the following separate debt agreements *a* through *f*:

| Case | Single Future Payment | Number of Periods | Interest Rate |
|------|----------------------|-------------------|---------------|
| a. ........ | $40,000 | 3 | 4% |
| b. ........ | 75,000 | 7 | 8 |
| c. ........ | 52,000 | 9 | 10 |
| d. ........ | 18,000 | 2 | 4 |
| e. ........ | 63,000 | 8 | 6 |
| f. ........ | 89,000 | 5 | 2 |

---

**Exercise B-13**
Present values of annuities

P3

C&H Ski Club recently borrowed money and agrees to pay it back with a series of six annual payments of $5,000 each. C&H subsequently borrows more money and agrees to pay it back with a series of four annual payments of $7,500 each. The annual interest rate for both loans is 6%.

**1.** Use Table B.1 to find the present value of these two separate annuities. (Round amounts to the nearest dollar.)

**2.** Use Table B.3 to find the present value of these two separate annuities.

---

**Exercise B-14**
Present value with semiannual
compounding

C1   P3

Otto Co. borrows money on April 30, 2005, by promising to make four payments of $13,000 each on November 1, 2005; May 1, 2006; November 1, 2006; and May 1, 2007.

**1.** How much money is Otto able to borrow if the interest rate is 8%, compounded semiannually?

**2.** How much money is Otto able to borrow if the interest rate is 12%, compounded semiannually?

**3.** How much money is Otto able to borrow if the interest rate is 16%, compounded semiannually?

---

**Exercise B-15**
Future value
of an amount   P2

Mark Welsch deposits $7,200 in an account that earns interest at an annual rate of 8%, compounded quarterly. The $7,200 plus earned interest must remain in the account 10 years before it can be withdrawn. How much money will be in the account at the end of 10 years?

---

**Exercise B-16**
Future value
of an annuity   P4

Kelly Malone plans to have $50 withheld from her monthly paycheck and deposited in a savings account that earns 12% annually, compounded monthly. If Malone continues with her plan for two and one-half years, how much will be accumulated in the account on the date of the last deposit?

---

**Exercise B-17**
Future value of
an amount plus
an annuity   P2   P4

Starr Company decides to establish a fund that it will use 10 years from now to replace an aging production facility. The company will make a $100,000 initial contribution to the fund and plans to make quarterly contributions of $50,000 beginning in three months. The fund earns 12%, compounded quarterly. What will be the value of the fund 10 years from now?

---

**Exercise B-18**
Future value of
an amount   P2

Catten, Inc., invests $163,170 today earning 7% per year for nine years. Use Table B.2 to compute the future value of the investment nine years from now.

For each of the following situations, identify (1) the case as either (*a*) a present or a future value and (*b*) a single amount or an annuity, (2) the table you would use in your computations (but do not solve the problem), and (3) the interest rate and time periods you would use.

**a.** You need to accumulate $10,000 for a trip you wish to take in four years. You are able to earn 8% compounded semiannually on your savings. You plan to make only one deposit and let the money accumulate for four years. How would you determine the amount of the one-time deposit?

**b.** Assume the same facts as in part (*a*) except that you will make semiannual deposits to your savings account.

**c.** You want to retire after working 40 years with savings in excess of $1,000,000. You expect to save $4,000 a year for 40 years and earn an annual rate of interest of 8%. Will you be able to retire with more than $1,000,000 in 40 years? Explain.

**d.** A sweepstakes agency names you a grand prize winner. You can take $225,000 immediately or elect to receive annual installments of $30,000 for 20 years. You can earn 10% annually on any investments you make. Which prize do you choose to receive?

**Exercise B-19**
Using present and future value tables

C1  P1  P2  P3  P4

## Table B.1

Present Value of 1

$$p = 1/(1 + i)^n$$

| Periods | 1% | 2% | 3% | 4% | 5% | 6% | 7% | 8% | 9% | 10% | 12% | 15% |
|---|---|---|---|---|---|---|---|---|---|---|---|---|
| 1 | 0.9901 | 0.9804 | 0.9709 | 0.9615 | 0.9524 | 0.9434 | 0.9346 | 0.9259 | 0.9174 | 0.9091 | 0.8929 | 0.8696 |
| 2 | 0.9803 | 0.9612 | 0.9426 | 0.9246 | 0.9070 | 0.8900 | 0.8734 | 0.8573 | 0.8417 | 0.8264 | 0.7972 | 0.7561 |
| 3 | 0.9706 | 0.9423 | 0.9151 | 0.8890 | 0.8638 | 0.8396 | 0.8163 | 0.7938 | 0.7722 | 0.7513 | 0.7118 | 0.6575 |
| 4 | 0.9610 | 0.9238 | 0.8885 | 0.8548 | 0.8227 | 0.7921 | 0.7629 | 0.7350 | 0.7084 | 0.6830 | 0.6355 | 0.5718 |
| 5 | 0.9515 | 0.9057 | 0.8626 | 0.8219 | 0.7835 | 0.7473 | 0.7130 | 0.6806 | 0.6499 | 0.6209 | 0.5674 | 0.4972 |
| 6 | 0.9420 | 0.8880 | 0.8375 | 0.7903 | 0.7462 | 0.7050 | 0.6663 | 0.6302 | 0.5963 | 0.5645 | 0.5066 | 0.4323 |
| 7 | 0.9327 | 0.8706 | 0.8131 | 0.7599 | 0.7107 | 0.6651 | 0.6227 | 0.5835 | 0.5470 | 0.5132 | 0.4523 | 0.3759 |
| 8 | 0.9235 | 0.8535 | 0.7894 | 0.7307 | 0.6768 | 0.6274 | 0.5820 | 0.5403 | 0.5019 | 0.4665 | 0.4039 | 0.3269 |
| 9 | 0.9143 | 0.8368 | 0.7664 | 0.7026 | 0.6446 | 0.5919 | 0.5439 | 0.5002 | 0.4604 | 0.4241 | 0.3606 | 0.2843 |
| 10 | 0.9053 | 0.8203 | 0.7441 | 0.6756 | 0.6139 | 0.5584 | 0.5083 | 0.4632 | 0.4224 | 0.3855 | 0.3220 | 0.2472 |
| 11 | 0.8963 | 0.8043 | 0.7224 | 0.6496 | 0.5847 | 0.5268 | 0.4751 | 0.4289 | 0.3875 | 0.3505 | 0.2875 | 0.2149 |
| 12 | 0.8874 | 0.7885 | 0.7014 | 0.6246 | 0.5568 | 0.4970 | 0.4440 | 0.3971 | 0.3555 | 0.3186 | 0.2567 | 0.1869 |
| 13 | 0.8787 | 0.7730 | 0.6810 | 0.6006 | 0.5303 | 0.4688 | 0.4150 | 0.3677 | 0.3262 | 0.2897 | 0.2292 | 0.1625 |
| 14 | 0.8700 | 0.7579 | 0.6611 | 0.5775 | 0.5051 | 0.4423 | 0.3878 | 0.3405 | 0.2992 | 0.2633 | 0.2046 | 0.1413 |
| 15 | 0.8613 | 0.7430 | 0.6419 | 0.5553 | 0.4810 | 0.4173 | 0.3624 | 0.3152 | 0.2745 | 0.2394 | 0.1827 | 0.1229 |
| 16 | 0.8528 | 0.7284 | 0.6232 | 0.5339 | 0.4581 | 0.3936 | 0.3387 | 0.2919 | 0.2519 | 0.2176 | 0.1631 | 0.1069 |
| 17 | 0.8444 | 0.7142 | 0.6050 | 0.5134 | 0.4363 | 0.3714 | 0.3166 | 0.2703 | 0.2311 | 0.1978 | 0.1456 | 0.0929 |
| 18 | 0.8360 | 0.7002 | 0.5874 | 0.4936 | 0.4155 | 0.3503 | 0.2959 | 0.2502 | 0.2120 | 0.1799 | 0.1300 | 0.0808 |
| 19 | 0.8277 | 0.6864 | 0.5703 | 0.4746 | 0.3957 | 0.3305 | 0.2765 | 0.2317 | 0.1945 | 0.1635 | 0.1161 | 0.0703 |
| 20 | 0.8195 | 0.6730 | 0.5537 | 0.4564 | 0.3769 | 0.3118 | 0.2584 | 0.2145 | 0.1784 | 0.1486 | 0.1037 | 0.0611 |
| 25 | 0.7798 | 0.6095 | 0.4776 | 0.3751 | 0.2953 | 0.2330 | 0.1842 | 0.1460 | 0.1160 | 0.0923 | 0.0588 | 0.0304 |
| 30 | 0.7419 | 0.5521 | 0.4120 | 0.3083 | 0.2314 | 0.1741 | 0.1314 | 0.0994 | 0.0754 | 0.0573 | 0.0334 | 0.0151 |
| 35 | 0.7059 | 0.5000 | 0.3554 | 0.2534 | 0.1813 | 0.1301 | 0.0937 | 0.0676 | 0.0490 | 0.0356 | 0.0189 | 0.0075 |
| 40 | 0.6717 | 0.4529 | 0.3066 | 0.2083 | 0.1420 | 0.0972 | 0.0668 | 0.0460 | 0.0318 | 0.0221 | 0.0107 | 0.0037 |

## Table B.2

Future Value of 1

$$f = (1 + i)^n$$

| Periods | 1% | 2% | 3% | 4% | 5% | 6% | 7% | 8% | 9% | 10% | 12% | 15% |
|---|---|---|---|---|---|---|---|---|---|---|---|---|
| 0 | 1.0000 | 1.0000 | 1.0000 | 1.0000 | 1.0000 | 1.0000 | 1.0000 | 1.0000 | 1.0000 | 1.0000 | 1.0000 | 1.0000 |
| 1 | 1.0100 | 1.0200 | 1.0300 | 1.0400 | 1.0500 | 1.0600 | 1.0700 | 1.0800 | 1.0900 | 1.1000 | 1.1200 | 1.1500 |
| 2 | 1.0201 | 1.0404 | 1.0609 | 1.0816 | 1.1025 | 1.1236 | 1.1449 | 1.1664 | 1.1881 | 1.2100 | 1.2544 | 1.3225 |
| 3 | 1.0303 | 1.0612 | 1.0927 | 1.1249 | 1.1576 | 1.1910 | 1.2250 | 1.2597 | 1.2950 | 1.3310 | 1.4049 | 1.5209 |
| 4 | 1.0406 | 1.0824 | 1.1255 | 1.1699 | 1.2155 | 1.2625 | 1.3108 | 1.3605 | 1.4116 | 1.4641 | 1.5735 | 1.7490 |
| 5 | 1.0510 | 1.1041 | 1.1593 | 1.2167 | 1.2763 | 1.3382 | 1.4026 | 1.4693 | 1.5386 | 1.6105 | 1.7623 | 2.0114 |
| 6 | 1.0615 | 1.1262 | 1.1941 | 1.2653 | 1.3401 | 1.4185 | 1.5007 | 1.5869 | 1.6771 | 1.7716 | 1.9738 | 2.3131 |
| 7 | 1.0721 | 1.1487 | 1.2299 | 1.3159 | 1.4071 | 1.5036 | 1.6058 | 1.7138 | 1.8280 | 1.9487 | 2.2107 | 2.6600 |
| 8 | 1.0829 | 1.1717 | 1.2668 | 1.3686 | 1.4775 | 1.5938 | 1.7182 | 1.8509 | 1.9926 | 2.1436 | 2.4760 | 3.0590 |
| 9 | 1.0937 | 1.1951 | 1.3048 | 1.4233 | 1.5513 | 1.6895 | 1.8385 | 1.9990 | 2.1719 | 2.3579 | 2.7731 | 3.5179 |
| 10 | 1.1046 | 1.2190 | 1.3439 | 1.4802 | 1.6289 | 1.7908 | 1.9672 | 2.1589 | 2.3674 | 2.5937 | 3.1058 | 4.0456 |
| 11 | 1.1157 | 1.2434 | 1.3842 | 1.5395 | 1.7103 | 1.8983 | 2.1049 | 2.3316 | 2.5804 | 2.8531 | 3.4785 | 4.6524 |
| 12 | 1.1268 | 1.2682 | 1.4258 | 1.6010 | 1.7959 | 2.0122 | 2.2522 | 2.5182 | 2.8127 | 3.1384 | 3.8960 | 5.3503 |
| 13 | 1.1381 | 1.2936 | 1.4685 | 1.6651 | 1.8856 | 2.1329 | 2.4098 | 2.7196 | 3.0658 | 3.4523 | 4.3635 | 6.1528 |
| 14 | 1.1495 | 1.3195 | 1.5126 | 1.7317 | 1.9799 | 2.2609 | 2.5785 | 2.9372 | 3.3417 | 3.7975 | 4.8871 | 7.0757 |
| 15 | 1.1610 | 1.3459 | 1.5580 | 1.8009 | 2.0789 | 2.3966 | 2.7590 | 3.1722 | 3.6425 | 4.1772 | 5.4736 | 8.1371 |
| 16 | 1.1726 | 1.3728 | 1.6047 | 1.8730 | 2.1829 | 2.5404 | 2.9522 | 3.4259 | 3.9703 | 4.5950 | 6.1304 | 9.3576 |
| 17 | 1.1843 | 1.4002 | 1.6528 | 1.9479 | 2.2920 | 2.6928 | 3.1588 | 3.7000 | 4.3276 | 5.0545 | 6.8660 | 10.7613 |
| 18 | 1.1961 | 1.4282 | 1.7024 | 2.0258 | 2.4066 | 2.8543 | 3.3799 | 3.9960 | 4.7171 | 5.5599 | 7.6900 | 12.3755 |
| 19 | 1.2081 | 1.4568 | 1.7535 | 2.1068 | 2.5270 | 3.0256 | 3.6165 | 4.3157 | 5.1417 | 6.1159 | 8.6128 | 14.2318 |
| 20 | 1.2202 | 1.4859 | 1.8061 | 2.1911 | 2.6533 | 3.2071 | 3.8697 | 4.6610 | 5.6044 | 6.7275 | 9.6463 | 16.3665 |
| 25 | 1.2824 | 1.6406 | 2.0938 | 2.6658 | 3.3864 | 4.2919 | 5.4274 | 6.8485 | 8.6231 | 10.8347 | 17.0001 | 32.9190 |
| 30 | 1.3478 | 1.8114 | 2.4273 | 3.2434 | 4.3219 | 5.7435 | 7.6123 | 10.0627 | 13.2677 | 17.4494 | 29.9599 | 66.2118 |
| 35 | 1.4166 | 1.9999 | 2.8139 | 3.9461 | 5.5160 | 7.6861 | 10.6766 | 14.7853 | 20.4140 | 28.1024 | 52.7996 | 133.176 |
| 40 | 1.4889 | 2.2080 | 3.2620 | 4.8010 | 7.0400 | 10.2857 | 14.9745 | 21.7245 | 31.4094 | 45.2593 | 93.0510 | 267.864 |

$$p = \left[1 - \frac{1}{(1 + i)^n}\right]/i$$

## Table B.3

Present Value of an Annuity of 1

| Periods | 1% | 2% | 3% | 4% | 5% | 6% | 7% | 8% | 9% | 10% | 12% | 15% |
|---|---|---|---|---|---|---|---|---|---|---|---|---|
| 1 | 0.9901 | 0.9804 | 0.9709 | 0.9615 | 0.9524 | 0.9434 | 0.9346 | 0.9259 | 0.9174 | 0.9091 | 0.8929 | 0.8696 |
| 2 | 1.9704 | 1.9416 | 1.9135 | 1.8861 | 1.8594 | 1.8334 | 1.8080 | 1.7833 | 1.7591 | 1.7355 | 1.6901 | 1.6257 |
| 3 | 2.9410 | 2.8839 | 2.8286 | 2.7751 | 2.7232 | 2.6730 | 2.6243 | 2.5771 | 2.5313 | 2.4869 | 2.4018 | 2.2832 |
| 4 | 3.9020 | 3.8077 | 3.7171 | 3.6299 | 3.5460 | 3.4651 | 3.3872 | 3.3121 | 3.2397 | 3.1699 | 3.0373 | 2.8550 |
| 5 | 4.8534 | 4.7135 | 4.5797 | 4.4518 | 4.3295 | 4.2124 | 4.1002 | 3.9927 | 3.8897 | 3.7908 | 3.6048 | 3.3522 |
| 6 | 5.7955 | 5.6014 | 5.4172 | 5.2421 | 5.0757 | 4.9173 | 4.7665 | 4.6229 | 4.4859 | 4.3553 | 4.1114 | 3.7845 |
| 7 | 6.7282 | 6.4720 | 6.2303 | 6.0021 | 5.7864 | 5.5824 | 5.3893 | 5.2064 | 5.0330 | 4.8684 | 4.5638 | 4.1604 |
| 8 | 7.6517 | 7.3255 | 7.0197 | 6.7327 | 6.4632 | 6.2098 | 5.9713 | 5.7466 | 5.5348 | 5.3349 | 4.9676 | 4.4873 |
| 9 | 8.5660 | 8.1622 | 7.7861 | 7.4353 | 7.1078 | 6.8017 | 6.5152 | 6.2469 | 5.9952 | 5.7590 | 5.3282 | 4.7716 |
| 10 | 9.4713 | 8.9826 | 8.5302 | 8.1109 | 7.7217 | 7.3601 | 7.0236 | 6.7101 | 6.4177 | 6.1446 | 5.6502 | 5.0188 |
| 11 | 10.3676 | 9.7868 | 9.2526 | 8.7605 | 8.3064 | 7.8869 | 7.4987 | 7.1390 | 6.8052 | 6.4951 | 5.9377 | 5.2337 |
| 12 | 11.2551 | 10.5753 | 9.9540 | 9.3851 | 8.8633 | 8.3838 | 7.9427 | 7.5361 | 7.1607 | 6.8137 | 6.1944 | 5.4206 |
| 13 | 12.1337 | 11.3484 | 10.6350 | 9.9856 | 9.3936 | 8.8527 | 8.3577 | 7.9038 | 7.4869 | 7.1034 | 6.4235 | 5.5831 |
| 14 | 13.0037 | 12.1062 | 11.2961 | 10.5631 | 9.8986 | 9.2950 | 8.7455 | 8.2442 | 7.7862 | 7.3667 | 6.6282 | 5.7245 |
| 15 | 13.8651 | 12.8493 | 11.9379 | 11.1184 | 10.3797 | 9.7122 | 9.1079 | 8.5595 | 8.0607 | 7.6061 | 6.8109 | 5.8474 |
| 16 | 14.7179 | 13.5777 | 12.5611 | 11.6523 | 10.8378 | 10.1059 | 9.4466 | 8.8514 | 8.3126 | 7.8237 | 6.9740 | 5.9542 |
| 17 | 15.5623 | 14.2919 | 13.1661 | 12.1657 | 11.2741 | 10.4773 | 9.7632 | 9.1216 | 8.5436 | 8.0216 | 7.1196 | 6.0472 |
| 18 | 16.3983 | 14.9920 | 13.7535 | 12.6593 | 11.6896 | 10.8276 | 10.0591 | 9.3719 | 8.7556 | 8.2014 | 7.2497 | 6.1280 |
| 19 | 17.2260 | 15.6785 | 14.3238 | 13.1339 | 12.0853 | 11.1581 | 10.3356 | 9.6036 | 8.9501 | 8.3649 | 7.3658 | 6.1982 |
| 20 | 18.0456 | 16.3514 | 14.8775 | 13.5903 | 12.4622 | 11.4699 | 10.5940 | 9.8181 | 9.1285 | 8.5136 | 7.4694 | 6.2593 |
| 25 | 22.0232 | 19.5235 | 17.4131 | 15.6221 | 14.0939 | 12.7834 | 11.6536 | 10.6748 | 9.8226 | 9.0770 | 7.8431 | 6.4641 |
| 30 | 25.8077 | 22.3965 | 19.6004 | 17.2920 | 15.3725 | 13.7648 | 12.4090 | 11.2578 | 10.2737 | 9.4269 | 8.0552 | 6.5660 |
| 35 | 29.4086 | 24.9986 | 21.4872 | 18.6646 | 16.3742 | 14.4982 | 12.9477 | 11.6546 | 10.5668 | 9.6442 | 8.1755 | 6.6166 |
| 40 | 32.8347 | 27.3555 | 23.1148 | 19.7928 | 17.1591 | 15.0463 | 13.3317 | 11.9246 | 10.7574 | 9.7791 | 8.2438 | 6.6418 |

$$f = [(1 + i)^n - 1]/i$$

## Table B.4

Future Value of an Annuity of 1

| Periods | 1% | 2% | 3% | 4% | 5% | 6% | 7% | 8% | 9% | 10% | 12% | 15% |
|---|---|---|---|---|---|---|---|---|---|---|---|---|
| 1 | 1.0000 | 1.0000 | 1.0000 | 1.0000 | 1.0000 | 1.0000 | 1.0000 | 1.0000 | 1.0000 | 1.0000 | 1.0000 | 1.0000 |
| 2 | 2.0100 | 2.0200 | 2.0300 | 2.0400 | 2.0500 | 2.0600 | 2.0700 | 2.0800 | 2.0900 | 2.1000 | 2.1200 | 2.1500 |
| 3 | 3.0301 | 3.0604 | 3.0909 | 3.1216 | 3.1525 | 3.1836 | 3.2149 | 3.2464 | 3.2781 | 3.3100 | 3.3744 | 3.4725 |
| 4 | 4.0604 | 4.1216 | 4.1836 | 4.2465 | 4.3101 | 4.3746 | 4.4399 | 4.5061 | 4.5731 | 4.6410 | 4.7793 | 4.9934 |
| 5 | 5.1010 | 5.2040 | 5.3091 | 5.4163 | 5.5256 | 5.6371 | 5.7507 | 5.8666 | 5.9847 | 6.1051 | 6.3528 | 6.7424 |
| 6 | 6.1520 | 6.3081 | 6.4684 | 6.6330 | 6.8019 | 6.9753 | 7.1533 | 7.3359 | 7.5233 | 7.7156 | 8.1152 | 8.7537 |
| 7 | 7.2135 | 7.4343 | 7.6625 | 7.8983 | 8.1420 | 8.3938 | 8.6540 | 8.9228 | 9.2004 | 9.4872 | 10.0890 | 11.0668 |
| 8 | 8.2857 | 8.5830 | 8.8923 | 9.2142 | 9.5491 | 9.8975 | 10.2598 | 10.6366 | 11.0285 | 11.4359 | 12.2997 | 13.7268 |
| 9 | 9.3685 | 9.7546 | 10.1591 | 10.5828 | 11.0266 | 11.4913 | 11.9780 | 12.4876 | 13.0210 | 13.5795 | 14.7757 | 16.7858 |
| 10 | 10.4622 | 10.9497 | 11.4639 | 12.0061 | 12.5779 | 13.1808 | 13.8164 | 14.4866 | 15.1929 | 15.9374 | 17.5487 | 20.3037 |
| 11 | 11.5668 | 12.1687 | 12.8078 | 13.4864 | 14.2068 | 14.9716 | 15.7836 | 16.6455 | 17.5603 | 18.5312 | 20.6546 | 24.3493 |
| 12 | 12.6825 | 13.4121 | 14.1920 | 15.0258 | 15.9171 | 16.8699 | 17.8885 | 18.9771 | 20.1407 | 21.3843 | 24.1331 | 29.0017 |
| 13 | 13.8093 | 14.6803 | 15.6178 | 16.6268 | 17.7130 | 18.8821 | 20.1406 | 21.4953 | 22.9534 | 24.5227 | 28.0291 | 34.3519 |
| 14 | 14.9474 | 15.9739 | 17.0863 | 18.2919 | 19.5986 | 21.0151 | 22.5505 | 24.2149 | 26.0192 | 27.9750 | 32.3926 | 40.5047 |
| 15 | 16.0969 | 17.2934 | 18.5989 | 20.0236 | 21.5786 | 23.2760 | 25.1290 | 27.1521 | 29.3609 | 31.7725 | 37.2797 | 47.5804 |
| 16 | 17.2579 | 18.6393 | 20.1569 | 21.8245 | 23.6575 | 25.6725 | 27.8881 | 30.3243 | 33.0034 | 35.9497 | 42.7533 | 55.7175 |
| 17 | 18.4304 | 20.0121 | 21.7616 | 23.6975 | 25.8404 | 28.2129 | 30.8402 | 33.7502 | 36.9737 | 40.5447 | 48.8837 | 65.0751 |
| 18 | 19.6147 | 21.4123 | 23.4144 | 25.6454 | 28.1324 | 30.9057 | 33.9990 | 37.4502 | 41.3013 | 45.5992 | 55.7497 | 75.8364 |
| 19 | 20.8109 | 22.8406 | 25.1169 | 27.6712 | 30.5390 | 33.7600 | 37.3790 | 41.4463 | 46.0185 | 51.1591 | 63.4397 | 88.2118 |
| 20 | 22.0190 | 24.2974 | 26.8704 | 29.7781 | 33.0660 | 36.7856 | 40.9955 | 45.7620 | 51.1601 | 57.2750 | 72.0524 | 102.444 |
| 25 | 28.2432 | 32.0303 | 36.4593 | 41.6459 | 47.7271 | 54.8645 | 63.2490 | 73.1059 | 84.7009 | 98.3471 | 133.334 | 212.793 |
| 30 | 34.7849 | 40.5681 | 47.5754 | 56.0849 | 66.4388 | 79.0582 | 94.4608 | 113.283 | 136.308 | 164.494 | 241.333 | 434.745 |
| 35 | 41.6603 | 49.9945 | 60.4621 | 73.6522 | 90.3203 | 111.435 | 138.237 | 172.317 | 215.711 | 271.024 | 431.663 | 881.170 |
| 40 | 48.8864 | 60.4020 | 75.4013 | 95.0255 | 120.800 | 154.762 | 199.635 | 259.057 | 337.882 | 442.593 | 767.091 | 1,779.09 |

*"To build a great company you have to build a great team of people—people that are completely focused, who see this as their opportunity to achieve their lifelong financial goals"*—Ralph Cruz (on right; Bill Cruz on left)

# Reporting and Analyzing Investments and International Operations

## A Look at This Appendix

This appendix focuses on investments in securities. We explain how to identify, account for, and report investments in both debt and equity securities. We also introduce foreign exchange rates and describe accounting for transactions listed in a foreign currency.

# CAP

## Conceptual

**C1** Distinguish between debt and equity securities and between short-term and long-term investments. *(p. C-2)*

**C2** Identify and describe the different classes of investments in securities. *(p. C-3)*

**C3** Describe how to report equity securities with controlling influence. *(p. C-9)*

## Analytical

**A1** Compute and analyze the components of return on total assets. *(p. C-10)*

## Procedural

**P1** Account for trading securities. *(p. C-5)*

**P2** Account for held-to-maturity securities. *(p. C-6)*

**P3** Account for available-for-sale securities. *(p. C-6)*

**P4** Account for equity securities with significant influence. *(p. C-7)*

## Decision Feature

# Sound of Success

PLANTATION, FL—Bill and Ralph Cruz remember it as if it were yesterday. The Cruz brothers, then teenagers, combined their life savings of $2,400 and invested in securities. By week's end, they had amassed a $400 profit. "At the time we were poor, starving musicians," said Bill; "$400 seemed like we were set for life." However, success in trading securities can be short lived, and by the next week they had lost their profit and much of their original investment.

Although that first experience was unprofitable, the young musicians were hooked. The Cruz brothers had dreamed of becoming violinists but their attention turned to trading securities. "A lot of what we learned then [in music] we transferred to our business," says Bill. That business, now called the **TradeStation Group [TradeStation.com],** is based on an award-winning trading platform which enables very active individual and professional traders to design custom trading strategies, and then test, refine and automate the execution of those strategies. "The TradeStation trading platform monitors all the markets for you and the minute it spots buy or sell opportunities based on your criteria, it generates a real time buy or sell order that is usually executed instanta-

neously through our direct-access order execution technology," says Ralph.

The Cruz brothers also recognize the importance of knowing the accounting and reporting requirements for investments. The Cruzes point out that accounting rules for recognizing gains and losses for different portfolios can affect the trading strategies and successes of traders. It is important for investors to understand these rules to not inadvertently hurt their trading profits or accelerate gains recognition. This knowledge extends to investments in both equity and debt securities.

Bill Cruz says a future goal is to further their international brokerage base. "There's really no reason that a good portion of our revenue shouldn't come from active traders outside the U.S. who trade futures and NYSE and Nasdaq securities," says Bill. He also highlights unique accounting and reporting requirements that international traders in securities must consider. The one-time musicians have set lofty plans. "Our goal," says Bill, "is to be one of the largest online brokerages." Smart money says don't bet against them.

[Sources: *TradeStation Website*, January 2004, *Hispanic Magazine*, April 2003; *South Florida Business Journal Website Archive*, June 2003.]

This appendix's main focus is investments in securities. Many companies have investments, and many of these are in the form of debt and equity securities issued by other companies. We describe investments in these securities and how to account for them. An increasing number of companies also invest in international operations. We explain how to account for and report international transactions listed in foreign currencies.

## Reporting and Analyzing Investments and International Operations

### Basics of Investments
- Motivation for investments
- Short-term versus long-term investments
- Classification and reporting
- Basics of investment accounting

### Noninfluential Investments
- Trading securities
- Held-to-maturity securities
- Available-for-sale securities

### Influential Investments
- Securities with significant influence
- Securities with controlling influence
- Accounting summary for investments

# Basics of Investments

**C1** Distinguish between debt and equity securities and between short-term and long-term investments.

**Point:** Reporting securities at market value is referred to as *mark-to-market* accounting.

This section describes the motivation for investments, the distinction between short- and long-term investments, and the different classes of investments.

## Motivation for Investments

Companies make investments for at least three reasons. First, companies transfer *excess cash* into investments to produce higher income. Second, some entities, such as mutual funds and pension funds, are set up to produce income from investments. Third, companies make investments for strategic reasons. Examples are investments in competitors, suppliers, and even customers. Exhibit C.1 shows short-term (S-T) and long-term (L-T) investments as a percent of total assets for several companies.

## Exhibit C.1

Investments of Selected Companies

Percent of total assets

## Short-Term versus Long-Term Investments

Cash equivalents are investments that are both readily converted to known amounts of cash and mature within three months. Many investments, however, mature between 3 and 12 months. These investments are **short-term investments,** also called *temporary investments* and *marketable securities*. Specifically, short-term investments are securities that (1) management intends to convert to cash within one year or the operating cycle, whichever is longer, and (2) are readily convertible to cash. Short-term investments are reported under current assets and serve a purpose similar to cash equivalents.

**Long-term investments** in securities are defined as those securities that are not readily convertible to cash or are not intended to be converted into cash in the short term. Long-term investments can also include funds earmarked for a special purpose, such as bond sinking funds and investments in land or other assets not used in the company's operations. Long-term investments are reported in the noncurrent section of the balance sheet, often in its own separate line titled *Long-Term Investments*.

Investments in securities can include both debt and equity securities. *Debt securities* reflect a creditor relationship such as investments in notes, bonds, and certificates of deposit;

Topic Tackler C-1

they are issued by governments, companies, and individuals. *Equity securities* reflect an owner relationship such as shares of stock issued by companies.

## Classes of and Reporting for Investments

Accounting for investments in securities depends on three factors: (1) security type, either debt or equity, (2) the company's intent to hold the security either short term or long term, and (3) the company's (investor's) percent ownership in the other company's (investee's) equity securities. Exhibit C.2 identifies five classes of securities using these three factors. It describes each of these five classes of securities and the reporting required under each class.

**C2** Identify and describe the different classes of investments in securities.

Exhibit C.2

Investments in Securities

<sup>a</sup> Holding less than 20% of voting stock (equity securities only).   <sup>b</sup> Holding 20% or more, but not more than 50%, of voting stock.
<sup>c</sup> Holding more than 50% of voting stock.
* Unrealized gains and losses reported on the income statement.
** Unrealized gains and losses reported in the equity section of the balance sheet and in comprehensive income.

## Basics of Accounting for Investments

This section introduces the accounting basics for investments, including that for acquisition, disposition, and any interest or dividends.

**Accounting Basics for Debt Securities**   Debt securities are recorded at cost when purchased. Interest revenue for investments in debt securities is recorded when earned.

**Acquisition.**   Assume that Music City paid $29,500 plus a $500 brokerage fee on September 1, 2005, to buy Dell's 7%, two-year bonds payable with a $30,000 par value. The bonds pay interest semiannually on August 31 and February 28. Music City intends to hold the bonds until they mature on August 31, 2007, called held-to-maturity (HTM) securities. The entry to record this purchase is

**Example:** What is cost per share? *Answer:* Cost per share is the total cost of acquisition, including broker fees, divided by number of shares acquired.

| 2005 | | | |
|---|---|---|---|
| Sept. I | Long-Term Investments—HTM (Dell) ......... | 30,000 | |
| | Cash ............................. | | 30,000 |
| | *Purchased bonds to be held to maturity.* | | |

Assets = Liabilities + Equity
+30,000
−30,000

**Interest earned.**   On December 31, 2005, at the end of its accounting period, Music City accrues interest receivable as follows:

| Dec. 31 | Interest Receivable ...................... | 700 | |
|---|---|---|---|
| | Interest Revenue .................... | | 700 |
| | *Accrued interest earned ($30,000 × 7% × ⁴/₁₂).* | | |

Assets = Liabilities + Equity
+700                          +700

The $700 reflects 4/6 of the semiannual cash receipt of interest—the portion Music City earned as of December 31. Relevant sections of Music City's financial statements at December 31, 2005, are shown in Exhibit C.3.

## Exhibit C.3

Financial Statement Presentation of Debt Securities

| | |
|---|---:|
| On the income statement for year 2005: | |
| **Interest revenue** ................................................................. | **$ 700** |
| On the December 31, 2005, balance sheet: | |
| **Long-term investments—Held-to-maturity securities (at amortized cost)** ....... | **$30,000** |

On February 28, 2006, Music City records receipt of semiannual interest:

Assets  = Liabilities + Equity
+1,050             +350
  −700

| Feb. 28 | Cash ................................... | 1,050 | |
|---|---|---|---|
| | Interest Receivable ................... | | 700 |
| | Interest Revenue ..................... | | 350 |
| | *Received six months' interest on Dell bonds.* | | |

**Disposition.** When the bonds mature, the proceeds (not including the interest entry) are recorded as:

Assets  = Liabilities + Equity
+30,000
−30,000

| 2007 | | | |
|---|---|---|---|
| Aug. 31 | Cash ................................... | 30,000 | |
| | Long-Term Investments—HTM (Dell) ...... | | 30,000 |
| | *Received cash from matured bonds.* | | |

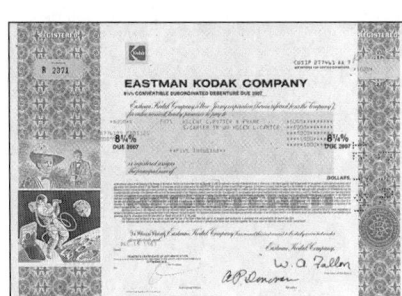

The cost of a debt security can be either higher or lower than its maturity value. When the investment is long term, the difference between cost and maturity value is amortized over the remaining life of the security. We assume for ease of computations that the cost of a long-term debt security equals its maturity value.

### Accounting Basics for Equity Securities

Equity securities are recorded at cost when acquired, including commissions or brokerage fees paid. Any cash dividends received are credited to Dividend Revenue and reported in the income statement. When the securities are sold, sale proceeds are compared with the cost, and any gain or loss is recorded.

**Acquisition.** Assume that Music City purchases 1,000 shares of Intex common stock at par value for $86,000 on October 10, 2005. It records this purchase of available-for-sale (AFS) securities as follows:

Assets  = Liabilities + Equity
+86,000
−86,000

| Oct. 10 | Long-Term Investments—AFS (Intex) ......... | 86,000 | |
|---|---|---|---|
| | Cash ............................. | | 86,000 |
| | *Purchased 1,000 shares of Intex.* | | |

**Dividend earned.** On November 2, Music City receives a $1,720 quarterly cash dividend on the Intex shares, which it records as:

Assets  = Liabilities + Equity
+1,720             +1,720

| Nov. 2 | Cash ................................... | 1,720 | |
|---|---|---|---|
| | Dividend Revenue .................... | | 1,720 |
| | *Received dividend of $1.72 per share.* | | |

**Disposition.** On December 20, Music City sells 500 of the Intex shares for $45,000 cash and records this sale as:

Assets  = Liabilities + Equity
+45,000             +2,000
−43,000

| Dec. 20 | Cash ................................... | 45,000 | |
|---|---|---|---|
| | Long-Term Investments—AFS (Intex) ...... | | 43,000 |
| | Gain on Sale of Long-Term Investments..... | | 2,000 |
| | *Sold 500 Intex shares ($86,000 × 500/1,000).* | | |

# Accounting for *Non*influential Investments

Companies must value and report most noninfluential investments at *fair market value,* or simply *market value.* The exact reporting requirements depend on whether the investments are classified as (1) trading, (2) held-to-maturity, or (3) available-for-sale.

**P1**   Account for trading securities.

**Trading Securities**   **Trading securities** are *debt and equity securities* that the company intends to actively manage and trade for profit. Frequent purchases and sales are expected and are made to earn profits on short-term price changes.

**Point:** Trading securities are *always* reported under current assets.

***Valuing and reporting trading securities.***   The entire portfolio of trading securities is reported at its market value; this requires a "market adjustment" from the cost of the portfolio. The term *portfolio* refers to a group of securities. Any **unrealized gain (or loss)** from a change in the market value of the portfolio of trading securities is reported on the income statement. Most users believe accounting reports are more useful when changes in market value for trading securities are reported in income.

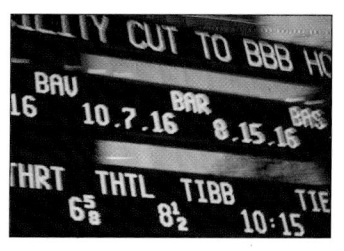

**Point:** The phrase *unrealized gain (or loss)* refers to a change in market value that is not yet realized through an actual sale.

To illustrate, TechCom's portfolio of trading securities had a total cost of $11,500 and a market value of $13,000 on December 31, 2005, the first year it held trading securities. The difference between the $11,500 cost and the $13,000 market value reflects a $1,500 gain. It is an unrealized gain because it is not yet confirmed by actual sales. The market adjustment for trading securities is recorded with an adjusting entry at the end of each period to equal the difference between the portfolio's cost and its market value. TechCom records this gain as:

**Point:** Market Adjustment—Trading is a *permanent account,* shown as a deduction or addition to Short-Term Investments—Trading.

| Dec. 31 | Market Adjustment—Trading . . . . . . . . . . . . . . . | 1,500 | |
|---------|-------------------------------------------------------|-------|-------|
| | Unrealized Gain—Income . . . . . . . . . . . . . | | 1,500 |
| | *To reflect an unrealized gain in market values of trading securities.* | | |

Assets = Liabilities + Equity
+1,500                    +1,500

The Unrealized Gain (or Loss) is reported in the Other Revenues and Gains (or Expenses and Losses) section on the income statement. The total cost of the trading securities portfolio is maintained in one account, and the market adjustment is recorded in a separate account. For example, TechCom's investment in trading securities is reported in the current assets section of its balance sheet as follows:

**Point:** Unrealized Gain (or Loss)—Income is a *temporary account* that is closed to Income Summary at the end of each period.

**Example:** If TechCom's trading securities have a cost of $14,800 and a market of $16,100 at Dec. 31, 2006, its adjusting entry is
Unrealized Loss—Income . . . . 200
   Market Adj.—Trading . . . . .     200
This is computed as: $1,500 Beg. Dr. + $200 Cr. = $1,300 End. Dr.

| **Current Assets** | | |
|---|---|---|
| Short-term investments—Trading (at cost) . . . . . . . . . . . . . . . . . . . . | $11,500 | |
| Market adjustment—Trading . . . . . . . . . . . . . . . . . . . . . . . . . . . . | 1,500 | |
| Short-term investments—Trading (at market) . . . . . . . . . . . . . . . . . | | $13,000 |
| | | |
| *or simply* | | |
| | | |
| Short-term investments—Trading (at market; cost is $11,500) . . . . . . . | | $13,000 |

***Selling trading securities.***   When individual trading securities are sold, the difference between the net proceeds (sale price less fees) and the cost of the individual trading securities that are sold is recognized as a gain or a loss. Any prior period market adjustment is *not* used to compute the gain or loss from sale. A gain is reported in the Other Revenues and Gains section on the income statement, whereas a loss is shown in Other Expenses and Losses. When the period-end market adjustment for trading securities is computed, it excludes the cost and market value of securities sold.

**Point:** Security prices are sometimes listed in fraction form. For example, a debt security with a price of $22\frac{1}{4}$ is the same as $22.25.

**Decision Insight**

**Flip-Flop**   About 70 years ago banks switched from reporting market values for short-term investments to reporting them at cost. We now see a return to market value reporting driven by S&L and banking failures that many allege could have been mitigated through the disclosure of market value changes.

**P2** Account for held-to-maturity securities.

**Held-to-Maturity Securities** **Held-to-maturity (HTM) securities** are *debt* securities a company intends and is able to hold until maturity. They are reported in current assets if their maturity dates are within one year or the operating cycle, whichever is longer. HTM securities are reported in long-term assets when the maturity dates extend beyond one year or the operating cycle, whichever is longer. All HTM securities are recorded at cost when purchased, and interest revenue is recorded when earned.

The portfolio of HTM securities is reported at (amortized) cost, which is explained in advanced courses. There is no market adjustment to the portfolio of HTM securities—neither to the short-term nor long-term portfolios. The basics of accounting for HTM securities were described earlier in this appendix.

**Point:** Only debt securities can be classified as *held-to-maturity;* equity securities have no maturity date.

**P3** Account for available-for-sale securities.

**Available-for-Sale Securities** **Available-for-sale (AFS) securities** are *debt and equity securities* not classified as trading or held-to-maturity securities. AFS securities are purchased to yield interest, dividends, or increases in market value. They are not actively managed like trading securities. If the intent is to sell AFS securities within the longer of one year or operating cycle, they are classified as short-term investments. Otherwise, they are classified as long-term.

**Point:** Many users believe that since AFS securities are not actively traded, reporting market value changes in income would unnecessarily increase income variability and decrease usefulness.

***Valuing and reporting available-for-sale securities.*** As with trading securities, companies adjust the cost of the portfolio of AFS securities to reflect changes in market value. This is done with a market adjustment to its total portfolio cost. However, any unrealized gain or loss for the portfolio of AFS securities is *not* reported on the income statement. Instead, it is reported in the equity section of the balance sheet (and is part of *comprehensive income,* explained later). To illustrate, assume that Music City had no prior period investments in available-for-sale securities other than those purchased in the current period. Exhibit C.4 shows both the cost and market value of those investments on December 31, 2005, the end of its reporting period.

## Exhibit C.4

Cost and Market Value of Available-for-Sale Securities

| | Cost | Market Value | Unrealized Gain (Loss) |
|---|---|---|---|
| Improv bonds .................... | $30,000 | $29,050 | $ (950) |
| Intex common stock, 500 shares ....... | 43,000 | 45,500 | 2,500 |
| Total ......................... | $73,000 | $74,550 | $1,550 |

**Example:** If market value in Exhibit C.4 is $70,000 (instead of $74,550), what entry is made? *Answer:*
Unreal. Loss—Equity ... 3,000
  Market Adj.—AFS .... 3,000

Assets = Liabilities + Equity
+1,550           +1,550

The year-end adjusting entry to record the market value of these investments follows:

| Dec. 31 | Market Adjustment—Available-for-Sale (LT) ..... | 1,550 | |
|---|---|---|---|
| |     Unrealized Gain—Equity .............. | | 1,550 |
| | *To record adjustment to market value of available-for-sale securities.* | | |

**Point:** Unrealized Loss—Equity and Unrealized Gain—Equity are *permanent* (balance sheet) *accounts* reported in the equity section.

Exhibit C.5 shows the December 31, 2005, balance sheet presentation—it assumes these investments are long term, but they can also be short term. It is also common to combine the cost of investments with the balance in the Market Adjustment account and report the net as a single amount.

| | | |
|---|---:|---:|
| Long-term investments—Available-for-sale (at cost) . . . . . . . . . . . . . . . . . . . . . . . . | $73,000 | |
| Market adjustment— Available-for-sale . . . . . . . . . . . . . . . . . . . . . . . . . . . . . . . . | 1,550 | |
| Long-term investments—Available-for-sale (at market) . . . . . . . . . . . . . . . . . . . . . . | | $74,550 |

or simply

| | |
|---|---:|
| Long-term investments—Available-for-sale (at market; cost is $73,000) . . . . . . . . . . . . | $74,550 |
| **Equity** | |

... usual equity accounts ...

| | |
|---|---:|
| Add unrealized gain on available-for-sale securities* . . . . . . . . . . . . . . . . . . . . . . . . | $ 1,550 |

*Exhibit C.5*

Balance Sheet Presentation of Available-for-Sale Securities

\* Often included under the caption Accumulated Other Comprehensive Income.

Let's extend this illustration and assume that at the end of its next calendar year (December 31, 2006), Music City's portfolio of long-term AFS securities has an $81,000 cost and an $82,000 market value. It records the adjustment to market value as follows:

**Point:** Income can be window-dressed upward by selling AFS securities with unrealized gains; income is reduced by selling those with unrealized losses.

| Dec. 31 | Unrealized Gain—Equity . . . . . . . . . . . . . . . . . . . | 550 | |
|---|---|---|---|
| | Market Adjustment—Available-for-Sale (LT) . . | | 550 |
| | *To record adjustment to market value of available-for-sale securities.* | | |

Assets = Liabilities + Equity
−550                        −550

The effects of the 2005 and 2006 securities transactions are reflected in the following T-accounts:

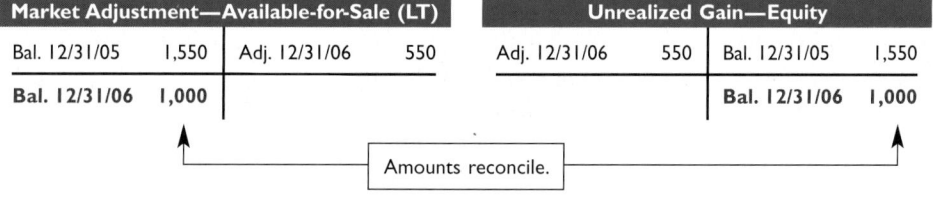

**Market Adjustment—Available-for-Sale (LT)**

| Bal. 12/31/05 | 1,550 | Adj. 12/31/06 | 550 |
|---|---|---|---|
| **Bal. 12/31/06** | **1,000** | | |

**Unrealized Gain—Equity**

| Adj. 12/31/06 | 550 | Bal. 12/31/05 | 1,550 |
|---|---|---|---|
| | | **Bal. 12/31/06** | **1,000** |

Amounts reconcile.

**Example:** If cost is $83,000 and market is $82,000 at Dec. 31, 2006, it records the following adjustment:
Unreal. Gain—Equity . . . 1,550
Unreal. Loss—Equity . . . 1,000
  Mkt. Adj.—AFS . . . .          2,550

**Selling available-for-sale securities.**   Accounting for the sale of individual AFS securities is identical to that described for the sale of trading securities. When individual AFS securities are sold, the difference between the cost of the individual securities sold and the net proceeds (sale price less fees) is recognized as a gain or loss.

**Point:** Market Adjustment—Available-for-Sale is a permanent account, shown as a deduction or addition to the Investment account.

## Quick Check

1. How are short-term held-to-maturity securities reported (valued) on the balance sheet?
2. How are trading securities reported (valued) on the balance sheet?
3. Where are unrealized gains and losses on available-for-sale securities reported?
4. Where are unrealized gains and losses on trading securities reported?

Answers—p. C-18

# Accounting for Influential Investments

## Investment in Equity Securities with Significant Influence

A long-term investment classified as **equity securities with significant influence** implies that the investor can exert significant influence over the investee. An investor that owns 20% or more (but not more than 50%) of a company's voting stock is usually presumed to have a significant influence over the investee. In some cases, however, the 20% test of significant influence is overruled by other, more persuasive, evidence. This evidence

P4   Account for equity securities with significant influence.

can either lower the 20% requirement or increase it. The **equity method** of accounting and reporting is used for long-term investments in equity securities with significant influence, which is explained in this section.

Long-term investments in equity securities with significant influence are recorded at cost when acquired. To illustrate, Micron Co. records the purchase of 3,000 shares (30%) of Star Co. common stock at a total cost of $70,650 on January 1, 2005, as follows:

Assets  = Liabilities + Equity
+70,650
−70,650

| Jan. 1 | Long-Term Investments—Star . . . . . . . . . . . . . . . | 70,650 | |
| | Cash. . . . . . . . . . . . . . . . . . . . . . . . . . . . . | | 70,650 |
| | *To record purchase of 3,000 Star shares.* | | |

The investee's (Star) earnings increase both its net assets and the claim of the investor (Micron) on the investee's net assets. Thus, when the investee reports its earnings, the investor records its share of those earnings in its investment account. To illustrate, assume that Star reports net income of $20,000 for 2005. Micron then records its 30% share of those earnings as follows:

Assets  = Liabilities +  Equity
+6,000                +6,000

| Dec. 31 | Long-Term Investments—Star . . . . . . . . . . . . . . . | 6,000 | |
| | Earnings from Long-Term Investment . . . . . . | | 6,000 |
| | *To record 30% equity in investee earnings.* | | |

The debit reflects the increase in Micron's equity in Star. The credit reflects 30% of Star's net income that appears on Micron's income statement. If the investee incurs a net loss instead of a net income, the investor records its share of the loss and reduces (credits) its investment account. The investor closes this earnings or loss account to Income Summary.

The receipt of cash dividends is not revenue under the equity method because the investor has already recorded its share of the investee's earnings. Instead, cash dividends received by an investor from an investee are viewed as a conversion of one asset to another; that is, dividends reduce the balance of the investment account. To illustrate, Star declares and pays $10,000 in cash dividends on its common stock. Micron records its 30% share of these dividends received on January 9, 2006 as:

**Point:** *Insider trading* usually refers to officers and employees who buy or sell shares in their firm based on information unavailable to the public. Generally, insider trading is illegal in the U.S., but some countries permit it.

Assets  = Liabilities + Equity
+3,000
−3,000

| Jan. 9 | Cash . . . . . . . . . . . . . . . . . . . . . . . . . . . . . . | 3,000 | |
| | Long-Term Investments—Star. . . . . . . . . . . | | 3,000 |
| | *To record share of dividend paid by Star.* | | |

The book value of an investment under the equity method equals the cost of the investment plus (minus) the investor's equity in the *undistributed* (*distributed*) earnings of the investee. Once Micron records these transactions, its Long-Term Investments account appears as in Exhibit C.6.

## Exhibit C.6

Investment in Star Common Stock (Ledger Account)

| Date | Explanation | Debit | Credit | Balance |
|---|---|---|---|---|
| **2005** | | | | |
| Jan. 1 | Investment acquisition | 70,650 | | 70,650 |
| Dec. 31 | Share of earnings | 6,000 | | 76,650 |
| **2006** | | | | |
| Jan. 9 | Share of dividend | | 3,000 | 73,650 |

Micron's account balance on January 9, 2006, for its investment in Star is $73,650. This is the investment's cost *plus* Micron's equity in Star's earnings since its purchase *less* Micron's equity in Star's cash dividends since its purchase. When an investment in equity securities is sold, the gain or loss is computed by comparing proceeds from the sale with the book value of the investment on the date of sale. If Micron sells its Star stock for $80,000 on January 10, 2006, it records the sale as:

| Jan. 10 | Cash | 80,000 | |
|---|---|---|---|
| | Long-Term Investments—Star | | 73,650 |
| | Gain on Sale of Investment | | 6,350 |
| | *Sold 3,000 shares of stock for $80,000.* | | |

Assets = Liabilities + Equity
+80,000                +6,350
−73,650

## Investment in Equity Securities with Controlling Influence

A long-term investment classified as **equity securities with controlling influence** implies that the investor can exert a controlling influence over the investee. An investor who owns more than 50% of a company's voting stock has control over the investee. This investor can dominate all other shareholders in electing the corporation's board of directors and has control over the investee's management. In some cases, controlling influence can extend to situations of less than 50% ownership. Exhibit C.7 summarizes the accounting for investments in equity securities based on an investor's ownership in the stock.

**C3**  Describe how to report equity securities with controlling influence.

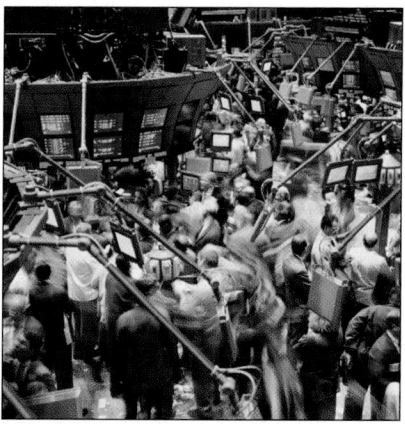

Equity Method with Consolidation (50%+)

Equity Method (20%–50%)

Market Value Method (Under 20%)

**Exhibit C.7**

Accounting for Equity Investments by Percent of Ownership

The *equity method with consolidation* is used to account for long-term investments in equity securities with controlling influence. The investor reports *consolidated financial statements* when owning such securities. The controlling investor is called the **parent,** and the investee is called the **subsidiary.** Many companies are parents with subsidiaries. Examples are (1) **McGraw-Hill**, the parent of *Business Week,* Standard & Poor's, and Compustat; (2) **Gap, Inc.**, the parent of Gap, Old Navy, and Banana Republic; and (3) **Brunswick**, the parent of Mercury Marine, Sea Ray, and U.S. Marine. A company owning all the outstanding stock of a subsidiary can, if it desires, take over the subsidiary's assets, retire the subsidiary's stock, and merge the subsidiary into the parent. However, there often are financial, legal, and tax advantages if a business operates as a parent controlling one or more subsidiaries. When a company operates as a parent with subsidiaries, each entity maintains separate accounting records. From a legal viewpoint, the parent and each subsidiary are separate entities with all rights, duties, and responsibilities of individual companies.

**Consolidated financial statements** show the financial position, results of operations, and cash flows of all entities under the parent's control, including all subsidiaries. These statements are prepared as if the business were organized as one entity. The parent uses the equity method in its accounts, but the investment account is *not* reported on the parent's financial statements. Instead, the individual assets and liabilities of the parent and its subsidiaries are combined on one balance sheet. Their revenues and expenses also are combined on one income statement, and their cash flows are combined on one statement of cash flows. The procedures for preparing consolidated financial statements are in advanced courses.

## Accounting Summary for Investments in Securities

Exhibit C.8 summarizes the accounting for investments in securities. Recall that many investment securities are classified as either short term or long term depending on management's

## Exhibit C.8

Accounting for Investments in Securities

| Class of Investment Securities | Accounting Method |
| --- | --- |
| **Short-Term Investment in Securities** | |
| Held-to-maturity (debt) securities | Cost (without any discount or premium amortization) |
| Trading (debt and equity) securities | Market value (with market adjustment to income) |
| Available-for-sale (debt and equity) securities | Market value (with market adjustment to equity) |
| **Long-Term Investment in Securities** | |
| Held-to-maturity (debt) securities | Cost (with any discount or premium amortization) |
| Available-for-sale (debt and equity) securities | Market value (with market adjustment to equity) |
| Equity securities with significant influence | Equity method |
| Equity securities with controlling influence | Equity method (with consolidation) |

intent and ability to convert them in the future. Understanding the accounting for these investments enables us to draw better conclusions from financial statements in making business decisions.

**Comprehensive Income** The term **comprehensive income** refers to all changes in equity for a period except those due to investments and distributions to owners. This means that it includes (1) the revenues, gains, expenses, and losses reported in net income *and* (2) the gains and losses that bypass net income but affect equity. An example of an item that bypasses net income is unrealized gains and losses on available-for-sale securities. These items make up *other comprehensive income* and are usually reported as a part of the statement of stockholders' equity. (Two other options are as a second separate income statement or as a combined income statement of comprehensive income; these less common options are described in advanced courses.) Most often this simply requires one additional column for Other Comprehensive Income in the usual columnar form of the statement of stockholders' equity (the details of this are left for advanced courses). The FASB encourages, but does *not* require, other comprehensive income items to be grouped under the caption *Accumulated Other Comprehensive Income* in the equity section of the balance sheet, which would include unrealized gains and losses on available-for-sale securities. For instructional benefits, we use actual account titles for these items in the equity section instead of this general, less precise caption.

### Quick Check

5. Give at least two examples of assets classified as long-term investments.
6. What are the requirements for an equity security to be listed as a long-term investment?
7. Identify similarities and differences in accounting for long-term investments in debt securities that are held-to-maturity versus those available-for-sale.
8. What are the three possible classifications of long-term equity investments? Describe the criteria for each class and the method used to account for each.

Answers—p. C-18

## Decision Analysis Components of Return on Total Assets

A1 Compute and analyze the components of return on total assets.

A company's **return on total assets** (or simply *return on assets*) is important in assessing financial performance. The return on total assets can be separated into two components, profit margin and total asset turnover, for additional analyses. Exhibit C.9 shows how these two components determine return on total assets.

## Exhibit C.9

Components of Return on Total Assets

$$\text{Return on total assets} = \text{Profit margin} \times \text{Total asset turnover}$$

$$\frac{\text{Net income}}{\text{Average total assets}} = \frac{\text{Net income}}{\text{Net sales}} \times \frac{\text{Net sales}}{\text{Average total assets}}$$

Profit margin reflects the percent of net income in each dollar of net sales. Total asset turnover reflects a company's ability to produce net sales from total assets. All companies desire a high return on total assets. By considering these two components, we can often discover strengths and weaknesses not revealed by return on total assets alone. This improves our ability to assess future performance and company strategy.

To illustrate, consider return on total assets and its components for **Reebok** in Exhibit C.10.

| Year | Return on Total Assets | = | Profit Margin | × | Total Asset Turnover |
|------|------------------------|---|---------------|---|----------------------|
| 2002 | 7.4% | = | 4.0% | × | 1.84 |
| 2001 | 6.8% | = | 3.4% | × | 1.99 |
| 2000 | 5.3% | = | 2.8% | × | 1.89 |
| 1999 | 0.7% | = | 0.4% | × | 1.78 |

### Exhibit C.10

Reebok's Components of Return on Total Assets

At least three findings emerge. First, Reebok's return on total assets steadily improved from 1999 through 2002. Second, total asset turnover might have slightly improved but nothing noteworthy. Third, Reebok's profit margin sharply rose between 1999 and 2002. These components reveal the dual role of profit margin and total asset turnover in determining return on total assets. They also reveal that the driver of Reebok's rebound is not total asset turnover but profit margin.

Generally, if a company is to maintain or improve its return on total assets, it must meet any decline in either profit margin or total asset turnover with an increase in the other. If not, return on assets will decline. Companies consider these components in planning strategies. A component analysis can also reveal where a company is weak and where changes are needed, especially in a competitor analysis. If asset turnover is lower than the industry norm, for instance, a company should focus on raising asset turnover at least to the norm. The same applies to profit margin.

### Decision Maker

**Retailer**  You are an entrepreneur and owner of a retail sporting goods store. The store's recent annual performance reveals (industry norms in parentheses): return on total assets = 11% (11.2%); profit margin = 4.4% (3.5%); and total asset turnover = 2.5 (3.2). What does your analysis of these figures reveal?

Answer—p. C-18

# Demonstration Problem—1

Garden Company completes the following selected transactions related to its short-term investments during 2005:

May 8  Purchased 300 shares of FedEx stock as a short-term investment in available-for-sale securities at $40 per share plus $975 in broker fees.

Sept. 2  Sold 100 shares of its investment in FedEx stock at $47 per share and held the remaining 200 shares; broker's commission was $225.

Oct. 2  Purchased 400 shares of Ajay stock for $60 per share plus $1,600 in commissions. The stock is held as a short-term investment in available-for-sale securities.

**Required**

1. Prepare journal entries for the above transactions of Garden Co. for 2005.

2. Prepare an adjusting journal entry as of December 31, 2005, if the market prices of the equity securities held by Garden Company are $48 per share for FedEx and $55 per share for Ajay. (Year 2005 is the first year Garden Co. acquired short-term investments.)

## Solution to Demonstration Problem—1

1.

| | | | |
|---|---|---|---|
| May 8 | Short-Term Investments—AFS (FedEx)......... | 12,975 | |
| | Cash............................. | | 12,975 |
| | *Purchased 300 shares of FedEx stock* | | |
| | *(300 × $40) + $975.* | | |

[continued on next page]

[continued from previous page]

| | | | |
|---|---|---|---|
| Sept. 2 | Cash . . . . . . . . . . . . . . . . . . . . . . . . . . . . . . . . . . . | 4,475 | |
| | Gain on Sale of Short-Term Investment. . . . . | | 150 |
| | Short-Term Investments—AFS (FedEx) . . . . . | | 4,325 |
| | *Sold 100 shares of FedEx for $47 per share less* | | |
| | *a $225 commission. The original cost is* | | |
| | *($12,975 × 100/300).* | | |
| Oct. 2 | Short-Term Investments—AFS (Ajay) . . . . . . . . . | 25,600 | |
| | Cash. . . . . . . . . . . . . . . . . . . . . . . . . . . . . | | 25,600 |
| | *Purchased 400 shares of Ajay for $60 per share* | | |
| | *plus $1,600 in commissions.* | | |

**2.** Computation of unrealized gain or loss:

| Short-Term Investments in Available-for-Sale Securities | Shares | Cost per Share | Total Cost | Market Value per Share | Total Market Value | Unrealized Gain (Loss) |
|---|---|---|---|---|---|---|
| FedEx . . . . . . . . . . . . . . . . . | 200 | $43.25 | $ 8,650 | $48.00 | $ 9,600 | |
| Ajay . . . . . . . . . . . . . . . . . | 400 | 64.00 | 25,600 | 55.00 | 22,000 | |
| Total . . . . . . . . . . . . . . . . | | | $34,250 | | $31,600 | $(2,650) |

Adjusting entry:

| | | | |
|---|---|---|---|
| Dec. 31 | Unrealized Loss—Equity . . . . . . . . . . . . . . . . . . | 2,650 | |
| | Market Adjustment—Available-for-Sale (ST). . | | 2,650 |
| | *To reflect an unrealized loss in market values* | | |
| | *of available-for-sale securities.* | | |

# Demonstration Problem—2

The following transactions relate to Brown Company's long-term investments during 2005 and 2006. Brown did not own any long-term investments prior to 2005. Show (1) the appropriate journal entries and (2) the relevant portions of each year's balance sheet and income statement that reflect these transactions for both 2005 and 2006.

*2005*

Sept.  9   Purchased 1,000 shares of Packard, Inc., common stock for $80,000 cash. These shares represent 30% of Packard's outstanding shares.
Oct.   2   Purchased 2,000 shares of AT&T common stock for $60,000 cash. These shares represent less than a 1% ownership in AT&T.
      17   Purchased as a long-term investment 1,000 shares of Apple Computer common stock for $40,000 cash. These shares arc less than 1% of Apple's outstanding shares.
Nov.   1   Received $5,000 cash dividend from Packard.
      30   Received $3,000 cash dividend from AT&T.
Dec.  15   Received $1,400 cash dividend from Apple.
      31   Packard's 2002 net income is $70,000.
      31   Market values for the investments in equity securities are Packard, $84,000; AT&T, $48,000; and Apple Computer, $45,000.
      31   For preparing financial statements, note the following post-closing account balances: Common Stock, $500,000, and Retained Earnings, $350,000.

*2006*

Jan.   1   Sold Packard, Inc., shares for $108,000 cash.
May   30   Received $3,100 cash dividend from AT&T.
June  15   Received $1,600 cash dividend from Apple.

Aug. 17 Sold the AT&T stock for $52,000 cash.

19 Purchased 2,000 shares of Coca-Cola common stock for $50,000 cash as a long-term investment. The stock represents less than a 5% ownership in Coca-Cola.

Dec. 15 Received $1,800 cash dividend from Apple.

31 Market values of the investments in equity securities are Apple, $39,000, and Coca-Cola, $48,000.

31 For preparing financial statements, note the following post-closing account balances: Common Stock, $500,000, and Retained Earnings, $410,000.

## Planning the Solution

- Account for the investment in Packard under the equity method.
- Account for the investments in AT&T, Apple, and Coca-Cola as long-term investments in available-for-sale securities.
- Prepare the information for the two years' balance sheets by including the appropriate asset and equity accounts.

## Solution to Demonstration Problem—2

**1.** Journal entries for 2005

| | | | |
|---|---|---|---|
| Sept. 9 | Long-Term Investments—Packard . . . . . . . . . . . . | 80,000 | |
| | Cash. . . . . . . . . . . . . . . . . . . . . . . . . . . . . | | 80,000 |
| | *Acquired 1,000 shares, representing a 30% equity in Packard.* | | |
| Oct. 2 | Long-Term Investments—AFS (AT&T) . . . . . . . . . | 60,000 | |
| | Cash. . . . . . . . . . . . . . . . . . . . . . . . . . . . . | | 60,000 |
| | *Acquired 2,000 shares as a long-term investment in available-for-sale securities.* | | |
| Oct. 17 | Long-Term Investments—AFS (Apple) . . . . . . . . . | 40,000 | |
| | Cash. . . . . . . . . . . . . . . . . . . . . . . . . . . . . | | 40,000 |
| | *Acquired 1,000 shares as a long-term investment in available-for-sale securities.* | | |
| Nov. 1 | Cash . . . . . . . . . . . . . . . . . . . . . . . . . . . . . | 5,000 | |
| | Long-Term Investments—Packard . . . . . . . . | | 5,000 |
| | *Received dividend from Packard.* | | |
| Nov. 30 | Cash . . . . . . . . . . . . . . . . . . . . . . . . . . . . . | 3,000 | |
| | Dividend Revenue . . . . . . . . . . . . . . . . . . . . | | 3,000 |
| | *Received dividend from AT&T.* | | |
| Dec. 15 | Cash . . . . . . . . . . . . . . . . . . . . . . . . . . . . . | 1,400 | |
| | Dividend Revenue . . . . . . . . . . . . . . . . . . . . | | 1,400 |
| | *Received dividend from Apple.* | | |
| Dec. 31 | Long-Term Investments—Packard . . . . . . . . . . . . | 21,000 | |
| | Earnings from Investment (Packard). . . . . . . . | | 21,000 |
| | *To record 30% share of Packard's annual earnings of $70,000.* | | |
| Dec. 31 | Unrealized Loss—Equity . . . . . . . . . . . . . . . . . . | 7,000 | |
| | Market Adjustment—Available-for-Sale (LT)* . | | 7,000 |
| | *To record change in market value of long-term available-for-sale securities.* | | |

\* Market adjustment computations:

| | Cost | Market Value | Unrealized Gain (Loss) | | Required balance of the Market Adjustment—Available-for-Sale | |
|---|---|---|---|---|---|---|
| AT&T | $ 60,000 | $48,000 | $(12,000) | | (LT) account . . . . . . . . . . . . . . | $(7,000) |
| Apple | 40,000 | 45,000 | 5,000 | | Existing balance . . . . . . . . . . . . . . | 0 |
| Total | $100,000 | $93,000 | $ (7,000) | | Necessary adjustment (credit) . . . . . | $(7,000) |

**2.** The December 31, 2005, selected balance sheet items appear as follows:

**Assets**

Long-term investments

| | |
|---|---|
| Available-for-sale securities (at market; cost is $100,000) . . . . . . . . | $93,000 |
| Investment in equity securities . . . . . . . . . . . . . . . . . . . . . . . . . | 96,000 |
| Total long-term investments . . . . . . . . . . . . . . . . . . . . . . . . | $189,000 |

**Stockholders' Equity**

| | |
|---|---|
| Common stock . . . . . . . . . . . . . . . . . . . . . . . . . . . . . . . . . . | 500,000 |
| Retained earnings . . . . . . . . . . . . . . . . . . . . . . . . . . . . . . . | 350,000 |
| Unrealized loss—Equity . . . . . . . . . . . . . . . . . . . . . . . . . . . | (7,000) |

The relevant income statement items for the year ended December 31, 2005, follow:

| | |
|---|---|
| Dividend revenue . . . . . . . . . . . . . | $ 4,400 |
| Earnings from investment . . . . . . . | 21,000 |

**1.** Journal entries for 2006

| | | | |
|---|---|---|---|
| Jan. 1 | Cash . . . . . . . . . . . . . . . . . . . . . . . . . . . . . . . . . . . | 108,000 | |
| | Long-Term Investments—Packard . . . . . . . . . | | 96,000 |
| | Gain on Sale of Long-Term Investments . . . . . | | 12,000 |
| | *Sold 1,000 shares for cash.* | | |
| May 30 | Cash . . . . . . . . . . . . . . . . . . . . . . . . . . . . . . . . . . . | 3,100 | |
| | Dividend Revenue . . . . . . . . . . . . . . . . . . . . | | 3,100 |
| | *Received dividend from AT&T.* | | |
| June 15 | Cash . . . . . . . . . . . . . . . . . . . . . . . . . . . . . . . . . . . | 1,600 | |
| | Dividend Revenue . . . . . . . . . . . . . . . . . . . . | | 1,600 |
| | *Received dividend from Apple.* | | |
| Aug. 17 | Cash . . . . . . . . . . . . . . . . . . . . . . . . . . . . . . . . . . . | 52,000 | |
| | Loss on Sale of Long-Term Investments . . . . . . . . | 8,000 | |
| | Long-Term Investments—AFS (AT&T) . . . . . . | | 60,000 |
| | *Sold 2,000 shares for cash.* | | |
| Aug. 19 | Long-Term Investments—AFS (Coca-Cola) . . . . . . | 50,000 | |
| | Cash . . . . . . . . . . . . . . . . . . . . . . . . . . . . | | 50,000 |
| | *Acquired 2,000 shares as a long-term investment in available-for-sale securities.* | | |
| Dec. 15 | Cash . . . . . . . . . . . . . . . . . . . . . . . . . . . . . . . . . . . | 1,800 | |
| | Dividend Revenue . . . . . . . . . . . . . . . . . . . . | | 1,800 |
| | *Received dividend from Apple.* | | |
| Dec. 31 | Market Adjustment—Available-for-Sale (LT)*. . . . . | 4,000 | |
| | Unrealized Loss—Equity . . . . . . . . . . . . . . | | 4,000 |
| | *To record change in market value of long-term available-for-sale securities.* | | |

\* Market adjustment computations:

| | Cost | Market Value | Unrealized Gain (Loss) |
|---|---|---|---|
| Apple | $40,000 | $39,000 | $(1,000) |
| Coca-Cola | 50,000 | 48,000 | (2,000) |
| Total | $90,000 | $87,000 | $(3,000) |

| | |
|---|---|
| Required balance of the Market Adjustment—Available-for-Sale (LT) account . . . . . . . . . . . . . . . | $(3,000) |
| Existing balance (credit) . . . . . . . . | (7,000) |
| Necessary adjustment (debit) . . . . . . | $ 4,000 |

**2.** The December 31, 2006, balance sheet items appear as follows:

**Assets**

Long-term investments

Available-for-sale securities (at market; cost is $90,000) . . . . . . .  $ 87,000

**Stockholders' Equity**

Common stock . . . . . . . . . . . . . . . . . . . . . . . . . . . . . . . . .  500,000

Retained earnings . . . . . . . . . . . . . . . . . . . . . . . . . . . . . . .  410,000

Unrealized loss— Equity . . . . . . . . . . . . . . . . . . . . . . . . . .  (3,000)

The relevant income statement items for the year ended December 31, 2006, follow:

Dividend revenue . . . . . . . . . . . . . . . . . . . . . . . .  $ 6,500

Gain on sale of long-term investments . . . . . . . .  12,000

Loss on sale of long-term investments . . . . . . . .  (8,000)

---

**APPENDIX**

# Investments in International Operations

C-A

Many entities from small entrepreneurs to large corporations conduct business internationally. Some entities' operations occur in so many different countries that the companies are called **multinationals.** Many of us think of **Coca-Cola** and **McDonald's**, for example, as primarily U.S. companies, but most of their sales occur outside the United States. Exhibit C-A.1 shows the percent of international sales and income for selected U.S. companies. Managing and accounting for multinationals presents challenges. This section describes some of these challenges and how to account for and report these activities.

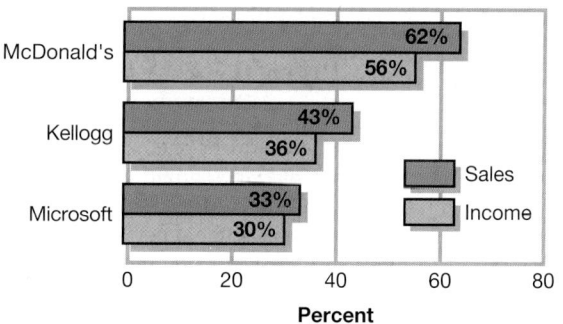

**Exhibit C-A.1**

International Sales and Income as a Percent of Their Totals

Topic Tackler C-2

Two major accounting challenges that arise when companies have international operations relate to transactions that involve more than one currency. The first is to account for sales and purchases listed in a foreign currency. The second is to prepare consolidated financial statements with international subsidiaries. For ease in this discussion, we use companies with a U.S. base of operations and assume the need to prepare financial statements in U.S. dollars. This means the *reporting currency* of these companies is the U.S. dollar.

**Point:** Transactions *listed* or *stated* in a foreign currency are said to be *denominated* in that currency.

## Exchange Rates between Currencies

Markets for the purchase and sale of foreign currencies exist all over the world. In these markets, U.S. dollars can be exchanged for Canadian dollars, British pounds, Japanese yen, Euros, or any other legal currencies. The price of one currency stated in terms of another currency is called a **foreign exchange rate.** Exhibit C-A.2 lists recent exchange rates for selected currencies. The exchange rate for British pounds and U.S. dollars is $1.6152, meaning 1 British pound could be purchased for $1.6152. On that same day, the exchange rate between Mexican pesos and U.S. dollars is $0.1063, or 1 Mexican peso can be purchased for $0.1063. Exchange rates

**C4** Explain foreign exchange rates between currencies.

**Decision Insight**

**Rush to Russia**  Investors are still eager to buy Russian equities even in the face of rampant crime, corruption, and slow economic growth. Why? Many argue Russia remains a bargain-priced, if risky, bet on future growth. Some analysts argue that natural-resource-rich Russia is one of the least expensive emerging markets.

## Exhibit C-A.2

Foreign Exchange Rates for
Selected Currencies*

| Source (unit) | Price in $U.S. | Source (unit) | Price in $U.S. |
|---|---|---|---|
| Britain (pound) ....... | $1.6152 | Canada (dollar) ........ | $0.7400 |
| Mexico (peso) ........ | 0.1063 | Japan (yen) ........... | 0.0085 |
| Taiwan (dollar) ........ | 0.0305 | Europe (Euro) ......... | 1.1703 |

\* Rates will vary over time based on economic, political, and other changes.

**Point:** For currency conversion, see XE.com

fluctuate due to changing economic and political conditions, including the supply and demand for currencies and expectations about future events.

## Sales and Purchases Listed in a Foreign Currency

**P5**  Record transactions listed in a foreign currency.

When a U.S. company makes a credit sale to an international customer, accounting for the sale and the account receivable is straightforward if sales terms require the international customer's payment in U.S. dollars. If sale terms require (or allow) payment in a foreign currency, however, the U.S. company must account for the sale and the account receivable in a different manner.

To illustrate, consider the case of the U.S.-based manufacturer Boston Company, which makes credit sales to London Outfitters, a British retail company. A sale occurs on December 12, 2005, for a price of £10,000 with payment due on February 10, 2006. Boston Company keeps its accounting records in U.S. dollars. To record the sale, Boston Company must translate the sales price from pounds to dollars. This is done using the exchange rate on the date of the sale. Assuming the exchange rate on December 12, 2005, is $1.80, Boston records this sale as follows:

### Decision Insight

**Global Greenback**  What do changes in foreign exchange rates mean? A decline in the price of the U.S. dollar against other currencies usually yields increased international sales for U.S. companies, without hiking prices or cutting costs, and puts them on a stronger competitive footing abroad. At home, they can raise prices without fear that foreign rivals will undercut them.

Assets = Liabilities + Equity
+18,000                +18,000

| Dec. 12 | Accounts Receivable—London Outfitters....... | 18,000 | |
|---|---|---|---|
| | Sales* ............................. | | 18,000 |
| | *To record a sale at £10,000, when the exchange rate equals $1.80.* * (£10,000 × $1.80) | | |

When Boston Company prepares its annual financial statements on December 31, 2005, the current exchange rate is $1.84. Thus, the current dollar value of Boston Company's receivable is $18,400 (10,000 × $1.84). This amount is $400 higher than the amount recorded on December 12. Accounting principles require a receivable to be reported in the balance sheet at its current dollar value. Thus, Boston Company must make the following entry to record the increase in the dollar value of this receivable at year-end:

Assets = Liabilities + Equity
+400                   +400

| Dec. 31 | Accounts Receivable—London Outfitters....... | 400 | |
|---|---|---|---|
| | Foreign Exchange Gain................ | | 400 |
| | *To record the increased value of the British pound for the receivable.* | | |

**Point:** Foreign exchange gains are credits, and foreign exchange losses are debits.

On February 10, 2006, Boston Company receives London Outfitters' payment of £10,000. It immediately exchanges the pounds for U.S. dollars. On this date, the exchange rate for pounds is $1.78. Thus, Boston Company receives only $17,800 (£10,000 × $1.78). It records the cash receipt and the loss associated with the decline in the exchange rate as follows:

Assets = Liabilities + Equity
+17,800                −600
−18,400

| Feb. 10 | Cash .................................. | 17,800 | |
|---|---|---|---|
| | Foreign Exchange Loss .................... | 600 | |
| | Accounts Receivable—London Outfitters ... | | 18,400 |
| | *Received foreign currency payment of an account and converted it into dollars.* | | |

Gains and losses from foreign exchange transactions are accumulated in the Foreign Exchange Gain (or Loss) account. After year-end adjustments, the balance in the Foreign Exchange Gain (or Loss) account is reported on the income statement and closed to the Income Summary account.

Accounting for credit purchases from an international seller is similar to the case of a credit sale to an international customer. In particular, if the U.S. company is required to make payment in a foreign currency, the account payable must be translated into dollars before the U.S. company can record it. If the exchange rate is different when preparing financial statements and when paying for the purchase, the U.S. company must recognize a foreign exchange gain or loss at those dates.

**Example:** Assume that a U.S. company makes a credit purchase from a British company for £10,000 when the exchange rate is $1.62. At the balance sheet date, this rate is $1.72. Does this imply a gain or loss for the U.S. company? *Answer:* A loss.

## Consolidated Statements with International Subsidiaries

A second challenge in accounting for international operations involves preparing consolidated financial statements when the parent company has one or more international subsidiaries. Consider a U.S.-based company that owns a controlling interest in a French subsidiary. The reporting currency of the U.S. parent is the dollar. The French subsidiary maintains its financial records in euros. Before preparing consolidated statements, the parent must translate financial statements of the French company into U.S. dollars. After this translation is complete (including that for accounting differences), it prepares consolidated statements the same as for domestic subsidiaries. Procedures for translating an international subsidiary's account balances depend on the nature of the subsidiary's operations. The process requires the parent company to select appropriate foreign exchange rates and to apply those rates to the foreign subsidiary's account balances. This is described in advanced courses.

> ### Decision Maker
>
> **Entrepreneur**   You are a U.S. home builder that purchases lumber from mills in both the U.S. and Canada. The price of the Canadian dollar in terms of the U.S. dollar jumps from US$0.70 to US$0.80. Are you now more or less likely to buy lumber from Canadian or U.S. mills?

Answer—p. C-18

**Global:** A weaker U.S. dollar often increases global sales for U.S. companies.

## Summary

**C1  Distinguish between debt and equity securities and between short-term and long-term investments.** *Debt securities* reflect a creditor relationship and include investments in notes, bonds, and certificates of deposit. *Equity securities* reflect an owner relationship and include shares of stock issued by other companies. Short-term investments in securities are current assets that meet two criteria: (1) They are expected to be converted into cash within one year or the current operating cycle of the business, whichever is longer and (2) they are readily convertible to cash, or *marketable*. All other investments in securities are long-term. Long-term investments also include assets not used in operations and those held for special purposes, such as land for expansion.

**C2  Identify and describe the different classes of investments in securities.** Investments in securities are classified into one of five groups: (1) trading securities, which are always short-term, (2) debt securities held-to-maturity, (3) debt and equity securities available-for-sale, (4) equity securities in which an investor has a significant influence over the investee, and (5) equity securities in which an investor has a controlling influence over the investee.

**C3  Describe how to report equity securities with controlling influence.** If an investor owns more than 50% of another company's voting stock and controls the investee, the investor's financial reports are prepared on a consolidated basis. These reports are prepared as if the company were organized as one entity.

**C4^A  Explain foreign exchange rates between currencies.** A foreign exchange rate is the price of one currency stated in terms of another. An entity with transactions in a foreign currency when the exchange rate changes between the transaction dates and their settlement will experience exchange gains or losses.

**A1  Compute and analyze the components of return on total assets.** Return on total assets has two components: profit margin and total asset turnover. A decline in one component must be met with an increase in another if return on assets is to be maintained. Component analysis is helpful in assessing company performance compared to that of competitors and its own past.

**P1  Account for trading securities.** Investments are initially recorded at cost, and any dividend or interest from these investments is recorded in the income statement. Investments classified as trading securities are reported at market value. Unrealized gains and losses on trading securities are reported in income. When investments are sold, the difference between the net proceeds from the sale and the cost of the securities is recognized as a gain or loss.

**P2  Account for held-to-maturity securities.** Debt securities held-to-maturity are reported at cost when purchased. Interest revenue is recorded as it accrues. The cost of long-term held-to-maturity securities is adjusted for the amortization of any difference between cost and maturity value.

**P3  Account for available-for-sale securities.** Debt and equity securities available-for-sale are recorded at cost when purchased. Available-for-sale securities are reported at their market values on the balance sheet with unrealized gains or losses shown in the equity section. Gains and losses realized on the sale of these investments are reported in the income statement.

**P4  Account for equity securities with significant influence.** The equity method is used when an investor has a significant influence over an investee. This usually exists when an investor owns 20% or more of the investee's voting stock but not more than 50%. The equity method means an investor records its share of investee earnings with a debit to the investment account and a credit to a revenue account. Dividends received reduce the investment account balance.

**P5**<sup>A</sup> **Record transactions listed in a foreign currency.** When a company makes a credit sale to a foreign customer and sales terms call for payment in a foreign currency, the company must translate the foreign currency into dollars to record the receivable. If the exchange rate changes before payment is received, exchange gains or losses are recognized in the year they occur. The same treatment is used when a company makes a credit purchase from a foreign supplier and is required to make payment in a foreign currency.

## Guidance Answers to **Decision Maker** and **Decision Ethics**

**Money Manager** If you have investments in fixed-rate bonds and notes when interest rates fall, the value of your investments increases. This is so because the bonds and notes you hold continue to pay the same (high) rate while the market is demanding a new lower interest rate. Your strategy is to continue holding your investments in bonds and notes, and, potentially, to increase these holdings through additional purchases.

**Retailer** Your store's return on assets is 11%, which is similar to the industry norm of 11.2%. However, disaggregation of return on assets reveals that your store's profit margin of 4.4% is much higher than the norm of 3.5%, but your total asset turnover of 2.5 is much lower than the norm of 3.2. These results suggest that, as compared with competitors, you are less efficient in using assets. You need to focus on increasing sales or reducing assets. You might consider reducing prices to increase sales, provided such a strategy does not reduce your return on assets. For instance, you could reduce your profit margin to 4% to increase sales. If total asset turnover increases to more than 2.75 when profit margin is lowered to 4%, your overall return on assets is improved.

**Entrepreneur** You are now less likely to buy Canadian lumber because it takes more U.S. money to buy a Canadian dollar (and lumber). For instance, the purchase of lumber from a Canadian mill with a $1,000 (Canadian dollars) price would have cost the U.S. builder $700 (U.S. dollars, computed as C$1,000 × US$0.70) before the rate change, and $800 (US dollars, computed as C$1,000 × US$0.80) after the rate change.

## Guidance Answers to **Quick Checks**

**1.** Short-term held-to-maturity securities are reported at cost.

**2.** Trading securities are reported at market value.

**3.** The equity section of the balance sheet (and in comprehensive income).

**4.** The income statement.

**5.** Long-term investments include (1) long-term funds earmarked for a special purpose, (2) debt and equity securities that do not meet current asset requirements, and (3) long-term assets not used in the regular operations of the business.

**6.** An equity investment is classified as long term if it is not marketable or, if marketable, it is not held as an available source of cash to meet the needs of current operations.

**7.** Debt securities held-to-maturity and debt securities available-for-sale are both recorded at cost. Also, interest on both is accrued as earned. However, only long-term securities held-to-maturity require amortization of the difference between cost and maturity value. In addition, only securities available-for-sale require a period-end adjustment to market value.

**8.** Long-term equity investments are placed in one of three categories and accounted for as follows: (a) **available-for-sale** (noninfluential, less than 20% of outstanding stock)—market value; (b) **significant influence** (20% to 50% of outstanding stock)—equity method; and (c) **controlling influence** (holding more than 50% of outstanding stock)—equity method with consolidation.

## Key Terms

Key Terms are available at the book's Website for learning and testing in an online Flashcard Format.

Available-for-sale (AFS) securities (p. C-6)
Comprehensive income (p. C-10)
Consolidated financial statements (p. C-9)
Equity method (p. C-8)
Equity securities with controlling influence (p. C-9)
Equity securities with significant influence (p. C-7)

Foreign exchange rate (p. C-15)
Held-to-maturity (HTM) securities (p. C-6)
Long-term investments (p. C-2)
Multinational (p. C-15)
Parent (p. C-9)

Return on total assets (p. C-10)
Short-term investments (p. C-2)
Subsidiary (p. C-9)
Trading securities (p. C-5)
Unrealized gain (loss) (p. C-5)

## Personal Interactive Quiz

Personal Interactive Quizzes A and B are available at the book's Website to reinforce and assess your learning.

*Superscript <sup>A</sup> denotes assignments based on Appendix C-A.*

## Discussion Questions

**1.** Under what two conditions should investments be classified as current assets?

**2.** On a balance sheet, what valuation must be reported for short-term investments in trading securities?

**3.** If a short-term investment in available-for-sale securities costs $6,780 and is sold for $7,500, how should the difference between these two amounts be recorded?

**4.** Identify the three classes of noninfluential and two classes of influential investments in securities.

**5.** Under what conditions should investments be classified as current assets? As long-term assets?

**6.** If a company purchases its only long-term investments in available-for-sale debt securities this period and their market value is below cost at the balance sheet date, what entry is required to recognize this unrealized loss?

**7.** On a balance sheet, what valuation must be reported for debt securities classified as available-for-sale?

**8.** Under what circumstances are long-term investments in debt securities reported at cost and adjusted for amortization of any difference between cost and maturity value?

**9.** For investments in available-for-sale securities, how are unrealized (holding) gains and losses reported?

**10.** In accounting for investments in equity securities, when should the equity method be used?

**11.** Under what circumstances does a company prepare consolidated financial statements?

**12.**<sup>A</sup>What are two major challenges in accounting for international operations?

**13.**<sup>A</sup>Assume a U.S. company makes a credit sale to a foreign customer that is required to make payment in its foreign currency. In the current period, the exchange rate is $1.40 on the date of the sale and is $1.30 on the date the customer pays the receivable. Will the U.S. company record an exchange gain or loss?

**14.**<sup>A</sup>If a U.S. company makes a credit sale to a foreign customer required to make payment in U.S. dollars, can the U.S. company have an exchange gain or loss on this sale?

**15.** What amount does **Krispy Kreme** report as  Accumulated Other Comprehensive Income on its balance sheet as of February 2, 2003, and February 3, 2002?

**16.** Refer to the balance sheet of **Tastykake** in  Appendix A. How can you tell that Tastykake uses the consolidated method of accounting?

**17.** Refer to the financial statements of **Harley-Davidson** in Appendix A. Compute its return on total assets for the year ended December 31, 2002.

### *Red numbers denote Discussion Questions that involve decision-making.*

*Homework Manager repeats all numerical Quick Studies on the book's Website with new numbers.*

On April 18, Dice Co. made a short-term investment in 500 common shares of XLT Co. The purchase price is $45 per share and the broker's fee is $150. The intent is to actively manage these shares for profit. On May 30, Dice Co. receives $1 per share from XLT in dividends. Prepare the April 18 and May 30 journal entries.

## QUICK STUDY

**QS C-1**
Short-term equity investments    C2  P1

Fender Co. purchased short-term investments in available-for-sale securities at a cost of $100,000 on November 25, 2005. At December 31, 2005, these securities had a market value of $94,000. This is the first and only time the company has purchased such securities.

**1.** Prepare the December 31, 2005, year-end adjusting entry for the securities' portfolio.

**2.** For each account in the entry for part 1, explain how it is reported in financial statements.

**3.** Prepare the April 6, 2006, entry when Fender sells one-half of these securities for $52,000.

**QS C-2**
Available-for-sale securities

C2   P3

Prepare Hoffman Company's journal entries to reflect the following transactions for the current year:

May 7   Purchases 100 shares of Lov stock as a short-term investment in available-for-sale securities at a cost of $25 per share plus $200 in broker fees.

June 6   Sells 100 shares of its investment in Lov stock at $28 per share. The broker's commission on this sale is $75.

**QS C-3**
Available-for-sale securities

C2   P3

**QS C-4**

Available-for-sale securities

C2  P3

Galaxy Company completes the following transactions during the current year:

May   9   Purchases 400 shares of X&O stock as a short-term investment in available-for-sale securities at a cost of $50 per share plus $400 in broker fees.

June  2   Sells 200 shares of its investment in X&O stock at $56 per share. The broker's commission on this sale is $180.

Dec. 31   The closing market price of the X&O stock is $46 per share.

Prepare the May 9 and June 2 journal entries and the December 31 adjusting entry. This is the first and only time the company purchased such securities.

---

**QS C-5**

Identifying long-term investments

C1

Which of the following statements are true of long-term investments?

**a.** They can include investments in trading securities.

**b.** They are always easily sold and therefore qualify as being marketable.

**c.** They can include debt and equity securities available-for-sale.

**d.** They are held as an investment of cash available for current operations.

**e.** They can include debt securities held-to-maturity.

**f.** They can include bonds and stocks not intended to serve as a ready source of cash.

**g.** They can include funds earmarked for a special purpose, such as bond sinking funds.

---

**QS C-6**

Describing investments in securities

C1  C2  C3

Complete the following descriptions by filling in the blanks.

**1.** Accrual of interest on bonds held as long-term investments requires a credit to _____ _____.

**2.** The controlling investor (more than 50% ownership) is called the _____, and the investee company is called the _____.

**3.** Trading securities are classified as _____ assets.

**4.** Equity securities giving an investor significant influence are accounted for using the _____ _____.

**5.** Available-for-sale debt securities are reported on the balance sheet at _____ _____.

---

**QS C-7**

Debt securities transactions

C2  P2

On February 1, 2005, Charo Mendez purchased 6% bonds issued by CR Utilities at a cost of $30,000, which is their par value. The bonds pay interest semiannually on July 31 and January 31. For 2005, prepare entries to record the July 31 receipt of interest and the December 31 year-end interest accrual.

---

**QS C-8**

Recording equity securities

C2  P3

On May 20, 2005, Allegra Co. paid $750,000 to acquire 25,000 common shares (10%) of TKR Corp. as a long-term investment. On August 5, 2006, Allegra sold one-half of these shares for $475,000. What valuation method should be used to account for this stock investment? Prepare entries to record both the acquisition and the sale of these shares.

---

**QS C-9**

Equity method transactions

C2  P4

Assume the same facts as in QS C-8 except that the stock acquired represents 40% of TKR Corp.'s outstanding stock. Also assume that TKR Corp. paid a $125,000 dividend on November 1, 2005, and reported a net income of $550,000 for 2005. Prepare the entries to record the receipt of the dividend and the December 31, 2005, year-end adjustment required for the investment account.

---

**QS C-10**

Recording market adjustment for securities

P3

During the current year, Patton Consulting Group acquired long-term available-for-sale securities at a $35,000 cost. At its December 31 year-end, these securities had a market value of $29,000. This is the first and only time the company purchased such securities.

**1.** Prepare the necessary year-end adjusting entry related to these securities.

**2.** Explain how each account used in part 1 is reported in the financial statements.

---

**QS C-11**

Return on total assets   A1

How is return on total assets computed? What does this ratio reflect?

---

**QS C-12**

Component return on total assets   A1

Write the formula to separate the return on total assets into its components. Explain how components of the return on total assets are helpful to financial statement users.

A U.S. company sells a British company a product with the transaction listed in British pounds. On the date of the sale, the transaction of $16,000 is billed as £10,000, reflecting an exchange rate of 1.60 (that is, $1.60 per pound). Prepare the entry to record (1) the sale and (2) the receipt of payment in pounds when the exchange rate is 1.50.

**QS C-13<sup>A</sup>**
Foreign currency transactions
P5

On March 1, 2005, a U.S. company made a credit sale requiring payment in 30 days from a Malaysian company, Hamac Sdn. Bhd., in 20,000 Malaysian ringgits. Assuming the exchange rate between Malaysian ringgits and U.S. dollars is $0.6811 on March 1 and $0.6985 on March 31, prepare the entries to record the sale on March 1 and the cash receipt on March 31.

**QS C-14<sup>A</sup>**
Foreign currency transactions
P5

 *Homework Manager* repeats all numerical Exercises on the book's Website with new numbers.

Prepare journal entries to record the following transactions involving the short-term securities investments of Smart Co., all of which occurred during year 2005:

**a.** On February 15, paid $100,000 cash to purchase FTR's 90-day short-term debt securities ($100,000 principal), dated February 15, that pay 8% interest (categorized as held-to-maturity securities).

**b.** On March 22, purchased 700 shares of FIX Company stock at $30 per share plus a $150 brokerage fee. These shares are categorized as trading securities.

**c.** On May 16, received a check from FTR in payment of the principal and 90 days' interest on the debt securities purchased in transaction *a*.

**d.** On August 1, paid $60,000 cash to purchase Better Buy's 10% debt securities ($60,000 principal), dated July 30, 2005, and maturing January 30, 2006 (categorized as available-for-sale securities).

**e.** On September 1, received a $1.00 per share cash dividend on the FIX Company stock purchased in transaction *b*.

**f.** On October 8, sold 350 shares of FIX Co. stock for $40 per share, less a $140 brokerage fee.

**g.** On October 30, received a check from Better Buy for 90 days' interest on the debt securities purchased in transaction *d*.

**EXERCISES**

**Exercise C-1**
Accounting for transactions in short-term securities

C2  P1  P2  P3

**Check**    (c) Dr. Cash $102,000

(f) Dr. Cash $13,860

Forex Co. purchases investments in trading securities at a cost of $56,000 on December 27, 2005. (This is its first and only purchase of such securities.) At December 31, 2005, these securities had a market value of $66,000.

**1.** Prepare the December 31, 2005, year-end adjusting entry for the trading securities' portfolio.

**2.** Explain how each account in the entry of part 1 is reported in financial statements.

**3.** Prepare the January 3, 2006, entry when Forex sells one-half of these securities for $30,000.

**Exercise C-2**
Accounting for trading securities

C1  P1

**Check**    (3) Gain, $2,000

On December 31, 2005, Rollo Company held the following short-term investments in its portfolio of available-for-sale securities. Rollo had no short-term investments in its prior accounting periods. Prepare the December 31, 2005, adjusting entry to report these investments at market value.

**Exercise C-3**
Adjusting available-for-sale securities to market

C2  P3

| | Cost | Market Value |
|---|---|---|
| Vicks Corporation bonds payable . . . . . . . . . . . | $79,600 | $90,600 |
| Pace Corporation notes payable . . . . . . . . . . . . | 60,600 | 52,900 |
| Lake Lugano Company common stock . . . . . . . | 85,500 | 82,100 |

**Check**    Unrealized loss, $100

Prepare journal entries to record the following transactions involving both the short- and long-term investments of Sophia Corp., all of which occurred during calendar year 2005. Use the account Short-Term Investments for any transactions that you determine are short term.

**a.** On February 15, paid $150,000 cash to purchase American General's 120-day short-term notes at par, which are dated February 15 and pay 10% interest (classified as held-to-maturity).

**b.** On March 22, bought 700 shares of Fran Industries common stock at $25 cash per share plus a $250 brokerage fee (classified as long-term available-for-sale securities).

**c.** On June 15, received a check from American General in payment of the principal and 120 days' interest on the notes purchased in transaction *a*.

**d.** On July 30, paid $50,000 cash to purchase MP3 Electronics' 8% notes at par, dated July 30, 2005, and maturing on January 30, 2006 (classified as trading securities).

**Exercise C-4**
Transactions in short- and long-term investments

C1  C2

**e.** On September 1, received a $0.50 per share cash dividend on the Fran Industries common stock purchased in transaction *b*.

**f.** On October 8, sold 350 shares of Fran Industries common stock for $32 cash per share, less a $175 brokerage fee.

**g.** On October 30, received a check from MP3 Electronics for three months' interest on the notes purchased in transaction *d*.

---

## Exercise C-5
Market adjustment to available-for-sale securities

P3

On December 31, 2005, Manhattan Co. held the following short-term available-for-sale securities:

|  | Cost | Market Value |
|---|---|---|
| Nintendo Co. common stock . . . . . . . . . . . | $68,900 | $75,300 |
| Atlantic Richfield Co. bonds payable . . . . . . | 24,500 | 22,800 |
| Kellogg Co. notes payable . . . . . . . . . . . . . | 50,000 | 47,200 |
| McDonald's Corp. common stock . . . . . . . . | 91,400 | 86,600 |

Manhattan had no short-term investments prior to the current period. Prepare the December 31, 2005, year-end adjusting entry to record the market adjustment for these securities.

---

## Exercise C-6
Market adjustment to available-for-sale securities

P3

Berroa Co. began operations in 2004. The cost and market values for its long-term investments portfolio in available-for-sale securities are shown below. Prepare Berroa's December 31, 2005, adjusting entry to reflect any necessary market adjustment for these investments.

|  | Cost | Market Value |
|---|---|---|
| December 31, 2004 . . . . . . . . | $79,483 | $72,556 |
| December 31, 2005 . . . . . . . . | 85,120 | 90,271 |

---

## Exercise C-7
Multi-year market adjustments to available-for-sale securities

P3

Ticker Services began operations in 2003 and maintains long-term investments in available-for-sale securities. The year-end cost and market values for its portfolio of these investments follow. Prepare journal entries to record each year-end market adjustment for these securities.

|  | Cost | Market Value |
|---|---|---|
| December 31, 2003 . . . . . . . | $374,000 | $362,560 |
| December 31, 2004 . . . . . . . | 426,900 | 453,200 |
| December 31, 2005 . . . . . . . | 580,700 | 686,450 |
| December 31, 2006 . . . . . . . | 875,500 | 778,800 |

---

## Exercise C-8
Classifying investments in securities; recording market values

C1  C2  P2  P3  P4

Information regarding Central Company's individual investments in securities during its calendar-year 2005, with the December 31, 2005, market values, follows:

**a.** Investment in Beeman Company bonds: $418,500 cost, $455,000 market value. Central intends to hold these bonds until they mature in 2008.

**b.** Investment in Baybridge common stock: 29,500 shares; $332,450 cost; $361,375 market value. Central owns 32% of Baybridge's voting stock and has a significant influence over Baybridge.

**c.** Investment in Carrollton common stock: 12,000 shares; $169,750 cost; $183,000 market value. This investment amounts to 3% of Carrollton's outstanding shares, and Central's goal with this investment is to earn dividends over the next few years.

**d.** Investment in Newtech common stock: 3,500 shares; $95,300 cost; $93,625 market value. Central's goal with this investment is to reap an increase in market value of the stock over the next three to five years. Newtech has 30,000 common shares outstanding.

**e.** Investment in Flockhart common stock: 16,300 shares; $102,860 cost; $109,210 market value. This stock is marketable and is held as an investment of cash available for operations.

Identify whether each investment should be classified as a short-term or long-term investment. For each long-term investment, indicate in which of the long-term investment classifications it should be placed. Prepare a journal entry dated December 31, 2005, to record the market value adjustment of the long-term investments in available-for-sale securities. Central had no long-term investments prior to year 2005.

**Check**  Unrealized gain, $11,575

---

Prepare journal entries to record the following transactions and events of Kash Company.

**2005**

Jan.   2   Purchased 30,000 shares of Bushtex Co. common stock for $204,000 cash plus a broker's fee of $3,480 cash. Bushtex has 90,000 shares of common stock outstanding and its policies will be significantly influenced by Kash.

Sept.  1   Bushtex declared and paid a cash dividend of $3.10 per share.

Dec. 31   Bushtex announced that net income for the year is $624,900.

**2006**

June  1   Bushtex declared and paid a cash dividend of $3.60 per share.

Dec. 31   Bushtex announced that net income for the year is $699,750.

Dec. 31   Kash sold 10,000 shares of Bushtex for $162,500 cash.

**Exercise C-9**
Securities transactions; equity method

P4  C2

---

The following information is available from the financial statements of Wright Industries. Compute Wright's return on total assets for 2005 and 2006. (Round percentages to one decimal place.) Comment on the company's efficiency in using its assets in 2005 and 2006.

**Exercise C-10**
Return on total assets

A1

| File Edit View Insert Format Tools Data Window Help | | | |
|---|---|---|---|
| **A** | **B** | **C** | **D** |
| 1 | **2004** | **2005** | **2006** |
| 2  Total assets, December 31 | $190,000 | $320,000 | $750,000 |
| 3  Net income | 28,200 | 36,400 | 58,300 |
| 4 | | | |

---

Desi of New York sells its products to customers in the United States and the United Kingdom. On December 16, 2005, Desi sold merchandise on credit to Bronson Ltd. of London at a price of 17,000 pounds. The exchange rate on that day for £1 was $1.5238. On December 31, 2005, when Desi prepared its financial statements, the rate was £1 for $1.4990. Bronson paid its bill in full on January 15, 2006, at which time the exchange rate was £1 for $1.5156. Desi immediately exchanged the 17,000 pounds for U.S. dollars. Prepare Desi's journal entries on December 16, December 31, and January 15 (round to the nearest dollar).

**Exercise C-11**[A]
Foreign currency transactions

P5

---

On May 8, 2005, Jett Company (a U.S. company) made a credit sale to Lopez (a Mexican company). The terms of the sale required Lopez to pay 800,000 pesos on February 10, 2006. Jett prepares quarterly financial statements on March 31, June 30, September 30, and December 31. The exchange rates for pesos during the time the receivable is outstanding follow:

| | |
|---|---|
| May 8, 2005 . . . . . . . . . . . . | $0.1984 |
| June 30, 2005 . . . . . . . . . . . | 0.2013 |
| September 30, 2005 . . . . . . . | 0.2029 |
| December 31, 2005 . . . . . . . . | 0.1996 |
| February 10, 2006 . . . . . . . . | 0.2047 |

**Exercise C-12**[A]
Computing foreign exchange gains and losses on receivables

C4  P5

Compute the foreign exchange gain or loss that Jett should report on each of its quarterly income statements for the last three quarters of 2005 and the first quarter of 2006. Also compute the amount reported on Jett's balance sheets at the end of each of its last three quarters of 2005.

## PROBLEM SET A

### Problem C-1A

Recording transactions and market adjustments for trading securities

C2   P1

Ryder Company, which began operations in 2005, invests its idle cash in trading securities. The following transactions are from its short-term investments in its trading securities:

**2005**

Jan.  20   Purchased 900 shares of Ford Motor Co. at $36 per share plus a $125 commission.
Feb.   9   Purchased 4,400 shares of Lucent at $10 per share plus a $200 commission.
Oct.  12   Purchased 500 shares of Z-Seven at $8 per share plus a $100 commission.

**2006**

Apr.  15   Sold 900 shares of Ford Motor Co. at $39 per share less a $185 commission.
July   5   Sold 500 shares of Z-Seven at $10.25 per share less a $100 commission.
      22   Purchased 800 shares of Hunt Corp. at $30 per share plus a $225 commission.
Aug.  19   Purchased 1,000 shares of Donna Karan at $12 per share plus a $100 commission.

**2007**

Feb.  27   Purchased 3,400 shares of HCA at $22 per share plus a $220 commission.
Mar.   3   Sold 800 shares of Hunt at $25 per share less a $125 commission.
June  21   Sold 4,400 shares of Lucent at $8 per share less a $180 commission.
      30   Purchased 1,000 shares of Black & Decker at $47.50 per share plus a $195 commission.
Nov.   1   Sold 1,000 shares of Donna Karan at $22 per share less a $208 commission.

**Required**

1. Prepare journal entries to record these short-term investment activities for the years shown. (Ignore any year-end adjusting entries.)

**Check**  (2) Dr. Market
Adjustment—Trading $2,385

2. On December 31, 2007, prepare the adjusting entry to record any necessary market adjustment for the portfolio of trading securities when HCA's share price is $24 and Black & Decker's share price is $43.50. (The Market Adjustment—Trading account had an unadjusted balance of zero.)

### Problem C-2A

Recording, adjusting, and reporting short-term available-for-sale securities

C2   P3

Perry Company had no short-term investments prior to year 2005. It had the following transactions involving short-term investments in available-for-sale securities during 2005:

Apr.  16   Purchased 8,000 shares of Gem Co. stock at $24.25 per share plus a $360 brokerage fee.
May    1   Paid $200,000 to buy 90-day U.S. Treasury bills (debt securities): $200,000 principal amount, 6% interest, securities dated May 1.
July   7   Purchased 4,000 shares of PepsiCo stock at $49.25 per share plus a $350 brokerage fee.
      20   Purchased 2,000 shares of Xerox stock at $16.75 per share plus a $410 brokerage fee.
Aug.   3   Received a check for principal and accrued interest on the U.S. Treasury bills that matured on July 29.
      15   Received an $0.85 per share cash dividend on the Gem Co. stock.
      28   Sold 4,000 shares of Gem Co. stock at $30 per share less a $450 brokerage fee.
Oct.   1   Received a $1.90 per share cash dividend on the PepsiCo shares.
Dec.  15   Received a $1.05 per share cash dividend on the remaining Gem Co. shares.
      31   Received a $1.30 per share cash dividend on the PepsiCo shares.

**Required**

1. Prepare journal entries to record the preceding transactions and events.

**Check**  (2) Cost = $328,440

2. Prepare a table to compare the cost and market values of Perry's short-term investments in available-for-sale securities. The year-end market values per share are Gem Co., $26.50; PepsiCo, $46.50; and Xerox, $13.75.

(3) Dr. Unrealized Loss—
Equity $8,940

3. Prepare an adjusting entry, if necessary, to record the market adjustment for the portfolio of short-term investments in available-for-sale securities.

*Analysis Component*

4. Explain the balance sheet presentation of a market adjustment for these short-term investments.

5. How do these short-term investments affect Perry's (a) income statement for year 2005 and (b) the equity section of its balance sheet at year-end 2005?

Shaq Security, which began operations in 2005, invests in long-term available-for-sale securities. Following is a series of transactions and events determining its long-term investment activity:

**2005**

Jan.  20   Purchased 900 shares of Johnson & Johnson at $18.75 per share plus a $590 commission.
Feb.   9   Purchased 2,200 shares of Sony at $46.88 per share plus a $2,578 commission.
June 12   Purchased 500 shares of Mattel at $55.50 per share plus a $832 commission.
Dec. 31   Per share market values for stocks in the portfolio are Johnson & Johnson, $20.38; Mattel, $57.25; Sony, $39.00.

**2006**

Apr. 15   Sold 900 shares of Johnson & Johnson at $21.75 per share less a $685 commission.
July   5   Sold 500 shares of Mattel at $49.13 per share less a $491 commission.
July 22   Purchased 1,600 shares of Sara Lee at $36.25 per share plus a $1,740 commission.
Aug. 19   Purchased 1,800 shares of Eastman Kodak at $28.00 per share plus a $1,260 commission.
Dec. 31   Per share market values for stocks in the portfolio are Kodak, $31.75; Sara Lee, $30.00; Sony, $36.50.

**2007**

Feb. 27   Purchased 3,400 shares of Microsoft at $23.63 per share plus a $1,606 commission.
June 21   Sold 2,200 shares of Sony at $40.00 per share less an $2,640 commission.
June 30   Purchased 1,200 shares of Black & Decker at $47.50 per share plus a $1,995 commission.
Aug.  3   Sold 1,600 shares of Sara Lee at $31.25 per share less a $1,750 commission.
Nov.  1   Sold 1,800 shares of Eastman Kodak at $42.75 per share less a $2,309 commission.
Dec. 31   Per share market values for stocks in the portfolio are Black & Decker, $56.50; Microsoft, $28.00.

**Required**

**1.** Prepare journal entries to record these transactions and events and any year-end market adjustments to the portfolio of long-term available-for-sale securities.

**2.** Prepare a table that summarizes the (*a*) total cost, (*b*) total market adjustment, and (*c*) total market value of the portfolio of long-term available-for-sale securities at each year-end.

**3.** Prepare a table that summarizes (*a*) the realized gains and losses and (*b*) the unrealized gains or losses for the portfolio of long-term available-for-sale securities at each year-end.

**Problem C-3A**
Recording, adjusting, and reporting long-term available-for-sale securities

C2   P3

**Check**   (2b) Market adjustment: 12/31/05, $(18,994); 12/31/06; $(31,664)

(3b) Unrealized Gain for 2007, $22,057

---

Park Co.'s long-term available-for-sale portfolio at December 31, 2004, consists of the following:

| Available-for-Sale Securities | Cost | Market Value |
|---|---|---|
| 80,000 shares of Company A common stock . . . . . . . . | $1,070,600 | $ 980,000 |
| 14,000 shares of Company B common stock . . . . . . . . | 318,750 | 308,000 |
| 35,000 shares of Company C common stock  . . . . . . . | 1,325,500 | 1,281,875 |

**Problem C-4A**
Long-term investment transactions; unrealized and realized gains and losses

C2   C3   P3   P4

Park enters into the following long-term investment transactions during year 2005.

Jan.  29   Sold 7,000 shares of Company B common stock for $158,375 less a brokerage fee of $3,100.
Apr.  17   Purchased 20,000 shares of Company W common stock for $395,000 plus a brokerage fee of $6,800. The shares represent a 30% ownership in Company W.
July   6   Purchased 9,000 shares of Company X common stock for $253,125 plus a brokerage fee of $3,500. The shares represent a 10% ownership in Company X.
Aug. 22   Purchased 100,000 shares of Company Y common stock for $750,000 plus a brokerage fee of $8,200. The shares represent a 51% ownership in Company Y.
Nov. 13   Purchased 17,000 shares of Company Z common stock for $533,800 plus a brokerage fee of $6,900. The shares represent a 5% ownership in Company Z.
Dec.   9   Sold 80,000 shares of Company A common stock for $1,030,000 less a brokerage fee of $4,100.

The market values of its investments at December 31, 2005, are B, $162,750; C, $1,220,625; W, $382,500; X, $236,250; Y, $1,062,500; Z, $557,600.

**Required**

**1.** Determine the amount Park should report on its December 31, 2005, balance sheet for its long-term investments in available-for-sale securities.

**2.** Prepare any necessary December 31, 2005, adjusting entry to record the market value adjustment for the long-term investments in available-for-sale securities.

**3.** What amount of gains or losses on transactions relating to long-term investments in available-for-sale securities should Park report on its December 31, 2005, income statement?

---

## Problem C-5A

Accounting for long-term investments in securities; with and without significant influence

C2   P3   P4

Pillar Steel Co., which began operations on January 4, 2005, had the following subsequent transactions and events in its long-term investments:

**2005**

Jan.   5    Pillar purchased 30,000 shares (20%) of Kildaire's common stock for $780,000.
Oct. 23    Kildaire declared and paid a cash dividend of $1.60 per share.
Dec. 31    Kildaire's net income for 2005 is $582,000, and the market value of its stock at December 31 is $27.75 per share.

**2006**

Oct. 15    Kildaire declared and paid a cash dividend of $1.30 per share.
Dec. 31    Kildaire's net income for 2006 is $738,000, and the market value of its stock at December 31 is $30.45 per share.

**2007**

Jan.   2    Pillar sold all of its investment in Kildaire for $947,000 cash.

### Part 1

Assume that Pillar has a significant influence over Kildaire with its 20% share of stock.

**Required**

**1.** Prepare journal entries to record these transactions and events for Pillar.

**2.** Compute the carrying (book) value per share of Pillar's investment in Kildaire common stock as reflected in the investment account on January 1, 2007.

**3.** Compute the net increase or decrease in Pillar's equity from January 5, 2005, through January 2, 2007, resulting from its investment in Kildaire.

### Part 2

Assume that although Pillar owns 20% of Kildaire's outstanding stock, circumstances indicate that it does not have a significant influence over the investee and that it is classified as an available-for-sale security investment.

**Required**

**1.** Prepare journal entries to record the preceding transactions and events for Pillar. Also prepare an entry dated January 2, 2007, to remove any balance related to the market adjustment.

**2.** Compute the cost per share of Pillar's investment in Kildaire common stock as reflected in the investment account on January 1, 2007.

**3.** Compute the net increase or decrease in Pillar's equity from January 5, 2005, through January 2, 2007, resulting from its investment in Kildaire.

---

## Problem C-6A[A]

Foreign currency transactions

C4   P5

Roundtree Co., a U.S. corporation with customers in several foreign countries, had these selected transactions for 2005 and 2006:

**2005**

Apr.   8    Sold merchandise to Salinas & Sons of Mexico for $7,938 cash. The exchange rate for pesos is $0.1323 on this day.

July 21    Sold merchandise on credit to Sumito Corp. in Japan. The price of 1.5 million yen is to be paid 120 days from the date of sale. The exchange rate for yen is $0.0096 on this day.

Oct.  14  Sold merchandise for 19,000 pounds to Smithers Ltd. of Great Britain, payment in full to be received in 90 days. The exchange rate for pounds is $1.5181 on this day.

Nov.  18  Received Sumito's payment in yen for its July 21 purchase and immediately exchanged the yen for dollars. The exchange rate for yen is $0.0091 on this day.

Dec.  20  Sold merchandise for 17,000 ringgits to Hamid Albar of Malaysia, payment in full to be received in 30 days. On this day, the exchange rate for ringgits is $0.6852.

Dec.  31  Recorded adjusting entries to recognize exchange gains or losses on Roundtree's annual financial statements. Rates for exchanging foreign currencies on this day follow:

| | |
|---|---|
| Pesos (Mexico) ......... | $0.1335 |
| Yen (Japan) ............ | 0.0095 |
| Pounds (Britain) ........ | 1.5235 |
| Ringgits (Malaysia) ....... | 0.6807 |

**2006**

Jan.  12  Received full payment in pounds from Smithers for the October 14 sale and immediately exchanged the pounds for dollars. The exchange rate for pounds is $1.5314 on this day.

Jan.  19  Received Hamid Albar's full payment in ringgits for the December 20 sale and immediately exchanged the ringgits for dollars. The exchange rate for ringgits is $0.6771 on this day.

### Required

**1.** Prepare journal entries for the Roundtree transactions and adjusting entries (round amounts to the dollar).

**2.** Compute the foreign exchange gain or loss to be reported on Roundtree's 2005 income statement.

**Check**  (2) 2005 total foreign exchange loss, $723

### Analysis Component

**3.** What actions might Roundtree consider to reduce its risk of foreign exchange gains or losses?

---

Deal Co., which began operations in 2005, invests its idle cash in trading securities. The following transactions relate to its short-term investments in its trading securities.

**2005**

Mar.  10  Purchased 1,200 shares of AOL at $59.15 per share plus a $773 commission.
May  7  Purchased 2,500 shares of MTV at $36.25 per share plus a $1,428 commission.
Sept.  1  Purchased 600 shares of UPS at $57.25 per share plus a $625 commission.

**2006**

Apr.  26  Sold 2,500 shares of MTV at $34.50 per share less a $1,025 commission.
27  Sold 600 shares of UPS at $60.50 per share less a $894 commission.
June  2  Purchased 1,800 shares of SPW at $172 per share plus a $1,625 commission.
14  Purchased 450 shares of Wal-Mart at $50.25 per share plus a $541.50 commission.

**2007**

Jan.  28  Purchased 1,000 shares of PepsiCo at $43 per share plus a $1,445 commission.
31  Sold 1,800 shares of SPW at $168 per share less a $1,020 commission.
Aug.  22  Sold 1,200 shares of AOL at $56.75 per share less a $1,240 commission.
Sept.  3  Purchased 750 shares of Vodaphone at $40.50 per share plus a $840 commission.
Oct.  9  Sold 450 shares of Wal-Mart at $53.75 per share less a $610.50 commission.

### Required

**1.** Prepare journal entries to record these short-term investment activities for the years shown. (Ignore any year-end adjusting entries.)

**2.** On December 31, 2007, prepare the adjusting entry to record any necessary market adjustment for the portfolio of trading securities when PepsiCo's share price is $41 and Vodaphone's share price is $37. (The Market Adjustment—Trading account had an unadjusted balance of zero.)

## PROBLEM SET B

### Problem C-1B
Recording transactions and market adjustments for trading securities

C2  P1

**Check**  (2) Cr. Market Adjustment—Trading $6,910

## Problem C-2B

Recording, adjusting, and
reporting short-term
available-for-sale securities

C2  P3

Day Systems had no short-term investments prior to 2005. It had the following transactions involving short-term investments in available-for-sale securities during 2005.

Feb.  6   Purchased 1,700 shares of Nokia stock at $41.25 per share plus a $1,500 brokerage fee.
      15   Paid $10,000 to buy six-month U.S. Treasury bills (debt securities): $10,000 principal amount, 6% interest, securities dated February 15.
Apr.  7   Purchased 600 shares of Dell Co. stock at $39.50 per share plus a $627 brokerage fee.
June  2   Purchased 1,250 shares of Merck stock at $72.50 per share plus a $1,945 brokerage fee.
      30   Received a $0.19 per share cash dividend on the Nokia shares.
Aug. 11   Sold 425 shares of Nokia stock at $46 per share less a $525 brokerage fee.
      16   Received a check for principal and accrued interest on the U.S. Treasury bills purchased February 15.
      24   Received a $0.10 per share cash dividend on the Dell shares.
Nov.  9   Received a $0.20 per share cash dividend on the remaining Nokia shares.
Dec. 18   Received a $0.15 per share cash dividend on the Dell shares.

### Required

**1.** Prepare journal entries to record the preceding transactions and events.

**Check**  (2) Cost = $170,616

**2.** Prepare a table to compare the cost and market values of the short-term investments in available-for-sale securities. The year-end market values per share are Nokia, $40.25; Dell, $41; and Merck, $59.

(3) Dr. Unrealized
Loss—Equity, $20,947

**3.** Prepare an adjusting entry, if necessary, to record the market adjustment for the portfolio of short-term investments in available-for-sale securities.

### Analysis Component

**4.** Explain the balance sheet presentation of a market adjustment to these short-term investments.

**5.** How do these short-term investments affect (*a*) its income statement for year 2005 and (*b*) the equity section of its balance sheet at the 2005 year-end?

## Problem C-3B

Recording, adjusting, and
reporting long-term
available-for-sale securities

C2  P3

Venice Enterprises, which began operations in 2005, invests in long-term available-for-sale securities. Following is a series of transactions and events involving its long-term investment activity:

### 2005

Mar. 10   Purchased 2,400 shares of Apple Computer at $33.25 per share plus $1,995 commission.
Apr.  7   Purchased 5,000 shares of Ford at $17.50 per share plus $2,625 commission.
Sept.  1   Purchased 1,200 shares of Polaroid at $49.00 per share plus $1,176 commission.
Dec. 31   Per share market values for stocks in the portfolio are Apple, $35.50; Ford, $17.00; Polaroid, $51.75.

### 2006

Apr. 26   Sold 5,000 shares of Ford at $16.38 per share less a $2,237 commission.
June  2   Purchased 3,600 shares of Duracell at $18.88 per share plus a $2,312 commission.
June 14   Purchased 900 shares of Sears at $24.50 per share plus a $541 commission.
Nov. 27   Sold 1,200 shares of Polaroid at $52 per share less a $1,672 commission.
Dec. 31   Per share market values for stocks in the portfolio are Apple, $35.50; Duracell, $18.00; Sears, $26.00.

### 2007

Jan. 28   Purchased 2,000 shares of Coca-Cola Co. at $41 per share plus a $3,280 commission.
Aug. 22   Sold 2,400 shares of Apple at $29.75 per share less a $2,339 commission.
Sept.  3   Purchased 1,500 shares of Motorola at $29.00 per share plus an $870 commission.
Oct.  9   Sold 900 shares of Sears at $27.50 per share less a $619 commission.
Oct. 31   Sold 3,600 shares of Duracell at $16.00 per share less a $1,496 commission.
Dec. 31   Per share market values for stocks in the portfolio are Coca-Cola, $46.00; Motorola, $22.00.

## Required

**1.** Prepare journal entries to record these transactions and events and any year-end market adjustments to the portfolio of long-term available-for-sale securities.

**2.** Prepare a table that summarizes the (*a*) total cost, (*b*) total market adjustment, and (*c*) total market value for the portfolio of long-term available-for-sale securities at each year-end.

**3.** Prepare a table that summarizes (*a*) the realized gains and losses and (*b*) the unrealized gains or losses for the portfolio of long-term available-for-sale securities at each year-end.

**Check**  (2b) Market adjustment:
12/31/05, $404; 12/31/06, $(1,266)

(3b) Unrealized loss for 2007, $4,650

---

Capollo's long-term available-for-sale portfolio at December 31, 2004, consists of the following:

| Available-for-Sale Securities | Cost | Market Value |
|---|---|---|
| 45,000 shares of Company R common stock ....... | $1,118,250 | $1,198,125 |
| 17,000 shares of Company S common stock ........ | 616,760 | 586,500 |
| 22,000 shares of Company T common stock ........ | 294,470 | 303,600 |

**Problem C-4B**
Long-term investment transactions; unrealized and realized gains and losses

C2  C3  P3  P4

Capollo enters into the following long-term investment transactions during year 2005:

Jan.  13  Sold 4,250 shares of Company S common stock for $144,500 less a brokerage fee of $2,390.

Mar.  24  Purchased 31,000 shares of Company U common stock for $565,750 plus a brokerage fee of $9,900. The shares represent a 62% ownership in Company U.

Apr.  5  Purchased 85,000 shares of Company V common stock for $267,750 plus a brokerage fee of $4,500. The shares represent a 10% ownership in Company V.

Sept.  2  Sold 22,000 shares of Company T common stock for $313,500 less a brokerage fee of $5,400.

Sept. 27  Purchased 5,000 shares of Company W common stock for $101,000 plus a brokerage fee of $2,100. The shares represent a 25% ownership in Company W.

Oct.  30  Purchased 10,000 shares of Company X common stock for $97,500 plus a brokerage fee of $2,340. The shares represent a 13% ownership in Company X.

The market values of its investments at December 31, 2005, are R, $1,136,250; S, $420,750; U, $545,600; V, $269,875; W, $109,375; X, $91,250.

## Required

**1.** Determine the amount Capollo should report on its December 31, 2005, balance sheet for its long-term investments in available-for-sale securities.

**2.** Prepare any necessary December 31, 2005, adjusting entry to record the market value adjustment of the long-term investments in available-for-sale securities.

**3.** What amount of gains or losses on transactions relating to long-term investments in available-for-sale securities should Capollo report on its December 31, 2005, income statement?

**Check**  (2) Dr. Unrealized Loss—
Equity, $34,785; Cr. Market Adjustment,
$93,530

---

Bengal Company, which began operations on January 3, 2005, had the following subsequent transactions and events in its long-term investments.

**Problem C-5B**
Accounting for long-term investments in securities; with and without significant influence

C2  P3  P4

### 2005

Jan.  5  Bengal purchased 15,000 shares (25%) of Bloch's common stock for $187,500.
Aug.  1  Bloch declared and paid a cash dividend of $0.95 per share.
Dec. 31  Bloch's net income for 2005 is $92,000, and the market value of its stock is $12.90 per share.

### 2006

Aug.  1  Bloch declared and paid a cash dividend of $1.25 per share.
Dec. 31  Bloch's net income for 2006 is $76,000, and the market value of its stock is $13.55 per share.

### 2007

Jan.  8  Bengal sold all of its investment in Bloch for $204,750 cash.

### Part 1

Assume that Bengal has a significant influence over Bloch with its 25% share.

**Required**

1. Prepare journal entries to record these transactions and events for Bengal.

2. Compute the carrying (book) value per share of Bengal's investment in Bloch common stock as reflected in the investment account on January 7, 2007.

3. Compute the net increase or decrease in Bengal's equity from January 5, 2005, through January 8, 2007, resulting from its investment in Bloch.

**Part 2**

Assume that although Bengal owns 25% of Bloch's outstanding stock, circumstances indicate that it does not have a significant influence over the investee and that it is classified as an available-for-sale security investment.

**Required**

1. Prepare journal entries to record these transactions and events for Bengal. Also prepare an entry dated January 8, 2007, to remove any balance related to the market adjustment.

2. Compute the cost per share of Bengal's investment in Bloch common stock as reflected in the investment account on January 7, 2007.

3. Compute the net increase or decrease in Bengal's equity from January 5, 2005, through January 8, 2007, resulting from its investment in Bloch.

---

## Problem C-6B[A]
Foreign currency transactions

C4   P5

Datamix, a U.S. corporation with customers in several foreign countries, had these selected transactions for 2005 and 2006:

**2005**

May 26   Sold merchandise for 6.5 million yen to Fuji Company of Japan, payment in full to be received in 60 days. On this day, the exchange rate for yen is $0.0094.

June 1   Sold merchandise to Fordham Ltd. of Great Britain for $72,613 cash. The exchange rate for pounds is $1.5277 on this day.

July 25   Received Fuji's payment in yen for its May 26 purchase and immediately exchanged the yen for dollars. The exchange rate for yen is $0.0090 on this day.

Oct. 15   Sold merchandise on credit to Martinez Brothers of Mexico. The price of 373,000 pesos is to be paid 90 days from the date of sale. On this day, the exchange rate for pesos is $0.1340.

Dec. 6   Sold merchandise for 242,000 yuans to Chi-Ying Company of China, payment in full to be received in 30 days. The exchange rate for yuans is $0.1975 on this day.

Dec. 31   Recorded adjusting entries to recognize exchange gains or losses on Datamix's annual financial statements. Rates of exchanging foreign currencies on this day follow:

| | |
|---|---|
| Yen (Japan) . . . . . . . . . . . | $0.0094 |
| Pounds (Britain) . . . . . . . | 1.5318 |
| Pesos (Mexico) . . . . . . . . | 0.1560 |
| Yuans (China) . . . . . . . . . | 0.2000 |

**2006**

Jan. 5   Received Chi-Ying's full payment in yuans for the December 6 sale and immediately exchanged the yuans for dollars. The exchange rate for yuans is $0.2060 on this day.

Jan. 13   Received full payment in pesos from Martinez for the October 15 sale and immediately exchanged the pesos for dollars. The exchange rate for pesos is $0.1420 on this day.

**Required**

1. Prepare journal entries for the Datamix transactions and adjusting entries.

2. Compute the foreign exchange gain or loss to be reported on Datamix's 2005 income statement.

*Analysis Component*

3. What actions might Datamix consider to reduce its risk of foreign exchange gains or losses?

---

## PROBLEM SET C

Problem Set C is available at the book's Website to reinforce and assess your learning.

*(This serial problem began in Chapter 1 and continues through most of the book. If previous chapter segments were not completed, the serial problem can begin at this point. It is helpful, but not necessary, for you to use the Working Papers that accompany the book.)*

## SERIAL PROBLEM

Success Systems

While reviewing the March 31, 2005, balance sheet of Success Systems, Kay Breeze notes that the business has built a large cash balance of $77,845. Its most recent bank money market statement shows that the funds are earning an annualized return of 0.75%. Breeze decides to make several investments with the desire to earn a higher return on the idle cash balance. Accordingly, in April 2005, Success Systems makes the following investments in trading securities:

April 16   Purchases 200 shares of Johnson & Johnson stock at $55 per share plus $240 commission.
April 30   Purchases 100 shares of Starbucks Corporation at $24 per share plus $120 commission.

On June 30, 2005, the per share market price of the Johnson & Johnson shares is $60 and the Starbucks shares is $21.

**Required**

**1.** Prepare journal entries to record the April purchases of trading securities.
**2.** On June 30, 2005, prepare the adjusting entry to record any necessary market adjustment to its portfolio of trading securities.

## BEYOND THE NUMBERS

**BTN C-1**   Refer to **Krispy Kreme**'s financial statements in Appendix A to answer the following:

**1.** Are Krispy Kreme's financial statements consolidated? How can you tell?
**2.** What is Krispy Kreme's *comprehensive income* for the year ended February 2, 2003?
**3.** Does Krispy Kreme have any foreign operations? How can you tell?
**4.** Compute Krispy Kreme's return on total assets for the year ended February 2, 2003.

*Roll On*

**5.** Access Krispy Kreme's annual report for a fiscal year ending after February 2, 2003, from either its Website (**KrispyKreme.Com**) or the SEC's EDGAR database (**www.SEC.gov**). Recompute Krispy Kreme's return on total assets for the years subsequent to February 2, 2003.

### REPORTING IN ACTION

C3  C4  A1

**BTN C-2**   Key comparative figures ($ millions) for **Krispy Kreme** and **Tastykake** follow:

| Key Figures | Krispy Kreme | | | Tastykake | | |
|---|---|---|---|---|---|---|
| | Current Year | 1 Year Prior | 2 Years Prior | Current Year | 1 Year Prior | 2 Years Prior |
| Net income ........ | $ 33,478 | $ 26,378 | $ 14,725 | $ 2,000* | $ 8,048* | $ 8,144 |
| Net sales .......... | 491,549 | 394,354 | 300,715 | 162,263 | 166,245 | 162,877 |
| Total assets ........ | 410,487 | 255,376 | 171,493 | 116,560 | 116,137 | 112,192 |

\* Restructuring charges are removed from income.

**Required**

**1.** Compute return on total assets for Krispy Kreme and Tastykake for the two most recent years.
**2.** Separate the return on total assets computed in part 1 into its components for both companies and both years according to the formula in Exhibit C.9.
**3.** Which company has the higher total return on assets? The higher profit margin? The higher total asset turnover? What does this comparative analysis reveal?

### COMPARATIVE ANALYSIS

A1

**BTN C-3**   Kendra Wecker is the controller for Wildcat Company, which has numerous long-term investments in debt securities. Wildcat's investments are mainly in 10-year bonds. Wecker is preparing its year-end financial statements. In accounting for long-term debt securities, she knows that each long-term investment must be designated as a held-to-maturity or an available-for-sale security.

### ETHICS CHALLENGE

C2  P2  P3

Interest rates rose sharply this past year causing the portfolio's market value to substantially decline. The company does not intend to hold the bonds for the entire 10 years. Wecker also earns a bonus each year, which is computed as a percent of net income.

**Required**

1. Will Wecker's bonus depend in any way on the classification of the debt securities?
2. What criteria must Wecker use to classify the securities as held-to-maturity or available-for-sale?
3. Is there likely any company oversight of Wecker's classification of the securities?

## COMMUNICATING IN PRACTICE

C2  P4

**BTN C-4**    Assume that you are Jackson Company's accountant. Company owner Abel Terrio has reviewed the 2006 financial statements you prepared and questions the $6,000 loss reported on the sale of its investment in Blackhawk Co. common stock. Jackson acquired 50,000 shares of Blackhawk's common stock on December 31, 2004, at a cost of $500,000. This stock purchase represented a 40% interest in Blackhawk. The 2005 income statement reported that earnings from all investments were $126,000. On January 3, 2006, Jackson Company sold the Blackhawk stock for $575,000. Blackhawk did not pay any dividends during 2005 but reported a net income of $202,500 for that year. Terrio believes that because the Blackhawk stock purchase price was $500,000 and was sold for $575,000, the 2006 income statement should report a $75,000 gain on the sale.

**Required**

Draft a one-half page memorandum to Terrio explaining why the $6,000 loss on sale of Blackhawk stock is correctly reported.

## TAKING IT TO THE NET

C1  C2

mhhe.com/wild3e

**BTN C-5**    Access the September 6, 2002, 10-K filing (for year-end June 30, 2002) of **Microsoft** (MSFT) at www.sec.gov. Review footnote 4, "Cash and Short-term Investments."

**Required**

1. How does the total for cash and short-term investments held as of June 30, 2002, compare to the prior year–end amount?
2. Identify the five types of short-term investments held by Microsoft as of June 30, 2002.
3. What were Microsoft's gains and losses from cash and short-term investments sold in 2002?
4. Was the cost or market of the short-term investments higher as of June 30, 2002?

## TEAMWORK IN ACTION

C1  C2  C3  P1  P2  P3  P4

**BTN C-6**    Each team member is to become an expert on a specific classification of long-term investments. This expertise will be used to facilitate other teammates' understanding of the concepts and procedures relevent to the classification chosen.

1. Each team member must select an area for expertise by choosing one of the following classifications of long-term investments.
   a. Held-to-maturity debt securities
   b. Available-for-sale debt and equity securities
   c. Equity securities with significant influence
   d. Equity securities with controlling influence
2. Learning teams are to disburse and expert teams are to be formed. Expert teams are made up of those who select the same area of expertise. The instructor will identify the location where each expert team will meet.
3. Expert teams will collaborate to develop a presentation based on the following requirements. Students must write the presentation in a format they can show to their learning teams in part (4).

**Requirements for Expert Presentation**

   a. Write a transaction for the acquisition of this type of investment security. The transaction description is to include all necessary data to reflect the chosen classification.
   b. Prepare the journal entry to record the acquisition.
   [*Note:* The expert team on equity securities with controlling influence will substitute requirements (*d*) and (*e*) with a discussion of the reporting of these investments.]
   c. Identify information necessary to complete the end-of-period adjustment for this investment.

**d.** Assuming that this is the only investment owned, prepare any necessary year-end entries.

**e.** Present the relevant balance sheet section(s).

**4.** Re-form learning teams. In rotation, experts are to present to their teams the presentations they developed in part 3. Experts are to encourage and respond to questions.

---

**BTN C-7** Read the article "Accounting: Bringing the Future into Play" in the March 11, 2002, issue of *Business Week*. (This book's Website provides a free link.)

**BUSINESS WEEK ACTIVITY**

C2

mhhe.com/wild3e

**Required**

**1.** On what types of data do accountants focus? How does this compare with the data desired by investors?

**2.** Explain the phrase "marking to market."

**3.** What ideas have been proposed to allow marking to market that will also limit fraud by insiders?

**4.** How do accountants respond to the economists' argument that mark-to-market accounting will result in "asymmetrical" information for investors?

**5.** What is the best argument for mark-to-market accounting?

---

**BTN C-8** Bill and Ralph Cruz, of **TradeStation Group**, know it is important for their clients to understand the accounting rules for recognizing gains and losses on investments in securities. Several clients, with little experience in investing, recently expressed confusion in the difference between un-realized and realized gains and losses. They also expressed concern about the low yields on their cer-tificate of deposit (CD) investments and inquired about investment alternatives.

**ENTREPRENEURIAL DECISION**

C1  C2  P3

**Required**

**1.** Assume that you are an assistant to Ralph Cruz. He asks you to prepare a brief email to his busi-ness client Andy Iglesias of Iglesias Company, explaining the difference between unrealized and realized gains and losses on securities. Prepare this email.

**2.** If the client, Iglesias Company, purchases available-for-sale securities, will any unrealized gains or losses on those securities affect its income statement? Explain.

**3.** Cruz asks you to email another client, Gloria Perez, explaining the benefits of long-term invest-ments in stocks rather than CDs. Prepare this brief email.

---

**BTN C-9ᴬ** Assume that you are planning a spring break trip to Europe. Identify three locations where you can find exchange rates for the dollar relative to the Euro or other currencies.

**HITTING THE ROAD** C4

---

**BTN C-10** Grupo Bimbo, Krispy Kreme, and Tastykake are competitors in the global marketplace.

**GLOBAL DECISION**

A1

| Key Figure | Grupo Bimbo (millions of pesos) | | | Krispy Kreme | | Tastykake | |
|---|---|---|---|---|---|---|---|
| | Current Year | One Year Prior | Two Years Prior | Current Year | Prior Year | Current Year | Prior Year |
| Net income ........ | 1,002.7 | 1,682.0 | 2,004.9 | — | — | — | — |
| Total assets ......... | 31,718.6 | 23,781.3 | 25,035.1 | — | — | — | — |
| Net sales .......... | 41,373.3 | 34,968.1 | 32,007.8 | — | — | — | — |
| Profit margin ....... | ? | ? | — | 6.80% | 6.70% | 1.20% | 4.80% |
| Total asset turnover .. | ? | ? | — | 1.48 | 1.85 | 1.39 | 1.46 |

**Required**

**1.** Compute Grupo Bimbo's return on total assets for the most recent two years using the data shown.

**2.** Which of these three companies has the highest return on total assets? Profit margin? Total asset turnover?

# Glossary

**Absorption costing** Costing method that assigns both variable and fixed costs to products. *(p. 745)*

**Accelerated depreciation method** Method that produces larger depreciation charges in the early years of an asset's life and smaller charges in its later years. *(p. 316)*

**Account** Record within an accounting system in which increases and decreases are entered and stored in a specific asset, liability, equity, revenue, or expense. *(p. 49)*

**Account balance** Difference between total debits and total credits (including the beginning balance) for an account. *(p. 53)*

**Account form balance sheet** Balance sheet that lists assets on the left side and liabilities and equity on the right. *(p. 18)*

**Account payable** Liability created by buying goods or services on credit; backed by the buyer's general credit standing. *(p. 50)*

**Accounting** Information and measurement system that identifies, records, and communicates relevant information about a company's business activities. *(p. 4)*

**Accounting cycle** Recurring steps performed each accounting period, starting with analyzing transactions and continuing through the post-closing trial balance (or reversing entries). *(p. 109)*

**Accounting equation** Equality involving a company's assets, liabilities, and equity; Assets = Liabilities + Equity; also called *balance sheet equation*. *(p. 12)*

**Accounting information system** People, records, and methods that collect and process data from transactions and events, organize them in useful forms, and communicate results to decision makers. *(p. E-2)*

**Accounting period** Length of time covered by financial statements; also called *reporting period*. *(p. 92)*

**Accounts payable ledger** Subsidiary ledger listing individual creditor (supplier) accounts. *(p. E-7)*

**Accounting rate of return** Rate used to evaluate the acceptability of an investment; equals the after-tax periodic income from a project divided by the average investment in the asset; also called *rate of return on average investment*. *(p. 853)*

**Accounts receivable** Amounts due from customers for credit sales; backed by the customer's general credit standing. *(p. 278)*

**Accounts receivable ledger** Subsidiary ledger listing individual customer accounts. *(p. E-7)*

**Accounts receivable turnover** Measure of both the quality and liquidity of accounts receivable; indicates how often receivables are received and collected during the period; computed by dividing net sales by average accounts receivable. *(p. 292)*

**Accrual basis accounting** Accounting system that recognizes revenues when earned and expenses when incurred; the basis for GAAP. *(p. 93)*

**Accrued expenses** Costs incurred in a period that are both unpaid and unrecorded; adjusting entries for recording accrued expenses involve increasing expenses and increasing liabilities. *(p. 99)*

**Accrued revenues** Revenues earned in a period that are both unrecorded and not yet received in cash (or other assets); adjusting entries for recording accrued revenues involve increasing assets and increasing revenues. *(p. 101)*

**Accumulated depreciation** Cumulative sum of all depreciation expense recorded for an asset. *(p. 97)*

**Acid-test ratio** Ratio used to assess a company's ability to settle its current debts with its most liquid assets; defined as quick assets (cash, short-term investments, and current receivables) divided by current liabilities. *(p. 167)*

**Activity-based budgeting (ABB)** Budget system based on expected activities. *(p. 783)*

**Activity-based costing (ABC)** Cost allocation method that focuses on activities performed; traces costs to activities and then assigns them to cost objects. *(p. 700)*

**Activity cost pool** Temporary account that accumulates costs a company incurs to support an activity. *(p. 700)*

**Adjusted trial balance** List of accounts and balances prepared after period-end adjustments are recorded and posted. *(p. 103)*

**Adjusting entry** Journal entry at the end of an accounting period to bring an asset or liability account to its proper amount and update the related expense or revenue account. *(p. 95)*

**Aging of accounts receivable** Process of classifying accounts receivable by how long they are past due for purposes of estimating uncollectible accounts. *(p. 286)*

**Allowance for Doubtful Accounts** Contra asset account with a balance approximating uncollectible accounts receivable; also called *Allowance for Uncollectible Accounts*. *(p. 283)*

**Allowance method** Procedure that (a) estimates and matches bad debts expense with its sales for the period and/or (b) reports accounts receivable at estimated realizable value. *(p. 282)*

**Amortization** Process of allocating the cost of an intangible asset to expense over its estimated useful life. *(p. 326)*

**Annual financial statements** Financial statements covering a one-year period; often based on a calendar year, but any consecutive 12-month (or 52-week) period is acceptable. *(p. 93)*

**Annual report** Summary of a company's financial results for the year with its current financial condition and future plans; directed to external users of financial information. *(p. A-1)*

**Annuity** Series of equal payments at equal intervals. *(p. 418)*

**Appropriated retained earnings** Retained earnings separately reported to inform stockholders of funding needs. *(p. 461)*

**Assets** Resources a business owns or controls that are expected to provide current and future benefits to the business. *(p. 12)*

**Audit** Analysis and report of an organization's accounting system, its records, and its reports using various tests. *(p. 9)*

**Authorized stock** Total amount of stock that a corporation's charter authorizes it to issue. *(p. 443)*

**Available-for-sale (AFS) securities** Investments in debt and equity securities that are not classified as trading securities or held-to-maturity securities. *(p. C-6)*

**Average cost** See *weighted average. (p. 202)*

**Avoidable expense** Expense (or cost) that is relevant for decision making; expense that is not incurred if a department, product, or service is eliminated. *(p. 866)*

**Bad debts** Accounts of customers who do not pay what they have promised to pay; an expense of selling on credit; also called *uncollectible accounts. (p. 281)*

**Balance column account** Account with debit and credit columns for recording entries and another column for showing the balance of the account after each entry. *(p. 56)*

**Balance sheet** Financial statement that lists types and dollar amounts of assets, liabilities, and equity at a specific date. *(p. 17)*

**Balance sheet equation** (See *accounting equation.) (p. 12)*

**Bank reconciliation** Report that explains the difference between the book (company) balance of cash and the cash balance reported on the bank statement. *(p. 250)*

**Bank statement** Bank report on the depositor's beginning and ending cash balances, and a listing of its changes, for a period. *(p. 248)*

**Basic earnings per share** Net income less any preferred dividends and then divided by weighted-average common shares outstanding. *(p. 458)*

**Batch processing** Accumulating source documents for a period of time and then processing them all at once such as once a day, week, or month. *(p. E-17)*

**Bearer bonds** Bonds made payable to whoever holds them (the *bearer*); also called *unregistered bonds. (p. 398)*

**Benchmarking** Practice of comparing and analyzing company financial performance or position with other companies or standards. *(p. 542)*

**Betterments** Expenditures to make a plant asset more efficient or productive; also called *improvements. (p. 321)*

**Bond** Written promise to pay the bond's par (or face) value and interest at a stated contract rate; often issued in denominations of $1,000. *(p. 396)*

**Bond certificate** Document containing bond specifics such as issuer's name, bond par value, contract interest rate, and maturity date. *(p. 399)*

**Bond indenture** Contract between the bond issuer and the bondholders; identifies the parties' rights and obligations. *(p. 399)*

**Bookkeeping** (See *recordkeeping.) (p. 5)*

**Book value** Asset's acquisition costs less its accumulated depreciation (or depletion, or amortization); also sometimes used synonymously as the *carrying value* of an account. *(p. 98 & 315)*

**Book value per common share** Recorded amount of equity applicable to common shares divided by the number of common shares outstanding. *(p. 462)*

**Book value per preferred share** Equity applicable to preferred shares (equals its call price [or par value if it is not callable] plus any cumulative dividends in arrears) divided by the number of preferred shares outstanding. *(p. 462)*

**Break-even point** Output level at which sales equals fixed plus variable costs; where income equals zero. *(p. 744)*

**Break-even time (BET)** Time-based measurement used to evaluate the acceptability of an investment; equals the time expected to pass before the present value of the net cash flows from an investment equals its initial cost. *(p. 868)*

**Budget** Formal statement of future plans, usually expressed in monetary terms. *(p. 770)*

**Budget report** Report comparing actual results to planned objectives; sometimes used as a progress report. *(p. 808)*

**Budgetary control** Management use of budgets to monitor and control company operations. *(p. 808)*

**Budgeted balance sheet** Accounting report that presents predicted amounts of the company's assets, liabilities, and equity balances as of the end of the budget period. *(p. 782)*

**Budgeted income statement** Accounting report that presents predicted amounts of the company's revenues and expenses for the budget period. *(p. 782)*

**Budgeting** Process of planning future business actions and expressing them as formal plans. *(p. 770)*

**Business** An organization of one or more individuals selling products and/or services for profit. *(p. 10)*

**Business entity principle** Principle that requires a business to be accounted for separately from its owner(s) and from any other entity. *(p. 10)*

**Business segment** Part of a company that can be separately identified by the products or services that it provides or by the geographic markets that it serves; also called *segment. (p. 456)*

**C corporation** Corporation that does not qualify for nor elect to be treated as a proprietorship or partnership for income tax purposes and therefore is subject to income taxes; also called *C corp. (p. D-4)*

**Call price** Amount that must be paid to call and retire a callable preferred stock or a callable bond. *(p. 449)*

**Callable bonds** Bonds that give the issuer the option to retire them at a stated amount prior to maturity. *(p. 398)*

**Callable preferred stock** Preferred stock that the issuing corporation, at its option, may retire by paying the call price plus any dividends in arrears. *(p. 449)*

**Canceled checks** Checks that the bank has paid and deducted from the depositor's account. *(p. 249)*

**Capital budgeting** Process of analyzing alternative investments and deciding which assets to acquire or sell. *(p. 850)*

**Capital expenditures** Additional costs of plant assets that provide material benefits extending beyond the current period; also called *balance sheet expenditures. (p. 320)*

**Capital expenditures budget** Plan that lists dollar amounts to be both received from disposal of plant assets and spent to purchase plant assets. *(p. 779)*

**Capital leases** Long-term leases in which the lessor transfers substantially all risk and rewards of ownership to the lessee. *(p. 421)*

**Capital stock** General term referring to a corporation's stock used in obtaining capital (owner financing). *(p. 443)*

**Capitalize** Record the cost as part of a permanent account and allocate it over later periods. *(p. 320)*

**Carrying value of bonds** Net amount at which bonds are reported on the balance sheet; equals the par value of the bonds less any unamortized discount or plus any unamortized premium; also called *carrying amount* or *book value. (p. 401)*

**Cash** Includes currency, coins, and amounts on deposit in bank checking or savings accounts. *(p. 240)*

**Cash basis accounting** Accounting system that recognizes revenues when cash is received and records expenses when cash is paid. *(p. 93)*

**Cash budget** Plan that shows expected cash inflows and outflows during the budget period, including receipts from loans needed to maintain a minimum cash balance and repayments of such loans. *(p. 780)*

**Cash disbursements journal** Special journal normally used to record all payments of cash; also called *cash payments journal. (p. E-14)*

**Cash discount** Reduction in the price of merchandise granted by a seller to a buyer when payment is made within the discount period. *(p. 155)*

**Cash equivalents** Short-term, investment assets that are readily convertible to a known cash amount or sufficiently close to their maturity date (usually within 90 days) so that market value is not sensitive to interest rate changes. *(p. 240)*

**Cash flow on total assets** Ratio of operating cash flows to average total assets; not sensitive to income recognition and measurement; partly reflects earnings quality. *(p. 510)*

**Cash Over and Short** Income statement account used to record cash overages and cash shortages arising from errors in cash receipts or payments. *(p. 241)*

**Cash receipts journal** Special journal normally used to record all receipts of cash. *(p. E-11)*

**Change in an accounting estimate** Change in an accounting estimate that results from new information, subsequent developments, or improved judgment that impacts current and future periods. *(p. 319 & 461)*

**Chart of accounts** List of accounts used by a company; includes an identification number for each account. *(p. 52)*

**Check** Document signed by a depositor instructing the bank to pay a specified amount to a designated recipient. *(p. 247)*

**Check register** Another name for a cash disbursements journal when the journal has a column for check numbers. *(p. 258 & E-15)*

**Classified balance sheet** Balance sheet that presents assets and liabilities in relevant subgroups, including current and noncurrent classifications. *(p. 110)*

**Clock card** Source document used to record the number of hours an employee works and to determine the total labor cost for each pay period. *(p. 625)*

**Closing entries** Entries recorded at the end of each accounting period to transfer end-of-period balances in revenue, gain, expense, loss, and dividend accounts to the retained earnings account. *(p. 106)*

**Closing process** Necessary end-of-period steps to prepare the accounts for recording the transactions of the next period. *(p. 104)*

**Columnar journal** Journal with more than one column. *(p. E-8)*

**Common stock** Corporation's basic ownership share; also generically called *capital stock. (p. 11, 51 & 442)*

**Common-size financial statement** Statement that expresses each amount as a percent of a base amount. In the balance sheet, total assets is usually the base and is expressed as 100%. In the income statement, net sales is usually the base. *(p. 547)*

**Comparative financial statement** Statement with data for two or more successive periods placed in side-by-side columns, often with changes shown in dollar amounts and percents. *(p. 543)*

**Compatibility principle** Information system principle that requires an accounting system to conform with a company's activities, personnel, and structure. *(p. E-3)*

**Complex capital structure** Capital structure that includes outstanding rights or options to purchase common stock, or securities that are convertible into common stock. *(p. 460)*

**Composite unit** Generic unit consisting of a specific number of units of each product; unit comprised in proportion to the expected sales mix of its products. *(p. 750)*

**Compound journal entry** Journal entry that affects at least three accounts. *(p. 59)*

**Comprehensive income** Net change in equity for a period, excluding owner investments and distributions. *(p. C-10)*

**Computer hardware** Physical equipment in a computerized accounting information system. *(p. E-17)*

**Computer network** Linkage giving different users and different computers access to common databases and programs. *(p. E-17)*

**Computer software** Programs that direct operations of computer hardware. *(p. E-16)*

**Conservatism principle** Principle that prescribes the less optimistic estimate when two estimates are about equally likely. *(p. 206)*

**Consignee** Receiver of goods owned by another who holds them for purposes of selling them for the owner. *(p. 196)*

**Consignor** Owner of goods who ships them to another party who will sell them for the owner. *(p. 196)*

**Consistency principle** Principle that prescribes use of the same accounting method(s) over time so that financial statements are comparable across periods. *(p. 204)*

**Consolidated financial statements** Financial statements that show all (combined) activities under the parent's control, including those of any subsidiaries. *(p. C-9)*

**Continuous budgeting** Practice of preparing budgets for a selected number of future periods and revising those budgets as each period is completed. *(p. 772)*

**Continuous improvement** Concept requiring every manager and employee continually to look to improve operations. *(p. 584)*

**Contingent liability** Obligation to make a future payment if, and only if, an uncertain future event occurs. *(p. 364)*

**Contra account** Account linked with another account and having an opposite normal balance; reported as a subtraction from the other account's balance. *(p. 97)*

**Contract rate** Interest rate specified in a bond indenture (or note); multiplied by the par value to determine the interest paid each period; also called *coupon rate, stated rate,* or *nominal rate. (p. 400)*

**Contributed capital** Total amount of cash and other assets received from stockholders in exchange for stock; also called *paid-in capital.* (p. 13 & 444)

**Contributed capital in excess of par value** Difference between the par value of stock and its issue price when issued at a price above par. (p. 444)

**Contribution margin** Sales revenue less total variable costs. (p. 595)

**Contribution margin income statement** Income statement that separates variable and fixed costs; highlights the contribution margin, which is sales less variable expenses. (p. 744)

**Contribution margin per unit** Amount that the sale of one unit contributes toward recovering fixed costs and earning profit; defined as sales price per unit minus variable expense per unit. (p. 744)

**Contribution margin ratio** Product's contribution margin divided by its sale price. (p. 595 & 744)

**Control** Process of monitoring planning decisions and evaluating the organization's activities and employees. (p. 581)

**Control principle** Information system principle that requires an accounting system to aid managers in controlling and monitoring business activities. (p. E-2)

**Controllable costs** Costs that a manager has the power to control or at least strongly influence. (p. 586 & 711)

**Controllable variance** Combination of both overhead spending variances (variable and fixed) and the variable overhead efficiency variance. (p. 821)

**Controlling account** General ledger account, the balance of which (after posting) equals the sum of the balances in its related subsidiary ledger. (p. E-7)

**Conversion costs** Expenditures incurred in converting raw materials to finished goods; includes direct labor costs and overhead costs. (p. 591)

**Convertible bonds** Bonds that bondholders can exchange for a set number of the issuer's shares. (p. 398)

**Convertible preferred stock** Preferred stock with an option to exchange it for common stock at a specified rate. (p. 449)

**Copyright** Right giving the owner the exclusive privilege to publish and sell musical, literary, or artistic work during the creator's life plus 70 years. (p. 327)

**Corporation** Business that is a separate legal entity under state or federal laws with owners called *shareholders* or *stockholders.* (p. 11 & 440)

**Cost** All normal and reasonable expenditures necessary to get an asset in place and ready for its intended use. (p. 311)

**Cost accounting system** Accounting system for manufacturing activities based on the perpetual inventory system. (p. 620)

**Cost-benefit principle** Information system principle that requires the benefits from an activity in an accounting system to outweigh the costs of that activity. (p. E-3)

**Cost center** Department that incurs costs but generates no revenues; common example is the accounting or legal department. (p. 704)

**Cost driver** Variable that causes an activity's cost to go up or down; a causal factor. (p. 700)

**Cost object** Product, process, department, or customer to which costs are assigned. (p. 585)

**Cost of goods available for sale** Consists of beginning inventory plus net purchases of a period. (p. 153)

**Cost of goods sold** Cost of inventory sold to customers during a period; also called *cost of sales.* (p. 153)

**Cost principle** Accounting principle that prescribes financial statement information to be based on actual costs incurred in business transactions. (p. 9)

**Cost variance** Difference between the actual incurred cost and the standard cost. (p. 815)

**Cost-volume-profit (CVP) analysis** Planning method that includes predicting the volume of activity, the costs incurred, sales earned, and profits received. (p. 738)

**Coupon bonds** Bonds with interest coupons attached to their certificates; bondholders detach coupons when they mature and present them to a bank or broker for collection. (p. 398)

**Credit** Recorded on the right side; an entry that decreases asset and expense accounts, and increases liability, revenue, and most equity accounts; abbreviated Cr. (p. 53)

**Credit memorandum** Notification that the sender has credited the recipient's account in the sender's records. (p. 161)

**Credit period** Time period that can pass before a customer's payment is due. (p. 155)

**Credit terms** Description of the amounts and timing of payments that a buyer (debtor) agrees to make in the future. (p. 155)

**Creditors** Individuals or organizations entitled to receive payments. (p. 50)

**Cumulative preferred stock** Preferred stock on which undeclared dividends accumulate until paid; common stockholders cannot receive dividends until cumulative dividends are paid. (p. 447)

**Current assets** Cash and other assets expected to be sold, collected, or used within one year or the company's operating cycle, whichever is longer. (p. 112)

**Current liabilities** Obligations due to be paid or settled within one year or the company's operating cycle, whichever is longer. (p. 112 & 353)

**Current portion of long-term debt** Portion of long-term debt due within one year or the operating cycle, whichever is longer; reported under current liabilities. (p. 361)

**Current ratio** Ratio used to evaluate a company's ability to pay its short-term obligations, calculated by dividing current assets by current liabilities. (p. 113)

**Curvilinear cost** Cost that changes with volume but not at a constant rate. (p. 740)

**Customer orientation** Company position that its managers and employees be in tune with the changing wants and needs of consumers. (p. 583)

**CVP chart** Graphic representation of cost-volume-profit relations. (p. 745)

**Date of declaration** Date the directors vote to pay a dividend. *(p. 450)*

**Date of payment** Date the corporation makes the dividend payment. *(p. 450)*

**Date of record** Date directors specify for identifying stockholders to receive dividends. *(p. 450)*

**Days' sales in inventory** Estimate of number of days needed to convert inventory into receivables or cash; equals ending inventory divided by cost of goods sold and then multiplied by 365; also called *days' stock on hand.* (p. 208)

**Days' sales uncollected** Measure of the liquidity of receivables computed by dividing the current balance of receivables by the annual credit (or net) sales and then multiplying by 365; also called *days' sales in receivables.* (p. 253)

**Debit** Recorded on the left side; an entry that increases asset and expense accounts, and decreases liability, revenue, and most equity accounts; abbreviated Dr. *(p. 53)*

**Debit memorandum** Notification that the sender has debited the recipient's account in the sender's records. *(p. 156)*

**Debt ratio** Ratio of total liabilities to total assets; used to reflect risk associated with a company's debts. *(p. 67)*

**Debtors** Individuals or organizations that owe money. *(p. 49)*

**Declining-balance method** Method that determines depreciation charge for the period by multiplying a depreciation rate (often twice the straight-line rate) by the asset's beginning-period book value. *(p. 316)*

**Deferred income tax liability** Corporation income taxes that are deferred until future years because of temporary differences between GAAP and tax rules. *(p. 375)*

**Degree of operating leverage (DOL)** Ratio of contribution margin divided by pretax income; used to assess the effect on income of changes in sales. *(p. 751)*

**Departmental accounting system** Accounting system that provides information useful in evaluating the profitability or cost effectiveness of a department. *(p. 703)*

**Departmental contribution to overhead** Amount by which a department's revenues exceed its direct expenses. *(p. 710)*

**Depletion** Process of allocating the cost of natural resources to periods when they are consumed and sold. *(p. 325)*

**Deposit ticket** Lists items such as currency, coins, and checks deposited and their corresponding dollar amounts. *(p. 247)*

**Deposits in transit** Deposits recorded by the company but not yet recorded by its bank. *(p. 250)*

**Depreciable cost** Cost of a plant asset less its salvage value. *(p. 314)*

**Depreciation** Expense created by allocating the cost of plant and equipment to periods in which they are used; represents the expense of using the asset. *(p. 97 & 313)*

**Diluted earnings per share** Earnings per share calculation that requires dilutive securities be added to the denominator of the basic EPS calculation. *(p. 460)*

**Dilutive securities** Securities having the potential to increase common shares outstanding; examples are options, rights, convertible bonds, and convertible preferred stock. *(p. 460)*

**Direct costs** Costs incurred for the benefit of one specific cost object. *(p. 585)*

**Direct expenses** Expenses traced to a specific department (object) that are incurred for the sole benefit of that department. *(p. 705)*

**Direct labor** Efforts of employees who physically convert materials to finished product. *(p. 591)*

**Direct labor costs** Wages and salaries for direct labor that are separately and readily traced through the production process to finished goods. *(p. 591)*

**Direct material** Raw material that physically becomes part of the product and is clearly identified with specific products or batches of product. *(p. 590)*

**Direct material costs** Expenditures for direct material that are separately and readily traced through the production process to finished goods. *(p. 590)*

**Direct method** Presentation of net cash from operating activities for the statement of cash flows that lists major operating cash receipts less major operating cash payments. *(p. 498)*

**Direct write-off method** Method that records the loss from an uncollectible account receivable at the time it is determined to be uncollectible; no attempt is made to estimate bad debts. *(p. 282)*

**Discount on bonds payable** Difference between a bond's par value and its lower issue price or carrying value; occurs when the contract rate is less than the market rate. *(p. 400)*

**Discount on note payable** Difference between the face value of a note payable and the (lesser) amount borrowed; reflects the added interest to be paid on the note over its life.

**Discount on stock** Difference between the par value of stock and its issue price when issued at a price below par value. *(p. 445)*

**Discount period** Time period in which a cash discount is available and the buyer can make a reduced payment. *(p. 155)*

**Discount rate** Expected rate of return on investments; also called *cost of capital, hurdle rate,* or *required rate of return.* (p. B-2)

**Discounts lost** Expenses resulting from not taking advantage of cash discounts on purchases. *(p. 259)*

**Dividend in arrears** Unpaid dividend on cumulative preferred stock; must be paid before any regular dividends on preferred stock and before any dividends on common stock. *(p. 448)*

**Dividend yield** Ratio of the annual amount of cash dividends distributed to common shareholders relative to the common stock's market value (price). *(p. 463)*

**Dividends** Corporation's distributions of assets to its owners. *(p. 13, 51 & 450)*

**Double-declining-balance (DDB) depreciation** Depreciation equals beginning book value multiplied by 2 times the straight-line rate. *(p. 316)*

**Double-entry accounting** Accounting system in which each transaction affects at least two accounts and has at least one debit and one credit. *(p. 53)*

**Double taxation** Corporate income is taxed and then its later distribution through dividends is normally taxed again for shareholders. *(p. 11)*

**Earnings** (See *net income.*) *(p. 13)*

**Earnings per share (EPS)** Amount of income earned by each share of a company's outstanding common stock; also called *net income per share.* (p. 458)

**Effective interest method** Allocates interest expense over the bond life to yield a constant rate of interest; interest expense for a period is found by multiplying the balance of the liability at the beginning of the period by the bond market rate at issuance; also called *interest method. (p. 419)*

**Efficiency** Company's productivity in using its assets; usually measured relative to how much revenue a certain level of assets generates. *(p. 541)*

**Efficiency variance** Difference between the actual quantity of an input and the standard quantity of that input. *(p. 820)*

**Electronic funds transfer (EFT)** Use of electronic communication to transfer cash from one party to another. *(p. 248)*

**Employee benefits** Additional compensation paid to or on behalf of employees, such as premiums for medical, dental, life, and disability insurance, and contributions to pension plans. *(p. 361)*

**Employee earnings report** Record of an employee's net pay, gross pay, deductions, and year-to-date payroll information. *(p. 372)*

**Enterprise resource planning (ERP) software** Programs that manage a company's vital operations, which range from order taking to production to accounting. *(p. E-17)*

**Entity** Organization that, for accounting purposes, is separate from other organizations and individuals. *(p. 10)*

**EOM** Abbreviation for *end of month;* used to describe credit terms for credit transactions. *(p. 155)*

**Equity** Owner's claim on the assets of a business; equals the residual interest in an entity's assets after deducting liabilities; also called *net assets. (p. 12)*

**Equity method** Accounting method used for long-term investments when the investor has "significant influence" over the investee. *(p. C-8)*

**Equity ratio** Portion of total assets provided by equity, computed as total equity divided by total assets. *(p. 555)*

**Equity securities with controlling influence** Long-term investment when the investor is able to exert controlling influence over the investee; investors owning 50 percent or more of voting stock are presumed to exert controlling influence. *(p. C-9)*

**Equity securities with significant influence** Long-term investment when the investor is able to exert significant influence over the investee; investors owning 20 percent or more (but less than 50 percent) of voting stock are presumed to exert significant influence. *(p. C-7)*

**Equivalent units of production (EUP)** Number of units that would be completed if all effort during a period had been applied to units that were started and finished. *(p. 664)*

**Estimated liability** Obligation of an uncertain amount that can be reasonably estimated. *(p. 361)*

**Estimated line of cost behavior** Line drawn on a graph to visually fit the relation between cost and sales. *(p. 742)*

**Ethics** Codes of conduct by which actions are judged as right or wrong, fair or unfair, honest or dishonest. *(p. 8)*

**Events** Happenings that both affect an organization's financial position and can be reliably measured. *(p. 13)*

**Expanded accounting equation** Assets = Liabilities + Equity; Equity equals [Contributed Capital + Retained Earnings + Revenues − Expenses] for a corporation where Dividends are subtracted from Retained Earnings. *(p. 13)*

**Expenses** Outflows or using up of assets as part of operations of a business to generate sales. *(p. 13)*

**External transactions** Exchanges of economic value between one entity and another entity. *(p. 13)*

**External users** Persons using accounting information who are not directly involved in running the organization. *(p. 5)*

**Extraordinary gains or losses** Gains or losses reported separately from continuing operations because they are both unusual and infrequent. *(p. 456)*

**Extraordinary repairs** Major repairs that extend the useful life of a plant asset beyond prior expectations; treated as a capital expenditure. *(p. 321)*

**Factory overhead** Factory activities supporting the production process that are not direct material or direct labor; also called *overhead* and *manufacturing overhead. (p. 591)*

**Factory overhead costs** Expenditures for factory overhead that cannot be separately or readily traced to finished goods; also called *overhead costs. (p. 591)*

**Favorable variance** Difference in actual revenues or expenses from the budgeted amount that contributes to a higher income. *(p. 810)*

**Federal depository bank** Bank authorized to accept deposits of amounts payable to the federal government. *(p. 370)*

**Federal Insurance Contributions Act (FICA) Taxes** Taxes assessed on both employers and employees; for Social Security and Medicare programs. *(p. 358)*

**Federal Unemployment Taxes (FUTA)** Payroll taxes on employers assessed by the federal government to support its unemployment insurance program. *(p. 360)*

**Financial accounting** Area of accounting mainly aimed at serving external users. *(p. 5)*

**Financial Accounting Standards Board (FASB)** Independent group of full-time members responsible for setting accounting rules. *(p. 9)*

**Financial leverage** Earning a higher return on equity by paying dividends on preferred stock or interest on debt at a rate lower than the return earned with the assets from issuing preferred stock or debt; also called *trading on the equity. (p. 449)*

**Financial reporting** Process of communicating information relevant to investors, creditors, and others in making investment, credit, and business decisions. *(p. 541)*

**Financial statement analysis** Application of analytical tools to general-purpose financial statements and related data for making business decisions. *(p. 540)*

**Financial statements** Includes the balance sheet, income statement, statement of stockholders' equity, and statement of cash flows. *(p. 17)*

**Financing activities** Transactions with owners and creditors that include obtaining cash from issuing long-term debt, repaying amounts borrowed, and obtaining cash from or distributing cash to owners. *(p. 494)*

**Finished goods inventory** Account that controls the finished goods files, which acts as a subsidiary ledger (of the Inventory account) in which the costs of finished goods that are ready for sale are recorded. *(p. 589 & 623)*

**First-in, first-out (FIFO)** Method to assign cost to inventory that assumes items are sold in the order acquired; earliest items purchased are the first sold. *(p. 201)*

**Fiscal year** Consecutive 12-month (or 52-week) period chosen as the organization's annual accounting period. *(p. 93)*

**Fixed budget** Planning budget based on a single predicted amount of volume; unsuitable for evaluations if the actual volume differs from predicted volume. *(p. 809)*

**Fixed budget performance report** Report that compares actual revenues and costs with fixed budgeted amounts and identifies the differences as favorable or unfavorable variances. *(p. 809)*

**Fixed cost** Cost that does not change with changes in the volume of activity. *(p. 585)*

**Flexible budget** Budget prepared (using actual volume) once a period is complete that helps managers evaluate past performance; uses fixed and variable costs in determining total costs. *(p. 810)*

**Flexible budget performance report** Report that compares actual revenues and costs with their variable budgeted amounts based on actual sales volume (or other level of activity) and identifies the differences as variances. *(p. 812)*

**Flexibility principle** Information system principle that requires an accounting system be able to adapt to changes in the company, its operations, and needs of decision makers. *(p. E-3)*

**FOB** Abbreviation for *free on board;* the point when ownership of goods passes to the buyer; *FOB shipping point* (or *factory*) means the buyer pays shipping costs and accepts ownership of goods when the seller transfers goods to carrier; *FOB destination* means the seller pays shipping costs and buyer accepts ownership of goods at the buyer's place of business. *(p. 157)*

**Foreign exchange rate** Price of one currency stated in terms of another currency. *(p. C-15)*

**Form 940** IRS form used to report an employer's federal unemployment taxes (FUTA) on an annual filing basis. *(p. 370)*

**Form 941** IRS form filed to report FICA taxes owed and remitted. *(p. 368)*

**Form 10-K (or 10-KSB)** Annual report form filed with SEC by businesses (small businesses) with publicly-traded securities. *(p. A-1)*

**Form W-2** Annual report by an employer to each employee showing the employee's wages subject to FICA and federal income taxes along with amounts withheld. *(p. 370)*

**Form W-4** Withholding allowance certificate, filed with the employer, identifying the number of withholding allowances claimed. *(p. 372)*

**Franchises** Privileges granted by a company or government to sell a product or service under specified conditions. *(p. 328)*

**Full-disclosure principle** Principle that prescribes financial statements (including notes) to report all relevant information about an entity's operations and financial condition. *(p. 290)*

**GAPP** (See *generally accepted accounting principles.*) *(p. 9)*

**General accounting system** Accounting system for manufacturing activities based on the *periodic* inventory system. *(p. 620)*

**General and administrative expense budget** Plan that shows predicted operating expenses not included in the selling expenses budget. *(p. 778)*

**General and administrative expenses** Expenses that support the operating activities of a business. *(p. 165)*

**General journal** All-purpose journal for recording the debits and credits of transactions and events. *(p. 54 & E-6)*

**General ledger** (See *ledger.*) *(p. 49)*

**General partner** Partner who assumes unlimited liability for the debts of the partnership; responsible for partnership management. *(p. D-3)*

**General partnership** Partnership in which all partners have mutual agency and unlimited liability for partnership debts. *(p. D-3)*

**Generally accepted accounting principles (GAAP)** Rules that specify acceptable accounting practices. *(p. 9)*

**Generally accepted auditing standards (GAAS)** Rules that specify acceptable auditing practices. *(p. 5 & 9)*

**General-purpose financial statements** Statements published periodically for use by a variety of interested parties; includes the income statement, balance sheet, statement of stockholders' equity (or statement of retained earnings), statement of cash flows, and notes to these statements. *(p. 541)*

**Going-concern principle** Principle that requires financial statements to reflect the assumption that the business will continue operating. *(p. 10)*

**Goods in process inventory** Account in which costs are accumulated for products that are in the process of being produced but are not yet complete; also called *work in process inventory.* *(p. 589 & 622)*

**Goodwill** Amount by which a company's (or a segment's) value exceeds the value of its individual assets less its liabilities. *(p. 328)*

**Gross margin** (See *gross profit.*) *(p. 153)*

**Gross margin ratio** Gross margin (net sales minus cost of goods sold) divided by net sales; also called *gross profit ratio.* *(p. 167)*

**Gross method** Method of recording purchases at the full invoice price without deducting any cash discounts. *(p. 259)*

**Gross pay** Total compensation earned by an employee. *(p. 357)*

**Gross profit** Net sales minus cost of goods sold; also called *gross margin.* *(p. 153)*

**Gross profit method** Procedure to estimate inventory when the past gross profit rate is used to estimate cost of goods sold, which is then subtracted from the cost of goods available for sale. *(p. 218)*

**Held-to-maturity (HTM) securities** Debt securities that a company has the intent and ability to hold until they mature. *(p. C-6)*

**High-low method** Procedure that yields an estimated line of cost behavior by graphically connecting costs associated with the highest and lowest sales volume. *(p. 742)*

**Horizontal analysis** Comparison of a company's financial condition and performance across time. *(p. 542)*

**Hurdle rate** Minimum acceptable rate of return (set by management) for an investment. *(p. 858)*

**Impairment** Diminishment of an asset value. *(p. 327)*

**Imprest system** Method to account for petty cash; maintains a constant balance in the fund, which equals cash plus petty cash receipts. *(p. 244)*

**Inadequacy** Condition in which the capacity of plant assets is too small to meet the company's production demands. *(p. 313)*

**Income** (See *net income*.) *(p. 13)*

**Income statement** Financial statement that subtracts expenses from revenues to yield a net income or loss over a specified period of time; also includes any gains or losses. *(p. 17)*

**Income Summary** Temporary account used only in the closing process to which the balances of revenue and expense accounts (including any gains or losses) are transferred; its balance is transferred to the retained earnings account. *(p. 106)*

**Incremental cost** Additional cost incurred only if a company pursues a specific course of action. *(p. 862)*

**Indefinite useful life** Asset life that is not limited by legal, regulatory, contractual, competitive, economic, or other factors. *(p. 326)*

**Indirect costs** Costs incurred for the benefit of more than one cost object. *(p. 585)*

**Indirect expenses** Expenses incurred for the joint benefit of more than one department (or cost object). *(p. 705)*

**Indirect labor** Efforts of production employees who do not work specifically on converting direct materials into finished products and who are not clearly identified with specific units or batches of product. *(p. 591)*

**Indirect material** Material used to support the production process but not clearly identified with products or batches of product. *(p. 588)*

**Indirect method** Presentation that reports net income and then adjusts it by adding and subtracting items to yield net cash from operating activities on the statement of cash flows. *(p. 498)*

**Information processor** Component of an accounting system that interprets, transforms, and summarizes information for use in analysis and reporting. *(p. E-4)*

**Information storage** Component of an accounting system that keeps data in a form accessible to information processors. *(p. E-4)*

**Infrequent gain or loss** Gain or loss not expected to recur given the operating environment of the business. *(p. 456)*

**Input device** Means of capturing information from source documents that enables its transfer to information processors. *(p. E-4)*

**Installment note** Liability requiring a series of periodic payments to the lender. *(p. 409)*

**Intangible assets** Long-term assets (resources) used to produce or sell products or services; usually lack physical form and have uncertain benefits. *(p. 112 & 326)*

**Interest** Charge for using money (or other assets) loaned from one entity to another. *(p. 288)*

**Interim financial statements** Financial statements covering periods of less than one year; usually based on one-, three-, or six-month periods. *(p. 93 & 217)*

**Internal controls** or **Internal control system** All policies and procedures used to protect assets, ensure reliable accounting, promote efficient operations, and urge adherence to company policies. *(p. 236 & E-2)*

**Internal rate of return (IRR)** Rate used to evaluate the acceptability of an investment; equals the rate that yields a net present value of zero for an investment. *(p. 857)*

**Internal transactions** Activities within an organization that can affect the accounting equation. *(p. 13)*

**Internal users** Persons using accounting information who are directly involved in managing the organization. *(p. 6)*

**International Accounting Standards Board (IASB)** Group that identifies preferred accounting practices and encourages global acceptance; issues International Financial Reporting Standards (IFRS). *(p. 9)*

**Inventory** Goods a company owns and expects to sell in its normal operations. *(p. 153)*

**Inventory turnover** Number of times a company's average inventory is sold during a period; computed by dividing cost of goods sold by average inventory; also called *merchandise turnover*. *(p. 207)*

**Investing activities** Transactions that involve purchasing and selling of long-term assets, includes making and collecting notes receivable and investments in other than cash equivalents. *(p. 494)*

**Investment center** Center of which a manager is responsible for revenues, costs, and asset investments. *(p. 715)*

**Investment center return on total assets** Center net income divided by average total assets for the center. *(p. 715)*

**Invoice** Itemized record of goods prepared by the vendor that lists the customer's name, items sold, sales prices, and terms of sale. *(p. 256)*

**Invoice approval** Document containing a checklist of steps necessary for approving the recording and payment of an invoice; also called *check authorization*. *(p. 257)*

**Job** Production of a customized product or service. *(p. 620)*

**Job cost sheet** Separate record maintained for each job. *(p. 622)*

**Job lot** Production of more than one unit of a customized product or service. *(p. 621)*

**Job order cost accounting system** Cost accounting system to determine the cost of producing each job or job lot. *(p. 622 & 659)*

**Job order manufacturing** Production of special-order products; also called *customized production*. *(p. 620)*

**Joint cost** Cost incurred to produce or purchase two or more products at the same time. *(p. 714)*

**Journal** Record in which transactions are entered before they are posted to ledger accounts; also called *book of original entry*. *(p. 54)*

**Journalizing** Process of recording transactions in a journal. *(p. 54)*

**Just-in-time (JIT) manufacturing** Process of acquiring or producing inventory only when needed. *(p. 584)*

**Known liabilities** Obligations of a company with little uncertainty; set by agreements, contracts, or laws; also called *definitely determinable liabilities*. *(p. 354)*

**Land improvements** Assets that increase the benefits of land, have a limited useful life, and are depreciated. *(p. 312)*

**Large stock dividend** Stock dividend that is more than 25% of the previously outstanding shares. *(p. 451)*

**Last-in, first-out (LIFO)** Method to assign cost to inventory that assumes costs for the most recent items purchased are sold first and charged to cost of goods sold. *(p. 201)*

**Lean business model** Practice of eliminating waste while meeting customer needs and yielding positive company returns. *(p. 584)*

**Lease** Contract specifying the rental of property. *(p. 328 & 421)*

**Leasehold** Rights the lessor grants to the lessee under the terms of a lease. *(p. 328)*

**Leasehold improvements** Alterations or improvements to leased property such as partitions and storefronts. *(p. 328)*

**Least-squares regression** Statistical method for deriving an estimated line of cost behavior that is more precise than the high-low method and the scatter diagram. *(p. 743)*

**Ledger** Record containing all accounts (with amounts) for a business; also called *general ledger*. *(p. 49)*

**Lessee** Party to a lease who secures the right to possess and use the property from another party (the lessor). *(p. 328)*

**Lessor** Party to a lease who grants another party (the lessee) the right to possess and use its property. *(p. 328)*

**Liabilities** Creditors' claims on an organization's assets; involves a probable future payment of assets, products, or services that a company is obligated to make due to past transactions or events. *(p. 12)*

**Licenses** (See *franchises*.) *(p. 328)*

**Limited liability** Owner can lose no more than the amount invested. *(p. 11)*

**Limited liability company** Organization form that combines select features of a corporation and a limited partnership; provides limited liability to its members (owners), is free of business tax, and allows members to actively participate in management. *(p. D-4)*

**Limited liability partnership** Partnership in which a partner is not personally liable for malpractice or negligence unless that partner is responsible for providing the service that resulted in the claim. *(p. D-3)*

**Limited partners** Partners who have no personal liability for partnership debts beyond the amounts they invested in the partnership. *(p. D-3)*

**Limited partnership** Partnership that has two classes of partners, limited partners and general partners. *(p. D-3)*

**Liquid assets** Resources such as cash that are easily converted into other assets or used to pay for goods, services, or liabilities. *(p. 240)*

**Liquidating cash dividend** Distribution of assets that returns part of the original investment to stockholders; deducted from contributed capital accounts. *(p. 451)*

**Liquidation** Process of going out of business; involves selling assets, paying liabilities, and distributing remainder to owners. *(p. 867 & D-11)*

**Liquidity** Availability of resources to meet short-term cash requirements. *(p. 240 & 541)*

**List price** Catalog (full) price of an item before any trade discount is deducted. *(p. 154)*

**Long-term investments** Long-term assets not used in operating activities such as notes receivable and investments in stocks and bonds. *(p. 112 & C-2)*

**Long-term liabilities** Obligations not due to be paid within one year or the operating cycle, whichever is longer. *(p. 112 & 353)*

**Lower of cost or market (LCM)** Required method to report inventory at market replacement cost when that market cost is lower than recorded cost. *(p. 205)*

**Maker of the note** Entity who signs a note and promises to pay it at maturity. *(p. 288)*

**Management by exception** Management process to focus on significant variances and give less attention to areas where performance is close to the standard. *(p. 824)*

**Managerial accounting** Area of accounting mainly aimed at serving the decision-making needs of internal users; also called *management accounting*. *(p. 6 & 580)*

**Manufacturer** Company that uses labor and operating assets to convert raw materials to finished goods. *(p. 13)*

**Manufacturing budget** Plan that shows the predicted costs for direct materials, direct labor, and overhead to be incurred in manufacturing units in the production budget. *(p. 789)*

**Manufacturing statement** Report that summarizes the types and amounts of costs incurred in a company's production process for a period; also called *cost of goods manufacturing statement*. *(p. 593)*

**Margin of safety** Excess of expected sales over the level of break-even sales. *(p. 748)*

**Market prospects** Expectations (both good and bad) about a company's future performance as assessed by users and other interested parties. *(p. 541)*

**Market rate** Interest rate that borrowers are willing to pay and lenders are willing to accept for a specific lending agreement given the borrowers' risk level. *(p. 400)*

**Market value per share** Price at which stock is bought or sold. *(p. 443)*

**Master budget** Comprehensive business plan that includes specific plans for expected sales, product units to be produced, merchandise (or materials) to be purchased, expenses to be incurred, plant assets to be purchased, and amounts of cash to be borrowed or loans to be repaid, as well as a budgeted income statement and balance sheet. *(p. 774)*

**Matching principle** Prescribes expenses to be reported in the same period as the revenues that were earned as a result of the expenses. *(p. 94 & 282)*

**Materiality** Prescribes that accounting for items that significantly impact financial statement and any inferences from them adhere strictly to GAAP. *(p. 282)*

**Materials consumption report** Document that summarizes the materials a department uses during a reporting period; replaces materials requisitions. *(p. 661)*

**Materials ledger card** Perpetual record updated each time units are purchased or issued for production use. *(p. 624)*

**Materials requisition** Source document production managers use to request materials for production; used to assign materials costs to specific jobs or overhead. *(p. 624)*

**Maturity date of a note** Date when a note's principal and interest are due. *(p. 288)*

**Merchandise** (See *merchandise inventory*.) *(p. 152)*

**Merchandise inventory** Goods that a company owns and expects to sell to customers; also called *merchandise* or *inventory*. *(p. 153)*

**Merchandise purchases budget** Plan that shows the units or costs of merchandise to be purchased by a merchandising company during the budget period. *(p. 777)*

**Merchandiser** Entity that earns net income by buying and selling merchandise. *(p. 152)*

**Merit rating** Rating assigned to an employer by a state based on the employer's record of employment. *(p. 360)*

**Minimum legal capital** Amount of assets defined by law that stockholders must (potentially) invest in a corporation; usually defined as par value of the stock; intended to protect creditors. *(p. 443)*

**Mixed cost** Cost that behaves like a combination of fixed and variable costs. *(p. 739)*

**Modified Accelerated Cost Recovery System (MACRS)** Depreciation system required by federal income tax law. *(p. 318)*

**Monetary unit principle** Principle that assumes transactions and events can be expressed in money units. *(p. 10)*

**Mortgage** Legal loan agreement that protects a lender by giving the lender the right to be paid from the cash proceeds from the sale of a borrower's assets identified in the mortgage. *(p. 412)*

**Multinational** Company that operates in several countries. *(p. C-15)*

**Multiple-step income statement** Income statement format that shows subtotals between sales and net income, categorizes expenses, and often reports the details of net sales and expenses. *(p. 164)*

**Mutual agency** Legal relationship among partners whereby each partner is an agent of the partnership and is able to bind the partnership to contracts within the scope of the partnership's business. *(p. D-3)*

**Natural business year** Twelve-month period that ends when a company's sales activities are at their lowest point. *(p. 93)*

**Natural resources** Assets physically consumed when used; examples are timber, mineral deposits, and oil and gas fields; also called *wasting assets*. *(p. 325)*

**Net assets** (See *equity*.) *(p. 12)*

**Net income** Amount earned after subtracting all expenses necessary for and matched with sales for a period; also called *income, profit,* or *earnings*. *(p. 13)*

**Net loss** Excess of expenses over revenues for a period. *(p. 13)*

**Net method** Method of recording purchases at the full invoice price less any cash discounts. *(p. 259)*

**Net pay** Gross pay less all deductions; also called *take-home pay*. *(p. 358)*

**Net present value (NPV)** Dollar estimate of an asset's value that is used to evaluate the acceptability of an investment; computed by discounting future cash flows from the investment at a satisfactory rate and then subtracting the initial cost of the investment. *(p. 855)*

**Net realizable value** Expected selling price (value) of an item minus the cost of making the sale. *(p. 196)*

**Noncontrollable costs** Costs that a manager does not have the power to control or strongly influence. *(p. 586)*

**Noncumulative preferred stock** Preferred stock on which the right to receive dividends is lost for any period when dividends are not declared. *(p. 448)*

**Noninterest-bearing note** Note with no stated (contract) rate of interest; interest is implicitly included in the note's face value.

**Nonparticipating preferred stock** Preferred stock on which dividends are limited to a maximum amount each year. *(p. 448)*

**No-par value stock** Stock class that has not been assigned a par (or stated) value by the corporate charter. *(p. 444)*

**Nonsufficient funds (NSF) check** Maker's bank account has insufficient money to pay the check; also called *hot check*. *(p. 250)*

**Note** (See promissory note.) *(p. 287)*

**Note payable** Liability expressed by a written promise to pay a definite sum of money on demand or on a specific future date(s). *(p. 288)*

**Note receivable** Asset consisting of a written promise to receive a definite sum of money on demand or on a specific future date(s). *(p. 49)*

**Objectivity principle** Principle that prescribes independent, unbiased evidence to support financial statement information. *(p. 9)*

**Obsolescence** Condition in which, because of new inventions and improvements, a plant asset can no longer be used to produce goods or services with a competitive advantage. *(p. 313)*

**Off-balance-sheet financing** Acquisition of assets by agreeing to liabilities not reported on the balance sheet. *(p. 422)*

**Online processing** Approach to inputting data from source documents as soon as the information is available. *(p. E-17)*

**Operating activities** Activities that involve the production or purchase of merchandise and the sale of goods or services to customers, including expenditures related to administering the business. *(p. 493)*

**Operating cycle** Normal time between paying cash for merchandise or employee services and receiving cash from customers. *(p. 110)*

**Operating leases** Short-term (or cancelable) leases in which the lessor retains risks and rewards of ownership. *(p. 421)*

**Operating leverage** Extent, or relative size, of fixed costs in the total cost structure. *(p. 751)*

**Opportunity cost** Potential benefit lost by choosing a specific action from two or more alternatives. *(p. 586)*

**Ordinary repairs** Repairs to keep a plant asset in normal, good operating condition; treated as a revenue expenditure and immediately expensed. *(p. 321)*

**Organization expenses (costs)** Costs such as legal fees and promoter fees to bring an entity into existence. *(p. 441)*

**Out-of-pocket cost** Cost incurred or avoided as a result of management's decisions. *(p. 586)*

**Output devices** Means by which information is taken out of the accounting system and made available for use. *(p. E-5)*

**Outsourcing** Manager decision to buy a product or service from another entity; part of a *make-or-buy* decision; also called *make or buy*. *(p. 863)*

**Outstanding checks** Checks written and recorded by the depositor but not yet paid by the bank at the bank statement date. *(p. 250)*

**Outstanding stock** Corporation's stock held by its shareholders. *(p. 453)*

**Overapplied overhead** Amount by which the overhead applied to production in a period using the predetermined overhead rate exceeds the actual overhead incurred in a period. *(p. 632)*

**Overhead cost variance** Difference between the total overhead cost applied to products and the total overhead cost actually incurred. *(p. 820)*

**Owner investment** Assets put into the business by the owner. *(p. 13)*

**Owners' equity** (See *equity* or *stockholders' equity*.) *(p. 12)*

**Owner withdrawals** (See *withdrawals*.) *(p. 13)*

**Paid-in capital** (See *contributed capital*.) *(p. 13 & 444)*

**Par value** Value assigned a share of stock by the corporate charter when the stock is authorized. *(p. 443)*

**Par value of a bond** Amount the bond issuer agrees to pay at maturity and the amount on which cash interest payments are based; also called *face amount* or *face value* of a bond. *(p. 396)*

**Par value stock** Class of stock assigned a par value by the corporate charter. *(p. 443)*

**Parent** Company that owns a controlling interest in a corporation (requires more than 50% of voting stock). *(p. C-9)*

**Participating preferred stock** Preferred stock that shares with common stockholders any dividends paid in excess of the percent stated on preferred stock. *(p. 448)*

**Partner return on equity** Partner net income divided by average partner equity for the period. *(p. D-14)*

**Partnership** Unincorporated association of two or more persons to pursue a business for profit as co-owners. *(p. 10 & D-2)*

**Partnership contract** Agreement among partners that sets terms under which the affairs of the partnership are conducted; also called *articles of partnership*. *(p. D-2)*

**Partnership liquidation** Dissolution of a partnership by (1) selling noncash assets and allocating any gain or loss according to partners' income-and-loss ratio, (2) paying liabilities, and (3) distributing any remaining cash according to partners' capital balances. *(p. D-12)*

**Patent** Exclusive right granted to its owner to produce and sell an item or to use a process for 17 years. *(p. 327)*

**Payback period (PBP)** Time-based measurement used to evaluate the acceptability of an investment; equals the time expected to pass before an investment's net cash flows equal its initial cost. *(p. 851)*

**Payee of the note** Entity to whom a note is made payable. *(p. 288)*

**Payroll bank account** Bank account used solely for paying employees; each pay period an amount equal to the total employees' net pay is deposited in it and the payroll checks are drawn on it. *(p. 374)*

**Payroll deductions** Amounts withheld from an employee's gross pay; also called *withholdings*. *(p. 358)*

**Payroll register** Record for a pay period that shows the pay period dates, regular and overtime hours worked, gross pay, net pay, and deductions. *(p. 370)*

**Pension plan** Contractual agreement between an employer and its employees for the employer to provide benefits to employees after they retire; expensed when incurred. *(p. 423)*

**Period costs** Expenditures identified more with a time period than with finished products costs; includes selling and general administrative expenses. *(p. 586)*

**Periodic inventory system** Method that records the cost of inventory purchased but does not continuously track the quantity available or sold to customers; records are updated at the end of each period to reflect the physical count and costs of goods available. *(p. 154)*

**Permanent accounts** Accounts that reflect activities related to one or more future periods; balance sheet accounts whose balances are not closed; also called *real accounts*. *(p. 106)*

**Perpetual inventory system** Method that maintains continuous records of the cost of inventory available and the cost of goods sold. *(p. 153)*

**Petty cash** Small amount of cash in a fund to pay minor expenses; accounted for using an imprest system. *(p. 244)*

**Planning** Process of setting goals and preparing to achieve them. *(p. 580)*

**Plant assets** Tangible long-lived assets used to produce or sell products and services; also called *property, plant and equipment (PP&E)* or *fixed assets*. *(p. 97 & 310)*

**Pledged assets to secured liabilities** Ratio of the book value of a company's pledged assets to the book value of its secured liabilities. *(p. 413)*

**Post-closing trial balance** List of permanent accounts and their balances from the ledger after all closing entries are journalized and posted. *(p. 109)*

**Posting** Process of transferring journal entry information to the ledger; computerized systems automate this process. *(p. 54)*

**Posting reference (PR) column** A column in journals in which individual ledger account numbers are entered when entries are posted to those ledger accounts. *(p. 55)*

**Predetermined overhead rate** Rate established prior to the beginning of a period that relates estimated overhead to another variable, such as estimated direct labor, and is used to assign overhead cost to production. *(p. 627)*

**Preemptive right** Stockholders' right to maintain their proportionate interest in a corporation with any additional shares issued. *(p. 442)*

**Preferred stock** Stock with a priority status over common stockholders in one or more ways, such as paying dividends or distributing assets. *(p. 447)*

**Premium on bonds** Difference between a bond's par value and its higher carrying value; occurs when the contract rate is higher than the market rate; also called *bond premium*. *(p. 403)*

**Premium on stock** (See *contributed capital in excess of par value*.) *(p. 444)*

**Prepaid expenses** Items paid for in advance of receiving their benefits; classified as assets. *(p. 95)*

**Price-earnings (PE) ratio** Ratio of a company's current market value per share to its earnings per share; also called *price-to-earnings*. *(p. 463)*

**Price variance** Difference between actual and budgeted revenue or cost caused by the difference between the actual price per unit and the budgeted price per unit. *(p. 812)*

**Prime costs** Expenditures directly identified with the production of finished goods; include direct materials costs and direct labor costs. *(p. 591)*

**Principal of a note** Amount that the signer of a note agrees to pay back when it matures, not including interest. *(p. 288)*

**Principles of internal control** Principles prescribing management to establish responsibility, maintain records, insure assets, separate recordkeeping from custody of assets, divide responsibility for related transactions, apply technological controls, and perform reviews. *(p. 237)*

**Stated value stock** No-par stock assigned a stated value per share; this amount is recorded in the stock account when the stock is issued. *(p. 444)*

**Statement of cash flows** A financial statement that lists cash inflows (receipts) and cash outflows (payments) during a period; arranged by operating, investing, and financing. *(p. 492)*

**Statement of partners' equity** Financial statement that shows total capital balances at the beginning of the period, any additional investment by partners, the income or loss of the period, the partners' withdrawals, and the partners' ending capital balances; also called *statement of partners' capital*. *(p. D-7)*

**Statement of retained earnings** Report of changes in retained earnings over a period; adjusted for increases (net income), for decreases (dividends and net loss), and for any prior period adjustment. *(p. 17 & 461)*

**Statement of shareholders' equity** (See *statement of stockholders' equity;* also called *statement of owners' equity.*)

**Statement of stockholders' equity** Financial statement that lists the beginning and ending balances of each major equity account and describes all changes in those accounts. *(p. 461)*

**Statements of Financial Accounting Standards (SFAS)** FASB publications that establish U.S. GAAP. *(p. 9)*

**Step-wise cost** Cost that remains fixed over limited ranges of volumes but changes by a lump sum when volume changes occur outside these limited ranges. *(p. 740).*

**Stock** (See *shares.*) *(p. 11)*

**Stock dividend** Corporation's distribution of its own stock to its stockholders without the receipt of any payment. *(p. 451)*

**Stock options** Rights to purchase common stock at a fixed price over a specified period of time. *(p. 460)*

**Stock split** Occurs when a corporation calls in its stock and replaces each share with more than one new share; decreases both the market value per share and any par or stated value per share. *(p. 453)*

**Stock subscription** Investor's contractual commitment to purchase unissued shares at future dates and prices. *(p. 446)*

**Stockholders' equity** A corporation's equity; also called *shareholders' equity* or *corporate capital*. *(p. 444)*

**Stockholders** (See *shareholders.*) *(p. 11)*

**Straight-line depreciation** Method that allocates an equal portion of the depreciable cost of plant asset (cost minus salvage) to each accounting period in its useful life. *(p. 97 & 314)*

**Straight-line bond amortization** Method allocating an equal amount of bond interest expense to each period of the bond life. *(p. 401)*

**Subsidiary** Entity controlled by another entity (parent) in which the parent owns more than 50% of the subsidiary's voting stock. *(p. C-9)*

**Subsidiary ledger** List of individual sub-accounts and amounts with a common characteristic; linked to a controlling account in the general ledger. *(p. E-6)*

**Sunk cost** Cost already incurred and cannot be avoided or changed. *(p. 586)*

**Supplementary records** Information outside the usual accounting records; also called *supplemental records*. *(p. 158)*

**Supply chain** Linkages of services or goods extending from suppliers, to the company itself, and on to customers. *(p. 584)*

**T-account** Tool used to show the effects of transactions and events on individual accounts. *(p. 53)*

**Temporary accounts** Accounts used to record revenues, expenses, and dividends; they are closed at the end of each period; also called *nominal accounts*. *(p. 104)*

**Term bonds** Bonds scheduled for payment (maturity) at a single specified date. *(p. 398)*

**Time period principle** Assumption that an organization's activities can be divided into specific time periods such as months, quarters, or years. *(p. 92)*

**Time ticket** Source document used to report the time an employee spent working on a job or on overhead activities and then to determine the amount of direct labor to charge to the job or the amount of indirect labor to charge to overhead. *(p. 625)*

**Times interest earned** Ratio of income before interest expense (and any income taxes) divided by interest expense; reflects risk of covering interest commitments when income varies. *(p. 365)*

**Total asset turnover** Measure of a company's ability to use its assets to generate sales; computed by dividing net sales by average total assets. *(p. 329)*

**Total quality management (TQM)** Concept calling for all managers and employees at all stages of operations to strive toward higher standards and reduce number of defects. *(p. 584)*

**Trade discount** Reduction from a list or catalog price that can vary for wholesalers, retailers, and consumers. *(p. 154)*

**Trademark** or **Trade (Brand) name** Symbol, name, phrase, or jingle identified with a company, product, or service. *(p. 328)*

**Trading on the equity** (See *financial leverage.*) *(p. 449)*

**Trading securities** Investments in debt and equity securities that the company intends to actively trade for profit. *(p. C-5)*

**Transaction** Exchange of economic consideration affecting an entity's financial position that can be reliably measured. *(p. 13)*

**Treasury stock** Corporation's own stock that it reacquired and still holds. *(p. 454)*

**Trial balance** List of accounts and their balances at a point in time; total debit balances equal total credit balances. *(p. 63)*

**Unadjusted trial balance** List of accounts and balances prepared before accounting adjustments are recorded and posted. *(p. 103)*

**Unavoidable expense** Expense (or cost) that is not relevant for business decisions; an expense that would continue even if a department, product, or service is eliminated. *(p. 866)*

**Unclassified balance sheet** Balance sheet that broadly groups assets, liabilities, and equity accounts. *(p. 110)*

**Uncontrollable costs** Costs that a manager does not have the power to determine or strongly influence. *(p. 712)*

**Underapplied overhead** Amount by which overhead incurred in a period exceeds the overhead applied to that period's production using the predetermined overhead rate. *(p. 631)*

**Unearned revenue** Liability created when customers pay in advance for products or services; earned when the products or services are later delivered. *(p. 51 & 98)*

**Unfavorable variance** Difference in revenues or costs, when the actual amount is compared to the budgeted amount, that contributes to a lower income. *(p. 810)*

**Unit contribution margin** Amount a product's unit selling price exceeds its total unit variable cost. *(p. 595)*

**Units-of-production depreciation** Method that charges a varying amount to depreciation expense for each period of an asset's useful life depending on its usage. *(p. 315)*

**Unlimited liability** Legal relationship among general partners that makes each of them responsible for partnership debts if the other partners are unable to pay their shares. *(p. D-3)*

**Unrealized gain (loss)** Gain (loss) not yet realized by an actual transaction or event such as a sale. *(p. C-5)*

**Unsecured bonds** Bonds backed only by the issuer's credit standing; almost always riskier than secured bonds; also called *debentures*. *(p. 397)*

**Unusual gain or loss** Gain or loss that is abnormal or unrelated to the company's ordinary activities and environment. *(p. 456)*

**Useful life** Length of time an asset will be productively used in the operations of a business; also called *service life*. *(p. 313)*

**Value chain** Sequential activities that add value to an entity's products or services; includes design, production, marketing, distribution, and service. *(p. 592)*

**Variable cost** Cost that changes in proportion to changes in the activity output volume. *(p. 585)*

**Variance analysis** Process of examining differences between actual and budgeted revenues or costs and describing them in terms of price and quantity differences. *(p. 812)*

**Vendee** Buyer of goods or services. *(p. 256)*

**Vendor** Seller of goods or services. *(p. 256)*

**Vertical analysis** Evaluation of each financial statement item or group of items in terms of a specific base amount. *(p. 542)*

**Volume variance** Difference between two dollar amounts of fixed overhead cost; one amount is the total budgeted overhead cost, and the other is the overhead cost allocated to products using the predetermined fixed overhead rate. *(p. 821)*

**Voucher** Internal file used to store documents and information to control cash disbursements and to ensure that a transaction is properly authorized and recorded. *(p. 243)*

**Voucher system** Procedures and approvals designed to control cash disbursements and acceptance of obligations. *(p. 243)*

**Wage bracket withholding table** Table of the amounts of income tax withheld from employees' wages. *(p. 372)*

**Warranty** Agreement that obligates the seller to correct or replace a product or service when it fails to perform properly within a specified period. *(p. 362)*

**Weighted average** Method to assign inventory cost to sales; the cost of available-for-sale units is divided by the number of units available to determine per unit cost prior to each sale that is then multiplied by the units sold to yield the cost of that sale. *(p. 202)*

**Wholesaler** Intermediary that buys products from manufacturers or other wholesalers and sells them to retailers or other wholesalers. *(p. 152)*

**Withdrawals** Payment of cash or other assets from a proprietorship or partnership to its owner or owners. *(p. 13)*

**Work sheet** Spreadsheet used to draft an unadjusted trial balance, adjusting entries, adjusted trial balance, and financial statements. *(p. 119)*

**Working capital** Current assets minus current liabilities at a point in time. *(p. 551)*

**Working papers** Analyses and other informal reports prepared by accountants and managers when organizing information for formal reports and financial statements. *(p. 119)*

# Credits

# Index

Note: Page numbers followed by *n* indicate material found in footnotes; items in **boldface** indicate defined terms; <u>underlined</u> items are URLs.

# Chart of Accounts

Following is a typical chart of accounts. Each company has its own unique accounts and numbering system.

## Assets

### Current Assets

101 Cash
102 Petty cash
103 Cash equivalents
104 Short-term investments
105 Market adjustment, _____ securities (S-T)
106 Accounts receivable
107 Allowance for doubtful accounts
108 Legal fees receivable
109 Interest receivable
110 Rent receivable
111 Notes receivable
119 Merchandise inventory
120 _____ inventory
121 _____ inventory
124 Office supplies
125 Store supplies
126 _____ supplies
128 Prepaid insurance
129 Prepaid interest
131 Prepaid rent
132 Raw materials inventory
133 Goods in process inventory, _____
134 Goods in process inventory, _____
135 Finished goods inventory

### Long-Term Investments

141 Long-term investments
142 Market adjustment, _____ securities (L-T)
144 Investment in _____
145 Bond sinking fund

### Plant Assets

151 Automobiles
152 Accumulated depreciation—Automobiles
153 Trucks
154 Accumulated depreciation—Trucks
155 Boats
156 Accumulated depreciation—Boats
157 Professional library
158 Accumulated depreciation—Professional library
159 Law library
160 Accumulated depreciation—Law library
161 Furniture
162 Accumulated depreciation—Furniture
163 Office equipment
164 Accumulated depreciation—Office equipment
165 Store equipment
166 Accumulated depreciation—Store equipment
167 _____ equipment

168 Accumulated depreciation—_____ equipment
169 Machinery
170 Accumulated depreciation—Machinery
173 Building _____
174 Accumulated depreciation—Building _____
175 Building _____
176 Accumulated depreciation—Building _____
179 Land improvements _____
180 Accumulated depreciation—Land improvements _____
181 Land improvements _____
182 Accumulated depreciation—Land improvements _____
183 Land

### Natural Resources

185 Mineral deposit
186 Accumulated depletion—Mineral deposit

### Intangible Assets

191 Patents
192 Leasehold
193 Franchise
194 Copyrights
195 Leasehold improvements
196 Licenses
197 Accumulated amortization—_____

## Liabilities

### Current Liabilities

201 Accounts payable
202 Insurance payable
203 Interest payable
204 Legal fees payable
207 Office salaries payable
208 Rent payable
209 Salaries payable
210 Wages payable
211 Accrued payroll payable
214 Estimated warranty liability
215 Income taxes payable
216 Common dividend payable
217 Preferred dividend payable
218 State unemployment taxes payable
219 Employee federal income taxes payable
221 Employee medical insurance payable
222 Employee retirement program payable
223 Employee union dues payable
224 Federal unemployment taxes payable
225 FICA taxes payable
226 Estimated vacation pay liability

### Unearned Revenues

230 Unearned consulting fees
231 Unearned legal fees
232 Unearned property management fees
233 Unearned _____ fees
234 Unearned _____ fees
235 Unearned janitorial revenue
236 Unearned _____ revenue
238 Unearned rent

### Notes Payable

240 Short-term notes payable
241 Discount on short-term notes payable
245 Notes payable
251 Long-term notes payable
252 Discount on long-term notes payable

### Long-Term Liabilities

253 Long-term lease liability
255 Bonds payable
256 Discount on bonds payable
257 Premium on bonds payable
258 Deferred income tax liability

## Equity

### Owner's Equity

301 _____, Capital
302 _____, Withdrawals
303 _____, Capital
304 _____, Withdrawals
305 _____, Capital
306 _____, Withdrawals

### Contributed Capital

307 Common stock, $ _____ par value
308 Common stock, no-par value
309 Common stock, $ _____ stated value
310 Common stock dividend distributable
311 Contributed capital in excess of par value, Common stock
312 Contributed capital in excess of stated value, No-par common stock
313 Contributed capital from retirement of common stock
314 Contributed capital, Treasury stock
315 Preferred stock
316 Contributed capital in excess of par value, Preferred stock

## Retained Earnings

318 Retained earnings
319 Cash dividends (or Dividends)
320 Stock dividends

## Other Equity Accounts

321 Treasury stock, Common
322 Unrealized gain—Equity
323 Unrealized loss—Equity

# Revenues

401 _____ fees earned
402 _____ fees earned
403 _____ services revenue
404 _____ services revenue
405 Commissions earned
406 Rent revenue (or Rent earned)
407 Dividends revenue (or Dividend earned)
408 Earnings from investment in _____
409 Interest revenue (or Interest earned)
410 Sinking fund earnings
413 Sales
414 Sales returns and allowances
415 Sales discounts

# Cost of Sales

## Cost of Goods Sold

502 Cost of goods sold
505 Purchases
506 Purchases returns and allowances
507 Purchases discounts
508 Transportation-in

## Manufacturing

520 Raw materials purchases
521 Freight-in on raw materials
530 Factory payroll
531 Direct labor
540 Factory overhead
541 Indirect materials
542 Indirect labor
543 Factory insurance expired
544 Factory supervision
545 Factory supplies used
546 Factory utilities
547 Miscellaneous production costs
548 Property taxes on factory building
549 Property taxes on factory equipment
550 Rent on factory building
551 Repairs, factory equipment
552 Small tools written off
560 Depreciation of factory equipment
561 Depreciation of factory building

## Standard Cost Variance

580 Direct material quantity variance
581 Direct material price variance
582 Direct labor quantity variance
583 Direct labor price variance
584 Factory overhead volume variance
585 Factory overhead controllable variance

# Expenses

## Amortization, Depletion, and Depreciation

601 Amortization expense—_____
602 Amortization expense—_____
603 Depletion expense—_____
604 Depreciation expense—Boats
605 Depreciation expense—Automobiles
606 Depreciation expense—Building _____
607 Depreciation expense—Building _____
608 Depreciation expense—Land improvements _____
609 Depreciation expense—Land improvements _____
610 Depreciation expense—Law library
611 Depreciation expense—Trucks
612 Depreciation expense—_____ equipment
613 Depreciation expense—_____ equipment
614 Depreciation expense—_____
615 Depreciation expense—_____

## Employee-Related Expenses

620 Office salaries expense
621 Sales salaries expense
622 Salaries expense
623 _____ wages expense
624 Employees' benefits expense
625 Payroll taxes expense

## Financial Expenses

630 Cash over and short
631 Discounts lost
632 Factoring fee expense
633 Interest expense

## Insurance Expenses

635 Insurance expense—Delivery equipment
636 Insurance expense—Office equipment
637 Insurance expense—_____

## Rental Expenses

640 Rent expense
641 Rent expense—Office space
642 Rent expense—Selling space
643 Press rental expense
644 Truck rental expense
645 _____ rental expense

## Supplies Expenses

650 Office supplies expense
651 Store supplies expense
652 _____ supplies expense
653 _____ supplies expense

## Miscellaneous Expenses

655 Advertising expense
656 Bad debts expense
657 Blueprinting expense
658 Boat expense
659 Collection expense
661 Concessions expense
662 Credit card expense
663 Delivery expense
664 Dumping expense
667 Equipment expense
668 Food and drinks expense
671 Gas and oil expense
672 General and administrative expense
673 Janitorial expense
674 Legal fees expense
676 Mileage expense
677 Miscellaneous expenses
678 Mower and tools expense
679 Operating expense
680 Organization expense
681 Permits expense
682 Postage expense
683 Property taxes expense
684 Repairs expense—_____
685 Repairs expense—_____
687 Selling expense
688 Telephone expense
689 Travel and entertainment expense
690 Utilities expense
691 Warranty expense
695 Income taxes expense

# Gains and Losses

701 Gain on retirement of bonds
702 Gain on sale of machinery
703 Gain on sale of investments
704 Gain on sale of trucks
705 Gain on _____
706 Foreign exchange gain or loss
801 Loss on disposal of machinery
802 Loss on exchange of equipment
803 Loss on exchange of _____
804 Loss on sale of notes
805 Loss on retirement of bonds
806 Loss on sale of investments
807 Loss on sale of machinery
808 Loss on _____
809 Unrealized gain—Income
810 Unrealized loss—Income

# Clearing Accounts

901 Income summary
902 Manufacturing summary

# A Rose by Any Other Name

**The same financial statement sometimes receives different titles. Below are some of the more common aliases.**[†]

| | |
|---|---|
| **Balance Sheet** | Statement of Financial Position |
| | Statement of Financial Condition |
| | |
| **Income Statement** | Statement of Income |
| | Operating Statement |
| | Statement of Operations |
| | Statement of Operating Activity |
| | Earnings Statement |
| | Statement of Earnings |
| | Profit and Loss (P&L) Statement |
| | |
| **Statement of Cash Flows** | Statement of Cash Flow |
| | Cash Flows Statement |
| | Statement of Changes in Cash Position |
| | Statement of Changes in Financial Position |
| | |
| **Statement of Owner's Equity** | Statement of Changes in Owner's Equity |
| | Statement of Changes in Owner's Capital |
| | |
| | Statement of Shareholders' Equity* |
| | Statement of Changes in Shareholders' Equity* |
| | Statement of Changes in Capital Accounts* |

[†] The term "**Consolidated**" often precedes or follows these statement titles to reflect the combination of different entities, such as a parent company and its subsidiaries.

* Corporation only.

*We thank Dr. Louella Moore from Arkansas State University for suggesting this listing.*

# MANAGERIAL ANALYSES AND REPORTS

## ① Cost Types

| | |
|---|---|
| Variable costs = cost changes in proportion to volume of activity | p. 739 |
| Fixed costs = cost does not change in proportion to volume of activity | p. 738 |
| Mixed costs = cost consists of both a variable and a fixed element | p. 739 |

## ② Cost Sources

| | |
|---|---|
| Direct materials = Raw materials directly linked to finished product | p. 590 |
| Direct labor = Employee work directly linked to converting materials into finished product | p. 591 |
| Overhead = Costs indirectly linked to processing finished product | p. 591 |

## ③ Costing Systems

| | |
|---|---|
| Job order costing = Costs assigned to each unit or batch of units | p. 629 |
| Process costing = Costs assigned to similar products that are mass-produced in a continuous manner | p. 670 |

## ④ Costing Ratios

| | |
|---|---|
| Contribution margin ratio = (Net sales − Variable costs)/Net sales | p. 744 |
| Predetermined overhead rate = Estimated overhead costs/Estimated "factor" costs | p. 628 |
| Costs per unit = Material, labor, and overhead costs per unit | p. 664 |
| Break-even point in units = Fixed costs/Contribution margin per unit | p. 744 |

## ⑤ Planning and Control Metrics

| | |
|---|---|
| Cost variance = Actual cost − Standard (budgeted) cost | p. 815 |
| Sales (revenue) variance = Actual sales − Standard (budgeted) sales | p. 827 |

## ⑥ Capital Budgeting

| | |
|---|---|
| Payback period = Time expected to recover investment cost | p. 852 |
| Accounting rate of return = Expected annual net income/Average annual investment | p. 854 |
| Net present value (NPV) = Present value of cash flows − Investment cost | p. 855 |
| NPV rule: 1. Compute net present value (NPV in $) | p. 855 |

NPV rule: 2. If NPV ≥ 0, then accept project; If NPV < 0, then reject project

Internal rate 1. Compute internal rate of return (IRR in %)
of return: 2. If IRR ≥ hurdle rate, accept project; If IRR < hurdle rate, reject project

## ⑦ Costing Terminology

| | | |
|---|---|---|
| Relevant range: | Organization's normal range of operating activity. | p. 740 |
| Direct cost: | Cost incurred for the benefit of one cost object. | p. 585 |
| Indirect cost: | Cost incurred for the benefit of more than one cost object. | p. 585 |
| Product cost: | Cost that is necessary and integral to finished products. | p. 586 |
| Period cost: | Cost identified more with a time period than with finished products. | p. 586 |
| Overhead cost: | Cost not separately or directly traceable to a cost object. | p. 591 |
| Relevant cost: | Cost that is pertinent to a decision. | p. 861 |
| Opportunity cost: | Benefit lost by choosing an action from two or more alternatives. | p. 586 |
| Sunk cost: | Cost already incurred that cannot be avoided or changed. | p. 586 |
| Standard cost: | Cost computed using standard price and standard quantity. | p. 813 |
| Cost variance: | Difference between actual cost and budgeted (standard) cost. | p. 815 |
| Budget: | Formal statement of an organization's future plans. | p. 770 |
| Break-even point: | Sales level at which an organization earns zero profit. | p. 744 |
| Incremental cost: | Cost incurred only if the organization undertakes certain action. | p. 862 |

## ⑧ Standard Cost Variances

| | | |
|---|---|---|
| **Total materials variance** = | Materials price variance + Materials quantity variance | p. 816 |

| | | |
|---|---|---|
| **Total labor variance** = | Labor (rate) variance + Labor efficiency (quantity) variance | p. 818 |

| | | |
|---|---|---|
| **Total overhead variance** = | Overhead controllable variance + Fixed overhead volume variance | p. 821 |

Variable overhead variance = Variable overhead spending variance + Variable overhead efficiency variance ⎫
Fixed overhead variance = Fixed overhead spending variance + Fixed overhead volume variance ⎬ = Total overhead variance

Overhead controllable overhead = Variable overhead spending variance + Variable overhead efficiency variance + Fixed overhead spending variance

**Materials price variance** = [AQ × AP] − [AQ × SP]

**Materials quantity variance** = [AQ × SP] − [SQ × SP]

**Labor (rate) variance** = [AH × AR] − [AH × SR]

**Labor efficiency (quantity) variance** = [AH × SR] − [SH × SR]

Variable overhead spending variance = [AH × AVR] − [AH × SVR]

Variable overhead efficiency variance = [AH × SVR] − [SH × SVR]

Fixed overhead spending variance = Actual overhead − Budgeted overhead

Fixed overhead volume variance = Budgeted overhead − Applied overhead

where
AQ is actual quantity of materials; AP is actual price of materials; AH is actual hours of labor; AR is actual rate of wages; AVR is actual variable rate of overhead; SQ is standard quantity of materials; SP is standard price of materials; SH is standard hours of labor; SR is standard rate of wages; SVR is standard variable rate of overhead.

---

### Manufacturing Statement
### For _period_ Ended _date_

| | | |
|---|---|---|
| Direct materials | | |
| Raw materials inventory, Beginning | $ # | |
| Raw materials purchases | # | |
| Raw materials available for use | # | |
| Raw materials inventory, Ending | (#) | |
| Direct materials used | | # |
| Direct labor | | # |
| Overhead costs | | |
| Total overhead costs | | # |
| Total manufacturing costs | | # |
| Add goods in process inventory, Beginning | | # |
| Total cost of goods in process | | # |
| Deduct goods in process inventory, Ending | | (#) |
| Cost of goods manufactured | | $ # |

---

### Contribution Margin Income Statement
### For _period_ Ended _date_

| | |
|---|---|
| Net sales (revenues) | $ # |
| Total variable costs | # |
| Contribution margin | # |
| Total fixed costs | # |
| Net income | $ # |

---

### Flexible Budget
### For _period_ Ended _date_

| | Flexible Budget | | Flexible Budget for Unit Sales of # |
|---|---|---|---|
| | Variable Amount per Unit | Fixed Cost | |
| Sales (revenues) | $ # | | $ # |
| Variable costs | | | |
| Examples: Direct materials, Direct labor, | | | |
| Other variable costs | # | | # |
| Total variable costs | # | | # |
| Contribution margin | $ # | | # |
| Fixed costs | | | |
| Examples: Depreciation, Manager | | $ # | # |
| salaries, Administrative salaries | | # | # |
| Total fixed costs | | $ # | # |
| Income from operations | | | $ # |

---

### Fixed Budget Performance Report
### For _period_ Ended _date_

| | Fixed Budget | Actual Performance | Variances[†] |
|---|---|---|---|
| Sales: In units | # | # | |
| In dollars | $ # | $ # | $ # F or U |
| Cost of sales | | | |
| Direct costs | # | # | # F or U |
| Indirect costs | # | # | # F or U |
| Selling expenses | | | |
| (Examples: Commissions, | # | # | # F or U |
| Shipping expenses) | # | # | # F or U |
| General and administrative expenses | | | |
| (Examples: Administrative salaries) | # | # | # F or U |
| Total expenses | $ # | $ # | $ # F or U |
| Income from operations | $ # | $ # | $ # F or U |

[†] F = Favorable variance; U = Unfavorable variance.

---

### Master Budget Sequence

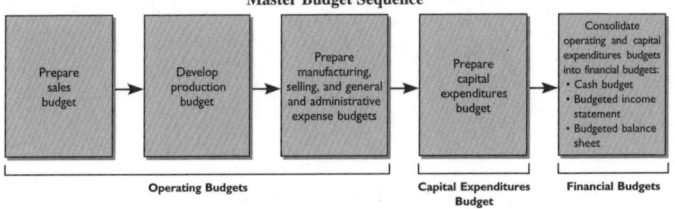

Prepare sales budget → Develop production budget → Prepare manufacturing, selling, and general and administrative expense budgets → Prepare capital expenditures budget → Consolidate operating and capital expenditures budgets into financial budgets:
- Cash budget
- Budgeted income statement
- Budgeted balance sheet

Operating Budgets     Capital Expenditures Budget     Financial Budgets

# FUNDAMENTALS

## ① Accounting Equation

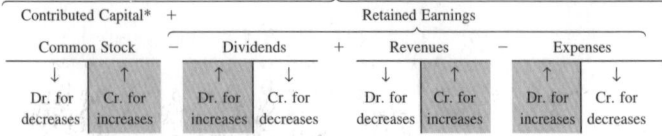

| Assets | = | Liabilities | + | Equity |
|---|---|---|---|---|
| ↑ Debit for increases | ↓ Credit for decreases | ↓ Debit for decreases | ↑ Credit for increases | ↓ Debit for decreases | ↑ Credit for increases |

| Contributed Capital* | + | Retained Earnings | | | |
|---|---|---|---|---|---|
| Common Stock | − Dividends | + Revenues | − Expenses | | |
| ↓ Dr. for decreases | ↑ Cr. for increases | ↑ Dr. for increases | ↓ Cr. for decreases | ↓ Dr. for decreases | ↑ Cr. for increases | ↑ Dr. for increases | ↓ Cr. for decreases |

Indicates normal balance.

*Includes common stock and any preferred stock.

## ② Accounting Cycle

1. Analyze transactions
10. Reverse Optional
9. Prepare post-closing trial balance
8. Close
2. Journalize
7. Prepare statements
3. Post
4. Prepare unadjusted trial balance
5. Adjust
6. Prepare adjusted trial balance

## ③ Adjustments and Entries

| Type | Adjusting Entry | |
|---|---|---|
| Prepaid Expenses | Dr. Expense | Cr. Asset* |
| Unearned Revenues | Dr. Liability | Cr. Revenue |
| Accrued Expenses | Dr. Expense | Cr. Liability |
| Accrued Revenues | Dr. Asset | Cr. Revenue |

*For depreciation, credit Accumulated Depreciation (contra asset).

## ④ 4-Step Closing Process

<1>Transfer revenue and gain account balances to Income Summary.
<2>Transfer expense and loss account balances to Income Summary.
<3>Transfer Income Summary balance to Retained Earnings.
<4>Transfer Dividends balance to Retained Earnings.

## ⑤ Accounting Concepts

| Characteristics | Assumptions | Principles | Constraints |
|---|---|---|---|
| Relevance | Business entity | Historical cost | Cost-benefit |
| Reliability | Going concern | Revenue recognition | Materiality |
| Comparability | Monetary unit | Matching | Industry practice |
| Consistency | Periodicity | Full disclosure | Conservatism |

## ⑥ Ownership of Inventory

| | Ownership transfers when goods passed to | Transportation costs paid by |
|---|---|---|
| FOB Shipping Point | Carrier | Buyer |
| FOB Destination | Buyer | Seller |

## ⑦ Inventory Costing Methods

Specific Identification
First-In, First-Out (FIFO)
Last-In, First-Out (LIFO)
Weighted-Average

## ⑧ Depreciation and Depletion

Straight-Line: $\dfrac{\text{Cost} - \text{Salvage value}}{\text{Useful life in periods}} \times \text{Periods expired}$

Units-of-Production: $\dfrac{\text{Cost} - \text{Salvage value}}{\text{Useful life in units}} \times \text{Units produced}$

Declining-Balance: Rate* × Beginning-of-period book value
*Rate is often double the straight-line rate, or $2 \times (1/\text{useful life})$

Depletion: $\dfrac{\text{Cost} - \text{Salvage value}}{\text{Total capacity in units}} \times \text{Units extracted}$

## ⑨ Interest Computation

Interest = Principal (face) × Rate × Time

## ⑩ Accounting for Investment Securities

Trading (debt and equity) securities . . . . . . . . . . Market value (with market adjustment to income)

Held-to-maturity (debt) securities
  Short-term . . . . . . . . . . . . . . . . . . . . . . . Cost (without any discount or premium amortization)
  Long-term . . . . . . . . . . . . . . . . . . . . . . . Cost (with any discount or premium amortization)

Available-for-sale (debt and equity) securities . . . Market value (with market adjustment to equity)

Equity securities with significant influence . . . . . Equity method

# ANALYSES

## ① Liquidity and Efficiency

Current ratio $= \dfrac{\text{Current assets}}{\text{Current liabilities}}$    p. 113

Working capital = Current assets − Current liabilities    p. 551

Acid-test ratio $= \dfrac{\text{Cash} + \text{Short-term investments} + \text{Current receivables}}{\text{Current liabilities}}$    p. 167

Accounts receivable turnover $= \dfrac{\text{Net sales}}{\text{Average accounts receivable}}$    p. 292

Credit risk ratio $= \dfrac{\text{Allowance for doubtful accounts}}{\text{Accounts receivable}}$    p. 292

Inventory turnover $= \dfrac{\text{Cost of goods sold}}{\text{Average inventory}}$    p. 207

Days' sales uncollected $= \dfrac{\text{Accounts receivable}}{\text{Net sales}} \times 365^*$    p. 253

Days' sales in inventory $= \dfrac{\text{Ending inventory}}{\text{Cost of goods sold}} \times 365^*$    p. 208

Total asset turnover $= \dfrac{\text{Net sales}}{\text{Average total assets}}$    p. 329

Plant asset useful life $= \dfrac{\text{Plant asset cost}}{\text{Depreciation expense}}$    p. 329

Plant asset age $= \dfrac{\text{Accumulated depreciation}}{\text{Depreciation expense}}$    p. 329

Days' cash expense coverage $= \dfrac{\text{Cash and cash equivalents}}{\text{Average daily cash expenses}}$    p. 241

*360 days is also commonly used.

## ② Solvency

Debt ratio $= \dfrac{\text{Total liabilities}}{\text{Total assets}}$    Equity ratio $= \dfrac{\text{Total equity}}{\text{Total assets}}$    p. 67 & p. 555

Pledged assets to secured liabilities $= \dfrac{\text{Book value of pledged assets}}{\text{Book value of secured liabilities}}$    p. 555

Times interest earned $= \dfrac{\text{Income before interest expense and income taxes}}{\text{Interest expense}}$    p. 365

Cash coverage of growth $= \dfrac{\text{Operating cash flow}}{\text{Cash outflow for plant assets}}$    p. 510

Cash coverage of debt $= \dfrac{\text{Cash flow from operations}}{\text{Total noncurrent liabilities}}$    p. 509

## ③ Profitability

Profit margin ratio $= \dfrac{\text{Net income}}{\text{Net sales}}$    p. 113

Gross margin ratio $= \dfrac{\text{Net sales} - \text{Cost of goods sold}}{\text{Net sales}}$    p. 167

Return on total assets $= \dfrac{\text{Net income}}{\text{Average total assets}}$    p. 20

$= \text{Profit margin ratio} \times \text{Total asset turnover}$    p. 557

Return on total equity $= \dfrac{\text{Net income}}{\text{Average total equity}}$    p. 397

Return on common stockholders' equity $= \dfrac{\text{Net income} - \text{Preferred dividends}}{\text{Average common stockholders' equity}}$    p. 557

Book value per common share $= \dfrac{\text{Stockholders' equity applicable to common shares}}{\text{Number of common shares outstanding}}$    p. 462

Basic earnings per share $= \dfrac{\text{Net income} - \text{Preferred dividends}}{\text{Weighted-average common shares outstanding}}$    p. 458

Cash flow on total assets $= \dfrac{\text{Cash flow from operations}}{\text{Average total assets}}$    p. 510

Payout ratio $= \dfrac{\text{Cash dividends declared on common stock}}{\text{Net income}}$    p. 463

## ④ Market

Price-earnings ratio $= \dfrac{\text{Market price per common share}}{\text{Earnings per share}}$    p. 558

Dividend yield $= \dfrac{\text{Annual cash dividends per share}}{\text{Market price per share}}$    p. 558